CW00322741

AA

HOTELS AND RESTAURANTS IN EUROPE 1990

GAZETTEER: Compiled by the AA's Research Unit. Information Control in co-operation
with AA Hotels Services, and generated by the AA's Establishment Data-base.
Additional contributions from Gerry Crawshaw.
MAPS: Prepared by the Cartographic Department of The Automobile Association
© The Automobile Association 1990
COVER DESIGN: The Paul Hampson Partnership
BLACK AND WHITE ILLUSTRATIONS: Lynda Roberts
ADDITIONAL RESEARCH: J. R. Parr
HEAD OF ADVERTISEMENT SALES: Christopher Heard   Tel 0256 20123 (ext 21544)
ADVERTISEMENT PRODUCTION: Karen Weeks   Tel 0256 20123 (ext 21545)
Gazetteer typeset by Page Bros, Norwich
All other text typeset by Tradespools, Frome, Somerset
Printed and bound in Great Britain by
Richard Clay Ltd, Bungay, Suffolk

EUROPEAN YEAR OF TOURISM 1990

Every effort is made to ensure accuracy, but the publishers do not hold themselves responsible for any consequences that may arise from errors or omissions. Whilst the contents are believed correct at the time of going to press, changes may have occurred since
that time or will occur during the currency of this book.

© The Automobile Association 1990.

All rights reserved. No part of this publication may be reproduced, stored in a retrieval
system, or transmitted in any form or by any means – electronic, mechanical, photocopy-
ing, recording or otherwise – unless the written permission of the Publisher has been
given beforehand.

A CIP Catalogue record – for this book is available from the British Library.

Published by The Automobile Association, Basingstoke, Hampshire RG21 2EA.

ISBN 0 7495 0027 1

CONTENTS

EUROPEAN
A B C

MOTORING AND GENERAL INFORMATION

The ABC provides a wide background of motoring regulations and general information, and is designed to be read in conjuction with the relevant country section

Motoring laws in Europe are just as wide-ranging and complex as those in the UK, but they should cause little difficulty to the average British motorist. You should, however, take more care and extend greater courtesy than you would normally do at home, and bear in mind the essentials of good motoring – avoiding any behaviour likely to obstruct traffic, endanger persons or cause damage to property. It is also important to remember that tourists are subject to the laws of the country in which they travel.

Road signs are mainly international and should be familiar, but in every country there are a few exceptions. One should particularly watch for signs indicating crossings and speed limits. Probably the most unusual aspect of motoring abroad to the British motorist is the rule giving priority to traffic coming from the right (**except in the Republic of Ireland**), and unless this priority is varied by signs, it must be strictly observed.

As well as a current passport (except for Republic of Ireland, see *Passports* page 20), a tourist temporarily importing a motor vehicle should always carry a full valid national driving licence (even when an International Driving Permit is held), the registration document of the car and evidence of insurance. The proper international distinguishing sign should be affixed to the rear of the vehicle. The appropriate papers must be carried at all times, and secured against loss. The practice of spot checks on foreign cars is widespread and, to avoid inconvenience or a *police fine*, ensure that your papers are in order and that the international distinguishing sign is of the approved standard design.

Make sure that you have clear all-round vision. See that your seat belts are securely mounted and not damaged, and remember that in most European countries their use is compulsory. If you are carrying skis, remember that their tips should point to the rear.

Make sure that your vehicle complies with the regulations concerning dimensions for all the countries you intend to pass through (see *ABC* and relevant *Country sections*). This is particularly necessary if you are towing a trailer of any sort. If you are planning to tow a caravan, you will find advice and information in the AA guide *Camping and Caravanning in Europe*.

Mechanical repairs and replacement parts can be very expensive abroad. While not all breakdowns are avoidable, a vast number occur because the vehicle has not been prepared properly before the journey. A holiday abroad involves many miles of hard driving over unfamiliar roads, perhaps without the facilities you are accustomed to. Therefore, you should give serious consideration to *preparing your vehicle for a holiday abroad*.

We recommend that your car undergoes a major service by a franchised dealer shortly before you holiday or tour abroad. In addition, it is advisable to carry out your own general check for any audible or visible defects.

It is not practical to provide a complete list of points to look for, but the *ABC* contains information under the following headings:

Automatic gearboxes
Automatic transmission fluid
Brakes
Cold weather touring
Direction indicators
Electrical
Engine and mechanical
Lights
Spares
Tyres
Warm climate touring

These, used in conjunction with the manufacturer's handbook, should ensure that no obvious faults are missed.

AA members can have their car thoroughly checked by one of the AA's experienced engineers; any AA Centre can arrange this at a

THE BYPASS TO
HOLIDAY FRANCE & SPAIN

CONVENIENT DEPARTURES

CIVILISED SHIPS

DIRECT TO BRITTANY,
NORMANDY & SPAIN

FAST, UNCROWDED ROADS

GREAT VALUE
BARGAIN RETURN FARES

HUNDREDS OF BREAKS,
GITES & MOTORING HOLIDAYS

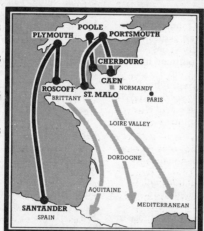

BYPASS BUSY LONDON

BYPASS JAMMED M2 & M20

BYPASS TEEMING DOVER

BYPASS 'RUSH-HOUR' FERRIES

BYPASS DISTANT CALAIS

BYPASS CONGESTED LE HAVRE

Brittany Ferries
The Holiday Fleet

THE BETTER VALUE WAY, AND ALL FOR THE PRICE OF AN ORDINARY FERRY.

FOR BROCHURES: RING PORTSMOUTH **(0705) 751708** OR PLYMOUTH **(0752) 269926** NOW.
RESERVATIONS RING PORTSMOUTH **(0705) 827701** OR PLYMOUTH **(0752) 221321**
OR CONTACT YOUR TRAVEL AGENT OR MOTORING ORGANISATION TODAY.

few days' notice. Our engineer will submit a written report, complete with a list of repairs required. There is a fee for this service. For more information, please ask for our leaflet Tech 8.

AA Service, including Port Agents

The Association does not maintain any offices abroad outside France, but it is represented by allied motoring clubs and other organisations throughout Europe. Additionally, it has appointed port agents on the Continent to assist and advise motorists embarking and disembarking. European motoring clubs allied to the AA will extend a courtesy service to AA members, insofar as their facilities will allow. See also *Country sections for France, Gibraltar* and *Spain.*

Accidents (See also Country sections)

The country sections give regulations for individual countries and information on summoning the emergency services. The international regulations are similar to those in the UK; the following action is usually required or advisable:

If you are involved in an accident you *must* stop. A warning triangle should be placed on the road at a suitable distance to warn following traffic of the obstruction. The use of hazard warning lights in no way affects the regulations governing the use of warning triangles. Medical assistance should be obtained for persons injured in the accident. If the accident necessitates calling the police, leave the vehicle in the position in which it came to rest; should it seriously obstruct other traffic, mark the position of the vehicle on the road and get the details confirmed by independent witnesses before moving it.

The accident must be reported to the police – if it is required by law, if the accident has caused death or bodily injury, or if an unoccupied vehicle or property has been damaged and there is no one present to represent the interests of the party suffering damage. Notify your insurance company (by letter, if possible), within 24 hours of the accident; see the conditions of your policy. If a third party is injured, the insurance company or

bureau, whose address is given on the back of your Green Card or frontier insurance certificate, should be notified; the company or bureau will deal with any claim for compensation to the injured party.

Make sure that all the essential particulars are noted, especially details concerning third parties, and co-operate with police, or other officials taking on-the-spot notes, by supplying your name, address or other personal details as required. It is also a good idea to take photographs of the scene; try to get good shots of other vehicles involved, their registration plates and any background which might help later enquiries. This record may be useful when completing the insurance company's accident form.

If you are not involved in the accident but feel your assistance as a witness or in any other useful capacity would be helpful, then stop and park your car carefully, well away from the scene. If all the help necessary is at the scene; then do not stop out of curiosity or park your car at the site.

Automatic gearboxes

When towing a caravan, the fluid in the automatic gearbox becomes hotter and thinner, so there is more slip and more heat generated in the gearbox. Many manufacturers recommend the fitting of a gearbox oil cooler. Check with the manufacturer as to what is suitable for your car.

Automatic transmission fluid

Automatic transmission fluid is not always readily available, especially in some of the more remote areas of Western Europe, and tourists are advised to carry an emergency supply.

BBC World Service

The BBC World Service transmits English language broadcasts which can be heard in many European countries. A full programme including current affairs, sport and music is available, with world news at approximately every hour. Most car radios operate on medium and long wave, so BBC World Service

programmes may normally be obtained in north-western Europe by tuning to the following frequencies between the times mentioned.

KHz	Metres	Summer broadcasting times – GMT	
1296	231	03.00–03.30, 17.00–19.00,	06.00–06.30, 22.00–23.15
648*	463	04.45–05.30, 11.00–16.15,	06.00–10.30, 19.00–02.15,
198	1515	02.30–03.15	23.45–04.50

*BBC 648 is Europe's first trilingual radio station. It carries World Service programmes in English for most of the day, but includes French and German sequences, news for Europe and 'English by Radio' at certain times.

In some Western European countries, it may be possible to receive BBC national services with the exception of Radio 3. For more comprehensive information on BBC transmissions throughout Europe, write to BBC World Information Centre and Shop, Bush House, Strand, London WC2B 4PH.

Boats

All boats taken abroad by road should be registered in the UK, except for very small craft to be used close inshore in France*. You must take the original Certificate of Registry with you, not a photocopy. Registration may be carried out through the Royal Yachting Association at a current fee of £10. A Helmsman's Overseas Certificate of Competence is required for Germany (Federal Republic), Italy (in some parts), Netherlands (if using a speedboat), Portugal, Spain and Yugoslavia. All applications to the Royal Yachting Association, RYA House, Romsey Road, Eastleigh, Hampshire SO5 4YA ☎ (0703) 629962. See also *Carnet de Passages* under *Customs regulations for European Countries*, page 10–11; *Identification plate*, page 15; and *Insurance*, page 15.

In France, very small craft are exempt from registration and the dividing line falls approximately between a Laser dinghy (which should be registered) and a Topper (which need not). The precise details are available from the RYA.

Brakes

Car brakes must always be in peak condition. Check both the level in the brake fluid reservoir, and the thickness of the brake lining/pad material. The brake fluid should be completely changed in accordance with the manufacturer's instruction, or at intervals of not more than 18 months or 18,000 miles.

However, it is always advisable to change the brake fluid before starting a Continental holiday, particularly if the journey includes travelling through a hilly or mountainous area.

Breakdown (See also Country sections)

If your car breaks down, try to move it to the side of the road, or to a position where it will obstruct the traffic flow as little as possible. Place a warning triangle at the appropriate distance on the road behind the obstruction. Bear in mind road conditions and, if near or on a bend, the triangle should be placed where it is clearly visible to following traffic. If the car is fitted with hazard warning lights, these may be switched on, but remember that they will only be effective on straight roads, and will have no effect at bends or rises in the road. If the fault is electrical, the lights may not operate, and it is for these reasons that they cannot take the place of a triangle. Having first taken these precautions, seek assistance if you cannot deal with the fault yourself.

Motorists are advised to take out *AA 5-Star Service*, the overseas motoring emergency cover, which includes breakdowns and accident benefits, and personal travel insurance. It offers security and peace of mind to motorists travelling in Europe. Cover may be purchased by any motorist, although non-members pay a small additional premium. Details and brochures are available from AA Centres, or telephone 021-550 7648.

Note: Members who have not purchased *AA 5-Star Service* prior to departure, and who subsequently require assistance, may request spare parts or vehicle recovery. But the AA will require a deposit to cover estimated costs and a service fee prior to providing the service. All expenses must be reimbursed to the AA in addition to the service fee.

British Embassies/Consulates

In most European countries, there is usually more than one British Consulate, and degrees of status vary. The functions and office hours of Vice-Consulates and Honorary Consuls are naturally more restricted. Generally, Consulates (and consular sections of the Embassy) are ready to help British travellers overseas, but there are limits to what they can do. A Consulate cannot pay your hotel, medical or any other bills, nor will they do the work of travel agents, information bureaux or police. Any loss or theft of property should be reported to the local police not the Consulate, and a statement obtained confirming the loss or theft. If you still need help (such as the issue of an emergency passport or guidance on how to transfer funds), contact the Consulate. See respective *Country sections* for addresses and locations of British Embassies and Consulates.

Camping and caravanning

Information is given separately in the AA guide *Camping and Caravanning in Europe*, on sale at most AA Centres and good bookshops.

Caravan and luggage trailers

Take a list of contents, especially if any valuable or unusual equipment is being carried, as this may be required at a frontier. A towed vehicle should be readily identifiable by a plate in an accessible position showing the name of the maker of the vehicle and production or serial number. See *Identification plate* page 15. See also *Principal mountain passes* page 39.

Claims against third parties

The law and levels of damage in foreign countries are generally different to our own. It is important to remember this when considering making a claim against another motorist, arising out of an accident abroad. Certain types of claims invariably present difficulties, the most common probably relating to the recovery of car-hire charges. Rarely are they fully recoverable, and in some countries they may be drastically reduced or not recoverable at all. General damages for pain and suffering are not recoverable in certain countries, but even in those countries where they are, the level of damages is usually lower than our own.

The negotiation of claims against foreign insurers is extremely protracted, and translation of all documents slows down the process. A delay of three months between sending a letter and receiving a reply is not uncommon.

If you take out the AA's 5-*Star Service* cover, this includes a discretionary service in respect of certain matters arising abroad requiring legal assistance, including the pursuit of uninsured loss claims against third parties arising out of a road accident. In this event, members should seek guidance and/or assistance from the AA.

Cold-weather touring

If you are planning a winter tour, fit a high-temperature (winter) thermostat, and make sure that the strength of your anti-freeze mixture is correct for the low temperatures likely to be encountered.

If travelling through snow-bound regions, it is important to remember that for many resorts and passes the authorities insist on wheel chains, or spiked or studded tyres. However, as wheel chains and spiked or studded tyres can damage bare road surfaces there are limited periods when these may be used, and in certain countries the use of spiked or studded tyres is illegal. Signposts usually indicate if wheel chains or spiked or studded tyres are compulsory.

In fair weather, wheel chains or spiked or studded tyres are only necessary on the higher passes, but (as a rough guide) in severe weather you will probably need them at altitudes above 2,000ft.

If you think you will need wheel chains, it is better to take them with you from home. They may be hired from the AA, and further details are available from your nearest AA Centre. Information on hiring wheel chains (where such a service exists) in the countries where they are most needed is given in the *Country sections*.

Wheel chains fit over the driving wheels to enable them to grip on snow or icy surfaces. They are sometimes called *snow chains* or *anti-skid chains*. Full-length chains which fit right round the tyre are the most satisfactory, but they must be fitted correctly. Check that the

TURN EVERY CROSSING INTO A CRUISE.

Cruise across to the Continent with P&O European Ferries.

That way, your holiday will start as soon as you step aboard.

On our 2 superferries from Dover to Calais, even the time passes quicker as you browse around the new supershop and duty free store.

On the longer crossings, you'll be able to stretch your legs in Club Class as our stewards serve you.

You can set your own course in the carvery, waiter service or self-service restaurants.

Or, snooze across in one of our luxury cabins.

We've done everything to smooth the way. So you can get your holiday off to a flying start.

Find out more in our free colour brochure from the AA or Brochure Department, P&O European Ferries, PO Box 12, Dover, Kent CT16 1LD or Tel (0304) 203388.

P&O
European Ferries

Dover-Calais, Dover-Boulogne, Dover-Zeebrugge, Dover-Ostend, Felixstowe-Zeebrugge, Portsmouth-Le Havre, Portsmouth-Cherbourg, Cairnryan-Larne.

chains do not foul your vehicle bodywork; if your vehicle has front-wheel drive, then put the steering on full lock while checking. If your vehicle has radial tyres, it is essential that you contact the manufacturers of your vehicle and tyres for their recommendations to avoid damage to your tyres. Chains should only be used when compulsory or necessary, as prolonged use on hard surfaces will damage the tyres. See also *Country sections* for *Andorra, Austria, France, Germany, Italy, Norway, Portugal, Sweden, Switzerland* and *Yugoslavia*.

Spiked or studded tyres are sometimes called *snow tyres*. They are tyres with rugged treads on which spikes or studs have been fitted. For the best grip, they should be fitted to all wheels. The correct type of spiked or studded winter tyres will generally be more effective than chains. See also *Country sections*.

Note: The above guidelines do not apply where extreme winter conditions prevail. For extreme conditions it is doubtful whether the cost of preparing a car normally used in the UK would be justified for a short period. However, the AA's *Technical Services Department* can advise on specific enquiries.

Compulsory equipment

All countries have different regulations on how vehicles should be equipped, but generally domestic laws are not enforced on visiting foreigners. However, where a country considers aspects of safety or other factors are involved, they will impose some regulations on visitors, and these will be mentioned in the *Country sections*.

Crash, or safety helmets

All countries in this guide require visiting motorcyclists and their passengers to wear crash, or safety helmets (except Belgium, where they are strongly recommended).

Credit/charge cards

Credit/charge cards may be used abroad, but their use is subject to the 'conditions of use' set out by the issuing company who, on request, will provide full information. Establishments display the symbols of cards they accept, but it is not possible to provide any detailed lists. However, hotels which accept credit/charge cards are indicated in the gazetteer; see page 50 for further information. See also *Country*

sections under *Petrol* for information on using credit cards to purchase fuel.

Currency and banking hours (See also *Country sections*)

There is no limit to the amount of sterling notes you may take abroad, but it is best to carry only enough currency for immediate expenses.

As many countries have regulations controlling the import and export of currency, you are advised to consult your bank for full information before making final arrangements.

Customs regulations for European countries (other than the UK)

Bona fide visitors to the countries listed in this guide may generally assume that they can *temporarily* import *personal articles* duty free, providing the following conditions are met:

a   that the articles are for personal use, and are not to be sold or otherwise disposed of;

b   that they may be considered as being in use, and in keeping with the personal status of the importer;

c   that they are taken out when the importer leaves the country, or

d   that the goods stay for no more than 6 months in any 12-month period, whichever is earlier.

All dutiable articles must be declared when you enter a country, otherwise you will be liable to penalties. If you are taking a large number of personal effects with you, it would be wise to prepare an inventory to present to the Customs authorities on entry. Customs officers may withhold concessions at any time, and ask the traveller to deposit enough money to cover possible duty, especially on portable items of apparent high value such as television sets, radios, cassette recorders, pocket calculators, musical instruments, etc, all of which must be declared. Any deposit paid (for which a receipt must be obtained) is likely to be high; it is recoverable (but only at the entry point at which it was paid) on leaving the country and exporting the item. Alternatively, the Customs may enter the item in the traveller's passport; in these circumstances, it is important to remember to get the entry cancelled when the item is exported. Duty and tax-free allowances may not apply (except in EEC countries) if the traveller enters the country more than once a month, or is under 17 years of age (an alternative age may apply in some countries). However, residents of the Channel Islands and

the Isle of Man do not benefit from EEC allowances due to their fiscal regimes.

A *temporarily imported motor vehicle, caravan, boat* or any other type of *trailer* is subject to strict control on entering a country, attracting Customs duty and a variety of taxes; much depends upon the circumstances and the period of the import, and also upon the status of the importer. People entering a country in which they are not resident, with a private vehicle for holiday or recreational purposes, and intending to export the vehicle within a short period, enjoy special privileges, and the normal formalities are reduced to an absolute minimum in the interests of tourism. However, a Customs *Carnet de Passages en Douane* is required under certain circumstances when temporarily importing a trailer or boat into some countries (see *Country sections* for *Belgium and Luxembourg*). The *Carnet* (for which charge is made), is a valuable document issued by the AA to its members, or as part of the AA *5-Star Service* – further information is available from most AA Centres. If you are issued with a *Carnet*, you must ensure that it is returned to the AA correctly discharged in order to avoid inconvenience and expense, possibly including payment of customs charges, at a later date. A temporarily imported vehicle, etc should not:

a be left in the country after the importer has left;

b be put at the disposal of a resident of the country;

c be retained in the country longer than the permitted period;

d be lent, sold, hired, given away, exchanged or otherwise disposed of.

People entering a country with a motor vehicle for a period of generally more than six months (see also *Visas*, page 26) or to take up residence, employment, any commercial activity or with the intention of disposing of the vehicle, should seek advice concerning their position well in advance of their departure. Most AA Centres will be pleased to help.

Customs regulations for the United Kingdom

If, when leaving Britain, you *export* any items of new appearance, for example watches, items of jewellery, cameras, etc, particularly of foreign manufacture, which you bought in the UK, it is a good idea to carry the retailer's receipts with you, if they are available. In the absence of such receipts, you may be asked to make a written declaration of where the goods were obtained.

Goods obtained duty and tax free in the EEC, or duty and tax free on a ship or aircraft, or goods obtained outside the EEC	Duty and tax-free allowances	Goods obtained duty and tax paid in the EEC
	Tobacco products	
200	Cigarettes	300
	or	
100	Cigarillos	150
	or	
50	Cigars	75
	or	
250g	Tobacco	400g
	Alcoholic drinks	
2 litres	Still table wine	5 litres
1 litre	Over 22% vol. (eg spirits and strong liqueurs)	1½ litres
	or	
2 litres	Not over 22% vol (eg low strength liqueurs or fortified wines or sparkling wines)	3 litres
	or	
2 litres	Still table wine	3 litres
50g	**Perfume**	75g
250cc	**Toilet water**	375cc
£32	**Other goods** but no more than: 50 litres of beer and 25 mechanical lighters	£250

Note

i The tobacco allowances in the left-hand column are doubled for persons who live outside Europe.

ii Persons under 17 are not entitled to tobacco and drinks allowances.

The *exportation* of certain goods *from the United Kingdom* is prohibited or restricted. These include: controlled drugs; most animals, birds and some plants; firearms and ammunition; strategic and technological equipment (including computers); and items manufactured more than 50 years before the date of exportation.

When you *enter the United Kingdom*, you will pass through Customs. You must declare everything in excess of the duty and tax free allowance (see above) which you have obtained outside the United Kingdom, or on the journey, and everything previously obtained free of duty or tax in the United Kingdom. You may not mix allowances between duty-free and non-duty-free sources within each heading, except for alcohol, which allows, for example, 1 litre of

duty and tax-free spirits in addition to 5 litres of duty and tax-paid still wine. Currently, as a concession only, travellers may use their entitlement of alcoholic drinks not over 22 per cent vol to import table wine in addition to the set table wine allowance. You must also declare any prohibited or restricted goods, and goods for commercial purposes. **Do not** be tempted to hide anything or mislead the Customs! The penalties are severe, and articles which are not properly declared may be forfeit. If articles are hidden in a vehicle, that, too, becomes liable to forfeiture. Customs officers are legally entitled to examine your luggage. Please co-operate with them if they ask to examine it. You are responsible for opening, unpacking and repacking your luggage.

The *importation* of certain goods *into the United Kingdom* is prohibited or restricted. These include: controlled drugs such as opium, morphine, heroin, cocaine, cannabis, amphetamines, barbiturates and LSD (lysergide); counterfeit currency; firearms (including gas pistols, electric shock batons and similar weapons), ammunition, explosives (including fireworks) and flick knives, swordsticks, butterfly knives and certain other offensive weapons; horror comics, indecent or obscene books, magazines, films, video tapes and other articles; animals* and birds, whether alive or dead (eg stuffed); certain articles derived from endangered species, including fur skins, ivory, reptile leather and goods made from them; meat and poultry and their products (including ham, bacon, sausage, pâté, eggs, milk and cream) but 1kg per passenger of fully cooked meat or poultry meat products in cans or other hermetically sealed containers of glass or foil (but not plastic) is permitted; plants, parts thereof and plant produce, including trees and shrubs, potatoes and certain other vegetables, fruit, bulbs and seeds; wood with bark attached; certain fish and fish eggs (whether live or dead); bees; radio transmitters (eg citizens' band radios, walkie-talkies, cordless telephones, etc) not approved for use in the United Kingdom.

---

*Note: Cats, dogs and other mammals must not be landed unless a British import licence (rabies) has previously been issued.

Customs Notice No. 1 is available to all travellers at the point of entry, or on the boat, and contains useful information of which returning tourists should be aware. Details for drivers going through the red and green *channels are enclosed in Notice No. 1.* Copies of this can be obtained from HM Customs and Excise, CDE, Room 201, Dorset House, Stamford Street, London SE1 9PS.

Dimensions and weight restrictions

For an ordinary private car, a height limit of 4 metres and a width limit of 2.50 metres is generally imposed. However, see *Country sections* for full details. Apart from a laden weight limit imposed on commercial vehicles, every vehicle, private or commercial, has an individual weight limit. For information on how this affects private cars, see *Overloading* page 18. See also *Major road tunnels*, page 36, as some dimensions are restricted by the shape of tunnels. If you have any doubts, consult the AA.

Direction indicators

All direction indicators should be working at 60–120 flashes per minute. Most standard car-flasher units will be overloaded by the extra lamps of a caravan or trailer and a special heavy duty unit or a relay device should be fitted.

Drinking and driving

There is only one safe rule – **if you drink, don't drive**. The laws are strict and penalties severe.

Driving licence and International Driving Permit

You should carry your national driving licence with you when motoring abroad. If an International Driving Permit (IDP) is necessary (see *IDP requirements* below), it is strongly recommended that you still carry your national driving licence. In most of the countries covered by this guide, a visitor may use a temporarily imported car or motorcycle without formality for up to three months with a valid full licence (not provisional) issued in the United Kingdom or Republic of Ireland, subject to the minimum age requirements of the country concerned (see *Country sections*). If you wish to drive a hired or borrowed car in the country you are visiting, make local enquiries.

If your licence is due to expire before your

anticipated return, it should be renewed in good time prior to your departure. The Driver and Vehicle Licensing Centre (in Northern Ireland the Licensing Authority) will accept an application two months before the expiry of your old licence.

An **International Driving Permit (IDP)** is an internationally recognised document which enables the holder to drive for a limited period in countries where their national licences are not recognised (see *Austrian, Greek,* and *Spanish Country sections* under *Driving licence*). The permit, for which a statutory charge is made, is issued by the AA to an applicant who holds a valid full British driving licence and who is over 18 years old. It is valid for 12 months and cannot be renewed. Application forms are available from any AA Centre. The permit cannot be issued to the holder of a foreign licence, who must apply to the appropriate authority in the country where the driving licence was issued. *Note:* Residents of the Republic of Ireland, Channels Islands and the Isle of Man should apply to their local AA Centre for the relevant application form.

'E' Card

This card may be displayed on the windscreen of your vehicle to assist the traffic flow across certain frontiers within the European Community. Full conditions of use are given on the card which may be obtained from AA Centres.

Electrical information

General: The public electricity supply in Europe is predominantly AC (alternating current) of 220 volts (50 cycles), but can be as low as 110 volts. In some isolated areas, low voltage DC (direct current) is provided. European circular two-pin plugs and screw-type bulbs are usually the rule. Useful electrical adaptors (not voltage transformers) which can be used in Continental shaver points and light bulb sockets are available in the United Kingdom, usually from the larger electrical appliance retailers.

Vehicle: Check that all the connections are sound, and that the wiring is in good condition. If problems arise with the charging system, it is essential to obtain the services of a qualified auto-electrician.

Emergency messages to tourists

In cases of emergency, the AA will assist in the passing on of messages to tourists in Austria, Belgium, Denmark, France, Germany (Federal Republic of), Gibraltar, Greece, Irish Republic, Italy, Luxembourg, Netherlands, Norway, Portugal, Spain, Sweden, Switzerland and Yugoslavia.

The AA can arrange for messages to be published in overseas editions of the *Daily Mail*, and in an extreme emergency, (death or serious illness concerning next-of-kin) can arrange to have personal messages broadcast on overseas radio networks. Anyone wishing to use this service should contact their nearest AA Centre.

Before you leave home, make sure your relatives understand the procedures to follow if an emergency occurs.

If you have any reason to expect a message from home*, information about radio frequencies and broadcast times are given in the *Country sections*. If you require further information, contact the tourist office or motoring club of the country you are staying in.

No guarantee can be given, either by the AA or by the *Daily Mail*, to trace the person concerned, and no responsibility can be accepted for the authenticity of messages.

*Emergency 'SOS' messages concerning the dangerous illness of a close relative may be broadcast on BBC Radio 4 long wave transmitters on 1515m/198KHz at 06.59 and 17.59 hrs BST (see *BBC World Service*, page 6). Such messages should be arranged through the local police or hospital authorities.

Engine and mechanical

Consult your vehicle handbook for servicing intervals. Unless the engine oil has been changed recently, drain and refill with fresh oil and fit a new filter. Deal with any significant leaks by tightening up loose nuts and bolts and renewing faulty joints and seals.

Brands and grades of *engine oil* familiar to the British motorist are usually available in Western Europe, but may be difficult to find in remote country areas. When available, they will be much more expensive than in the UK and generally packed in 2-litre cans (3½ pints). Motorists can usually assess the normal

consumption of their car, and are strongly advised to carry what oil they may require for the trip.

If you suspect that there is anything wrong with the engine, however insignificant it may seem, it should be dealt with straight away. Even if everything seems in order, do not neglect such common-sense precautions as checking valve clearances, sparking plugs and contact breaker points where fitted, and making sure that the distributor cap is sound. The fan belt should be checked for fraying and slackness. If any of these items are showing signs of wear, you should replace them.

Any obvious mechanical defects should be attended to at once. Look particularly for play in steering connections and wheel bearings and, where applicable, ensure that they are adequately greased. A car that has covered many miles will have absorbed a certain amount of dirt into the fuel system, and as breakdowns are often caused by dirt, it is essential that all filters (fuel and air) should be cleaned or renewed.

Owners should seriously reconsider towing a caravan with a car that has already given appreciable service. Hard driving on motorways and in mountainous country puts an extra strain on ageing parts, and items such as a burnt-out clutch can be very expensive.

The cooling system should be checked for leaks, the correct proportion of anti-freeze ascertained and any perished hoses or suspect parts replaced.

Eurocheques

The *Eurocheque* scheme is a flexible money-transfer system operated by a network of European banks. All the major UK banks are part of the Uniform Eurocheque scheme, and they can provide a multi-currency chequebook enabling you to write cheques in the currency of the country you are visiting. Most European banks will cash Eurocheques and retailer acceptance is widespread (over 5,000,000 through Europe). Approach your bankers well in advance of your departure for further information.

Ferry crossings

From Britain, the shortest sea crossing from a southern port to the Continent is the obvious but not always the best choice, depending on how the Continental port is serviced by main roads leading to your destination. Your starting point is important, too, because, if you have a long journey to a southern port, a service from an eastern port might be more convenient. It is worth considering the *Motorail* service to the south to save time and possibly an overnight stop. In some circumstances, the south-western ports may offer a convenient service. Before making bookings, it is worthwhile seeking advice so that your journey is as economic and as comfortable as possible. Similarly, for crossings to Ireland, there are several departure points along the west coast, and much depends on your starting location and ultimate destination for the most convenient ferry service.

The AA provides a full information service on all sea, motorail and hovercraft services, and instant confirmation is available on many by ringing one of the numbers listed below (Mon–Fri, 09.00–17.00hrs). Ring these numbers, too, if you want information and booking on Continental car-sleeper and ferry services.

UK ☎ 021-550 7848
Republic of Ireland ☎ *Dublin (0001) 833656*

Fire extinguisher

It is a wise precaution (compulsory in Greece) to equip your vehicle with a fire extinguisher when motoring abroad. A fire extinguisher may be purchased from the AA.

First-aid kit

It is another wise precaution (compulsory in Austria, Greece and Yugoslavia) to equip your vehicle with a first-aid kit when motoring abroad. A first-aid kit may be purchased from the AA.

Holiday traffic

For information relating to holiday traffic, see

Road conditions, page 24 and the Austrian, French, German, Spanish and Swiss Country sections under the Roads including holiday traffic heading. Further information on holiday traffic can be obtained from Teletext 'Oracle', the AA's Recorded Information Directory and AA Information Centres.

Horn

In built-up areas, the general rule is not to use horns unless safety demands it; in many large towns and resorts, as well as in areas indicated by the international sign (a horn in a red circle, crossed through), the use of the horn is totally prohibited. See also Country sections for Austria, Gibraltar, Ireland, Italy and Luxembourg.

Identification plate

If a boat, caravan or trailer is taken abroad, it must have a unique chassis number for identification purposes. If your boat, caravan or trailer does not have a number, an identification plate may be purchased from the AA. Boats registered on the Small Ships Register (see Boats page 7) are issued with a unique number which must be permanently displayed.

Insurance, including caravan insurance

Motor insurance is compulsory by law in all the countries covered in this guide, and you must make sure you are adequately covered for all countries in which you will travel. Temporary policies are available at all frontiers, except the Republic of Ireland, but this is a very expensive way of effecting cover. It is best to seek the advice of your insurer regarding the extent of cover and full terms of your existing policy. Some insurers may not be willing to offer cover in the countries that you intend to visit, and it may be necessary to seek a new, special policy for the trip from another insurer. If you have

any difficulty, AA Insurance Services will be pleased to help you. *Note:* Extra insurance is recommended when visiting Spain (see Spain–Bail Bond). Third-party insurance is compulsory for boats in Italy and Switzerland (see Italy and Switzerland–Boats) and is recommended elsewhere for all boats used abroad. It is compulsory for trailers temporarily imported into Austria (see Austria–Insurance).

An international motor insurance certificate or Green Card is recognised in most countries as evidence that you are covered to the minimum extent demanded by law. Compulsory in Andorra and Yugoslavia, the AA **strongly advises its use elsewhere**. It will be issued by your own Insurer upon payment of an additional premium, although some insurers now provide one free of charge too existing policy holders. A Green Card extends your UK policy cover to apply in those countries you intend visiting. It will name the countries for which it is valid. The document should be signed on receipt as it will not be accepted without the signature of the Insured. Green Cards are internationally recognised by police and other authorities, and may save a great deal of inconvenience in the event of an accident. If you are towing a caravan or trailer, it will need separate insurance, and mention on your Green Card. Remember, the cover on a caravan or on a trailer associated with a Green Card is normally limited to third-party towing risks, so a separate policy (see AA Caravan Plus, below) is advisable to cover accidental damage, fire or theft.

In accordance with a Common Market Directive, the production and inspection of Green Cards at the frontiers of Common Market countries are no longer legal requirements, and this principle has been accepted by other European countries who are not members of the EEC. However, the fact that Green Cards will not be inspected does not remove the necessity of having insurance cover as required by law in the countries concerned.

Motorists can obtain expert advice through AA Insurance Services for all types of insurance. Several special schemes have been arranged with leading insurers to enable motorists to obtain wide insurance cover at economic premiums. One of these schemes, AA Caravan Plus, includes damage cover for caravans and their contents, including personal effects. While detached from the towing vehicle, protection against your legal liability to other persons arising out of the use of the

caravan is also provided. Cover is also extended to most European countries for up to 60 days in any period of insurance without extra charge. *AA Caravan Plus* also provides cover for camping equipment. Full details of *AA Caravan Plus* may be obtained from any AA Centre or direct from AA Insurance Services Ltd, PO Box 2AA, Newcastle upon Tyne NE99 2AA.

Finally, make sure that you are covered against damage in transit (eg on the ferry or motorail). Most comprehensive motor insurance policies provide adequate cover for transit between ports in the UK, but need to be extended to give this cover if travelling abroad. You are advised to check this aspect with your insurer before setting off on your journey.

International distinguishing sign

An international distinguishing sign of the approved pattern (oval with black letters on a white background), and size (GB – at least 6.9in by 4.5in), must be displayed on a vertical surface at the rear of your vehicle (and caravan or trailer if you are towing one). These distinguishing signs indicate the country of registration of the vehicle. On the Continent checks are made to ensure that a vehicle's nationality plate is in order. Fines are imposed for failing to display a nationality plate, or for not displaying the correct nationality plate; see *Police fines*, page 21).

Level crossings

Practically all level crossings are indicated by international signs. Most guarded ones are the lifting barrier type, sometimes with bells or flashing lights to give a warning of an approaching train.

Lights (See also Country sections)

For driving abroad (except in the Republic of Ireland), headlights should be altered so that the dipped beam does not dazzle oncoming drivers. The alteration can be made by fitting headlamp converters (PVC mask sheets) or beam deflectors (clip-on lenses), on sale at AA Centres. However, it is important to remove the headlamp converters or beam deflectors as soon as you return to the UK.

Dipped headlights should also be used in conditions of fog, snowfall, heavy rain, and when passing through a tunnel, irrespective of its length and lighting. In some countries, police will wait at the end of a tunnel to check this requirement.

Headlight flashing is used only as a warning of approach or as a passing signal at night. In other circumstances, it is accepted as a sign of irritation, and should be used with caution to avoid misunderstanding. It is a wise precaution (compulsory in Spain and Yugoslavia and recommended in France, Italy and Norway) to equip your vehicle with a set of replacement bulbs when motoring abroad. An AA Emergency Auto Bulb Kit suitable for most makes of car can be purchased from the AA. Alternatively a Spares Kit or Motoring Emergency Pack, both of which contain spare bulbs, may be hired from the AA.

Note: Remember to have the lights set to compensate for the load being carried.

Liquified Petroleum Gas (LPG)

The availability of this gas in Europe makes a carefully planned tour, with a converted vehicle, limited but feasible. The gas is retailed by several companies in Europe, who will supply information on where their product may be purchased. Motorists regularly purchasing this fuel in the UK may be able to get lists of European addresses from their retailer.

Hours of opening of filling stations vary from country to country, but generally they operate during normal business hours, except for holidays and saints' days. At weekends LPG users are well advised to fill up on Saturdays and not rely on Sunday opening. A reducer nipple should be carried as a precautionary measure – this accessory can normally be obtained from the importer/manufacturer of the LPG unit at minimal cost.

When booking a ferry crossing, it is advisable to point out to the booking agent/ferry company that the vehicle runs on a dual-fuel system.

Medical treatment

Travellers who normally take certain medicines should ensure they have a sufficient supply to last the trip, since they may be very difficult to get abroad.

Those with certain medical conditions (diabetes or coronary artery diseases, for example) should get a letter from their doctor giving treatment details. Some Continental doctors will understand a letter written in English, but it is better to have it translated into the language of the country you intend to visit. The AA cannot make such a translation.

Travellers who, for legitimate health reasons, carry drugs or appliances (eg hypodermic syringe) may have difficulty with Customs or other authorities. Or it may be difficult to make hotel or restaurant staff understand any special dietary requirements. People with special conditions should carry translations of specific requirements to facilitate appropriate treatment and passage through Customs.

The National Health Service is available in the United Kingdom only, and medical expenses incurred overseas cannot generally be reimbursed by the United Kingdom Government. There are reciprocal health agreements with most of the countries covered by this guide, but you should not rely exclusively on these arrangements, as the cover provided under the respective national schemes is not always comprehensive. (For instance, the cost of bringing a person back to the UK in the event of illness or death is never covered, nor is the cost of any medical care needed as a result of a road accident in the Republic of Ireland.) The full costs of medical care must be paid in Andorra, Liechtenstein, Monaco, San Marino and Switzerland. Therefore, as facilities and financial cover can vary considerably, you are strongly advised to take out comprehensive and adequate insurance cover before leaving the UK (such as that offered under the *AA's 5-Star Service*, personal insurance section).

Urgent medical treatment in the event of an accident or unforeseen illness can be obtained by most visitors, free of charge or at reduced cost, from the health care schemes of those countries with whom the UK has health-care arrangements. Details are in the Department of Health leaflet *SA40, The Travellers' Guide to Health – Before You Go*. Free copies are available from local offices of the Department of Social Security or from Health Publications Unit, No 2 Site, Manchester Road, Heywood, Lancs OL10 2PZ. In some of these countries, visitors can obtain urgently needed treatment by showing their UK passport, but in others an NHS medical card must be produced, and in most European Community countries a certificate of entitlement (*E111*) is necessary. A form to obtain this certificate is included in the DH *SA40*. Applicants should allow at least one month for the form to be processed, although in an emergency the *E111* can be obtained over the counter of the local DH office (residents of the Republic of Ireland must apply to their Regional Health Board for an *E111*). The DH *SA40* also gives advice about health precautions and international vaccination requirements.

Further information about health care precautions and how to deal with an emergency abroad is given in the DH leaflet *SA41, The Travellers' Guide to Health – While You're Away*. A free copy is also available from Health Publications Unit, No 2 Site, Manchester Road, Heywood, Lancs OL10 2PZ or by ringing ☎0800 555777.

Minibus

A minibus constructed and equipped to carry 10 or more persons (including the driver*) and used outside the UK is subject to the regulations governing international bus and coach journeys. This will generally mean that the vehicle must be fitted with a tachograph, and documentation, in the form of a driver's certificate, model control document and waybill obtained. For vehicles registered in Great Britain (England, Scotland and Wales), contact the authorities as follows:

a   for driver's certificate and details of approved tachograph installers, apply to the local Traffic Area Office of the Department of Transport;

b   for model control document and waybill, apply to the Bus and Coach Council, Sardinia House, 52 Lincoln's Inn Fields, London WC2A 3LZ ☎01 (071 from 6 May)-831 7546.

For vehicles registered in Northern Ireland, contact the Department of the Environment for

Northern Ireland, Road Transport Department, Upper Galwally, Belfast BT8 4FY ☎(0232) 649044.

For vehicles registered in the Republic of Ireland, contact the Department of Labour, Mespil Road, Dublin 4 for details about tachographs, and the Government Publications Sales Office, Molesworth Street, Dublin 2 for information about documentation.

The above authorities should be contacted well in advance of your departure.

Note: A minibus driver must be at least 21 years of age and hold a full driving licence valid for group 'A' or, if automatic transmission, group 'B'.

Mirrors

When driving abroad on the right, it is essential (as when driving on the left in the UK and Republic of Ireland) to have clear all-round vision. Ideally, external rear-view mirrors should be fitted to both sides of your vehicle, but certainly on the left, to allow for driving on the right.

Motoring clubs in Europe

The *Alliance Internationale de Tourisme (AIT)* is the largest confederation of touring associations in the world, and it is through this body that the AA is able to offer its members the widest possible touring information service. Its membership consists not of individuals, but of associations or groups of associations with an interest in touring. The Alliance was formed in 1919 – the AA was a founder member, and is represented on its Administrative Council and Management Committee. The General Secretariat of the *AIT* is in Geneva.

Tourists visiting a country where there is an AIT club may use its touring advisory service upon furnishing proof of membership of their home *AIT* club. AA members making overseas trips should, whenever possible, seek the advice of the AA before setting out, and should only approach the overseas *AIT* clubs when necessary.

Motorways (See also Country sections)

Most of the countries in this guide have motorways, varying from a few short stretches to a comprehensive system. Tolls are payable on many of them. Motorway leaflets (containing information on tolls, etc for France, Italy,

Portugal and Spain are available to AA members. See also *Tolls*, page 25.

Orange badge scheme for disabled drivers

Some European countries which operate national schemes of parking concessions for the disabled have reciprocal arrangements whereby disabled visitors can enjoy the concessions of the host country by displaying the badge of their own scheme. Information, where available, is given in the appropriate *Country section*. However, in some countries responsibility for introducing the concessions rests with individual local authorities, and in some cases they may not be generally available. Under these circumstances, badge holders should enquire locally, as they should whenever they are in doubt as to their entitlement. As in the UK, the arrangements apply only to badge holders themselves, and the concessions are not for the benefit of able-bodied friends or relatives. A non-entitled person who seeks to take advantage of the concessions in Europe by wrongfully displaying an orange badge will be liable to whatever penalties apply for unlawful parking in the country in question.

Overloading

This can create safety risks, and in most countries committing such an offence can involve *on-the-spot* fines (see *Police fines*, page 21). And it would be very inconvenient, because if your car was stopped because of overloading you would not be allowed to proceed until the load had been reduced. The maximum loaded weight and its distribution between front and rear axles are decided by the vehicle manufacturer, and if your owner's handbook does not gives these facts you should contact the manufacturer direct. There is a public weighbridge in all districts, and when the car is fully loaded (not forgetting the passengers, of course), use this to check that the vehicle is within the limits. Load your vehicle carefully so that no lights, reflectors or number plates are masked, and the driver's view is not impaired. All luggage loaded on a roof rack must be tightly secured, and should not upset

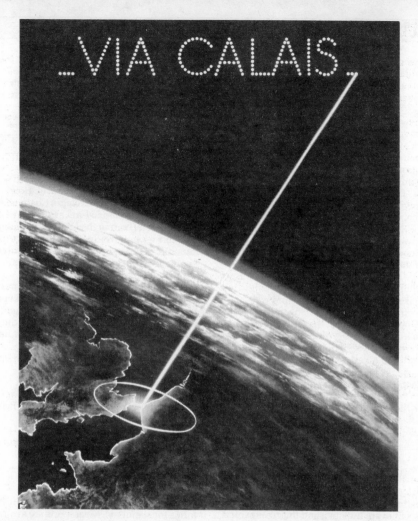

CALAIS—So close you could touch it. Once the only landfall for Britons bound for the Continent and far and away the best route today.

Seven modern jumbo size car ferries plus giant hovercraft provide a choice of over 100 crossings daily during the Summer and never less than 58 off Peak.

Dover Calais, the shortest sea route—from 75 minutes by car ferry and from 30 minutes by hovercraft.

By far the <u>fastest</u> and the <u>best</u> way to go and come back

the stability of the vehicle. Any projections beyond the front, rear, or sides of a vehicle, that might not be noticed by other drivers, must be clearly marked.

Overtaking

When overtaking on roads with two lanes or more in each direction, always signal your intention in good time, and after the manoeuvre, signal and return to the inside lane. Do NOT remain in any other lane. Failure to comply with this regulation, particularly in France, will incur an *on-the-spot* fine (see *Police Fines*, page 21).

Always overtake on the left (on the right in the Republic of Ireland) and use your horn to warn the driver of the vehicle being overtaken (except in areas where the use of the horn is prohibited). Do not overtake while being overtaken or when a vehicle behind is preparing to overtake. Do not overtake at level crossings, intersections, the crest of a hill or at pedestrian crossings. When being overtaken, keep well to the right (left in the Republic of Ireland) and reduce speed if necessary – *never increase speed*. See also *Overtaking* under *Luxembourg, Portugal, Spain* and *Sweden*.

Parking *(See also Country sections)*

Parking is a problem everywhere in Europe, and the police are extremely strict with offenders. Heavy fines are inflicted, and unaccompanied offending cars can be towed away. Besides being inconvenient, heavy charges are imposed for the recovery of impounded vehicles. Find out about local parking regulations and try to understand all relative signs. As a rule, always park on the right-hand side of the road (left-hand side in the Republic of Ireland) or at an authorised place. As far as possible, park off the main carriageway, but not on cycle tracks or tram tracks.

Passengers *(See also Country sections)*

It is an offence in all countries to carry more passengers in a car than the vehicle is constructed to seat, but some have regulations as to how the passengers shall be seated, particularly in the case of young children. The

paragraph entitled 'Children in Cars' in the Country Sections give full details.

For passenger-carrying vehicles constructed and equipped to carry more than 10 passengers including the driver, there are special regulations. See *Minibus* page 17).

Passports

Each person must hold, or be named on, an *up-to-date* passport valid for all the countries through which he intends to travel. However, the UK, the Republic of Ireland, Channel Islands and Isle of Man form a Common Travel Area. Persons born in the UK do not require a passport when travelling from the UK to the Republic of Ireland; similarly, citizens of the Republic of Ireland may travel to the UK without holding a passport.

Passports should be carried at all times and, as an extra precaution, a separate note kept of the number, date and place of issue. There are various types of British passport, including the standard or regular passport and the limited British Visitor's Passport.

Standard UK passports are issued to British Nationals, ie British Citizens, British Dependent Territories Citizens, British Overseas Citizens, British Nationals (Overseas), British Subjects, and British Protected Persons. Normally issued for a period of 10 years, a standard UK passport is valid for travel to all countries in the world. A related passport may cover the holder and children under 16. Children under 16 may be issued with a separate passport valid for five years and renewable for a further five years on application. Full information and application forms for standard UK passports are available from a main post office or from one of the Passport Offices in Belfast, Douglas (Isle of Man), Glasgow, Liverpool, London, Newport (Gwent), Peterborough, St Helier (Jersey) and St Peter Port (Guernsey). Application for a standard passport should be made to the Passport Office appropriate for the area concerned, allowing at least one month, or between February and August (when most people apply for passports), three months for passport formalities to be completed, and should be accompanied by the necessary documents and fees.

British Visitor's Passports are issued to British Citizens, British Dependent Territories Citizens or British Overseas Citizens over the age of eight, resident in the UK, Isle of Man or Channel Islands. Valid for one year only and

acceptable for travel in Western Europe and West Berlin, they cannot be used for overland travel through the German Democratic Republic (East Germany) to West Berlin. A British Visitor's Passport issued to cover the holder, spouse and children under 16 may only be used by the first person named on the passport to travel alone. Children under eight cannot have their own Visitor's Passport. Full information and application forms may be obtained from main post offices in Great Britain (England, Scotland and Wales) or Passport Offices in the Channel Islands, Isle of Man and Northern Ireland. However, Visitor's Passports or application forms for Visitor's Passports are NOT obtainable from Passport Offices in Great Britain. All applications for a Visitor's Passport must be submitted in person to a main post office or Passport Office as appropriate. Provided the documents are in order and the fee is paid, the passport is issued immediately.

Irish citizens resident in the Dublin Metropolitan area or in Northern Ireland should apply to the Passport Office, Dublin; if resident elsewhere in the Irish Republic, they should apply through the nearest Garda station. Irish citizens resident in Britain should apply to the Irish Embassy in London.

Petrol (See also Country sections)

In Western Europe, and indeed throughout the world, grades of petrol compare favourably with those in the UK. Internationally known brands are usually available on main tourist and international routes, but in remote districts familiar brands may not be readily available. The minimum amount of petrol which may be purchased is usually five litres (just over one gallon). You should keep the petrol tank topped up, particularly in remote areas or if you want to make an early start when garages may be closed, but use a lockable filler cap as a security measure. Some garages may close between 12.00 and 15.00hrs for lunch. Generally, petrol is readily available, and in most of the countries featured in this guide, you will find that petrol stations on motorways provide a 24-hour service.

In the UK, motorists use either unleaded or leaded fuel as recommended by the vehicle manufacturer, and this is related to the minimum octane requirement. For unleaded this usually will be the single grade, Premium of 95 octane, but for leaded the recommendation may be 90 octane – 2 star, 93 Octane – 3 star or 97 octane – 4-star.

Overseas both unleaded and leaded petrol is graded as Normal and Super and the local definitions are given in the respective Country sections, together with the octane ratings. You should be careful to use the recommended type of fuel, particularly if your car has a catalytic converter, and the octane grade should be the same or higher. If your car is designed only for leaded petrol do not panic if you accidentally use unleaded; it will not do any harm, but ensure that the next fill is of the correct type and grade. A low lead petrol is being sold in Denmark, Norway and Sweden, but we suggest that this is only used if you know that your car is suitable for unleaded petrol. Any queries regarding the suitability of a vehicle for the different fuels should be directed to the vehicle manufacturer or his agent. A leaflet containing further information Unleaded Petrol in Europe is available through AA Centres.

Petrol prices at filling stations on motorways will be higher than elsewhere; self-service pumps will be slightly cheaper. Although petrol prices are not quoted, the current position can be checked with the AA. Petrol price concessions in the form of petrol coupons are available for Italy and Yugoslavia (see these Country sections under Petrol) – check with the AA for the latest position.

The petrol contained in a vehicle tank may be imported duty-free. In some countries, an additional quantity in cans may be imported duty-free, while others impose a duty or forbid the carrying of petrol in cans in a vehicle; see Country sections for further information. If you intend carrying a reserve supply of petrol in a can, remember that on sea and air ferries and European car-sleeper trains, operators insist that spare cans must be empty. *Note:* A roof-rack laden with luggage increases petrol consumption, so take this into consideration when calculating mileage per gallon.

Photography

Photography in European countries is generally allowed without restriction, with the exception of photographs taken within the vicinity of military or government establishments.

Signs are usually prominent where the use of cameras is prohibited, and are often a picture of a camera crossed by a diagonal line.

Police fines

Some countries impose on-the-spot fines for minor traffic offences, which vary in amount

according to the offence committed and the country concerned. Other countries, eg France, impose an immediate deposit, and subsequently levy a fine which may be the same as, or greater or lesser than, this sum. Fines are either paid in cash to the police or at a local post office against a *ticket* issued by the police. They must usually be paid in the currency of the country concerned, and can vary in amount from £3–£690 (approximately). The reason for the fines is to penalise and, at the same time, keep minor motoring offences out of the courts. Disputing the fine usually leads to a court appearance, delays and additional expense. If the fine is not paid, legal proceedings will usually follow. Some countries immobilise vehicles until a fine is paid, and may sell it to pay the penalty imposed.

Once paid, a fine cannot be recovered, but a receipt should always be obtained as proof of payment. AA members who need assistance in any motoring matter involving local police should apply to the legal department of the relevant national motoring organisation.

Pollution

Tourists should be aware that pollution of the sea-water at European coastal resorts, including the Mediterranean, may still represent a severe health hazard, although the general situation has improved in recent years. A number of countries publish detailed information on the quality of their bathing beaches, including maps, which are available from national authorities. Furthermore, in many, though not all, popular resorts where the water quality may present dangers, signs (generally small) are erected, which forbid bathing. These signs are as follows:

	French
No bathing	*Défense de se baigner*
Bathing prohibited	*Il est défendu de se baigner*

	Italian
No bathing	*Vietato bagnàrsi*
Bathing prohibited	*È vietato bagnàrsi*

	Spanish
No bathing	*Prohibido bañarse*
Bathing prohibited	*Se prohibe bañarse*

Postcheques (See also *Country sections*)

Girobank current account holders who have a cheque guarantee card can use the *Girobank*

Postcheque service when travelling in any of the countries covered by this guide. The service enables account holders to cash Postcheques, up to the local currency equivalent of about £100, at most post offices. Further information may be obtained from: International Division, Girobank plc, Bootle, Merseyside GIR 0AA. ☎051-933 3330.

Poste restante

If you are uncertain of having a precise address, you can be contacted through the local *poste restante*. Before leaving the United Kingdom, notify your friends of your approximate whereabouts abroad at given times. If you expect mail, call with your passport at the main post office of the town where you are staying. To ensure that the arrival of correspondence will coincide with your stay, your correspondent should check with the Post Office before posting, as delivery times differ throughout Europe, and appropriate allowance must be made. It is most important that the recipient's name be written in full, for example: Mr Lazarus Perkins, Poste Restante, Turnhout, Belgium.
Do not use 'Esq'.
Italy Correspondence can be addressed 'c/o post office', by adding *Fermo in Posta* to the name of the locality. It will be handed over at the local central post office upon identification of the addressee by passport.
Spain Letters should be addressed as follows: Name of addressee, *Liste de Correos*, name of town or village, name of province in brackets, if necessary. Letters can be collected from the main post office in the town concerned upon identification of the addressee by passport.

For all other countries, letters should be addressed as in the example.

Priority including roundabouts
(See also *Country sections*)

The general rule is to *give way to traffic entering a junction from the right* (except in the Republic of Ireland), but this is sometimes varied at roundabouts (see below). This is one aspect of European driving which may cause British drivers the most confusion, because their whole training and experience makes it unnatural. Road signs indicate priority or loss of priority, and tourists must be sure that they understand such signs.

Great care should be taken at intersections, and tourists should never rely on receiving the

right of way, particularly in small towns and villages where local traffic, often slow-moving, such as farm tractors, etc, will assume right of way regardless of oncoming traffic. Always give way to public service and military vehicles. Blind or disabled people, funerals and marching columns must always be allowed right of way. Vehicles such as buses and coaches carrying large numbers of passengers will expect, and should be allowed, priority.

Generally, priority at roundabouts is given to vehicles *entering* the roundabout unless signposted to the contrary (see *France – Priority including Roundabouts*). This is a complete reversal of the United Kingdom and Republic of Ireland rule, and particular care should be exercised when manoeuvring while circulating in an anti-clockwise direction on a roundabout. It is advisable to keep to the outside lane on a roundabout, if possible, to make your exit easier.

Public holidays
(See also Country sections)

Public holidays (when banks, offices and shops are closed) vary from country to country, but generally fall into two categories: those which are fixed on the calendar by some national festival or religious date and those which are movable. The latter, usually religious, are based on a movable Easter Sunday, and the dates are given in the *Country sections*. For information about annual holidays and festivals, contact the appropriate Tourist Office; see under *Tourist information* in *Country section* for address.

Radio telephones/Citizens' band radios and transmitters in tourist cars abroad

Many countries exercise controls on the temporary importation and subsequent use of radio transmitters and radio telephones. So if your vehicle contains such equipment, whether fitted or portable, you should contact the AA for guidance.

Registration document

You must carry the original vehicle registration document with you. If, for any reason, your registration document has to be sent to the licensing authorities, you should remember that processing can take some while and the document may not be available in time for your departure. Under these circumstances, a *Certificate of Registration (V379)* will normally be issued to cover the vehicle for international circulation purposes. It can be obtained free from your nearest Vehicle Registration Office upon production of proof of identity (eg driving licence) and proof of ownership (eg bill of sale).

If you plan to use a borrowed, hired or leased vehicle, you should be aware that:

a for a borrowed vehicle, the registration document must be accompanied by a letter of authority to use the vehicle from the registered keeper (for Yugoslavia, this letter must be countersigned by the AA; for Portugal, a special certificate is required; and this is available *free* from the AA);

b for a UK registered hired or leased vehicle, the registration document will normally be retained by the hiring company. Under those circumstances, a *Hired/Leased Vehicle Certificate (VE103A)*, which may be purchased from the AA, should be used in its place (for Portugal, the certificate should be accompanied by an officially authenticated photocopy of the registration document).

Religious services

Refer to your religious organisation in the British Isles. A directory of British Protestant churches in Europe, North Africa and the Middle East entitled *English Speaking Churches*, can be purchased from Intercon (Intercontinental Church Society), 175 Tower Bridge Road, London SE1 2AQ ☎01 (071 from 6 May)-407 4588. See also the Belgian, French, Dutch, Spanish and Swiss *Country sections* for details of English-speaking church services in those countries.

Report forms

We would appreciate your comments on accommodation, garages and roads to help us to prepare future publications. Please list your comments on the report forms provided at the back of this guide. The accommodation report form is for your comments on hotels and motels which you have used, whether they are listed in this guide or not.

Similarly, the garage report form is for your reports on garages which you have used. The road report form is for reporting particularly bad stretches and road works.

Road conditions

Main roads are usually in good condition, but often not finished to British standards. The camber is often steeper than that usually found in the UK, and edges may be badly corrugated or surfaces allowed to wear beyond the customary limits before being repaired. In France, such stretches are sometimes signposted *Chausée déformée*. However, there are extensive motorway systems in France, Germany and Italy, and many miles of such roads in other countries. When roads under repair are closed, you must follow diversion signs – often inadequate – such as *déviation* (French) and *Umleitung* (German). To avoid damage to windscreens or paintwork, drive slowly over loose grit, and take care when overtaking.

July and August are the peak touring months, particularly in Austria, Belgium, France and Germany when the school holidays start, and during this period motorways and main roads are heavily congested. Further information on weather conditions can be obtained from Teletext 'Oracle', the AA's Recorded Information Directory and AA Information Centres.

Throughout the summer, there is a general exodus from the cities, particularly at weekends when tourists should be prepared for congested roads and consequent hold-ups. See also *Roads* and *Motorways* in *Country sections*.

Road signs

Most road signs throughout Europe are internationally agreed, and most will be familiar. Watch for road markings – do not cross a solid white or yellow line marked on the road centre. In Belgium, there are two official languages, and signs will be in Flemish or French (see *Belgium – Roads*, for further information). In the Basque and Catalonian areas of Spain, local and national placenames appear on signposts (see *Spain – Road signs* for further information). For Germany, Greece, Netherlands and Yugoslavia, see also *Country sections*.

Rule of the road

In all countries in this guide except Ireland, drive on the right and overtake on the left; in Ireland drive on the left and overtake on the right.

Seat belts

All countries in this guide (except *Gibraltar* where they are *strongly recommended*) require wearing of seat belts. If your car is fitted with belts, in the interests of safety, wear them; you also avoid the risk of a police fine.

Spares

The problem of what spares to carry is a difficult one; it depends on the vehicle and how long you are likely to be away. However, you should consider hiring an AA Spares Kit for your car; full information about this service is available from any AA Centre. AA Emergency Windscreens are also available for hire or purchase.

In addition to the items contained in the spares kit, the following are useful:

- a pair of windscreen wiper blades;
- a torch;
- a length of electrical cable;
- a fire extinguisher;
- an inner tube of the correct type;
- a tow rope;
- a roll of insulating or adhesive tape.

Remember that when ordering spare parts for dispatch abroad, you must be able to identify them as clearly as possible (by the manufacturer's part number, if known). When ordering spares, always quote the engine and chassis numbers of your car. See also *Lights*, page 16).

Speed limits (See also *Country sections*)

It is important to observe speed limits at all times. Offenders may be fined, and driving licences confiscated on the spot, causing great inconvenience and possible expense. The limits may be varied by road signs, and where such signs are displayed, the lower limit should be accepted. At certain times, limits may also be temporarily varied, and information should be available at the frontier. It can be an offence to travel without good reason at so slow a speed as obstruct traffic flow.

Telephones (See also Country sections)

It is no more difficult to use the telephone abroad than it is at home. It only appears to be so because of unfamiliarity with the language and equipment. In most Continental countries, the ringing tone consists of a single tone of about 1–1½ seconds repeated at intervals of between 3 and 10 seconds (depending upon the country). The engaged tone is similar to the UK or faster. The information in the *Country sections* will be helpful with elementary principles when making calls from public callboxes, but try to get assistance in case you encounter language difficulties.

International Direct Dial (IDD) calls can be made from many public callboxes abroad, thus avoiding the addition of surcharges imposed by most hotels. Types of callboxes from which *IDD* calls can be made are identified in the *Country sections*. You will need to dial the international code, international country code (for the UK it is 44), the telephone dialling code (omitting the initial '0'), followed by the number. For example, to call the AA Basingstoke (0256) 20123 from Italy, dial 00 44 256 20123. Use higher-denomination coins for *IDD* calls to ensure reasonably lengthy periods of conversation before the coin expiry warning. The equivalent of £1 should allow a reasonable period of uninterrupted conversation.

Note: Cardphones are in use in Austria, Belgium, France, Italy, Netherlands, Portugal and Switzerland; the cards to operate them are available from a post office or shop in the vicinity.

Tolls

Tolls are charged on most motorways in France, Italy, Portugal, Spain and on sections in Austria, Greece and Yugoslavia. Over long distances, the toll charges can be quite considerable. It is advisable to weigh the cost against time and convenience (eg overnight stops), particularly as some of the all-purpose roads are often fast. Always have some currency of the country in which you are travelling ready to pay the tolls, as travellers' cheques etc are not accepted at toll booths. All toll charges quoted in this book should be used as a guide only, as

they are subject to change. Also see *Motorways* page 18.

Note: In Switzerland the authorities charge an annual motorway tax. See *Switzerland – Motorways*, for further information.

Tourist information
(See also Country sections)

National tourist offices are specially equipped to deal with enquiries relating to their countries. They are particularly useful for information on current events, tourist attractions, car hire, equipment hire and specific activities such as skin-diving, gliding, horse-riding etc.

The offices in London are most helpful, but the local offices overseas merit a visit when you arrive at your destination because they have information not available elsewhere. Hotels etc, will be able to supply the local address.

Traffic lights

In principal cities and towns, traffic lights operate in a way similar to those in the UK, although they are sometimes suspended over the roadway. The density of the light may be so poor that lights could be missed – especially those overhead. There is usually only one set on the right-hand side of the road some distance before the road junction, and if you stop too close to the corner, the lights will not be visible. Watch out for 'filter' lights which will enable you to turn right at a junction against the main lights. If you wish to go straight ahead, do not enter a lane leading to 'filter' lights or you may obstruct traffic wishing to turn. See also the *Country sections* for Austria, Belgium, France, Germany, Ireland and Spain.

Trams

Trams take priority over other vehicles. Always give way to passengers boarding and alighting. Never position a vehicle so that it impedes the free passage of a tram. Trams must be overtaken on the right, except in one-way streets. See also *Country sections* for Norway and Sweden.

Traveller's cheques

We recommend you take *Traveller's Cheques*. You can use them like cash, or change them for currency in almost any country in the world.

Tyres

Inspect your tyres carefully; if you think they are likely to be more than three-quarters worn before you get back, it is better to replace them before you leave. If you notice uneven wear, scuffed treads or damaged walls, expert advice should be sought on whether the tyres are suitable for further use. In some European countries, drivers can be fined if tyres are badly worn. The regulations in the UK governing tyres call for a minimum tread depth of 1 mm over 75 per cent of the width of the tyre all around the circumference, with the original tread pattern clearly visible on the remainder. European regulations are stricter: a minimum tread depth of 1 mm or 1.6 mm over the whole width of the tyre around the circumference.

When checking tyre pressures, remember that if the car is heavily loaded the recommended pressures may have to be raised; this may also be required for high-speed driving. Check the recommendations in your handbook, but remember pressures can only be checked accurately when the tyres are cold. Do not forget the spare tyre.

Valuables

Tourists should pay particular attention to the security of their money and items of value while touring. Whenever possible, any excess cash and traveller's cheques should be left with the hotel management **against a receipt**. In some areas, children and youths cause a diversion to attract tourists' attention while pickpockets operate in organised gangs. Avoid stopping to watch unusual incidents, which are more likely to occur in crowded markets or shopping centres.
Note: It cannot be stressed too strongly that all valuables should be **removed** from a parked car even if it is parked in a supervised car park or lock-up garage.

Vehicle excise licence

When taking a vehicle out of the UK for a temporary visit (eg holiday or business trip) you must remember that the vehicle excise licence (tax disc) needs to be valid on your return. Therefore, if your tax disc is due to expire whilst you are abroad, you may apply by post before you leave to the post office, for a tax disc up to 42 days in advance of the expiry date of your present disc. You should explain why you want the tax disc in advance, and ask for it to be posted to you before you leave or to an address you will be staying at abroad. However, your application form must always be completed with your UK address.

To find out which post office in your area offers this service, you should contact your local Post Office Customer Service Unit on the number listed in your local telephone directory.

Visas

A visa is not normally required by United Kingdom and Republic of Ireland passport holders when visiting Western European countries for periods of three months or less. However, if you hold a passport of any other nationality, a UK passport not issued in this country, or are in any doubt at all about your position, check with the embassies or consulates of the countries you intend to visit.

Visitors' registration

All visitors to a country must register with the local police. This formality is usually satisfied by the completion of a card or certificate when booking into a hotel, camp site or place offering accommodation. If staying with friends or relatives, it is usually the responsibility of the host to seek advice from the police within 24 hours of the arrival of guests.

For short holiday visits, the formalities are very simple, but most countries place a time limit on the period that tourists may stay, after which a firmer type of registration is imposed. Therefore, if you intend staying in any one country for longer than three months (Portugal, 60 days see *Country section*), you should make the appropriate enquiries before departure from the UK.

Warm climate touring

In hot weather and at high altitudes, excessive heat in the engine compartment can cause carburation problems. It is advisable, if you are taking a caravan, to consult the manufacturers

IF YOU THINK REGULAR FERRY MOTORISTS DESERVE LOWER FARES, JOIN THE CLUB.

Announcing a club for motorists who travel abroad.

The Sealink Auto Club.

As a member, each time you sail on a Sealink standard fare motorist ticket, we'll send you an Auto Club cheque worth 20% of your fare. A saving you can put towards your next Sealink trip.*

Alternatively, collect five excursion tickets within twelve months, and we'll send you a cheque for 20% of their combined value to put towards your next excursion fare.** But the perks don't stop there.

We're also offering generous discounts on over 200 Campanile hotels throughout France, Belgium and the UK. And 10% off a wide range of Sealink holidays of 6 days or more.

And the cost? Not a penny, centime, lira, or pfennig. Membership is free – but limited. So clip the coupon or contact your local travel agent or motoring organisation today. Before you miss the boat.

*Excludes Isle of Wight services. **Excludes Isle of Wight and Irish routes, and not available on all excursion fares.

Please enrol me as a member of the Sealink Autoclub and send me full details of the scheme. Allow 28 days for delivery. New membership limited to 50,000 in 1990. UK and Ireland residents only.

Name_____

Address_____

_____ Postcode_____

Signature_____ Date_____

Sealink Autoclub, PO Box 14, Horley, Surrey RH6 8DW

SEALINK BRITISH FERRIES

You'll always want to come back.

of your towing vehicle about the limitations of the cooling system, and the operating temperature of the gearbox fluid if automatic transmission is fitted. See also *Automatic gearboxes* page 6).

Warning triangle/hazard warning lights (See also Country sections)

The use of a warning triangle is compulsory in most European countries, and is always a wise precaution. It should be placed on the road behind a stopped vehicle to warn traffic approaching from the rear of an obstruction ahead. The triangle should be used when a vehicle has stopped for any reason – not just breakdowns. It should be placed in such a position as to be clearly visible up to 100m (110yds) by day and by night, about 2ft from the edge of the road, but not in such a position as to present a danger to oncoming traffic. It should be set about 30m (33yds) behind the obstruction, but this distance should be increased up to 100m (110yds) on motorways. A warning triangle is not required for two-wheeled vehicles. An AA Warning Triangle, which complies with the latest International and European standards, can be purchased from the AA. Alternatively, a warning triangle forms part of the Motoring Emergency Pack which may be hired from the AA.

Although four flashing indicators are allowed in the countries covered by this guide, they in no way affect the regulations governing the use of warning triangles. Generally, hazard warning lights should not be used in place of a triangle, although they may complement it in use; but see *Country sections* for *France, Netherlands* and *Switzerland*. See also *Breakdowns* page 7.

Weather information, including winter conditions

Members of the public may telephone or call in at one of the Met Office Weather Centres listed below, except where indicated otherwise. The centres can provide information about local, national and Continental weather forecasts, but **not** road conditions.

Aberdeen
Seaforth Centre, Lime Street
☎(0224) 210574
Belfast (*telephone calls only*)
☎(08494) 22339

Bristol
The Gaunts House, Denmark Street
☎(0272) 279298
Cardiff
Southgate House, Wood Street ☎(0222) 397020
Glasgow
33 Bothwell Street ☎041-248 3451
Leeds
Oak House, Park Lane ☎(0532) 451990
London
284–286 High Holborn ☎01 (071 from 6 May)-836 4311
Manchester
Exchange Street, Stockport ☎061-477-1060
Newcastle upon Tyne
7th Floor, Newgate House, Newgate Street
☎091-232 6453
Norwich
Rouen House, Rouen Road ☎(0603) 660779
Nottingham
Main Road, Watnall ☎(0602) 384092
Plymouth *telephone calls only*)
☎(0752) 402534
Southampton
160 High Street-below-bar ☎(0703) 228844

A Met Office Weather Centre is also being established in Birmingham, but full details are not yet available.

If you require information about climate when planning your holidays, you should contact the national tourist offices of the countries concerned. When you are abroad, you should contact the nearest office of the appropriate national motoring club for weather details (see *Country sections*). it is advisable to check on conditions ahead as you go along, and hotels and garages are often helpful in this respect.

Winter conditions Motoring in Europe during the winter months is restricted because of the vast mountain ranges – the Alps sweeping in an arc from the French Riviera, through Switzerland, northern Italy and Austria to the borders of Yugoslavia, and the Pyrenees which divide France and Spain. Extensive areas of Spain, France and Germany are at an altitude of well over 1,000ft. However, matters have eased with improved communications and modern snow-clearing apparatus.

Reports on the accessibility of mountain passes in Austria, France, Italy and Switzerland are received by the AA from the *European Road Information Centre* in Geneva. Additionally, during the winter months, and also under certain weather conditions, the AA in France collects information regarding the state of

approach roads to the Continental Channel ports. AA members can obtain information during office hours, by ringing ☎0345 500 600, or enquiring at the AA Port Service Centre before embarking.

Details of road and rail tunnels which can be used to pass under the mountains are given pages 36–38; the periods when the most important mountain passes are usually closed are detailed on pages 39–48. If you want a conventional seaside holiday between October and March, you will probably have to travel at least as far south as Lisbon, Valencia, or Naples to be reasonably certain of fine weather.

See also *Country sections* for Austria, Belgium, France, Germany, Italy, Norway, Spain, Sweden and Switzerland. Further information is given in the leaflet entitled *Continental Weather and Motoring in Winter* which is available from the AA. Further information on weather conditions can be obtained from Teletext 'Oracle', the AA's Recorded Information Directory and AA Information Centres.

AA **For travel throughout Europe, consult AA Road Maps**

Series includes:
Austria, Italy and Switzerland
Benelux and Germany
France
Great Britain and Ireland
Spain and Portugal

These invaluable maps feature a special fold coding system, making it easy to find the section you need. Produced to the AA's traditionally high standards of mapping, *Europe Road Maps* are ideal for planning your route and for touring.

Featuring:
Up-to-date road information
Scenic routes and viewpoints
Contours and gradients
Full colour, 16 to 24 miles to 1 inch
Available at good bookshops and AA Centres
Don't leave home without one

EUROPEAN ROUTES SERVICE

Individually prepared routes to your own requirements

The AA's Overseas Routes Unit has a comprehensive and unique database of road and route information built into the very latest computerised equipment. The database holds all the relevant information needed for an enjoyable trouble-free route, including distances in miles and kilometres for estimating journey times. A prepared route gives route numbers, road signs to follow, motorway services, landmarks, road and town descriptions, frontier opening times, etc.

Overseas Routes can supply you with any route you may require; scenic routes – direct routes – by-way routes – fast routes – coach routes – caravan routes – motorway routes – non-motorway routes – touring routes – special interest routes – and more.

You may believe you know the best route – we can confirm if you are correct or tell you if we believe you are wrong – and probably save you time and money.

Can we help you further?

If we can, please contact any AA Centre for a European Route application form. Alternatively, telephone Overseas Routes at Basingstoke (0256) 493748 or (0256) 493907 for credit card requests, or complete the application form below, and we will send you full details of the European Routes Service and the prices charged. Notice of 21 days is needed.

Send the form below to:
Overseas Routes, The Automobile Association, Fanum House, Basingstoke RG21 2EA.

✂ ─

Application form for details of the European Routes service
(Complete in BLOCK CAPITALS)

Mr/Mrs/Ms/Miss/Title: Initials: Surname:

Address:

_____

_____

_____

_____ Postcode: _____

Membership number (or 5-Star number):

Date of request:

(If you are not a member of the AA an additional fee is payable unless you have paid the 5-Star non-member's service fee.)

Countries/places you will visit:

_____

Date of departure:

CUSTOMS OFFICES

Many Customs offices at the main frontier crossings are open 24 hours daily to deal with touring documents.

Major offices with restricted opening times are listed below. During these hours, the Customs handle normal tourist entry into their country. However, persons with dutiable items to declare, or other business to transact, should cross the frontier during normal business hours only. For additional information, see also *Customs regulations for European Countries* page 10.

The table can be read in either direction, eg for France–Belgium read from left to right, for Belgium–France read from right to left.

Nearest town	Road no.	Frontier post	Opening times		Frontier post	Road no.	Nearest town
FRANCE					**BELGIUM**		
Dunkirk	D916A	Oost-Cappel	08.00–20.00	08.00–20.00	Kapelhoek	N9	**Ypres (Ieper)**
Lille	D941	Baisieux	07.00–19.00 Mon–Fri	08.00–16.00	Hertain	N8	**Tournai**
Valenciennes	D169	Maulde	06.00–22.00		Bléharies	N71	**Tournai**
Maubeuge	D936	Cousoire	07.00–21.00	08.00–18.00 Mon–Fri Sat, Sun and public holidays, 07.00–21.00 between 1 Apr–30 Sep, 08.00–18.00 between 1 Oct–31 Mar	Leugnies	N36	**Beaumont**
Avesnes	D962	Hestrud	07.00–22.00	07.00–19.00	Grandrieu	N21	**Beaumont**
Givet	D949	Givet	09.00–17.30	08.00–18.00 Mon–Fri, 09.00–17.00 Sat, Sun and public holidays	Petit Doische	N46	**Philippeville**
Givet	D949	Givet	09.00–17.30	08.00–18.00 Mon–Fri, 09.00–17.00 Sat, Sun and public holidays	Dion	N46	**Beauraing**
FRANCE					**GERMANY**		
Seltz	D28	Seltz Bac	03.00–19.00		Rheinfähre Plittersdorf	Unclass	**Rastatt**
Erstein	D426	Gerstheim	03.00–19.00		Nonnenweier	Unclass	**Lahr**
Benfeld	D5	Rhinou Bac	03.00–19.00		Rheinfähre Kappel-Grafenhausen	Unclass	**Ettenheim**
Metz	D954	Villing	06.00–22.00		Ittersdorf Villinger Strasse	269	**Saarlouis**
FRANCE					**SPAIN**		
Bayonne	D20	Ainhoa	1 May–30 Sep 07.00–24.00, 1 Oct–30 Apr 07.00–22.00		Dancharinea	N121	**Pamplona**
St-Jean-Pied-de-Port	D949	St Etienne de Baigomy	16 Jun–15 Sep 13.00–20.00 (closed 16 Sep–15 Jun)	1 Jun–15 Sep 08.00–22.00, 16 Sep–31 May 09.00–21.00	Errazu	NAGZO	**Pamplona**
St-Jean-Pied-de-Port	D933	Arnéguy	as above		Valcarlos	C135	**Pamplona**
Mauleon Lichorre	D26	Larrau	16 Jun–31 Aug 09.00–22.00,	1 Jun–15 Sep 08.00–22.00	Ochagavia	Unclass	**Pamplona**

CUSTOMS OFFICES

Nearest town	Road no.	Frontier post	Opening times	Frontier post	Road no.	Nearest town
Oloron-Ste-Marie	D132	Arette	1 Sep–31 Oct 09.00–18.00 (closed Nov–15 Jun) 16 Jun–20 Jun 09.00–18.00, 1 Jul–31 Aug 09.00–20.00, 1 Sep–31 Oct 09.00–18.00 (closed Nov–15 Jun) / 16 Sep–31 Oct 09.00–19.00 15 Jun–15 Sep 08.00–22.00, 31 Oct–14 Jun 09.00–19.00	Isaba	C137	Jaca
Oloron-Ste-Marie	N134	Urdos	16 Jun–30 Sep always 1 Oct–15 Jun Mon–Thu 08.00–21.00, Fri, Sat and Sun 08.00–22.00	Canfranc (Candanchú)	N330	Jaca
Pau	D934	Les Eaux-Chaudes Col du Pourtalet	1 Apr–31 May 08.00–20.00 1 Jun–31 Oct 07.00–24.00, 1 Nov–23 Dec 08.00–20.00 (closed 24 Dec–31 Mar)	Sallent-de Gállego	C136	Huesca
Bagnères de Luchon	D618	Bagnères de Luchon	08.00–22.00	Bossost	C141	Viella
Montréjeau	N125	Melles Pont du Roi	1 Oct–30 Apr 08.00–24.00, 1 May–30 Sep always	Lés	N230	Viella
Amélie-les-Bains	D115	Prats-de Mollo	1 Jun–30 Sep 08.00–20.00, Mon–Sat 07.00–24.00, Sun and public holidays 1 Oct–31 May 08.00–20.00 / 08.00–20.00 (holidays 07.00–24.00)	Camprodón	C151	Ripoll

BELGIUM* — NETHERLANDS*

Nearest town	Road no.	Frontier post	Opening times	Frontier post	Road no.	Nearest town
Maldegem	N410	Strooibrug	07.00–19.00 Mon–Fri, 07.00–14.00 Sat, 10.00–18.00 Sun and public holidays / 1 Apr–30 Sep 07.00–24.00, 1 Oct–31 Mar 07.00–21.00	Eede	Unclass	Breskens
Gent	N456	Watervliet	07.00–17.00 Mon–Fri (closed Sat Sun and public holidays) / 07.00–19.00	Veldzicht	Unclass	Breskens
Turnhout	N119	Weelde	06.00–22.00 Mon–Fri, 07.00–14.00 Sat (closed Sun and public holidays) / 07.00–24.00	Baarle Hertog	Unclass	Breda

*Note All customs offices on the Belgian/Dutch frontier may be passed at any time of day, regardless of whether they are open or not, on condition that the visitor has no goods to declare.

NETHERLANDS — GERMANY

Nearest town	Road no.	Frontier post	Opening times	Frontier post	Road no.	Nearest town
Emmen	N37	Zwartemeer	06.00–24.00	Hebelermeer	Unclass	Meppen
Emmen	Unclass	Coevorden	06.00–24.00	Eschebrügge	403	Nordhorn
Venlo	Unclass	Herungerweg	06.00–22.00	Niederdorf	60	Moers

ITALY — SWITZERLAND

Nearest town	Road no.	Frontier post	Opening times	Frontier post	Road no.	Nearest town
Domodossola	SS337	Ponte Ribellasca	05.00–24.00	Cámedo	69	Locarno

Nearest town	Road no.	Frontier post	Opening times		Frontier post	Road no.	Nearest town
Luino	SS394	Zenna	05.00–24.00	1 Apr–30 Sep 05.00–01.00, 1 Oct–31 Mar Mon–Fri 05.00–24.00, Sat, Sun, holidays and fast days 05.00–01.00	Dirinella	Unclass	Locarno
Luino	Unclass	Fornasette	05.00–24.00	05.00–24.00 (Sun, holidays) and fast days 1 May–30 Sep, 05.00–01.00)	Fornasette	Unclass	Lugano
Chiavenna	SS36	Montespluga	spring–30 Jun 06.00–22.00, 1 Jul–31 Aug 05.00–24.00, 1 Sep–Autumn 06.00–22.00 (autumn–spring closed	spring–31 May 06.00–22.00, 1 Jun–30 Jun 05.00–22.00, 1 Jul–30 Sep 05.00–24.00, 1 Oct–autumn 06.00–22.00	Splugen Pass	64	Thusis
Tirano	SS38A	Piattamala	05.00–00.30	05.00–23.00 05.00–02.00 Christmas and Easter	Campo-cologno	29 via Bernina Pass	Pontresina
Bórmio	SS38	Giogo di Santa Maria (Stelvio)	1 Jul–31 Aug 06.00–22.00	spring–30 Jun 06.00–20.00, 1 Jul–31 Aug 06.00–22.00, 1 Sep–autumn 06.00–20.00 (closed in winter)	Umbrail Pass	66	Santa Maria
Glorenza	SS41	Tubre	06.00–24.00	1 May–31 Oct 04.00–24.00 Mon–Fri (always Sat–Sun) 1 Nov–30 Apr 05.00–24.00	Mustair	28	Santa Maria

SWITZERLAND _____ **AUSTRIA** _____

Zernez	27	Martina	05.00–24.00	always	Nauders (Zollhaus)	185	Nauders

ITALY _____ **AUSTRIA** _____

Merano	SS44b	Passo del Rombo	1 May––31 Oct 07.00–20.00 (closed in winter)		Timmelsjoch	186	Sölden

PORTUGAL _____ **SPAIN** _____

Valenca do Minho	N301	Sào Gregório	1 May–31 Oct 07.00–24.00, 1 Nov–28 Feb 07.00–21.00	1 May–31 Oct 08.00–01.00, 1 Nov–28 Feb 08.00–22.00	Ponte Barxas	Unclass	Orense
Chaves	N103–5	Vila Verde Da Raia	12 Mar and 17 Mar–2 Apr 29 Oct–1 Nov 19 Dec–7 Jan always. At other times 07.00–24.00	12 Mar and 17 Mar–2 Apr 1 Jul–30 Sep 29 Oct–1 Nov 19 Dec–7 Jan always. At other times 08.00–01.00	Feces de Abajo	C532	Orense
Bragança	N103–7	Portelo	19 Mar–28 Mar 13 May–14 May 29 Jul–6 Aug 7 Sep–8 Sep 18 Dec–23 Dec always. At other times between 1 June–30 Sep	19 Mar–28 Mar 13 May–14 May 29 Jul–6 Aug 7 Sep–8 Sep 18 Dec–23 Dec always. At other times between 1 Oct–31 May	Calabor	C622	Puebla de Sanabria

CUSTOMS OFFICES

Nearest town	Road no.	Frontier post	Opening times		Frontier post	Road no.	Nearest town
			07.00–23.00, 1 Oct–31 May 07.00–21.00	08.00–22.00. 1 Jun–28 Jul 7 Aug–30 Sep 08.00–24.00			
Bragança	N218–1	Quintanilha	19 Mar–28 Mar 29 Jul–3 Aug 18 Dec–23 Dec always. At other times between 1 Jun–30 Sep 07.00–23.00, 1 Oct–31 Mar 07.00–21.00	19 Mar–28 Mar 29 Jul–3 Aug 18 Dec–23 Dec always. At other times betwéen 1 Jun–28 Jul 4 Aug–30 Sep 08.00–24.00, 1 Oct–31 May 08.00–22.00	San Martin del Pedroso/ Alcañices	N122	**Zamora**
Bragança	N218	Mirando do Douro	19 Mar–28 Mar 27 Jun–28 Jun 29 Jul–3 Aug 18 Aug–20 Aug 18 Dec–23 Dec always. At other times 07.00–23.00	19 Mar–28 Mar 27 Jun–29 Jun 29 Jul–3 Aug 18 Aug–20 Aug 18 Dec–23 Dec always. At other times 08.00–24.00	Torregamones	Unclass	**Zamora**
Mogadouro	N221–7	Bemposta	19 Mar–28 Mar 15 Jul–31 Aug 18 Dec–23 Dec always. At other times between 1 Jun–30 Sep 07.00–23.00, 1 Oct–31 May 07.00–21.00	19 Mar–28 Mar 29 Jun–3 Aug 18 Dec–23 Dec always. At other times between 1 Jun–28 Jul 4 Aug–30 Sep 08.00–24.00 1 Oct–31 May 08.00–24.00	Fermoselle	C527	**Zamora**
Castelo Branco	N355	Segura	1 Mar–31 Oct 07.00–24.00, 1 Nov–28 Feb 07.00–21.00	1 Mar–31 Oct 08.00–01.00, 1 Nov–28 Feb 08.00–22.00	Piedras Albas	C523	**Cáceres**
Portalegre	N246–1	Galegos Marvào	1 Mar–31 Oct 07.00–24.00, 1 Nov–28 Feb 07.00–21.00	1 Mar–31 Oct 08.00–01.00, 1 Nov–28 Feb 08.00–22.00	Valencia de Alcántara	N521	**Cáceres**
Mourão	N256–1	São Leonardo	31 Jan–4 Feb 23 May–25 May 11 Jun–13 Jun 22 Aug–30 Aug and 31 Dec always. At other fimes between 1 Mar–31 Oct 07.00–24.00, 1 Nov–28 Feb 07.00–21.00	31 Jan–4 Feb 23 May–25 May 11 Jun–13 Jun 22 Aug–30 Aug and 31 Dec always. At other times between 1 Mar–31 Oct 08.00–01.00, 1 Nov–28 Feb 08.00–22.00	Villaneuva del Fresno	C436	**Zafra**
Beja	N260	Vila Verde de Ficalho	24 Mar–26 Mar always. At other times between 1 Mar–31 Oct 07.00–24.00, 1 Nov–28 Feb 07.00–21.00	24 Mar–26 Mar always. At other times between 1 Mar–31 Oct 08.00–01.00 1 Nov–28 Feb 08.00–22.00	Rosal de la Frontera	N433	**Seville**
Faro	N125	Vila Real de Santo António	12 Mar–2 Apr 1 Jul–30 Sep 12 Dec–10 Jan always. At other times 07.00–23.00	12 Mar–2 Apr 1 Jul–30 Sep 12 Dec–10 Jun always. At other times 08.00–24.00	Ayamonte	N431	**Huelva**

CUSTOMS OFFICES

Nearest town	Road no.	Frontier post	Opening times	Frontier post	Road no.	Nearest town
DENMARK				**GERMANY**		
Padborg	Unclass	Oksevejen	06.00–24.00	Harrislee	Unclass	**Flensburg**
Tønder	Unclass	Rudbøl	08.00–22.00	Fischerhäuser	Unclass	**Niebüll**
Tønder	Unclass	Møllehus	08.00–22.00	Aventoft	Unclass	**Niebüll**
SWEDEN*				**NORWAY***		
Hallavadsholm	165	Vassbotten	09.00–16.00 Mon–Fri, 09.00–13.00 Sat	Vassbotten	22	**Halden**
Torsby	239	Vittjärn	07.00–21.00 Mon–Fri, 09.00–16.00 Sat	Vittjärn	204	**Kongsvinger**
Sälen	Unclass	Østby	07.00–21.00	Østby	25	**Elverum**
Idre	70	Flötningen	08.00–18.00 Mon–Sat	Flötningen	218	**Drevsjø**
Östersund	Unclass	Ådalsvollen	09.00–16.00	Ådalsvollen	72	**Levanger**
Gäddede	342	Gäddede	07.00–21.00	Gäddede	74	**Grong**
Tärnaby	E79	Tärnaby	07.00–21.00	Tärnaby	E79	**Mo-i-Rana**
Arjeplog	95	Junkerdal	08.00–21.00 Mon–Fri, 08.00–15.00 Sat	Junkerdal	77	**Storjord**
Kiruna	98	Björkliden	08.00–21.00 Mon–Fri, 08.00–15.00 Sat	Björkliden	70	**Narvik**

*Note All Customs offices on the Swedish/Norwegian frontier may be passed at any time of the day, regardless of whether they are open or not, on condition that the visitor has no goods to declare

JOURNEY TIMES

As there are several aspects of a journey to consider, it is difficult to estimate accurately how long a journey will take. Customs clearance, traffic and weather conditions, the time of day, the negotiating of mountain passes and other factors will affect calculations. However, an approximate travelling time can be arrived at by considering the kilometre distance as minutes: ie 60km (37½ miles) takes about 60 minutes. Thus to travel 300km will take about 300 minutes or 5 hours. Allowance will, of course, have to be made in the light of your experience when travelling along motorways (where an average speed of 55mph is possible) and secondary roads.

The table below is a guide to journey times at average speeds expressed in kilometres.

Distance in kilometres	Average speed in mph									
	30		40		50		60		70	
	hrs	mins	hrs	mins	hrs	mins	hrs	mins	hrs	mins
20		25		19		15		13		11
30		37		28		22		19		16
40		50		37		30		25		21
50	1	2		47		37		31		27
60	1	15		56		45		38		32
70	1	25	1	5		52		43		36
80	1	39	1	15	1	0		50		42
90	1	52	1	24	1	7		56		48
100	2	4	1	33	1	15	1	2		53
150	3	6	2	20	1	52	1	33	1	20
200	4	8	3	6	2	30	2	4	1	46
250	5	10	3	53	3	7	2	35	2	13
300	6	12	4	40	3	44	3	6	2	40
350	7	14	5	27	4	21	3	37	3	7
400	8	16	6	12	5	0	4	8	3	32
450	9	18	6	59	5	37	4	39	3	59
500	10	20	7	46	6	14	5	10	4	26

MAJOR ROAD TUNNELS

See also *Lights* page 16. There are also minimum and maximum speed limits in operation in the tunnels. **All charges listed below should be used as guide only**.

Bielsa France–Spain

The trans-Pyrenean tunnel is 3km (2 miles) long, and runs nearly 6,000ft above sea level between Aragnouet and Bielsa. The tunnel is usually closed from October to Easter.

Cadí Spain

A new road tunnel has been opened in Catalonia (road number C1411), between the villages of Bellver de Cerdanya and Bagá, and to the west of the Toses (Tosas) Pass.

The tunnel is 5km (3 miles) long and runs at about 4,000ft above sea level under the Sierra del Cadí mountain range. 18km (11 miles) of new access roads have also been completed.

Charges (in *Pesetas*)

	single
cars (with or without caravan)	670

Fréjus France–Italy

This tunnel is over 4,000ft above sea level; it runs between Modane and Bardonecchia. The tunnel is 12.8km (8 miles) long, 4.5m (14ft 9in) high, and the two-lane carriageway is 9m (29ft 6in) wide. The *minimum* speed is 60kph (37mph) and the *maximum* 80kph (49mph). **Toll charges as Mont Blanc Tunnel (see below)**.

Mont Blanc Chamonix (France)– Courmayeur (Italy)

The tunnel is over 4,000ft above sea level. It is 11.6km (7 miles) long. Customs and passport control are at the Italian end. The permitted maximum dimensions of vehicles are: height 4.20m (13ft 8in); length 19m (62ft 4in); width 2.60m (8ft 5in). Total weight 35 metric tons (34 tons 9 cwt); axle weight 13 metric tons (12 tons 16 cwt). The minimum speed is 50kph (31mph) and the maximum 70kph (43mph). Do not stop, overtake, sound your horn or make U-turns. Use only side/rear lights, not headlights, and keep 100m (110yds) distance between vehicles. Make sure you have sufficient petrol for the journey, 30km (19 miles).

Charges (in *French francs*)
The tolls are calculated on the wheelbase.

motorcycle	70
cars wheelbase less than 2.30m(7ft 6½in)	70
wheelbase from 2.30m but less than 2.63m (7ft 6½in to 8ft 7½in	105
wheelbase from 2.63m to a maximum of 3.30m (8ft 7½in to 10ft 10in)	140
caravans	140
wheelbase over 3.30m (10ft 10in)	350
vehicles with three axles	530
with four, or more axles	700

Grand St Bernard Switzerland–Italy

The tunnel is over 6,000ft above sea level; although there are covered approaches, wheel chains may be needed to reach it in winter. The Customs, passport control, and toll offices are at the entrance. The tunnel is 5.9km (3½ miles) long. The permitted maximum dimensions of vehicles are: height 4m (13ft 1in), width 2.5m (8ft 2½in). The minimum speed is 40kph (24mph) and the maximum is 80kph (49mph). Do not stop or overtake. There are breakdown bays with telephones on either side.

Charges (in *Swiss francs*)
The toll charges are calculated according to the wheelbase.

	single
motorcycles	5
cars wheelbase up to 2.08m (6ft 10in)	15
wheelbase from 2.08m to 3.20m (6ft 10in to 10ft 6in)	22.50
wheelbase over 3.20m (10ft 6in)	34
with caravan	34
minibuses	34
vehicles with three axles	67.50
with four or more axles	112.50

St Gotthard Switzerland

The world's longest road tunnel. The tunnel is about 3,800ft above sea level; it runs under the St Gotthard Pass from Göschenen, on the northern side of the Alps, to Airolo in the Ticino. The tunnel is 16.3km (10 miles) long, 3.4m (14ft 9in) high, and the two-lane carriageway is 7.5m (25ft) wide. The maximum speed is 80kph (49mph). Forming part of the Swiss national motorway network, the tunnel is subject to the annual motorway tax, and the tax

disc must be displayed (see Switzerland – Motorways).

From December to February, wheel chains may occasionally be required on the approaches to the tunnel, but they are **NOT** allowed to be used in the tunnel. (Lay-bys are available for the removal and refitting of wheel chains.)

San Bernardino Switzerland

This tunnel is over 5,000ft above sea level. It is 6.6km (4 miles) long, 4.8m (15ft 9in) high, and the carriageway is 7m (23ft) wide. Do not stop or overtake in the tunnel. Keep 100m (110yds) distance between vehicles. There are breakdown bays with telephones. Forming part of the Swiss national motorway network, the tunnel is subject to the annual motorway tax, and the tax disc must be displayed (see *Switzerland – Motorways*).

From November to March, wheel chains may occasionally be required on the approaches to the tunnel.

Arlberg Austria

This tunnel is 14km (8¾ miles) long and runs at about 4,000ft above sea level, to the south of and parallel to the Arlberg Pass.
Charges
The toll charges are: cars (with or without caravans) **150** *Austrian schillings*, motorcycles **90** *Austrian schillings*.

Bosruck Austria

This tunnel (opened October 1983) is 2,434ft above sea level. It is 5.5km (3½ miles) long and runs between Spital am Pyhrn and Selzthal, to the east of the Pyhrn Pass. With the Gleinalm Tunnel (see below) it forms an important part of the A9 Pyhrn Autobahn between Linz and Graz, now being built in stages.
Charges
The toll charges are: cars (with or without caravans) or motorcycles, **70** *Austrian schillings* for a single journey.

Felbertauern Austria

This tunnel is over 5,000ft above sea level; it runs between Mittersill and Matrei, west of and parallel to the Grossglockner Pass.

The tunnel is 5.3km (3¼ miles) long, 4.5m (14ft 9in) high, and the two-lane carriageway is 7m (23ft) wide. From November to April, wheel

chains may be needed on the approach to the tunnel.
Charges (in *Austrian schillings*)

		single
cars	summer rate (May–Oct)	**180**
motorcycles	winter rate (Nov–Apr)	**100**
caravans		**free**

Gleinalm Austria

This tunnel is 2,680ft above sea level, 8.3km (5 miles) long and runs between St Michael and Friesach, near Graz. The tunnel forms part of the A9 Pyhrn Autobahn which will, in due course, run from Linz, via Graz, to Yugoslavia.
Charges (in *Austrian schillings*)

	single
cars (with or without caravan)	**130**
motorcycles	**90**

Karawanken Austria–Yugoslavia

This new motorway tunnel under the Karawanken mountain range is now due to open in 1991.

The tunnel is 8km (5 miles) long and runs at about 2,000ft above sea level between Rosenbach in Austria and Jesenice in Yugoslavia. There will probably be a toll charge.

Tauern Autobahn (*Katschberg* and *Radstädter*) Austria

Two tunnels, the Katschberg and the Radstädter Tauern, form the key elements of this toll motorway between Salzburg and Carinthia.

The **Katschberg** tunnel is 3,642ft above sea level. It is 5.4km (3½ miles) long, 4.5m (14ft 9in) high, and the two-lane carriageway is 7.5m (25ft) wide.

The **Radstädter Tauern** tunnel is 4,396ft above sea level and runs to the east of and parallel to the Tauern railway tunnel. The tunnel is 6.4km (4 miles) long, 4.5m (14ft 9in) high, and the two-lane carriageway is 7.5m (25ft) wide.

On both sections, a second tunnel is being built to allow for dual-carriageway throughout. Work should be completed by 1993.
Charges (in *Austrian schillings*) for the whole toll section between Flachau and Rennweg

		single
cars	summer rate (May–Oct)	**190**
	winter rate (Nov–Apr)	**110**
caravans		**free**
motorcycles	summer/winter rate	**90**

MAJOR RAIL TUNNELS

Vehicles are conveyed throughout the year through the **Simplon Tunnel** (Brig-Iselle) and the **Lötschberg Tunnel** (Kandersteg–Goppenstein). It is also possible to travel all the way from Kandersteg to Iselle by rail via both the Lötschberg and Simplon Tunnels. Total journey time is about 1–1½ hours. Services are frequent with no advance booking necessary; the actual transit time is 15/20 minutes for each tunnel but loading and unloading formalities can take some time.

The operating company issues a full timetable and tariff list which is available from the Swiss National Tourist Office (see *Switzerland – Tourist information*) **or at most Swiss frontier crossings.**

Albula Tunnel Switzerland

Thusis (2,372ft)–**Samedan** (5,650ft)
The railway tunnel is 5.9km (3½ miles) long. Motor vehicles can be conveyed through the tunnel, but you are recommended to give notice. **Thusis** ☎(081) 811113 and **Samedan** ☎(082) 65404.
Journey time 90 minutes.

Services
Nine trains daily going *south*; 6 trains daily *north*.

Charges
These are given in *Swiss francs* and are likely to increase.
cars (including driver)————————70
additional passengers————————8.80
car and caravan————————140

Furka Tunnel Switzerland

Oberwald (4,482ft)–**Realp** (5,046ft)
The railway tunnel is 15.3km (9½ miles) long. Journey time 20 minutes.

Services
Hourly from 06.50–21.00hrs

Charges
These are in *Swiss francs*.
cars (including passengers)————————18
car and caravan————————36

Oberalp Railway Switzerland

Andermatt (4,737ft)–**Sedrun** (4,728ft)
Journey time 50 minutes.

Booking
Advance booking is necessary. **Andermatt** ☎(044) 67220 and **Sedrun** ☎(086) 91137.

Services
2–4 trains daily, winter only (Oct–Apr).

Charges
These are in *Swiss francs*.
cars (including driver)————————51
additional passengers————————8.40
car and caravan————————102

Tauern Tunnel Austria

Böckstein (3,711ft) (near Badgastein)–**Mallnitz** 8.5km (5½ miles) long.
Maximum dimensions for caravans and trailers: height 8ft 10½in, width 8ft 2½in.

Booking
Advance booking is unnecessary (except for request trains), but motorists must report at least 30 minutes before the train is due to leave. Drivers must drive their vehicle on and off the wagon.

Services
At summer weekends, trains run approximately every half-hour in both directions, 06.30–22.30hrs; and every hour during the night. During the rest of the year, there is an hourly service from 06.30 to 22.30hrs (23.30hrs Fri and Sat, 7 Jul–9 Sep). Journey time 12 minutes.

Charges
These are given in *Austrian schillings* and are for a single journey.
cars (including passengers————————160
motorcycles (with or without sidecar)————30
caravans————————free

PRINCIPAL MOUNTAIN PASSES

It is best not to attempt to cross mountain passes at night, and daily schedules should make allowance for the comparatively slow speeds inevitable in mountainous areas. Gravel surfaces (such as grit and stone chips) vary considerably; they are dusty when dry, slippery when wet. Where known to exist, this type of surface has been noted. Road repairs can be carried out only during the summer, and may interrupt traffic. Precipitous sides are rarely, if ever, totally unguarded; on the older roads, stone pillars are placed at close intervals. Gradient figures take the mean figure of hairpin bends, and may be steeper on the insides of the curves, particularly on the older roads.

Before attempting late evening or early morning journeys across frontier passes, check the times of opening of the Customs offices, as a number of offices close at night (see *Customs Offices*, pages 31–35).

Always engage a low gear before either ascending or descending steep gradients, keep well to the right side of the road and avoid cutting corners. Avoid excessive use of brakes. If the engine overheats, pull off the road, making sure you do not cause an obstruction, leave the engine idling, and put the heater controls, including the fan, into the *maximum* heat position. Under no circumstances remove the radiator cap until the engine has cooled down. Do not fill the coolant system of a hot engine with cold water.

Always engage a lower gear before taking a hairpin bend, give priority to vehicles ascending and remember that, as your altitude increases, so your engine power decreases. Priority must always be given to postal coaches travelling in either direction. Their route is usually signposted.

Caravans

Passes *suitable for caravans* are indicated in the table on the following pages. Those shown to be *negotiable by caravans* are best used only by experienced drivers of cars with ample power. The remainder are probably best avoided. A correct power-to-load ratio is always essential.

Conditions in winter

Winter conditions are given in italics in the last column. *UO* means usually open although a severe fall of snow may temporarily obstruct the road for 24–48 hours, and wheel chains are often necessary; *OC* means 'occasionally closed between the dates stated', and *UC* 'usually closed between the dates stated'. Dates for opening and closing the passes are approximate only. Warning notices are usually posted at the foot of a pass if it is closed, or if chains or snow tyres should or must be used.

Wheel chains may be needed early and late in the season, and between short spells (a few hours) of obstruction. At these times, conditions are usually more difficult for caravans.

In fair weather, wheel chains or snow tyres are only necessary on the higher passes, but in severe weather you will probably need them (as a rough guide) at altitudes exceeding 2,000ft. Further information on conditions in winter can be obtained from Teletext 'Oracle' and AA Information Centres.

Conversion table gradients

All steep hill signs show the grade in percentage terms. The following conversion table may be used as a guide:

30%	1 in 3	14%	1 in 7
25%	1 in 4	12%	1 in 8
20%	1 in 5	11%	1 in 9
16%	1 in 6	10%	1 in 10

PRINCIPAL MOUNTAIN PASSES

PASS AND HEIGHT	FROM TO	DISTANCES FROM SUMMIT AND MAX GRADIENT		MIN WIDTH OF ROAD	CONDITIONS (See page 39 for key to abbreviations)
*Albula 7,595ft (2315m) Switzerland	Tiefencastel (2,821ft) La Punt (5,546ft)	30km 9km	1 in 10 1 in 10	12ft	UC Nov–early Jun. An inferior alternative to the Julier; tar and gravel; fine scenery. Alternative rail tunnel.
Allos 7,382ft (2250m) France	Barcelonnette (3,740ft) Colmars (4,085ft)	20km 24km	1 in 10 1 in 12	13ft	UC early Nov–early Jun. Very winding, narrow, mostly unguarded but not difficult otherwise; passing bays on southern slope, poor surface (maximum width vehicles 5ft 11in).
Aprica 3,858ft (1176m) Italy	Tresenda (1,220ft) Edolo (2,264ft)	14km 15km	1 in 11 1 in 16	13ft	UO. Fine scenery; good surface, well graded; suitable for caravans.
Aravis 4,915ft (1498m) France	La Clusaz (3,412ft) Flumet (3,008ft)	8km 12km	1 in 11 1 in 11	13ft	OC Dec–Mar. Oustanding scenery, and a fairly easy road.
Arlberg 5,912ft (1802m) Austria	Bludenz (1,905ft) Landeck (2,677ft)	35km 35km	1 in 8 1 in 7½	20ft	OC Dec–Apr. Modern road; short steep stretch from west easing towards the summit; heavy traffic; parallel toll road tunnel available (see page 37). Suitable for caravans, using tunnel. Pass road closed to vehicles towing trailers.
Aubisque 5,610ft (1710m) France	Eaux Bonnes (2,461ft) Argelès-Gazost (1,519ft)	11km 32km	1 in 10 1 in 10	11ft	UC mid Oct–Jun. A very winding road; continuous but easy ascent; the descent incorporates the Col de Soulor (4,757ft); 8km of very narrow, rough, unguarded road, with a steep drop.
Ballon d'Alsace 3,865ft (1178m) France	Giromagny (1,830ft) St-Maurice-sur-Moselle (1,800ft)	17km 9km	1 in 9 1 in 9	13ft	OC Dec–Mar. A fairly straightforward ascent and descent, but numerous bends; negotiable by caravans.
Bayard 4,094ft (1248m) France	Chauffayer (2,988ft) Gap (2,382ft)	18km 8km	1 in 12 1 in 7	20ft	UO. Part of the Route Napoléon. Fairly easy, steepest on the southern side; negotiable by caravans from north to south
*Bernina 7,644ft (2330m) Switzerland	Pontresina (5,915ft) Poschiavo (3,317ft)	15.5km 19km	1 in 10 1 in 8	16ft	OC Dec–Mar. A good road on both sides; negotiable by caravans.
Bonaigua 6,797ft (2072m) Spain	Viella (3,150ft) Esterri d'Aneu (3,140ft)	23km 21km	1 in 12 1 in 12	14ft	UC Nov–Apr. A sinuous and narrow road with many hairpin bends and some precipitous drops, the alternative route to Lleida (Lérida) through the Viella tunnel is open in winter.
Bracco 2,011ft (613m) Italy	Riva Trigoso (141ft) Borghetto di Vara (318ft)	15km 18km	1 in 7 1 in 7	16ft	UO. A two-lane road with continuous bends; passing usually difficult; negotiable by caravans; alternative toll motorway available.
Brenner 4,508ft (1374m) Austria–Italy	Innsbruck (1,883ft) Vipiteno (3,110ft)	38km 15km	1 in 12 1 in 7	20ft	UO. Parallel toll motorway open; heavy traffic may delay at Customs; suitable for caravans using toll motorway. Pass road closed to vehicles towing trailers.

*Permitted maximum width of vehicles 7ft 6in

PASS AND HEIGHT	FROM TO	DISTANCES FROM SUMMIT AND MAX GRADIENT		MIN WIDTH OF ROAD	CONDITIONS (See page 39 for key to abbreviations)
†Brunig 3,304ft (1007m) Switzerland	Brienzwiler Station (1,886ft) Giswil (1,601ft)	6km 13km	1 in 12 1 in 12	20ft	*UO*. An easy but winding road; heavy traffic at weekends; *suitable for caravans.*
Bussang 2,365ft (721m) France	Thann (1,115ft) St-Maurice-sur-Moselle (1,800ft)	22km 8km	1 in 10 1 in 14	13ft	*UO*. A very easy road over the Vosges; beautiful scenery; *suitable for caravans.*
Cabre 3,871ft (1180m) France	Luc-en-Diois (1,870ft) Aspres-sur-Buëch (2,497ft)	22km 17km	1 in 11 1 in 14	18ft	*UO*. An easy pleasant road; *suitable for caravans.*
Campolongo 6,152ft (1875m) Italy	Corvara in Badia (5,145fr) Arabba (5,253ft)	6km 4km	1 in 8 1 in 8	16ft	*OC Dec–Mar.* A winding but easy ascent; long level stretch on summit followed by easy descent; good surface; *suitable for caravans.*
Cayolle 7,631ft (2326m) France	Barcelonnette (3,740ft) Guillaumes (2,687ft)	32km 33km	1 in 10 1 in 10	13ft	*UC early Nov–early Jun.* Narrow and winding road with hairpin bends; poor surface and broken edges; steep drops. Long stretches of single track road with passing places.
Costalunga (Karer) 5,751ft (1753m) Italy	Cardano (925ft) Pozza (4,232ft)	24km 10km	1 in 8 1 in 7	16ft	*OC Dec–Apr.* A good, well-engineered road but mostly winding; *caravans prohibited.*
Croix 5,833ft (1778m) Switzerland	Villars-sur-Ollon (4,111ft) Les Diablerets (3,789ft)	8km 9km	1 in 7½ 1 in 11	11ft	*UC Nov–May.* A narrow and winding route but extremely picturesque.
Croix-Haute 3,858ft (1176m) France	Monestier-de-Clermont (2,776ft) Aspres-sur-Buëch (2,497ft)	36km 28km	1 in 14 1 in 14	18ft	*UO*. Well-engineered; several hairpin bends on the north side; *suitable for caravans.*
Envalira 7,897ft (2407m) Andorra	Pas de la Casa (6,851ft) Andorra (3,375ft)	5km 29km	1 in 10 1 in 8	20ft	*OC Nov–Apr.* A good road with wide bends on ascent and descent; fine views; *negotiable by caravans.* (Max height vehicles 11ft 6in on northern approach near L'Hospitalet).
Falzárego 6,945ft (2117m) Italy	Cortina d'Ampezzo (3,983ft) Andraz (4,622ft)	17km 9km	1 in 12 1 in 12	16ft	*OC Dec–Apr.* Well-engineered bitumen surface; many hairpin bends on both sides; *negotiable by caravans.*
Faucille 4,341ft (1323m) France	Gex (1,985ft) Morez (2,247ft)	11km 28km	1 in 10 1 in 12	16ft	*UO*. Fairly wide, winding road across the Jura mountains; *negotiable by caravans,* but it is probably better to follow La Cure–St-Cerque-Nyon.
Fern 3,967ft (1209m) Austria	Nassereith (2,766ft) Lermoos (3,244ft)	9km 10km	1 in 10 1 in 10	20ft	*UO*. An easy pass, but slippery when wet; heavy traffic at summer weekends; *suitable for caravans.*

†Permitted maximum width of vehicles 8ft 2½in.

PASS AND HEIGHT	FROM TO	DISTANCES FROM SUMMIT AND MAX GRADIENT		MIN WIDTH OF ROAD	CONDITIONS (See page 39 for key to abbreviations)
Flexen 5,853ft (1784m) Austria	Lech (4,747ft) Rauzalpe (near Arlberg Pass) (5,341ft)	6.5km 3.5km	1 in 10 1 in 10	18ft	*UO.* The magnificent 'Flexenstrasse', a well-engineered mountain road with tunnels and galleries. The road from Lech to Warth, north of the pass, is usually closed between November and April due to danger of avalanches.
***Flüela** 7,818ft (2383m) Switzerland	Davos-Dorf (5,174ft) Susch (4,659ft)	13km 13km	1 in 10 1 in 8	16ft	*OC Nov–May.* Easy ascent from Davos; some acute hairpin bends on the eastern side; bitumen surface; *negotiable by caravans.*
†Forclaz 5,010ft (1527m) Switzerland France	Martigny (1,562ft) Argentière (4,111ft)	13km 19km	1 in 12 1 in 12	16ft	*UO Forclaz; OC Montets Dec–early Apr.* A good road over the pass and to the frontier; in France, narrow and rough over Col des Montets (4,793ft); *negotiable by caravans.*
Foscagno 7,516ft (2291m) Italy	Bormio (4,019ft) Livigno (5,958ft)	24km 14km	1 in 8 1 in 8	11ft	*OC Nov–Apr.* Narrow and winding through lonely mountains; generally poor surface. Long winding ascent with many blind bends; not always well guarded. The descent includes winding rise and fall over the Passo d'Eira (7,218ft).
Fugazze 3,802ft (1159m) Italy	Rovereto (660ft) Valli del Pasubio (1,148ft)	27km 12km	1 in 7 1 in 7	10ft	*UO.* Very winding with some narrow sections, particularly on northern side. The many blind bends and several hairpin bends call for extra care.
***Furka** 7,976ft (2431m) Switzerland	Gletsch (5,777ft) Realp (5,046ft)	10km 13km	1 in 10 1 in 10	13ft	*UC Oct–Jun.* A well-graded road, with narrow sections and several sharp hairpin bends on both ascent and descent. Fine views of the Rhône Glacier. Alternative rail tunnel available.
Galibier 8,678ft (2645m) France	Lautaret Pass (6,752ft) St-Michel-de-Maurienne (2,336ft)	7km 34km	1 in 14 1 in 8	10ft	*UC Oct–Jun.* Mainly wide, well-surfaced but unguarded. Ten hairpin bends on descent then 5km narrow and rough. Rise over the Col du Télégraphe (5,249ft), then 11 more hairpin bends. (Tunnel under the Galibier summit is closed.)
Gardena (Grödner-Joch) 6,959ft (2121m) Italy	Val Gardena (6,109ft) Corvara in Badia (5,145ft)	6km 10km	1 in 8 1 in 8	16ft	*OC Dec–Jun.* A well-engineered road, very winding on descent.
Gavia 8,599ft (2621m) Italy	Bormio (4,019ft) Ponte di Legno (4,140ft)	25km 16km	1 in 5½ 1 in 5½	10ft	*UC Oct–Jul.* Steep and narrow, but with frequent passing bays; many hairpin bends and a gravel surface; not for the faint-hearted; extra care necessary (maximum width, vehicles 5ft 11in).
Gerlos 5,341ft (1628m) Austria	Zell am Ziller (1,886ft) Wald (2,904ft)	29km 15km	1 in 12 1 in 12	14ft	*UO.* Hairpin ascent out of Zell to modern toll road; the old steep, narrow, and winding route with passing bays and 1-in-7 gradient is not recommended, but is negotiable with care; *caravans prohibited.*

*Permitted maximum width of vehicles 7ft 6in
†Permitted maximum width of vehicles 8ft 2½in

PASS AND HEIGHT	FROM TO	DISTANCES FROM SUMMIT AND MAX GRADIENT		MIN WIDTH OF ROAD	CONDITIONS (See page 39 for key to abbreviations)
†Grand St Bernard 8,114ft (2473m) Switzerland Italy	Martigny (1,562ft) Aosta (1,913ft)	44km 33km	1 in 9 1 in 9	13ft	*UC Oct–Jun.* Modern road to entrance of road tunnel (usually open; see page 36); then narrow, but bitumen surface over summit to frontier; also good in Italy; *suitable for caravans, using tunnel.* Pass road closed to vehicles towing trailers.
*Grimsel 7,100ft (2164m) Switzerland	Innertkirchen (2,067ft) Gletsch (5,777ft)	25km 6km	1 in 10 1 in 10	16ft	*UC mid Oct–late Jun.* A fairly easy, modern road, but heavy traffic at weekends. A long, winding ascent, finally hairpin bends; then a terraced descent with six hairpins into the Rhône valley.
Grossglockner 8,212ft (2503m) Austria	Bruck an der Glocknerstrasse (2,480ft) Heiligenblut (4,268ft)	33km 15km	1 in 8 1 in 8	16ft	*UC late Oct–early May.* Numerous well-engineered hairpin bends; moderate but very long ascents; toll road; very fine scenery; heavy tourist traffic; *negotiable, preferably from south to north, by caravans.*
Hochtannberg 5,509ft (1679m) Austria	Schröcken (4,163ft) Warth (near Lech) (4,921ft)	5.5km 4.5km	1 in 7 1 in 11	13ft	*OC Jan–Mar.* A reconstructed modern road.
Ibañeta (Roncesvalles) 3,468ft (1057m) France–Spain	St-Jean-Pied-de-Port (584ft) Pamplona (1,380ft)	26km 52km	1 in 10 1 in 10	13ft	*UO.* A slow and winding, scenic route; *negotiable by caravans.*
Iseran 9,088ft (2770m) France	Bourg-St-Maurice (2,756ft) Lanslebourg (4,587ft)	49km 33km	1 in 12 1 in 9	13ft	*UC mid Oct–late Jun.* The second highest pass in the Alps. Well-graded with reasonable bends; average surface; several unlit tunnels on northern approach.
Izoard 7,743ft (2360m) France	Guillestre (3,248ft) Briançon (4,396ft)	32km 20km	1 in 8 1 in 10	16ft	*UC late Oct–mid Jun.* A winding and, at times, narrow road with many hairpin bends. Care required at several unlit tunnels near Guillestre.
*Jaun 4,951ft (1509m) Switzerland	Broc (2,378ft) Reidenbach (2,769ft)	25km 8km	1 in 10 1 in 10	13ft	*UO.* A modernised but generally narrow road; some poor sections on ascent, and several hairpin bends on descent; *negotiable by caravans.*
†Julier 7,493ft (2284m) Switzerland	Tiefencastel (2,821ft) Silvaplana (5,958ft)	36km 7km	1 in 10 1 in 7½	13ft	*UO.* Well-engineered road approached from Chur by Lenzerheide Pass (5,098ft); *negotiable by caravans, preferably from north to south.*
Katschberg 5,384ft (1641m) Austria	Spittal (1,818ft) St Michael (3,504ft)	35km 6km	1 in 5 1 in 6	20ft	*UO.* Steep though not particularly difficult; parallel toll motorway, including tunnel available; *negotiable by light caravans, using tunnel (see page 37).*
*Klausen 6,391ft (1948m) Switzerland	Altdorf (1,512ft) Linthal (2,126ft)	25km 23km	1 in 11 1 in 11	16ft	*UC late Oct–Early Jun.* Narrow and winding in places, but generally easy, in spite of a number of sharp bends; *no through route for caravans as they are prohibited from using the road between Unterschächen and Linthal.*

*Permitted maximum width of vehicles 7ft 6in
†Permitted maximum width of vehicles 8ft 2½in

PRINCIPAL MOUNTAIN PASSES

PASS AND HEIGHT	FROM TO	DISTANCES FROM SUMMIT AND MAX GRADIENT		MIN WIDTH OF ROAD	CONDITIONS (See page 39 for key to abbreviations)
Larche (della Maddalena) 6,542ft (1994m) France–Italy	Condamine (4,291ft) Vinadio (2,986ft)	19km 32km	1 in 12 1 in 12	10ft	OC Dec–Mar. An easy, well-graded road; narrow and rough on ascent, wider with better surface on descent; *suitable for caravans.*
Lautaret 6,752ft (2058m) France	Le Bourg-d'Oisans (2,359ft) Briançon (4,396ft)	38km 28km	1 in 8 1 in 10	14ft	OC Dec–Mar. Modern, evenly graded, but winding, and unguarded in places; very fine scenery; *suitable for caravans.*
Loibl (Ljubelj) 3,500ft (1067m) Austria–Yugoslavia	Unterloibl (1,699ft) Kranj (1,263ft)	10km 29km	1 in 5½ 1 in 8	20ft	UO. Steep rise and fall over Little Loibl. Pass to tunnel (1.6km long) under summit; from south to north *just negotiable by experienced drivers with light caravans.* The old road over the summit is closed to through traffic.
*Lukmanier (Lucomagno) 6,286ft (1916m) Switzerland	Olivone (2,945ft) Disentis (3,772ft)	18km 22km	1 in 11 1 in 11	16ft	UC Nov–late May. Rebuilt, modern road; *no throughroute for caravans as they are prohibited* from using the road between the Lukmanier Pass and Olivone.
†Maloja 5,955ft (1815m) Switzerland	Silvaplana (5,958ft) Chiavenna (1,083ft)	11km 32km	level 1 in 11	13ft	UO. Escarpment facing south; fairly easy, but many hairpin bends on descent; *negotiable by caravans, possibly difficult on ascent.*
Mauria 4,258ft (1298m) Italy	Lozzo Cadore (2,470ft) Ampezzo (1,837ft)	14km 31km	1 in 14 1 in 14	16ft	UO. A well-designed road with easy, winding ascent and descent; *suitable for caravans.*
Mendola 4,472ft (1363m) Italy	Appiano (Eppan) (1,348ft) Sarnonico (3,208ft)	15km 8km	1 in 8 1 in 10	16ft	UO. A fairly straightforward, but winding road; well-guarded; *suitable for caravans.*
Monte Cenis 6,834ft (2083m) France–Italy	Lanslebourg (4,587ft) Susa (1.642ft)	11km 28km	1 in 10 1 in 8	16ft	UC Nov–May. Approach by industrial valley. An easy, broad highway, but with poor surface in places; *suitable for caravans.* Alternative Fréjus road tunnel available (see page 36).
Monte Croce di Comélico (Kreuzberg) 5,368ft (1636m) Italy	San Candido (3,874ft) Santo Stefano di Cadore (2,979ft)	15km 21km	1 in 12 1 in 12	16ft	UO. A winding road with moderate gradients; beautiful scenery; *suitable for caravans.*
Montegenèvre 6,070ft (1850m) France–Italy	Briançon (4,334ft) Cesana Torinese (4,429ft)	12km 8km	1 in 14 1 in 11	16ft	UO. An easy, modern road; *suitable for caravans.*
Monte Giovo (Jaufen) 6,870ft (2094m) Italy	Merano (1,063ft) Vipiteno (3,115ft)	40km 19km	1 in 8 1 in 11	13ft	UC Nov–May. Many well-engineered hairpin bends; *caravans prohibited.*
Montets (see Forclaz)					
Morgins 4,491ft (1369m) France– Switzerland	Abondance (3,051ft) Monthey (1,391ft)	14km 15km	1 in 11 1 in 7	13ft	UO. A lesser-used route through pleasant, forested countryside, crossing the French/ Swiss border.

*Permitted maximum width of vehicles 7ft 6in
†Permitted maximum width of vehicles 8ft 2½in

PASS AND HEIGHT	FROM TO	DISTANCES FROM SUMMIT AND MAX GRADIENT		MIN WIDTH OF ROAD	CONDITIONS (See page 39 for key to abbreviations)
*Mosses 4,740ft (1445m) Switzerland	Aigle (1,378ft) Château-d'Oex (3,153ft)	18km 15km	1 in 12 1 in 12	13ft	UO. A modern road; suitable for caravans.
Nassfeld (Pramollo) 5,020ft (1530m) Austria–Italy	Tröpolach (1,972ft) Pontebba (1,841ft)	10km 10km	1 in 5 1 in 10	13ft	OC late Nov–Mar. The winding descent in Italy has been improved.
*Nufenen (Novena) 8,130ft (2478m) Switzerland	Ulrichen (4,416ft) Airolo (3,747ft)	13km 24km	1 in 10 1 in 10	13ft	UC mid Oct–mid Jun. The approach roads are narrow, the tight bends, but the road over the pass is good; negotiable by light caravans (limit 1.5 tons).
*Oberalp 6,706ft (2044m) Switzerland	Andermatt 4,737ft) Disentis (3,772ft)	10km 22km	1 in 10 1 in 10	16ft	UC Nov–late May. A much improved and widened road with a modern surface; many hairpin bends, but long, level stretch on summit; negotiable by caravans. Alternative rail tunnel during the winter.
*Ofen (Fuorn) 7,051ft (2149m) Switzerland	Zernez (4,836ft) Santa Maria im Münstertal (4,547ft)	22km 14km	1 in 10 1 in 8	12ft	UO. Good, fairly easy road through the Swiss National Park; suitable for caravans.
Petit St Bernard 7,178ft (2188m) France–Italy	Bourg-St-Maurice (2,756ft) Pré St-Didier (3,335ft)	31km 23km	1 in 16 1 in 12	16ft	UC mid Oct–Jun. Outstanding scenery; a fairly easy approach, but poor surface and unguarded broken edges near the summit; good on the descent in Italy; negotiable by caravans.
Peyresourde 5,128ft (1563m) France	Arreau (2,310ft) Luchon (2,067ft)	18km 14km	1 in 10 1 in 10	13ft	UO. Somewhat narrow with several hairpin bends, though not difficult.
*Pillon 5,072ft (1546m) Switzerland	Le Sépey (3,212ft) Gsteig (2,911ft)	14km 7km	1 in 11 1 in 11	13ft	OC Jan–Feb. A comparatively easy modern road; suitable for caravans.
Plöcken (Monte Croce–Carnico) 4,468ft (1362m) Austria–Italy	Kötschach (2,316ft) Paluzza (1,968ft)	14km 17km	1 in 7 1 in 14	16ft	OC Dec–Apr. A modern road with long reconstructed sections; heavy traffic at summer weekends; delay likely at the frontier; negotiable by caravans.
Pordoi 7,346ft (2239m) Italy	Arabba (5,253ft) Canazei (4,806ft)	9km 12km	1 in 10 1 in 10	16ft	OC Dec–Apr. An excellent modern road with numerous hairpin bends; negotiable by caravans.
Port 4,098ft (1249m) France	Tarascon (1,555ft(Massat (2,133ft)	18km 13km	1 in 10 1 in 10	14ft	OC Nov–Mar. A fairly easy road, but narrow on some bends; negotiable by caravans.
Portet-d'Aspet 3,507ft (1069m) France	Audressein (1,625ft) Fronsac (1,548ft)	18km 29km	1 in 7 1 in 7	11ft	UO. Approached from the west by the easy Col des Ares (2,611ft) and Col de Buret (1,975ft); well-engineered road, but calls for particular care on hairpin bends; rather narrow.

*Permitted maximum width of vehicles 7ft 6in

PRINCIPAL MOUNTAIN PASSES

PASS AND HEIGHT	FROM TO	DISTANCES FROM SUMMIT AND MAX GRADIENT		MIN WIDTH OF ROAD	CONDITIONS (See page 39 for key to abbreviations)
Pötschen 3,221ft (982m) Austria	Bad Ischl (1,535ft) Bad Aussee (2,133ft)	19km 10km	1 in 11 1 in 11	23ft	*UO. A modern road; suitable for caravans.*
Pourtalet 5,879ft (1792m) France–Spain	Eaux-Chaudes (2,152ft) Biescas (2,821ft)	23km 34km	1 in 10 1 in 10	11 ft	*UC late Oct–early Jun.* A fairly easy, unguarded road, but narrow in places.
Puymorens 6,283ft (1915m) France	Ax-les-Thermes (2,362ft) Bourg-Madame (3,707ft)	28km 27km	1 in 10 1 in 10	18ft	*OC Nov–Apr.* A generally easy, modern tarmac road, but narrow, winding, and with a poor surface in places; not suitable for night driving; *suitable for caravans* (max height vehicles 11ft 6in). Alternative rail service available between Ax-les-Thermes and Latour-de-Carol.
Quillane 5,623ft (1714m) France	Quillan (955ft) Mont-Louis (5,135ft)	63km 5km	1 in 12 1 in 12	16ft	*OC Nov–Mar.* An easy, straightforward ascent and descent; *suitable for caravans.*
Radstäder-Tauern 5,702ft (1739m) Austria	Radstad (2,808ft) Mauterndorf (3,681ft)	21km 17km	1 in 6 1 in 7	16ft	*OC Jan–Mar.* Northern ascent steep, but not difficult otherwise; parallel toll motorway with tunnel (see page 37); *negotiable by light caravans, using tunnel.*
Résia (Reschen) 4,934ft (1504m) Italy–Austria	Spondigna (2,903ft) Pfunds (3,182ft)	29km 20km	1 in 10 1 in 10	20ft	*UO.* A good, straightforward alternative to the Brenner Pass; *suitable for caravans.*
Restefond (La Bonette) 9,193ft (2802m) France	Jausiers (near Barcelonnette) (3,986ft) St-Etienne-de-Tinée (3,766ft)	23km 27km	1 in 9 1 in 9	10ft	*UC Oct–Jun.* The highest pass in the Alps. Narrow, rough, unguarded ascent with many blind bends, and nine hairpins. Descent easier; winding with 12 hairpin bends.
Rolle 4,463ft (1970m) Italy	Predazzo (3,337ft) Mezzano (2,098ft)	21km 25km	1 in 11 1 in 14	16ft	*OC Dec–Mar.* Very beautiful scenery; bitumen surface; a well-engineered road; *negotiable by caravans.*
Rombo (see Timmelsjoch)					
Route des Crêtes 4,210ft (1283m) France	St-Dié (1,125ft) Cernay (902ft)	— —	1 in 8 1 in 8	13ft	*UC Nov–Apr.* A renowned scenic route crossing seven ridges, with the highest point at 'Hôtel du Grand Ballon'.
†St Gotthard (San Gottardo) 6,916ft (2108m) Switzerland	Göschenen (3,629ft) Airolo (3,747ft)	19km 15km	1 in 10 1 in 10	20ft	*UC mid Oct–early Jun.* Modern, fairly easy two or three-lane road. Heavy traffic; *negotiable by caravans* (max height vehicles 11ft 9in). Alternative road tunnel available (see page 36).
*San Bernardino 6,778ft (2066m) Switzerland	Mesocco (2,549ft) Hinterrhein (5,328ft)	22km 9.5km	1 in 10 1 in 10	13ft	*UC Oct–late Jun.* Easy, modern roads on northern and southern approaches to tunnel (see page 37); narrow and winding over summit; via tunnel *suitable for caravans.*

*Permitted maximum width of vehicles 7ft 6in
†Permitted maximum width of vehicles 8ft 2½in

46

PASS AND HEIGHT	FROM TO	DISTANCES FROM SUMMIT AND MAX GRADIENT		MIN WIDTH OF ROAD	CONDITIONS (See page 39 for key to abbreviations)
Schlucht 3,737ft (1139m) France	Gérardmer (2,182ft) Munster (1,250ft)	15km 17km	1 in 14 1 in 14	16ft	UO. An extremely picturesque route crossing the Vosges mountains, with easy, wide bends on the descent; *suitable for caravans.*
Seeberg (Jezersko) 3,996ft (1218m) Austria–Yugoslavia	Eisenkappel (1,821ft) Kranj (1,263ft)	14km 33km	1 in 8 1 in 10	16ft	UO. An alternative to the steeper Loibl and Wurzen passes; moderate climb with winding, hairpin ascent and descent.
Sella 7,349ft (2240m) Italy	Plan (5,269ft) Canazei (4,806ft)	9km 13km	1 in 9 1 in 9	16ft	OC Dec–Jun. A finely engineered, winding road; exceptional view of the Dolomites.
Semmering 3,232ft (985m) Austria	Mürzzuschlag im Mürztal (2,205ft) Gloggnitz (1,427ft)	14km 17km	1 in 16 1 in 16	20ft	UO. A fine, well-engineered highway; *suitable for caravans.*
Sestriere 6,670ft (2033m) Italy	Cesana Torinese (4,429ft) Pinerolo (1,234ft)	12km 55km	1 in 10 1 in 10	16ft	UO. Mostly bitumen surface; *negotiable by caravans.*
Silvretta (Blielerhöhe) 6,666ft (2032m) Austria	Partenen (3,448ft) Galtür (5,197ft)	16km 10km	1 in 9 1 in 9	16ft	UC late Oct–early Jun. For the most part reconstructed; 32 easy, hairpin bends on western ascent; eastern side more straightforward. Toll road; *caravans prohibited.*
†Simplon 6,578ft (2005m) Switzerland–Italy	Brig (2,231ft) Domodóssola (919ft)	22km 41km	1 in 9 1 in 11	23ft	OC Nov–Apr. An easy, reconstructed modern road, but 13 miles long, continuous ascent to summit; *suitable for caravans.* Alternative rail tunnel (see page 38).
Somport 5,354ft (1632m) France–Spain	Bedous (1,365ft) Jaca (2,687ft)	31km 30km	1 in 10 1 in 10	12ft	UO. A favoured, old-established route; generally easy, but in parts narrow and unguarded; fairly good-surfaced road; *suitable for caravans.*
*Splügen 6,932ft (2113m) Switzerland–Italy	Splügen (4,780ft) Chiavenna (1,083ft)	9km 30km	1 in 9 1 in 7½	10ft	UC Nov–Jun. Mostly narrow and winding, with many hairpin bends, and not well-guarded; care also required at many tunnels and galleries (max height vehicles 9ft 2in).
††Stelvio 9,045ft (2757m) Italy	Bormio (4,019ft) Spondigna (2,903ft)	22km 28km	1 in 8 1 in 8	13ft	UC Oct–late Jun. The third highest pass in the Alps; the number of acute hairpin bends, all well-engineered, is exceptional–from 40 to 50 on either side; their surface is good, the traffic heavy. Hairpin bends are too acute for long vehicles.
†Susten 7,297ft (2224m) Switzerland	Innertkirchen (2,067ft) Wassen (3,005ft)	28km 19km	1 in 11 1 in 11	20ft	UC Nov–Jun. A very scenic and well-guarded mountain road; easy gradients and turns; heavy traffic at weekends; *negotiable by caravans.*
Tenda (Tende) 4,334ft (1321m) Italy–France	Borgo S Dalmazzo (2,103ft) La Giandola (1,010ft)	24km 29km	1 in 11 1 in 11	18ft	UO. Well-guarded, modern road with several hairpin bends; road tunnel at summit; *suitable for caravans,* but *prohibited during the winter.*

*Permitted maximum width of vehicles 7ft 6in
†Permitted maximum width of vehicles 8ft 2½in

††Maximum length of vehicles 30ft

PRINCIPAL MOUNTAIN PASSES

PASS AND HEIGHT	FROM TO	DISTANCES FROM SUMMIT AND MAX GRADIENT		MIN WIDTH OF ROAD	CONDITIONS (See page 39 for key to abbreviations)
Thurn 4,180ft (1274m) Austria	Kitzbühel (2,500ft) Mittersill (2,588ft)	19km 10km	1 in 12 1 in 16	16ft	UO. A good road with narrow stretches; northern approach rebuilt; *suitable for caravans.*
Timmelsjoch (Rombo) 8,232ft (2509m) Austria–Italy	Obergurgl (6,322ft) Moso (3,304ft)	14km 21km	1 in 7 1 in 8	12ft	UC mid Oct–late Jun. The pass is open to private cars (without trailers) **only**, as some tunnels on the Italian side are too narrow for larger vehicles; toll road. *Roadworks on Italian side still in progress.*
Tonale 6,178ft (1883m) Italy	Edolo (2,264ft) Dimaro (2,513ft)	30km 27km	1 in 14 1 in 8	16 ft	UO. A relatively easy road; *suitable for caravans.*
Toses (Tosas) 5,905ft (1800m) Spain	Puigcerdá (3,708ft) Ribes de Freser (3,018ft)	25km 25km	1 in 10 1 in 10	16ft	UO. Now a fairly straightforward, but continuously winding, two-lane road with many sharp bends; some unguarded edges; *negotiable by caravans.*
Tourmalet 6,936ft (2114m) France	Luz (2,333ft) Ste-Marie-de-Campan (2,811ft)	19km 17km	1 in 8 1 in 8	14ft	UC Oct–mid Jun. The highest of the French Pyrenees routes; the approaches are good, though winding and exacting over summit; sufficiently guarded.
Tre Croci 5,935ft (1809m) Italy	Cortina d'Ampezzo (3,983ft) Auronzo di Cadore (2,835ft)	7km 26km	1 in 9 1 in 9	16ft	OC Dec–Mar. An easy pass; very fine scenery; *suitable for caravans.*
Turracher Höhe 5,784ft (1763m) Austria	Preditz (3,024ft) Ebene-Reichenau (3,563ft)	20km 8km	1 in 5½ 1 in 4½	13ft	UO. Formerly one of the steepest mountain roads in Austria; now much improved; steep, fairly straightforward ascent, followed by a very steep descent; good surface and mainly two-lane width; fine scenery.
***Umbrail** 8,205ft (2501m) Switzerland–Italy	Santa Maria im Münstertal (4,547ft) Bormio (4,019ft)	13km 19km	1 in 11 1 in 11	14ft	UC early Nov–early Jun. Highest of the Swiss passes; narrow; mostly gravel surfaced with 34 hairpin bends, but not too difficult.
Vars 6,919ft (2109m) France	St-Paul-sur-Ubaye (4,823ft) Guillestre (3,248ft)	8km 20km	1 in 10 1 in 10	16ft	OC Dec–Mar. Easy winding ascent with seven hairpin bends; gradual winding descent with another seven hairpin bends; good surface; *negotiable by caravans.*
Wurzen (Koren) 3,520ft (1073m) Austria–Yugoslavia	Riegersdorf (1,775ft) Kranjska Gora (2,657ft)	8km 5km	1 in 5½ 1 in 5½	13ft	UO. A steep two-lane road, which otherwise is not particularly difficult; heavy traffic at summer weekends; delay likely at the frontier; *caravans prohibited.*
Zirler Berg 3,310ft (1009m) Austria	Seefeld (3,871ft) Zirl (2,041ft)	7km 5km	1 in 7 1 in 6	20ft	UO. An escarpment facing south, part of the route from Garmisch to Innsbruck; a good, modern road, but heavy tourist traffic and a long steep descent, with one hairpin bend, into the Inn Valley. Steepest section from the hairpin bend down to Zirl; *caravans prohibited.*

*Permitted maximum width of vehicles 7ft 6in

ABOUT THE GAZETTEER

AA signs

The AA issues signs on request to hotels listed in this guide. You are advised, however, not to rely solely on the signs exhibited, but to check that the establishment still appears in this edition.

Charges

No prices are shown against individual hotels, but a price-banding chart appears at the beginning of the gazetteer for each country section. This shows the average *minimum* and *maximum* prices for *single* and *double* rooms within each classification, plus the average cost of breakfast and lunch/dinner. All average prices are expressed in **the currency of the country**, based on the rate of exchange at the time of going to press. For comparison, the current rate may be obtained from banks or from the national press. In the main, the average prices quoted should give a fairly accurate guide to hotel costs, but you are likely to find that accommodation is generally more expensive in capital cities and some of the larger, more popular towns.

In France, **DPn** indicates *demi-pension* (half-board) terms *only* available. This means that, in addition to the charge for rooms, guests are expected to pay for one main meal whether it is taken or not. **Pn** indicates *full pension* (full board) terms *only* available.

Hotels are not required by law to exchange traveller's cheques for guests, and many small hotels are unable to do so. You must expect to pay a higher rate of commission for this service at a hotel than you would at a bank.

Classification

Although the system of classification used in this guide is similar to that employed by the AA in this country, the variations in the traditions

---

EXAMPLE OF A GAZETTEER ENTRY

The gazetteer entries are compiled from information which is supplied by the proprietors of the establishments concerned, and every effort is made to ensure that the information given is up-to-date. Where this has not been possible, *establishment names have been printed in italics to show that particulars have not been confirmed by the management.*

Town name appears in bold type in alphabetical order

Hotel name, if hotel forms part of a group this is indicated by initials after name or by name itself, see **Hotel Groups** page 50.

Province

Classification see above

Address: street name followed by street number on the Continent.

SALZBURG
Salzburg **See Plan**

★ ★ ★ ★ ★ **Schoberschloss** (ABC)
Mönchsberg 62 ☎(0662) 413163
tx654321

Area telephone code and number

Etr—Oct: Rest closed sun pm
rm100 (⇥♓70) A5rm 🛏 **P**15 Lift ℂ
𝒫 ▭ ⌇ ♓ Ü Mountain
Creditcards ①③⑤

Opening dates (inclusive) and occasional restaurant closure (Etr = Easter, Whit = Whitsun). When no dates are shown, the establishment is open all year.

Specific accommodation details and facilities. The information in brackets gives number of rooms with facilities, private bath and/or private shower. See *Credit/charge cards* page 50 and *Symbols and Abbreviations*, page 56–57.

and customs of hotel-keeping abroad often make identical grading difficult.

Hotels and motels are classified by stars. The definitions are intended to indicate the type of hotel rather than the degree of merit. Meals, service, and hours of service should be in keeping with the classification, and all establishments with restaurants must serve meals to non-residents and are expected to give good value for money.

> ★ Hotels simply furnished, but clean and well kept; **all** bedrooms with hot and cold running water; adequate bath and lavatory facilities.
>
> ★ ★ Hotels offering a higher standard of accommodation; adequate bath and lavatory facilities on all main floors, and some private bathrooms and/or showers.
>
> ★ ★ ★ Well-appointed hotels, with a large number of bedrooms with private bathrooms/showers.
>
> ★ ★ ★ ★ Exceptionally well-appointed hotels offering a very high standard of comfort and service with **all** bedrooms providing private bathrooms/showers.
>
> ★ ★ ★ ★ ★ Luxury hotels offering the highest international standards.

Complaints

You are advised to bring any criticism to the notice of the hotel management immediately. This will enable the matter to be'dealt with promptly to the advantage of all concerned. If a personal approach fails, members should inform the AA. Please state whether or not your name may be disclosed in any enquiries we may make.

Credit/charge cards

The numbered boxes below indicate the credit/charge cards which the hotels accept

1 Access/Eurocard/Mastercard
2 American Express
3 Visa/Carte Bleue
4 Carte Blanche
5 Diners

It is advisable to check when booking to ensure that the cards are still accepted.

Hotels

The lists of hotels for each country have been compiled from information given by members,

by the motoring organisations and tourist offices of the countries concerned, and from many other sources.

Your comments concerning the whole range of hotel information – whether included in this guide or not, and whether in praise or in criticism – will always be most welcome; a special form will be found at the back of this book, and all information will be treated in the strictest confidence.

Hotel discounts

Travellers Discount Card This card, on sale at AA Centres (£5 to AA members and 5-Star purchasers and £6 to non-members) entitles holders to 10 per cent off the standard room rate at over 2,000 hotels in Europe. It also automatically provides third-party liability insurance cover for you and your party during your stay at participating hotels. The hotels at which the card is valid and listed in a booklet issued with the card, and these hotels will accept the card as an identity paper, which can be left with hotel reception during your stay instead of a passport.

The ITC is not valid in the country of issue; it is valid only for hotels abroad.

Hotel groups

Below is a list of hotel groups and consortia.

Key to abbreviations and company/consortia reservation telephone numbers:

COMPANY	TELEPHONE
Ambassador	01-541 0033
Altea	01-621 1962
Arcade	01-621 1962
Astir	01-636 0818
Best Western (BW)	01-541 0033
Climat de France	01-494 2261
Crest*	0800 200500
Dorint	01-978 5212
Fah/Minotel	(0253) 594185
Forum	01-741 9000
Gast im Schloss (GS)	01-408 0111
Golden Tulip (GT)	01-847 3951
Hilton International	01-780 1155
Holiday Inns	01-722 7755
Ibis	01-724 1000
Inter Continental (Intercont)	01-741 9000
Inter DK	01-351 7292
Inter S	01-351 7292
Italian Grand Hotels (CIGA)	01-930 4147
Jolly Hotels	0800 282729
L'Horset	01-951 3990

COMPANY	TELEPHONE
MAP Hotels (MAP)	01-541 0033
Melia	0800 282720
Mercure	01-724 1000
Minorel	(0252) 594185
Mövenpick	0800 894517
Novotel	01-724 1000
Pullman	01-621 1962
Queens Moat House (Hotels) Ltd	
(Queens Moat/QM)	(0423) 52644 & (0800) 289 330
Ramada	01-235 5264 & (0800) 181 737
Romantik (ROM)	01-408 0111
Sheraton	0800 353535
Sofitel	01-724 1000
Steigenberger (SRS)	01-486 5754
Trusthouse Forte (THF)	01-567 3444 & (0345) 500 400

*Crest Hotels offer AA members the opportunity to book a double room at the normal single rate (for double occupancy). For further information, please contact the central reservations office ☎(0295) 67733.

Note: London telephone codes are due to change on 6th May 1990.

Location maps

These are to be found at the beginning of each country section, except those for Luxembourg, Portugal and Sweden which are incorporated in the Belgian, Spanish and Norwegian maps respectively. The location maps are intended to assist the reader who wishes to stay in a certain area, by showing only those towns for which there is an entry in the gazetteer. Thus, someone wishing to stay in the Innsbruck area will be able to select suitable towns by looking at the map. The location maps in this book use the symbols in the box (next column) to indicate adjoining countries: It must be emphasised that these maps are not intended to be used to find your way around the country, and we recommend that readers should obtain the *AA Big Road Atlas Europe* on sale at AA Centres and good bookshops.

Reservations

The practice is the same on the Continent as it is in this country – rooms are booked subject to their still being available when confirmation is received. It is therefore most important that written confirmation be given to the hotel as soon as possible after rooms have been offered. Regrettably, many hotels will **not** accept

SYMBOLS USED FOR COUNTRY IDENTIFICATION

All location maps in this book use the following symbols to indicate adjoining countries

AL Albania		**I** Italy
AND Andorra		**FL** Liechtenstein
A Austria		**L** Luxembourg
B Belgium		**NL** Netherlands
BG Bulgaria		**N** Norway
CS Czechoslovakia		**PL** Poland
DK Denmark		**P** Portugal
SF Finland		**RO** Romania
F France		**E** Spain
D Germany (Fed Rep of)		**S** Sweden
DDR Germany (DDR)		**CH** Switzerland
GR Greece		**TR** Turkey
H Hungary		**SU** USSR
IRL Ireland (Rep of)		**YU** Yugoslavia

bookings for **one** or **two** nights only. Sometimes, a deposit is required, which can be arranged through your bank. Many hotels do not hold reservations after 19.00hrs, and you should advise hotels if you anticipate a late arrival, or if you are unable to take up your booking for any reason. Unwanted rooms can then often be relet, and you will be saved the expense of paying for them, as a written, confirmed booking represents a legal contract.

Hotel telephone numbers are given in the gazetteer. In some entries, the name of the group operating the hotel is indicated, and a key to the abbreviations used may be found on page 00, together with the telephone numbers for reservations. **Hotels belonging to a group or consortium (shown in the gazetteer entry) may usually be booked in the United Kingdom.**

Please see pages 50–51 for UK reservation numbers.

ABOUT THE GAZETTEER

When writing direct to hotels abroad, it is advisable to enclose an *International Reply Coupon*; these are available from any post office. Specimen letters appear on page 54.

Double rooms may not be reduced in price when let to one person; however, a double room is generally cheaper than two rooms. Accommodation in an annexe may be of different standard from rooms in the main hotel building; it is advisable to check the exact nature of the accommodation at the time of reservation.

Town plans

Listed below are major towns and cities for which town plans are included within the gazetteer. A list of hotels showing the plan number can be found adjacent to the relevant plan.

Innsbruck, Austria
Salzburg, Austria
Wien (Vienna), Austria
Bruxelles-Brussel (Brussels), Belgium
Oostende (Ostend), Belgium
København (Copenhagen), Denmark
Boulogne, France
Calais, France
Cherbourg, France
Dieppe, France
Le Havre, France
Nice, France
Paris, France
Bonn, Germany
Köln (Cologne), Germany
München (Munich), Germany
Gibraltar
Athinai (Athens), Greece
Dublin, Ireland (Rep of)
Firenze (Florence), Italy
Milano (Milan) Italy
Roma (Rome), Italy
Luxembourg
Amsterdam, Netherlands
Oslo, Norway
Lisboa (Lisbon), Portugal
Barcelona, Spain
Madrid, Spain
Santander, Spain
Stockholm, Sweden
Basel-Bâle-Basle (Basel), Switzerland
Bern (Berne), Switzerland
Genève (Geneva), Switzerland
Luzern (Lucerne), Switzerland
Zürich, Switzerland
Beograd (Belgrade), Yugoslavia

GARAGES

Garages(*See also under France and Spain*). The garages listed in the gazetteer for each country are those which are most likely to be of help to members on tour, because of their situation and the services they have stated they can provide. Although the AA cannot accept responsibility for difficulties over repairs to members' cars, any unsatisfactory cases will be noted for amendment in future editions of the guide.
It cannot be emphasised too strongly that disputes with garages on the Continent must be settled on the spot. It has been the AA's experience that subsequent negotiations can seldom be brought to a satisfactory conclusion.

In selecting garages, preference has been given to those which provide a breakdown service (see below) and those accepting *AIT Credit Vouchers*. The number of garages holding each agency reflects, as far as possible, the relative popularity of the various makes of cars. Although firms normally specialise in the makes for which they are accredited agents, they do not necessarily hold stocks of spare parts. Certain garages will repair only the make of car for which they are officially agents as indicated in the text. The symbol 'P' indicates that the establishments undertake the garaging of cars.
A complete list of service agencies for your make of car is generally available through your own dealer. It has been found that some garages in Europe occasionally make extremely high charges for repairing tourists' cars; always ask for an estimate before authorising a repair.

Breakdown service

The breakdown service of garages listed in the gazetteer is not free, and any assistance obtained must be paid for. The AA's free breakdown service for members operates in the United Kingdom and Republic of Ireland only. Therefore, motorists travelling in Europe are advised to purchase *AA 5-Star Service*; see *Breakdown* page 7 for further information.

Hours of opening

In most European countries, business hours are

08.00–18.00hrs; these times may be altered on Sundays and public holidays, when repairs, breakdown service, and petrol are often unobtainable.

In many countries, especially France, it may be difficult to get a car repaired during August, because many garages close down for annual holidays.

Alf	Alfa Romeo	**Fia**	Fiat	**Mit**	Mitsubishi	**Saa**	Saab
Ast	Aston Martin	**For**	Ford	**Nis**	Nissan	**Sko**	Skoda
Aud	Audi	**Hon**	Honda	**Ope**	Opel	**Tal**	Talbot
BMW	BMW	**Lan**	Lancia	**Peu**	Peugeot	**Toy**	Toyota
RR	Bentley	**LR**	Land Rover	**Por**	Porsche	**Vau**	Vauxhall
Cit	Citroen	**Lot**	Lotus	**Ren**	Renault	**VW**	Volkswagen
Dai	Daihatsu	**Maz**	Mazda	**RR**	Rolls-Royce	**Vol**	Volvo
Dj	Daimler/Jaguar	**Mer**	Mercedes-Benz	**Rov**	Rover Group		

MOTORING IN EUROPE?

IF SO YOU NEED AA 5-STAR SERVICE

If you are taking a European motoring holiday let AA 5-Star Service give you the added peace of mind of knowing that you, your family and your car are well cared for by the world's No. 1 motoring organisation.

AA 5-Star Service gives you roadside assistance, vehicle recovery, medical expenses and lots more besides – no wonder over 300,000 cars and over 800,000 people were covered last year.

So why not contact your local AA Centre or phone 021-550 7648 and ask for details now.

Have the Best – Don't Hope for The Best

ABOUT THE GAZETTEER: Specimen letters for booking hotels

Please use **block letters** and enclose an **International Reply Coupon**, obtainable from the Post office.

English

Dear sir
Please send me by return your terms with tax and service included, and confirm availability of accommodation with: Full board/Half Board/ Bed and Breakfast*
I would arrive on . . . .
and leave on . . . .
I would need . . . . rooms with single bed with/without* bath/shower*
. . . . rooms with double bed with/without* bath/shower*
. . . . rooms with twin beds with/without* bath/shower*
. . . . cots in parents' room
We are . . . . adults
Our party also includes . . . . children . . . . .
boys aged . . . . . . years and . . . . . . girls aged . . . . years.
I look forward to receiving your reply and thank you in advance.

German

Sehr geehrter Herr
Bitte senden Sie mir umgehend Angaben Ihrer Preise, einschl. Steuer-und. Bedienungskosten, und bestätigen, ob Sie Zimmer frei haben, für eine Unterbringung mit: Vollpension/Halbpension/Zimmer mit Frühstück*
Ankunftsdatum . . . .
Abfahrtsdatum . . . .
Ich möchte . . . . . Einzelzimmer mit/ohne* Bad/Dusche*
. . . . Zimmer mit Doppelbett mit/ohne* Bad/Dusche*
. . . . Zimmer mit zwei Betten mit/ohne* Bad/Dusche*
. . . . Kinderbettchen im Elternzimmer
Wir sind . . . . Erwachsene und zusätzlich . . . . . Kinder . . . . . Jungen
. . . . Jahre und . . . . Mädchen . . . . Jahre.
Ich sehe ihre Antwort gern entgegen und danke Ihnen im voraus für Ihre Bemühungen.

French

Monsieur
Pourriez vous m'indiquer par retour si vous pouvez réserver et à quel tarif, taxe et service comprise, pour un séjour en: Pension/Demi-pension/ Chambre et petit déjeuner*
J'arriverais le . . . .
et je repartirais le . . . .
Il me faudrait . . . . . chambres à un lit d'une personne avec/sans* bain/douche*
. . . . chambres à grand lit avec/sans* bain/douche*
. . . . chambres à deux lits avec/sans* bain/douche*
. . . . lits d'enfants dans la chambre des parents
Nous sommes . . . . adultes
accompagnés de . . . . . . enfants; . . . .
garçons de . . . . ans et . . . .
filles de . . . . ans.
J'attends vos renseignements et vous remercie par avance.

Italian

Eregio Direttore
Potrebbe indicarmi a ritorno di posta le condizioni d'alloggio con tasse e servizo inclusi, e se é possible riservare con: Pensione completa/ mezza pensione/camera e colazione*
Data d'arrivo . . . .
data di partenza . . . .
Vorrei riservare . . . . camera con letto singolo e con/senza* bagno/doccia*
. . . . camera con letto matrimoniale e con/senza* bagno/doccia*
. . . . camera a due letti e con/senza* bagno/doccia*
. . . . lettino nella camera dei genitori
Saimo . . . . adulti
accompagnati da . . . . bambini di
. . . . anni e . . . . . . bambini di . . . . . anni.
Resto in attesa di una sua cortese risposta e la ringrazio.

Spanish

Muy Señor mio
Sirvase comunicarme a vuelta de correo sus condiciones de alojamiento con impuestos y servicio incluidos, y si pudeo reservar con: Pensión completa/media pensión/habitación y desayuno*
Fecha de ilegada . . . .
Fecha de salida . . . .
Necesitaria . . . . habitaciones de una sola cama con/sin* baño/ducha*
. . . . habitaciones con cama de matrimonio con/sin* baño/ducha*
. . . . habitaciones de dos camas con/sin* baño/ducha*
. . . . camita en la habitación de los padres
Somos . . . . adultos
Acompañados por . . . . . . niños de . . . . . .
años y . . . . ninas de . . . . años.
Quedo a là espera de sus noticias y le doy las gracias.
**delete where inapplicable.*

54

The City Centre Hotel!

Also in Montréal
CANADA

Hambourg

Hull

Portsmouth
Zeebrugge Anvers
Dover Ostende Gand
Calais Hasselt
Lille Louvain
Boulogne-sur-Mer Bruxelles

Bochum
Essen
Düsseldorf
Cologne
Bonn

Cherbourg Caen Le Havre

Saint-Malo

Rouen Compiègne
Reims

Francfort
Wiesbaden
Heidelberg
Heilbronn
Strasbourg Regensbourg

Brest

Dreux Paris *

Laval Troyes
Orléans Sens Relais
Le Mans
Auxerre

Colmar
Mulhouse

Augsbourg
Munich

Lorient

Nantes Blois
Tours Dijon Relais
Besançon
Poitiers Beaune
Bourges Relais
Châteauroux Relais

La Rochelle
Rochefort Vichy
Limoges Lyon
Angoulême Clermont-Frd.
Relais Vienne
Périgueux Grenoble Relais

Villefranche-sur-Saône

Bordeaux

Montauban Relais
Toulouse Avignon
Pau Sète Montpellier Cannes
Lourdes Carcassonne Marseille
Hyères

Andorre

Ajaccio
Relais

RESERVATIONS/INFORMATIONS

UNITED KINGDOM
Tel.: 01/621.19.62
Fax: 01/283.57.52
Telex: 881.36.08

FRANCE
Tel.: 1/42.68.23.45

BELGIUM
Tel.: 02/218.26.46

W. GERMANY
Tel.: 069/23.08.58

HOTEL ARCADE
member of
PULLMAN INTERNATIONAL HOTELS

* PARIS AND SURROUNDINGS

Paris Bastille
Paris Bercy
Paris Cambronne
Paris Montparnasse
Paris la Villette
Paris Mairie-d'Issy
Corbeil
Evry
Juvisy-S/-Orge
Orly-Aéroport
Poissy
Rueil-Malmaison
Cergy-Pontoise
Sarcelles
Roissy-Aéroport
Marne-la-Vallée

SYMBOLS & ABBREVIATIONS

English

★★★	Hotel classification
O	Hotel likely to be open during the currency of this annual guide
⇄	Private baths
♠	Private showers
P	Parking for cars
☎	Garage and/or lock-up
☽	Night porter
♪	Tennis court(s) (private)
►	Golf (private)
�	Riding stables (private)
▣	Indoor swimming pool
⊇	Outdoor swimming pool
➹	Breakdown service
☎	Telephone number
DPn	Demi-pension
Pn	Full pension
(n.rest)	Hotel does not have its own restaurant
tx	Telex
rm	Number of bedrooms (including annexe)
A	Annexe, followed by number of rooms
Ŀ	Logis de France
M/c	Motorcycle repairs undertaken
Beach	Hotel has private beach
Sea/Moun-tain/Lake	Rooms overlook sea, mountain(s) or a lake
→	Entry continued overleaf
Credit cards	(see page 50)

For a more detailed explanation refer to 'About the Gazetteer' pages 49–54

Français

★★★	Classement des hôtels
O	Hôtels qui doivent ouvrir prochainement
⇄	Salles de bain privées
♠	Douches privées
P	Parking pour voitures
☎	Garage et/ou garage avec serrure
☽	Portier de nuit
♪	Court(s) de tennis (privè)(s)
►	Golf (privè)
♁	Equitation (privée)
▣	Piscine couverte
⊇	Piscine en plein air
➹	Service dépannage
☎	Numèro de téléphone
DPn	Demi-pension
Pn	Pension complète
(n.rest)	Hôtel sans restaurant
tx	Télex
rm	Nombre de chambres (annexes comprises)
A	Annexe suivie par nornbre de chambres
Ŀ	Logis de France
M/c	Réparations de cyclomoteurs possibles
Beach	Hôtel a une plage privée
Sea/Moun-tain/Lake	Chambres avec vue sur la mer, les montagnes ou un lac
→	Suite au verso
Cartes de crédit	(voir page 50)

Pour plus amples informations veuillez vous référer à 'About the Gazetteer' voir pages 49–54

Deutsch

★★★	Hotelklassitizierung
O	Hotel wird während der Laufzeit dieses Führers eröffnet
⇄	Privatbad
♠	Privatdusche
P	Parken
☎	Garage bzw verschliessbare Parkeinheit
☽	Nachtportier
♪	Tennisplatz (Privat)
►	Golfplatz (Privat)
♁	Reitgelegenheiten (Privat)
▣	Hallenbad
⊇	Freibad
➹	Pannendienst
☎	Telefonnummer
DPn	Demipension
Pn	Vollpension
(n.rest)	Hotel ohne eigenes Restaurant
tx	Telex
rm	Zimmeranzahl (einschliesslich Nebengebaude)
A	Nebengebaude und danach Zimmeranzahl
Ŀ	Logis de Frar ce
M/c	Motorradreparaturen
Beach	Hotel hat Privatstrand
Sea/Moun-tain/Lake	Zimmer mit einem Blick auf das Meer, die Gebirge oder einen See
→	Fortsetzung siehe umseitig
Kreditkarten	(siehe Seite 50)

Für weitere Angaben beziehen Sie sich auf 'About the Gazetteer' siehe Seiten 49–54

Italiano

★★★	Classificazione alberghi
O	Alberghi che saranno aperti durante il periodo di validita della guida
⇄	Bagni privati
♠	Docce private
P	Parcheggio macchine
☎	Garage e/o box
☽	Portiere notturno
♪	Campi da tennis (privati)
►	Golf (privato)
♁	Scuola d'equitazione (privata)
▣	Piscina coperta
⊇	Piscina all'aperto
➹	Servizio assistenza stradale
☎	Numero telefonico
DPn	Mezza pensione
Pn	Pensione completa
(n.rest)	Albergo senza ristorante
tx	Telex
rm	Numero di camere (compresa la dependance)
A	Dependence, seguita dal numero di camere
Ŀ	Logis de France
M/c	Si riparano motociclette
Beach	L'albergo è provvisto di spiaggia privata
Sea/Moun-tain/Lake	Le camere guardano sul mare/i mont/il lago
→	La lista delle voici continua a tergo
Carte di credito	(vedere pagine 50)

Per una splegazione plé dettagliata, consultare la sezione 'About the Gazetteer' vedere pags 49–54

SYMBOLS & ABBREVIATIONS

Español

★★★   Clasificación de hoteles
○   Hoteles a ser inaugurados durante la vigencia de estaguia
⇄   Baños en cada habitación
🏠   Duchas en cada habitación
P   Aparcamiento para automóviles
🏠   Garaje y/o garaje individual con cerradura
☽   Conserje nocturno
♀   Pistas de tenis (privadas)
▶   Golf (privado)
∪   Escuela hípica (privada)
▣   Piscina cubierta
⌾   Piscina al aire libre
🗠   Servicio de asistencia avenas
☎   Número de teléfono
DPn   Media pensión
Pn   Pensión completa

(n.rest)   El hotel no tiene restaurante
tx   Telex
rm   Número de habitaciones (incluso el edificio anexo)
A   Edificio anexo, seguido por el número de habitaciones
Ⱡ   Logis de France
M/c   Se reparan motocicletas
Beach   El hotel tiene playa privada
Sea/Mountain/Lake   Las habitaciones tienen vista al mar/a las montañas/al lago
→   La lista de símbolos continúa a la vuelta
Plan   El número indica la posición del hotel en el plano de la ciudad
Tarjetas de crédito   (véase página 50)

Para una explicación más detallada, consúltese la sección 'About the Gazetteer' (véase el índice de materias) véase paginas 49–54

AA

DIRECTORY

Motoring abroad

Phone before you go

Ring our recorded information service for the latest news on ferries and crossing conditions, as well as traffic and roadworks around the Channel ports and on Continental motorways and main roads.

ROADWATCH EUROPE

Continental Roadwatch Update

0836-401-904

For your free copy of the complete AA Directory, call 0256 491648.

Messages are charged at 25p per minute cheap rate, 38p per minute at all other times (including VAT); callers pay only for the time they use. Prices for mobile calls can vary – see your service provider.

We're all you need to know.

AA

W hether you are seeking peace and relaxation, fun and activity, or would rather spend your time exploring beautiful and fascinating cities and towns, Austria cannot fail to delight. You can take to the meadows and mountains, either alone or with a guide, following beautiful marked trails which reveal the splendour of the unspoiled countryside. Or you can scale great mountains by chairlift or mountain railway and be rewarded with a magnificent panorama of peaks and a land full of forests, lakes and meadows.

For the more active, Austria offers an enormous range of sports facilities and amenities throughout the year. In winter, skiers head for Austria's slopes and are pampered in some of the world's finest winter holiday resorts, while summer visitors can enjoy wind-surfing, golf, tennis, sailing, water-skiing, para-sailing, cycling, horse-riding, hang-gliding, walking and hiking, swimming, fishing, canoeing and rafting.

Then there are the cities – Vienna, the cultural showcase of Europe, where old-world charm is blended with imperial splendour; Salzburg, stunningly located at the foot of the snow-capped Austrian Tyrol; and Innsbruck, which preserves its delightful medieval core.

AUSTRIA

Language
German

Local Time
GMT + 1 hour (Summer GMT + 2 hours)

Currency
Austrian *schilling*, divided into 100 *groschen*. At the time of going to press
£1 = ASch 21.85
US $1 = ASch 13.16

Emergency numbers
Fire 122   Police 133
Ambulance 144

Information In Britain
Austrian National Tourist Organisation, 30 St George Street, London. W1R 0AL
☎01-629 0461 (☎071-629 0461 from 6th May 1990)

Information in the USA
Austrian National Tourist Office, 500 Fifth Avenue, New York, NY 10110
☎212 944 6880

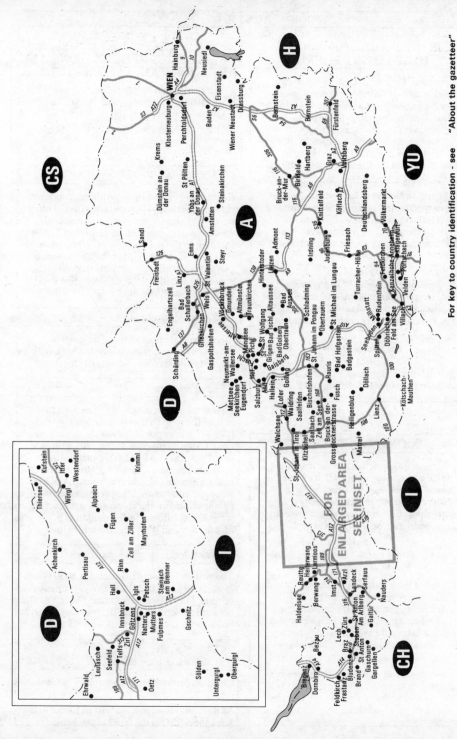

For key to country identification - see   "About the gazetteer"

Map labels (main map):

H

CS

YU

A

D

I

CH

Hainburg
9
Neusiedl
10
WIEN
Klosterneuburg
Perchtoldsdorf
S3 A22
Baden
Eisenstadt
Draßburg
Wiener Neustadt
A2
Bernstein
Bernstein
307
Fürstenfeld
65
S6
Hartberg
Birkfeld
306
Graz
A2
Wolfsberg
A9
Krems
Dürnstein an
der Donau
St Pölten
A1
Steinakirchen
Ybbs an
der Donau
Amstetten
Bruck-an-
der-Mur
116
A9
Knittelfeld
Köflach
Deutschlandsberg
Sandl
125
Ems
Steyr
Linz A1
St Valentin
S5
Admont
Irdning
112
Judenburg
Friesach
83
Völkermarkt
20
Freistadt
Hinterstoder
Liezen
A9
Turracher-Höhe
Klagenfurt
138
Engelhartszell
Bad
Schallerbach
Wels
Altmünster
Bad
Aussee
Schladming
94
Feldkirchen
Velden
16
Tarvisch
137
Grieskirchen
Vöcklabruck
Gmunden
Traunkirchen
Altaussee
A10
Klanzelhöhe-Annenheim
Villach
A2
Schärding
A8
Gaspoltshofen
Attersee
Mondsee
St Gilgen Bad Ischl
St Wolfgang
Bad
Oberau
St Johann im Pongau
St Michael im Lungau
Spital
Döbriach
Seeboden
Feld am See
Neumarkt-am-
Seekirchen Wallersee
Pichl
Golling
163
Obertauern
Millstatt
Radenthein
Eugendorf
Mattsee
Salzburg
Gaisberg
Hallein
Waldring
Bischofshofen
Rauris
Bad Hofgastein
Döllach
Kötschach-
Mauthen
Walchsee
Lofer
312
Saalfelden
Zell am See
168
Fusch
Badgastein
Lienz
108
100
Kitzbühel
Saalbach
Bruck an der-
Grossglocknerstrasse
Heiligenblut
100
St Johann in Tirol
Matrei

ENLARGED AREA
FOR
SEE INSET

A12
313
A12
189

Reutte
Hartenwang
Heiterwang
Berwang
Lermoos
Imst
171
Arzl
316
Landeck
Serfaus
Nauders
Haldensee
Bregenz
A14
Bezau
Lech Zürs
Braz
St Anton
Stuben
Am Arlberg
St Christoph
Gaschurn
Gargellen
Dornbirn
Feldkirch
Frastanz
Bludenz
Brand
Galtür

Inset map labels:

D

I

CH

Kufstein
312
Itter
Westendorf
Thiersee
Wörgl
Alpbach
Krimml
Achenkirch
A12
Fügen
Pertisau
Rinn
Zell am Ziller
Mayrhofen
A12
Hall
Igls
Steinach
am Brenner
Seefeld
Telfs
313
Zirl
Innsbruck
Götzens
Natters
Patsch
Mutters
Fulpmes
A13
Gschnitz
Leutasch
Ehrwald
A12
171
189
A12
Oetz
Sölden
Untergurgl
Obergurgl

59

HOW TO GET THERE

The usual Continental Channel ports for this journey are Calais, Oostende (Ostend) or Zeebrugge. *For Salzburg and central Austria* drive through Belgium to *Aachen* then via *Köln* (Cologne), *Frankfurt*, *Nürnberg* and *München* (Munich). *For Innsbruck and The Tirol* as above to *Frankfurt*, then via *Karlsruhe* and *Stuttgart*.

As an alternative, you could cross to Dieppe, Le Havre or Cherbourg and drive through northern France via **Strasbourg** and **Stuttgart**, or via **Basle** and northern Switzerland. But see 'Motorways' in the Switzerland section for details of motorway tax.

Distance
From the Continental Channel ports, Salzburg is about 1130km (700 miles) and Vienna is about 1450km (900 miles), and you would normally need one overnight stop on the way.

Car sleeper trains
Services are available in summer from Brussels in Belgium and 's-Hertogenbosch in the Netherlands to Salzburg and Villach.

MONEYMATTERS

There are no restrictions on the amount of foreign or Austrian currency that a bona fide tourist can take into the country. No more than ASch 50,000 in local currency can be taken out of Austria, but there is no such restriction on foreign currency.

Banking Hours
Monday–Friday 08.00–12.30hrs and 13.30–15.00hrs (17.30hrs on Thursdays)

There is a bank counter at the head office of the Austrian motoring club (ÖAMTC) which is open during office hours (see under Motoring Club). Exchange offices at some main railway stations are open at weekends and on public holidays.

Postcheques
may be cashed at all post offices for any amount up to ASch 2,500 per cheque. Go to the counter with the 'Postcheque' window sticker.

MOTORING REGULATIONS AND GENERAL INFORMATION

The information given here is specific to Austria. It **must** be read in conjunction with the European ABC at the front of the book, which covers those regulations which are common to many countries.

Accidents*

If you are involved in an accident, you must stop and exchange particulars with the other party. If anyone is injured, you *must* obtain medical assistance, and immediately report the incident to the police. Anyone who arrives at the scene of an accident is obliged to render assistance unless it is obvious that everything necessary has already been done. See also *Warning triangle below.*

Boats*

Motorboats are now allowed on most of Austria's lakes. It is advisable to check with the Tourist Office before taking boats to Austria.

Breakdown*

If your car breaks down, try to move it to the side of the road so that it obstructs the traffic flow as little as possible. The Austrian motoring club, *Österreichischer Automobil-Motorrad-und Touring Club* (ÖAMTC), maintains a roadside assistance service (Pannenhilfe) and a towing service (Abschleppdienst). A patrol service (Strassenwacht) operates around Wien (Vienna), and on the south and west motorways when the volume of traffic demands it. See also *Motorways* and *Warning triangle* below.

British Embassy/Consulates*

The British Embassy is located at 1030 Wien, Jaurègasse 12 ☏(0222) 7131575/9; consular section, Jaurègasse 10 ☏(0222) 756117/8. There are British Consulates with Honorary Consuls in Bregenz, Graz, Innsbruck and Salzburg.

Children in cars
(See also European ABC)

Children under 12 must not travel in front seats

*Additional information will be found in the European ABC at the front of the book.

unless they are using special seats, or safety belts which are suitable for children.

Dimensions and weight restrictions

Private **cars** and towed **trailers** or **caravans** are restricted to the following dimensions – height, 4 metres; width, 2.50 metres; length, 12 metres. The maximum permitted overall length of vehicle/trailer or caravan combinations is 18 metres.

Trailers without brakes may weigh up to 750kg and may have a total weight of up to 50% of the towing vehicle.

Driving licence*

A valid UK licence is acceptable in Austria, and although language difficulties may give rise to misunderstanding in a few isolated cases, it is legally valid. The minimum age at which a visitor may use a temporarily imported motorcycle (exceeding 50cc) or car is 18 years. The Austrian motoring club (ÖAMTC) will supply a free translation of your licence into German, but this is only available from their head office in Wien (Vienna), and therefore will only be of use if touring in eastern Austria. However, an International Driving Permit is required by the holder of a licence issued in the Republic of Ireland – compulsory if it is a red three-year licence and recommended if it is a pink EC type licence.

Emergency messages to tourists*

Emergency messages to tourists are broadcast daily by Austrian Radio in the *Autofahrer unterwegs* programme. These messages are transmitted in German on VHF between 11.30–12.45hrs Monday to Saturday and 12.00–13.00hrs on Sundays and public holidays.

First-aid kit*

In Austria, all vehicles (including motorcycles) must be, by law, be equipped with a first-aid kit, and visitors are expected to comply. This item will not be checked at the frontier, but motorists can be stopped at the scene of an accident and their first-aid kit demanded; if you do not have one, the police may take action.

Hitch-hiking

In Austria, hitch-hiking is generally prohibited on motorways and highways. In Upper Austria,

Styria, Burgenland and Vorarlberg, hitch-hiking is prohibited for persons under the age of 16.

Horn, use of

The horn must not be used where the relevant sign is displayed. Generally, the use of the horn is prohibited at night in large towns and resort areas; it is prohibited at all times in Wien (Vienna).

Insurance*

All temporarily-imported trailers must be covered by a separate policy, not the policy covering the towing vehicle.

Lights

Although it is prohibited to drive with undipped headlights in built-up areas, motorists may give warning of their approach by flashing their lights. It is prohibited to drive on unlit urban motorways and outside built-up areas with sidelights only. In poor visibility, motorists may use fog lamps in conjunction with both sidelights and dipped headlights. Parking lights are not required if the vehicle can be seen from 50 metres (55yds). Lights on lamp-posts which are ringed with red do not stay on all night and parking lights will be required. It is compulsory for *motorcyclists* to use dipped headlights during the day.

Motoring club*

 The **Österreichischer Automobil-Motorrad-un Touring Club** (ÖAMTC) has its headquarters at 1010 Wien, Schubertring 1–3 ☎(0222) 71199–0 (located on the plan of Wien within the gazetteer). It also has offices at the major frontier crossings, and is represented in most towns either direct or through provincial motoring clubs. The offices are usually open between 08.30 and 18.00hrs weekdays, 09.00 to 12.00hrs on Saturdays and are closed on Sundays and public holidays.

Motorways

About 875 miles of motorway (*Autobahn*) are open, and more stretches are under construction. A network of just over 1,000 miles

*Additional information will be found in the European ABC at the front of the book.

is planned. Only three motorways carry a toll: the Brenner Autobahn, the Tauern Autobahn and the Pyhrn Autobahn (Gleinalm and Bosruck Tunnels). For details of tolls, see Major Road Tunnels in the Route Planning section of the book.

There are *emergency telephones* at 2km (1¼m) intervals and small triangles on the guard-rails or limitation posts point towards the nearest. To use the telephone, lift the speaking flap and you will be automatically connected to the motorway control. The location of the post is printed inside the speaking flap; read this into the telephone, standing 6 to 8in away from the microphone. If you ask for help and then find you do not need it, you must tell the motorway control. On the Brenner motorway, emergency call posts of a different type have been installed. They are coloured red and orange and have a speaking tube and four levers bearing the symbols for police, Red Cross, repair service and telephone connection. By pressing the appropriate lever, you will be connected with the required emergency service. When one of the first three levers is used, sufficient indication of what type of help is needed is conveyed to the headquarters in Innsbruck; when the telephone connection lever is used you can talk direct to the headquarters, who will then send help if required.

At the top of each telephone post, there is an orange/yellow light, which flashes if there is danger on that stretch of the motorway.

Orange badge scheme for disabled drivers*

In Austria, badge holders are allowed to park without any time limit in areas where restricted or prohibited parking signs appear (red rings and bars with blue background). In some areas, the local authority provides special parking places for disabled persons' vehicles near hospitals and public service facilities.

Parking

Before you leave your vehicle, make sure it does not contravene parking regulations; cars must be parked in the direction of the traffic flow. Parking is forbidden on a main road or one carrying fast-moving traffic. In addition, parking is prohibited wherever there is a sign reading *Beschränkung für Halten oder Parken* (restriction for stopping or parking).

There is a total ban on stopping on roads

which have priority (as a rule, Federal roads), in case of fog or any other impediment to visibility. It is forbidden to leave a caravan trailer without its towing vehicle in a public parking place. Spending the night in a vehicle or trailer on the roadside is prohibited.

Blue Zones are areas where short-term parking is allowed. They are indicated by a No Parking sign bearing the words *Zone* or *Kurzparkzone*, and sometimes blue road markings, and, unless the sign indicates otherwise, parking is allowed for up to 3 hours. Parking tickets must be purchased in advance from the ÖAMTC, from banks or tobacconists, and the date and time of arrival indicated on the ticket. You should note that the only signs are those which mark the beginning of the zone and there are no further reminders. In Baden, Bludenz, Bregenz, Feldkirch, Graz, Innsbruck, Klagenfurt, Krems, Linz, St Polten, St Veit/Glan, Schwaz, Villach, Volkermaskt, Wien (Vienna) and Wiener Neustadt a charge is made for parking if more than two wheels of the vehicle are parked within the Blue Zone.

In other towns you can park free for up to 90 minutes in a Blue Zone, but you must display a parking disc which is available free of charge from any tobacconist.

Between 15 December and 31 March, parking is prohibited at night on any roads with tram lines.

Petrol*

Credit cards Petrol stations generally accept recognised credit cards.
Duty-free petrol In addition to the petrol in the vehicle tank, up to 10 litres in a can may be imported free of customs duty and tax.
Petrol (leaded) Super benzin (98 octane) grade is available.
Petrol (unleaded) is sold in Austria as *Normal benzin* (91 octane) and *Eurosuper benzin* (95 octane) grades. Pumps dispensing unleaded petrol are marked with a green point or label indicating *Euro 95* or *Eurosuper* or *bleifrei*. The octane rating is clearly marked on the individual pumps, except for those in a few non-brand garages.

Postal information

Mail Postcards ASch5, letters up to 20gm ASch6, at the time of going to press.

*Additional information will be found in the European ABC at the front of the book.

Post offices There are 2,300 post offices in
Austria. Opening hours in major towns are
08.00–17.00hrs Monday to Friday, 08.00–
10.00hrs Saturday. Elsewhere, they are open
08.00–12.00hrs and 14.00–16.00hrs Monday to
Friday. Some large offices are open longer.

Priority*

Vehicles which continue straight ahead or
make a right-hand turn at a crossroads or
intersection have priority over oncoming
vehicles turning left, providing that there are no
signs to the contrary; in this case even trams
cede priority. If you wish to turn across the flow
of traffic at a junction controlled by a
policeman, pass in front of him unless
otherwise directed.

Public holidays 1990*

Official public holidays in Austria for 1990 are
given below.
   January 1† (New Year's Day)
   January 6 (Epiphany)
   April 16 (Easter Monday)
   May 1 (Labour Day)
   May 24 (Ascension Day)
   June 4 (Whit Monday)
   June 14 (Corpus Christi)
   August 15 (Assumption)
   October 26 (National Day)
   November 1 (All Saints' Day)
   December 8† (Immaculate Conception)
   December 25 (Christmas Day)
   December 26 (St Stephen's Day)
†Saturday

Roads including holiday traffic

Austria has a network of well-engineered roads.
   The main traffic artery runs from Bregenz in
the west to Wien (Vienna) in the east, via the
Arlberg Tunnel (Toll: see Major Road Tunnels
with the Route Planning section of the book),
Innsbruck, Salzburg, and Linz. Most of the
major alpine roads are excellent, and a
comprehensive tour can be made through the
Tirol, Salzkammergut and Carinthia without
difficulty. Service stations are fairly frequent,
even on mountain roads.
   In July and August, several roads across the
frontier become congested, mainly on the
Lindau–Bregenz road; at the Brenner Pass
(possible alternative – the Resia Pass); at
Kufstein; on the München (Munich)–Salzburg
Autobahn and on the Villach–Tarvisio road.

Details of mountain passes can be found within
the Route Planning section of the book. See also
Road conditions in the European ABC.

Shopping hours

Generally, shops are open 08.00–18.00hrs
Monday–Friday with a one or two-hour break
for lunch, except in central Wien (Vienna),
where shops do not close for lunch; on
Saturday, most shops close at 12.00 or 12.30hrs.
   Some shops operate a tax-free service
whereby, on leaving the country, visitors are
reimbursed for VAT paid. A special form *(U34)*
must be obtained, completed and stamped,
from the shop and presented to the Austrian
customs when crossing the border. Look for
shops displaying the blue 'Tax-free Shopping'
sign, or go to the local tourist information or
ÖAMTC office for address lists.

Speed limits*

The beginning of a built-up area is indicated by
the sign *Ortsanfang*, and the end by a sign
bearing the inscription *Ortsende* (end of area)
followed by the name of the place. In these
areas, the maximum speed for all vehicles
(except mopeds) is 50kph (31mph); mopeds
40kph (24mph). Outside built-up areas, private
cars are subject to a speed limit of 100kph
(62mph), which is increased to 130kph
(80mph) on motorways, unless lower speed
limits are indicated. Private vehicles towing
trailers with a total weight of less than 750kg*
(1,650lb) are restricted to 100kph (62mph) on
all roads, including motorways, outside
built-up areas. If the trailer is over 750kg*, then
the limit is 100kph on motorways and 80kph
(49mph) on main roads outside built-up areas.
At certain periods during the summer, lower
speed restrictions are imposed.
   *If the weight of the trailer exceeds that the
towing vehicle (or if the total weight of the two
vehicles exceeds 3,500kg), the limit outside
built-up areas is 60kph (37mph) and 70kph
(43mph) on motorways. **Note** When the total
weight of the two vehicles exceeds 3,500kg, it is
not permissible to tow with a motorcar driving
licence.

Spiked or studded tyres

Spiked tyres May generally be used on many

***Additional information will be found in the
European ABC at the front of the book.**

Austrian roads between November and April. Exact dates are published by the national authorities, though there may be local variations. They may only be used on vehicles with a maximum total authorised weight no exceeding 3,500kg. Spiked tyres must be fitted on all wheels, or on two wheels if the drive wheels are fitted with wheel chains. Speed must be restricted to 80kph (49mph) outside built-up areas and 100kph (62mph) on motorways.

Telephone*

You will find instructions in English in many callboxes.
Insert coin **after** lifting the receiver.
Use ASch1, 5 or 10 coins for local calls and ASch10 or 20 coins for national and international calls.
International callboxes have payphones with three/four coin slots.
Cardphones can also be used for international calls.

Telephone codes

UK to Austria	010 43
Austria to UK	00 44
Austria to Republic of Ireland	00 353
Austria to the USA	00 1

Traffic lights*

A flashing green light indicates that the green phase is about to end; an orange light with the red light indicates that the green phase is about to begin.

Warning triangle*

The use of a warning triangle is compulsory in the event of accident or breakdown. The triangle must be placed on the road an adequate distance behind the vehicle or obstacle, and must be clearly visible from 200 metres (220yds).

Wheel chains

If you plan to motor in areas of high altitude during winter, you may find wheel chains are compulsory in certain local conditions. It is probably better to consider hiring or purchasing these at home before you leave; they can be hired from the AA (allow at least 28 days prior to departure date) or purchased from a car accessory shop (allow 6–8 weeks for delivery). This will have the advantage of ensuring a proper fit. Alternatively, they may be hired from the ÖAMTC for a maximum period of 60 days, but a deposit will have to be paid. They are delivered packaged; if they are returned unused the deposit is returned, less a percentage reduction according to the length of hire. The conditions of hire are fully described in a leaflet issued by the ÖAMTC from any of their offices. See also *Cold-weather touring* in the European ABC.

Winter conditions*

Entry from southern Germany The main approaches to Innsbruck and Salzburg and Wien (Vienna) are not affected.

Entry from Switzerland Vorarlberg and the Tirol are accessible at all times through the Arlberg Tunnel (toll).

From Austria to Italy The Resia and Brenner Passes are usually open throughout the year, but snow chains may be necessary in severe weather. The Plöcken Pass is occasionally closed in winter. Roads entering Italy at Dobbiaco and Tarvisio are usually clear, providing an unobstructed through-route from Wien (Vienna) to Venezia (Venice).

From Austria to Yugoslavia It is best to travel via Lavamünd and Dravograd, or via Graz and Maribor. Entry via the Wurzen and Seeberg Passes and the Liobl Pass road tunnel is possible but not advised.

Within Austria In the provinces of Upper Austria, Lower Austria and Burgenland, motoring is unaffected by winter conditions; elsewhere, because of the altitude, it is restricted.
When the Grossglockner Pass is closed, Ost Tirol and Carinthia can be reached by either the Felbertauern road tunnel, the Tauern Autobahn or the Tauern railway tunnel between Böckstein (near Badgastein) and Mallnitz (see Major Road Tunnels within the Route Planning section of the book).

Winter sports resorts The main approach roads are swept, and are closed only in the most severe weather. Zürs and Lech can be reached via the Arlberg Pass only.

*Additional information will be found in the European ABC at the front of the book.

ACCOMMODATION

Hotels are officially classified from five star (luxury) to one star (simple hotels) and the charges for the room, pension, service and heating charges are displayed in the bedrooms

The prices shown below are an average for each classification. Accommodation is likely to be more expensive in Wien (Vienna) and in some of the more popular tourist areas.

At the time of going to press, £1 *Sterling = ASch21.85 and US$1 = ASch13.16* but you should check the rate of exchange before your departure.

AVERAGE PRICES

	Single Room	Double Room	Breakfast	Lunch/Dinner
★★★★★	ASch1775–2470	ASch2420–3590	ASch149–258	ASch223–614
★★★★	ASch967–1338	ASch1280–1834	ASch80–90	ASch198–477
★★★	ASch607–918	ASch928–1796	ASch81–117	ASch132–265
★★	ASch449–665	ASch706–1044	ASch66–94	ASch115–199
★	ASch335–432	ASch513–707	ASch57–184	ASch99–189

Abbreviations:
pl   platz
str   strasse

ACHENKIRCH AM ACHENSEE
Tirol
★**Sporthotel Imhof** ☎(05246)6309
20 Dec-Oct
⏴ℿ30 ☒ P30 Lift Mountain
Credit Card ①
⏴ **F Moser** Nr 497 ☎(05246) 6269 For

ADMONT
Steiermark
★★**Post** ☎(03613)2416
rm35(⏴ℿ30) ☒ P Mountain

AIGEN
See SALZBURG

ALPBACH
Tirol
★★★★**Böglerhof** (ROM) Dorfpl ☎(05336)5227 tx 051160
mid May-mid Oct
⏴ℿ46 ☒ P2 Lift ⚲ ☐ ☒ Mountain
Credit Cards ① ③
★★★**Alpbacher-Hof** ☎(05336)5237
12 May-Sep & 10 Dec-Mar
⏴ℿ55 ☒ P2 Lift ☐ Mountain
Credit Card ③

ALTAUSSEE
Steiermark
★★★**Tyrol** (n.rest) ☎(06152)71636
⏴ℿ21 ☒ P30 Lift ☾ Mountain Lake
Credit Cards ① ② ③ ④ ⑤
★★**Hubertushof** Puchen 86 (n.rest)
☎(06152)71280
27 Dec-10 Jan, Feb & 20 May-Sep
⏴ℿ9 A1rm ☒ P2 ☒ Mountain Lake
Credit Cards ① ③ ⑤

ALTMÜNSTER
Oberösterreich
★★**Reiberstorfer** Maximilianstrabe 2
☎(07612)8338
⏴ℿ37 ☒ P70 Lift Beach Mountain Lake
Credit Cards ① ② ③ ⑤

AMSTETTEN
Niederösterreich
★★★**Hofmann** Bahnhofstr 2 ☎(07472)2516 tx 19212
rm56(⏴ℿ44) ☒ P25 Lift
Credit Cards ① ② ③ ⑤

ANIF
Salzburg
★★**Schlosswirt** (ROM) ☎(06246)2175
⏴ℿ36 A17rm ☒ P Mountain

ARZL IM PITZTAL
Tirol
★★**Post** ☎(05412)3111 tx 58240
⏴ℿ70 A30rm ☒ P20 Lift Mountain

ATTERSEE
Oberösterreich
★★**Oberndorfer** Hauptstr 18 ☎(07666)364
Mar-Nov :Rest closed Nov
⏴ℿ24 ☒ P55 ☒ Beach Mountain Lake
Credit Cards ① ③
★★★**Erzherzog Johann** Kurhauspl 62
☎(06152)2507 tx 38327
⏴ℿ62 ☒ Lift ☾ ☐ Mountain
Credit Cards ① ② ③ ⑤
★★**Kristina** Altausseerstr 54 ☎(06152)2017
⏴ℿ12 ☒ P15 ☾ Mountain
Credit Cards ① ② ③ ⑤
★**Stadt Wien** ☎(06152)2068
May-15 Nov
rm15(ℿ4) P20 Mountain
Credit Cards ① ②

BAD
Each name preceded by 'Bad' is listed under the name that follows it.

BADEN BEI WIEN
Niederösterreich
★★★**Herzoghof** (BW) Theresiengasse 5
☎(02252)48395 tx 14480
⏴ℿ86 Lift ☾ ☐ ☒
Credit Cards ① ② ③ ④ ⑤
★★★**Krainerhütte** Helenental ☎(02252)44511 tx 14303
⏴ℿ66 ☒ P160 Lift ☾ ⚲ ☐ Mountain
Credit Cards ① ⑤
★★★**Schloss Weikersdorf** Schlossgasse 9-11
☎(02252)48301 tx 14420
⏴ℿ103 A26rm Lift ☾ ⚲ ☐
Credit Cards ① ② ③ ⑤

BADGASTEIN
Salzburg
★★★★**Elisabethpark** ☎(06434)2551 tx 67518
20 Dec-Mar & 15 May-Sep
⏴ℿ125 P Lift ☾ ☐ Mountain

★★★★**Habsburgerhof** Kaiser Wilhelm Promenade (n.rest) ☎(06434)2561 tx 67528
18 Dec-25 Mar & Jun-Sep
⏴ℿ45 Lift ☾ ☐ Mountain Lake
★★★**Europäischer Hof** (BW) ☎(06434)2526 tx 67556
⏴ℿ130 ☒ P200 Lift ☾ ⚲ ☐ Mountain
Credit Cards ① ② ③ ⑤
★★★**Parkhotel Bellevue** ☎(06434)25710 tx 67524
19 Dec-25 Oct
rm126(⏴108) P50 Lift ☾ ☐ ☒ Mountain
Credit Card ①
★★★**Savoy** ☎(06434)2588 tx 67668
17 Dec-15 May & 5 Apr-5 Oct
⏴ℿ67 ☒ P40 Lift ☾ ☐ Mountain
Credit Cards ① ② ③ ⑤
★★**Bristol** ☎(06434)2219
Dec-Apr & Jun-Sep
⏴ℿ44 A20rm ☒ P15 Lift Mountain
★★**Grüner Baum** (ROM/Relais et Châteaux) (n.rest) ☎(06434)25160 tx 67516
5 May-21 Oct & 20 Dec-1 Apr
⏴ℿ19 A75rm ☒ ⚲ ☐ ☒ Mountain
Credit Cards ① ② ③ ④ ⑤
★★**Kurhotel Eden** ☎(06434)2076
rm37(⏴11) P Lift Mountain

BERNSTEIN
Burgenland
★★★**Burg Bernstein** ☎(03354)220
Etr-Oct
⏴ℿ10 ☒ P10 ☒ Mountain
Credit Cards ② ③ ⑤

BERWANG
Tirol
★★★**Singer** (Relais et Châteaux) Haus Am Sonnenhang ☎(05674)8181 tx 55544
Closed 8 Dec & 5 Apr-16 May
⏴ℿ60 P40 Lift Mountain
Credit Cards ③ ⑤

BEZAU
Vorarlberg
★**Post** ☎(05514)21207 tx 59142
20 Dec-26 Oct
⏴ℿ42 A11rm ☒ P30 Lift ☐ Mountain

BIRKFELD
Steiermark
⏴ **K & M Friesenbichler** Edelsee 332 ☎(03174) 4544 **P** For Peu Tal

BISCHOFSHOFEN
Salzburg
★**Tirolerwirt** Gasteinerstr 3 ☎(06462)2776
◗↰9 A1rm ☘ P7
H Wildmann Gasteiner Str 58 ☎(06462) 2513 **P**
For

BLUDENZ
Vorarlberg
★★**Schlosshotel** ☎(05552)63016 tx 52175
◗↰37 A7rm ☘ P35 Mountain
Credit Cards ①②③⑤
At NÜZIDERS(2.5km NW)
◖◗ S Amann Walgaustr 83 ☎(05552) 62387 **P**
Nis Saa

BRAND
Vorarlberg
★★★**Scesaplana** ☎(05559)221 tx 52193
◗↰63 P50 Lift ॰ ☐ ☐ Mountain
Credit Cards ①②③④⑤
★★**Hämmerle** (n.rest) ☎(05559)213
mid Dec-Sep
◗↰24 P20 Lift Mountain
★*Zimba* ☎(05559)351
15 Dec-15 Oct
◗↰21 A5rm ☘ P30 Mountain

BRAZ
Vorarlberg
★**Landhaus Walch DPn** ☎(05552)8102
Dec-15 Oct
◗↰10 ☘ P10 Mountain
Credit Cards ①②

BREGENZ
Vorarlberg
★★**Weisses Kreuz** (BW) Römerstr 5
☎(05574)22488 tx 57741
◗↰44 Lift ℂ
Credit Cards ①②③⑤

BRUCK AN DER GROSSGLOCKNERSTRASSE
Salzburg
★★**Lukashansl** ☎(06545)458
◗↰90 ☘ P40 Lift
★**Höllern** ☎(06545)240 tx 066697
15 Dec-Sep
◗↰45 ☘ P50 Lift ☐ Mountain
Credit Cards ①②③⑤

BRUCK AN DER MUR
Steiermark
★★*Bauer 'Zum Schwarzen Adler'* Mittergasse
23 ☎(03862)51331
◗↰60 ☘ P13 Lift
Credit Cards ①②
★★**Bayer** ☎(03862)51218 tx 36521
rm33(◗↰16) P Mountain
Credit Cards ①②③⑤
◖◗ *R Reichel* Grazer Str 17 ☎(03862) 51633 M/C
For

DEUTSCHLANDSBERG
Steiermark
◖◗ Hermann Dr Verdross-Str 1 ☎(03462) 3596
M/C **P** Ope

DÖBRIACH
Kärnten
◖◗ *F Burgstaller* Hauptstr 49 ☎(04246) 7736 M/C
For

DÖLLACH
Kärnten
★★**Schlosswirt** ☎(04825)211 tx 48180
◗↰22 ☘ P40 ॰ ☐ ∪ Mountain
Credit Cards ①②③⑤

DORNBIRN
Vorarlberg
★★★**Park** Goethestr 6 ☎(05572)62691 tx 059109
◗↰35 P Lift ℂ

★★*Hirschen* Haselstanderstr 31 ☎(05572)66363
◗↰45 A15rm ☘ P ℂ Mountain
◖◗ E Bohle Im Schwefel Nr 44 ☎(05572) 62824
Rov Mit
◖◗ *Gerster* Schwefel 84 ☎(05572) 65551 Ope
◖◗ L Winder Hatlerstr 27 ☎(05572) 62094 Ren
◖◗ W Luger Maosmahdstr 10a ☎(05572) 60300
M/C Hon

DRASSBURG
Burgenland
★★★*Schloss Drassburg* ☎(02686)2220 tx
17604
Mar-Nov
rm34(◗↰16) A18rm ☘ P20 ॰ ☐ ☐ ∪
Credit Cards ①③⑤

DÜRNSTEIN AN DER DONAU
Niederösterreich
★★★**Schloss Dürnstein** (Relais et Châteaux)
☎(02711)212 tx 71147
Apr-8 Nov
◗↰37 ☘ P45 Lift ℂ ☐
Credit Cards ①②③④⑤
★★*Richard Löwenherz* ☎(02711)222 tx 071199
Mar-Nov
◗↰46 P ℂ ☐

EHRWALD
Tirol
★★★*Schönruh* ☎(05673)2322
Closed 15 Oct-18 Dec
◗↰40 ☘ P25 ॰ Mountain
Credit Cards ②③
★★**Halali DPn** ☎(05673)2101
20 Dec-15 Oct
◗↰15 ☘ P20 Mountain
★★**Sonnenspitze DPn** Kirchpl 14 ☎(05673)2208
30 Apr-10 Oct & 15 Dec-Mar
rm30(◗↰26) P30 Mountain
Credit Cards ①②③⑤
★★**Spielmann** Wettersteinstr 24 ☎(05673)2225
Dec-Apr & May-Oct
◗↰30 ☘ P30 ℂ ☐ ∪ Mountain
Credit Cards ①②③

EISENSTADT
Burgenland
★★★**Burgenland** Schubertpl 1 ☎(02682)5521 tx
17527
◗↰88 P50 Lift ℂ ☐
Credit Cards ①②③⑤
◖◗ *F Stolovitz* Mattersburger Str 28 ☎(02682)
5163 **P** Col

ENGELHARTSZELL
Oberösterreich
★★*Ronthalerhof* Nibelungenstr ☎(07717)8083
◗↰24 ☘ P24 Mountain
Credit Cards ①②③⑤

ENNS
Oberösterreich
★★**Lauriacum** Wiener Str 5-7 ☎(07223)2315 tx
21947
7 Jan-22 Dec :Rest closed Sat
◗↰60 P25 Lift ℂ
Credit Cards ①②③④

EUGENDORF
Salzburg
★★**Wallersee** ☎(06212)18282
◗↰12 ☘ P20 Mountain
Credit Cards ①②③⑤

FELD AM SEE
Kärnten
★★*Lindenhof* ☎(04246)2274
Apr-Oct & 20 Dec-28 Feb : Rest closed 15-30 Oct
& 10 Jan-Feb
◗↰25 P20 ॰ Mountain Lake
Credit Cards ①⑤

FELDKIRCH
Vorarlberg
★★★*Central-Löwen* Neustadt 17 ☎(05522)22070
tx 52311
◗↰50 P Lift ℂ Mountain
★★★*Ill Park* ☎(05522)24600 tx 2119
◗↰92 P Lift ℂ ☐ Mountain
★★**Alpenrose** Rosengasse 6 (n.rest)
☎(05522)22751-0
◗↰24 ☘ P18 Lift
Credit Cards ①②③④⑤

FELDKIRCHEN
Kärnten
★★*Dauke* ☎(04276)2413
◗↰24 P ℂ Mountain
◖◗ Auto Stranig Industriestr 16 ☎(04276) 3424
M/C **P** For
◖◗ *Pirker* Dr-A-Lemisch-Str 6 ☎(04276) 2345 M/C
P Ope
◖◗ *R Truppe* Ossiacher Bundesstr 14 ☎(04276)
2294 M/C **P** BMW Toy

FRASTANZ
Vorarlberg
★★*Stern* ☎(05522)51517 tx 52502
5 Dec-4 Nov : Rest closed Wed
rm50(◗↰48) A20rm ☘ P50 Lift Mountain
Credit Cards ①②③④⑤

FREISTADT
Oberösterreich
★★**Goldener Hirsch** Böhmerg 8 ☎(07942)2258
◗↰24 P8
Credit Card ⑤

FRIESACH
Kärnten
◖◗ *M Baier* Neumarkterstr 56 ☎(04268) 2389 M/C
P Ope

FÜGEN
Tirol
★*Post* ☎(05288)3212
Closed Nov
◗↰54 P35 Lift ☐ Mountain

FULPMES
Tirol
★★*Alphof* Herrengasse ☎(05225)3163
◗↰30 P20 Lift ॰ Mountain
Credit Cards ①②

FÜRSTENFELD
Steiermark
★★*Hitzl* ☎(03382)2144
Rest closed Mon
rm35(◗↰25) ☘ P25
Credit Cards ①②③④⑤
◖◗ *M Koller* Fehringesstr 13 ☎(03382) 2527 M/C
P For Mer

FUSCH
Salzburg
★★*Post Hofer* ☎(06546)226
15 May-15 Oct
◗↰50 A10rm ☘ P40 ॰ Mountain
★*Gasthof Lampen Haus'l* Grossglocknerstrasse
15 ☎(06546)215
15 Dec-Oct
◗↰34 ☘ P100 ॰ ☐ Mountain

FUSCHL AM SEE
Salzburg
★★★*Parkhotel Waldhof* ☎(06226)264 tx 632487
20 Mar-10 Jan
rm68(◗↰58) P60 Lift ॰ ☐ ☐ Mountain Lake
Credit Card ②
★★*Hochlackenhof* Ellmau 7 ☎(06226)330
May-Sep :Rest closed Tue
rm20(◗↰10) P20 ☐ Mountain

★★**Seehotel Schlick** ☎(06226)237 tx 632795
◀♠40 ☎ P30 Lift Mountain Lake
Credit Cards ① ② ③ ④ ⑤

GAISBERG
Salzburg

★★★**Zistelalm** ☎(0662)20105/641068
20 Dec-20 Oct
rm31(◀♠20) ☎ P ⊇ Mountain
Credit Cards ① ② ③ ④ ⑤

GALTÜR
Tirol

★★**Berghaus Franz Lorenz** ☎(05443)206
Dec-Apr & 15 Jun-Sep
◀♠22 ☎ P Lift Mountain

★★**Fluchthorn** ☎(05443)202 tx 58271
Jun-Oct & Dec-Apr
◀♠50 ☎ P40 Lift ℂ Mountain

GARGELLEN
Vorarlberg

★★**Alpenrose** ☎(05557)6314
15 Dec-15 Apr & Jun-15 Oct
◀♠19 ☎ P20 Mountain

GASCHURN
Vorarlberg

★★★**Sporthotel Epple** ☎(05558)8251 tx 52389
Dec-Apr
◀♠70 ☎ P30 Lift ℂ ℀ ◫ Mountain

GASPOLTSHOFEN
Oberösterreich

๖ R Danner Jeding 17 ☎(07735) 6711 P For

GMUNDEN
Oberösterreich

★★★**Parkhotel Am See** Schiffslände 17
☎(07612)4230 tx 24515
19 May-23 Sep
rm50(◀♠43) ☎ P30 Lift ℂ ℀ Mountain Lake
Credit Cards ① ② ③ ⑤

๖ G Esthofer Bahnhofstr 46 ☎(07612) 2441 M/C
P Aud Por VW

๖ L Woffsgruber Kuferzeile 14-16 ☎(07612)
4629 Nis Saa Sko

GOISERN, BAD
Oberösterreich

★★**Agathawirt** ☎(06135)8341 tx 68186
◀♠45 ☎ P50 ⊇ Mountain
Credit Cards ① ② ③ ⑤

GOLLING
Salzburg

★**Goldener Stern** Hauptstr ☎(06244)2200
Dec-Oct :Rest closed Mon
◀♠40 A22rm ☎ P15 ◫ ⊇ Mountain
Credit Cards ① ② ③ ⑤

GÖTZENS
Tirol

★**Haus Elisabeth** (n.rest) ☎(05234)32225
rm15(◀♠11) P15 Mountain

GRAZ
Steiermark

★★★**Alba Wiesler Graz** Grieskai 4
☎(0316)913241 tx 311130
◀♠98 ☎ P50 Lift ℂ
Credit Cards ① ② ③ ④ ⑤

★★★**Daniel** (BW) Europapl 1 ☎(0316)911080 tx
311182
10 Jan-20 Dec
rm100(◀♠94) ☎ P100 Lift ℂ
Credit Cards ① ② ③ ④ ⑤

★★★**Park** Leonhardstr 8 ☎(0316)33511 tx
311498
◀♠65 ☎ P60 Lift ℂ
Credit Cards ① ② ③ ⑤

★★★**Steirerhof** Jakominipl 12 ☎(0316)826356 tx
0311282
◀♠89 P9 Lift ℂ
Credit Cards ① ② ③ ⑤

★★★**Weitzer** Grieskai 12-14 ☎(0316)913801 tx
311284
rm209(◀♠192) P40 Lift ℂ
Credit Cards ① ② ③ ④ ⑤

★★**Mariahilf** Mariahilfer Str 9 ☎(0316)913163 tx
311087
:Rest closed Sun
rm44(◀♠33) ☎ Lift ℂ
Credit Cards ① ② ③ ⑤

๖ A Gaberszik Fabriksgasse 15 ☎(0316)
911605 P For

๖ H Krajacic Idlhofgasse 17 ☎(0316) 912823 P
AR Dat

๖ J Jacomini Kärntner Str 115 ☎(0316) 271474
AR DJ Hon

GRIESKIRCHEN
Oberösterreich

๖ R Danner Schlüsslberg ☎(07248) 32110 P For

GSCHNITZ
Tirol

★★**Gschnitzer Hof** ☎(05276)213
Jan-10 Apr & Jun-Sep
◀♠29 ⊇ Mountain
Credit Cards ① ②

HAAG
See **LINZ**

HAINBURG
Burgenland

๖ G Bauer Hummelstr 1 ☎(02165) 2366 M/C P
Hon Mer

HALDENSEE
Tirol

★★**Rot-Fluh** ☎(05675)6431 tx 055546
◀♠100 ☎ P120 Lift ℂ ℀ ◫ ⊇ Mountain Lake
Credit Cards ① ② ③ ④ ⑤

HALLEIN
Salzburg

★**Stern** (n.rest) ☎(06245)2610
May-Sep
rm35(◀♠14) P10 Mountain

๖ Voith R-Winkler-Str 33a ☎(06245) 2992 P For

HALL IN TIROL
Tirol

★★★**Tyrol** ☎(05223)6621 tx 534223
◀♠38 ☎ P30 Lift ⊇ Mountain
Credit Cards ① ② ③ ⑤

๖ F Autherith Burgfrieden 5 ☎(05223) 7571 M/C
All makes

๖ Hollaus Burgfrieden 2 ☎(05223) 6560 M/C P
Ope

HARTBERG
Steiermark

๖ Kappler Ressavarstr 64 ☎(03332) 2754 M/C
P All makes

HEILIGENBLUT
Kärnten

★★★★**Glocknerhof** ☎(04824)2244 tx 048154
Jun-Sep & 20 Dec-15 Apr
rm52(◀♠50) ☎ P20 Lift ◫ Mountain

★★★**Kaiser Franz Josef Haus** ☎(04824)2512 tx
48270
15 May-10 Oct
◀♠50 ☎ P40 ℂ
Credit Cards ① ② ③ ⑤

★★★**Post** ☎(04824)2245 tx 3476201
Closed Oct-Nov
◀♠51 ☎ P10 Lift ℂ ◫ Mountain

๖ M Kramser Pockhorn 29 ☎(04824) 2122 M/C
P Ope

HEITERWANG
Tirol

★**Fischer-am-See** ☎(05674)5116
10 May-10 Oct,20 Dec-10 Jan & Feb-10 Apr
◀♠12 ☎ P20 Beach Mountain Lake

HINTERSTODER
Oberösterreich

★★★**Berghotel** ☎(07564)5421
15 Dec-Apr & 17 Jun-15 Sep
◀♠26 P30 Lift ℀ Mountain

★**Dietlgut** ☎(07564)5248
15 Dec-20 Oct
rm22(◀♠19) A4rm P ⊇ Mountain
Credit Card ①

HOF BEI SALZBURG
Salzburg

★★★★**Schloss Fuschl** (Relais et Châteaux)
☎(06229)22530 tx 633454
◀♠84 A61rm ☎ P30 Lift ℂ ℀ ◫ ⋔⋔ Mountain
Lake
Credit Cards ① ② ⑤

HOFGASTEIN, BAD
Salzburg

★★★**Grand Park** Kurgarten Str 26
☎(06432)63560 tx 67756
rm92(◀♠87) ☎ P60 Lift ℂ ◫ Mountain
Credit Cards ② ⑤

★★**Österreichischer Hof** Kurgartenstr 9
☎(06432)62160
20 Dec-Mar & May-10 Oct
◀♠58 ☎ P14 Lift ◫ Mountain

IGLS
Tirol

★★★★**Sporthotel** ☎(05222)77241 tx 53314
◀♠90 ☎ P50 Lift ℂ ℀ ◫ ⋔ ⋔ Mountain
Credit Cards ① ② ③ ⑤

★★★**Aegidihof** Bilgeristr 1 ☎(05222)77108 tx
54123
Closed Nov
◀♠29 ☎ P6 Lift Mountain
Credit Cards ① ② ③ ④ ⑤

★★★**Alpenhof** (BW) Iglerstr 47 ☎(05222)77491
tx 534119
21 May-Sep & 21 Dec-2 Apr
◀♠36 ☎ P Lift ℂ Mountain
Credit Cards ① ② ③ ④ ⑤

★★★**Park** ☎(50222)77035 tx 53576
Closed Nov
rm65(◀♠60) ☎ P30 Lift ℂ ℀ ⊇ Mountain
Credit Cards ① ② ③ ④

★★**Batzenhäusl** ☎(05222)77104 tx 0533495
15 Dec-15 Oct
◀♠33 ☎ P25 Lift Mountain
Credit Cards ① ② ③ ④

★★**Romedihof** ☎(05222)77141
Jul-Aug
◀♠22 P14 Mountain

★★**Waldhotel** ☎(05222)77272 tx 533197
May-Oct & Dec-Mar
◀♠19 P15 Lift ◫ Mountain
Credit Cards ① ② ③ ⑤

★**Bon-Alpina** Hilberstr 8 ☎(05222)77219 tx
533509
Dec-Oct
◀♠100 ☎ P40 Lift ℂ ◫ Mountain
Credit Cards ① ② ③ ⑤

★**Gothensitz** (n.rest) ☎(05222)77211
Closed Nov
rm15(◀♠10) ☎ P10 Mountain
Credit Card ②

IMST
Tirol

★★**Post** (ROM) Postpl 3 ☎(05412)2554
Feb-1 Nov
◀♠40 ☎ P50 Lift ◫ Mountain
Credit Cards ① ② ③ ⑤

🛥 **Autohof Imst** T-Walch-Str 45 ☎(05412) 3182
P Ope
🛥 **H Eisenrigler** T-Walchstr 43 ☎(05412) 2410
Aud VW
🛥 **J Schöpf** Bundesstr ☎(05412) 4526 M/C **P**
Ren

INNSBRUCK
Tirol

See plan The area around the
Herzog-Friedrich Str is a
pedestrian precinct and only
open to vehicular traffic at certain
times of the day.
Innsbruck, a well preserved
ancient city in the heart of the
Austrian Tyrol, is set against a
majestic backdrop of Alps.
A good place to begin a tour is
the *Goldenes Dachl* (Golden Roof),
where the Olympic Museum
features video tapes of the
Innsbruck Winter Olympics.
Other notable attractions include
the Imperial Palace (*Hofburg*) the
Imperial Church *Hofkirche*, which
was built as a mausoleum for
Maximilian and the Tyrolean Folk
Art Museum (*Tiroler
Volkskunstmuseum*) which
displays costumes, rustic
furniture and farmhouse rooms
decorated in various styles. Also
worth visiting is the
Ferdinandeum, which exhibits
Austria's largest collection of
Gothic art, together with 19th-
and 20th-century paintings.
When shopping for souvenirs,
look out for Tyrolean hats, Loden
cloth and wood carvings.

EATING OUT Hearty,
unpretentious food tends to be
the order of the day in
Innsbruck. Most establishments
prepare delicious soups, such as
bohnensuppe, bean soup often
served with chunks of sausage or
bacon; and a chicken or beef
soup with dumplings and bacon
known as *knodelsuppe*. Another
local speciality is *Tyrolean grostl*,
beef or pork sauteed with
potatoes, chives and other herbs.
The *Schwarzer Adler*, in
Kaiserjagerstrasse, is one of the
most atmospheric restaurants in
Innsbruck, and serves specialities
such as dumplings and pot
roasts. Another long-standing
favourite with residents and
visitors is the charming *Ottoburg*,
in Herzog-Friedrich-Strasse,
while for inexpensive food in a

lively, convivial atmosphere, the
wine tavern *Goethstube*, in the
same street as *Ottoburg*, is highly
recommended.

INNSBRUCK
Tirol

★★★★**Europa Tyrol** (CIGA) Südtirolerpl 2
☎(05222)35571 tx 533424
🛏132 🍴 P42 Lift ℂ Mountain
Credit Cards ①②③④⑤
★★★**Goldener Adler** Herzog-Friedrichstr 6
☎(05222)586334 tx 533415
🛏34 Lift ℂ Mountain
Credit Cards ①②③④⑤
★★★**Greif** Leopoldstr 3 ☎(05222)587401 tx
533111
🛏66 P Lift ℂ Mountain
Credit Cards ①②③④⑤
★★★**Maria Theresia** (BW) Maria Theresienstr 31
☎(05222)5933 tx 533300
🛏105 🍴 P130 Lift ℂ Mountain
Credit Cards ①②③④⑤
★★★**Schwarzer Adler** (ROM) Kaiserjagerstr 2
☎(0512)587109 tx 61-3522250
:Rest closed Tue & Jan
🛏26 🍴 P5 Lift ℂ Mountain
Credit Cards ①②③⑤
★★**Binder** Dr-Glatzstr 20 ☎(05222)42236 tx
534404
rm36(🛏16) 🍴 P14 ℂ Mountain
★★**Central** Glimstr 5 ☎(0512)5920 tx 533824
🛏87 Lift ℂ 🖃 Mountain
Credit Cards ①②③④⑤
★★**Grauer Bär** Universitätstr 5-7 ☎(05222)5924
tx 533387
rm123(🛏115) A81rm P25 Lift ℂ Mountain
Credit Cards ①②③⑤
★★**Ibis** Schutzenstr 43 ☎(05222)65544 tx 534433
🛏96 P Lift
Credit Cards ①③
★**Paula** Weiherburggasse 15 (n.rest)
☎(0512)892262
rm13(🛏6) P10 Mountain
At **VÖLS**(5km W on 1A)
🛥 **Auto-Meisinger** Postfach 13 ☎(05222)
303132 **P** Alf DJ LR Peu

IRDNING
Steiermark

★★★**Schloss Pichlarn** Gatschen 28
☎(03682)2841 tx 38190
Closed Nov-19 Dec
🛏72 🍴 P70 Lift ℂ 🗙 🖃 ➘ 🏌 🏌 U Mountain
Credit Cards ①②③⑤

ISCHL, BAD
Oberösterreich

★★★★**Kurhotel** (BW) Voglhuberstr 10
☎(06132)4271 tx 68127
🛏115 Lift ℂ 🖃 Mountain
Credit Cards ①②③⑤
★★**Freischütz** Rottenbach 96 ☎(06132)3354
Apr-Oct
rm25(🛏8) 🍴 P30 Mountain

ITTER
Tirol

★★**Tirolerhof** ☎(05335)2690
Rest closed Apr-May & Oct-18 Dec
🛏62 A14rm Lift ➘ Mountain
Credit Cards ①③

JUDENBURG
Steiermark

🛥 **Klenzl** Bürggasse 103 ☎(03572) 3572 **P** For

KANZELHOHE-ANNENHEIM
Kärnten

★★★**Sonnenhotel** ☎(04248)2713
20 Dec-10 Apr & 5 Jun-Sep
🛏32 P25 Lift ℂ 🖃 Mountain Lake
Credit Card ②

KITZBÜHEL
Tirol

★★★★**Hirzingerhof** Schwarzsee Str 8
☎(05356)3211
🛏26 🍴 P20 Lift Mountain
Credit Cards ①②③⑤
★★★★**Tennerhof** (ROM) Griesenauweg 26
☎(05356)3181 tx 51766
19 Dec-Mar & Jun-8 Oct
🛏42 🍴 P25 Lift ℂ 🖃 ➘ Mountain
Credit Cards ①③⑤
★★★**Goldener Greif** ☎(05356)4311 tx 51-748
Jun-Sep & Dec-Mar
🛏55 Lift ℂ Mountain
Credit Cards ②③⑤
★★★**Schloss Lebenberg** Lebenbergstr 17
☎(05356)4301 tx 51759
end Dec-mid Oct
🛏109 A5rm 🍴 P50 Lift ℂ 🖃 Mountain
Credit Cards ①②③⑤
★★**Erika** J-Pirchistr 21 ☎(05356)4885 tx 511264
Dec-15 Apr & May-Oct
🛏36 P Lift 🖃 Mountain
Credit Cards ①②③⑤
★★**Klausner** Bahnhofstr ☎(05356)2136 tx
5118418
Dec-Mar & Jun-Sep
🛏45 🍴 P20 Lift ℂ Mountain
Credit Cards ①②⑤
★★**Schweizerhof** Hahnenkampstr 4
☎(05356)2735 tx 51370
10 May-5 Oct & 18 Dec-5 Apr
rm42(🛏41) 🍴 P Mountain
Credit Cards ①②③⑤
🛥 **Herz Garage KG** J-Pirchl-Str 30 ☎(05356)
4638 For

KLAGENFURT
Kärnten

★★★**Sandwirt** (BW) Pernhartgasse 9
☎(0463)56209 tx 422329
rm45(🛏40) 🍴 P30 Lift ℂ
Credit Cards ①②③⑤
★★**Kurhotel Carinthia** 8 Mai Str 41 (n.rest)
☎(0463)511645 tx 422399
🛏28 Lift ℂ Mountain
Credit Cards ①②③⑤
🛥 **A Wiesner** Rosenthalerstr 205 ☎(0463)
281913 **P** Rov
🛥 **J Sintschrinig** Sudbahngürtel 8 ☎(0463)
32144 **P** For
🛥 **Joweinig** Sudbahngürtel 14 ☎(0463) 32307 **P**
Nis Saa Sko
🛥 **Kaposi** Pischeldorfer Str 219 ☎(0463) 42200
M/C **P** For
🛥 **Luger** Volkermarkterstr 58 ☎(0463) 31684 M/
C **P** Peu DJ Tal

KLOSTERNEUBURG
Niederösterreich

★★★**Martinschloss** Martinstr 34-36
☎(02243)7426 tx 114257
🛏26 A6rm P20 ℂ ➘ Mountain
Credit Cards ①②③④⑤
🛥 **F Nagl** Wiener Str 152 ☎(02243) 2392 **P** Ope

KNITTELFELD
Steiermark

🛥 **Weidlinger** Wienerstr 40 ☎(03512) 2789 Ren

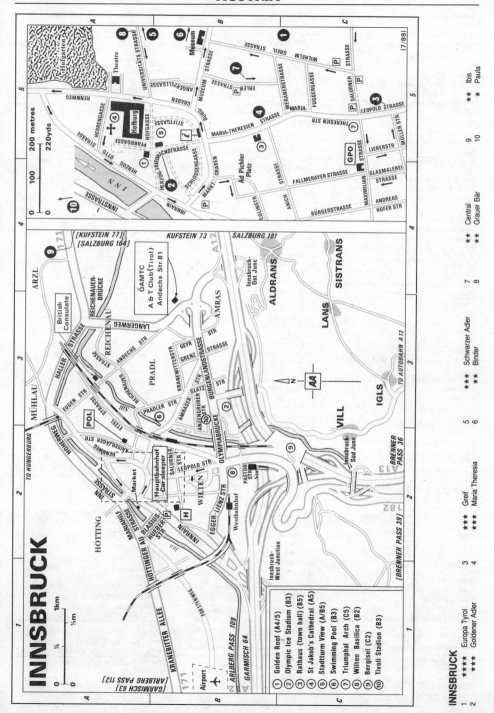

INNSBRUCK

(7/89)

INNSBRUCK

1 ★★★★ Europa Tyrol
2 ★★★ Goldener Adler

3 ★★★ Greif
4 ★★★ Maria Theresia

5 ★★★ Schwarzer Adler
6 ★★ Binder

7 ★★ Central
8 ★★ Grauer Bär

9 ★ Ibis
10 ★ Paula

① Golden Roof (A4/5)
② Olympic Ice Stadium (B3)
③ Rathaus (town hall) (B5)
④ St Jakob's Cathedral (A5)
⑤ Stadtturm View (A/B5)
⑥ Swimming Pool (B3)
⑦ Triumphal Arch (C5)
⑧ Wilten Basilica (B2)
⑨ Bergisel (C2)
⑩ Tivoli Stadion (B3)

British Consulate

ÖAMTC
A & T Club (Tirol)
Andechs Str 81

[KUFSTEIN 77]
[SALZBURG 164]

KUFSTEIN 73   SALZBURG 181

TO AUTOBAHN A13

[BRENNER PASS 39]

BRENNER
PASS 36

[GARMISCH 63]
[ARLBERG PASS 112]

ARLBERG PASS 109
GARMISCH 64

200 metres
220yds

KÖFLACH
Steiermark

H Mayer Lagerstr 10 ☎(03144) 2195 **P** Toy

KÖTSCHACH-MAUTHEN
Kärnten

★★**Post** ☎(04715)221
🍴♨30 ☎ P20 ⊇ Mountain
Credit Cards [1][2][3]

J Schwarzenbacher Nr 181 ☎(04715) 343 M/
C P Ope

KREMS
Niederösterreich

★★★**Park** E-Hofbauerstr 19 ☎(02732)7565
🍴72 Lift ℂ

J Auer Wienerstr 78-82 ☎(02732) 135010 M/C
Ope Vol

H Kneth Hafernsstr 65 ☎(02732) 3662 **P** For

K Teuschl Hafenstr 50 ☎(02732) 3428 **P** Alf
Col AR DJ

KRIMML
Salzburg

★★**Klockerhaus** ☎(06564)208 tx 66552
Closed Nov
rm47(🍴43) P30 Lift ⊇ Mountain Lake
Credit Cards [2][5]

KUFSTEIN
Tirol

A Reibmayr Fischergries 16 ☎(05372) 2141
Ope

LANDECK
Tirol

★★**Post** Malserstr 19 ☎(05442)2383 tx 058131
🍴88 ☎ P20 Lift ℂ Mountain
At **ZAMS**(2km NE)

Auto Plaseller Buntweg 8 ☎(05442) 2304 **P**
For

LECH AM ARLBERG
Vorarlberg

★★★**Post** (ROM/Relais et Châteaux)
☎(05583)22060 tx 52677
25 Jun-28 Sep
🍴40 ☎ P40 Lift ℂ ⊡ Mountain
Credit Cards [2][3]

★★★**Tannbergerhof** ☎(05583)2202 tx 52676
25 Jun-21 Sep & 3 Dec-22 Apr
🍴30 ☎ P5 Lift ℂ Mountain

★★**Arlberg** ☎(05583)21340 tx 52679
Dec-Apr & Jul-Sep
🍴56 ☎ P Lift ℂ ♨ ⊡ ⊇ Mountain

★★**Schneider-Almhof** ☎(05583)3500-0 tx 52674
2 Dec - 22 Apr
🍴70 ☎ P30 Lift ℂ ♨ ⊡ ⊇ Mountain

LERMOOS
Tirol

★★★**Drei Mohren** Innsbrückerstr 40
☎(05673)2362 tx 55558
May-20 Oct & 20 Dec-20 Mar
rm50(🍴36) ☎ P30 Lift Mountain
Credit Cards [1][2][3][5]

★★**Post** ☎(05673)2281
Dec-Apr & May-Oct
🍴53 A26rm ☎ P30 Lift ⊡

★**Sporthotel Loisach** Unterdorf 6 ☎(05673)2394
Closed Nov
🍴46 ☎ P50 Lift Mountain

Hundertpfund Silbergasse 8 ☎(05673) 2411
M/C **P** Toy

LEUTASCH
Tirol

★**Waldheim** ☎(05214)6288
rm12(🍴6) P Mountain

LIENZ
Tirol

★★★**Traube** (ROM/Relais et Châteaux) Haupt Pl
14 ☎(04852)64444 tx 46515
15 Dec-Oct
rm54(🍴50) P10 Lift ℂ ⊡ Mountain
Credit Cards [1][2][3][4][5]

★★**Glocknerhof** Schillerstr 4 ☎(04852)2167
15 May-Oct & Dec-Apr
🍴16 P25 ℂ ⊇ Mountain
Credit Cards [1][2][3][5]

★★**Post** Südtirolerpl 7 ☎(04852)2505
🍴26 P ℂ Mountain

★★**Sonne** (BW) Südtirolerpl ☎(04852)63311 tx
46661
🍴56 ☎ P12 Lift ℂ Mountain
Credit Cards [1][2][3][4][5]

W Rogen Kärntner Str 36 ☎(04852) 62335 M/
C P Ope Vau

G Troger Dr-K-Renner Str 12 ☎(04852) 3411
P For

LIEZEN
Steiermark

★★**Karow** Bahnhofstr 3 ☎(03612)22381
rm33(🍴15) ☎

LINZ
Oberösterreich

★★★★**Schillerpark** Rainerstr 2-4 ☎(0732)554050
tx 22107
🍴111 Lift ℂ
Credit Cards [1][2][3][4][5]

★★★★**Spitz** K-Fiedlerstr 6 ☎(0732)2364410 tx
22784
:Rest closed Sun
🍴56 ☎ P Lift ℂ
Credit Cards [1][2][3][5]

★★★★**Trend Linz** Untere Donaulände 9
☎(0732)2750750 tx 21962
🍴180 ☎ P40 Lift ℂ ⊡ Lake
Credit Cards [1][2][3][4][5]

★★★**Ebelsbergerhof** Wiener Str 485
☎(0732)311731 tx 229260
🍴38 ☎ P40 Lift ℂ
Credit Cards [1][2][3][5]

★★★**Mercure** Wankmüllerhofstr 39
☎(0732)42361 tx 21795
🍴105 ☎ P100 Lift ℂ
Credit Cards [1][2][3][5]

★★★**Novotel** Wankmüllerhofstr 37 ☎(0732)47281
tx 22618
🍴115 P150 Lift ℂ ♨ ⊇
Credit Cards [1][2][3][5]

★★**Wolfinger** ☎(0732)2732310
rm21(🍴17) ☎ P Lift
Credit Cards [1][2][3][5]

Günther Hamerlingstr 13-15 ☎(0732) 55025
M/C **P** Ope
At **HAAG**(6km SW)

Tarbuk Autohaus Gesellschaft Welser Str
17-19 ☎(0732) 56461 **P** Alf Dat LR Saa
At **PASCHING**(10km SW)

F Mitterbauer Wagram 195 ☎(0732) 61028 **P**
Toy

LOFER
Salzburg

★★★★**St-Hubertus** ☎(06588)266 tx 66547
Closed 21 Oct-14 Dec
🍴56 ☎ P50 ⊡ Mountain
Credit Cards [1][2][3][5]

★★**Bräu** Hauptstr ☎(06588)2070 tx 66535
🍴27 ☎ P Lift Mountain

★★**Post** Hauptpl ☎(06588)3030
rm44(🍴23) P39 ⊇ Mountain
Credit Cards [1][2][3][4][5]

★**Lintner** ☎(06588)240 tx 751200
10 May-20 Oct & 20 Dec-5 Apr
rm23(🍴17) ☎ P20 ♨ Mountain
Credit Cards [1][2][3][5]

LOIBICHL
See **MONDSEE**

MATREI
Tirol

J Mayr Lienzer Str 38 ☎(04875) 6554 M/C **P**
Ope

MATTSEE
Salzburg

★★**Gasthof Post** ☎(06217)207
Apr-Nov :Rest closed Mon
A5rm
Credit Card [2]

MAUERBACH
See **WIEN (VIENNA)**

MAYRHOFEN
Tirol

★★★**Krammerwirt** ☎(05285)2615 tx 534589
15 Dec- Nov
🍴72 A7rm ☎ P30 Lift Mountain

Mayrhofen Stumpfau 683 ☎(05285) 8154 M/C
Col For

MILLSTATT
Kärnten

★★**Forelle** ☎(04766)2050
May-15 Oct
🍴50 P35 Lift ℂ ♨ ⊇ Mountain Lake

MONDSEE
Oberösterreich

★★★**Altea Mondsee** Innerschwandt 150
☎(06232)2876 tx 633357
🍴46 P Lift ℂ ⊇ Mountain Lake
Credit Cards [1][2][5]

★★★**Mondsee** (n.rest) ☎(06232)2154
rm25(🍴22) ☎ P40 ℂ ⊇ Mountain
Credit Cards [2][3][5]

★**Leitnerbräu** Marktpl 9 ☎(06232)2219
rm9(🍴6) P
Credit Cards [1][2][3][5]

M Stabauer Herzog-Odilo-Str 82 ☎(06232)
2476 For

M Widlrolther Südtirolerstr 4 ☎(06232) 2612
M/C AR Toy
At **LOIBICHL**(14km SE)

★★**Seehof Am Mondsee** ☎(06232)2550
11 May-20 Sep
🍴25 ☎ P60 ♨ ⊇ Mountain Lake
Credit Cards [1][2][3][5]

MUTTERS
Tirol

★★**Muttererhof** ☎(05222)587491 tx 533932
23 Dec-22 Apr,12 May-20 Oct
🍴20 ☎ P ⊡ Mountain
Credit Cards [1][2][3]

NATTERS
Tirol

★**Eichhof** ☎(05222)575637
May-Oct
rm20(🍴10) ☎ Mountain

★**Steffi** ☎(05222)589402
15 Jun-15 Sep
🍴10 P Mountain

NAUDERS
Tirol

★★★**Tirolerhof** ☎(05473)255 tx 58172
May-Oct
🍴68 ☎ P40 Lift ℂ ⊡ Mountain
Credit Cards [1][2][3][5]

★**Post** ☎(05743)202
18 Dec-20 Apr & 25 May-Sep
rm38(➔♠29) A32rm ☎ P30 Mountain
Credit Card ②

★**Verzasca** (n.rest) ☎(05473)237
15 Dec-15 Apr & Jun-Sep
rm18(➔♠10) ☎ P14 Mountain

NEUMARKT AM WALLERSEE
Salzburg

★**Lauterbacher** ☎(06216)456
➔♠10 ☎ P20 Mountain Lake

NEUSIEDL AM SEE
Burgenland

★★★**Wende** (BW) Seestr 40-42 ☎(02167)8111 tx 18182
:Rest closed 24-25 Dec
➔♠105 ☎ P50 Lift ℂ ९ ☒ ⊃ ∪
Credit Cards ① ⑤

NÜZIDERS
See BLUDENZ

OBERGURGL
Tirol

★★★**Edelweiss & Gurgl** ☎(05256)223 tx 534347
mid May-mid Oct & mid Nov-mid Apr
➔♠97 ☎ P100 Lift ℂ ☒ Mountain
Credit Cards ① ② ⑤

★★**Gasthof Mühle** am Königsrain ☎(05256)230
tx 0533995
Dec- 20 Apr & 26 Jun- 10 Oct
➔♠50 P50 Lift ☒ Mountain
Credit Card ⑤

OBERTAUERN
Salzburg

★★**Pohl** ☎(06456)209
3 Dec-24 Apr & 30 Jun-16 Sep
➔♠17 P Mountain
Credit Card ⑤

OBERTRAUN
Oberösterreich

★★**Berghotel Krippenstein** ☎(06135)7129 tx 68143
May-15 Oct & 20 Dec-12 Apr
rm38(♠26) P50 Lift Mountain
Credit Cards ② ⑤

OETZ
Tirol

★★★**Alpenhotel Oetz** Bielefeldstr 4 ☎(05252)6232
May-15 Oct & 15 Dec-1 Apr
➔♠46 ☎ P Lift Mountain
Credit Card ②

★★**Drei Mohren** Haupstr ☎(05252)6301
➔♠22 Lift ९ Mountain
Credit Cards ① ② ③ ⑤

PASCHING
See LINZ

PATSCH
Tirol

★★**Grünwalderhof** ☎(05222)77304
15 May-Sep & 18 Dec-15 Mar
➔♠30 ☎ P ९ ⊃ Mountain

PERCHTOLDSDORF
Niederösterreich

☙● **K Skala** Vierbatzstr 3 ☎(0222) 862345 M/C Ren

PERTISAU AM ACHENSEE
Tirol

★★**Pfandler** ☎(05243)5223 tx 54180
15 Dec-15 Oct
➔♠54 P Lift Mountain Lake

PICHLING
See KÖFLACH

PÖRTSCHACH AM WÖRTHERSEE
Kärnten

★★★★**Park** Elisabethstr 22 ☎(04272)2621-0 tx 422344
May-Oct
➔♠182 ☎ P200 Lift ℂ ९ ☒ ♠♠ Beach Mountain Lake
Credit Cards ② ③ ⑤

★★★**Schloss Leonstein** ☎(04272)2816 tx 0422019
May-Sep
➔♠36 ☎ P25 ℂ ९ ♠♠ ∪ Beach
Credit Cards ② ③ ⑤

★★**Schloss Seefels** (Relais et Châteaux) Töschling 1 ☎(04272)2377 tx 0422153
20 Dec-Oct
rm88(➔♠81) ☎ P150 ℂ ९ ☒ ⊃ ♠♠ Mountain Lake
Credit Cards ① ② ③ ⑤

★**Sonnengrund** Annastr 9 ☎(04272)2343
20 Apr-20 Oct
➔♠48 A3rm ☎ P28 Lift Mountain Lake

★★★**Werzer Astoria** Werzerpromenade 8 ☎(04272)2231 tx 422940
May-Oct
➔♠132 P100 Lift ℂ ९ ⊃ ♠♠ Mountain Lake
Credit Cards ② ③ ⑤

RADENTHEIN
Kärnten

★★**Metzgerwirt** ☎(04246)2052 tx 45671
➔♠38 ☎ P18 ⊃ Mountain
Credit Cards ① ③ ⑤

RAURIS
Salzburg

★**Raurisserhof** ☎(06544)213
➔♠94 Lift ⊃

REITH
See SEEFELD

REUTTE
Tirol

★★**Tirolerhof** Bahnhofstr 16 ☎(05672)2557
15 Dec-5 Nov
➔♠37 ☎ P Lift Mountain

☙● **Auto-Schlaffer** Allgäuerstr 68 ☎(05672) 2622 Cit Toy

RINN
Tirol

At JUDENSTEIN(1km N)

★★**Judenstein** ☎(05223)8168 tx 534381
rm70(➔♠30) P100 Lift ⊃ Mountain
Credit Cards ① ③ ⑤

SAALBACH
Salzburg

★★★**Bergers Sporthotel** Dorfstr 33 ☎(06541)577 tx 66504
Closed Oct & Nov
➔♠55 ☎ P30 Lift ℂ ☒ Mountain
Credit Cards ① ② ③ ⑤

★★★**Kendler** ☎(06541)225 tx 066508
23 May-3 Oct
➔♠52 ☎ P30 Lift ☒ Mountain

★★**Saalbacherhof** ☎(06541)7111 tx 66502
Dec-15 Nov
➔♠100 ☎ P60 Lift ℂ ९ ⊃ Mountain
Credit Cards ② ⑤

SAALFELDEN
Salzburg

★★**Dick** Bahnhofstr 106 ☎(06582)2215
rm30(➔♠26) ☎ P25 ⊃ ∪ Mountain

★★**Schoerhof** ☎(06582)2210
➔♠32 ☎ P60 Lift ⊃ ♠♠ Mountain
Credit Cards ① ② ③ ⑤

☙● **G Altendorfer** Loferer Bundesstr 13 ☎(06582) 2085 Ope Vau

ST ANTON
Vorarlberg

★★★**Adler** ☎(05552)7118
10 Dec-20 Oct
➔♠30 ☎ P30 Lift ☒ Mountain

ST ANTON AM ARLBERG
Tirol

★★★**Alte Post** ☎(05446)225530 tx 58265
Dec-Apr
➔♠56 P30 Lift ℂ
Credit Cards ① ② ③ ⑤

★★**Montjola** ☎(05466)2302 tx 5817525
Dec-15 Apr & 15 Jun-15 Sep
rm18(➔♠16) A8rm P6 Mountain
Credit Cards ① ② ③ ⑤

★**Bergheim** (n.rest) ☎(05446)2255
Dec-May
➔♠30 ☎ P12 Mountain

ST GILGEN AM WOLFGANGSEE
Salzburg

★★★**Parkhotel Billroth** ☎(06227)217
May-Sep
➔♠44 P40 ℂ ९ Mountain Lake
Credit Cards ① ② ③ ④ ⑤

★**Alpenland am See** (n.rest) ☎(06227)330
Jun-15 Sep
rm14(➔♠13) ☎ P10 Mountain Lake

★**Hollweger** Mondseer Bundesstr 2 ☎(06227)226
Closed Nov-20 Dec
➔♠40 ☎ P30 Lift Beach Mountain Lake
Credit Card ②

★★**Radetzky** Streicherpl 1 ☎(06227)232
May-10 Oct
rm20(➔♠17) P4

★**Mozartblick** (n.rest) ☎(06227)403
➔♠27 A12rm ☎ P14 Mountain Lake

ST JOHANN IM PONGAU
Salzburg

★★★**Prem** ☎(06142)6320
➔♠38 A7rm ☎ P Lift ९ Mountain
Credit Cards ① ②

ST JOHANN IN TIROL
Tirol

★★**Kaiserhof** ☎(05352)25450
10 Dec-15 Oct
➔♠30 ☎ P30 Lift Mountain
Credit Cards ① ③ ⑤

☙● **Auto-Sparer** Innsbrucker Str 21 ☎(05352) 23850 M/C Ope Vau

☙● **E Foidl** Pass-Thurn-Str II ☎(05352) 2129 M/C P AR Dat DJ

☙● **F Reiter** Fieberbrunner Str 35 ☎(05352) 2417 P For

ST MICHAEL IM LUNGAU
Salzburg

☙● **H Neubauer** Hof Nr 39 ☎(06477) 260 P Ope

ST PÖLTEN
Niederösterreich

☙● **M Hänfling** Kremser Landstr 67 ☎(02742) 62838 AR Dai Hon

☙● **Schirak** Porschestr 19 ☎(02742) 67531 P Alf AR Dat DJ LR Saa

☙● **Schwarzimüller** Porschestr 17 ☎(02742) 67578 For

ST VALENTIN
Niederösterreich

★★★**St Valentin** Westautobahn ☎(07435)2002 tx 19275
➔♠49 ☎ P200 ℂ
Credit Cards ① ② ③ ⑤

☙● **F Stelzhammer** Werkstr 44 ☎(07435) 2285 P Alf Peu Ren

SALZBURG

1	★★★★★	Schloss Mönchstein
2	★★★★	Europa
3	★★★★	Österreichischer Hof
4	★★★★	Winkler
5	★★★	Auersperg
6	★★★	Gablerbräu
7	★★★	Goldener Hirsch
8	★★★	Doktorwirt (At Aigen)
9	★★★	Kasererhof
10	★★★	Schlosshotel St-Rupert
11	★★	Corvin Residenz Salzburg
12	★★	Gastein
13	★★	Markus Sittikus
14	★★	Pitter
15	★★	Schwarzes Rössl
16	★★	Stein
17	★★	Traube
18	★★	Weisse Taube
19	★	Elefant

ST WOLFGANG AM WOLFGANGSEE
Oberösterreich

★★★**Romatikhotel um Weissen Rössl** (ROM)
☎(06138)2306-0 tx 68148
Closed 6 Nov-16 Dec
➡ᴿ68 ☎ P35 Lift ℂ ♗ ⌷ ⌷ Beach Lake
Credit Cards ⟦1⟧⟦2⟧⟦3⟧⟦5⟧

★★*Appesbach* ☎(06138)2209
May-Oct
➡ᴿ27 A7rm ☎ P30 ℂ ♗ Mountain Lake
Credit Cards ⟦1⟧⟦3⟧⟦4⟧⟦5⟧

★★*Post & Schloss Eibenstein* ☎(06138)2346
Apr-Oct
➡ᴿ150 P50 Lift ⌷ ⌷ Mountain
Credit Cards ⟦1⟧⟦2⟧⟦3⟧⟦5⟧

SALZBURG
Salzburg

See plan
This city of quaint streets, graceful mansions, busy squares and peaceful churches reclines on the banks of the River Salzburg, protected by a lofty 900-year-old fortress.
As befits the birthplace of Wolfgang Amadeus Mozart, Salzburg offers a wide choice of concerts, and hosts international festivals, but music of a different kind brought more recent fame to the city when the *Sound of Music* was filmed on location at the Leopoldskron Palace. The galleries and museums display works by Rembrandt, Titian and Rubens, and the Mirabelle gardens are a delight.

EATING OUT Soups are popular, such as *knodelsuppe* - chicken broth with spicy bacon and garlic dumplings. The meat dishes are hearty and flavoursome. Try *Troler grostl*, beef sauteed with potatoes and herbs, or the *schnitzels* - veal

SALZBURG

0 — ½ — 1km
0 — ½m

① Cathedral (A2)
② Glockenspiel (A3)
③ Hohensalzburg Fortress (D3/D4)
④ Marionette theatre (C3)
⑤ Mozart's birthplace (A2)
⑥ New Festival theatre (A2)
⑦ Rathaus (town hall) (A2)
⑧ Stadion Lehen (A2)

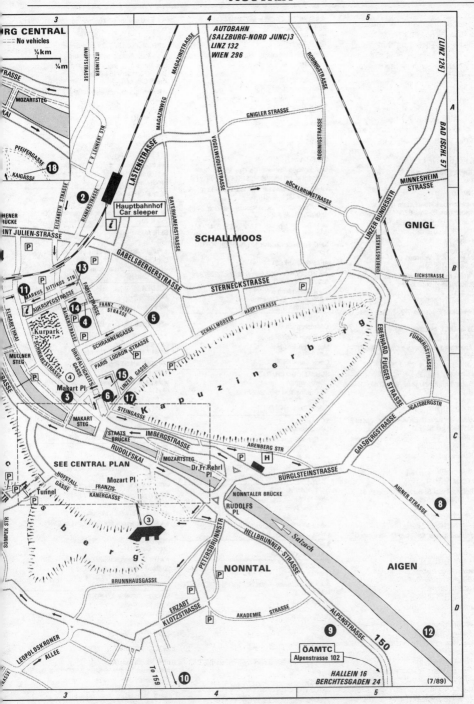

RG CENTRAL
No vehicles
¼ km
¼ m

MOZARTSTEG
PFEIFERGASSE
KAIGASSE
18

AUTOBAHN
(SALZBURG-NORD JUNC)3
LINZ 132
WIEN 296

[LINZ 125]

BAD ISCHL 57

MINNESHEIM STRASSE

GNIGL

GNIGLER STRASSE

ROBINIGSTRASSE

RÜCKLBRUNNSTRASSE

EICHSTRASSE

FÜRBERGSTRASSE

LINZER BUNDESSTR

MAGAZINSTRASSE

MAGAZINWEG

VOGELWEIDERSTRASSE

BAYERHAMERSTRASSE

LASTENSTRASSE

F. V. LEINERT STR

ITZLINGER

HAUPTSTRASSE

2

RAINERSTRASSE

ELISABETHSTRASSE

Hauptbahnhof
Car sleeper

SCHALLMOOS

INT JULIEN-STRASSE

HENER
RÜCKE

STRASSE

13

GABELSBERGERSTRASSE

STERNECKSTRASSE

SCHALLMOOSER HAUPTSTRASSE

HAUPTSTRASSE

FÜRBERGSTRASSE

EBERHARD FUGGER STRASSE

11 MARKUS SITTIKUS STR

AUERSPEGSTRASSE

FABERSTRASSE

14

FRANZ JOSEF STRASSE

5

4

RAINERSTRASSE

Kurpark

SCHRANNENGASSE

PARIS LODRON STRASSE

DREIFALTIGKEITS GASSE

SCHWARZSTRASSE

ELISABETHKAI

MÜLLNER STEG

4

15

LINZER GASSE

K a p u z i n e r b e r g

GAISBERGSTR

GAISBERGSTRASSE

3 Makart Pl

6

17

STEINGASSE

MAKART STEG

STAATS BRÜCKE

IMBERGSTRASSE

ARENBERG STR

BÜRGLSTEINSTRASSE

AIGNER STRASSE

8

RUDOLFSKAI

SEE CENTRAL PLAN

MOZARTSTEG

Dr.Fr.Rehrl Pl

H

SÖMPEK STR

HOFSTALL GASSE

Tunnel

FRANZIS.

KANERGASSE

Mozart Pl

3

s b e r g

NONNTALER BRÜCKE

RUDOLFS PL

Salzach

HELLBRUNNER STRASSE

PETERSBRUNNSTR

NONNTAL

AIGEN

BRUNNHAUSGASSE

ERZABT KLOTZSTRASSE

AKADEMIE STRASSE

ALPENSTRASSE

150

12

LEOPOLDSKRONER ALLEE

9

ÖAMTC
Alpenstrasse 102

To 159

10

HALLEIN 16
BERCHTESGADEN 24

(7/89)

73

AUSTRIA

coated in breadcrumbs. Austrian pastries *küchen* and *torten* are irresistible, including things such as apples, cherries, nuts and chocolate; as well as the classic *apfelstrudel*.
Of Salzburg's many acclaimed restaurants, the *Alt Salzburg*, in Burgerspitalgasse, is one of the best. Also highly recommended is the *Zum Eulenspiegel*, located in an old city house in Hagenauerplatz. For pastries and cakes the *Ratzka*, in Imbergstrasse, is outstanding.

SALZBURG
★★★★★**Schloss Mönchstein** (BW) Mönchsbergpark 26 ☎(0662)848555 tx 632080
↵17 ≩ P20 Lift (℃ Mountain
Credit Cards 1 2 3 5
★★★★**Europa** Rainerstr 31 ☎(0662)73293 tx 633424
↵104 P45 Lift (Mountain
Credit Cards 1 2 3 4 5
★★★★*Österreichischer Hof* (SRS) Schwarzstr 5-7 ☎(0662)72541 tx 633590
↵120 ≩ Lift (
Credit Cards 1 2 3 5
★★★★**Winkler** F-Josefstr 7-9 ☎(0622)73513 tx 633961
↵103 ≩ Lift (Mountain
Credit Cards 1 2 3 5
★★★**Auersperg** Auerspergstr 61 ☎(0662)71721 tx 633817
rm57(↵55) ≩ P20 Lift (
Credit Cards 1 2 3 5
★★★**Gablerbräu** Linzergasse 9 ☎(0662)73441 tx 631067
↵52 Lift (
Credit Cards 1 2 3 4 5
★★★**Goldener Hirsch** (CIGA) Getreidegasse 37 ☎(0662)848511 tx 632967
↵74 ≩ P20 Lift (
Credit Cards 1 2 3 5
★★★**Kasererhof** (BW) Alpenstr 6 ☎(0662)21265 tx 633477
↵53 P100 Lift (Mountain
Credit Cards 1 2 3 5
★★*Corvin Residenz Salzburg* M-Sittikusstr 3 ☎(0662)74343
↵28 P10 (
Credit Cards 1 2 3 4 5
★★**Gastein** Ignaz Rieder Kai 25 (n.rest) ☎(0662)29890 tx 632760
↵13 ≩ P12 Mountain
★★**Markus Sittikus** M-Sittikusstr 20 (n.rest) ☎(0662)71121 tx 632720
rm41(↵38) P10 Lift (
Credit Cards 1 2 3 5
★★**Pitter** Rainerstr 6-8 ☎(0662)785710 tx 633532
↵200 P10 Lift (
Credit Cards 1 2 3 4 5
★★**Schwarzes Rössl** Priesterhausgasse 6 ☎(0662)74426 tx 114832
Jul-Sep
rm51(↵4) Lift (
Credit Cards 1 2 3 5

★★**Stein** Staatsbrücke ☎(0662)74346
22 Dec-25 Oct
rm70(↵41) Lift (Mountain
Credit Card 2
★★**Traube** Linzergasse 4 (n.rest) ☎(0662)74062 tx 132474
Jul-Sep
rm40(↵22) Lift (
Credit Cards 1 2 3 5
★★**Weisse Taube** Kaigasse 9 (n.rest) ☎(0662)842404 tx 633065
rm30(↵28) Lift
Credit Cards 1 2 3 5
★*Elefant* S-Haffnergasse 4 ☎(0662)843397 tx 632725
↵36 ≩ Lift (
Credit Cards 1 2 3 5
⭗ **Autohaus Fieber & Co Ges MHB** Wasserfeldtstr 15 ☎(0662) 50515 P Rov DJ LR
⭗ **Autohaus Grasser** Sterneckstr 28-30 ☎(0662) 72610 Rov DJ Maz RR
⭗ **E Scheidinger** Schallmooser Hauptstr 24-26 ☎(0662) 71176 For
⭗ **M Decker** Alpenstr 142 ☎(0662) 20477 M/C P Ope Vau
⭗ *O Schmidt* Alpenstr 122 ☎(0662) 20531 M/C For

At **AIGEN**(3km SE)
★★★*Doktorwirt* Glaserstr 9 ☎(0662)22973 tx 632938
:Rest closed Mon & Nov
↵39 ≩ P30 ⊃ Mountain
Credit Cards 1 2 3 5

SANDL
Oberösterreich
★★*Braun* ☎(07944)250
May-Oct & Dec-Mar
↵18 P10
Credit Cards 2 5

SCHALLERBACH, BAD
Oberösterreich
★★**Grünes Türl** ☎(07249)8163
↵30 ≩ P80 ↵
Credit Cards 1 2 3 5

SCHÄRDING
Oberösterreich
★★*Schärdinger Hof* Innsbruckstr 8 ☎(07712)2651 tx 027459
↵31 ≩ P
⭗ *F Psotka* Haraberg 12 ☎(07712) 2647 P For
⭗ *F Schachner* Haid 21 ☎(07712) 2845 AR Dat

SCHLADMING
Steiermark
★★★*Alte Post* (ROM) ☎(03687)22571 tx 38282
Closed 27 Oct-4 Dec
↵40 ≩ P20 Lift Mountain
Credit Cards 1 2 3 5

SCHWECHAT
See **WIEN (VIENNA)**

SEEBODEN
Kärnten
★★★★*Sporthotel Royal Seehof* ☎(04762)81714 tx 048122
16 Apr-2 Oct
↵60 A25rm ≩ P60 Lift ℃ ⊠ ⊃ Mountain Lake
Credit Card 5
★★*Seehotel Steiner* ☎(04762)81713
May-Oct
rm50(↵49) A4rm ≩ P40 (℃ ⊠ ⊃ Mountain Lake

SEEFELD
Tirol
★★★★*Astoria* ☎(05212)22720 tx 534041
17 Dec-Mar & 24 May-27 Sep
↵54 ≩ P50 Lift (⊠ ⊃ Mountain

★★★★*Gartenhotel Tümmlerhof* ☎(05212)25710 tx 613522350
Jun-Oct & Dec-Apr
↵66 ≩ P50 Lift (℃ ⊠ ⊃ Mountain
★★★*Park* (n.rest) ☎(05212)2484
Dec-Mar & May-Sep
↵32 A5rm ≩ P15 Lift ⊠ Mountain
Credit Cards 1 5
★★★*Philipp* Münchnerstr 68 ☎(05212)2301 tx 534044
May-Oct
rm60(↵57) ≩ P10 Lift (Mountain
Credit Cards 1 2 3 4 5
⭗ **Auto-Nemeth** Münchner Str 75 ☎(05212) 2407 P For

At **REITH**(2km S)
★★★*Alpenkönig* ☎(05212)3320 tx 0534665
↵150 ≩ P10 Lift (℃ ⊠ ⊃ Mountain
Credit Cards 1 2 3 5

SEEKIRCHEN
Salzburg
⭗ **I & J Heiss-Hutticher** Hauptstr 14 ☎(06212) 236 P Toy

SERFAUS
Tirol
★*Furgler* ☎(05476)6201 tx 0581275
Dec-Oct
↵42 ≩ P25 Lift ⊠ Mountain
Credit Card 5

SÖLDEN
Tirol
★★★*Central* ☎(05254)2260 tx 0533353
15 Jul-Etr
↵70 P100 Lift (℃ ⊠ Lake
★★★*Sonne* ☎(05254)2203
Jan-Apr & Jun-Dec
↵64 A46rm P25 ℃ Mountain

SPITTAL AN DER DRAU
Kärnten
★★★*Salzburg* Tirolerstr 12 ☎(04762)3165 tx 48111
↵85 ≩ P15 Lift (⊠ Mountain
Credit Cards 1 2 3 5
⭗ *J Buchleitner* Neuer Pl 21 ☎(04762) 3421 M/C Ope Vau
⭗ **W Riebler** Villacher Str ☎(04762) 2561 Nis

STEINACH AM BRENNER
Tirol
★★★*Post* ☎(05272)6239 tx 53245
Nov-Sep
↵34 A4rm ≩ P25 (Mountain
★★★*Weisses Rössl* ☎(05272)6206 tx 534531
20 Dec-16 Oct
↵44 ≩ P20 Lift ⊠ Mountain
★★*Steinacherhof* ☎(05272)5241 tx 534440
Jan-12 Oct
↵60 ≩ P35 Lift (℃ ⊠ Mountain
Credit Cards 1 2 3 5
★★*Wilder Mann* ☎(05272)6210-0
20 Dec-10 Apr & 11 May-25 Oct
↵51 A4rm ≩ P20 Lift ⊠ Mountain
Credit Card 2

STEINAKIRCHEN AM FORST
Niederösterreich
★★★*Schloss Ernegg* ☎(07488)214 tx 019289
May-Oct
rm20(↵18) P30 ↳ U
Credit Cards 1 3 5

STEYR
Oberösterreich
★★★*Mader* Stadtpl 36 ☎(07252)23358 tx 028302
:Rest closed Sun Nov-Apr
rm53(↵52) ≩ Lift
Credit Cards 1 3

★★*Minichmayr* Haratzmllerstr 1 ☎(07252)23410
tx 028134
🛏51 P15 Lift ℂ Lake
Credit Cards [2] [3] [5]
🕪 *F Hilbert* Madelsederstr 1 ☎(07252) 63460 M/
C For

STUBEN
Vorarlberg
★★*Post* ☎(05582)761 tx 052459
🛏47 A19rm P5 Mountain
Credit Cards [1] [3]

TELFS
Tirol
★*Hohe Munde* Untermarktstr 17 ☎(05262)2408
🛏21 🏠 P Mountain
Credit Cards [1] [2] [3] [5]
🕪 *Prantl* Untermarkt 72 ☎(05262) 2551 Ope

THIERSEE
Tirol
★★*Haus Charlotte* ☎(05376)5500
Dec-Oct
rm33(🛏29) 🏠 P45 Lift 🖃 Mountain Lake
Credit Card [5]

TRAUNKIRCHEN AM TRAUNSEE
Oberösterreich
★★*Post* ☎(07617)2307 tx 24555
🛏60 Lift 🛥 Mountain Lake
Credit Cards [1] [2] [3] [4] [5]

TURRACHER-HÖHE
Kärnten
★*Hochschober* ☎(04275)8213 tx 422152
Closed 1-13 Jun & 20 Oct-18 Dec
🛏83 🏠 P ⚬ 🖃 Mountain Lake

UNTERGURGL
Tirol
★★*Alpenglühn* (n.rest) ☎(05256)301
Oct-May
🛏12 P12 Mountain

VELDEN AM WÖRTHERSEE
Kärnten
★★★*Schloss Velden* am Corso 24
☎(04274)2655
May-Sep
rm120(🛏100) P120 ℂ ⚬ 🛥 Mountain Lake
Credit Card [2]

★★★*Seehotel Europa* (BW) Wrannpark 1-3
☎(04274)2770 tx 422608
May-Oct
🛏70 A18rm P100 Lift ℂ ⚬ Beach Mountain
Lake
Credit Cards [1] [2] [3] [5]
★★*Alte Post-Wrann* Europapl 4 ☎(04274)2141
tx 422608
🛏37 🏠 P35 ⚬ 🛥
Credit Cards [1] [2] [3] [5]
★★*Seehotel Hubertushof* ☎(04274)2676
Etr-mid Oct
🛏48 P30 ⚬ 🖃 🛥 Lake
Credit Card [5]
★★*Servus* (n.rest) ☎(04274)2262
Jan-Oct
🛏12 🏠 P20 🖃 Mountain
Credit Card [1]

VIENNA
SeeWIEN

VILLACH
Kärnten
★★★*City* Bahnhofpl 3 (n.rest) ☎(04242)27896 tx
45602
🛏62 P30 Lift ℂ Mountain
Credit Cards [1] [2] [3] [4] [5]
★★★*Parkhotel* Moritzschstr 2 ☎(04242)23300 tx
045582
🛏170 P100 Lift ℂ Mountain
Credit Cards [1] [2] [3] [4] [5]
★★*Mosser* Bahnhofstr 9 ☎(04242)24115 tx
45728
🛏30 P100 ℂ
Credit Cards [1] [2] [3] [4] [5]
★★*Post* (ROM) Hauptpl 26 ☎(04242)26101 tx
45723
🛏77 🏠 P28 Lift ℂ
Credit Cards [1] [2] [3] [4] [5]
🕪 *R Prohining* Pogoriacherstr 175 ☎(04242)
28186 M/C P Rov
🕪 *R Thalmeiner* Tiroler Str 19 ☎(04242) 24590
Ope
🕪 *S Papp* Steinwenderstr 15 ☎(04242) 24826 M/
C P For

At WARMBAD(5km S)
★★★*Josefinenhof* ☎(04242)25531 tx 45652
20 Dec-Nov
rm61(🛏50) P80 Lift ℂ ⚬ 🖃 Mountain
Credit Cards [3] [5]

VÖCKLABRUCK
Oberösterreich
🕪 *Autohandels* R- Kunz Str 3 ☎(07682) 8006
M/C P Nis Fia

VOITSBERG
Steiermark
🕪 *Rossmann* Grazer Vorstadt 72 ☎(03142)
2670 For

VÖLKERMARKT
Kärnten
🕪 *R Pribasnig* Grifferstr 11 ☎(04232) 2229 M/C
Ope Vau

VÖLS
See INNSBRUCK

VÖSENDORF
See WIEN (VIENNA)

WAIDRING
Tirol
★★*Tiroler Adler* ☎(05353)5311
Dec-10 Apr & May-20 Oct
🛏33 🏠 P10 Lift Mountain
Credit Cards [1] [2] [5]

WALCHSEE
Tirol
🕪 *A Greiderer* Dorf 1b ☎(05374) 5620 M/C P
For

WARMBAD
See VILLACH

WELS
Oberösterreich
★★★*Rosenberger* (BW) Adlerstr 1
☎(07242)62236 tx 3732211
🛏106 🏠 Lift ℂ
Credit Cards [1] [2] [3] [5]
🕪 *Mühlbachler* Eferdingerstr 69 ☎(07242) 82902
AR Hon
🕪 *Reiter* Salzburgerstr 178 ☎(07242) 6590 M/C
P Toy

WESTENDORF
Tirol
★*Jakobwirt* ☎(05334)6245
Dec-Mar & May-Sep
🛏50 P20 Lift 🖃 Mountain
Credit Cards [2] [5]

WIEN *(VIENNA)*

See Plan page 78 *Population* 1,531,300 *Local tourist office* Wiener Fremdenverkehreverband, Kinderspitalgasse 5 tel (0222) 431608

Wien is a city of legends, elegance and grace, of mouth-watering *sachertorte* and delicious coffee. It has fine traditions, beautiful woods and spectacular architecture. Wien has also been called the musical capital of the world, and with good reason. Synonymous with Strauss, Schubert and Mozart, it offers a setting every bit as capital. Along its great boulevards - the Ring - are the grand façades of museums and parliament buildings and the state theatre (*Burgtheatre*).

In addition to the musical mementos littering the city there are concert halls and an opera house (*Staatsoper*) that is known throughout the world. Even the native tongue is spoken with a musical lilt, and there are accordian players in the cafés and concerts in the Stadtpark in summer.

Among Wien's many interesting sights are impressive historic residences, from the Schonbrunn Palace, to the personal homes of Freud, Schubert, Mozart, Strauss and Beethoven; and art galleries such as the Museum of Fine Arts (*Kunsthistorisches Museum*) and the Belvederes. A 'must' is a visit to the famous Spanish Riding School (*Spanische Reitschule*) housed in the Hofburg, the Hapsburgs' winter palace, while a popular outing is a visit to the Vienna Woods where one can take a boat trip on Europe's largest subterranean lake. St Stephen's Cathedral (*Stephansdom*), the south spire of which rises to 450ft, is the most important Gothic building in Austria.

Wien's finest shops lie between Graben and Karntner-Strasse, and they open on weekdays and Saturday mornings. Viennese specialities include Loden clothing for men and women, petit-point embroidery and Austrian jade. The *Naschmarkt*, near Karlplatz, is the best known of the city markets.

EATING OUT Good restaurants and wine taverns can be found throughout the centre of the city. Bohemian dumplings, Hungarian goulash and Polish stuffed cabbage feature prominently on Viennese menus, along with local specialities such as *wienerschnitzel*, a thin cutlet of veal cooked with a coating of breadcrumbs, and *tafelspitz* (boiled beef). The city is justly famous for its pastries, and you can try the genuine *sachertorte* at the Hotel Sacher.

The Viennese claim - and with some justification - that the best pastries in the world are served at the *Konditorei Oberlaa*, in Neuer Markt; while those looking for atmosphere should seek out the *Glacis-Beisl* restaurant in the Messepalast, complete with delightful, vine-filled garden.

WIEN (VIENNA)
Bezirk I

★★★★★**Ambassador** Neuer Markt 5
☎(0222)51466 tx 111906
◀️107 P3 Lift ℂ
Credit Cards ①②③④⑤

★★★★**Bristol** (CIGA) Kärntner Ring 1
☎(0222)515160 tx 112474
◀️152 Lift ℂ
Credit Cards ①②③⑤

★★★★**Imperial** (CIGA) Kärntner Ring 16
☎(0222)50110 tx 112630
◀️158 ⚘ P Lift ℂ
Credit Cards ①②③⑤

★★★★**Sacher** Philharmonikerstr 4
☎(0222)51456 tx 112520
rm126(◀️123) Lift ℂ
Credit Cards ①②③⑤

★★★**Europa** Neuer Markt 3 ☎(0222)515940 tx 1122
◀️102 Lift ℂ
Credit Cards ①②③④⑤

★★★★**Parkring** (BW) Parkring 12
☎(0222)526524 tx 113420
◀️64 ⚘ Lift ℂ
Credit Cards ①②③⑤

★★★★**Royal** Singerstr 3 ☎(0222)524631 tx 112870
◀️81 Lift ℂ
Credit Cards ①②③④⑤

★★★★**Stephansplatz** Stephanspl 9
☎(0222)53405-0 tx 114334
◀️62 Lift ℂ
Credit Cards ①②③⑤

★★★**Amadeus** Wildpretmarkt 5 (n.rest)
☎(0222)638738 tx 111102
27 Dec-23 Dec
◀️30 Lift ℂ

★★★**Astoria** Kärntnerstr 32 ☎(0222)515770 tx 112856
◀️108 Lift ℂ
Credit Cards ①②③④⑤

★★★**Kärntnerhof** Grashofgasse 4 (n.rest)
☎(0222)5121923 tx 112535
rm45(◀️36) P7 Lift ℂ
Credit Cards ①②③④⑤

★★★**Römischer Kaiser** (ROM/BW) Anngasse 16
(n.rest) ☎(0222)51277510 tx 113696
◀️24 P3 Lift ℂ
Credit Cards ①②③⑤

★★**Austria** Wolfengasse 3 (n.rest) ☎(0222)51523 tx 112848
rm51(◀️40) P Lift ℂ
Credit Cards ①②③④⑤

★★**Graben** Dorotheergasse 3 ☎(0222)5121531 tx 114700
◀️46 Lift ℂ
Credit Cards ①②③④⑤

Bezirk II

🍴 **E Glaser** Czerningasse 11 ☎(0222) 2143748 Rov LR

Bezirk III

★★★★★**Hilton International** am Stadtpark
☎(0222)752652 tx 136799
◀️614 ⚘ P306 Lift ℂ
Credit Cards ①②③④⑤

★★★★★**Inter-Continental** Johannesgasse 28
☎(0222)711220 tx 131235
◀️498 ⚘ P240 Lift ℂ 🍴
Credit Cards ①②③④⑤

★★★**Palais Schwarzenberg** (Relais et Châteaux)
Schwarzenbergpl 9 ☎(0200)784515 tx 136124
◀️38 ⚘ P100 Lift ℂ
Credit Cards ①②③⑤

★★★**Pullman Belvedere** am Heumarkt 35-37
☎(0222)752535 tx 111822
◀️211 ⚘ P38 Lift ℂ

Bezirk IV

★★★★**Erzherzog Rainer** (BW) Wiedner Hauptstr 27-29 ☎(0222)50111 tx 132349
◀️84 Lift ℂ
Credit Cards ①②③④⑤

★★★★**Prinz Eugen** Wiedner Gürtel 14
☎(0222)5051741 tx 132483
◀️106 Lift ℂ
Credit Cards ①②③④⑤

★★★**Kaiserhof** (BW) Frankenberggasse 10
☎(0222)5051701 tx 136872
◀️76 Lift ℂ
Credit Cards ①②③⑤

Bezirk V

★★★**Alba** Margaretenstr 53 ☎(0222)58850 tx 113264
◀️46 ⚘ Lift ℂ
Credit Cards ①②③④⑤

Bezirk VI

★★★**Tyrol** Mariahilferstr 15 ☎(0222)5875415 tx 111885
◀️37 Lift ℂ
Credit Cards ①③

★★**Ibis** M-Hilfergurtel 22-24 ☎(0222)565626 tx 133833
◀️341 P Lift ℂ
Credit Cards ①②③④⑤

★★**Ibis Wien** Marie Hilfergurtel 22-24,Mariahilfer Gurtel ☎(0222)565626 tx 133833
rm341(◀️241) P147 Lift ℂ
Credit Cards ①②③⑤

Bezirk IX

★★★**Bellevue** Althanstr 5 ☎(0222)3456310 tx 114906
◀️160 ⚘ P12 Lift ℂ
Credit Cards ①②③④⑤

★★★**Regina** Rooseveltpl 15 ☎(0222)427681-0 tx 114700
◀️130 Lift ℂ
Credit Cards ①②③④⑤

Bezirk XIII

★★★**Parkhotel Schönbrunn** (SRS) Hietzinger Hauptstr 10-14 ☎(0222)822676 tx 132513
◀️500 ⚘ P Lift ℂ ☐
Credit Cards ①②③④⑤

Bezirk XIV

★★★**Novotel Wien West** Autobahnstation Auhof
☎(0222)972542 tx 135584
◀️114 P300 Lift ℂ ⌐
Credit Cards ①②③⑤

Bezirk XV

★★**Stieglbräu** Mariahilferstr 156 (n.rest)
☎(0222)833621 tx 133636
◀️54 Lift ℂ

Bezirk XVII

🍴 **P Reimann** Bergsteiggasse 48 ☎(0222) 424472 Toy

🍴 **R Moser** Hernalser Hauptstr 220 ☎(0222) 463190

Bezirk XIX

★★★**Kahlenberg** Kahlenberg,Josefsdorf 1
☎(0222)321251 tx 74970
rm32(◀️30) P20 Lift
Credit Cards ①②③⑤

Bezirk XX

Stahl Heistergasse 4-6 ☎(0222) 334601 AR Dai Hon

Bezirk XXIII

🍴 **E Hanzl** Draschestr 36 ☎(0222) 671159 **P** Toy

🍴 **H Hölbl** Dr-Hanswenzlgasse 20 ☎(0222) 691329 **P** Toy

🍴 **J Holzer** Gregorygasse 8 ☎(0222) 842561 **P** Toy

🍴 **Wöhrer** R-Strauss-Str 17 ☎(0222) 612525 M/ C Hon

At MAUERBACH(8km W)

★★★**Tulbingerkogel** Mauerbach ☎(02273)7391 tx 113756
◀️37 P Lift Mountain
Credit Cards ①②③⑤

At SCHWECHAT(10km SE)

★★★**Novotel** ☎(0222)776666 tx 11566
◀️127 P50 Lift ℂ ⌐
Credit Cards ①②③⑤

At VÖSENDORF(10km SE)

★★★**Novotel Wien Süd** ☎(0222)692601 tx 134793
◀️102 P150 Lift ℂ ⌐ Mountain
Credit Cards ①②③⑤

WIENER NEUSTADT
Niederösterreich

★★★**Corvinus** F-Porsche Ring ☎(02622)24134 tx 16724
◀️68 P60 Lift ℂ Mountain Lake
Credit Cards ①②③⑤

🍴 **Auto-Vertriebsges** Wienerstr 103 ☎(02622) 24705 Ren

F Czeczelits Zehnergürtel 40-52 ☎(02622) 22918 P For Tal

Strum Zehnergürtel 8-10 ☎(02622) 8651 P Dat Saa

WÖRGL
Tirol

★★★**Angath Rosenberger** (BW) ☎(05332)4375 tx 51135
📞45 P300 Lift ℂ Mountain
Credit Cards ① ② ③ ⑤

★★**Central** Bahnhofstr 27 ☎(05332)2549
📞55 A7rm P Lift ⌂ Mountain

F Holzknecht Innsbrucker Str 64 ☎(05332) 2928 P Ope

Scheffold Salzburgerstr 33 ☎(05332) 3711 M/ C P For Hon Mer

YBBS AN DER DONAU
Niederösterreich

★**Steiner** Burgpl 2 ☎(07412)2629
📞20 ⌂ P12

ZAMS
See **LANDECK**

ZELL AM SEE
Salzburg

★★★★★**Salzburger Hof** Auerspergstr 11 ☎(06542)28280 tx 66695
📞60 ⌂ P20 Lift ℂ ⌂ Mountain Lake
Credit Cards ② ⑤

★★★**St Georg** (BW) Schillerstr ☎(06542)3533 tx 66706
20 Dec-10 Apr & Jun-Oct
📞37 ⌂ P30 Lift ℂ ⌂ Mountain
Credit Cards ① ② ③ ⑤

★★**Berner** N-Gassner-Promenade 1 ☎(06542)2557
17 Dec-2 Apr & 20 May-1 Oct
📞30 P20 Lift Mountain Lake
Credit Cards ② ③

ZELL AM ZILLER
Tirol

★★★**Tirolerhof** ☎(05282)2227
22 Dec-9 Oct
📞40 P Lift Mountain

W Haidacher An der Umfahrungsstr ☎(05282) 3112 M/C P Cit Fia Hon

ZIRL
Tirol

★★★**Goldener Löwe** (BW) Kirchstr 2 ☎(05238)2330 tx 533550
📞28 P50 Lift Mountain
Credit Cards ① ② ③ ④ ⑤

ZÜRS AM ARLBERG
Vorarlberg

★★★**Zürserhof** ☎(05583)2513 tx 5239114
Dec-15 Apr
📞114 ⌂ P60 ⚲ Mountain

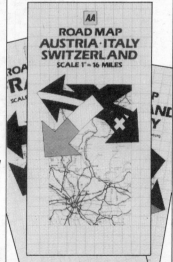

AA | Road Map – Austria, Italy and Switzerland

Featuring:
- **Up-to-date road information**
- **Scenic routes and viewpoints**
- **Contours and gradients**
- **Distances between towns**
- **Full colour, 16 miles to 1 inch**

An ideal map for route-planning and touring — available at good book-shops and AA Centres

Don't leave the country without one

WIEN (VIENNA)

			Bezirk
1	★★★★★	Ambassador	I
2	★★★★★	Bristol	I
3	★★★★★	Hilton International	III
4	★★★★★	Imperial	I
5	★★★★★	Inter-Continental	III
6	★★★★★	Sacher	I
7	★★★★	Erzherzog Rainer	IV
8	★★★★	Europa	I
9	★★★★	Parkring	I
10	★★★★	Prinz Eugen	IV
11	★★★★	Royal	I
12	★★★★	Stephansplatz	I
13	★★★	Alba	V
14	★★★	Amadeus	I
15	★★★	Astoria	I
16	★★★	Bellevue	IX
18	★★★	Kahlenberg	XIX
19	★★★	Kaiserhof	IV
20	★★★	Kärntnerhof	I
21	★★★	Palais Schwarzenberg	III
22	★★★	Parkhotel Schönbrunn	XII
22A	★★★	Pullman Belvedere	III
23	★★★	Regina	IX
24	★★★	Römischer Kaiser	I
25	★★★	Tyrol	VI
26	★★	Austria	I
27	★★	Graben	I
28	★★	Ibis	VI
29	★★	Stieglbräu	XV

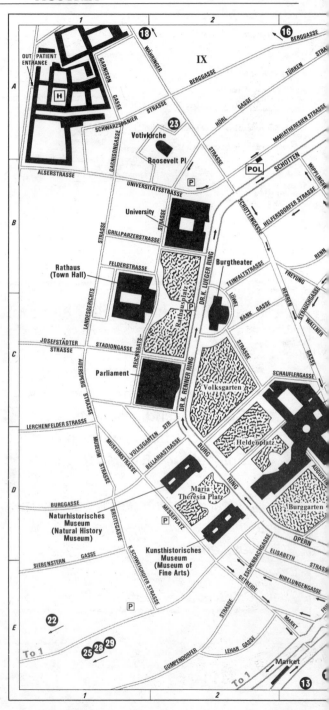

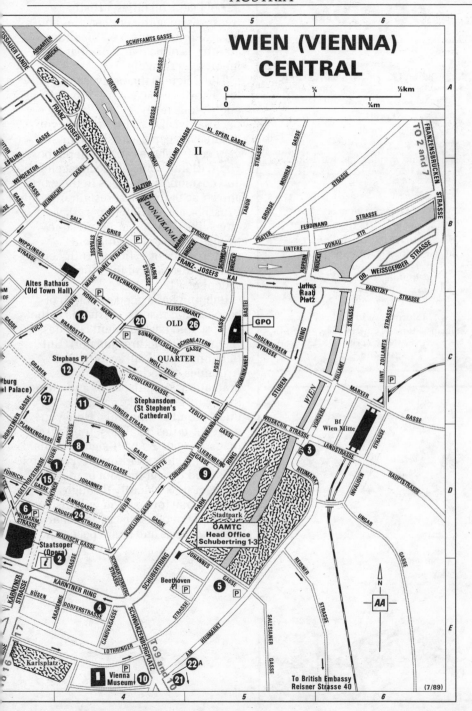

WIEN (VIENNA) CENTRAL

0 — ¼ — ½km
0 — ¼m

SCHIFFAMTS GASSE

DONAUSAUER LANDE

AUGARTEN BRUCKE

GROSSE GASSE

KI. SPERL GASSE

II

HOLLAND STRASSE

GASSE

MOHREN STRASSE

STRASSE

FRANZ JOSEFS KAI

DONAU

SALZTOR BRUCKE

DONAUKANAL

TABOR STRASSE

FERDINAND STRASSE

PRATER STRASSE

UNTERE DONAU STR.

ASPERN BRUCKE

TO 2 and 7

FRANZENSBRUCKEN STRASSE

OB. WEISSGERBER STRASSE

RADETZKY STRASSE

WIPPLINGER STRASSE

SALZ GASSE

SALZTORG

VORLAUF STRASSE

GRIES

MARC AUREL STRASSE

FLEISCHMARKT

RABEN STRASSE

FRANZ- JOSEFS KAI

SCHWEDEN BRUCKE

MAREN STRASSE

Julius Raab Platz

Altes Rathaus (Old Town Hall)

HOHER MARKT

LAUBEN GASSE

FLEISCHMARKT

14

20

OLD

26

SONNENFELSGASSE

SCHONLATERN GASSE

GASSE

GPO

ROSENBURSEN STRASSE

BASTEI

WIEN

TUCH GASSE

BRANDSTÄTTE

QUARTER

WOLL – ZEILE

POST GASSE

DOMINIKANER BASTEI

STUBEN RING

VORDERE ZOLLAMT STRASSE

HINT. ZOLLAMTS STRASSE

P

MARXER GASSE

GRABEN

Stephans Pl

12

SCHULERSTRASSE

WEISKIRCHN STRASSE

STUBENBASTEI

Bf Wien Mitte

burg (al Palace)

27

11

Stephansdom (St Stephen's Cathedral)

SINGER STRASSE

ZEDLITZ GASSE

STUBENBASTEI

LIEBENBERG GASSE

GASSE

LANDSTRASSE

GASSE

HAUPTSTRASSE

DOROTHEER GASSE

PLANKENGASSE

WEIHBURG GASSE

I

8

HIMMELPFORTGASSE

STATTE GASSE

COBURGBASTEI

GASSE

9

3

INVALIDEN GASSE

UNGAR GASSE

FÜHRICH GASSE

TEGETTHOFSTRASSE

FEUER

1

JOHANNES GASSE

SEILER STÄTTE

GASSE

PARK

Stadtpark

HEUMARKT

REISNER GASSE

15

ANNAGASSE

KARNTNER STRASSE

KRUGER STRASSE

24

SCHELLING GASSE

GASSE

ÖAMTC Head Office Schubertring 1-3

6

PHILHARM. STRASSE

P

WALFISCH GASSE

SCHWARZENBERG STRASSE

SCHUBERTRING

JOHANNES GASSE

5

GASSE

SALESIANER GASSE

Staatsoper (Opera)

2

KARNTNER RING

BÜSEN

AKADEMIE

DORFERSTRASSE

4

SCHWARZENBERGPLATZ

SCHUBERTRING

Beethoven Pl

N

AA

KARLNTER STRASSE

CANOVAGASSE

LOTHRINGER STRASSE

TO 9 and

Karlsplatz

Vienna Museum

10

22 A

21

AM HEUMARKT

To British Embassy Reisner Strasse 40

(7/89)

BELGIUM

Language
French and Flemish (Dutch) are the official languages. Walloon and German are widely used in certain areas.

Local Time
GMT + 1 hour (summer GMT + 2 hours)

Currency
Belgian franc, divided into 100 centimes. At time of going to press.
£1 = BFr65.05
US$1 = BFr39.18

Emergency numbers
Fire and ambulance ☎100; Police ☎101

Information in Britain
Belgian Tourist Organisation, Premier House, 2 Gayton Road, Harrow, Middlesex HA1 2XO
☎01–861 3300 (081–861 3300 after 6 May 1990).

Information in the USA
Belgian National Tourist Office, 745 Fifth Avenue, New York, NY10151
☎212 758 8130.

*B*elgium has more than its fair share of beautiful cities, artistic treasures, magnificent beaches and lovely countryside, yet this little country is often overlooked and ignored by so many.

The Belgians themselves are a jolly lot. They love pageantry, processions and riotous festivals and they have a peculiar weakness for funfairs; you might even come across one in the very centre of the capital. Here, too, you will find some of the most elegant and cosmopolitan shops in the world and some of the finest restaurants. In Brussels, and in Belgium's great art cities like Ghent and picturesque Brugge, there are magnificent masterpieces of 15th and 16th-century architecture, and of the Flemish school of art.

Belgium has a good selection of beaches and resorts. Oostende is the biggest, and has excellent beaches, a casino and a picturesque port. But Belgium's best-kept secret is the Ardennes, a land of deep forests, dramatic waterfalls, lakes and awe-inspiring grottos like great underground cathedrals. Here you can drive for miles on almost traffic-free roads, or walk on well-signed paths following clear sparkling rivers which twist and turn at the foot of rocky cliffs, or flow placidly through picturesque towns. You will discover magnificent cliff-top castles, charming rustic villages and a rare peace and tranquillity.

NORTH SEA

NL

B
BRUXELLES

D

L
LUXEMBOURG

F

Knokke-Heist
Blankenberge
De Haan
Wenduine
Bredene
Oostende
Westende
Koksijde
De Panne
Diksmuide
Ieper
Menen
Kortrijk
Torhout
Brugge
Deurle
Eeklo
Aalter
Gent
Lokeren
St-Niklaas
Beveren
Antwerpen
Brasschaat
Turnhout
Kasterlee
Geel
Zolder
Hasselt
Genk
Diest
Tienen
Leuven
Mechelen
Zaventem
Aalst
Enghien
Masnuy
St-Jean
Casteau
Mons
La Louvière
Leuze
Tournai
Philippeville
Profondeville
Yvoir
Dinant
Houyet
Namur
Wepion
Huy
Wavre
St-Truiden
Tongeren
Liège
Chaudfontaine
Verviers
Spa
Eupen
Francorchamps
Malmedy
Ligneuville
Amel
Heinerscheid
Houffalize
Clervaux
Kautenbach
Vianden
Diekirch
Ettelbruck
Grundhof
Echternach
Beaufort
Berdorf
Larochette
Haller
Grevenmacher
Mersch
Dommeldange
Arlon
Martelange
Bastogne
Remouchamps
La Roche-
en-Ardenne
Marche-
en-Famenne
Villers-sur-Lesse
Rochefort
Han-sur-Lesse
Bouillon
Florenville
Esch-sur-
Alzette
Mondorf
Ehnen

E34
E19
E17
E40
N31
N33
A10
N34
N39
E313
E314
E313
A2
A54
E19
E42
E411
E19
E42
E40
E42
A17
N5
923
E25
N4
E411
N33
N6
N2
E25
E25

For key to country identification - see "About the gazetteer"

HOW TO GET THERE

Many ferries operate services direct to
Belgium:
To *Oostende* (Ostend) from *Dover*
takes 3¾–4 hours.

To *Zeebrugge* from *Dover*
takes 4–4½ hours
from *Felixstowe*
takes 5¼ hours (8–9 hours at night).
from *Hull*
takes 14 hours.

Alternatively, you could take a shorter
crossing by ferry or hovercraft to Calais
or Boulogne in France and drive along
the coast road to Belgium.

MONEYMATTERS

There are no restrictrions on the amount
of Belgian or foreign currency that can be
taken in or out of Belgium.

Banking hours
Monday–Friday 09.00–15.30hrs.
Some banks close for lunch and some
remain open until 16.00hrs on Fridays.

Currency exchanges are open at the Gare
du Nord and the Gare du Midi in
Bruxelles (Brussels) from 07.00–22.00hrs
daily, and at Zaventem Airport from
07.30–22.00hrs daily.

Postcheques
can be cashed for any amount up to
BFr7,000 per cheque, but only at main
post offices. Go to the counter marked
'Cheques Postaux' or 'postchecks'.

MOTORING REGULATIONS AND GENERAL INFORMATION

The information given here is specific to
Belgium. It must be read in conjunction
with the European ABC at the front of the
book, which covers those regulations
which are common to many countries.

Accidents*

The police must be called if an unoccupied
stationary vehicle is damaged, or if anyone is
injured. If injury is involved, the vehicle must
not be moved.

Breakdown*

The Belgian motoring club, Touring Club Royal
de Belgique (TCB) maintains an efficient 24-
hour breakdown service known as Touring
Secours/Touring Wegenhulp.
   The Flemish Automobile Club (VAB-VTB)
which operates only in the Flemish area, and
the Royal Automobile Club of Belgium (RACB)
have patrol cars displaying the signs 'Wacht op
de Weg' or 'RACB'. However, neither is
associated with the AA, and motorists will have
to pay for all services. See also *Warning triangle
below*.

British Embassy/Consulates*

The British Embassy is at 1040 Bruxelles,
Britannia House, 28 rue Joseph II
☎(02) 2179000; consular section 32 rue Joseph
II ☎(02) 2179000. Both are located on the town
plan of Bruxelles (Brussels) within the
gazetteer. There are British Consulates with
Honorary Consuls in Antwerpen (Antwerp) and
Liège.

Children in Cars

Children under 12 are not permitted to travel in
a vehicle as front seat passengers except when
using special seats or when rear seats are
already occupied by children.

Customs regulations*

A *Customs Carnet de Passages en Douane* is
required for all trailers not accompanied by the
towing vehicle.

***Additional information will be found in the
European ABC at the front of the book.**

Dimensions and weight restrictions

Private **cars** and towed **trailers** or **caravans** are restricted to the following dimensions – height, 4 metres; width, 2.50 metres; length (including any coupling device), up to 2,500kg, 8 metres, over 2,500kg, 10 metres. The maximum permitted overall length of vehicle/trailer or caravan combinations is 18 metres.

Trailers without brakes may have a total maximum weight of 750kg.

Driving licence*

A valid UK or Republic of Ireland licence is acceptable in Belgium. The minimum age at which a visitor may use a temporarily imported car or motorcycle is 18 years.

Emergency messages to tourists*

Emergency messages to tourists are broadcast daily on Belgian Radio in French and Dutch.

Radio Television Belge transmitting on 483 metres medium wave broadcasts these messages in French during the news at 14.00hrs, and after the news at 19.00hrs Monday to Friday and 13.00 and 19.00hrs on Saturday and Sunday.

Belgische Radio en Televisie (BRT1) transmitting on 323.6 metres medium wave broadcasts the messages daily in Dutch after the news at 07.00, 08.00, 12.00, 17.00, 19.00 and 22.00hrs.

Radio Television Belge (RTBF) transmitting on 16 and 49 metres short wave broadcasts the messages daily in French at 12.45hrs.

Belgische Radio en Televisie (BRT) transmitting on 50.89 metres short wave broadcasts the messages in Dutch after the news at 09.00hrs Monday to Friday, and on 198.4 metres medium wave between 19.00–22.00hrs Monday to Saturday and 19.00hrs on Sunday.

Lights*

Between dusk and dawn, and in all cases where visibility is restricted to 200m (220yds), dipped or full headlights must be used. However, headlights must be dipped: where street lighting is continuous, permitting clear vision for 100m (110yds); at the approach of oncoming traffic (including vehicles on rails); when following another vehicle at a distance of less than 50m (55yds); and, where the road is adjacent to water, at the approach of oncoming craft if the pilot is likely to be dazzled. It is compulsory for *motorcyclists* to use dipped headlights during the day.

Vehicles parked on the public highway must use front and rear side lights both day and night if vehicles are not visible from 100 metres.

In built-up areas, the position lights may be replaced by a single parking light displayed on the side nearest to the centre of the road, providing the vehicle is not more than 6 metres long and 2 metres wide, has no trailer attached to it and its maximum carrying capacity is not more than eight persons, excluding the driver.

Motoring club*

 The **Touring Club Royal de Belgique** (TCB) has its head office at 1040 Bruxelles, 44 rue de la Loi ☎(02) 2332211, located on the town plan of Bruxelles (Brussels) within the gazetteer. It is open weekdays 09.00–18.00hrs; Saturday 09.00–12.00hrs. There are branch offices in most towns and they are open weekdays 09.00–12.30hrs (Monday from 09.30hrs) and 14.00–18.00hrs; Saturday 09.00–12.00hrs. All offices are closed on Saturday afternoons and Sundays.

Motorways

There is a comprehensive system of toll free motorways linking major towns and adjoining countries. Two numbering systems are in force, a national network (white and black numbers with prefix 'A'), and an international network (green and white signs with the prefex 'E').

Nearly all motorways are part of the European international network, and carry only an 'E' number in preference to the 'A' number, which is used for the remainder of the motorway network. In 1986 a new numbering system of the European international network was introduced. Below is a list of the old and new 'E' numbers:

Old No.	Route	New No.
E3	Kortrijk – Gent – Antwerpen	E17
E3	Antwerpen – Dutch Fronter (Eindhoven)	E34
E5	Veurne – Brussel – Liège – Aachen (D)	E40
E9	Maastricht (NL) – Liège – Arlon – Luxembourg	E25

*Additional information will be found in the European ABC at the front of the book.

Old No.	Route	New No.
E10	Valenciennes (F) – Brussel – Dutch Frontier (Breda)	E19
E39	Antwerpen – Lummen (nr. Hasselt)	E313
E39	Lummen (nr. Hasselt) – Dutch Frontier (Heerlen)	E314
E40	Brussel – Arlon	E411
E41	Mons – Liège	E42
–	Lummen (nr. Hasselt) – Liège	E313/A13
–	Tournai – Mons	E42/A16
–	Verviers – St Vith	E42/A27

Orange badge scheme for disabled drivers*

In Belgium, special parking places are reserved for disabled drivers and are indicated by a parking sign (white letter on blue panel) with the international disabled symbol. Badge holders may also park without time limit in *blue zones* and by road signs where parking time is otherwise restricted. In addition, many local authorities do not require badge holders to pay at parking meters. However, badge holders are not allowed to park in places where parking is otherwise prohibited.

Parking*

Regulations differentiate between waiting (long enough to load or unload goods or for passengers to get in or out) and *parking*. Vehicles must be parked on the right-hand side of the road, except in one-way streets when they can be parked on either side. Where possible, the vehicle must be parked on the level shoulder inside built-up areas and on the shoulder, level or otherwise, outside these areas. If the shoulder is used by pedestrians, then at least 1 metre must be left for them on the side farthest away from the traffic. Parking restrictions are similar to those in the UK. Before leaving your vehicle, make sure it does not restrict the movement of other road users. Do not park on major roads outside built-up areas; on a carriageway marked in traffic lanes or where broken yellow lines are painted; opposite another stationary vehicle if this would hamper the crossing of **two** other vehicles or on the central reservation of dual-carriageways.

In many towns and cities, there are short-term parking areas known as *blue zones* where parking discs must be displayed. Outside these areas, a parking disc must be used where the parking sign has an additional panel showing a parking disc. In some areas there are parking meters and a parking disc is not valid in the meter bay. Instructions for use will be on the meter. In Antwerpen and Gent wheel clamps are used on illegally parked vehicles.

Petrol*

Credit cards Some petrol stations will accept 'Diners Club International' and 'Visa'
Duty-free petrol In addition to the petrol in the vehicle tank, up to 10 litres in a can may be imported free of customs duty and tax.
Petrol (leaded) Super (98–99 octane) is available.
Petrol (unleaded) is sold in Belgium both as the regular (92 octane) and super (95 octane) grades. Pumps dispensing unleaded petrol are marked either 2085 or display a white disc and the words *normale sans plomb* or *normale ongelood* or *normal unverbleit* in green letters.

Postal information

Mail Postcards BFr13.00; letters up to 20g BFr13.00.
Post Offices There are 1,800 post offices in Belgium. The opening hours of larger offices are from 09.00–17.00hrs Monday to Thursday and 09.00–19.00hrs Friday. Some large offices are also open on Saturdays 09.00–12.00hrs. The smaller offices open from 09.00–12.30hrs and 14.00–16.00hrs Monday to Friday.

Priority*

In built-up areas, you must give way to bus drivers indicating their intention to drive away from a bus stop. Trams have priority from both right and left.

Public holidays*

Official public holidays in Belgium for 1990 are given below.
January 1 (New Year's Day)
April 16 (Easter Monday)
May 1 (Labour Day)
May 24 (Ascension Day)
June 4 (Whit Monday)
July 21†† (National Day)

*Additional information will be found in the European ABC at the front of the book.

August 15 (Assumption Day)
November 1 (All Saint's Day)
November 11† (Armistice Day)
December 25 (Christmas Day)
††Saturday, †Sunday

Religious services*

The Intercontinental Church Society welcomes
visitors from any denomination to English
language services in the following centres:
8400 Oostende The Rev Canon M Hart, The
English Chaplaincy, Van Iseqhemlaan 83, bis 2
☎(059) 702859. (The English Chaplaincy also
provides services in Brugge and Knokke).
1180 Bruxelles The Ven John Lewis, 116 rue
du Chateau d'Eau ☎(02) 5117183.

Roads

A good road system is available. However, one
international route that has given more cause
for complaints than any other is, without doubt,
that from Calais (France) through Belgium to
Köln/Cologne (Germany). The problem is
aggravated by the fact that there are two official
languages in Belgium; in the Flemish part of
Belgium all signs are in Flemish only, while in
Wallonia, the French-speaking half of the
country, the signs are all in French. Brussels
(Bruxelles-Brussel) seems to be the only netural
ground where the signs show the two
alternative spellings of placenames
(Antwerpen-Anvers; Gent-Gand; Liège-Luik;
Mons-Bergen; Namur-Namen; Oostende-
Ostende; Tournai-Doornik). From the Flemish
part of the country, Dunkirk (Dunkerque) in
France is signposted *Duinkerke* and Lille is
referred to as *Rijsel*, and even Paris is shown as
Parijs.

Road number changes. A new numbering
system, retaining the prefix N, has been
introduced for Belgian main roads, with the
exception of N1–N5 which retain their original
numbers. The change-over took place during
1986, but some irregularities may still occur
when the same road may have signs showing
two different numbers.

Shopping hours

All shops are usually open 09.00–18.00, 19.00
or 20.00hrs from Monday to Saturday; however,
food shops may close 1 hour later.

Speed limits*

The following limits apply even if they are not
indicated unless there are signs to the contrary.
The beginning of a built-up area is indicated by
a sign bearing the place-name in black letters on
a white background:

Car/caravan/trailer
Built-up area 60kph (37mph)
Other roads 90kph (56mph)
Motorways and 4 lane roads 120kph (74mph)

Minimum speed on *motorways* on straight level
stretches is 70kph (43mph). Vehicles being
towed after an accident or breakdown are
limited to 25kph (15mph) on all roads and, if on
a motorway, must leave at the first exit.

Spiked or studded tyres

Spiked tyres Are permitted between 1
November and 31 March on vehicles under 3.5
tonnes. They must be fitted to all four wheels,
and also to a trailer over 500kg. Speed should
not exceed 90kph (56mph) on motorways and
other roads having four or more lanes, and
60kph (37mph) on all other public roads. See
also *Cold-weather touring* in the European
ABC.

Telephone*

Insert coin **after** lifting the receiver; the dialling
tones is the same as in the UK. Use BFr5 coins
for local calls and BFr5 (BFr20 in some boxes)
or coins for national and international calls.

International callboxes are identified with
European flags.
Cardphones can also be used for international
calls.
A telephone call to the UK costs BFr25 for each
minute.
Telephone codes
UK to Belgium	010 32
Belgium to UK	00*44
Belgium to Republic of Ireland	00*353
Belgium to USA	00*1

*Wait for the second dialling tone or see
instructions in callbox.

Town names

Some of the town names in the gazetteer are
shown in both Flemish and French, the first

***Additional information will be found in the
European ABC at the front of the book.**

being the one used locally. Brussels (Bruxelles/Brussel) is officially bi-lingual. See also *Roads* for the effect on signposting.

Traffic lights*

The three-colour traffic light system operates in Belgium. However, the lights may be replaced by arrows of the individual colours and these have the same meaning as the lights, but only in the direction in which the arrow points.

Warning triangle*

The use of a warning triangle is compulsory in the event of accident or breakdown. The triangle must be placed 30 metres (33yds) behind the vehicle on ordinary roads and 100 metres (110yds) on motorways to warn

following traffic of any obstruction; it must be visible at a distance of 50 metres (55yds).

Winter conditions*

Motoring is rarely restricted by weather conditions, although you may find snow and ice in the Ardennes when the weather is very severe. From 1 November to 31 March, information on road conditions in Belgium and on main routes abroad can be obtained by telephoning (02) 2332587 between 09.00 and 18.00hrs daily; from April to 31 October, information may be obtained 09.00–18.00hrs Monday to Friday and 09.00–12.00hrs on Saturday by telephoning (02) 2332211.

*Additional information will be found in the European ABC at the front of the book.

ACCOMMODATION

Hotels are classified from five star (luxury) to one star (simple hotels) in accordance with AA standards. However, you will find that the local system of classification in the Benelux Countries is from one to four stars. Room prices are exhibited in hotel reception areas and full details of charges, including service and taxes, are shown in each room. Belgium Tourist Reservation (BTR) provides a free hotel booking service throughout the country. Their address is BP41, 1000 Bruxelles 23 ☎(02) 2305029; telex

65888. Tourist offices in major towns can also arrange hotel bookings for visitors. The service is free, but a deposit is payable, which will be deducted from the final bill.

The prices shown below are an average for each classification, but accommodation is likely to be more expensive in Bruxelles (Brussels) and some of the more popular tourist areas. At the time of going to press £1 Sterling = BFr65.05; US$1 = BFr39.18, but you should check the rate of exchange before your departure.

AVERAGE PRICES

	Single Room	Double Room	Breakfast	Lunch/Dinner
★★★★★	BFr3145–7100	BFr7850–8300	from BFr395	from BFr575
★★★★	BFr3136–4573	from BFr4865	from BFr317	BFr850–1100
★★★	BFr2029–2379	BFr2646–3146	BFr276–326	BFr588–1176
★★	BFr1650	BFr2029–2927	BFr209–227	BFr219–1240
★	BFr1014–1316	BFr1730–2129	BFr132–137	BFr522–910

Abbreviations:
av	avenue	esp	esplanade
r	rue	str	straat
bd	boulevard	pl	place,
rte	route		plein

Belgium is divided into the Flemish region in the north and the French-speaking Walloon region in the south. Some of the town names in the gazetteer show both languages and that shown first is the one used locally. Brussels (Bruxelles/Brussel) is officially bi-lingual.

AALST (ALOST)
Oost-Vlaanderen

★*Borse van Amsterdam* Grote Markt 26
☎(053)211581
Closed 2-4 Jul
rm6(➜1)

AALTER
Oost-Vlaanderen
★★**Memling** Markt 11 (n.rest) ☎(091)741013
Closed 16 Dec-7 Jan
➜17 P1 ℂ
Credit Cards ①②③⑤

AARLEN
See **ARLON**

ALBERT PLAGE
See **KNOKKE-HEIST**

AMEL (AMBLEVE)
Liège
★*Oos Heem* Deidenberg 124 ☎(080)349692
rm17(➜4) P ⌂

ANTWERPEN (ANVERS)
Antwerpen

Antwerpen is a bustling international sea port, rich in art and culture. Its favourite son, Rubens, lived and worked here, drawing his inspiration from the city; visitors can still see his house, and his work is displayed in churches and galleries. For a nautical flavour take a harbour cruise and visit the

National Maritime Museum, housed in a 12th-century fortress which was also once a prison. The Cathedral of Our Lady (*Onze Leive Vrouwekahedraal*) has glorious stained glass windows, as well as Rubens' masterpieces, including the *Descent from the Cross*.

Visitors should be sure to visit the diamond centres for which the city is world famous. Even if one has no intention of buying, the complex process which transforms dull stones to sparkling gems is fascinating. Antwerpen takes great pride in its zoo, which houses such unusual inmates as tree kangaroos and electric eels. There is also a dolphinarium, aquarium and baby zoo.

Shoppers will enjoy the animals, plants and food on sale at the bird market and the antiques and curiosities on offer at the North Gate of the cathedral. There are also super modern shopping centres and attractive shopping streets such as the Meir and De Keyserlei.

EATING OUT Especially good value are the restaurants in the Suikerrui and Handschoenmarkt area, near the cathedral. Mussels, eels and rabbit are tasty specialities, as are *Antwerpse handges* - biscuits and pastries. You can dine in restaurants overlooking the Schelde and enjoy the view as much as the food. Of the city's many fine restaurants, *La Rade* in Van Dyckkai, and the *Criterium* in De Keyserlei, enjoy outstanding reputations. *Rooden Hoed*, Oud Koornmarkt, near the cathedral, is Antwerpen's most ancient restaurant and specialises in various preparations of eel and mussels.

Belgium produces hundreds of quality beers and lagers, with even small bars stocking at least 20 or so. If you fancy something stronger, try *jenever* (Antwerp gin).

ANTWERPEN (ANVERS)
Antwerpen

★★★★**Crest** G-Lagrellelaan 10 ☎(03)2372900 tx 33843
📶253 ⌷ P200 Lift ℂ
Credit Cards ①②③④⑤

★★★**Columbus** Frankyklei 4 (n.rest) ☎(03)2330390 tx 71354
rm27(📶25) Lift ℂ
Credit Cards ①②③⑤

★★★**Novotel Antwerpen Nord** Luihagen-Haven 6 ☎(03)5420320 tx 32488
📶119 P Lift ⌷ ⌷
Credit Cards ②③⑤

★★★**Plaza** Charlottalei 43 (n.rest) ☎(03)2189240 tx 31531
📶79 ⌷ Lift ⌷
Credit Cards ①②③④⑤

★★★**Switel** (QM) Copernicuslaan 2 ☎(03)2316780 tx 33965
rm350(📶335) ⌷ P100 Lift ℂ ⌷ ⌷
Credit Cards ①②③⑤

★★**Arcade** Meistraat 39 (n.rest) ☎(03)2318830 tx 31104
📶150 Lift
Credit Cards ①③

🍴 *Etabl J Lins* Tunnelpl 3-5-7 ☎(03) 2339928 P AR Dat LR RR

🍴 *New Antwerp Car Service PVBA* Ijzelaan 52 ☎(03) 2329830 P Lot Peu Toy

At BORGERHOUT

★★★**Scandic Crown** L-Lippenslaan 66 ☎(03)2359191 tx 34479
📶205 P150 Lift ℂ ⌷
Credit Cards ①②③⑤

ARLON (AARLEN)
Luxembourg

★★**Nord** r des Faubourgs 2 ☎(063)220283 rm23(📶12) P

🍴 *Beau Site* av de Longwy 163-167 ☎(063) 220389 For

BALMORAL
See **SPA**

BASTOGNE
Luxembourg

★★**Lebrun** 8 r de Marché ☎(062)215421 :Rest closed Mon (out of season)
rm20(📶12) ⌷ P10
Credit Cards ①②③⑤

🍴 *F Luc-Nadin* 16 r des Scieries ☎(062) 211806 P AR

BERGEN
See **MONS**

BEVEREN-WAAS
Oost-Vlaanderen

★★★**Beveren** Gentseweg 280 ☎(03)7758623
📶29 P ⌷

BIERGES
See **WAVRE**

BLANKENBERGE
West-Vlaanderen

★★★**Ideal** Zeedijk 244 ☎(050)429474 tx 26937
Apr-20 Sep & Oct 27-Nov 4 :Rest closed Tue
📶50 ⌷ Lift ℂ ⌷ ⌷ Sea
Credit Card ③

★★**Marie-José** av Maria-José 2 ☎(050)411639
Apr-Sep
📶49 A11rm Lift ℂ
Credit Cards ①②③⑤

★★**Pacific** J-de-Troozlaan 48 ☎(050)411542
Closed 16-31 Oct
rm24(📶12) Lift

BORGERHOUT
See **ANTWERPEN (ANVERS)**

BOUILLON
Luxembourg

★★**Panorama** r au Dessus de la Ville 25 ☎(061)466138
rm45(📶32) ⌷ P8 Lift
Credit Cards ①②③⑤

★★**Poste** pl St-Arnould 1 ☎(061)466506 tx 41678
rm80(📶57) ⌷ P6 Lift ℂ Mountain
Credit Cards ①②③⑤

★**Semois** r du Collège 46 ☎(061)466027
rm45(📶36) ⌷ P40 Lift
Credit Cards ①②③⑤

BOUVIGNES
See **DINANT**

BRASSCHAAT-POLYGOON
Antwerpen

★★**Dennenhof** Bredabaan 940 ☎(031)6630509
📶64 P ⌷

BREDENE
West-Vlaanderen

★**Zomerlust** P-Benoitlaan 26 ☎(059)320340 rm20

🍴 *Oostende International Depannage Service* Brugsesteenweg 45 ☎(059) 322105 P

BRUGGE (BRUGES)
West-Vlaanderen

Brugge is a picture-postcard town of pretty gabled houses and quiet backwaters crossed by arched bridges and overhung with willows. It has a reputation as the best preserved medieval town in Europe, and it is easy to understand why. Savour this 'Venice of the North', with its distinctive 16th-century merchants' houses, on a peaceful cruise along the canals and the Lake of Love, or wend your way through the cobbled streets in a horse-drawn carriage. Or simply stroll along quiet lanes and quaysides. The main square is dominated by the 225ft belfry, from where the carillon peals out across the town, and which offers a panoramic view of the surroundings.

EATING OUT Brugge has a range of restaurants which cater for all tastes and budgets and which live up to the high reputation of Belgian cuisine. Being so close to the coast, fresh fish and seafood are delicious specialities, and there is plenty to satisfy the heartiest appetite. If money is no object, *De Witte Poorte*, in Jan Van Eyckplein, is highly recommended. It specialises in fresh fish and game in season. The moderately-priced *Oud Brugge* is located in an ancient, vaulted building in Kuiperstraat, while for inexpensive local dishes and Flemish ambience the *Gistelhof*, in West Gistelhof, is justly popular.

BRUGGE (BRUGES)
West-Vlaanderen

★★★★**Holiday Inn** Boeveriestr 2 ☎(050)340971 tx 81369
◣♪155 ☎ Lift ℂ ☒
Credit Cards ①②③⑤

★★★**Navarra** St-Jacobsstr 41 (n.rest)
☎(050)340561 tx 81037
rm80(◣♪69) A6rm P30 Lift ℂ ☒
Credit Cards ①②③⑤

★★★**Novotel** Chartreuseweg 20 ☎(050)382851 tx 81507
◣♪101 P250 Lift ☐
Credit Cards ①②③⑤

★★★**Park** t'Zand Vrydagmarkt 5 (n.rest)
☎(050)333364 tx 81686
◣♪61 Lift ℂ

★★**Campanile** Jagerstr 20 ☎(050)381360 tx 81402
◣♪50 P35
Credit Card ③

★★**Climat** J-Wauterstr ☎(050)380988
◣♪48 P ℂ

★★**Duc de Bourgogne** Huidenvettersspl 12
☎(050)332038
Seasonal :Rest closed Mon & Tue lunch
◣♪10

★★**Europ** Augustÿnenrei 18 (n.rest)
☎(050)337975 tx 82490
Mar-15 Nov
rm30(◣♪27) ☎ Lift ℂ
Credit Cards ①②③⑤

★★**Sablon** Noordzandstr 21 ☎(050)333902 tx 83033
rm46(◣♪21) Lift ℂ
Credit Cards ①②③

★**Févéry** Collaert Mansionstr 3 (n.rest)
☎(050)331269
◣♪11 Lift

★**Lybeer** Korte Vuldersstr 31 (n.rest)
☎(050)334355
Mar-Oct
rm24 ℂ
Credit Cards ①②③

⚙ **Garage Canada** St-Pieterskaai 15 ☎(050)317370 For

BRUXELLES-BRUSSEL (BRUSSELS)

See Plan page 90 *Population* 990,000 *Local Tourist Office* 61 rue Marché-aux-Herbes ☎(02) 5123030
Bruxelles is one of the relatively undiscovered capitals of Europe and has a genuinely friendly and cosmopolitan atmosphere. Its international flavour is born partly from playing host to the headquarters of NATO, the EEC and the European Parliament, and partly from its trading heritage at the crossroads of Europe.
This is a bi-lingual city, the natives switching from Fench to Flemish with nonchalant ease. The best known symbol of its international appeal is the Atomium, built in 1958 for the World Fair and representing an iron molecule magnified 20 billion times. Much of Bruxelles' charm lies in its old-world atmosphere, however, and this is epitomised in the Grand Place which ranks among the most beautiful squares in the world, and in the Baroque architecture of the merchants' houses and the Town Hall. The wealth of museums and art galleries includes a Brewery Museum, a Museum of Costume and Lace, the Autoworld Motor Museum and a magnificent collection of paintings by such masters as Rubens and Breugel in the Gallery of Ancient Art.
The city offers the best of both worlds for shopping - the small shops in the narrow streets of the old quarter and department stores in the modern arcades. Souvenirs include luxurious confectionary, spicy gingerbread, crystal and Brussels lace.

EATING OUT Among the experts of the gourmet world Bruxelles is held in very high esteem. You will find the highest standards in restaurants of modest appearance, but even at inexpensive places you will find speciality dishes of remarkable value. Seafood, especially mussels, is a great favourite, and the meat dishes are unusual and extremely tasty, particularly Flemish *carbonnade* - beef braised in beer. There are creamy cheeses and syrupy waffles, and it is difficult to resist the chocolates and pralines. There are self-service restaurants in large stores which provide excellent meals at reasonable prices. The restaurants of the Rue des Bouchers, just off the Grand Place in the centre of the city, have excellent reputations, as do those at Sainte Catherine near the old fish market.

BRUXELLES (BRUSSELS)

★★★★★**Brussels Sheraton** pl Rogier 3
☎(02)2193400 tx 26887
◣♪523 ☎ Lift ℂ ☒
Credit Cards ①②③④⑤

★★★★★**Hilton International** bd de Waterloo 38
☎(02)5138877 tx 22744
◣♪369 ☎ P120 Lift ℂ
Credit Cards ①②③④⑤

★★★★**Amigo** r de l'Amigo 1-3 ☎(02)5115910 tx 21618
◣♪183 ☎ P60 Lift ℂ
Credit Cards ①②③⑤

★★★★**Belson** Leuvense Steenweg 805 (n.rest)
☎(02)7350000 tx 64921
◣♪87 ☎ Lift ℂ

★★★★**Brussels Europa** Rue de la Loi/Wetstr 107 ☎(02)2301333 tx 25121
◣♪240 ☎ P20 Lift ℂ
Credit Cards ①②③⑤

★★★★**Mayfair Crest** av Louise 381-383
☎(02)6499800 tx 24821
◣♪99 Lift ℂ
Credit Cards ①②③④⑤

★★★★**Palace** Rue Gineste 3 ☎(02)2176200 tx 65604
◣♪352 Lift ℂ
Credit Cards ①②③④⑤

★★★★**Pullman Astoria** r Royale 103
☎(02)2176290 tx 25040
◣♪128 Lift ℂ
Credit Cards ①②③⑤

★★★★**Royal Windsor** (SRS) Duquesnoystr 5
☎(02)5114215 tx 62905
◣♪300 ☎ Lift ℂ
Credit Cards ①②③⑤

★★★★**Sofitel Brussels** 40 Av de la Toison d'Or
☎(02)5142200 tx 63547
◣♪171 Lift ℂ
Credit Cards ①②③

★★★**Arenberg** r d'Assaut 15 ☎(02)5110770 tx 25660
◣♪155 ☎ Lift ℂ
Credit Cards ①②③④⑤

★★★**Bedford** (MAP) r du Midi 135 ☎(02)5127840 tx 24059
◣♪275 ☎ Lift

★★★**Delta** chaussée de Charleroi 17
☎(02)5390160 tx 63225
◣♪253 ☎ Lift ℂ
Credit Cards ①②③⑤

★★★**Jolly Atlanta** bd A-Max (n.rest)
☎(02)2170120 tx 21475
◣♪242 ☎ Lift ℂ
Credit Cards ①②③④⑤

★★★**Président Nord** (MAP) bd A-Max 107 (n.rest) ☎(02)2190060 tx 61417
◣♪63 Lift ℂ
Credit Cards ①②③⑤

★★★**Ramada** Charleroisesteenweg 38
☎(02)5393000 tx 25539
◣♪201 ☎ Lift ℂ
Credit Cards ①②③④⑤

★★**Arcade** pl Ste-Catherine (n.rest)
☎(02)5137620 tx 22476
◣♪234 Lift ℂ
Credit Cards ①②③

★★**Fimotel Expositions** av Imperatrice Charlotte
☎(02)4791910 tx 20907
◣♪80 P Lift ⚙
Credit Cards ①②③⑤

★★**Ibis Brussels Centre** Grasmarkt,100 r du
Marché aux Herbes ☎(02)5144040 tx 25490
↩170 Lift ℂ
Credit Cards ①②③⑤

★★**Noga** r de Béguinage 38 (n.rest)
☎(02)2186763
↩19 Lift

★★**Queen Anne** bd E-Jacqmain 110 (n.rest)
☎(02)2171600 tx 22676
↩59 Lift ℂ
Credit Cards ①②③⑤

★★**Scheers** bd A-Max 132 ☎(02)2177760 tx
21675
↩62 Lift

★★**Van Belle** chaussée de Mons 39
☎(02)5213516 tx 63840
↩146 ☎ Lift ℂ
Credit Cards ①②③⑤

★**Concorde-Louise** r de la Concorde 59 (n.rest)
☎(02)5133886
↩20 Lift ℂ
Credit Card ③

★**Pacific** r A-Dansaert 57 ☎(02)5118459
rm15 Lift

BRUXELLES-BRUSSEL AIRPORT

At **DIEGEM**(8km NE)

★★★★**Holiday Inn** Holidaystr 7 ☎(02)7205865 tx
24285
↩309 P300 Lift ℂ ⬚ ⬚
Credit Cards ①②③⑤

★★★★**Sofitel** Bessenveldstr 15 ☎(02)7251160 tx
26595
↩125 P300 Lift ℂ ⬚
Credit Cards ①②③⑤

★★★**Novotel Brussels Airport** Olmenstr
☎(02)7205830 tx 26751
↩161 Lift ⬚
Credit Cards ①②③④⑤

★**Fimotel** Berkenlaan ☎(02)7253380 tx 20906
↩79 P70 Lift ℂ
Credit Cards ①②③⑤

At **KRAAINEM**(14km NE)

Arema av de Kraainem 33 ☎(020) 7317140 P
Saa

At **OVERIJSE**(14km SE)

R Lamal Steanwag op Waver 117 ☎(02)
6877341 For

CASTEAU
Hainaut

★★★**Casteau Moat House** (QM) chaussée de
Bruxelles 38 ☎(065)728741 tx 57164
rm71(↩35) P200 ℂ ℚ
Credit Cards ①②③④⑤

CHAUDFONTAINE
Liège

★★**Palace** esp 2 ☎(041)650070
rm24(↩20) P Lift

COQ, LE
See **HAAN, DE**

COURTRAI
See **KORTRIJK**

COXYDE-SUR-MER
See **KOKSIJDE**

CUESMES
See **MONS (BERGEN)**

DEURLE
Oost-Vlaanderen

★★**Auberge de Pêcheur** Pontstr 42
☎(091)823144 tx 13867
↩19 A6rm ☎ P150 Lift ℂ ℚ Lake

DIEGEM
See **BRUXELLES-BRUSSEL AIRPORT**

DIEST
Brabant

★★**Modern** Leuvensesteenweg 93 ☎(013)311066
Closed Jul
↩13 P

Garage Meelbergs NV Leuvensesteenweg
108 ☎(013) 333386 P For

DIKSMUIDE (DIXMUDE)
West-Vlaanderen

Durie Esenweg 72 ☎(051) 502501 For

DINANT
Namur

★★**Couronne** r A-Sax 1 ☎(082)222441
Feb-14 Nov & Dec-14 Jan.Closed Mon low
season:Rest closed Mon Jul-Apr
rm10(↩7) Lift

★**Gare** de la Station 39 ☎(082)222056
rm27(↩7) ☎ P Lift

★**Plateau** Plat de la Citadelle 15 ☎(082)222834
rm11(↩2) P ℚ

Dinant Motors rte de Bouvignes 53 ☎(082)
223026 P Ope

Ets Robert Michaux S.P.R.L La Chaussee
d'Yvoir ☎082 223545 P Ren

At **BOUVIGNES**(2km NW)

★★**Auberge de Bouvignes** r Fétis 112
☎(082)611600
rm6(↩3) ☎ P

DOORNIK
See **TOURNAI**

EEKLO
Oost-Vlaanderen

★**Rembrandt** Koningin Astridpl 2 ☎(091)772570
rm8(↩2)

Etn B de Baets Pvbm Koning Albertstr 106
☎(091) 771285 P Aud VW

ENGHIEN
Hainaut

Garage de la Chapelle r d'Hoves 132 ☎(02)
3953758 Cit

EUPEN
Liège

★★**Bosten** Verviersestr 2 ☎(087)742209
Closed 24-26 Dec :Rest closed Mon Jul & Aug
rm11(↩6) ☎ P6
Credit Cards ①②③④⑤

FLORENVILLE
Luxembourg

★**France** r des Généraux Cuvelier 26
☎(061)311032
16 Feb-20 Sep & Oct-Dec
rm35(↩11) ☎ P Lift

FRANCORCHAMPS
Liège

★★★**Roannay** rte de Spa 155 ☎(087)275311 tx
49031
Closed 12-28 Mar & 19 Nov-19 Dec
↩18 ☎ P28 ⬚ Mountain
Credit Cards ①②③⑤

GEEL
Antwerpen

Dierckx P V B A Passtr 170 ☎(014) 588020 P
BMW

GENK
Limburg

N V Genk Motor Etabl de Schaetzen
Hasseltweg 131 ☎(011) 354180 For

GENT (GAND)
Oost-Vlaanderen

The former capital of the Counts
of Flanders, Gent has had a
fascinating history from which it
has emerged as a very beautiful
city, with numerous medieval
buildings, churches and art
galleries; it has as many canals as
Brugge and these all lead in the
direction of the picturesque old
port area of Graslei.
Beside the canals of the Graslei
area stand a wealth of beautifully
preserved medieval merchants'
houses and guild halls, the
Butchers' Hall, the Korenlei, and
the Fishmongers' Hall are
particularly interesting. The
countryside around the town
forms a coloured carpet of
flowers tended by horticulturists
who have made the garden fields
of Gent famous.

EATING OUT *Carbonnades
flamandes*, a dish of beef cooked
in beer, is generally better here
than in most other regions of
Belgium. Other specialities
include *waterzooi* - a delicious
fish stew with herbs, leeks and
cream - and *gentse hutsepot*,
containing all sorts of meats and
virtually all the vegetables
Flanders produces.

GENT (GAND)
Oost-Vlaanderen

★★★★**Holiday Inn** Ottergemsesteenweg 600
☎(091)225885 tx 11756
↩167 P180 Lift ℂ ℚ ⬚
Credit Cards ①②③⑤

★★★**Europa** Gordunakaai 59 ☎(091)226071 tx
11547
:Rest closed Sun
↩39 ☎ P25 Lift
Credit Cards ①②③⑤

★★★**Novotel Gent Centrum** Gouden Leeuwpl 7
☎(091)242230 tx 11400
↩117 ☎ Lift ⬚
Credit Cards ①②③⑤

★★**Arcade** Nederkouter 24/26 (n.rest)
☎(091)250707 tx 11655
↩134 ☎ Lift ℂ
Credit Cards ①③

★**Condor** (BW) Ottergemsesteenweg 703
☎(091)218041 tx 13887
↩48 P200 Lift ℂ
Credit Cards ①②③⑤

★★**St-Jorishof** Botermarkt 2 ☎(091)242424 tx
12738
Closed 3 wks Jul & Xmas :Rest closed Sun & BH
↩37 A27rm ☎ P5 Lift ℂ
Credit Cards ①②③⑤

Garage A Martens Kuitendgstr 42 ☎(091)
530517 P Col

N.V. Vandersmissen Brusselsesteenweg 506
☎(091) 313303 For

🛏 **Vernaeve N V** Doornzelestr 31 ☎(091) 230384
AR LR

HAAN, DE (LE COQ)
West-Vlaanderen

★★★*Dunes* Leopoldpl 5 (n.rest) ☎(059)233146
15 Mar-15 Oct
🛏🆁27 P Lift

★★*Auberge des Rois* Zeedijk 1 ☎(059)233018
Closed 11 Nov-22 Dec & 7-24 Jan
rm28(🛏🆁24) 🕿 P14 Lift Sea
Credit Cards ① ⑤

★★*Bellevue* Koningspl 5 ☎(059)233439
20 Apr-15 Oct
rm50(🛏🆁30) P Lift

HAN-SUR-LESSE
Namur

★★*Voyageurs* r de C-Ardennais 1 ☎(084)377237
tx 42079
rm42(🛏🆁31) P Lift

HASSELT
Limburg

★*Century* Leopoldpl 1 ☎(011)224799
rm17(🛏🆁6)
Credit Cards ① ② ③ ⑤

🛏 *Etabl Hoffer* Demerstr 66 ☎(011) 224911 Ren

HERSTAL
See **LIÈGE (LUIK)**

HOEI
See **HUY**

HOUFFALIZE
Luxembourg

★*Clé des Champs* rte de Libramont 22
☎(062)288044
rm13(🆁8) 🕿 P

🛏 **Garage Lambin SPRL** 10 rte de Liege ☎(062)
288035 P Toy

BRUXELLES (BRUSSELS)

1	Brussels Sheraton	★★★★★
2	Hilton International	★★★★★
3	Amigo	★★★★
4	Brussels Europa	★★★★
5	Holiday Inn see Bruxelles Airport (At Diegem)	★★★★
6	Mayfair Crest	★★★★
7	Palace	★★★★
8	Pullman Astoria	★★★★
9	Royal Windsor	★★★★
10	Sofitel see Bruxelles Airport (At Diegem)	★★★★
11	Arenberg	★★★
12	Bedford	★★★
13	Delta	★★★
14	Jolly Atlanta	★★★
15	Novotel Brussels Airport see Bruxelles Airport (At Diegem)	★★★
16	President Nord	★★★
17	Ramada	★★★
18	Sofitel Brussels	★★★
19	Arcade	★★
20	Fimotel Expositions	★★
21	Fimotel see Bruxelles Airport (At Diegem)	★★
21A	Ibis Centre	★★
22	Noga	★★
23	Queen Anne	★★
24	Scheers	★★
25	Concorde-Louise	★★
26	Pacific	★

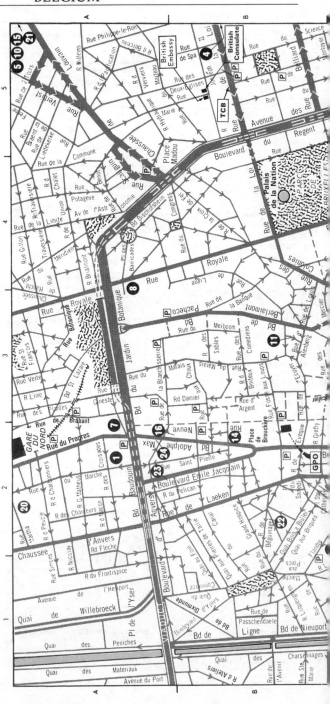

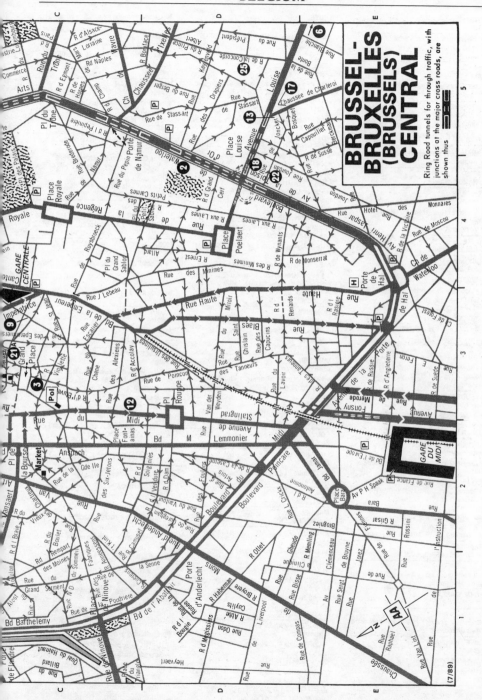

BRUSSEL-BRUXELLES (BRUSSELS) CENTRAL

Ring Road tunnels for through traffic, with junctions at the major cross roads, are shown thus ▬█▬

(7/89)

BELGIUM

HOUYET
Namur

★**Marquisette** rte de Dinant ☎(082)666429
Closed 20 Jun-10 Jul
⇘⋔10 ☎ P

HUY (HOEI)
Liège

★★**Fort** chaussée Napoléon 5-6 ☎(085)212403
rm22(⇘12)

IEPER (YPRES)
West-Vlaanderen

★**St Nicolas** G-de Stuerstr 6 ☎(057)200622
Closed 17 Jul-6 Aug :Rest closed Sun pm & Mon
rm8(⇘4)

⇘ Garage Devos & Dewanckel Industrielaan 2
☎057 201335 P For

JAMBES
See **NAMUR (NAMEN)**

KASTERLEE
Antwerpen

★★**Dennen** Lichtaarsebaan 79 ☎(014)556107
Closed 1-14 Jan
rm12(⇘⋔9) P25

KNOKKE
See **KNOKKE-HEIST**

KNOKKE-HEIST
West-Vlaanderen

At **ALBERT PLAGE**

★★★**Lido DPn** Zwaluwenlaan 18 ☎(050)601925
Etr-Sep Closed Tue-Thu Oct-Etr
⇘⋔40 ☎ P8 Lift ℂ

At **KNOKKE**

★★**Bristol** Zeedijk 291 ☎(050)511220
Etr-Sep
rm30(⇘⋔23) Lift

At **ZOUTE, LE**

★★★**Majestic** Zeedijk 697 ☎(051)611144
Apr-Sep
rm61(⇘52) ☎ Lift

KOKSIJDE (COXYDE-SUR-MER)
West-Vlaanderen

★★**Royal** Zeedijk 65 ☎(058)511300
Apr-5 Sep
rm29(⇘7) Lift

KORTRIJK (COURTRAI)
West-Vlaanderen

★★**Climat** Kennedy Park 1 ☎(056)200687 tx
85461
⇘⋔48 Lift ℂ

★★**Damier** Grote Markt 41 ☎(056)221547 tx
86320
⇘⋔51 Lift ℂ
Credit Cards ① ② ③ ⑤

⇘ **Vanneste & Zonen N.V.** Kortrijksteenweg
405,Harelbeke ☎(056) 201000 Dat Fia Lan

KRAAINEM
See **BRUXELLES-BRUSSEL**

LA
Each name preceded by 'La' is listed under the
name that follows it.

LAC-DE-WARFAZ
See **SPA**

LE
Each name preceded by 'Le' is listed under the
name that follows it.

LEUVEN (LOUVAIN)
Brabant

At **WINKSELE**(3km NW)

⇘ **Hergon** Brusselsesteenweg 57 ☎(016) 223506
For

LEUZE
Hainaut

★**Couronne** pl de la Gare 18 ☎(069)622166
Closed Aug
rm10

LIÈGE (LUIK)
Liège

★★★★**Palais des Congres Liege** (QM) esp de
l'Europe 2 ☎(041)426020 tx 41156
⇘⋔219 ☎ P250 Lift ℂ ▱
Credit Cards ① ② ③ ④ ⑤

★★★★**Ramada** bd de la Sauvenière 100
☎(041)224910 tx 41896
⇘⋔105 ☎ P35 Lift ℂ
Credit Cards ① ② ③ ④ ⑤

★★**Cygne d'Argent** r Beekman 49
☎(041)237001 tx 42617
⇘⋔27 ☎ Lift
Credit Cards ① ② ③ ⑤

★★**Urbis** 41 pl de la République,Francaise
(n.rest) ☎(041)236085 tx 42369
rm80(⇘⋔78) Lift ℂ
Credit Cards ① ② ③ ⑤

⇘ **Ets des Grosses Battes S.A.** 117 quai des
Ardennes ☎(041) 653990 For

⇘ **S A Sodia** r L-Boumal 24 ☎(041) 526862 P
AR LR

At **HERSTAL**(8km NE on E25)

★★★**Post House** (THF) r Hurbise (SE5 at exit 34
Hermée-Hauts-Sarts) ☎(041)646400 tx 41103
⇘⋔100 P100 ▱
Credit Cards ① ② ③ ⑤

LIGNEUVILLE
Liège

★★**Moulin** r de Centre 91 ☎(080)570081
Closed Nov-21 Dec
⇘⋔14 ☎ P

LOKEREN
Oost-Vlaanderen

★★**Park** Antwerpsesteenweg 1 ☎(091)482046
10 Jan-10 Jul & 4 Aug-10 Jan :Rest closed Sun &
Mon
⇘⋔9 P100
Credit Cards ① ② ③ ⑤

⇘ **Siau NV** Weverslaan 14 ☎(091) 481400 BMW

LOUVAIN
See **LEUVAN**

LOUVIÈRE, LA
Hainaut

⇘ **J Dupire** r L-Dupuis 10 ☎(064) 224031 P
ROV DJ LR

LUIK
See **LIÈGE**

MALINES
See **MECHELEN**

MALMÉDY
Liège

⇘ **E Nachsem-Lejoly** Baugnez 94 ☎(080)
338301 P Toy

At **XHOFFRAIX**(5km N on N28)

★★**Trôs Marets** (Relais et Châteaux) rte de Trôs
Marets 2 ☎(080)337917
Closed 16 Nov-21 Dec
⇘⋔11 ☎ P40 ℂ ▱
Credit Cards ① ② ③ ⑤

MARCHE-EN-FAMENNE
Luxembourg

★**Alfa** Porte de Rochefort 11 ☎(084)311793
rm21(⇘⋔15) Lift
Credit Cards ① ② ③ ④

⇘ **Est Leunen & Cie Sprl** rte de Bastogne 51A
☎(084) 311582 P Fia

⇘ **Garage Marlair S P R L** 19 Chaussée de
Liège ☎(084) 312084 Ope Vau

⇘ **Garage Verhulst** rte de Liège 50 ☎(084)
311673 P AR LR

MARTELANGE
Luxembourg

★**Maison Rouge** rte d'Arlon 5 ☎(063)64006
Closed Oct
rm12 ☎ P

MASNUY-ST-JEAN
Hainaut

★★★**Amigo** chaussée Brunehault 3
☎(065)728721 tx 57313
⇘⋔52 P40 Lift ℂ ▱
Credit Cards ① ② ③ ⑤

MECHELEN (MALINES)
Antwerpen

★**Claes** O.L.Vrouwstr 51 ☎(015)412866
Etr-Oct Closed wknds Nov-Etr:Rest closed Sun
rm15

⇘ **Etn Festraets NV** M-Sabbestr 123 ☎(015)
202752 Fia Lan Vau

MENEN (MENIN)
West-Vlaanderen

⇘ **N V Imecar S A** Kortrijkst 269 ☎(056) 513535
Ren

MONS (BERGEN)
Hainaut

⇘ **Willems** 39 bd Sainctelette ☎(0659) 346363
Ope vau

At **CUESMES**(4km SW)

⇘ **Auto Mons** r de Chemin de Fer 163 ☎(065)
311128 P For

NAMUR (NAMEN)
Namur

At **JAMBES**

⇘ **Jambes** pl Charlotte 18 ☎(081) 301451 P For

NIVELLES (NIJVEL)
Brabant

★★**Nivelles-Sud** chaussée de Mons 22
☎(067)218721 tx 57788
⇘⋔115 P Lift ℂ ▱
Credit Cards ① ② ③ ⑤

⇘ **Flash Service Sprl** 63 chaussée de Namur
☎(067) 211025 P All makes

⇘ **Nivelles Motors S.A.** 68 faubourg de Mons
☎(067) 213023 M/C Ope

OOSTENDE (OSTENDE)
West-Vlaanderen

See Plan page 94
Oostende is the largest resort on
the Belgian coast, offering
extensive sandy beaches, an
attractive promenade,
picturesque yacht harbour and
excellent hotels, restaurants and
visitor facilities. The five main
beaches are free except for the
Lido Beach, where the small
entrance fee includes the use of
deck chairs. The Dolphin's Beach
next to the Lido is reserved
exclusively for children under 14.
The centre of Oostende has large
traffic-free shopping precincts
with a range of boutiques and
stores to match any major city.
The town square is lined with
flower-decked pavement cafés
where you can sit and listen to

the band while enjoying a drink or a celebrated Belgian waffle with fresh strawberries and cream.

EATING OUT The Casino's restaurant, *Périgord*, is one of the most fasionable places to eat.

OOSTENDE (OSTENDE)
West-Vlaanderen
★★★**Bellevue-Britannia** Prom Albert 1 55-56 (n.rest) ☎(059)706373 tx 81378
16 Dec-14 Nov
�¶61 P12 Lift ℂ Sea
Credit Cards ① ② ③ ⑤
★★★**Prado** Leopold II Laan 22 (n.rest)
☎(059)705306 tx 82237
➶32 Lift ℂ
Credit Cards ① ② ③ ⑤
★★★**Ter Streep** Leopold II Laan 14 (n.rest)
☎(059)700912 tx 82261
➶35 Lift
★★★**Westminster** van Iseghemlaan 22
☎(059)702411 tx 81869
➶60 Lift ℂ
Credit Cards ① ② ③ ④ ⑤
★★**Ambassadeur** Wapenpl 8A ☎(059)700941 tx 81415
➶23 ⌂ P Lift
★★**Bero** Hofstr 1A ☎(059)702335 tx 82163
➶60 ⌂ Lift ℂ 🖃
Credit Cards ① ② ③ ⑤
★★**Europe** Kapucijnenstr 52 ☎(059)701012 tx 81659
Mar-15 Oct
➶65 Lift ℂ
Credit Cards ② ③
★★**Lido** L-Spilliaetstr 1 ☎(059)700806 tx 83006
Mar-27 Dec
➶66 Lift ℂ
Credit Cards ① ② ③ ⑤
★★**Parc** M-Josépl 3 (n.rest) ☎(059)706580
rm44(➶27) ℂ Sea
Credit Cards ① ② ③ ⑤
★**Glenmore** Hofstr 25 ☎(059)702022 tx 82389
Closed Jan
➶40 Lift ℂ Sea
Credit Cards ① ② ③ ⑤
★**Nieuwe Sportman** de Smet de Naeyerlaan 9 (n.rest) ☎(059)702384
rm10
★**Pacific** Hofstr 11 ☎(059)701507
Apr-15 Oct
rm51(➶35) ⌂ Lift
★**Strand** Visserskaai 1 ☎(059)703383 tx 81357
Feb-Nov
➶21 Lift ℂ
Credit Cards ① ② ③ ⑤
➹ **F Stoops** chaussée de,Torhoutsteenweg 597
☎(059) 702472 Toy
➹ **Garage Casino Kursaal** Torhoutsesteenweg 684 ☎(059) 703240 P Peu Tal
➹ **Garage Delta** Steenweg op Torhout 529
☎(059) 801503 For
➹ **Garage Royal-Auto** Koninginnelaan 52
☎(059) 707635 M/C P Fia Lan

OVERIJSE
See **BRUXELLES-BRUSSEL**

PANNE, DE (LA PANNE)
West-Vlaanderen
★★**Regina Maris** Bortierlaan 13 ☎(058)411222
Apr-Sep & 20 Dec-3 Jan
➶72 Lift 🖃
Credit Cards ① ② ③

★**Strand** Niewpoortlaan 153 (n.rest)
☎(058)411196
Apr-Nov
rm51(➶43) ⌂ P42 Beach Sea
Credit Cards ③ ⑤

PHILIPPEVILLE
Namur
★**Croisée** r de France 45 ☎(071)666231
14 Feb-26 Aug & 15 Sep-Dec
rm12(➶5) ⌂ P

PROFONDEVILLE
Namur
★**Auberge d'Alsace** av Gl-Garcia 42
☎(081)412228
➶6 P

REMOUCHAMPS
Liège
★★**Royal Étrangers** r de la Reffe 26
☎(041)844006
Closed 16 Nov-9 Dec
rm15(➶5) ⌂ P

ROCHE-EN-ARDENNE, LA
Luxembourg
★★★**Air Pur** rte d'Houffalize 11, Villez
☎(084)411223
Closed 25 Jun-12 Jul :Rest closed Tue & Wed
rm11(➶10) ⌂ P10
Credit Cards ① ② ③
★★★**Ardennes DP**n r de Beausain 2
☎(084)411112
15 Mar-20 Nov & 20 Dec-2 Jan :Rest closed Mon out of season
➶12 ⌂ P8
Credit Cards ① ② ③ ⑤
★★**Belle Vue** rue de la Gare 10 ☎(084)411187
rm10(➶6) P6 ℂ Lake
Credit Cards ② ⑤

ROCHEFORT
Namur
★**Fayette** r Jacquet 87 ☎(084)214273
rm9(➶2) ⌂ P15
Credit Cards ① ② ③ ⑤
★**Limbourg** pl Roi Albert 21 ☎(084)211036
Mar-28 Aug & Sep-Jan
rm6(➶5) P

SINT NIKLAAS (ST-NICOLAS)
Oost-Vlaanderen
★★**Serwir** Koningin Astridlaan 49 ☎(03)7780511 tx 32422
Closed 8-28 Jul
➶27 P250 Lift ℂ
Credit Cards ① ② ③ ⑤
➹ **Central Garage** Dalstr 28 ☎(03) 7763830 For
➹ **Garage Sint Christoffel** Wegvoeringstr 88
☎(03) 7761338 ROV LR

SINT TRUIDEN (ST-TROND)
Limburg
➹ **Celis** Naamsestweg 239 ☎011 689951 Vol
➹ **Milou** Tiensesteenweg 109 ☎(011) 683941 P
Fia Ren

SPA
Liège
At **BALMORAL**(3km N)
★★★**Dorint Spa Balmoral** rte de Balmoral 33
☎(087)772581 tx 49209
➶97 P80 Lift ℂ ℴ 🖃 ⇌ ☏ Lake
Credit Cards ① ② ③ ④ ⑤
At **LAC-DE-WARFAZ**(2.5km NE)
★★**Lac DP**n av A-Hesse 45 ☎(087)771074
:Rest closed Tue
rm11(➶8) ⌂ Mountain Lake
Credit Cards ① ② ③ ⑤

At **TIÈGE-LEZ-SPA**(5km NE)
★★★**Charmille** r de Tiège ☎(087)474313
Apr-15 Nov
➶33 ⌂ P Lift

THOUROUT
See**TORHOUT**

TIÈGE-LEZ-SPA
See **SPA**

TIENEN (TIRLEMONT)
Brabant
➹ **Garage Delaisse** Leuvensestr 115-117 ☎(016) 811077 P Toy
➹ **Standaert Motors PVBA** Hamelendreef 65
☎016 814646 P For

TONGEREN
Limburg
★**Lido** Grote Markt 19 ☎(012)231948
➶9

TORHOUT (THOUROUT)
West-Vlaanderen
➹ **Garage Deketelaere** Vredelaan 69 ☎(050) 212623 Hon Vau
At **WYNENDALE**(3km)
★★**t'Gravenhof** Oostendestr 343 ☎(050)212314
:Rest closed Tue & Wed
➶10 P20

TOURNAI (DOORNIK)
Hainaut
➹ **Ets Lintermans S P R L** 14-16 quai Staline
☎(069) 222116 P Ope Vau

TURNHOUT
Antwerpen
➹ **Perfect** Nieuwekaai 9-11 ☎(014) 413588 Ren

VERVIERS
Liège
★★★**Amigo** r Herla 1 ☎(087)316767 tx 49128
➶54 P30 Lift ℂ 🖃
Credit Cards ① ② ③ ⑤

VILLERS-SUR-LESSE
Namur
★**Beau Séjour** r des Platanes ☎(084)377115
Mar-15 Jan
➶19 ⌂ P ⇌

WAVRE
Brabant
At **BIERGES**(2km SW)
➹ **Lescot-Wavre** bd de l'Europe,ZI ☎(010) 419496 P For

WENDUINE
West-Vlaanderen
★★**Mouettes** Zeedijk ☎(050)411514
15 Apr-Sep
➶30 Lift Sea

WEPION
Namur
★★★★**Novotel Namur** chaussée de Dinant 1449
☎(081)460811 tx 59031
➶110 ⌂ P125 🖃 ⇌
Credit Cards ① ② ③ ④ ⑤
★**Frisia** chaussée de Dinant 1455 ☎(081)411106
15 Mar-Oct
rm10(➶7) P Sea

WESTENDE
West-Vlaanderen
★★**Rotonda** Zeedijk 300 ☎(059)300495
Mar-Dec
rm18(➶10) ⌂ P

WINKSELE
See **LEUVEN (LOUVAIN)**

WYNENDALE
See **TORHOUT (THOUROUT)**

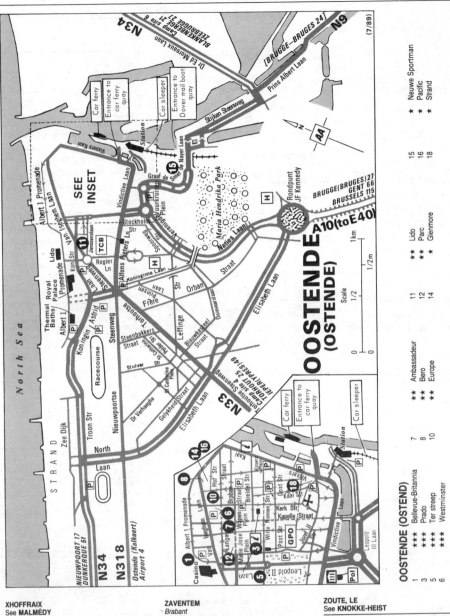

(7/89)

OOSTENDE (OSTEND)

1	★★★	Bellevue-Britannia	
3	★★★	Prado	
5	★★★	Ter streep	
6	★★★	Westminster	
7	★★	Ambassadeur	
8	★★	Bero	
10	★★	Europe	
11	★★	Lido	
12	★★	Parc	
14	★	Glenmore	
15	★	Neuwe Sportman	
16	★	Pacific	
18	★	Strand	

XHOFFRAIX
See **MALMÉDY**

YPRES
See **IEPER**

YVOIR
Namur
★★*Vachter* chaussée de Namur 140
☎(082)611314
rm9(⇥8) ☎ P

ZAVENTEM
Brabant

👜 *Garage Abeloos Bvba* Mechelsesteenweg
297 ☎(02) 7312657 P For

ZOLDER
Limburg
★*Pits* Omloop Terlaemen ☎(011)251899
⇥12 P

ZOUTE, LE
See **KNOKKE-HEIST**

*T*his land of fairytales is also the land that loves children and where everyone seems to live life to the full. Denmark has pretty countryside, a marvellous coastline with vast sandy beaches ideal for watersports of all kinds, and fun-filled leisure attractions that have wide appeal. Wherever you go in this ancient kingdom, famed for its warmth and hospitality, you will never be more than 30 miles from the sea, and all around will be lovely countryside of forests and heather-clad moors, rolling meadowlands or nature reserves.

Denmark is divided into three distinct regions and, although the country is not large, there is considerable water between them. The 'garden island' of Fyn in the middle separates mainland Jylland to the west and in the other direction Sjaelland, with København its main target for visitors. The undeniable attractions of the capital tend to obscure the rest of Denmark – and quite unfairly. Like most capitals, Copenhagen is not typical of the country, and any balanced visit should include one or more of the other centres.

DENMARK

Language
Danish

Local time
GMT + 1 (Summer GMT + 2)

Currency
Danish krone, divided into 100 øre. At the time of going to press.
£1 = Dkk12.10
US$1 = Dkk7.28

Emergency numbers
Fire, police, ambulance ☎000

Information in English
Danish Tourist Board Information Office, Sceptre House, 169/173 Regent Street, London W1R 8PY
☎*01-734 2637/8
*071 from 6 May

Information in the USA
Scandinavian National Tourist Office, 655 Third Avenue, New York, NY 10017
☎212 949 2333

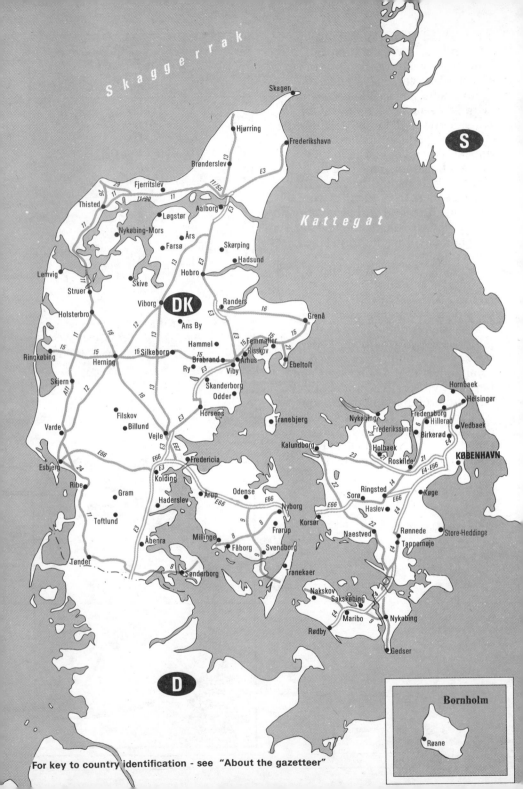

Skaggerrak

Skagen

Hjørring

Frederikshavn

Brønderslev

E3

Fjerritslev 29

11/55

11 11/20

Thisted 26

11

Aalborg E3

Løgstør

Kattegat

Nykøbing-Mors

Års

Farsø

Skørping

Hadsund

Lemvig

Hobro

Struer

Skive

Viborg Randers

16

Holsterbro

DK

Ans By

Grenå

12

15 Femmøller 15

Hammel Risskov 15

18

Silkeborg Brabrand Århus 21

Ringkøbing 15 15 Herning 13 Ry E3 Viby Ebeltoft

Skjern A11 Skanderborg

12 Odder

18 Horsens

Filskov

Tranebjerg

Hornbæk

Varde Billund E3 Helsingør

Vejle Nykøbing Fredensborg

Frederikssund Hillerød Vedbæk

E66 E67 Birkerød E4

Esbjerg 24 E66 Fredericia Kalundborg Holbæk

Ribe E3 Kolding Roskilde 21 KØBENHAVN

Gram 23 E4-E66

Haderslev Arup 22 Sorø Ringsted 14 Køge

Toftlund Odense E66

11 E66 Haslev E4

Åbenrå 9 Nyborg Næstved Rønnede Store-Heddinge

Millinge 8 8 Frørup E66 22 Tappernøje

Tønder Fåborg Svendborg Korsør

8 9 Tranekær

Sønderborg

Nakskov

Sakskøbing

E4 Maribo 9 Nykøbing

Rødby

Gedser

D

Bornholm

Røane

For key to country identification - see "About the gazetteer"

HOW TO GET THERE

There are three direct ferry routes to Denmark: To **Esbjerg**, in western Jutland, from **Harwich** takes 15–20 hours; from **Newcastle** (summer only) takes 19–22 hours; To **Hirtshals** in northern Jutland, from **Newcastle** takes 25 hours

Alternatively you could take one of the short Channel crossings to France or Belgium and drive through the Netherlands and northern Germany.

Distance

From the Channel ports to København (Copenhagen) is roughly 1,060km (660 miles).

Another possibility is to use the ferry operating between Harwich and Hamburg (19¼–21½ hours) and drive the short distance to southern Denmark.

Inter-island travel is made easier by either bridge links or frequent vehicle ferries.

MONEYMATTERS

There are no restrictions on the amount of foreign or Danish currency that visitors may import or export. However, if the Danish currency exported exceeds *Dkk*50,000 it must be proved that the amount was imported or obtained by conversion of imported foreign currency.

Banking hours

In København: 09.30–16.00hrs Monday, Tuesday, Wednesday and Friday (18.00hrs on Thursdays). At the Central Railway Station and the Air Terminal banks are open until 22.00hrs.
Outside København: generally 09.30–12.00hrs and 14.00–16.00hrs.

All banks are closed on Saturdays, except Exchange offices on the Danish/German border which close between 13.00 and 15.00hrs. These offices may also open on summer Sundays.

Postcheques

may be cashed at all but the smallest post offices, up to a maximum of *Dkk*1,500 per cheque. Go to the counter marked *Postcheques* or *Postsparebank* and showing the flag of the issuing country.

MOTORING REGULATIONS AND GENERAL INFORMATION

The information given here is specific to Denmark. It **must** be read in conjunction with the European ABC at the front of the book, which covers those regulations which are common to many countries.

Accidents*

If you are involved in an accident, you must stop and exchange particulars with the other party. If anyone is injured you *must* obtain medical assistance and immediately report the incident to the police. See also *Warning triangle* below

Breakdown*

If you car breaks down, try to move it to the side of the road so that it obstructs the traffic flow as little as possible. The Danish Motoring Club (FDM) is unable to provide roadside assistance. In the event of a breakdown assistance may be obtained from either the *Falck Organisation* or *Dansk Autohjaelp* (Danish Automobile Association), both of which operate a 24-hour service. (See local telephone directory for number of nearest station.) If you break down on a motorway and call for assistance from an emergency telephone, you must specify whether help is required from Falck or Dansk Autohjaelp. Any service received must be paid for. See *Warning triangle* below.

British Embassy/Consulate*

The British Embassy together with its consular section is located at DK-2100 København ø, Kastelsvej 36–40 ☎(31) 26 4600 and is located on the plan of København in the gazetteer. There are British Consulates with Honorary Consuls in Åbenrå, Ålborg, Århur, Bornholm, Esbjerg, Fredericia and Odense.

Dimensions and weight restrictions

Private **cars** and towed **trailers** or **caravans** are restricted to the following dimensions – height, 4 metres; width, 2.50 metres; length, 12 metres. The maximum permitted overall length of vehicle/trailer or caravan combinations is 18 metres.

*Additional information will be found in the European ABC at the front of the book.

Trailers without brakes may have a total weight of up to 50% of the weight of the towing vehicle; trailers with brakes may have a total weight up to 90% of the weight of the towing vehicle.

Driving licence*

A valid UK or Republic of Ireland licence is acceptable in Denmark. The minimum age at which a visitor may use a temporarily imported car or motorcycle is 17 years.

Emergency messages to tourists*

Emergency messages to tourists are broadcast daily on *Radio Denmark*. The messages are transmitted in English on 245Khz long wave and 1062Khz medium wave between 08.15–08.20hrs.

Lights

Headlights should be dipped early when meeting another vehicle, as the lighting of Danish-registered vehicles is of lower density than that of UK-registered vehicles. Driving with only one headlight or spotlight is not allowed. Fog lamps may be used in pairs in conjunction with sidelights (but not headlights). It is compulsory for *motorcyclists* to use dipped headlights during the day.

Motoring club*

 The **Forenede Danske Motorejere** (FDM) has its headquarters at 2800 Lyngby, Firskovvej 32 ☎(45) 930800 and branch offices are maintained in major towns throughout the country. The offices are usually open between 09.00 and 17.00hrs from Monday to Friday. During the summer, the headquarters and many branch offices are open on Saturday to personal callers between 09.00 and 12.00hrs. See the *Town Plan of København* within the gazetteer.

Motorways

Approximately 400 miles of toll-free motorways (*motorvej*) are at present open, and more stretches of the planned 560-mile network are under construction. Nearly all motorways are part of the European international network of *E-roads*, which are marked with green and white signs with the prefix 'E'.

Orange badge scheme for disabled drivers*

Concessions are extended to badge holders who are allowed to park for up to 1 hour where a shorter time limit applies to other motorists. Unlimited parking is permitted where a time limit of 1 hour or longer would otherwise apply.

Parking*

Regulations are similar to those in the UK, but it is advisable to use public car parks. In central København kerbside parking is restricted to one hour (three hours where there are parking meters). Vehicles illegally parked will be removed by the police at the owner's expense and a fine will be imposed. Parking discs, which are obtainable from the police, FDM offices, service stations, post offices and some banks are obligatory. These discs are set at the time of parking, and show when the parking time expires according to the time limit allowed in the district. Failure to observe zonal regulations could result in a fine or the vehicle being towed away.

Parking lights must be used in badly lit areas, and when visibility is poor.

Petrol*

Credit cards Some recognised credit cards are accepted at petrol stations.
Duty-free petrol In addition to the petrol in the vehicle tank, up to 10 litres in a can may be imported free of customs duty and tax.
Petrol (leaded) Super Benzin (98 octane) grade.
Petrol (low lead) is sold as the 96 octane grade.
Petrol (unleaded) is sold in Denmark. It is available with an octane rating of either 92 or 95 which is indicated on the pump, together with the word ***blyfri*** (lead free).

Postal information

Mail Postcards Dkk3.20, letters up to 20gm Dkk3.20.
Post offices There are 300 post offices in Denmark. Large offices are open 09.00–17.00hrs or 10.00–17.00hrs Monday to Friday, and 09.00–12.00hrs or 10.00–12.00hrs Saturday. Opening hours for small offices vary. In København the head Post Office is open 09.00–

*Additional information will be found in the European ABC at the front of the book.

19.00hrs Monday to Friday and 09.00–13.00hrs Saturday. The post office at the Central Station is open 09.00–21.00hrs Monday to Friday, 09.00–18.00hrs Saturday and 10.00–16.00hrs Sundays and public holidays.

Priority*

A line of white triangles painted across the road indicates that you must give way to traffic on the road you are entering.

Public holidays*

Official public holidays in Denmark for 1990 are given below.
January 1 (New Year's Day)
April 12 (Maundy Thursday)
April 13 (Good Friday)
April 16 (Easter Monday)
May 11 (Store Bededag or Great Prayer Day)
May 24 (Ascension Day)
June 5† (Constitution Day)
December 24† (Christmas Eve)
December 25 (Christmas Day)
December 26 (Boxing Day)
December 31† (New Year's Eve)
†Officially a public holiday from noon, but banks remain closed all day

Roads

The roads in Denmark are generally of a very high standard and well signposted. They are classified into three categories, showing E-roads (green and white signs with prefix 'E'), primary roads (one or two-digit black numbers on yellow boards) and secondary roads (three-digit black numbers on white boards). See also Road conditions in the European ABC.

Shopping hours

Shops are usually open between 09.00 and 17.30hrs (19.00 or 20.00hrs on Friday). Most shops are closed on Saturday afternoons.

Speed limits*

Unless indicated by signs the following limits apply:

	Built-up area (indicated on white plates with 'town silhouettes')
Car	50kph (31mph)
Car/caravan/trailer	50kph (31mph)
	Other roads
Car	80kph (49mph)
Car/caravan/trailer	70kph (43mph)
	Motorways
Car	100kph (62mph)
Car/caravan/trailer	70kph (43mph)

Even minor infringement of these limits can result in a fine.

Spiked or studded tyres

Spiked or studded tyres may be used between 1 October and 30 April. When spiked tyres are used no special speed limits apply, but the spiked tyres must be fitted to all wheels. Generally, motoring in Denmark is rarely restricted by bad weather.

Telephone*

Insert coin **after** lifting receiver; dialling tone is a continuous tone. When making calls to subscribers within Denmark, precede the number with the relevant area code (shown in parentheses before hotel/garage enquiry number in gazetteer). Use Dkk1 coin or two 25øre coins for local calls, and Dkk1 or Dkk5 coins for national and international calls. Coins inserted in a callbox are not returned even if the number is engaged, but repeat attempts may be made until the time runs out.
International calls can be made from all payphones.
A telephone call to the UK costs Dkk3.60 for each minute.
Telephone codes
UK to Denmark	010 45
Denmark to UK	009 44
Denmark to Republic of Ireland	009 353
Denmark to the USA	009 1

Warning triangle*

The use of a warning triangle is compulsory in the event of accident or breakdown. The triangle must be placed at least 50 metres (55yds) behind the vehicle on ordinary roads, and 100 metres (110yds) on motorways, to warn following traffic of any obstruction.

*Additional information will be found in the European ABC at the front of the book.

ACCOMMODATION

The hotel accommodation prices listed below are an average for each classification from five to one star. Hotel charges generally include VAT (22%) and service (15½%). Accommodation is likely to be more expensive in København (Copenhagen) and some of the more popular tourist areas.

At the time of going to press, £1 *Sterling = Dkk12.10 and US$1 = Dkk7.28* but you should check the rate of exchange before your departure.

AVERAGE PRICES

	Single Room	Double Room	Breakfast	Lunch/Dinner
★★★★★	Dkk1520–1809	Dkk1769–2034	Dkk90–125	—
★★★★	Dkk705–842	Dkk1020–1412	Dkk63–76	Dkk76–139
★★★	Dkk560–681	Dkk732–927	from Dkk52	Dkk107–184
★★	Dkk407–569	Dkk596–768	Dkk47–53	Dkk88–169
★	Dkk244–355	Dkk417–507	Dkk51–61	Dkk135–155

The Danish alphabet differs from the English one in that the last letters after Z are Æ,Ø,Å; this must be borne in mind when using Danish reference books. Some Danish telephone numbers are likely to change during the currency of this guide.

AALBORG
Jylland
★★★★**Hvide Hus** Vesterbro 2 ☎(98)138400 tx 69690
⇔♠201 ⌂ P Lift ℂ ➩
Credit Cards 1 2 3 4 5

★★★**Limfjordshotellet** Ved Stranden 14-16 ☎(98)164333 tx 69516
⇔♠180 ⌂ P60 Lift ℂ
Credit Cards 1 2 3 4 5

★★★**Phønix** Vesterbro 77 ☎(98)120011 tx 69782
⇔♠183 P70 Lift ℂ
Credit Cards 1 2 3 5

★★★**Scheelsminde** (Inter DK) Scheelsmindevej 35 ☎(98)183233 tx 60118
rm70 P50 ℂ ⌖ ▱
Credit Cards 1 2 3 4 5

★★**Park** Boulevarden 41 ☎(98)123133
⇔♠81 Lift ℂ
Credit Cards 1 2 3 4 5

ÅBENRA
Jylland
★★★**Hvide Hus** Flensborgvej 50 ☎(74)624700 tx 52182
⇔♠67 A15rm ⌂ P50 ℂ Sea
Credit Cards 1 2 3 4 5

➦ **Automobilfordhandler** Vestermarksvej 7-9 ☎(04) 622028 Peu

➦ **I M Jensen** Flensborgvej 2 ☎(04) 621355 Ope

➦ **Skifter Andersen** Langrode,Vestvejen ☎(04) 621333 Vol

ALBERTSLUND
See **KØBENHAVN (COPENHAGEN)**

ANS BY
Jylland
At **KONGENSBRO**(5km SE)
★★**Kongensbro Kro** Gl-Kongevej 70 ☎(86)870177
14 Jan-20 Dec
⇔♠15 ⌂ P50 Lake
Credit Cards 1 2 3 5

ÅRHUS
Jylland

Denmark's second city is a pleasant university town of character, located on Jylland's east coast and surrounded by woods and rich farmland. Attractions include a fascinating open-air museum, a nightlife of more than 200 bars, restaurants and discotheques - and a serious programme of theatre, ballet and opera. Of special interest is the 13th-century Domkirke, Scandinavia's longest church, which houses a fine early 18th-century organ. For a panoramic view of the town, a trip up the 200ft tower of the *Rådhuset* (Town Hall) is rewarding. Built between 1938 and 1942 as a showpiece of Danish architecture, it features a huge carpet depicting the city map.

Århus' open-air museum, known as *Den gamle By* (the Old Town), features 65 half-timbered houses, a mill and a millstream. The period interiors give the atmosphere of a Danish market town as Hans Christian Andersen might have seen it. Nearby Ebeltoft, a fairy-tale village steeped in medieval history, Grenå and Randers are also well worth visiting.

EATING OUT Excellent French cuisine can be enjoyed at *De 4 Arstider*, in Aboulevarden.

ÅRHUS
Jylland
★★★★**Atlantic** Europaplads ☎(0045)131111 tx 64301
2 Jan-22 Dec
⇔♠101 ⌂ P100 Lift ℂ Sea
Credit Cards 1 2 3 4 5

★★★**Marselis** Strandvejen 25 ☎(86)144411 tx 68751
2 Jan-19 Dec
⇔♠102 ⌂ P100 Lift ℂ Beach Sea
Credit Cards 1 2 3 5

★★★**Ritz** Banegårdspl 12 ☎(06)134444
Closed 24-31 Dec
⇔♠63 P8 Lift ℂ
Credit Cards 1 2 3 5

★★**Missions** Banegårdspl 14,Postboks 34 ☎(86)124122
rm170(⇔157) ⌂ P20 Lift ℂ
Credit Cards 1 3 5

★★**Royal** Store Torv 4 ☎(86)120011 tx 64500
⇔♠104 Lift ℂ
Credit Cards 1 2 3 4 5

At **HØJBJERG**(3km SE)
★★★★**Scanticon** Ny Moesgaarden ☎(86)273233 tx 68715
⇔♠110 P200 Lift ℂ Sea
Credit Cards 1 2 3 4 5

ÅRS
Jylland
➦ **Aars Autocentrum** Vestre Boulevard 21 ☎(08) 621511 P

ÅRUP
Fyn
➦ **H Obelitz** Holmelund 32 ☎(09) 431005 P Ren Vol

BILLUND
Jylland
★★ **Vis-a-Vis** Åstvej 10 ☎(05)331244 tx 60717
⇔♠108 P200 Lift ℂ
Credit Cards 1 2 3 4 5

BIRKERØD
Sjælland
➦ **M Klingsholm** Kongevejen 74-76 ☎(02) 810080 Ope

BLOMMENSLYST
See **ODENSE**

BRABRAND
Jylland
★★**Århus Stor Kro** Silkeborgvej 900 (n.rest)
☎(06)260577 tx 260765
◾✿80 P200 ⌂ Mountain
Credit Cards 1 2 3 5

BRØNDERSLEV
Jylland
◾✿ **J Andersen** Ostergade ☎(02) 820588 P Ope

COPENHAGEN
See **KØBENHAVN**

EBELTOFT
Jylland
★★★★**Ebeltoft Strand** Nordre Strandvej 3
☎(06)343300 tx 60967
◾✿68 ⌘ P250 Lift ℂ ⌂ Sea Mountain
Credit Cards 1 2 3 5
★★**Vigen** Adelgade 5 ☎(06)344800
Seasonal
rm30(◾✿18) ⌘ P15 Lift ℂ
Credit Cards 2 3 4

ELSINORE
See **HELSINGØR**

ESBJERG
Jylland
★★★**Britannia** Torvet ☎(75)130111
Closed 25-26 Dec
◾✿79 P60 Lift ℂ
Credit Cards 1 2 3 4 5
★★**Ansgar** Skolegade 36 ☎(75)128244
rm63(◾✿51) P45 Lift ℂ
Credit Cards 1 2 3 5
★★**Palads** Skolegade 14 ☎(05)123000
rm48(◾✿30) P Lift ℂ
Credit Cards 1 2 3 5

FÅBORG
Fyn
★★**Faaborg Fjord** ☎(62)611010 tx 50312
7 Jan-20 Dec :Rest closed Sun & 3 wks in
summer
◾✿131 A5rm P150 ℂ ⌂ Beach
Credit Cards 1 2 3 5
◾✿ **Oddershede** Assenvej 2-4 ☎(09) 611501 For

FARSØ
Jylland
◾✿ **M Nielsen** Norregade 18-20 ☎(08) 831600 M/
C P Ope

FEMMØLLER
Jylland
★★**Molskroen** Femmller Strand ☎(06)362200
◾✿26 P ℂ Sea
★★**Vaegtergarden** Femmller Strand
☎(06)362211
rm26(◾✿13) P50
Credit Cards 1 3 4 5

FILSKOV
Jylland
★**Filskov Kro** ☎(75)348111
Closed 22 Dec-6 Jan
rm45(◾✿42) A3rm P40 ℚ ⌐
Credit Cards 1 2 3 5

FJERRITSLEV
Jylland
◾✿ **Auto-Centralen** Sondergade 15 ☎(08) 211666
Ope

FREDENSBORG
Sjælland
★★★★**Store Kro** Slotsgade 6 ☎(42)280047 tx
40971
5 Jan-20 Dec
◾✿49 A16rm P30 Lift ℂ
Credit Cards 1 2 3 4 5

FREDERICIA
Jylland
★★★**Landsoldaten** Norgesgade 1 ☎(05)921555
tx 51100
2 Jan-21 Dec
◾✿59 Lift ℂ
Credit Cards 1 2 3 4 5
★★★**Postgaarden** Oldenborggade 4 (n.rest)
☎(05)921855
15 Jan-20 Dec
◾✿24 P ℂ
Credit Cards 1 2 3 5
◾✿ **Fredericia Automobilhandel** Vejlevej 30
☎(05) 920211 P For

FREDERIKSHAVN
Jylland
★★★**Jutlandia** Havnepladsen 1 ☎(98)424200 tx
67142
3 Jan-21 Dec
◾✿104 ⌘ P Lift ℂ Sea
Credit Cards 1 2 3 5
★★**Hoffmans** Tordenslejoldsg 3 (n.rest)
☎(98)422166
Closed 23 Dec-1 Jan
rm54(◾✿38) P20 Lift ℂ
Credit Cards 1 2 3 5
◾✿ **A Precht-Jensen** Hjrringvej 12-14 ☎(08)
423366 Saa
◾✿ **B Srensen** Grnlandsvej 10 ☎(08) 422877 P
Rov LR Ren

FREDERIKSSUND
Sjaelland
◾✿ **Autohuset** Vlundsvej 11 ☎(02) 315556 For

FRØRUP
Fyn
★★**Øksendrup Kro** Svendborg Landevej
30,Oksendrup ☎(09)371057
◾✿15 P10

GAMMEL SKAGEN
See **SKAGEN**

GEDSER
Falster
★**Gedser** Langgade 59 ☎(03)879302
rm15(◾✿12) P10
Credit Cards 1 2 3

GENTOFTE
See **KØBENHAVN (COPENHAGEN)**

GLOSTRUP
See **KØBENHAVN (COPENHAGEN)**

GRAM
Jylland
★★**Gamle Kro** Slotsvej 47 ☎(74)821620
rm33(◾✿25) A12rm P45 ℚ Lake
Credit Cards 1 2 3 4 5

GRENÅ
Jylland
★★★**Nord** (Inter DK) Kystvej 25 ☎(06)322500 tx
63480
◾✿100 P Lift ℂ ⌐ Sea
Credit Cards 1 2 3 5

HADERSLEV
Jylland
★★★**Norden** (Inter DK) Storegade 55
☎(74)524030
◾✿67 P ℂ ⌂ Lake
Credit Cards 1 2 3 5
★★**Haderslev** Damparken ☎(74)526010 tx 51599
◾✿70 P100 Lift Lake
Credit Cards 1 2 3 5
◾✿ **Skifter Anderson** Bygnaf 4 ☎(04) 520353
Ren Vol

HADSUND
Jylland
★**Øster Hurup** Kystvegen 57 ☎(08)588014
rm13 ⌘ P

HAMMEL
Jylland
◾✿ **J B Winter** Anbaekvej 36 ☎(06) 933855 Ren
Vol

HASLEV
Sjælland
◾✿ **Thomsen's** Finlandsgade 21 ☎(03) 693200
For

HELSINGØR (ELSINORE)
Sjælland
★★★★**Marienlyst** (SRS) Nordre Strandvej 2
☎(42)101042 tx 41116
◾✿208 A76rm P200 Lift ℂ ⌂ Beach Sea
Credit Cards 1 2 3 4 5
★**Hamlet** Bramstraede 5 ☎(49)210591 tx 41178
◾✿36 P Lift ℂ
Credit Cards 1 2 3 5
◾✿ **Sommer Automobiler Helsingr** Kongevej 101
☎(02) 213111 Ren Vol

HERNING
Jylland
★★★**Eyde** (Inter DK) Torvet 1 ☎(97)221800 tx
62195
Jul-Etr
◾✿96 P60 Lift ℂ
Credit Cards 2 5
At LIND(3km S)
★**Lynggarden** ☎(07)223000
◾✿58 P90 ℂ
Credit Cards 1 2 3 4 5

HILLERØD
Sjælland
◾✿ **Hvam** Frejasvej 40 ☎(02) 264533 For

HIMMELEV
See **ROSKILDE**

HJØRRING
Jylland
◾✿ **L Karlborg** Frederikshavnsvej 76 ☎(08)
923011 Ren Vol

HOBRO
Jylland
◾✿ **E Nielson** Hovedvej A10 Nord ☎(08) 523111
P BMW Hon

HØJBJERG
See **ÅRHUS**

HOLBÆK
Sjælland
★★**Strandparken** Kalundborgvej 58 ☎(03)430616
◾✿31 P125 ℂ ⌐ Beach Sea
Credit Cards 1 3 5
◾✿ **Trekanten** Taastrup Mollevej 6 ☎(03) 431313
Cit Mit

HOLSTEBRO
Jylland
★★★**Bel Air** ☎(07)426666
◾✿57 P300 Lift ℂ
Credit Cards 1 3 5
★★**Schaumburg** Norregade 26 ☎(07)423111
rm37(◾✿20) P50
Credit Cards 1 2 3 5

HORNBÆK
Sjælland
★★★**Trouville** Kystvej 20 ☎(72)202200 tx 41241
◾✿50 P100 Lift ℂ ⌂ ≋ Sea
Credit Cards 1 3 5

HORNDRUP
See **SKANDERBORG**

DENMARK

HORSENS
Jylland

★★★**Bygholm Park** Schüttesvej 6 ☎(05)622333
rm148(➜130) P500 Lift ℂ ⬒
Credit Cards ①②③⑤

★★**Postgarden** Gl-Jernbanegade 6 ☎(05)621800
rm50 ☎ P

❤ Horsens Motor Compagni Ormhjgaardvej 2
☎(05) 648000 For

HVIDOVRE
See **KØBENHAVN (COPENHAGEN)**

KASTRUP AIRPORT
See **KØBENHAVN (COPENHAGEN)**

KØBENHAVN *(COPENHAGEN)*

See Plan page 105 *Population* 1,365,760 *Local Tourist Office* Danish Tourist Board, H C Andersens Boulevard 22 (opposite City Hall) ☎(33) 111325

The little mermaid, inspired by Hans Christian Andersen's story is a familiar image of København, a welcoming city of green parks and fairytale castles. The Amalienborg Palace (not open) is the royal residence, and also worth a visit are the Christiansborg Palace, the Stock Exchange and the university. For a spectacular view, climb the spiral ramp up one of the city's landmarks, the Round Tower (*Rundetårn*). You may glimpse that renowned Danish lager being delivered around the city in horse-drawn drays, and the Carlsberg and Tuborg breweries give interesting conducted tours explaining the production process - and offering tastings of the finished product.

The city's many other attractions include a zoo and museums of dolls, toys and puppets. The renowned Tivoli is a fantasy land built on the site of the ancient city walls, where the landscaped gardens are a myriad of lakes, fountains and flowers, lit after nightfall by twinkling fairy lights and fireworks. Here you can ride the switchback, listen to the music from the bandstands, laugh at the puppets and admire the show at the Mime Theatre. And when you have worked up an appetite, there are 22 restaurants from which to choose.

Souvenirs from Denmark are unusual and make interesting presents, especially silverware, porcelain, pipes, wooden toys and distinctive Scandinavian sweaters.

EATING OUT The fame of the Scandinavian buffet - *det store kolde bord* - has spread worldwide, and here in København is the genuine article. It is a mouth-watering array of cold and hot dishes, usually including fish such as herring, meats, cheeses, vegetables and salads. Also delicious are the desserts, such as *rodgrod* - a red fruit pudding. Open sandwiches (*smorrebrod*) are wonderful, too, while for substantial and simpler food seek out the basement cafés for the speciality of the day, known as *dagens ret*. Eating out can be expensive, but there are plenty of *frokost-restaurants* (lunch restaurants) along Stroget, offering light salads and *smorrebrod*, while hotdog stands are practically everywhere. Also look out for restaurants displaying the sign *Dan Menu*, which serve inexpensive two-course meals.

Number one seafood restaurant in København is *Den Gyldne Fortun - Fiskkaelderen*, in Ved Stannden, which specialises in the products of the waters around Denmark and Greenland. The moderately priced *Peder Oxe*, in Graabrode Torv, is charmingly located in the old part of town, with whitewashed walls, wooden floors and lots of atmosphere.

KØBENHAVN (COPENHAGEN)

★★★★★**Angleterre** (Intercont) Kongens Nytorv 34 ☎(33)120095 tx 15877
➜♠130 Lift ℂ
Credit Cards ①②③④⑤

★★★★★**Sheraton** Vester Sogade 6
☎(33)143535 tx 27450
➜♠471 Lift ℂ Lake
Credit Cards ①②③④⑤

★★★★★**SAS Royal** (SRS) Hammerichsgade 1
☎(33)141412 tx 27155
:Rest closed Sun
➜♠266 ☎ P70 Lift ℂ
Credit Cards ①②③④⑤

★★★★**Copenhagen Admiral** Toldbodgade 24
☎(33)118282 tx 15941
➜♠366 P80 Lift ℂ Sea
Credit Cards ①②③

★★★★**Imperial** (THF) Vester Farimagsgade 9
☎(01)128000 tx 15556
➜♠163 Lift ℂ
Credit Cards ①②③④⑤

★★★★**Mercur** Vester Farimagsgade 17
☎(33)125711 tx 19767
Rest closed Sun & Holidays
➜♠108 Lift ℂ ⚲
Credit Cards ①②③⑤

➜♠132 Lift ℂ ⚲
Credit Cards ①②③⑤

★★★★**Sophie Amalie** St-Annae Plads 21
☎(33)133400 tx 15815
➜♠134 P5 Lift ℂ
Credit Cards ①②③

★★★**Alexandra** H-C-Andersens bd 8
☎(33)172200
1 Mar-1 Dec
➜♠63 Lift ℂ
Credit Cards ①②③④⑤

★★★**Astoria** Banegaardspladsen 4 ☎(01)141419
tx 16319
➜♠91 Lift ℂ
Credit Cards ①②③⑤

★★★**Falkoner** (Inter DK) Falkoner Alle 9
☎(31)198001 tx 15550
Closed 24 Dec-1 Jan
➜♠166 ☎ Lift ℂ
Credit Cards ①②③⑤

★★★**Grand** Vesterbrogade 9 ☎(31)313600 tx
15343
:Rest closed Sun
➜♠142 Lift ℂ
Credit Cards ①②③④⑤

★★★**SAS Globetrotter** 171 Engvej ☎(31)551433
tx 31222
➜♠196 P Lift ℂ ⬒
Credit Cards ①②③④⑤

★★★**71 Nyhavn** Nyhavn 71 ☎(33)118585 tx
27558
:Rest closed 24-26 Dec
➜♠82 P7 Lift ℂ Sea
Credit Cards ①②③④⑤

★★**Missionshotellet Hebron** Helgolandsgade 4
☎(31)316906 tx 27416
4 Jan-23 Dec
➜♠111 Lift ℂ
Credit Cards ①②③⑤

★★**Viking** Bredgade 65 (n.rest) ☎(01)124550 tx
19590
rm90(➜19) Lift ℂ
Credit Cards ①②③④⑤

★**Vesterhus** Vestersogade 58 ☎(01)113870 tx
15708
rm44(➜34) Lift ℂ Lake
Credit Cards ①②③⑤

❤ Baunsoe Biler Middelfartgade 15 ☎(01)
297711

B P Parkringshuset Nyropsgade 6 ☎(01) 126765
P BMW

❤ Schibbye Automobiler Sylows Alle 1 ☎(01)
345200 For

At **ALBERTSLUND**(15km W on N1)
★**Wittrup** Roskildevej 251 ☎(42)649551
Closed 24 Dec-1 Jan
rm56(♠48) P60 ℂ
Credit Cards ①③⑤

At **GENTOFTE**(5km N1)

★★★**Gentofte** Gentoftegade 29 ☎(31)680911 tx 15610
⚓70 P80 Lift ℂ
Credit Cards ① ② ③ ④ ⑤

At **GLOSTRUP**(11km W on N1)

‰ Monk's Automobiler Vibeholmsvej 26-28 ☎(01) 4590000 Toy

At **HVIDOVRE**(6km SW)

★★★**Scandic** Kettevej 4 ☎(01)498222 tx 15517
⚓220 Lift ℂ

At **KASTRUP AIRPORT**(9km SE)

★★★**Dan** Kastruplundgade 15 Box 69 ☎(31)511400 tx 31111
⚓228 P50 Lift ℂ Sea
Credit Cards ① ② ③ ⑤

★★★**Scandic** Ljtegårdsvej 99 ☎(31)513033 tx 31240
⚓173 ℂ ▱ ▱
Credit Cards ① ② ③ ⑤

KØGE
Sjælland

★★★**Hvide Hus** Strandvejen 111 ☎(53)653690 tx 43501
⚓127 A22rm ♒ P200 ℂ Sea
Credit Cards ① ② ③ ④ ⑤

KOLDING
Jylland

★★★**Saxildhus** (Inter DK) Banegårdspl ☎(75)521200 tx 51446
Closed 20 Dec-2 Jan
⚓95 P100 Lift ℂ
Credit Cards ① ② ③ ④ ⑤

★★★**Tre Roser** Grnningen 2 Byparken ☎(75)532122
⚓95 P70 ℂ ▱
Credit Cards ① ② ③ ⑤

‰ H G Nielsen Vejlevej 108 ☎(05) 522555 For

KONGENSBRO
See **ANS BY**

KORSØR
Sjælland

‰ Bilhuset Korsr Tårnborgvej 170 ☎(03) 572900 Rov Sko Dai Sko

LEMVIG
Jylland

★★★**Nørre Vinkel** Sgådevejen 6,Vinkelhage ☎(07)822211
⚓26 P Lift ℂ Lake

LIND
See **HERNING**

LØGSTØR
Jylland

★★**Nord** Havnevej 38 ☎(08)671711
⚓21 P100 ▱ Beach Sea
Credit Cards ① ③ ④ ⑤

MARIBO
Lolland

★★★**Hvide Hus** Vestergade 27 ☎(53)881011 tx 40880
⚓69 A6rm ♒ P50 Lift ℂ ▱ Lake
Credit Cards ① ③ ⑤

MILLINGE
Fyn

★★**Falsled Kro** Assensvej 513,Falsled ☎(62)681111 tx 50404
Mar-18 Dec :Rest closed Mon lunchtime May-Aug
⚓14 P30 Sea
Credit Cards ① ② ③ ⑤

NÆSTVED
Sjælland

★★★**Mogenstrup Kro** Praest Landevej,Mogenstrup ☎(53)761130 tx 46201
⚓87 A4rm P
Credit Cards ① ② ③ ④ ⑤

★★★**Vinhuset** St-Peders Kirkepl 4 ☎(53)720807 tx 46279
⚓57 P30
Credit Cards ① ② ③ ⑤

NAKSKOV
Lolland

★★**Harmonien** Nybrogade 2 ☎(03)922100
⚓39

★★**Skoveridergården** Svingelen 4 ☎(53)920355
⚓10 A5rm P ℂ
Credit Cards ① ② ③ ④ ⑤

NYBORG
Fyn

★★★★**Hesselet** Christianslundsvej 119 ☎(09)313329 tx 9297122
Closed 2 wks Xmas
⚓46 P100 ℂ ▱ Sea
Credit Cards ① ③ ⑤

★★★**Nyborg Strand** (Inter DK) Osterovej 2 ☎(65)313131 tx 50371
⚓245 ♒ P250 Lift ℂ ▱ Beach Sea
Credit Cards ① ② ③ ④ ⑤

NYKØBING
Falster

‰ Breitenstein Biler A/S Randersvej 4 ☎(03) 852266 Maz Rov Saa

‰ A Hansen Randersvej 8 ☎(03) 850600 For

‰ Auto-Co Fisegade 31 ☎(03) 853155

At **SUNDBY**(2km N)

‰ Liselund Lundevej 22,Sundby ☎(03)851566
⚓24 P30
Credit Cards ① ③ ⑤

NYKØBING-MORS
Jylland

‰ H D Pedersen Limfjordsvej 44 ☎(07) 723044 Ren Vol

NYKØBING-SJÆLLAND
Sjælland

‰ P Tamstorf Kiakestraede 5 ☎(03) 411400 For

ODDER
Jylland

‰ Arne Rasmussen Automobiler Ballevej 14 ☎(06) 543000 Toy

ODENSE
Fyn

★★★**H C Andersen** Claus-Bergsgade 7 ☎(66)147800 tx 59694
⚓148 P140 Lift ℂ
Credit Cards ① ② ③ ④ ⑤

★★★**Grand** (SARA) Jernbanegade 18 ☎(66)117171 tx 59972
⚓139 P20 Lift ℂ
Credit Cards ① ② ③ ④ ⑤

★★★**Odense Plaza** Østre Stationsvej 24 ☎(66)117745 tx 59471
:Rest closed Sat & Sun
⚓70 P10 Lift ℂ
Credit Cards ① ② ③ ④ ⑤

★★★**Scandic** Hvidkaervej 25 ☎(09)172500 tx 291750
2 Jan-23 Dec
rm102 ℂ ⚷ ▱
Credit Cards ① ② ③ ⑤

★★**Odense** (Inter DK) Hunderupgade 2 ☎(66)114213
⚓62 P60 ℂ
Credit Cards ① ② ③ ④ ⑤

★★**Windsor** Vindegade 45 ☎(09)120652 tx 59662
⚓62 P Lift ℂ
Credit Cards ① ② ③ ④ ⑤

★**Ansgarhus** Kirkegårds-Alle 17-19 ☎(09)128800
Closed Oct
rm17(⚓4) ♒

‰ Fehr Svendborgvej 90 ☎(09) 141414 P For Fia

‰ V Hansen Odensevj 121 ☎(09) 117255 Ren Vol

‰ E M Jensen Odensevej 101 ☎(09) 115810 Rov Dai

‰ BMW Odense Dalumvej 67 ☎(09) 123333 BMW Hon

At **BLOMMENSLYST**(10km W A1/E66)

★★**Brasillia** (Inter DK) Middlefartvej 420 ☎(65)967012 tx 27459
5 Jan-24 Dec
⚓52 P100 ℂ
Credit Cards ① ② ③ ⑤

RANDERS
Jylland

★★★★**Randers** Torvegade 11 ☎(86)423422 tx 65135
3 Jan-23 Dec
⚓79 ♒ Lift ℂ
Credit Cards ① ② ③ ⑤

★★★**Scandic Kongens** Hadsundvej 2 ☎(86)430300 tx 65130
Closed Xmas
⚓130 Lift ℂ
Credit Cards ① ② ③ ⑤

‰ Blicher Grenavej 51 ☎(06) 431366 Saa

‰ Bohnstedt-Petersen Ny Grenåvej ☎(06) 425399 Col Mer

‰ J Madson Århusvej 108 ☎(06) 427800 Ope Vau

RIBE
Jylland

★★**Dagmar** (Inter DK) Torvet 1 ☎(75)420033
⚓50 P10 ℂ
Credit Cards ① ② ③ ⑤

RINGKØBING
Jylland

★★★**Fjordgaarden** (Inter DK) Vesterkaer 28 ☎(97)321700
Closed 22-30 Dec
⚓87 P140 ℂ
Credit Cards ① ② ③ ⑤

‰ N Hansens Enghavevej 11 ☎(07) 321133 For

RINGSTED
Sjælland

‰ H Larsen Huginsved 25 ☎(03) 612518 P For

RISSKOV
Jylland

‰ Egå Autohandel Grenåvej 351 ☎(06) 175500 For

RØDBY
Lolland

★★★**Danhotel** Havnegade 2 ☎(03)905366 tx 40890
⚓40 P100 Lift ℂ Sea
Credit Cards ① ② ③ ⑤

RØNNE
Isle of Bornholm

★★★**Fredensborg** (Inter/BW) Strandvejen 116 ☎(53)954444 tx 48188
⚓72 Lift ℂ ⚷ Sea
Credit Cards ① ② ③ ⑤

RØNNEDE
Sjælland

★**Axelved** Ronnedevej 1,Axelved ☎(03)711401 rm8

ROSKILDE
Sjælland
★★**Prindsen** Algade 13 ☎(42)358010 tx 43310
🍴38 P30 Lift ℂ
Credit Cards ① ② ③ ⑤
At **HIMMELEV**(3km N on N6)
★★**Roskilde Motor** Hovedvej A1 ☎(42)354385
Closed 24 Dec-3 Jan
rm15(🛏14) A13rm 🏖 P50 Lift
Credit Cards ① ③ ④ ⑤

RY
Jylland
★★**Ry Park Hotel DPn** Kyhnsvej 2 ☎(86)891911
🍴80 A21rm P30 ☐ Lake
Credit Cards ① ② ③ ⑤

SAKSKØBING
Lolland
🍴 *M Skotte* Nykobingvej 8 ☎(03) 894285 Ope
Vau

SILKEBORG
Jylland
★★★**Dania** Torvet 5 ☎(86)820111 tx 63269
:Rest closed 25 & 31 Dec
🍴47 ℂ
Credit Cards ① ② ③ ⑤
★★★*Impala* (Inter DK) Vester Ringvej
☎(06)820300
2 Jan-20 Dec
🍴60 A12rm P150 ℂ ☐ Lake
Credit Cards ① ② ③ ⑤

**KØBENHAVN
(COPENHAGEN)**

1	★★★★★	Angleterre
2	★★★★★	SAS Royal
3	★★★★★	Sheraton
4	★★★★	Sophie Amalie
5	★★★★	Copenhagen Admiral
6	★★★★	Dan (At Kastrup)
7	★★★★	Imperial
9	★★★★	Mercur
10	★★★	Richmond
11	★★★	Alexandra
12	★★★	Astoria
13	★★★	Falkoner
14	★★★	Gentofte (At Gentofte)
15	★★★	Grand
17	★★★	71 Nyhavn
18	★★★	SAS Globetrotter
19	★★★	Scandic (At Hvidovre)
20	★★★	Scandic (At Kastrup)
21	★★★	Missionshotellet Hebron
22	★★	Viking
23	★★	Vestersøhus
24	★	Wittrup (At Albertslund)

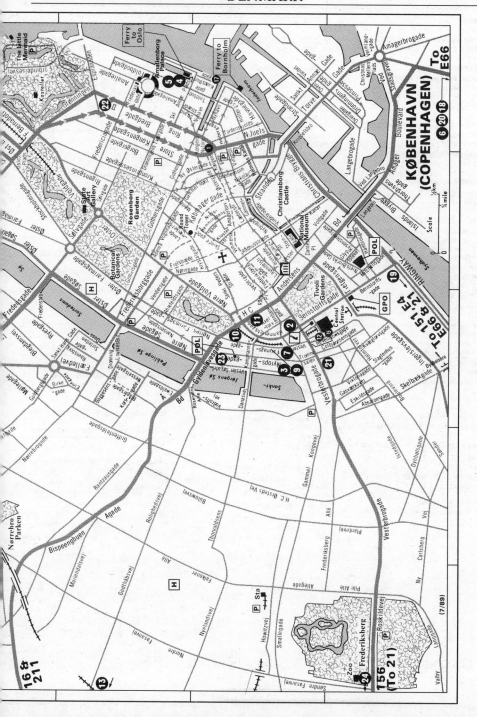

DENMARK

SKAGEN
Jylland
★★★**Skagen** Gammel Landevej ☎(98)442233
🛬🛏81 P70 ℂ ⊿
Credit Cards ① ③ ⑤
At **GAMMEL SKAGEN**(2km W)
★**Ruth's** H-Ruthsvej 1 ☎(08)441124
rm40(🛏7) P40 Sea
Credit Cards ① ③ ⑤

SKANDERBORG
Jylland
★★★**Skanderborghus** Dyre Haven ☎(86)520955
🛬🛏45 ℂ Lake
Credit Cards ① ② ③ ⑤
★**Slotskroen** Adelgade 23 ☎(06)520012
🛬🛏20 P20 ℂ Beach Lake
Credit Cards ① ② ③ ⑤
At **HORNDRUP**(10km S)
★★**Oasen** ☎(06)579228
🛬🛏12 🥢 Lake

SKIVE
Jylland
★★**GI Skivehus** (Inter DK) Sdr 1,stertorv
☎(07)521144 tx 66766
🛬🛏57 A6rm 🥢 P55 Lift ℂ
Credit Cards ① ② ③ ⑤
★★**Hilltop** Sondre-Boulevard ☎(07)523711
🛬🛏68 P100 ℂ
Credit Cards ① ② ③ ⑤
🚗 **J Fogh** Sdr Boulevard 9 ☎(07) 522100 P For

SKØRPING
Jylland
★★★**Rold Stor Kro** (Inter DK) Vlderskoven 13
☎(98)375100
rm53(🛬🛏42) 🥢 P100 ℂ ⊠ 🐾
Credit Cards ① ② ③ ⑤

SØNDERBORG
Jylland
★★★**Scandic** Rosengade ☎(04)421900 tx
9245353
2 Jan-22 Dec
rm95 ℂ ⊠
Credit Cards ① ② ③ ⑤
★★**City** Kongevej 64 ☎(04)421626 tx 16600
rm13(🛬3) P13
🚗 **M Iversen** Alsgade 60-62 ☎(04) 423640 For

SORØ
Jylland
★★**Postgården** Storgade 27 ☎(53)632222
8 Jan-22 Dec
🛬🛏26 P
Credit Cards ① ② ③ ⑤
🚗 **J Frandsen** Holbaekvej 1-3 ☎(03) 630100 For

STORE-HEDDINGE
Sjælland
🚗 **Stevns Motor** Hjerupvej 2 ☎(03) 702720 For

STRUER
Jylland
★★**Struer Grand** Østergade 24 ☎(97)850400
🛬🛏71 Lift ℂ Sea
Credit Cards ① ② ③ ⑤

SUNDBY
See **NYKØBING**

SVENDBORG
Fyn
★★★**Svendborg** (Inter DK) Voldgade 10
☎(62)211700 tx 58128
🛬🛏87 P40 Lift ℂ ⊠
Credit Cards ① ② ③ ⑤
🚗 **Bilhuset** Gronnemosevej 6 ☎(09) 221111 AR
Dai Fia
Bukkehave Lerchesvej 11 ☎(09) 211457 All
Makes
🚗 **Kjaer Svendborg** Gronnemasevej 6 ☎(09)
211700 P

TAPPERNØJE
Sjælland
🚗 **Tappenje Autoservice** Hovedvejen 67 ☎(53)
765099 Rov Dai

THISTED
Jylland
★★★**Ålborg** Storegade 29 ☎(07)923566
rm32(🛬22) 🥢 P50 ℂ Sea
Credit Cards ① ② ③ ⑤
🚗 **A P Anderson** Rosenkrantgade 1 ☎(07)
921600 P

TOFTLUND
Jylland
🚗 **P Henriksen** Østergade 23 ☎(04) 831122 P
Ope

TØNDER
Jylland
★★★**Tønderhus** Jomflustien 1 ☎(04)722222
rm31(🛬17) A18rm 🥢 P15 ℂ
Credit Cards ① ③ ⑤
★★**Hostrups** Søndergade 30 ☎(04)722129
3 Jan-22 Dec
rm27(🛬26) A5rm 🥢 P

TRANEBJERG
Sams
🚗 **Ole's Autoservice** Langgade 2 ☎(06) 590265
VW

TRANEKAER
Island of Langeland
★**Gjaestgivergaarden** Slotsgade 74
☎(09)591204
🛬🛏12 P20

VARDE
Jylland
🚗 **Varde Motor** V-Landevej 78 ☎(05) 220499 P
For

VEDÆK
Sjælland
★★★**Marina** Vedbæk Strandvej 391 ☎(42)891711
tx 37217
🛬🛏106 🥢 P200 Lift ℂ 🍴 Beach Sea
Credit Cards ① ② ⑤

VEJLE
Jylland
★★★★★**Scandic Hotel Australia** Daemningen 6
☎(75)824311 tx 61104
Closed 23 Dec-3 Jan
🛬🛏87 🥢 P200 Lift ℂ
Credit Cards ① ② ③ ④ ⑤
★★★★**Munkebjerg** Munkebjergvej 125
☎(75)723500 tx 61103
Closed 23 Dec-2 Jan
🛬🛏147 P250 Lift ℂ ⊠ Sea
Credit Cards ① ② ③ ④ ⑤
★★**Vejle** Dæmningen 52 ☎(75)823211
Feb-15 Dec :Rest closed Sun
rm55(🛬🛏42) P15 Lift
Credit Cards ① ③ ⑤
🚗 **Bje & Brchner** Boulevarden ☎(05) 826000
For
🚗 **M Kjaer** Boulevarden 54 ☎(05) 828255 Ope
Vau
🚗 **Neergaard** Vestre Engvej 7 ☎(05) 823366 M/
C P BMW Hon
🚗 **Vejle-Motor** Diskovej 1 ☎(05) 822100 AR Dai
LR

VIBORG
Jylland
★★★**Golf** Randersvej 2 ☎(86)610222 tx 61243
🛬🛏133 P200 Lift ℂ ⊠ Lake
Credit Cards ① ② ③ ④ ⑤
★★**Missionshotellet** St-Matthiasgade 5
☎(86)623700
🛬🛏60 🥢 P45 Lift ℂ
Credit Cards ① ② ③ ⑤
🚗 **V Slvsten** Mansk Stigsvej 9 ☎(06) 610066
Mer
🚗 **P Wraa** Falkevej 23 ☎(06) 624600 Aud VW

VIBY
Jylland
★★★**Mercur** Viby Torv ☎(06)141411 tx 68746
2 Jan-22 Dec
🛬🛏161 🥢 P200 Lift ℂ Lake
Credit Cards ① ② ③ ④ ⑤

AA

DIRECTORY

Motoring in Europe?

Phone before you go

Before taking your car abroad, ring our recorded information service for country-by-country advice on motoring and traffic regulations, equipment and documents you will need, and tips on currency and budgeting.

Austria	0836-401-866
Belgium	0836-401-867
Denmark	0836-401-868
France	0836-401-869
Germany (West)	0836-401-870
Gibraltar	0836-401-871
Greece	0836-401-872
Ireland (Republic)	0836-401-873
Italy	0836-401-874
Luxembourg	0836-401-875
Netherlands	0836-401-876
Norway	0836-401-877
Portugal	0836-401-878
Spain	0836-401-879
Sweden	0836-401-880
Switzerland	0836-401-881
Yugoslavia	0836-401-882
European fuel prices and availability	0836-401-883
French motorway toll information	0836-401-884

For your free copy of the complete AA Directory, call

0256 491648

Messages last from about 1 up to 7 minutes and are charged at 25p per minute cheap rate, 38p per minute at other times (including VAT); callers pay only for the time they use. Prices for mobile calls can vary — see your service provider.

We're all you need to know.

107

FRANCE

Language
French

Local time
GMT + 1 (Summer GMT + 2)

Currency
Franc, divided into 100 *centimes*. At the
time of going to press.
£1 = Fr10.52
US$1 = Fr6.33

Emergency numbers
Fire ☎18   Police ☎17
Ambulance: number given in telephone
box or, if no number given, call the
police (brigade de gendarmerie).

There are emergency telephone boxes
every 20km on some roadways. These are
connected directly to local police
stations. In larger towns emergency help
can be obtained from the *police secours*
(emergency assistance department).

Information in England
French Government Tourist Office, 178
Piccadilly, London W1V 0AL
☎†01-491 7622 general enquiries,
☎†01-499 6911 24hr recorded
information.
†071 from 6 May.

Information in the USA
French Government Tourist Office, 610
First Avenue, New York, NY10020
☎212 757 1125

With its endless variety of countryside and coastline, its legendary cuisine and fine wines, and diverse culture and heritage, France has long been a much-loved holiday destination. Every region of the country is steeped in its own unique character and traditions, offering something to suit all tastes.

Enchanting and romantic Paris, brimful of artistic treasures; the peaceful beauty of Brittany's coastline; the cosmopolitan glamour of the Riviera; the seemingly endless sands of the Languedoc-Rousillon and the spectacular scenery of the Savoie Alps.

From the rugged capes and deserted dunes of the Atlantic coast to the quiet coves and sandy beaches of the Channel resorts, there is every possible scenic variation. In the south the Alps and Pyrénées plunge down to the Mediterranean, creating some of the most dramatic coastal scenery in Europe. Inland there are mountain pastures, deserted plateaus, gentle river valleys and stony hillsides.

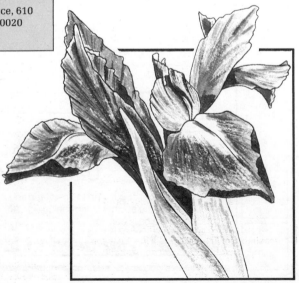

HOW TO GET THERE

Short ferry crossings
from **Dover** to **Boulogne** takes
1hr 40 mins
to **Calais** takes 1¼–1½hrs
from **Folkestone** to **Boulogne** takes
1hr 50mins

Longer ferry crossings from **Ramsgate** to **Dunkerque** (Dunkirk) takes 2¼hrs from **Newhaven** to **Dieppe** takes 4hrs from **Portsmouth** to **Le Havre** takes 5¾–7hrs to **Caen** takes 5¾–7hrs to †**Cherbourg** takes 4¾–6hrs to **St Malo** takes 9–11hrs from †**Poole** to **Cherbourg** takes 4½hrs from **Plymouth** to **Roscoff** takes 6–6½hrs from †**Weymouth** to **Cherbourg** takes 4–6hrs
†Summer service only

Fast hovercraft services
from **Dover** to **Boulogne** takes 40mins
to **Calais** takes 35mins

Car sleeper trains
Services operate from Boulogne, Calais and Dieppe to the south of the country.

MONEYMATTERS

There are no restrictions on the importation of foreign or French currency, but amounts exceeding Fr50,000 should be declared on arrival. Visitors may export up to Fr50,000 in foreign or French currency, but must produce a declaration for larger amounts.

Banking hours
In large towns, Monday–Friday 09.00–12.00hrs and 14.00–16.00hrs. In the provinces, Tuesday–Saturday as above.

Banks close at midday on the day before a national holiday, and all day on a Monday if the holiday falls on a Tuesday.

Traveller's cheques
can be cashed at the Crédit Lyonnais offices at the Invalides air terminal in Paris, and the Société Générale has two offices at Orly airport. Exchange facilities are also available at the Charles de Gaulle airport.

Postcheques
can be cashed at all post offices up to a maximum of Fr1,400 per cheque. Go to the counter marked *Parliament des mandats* or *Cheques postaux*.

MOTORING REGULATIONS AND GENERAL INFORMATION

The information given here is specific to France. It **must** be read in conjunction with the European ABC at the front of the book, which covers those regulations which are common to many countries.

AA Service including Port Agents

62201 Boulogne-sur-Mer The Automobile Association, Tour Damremont (18ème), Boulevard Chanzy BP No.21 ☎21872121
62100 Calais The Automobile Association, Terminal Est ☎21964720
50100 Cherbourg (Port Agent) Agence Maritime Tellier, Gare Maritime ☎33204338; port office (when ferries operating), car ferry terminal ☎33204274. See also *AA Service* page 60 and *Town Plans* of *Boulogne-sur-Mer*, *Calais* and *Cherbourg* below.

Accidents*

If you are involved in an accident you must complete a *constat à l'amiable* before the vehicle is moved. The *constat à l'amiable* was introduced by French insurance companies and represents the 'European Accident Statement Form'. It must be signed by the other party, and in the event of a dispute and a refusal to complete the form, you should immediately obtain a *constat d'huissier*. This is a written report from a bailiff (*huissier*). A bailiff can usually be found in any large town and will charge a fee of Fr400 for preparing the report.

The police are only called out to accidents when someone is injured, a driver is under the influence of alcohol or the accident impedes traffic flow. When attending an accident the police prepare a report known as a *procès verbal*. The French authorities, at their discretion, may request a surety payment to cover the court costs or fines. See also *Warning Triangle* below.

Breakdown*

If your car breaks down, try to move it to the side of the road so that it obstructs the traffic flow as little as possible.

You are advised to seek local assistance as,

*Additional information will be found in the European ABC at the front of the book.

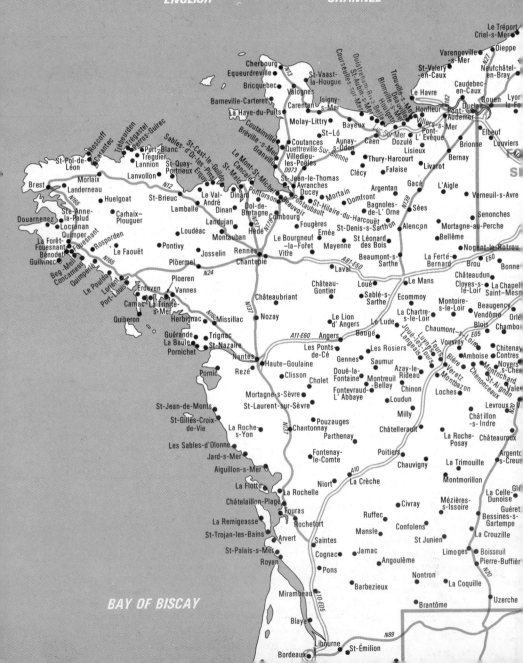

ENGLISH   CHANNEL   Berck Plage

Le Tréport
Criel-s-Mer
Varengeville   Dieppe
-s-Mer
Cherbourg   St-Vaast-   St-Valery-   Neufchâtel-
Equeurdreville   la-Hougue   en-Caux   en-Bray
           Bricquebec   Caudebec-
                      Valognes   en-Caux   Rouen   Lyor
Barneville-Carteret   Isigny-   Le Havre   la-Fo
  La-Haye-du-Puits   Carentan   s-Mer   Honfleur   Duclair
                                                              Pont-   Audemer
              Coutainville   Molay-Littry   Bayeux   Villers-s-   Elbeuf
           Bréville-s-Mer   St-Lô   Mer   L' Evêque   Louviers
  St-Pol-de-   Coutances   Aunay-   Caen   Dozulé   Lisieux
Léon   Quettreville-Sur-Sienne s-Odon   Villedieu- Thury-Harcourt Bernay   Brionne
Morlaix   Granville   les-Poêles   Clécy   Livarot
                        St-Jean-le-Thomas   Falaise   Gacé   L'Aigle
Brest   Landerneau   Avranches   Mortain   Argentan   Verneuil-s-Avre
Huelgoat   Dinard   Ducey   Domfront   Sées   Senonches
Ste-Anne-   Dinan   St-Hilaire-   Bagnoles-   Mortagne-au-Perche
la-Palud   Lamballe   Combourg du-Harcouët   Alençon   Bellême   Nogent-le-Rotrou
Douarnenez   Carhaix-   Loudéac   Hédé   Fougères Ernée   St Léonard   La Ferté-   Brou
Quimper   Plouguer   Montauban   Le Bourgneuf Mayenne   des Bois   Bernard
La Forêt-   Rosporden   Pontivy   –la–Forêt   Beaumont-s-
Fouesnant   Le Faouët   Josselin   Rennes   Vitré   Laval   Sarthe   Le Mans
Bénodet   Quimperlé   Ploërmel   Chantepie   A81-E50   Loué   Châteaudun
Guilvinec   N24   Château-   Sablé-s-   Ecommoy
Lorient   Vannes   Châteaubriant   Gontier   Sarthe   La Chartre-   Montoire-
Port-Louis   Erdeven   Nozay   Le Lion   s-le-Loir   s-le-Loir
Carnac   Missillac   d' Angers   Le Lude
La Trinité-   Herbignac   Angers   Les Rosiers
s-Mer   Trignac   Les Ponts-   Gennes   Saumur
Quiberon   Guérande   St-Nazaire   de-Cé
La Baule   Pornichet   Nantes   Doué-la-   Montreuil-
Pornic   Rezé   Haute–Goulaine   Fontaine   -Bellay   Chinon
St-Jean-de-Monts   Clisson   Cholet   Fontevraud-   Loudun
St-Gilles-Croix-   Mortagne-s-Sèvre   L' Abbaye
de-Vie   La Roche-   St-Laurent-sur-Sèvre   Milly
Les Sables-d'Olonne   s-Yon   Pouzauges   Chantonnay   Châtellerault
Jard-s-Mer   Parthenay   Poitiers
Aiguillon-s-Mer   Fontenay-   Chauvigny
La Flotte   le-Comte   Niort   La Crèche
Châtelaillon-Plage   La Rochelle   Montmorillon
La Remigeasse   Fouras   Rochefort   Ruffec   Mézières-
St-Trojan-les-Bains   Arvert   Saintes   Confolens   s-Issoire
St-Palais-s-Mer   Royan   Cognac   Jarnac   Mansle   St Junien   Limoges
Pons   Angoulême   Nontron   La Coquille
BAY OF BISCAY   Mirambeau   Barbezieux   Brantôme   Uzerche
Blaye
Libourne   St-Emilion
Bordeaux

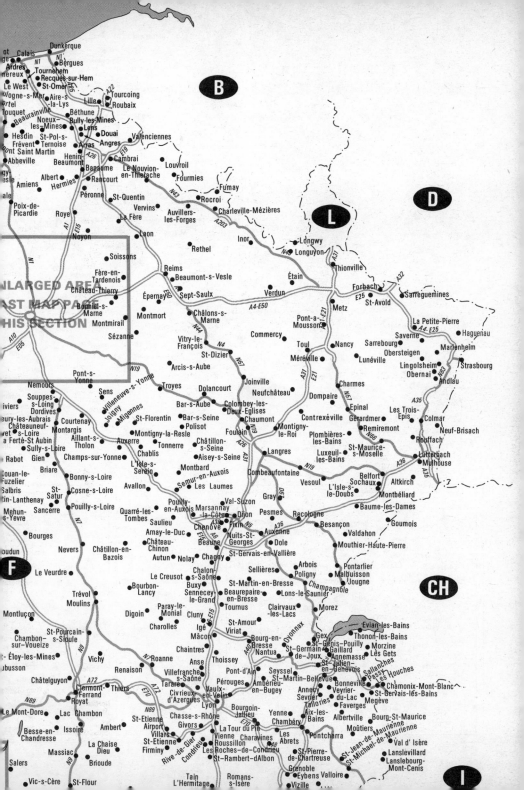

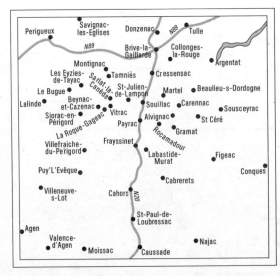

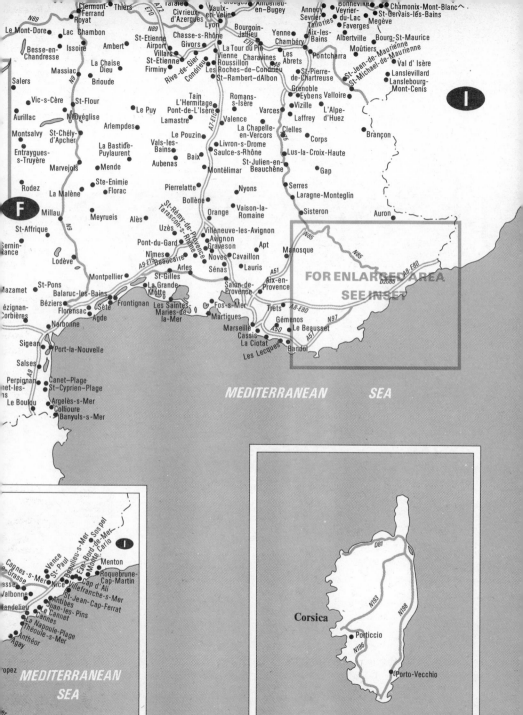

Le Mont-Dore • Lac Chambon • Clermont-Ferrand • Thiers • Tarare • E70 • Civrieux-d'Azergues • Vaulx-en-Velin • Amberieu-en-Bugey • Annecy • Sevrier • Veyrier-du-Lac • Talloires • Faverges • Chamonix-Mont-Blanc • Bonneville • St-Gervais-lès-Bains • Megève

Royat • Besse-en-Chandresse • Issoire • Ambert • St-Etienne Airport • Villars • Chasse-s-Rhône • Givors • Bourgoin-Jallieu • Yenne • Chambéry • Aix-les-Bains • Albertville • Bourg-St-Maurice • Moûtiers

Massiac • La Chaise Dieu • St-Etienne • Firminy • Rive-de-Gier • Condrieu • La Tour du Pin • Vienne • Charavines • Roussillon • Les Abrets • Pontcharra • St-Jean-de-Maurienne • St-Michel-de-Maurienne • Val d'Isère

Brioude • N9 • Les Roches-de-Condrieu • St-Rambert-d'Albon • St-Pierre-de-Chartreuse • Lanslevillard • Lanslebourg-Mont-Cenis

Salers • Vic-s-Cère • St-Flour • Neuvéglise • Le Puy • Tain • L'Hermitage • Pont-de-L'Isère • Romans-s-Isère • Grenoble • Eybens • Valloire • Vizille • Laffrey • L'Alpe-d'Huez

Aurillac • Arlempdes • Lamastre • Valence • Varces • Clelles • Corps • Briançon

Montsalvy • St-Chély-d'Apcher • La Bastide-Puylaurent • Le Pouzin • La Chapelle-en-Vercors • Livron-s-Drome • Lus-la-Croix-Haute • Laragne-Monteglin

Entraygues-s-Truyère • Marvejols • Mende • Vals-les-Bains • Baix • Saulce-s-Rhône • St-Julien-en-Beauchène • Gap

Rodez • La Malène • Ste-Enimie • Aubenas • Montélimar • Serres

Millau • Meyrueis • Florac • Pierrelatte • Nyons • Vaison-la-Romaine • Sisteron • Auron

St-Affrique • Alès • Bollène • Orange • St-Rémy-de-Provence • Tarascon-s-Rhône • Villeneuve-les-Avignon • Avignon • Manosque

Sernin-Mance • Lodève • Uzès • Pont-du-Gard • Graveson • Novès • Cavaillon • Apt

Mazamet • Montpellier • Nîmes • Beaucaire • Arles • Sénas • Lauris • Aix-en-Provence

St-Pons • Balaruc-les-Bains • St-Gilles • La Grande Motte • Salon-de-Provence • Trets

Béziers • Sète • Frontignan • Les Saintes-Maries-de-la-Mer • Fos-s-Mer • Gémenos • Le Beausset

Bézignan-Corbières • Florensac • Agde • Martigues • Marseille • Cassis • Bandol

Narbonne • Sigean • La Ciotat • Les Lecques

Salses • Port-la-Nouvelle

Perpignan • Canet-Plage • St-Cyprien-Plage • Le Boulou • Argelès-s-Mer • Collioure • Banyuls-s-Mer

FOR ENLARGED AREA SEE INSET

MEDITERRANEAN SEA

Cagnes-s-Mer • Vence • St-Paul • Beaulieu-s-Mer • Sospel • Eze-Bord-de-Mer • Monte-Carlo • Menton
Grasse • Nice • Villefranche-s-Mer • Roquebrune-Cap-Martin • Cap d'Ail
Valbonne • Antibes • St-Jean-Cap-Ferrat
Mandelieu • Juan-les-Pins
Cannes • Le Cannet
La Napoule-Plage • Théoule-s-Mer
Anthéor • Agay
Lopez

MEDITERRANEAN SEA

Corsica
D81
N193
N198
Porticcio
N196
Porto-Vecchio

For key to country identification - see "About the gazetteer"

at the present time, there is no nationwide road assistance service in France. see also *Warning triangle/Hazard warning lights* below.

British Embassy/Consulates*

The British Embassy is located at 75383 Paris, 35 rue du Faubourg St Honoré ☎42669142; consular section 75008 Paris, 16 rue d'Anjou ☎42669142. There are British Consulates in Bordeaux, Lille, Lyons and Marseilles; there are British Consulates with Honorary Consuls in Boulogne-sur-Mer, Calais, Cherbourg, Dunkerque (Dunkirk), Le Havre, Nantes, St Malo-Dinard and Toulouse.

Children in cars*

Children under 10 are not permitted to travel in a vehicle as front-seat passengers when rear seating is available.

Dimensions and weight restrictions

Private **cars** and towed **trailers** or **caravans** are restricted to the following dimensions – height, no restriction, but 4 metres is a recommended maximum; width, 2.50 metres; length, 12 metres (excluding towing device). The maximum permitted overall length of vehicle/trailer or caravan combinations is 18 metres.

If the weight of the trailer exceeds that of the towing vehicle, see also *Speed limits* below.

Driving licence*

A valid UK or Republic of Ireland licence is acceptable in France and Monaco. The minimum age at which a visitor may use a temporarily imported car is 18 years. In France a visitor may use a temporarily imported motorcycle of up to 80cc at 16 but must be at least 18 to use one over 80cc (in Monaco up to 125cc at 16, but 18 if over 125cc). See also *Speed limits* below.

Emergency messages to tourists*

Emergency messages to tourists are broadcast by France Inter on 1829 metres longwave, Monday to Saturday from 25 June to 31 August. The messages are transmitted in English and German after the news at 09.00hrs and 16.00hrs.

Garages*

All prices must be displayed on the premises so that they are clearly visible and legible. When you have had a repair carried out, you should receive an invoice stating the labour charge, ie the hourly rate (displayed) multiplied by the time spent or the time shown on the time schedule for each operation, and not just a lump sum. The price of supplies and spares should be shown separately. Parts which have been replaced must be returned to you, unless it is a routine replacement or the repair is carried out free during the guarantee period.

Lights*

It is obligatory to use headlights, as driving on sidelights *only* is not permitted. In fog, mist or poor visibility during the day, either two fog lamps or two dipped headlights must be switched on in addition to two sidelights. It is also compulsory for *motorcyclists* riding machines exceeding 125cc to use dipped headlights during the day. Failure to comply with these regulations will lead to an *on-the-spot* fine.

It is recommended that visiting motorists equip their vehicle with a set of replacement bulbs; drivers unable to replace a faulty bulb when requested to do so by the police may be fined. In France, a regulation requires all locally registered vehicles to be equipped with headlights which show a yellow beam and, in the interests of safety and courtesy, visiting motorists are advised to comply. If you are able to use beam deflectors to alter your headlights for driving abroad, you can purchase deflectors with yellow lenses. However, with headlamp converters, it is necessary to coat the outer surface of the headlamp glass with a yellow plastic paint which is removable with a solvent. The yellow headlamp paint can be purchased from the AA.

Motoring club*

 The AA is affiliated to the *Association Français des Automobilistes* (AFA) whose office is at F-75017 Paris, 9 rue Anatole-de-la-Forge ☎42278200.

*Additional information will be found in the European ABC at the front of the book.

Motorways

There are over 4,000 miles of motorway (*Autoroute*) open, and more are under construction or in preparation. To join a motorway, follow signs with the international motorway symbol, or signs with the words '*par Autoroute*' added. Signs with the added words '*Péage*' or '*par péage*' lead to toll roads. With the exception of a few sections into or around large cities, all autoroutes have a toll charged according to the distance travelled eg toll charges for a single journey from Calais to Nice are about £32 for a car and about £49 for a car with caravan. On the majority of toll motorways, a travel ticket is issued on entry and the toll is paid on leaving the motorway. The travel ticket gives all relevant information about the toll charges, including the toll category of your vehicle. At the exit point, the ticket is handed in and the amount due shows up on an illuminated sign at the toll booth. On some motorways, the toll collection is automatic; have the correct amount ready to throw into the collecting basket. If change is required, use the marked separate lane. A leaflet entitled *Motorways in France* is available to AA members.

Motorway restaurants The *L'Arche* restaurant chain was the first network of restaurants established on French motorways. The 21 restaurants are open all year from at least 07.00–22.30hrs, and offer the prospect of a relaxing stop-over. Change facilities, a telephone, a baby's corner and playgrounds for children are always to be found.

Motorway telephones For assistance on a motorway, use one of the telephone boxes sited at 2.4km (1½ mile) intervals; they are directly connected to police stations.

Orange badge scheme for disabled drivers*

There is no formal system of concessions in operation, and responsibility for parking in built-up areas rests with the local authorities. Any parking places reserved for the disabled are indicated by the international symbol. However, the police are instructed to show consideration where parking by the disabled is concerned. In some towns and cities including Paris, orange badge holders may be allowed to park at meter bays and pay only the initial charge.

Parking*

Regulations are similar to those in the UK. As a general rule, all prohibitions are indicated by road signs or by yellow markings on the kerb.

Blue zones are areas, in most principal towns, where short-term parking is permitted. Discs must be used, placed against the windscreen, every day except Sundays and Public Holidays, 09.00–12.30hrs and 14.30–19.00hrs. Discs are sold at police stations, but at tourist offices and some clubs and commercial firms they are available free of charge. They permit parking for up to one hour.

Grey zones are areas where parking meters are in use. A fee must be paid between 09.00 and 19.00hrs. The ticket, issued by an automatic machine, must be displayed behind the windscreen or nearside front window.

Green zones In some parts of the green zone parking is completely forbidden.

Alternate unilateral parking On some roads in built-up areas parking is allowed from the 1st to the 15th of the month on the side of the road where the buildings have odd numbers, and from the 16th to the end of the month on the side with even numbers.

In Paris cars towing caravans are prohibited from the blue zone between 14.00 and 20.30hrs. Cars towing trailers with an overall surface of 10 square metres or more may neither circulate nor park in the central green zone between 14.00–20.30hrs, except on Sundays and Public Holidays. Vehicle combinations with an overall surface exceeding 16 square metres may neither circulate nor park in the green zone between 08.00 and 20.30hrs. If you want to cross Paris during these hours with vehicle/trailer combinations you can use the Boulevard Pérphérique, although the route is heavily congested, except during Public holiday periods. It is prohibited to park caravans, even for a short period, in the green zone and most other areas of Paris.

In Paris and surrounding departments it is also prohibited to leave a vehicle parked in the same place for more than 24 consecutive hours.

Vehicles which are parked contrary to regulations are liable to be removed by the

*Additional information will be found in the European ABC at the front of the book.

police at the owner's risk, and the driver will be liable for any costs incurred, including a heavy fine. In Paris and some other large towns wheel clamps are used on all illegally parked cars.

Petrol*

Credit cards The most widely accepted credit cards at petrol stations in France are Access, Eurocard/Mastercard and Visa; these can be used for purchases of petrol at all main garages.
Duty-free petrol The petrol in the vehicle tank may be imported free of customs duty and tax. Additionally, if the vehicle is fitted with a catalytic converter, up to 10 litres of unleaded petrol in a can may be imported free of customs duty and tax.
Petrol (leaded) *Essence Normale* (90 octane) and *Essence Super* (98 octane) grades.
Petrol (unleaded) is sold in France as *Essence Super* (95 and 98 octane) grades. Pumps dispensing unleaded petrol are clearly marked with a sticker *essence sans plomb* (super grade unleaded).

Postal information

Mail Postcards Fr2; letters up to 20gm Fr2.20.
Post offices There are 17,500 post offices in France. They are open 09.00–12.00hrs and 14.00–17.00hrs Monday to Friday and 09.00–12.00hrs Saturday. Opening hours of small offices in rural areas may vary. In Paris, the office at 52 rue de Louvre is open 24 hours a day.

Priority including roundabouts*

In built-up areas, you must give way to traffic coming from the right – *priorité à droite*. However, at roundabouts with signs saying 'Vous n'avez pas la priorité' or 'Cedez le passage' traffic **on** the roundabout has priority; where there is no such sign traffic **entering** the roundabout has priority. Outside built-up areas all main roads of any importance have right of way. This is indicated by a red-bordered triangle showing a black cross on a white background with the words '*Passage Protege*' underneath: or a red-bordered triangle showing a pointed black upright with horizontal bar on a white background; or a yellow square within a white square with points vertical.

Public holidays*

Official Public holidays in France for 1990 are given below.

January 1 (New Year's Day)
April 15 (Easter Sunday)
April 16 (Easter Monday)
May 1 (Labour Day)
May 8 (VE Day)
May 24 (Ascension Day)
June 3 (Whit Sunday)
June 4 (Whit Monday)
July 14†† (National Holiday)
August 15 (Assumption)
November 1 (All Saints' Day)
November 11† (Armistice Day)
December 25 (Christmas Day)
††Saturday   †Sunday

Religious services*

The Intercontinental Church Society welcomes visitors from any denomination to English language services in the following centres:
06400 Cannes The Rev Canon Keith Anderson, Chaplain's Apartment, 'Residence Kent', rue Général Ferrie ☎93945461
60500 Chantilly The Rev John Fulton, 15F av Marie-Amelie ☎44585322
59140 Dunkerque The Rev Tony Rimmer, 130 rue de l'Ecole Maternelle ☎28633947
33310 Lormont The Rev Brian Eaves, 32 rue de Lormont Village (serving Bordeaux) ☎56063717
78600 Maisons-Laffitte The Rev Ben Eaton, 15 av Carnot (Paris area) ☎39623497
75008 Paris The Ven Brian Lea, 5 rue d'Aguesseau ☎47427088
69110 Sainte Foy-Les-Lyon The Rev Gerald Hovenden, Le Coteau, 38 Chemin de Taffignon (serving Lyon and Grenoble) ☎78596706
78000 Versailles The Rev Martin Oram, 31 rue du Pont Colbert ☎39514707

Roads, including holiday traffic

France has a very comprehensive network of roads, and surfaces are normally good; exceptions are usually signposted *Chaussée déformée*. The camber is often severe and the edges rough. See also *Road conditions* in the European ABC.
During July and August and especially at weekends, traffic on main roads is likely to be very heavy. Special signs are erected to indicate alternative routes with the least traffic congestion. Wherever they appear, it is usually advantageous to follow them, although you

*Additional information will be found in the European ABC at the front of the book.

FRANCE

cannot be absolutely sure of gaining time. The alternative routes are quiet, but they are not as wide as the main roads. They are **not** suitable for caravans.

A free road map showing the marked alternative routes, plus information centres and petrol stations open for 24 hours, is available from service stations displaying the *Bison Futé* poster (a Red Indian chief in full war bonnet). These maps are also available from *Syndicats d'Initiative* and information offices.

Road number changes Following the 1974–78 decentralisation, when many secondary National highways were transferred to the Departments ('N' and 'D' roads: N315 became D915, and N16 became D916, *etc*), further modifications to the road system are taking place. These latest changes involve about 4,000–5,000km on N-roads throughout France, and some irregularities may occur during the changeover period when the same road may have signs showing two different numbers.

Traffic lanes (Paris) There are special lanes for buses and taxis only in some streets; they are marked by a continuous yellow line painted one vehicle width from the kerb. Usually, buses and taxis in the special lane travel in the opposite direction to other traffic.

Shopping hours

Most shops, including department stores are open Monday to Saturday 09.00–18.30/19.00hrs; *food shops* open earlier at 07.00hrs, and some (bakers in particular), open on Sunday mornings. *Hypermarkets* generally remain open until 21.00/22.00hrs. However, outside the larger cities, you will find that many shops close all day, or a half-day, on Mondays. In *small towns* lunch-time closing can extend from 12.00 to 14.00hrs.

Speed limits*

The beginning of a built-up area is indicated by a sign with the placename in blue letters on a light background; the end by the placename sign with a thin red line diagonally across it. Unless otherwise signposted, speed limits are:

Built-up areas 60kph (37mph).
Outside built-up areas on normal roads 90kph (56mph); on *dual-carriageways* separated by a central reservation 110kph (68mph).
On motorways 130kph (80mph). **Note** The *minimum* speed in the fast lane on a level stretch of motorway during good daytime visibility is 80kph (49mph), and drivers travelling below this speed are liable to be fined. The *maximum* speed on the Paris ring road is 80kph (49mph) and, on other urban stretches of motorway, 100kph (68mph). In wet weather, speed limits outside built-up areas are reduced to 80kph (49mph), 100kph (62mph) and 110kph (68mph) on motorways.

These limits also apply to private cars towing a trailer or caravan, if the latter's weight does not exceed that of the car. However, if the weight of the trailer exceeds that of the car by less than 30% the speed limits is 65kph (39mph), if more than 30% the speed limit is 45kph (28mph). Additionally, these combinations must:

   i Display a disc at the rear of the caravan/trailer showing the maximum speed.
   ii Not be driven in the fast lane of a 3-lane motorway.

Both French residents and visitors to France who have held a driving licence for less than one year must not exceed 90kph (56mph) or any lower signposted limit when driving in France.

Spiked or studded tyres

Spiked or **studded tyres** may be used between November and March by vehicles with a total authorised laden weight not exceeding 3,500kg, provided that a speed of 90kph (56mph) is not exceeded. The speed-limitation disc bearing the figure '90' is only compulsory for French-registered vehicles.

Telephone*

Insert coin **after** lifting the receiver; the dialling tone is a continuous tone. Generally, to make a local call use a *Fr*1 coin, or *jeton* (special telephone coin bought from the point where the call is made), but 2 × 50 *centimes* are required in some callboxes. Coins accepted are 50 *centimes* and Fr1, 5 or 10.

Within France, to call one provincial number from another, or one Paris area number (Paris, Seine St Denis, Hauts de Seine and Val de Marne) from another, simply dial the 8-digit number. To call a Paris area number from the provinces, precede the 8-digit number with (161), and to call a provincial number from the Paris area, precede the 8-digit number with (16).

*Additional information will be found in the European ABC at the front of the book.

118

International callboxes have metallic grey payphones. Cardphones can also be used for international calls.

The charge for a call to the UK is Fr0.5 for 11 seconds, with a surcharge if the call is made from an hotel. A reduced rate is available for calls made between 21.00 and 08.00hrs.

Telephone codes

UK to France	010 33
France to UK	19 †44
France to Republic of Ireland	19 †353
France to the USA	19 †1

†Wait for second dialling tone.

Traffic lights*

The three-colour system is in operation, as in the United Kingdom, with the addition of miniatures set at eye-level and with the posts placed in irregular positions, sometimes overhead and possibly without a set on the opposite side of the junction. It must be stressed that the lights themselves are extremely dim, and easily missed.

A *flashing amber light* is a warning that the intersection or junction is particularly dangerous. A *flashing red light* indicates no entry, or may be used to mark obstacles.

Warning triangle/Hazard warning lights*

The use of a warning triangle or hazard warning lights is compulsory in the event of accident or breakdown. However, as hazard warning lights may be damaged or inoperative, it is recommended that a warning triangle always be carried. The triangle must be placed on the road 30 metres (33yds) behind the vehicle and clearly visible from 100 metres (110yds). For vehicles over 3,500kg, warning must be given by at least a warning triangle.

Note if your vehicle is equipped with hazard warning lights, it is also compulsory to use them if you are forced to drive temporarily at a greatly reduced speed. However, when slow moving traffic is established in an uninterrupted lane or lanes, this only applies to the last vehicle in the lane(s).

Wheel chains

These can be purchased from vehicle accessory shops in large towns. Wheel chains can be hired from some garages; however, they have only small supplies. See also *Cold-weather touring* in the European ABC.

Winter conditions*

Although there are five mountain regions – the Vosges, Jura, Massif Central, Alps and Pyrenees – motoring in winter is not severely restricted. The main routes for south-bound traffic wanting to avoid the Alps and Massif Central are the A7 and N7 route along the Rhône Valley, the N20 from Limoges to Toulouse, and the highways farther west. Roads into Belgium, Luxembourg and Germany are generally not affected by road closures in winter.

All-the-year-round approaches to Strasbourg and Basle avoiding the Vosges and Jura are the Paris–Strasbourg motorway (A4) and the Paris–Beaune–Belfort motorway (A6–A36) respectively. The approach to Switzerland via the A40, Mâcon–Geneva motorway, is always open. Italy can be entered via the Mont Blanc road tunnel, the Fréjus road tunnel, or along the French Riviera via Menton. The main routes to Spain via Biarritz and Perpignan avoid the Pyrenees.

Whenever possible, roads are swept and kept clear. However, during periods of thaw, some roads may only be used by certain classes of traffic at the driver's risk; passenger vehicles without trailers being used privately may proceed provided they do not exceed 80kph (49mph)

*Additional information will be found in the European ABC at the front of the book.

MONACO

The tiny Principality of Monaco covers 8 square miles. Although an independent, sovereign state, it is very much under the influence of France with laws similar to those of the major country. The official Monaco information centre in the UK is the Monaco Government Tourist and Convention Office, 50 Upper Brook Street, London W1Y 1PG ☎01-(071 from 6 May) 692 4712. Monaco is one large city-state, with Monaco Town and Monte Carlo the two towns.

Motoring regulations are generally the same as in France, but it should be stated that whilst caravans are permitted to pass through the Principality, they are not allowed to stop or park.

ACCOMMODATION

The French Ministry of Tourism classifies hotels into five categories, one to four-star and four-star *luxe*. Rates for rooms are usually officially controlled and must be displayed in each room, but this does not apply to the cost of meals, always displayed outside restaurants. Many hotels offer half-board only, as indicated in the gazetteer (Dpn).

The prices shown below are an average for each classification. Accommodation is likely to be more expensive in Paris and some of the more popular tourist areas.

At the time of going to press £1 *Sterling = Fr10.52 and US$1 = Fr6.33* but you should check the rate of exchange before your departure.

Gîtes de France This is furnished accommodation in rural France, often at farms, for those who prefer to cater for themselves. There are some 23,000 gîtes in 4,000 villages, created with the financial support of the French Government and governed by a charter laid down by the Fédération Nationale des Gîtes de France. For information on membership, write

to: Gîtes de France, Dept. TF, 178 Piccadilly, London W1V 9DB, enclosing details of preferred regions, choice of dates and a stamped addressed envelope.

Logis de France These are privately owned, mostly family-run hotels equivalent to one- and two star or sometimes three star, categories. They are generally located off the beaten track, and offer a high standard for their type and good value for money. There are more than 4,500 logis, some of which are listed in the gazetteer, and they are marked by the symbol **lE**. There are none in Paris. A copy of the Logis Hotel Guide may be obtained in early March from the French Government Tourist Office, 178 Piccadilly, London W1V 0AL (against payment of 50p in stamps to cover postage and packing).

Relais Routiers These are restaurants situated on main roads, some offering simple accommodation and providing a good meal at a reasonable price. The Relais Routiers Guide issued from February each year can be purchased through bookshops.

AVERAGE PRICES

	Single Room	Double Room	Breakfast	Lunch/Dinner
★★★★★	Fr1220–1783	Fr1494–5601	Fr85–123	Fr212–324
★★★★	Fr490–871	from Fr1246	Fr57–70	Fr165–294
★★★	Fr296–419	Fr373–487	Fr38–44	Fr123–373
★★	Fr185–248	Fr208–288	Fr27–32	Fr80–159
★	Fr124–200	Fr141–217	Fr23–30	Fr70–178

The department name follows the town name. For information on making internal local telephone calls see page 118.

Abbreviations:

av	avenue	pl	place
bd	boulevard	Prés	Président
Cpt	Capitaine	Prof	Professeur
Cdt	Commandant	prom	promenade
espl	esplanade	r	rue
fbg	faubourg	rte	route
Gl	Général	sq	square
Ml	Marshal,Maréchal		
Mon	Monseigneur		

ABBEVILLE
Somme
★★Ibis 234 rte d'Amiens ☎22248080 tx 145045
✈♠45 P50
Credit Cards 1 3
──────
★Condé DPn 14-16 pl de la Libération ☎22240633
✈♠7
Credit Cards 2 3 4
──────
★Jean Bart 5-7 r Ste-Catherine ☎22242171
Mar-Jan :Rest closed Sun
rm16(✈♠12) P8
Credit Cards 1 2 3

✈♠ *Abbeville Automobile* 29 chaussée d'Hocquet
☎ 22240854 P For
✈♠ *SADRA* 53 av R-Schumann ☎ 22243481 P
Aud VW
──────
ABRETS, LES
Isère
★Belle Etoile lE4 r V-Hugo ☎76320497
rm15(✈♠8) ♨ P Mountain
──────
★Hostellerie Abrésienne 34 r Gambetta (N75)
☎76320428
:Rest closed Tue
rm22(✈♠5) ♨ P12
Credit Cards 1 3
──────
AGAY
Var
✈♠ *Agay* av du Gratadis ☎ 94820616 All makes
At DRAMONT, LE(2km SW)
★★★Sol et Mar DPn ☎94952560
Etr-15 Oct
✈♠47 P40 Lift ♨ ⊇ Beach Sea Mountain
Credit Card 3
──────
AGDE
Hérault
✈♠ Four 12 av Gl-de-Gaulle ☎ 67941141 Peu Tal
✈♠ Gare 1 av V-Hugo ☎ 67942268 P All makes

At CAP-D'AGDE(7km SE)
★★★★*Matagor* r Trésor Royal ☎67260005 tx 480978
✈♠90 P60 Lift ⊇ Sea
Credit Cards 1 2 3 5
──────
★★Ibis r du Tambour (n.rest) ☎67264666 tx 490034
✈♠30 ♨ P Lift ℂ
Credit Cards 1 3
At TAMARISSIÈRE, LA(4km SW D32E)
★★*Tamarissière* 21 quai T-Cornu ☎67942087 tx 490225
15 Mar-Nov
✈♠34 A5rm ⊇ Sea
Credit Cards 1 2 3 5
──────
AGEN
Lot-et-Garonne
★★Château Jacobins lE1 pl Jacobins ☎53470331 tx 571162
✈♠15 P18 ℂ
Credit Cards 1 2 3
──────
★★Ibis 105 bd Carnot ☎53473123 tx 541331
:Rest closed Sun
✈♠56 P Lift ℂ
Credit Cards 1 3

★★*Périgord* **LE**42 pl XIV Juillet ☎53661001
⇌21 Lift
Credit Cards [1] [3]

➤ **F Tastets** 182 bd de la Liberté ☎ 53471063 DJ

AIGLE, L'
Orne

★★★**Dauphin** (MAP/BW) pl de la Halle ☎33244312 tx 170979
rm30(⇌28) P8 ☾
Credit Cards [1] [2] [3] [5]

AIGUEBELLE
Var

★★★★**Roches** (4 km on N599 to Le Lavandu) ☎94710507 tx 430023
Apr-early Oct
⇌45 ⌂ P30 ☾ ⩳ Beach Sea
Credit Cards [1] [2] [3]

★★**Plage DPn** 14 r des 3 Dauphins ☎94058074
Etr-Sep
rm53(⇌20) A31rm Sea

AIGUILLON-SUR-MER
Vendée

★★*Port* 2 r Belle Vue ☎51564008
Mar-Oct
⇌33 P ⚲ ⩳
Credit Card [3]

AINHOA
Pyrénées-Atlantiques

★★★**Argi-Eder** (MAP/BW) **DPn** rte de la Chapelle ☎59299104 tx 570067
Apr-15 Nov
⇌40 A4rm P80 ⚲ ⩳ Mountain
Credit Cards [1] [2] [3] [5]

AIRE-SUR-L'ADOUR
Landes

➤ **Tolerie** 65 av de Bordeaux ☎ 58716214 **P** Cit

AIRE-SUR-LA-LYS
Pas-de-Calais

★**Europ Hotel** 14 Grande Pl (n.rest) ☎21390432
rm14(⇌13) ⌂ P6
Credit Cards [1] [2] [3]

AISEY-SUR-SEINE
Côte-d'Or

★★**Roy LEDPn** ☎80932163
Closed Dec-1 Jan:Rest closed Tue
rm10(⇌8) P10
Credit Cards [1] [3]

AIX-EN-PROVENCE
Bouches-du-Rhône

★★★★*Pullman le Pigonnet* 5 av Pigonnet (off N8 towards Marseille) ☎42590290 tx 410629
⇌49 A14rm ⌂ P Lift ⩳
Credit Cards [1] [2] [3] [4] [5]

★★★**Manoir** 8 r d'Entrecasteaux (n.rest) ☎42262720 tx 441489
15 Feb-15 Jan
rm43(⇌38) Lift ☾
Credit Cards [1] [2] [3] [4] [5]

★★★*Novotel Beaumanoir* Résidence Beaumanoir (A8) ☎42274750 tx 400244
⇌102 P Lift ⩳
Credit Cards [1] [2] [3] [5]

★★★*Novotel Sud* Périphérique Sud,Arc de Meyran ☎42279049 tx 420517
⇌80 P100 Lift ⚲ ⩳
Credit Cards [1] [2] [3] [5]

★★★*Paul Cézanne* 40 av V-Hugo (n.rest) ☎42263473
18 Jan-20 Dec
⇌44 ⌂ P Lift ☾
Credit Card [2]

★★★**Résidence Rotonde** 15 av des Belges (n.rest) ☎42262988 tx 410777
15 Jan-15 Nov
⇌42 ⌂ P42 Lift ☾
Credit Cards [1] [2] [3] [5]

★★*Campanile* ZAC du Jas de Bouffan ☎42594073 tx 441273
⇌47 P80 Lift
Credit Card [3]

★★**Ibis** chemin des Infirmeries ☎42279820 tx 420519
⇌83
Credit Cards [1] [3]

★★*Renaissance* 4 bd de la République (n.rest) ☎42262422
⇌36 P
Credit Card [3]

At **EGUILLES**(11km NW)

★★*Belvédère* quartier des Landons ☎42925292 tx 403521
⇌38 A32rm P40 ⩳
Credit Cards [1] [2] [3] [5]

At **MILLES, LES**(5km S off D9)

★★*Climat* r Ampère ☎42203077 tx 612241
⇌38 P

AIX-LES-BAINS
Savoie

★★★*Iles Britanniques* pl de l'Establissement Thermal ☎79610377
May-Sep
⇌90 A10rm ⌂ P Lift ☾ Mountain Lake

★★★**International Rivollier** 18 av C-de-Gaulle ☎79352100 tx 320903
⇌60 ⌂ P12 Lift ☾ Mountain
Credit Cards [1] [2] [3] [4] [5]

★★★*Manoir* **LE**(Inter) 33 r Georges 1er ☎79614400 tx 980793
24 Jan-24 Dec
⇌72 ⌂ P10 Lift
Credit Cards [1] [3] [5]

★★★**Pastorale** 221 av Grand Port ☎79352536 tx 309709
Apr-Jan :Rest closed Mon
⇌30 P25 Lift Mountain
Credit Cards [1] [2] [3] [5]

★★*Campanile* av du Golf de Marlioz ☎79613066 tx 980090
⇌43 P43
Credit Card [3]

★★*Cecil* 20 av Victoria (n.rest) ☎79350412
rm18(⇌11) Lift Mountain

★★**Paix LE**11 r Lamartine,BP 513 ☎79350210 tx 980940
Mar-Nov
rm70(⇌60) Lift ☾ Mountain Lake
Credit Cards [3] [5]

★★*Parc* 28 r de Chambéry ☎79612911
mid Apr-Oct
rm50(⇌18) ⌂ Lift ☾ Mountain

★★**Pavillon Rivollier** pl Gare ☎79351904
2 May-14 Oct
rm42(⇌34) ⌂ P5 Lift ☾ Mountain
Credit Cards [2] [3] [5]

ALBERT
Somme

★**Basilique LEDPn** 3-5 r Gambetta ☎22750471
:Rest closed Sun
rm10(⇌8)
Credit Cards [1] [3]

★**Paix LE**43 r V-Hugo ☎22750164
Closed 1-16 Feb
rm15(⇌6) A3rm ⌂ P8
Credit Cards [1] [2] [3]

ALBERTVILLE
Savoie

★★★**Million** 8 pl de la Liberté ☎79322515 tx 306022
Closed 24 Apr-9 May & 18 Sep-3 Oct :Rest closed Mon & Sun evening
rm28(⇌27) ⌂ P12 Lift
Credit Cards [1] [2] [3] [5]

★★*Costaroche* 1 chemin P-du-Roy ☎79320202 :Rest closed Sun & Mon midday
⇌20 P20 Mountain
Credit Cards [1] [3]

ALBI
Tarn

★★★★**Hostellerie St-Antione** (MAP/BW) 17 r St-Antoine ☎63540404 tx 520850
⇌50 ⌂ P30 Lift ☾ ⚲ ⩳
Credit Cards [1] [2] [3] [5]

★★★**Chiffre** 50 r Séré de Rivières ☎63540460 tx 520411
⇌40 ⌂ P40 Lift ☾
Credit Cards [1] [2] [3] [5]

★★**Orléans** (FAH) pl Stalingrad ☎63541656 tx 521605
Closed 21 Dec-4 Jan : Rest closed Sun evening
⇌62 Lift ☾
Credit Cards [1] [2] [3] [5]

★**Vieil Alby DPn** 25 r T-Lautrec ☎63541469
15 Jan-25 Jun & 10 Jul-25 Dec :Rest closed Sun evening & Mon
rm10(⇌6) ⌂ P3
Credit Cards [1] [2] [3] [5]

At **FONVIALANE**(3km N on N606)

★★★★**Réserve** (Relais et Châteaux) **DPn** rte de Cordes ☎63607979 tx 520850
Apr-Oct
⇌24 ⌂ P50 ☾ ⚲ ⩳ Lake
Credit Cards [1] [2] [3] [5]

ALENCON
Orne
See also ST-LÉONARD-DES-BOIS

★★★**Grand Cerf** 21 r St-Blaise ☎33260051 tx 772212
Closed 15 Dec-15 Jan
rm33(⇌24) Lift ☾
Credit Cards [1] [2] [3] [4]

★★*Campanile* rte de Paris ☎33295385 tx 171908
⇌35 P35
Credit Card [3]

★★**France** 3 r St-Blaise (n.rest) ☎33262636
rm31(⇌24) ☾
Credit Cards [1] [3]

★★**Gare LE**50 av Wilson ☎33290393
Closed 27 Dec-4 Jan
rm22(⇌21) ⌂ P15
Credit Cards [1] [2] [3] [5]

★**Industrie LE**20-22 pl du Gl-de-Gaulle ☎33271930
rm9(⇌6) P15
Credit Cards [1] [3]

★**Paris** 26 r D-Papin (opposite station) ☎33290164
Rest closed Fri-Sun
rm17(⇌9) ⌂ P10
Credit Cards [1] [3]

ALÈS
Gard

★★★*Mercure* 18 r E-Quinet ☎66522707 tx 480830
Rest closed Sun
⇌75 P45 Lift
Credit Cards [1] [3] [5]

➤ **C Roux** av de Croupillac ☎ 66862626 **P** Peu

➤ *Prairie* 4 av J-Guesde ☎ 66520261 AR LR

ALPE-D'HUEZ, L'
Isère

★★★**Chamois d'Or DPn** r de Fontbelle
☎76803132
15 Dec-25 Apr
📶45 P25 Lift Mountain
Credit Card ③

★★★**Ours Blanc** (MAP) av des Jeux ☎76803111
tx 320807
20 Dec-20 Apr
📶37 ⌂ P40 Mountain
Credit Cards ①②③⑤

ALTKIRCH
Haut-Rhin

★★**Terrasse** ⓛ44-46 r du 3e Zouave
☎89409802
rm22(📶18)
Credit Cards ①③⑤

★**Sundgovienne** ⓛErte de Belfort (3.5km W on
D4) ☎89409718
Feb-23 Dec
📶31 ⌂ P50 Lift
Credit Cards ①②③⑤

At **WALHEIM**(3.5km NE D432)
🛏 **Schmitt** 63b Grand rue Walheim ☎ 89409162
P All makes

ALVIGNAC
Lot

★★★**Palladium** av de Padirac ☎65336023
Apr-mid Oct
📶25 A19rm P45 ⌂ Mountain
Credit Cards ①②③④⑤

AMBÉRIEU-EN-BUGEY
Ain

★★★**Savoie** (Inter-Hotels) (2km N on D36)
☎74380690
Feb-23 Dec
📶45 P Lift

AMBERT
Puy-de-Dôme

★★**Livradois DPn** 1 pl du Livradois ☎73821001
:Rest closed Mon (out of season)
rm14(📶7) ⌂ P4 Mountain
Credit Cards ①②③④⑤

★**Gare** 17 av de la Gare ☎73820027
15 Nov-15 Oct
rm22(📶14) ⌂ P12
Credit Cards ①②③⑤

AMBOISE
Indre-et-Loire

★★★**Novotel** 17 r des Sablonnières ☎47574207
tx 751203
📶121 P95 Lift ⌖ ⌂
Credit Cards ①②③⑤

★★**Château de Pray DPn** (2km NE on N751)
☎47572367
10 Feb-Dec
rm16(📶14) P50
Credit Cards ①②③⑤

★ **Ibis** La Boitardière ☎47231023 tx 752414
:Rest closed Sat & Sun Nov-Feb
📶70 P90
Credit Cards ①③

★**Lion d'Or** ⓛⒺDPn 17 quai C-Guinot
☎47570023
Feb-Nov :Rest closed Sun evening & Mon
rm23(📶19)
Credit Cards ①③

★★**Parc** ⓛⒺ8 r L-da-Vinci ☎47570693
Mar-Oct
rm19(📶18) A1rm P30
Credit Cards ①③

★**Brèche DPn** 26 r J-Ferry ☎47570079
Closed 23 Dec-Jan :Rest closed Mon & 14 Nov-
Etr
rm13(📶7) ⌂ P2
Credit Cards ①③

AMIENS
Somme

★★★**Grand Hotel de l'Univers** 2 r Noyon (n.rest)
☎22915251 tx 145070
📶41 P Lift ℂ
Credit Cards ①②③④⑤

★★★**Carlton-Belfort** 42 r de Noyon ☎22922644 tx
140754
📶36 Lift ℂ
Credit Cards ①②③④⑤

★★**Ibis** 'Le Centrum',r Ml-de-Lattre-de-Tassigny
☎22925733 tx 140765
📶94 ⌂ Lift
Credit Cards ①③

★★**Nord-Sud** 11 r Gresset ☎22915903
rm26(📶20)

★★**Paix** 8 r de la République (n.rest) ☎22913921
Closed mid Dec-mid Jan
rm26(📶11) P17

★★**Prieure** 17 r Porion ☎22922767 tx 140754
:Rest closed Sat midday
📶11

★**Normandie** 1 bis r Lamartine (n.rest)
☎22917499
rm26(📶23) ⌂ P9
Credit Card ③

🛏 **Anciens** 48 r Gauthier-de-Rumilly ☎
22953720 For

At **BOVES**(7km SE D934)
★★★**Novotel Amiens Est** (CD934) ☎22462222
tx 140731
📶93 P150 ⌂ P
Credit Cards ①②③⑤

AMILLY
See MONTARGIS

AMMERSCHWIHR
See COLMAR

ANDELYS, LES
Eure

★★★**Chaine d'Or** ⓛⒺ27 r Grande,pl St-Sauveur
☎32540031
Closed Jan
📶12 A1rm P12
Credit Card ③

★**Normandie Pn** 1 r Grande ☎32541052
Closed Dec: Rest closed Wed & Thu
rm11(📶6) P12
Credit Card ①

ANDLAU
Bas-Rhin

★★**Kastelberg** r du Gl-Koenig ☎88089783
Closed Xmas:Rest closed Nov-Mar
📶28 P28 Mountain
Credit Cards ①③

ANDRÉZIEUX-BOUTHÉON
See ST-ÉTIENNE AIRPORT

ANGERS
Maine-et-Loire

★★★**Anjou** (MAP/BW) 1 bd Ml-Foch ☎41882482
tx 720521
:Rest closed Sun
📶51 ⌂ P18 Lift ℂ
Credit Cards ①②③⑤

★★★**Mercure** pl M-France ☎41603481 tx 722139
📶86 ⌂ P60 Lift
Credit Cards ①②③⑤

★★**Boule d'Or** 27 bd Carnot ☎41437656 tx
720930
:Rest closed Fri
rm33(📶27) A5rm ⌂ P15
Credit Cards ①③

★★**Climat** r du Château-d'Orgemont ☎41663045
tx 722747
📶42 P40 ℂ
Credit Cards ①②③

★★**Fimotel** 23 r P-Bert ☎41881010 tx 722735
📶50 ⌂ P50 Lift
Credit Cards ①②③⑤

★★**France** (FAH) 8 pl de la Gare ☎41884942 tx
720895
📶57 Lift ℂ
Credit Cards ①②③⑤

★★**Ibis** r de la Poissonnerie ☎41861515 tx
720916
📶95 Lift ℂ
Credit Cards ①③

★★**Progrès** 26 r D-Papin (n.rest) ☎41881014 tx
720982
Closed 18 Dec-8 Jan
📶41 Lift ℂ
Credit Cards ①②③⑤

★★**Univers** 2 r de la Gare (n.rest) ☎41884358 tx
720930
📶45 Lift ℂ
Credit Cards ①②③⑤

🛏 **Clogenson** 30 r Coste-et-Bellonte ☎
41668266 P Peu Tal

🛏 **Rallye Service** 4 bis r St-Maurille ☎ 41880339
AR

ANGLET
Pyrénées-Atlantiques

★★★**Chiberta et du Golf** (Inter-Hotels) 104 bd
des Plages ☎59521516 tx 573412
Closed 20 Nov-19 Dec
📶98 A53rm P100 Lift ℂ ⌂ ⣫ Sea Lake
Credit Cards ①②③⑤

★★**Climat** bd du B.A.B ☎59529900 tx 572140
📶44 ⌂ P56
Credit Cards ①②③

★★**Ibis** 64 av d'Espagne (N10) ☎59034545 tx
560121
📶59 P Lift
Credit Cards ①③

★**Fauvettes** 69 r Moulin Barbot,à la Chambre
d'Amour ☎59037558
Apr-Sep: Rest for guests only
rm11(📶3) ⌂ Sea

🛏 **J Iribarren** av de Cambo,Quartier Sutar ☎
59423056 **P**

ANGOULÊME
Charente

★★★**Grand France** (Inter-Hotels) 1 pl des Halles
☎45954795 tx 791020
:Rest closed Sat & Sun am
rm60(📶47) ⌂ P10 Lift ℂ
Credit Cards ①②③⑤

★★**Epi d'Or** 66 bd R-Chabasse (n.rest)
☎45956764
📶32 P25 Lift ℂ
Credit Cards ①②③⑤

★**Flore** 414 rte de Bordeaux ☎45919946 tx
791573
rm40(📶14) A2rm ⌂ P20 ℂ
Credit Cards ①②③④⑤

🛏 **Mathieux Automobiles** rte de Paris,Le Gond
Pontouvre ☎ 45680255 P For

At **CHAMPNIERS**(7km NE)
★★★**Novotel Angoulême Nord** (N10)
☎45685322 tx 790153
📶100 Lift ⣫
Credit Cards ①②③⑤

★★**PM16** rte de Poitiers ☎45680322 tx 790345
📶41 P100 ℂ
Credit Cards ①②③⑤

ANGRES
Pas-de-Calais

★★**Captain** Place du Caumont,r J Bart
☎21450909 tx 134492
📶42 P Lift ⌖

ANNECY
Haute-Savoie
See also TALLOIRES; VEYRIER-DU-LAC
★★★**Mercure Annecy Sud** rte d'Aix,Seynod
(N201) ☎50520966 tx 385303
⊷ℕ69 P100 ⌫ Mountain
Credit Cards ①③④⑤
★★★**Splendid** 4 quai E-Chappuis (n.rest)
☎50452000 tx 385233
⊷ℕ50 P800 Lift Lake
Credit Cards ①③
★★**Campanile** Impasse de Crêts ☎50677466 tx
385565
⊷ℕ40 P40
Credit Card ③
★★**Faisan Doré** **LE**DPn 34 av d'Albigny
☎50230246
Closed 12 Dec-20 Jan
⊷ℕ40 ☎ P4 Lift
Credit Cards ①③
★★**Ibis** quartier de la Manufacture,12 r de la Gare
☎50454321 tx 385585
⊷ℕ83 Lift
Credit Cards ①③
➤ **Parmelan** av du Petit Port,Annecy-le-Vieux ☎
50231285 Ope

ANNEMASSE
Haute-Savoie
See also GAILLARD
★★★**Parc** (MAP/BW) 19 r de Genève (n.rest)
☎50384460 tx 309034
⊷ℕ30 ☎ P Lift ☾ Mountain
Credit Cards ①②③⑤
★★**Campanile** Parc d'Etremblères ☎50378485 tx
309511
⊷ℕ42 P42
Credit Card ③
★★**National** (Inter) 10 pl J-Deffault (n.rest)
☎50920644 tx 319003
rm45(⊷ℕ42) ☎ P17 Lift ☾ Mountain
Credit Cards ①②③⑤

ANSE
Rhône
➤ **M Salel** 59 r National ☎ 74670368

ANTHÉOR
Var
★★**Réserve d'Anthéor** (N98) ☎94448005
15 Feb-15 Oct
⊷ℕ13 P30 Beach Sea
Credit Cards ①②③⑤

ANTIBES
Alpes-Maritimes
★★★★**Tananarive** rte de Nice (N7) ☎93333000
⊷ℕ50 ☎ P30 Lift ☾ ⌫ Sea Mountain
★★★**First** 21 av des Chênes ☎93618737 tx
462466
Mar-Dec
⊷ℕ16 P ☾ Sea Mountain
Credit Cards ①②③④⑤
★★★**Mercator** 120 chemin des Groules,Quartier
de la Brague (4km N via N7) (n.rest) ☎93335075
15 Dec-15 Nov
⊷ℕ18 A2rm P20 ☹
Credit Cards ①②③⑤
★★**Fimotel** 2599 rte de Grasse (4.5km W)
☎93744636 tx 461181
⊷ℕ75 P60 Lift ☾ ⌫ Sea Mountain
Credit Cards ①②③⑤
➤ **Antibes Dépannage** chemin de St-Maymes ☎
93616203 P
➤ **Boschini** 1650 av J-Grec ☎ 93335086 P Peu
Tal
➤ **Dugommier** 16 bd Dugommier ☎ 93745999
Ope

At CAP-D'ANTIBES
★★★**Gardiole** DPn chemin de la Garoupe
☎93613503 tx 460000
Closed 6 Nov-Feb
⊷ℕ21 A4rm P35
Credit Cards ①②③⑤
★★**Beau Site** 141 bd Kennedy (n.rest)
☎93615343
Apr-Oct
rm26(⊷ℕ24) A6rm P30 Sea Mountain

ANTONY
Hauts-de-Seine
★★★**Fimotel** r M-Berthelot ☎46682022 tx 206037
⊷ℕ42 P40 Lift
Credit Cards ①②③⑤

APPOIGNY
See AUXERRE

APT
Vaucluse
★★★**Ventoux** **LE**DPn 67 av V-Hugo
☎90740758
⊷ℕ13 P6 Lift
Credit Cards ①②③⑤
➤ **Germain** 56 av V-Hugo ☎ 90741017 For

ARBOIS
Jura
★★**Messageries** **LE**2 r Courcelles (n.rest)
☎84661545
Mar-Nov
rm26(⊷ℕ14)
Credit Cards ①③
★**Paris** **LE**DPn 9 r de l'Hôtel-de-Ville
☎84660567 tx 361033
15 Mar-15 Nov :Rest closed Tue & Wed lunch ex
Sep
⊷ℕ18 A6rm ☎ P5 Lift
Credit Cards ①③⑤

ARCACHON
Gironde
See also PYLA-SUR-MER
★★★**Arc** 89 bd Plage (n.rest) ☎56830685 tx
571044
⊷ℕ30 P40 Lift ☾ ⌫ Sea
Credit Cards ①②③⑤
★★★**Tamarins** 253 bd Côte-d'Argent (n.rest)
☎56545096
⊷ℕ28 A5rm Lift
Credit Cards ①③

ARDRES
Pas-de-Calais
★★★**Grand Clément** pl du Gl-Leclerc (n.rest)
☎21822525
Closed 16 Jan-14 Feb:Rest closed Mon
⊷ℕ17 ☎ P12
Credit Cards ①②③⑤
★★**Relais** **LE**bd C-Senlecq ☎21354200 tx
130886
rm13(⊷ℕ12) A3rm P12
Credit Cards ①②③
★**Chaumière** 67 av de Rouville (n.rest)
☎21354124
⊷ℕ12 P6
Credit Cards ①③

ARGELÈS-GAZOST
Hautes-Pyrénées
★**Bernède** **LE**(FAH) 51 r Ml-Foch ☎62970664
tx 531040
Feb-Oct
rm43(⊷ℕ40) P25 Lift Mountain
Credit Cards ①②③
★**Mon Cottage** 3 r Yser ☎62970792
Apr-Sep
rm24(⊷18) A8rm P25 Lift Mountain

ARGELÈS-SUR-MER
Pyrénées-Orientales
★★★**Plage des Pins** allée des Pins ☎68810905
28 May-Sep
⊷ℕ49 ☎ P50 Lift ☾ ☹ ⌫ Sea Mountain
Credit Cards ①③
★**Grand Commerce** **LE**DPn 14 rte de Collioure
(N22) ☎68810033
4 Feb-20 Dec :Rest closed Mon also Sun eve in
winter
rm63(⊷ℕ46) A23rm ☎ P60 Lift ⌫
Credit Cards ①②③⑤

ARGENTAN
Orne
★★**Rennaissance** **LE**av de la 2E D-B
☎33361420
3 Jan-23 Jul & 11 Aug-23 Dec
rm15(⊷ℕ12) P30
Credit Cards ①②③⑤

ARGENTAT
Corrèze
★★**Gilbert** **LE**av J-Vachal ☎55280162
5 Mar-Dec
rm27(⊷ℕ20) P13 Lift Mountain
Credit Cards ①③⑤
➤ **Manaux** 1 rte de Tulle ☎ 55280332 P Peu

ARGENTEUIL
Val-d'Oise
★★**Climat** bd Lenine,angle r du Perreux
☎39619805 tx 609372
⊷ℕ45 P51
Credit Cards ①②③④
★★**Fimotel** 148 rte de Pontoise (N192)
☎34105200 tx 699681
⊷ℕ40 ☎ P80 Lift
Credit Cards ①②③⑤

ARGENTON-SUR-CREUSE
Indre
★★**Manoir de Boisvillers** 11 r Moulin-de-Bord
(n.rest) ☎54241388
Closed 21 Dec-14 Jan
rm14(⊷ℕ10) A5rm ☎ P12 ☾ Lake
Credit Cards ①②③⑤
★**France** **LE**8 r J-J-Rousseau ☎54240331
:Rest closed Sun
rm22(⊷13) A7rm ☎ P8
Credit Cards ①②③⑤

ARLEMPDES
Haute-Loire
★★**Manoir** **LE**☎71571714
Mar-Nov
rm17(ℕ11) Mountain

ARLES
Bouches-du-Rhône
★★★★**Jules César** (Relais et Châteaux) bd des
Lices ☎90934320 tx 400239
Closed early Nov-21 Dec
⊷ℕ55 ☎ P7 ☾ ☹
Credit Cards ①②③④⑤
★★★**Arlatan** 26 r Sauvage (n.rest) ☎90935666 tx
441203
⊷ℕ44 ☎ Lift ☾
Credit Cards ①②③⑤
★★★**Cantarelles** Ville Vieille ☎90964410 tx
401582
May-15 Nov
⊷ℕ35 P30 ☹
Credit Cards ①②③⑤
★★★**Forum** 10 pl Forum (n.rest) ☎90934895
Mar-30 Oct
⊷ℕ45 P25 Lift ☾ ⌫
★★★**Primotel** av de la 1er Division F-Libre,Face
de la Palais du Congrès ☎90939880 tx 401001
⊷ℕ148 P150 Lift ☾ ⌫
Credit Cards ①②③⑤

★★★**Select** 35 bd G-Clemenceau (n.rest)
☎90960831
₩🛏24 Lift
Credit Cards ①②③⑤

★★*Campanile* ZAD de Fourchon,r C-Chaplin
☎90499999 tx 403624
₩🛏40 P40
Credit Card ③

★★**Cloître** 18 r du Cloître (n.rest) ☎90962950
rm33(₩🛏27) A10rm ☎
Credit Cards ①②③

★★**Ibis** quartier de Fourchon ☎90931674 tx
440201
₩🛏91 P92 ⌿
Credit Cards ①③

★★*Mireille* 2 pl St-Pierre ☎90937074 tx 440308
Mar-15 Nov
₩🛏34 A4rm ☎ P60 ℂ ⌿
Credit Cards ①②③⑤

★★**Montmajour et Le Rodin** (Inter) 84 rte de
Tarason ☎90496910 tx 420776
:Rest closed Sun evening in winter
₩🛏46 A20rm ☎ P50 Lift ⌿
Credit Cards ①②③⑤

★*Mirador* (Inter) 3 r Voltaire (n.rest) ☎90962805
10 Feb-5 Jan
₩🛏15 ☎
Credit Cards ①②③

🍴 *Marguerite* 89 av de Stalingrad ☎ 90960309
P For

At **RAPHÈLE-LES-ARLES**(8km SE N453)

★★★**Auberge la Fenière** Voie Touristique 453
(8km SE on N453) ☎90984744 tx 441237
₩🛏25 ☎ P25
Credit Cards ①②③⑤

ARMBOUTS-CAPPEL
See **DUNKERQUE (DUNKIRK)**

ARNAGE
See **MANS, LE**

ARNAY-LE-DUC
Côte-d'Or

★*Terminus* **LE**Pn r Arquebuse ☎80900033
Closed 7 Jan-5 Feb:Rest closed Wed
rm12(₩🛏7) P12
Credit Cards ①③

ARRAS
Pas-de-Calais

★★★**Univers** (Inter) 3 pl Croix Rouge
☎21713401
rm36(₩🛏29) A1rm ☎ P25 ℂ
Credit Cards ①②③

★★*Astoria* 12 pl MI-Foch ☎21710814 tx 160768
rm31(₩🛏17) ℂ
Credit Cards ①②③⑤

★★**Commerce** 28 r Gambetta (n.rest)
☎21711007
rm40(₩🛏18) ☎ Lift ℂ
Credit Cards ①③

★★**Moderne** 1 bd Faidherbe (n.rest) ☎21233957
tx 133701
Closed 25 Dec-2 Jan
rm53(₩🛏50) Lift
Credit Cards ①②③④⑤

★*Chánzy* **LE**8 r Chánzy ☎21710202 tx 133010
rm20(₩🛏14) A9rm ☎
Credit Cards ①②③⑤

🍴 **Lievinoise Auto** 16 av P-Michonneau ☎
21554242 P For

At **ST-NICHOLAS**(N off N17)

★★*Campanile* Zone d'Emploi des Alouettes
☎21555630 tx 133616
₩🛏39 P50
Credit Cards ①③

ARREAU
Hautes-Pyrénées

★★**Angleterre LE**DPn rte de Luchon
☎62986330
Jun-10 Oct & 26 Dec-15 Apr
₩🛏25 P30 Mountain
Credit Cards ①③

At **CADÉAC**(2km S)

★★*Val d'Aure* rte de St-Lary ☎62986063
May-Sep 21 & Dec-15 Apr
₩🛏23 A4rm ☎ P30 ⚲ Mountain
Credit Cards ①③

ARTIGUES
See **BORDEAUX**

ARVERT
Charente-Maritime

★★**Villa Fantaisie LE**DPn ☎46364009
Closed Feb:Rest closed Sun & Mon
rm23(₩🛏17) A10rm P80
Credit Cards ①②③

ASCAIN
Pyrénées-Atlantiques

★★**Rhune Pn** pl d'Ascain ☎59540004 tx 570792
Closed 16 Jan-14 Mar
rm50(₩🛏48) A23rm P30 ⌿ Mountain
Credit Cards ①③

ASSEVILLERS
See **PÉRONNE**

ATHIS-MONS
See **PARIS AIRPORTS** under **ORLY AIRPORT**

AUBENAS
Ardèche

★★*Pinède* **LE**rte du Camping des Pins
☎75352588
₩🛏32 A10rm ☎ P80 ⚲
Credit Cards ①③

AUBRES
See **NYONS**

AUBUSSON
Creuse

★★*France* **LE**(FAH) **Pn** 6 r Désportés
☎55651022
₩🛏21 ☎
Credit Cards ①②③④⑤

★*Lion d'Or* **Pn** pl d'Espagne ☎55661388
:Rest closed Sun & Mon
rm11(₩🛏5) P

At **FOURNEAUX**(3km SW)

★★*Tuilerie* (Inter) **Pn** ☎55662809
May-Oct
₩🛏24
Credit Cards ①②③⑤

AUCH
Gers

★★★*France* **LE**(FAH) 2 pl de la Libération
☎62050044 tx 520474
:Rest closed Sun evening, Mon & Jan
₩🛏29 ☎ P5 Lift ℂ
Credit Cards ①②③⑤

AULNAT AÉROPORT
See **CLERMONT-FERRAND**

AULNAY-SOUS-BOIS
Seine

★★★*Novotel Paris Aulnay-sous-Bois* RN370
☎48662297 tx 230121
₩🛏138 P280 Lift ⌿
Credit Cards ①②③⑤

AUMALE
Seine-Maritime

★*Dauphin* **Pn** 27 r St-Lazare ☎35934192
Closed 24 Dec-17 Jan:Rest closed Sun
rm11(₩🛏10) P6
Credit Cards ①②③

🍴 **Fertun** av Foch 2 ☎ 35934121 P Peu

AUNAY-SUR-ODON
Calvados

★*Place* **LE**☎31776073
rm19(🛏10) P28
Credit Cards ①②③

★*St Michel* **LE**6 & 8 r de Caen ☎31776316
rm7(🛏3) P7
Credit Cards ①③

🍴 **l'Odon** r de Caen ☎ 31776288 P Fia Lan

AURILLAC
Cantal

★★**Grand Hotel de Boreaux LE**(MAP/BW) 2 av
de la République (n.rest) ☎71480184 tx
990316
Closed 16 Dec-14 Jan
₩🛏35 ☎ Lift
Credit Cards ①②③⑤

AURON
Alpes-Maritimes

★★★*Pilon* ☎93230015 tx 470300
20 Dec-15 Apr & Jul-Aug
₩🛏32 P30 Lift ℂ ⌿ Mountain
Credit Cards ①②③⑤

AUTUN
Saône-et-Loire

★★*Tête Noire* **LE**DPn 1-3 r de l'Arquebuse
☎85522539
rm19 ☎
Credit Card ③

AUVILLIERS-LES-FORGES
Ardennes

★★**Lenoir LE**Maubert ☎24543011
1 Mar-2 Jan :Rest closed Fri
rm21(₩🛏18) A21rm P8 Lift
Credit Cards ①②③④⑤

AUXERRE
Yonne

★★★*Clairions* **LE**av Worms ☎86468564 tx
800039
₩🛏62 P150 Lift ℂ ⚲ ⌿
Credit Cards ①②③

★★★*Maxime* **LE**2 quai de la Marine
☎86468564 tx 800039
₩🛏44 P Lift

★★**Cygne** 14 r du 24-Août (n.rest) ☎86522651
rm24(₩🛏20) ☎ P10
Credit Cards ①②③

★★**Normandie** (Inter) 41 bd Vauban (n.rest)
☎86525780
₩🛏47 ☎ Lift ℂ
Credit Cards ①②③④⑤

★*Seignelay* **LE**2 r Pont ☎86520348
Closed 15 Feb-16 Mar
rm21(₩🛏14)
Credit Cards ①③

At **APPOIGNY**(9.5km NW N6)

★★★*Mercure* CD319 Lieu-dit-le Chaumois
☎86532500 tx 800095
₩🛏82 P120 ⌿
Credit Cards ①②③⑤

★★*Climat* chemin des Ruelles ☎86532711 tx
351888
₩🛏26 P30
Credit Cards ①②③

AUXONNE
Côte-d'Or

★*Corbeau* **LE**1 r de Berbis ☎80311188
Closed 16 Dec-9 Jan:Rest closed Mon
₩🛏10 P10
Credit Cards ①②③④⑤

At **VILLERS-LES-POTS**(5km NW)

★★*Auberge du Cheval Rouge* **LE**☎80314488
:Rest closed Sat lunch & Sun evening
₩🛏10 P15
Credit Cards ①②③

AVALLON
Yonne
★★★★**Poste** (Relais et Châteaux) 13 pl Vauban
☎86340612 tx 351806
Mar-Nov :Rest closed Mon
rm23(⇌♠22) ☎ P12
Credit Cards ①③⑤

★★**Moulin des Ruats** DPn Vallée du Cousin
(4.5km W via D957 & D427) (n.rest) ☎86340774
15 Feb-15 Nov :Rest closed Mon & Tue in season
⇌♠27 P25
Credit Cards ①③⑤

★★**Relais Fleuri** LESortie Autoroute A6 (5km E
on N6) ☎86340285 tx 800084
⇌♠48 P50 ℁ ⊐
Credit Cards ①②③⑤

AVIGNON
Vaucluse
See also VILLENEUVE-LES-AVIGNON
★★★**Mercure Avignon Sud** rte Marseille-La
Barbière ☎90889110 tx 431994
⇌♠105 Lift ⊐
Credit Cards ①②③⑤

★★★**Novotel Avignon-Sud** rte de Marseille (N7)
☎90876236 tx 432878
⇌♠79 ⊐
Credit Cards ①②③⑤

★★**Angleterre** LE29 bd de Raspail (n.rest)
☎90863431
Closed 16 Dec-14 Jan
rm40(⇌♠36) P13 Lift
Credit Cards ①③

★★**Balladins** av du Grand Gigognan,Z.I. de
Courtine ☎90868892
⇌♠38 P
Credit Cards ①②③

★★**Ibis** angle av Montclar,bd St-Roch
☎90853838 tx 432502
⇌♠98 Lift
Credit Cards ①③

★★**Midi** (FAH) 25 r de la République (n.rest)
☎90821556 tx 431074
⇌♠57 Lift ℂ
Credit Cards ①②③④⑤

✎ **Auto Service** 4 bd Limbert,1 rte de Montfavet
☎ 90863958 P Rov

✎ **Automobile du Centre** 1 bis rte de Morières
☎ 90821676 For

✎ **EGSA** Centre des Affaires Cap Sud,rte de
Marseille ☎ 90876322 Aud

At **AVIGNON NORD AUTOROUTE JUNCTION
A7**(8km E by D942)
★★★★**Avignon Nord** ☎90311643 tx 432869
⇌♠100 P150 Lift ℁ ⊐
Credit Cards ①②③⑤

At **MONTFAVET**(5.5km E)
★★**Campanile** ZA du Clos de la Cristole
☎90899977 tx 432060
⇌♠42 P42
Credit Card ③

★★**Climat de l'Amandier** allée des Fenaisons
☎90881300
⇌♠30 ☎ P40 Lift

★★**Ibis** rte de Marseille (N 7),Zone de la Cristole
☎90871100 tx 432811
⇌♠69 Lift ⊐
Credit Cards ①③

AVIGNON NORD AUTOROUTE JUNCTION A7
See **AVIGNON**

AVON
See **FONTAINEBLEAU**

AVRANCHES
Manche
★★**Croix d'Or** DPn 83 r de la Constitution
☎33580488
mid Mar-mid Nov
rm30(⇌♠25) A4rm ☎ P15
Credit Cards ①③

★★**St-Michel** DPn 5 pl Gl-Patton ☎33580191
Etr-15 Nov :Rest closed Sun evening & Mon
rm24(⇌♠16) ☎ P15
Credit Cards ①③

AX-LES-THERMES
Ariège
★★★**Royal Thermal** (MAP/BW) espl de
Couloubret ☎61642251 tx 530955
rm68(⇌♠54) P30 Lift ℂ Mountain
Credit Cards ①②③⑤

★★**Moderne** LE20 av du Dr-Gomma
☎61642024
Feb-Oct
⇌♠22 ☎ Lift Mountain

★★**Roy René** LEDPn 11 av du Dr-Gomma
☎61642228
Jan-Oct
⇌♠29 ☎ P18 Lift Mountain
Credit Cards ①②③

★**Lauzeraie** prom du Couloubret (n.rest)
☎61642070
Feb-15 Nov
⇌♠33 Lift Mountain
Credit Cards ①③

AZAY-LE-RIDEAU
Indre-et-Loire
★★**Grand Monarque** LEDPn pl République
☎47454008
rm28(⇌♠25) P12
Credit Cards ①②③

BAGNÈRES-DE-BIGORRE
Hautes-Pyrénées
★★**Résidence** Pn Parc Thermal de Salut
☎62950397
Apr-15 Oct
⇌♠31 P70 ℁ Mountain
Credit Cards ①③

★★**Vignaux** LE16 r de la République
☎62950341
rm15(⇌♠2)

BAGNEUX
See **SAUMUR**

BAGNOLES-DE-L'ORNE
Orne
★★★**Lutetia-Reine Astrid** (FAH) DPn bd P-
Chalvet,pl du Gl-de-Gaulle ☎33379477
28 Mar-2 Nov
⇌♠34 A14rm
Credit Cards ①③⑤

★★**Bois Joli** (FAH) av P-du-Rozier ☎33379277
tx 171782
Etr-Oct
rm20(⇌♠17) P15 Lift Lake
Credit Cards ①②③⑤

★★**Ermitage** (Inter-Hotels) 24 bd P-Chalvet
(n.rest) ☎33379622 tx 77274
May-Sep
rm39(⇌♠29) ☎ P20 Lift
Credit Cards ①③

BAGNOLET
See **PARIS**

BAGNOLS-EN-FORÊT
Var
★★**Auberge Bagnolaise** LErte Fayence
☎94406024
May-Sep
⇌♠8 P Mountain

BAIX
Ardèche
★★★**Cardinale** (Relais et Châteaux) quai du
Rhône ☎75858040 tx 346143
Mar-2 Jan :Rest closed Thu & Fri
⇌♠15 A10rm ⊐ Mountain
Credit Cards ①②③⑤

BALARUC-LE-VIEUX
Hérault
★★**Balladins** Zone Commerciale de Balaruc
le,Vieux ☎67801980 tx 649394
⇌♠38 P28
Credit Cards ①②③

BANDOL
Var
★★★★**Pullman Ile Rousse** DPn bd L-Lumière
☎94294686 tx 400372
⇌♠53 ☎ P25 Lift ℂ ⊐ Beach Sea
Credit Cards ①②③⑤

★★**Baie** 62 r Marçon (n.rest) ☎94294082
⇌♠14 ℂ Sea
Credit Cards ①③

★★**Golf** Plage de Renécros (n.rest) ☎94294583
tx 400383
Etr-Oct
rm24(⇌♠23) P25 ℂ Beach Sea
Credit Cards ①③

★★**Provençal** DPn r des Écoles ☎94295211 tx
400308
:Rest closed Nov-Etr
rm22(⇌♠21) ℂ Sea
Credit Cards ①③

★★**Réserve** rte de Sanary ☎94294271
15 Jan-15 Nov
⇌♠16 P13 Sea
Credit Cards ①②③⑤

BANYULS-SUR-MER
Pyrénées-Orientales
★★★**Catalan** rte Cerbère ☎68880280
Apr-Oct
⇌♠36 Lift ℂ ℁ ⊐ Sea Mountain
Credit Cards ①②③⑤

BAPAUME
Pas-de-Calais
★**Paix** 11 av A-Guidet ☎21071103
Closed 21 Dec-4 Jan:Rest closed Sat
rm16(⇌♠9) ☎
Credit Cards ①②③

BARBEN, LA
See **SALON-DE-PROVENCE**

BARBEREY
See **TROYES AIRPORT**

BARBEZIEUX
Charente
★★**Boule d'Or** LE(Inter) 9 bd Gambetta
☎45782272
rm28(⇌♠20) ☎ P15 ℁ ⊐
Credit Cards ①②③

✎ **Alain Cougnon** rte de Chalais ☎ 45782976
Peu Tal

At **BOIS-VERT**(11km S on N10)
★★**Venta** ☎45784095
:Rest closed 15-31 Dec
⇌♠23 ☎ P80 Lift ℁ ⊐
Credit Cards ①③

BARBIZON
Seine-et-Marne
★★★★★**Bas-Breau** (Relais et Châteaux) DPn
Grande Rue ☎60664005 tx 690953
Closed 2 Jan-2 Feb
⇌♠19 ☎ P15 ℂ ℁ ▱ ⊐
Credit Cards ①②③

★★**Charmettes** Grande Rue ☎60664021
Closed Feb
⇌♠39 ☎ P26

BARBOTAN-LES-THERMES
Gers

★★*Château-de-Bégue* (2km SW on N656)
☎62695008 tx 531918
2 May-Sep
rm14(✦11) ☎ P50 Lift
Credit Card ③

BARENTIN
See **ROUEN**

BARNEVILLE-CARTERET
Manche

At **BARNEVILLE PLAGE**

★★*Isles* **LE**bd Maritime ☎33049076
Feb-25 Nov
rm35(✦32) Sea
Credit Cards ① ② ③ ⑤

At **CARTERET**

★★*Angleterre* **LE**4 r de Paris ☎33538604
15 Mar-5 Nov
rm43(✦23) P20 Sea
Credit Cards ① ② ③ ⑤

★★*Marine* **LE**2 r de Paris ☎33538331
15 Feb-15 Nov
✦31 A3rm P13 Sea
Credit Cards ① ③ ⑤

BARNEVILLE PLAGE
See **BARNEVILLE-CARTERET**

BAR-SUR-AUBE
Aube

★*Commerce* 38 r Nationale ☎25270876
Closed Jan
rm15(✦12) P15
Credit Cards ① ② ③ ⑤

BAR-SUR-SEINE
Aube

★★*Barséquanais* 7 av Gl-Leclerc ☎25298275
15 Jan-15 Dec :Rest closed Sun pm,Mon lunch ex
Jul&Aug
rm28(✦17) A10rm P40
Credit Cards ① ③

BASTIDE-PUYLAURENT, LA
Lozère

★★*Pins* ☎66460007
Feb-Nov
✦25 P20 Mountain
Credit Cards ① ③

BAUGÉ
Maine-et-Loire

★*Boule d'Or* **LEDP**n 4 r du Cygne ☎41898212
15 Feb-15 Jan :Rest closed Sun evening & Mon
rm12(✦8) ☎ P6
Credit Cards ① ③

BAULE, LA
Loire-Atlantique

★★★*Bellevue-Plage* 27 bd Océan ☎40602855 tx
710459F
Feb-Nov :Rest closed Mon out of season
✦34 P27 Lift ℂ Sea
Credit Cards ① ② ③ ⑤

★★★*Majestic* espl F-André (n.rest) ☎40602486
tx 701905
14 Apr-15 Oct
✦67 P30 Lift ℂ Sea
Credit Cards ② ③ ⑤

★★*Concorde* 1 av de la Concorde (n.rest)
☎40602309
Apr-Oct
✦47 ☎ P7 Lift Sea
Credit Cards ① ③

★★*Palmeraie* **LEP**n 7 allée Cormorans
☎40602441
26 Mar-Sep
✦23
Credit Cards ① ② ③ ⑤

★★*Riviera* 16 av des Lilas (n.rest) ☎40602897
May-Sep
rm20(✦16)
Credit Card ②

★★*Welcome* 7 av des Impairs (n.rest)
☎40603025
20 Mar-15 Oct
✦18 Sea
Credit Cards ① ③

◖◗ *St-Atlantic* 33 av G-Clemenceau ☎ 40602375
P AR

BAUME-LES-DAMES
Doubs

At **HYÈVRE-PAROISSE**(7km NE N83)

★★*Ziss* N83 ☎81840788
:Rest closed Sat lunch
✦21 ☎ P50 Lift Mountain
Credit Cards ① ② ③

BAVANS
See **MONTBÉLIARD**

BAYEUX
Calvados

★★★*Lion d'Or* **LEDP**n 71 r St-Jean
☎31920690
22 Jan-19 Dec
rm29(✦26) ☎ P14 ℂ
Credit Cards ① ② ③ ④ ⑤

★★*Bayeux* 9 r de Tardif (n.rest) ☎31927008 tx
171704
✦31 ☎ P5
Credit Cards ① ③

★★*Mogador* 20 r A-Chartier (n.rest) ☎31922458
✦14 ☎ P15
Credit Cards ① ③

BAYONNE
Pyrénées-Atlantiques

★★★*Agora* av J-Rostand ☎59633090 tx 550621
✦105 Lift
Credit Cards ① ② ③ ⑤

★★★*Capagorry* (MAP/BW) 14 r Thiers (n.rest)
☎59254822
rm48(✦35) ☎ P3 Lift ℂ
Credit Cards ① ② ③ ⑤

◖◗ *Sajons* 36 allée Marines ☎ 59254579 P All
makes

At **VILLEFRANQUE**(4km S)

★★★★*Château de Larraldia* ☎59442000 tx
540831
Jun-3 Oct
✦22 A4rm ℺ ◰ ◱ Mountain
Credit Cards ① ② ③ ⑤

BEAUCAIRE
Gard

★★★*Vignes Blanches* rte de Nîmes ☎66591312
tx 480690
Apr-15 Oct
✦62 P30 Lift ◱
Credit Card ③

BEAUGENCY
Loiret

★★*Ecu de Bretagne* **LE**pl du Martroi
☎38446760
7 Mar-30 Jan
rm26(✦17) A11rm ☎ P26
Credit Cards ① ② ③ ⑤

BEAULIEU-SUR-DORDOGNE
Corrèze

★★*Central* **LEDP**n ☎55910134
15 Mar-15 Nov
rm30(✦20) P20

★★*Chasselas-Farges* **LE**pl du Champ de Mars
☎55911104
rm18(✦11) A6rm ☎
Credit Cards ① ②

BEAULIEU-SUR-MER
Alpes-Maritimes

★★★★★*Réserve de Beaulieu* **DP**n 5 bd Gl-
Leclerc ☎93010001 tx 470301
23 Dec-19 Nov
✦50 ☎ P12 Lift ℂ ◱ Sea
Credit Cards ② ③ ⑤

★★★★*Métropole* (Relais et Châteaux) **P**n bd Gl-
Leclerc ☎93010008 tx 470304
20 Dec-20 Oct
✦50 P Lift ℂ ℺ ◰ Beach Sea

★★★*Victoria* 47 bd Marinoni ☎93010220 tx
470303
20 Dec-Sep
rm80(✦60) Lift ℂ Sea Mountain

BEAUMONT-SUR-SARTHE
Sarthe

★*Barque* 11 pl de la Libération ☎43970016
10 Jan-20 Dec
rm25(✦16) P12
Credit Cards ① ② ③

★*Chemin de Fer* **LE**La Gare ☎4397005
6 Nov-8 Feb & 3 Mar-15 Oct
rm15(✦9) A9rm ☎ P
Credit Cards ① ③

◖◗ *Thureau* rte Nationale 138 ☎ 43970033 P Peu
Tal

BEAUMONT-SUR-VESLE
Marne

★*Maison du Champagne* **LEDP**n ☎26039245
Nov-Jan & Mar-Sep :Rest closed Sun evening &
Mon
rm10(✦7) ☎ P12
Credit Cards ① ② ③ ⑤

BEAUNE
Côte-d'Or

★★★*Altea* Autoroute 6 ☎80214612 tx 350627
✦150 P150
Credit Cards ① ② ③ ⑤

★★★*Cep* 27 r Maufoux ☎80223548 tx 351256
14 Mar-Nov
✦46 A6rm ☎ P Lift ℂ
Credit Cards ① ② ③ ⑤

★★★*Poste* **P**n 5 bd Clemenceau ☎80220811 tx
350982
Apr-mid Nov
rm25(✦24) ☎ P8 Lift ℂ Mountain
Credit Cards ① ② ③ ⑤

★★*Arcade* av du Gl-de-Gaulle,Rond Point de
l'Europe ☎80227567 tx 351287
✦41 P22 Lift ℂ
Credit Cards ① ③

★★*Balladins* Zac de la Chartreuse ☎05355575
tx 649394
✦38 P30
Credit Cards ① ② ③ ⑤

★★*Bourgogne* **LE**av C-de-Gaulle ☎80222200
tx 350666
Feb-Dec
✦120 Lift ℂ
Credit Cards ① ② ③ ⑤

★★*Central* **LEDP**n 2 r V-Millot ☎80247724
Closed Jan
✦20
Credit Cards ① ③

★★*Climat* ZA de la Chartreuse ☎80227410 tx
351384
✦38 P38
Credit Cards ① ② ③

★★*Ibis* av Ch-de-Gaulle ☎80224675 tx 351410
✦103 P120 Lift ℂ ◱
Credit Cards ① ③

★★*Samotel* **P**n rte de Pommard (N74)
☎80223555 tx 350596
✦65 P65 ◱ Mountain
Credit Cards ① ② ③ ⑤

◖◗ *Biais* 30 bd Foch ☎ 80247172 P Peu Tal

👄 Bolatre 40 fbg Bretonnière ☎ 80222803 **P** Fia Lan

At **LADOIX-SERRIGNY**(5km NE)

★★Paulands (n.rest) ☎80264105 tx 351293
rm21(➜🛏20) P20 ⌐
Credit Cards 1 3

At **MONTAGNY-LES-BEAUNE**(3km SE)

★★Campanile rte de Verdun ☎80226550 tx 350156
➜🛏42 P42
Credit Card 3

BEAURAINVILLE
Pas-de-Calais

★Val de Canche LEPn ☎21903233
Jan 15-Dec 24 :Rest closed Mon
rm10(➜🛏4) 🏤
Credit Cards 1 3

BEAUREPAIRE
Isère

★★Fiard 25 r de la République ☎74846202
10 Feb-1 Jan
➜🛏15 ℂ
Credit Cards 1 2 3 5

BEAUSSET, LE
Var

★★Auberge de la Gruppi LEDPn 46 rte Nationale 8 ☎94987018
Mar-Jan :Rest closed Tue
rm12(🛏4)
Credit Cards 1 2 3 4 5

BEAUVAIS
Oise

★★★Chenal 63 bd Gl-de-Gaulle (n.rest) ☎44450355 tx 145223
➜🛏29 P6 Lift ℂ
Credit Cards 1 2 3 5

★★★Mercure av Montaigne,ZAC St-Lazare ☎44020336 tx 150210
➜🛏60 P120 ⌐
Credit Cards 1 2 3 5

★★Campanile av Descartes ☎44052700 tx 150992
➜🛏47 P47
Credit Card 3

★Commerce LE11 & 13 r Chambiges (n.rest) ☎44481784
rm14(🛏6) 🏤 P4

★Palais 9 r St-Nicolas (n.rest) ☎44451258
➜🛏15
Credit Cards 1 2 3 4

BEAUVALLON
Var
See also STE-MAXIME

★Marie Louise DPn Guerrevieille ☎94960605
➜🛏14 P15 Sea
Credit Cards 1 3 5

BEAUVOIR
Manche

★★Gué de Beauvoir Château de Beauvoir (n.rest) ☎33600923
Etr-Sep
rm21(➜🛏8) P30
Credit Cards 1 3

BEG-MEIL
Finistère

★★Bretagne ☎98949804
Apr-Sep :Rest closed Tue
rm38(➜6) A18rm P100
Credit Cards 1 3

★★Thalamot LE Le Chemin Creux Fouesnant ☎98949738
23 Apr-2 Oct
rm35(➜🛏29) A4rm
Credit Cards 1 2 3

BELFORT
Territoire-de-Belfort

★★★Altea du Lion 2 r G-Clemenceau ☎84210914
☎84211700 tx 360914
➜🛏82 P150 Lift ℂ
Credit Cards 1 2 3 5

★★Climat r G-Defferre ☎84220984 tx 361017
➜🛏46 P30 Lift Mountain
Credit Cards 1 2 3

At **BESSONCOURT**(7km NE)

★★Campanile Exchangeur Belfort Nord ☎84299442 tx 360724
➜🛏46 P46
Credit Card 3

At **DANJOUTIN**(3km S)

★★★Mercure r de Dr-Jacquot ☎84215501 tx 360801
➜🛏80 P150 Lift ⌐
Credit Cards 1 2 3 5

BELIN-BELIET
Gironde

★Aliénor d'Aquitaine LEDPn ☎56880123
Mar-Nov
➜🛏12 P15

👄 Firmin Burgana RN10 ☎ 56880139 **P** Peu

BELLÊME
Orne

★Relais St Louis 2 bd Bansart-des-Bois ☎33731221
20 Mar-Dec. :Rest closed Wed
rm9(➜🛏7) 🏤 P6

BELLERIVE-SUR-ALLIER
See VICHY

BENODET
Finistère

★★Ancre de Marine av l'Odet 6 ☎98570529
15 Mar-5 Nov
rm25(➜🛏14) Sea
Credit Cards 1 3

★★Poste (FAH) r Église 17 ☎98570109 tx 941818
:Rest closed Mon
rm36(➜🛏32) A17rm 🏤 P10
Credit Cards 1 2 3 4 5

BERCK-PLAGE
Pas-de-Calais

★★Homard Bleu DPn 44-48 pl de l'Entonnoir ☎21090465
:Rest closed Sun evening & Mon
➜🛏18
Credit Cards 1 2 3

BERGERAC
Dordogne

★★Bordeaux LE38 pl Gambetta ☎53571283 tx 550412
Feb-Nov
➜🛏42 Lift ℂ ⌐
Credit Cards 1 2 3 5

★★Commerce LE(FAH) 36 pl Gambetta ☎53273050 tx 541888
Mar-10 Feb :Rest closed Sun evening
➜🛏30 Lift
Credit Cards 1 2 3 5

👄 Ets Jean Geraud pl du Pont ☎ 53576272 Peu Tal

BERGUES
Nord
See also DUNKERQUE

★★Motel 25 Autoroute Lille-Dunkerque ☎28687900 tx 132309
➜🛏42 ℂ ⚓ Lake
Credit Cards 1 2 3 5

★Tonnelier 4 r de Mont-de-Piété ☎28687005
20 Jan-17 Aug & 4-31 Oct :Rest closed Fri
rm11(🛏7) 🏤 P5
Credit Cards 1 3 4

BERNAY
Eure

★Angleterre et Cheval Blanc LEDPn 10 r Gl-de-Gaulle ☎32431259
rm23(➜🛏3) P50
Credit Cards 1 2 3 5

👄 Ets Lefèvre rte de Broglie,RN138 ZI ☎ 32433428 **P** Peu Tal

BESANÇON
Doubs

★★★★Altea Parc Micaud 3 av E-Droz ☎81801444 tx 360268
➜🛏95 P100 Lift
Credit Cards 1 2 3 4 5

★★★Novotel 22 bis r de Trey ☎81501466 tx 360009
➜🛏107 Lift ⌐
Credit Cards 1 2 3 4 5

★★Arcade 21 r Gambetta (n.rest) ☎81835054 tx 361247
➜🛏49 🏤 P Lift
Credit Cards 1 3

★★Balladins r B-Russell ☎81515251
➜🛏28 P25
Credit Cards 1 2 3

★★Ibis 4 av Carnot ☎81803311 tx 361276
➜🛏66 Lift
Credit Cards 1 3

★★Paris 33 r des Granges ☎81813656 tx 361301
rm56(➜🛏40) 🏤 P38 ℂ
Credit Cards 1 2 3

★★Urbis 5 av Foch ☎81882726 tx 361576
➜🛏96 Lift ℂ
Credit Cards 1 3

★Gambetta 13 r Gambetta (n.rest) ☎81820233
rm26(➜🛏19)
Credit Cards 1 2 3 5

★Granvelle 13 r de G-Lecourbe (n.rest) ☎81813392
rm26(➜🛏22) P12 ℂ
Credit Cards 1 2 3 5

👄 Auto Dépannage 9 r A-Fanart ☎ 81501332 **P** Cit

👄 Est Auto 18 av Carnot ☎ 81807218 For

👄 M Morel 48 r de Vesoul ☎ 81503673 Peu

At **CHÂTEAU-FARINE**(6km SW)

★★★Epicure 159 r de Dôle (n.rest) ☎81520400 tx 360167
➜🛏59 P60 Lift ⌐
Credit Cards 1 2 5

At **ÉCOLE-VALENTIN**(4.5km NW)

★★Campanile ZAC de Valentin ☎81535222 tx 361172
➜🛏55 P55
Credit Card 3

★★Climat La Combe Oudotte ☎81880411 tx 361651
➜🛏43
Credit Cards 1 2 3

BESSE-EN-CHANDESSE
Puy-de-Dôme

★★Beffroy ☎73795008
Closed Nov
rm16(➜🛏14) 🏤 P

BESSINES-SUR-GARTEMPE
Haute-Vienne

★★★Toit de Chaume Rn 20-Rocade Bessines Sud (5km S on Limoges rd) ☎55760102 tx 580915
➜🛏20 🏤 P40 ⌐
Credit Cards 1 2 3 5

★★Vallée LEPn ☎55760166
Closed Feb: Rest closed Sun evening
rm20(➜🛏16) P6
Credit Cards 1 3

BESSONCOURT
See **BELFORT**

BÉTHUNE
Pas-de-Calais
★★**Vieux Beffroi** 48 Grand pl ☎21681500 tx 134105
rm65(➡♒59) A29rm P300 Lift ℂ ℚ
Credit Cards ① ② ③ ⑤
★**Bernard et Gare LE**3 pl de la Gare (n.rest) ☎21572002
rm33(➡♒23)
Credit Cards ① ③
At **BEUVRY**(4km SE)
★★★**France II** 11 r du Gl-Leclerc ☎21651100 tx 110691
➡♒54 ☎ P150 Lift
Credit Cards ① ② ③ ⑤

BEUVRY
See **BÉTHUNE**

BEYNAC-ET-CAZENAC
Dordogne
★★**Bonnet LEDPn** ☎53295001
14 Apr-15 Oct
rm22(➡♒20) ☎ P40
Credit Cards ① ③

BEYNOST
See **LYON**

BÉZIERS
Hérault
★★★**Imperator** (Inter-Hotels) 28 allée P-Riquet (n.rest) ☎67490225 tx 490608
➡♒45 ☎ Lift ℂ
Credit Cards ① ② ③ ⑤
★★**Ibis** Echangeur Béziers-Est ☎67625514 tx 480938
➡♒50 Lift
Credit Cards ① ③

BIARD
See **POITIERS**

BIARRITZ
Pyrénées-Atlantiques
★★★★★**Palais** 1 av de l'Imperatrice ☎59240940 tx 57000
15 Mar- Nov
➡♒138 P150 Lift ℂ ⊇ Sea
Credit Cards ① ② ③ ⑤
★★★★**Miramar** av de l'Imperatrice ☎59413000 tx 540831
➡♒126 ☎ P10 Lift ℂ ⊇ Sea Mountain
Credit Cards ① ② ③ ④ ⑤
★★★**Regina & Golf** 52 av de l'Imperatrice ☎59413300 tx 541330
➡♒70 P40 Lift ℂ ℚ ⊇ Sea Lake
Credit Cards ① ② ③ ④ ⑤
★★★**Windsor** (Inter-Hotels) Grande Plage ☎59240852
15 Mar-15 Oct
➡♒37 Lift ℂ Sea
Credit Cards ① ② ③ ④
★★**Beau-Lieu** 3 espl du Port-Vieux (n.rest) ☎59242359
15 Feb-Dec
rm26(➡♒22) Sea
Credit Cards ① ② ③
★★**Campanile** rte d'Espagne ☎59234041 tx 572120
➡♒41 P41
Credit Card ③
★**Palacito** 1 r Gambetta (n.rest) ☎59240489
➡♒26 Lift
Credit Cards ① ② ③
🛏 **Darrort** 4 r Loeb ☎ 59410063 **P** Rov

BIDART
Pyrénées-Atlantiques
★★★**Bidartea** (MAP/BW) rte d'Espagne N10 ☎59549468 tx 573441
16 Feb-1 Jan :Rest closed Mon & Sun in winter
➡♒36 A6rm ☎ P60 Lift ⊇ Sea Mountain
Credit Cards ① ② ③ ⑤

BLAGNAC
See **TOULOUSE AIRPORT**

BLANGY-SUR-BRESLE
Seine-Maritime
★**Poste Pn** 44 Grand r ☎35935020
15 Jan-15 Dec :Rest closed Mon lunch & Fri eve Nov-Mar
rm12 P10
Credit Cards ① ③
★**Ville Pn** 2 r Notre-Dame ☎35935157
Closed 6-26 Jul:Rest closed Sun
rm9(➡♒8) A3rm
Credit Card ③
🛏 *St-Denis* 6 r St-Denis ☎ 35935042 **P**

BLAYE
Gironde
★★**Citadelle** pl d'Armes ☎57421710 tx 540127
rm34(➡♒27) A13rm P80 ℂ ⊇ Sea
Credit Cards ① ② ③ ⑤

BLÉRE
Indre-et-Loire
★**Cher Pn** 9 r Pont ☎47579515
➡♒19 A8rm ☎ P10
Credit Cards ① ③

BLÉRIOT-PLAGE
Pas-de-Calais
★**Dunes Pn** N48 ☎21345430
rm13(➡♒8) ☎ P10
Credit Cards ② ③ ⑤

BLOIS
Loir-et-Cher
★★**Campanile** r de la Vallée Maillard ☎54744466 tx 751628
➡♒54 P54
Credit Card ③
★★**Ibis** 15 r de la Vallée Maillard ☎54746060 tx 750959
➡♒40 Lift
Credit Cards ① ③
★★**Urbis** 3 r Porte Côté (n.rest) ☎54740117 tx 752287
➡♒55 Lift ℂ
Credit Cards ① ② ③
★**Bellay LE**12 r Minimes (n.rest) ☎54782362 tx 750135
rm12(➡♒6) A2rm
★**St-Jacques** pl Gare (n.rest) ☎54780415
Closed 25 Dec-1 Jan
rm33(➡♒20) ℂ
Credit Cards ① ③
★**Viennois** 5 quai A-Contant (n.rest) ☎54741280
15 Jan-15 Dec
rm26(➡♒20) A15rm
🛏 **M Gueniot** 74 Leveé des Tuileries ☎ 54789463 **P**
At **CHAUSSÉE ST-VICTOR, LA**(4km N)
★★★**Novotel Blois l'Hermitage** ☎54783357 tx 750232
➡♒116 P105 Lift ⊇ Lake
Credit Cards ① ② ③ ⑤
At **ST-GERVAIS-LA-FORÊT**(3km SE)
★★**Balladins** r G-Melies ☎54426990
➡♒36 P30
Credit Cards ① ② ③

At **VINEUIL**(4km SE)
★★**Climat** 48 r des Quatre-Vents ☎54427022 tx 752302
➡♒58 P60
Credit Cards ① ② ③

BLONVILLE-SUR-MER
Calvados
★**Mer LE**93 av de la République (n.rest) ☎31879323
Feb-Nov
rm20(➡♒14) P20 Sea
Credit Cards ① ③

BOBIGNY
Seine-St-Denis
★★**Campanile** ZUP des Sablons,304 av P-V-Couturier ☎48313755 tx 233027
➡♒120 P Lift
Credit Card ③
★★**Ibis** 15 r H-Berlioz ☎48960730 tx 231452
➡♒80 P80 Lift
Credit Cards ① ③

BOCCA, LA
See **CANNES**

BOIS-GUILLAUME
See **ROUEN**

BOISSEUIL
Haute-Vienne
★**Relais** ☎55711183
Closed 10-31 Dec
➡♒13 A3rm P9

BOIS-VERT
See **BARBEZIEUX**

BOLLENBERG
See **ROUFFACH**

BOLLÈNE
Vaucluse
★★**Campanile** av T-Aubanel ☎90300042 tx 432017
➡♒30 P30
Credit Card ③

BONNEUIL-SUR-MARNE
Val-de-Marne
★★**Campanile** ZA des Petits Carreaux,2 av des Bleuets ☎43777029 tx 211251
➡♒50 P50
Credit Card ③

BONNEVAL
Eure-et-Loir
★★**Bois Guibert** rte Nationale 10 ☎37472233
rm17(➡♒8) ☎ P50
Credit Cards ① ② ③

BONNEVILLE
Haute-Savoie
★★**Sapeur** pl de l'Hôtel-de-Ville ☎50972068 :Rest closed Mon
➡♒18 P20 Lift Mountain
At **CONTAMINE-SUR-ARVE**(8km NW)
★**Tourne-Bride Pn** ☎50036218 :Rest closed Mon
rm7 P12
Credit Cards ① ③

BONNY-SUR-LOIRE
Loiret
★★**Fimotel-Val De Loire** rte 7 ☎38316462
➡♒46 P70
Credit Cards ② ③ ⑤
🛏 **Parot** 139 Grande Rue ☎ 38316332 **P** Ren

BORDEAUX
Gironde

Capital of Aquitaine, a region noted for its pleasant climate, beautiful scenery and superb beaches, Bordeaux lies in a sweeping plain beside the wine-producing district of Médoc. The city - which belonged to the English during the turbulent period from 1154-1453 - retains a wealth of monuments and sites from Roman and medieval times, though much of the present elegance dates from the 18th century.

EATING OUT Aquitaine's cuisine is rich and varied. Among the dishes to look out for are *entrecôte Bordelaise*, mushrooms, and all fish and shellfish dishes. Smoked chicken, turkey escalopes, turkey roasts and ragout of wild duck are typical delicacies in and around the city, as are oysters from Arcachon and young eels from the Adour river near Biarritz. The delicious smoked ham from Bayonne is used in a fish dish made from fresh mountain stream trout, cooked with shredded ham. For dessert, *gâteau Basque*, a rich, moist butter sponge cake flavoured with ground almonds or fruit, is particularly tasty, and stuffed walnuts are another speciality. Excellent fish dishes can be enjoyed at *Chez Philippe*, in Place du Parlement, and good regional fare at *Tulipa*, in rue Porte de la Monnaie.

BORDEAUX
Gironde
★★★★**Aquitania Sofitel** Parc des Expositions ☎56508380 tx 570557
⊶210 Lift ℃ ⌣ Lake
Credit Cards ① ② ③ ④ ⑤
★★★★**Mercure Bordeaux le Lac** quartier du Lac ☎56509030 tx 540077
⊶108 P Lift ℃ ⌣ Lake
Credit Cards ② ⑤
★★★★**Pullman Meriadeck** 5 r R-Lateulade ☎(33)56564343 tx 540565
⊶196 P Lift
Credit Cards ① ② ③ ⑤
★★★**Normandie** 7 cours 30-Juillet (n.rest) ☎56521680 tx 570481
⊶100 Lift ℃
Credit Cards ① ② ③ ⑤
★★★**Novotel Bordeaux-le-Lac** av J-G-Domergue ☎56509970 tx 570274
⊶176 Lift ⌣ Lake
Credit Cards ① ② ③ ⑤

★★★**Sofitel** Centre Hôtelier ☎56509014 tx 540097
⊶100 Lift ℃ ⌣
Credit Cards ① ② ③ ⑤
★★**Arcade** 60 r Eugéne le Roy ☎56914040 tx 550952
⊶140 ☎ P Lift
Credit Cards ① ③
★★**Bayonne** (Inter-Hotels) 15 cours de l'Intendance (n.rest) ☎56480088
Jan-15 Dec
rm37(**⊶**25) Lift
Credit Card ③
★★**Campanile** quartier du Lac ☎56395454 tx 560425
⊶150 P150 Lake
Credit Card ③
★★**Campaville** quartier du Lac (n.rest) ☎56399540 tx 572877
⊶41
Credit Card ③
★★**Hotel Campaville** Angle cours Clemenceau (n.rest) ☎56529898 tx 541079
⊶45
Credit Card ③
★★**Ibis** 8 r A-Becquerel,Parc Industriel,Pessac ☎56072784 tx 572294
⊶87 P80 Lift
Credit Cards ① ③
★★**Ibis Bordeaux-le-Lac** quartier du Lac ☎56509050 tx 550346
⊶119 Lift
Credit Cards ① ③
★★**Sèze** 23 allées Tourny (n.rest) ☎56526554 tx 572808
rm25(**⊶**22) Lift ℃
Credit Cards ① ② ③ ④ ⑤
★**Etche-Ona** 11 r Mautrec (n.rest) ☎56443649 tx 570362
⊶33 Lift ℃
Credit Cards ① ③
✿ **P Mercier** 162-166 r de la Benauge ☎56862133 DJ Maz RR
✿ **Ste Nouvelle** 107 r G-Bonnac ☎56968026 Peu Tal
✿ **SAFI 33** 486 rte de Toulouse ☎56378008 **P** For
At ARTIGUES(7km NE)
★★**Campanile** av J-F-Kennedy ☎56327332 tx 541745
⊶50 P50
Credit Card ③
At BOUSCAT, LE(4km NW)
★★**Campanile** rte du Médoc ☎56283384 tx 571622
⊶50 P50
Credit Card ③
At CESTAS(15km SW)
★**Campanile** Aire de Service de Bordeaux,Cestas A63 ☎56218068 tx 540408
⊶39 P39
Credit Card ③
At GRADIGNAN(6km SW)
★★**Beausoleil** ☎56890048 tx 540322
:Rest closed Sat & Sun evening
⊶32 P40 Lift
Credit Cards ① ② ③ ⑤
At LORMONT(5km NE)
★★**Climat** Carrefour des 4 Pavillons,(N10) ☎56329610 tx 612241
⊶38 P
At MÉRIGNAC(5km W on D106)
★★★**Novotel Bordeaux Aéroport** av du Près-Kennedy ☎56341025 tx 540320
⊶100 ⌣
Credit Cards ① ② ③ ⑤

★★**Campanile** av du Prés-Kennedy ☎56344362 tx 550496
⊶47 P47
Credit Card ③
★★**Fimotel** av du Près-Kennedy ☎56343308 tx 541315
⊶60 P50 Lift ℃ ⌣
Credit Cards ① ② ③ ⑤
★★**Ibis Bordeaux Aéroport** av du Prés-Kennedy ☎56341019 tx 541430
⊶64 P50 ℃
Credit Cards ① ③

BORMES-LES-MIMOSAS
Var
★★**Safari** rte Stade (n.rest) ☎94710983 tx 404603
Apr-15 Oct
rm32(**⊶**30) ☎ P50 ☎ ⌣ Sea
Credit Cards ① ② ③ ⑤
★**Belle Vue** L pl Gambetta ☎94711515
Feb-Sep
rm14(**⊶**13) Sea
Credit Card ①

BOSSONS, LES
See **CHAMONIX-MONT-BLANC**

BOULOGNE-BILLANCOURT
See **PARIS**

BOULOGNE-SUR-MER
Pas-de-Calais
See plan page 130 Agent:see page 109
See also **PORTEL, LE**
★★**Alexandra** 93 r Thiers ☎21305222
Feb-Dec
⊶20 P ℃
Credit Cards ① ② ③
★★**Arcade** Angle bd Ewvin,r Crte Neuve (n.rest) ☎42682345 tx 215059
⊶51 ☎ P Lift Sea
Credit Cards ① ③
★★**Climat** pl Rouget-de-Lisle ☎21801450 tx 135570
⊶47 Lift ℃
Credit Cards ① ③
★★**Faidherbe** 12 r Faidherbe (n.rest) ☎21316093
⊶35 ☎ P10 Lift ℃ Sea
Credit Cards ① ③
★★**Ibis** (Inter-Hotels) bd Diderot,quartier L-Danremont ☎21301240 tx 160485
⊶79 Lift
Credit Cards ① ③
★★**Lorraine** 7 pl de Lorraine (n.rest) ☎21313478
rm21(**⊶**17) ℃
Credit Cards ① ② ③
★★**Métropole** (Inter-Hotels) 51 r Thiers (n.rest) ☎21315430
5 Jan-20 Dec
rm27(**⊶**22) Lift ℃
Credit Cards ① ② ③ ④
★**Hamiot** 1 r Faidherbe ☎21314420
rm21 Lift
Credit Cards ① ③
★**Londres** 22 pl de France (n.rest) ☎21313563
rm20(**⊶**16) P8 Lift
Credit Cards ① ③
✿ **Auto Channel** bd de la Liane ☎21920330 AR
✿ **St-Christophe** 128 bd de la Liane ZI ☎21920911 Peu Tal
✿ **SNAB** 122 bd de la Liane ☎21806680 Aud Vol

BOULOU, LE
Pyrénées-Orientales
✿ **Noguer J** 1 r de Catalogne ☎68833057 Peu Tal

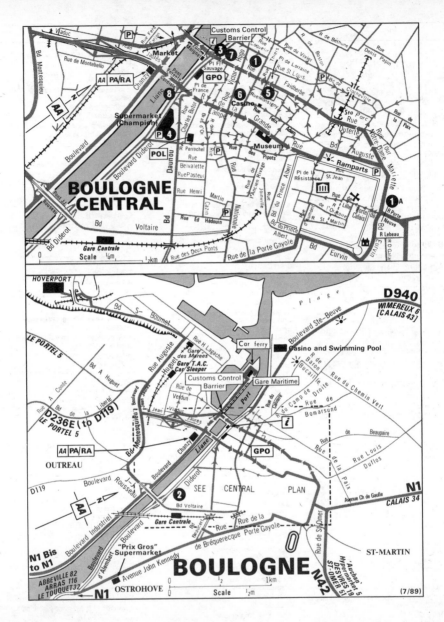

BOULOGNE

1	★★	Alexandra
1A	★★	Arcade
2	★★	Climat
3	★★	Faidherbe
4	★★	Ibis
5	★★	Lorraine
6	★★	Métropole
7	★	Hamiot
8	★	Londres

BOURBON-LANCY
Seine-et-Loire

★★**Raymond** LEDPn 8 r d'Autun ☎85891739
rm19(➜12) ᐠ P19
Credit Cards [1] [3] [5]

BOURDEILLES
See BRANTÔME

BOURG-EN-BRESSE
Ain

★★★**Logis de Brou** 132 bd Brou (n.rest)
☎74221155
➜30 ᐠ P10 Lift ℂ
Credit Cards [1] [2] [3] [5]

★★★**Prieuré** 49 bd de Brou (n.rest) ☎74224460
➜14 ᐠ P14 Lift ℂ
Credit Cards [1] [2] [3] [5]

★★**Chantecler** (MAP/BW) 10 av Bad Kreuznach
☎74224488 tx 380468
➜30 P30
Credit Cards [1] [2] [3] [4] [5]

★★**Ibis** ZAC de la Croix Blanche,bd Ch-de-Gaulle
☎74225266 tx 900471
➜63 P55 ℂ
Credit Cards [1] [2] [3]

⭐**Mevnier** rte de Strasbourg,Viriat ☎ 74222080
P Rov LR

BOURGES
Cher

★★**Christina** 5 r Halle (n.rest) ☎48705650
rm76(🛏52) A4rm Lift ☾
Credit Cards ①②③④⑤

★★**Monitel** 73 r Barbes ☎48502362 tx 783397
3 Jan-23 Dec :Rest closed Sat lunch Sun evening
🛏48 P20 Lift
Credit Cards ①②③⑤

★★**Poste** 22 r Moyenne (n.rest) ☎48700806
rm34(🛏22) A5rm ☎ P12 Lift ☾

★★**St-Jean** 23 av M-Dormoy (n.rest) ☎48241348
Mar-Jan
rm24(🛏🍴) ☎ P8 Lift
Credit Cards ①③

★★**Tilleuls** (Inter-Hotels) 7 pl de la Pyrotechnic
(n.rest) ☎48204904 tx 782026
🛏29 A9rm ☎ P20
Credit Cards ①③⑤

🚙 **Carrosserie Berthot** 136 bis rte de Nevers ☎
48504210 P Rov

At **ST-DOULCHARD**(2km S)

★★**Campanile** Le Detour du Pave ☎48702053 tx
780400
🛏42 P42
Credit Card ③

BOURGET AIRPORT, LE
See **PARIS AIRPORTS**

BOURG-LÈS-VALENCE
See **VALENCE**

BOURGNEUF-LA-FORÊT, LE
Mayenne

★ **Vielle Auberge** pl de l'Église ☎43371700
Feb-Dec :Rest closed Sun evening
rm8(🛏🍴2) ☎ P10
Credit Cards ①②③

BOURGOIN-JALLIEU
Isère

★★**Campanile** ZAC de St-Hubert l'Isle,d'Abeau
Est ☎74270122 tx 308232
🛏50
Credit Card ③

★★**Climat** 15 r E-Branly,ZAC de la Maladière
☎74285229 tx 308152
🛏42 P50
Credit Cards ①②③⑤

🚙 **Giroud** rte de Lyon,Domarin ☎ 74283244 P
AR

BOURG-ST-MAURICE
Savoie

★★**Petit St-Bernard** Petit St Bernard,2 av Stade
☎79070432
20 Dec-15 Apr & 28 Jun-15 Sep
rm24(🛏18) ☎ P20 Mountain
Credit Cards ②③⑤

BOUSCAT, LE
See **BORDEAUX**

BOVES
See **AMIENS**

BRANTÔME
Dordogne

★★★**Chabrol** DPn 59 r Gambetta ☎53057015
:Rest closed Sun & Mon in Winter
🛏20
Credit Cards ②③⑤

★★★**Moulin de l'Abbaye** ☎53058022 tx 560570
May-Oct
🛏12 A3rm ☎ P14
Credit Cards ①②③④

At **BOURDEILLES**(10km SW)

★★★**Griffons** ☎53037561
Apr-Sep :Rest closed evenings
🛏10 ☎ P10 ☀ ⌒ Lake
Credit Cards ①②③⑤

BREST
Finistère

★★★**Novotel de Brest** rte de Gouesnou,ZAC de
Kergaradec ☎98023283 tx 940470
🛏85 ⌒
Credit Cards ①②③⑤

★★★**Sofitel Océania** 82 r de Siam ☎98806666
tx 940951
🛏82 Lift
Credit Cards ①②③⑤

At **GOUESNOU**(6km N)

★★**Campanile** ZA d'Activities de Kergaradec,av
du Baron ☎98416341 tx 941413
🛏42 P42
Credit Card ③

At **PLOUGASTEL-DAOULAS**(9.5km SE)

★★**Balladins** ☎98403200 tx 649394
🛏38 P38
Credit Cards ①②③

★★**Ibis Brest** rte de Quimper,quartier de Ty-
Menez ☎98405028 tx 940731
🛏45 P50 ☾
Credit Cards ①③

🚙 **Caroff** 2 r de Portzmoguer ☎ 98403732 Peu
Tal

BRÉVILLE-SUR-MER
Manche

★★**Mougine des Moulins à Vent** Les Moulins à
Vent (n.rest) ☎33502241
🛏7 P30 Sea
Credit Cards ①③⑤

BRIANÇON
Hautes-Alpes

★★**Cristol** LEPn 6 rte d'Italie ☎92202011
15 Dec-15 Nov
🛏16 ☎ P5 Mountain
Credit Cards ①②③⑤

At **STE-CATHÉRINE**

★★★**Mont Brison** 1 av Gl-de-Gaulle (n.rest)
☎92211455
15 Dec-2 Nov
rm44(🛏33) ☎ P15 Lift Mountain
Credit Cards ①③

★★★**Vauban** DPn 13 av Gl-de-Gaulle
☎92211211
20 Dec-10 Nov
rm44(🛏38) ☎ P25 Lift Mountain
Credit Cards ①③

BRIARE
Loiret

★**Cerf** 22 bd Buyser ☎38370080
Mar-15 Feb :Rest closed Wed low season
rm20(🛏10) A8rm ☎ P15
Credit Cards ①③

🚙 **SARL Relais Briarois Autos** 17 av de Lattre-
de-Tassigny ☎ 38370161 P Aud

BRICQUEBEC
Manche

★**Vieux Château** LE4 cour du Château
☎33522449
🛏22 A8rm ☀
Credit Cards ①③

BRIDORÉ
See **LOCHES**

BRIONNE
Eure

★**Logis de Brionne** LEDPn 1 pl St-Denis
☎32448173
:Rest closed Sun evening/ Mon low season
🛏13 ☎ P10
Credit Cards ①③

★**Vieux Donjon** Pn 19 r de la Soie ☎32448062
Mar-15 Nov & 10 Dec-15 Feb :Rest closed Mon
rm8(🛏4) P25
Credit Cards ①③

BRIOUDE
Haute-Loire

★★**Brivas** rte Puy ☎71501049 tx 392589
29 Dec-19 Nov :Rest restricted Fri & Sat in
season
🛏30 P50 Lift ⌒ Mountain
Credit Cards ①②③⑤

★★**Moderne** LE(FAH) 12 av V-Hugo
☎71500730
🛏17 P17

BRIVE-LA-GAILLARDE
Corrèze

★★★★**Mercure** rte Objat 5.5km NW via av Turgot
☎55871503 tx 590096
🛏57 P80 Lift ☾
Credit Cards ①②③④⑤

★★**Campanile** av Gl-Pouyade ☎55868855 tx
590838
🛏42 P42

★★**Crémaillère** LE53 av de Paris ☎55743247
🛏12
Credit Cards ①③

★★**Truffe Noir** 22 bd A-France ☎55743532
🛏35 Lift ☾
Credit Cards ①②③⑤

★**Montauban** LE6 av E-Herriot ☎55240038
Feb-Dec :Rest closed Mon midday & Fri evening
rm18(🛏11) ☎ P18
Credit Cards ①②③

🚙 **G Cremoux** 20 av du Ml-Bugeaud ☎
55236922 P Rov

🚙 **M Taurisson** 21-123 av de Toulouse ☎
55742542 P BMW

At **VARETZ**(14km NW)

★★★**Château de Castel Novel** LE(Relais et
Châteaux) ☎55850001 tx 590065
7 May-15 Oct
🛏37 A10rm P100 Lift ☾ ☀ ⛳ Mountain
Credit Cards ①②③⑤

BRON
See **LYON**

BROU
Eure-et-Loir

★**Plat d'Etain** LEpl des Halles ☎37470398
rm20(🛏10) A7rm ☎ P10
Credit Cards ①③

BUC
Yvelines

★★**Climat** r L-Pasteur ☎39564811 tx 699220
🛏43 P50
Credit Cards ①②③

BUCHÈRES
See **TROYES**

BUGUE, LE
Dordogne

★★★**Royal Vezère** (MAP/BW) pl H-de-Ville
☎53072001 tx 540710
May-Sep :Rest closed midday Mon & Thu
🛏53 ☎ Lift ☾ ⌒
Credit Cards ①②③⑤

BULLY-LES-MINES
Pas-de-Calais

★**Moderne** 144 r de la Gare ☎21291422
🛏36 ☎ P10
Credit Cards ①②③

BUXY
Saône-et-Loire

★**Girardot** pl de la Gare ☎85920404
15 Mar-8 Feb
rm11(🛏7) ☎ P10 Lift
Credit Cards ①③

CABRERETS
Lot

★**Grottes** DPn ☎65312702
15 May-15 Oct :Rest closed Sat midday (15 May-Jun)
rm18(₩↑9) A6rm P20 ➚
Credit Cards ①③

CADÉAC
See **ARREAU**

CAEN
Calvados

★★★★**Relais des Gourmets** 15 r Geôle
☎31860601 tx 171657
₩↑28 ⓐ P300 Lift ℂ
Credit Cards ①②③④⑤

★★★**Malherbe** pl Ml-Foch (n.rest) ☎31844006 tx 170555
₩↑44 P100 Lift ℂ
Credit Cards ①②③④⑤

★★★**Novotel** av de la Côte-de-Nacre ☎31930588 tx 170563
₩↑126 P140 Lift ➚
Credit Cards ①②③⑤

★★**Balladins** ZI de la Sphere (CD 60),rte de Lion-sur-Mer ☎314740000 tx 649394
₩↑38 P38
Credit Cards ①②③

★★**Bristol** (Inter) 31 r du XI Novembre ☎31845976 tx 170234
rm25(₩↑24) Lift
Credit Cards ①②③

★★**Château** 5 av du 6-Juin (n.rest) ☎31861537
₩↑25 ⓐ P5 Lift ℂ
Credit Cards ①③

★★**Climat de France** av Montgomery,Quartier du Musée Memorial ☎31443636 tx 772141
₩↑43 P48
Credit Cards ①②③

★**Bernières** 50 r de Bernières (n.rest) ☎31860126
rm15(₩↑12) ℂ
Credit Cards ①③

★**St-Jean** 20 r des Martyrs (n.rest) ☎31862335
₩↑15 P7
Credit Cards ①③

At **HÉROUVILLE-ST-CLAIR**

★★**Campanile** Parc Tertiaire,bd du Bois ☎31952924 tx 170618
₩↑43 P43
Credit Card ③

★★**Ibis** 4 Quartier Savary ☎31956000 tx 170755
₩↑89 P70 Lift ℂ
Credit Cards ①③

At **MONDEVILLE**(3.5km SE)

★★**Fimotel** rte de Paris (N1) ☎31343700 tx 171514
₩↑42 P30 Lift
Credit Cards ①②③⑤

CAGNES-SUR-MER
Alpes-Maritimes

★★★**Cagnard** (Relais et Châteaux) r Pontis Long ☎93207321 tx 462223
₩↑20 A6rm P10 Lift Sea Mountain
Credit Cards ①②③⑤

★★★**Tierce** bd de la Plage/bd Kennedy ☎93200209
6 Dec-25 Oct
₩↑23 ⓐ P23 Lift ℂ Sea Mountain

❧ **Garage Amblard-Les Tritons** 115 rte de Nice ☎ 93310678 P Peu

At **CROS-DE-CAGNES**(2km SE)

★★**Horizon** 111 bd de la Plage (n.rest) ☎93310995
20 Dec-3 Nov
₩↑44 P30 Lift Sea Mountain
Credit Cards ②③⑤

At **VILLENEUVE-LOUBET-PLAGE**

★★**Méditerranée** N98 (n.rest) ☎93200007
Closed Nov
₩↑16 P16

CAHORS
Lot

★★★**Wilson** 72 r Prés-Wilson (n.rest) ☎65354180 tx 533721
₩↑36 P15 Lift
Credit Cards ①③④

★★**France** Ⓛ252 av J-Jaurès (n.rest) ☎65351676 tx 520394
₩↑80 ⓐ P20 Lift
Credit Cards ①②③⑤

★**Terminus** Ⓛ5 av C-de-Freycinet ☎65352450
₩↑31 ⓐ P7 Lift ℂ
Credit Cards ①③

❧ **Lacassagne** av A-de-Monsie ☎ 65354510 P

❧ **Recuperautos** rte de Villefranche ☎ 65351516

At **LAROQUE-DES-ARC**(5km N)

★**Beau Rivage** ☎65353058
Etr-Oct :Rest closed Feb & Tue low season
₩↑16 P40
Credit Cards ①②③

CAISSARGUES-BOUILLARGUES
See **NÎMES**

CALAIS
Pas-de-Calais

See plan page 134; Agent Ⓐ
see page 109

Calais, only 21 miles from Dover, is the nearest French town to England, the largest town of its *département*, an important port and a popular holiday resort. At the north end of the Boulevard Jacquard is the Place du Soldat-Inconnu, the Square of the Unknown Soldier, where Rodin's famous statue stands before the *Hôtel de Ville*.

The George V bridge leads to Calais-Nord, largely rebuilt since 1945. The rue Royale runs north and south through this district, the 13th-century *Tour du Guet* standing to its right.

North of the ruined church of Notre-Dame, currently being restored, is the lighthouse (1848), an octagonal tower 167ft high, visible 38 miles away. For shoppers, the Gro supermarket on the Place d'Armes is convenient for car-ferry users, while the *Maison du Fromage*, across the Square, offers a selection of more than 200 cheeses.

EATING OUT One of the best restaurants in town is the comfortable *Le Channel*, in Boulevard de la Résistance. Specialities include *terrine de langoustes*.

CALAIS
Pas-de-Calais

★★★**Meurice** 5 r E-Roche ☎21345703 tx 135671
₩↑40 A15rm ⓐ P20 Lift ℂ
Credit Cards ②③⑤

★★**Bellevue** 25 pl d'Armes (n.rest) ☎21345375 tx 136702
rm56(₩↑50) ⓐ P40 Lift ℂ
Credit Cards ①②③⑤

★★**Campanile** r de Maubeuge,ZAC du Beau Marais ☎21343070 tx 135229
₩↑42 P42
Credit Card ③

★★**Climat** Digue G-Berthe ☎21346464 tx 135300
₩↑44 P50 Sea
Credit Cards ①②③⑤

★★**George-V** (FAH/Inter-Hotels) 36 r Royale ☎21976800 tx 135159
rm45(₩↑44) P20 Lift ℂ
Credit Cards ①②③⑤

★★**Ibis** r Greuze,ZUP du Beau-Marais ☎21966969 tx 135004
₩↑55 P50 ℂ
Credit Cards ①③

★★**Pacific** 40 r de Duc-de-Guise (n.rest) ☎21345024
₩↑23 A3rm ⓐ P8 ℂ
Credit Cards ①②③⑤

★**Beffroi** 10 r A-Gerschel (n.rest) ☎21344751
rm20(₩↑13) P8 ℂ
Credit Cards ①③⑤

★**Richelieu** 17 r Richelieu ☎21346160 tx 130886
₩↑15 ⓐ P ℂ
Credit Cards ①②③⑤

★**Sole Meunière** 53 r de la Mer (n.rest) ☎21343608
₩↑14 P ℂ Sea
Credit Cards ①③

❧ **Calais Nord** 361 av de St-Exupéry ☎ 21967242 Peu Tal

❧ **George V** 2-4 bd Clemenceau ☎ 21344004 P Peu Tal

❧ **L'Europe** 58 rte de St-Omer ☎ 21343575 P For

CALIGNAC
Lot-et-Garonne

★**Palmiers** ☎59247772
₩↑25 P50 ➚

CAMBO-LES-BAINS
Pyrénées-Atlantiques

★**Bellevue** r des Terrasses ☎59297322
15 Nov-1 Feb
₩↑28 P Mountain
Credit Card ③

CAMBRAI
Nord

★★★**Beatus** 718 av de Paris (n.rest) ☎27814570 tx 820597
₩↑26 ⓐ P22 ℂ
Credit Cards ①②③④⑤

★★★**Château de la Motte Fenelon** Sq du Château ☎27836138 tx 120285
₩↑29 A22rm P70 Lift ℚ
Credit Cards ②③⑤

★★**Campanile** rte de Bapaume ☎27816200 tx 820992
₩↑42 P42
Credit Card ③

★**Ibis** rte de Bapaume,Fontaine Notre-Dame ☎27835454 tx 135074
₩↑51 P40
Credit Cards ①③

★★**Mouton Blanc** 33 r A-Lorraine ☎27813016 tx 133365
rm31(₩↑27) ⓐ P6 Lift
Credit Cards ①②③

FRANCE

★★**Poste** 58-60 av de la Victoire (n.rest)
☎27813469
rm33(✚📞32) ☎ P6 Lift
Credit Cards ① ③

★**France** 37 r Lille (n.rest) ☎27813880
Closed 26 Dec-1 Jan & 5 Aug-27 Aug
rm24(✚📞7)
Credit Cards ① ② ③

CAMP-ST-LAURENT
See TOULON

CANCALE
Ille-et-Vilaine

★★**Continental LEPn** quai au Thomas
☎99896016
20 Mar-14 Nov
✚📞20 Sea
Credit Cards ① ③

CANET-PLAGE
Pyrénées-Orientales

★★★**Sables** r Vallée-du-Rhône ☎68802363 tx
505213
✚📞41 A17rm P20 Lift ⊒
Credit Cards ① ② ③ ⑤

★★**Mar-I-Cel** pl Centrale ☎68803216 tx 500997
Mar-Nov
✚📞71 A11rm P30 Lift ℂ 🖂 ⊒ Sea Mountain
Credit Cards ① ③ ⑤

CANNES
Alpes-Maritimes

Cannes is a fashionable resort in the Alpes-Maritimes *département* of France, 13 miles south-west of Nice. Until 1834 it was a small fishing village nestling beneath the ruins of an 11th-century castle at the head of the Golfe de la Napoule, and sheltered from the mistral by the Esterel. That year Lord Brougham, Britain's Lord Chancellor, *en route* to Nice when an outbreak of cholera forced the authorities to freeze all travel, fell in love with Cannes and built a villa here as an annual refuge from the British winter; over the next century the English aristocracy, tsars, kings and princes followed his example, and Cannes became a centre for the international élite. The steep cobbled streets of le Suquet, the old town, are well worth exploring. The modern resort extends along the littoral behind the Boulevard de la Croisette. Almost all of Cannes' beaches are private, but can be used by visitors for a fee.

EATING OUT The *Mirabelle*, in Rue St-Antoine, in the old part of town, is one of the most popular restaurants in the resort, noted for its imaginative cuisine and regional and national specialities.

CANNES
Alpes-Maritimes

★★★★★**Carlton Intercontinental** (Intercont) 58 La Croisette ☎93689168 tx 470720
✚📞355 ☎ P150 Lift ℂ Beach Sea Mountain
Credit Cards ① ② ③ ④ ⑤

★★★★★**Majestic** (SRS) 163 bd Croisette
☎93689100 tx 470475
mid Dec-mid Nov
✚📞262 ☎ P70 Lift ℂ ९ 🖂 ⊒ ⌘⌘ Beach Sea
Credit Cards ① ② ③ ⑤

★★★★★**Martinez** 73 bd Croisette ☎93943030 tx 470708
20 Jan-Dec
✚📞420 ☎ P150 Lift ℂ ९ ⊒ Beach Sea Mountain
Credit Cards ① ② ③ ④ ⑤

★★★★**Grand** 45 bd Croisette ☎93381545 tx 470727
✚📞76 P36 Lift ℂ Beach Sea Mountain
Credit Cards ① ② ③

★★★★*Pullman Beach* 13 r du Canada
☎93945050 tx 470034
Jan-Oct
✚📞95 ☎ Lift ⊒

★★★★**Sofitel Méditerranée** 2 bd J-Hibert
☎93992275 tx 470728
Closed 20 Nov-21 Dec
✚📞150 ☎ P25 Lift ℂ ⊒ Sea
Credit Cards ① ② ③ ⑤

★★★**Embassy** 6 r de Bone ☎93387902 tx 470081
✚📞60 ☎ P10 Lift
Credit Cards ① ② ③ ④ ⑤

★★★**Savoy** 5 r F-Einesy ☎93381774
20 Dec-Oct
rm55(✚📞48) Lift ℂ
Credit Cards ② ⑤

★★**Campanile** Aérodrome de Cannes-Mandelieu ☎93486941 tx 461570
✚📞98 P60
Credit Card ③

★★**France** 85 r d'Antibes (n.rest) ☎93392334
✚📞34 Lift ℂ Mountain
Credit Cards ① ② ③

★★**Roches Fleuries** 92 r G-Clemenceau (n.rest)
☎93392878
28 Dec-13 Nov
rm24(✚📞15) Lift Sea Mountain

At BOCCA, LA

★★**Climat de France** 232 av F-Tonner
☎93902222 tx 970257
✚📞46 Lift ⊒
Credit Cards ① ② ③ ⑤

📞 *Romeo* 4 bd J-Hibert,22 av des Arlves ☎ 93475541 For

CANNET, LE
Alpes-Maritimes

★★**Ibis** 87 bd Carnot ☎93457976 tx 470095
✚📞40 Lift
Credit Cards ① ③

📞 *Europa* Bretelle Autoroute au Cannet ☎ 934351700 Alf Dai

CAPBRETON
Landes

★★**Ocean LE**av de la Plage ☎58721022
Mar-Oct :Rest closed Tue out of season
rm52(✚📞43) A20rm P40 Lift ℂ Sea
Credit Cards ① ③ ⑤

CAP-D'AGDE
See AGDE

CAP-D'AIL
Alpes-Maritimes

★★**Cigogne LE**r de la Gare ☎93782960
end Mar-Nov
✚📞20 Sea
Credit Card ③

★★**Miramar** 126 av du 3 Septembre ☎93780660
Closed 6-31 Jan
rm27(📞15) P12 Sea
Credit Card ③

CAP-D'ANTIBES
See ANTIBES

CAP FERRET
Gironde

★★**Frégate** 34 av de l'Océan (n.rest) ☎56604162
Etr-Sep
✚📞24 A4rm P8
Credit Cards ① ② ③ ⑤

CARANTEC
Finistère

★**Falaise** pl du Kelenn ☎98670053
Etr-20 Sep
rm24(✚📞18) ☎ P35 Sea

CARCASSONNE
Aude

★★★★**Domaine D'Auriac DPn** rte St-Hilaire,BP 554 ☎68257222 tx 500385
Feb-Jan :Rest closed Sun & Mon (mid Oct-Etr)
✚📞23 ☎ P80 Lift ℂ ९ ⊒ ⌘⌘
Credit Cards ① ② ③

★★★**Donjon LE**(MAP/BW) 2 r Comte Roger
☎68710880 tx 505012
✚📞36 ☎ P70 Lift ℂ Mountain
Credit Cards ① ② ③ ⑤

★★★**Terminus** (Inter-Hotels) 2 av Ml-Joffre
☎68252500 tx 500198
rm110(✚📞92) ☎ P6 Lift ℂ
Credit Cards ① ② ③ ⑤

★★★**Vicomte** 18 r Camille St-Saëns ☎68714545 tx 500303
:Rest closed Sun in low season
✚📞59 P60 Lift ℂ ⊒
Credit Cards ① ② ③ ④ ⑤

★★**Aragon** (FAH/Inter-Hotels) 15 Montée Combéléran (n.rest) ☎68471631 tx 505076
✚📞29 ☎ P27 ⊒
Credit Cards ① ② ③ ⑤

★★**Arcade** 5 sq Gambetta (n.rest) ☎68723737 tx 505227
✚📞48 P20 Lift
Credit Cards ① ③

★★*Balladins* ZI La Bouriette,3 alle de Roberval ☎68723434
✚📞38 P40
Credit Cards ① ② ③

★★**Campanile** Centre Commercial Salvaza,lieu-dit 'La Coustoune' ☎68724141 tx 505170
✚📞42 P42
Credit Card ③

★★**Climat** 8 r des Côteaux de Pech-Mary ☎68711620
✚📞26 P Mountain

★★**Croque Sel** rte Narbonne (N113) ☎68251415
✚📞11 P11
Credit Cards ② ③

★★**Ibis** rte de Barriac ☎68479835 tx 500554
✚📞60 P70 Lift
Credit Cards ① ③

★★**Montségur** 27 allée d'Léna ☎68253141 tx 505261
✚📞21 Lift ℂ
Credit Cards ① ② ③ ⑤

📞 *Salvaza Automobiles* rte de Montreal ☎ 68251150 P For

CARENNAC
Lot

★**Fenelon LEDPn** ☎65386767
10 Mar-25 Jan :Rest closed Fri & Sat lunch low season
rm19(✚📞13) P15 Lake
Credit Cards ① ③

CALAIS

1	★★★	Meurice
2	★★	Bellevue
3	★★	Campanile
5	★★	Climat
6	★★	George V
7	★★	Ibis
8	★★	Pacific
9	★	Beffroi
10	★	Richelieu
11	★	Sole Meunière

CARENTAN
Manche

At VEYS, LES(7km NE)

★★**Aire de la Baie** ☎33420099 tx 772085
🍴40 P40 ⚲
Credit Cards ①②③⑤

CARHAIX-PLOUGUER
Finistère

★★**Gradlon** 12 bd de la République ☎98931522
16 Jan-14 Dec :Rest closed Fri pm & Sat lunch
Oct-May
🍴45 P12 Lift ⚲
Credit Cards ①②③⑤

CARNAC
Morbihan

★★**Armoric DPn** 53 av de la Poste ☎97521347
Etr-15 Sep
🍴25 P50 ⚲
Credit Cards ① ③

At CARNAC-PLAGE

★★★**Novotel Tal-Ar-Mor** av de l'Atlantique
☎97521666 tx 950324
3 Jan-18 Nov
🍴106 P Lift ⌣
★★**Celtique** 17 av Kermario ☎97521149
Feb-Oct
rm35(🍴31) P22 ℂ
Credit Card ③

★★**Genêts DPn** 45 av Kermario ☎97521101
1 Jun-25 Sep
rm33(🍴26) A4rm
Credit Cards ① ③

CARNAC-PLAGE
See **CARNAC**

CARQUEFOU
See **NANTES**

CARQUEIRANNE
Var

★★**Plein Sud** av du Gl-de-Gaulle,rte des Salettes
(n.rest) ☎94585286
🍴17 P18 Sea
Credit Cards ① ③

CARTERET
See **BARNEVILLE-CARTERET**

CASSIS
Bouches-du-Rhône

★★★**Plage** pl Bestouan ☎420105870 tx 441287
20 Mar-25 Oct
🍴29 Lift ℂ Sea
Credit Cards ①②③⑤

CASTELJALOUX
Lot-et-Garonne

★**Grand Cadets de Gascogne** 🅛pl Gambetta
☎53930059
rm15(🍴10) ☎ P10 Lift
Credit Cards ①②③⑤

CASTELLANE
Alpes-de-Haute-Provence

★**Petit Auberge** pl M-Sauvaire ☎92836206
Mar-Nov
🍴18 P5 Mountain
Credit Cards ①②③

🚗 **Vincent** bd St-Michel ☎ 92836162 Peu

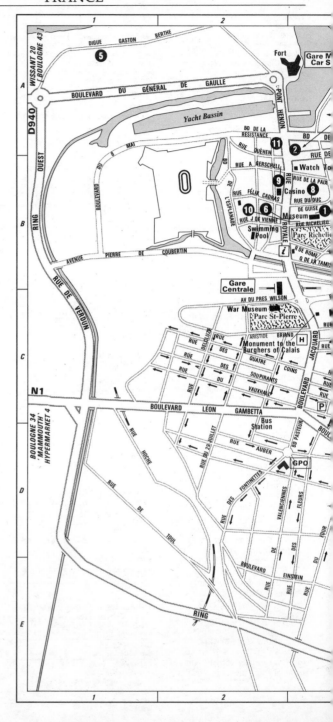

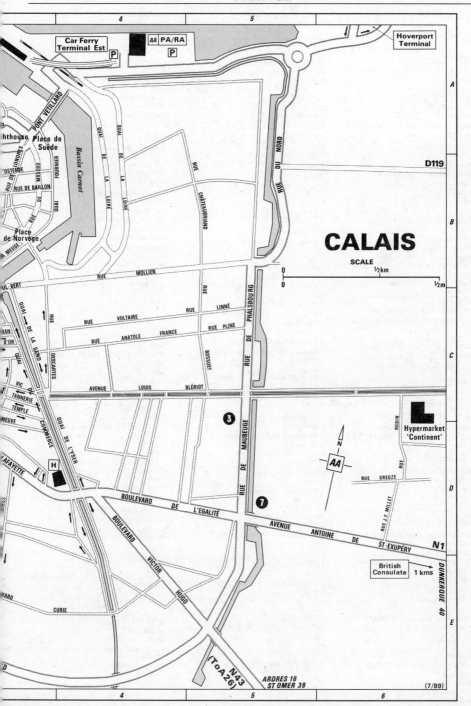

CASTELNAUDARY
Aude
★★*Palmes* (MAP/BW) 10 av Ml-Foch ☎231710 tx
500372
◆↑20 ⌂ Lift
Credit Cards ①②③⑤
★*Fourcade* 14 r des Carmes ☎6821302108
10 Feb-5 Jan
rm14(◆↑10) ⌂
Credit Cards ①②③④⑤

CASTELSARRASIN
Tarn-et-Garonne
★*Moderne* 54 r de l'Égalité (n.rest) ☎63323010
rm12(◆↑7) ⌂ P6

CASTÉRA-VERDUZAN
Gers
★★*Thermes* ☎62681307 tx 532915
Closed Jan :Rest closed Sat pm & Sun in winter
rm48(◆↑37) A8rm
Credit Cards ①②③⑤

CASTRES
Tarn
★★*Fimotel* ZI de la Chartreuse,(N622)
☎63598299
◆↑40 P52 Mountain
Credit Cards ①②③⑤
★★*Grand* (Inter) 11 r de la Libération
☎63590030
15 Jan-15 Dec :Rest closed Fri evening & Sat
rm40(◆↑37) Lift ☾ Mountain Lake
Credit Cards ①②③⑤

CAUDEBEC-EN-CAUX
Seine-Maritime
★★★*Marine* 18 quai Guilbaud ☎35962011 tx
770404
Closed 2-28 Jan
◆↑29 P15 Lift
Credit Cards ①②③
★★*Normandie* 𝐋Equai Guilbaud ☎35962511 tx
772684F
Closed Feb
◆↑16 P20
Credit Cards ①②③

CAUSSADE
Tarn-et-Garonne
★★*Dupont* 25 r Recollets ☎63650500
Closed 2 wks Feb & Nov :Rest closed Fri & Sat
(seasonal)
rm31(◆↑23) A8rm ⌂ P25
Credit Cards ①②③
★★*Larroque* 𝐋Eav de la Gare ☎63931014
20 Jan-20 Dec :Rest closed Sat midday & Sun
evening
rm27(◆↑24) ⌂ P20 ≏
Credit Cards ①②③⑤

CAVAILLON
Vaucluse
★★★*Christel* Digue de Gd-Jardin (2km S)
☎90710779 tx 431547
◆↑109 P Lift ⊡
★★*Toppin* 𝐋E(FAH) 70 cours Gambetta
☎90713042
◆↑32 ⌂ P20
Credit Cards ①②③⑤

CAVALAIRE-SUR-MER
Var
★★*Bonne Auberge* 400 av des Allies,rte
Nationale ☎94640296
Etr-Oct
rm31(◆↑24) P30

CAVALIÈRE
Var
★★★*Surplage* ☎94058019
12 May-12 Oct
◆↑60 Lift ☾ ⊡ Beach Sea
Credit Cards ①③

★★*Cap Nègre* ☎94058046
May-28 Sep
◆↑32 P30 Lift Beach Sea Mountain

CELLE-DUNOISE, LA
Creuse
★*Pascaud* 𝐋E☎55891066
Feb-Dec :Rest closed Sun evening & Mon Sep-
May
◆↑9 ⌂ P2 ⚲ ∪
Credit Card ③

CERGY
See **PONTOISE**

CESSON-SÉVIGNÉ
See **RENNES**

CESTAS
See **BORDEAUX**

CHABLIS
Yonne
★*Étoile* 4 r Moulins ☎86421050
Mar-Jan
rm15(◆↑8) ⌂ P1
Credit Cards ①②③

CHAGNY
Saône-et-Loire
★★★*Lameloise* 36 pl d'Armes ☎85870885 tx
801086
Closed 19 Dec-17 Jan
◆↑21 ⌂ P12 Lift ☾
Credit Cards ①③
★★*Capucines* 30 rte de Châlon ☎85870817
◆↑15 A4rm P50
Credit Cards ①③
★*Paris* 6 r de Beaune ☎85870838
15 Feb-15 Nov
rm11(◆↑6) P12

At **CHASSEY-LE-CAMP**(6km W)
★★*Auberge du Camp Romain* ☎85870991 tx
801583
Mar-Dec
rm26(◆↑22) ⌂ P50 ⚲ ≏ Mountain
Credit Cards ①③

CHAINTRÉ-LA-CHAPELLE-DE-GUINCHAY
See **MÂCON**

CHAISE-DIEU, LA
Haute-Loire
★★*Tremblant* 𝐋E(D906) ☎71000185
15 Apr-15 Nov
rm28(◆↑19) ⌂ P15 Mountain
Credit Cards ①③

CHALLES-LES-EAUX
Savoie
★★★*Château* (MAP/BW) Montée-du-Château
☎79728671 tx 309756
Feb-Nov
rm63(◆↑50) ⚲ ≏ Mountain
Credit Cards ①②③⑤
★★*Château de Trivier* ☎79850727
◆↑27 A13rm P150 Mountain
Credit Cards ①②③⑤

CHÂLONS-SUR-MARNE
Marne
★★*Angleterre* DPn 19 pl Mgr-Tissier ☎26682151
tx 842048
8 Jan-Jun & 23 Jul-21 Dec :Rest closed Sun
◆↑18 P9 ☾
Credit Cards ①②③⑤
★★*Bristol* 77 av P-Sémard (n.rest) ☎26682463
Closed Xmas
◆↑24 ⌂ P35 ☾
Credit Cards ①③
★★*Ibis* rte de Sedan,Complex Agricole
☎26651665 tx 830595
◆↑40 Lift
Credit Cards ①③

★★*Mont des Logès* r de Champagne
☎26673343
◆↑20 P150
Credit Cards ①②③⑤
★★*Pasteur* 46 r Pasteur (n.rest) ☎26681000
rm29(◆↑25) ⌂ P7
Credit Cards ①③
🚗 **Hall Automobiles** 34 av W-Churchill ☎
26644937 For
🚗 **G Poiret** 16 r du faubourg St-Antoine ☎
26680845 P Rov

At **COURTISOLS**(10.5km NE)
🚗 **Montel** 63 rte Nationale ☎ 26666004 P Ren

At **ÉPINE, L'**(8.5km E on N3)
★★*Armes de Champagne* ☎26669679 tx
830998
Closed 7 Jan-12 Feb
◆↑39 A16rm P4 ☾
Credit Cards ①③

CHALON-SUR-SAÔNE
Saône-et-Loire
★★★*Mercure* Centre Commercial de la Thalie,av
de l'Europe ☎85465189 tx 800132
◆↑85 P100 Lift ☾ ≏
Credit Cards ①②③⑤
★★*Royal* (MAP/BW) 8 r du Port Villiers
☎85481586 tx 801610
◆↑50 ⌂ P18 Lift ☾
Credit Cards ①②③⑤
★★★*St-Regis* (MAP/BW) 22 bd de la République
☎85480728 tx 801624
◆↑40 ⌂ P30 Lift ☾
Credit Cards ①②③⑤
★★★*St-Georges* 32 av J-Jaurès ☎85482705 tx
800330
◆↑48 ⌂ P15 Lift ☾
Credit Cards ①②③⑤
★★*Ibis* Carrefour des Moirots (n.rest) ☎85466462
tx 800381
◆↑62 Lift
Credit Cards ①③
★*Rotonde* 14 pl du Pont-Paron,St-Rémy (n.rest)
☎85483593
rm32(↑10) ⌂ P4
Credit Cards ①③
★★*St-Jean* 24 quai Gambetta (n.rest)
☎85484565
rm25(◆↑23) Sea
Credit Card ③
★*St-Rémy* 𝐋E89 r A-Martin,St-Rémy (n.rest)
☎85483804 tx 800175
◆↑40 P30
Credit Cards ①③⑤
🚗 **Moderne** r des P-d'Orient ☎ 85465212 Cit
🚗 **Soreva** 4 av Kennnedy ☎ 85464945 For

At **CHAMPFORGEUIL**(4km NW)
★★*Climat* ZAC des Blettrys (4km NW)
☎85644601 tx 692844
◆↑42

CHAMBÉRY
Savoie
★★★★*Grand Hotel* 6 pl de la Gare ☎79695454
tx 320910
◆↑50 ⌂ Lift ☾ Mountain
Credit Cards ①②③④⑤
★★★*Art-Hotel* 12 r Sommeiller (n.rest)
☎79623726
◆↑40 ⌂ Lift
Credit Cards ①②③④⑤
★★★*France* 22 fbg Réclus (n.rest) ☎79335118 tx
309689
◆↑48 ⌂ P40 Lift ☾ Mountain
Credit Cards ①②③⑤

★★★**Novotel** Joie rapide urbaine,Sortie 6,Z1 des Landiers ☎79692127 tx 320446
📞103 P100 Lift ⌿ Mountain
Credit Cards ①②③⑤

★★**Balladins** Z.I. Les Épinettes ☎79961122 tx 649394
📞38 P30 Mountain
Credit Cards ①②③④⑤

At CHAMNORD

★★**Ibis Chambéry** r E-Ducretet ☎79692836 tx 320457
📞87 Lift
Credit Cards ①③

CHAMBON, LAC
Puy-de-Dôme

★★**Bellevue** LE☎73886106
Apr-Sep
rm25(📞23) A8rm P20 Mountain Lake

★★**Grillon** LE☎73886066
Feb-Nov
rm20(📞18) P20 Mountain Lake
Credit Cards ①③

CHAMBON-SUR-VOUEIZE
Creuse

★★**Etonneries** LE41 av G-Clemenceau ☎55821466
Mar-20 Dec
rm10(📞6) P15 Mountain
Credit Cards ③⑤

CHAMBORD
Loir-et-Cher

★★**Grand St-Michel** LEDPn Face au Château ☎54203131
20 Dec-12 Nov
rm40(📞36) ♨ P22 ℂ ⌖
Credit Cards ①③

CHAMBOURCY
See ST-GERMAIN-EN-LAYE

CHAMBRAY-LES-TOURS
See TOURS

CHAMNORD
See CHAMBÉRY

CHAMONIX-MONT-BLANC
Haute-Savoie

★★★★**Croix Blanche** 7 r Vallot,BP135 ☎50530011 tx 385614
Jul-Apr
rm34(📞33) A20rm P14 Lift ℂ Mountain
Credit Cards ①②③⑤

★★★**Mont Blanc** Pn pl d'Église ☎50530564 tx 385614
15 Dec-15 Oct
📞50 Lift ℂ ⌖ ⌿ Mountain
Credit Cards ①②③④⑤

★★★**Richemond** 228 r Dr-Paccard ☎50530885 tx 389000
20 Dec-16 Apr & 17 Jun-17 Sep
📞53 P25 Lift ℂ Mountain
Credit Cards ①②③④⑤

★★★**Sapinière-Montana** DPn 102 r Mummery ☎50530763 tx 305551
Dec-Apr & Jun-Sep
📞30 ♨ P10 Lift ℂ Mountain
Credit Cards ①②③⑤

At BOSSONS, LES(3.5km S)

★★**Aiguille du Midi** DPn ☎50530065
Seasonal
rm50(📞42) A16rm P80 Lift ⌖ ⌿ Mountain
Credit Cards ①③

CHAMPAGNAC
Cantal

★★**Lavendès** LEDPn Château-le-Lavendès,D15 rte de Neuvic ☎71696279 tx 393160

Mar-Dec
📞8 P30 ⌿ Mountain
Credit Cards ①③

CHAMPAGNOLE
Jura

★★★**Ripotot** 54 r Ml-Foch ☎84521545
15 Apr-15 Oct
rm60(📞34) ♨ P25 Lift ℂ ⌖
Credit Cards ①②③⑤

CHAMPFORGEUIL
See CHALON-SUR-SAÔNE

CHAMPILLON
See ÉPERNAY

CHAMPNIERS
See ANGOULÊME

CHAMPS-SUR-MARNE
Seine-et-Marne

At ÉMERAINVILLE

★★**Climat** Le Pave Neuf -(CD 51) ☎60063834 tx 612241
📞38 P

CHAMPS-SUR-YONNE
Yonne

★★**Ibis** Aire du Soleil Levant,A6 Venoy (n.rest) ☎86403131 tx 351817
📞72 P50

CHANAS
See ROUSSILLON

CHANTEPIE
Ille-et-Vilaine

★★**Campanile** ZAC des Deux Ruisseaux,r de la Chalotais ☎99414444 tx 740436
📞39 P39
Credit Card ③

CHANTILLY
Oise

★★**Campanile** rte de Creil,(N16) ☎44573924 tx 140065
📞50 P50
Credit Card ③

★**Petit Vatel** ☎44570166
Closed end Dec & 1 wk Feb :Rest closed Fri & Sun eve out of season
rm15(📞3)
Credit Card ③

At GOUVIEUX(3km SW)

★★★**Château de Montvillar** Genne ☎44570514 tx 150212
📞164 P400 Lift ⌖ ⌱
Credit Cards ①②③

★★**Balladins** rte de Creil ☎44581312 tx 649394
📞38 P35
Credit Card ①

At LAMORLAYE(5km S)

★★★**Hostellerie du Lys** 7th Av ☎44212619 tx 150298
:Rest closed 2 wks Xmas
📞35 A21rm P70 ℂ
Credit Cards ①②③⑤

CHANTONNAY
Vendée

★★**Moulin Neuf** LE☎51943027
📞60 ♨ P80 ⌖ ⌿ Lake
Credit Card ③

★**Mouton** LE31 r Nationale ☎51943022
📞11 ♨ P5
Credit Cards ①②③⑤

CHAPELLE-EN-VERCORS, LA
Drôme

★**Bellier** DPn ☎75482003 tx 306022
18 Jun-25 Sep
rm12(📞11) Mountain
Credit Cards ①②③⑤

CHAPELLE-ST-MESMIN, LA
Loiret

★★**Campanile** "Bel Air",r de l'Aquitaine ☎38722323 tx 783799
📞52 P52
Credit Card ③

★★**Fimotel** 7 r de l'Aquitaine ☎38437144 tx 781265
📞42 P50 Lift
Credit Cards ①②③⑤

CHARAVINES
Isère

★★**Hostellerie Lac Bleu** LE☎76066048
15 Mar-15 Oct
rm15(📞10) P12 Mountain Lake
Credit Card ③

CHARBONNIÈRES-LES-BAINS
See LYON

CHARLES-DE-GAULLE AIRPORT
See PARIS AIRPORTS

CHARLEVILLE-MÉZIÈRES
Ardennes

★★★**Cleves** DPn 43 r de l'Arquebuse ☎24331075 tx 841164
📞49 P20 Lift
Credit Cards ①②③⑤

★★**Campanile** ZAC du Moulin Blanc,(N51) ☎24375455 tx 842821
📞51 P51
Credit Cards ③⑤

At VILLERS-SEMEUSE(5km E)

★★★**Mercure** r L-Michel ☎24375529 tx 840076
📞68 P100 ⌱
Credit Cards ①②③⑤

CHARMES
Vosges

★**Central** LE4 r des Capucins ☎29380240
Jan-15 Feb & 28 Feb-31 Dec
📞10 ♨ P
Credit Cards ①⑤

CHAROLLES
Saône-et-Loire

★★**Moderne** LE10 av de la Gare ☎85240702
Sep-28 Dec
rm18(📞16) ♨ P20 ⌱
Credit Cards ②③⑤

CHARTRES
Eure-et-Loir

★★★**Grand Monarque** (MAP/BW) 22 pl des Epars ☎37210072 tx 760777
📞46 A11rm ♨ P30 Lift ℂ
Credit Cards ①②③

★★★**Novotel** av M-Proust, Le Madeleine ☎37348030 tx 781298
📞78 P109 Lift ⌱
Credit Cards ①②③⑤

★★**Europ** 5 av M-Proust ☎37359111 tx 781284
📞47 P150
Credit Card ②

★★**Ibis Chartres Centre** pl de la Porte Drouaise ☎37360636 tx 789533
📞79 ♨ Lift ⌱
Credit Cards ①③

★★**Poste** LE3 r du Gl-König ☎37210427 tx 760573
rm60(📞57) ♨ P12 Lift
Credit Cards ①②③⑤

★**Ouest** 3 pl Sémard (n.rest) ☎37214327
rm29(📞14) P10
Credit Cards ①③

🅿️ **Mauger** 1 av de Sully,ZUP de la Madeleine ☎37344411 P Peu Tal

🅿️ **Paris-Brest** 80 r F-Lepine,Luisant ☎37281388 P For

At LUCÉ(3km SW on N23)
★★**Ibis** Impasse du Périgord (N 23) ☎37357600
tx 780348
⊷♠52 Lift
Credit Cards ①③
☎ **Chartres Auto Sport** rte d'Illiers ☎ 37352479
Rov

CHARTRE-SUR-LE-LOIR, LA
Sarthe
★★**France** ⌷**E**Pn 20 pl de la République
☎43444016
15 Dec-15 Nov
⊷♠28 A12rm P12 ⌕
Credit Cards ①③

CHASSENEUIL-DU-POITOU
See POITIERS

CHASSE-SUR-RHÔNE
Isère
★★★**Mercure Lyon Sud** CD4-Les Roues
☎78731394 tx 300625
⊷♠115 P250 Lift
Credit Cards ①②③⑤

CHASSEY-LE-CAMP
See CHAGNY

CHÂTEAU-ARNOUX
Alpes-de-Haute-Provence
★★★**Bonne Étape** (Relais et Châteaux) **DPn**
Chemin du Lac ☎92640009 tx 430605
mid Feb-Jan
⊷♠18 ☎ P16 ⌂ Mountain Lake
Credit Cards ①②③⑤

CHÂTEAUBRIANT
Loire-Atlantique
★★★**Hotellerie de la Ferrière** (FAH/Inter-Hotels)
rte de Nantes ☎40280028 tx 701353
rm25(⊷♠22) A14rm P200
Credit Cards ①②③⑤
★★**Châteaubriand** 30 r du II Novembre (n.rest)
☎40281414 tx 721154
⊷♠37 P20 Lift
Credit Cards ①②③⑤
★**Armor** 19 pl Motte (n.rest) ☎40811119
⊷♠20 Lift
Credit Cards ①②③⑤

CHÂTEAU-CHINON
Nièvre
★★**Vieux Morvan** ⌷**E**6 pl Gudin ☎86850501
rm24(⊷♠20) Mountain
Credit Cards ①③

CHÂTEAU-D'OLONNE
See SABLES-D'OLONNE, LES

CHÂTEAUDUN
Eure-et-Loir
★★**Armorial** 59 r Gambetta (n.rest) ☎37451957
:Rest closed Fri evenings Oct-Apr
rm16(⊷♠13)
Credit Cards ①③
★★**Beauce** (Inter) 50 r de Jallans (n.rest)
☎37451475
rm24(⊷♠18) ☎ P10
Credit Cards ①③
★**Rose** ⌷**E**DPn 12 r L-Licors ☎37452183
⊷♠7 ☎ P4
Credit Cards ①③⑤

CHÂTEAU-FARINE
See BESANÇON

CHÂTEAUNEUF
See NANS-LES-PINS

CHÂTEAUNEUF
See POUILLY-EN-AUXOIS

CHÂTEAUNEUF-GRASSE
Alpes-Maritimes
★★**Campanile** Pré du Lac ☎93425555 tx 470092
⊷♠41 P41
Credit Card ③

CHÂTEAUNEUF-SUR-LOIRE
Loiret
★★**Capitainerie** DPn 1 Grande r ☎38584216 tx
760712
Mar-Jan
rm14(⊷♠12) P14
Credit Cards ①③④⑤
★**Nouvel du Loiret** ⌷**E**DPn 4 pl A-Briand
☎38584228
rm20(⊷♠12) ☎
Credit Cards ①②③⑤

CHÂTEAUROUX
Indre
★**Central** 19 av de la Gare (n.rest) ☎54220100
5 Jan-22 Dec
rm11(♠8)
Credit Cards ①③

CHÂTEAU-THIERRY
Aisne
★★**Ile de France** (2km N on rte de Soissons)
☎23691012 tx 150666
Closed 21-28 Dec
rm56(⊷♠31) P100 Lift
Credit Cards ①②③⑤
★**Girafe** pl A-Briand (n.rest) ☎23830206
rm30(⊷♠12) ☎
Credit Cards ①③

CHÂTELAILLON-PLAGE
Charente-Maritime
★**Hermitage** 13 av Gl-Leclerc ☎46562097
⊷♠27 ☎ P20
Credit Cards ①②③
★★**Hostellerie Select** 1 r G-Musset ☎46562431
Closed Nov
⊷♠21 P15
Credit Cards ①②③④⑤
★★**Majestic** pl de St-Marsault ☎46562053
rm30(⊷♠29) P12
Credit Cards ①②③④⑤

CHÂTELGUYON
Puy-de-Dôme
★★★★**Splendid** (MAP/BW) 5-7 r d'Angleterre
☎73860480 tx 990585
25 Apr-15 Oct
⊷♠93 P100 Lift ℂ ⌂ Sea Lake
Credit Cards ①②③⑤
★★★**International** r A-Punnet ☎73860672
Closed 27 Apr-5 Oct
rm68(⊷♠57) Lift ℂ
Credit Cards ①②③⑤

CHÂTELLERAULT
Vienne
★★★**Moderne** (MAP/BW) 74 bd Blossac
☎49213011 tx 791801
rm33(⊷♠30) ☎ P5 Lift ℂ
Credit Cards ①②③④⑤
★★**Croissant** 19 av Kennedy ☎49210177
rm19(⊷♠16) P
Credit Cards ①③
★★**Ibis** av Camille Plage,Quartier de la Forêt
(n.rest) ☎49217577 tx 791488
⊷♠72 Lift
Credit Cards ①③
★★**Univers** 4 av G-Clemenceau ☎49212353
⊷♠30 ☎ Lift
Credit Cards ①②③⑤
☎ **Rousseau** 91 av L-Ripault ☎ 49210613 P Peu
☎ **Tardy** 40-42 bd d'Estrées ☎ 49214344 P For

CHÂTILLON-EN-BAZOIS
Nièvre
★**Poste** ⌷**E**DPn Grande r ☎86841468
9 Jan-end Nov
rm12(♠5) ☎ P25
Credit Card ④

CHÂTILLON-SUR-INDRE
Indre
★**Auberge de la Tour** ⌷**E**DPn ☎54387217
1 Feb-15 Dec
rm10(⊷♠7) ☎ P2
Credit Cards ①③

CHÂTILLON-SUR-SEINE
Côte-d'Or
★★**Côte d'Or** Pn r C-Ronot ☎80911329
12 Jan-12 Dec :Rest closed Sun pm & Mon (Jul-
Aug)
rm11(⊷♠8) ☎ P11
Credit Cards ①②③④⑤
★★**Sylvia** 9 av de la Gare (n.rest) ☎80910244
rm21(⊷♠15) A8rm ☎ P25
Credit Cards ①③
★**Jura** 19 r Dr-Robert (n.rest) ☎80912696
rm10(⊷♠8) P6
Credit Cards ①③

CHATTANCOURT
See VERDUN

CHAUMONT
Haute-Marne
★★★**Terminus Reine** (MAP/BW) pl du Gl-de-
Gaulle ☎25036666 tx 840920
rm68(⊷♠62) ☎ P20 Lift ℂ
Credit Cards ①②③⑤
★★**Grand Val** (Inter) rte de Langres (N19)
☎25039035
Jan-21 Dec
rm60(⊷♠35) ☎ P50 Lift
Credit Cards ①②③⑤
★**France** 25 r Toupot-de-Beveaux ☎25030111
rm40(⊷♠30) ☎ P
Credit Cards ①②③⑤
☎ **François** rte de Langres ☎ 25320888 M/C P
For

CHAUMONT-SUR-LOIRE
Loir-et-Cher
★★★**Château** DPn r du Ml-de-L-de-Tassigny
☎54209804
15 Mar-15 Nov
⊷♠15 P15 ⌂
Credit Cards ①②③⑤

CHAUSSÉE ST-VICTOR, LA
See BLOIS

CHAUVIGNY
See NANCY

CHAUVIGNY
Vienne
★**Lion d'Or** ⌷**E**8 r Marché ☎49463028
Closed 16 Dec-14 Jan
rm27(⊷♠22) A16rm P10
Credit Card ③

CHAVAGNE
See CRÈCHE, LA

CHAVELOT
See ÉPINAL

CHELLES
Seine-et-Marne
★★**Climat Paris Est** r du Château-Gaillard
☎60087558 tx 691149
⊷♠43 P43
Credit Cards ①②③

CHÊNEHUTTE-LES-TUFFEAUX
See SAUMUR

CHENONCEAUX
Indre-et-Loire
★★**Bon Laboureur et Château** 6 r Dr-
Bretonneau ☎47239002
Mar-Nov
⊷♠26 ☎ P20 *
Credit Cards ①②③⑤

★**Roy** 9 r Dr-Bretonneau ☎47239017
7 Feb-12 Nov
rm42(⋇24) A12rm P15
Credit Cards [1] [3]

CHENÔVE
Côte-d'Or

★★**Balladins** 18 r J-Moulin ☎80521511 tx
350282
⋇36 P14
Credit Cards [1] [2] [3] [5]

CHERBOURG
Manche

See plan page 140; Agent [AA]
see page 109
The port of Cherbourg, its
harbour created by the building
of a massive breakwater, is both
a naval base and an important
terminus of travel. There seems
to have been a castle here in
early medieval times, and a
Count of Cherbourg was with
William the Conqueror in 1066.
To the west of the Gare Maritime
and its jetty is the bathing beach.
Next to it is the Place Napoléon,
with an equestrian monument to
the Emperor, and the Church of
the Trinity (1423-1504), a good
example of Flamboyant Gothic
with a notable south porch.
Continuous with the Place
Napoléon is the Place de la
République, where the *Hôtel de
Ville* houses the Thomas Henry
Museum and its interesting
collection of paintings. From the
Hôtel de Ville the Rue de la Paix
runs west to the Rue de L'Abbé,
which skirts the Parc Emmanuel-
Lias, where there are many exotic
trees and shrubs, a natural
history museum, and a coin
collection.

EATING OUT *Le Vauban,* on
Quai de Caligny, has both a
snack bar and a restaurant, the
former offering a huge range of
reasonably priced *hors d'oeuvres*
as well as a *plat du jour* of meat
or fish.

CHERBOURG
Manche

★★**Beauséjour** 26 r Grande-Vallée (n.rest)
☎33531030
⋇27 ☎
Credit Cards [1] [3]

★★**Chantereyne** Port de Plaisance (n.rest)
☎33930220 tx 171137
⋇50 P30 Sea
Credit Cards [1] [2] [3] [5]

★★**France** LE41 r MI-Foch ☎33531024 tx
170764
8 Jan-20 Dec
rm50(⋇30) A9rm Lift
Credit Cards [1] [3]

★★**Louvre** 28 r de la Paix (n.rest) ☎33530228 tx
171132
Closed 24-31 Dec
rm42(⋇32) ☎ Lift ℂ
Credit Cards [1] [3]

★**Renaissance** 4 r de l'Église (n.rest) ☎33432390
⋇12 Sea
Credit Cards [1] [3]

Accessoirauto 124 r du Val-de-Saire ☎
33442591 M/C P

S A Lemasson ZI av de l'Al-Lemonnier ☎
33430522 For

At GLACERIE, LA(6km SE N13)

★★**Campanile** r Montmartre ☎33434343 tx
171074
⋇43 P43

CHESNAY
SeePARIS

CHINON
Indre-et-Loire

★**Boule d'Or** LE66 quai J-d'Arc ☎47930313
Feb-Nov
rm20(⋇13)
Credit Cards [1] [2] [3] [5]

★**Gargantua** Pn 73 r Voltaire ☎47930474
15 Apr-Dec
rm13(⋇9) A3rm ☎
Credit Cards [1] [2] [3] [5]

At MARCAY(7km S on D116)

★★★**Château de Marcay** ☎47930347 tx 751475
15 Mar-Dec
⋇38 A11rm P50 Lift ℂ ⌇ ⌇
Credit Cards [1] [3] [5]

CHISSAY-EN-TOURAINE
See MONTRICHARD

CHITENAY
Loir-et-Cher

★**Clé des Champs** rte de Fougères ☎54704203
Closed 12-21 Nov & 5 Jan-5 Feb
rm10(⋇3) P40
Credit Cards [1] [3]

CHOLET
Maine-et-Loire

★★★**Fimotel** av Sables d'Olonne (2km S)
☎41624545
⋇42 ☎ P100 Lift
Credit Cards [2] [3] [5]

★★**Campanile** Parc de Carteron,,sq de la
Nouvelle France ☎41628679 tx 720318
⋇43 P43
Credit Card [3]

CHONAS-L'AMBALLAN
See VIENNE

CIBOURE
See ST-JEAN-DE-LUZ

CIOTAT, LA
Bouches-du-Rhône

★★★**Rose-Thé** 4 bd Beau Rivage ☎42830923
Apr-15 Oct
rm22(⋇14) P22 ℂ Sea
Credit Cards [1] [2] [5]

★★**Rotonde** 44 bd de la République (n.rest)
☎42086750
rm32(⋇11) P8 Lift
Credit Card [3]

CIVRAY
Vienne

★★**Dravir** Comporte,St-Marcoux ☎49873195
⋇8 ☎ P30 ℂ Lake
Credit Cards [1] [3]

CIVRIEUX-D'AZERGUES
Rhône

★★**Roseraie** LE☎78430178
⋇10 ☎
Credit Card [1]

CLAIRVAUX-LES-LACS
Jura

★**Lac** Bonlieu ☎84255711
15 Dec-15 Nov
rm39(⋇6) P40 Mountain Lake
Credit Cards [1] [2] [3] [5]

CLAIX
See GRENOBLE

CLÉCY
Calvados

★★**Site Normand** LEDPn ☎31697105 tx
170234
1 Feb-21 Feb
rm13(⋇10) A6rm
Credit Cards [1] [2] [3] [4] [5]

CLELLES
Isère

★★**Ferrat** LEPn ☎76344270
Mar-Nov
⋇17 A10rm ☎ P20 ⌇ Mountain
Credit Card [1]

CLÉON
See ELBEUF

CLERMONT-FERRAND
Puy-de-Dôme

★★★★**Altea Gergovia** Pn 82 bd Gergovia
☎73930575 tx 392658
⋇124 ☎ Lift Mountain
Credit Cards [1] [2] [3] [5]

★★★**Gallieni** 51 r Bonnabaud ☎73935969 tx
392779
⋇80 P85 Lift Mountain
Credit Cards [1] [2] [3] [5]

★★★**PLM Arverne** 16 pl Delille ☎73919206 tx
392741
⋇57 ☎ P Lift Mountain

★★★**Relais Arcade** 19 r Colbert (n.rest)
☎73932566 tx 990125
⋇66 ☎ P Lift
Credit Cards [1] [3]

★★**Balladins** ZAC du Brezet-Est (n.rest)
☎05355575 tx 649394
rm38 P38
Credit Cards [1] [2] [3] [4] [5]

★★**Campanile** r C-Guichard ☎73918891 tx
394166
⋇43 P43 Lift
Credit Card [3]

★★**Ibis** bd A-Brugière,Quartière Montferrand
☎73230004 tx 392288
⋇52 P200 Lift
Credit Cards [1] [3]

★★**Minimes** 10 r des Minimes (n.rest)
☎73933149
rm28(⋇15) P ℂ Mountain
Credit Card [2]

★**Foch** 22 r MI-Foch (n.rest) ☎73934840
rm19(⋇1)
Credit Cards [1] [2] [3]

★**Ravel** 8 r de Maringues (n.rest) ☎73915133
rm19(⋇11)
Credit Card [3]

Auvergne Auto 3 r B-Palissy,ZI du Brezet ☎
73917656 Ope

At AULNAT AÉROPORT(5km E)

★★**Climat** ☎73927202
⋇42
Credit Cards [1] [2] [3] [5]

CLISSON
Loire-Atlantique

★**Auberge de la Cascade** Gervaux ☎40540241
rm10(⋇5) P Lake
Credit Cards [1] [3]

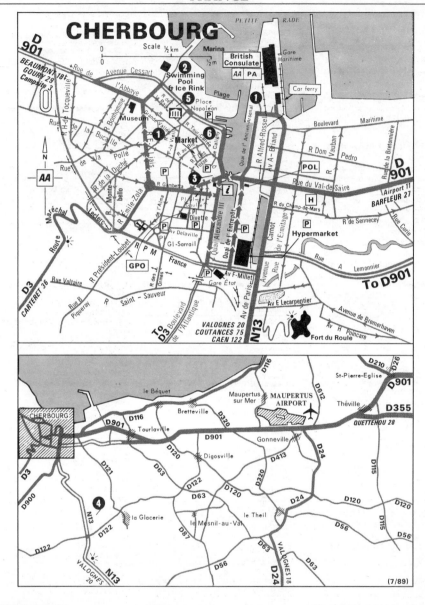

CLOYES-SUR-LE-LOIR
Eure-et-Loir

★★**St-Jacques** 35 r Nationale ☎37984008
Feb-15 Dec :Rest closed Sun pm & Mon, Oct-Apr
✠22 A5rm P13 Lift
Credit Cards ①③

★**St-Georges** 13 r du Temple ☎37985436
✠11 ☎ P8
Credit Card ②

◑**Cassonnet** 37 r Nationale ☎ 37985190 P Peu
Tal

CLUNY
Saône-et-Loire

★★**Bourgogne DPn** pl de l'Abbaye ☎85590058
15 Feb-15 Nov
rm16(✠15) ☎ P12
Credit Cards ①②③⑤

★★**Moderne DPn** Pont de l'Ètang ☎85590565
rm15(✠13) ☎ P15 Lake
Credit Cards ①②③⑤

CHERBOURG

1	★★	Beauséjour
2	★★	Chantereyne
3	★★	France
4	★★	Campanile (At La Glacerie)
5	★★	Louvre
6	★	Renaissance

140

★**Abbaye** ⎐**EDP**n av de la Gare ☎85591114
3 Mar-28 Nov
rm16(◕↾9) ♨ P15 Mountain
Credit Cards ①③

COGNAC
Charente

★★**Auberge** 13 r Plumejeau ☎45320870
rm22(◕↾20)
Credit Cards ①②③

★★**Moderne** ⎐E24 r Élysée-Mousnier,pl de la
Sous Préfecture (n.rest) ☎45821953 tx
793105
6 Jan-20 Dec
rm40(◕↾39) P15 Lift
Credit Cards ①③⑤

At **ST-LAURENT-DE-COGNAC**(6km W)

★★**Logis de Beaulieu** ⎐E45823050 tx
791020
◕↾21 ♨ P ℂ ℚ
Credit Cards ①②③⑤

COL-DE-CUREBOURSE
See **VIC-SUR-CÉRE**

COLLIOURE
Pyrénées-Orientales

★★**Madeloc** (Inter) r R-Rolland (n.rest)
☎68820756
Apr-15 Oct
◕↾22 P18 Mountain
Credit Cards ①②③⑤

COLLONGES-LA-ROUGE
Corrèze

★**Relais St-Jacques de Compostelle**
☎55254102 tx 283155
Feb-Nov
rm26(◕↾7) A9rm P20
Credit Cards ①②③⑤

COLMAR
Haut-Rhin

★★★**Altea Champs de Mars** 2 av de la Marne
(n.rest) ☎89415454 tx 880928
◕↾75 ♨ P12 Lift
Credit Cards ①②③⑤

★★★**Novotel** 49 rte de Strasbourg ☎89414914 tx
880915
◕↾66 P66 ♨ Mountain
Credit Cards ①②③⑤

★★★**Terminus Bristol** (MAP/BW) 7 pl de la Gare
☎89235959 tx 880248
◕↾70 P80 Lift ℂ
Credit Cards ①②③⑤

★★**Campanile** ZI Nord,r des Frères-Lumière
☎89241818 tx 394166
◕↾42 P42
Credit Card ③

★★**Climat** r du la 1 Armée Française ☎89411110
tx 880650
◕↾43 P30 Lift
Credit Cards ①②③⑤

★★**Ibis Colmar** 13 rte de Neuf-Brisach
☎89234646 tx 880294
◕↾62 ♨ P250 Lift ℂ
Credit Cards ①③

★★**Turenne** 10 rte Bâle (n.rest) ☎89411226 tx
880959
◕↾85 ♨ P Lift
Credit Cards ①②③⑤

✎ **Bolchert** 77 r Morat ☎ 89791125 For

At **AMMERSCHWIHR**(7km NW)

★**Arbre Vert** ⎐**EDP**n 7 r des Cigognes
☎89471223
25 Mar-10 Feb :Rest closed Thu
rm13(◕↾11) P50
Credit Cards ①②③

At **KAYSERSBERG**(1km NW)

★★**Remparts** ⎐Er de la Flieh (n.rest)
☎89471212

◕↾32 A6rm
Credit Cards ①②③

COLOMBEY-LES-DEUX-ÉGLISES
Haute-Marne

★★★**Dhuits** ⎐E(MAP/BW) N19 ☎25015010 tx
840920
◕↾30 ♨ P60
Credit Cards ①②③⑤

COLOMBIER
See **FRÉJUS**

COLOMIERS
Haute-Garonne

★★**Fimotel** pl de la Gare,rte d'Auch ☎61789292
tx 531782
◕↾42 P50 Lift
Credit Cards ①②③⑤

COMBEAUFONTAINE
Haute-Saône

★**Balcon** ⎐Erte de Paris ☎84921113
rm20(◕↾17) ♨ P40
Credit Cards ①②③④⑤

COMBOURG
Ille-et-Vilaine

★★**Château & Voyageurs** (FAH) 1 pl
Châteaubriand ☎99730038 tx 740901
20 Jan-15 Dec
rm31(◕↾30) A9rm ♨ P12 Lake
Credit Cards ①②③⑤

COMPIÈGNE
Oise

★★**Campanile** av de Huy (Rocade Sud)
☎44204235 tx 150088
◕↾55 P55
Credit Card ③

★★**Harlay** 3 r Harlay (n.rest) ☎44230150 tx
145923
6 Jan-15 Dec
◕↾20 P6 Lift
Credit Cards ①②③⑤

★★**Ibis** 18 r E-Branly,Quartier de l' Université
☎44231627 tx 145991
◕↾60 P60 ℂ
Credit Cards ①③

✎ **Thiry** Centre C-de-Venette ☎ 44832992

At **MARGNY**(2km W on D935)

✎ **Depan' Nord** 189 r de Beauvais ☎ 44832883
P Dat

✎ **Ille-de-France** 186 av O-Butin ☎ 44833232
For

CONCARNEAU
Finistère

★★**Grand** 1 av P-Guéguen (n.rest) ☎98970028
3 Apr-Aug
rm33(◕↾22) P12 ℂ Sea

★★**Sables Blancs** ⎐**EDP**n Plages des Sables
☎98970139
25 Mar-4 Nov
rm48(◕↾42) Sea
Credit Cards ②③④⑤

✎ **B Tilly** 106 av de la Gare ☎ 98973500 M/C P
For

CONCHE-DE-NAUZAN
See **ROYAN**

CONDOM
Gers

★★**Table des Cordeliers** ☎62280368
◕↾21 ♨ P12 ⊐
Credit Card ③

CONDRIEU
Rhône

★★★**Beau Rivage** (Relais et Châteaux) 2 r Beau-
Rivage ☎74595224 tx 308946
15 Feb-5 Jan
◕↾24 ♨ P30 Lake
Credit Cards ①②③⑤

CONFLANS-STE-HONORINE
Yvelines

★★**Campanile** Deviation RN184,r des Frères-
Dammes ☎39192100 tx 699149
◕↾50 P50
Credit Card ③

CONFOLENS
Charente

★**Belle Étoile** ⎐**EDP**n 151 bis rte Angoulême
☎45840235
Nov-Dec & Feb-Sep
rm14(◕↾6) ♨ P30

CONQUES
Aveyron

★**Ste-Foy** ☎65698403
Etr-Oct
◕↾21 P8
Credit Cards ①③

CONTAMINE-SUR-ARVE
See **BONNEVILLE**

CONTRES
Loir-et-Cher

★★**France** ⎐**EDP**n 37 r P-H-Mauger
☎54195014 tx 750826
Mar-Jan
◕↾37 P20 ℚ
Credit Cards ①③

CONTREXEVILLE
Vosges

★★**Campanile** rte du Lac-de-la-Folie ☎29080372
tx 960333
◕↾31 P31 Lake
Credit Card ③

★★**Douze Apôtres** 25 r G-Thomson ☎29080412
Apr-15 Oct
◕↾38 A12rm ♨ P7 ℂ

COQUILLE, LA
Dordogne

★★**Voyageurs** ⎐Er de la République (N21)
☎53528013
Apr-Oct
rm10(◕↾5) ♨ P10
Credit Cards ①②③⑤

CORBEIL-ESSONNES
Essonne
See also EVRY

★★**Campanile** av P-Mantenant ☎60894145 tx
600934
◕↾50 P50
Credit Card ③

✎ **Feray** 46 av du Mai 1945 ☎ 64979494 Ren

At **PLESSIS-CHENET, LE**(4km S)

★★**Climat** 2 r Panhard ☎64938536 tx 692844
◕↾50 P100
Credit Cards ①②③④

CORDES
Tarn

★★★**Grand-Ecuyer** r Voltaire ☎63560103
Etr-Oct :Rest closed Mon low season & holidays
◕↾13
Credit Cards ①②③⑤

★★**Hostellerie du Vieux Cordes** ⎐Er de la
République ☎63560012 tx 530955
1 Feb-2 Jan
◕↾21
Credit Cards ①②③⑤

CORNEVILLE-SUR-RISLE
See **PONT-AUDEMER**

CORPS
Isère

★★**Poste** ⎐Epl de la Mairie ☎76300003
Closed Dec-Jan
◕↾20 A10rm ♨ P10 Mountain
Credit Cards ①③④

R Rivière pl Napoléon ☎ 76300113 M/C **P**
Ren

CORSE (CORSICA)
PORTICCIO
Corse-du-Sud

★★★**Sofitel DPn** Golfe d'Ajaccio ☎95250034 tx
460708
Closed 2 Dec-7 Jan
⊷▮100 P100 Lift 《 ⊶ ⊃ Beach Sea
Credit Cards ①②③⑤

PORTO-VECCHIO
Corse-du-Sud

★★★**Ziglione** (5km E on N198) ☎95700983
15 May-20 Sep
⊷▮32 P45 《 Beach Sea Mountain

COSNE-SUR-LOIRE
Nièvre

★★**Grand Cerf DPn** 43 r St-Jaques ☎86280446
Closed 16 Dec-14 Jan
rm20(⊷▮13)
Credit Cards ①③

COULANDON
See **MOULINS**

COURBEVOIE
Hauts-de-Seine

★★★**Novotel Paris - La Défense** 2 bd de
Neuilly,Défense 1 ☎47781668 tx 630288
⊷▮280 Lift
Credit Cards ①②③⑤

★★★**Paris Penta** 18 r Baudin ☎47885051 tx
610470
⊷▮494 ⋒ Lift 《
Credit Cards ①②③⑤

COURSEULLES-SUR-MER
Calvados

★★**Crémaillère** LEbd de la Plage ☎31374673
tx 171952
⊷▮34 A25rm
Credit Cards ①②③⑤

★★**Paris** pl du 6-Juin ☎31374507 tx 170656
Apr-Sep
⊷▮30 P8 Sea
Credit Cards ①②③④⑤

COURTABOEUF
See **ORSAY**

COURTENAY
Loiret

Chenardière rte de Sens ☎ 38974194 **P**

COURTISOLS
See **CHÂLONS-SUR-MARNE**

COUTAINVILLE
Manche

★**Hardy** LEPn pl 28-Juillet ☎33470411
15 Feb-8 Jan :Rest closed Mon & out of season
⊷▮17 P30
Credit Cards ①②③⑤

COUTANCES
Manche

★★★**Cositel** (FAH) rte de Coutainville
☎33075164 tx 772003
⊷▮40 ⋒ P74
Credit Cards ①②③⑤

★**Moderne** (Inter) 25 bd Alsace-Lorraine
☎33451377
rm17(⊷▮11) ⋒ P25
Credit Cards ①③

CRÈCHE, LA
Deux-Sèvres

★★**Campanile** rte de Paris ☎49255622 tx
791216
⊷▮47 P47
Credit Card ③

At **CHAVAGNE**(4km SW)

★★★**Rocs** ☎49255038 tx 790632
⊷▮51 P1500 ⊶ ⊃
Credit Cards ①②③⑤

CRÈCHES-SUR-SAÔNE
See **MÂCON**

CREIL
Oise

★★**Climat** r H-Bessemer ☎44244692 tx 262629
⊷▮42 P60
Credit Cards ①③

Central 9 r J-Jaurès ☎ 44554197 **P** Rov

CRESSENSAC
Lot

★**Chez Gilles** rte National 20 ☎65377006
rm25(⊷▮13) A19rm ⋒ P12
Credit Cards ①②③⑤

CRÉTEIL
See **PARIS**

CREUSOT, LE
Saône-et-Loire

At **MONTCHANIN**(8km E off D28)

★★★**Novotel** r du Pont J-Rose ☎85785555 tx
800588
⊷▮87 P120 Lift 《 ⊃
Credit Cards ①②③⑤

At **TORCY**(4km SE)

★★**Balladins** 2 allée G-Defferre ☎60176309 tx
649394
⊷▮39 P40
Credit Cards ①②③

★★**Fimotel** bd de Beaubourg ☎42615014 tx
215269
⊷▮42 P Lift
Credit Cards ①②③⑤

CRIEL-SUR-MER
Seine-Maritime

★★★**Hostellerie de la Vielle Ferme** DPn 23 r de la
Mer ☎35867218 tx 770303
Closed 3-31 Jan
rm35(⊷▮33) ⊶
Credit Cards ①②③⑤

LA CROIX-VALMER
Var

★★★**Souleias** Plage de Gigaro ☎94796191 tx
970032
15 Apr-1 Nov
⊷▮47 ⋒ P25 Lift 《 ⊶ ⊃ Sea
Credit Cards ①②③⑤

★★**Thalotel** DPn bd de la Mer (2.5km SE on
N559) ☎94795615
rm36(⊷▮32) P20 《 ⊃ Mountain
Credit Cards ①②③⑤

CROS-DE-CAGNES
See **CAGNES-SUR-MER**

CROUZILLE, LA
Haute-Vienne

At **NANTIAT**

★★**Relais St-Europe** ☎55399121
⊷▮19 P19 Mountain
Credit Cards ①③

CUVILLY
See **RESSONS-SUR-MATZ**

DAMMARIE-LES-LYS
See **MELUN**

DANJOUTIN
See **BELFORT**

DARDILLY
See **LYON**

DEAUVILLE
Calvados

★★★★★**Normandy** r J-Mermoz ☎31986622 tx
170617
⊷▮300 Lift 《 ⊡ ⊩ Beach Sea
Credit Cards ①②③⑤

★★★★**Royal** ☎31986633 tx 170549
Mar-Nov
⊷▮300 P160 Lift 《 ⊃ ⊩ Beach Sea
Credit Cards ①②③⑤

★★★**Altea Port Deauville** bd Corniche (n.rest)
☎31886262 tx 170364
⊷▮72 Lift Sea
Credit Cards ①②③⑤

★★★**Golf** ☎31881901 tx 170448
10 Apr-Oct
⊷▮175 P Lift ⊶ ⊃ ⊩ Sea
Credit Cards ①②③⑤

★★**Ibis** 9 quai de la Marine ☎31983890 tx
171295
⊷▮94 ⋒ Lift
Credit Cards ①③

At **TOUQUES**(2.5km S)

★★★**Amirauté** (N834) ☎31889062 tx 171665
⊷▮120 P200 Lift ⊶ ⊃
Credit Cards ①②③④⑤

DÉFENSE, LA
See**PARIS**

DIEPPE
Seine-Maritime

See plan
Situated at the mouth of the river
Arques on the Channel coast,
Dieppe is one of the chief ferry
ports in France and a popular
seaside resort. At the western
end of the town on a cliff-edge is
the castle, a picturesque 15th-
century building which has now
been restored as a museum;
among the exhibits are a
collection of ivory and examples
of Impressionist paintings. The
cliff above the castle commands
striking panoramic views of land
and sea. On the nearby shore
lawns and playgrounds separate
the hotels of the broad Boulevard
de Verdun from the fine expanse
of beach that stretches towards
the mouth of the port.
In the town itself is the modern
church of Notre-Dame de Bon
Secours and the Church of St
James, a fine building of the 13th
and 14th centuries, flanked by a
square 15th-century tower.

EATING OUT Fish specialities
include *sole dieoppoise, harengs
marinés* (marinated herring),
soupe de poisin (fish soup) and
marmite dieppoise, a cream-based
bouillabaisse. La Marine, in
l'Arcade de la Poissonerie, off la
Grande Rue, is noted for its
seafood dishes.

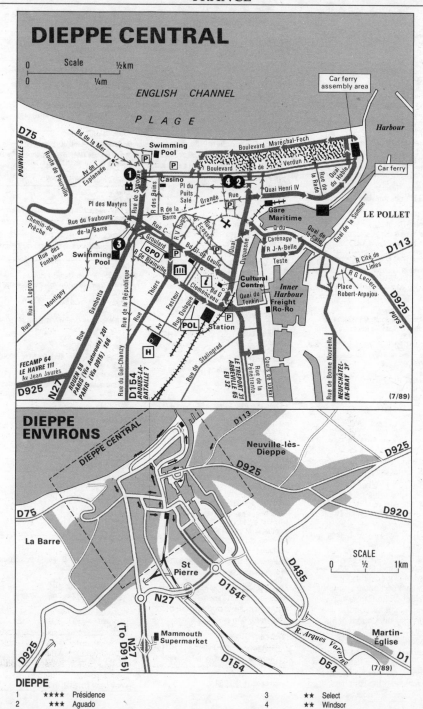

DIEPPE CENTRAL

Scale
0 — ½ km
0 — ¼ m

ENGLISH CHANNEL

PLAGE

Car ferry
assembly area

Harbour

D75

POURVILLE 5

Bd de la Mer

Route de Pourville

Av de l' Esplanade

Swimming Pool

Boulevard Maréchal-Foch

Car ferry

LE POLLET

Casino

Boulevard

de Verdun

Quai du Hâble

Quai de la Hâde

1

Pl du Puits Salé

4 2

Rue

Quai Henri IV

Rue de Sygogne

R des Bains

R de la Barre

Grande

Gare Maritime

Pl des Maytyrs

Rue du Faubourg-de-la-Barre

Rue C-

R V Hugo

Rue Ecossai

Quai

Duquesne

Q du

Quai de la Somme

D113

Chemin-du-Prêche

Rue des Fontaines

3

Swimming Pool

Groulard

Bd Gl-de-Gaulle

Carénage

R J-A-Belle

Teste

R Cité de Limes

R G Leclerc

Place Robert-Arpajou

D925

PUYS 3

Rue A Legros

Montigny

Rue

Gambetta

GPO

R de Blainville

Thiers

Pasteur

Bd G

Clemenceau

Cultural Centre

i

Inner Harbour Freight Ro-Ro

Rue de la République

Rue

Av

Quai du Tonkin

POL

Station

Cours de Vatar

H

Rue du Gal-Chanzy

Rue Dulague

Rue de Stalingrad

Rue de la Pénétrante

Rue de Bonne Nouvelle

NEUFCHÂTEL-EN-BRAY 3F

FECAMP 64
LE HAVRE 111
Av Jean Jaurès

ROUEN 58 (Via Autoroute) 20†
PARIS (Via Autoroute) 166
PARIS (Via D915) 166

D154
ARQUES-LA-BATAILLE 7

LE TRÉPORT 31
ABBEVILLE 65
EU 32

D925

N27

(7/89)

DIEPPE ENVIRONS

DIEPPE CENTRAL

D113

Neuville-lès-Dieppe

D925

D925

D75

D920

La Barre

St Pierre

D154E

N27

D485

D925

N27 (To D915)

Mammouth Supermarket

D154

R. Arques Varenne

D54

Martin-Église

D1

SCALE
0 — ½ — 1km

(7/89)

DIEPPE

1	★★★★	Présidence	3	★★	Select
2	★★★	Aguado	4	★★	Windsor

DIEPPE
Seine-Maritime

★★★★**Présidence** 1 bd de Verdun ☎35843131
tx 180865
🏃♿89 ♨ P52 Lift ℂ Sea
Credit Cards ①②③⑤

★★★**Aguado** 30 bd de Verdun (n.rest)
☎35842700
🏃♿56 Lift Sea
Credit Cards ①③

★★**Select** 1 r Toustain,pl de la Barre (n.rest)
☎35841466
rm25(♿24) A3rm P5 Lift
Credit Cards ①②③

★★**Windsor** 𝕃𝔼18 bd de Verdun ☎35841523
25 Jan-20 Dec
rm47(♿42) Lift Sea
Credit Cards ①②③⑤

DIGNE
Alpes-de-Haute-Provence

★★**Aiglon** 𝕃𝔼1 r de Provence ☎92310270
Feb-Nov
rm26(♿5) P8 Mountain
Credit Cards ①②③⑤

★★**Mistre** 65 bd Gassendi ☎92310016
10 Jan-10 Dec :Rest closed Sat
🏃♿19 ♨
Credit Cards ①②③

🍴 **J P Pavot** 21 av du MI-Juin ☎ 92313536 P
Peu

🍴 **Zerubia** ZI des Arches ☎ 92312551 Rov

DIGOIN
Saône-et-Loire

★**Gare** 79 av GI-de-Gaulle ☎85530304
Feb-Dec :Rest closed Wed (except Jul & Aug)
🏃♿13 A4rm P20
Credit Cards ①③⑤

★**Terminus** DPn 76 av du GI-de-Gaulle
☎85532528
Feb-15 Jan
rm15(♿12) ♨ P14
Credit Cards ①③

DIJON
Côte-d'Or

Dijon is an exceptionally rich city
of art with numerous facinating
monuments recalling the fact that
it was, under the reign of the
Dukes of Burgundy, the capital of
a state which united Flanders
and Bourgogne.
Be sure to visit the *Hôtel Ducal*
and the *Palais de Ducs et Palais
des Etats* (Palace of the Dukes and
Palace of the States of Burgundy),
dating from the 14th - 15th
centuries; the St Bénigne
Cathedral (13th century) with its
extremely rare Roman crypt; the
Church of Notre-Dame, a
masterpiece of Burgundian
Gothic; and the Church of St
Michel, a Renaissance jewel. Also
well worth visiting are the
courthouse, installed in a former
headquarters of the Parliament of
Burgundy, the many rich private
mansions; and the countless
well-restored old houses in the

pedestrian sector of the city.
Dijon's impressive museums
include the *Musée des Beaux Arts*
(Fine Arts Museum), one of the
richest in France, the Rude
Museum, the Museum of Sacred
Art and the Archaeological
Museum.

EATING OUT Widely considered
one of the best restaurants in
Dijon is the *Jean-Pierre Billoux*,
located in a delightfully restored
town house in Place Darcy. Good
regional cooking can be sampled
at *Vinarium*, in Place Bossuet,
housed in a 13th-century crypt.

DIJON
Côte-d'Or

★★★★**Altea Palais des Congrès** Face au Palais
des Congres-BP3 ☎80723113 tx 350293
🏃♿123 ♨ P100 Lift ⌇
Credit Cards ①②③⑤

★★★★**Cloche** 14 pl Darcy ☎80301232 tx 350498
:Rest closed Sun evening & Mon
🏃♿80 ♨ P60 Lift
Credit Cards ①②③⑤

★★★**Chapeau Rouge** (MAP/BW) 5 r Michelet
☎80302810 tx 350535
🏃♿33 ♨ P30 Lift ℂ
Credit Cards ①②③④⑤

★★★**Urbis Dijon** 3 pl Grangier ☎80304400 tx
350606
🏃♿90 Lift
Credit Cards ①③

★★**Arcade Relais Dijon** 15 bis av Albert 1er
☎80430112 tx 350515
🏃♿128 ♨ P Lift
Credit Cards ①③

★★**Hostellerie du Sauvage** 64 r Monge (n.rest)
☎80413121
rm21(♿10) ♨
Credit Card ③

★★**Jura** 14 av MI-Foch (n.rest) ☎80416112 tx
350485
🏃♿80 P20 Lift ℂ
Credit Cards ①②③⑤

★**Nord** Place Darcy ☎80305858 tx 351554
9 Jan-23 Dec
rm29(♿25) Lift ℂ
Credit Cards ①②③⑤

🍴 **Château d'Eau** 1 bd Fontaine des Suisses ☎
80654034 P Peu

🍴 **Dijon Nord** 2 r du Champsaux Feves,Z
Antisanale ☎ 80572523 P Ope Mit

🍴 **Lignier** 3 r des G-Champs ☎ 80663905 P For

🍴 **Monchpart** 12 r Gagnereaux ☎ 80734111 For

🍴 **Mont Blanc** 2 av du Mont-Blanc ☎ 80664514
P Peu

🍴 **SCA Bourgogne Auto** Dijon Nord,r de
Cracovie ☎ 80738116 Peu Tal

At HAUTEVILLE-LÈS-DIJON(7km NE D107)

★**Musarde** 𝕃𝔼DPn ☎80562282
rm11(♿8) P10
Credit Cards ①③⑤

At PERRIGNY-LÈS-DIJON(9km S on N74)

★★★**Novotel Dijon-Sud** rte de Beaune (N74)
☎80521422 tx 350728
🏃♿124 ⌇
Credit Cards ①②③⑤

★★**Ibis** rte de Lyon-Beaune ☎80528645 tx
351510
:Rest closed Sun & B H
🏃♿48 P45

At QUÉTIGNY(5km E CD 107b)

★★**Climat** 14 av de Bourgogne ☎80460446 tx
692844
🏃♿42 P
Credit Cards ①③

At ST-APOLLINAIRE(3km E)

★★**Campanile** rte de Gray ☎80724538 tx 350566
🏃♿50 P50
Credit Card ③

At SENNECEY-LE-DIJON(3km SW)

★★★**Flambée** (MAP/BW) Ancienne rte de Dole-
Genève (n.rest) ☎80473535 tx 350273
🏃♿23 P40 Lift
Credit Cards ①②③⑤

DINAN
Côtes-du-Nord

★★**Avaugour** 𝕃𝔼1 pl du Champs Clos
☎96390749 tx 950145
🏃♿27 Lift
Credit Cards ①②③④⑤

🍴 **Dinanaise Auto** rte de Ploubalay,Taden ☎
96396495 P For

DINARD
Ille-et-Vilaine

★★★★**Grand** 46 av George-V ☎99461028 tx
740522
🏃♿93 P30 Lift ℂ ⌇ Sea
Credit Cards ①②③

★★**Bains** 38 av George-V ☎99461311 tx 740802
15 Mar-15 Oct
rm39(♿35) Lift ℂ Sea
Credit Cards ②③⑤

★★**Climat** La Millière ☎99466955 tx 740300
🏃♿42 A16rm P35 Sea
Credit Cards ①③④

★★**Emeraude Plage** 1 bd Albert Ier ☎99461579
tx 740802
Etr-Sep
rm59(♿53) A5rm ♨ P20 Lift Sea

★★**Printania** 5 av Georges-V ☎99461307
Etr-Sep
🏃♿77 A30rm Sea
Credit Cards ②③

DIZY
See ÉPERNAY

DOLANCOURT
Aube

★★**Moulin du Landion** DPn ☎25261217/
25279217
Jan-Nov
🏃♿16 P36
Credit Cards ①③⑤

DOL-DE-BRETAGNE
Ille-et-Vilaine

★★**Bresche Arthur** 𝕃𝔼(Inter) DPn bd Deminiac
☎99480144 tx 741369
🏃♿24 P10
Credit Cards ①②③④⑤

★★**Bretagne** 𝕃𝔼17 pl Châteaubriand
☎99480203
Closed Oct
rm29(♿14) ♨ P8
Credit Cards ①③

DOLE
Jura

★★★**Chandioux** (MAP/BW) pl Grévy ☎84790066
tx 360498
🏃♿33 ♨ P23 ℂ
Credit Cards ①②③④⑤

DOMFRONT
Orne

★★**Poste** L̲E̲DPn 15 r Ml-Foch ☎33385100
25 Feb-15 Jan
rm29(🛏14) 🅿 P20
Credit Cards 1 2 3 5

★**France** L̲Er Mont St-Michel ☎33385144 tx
306022
14 Feb-6 Jan
rm22(🛏14) P30 ⚲
Credit Cards 1 3

DOMPAIRE
Vosges

★★**Commerce** L̲Epl Ml-Leclerc ☎29365028
🛏11
Credit Cards 1 2 3 4 5

DONZENAC
Corrèze

🚗 **J N Chamournie** La Pause ☎ 55857876 **P**
Peu Tal

At **ST-PARDOUX-L'ORTIGIER**(9km N off N20)
🚗 **M Dely** N20 ☎ 55845167 **P** Peu Tal

DORDIVES
Loiret

★★**César** L̲E8 r de la République ☎38927320
rm24(🛏14) 🅿 P24
Credit Cards 1 2 5

DOUAI
Nord

★★**Climat** pl du Brossolette ☎27882997 tx
820537
🛏42 P40
Credit Cards 1 3

★**Grand Cerf** 46 r St-Jacques ☎27887960
rm39(🛏30) P ☾
Credit Cards 1 2 3

★★**Urbis** pl St-Ame,r de la Fonderie ☎27872727
tx 820220
🛏42 🅿 P20 Lift
Credit Cards 1 3

DOUARNENEZ
Finistère

★★**Bretagne** 23 r Duguay-Trouin (n.rest)
☎98923044 tx 29100
🛏27 Lift

DOUÉ-LA-FONTAINE
Maine-et-Loire

★**Dagobert** L̲E̲DPn 14 pl Champ-de-Foire
☎41591444
Closed Dec & Jan
rm20(🛏16) P
Credit Card 3

DOURDAN
Essonne

★★★**Blanche de Castille** pl des Halles
☎64596892 tx 604902
🛏41 P30 Lift ☾
Credit Cards 1 2 3 5

DOUSSARD
See **FAVERGES**

DOZULÉ
Calvados

🚗 **R Marci** fbg du Pont Mousse ☎ 31792041 **P**
Peu Tal

🚗 **St-Christophe** 102 Grande rue ☎ 31792036 **P**
Ren

DRAGUIGNAN
Var

★★**Col de l'Ange** rte de Lorgues ☎94682301 tx
970423
🛏30 P30 ⌂ Mountain
Credit Cards 1 2 3 5

DRAMONT, LE
See **AGAY**

DREUX
Eure-et-Loir

★★**Auberge Normande** L̲E12 pl Metezeau
(n.rest) ☎37500203
🛏16
Credit Cards 1 3

★★**Balladins** rte des Anglais ☎05355575 tx
649394
rm38 P38
Credit Cards 1 2 3 4

★★**Campanile** av W-Churchill ☎37426484 tx
783578
🛏42 P42
Credit Card 3

🚗 **Ouest** 51 av des Fenots ☎ 37461145 Rov

🚗 **Perrin Freres** bd de l'Europe,Vernouillet ☎
37462331 **P** For

At **MONTREUIL**(8km NE)

★★**Auberge Gué des Grues** ☎37435025
rm3(🛏2) P Lift

DUCEY
Manche

★★**Ibis** St-Quentin-sur-Le-Homme ☎33604242 tx
171784
🛏42 P50 ☾
Credit Cards 1 3

DUCLAIR
Seine-Maritime

★★**Poste** L̲E̲DPn 286 quai de la Libération
☎35375004
:Rest closed Sun evening & Mon
🛏24
Credit Cards 1 2 3

DUNKERQUE (DUNKIRK)
Nord

★★★**Altea Reuze** r J-Jaurès (n.rest)
☎28591111 tx 110587
🛏122 P3 Lift Sea
Credit Cards 1 2 3 5

★★★**Borel** 6 r l'Hermitte (n.rest) ☎28665180 tx
820050
🛏48 Lift
Credit Cards 1 2 3 4 5

★★★**Europ** (MAP/BW) 13 r de Leughenaer
☎28662907 tx 120084
🛏130 🅿 Lift
Credit Cards 1 2 3 4 5

At **ARMBOUTS-CAPPEL**(6km S)

★★★**Mercure** Voie-Express,Bordure du Lac
☎28607060 tx 820916
🛏64 🅿 P100 ⛱ Lake
Credit Cards 1 2 3 5

★★**Campanile** Bordure du Lac ☎28646470 tx
132294
🛏42 P42

ÉCOLE-VALENTIN
See **BESANÇON**

ÉCOMMOY
Sarthe

★**Commerce** 19 pl République ☎43421034
15 Feb-Jan
rm13(🛏4) 🅿 P3
Credit Cards 1 3

ECOUEN
Val-d'Oise

★★**Campanile** La Redoute du Moulin (N16)
☎39944600 tx 699594
🛏50 P50
Credit Card 3

ECULLY
See **LYON**

EGUILLES
See **AIX-EN-PROVENCE**

ELBEUF
Seine-Maritime

At **CLÉON**(5km N)

★★**Campanile** r de l'Église ☎35813800 tx
172691
🛏42 P42
Credit Card 3

At **LONDE, LA**(5km NW D913)

🚗 **Maison Brulée** ☎ 35238055 **P** AR

ÉMERAINVILLE
See **CHAMPS-SUR-MARNE**

ENGLOS
See **LILLE**

ENTRAYGUES-SUR-TRUYÈRE
Aveyron

★★**Truyère** L̲E☎65445110
Apr-15 Nov :Rest closed Mon
🛏25 🅿 P25 Lift Mountain Lake
Credit Cards 1 3

ÉPERNAY
Marne

★★★**Berceaux** 13 r Berceaux ☎26553022 tx
842717
🛏29 Lift ☾
Credit Cards 1 2 3 5

★★★**Champagne** 30 r E-Mercier ☎26553022 tx
842068
🛏32 🅿 P6 Lift ☾
Credit Cards 1 2 5

★★**Climat** r de Lorraine ☎26541739 tx 842720
🛏33 P40 ☾
Credit Cards 1 3

★★**Pomme d'Or** 12 r E-Mercier (n.rest)
☎26531144 tx 841150
🛏26 Lift
Credit Card 1

At **CHAMPILLON**(6km N on N51)

★★★**Royal Champagne** (Relais et Châteaux)
Bellevue ☎26511151 tx 830111
Closed 3wks Jan
🛏23 P ☾
Credit Cards 1 2 3 4 5

At **DIZY**(3km N)

★★**Campanile** Les Terres Rouges ☎26553366 tx
842713
🛏42 P42
Credit Card 3

At **MOUSSY**(2.5km S)

★★**Auberge Champenoise** L̲EMoussy le Village
☎26540348 tx 842743
rm35(🛏30) A8rm 🅿 P40 ⚲
Credit Cards 1 3

At **VINAY**(6km S on n51)

★★★**Briqueterie** rte de Sézanne ☎26541122 tx
842007
2 Mar-Oct :Rest closed 5 Feb-2 Mar
🛏42 P75 ⛱
Credit Cards 1 2 3 4 5

ÉPINAL
Vosges

★★★**Mercure** 13 pl Stein ☎29351868 tx 960277
:Rest Closed Sat
🛏40 🅿 P10 Lift
Credit Cards 1 2 3 5

★★**Campanile** r du M-Blanc,Bois-de-la-Voivre
☎29313838 tx 961107
🛏41 P41
Credit Card 3

★★**Ibis** quai Ml-de-Contades ☎29642828 tx
850053
🛏60 🅿 P20 Lift
Credit Cards 1 3

🚗 **Grands Garages Spinaliens** 17 r du Ml-
Lyautey ☎ 29824747 For

🚗 **Sessa** r A-Vitu ☎ 29341864 Rov Vol

At CHAVELOT(8km N)

★★**Climat** ☎29313940
⇥✿26

ÉPINAY-SUR-ORGE
Essonne

★★**Campanile** r du Grand Vaux ☎64486020 tx
600148
⇥✿50 P50

ÉPINAY-SUR-SEINE
Seine-et-Denis

★★**Ibis** av du 18 Juin 1940 ☎48298341 tx
614354
⇥✿91 ✿ P25 Lift
Credit Cards ①③

ÉPINE, L'
See CHÂLONS-SUR-MARNE

EPONE
Yvelines

★★**Etape Coqvert** CD113 ☎30956870 tx 698286
⇥✿49 P50 ◑
Credit Card ③

EQUEUDREVILLE
Manche

★★**Climat** r de la Paix ☎33934294
⇥✿42 P40
Credit Cards ①②③⑤

ERDEVEN
Morbihan

★★**Auberge du Sous Bois** Ⓛ(FAH) rte de Pont
Lorois ☎97556610 tx 950581
Apr-10 Oct
⇥✿22 P50 ☾
Credit Cards ①②③⑤

ERMENONVILLE
Oise

★★**Auberge de la Crôix d'Or** ⒧Ⓔ**DPn** 2 r Prince
Radziwill ☎44540004
Closed 2-19 Jan:Rest closed Mon
rm11(⇥✿9) P15
Credit Cards ①③

ERNÉE
Mayenne

★★★**Relais de Poste** Ⓛ1 pl de l'Église
☎43052033 tx 730956
:Rest closed Sun Eve
⇥✿35 ✿ P Lift
Credit Cards ①③

ERQUY
Côtes-du-Nord

★**Beauregard** Ⓛbd de la Mer ☎96723003
rm17 A8rm P30 Sea
Credit Cards ①②⑤

ÉTAIN
Meuse

➽ **Beauguitte** 87 r Poincaré ☎ 29871290 **P** Ren

ETSAUT
Pyrénées-Atlantiques

★**Pyrénées** Ⓛ**DPn** ☎59348862
Jan-10 Nov
rm16(⇥✿12) Mountain
Credit Cards ③④

EVIAN-LES-BAINS
Haute-Savoie

★★★★**Royal** ☎50751400 tx 385759
10 Feb-15 Dec
⇥✿158 ✿ P102 Lift ☾ ◑ ▱ ⌂ ♤♤ Mountain
Lake
Credit Cards ①②③⑤

★★★**Bellevue** 6 r B-Moutardier ☎50750113
May-Sep
⇥✿50 Lift ☾ Lake
Credit Cards ①③

★★**Mateirons** (Inter-Hotels) ☎50750416
15 Mar-15 Oct
rm22(⇥✿18) P Mountain Lake
Credit Card ②

ÉVREUX
Eure

★★**Campanile** av W-Churchill ☎32337565 tx
771348
⇥✿42 P42
Credit Card ③

★★**Climat** Zone Tertiaire de la Madel ☎32311047
tx 770516
⇥✿42 P40
Credit Cards ①③

★★**France** Ⓛ29 r St-Thomas ☎32390925
⇥✿15 ✿ P4
Credit Cards ①②③⑤

★★**Grenoble** 17 r St-Pierre (n.rest) ☎32330731
Closed Etr & Xmas
rm19(⇥✿16) ✿ P7
Credit Cards ①③

★★**Ibis** av W-Churchill ☎32381636 tx 172748
⇥✿60 P60
Credit Cards ①③

★★**Normandy** 37 r E-Féray ☎32331440 tx
770411
:Rest closed Sun
⇥✿26 ✿ P15 ☾
Credit Cards ①③

★★**Orme** Ⓛ(FAH) 13 r Lombards (n.rest)
☎32393412
rm43(⇥✿37) Lift
Credit Cards ①②③

➽ **Hôtel-de-Ville** 4 r G-Bernard ☎ 32395863 For

ÉVRY
Essonne
See also CORBEIL-ESSONNES

★★**Arcade** 16 cours Blaise-Pascal ☎60782990 tx
601249
:Rest closed Fri lunch-Sun lunch
⇥✿100 Lift
Credit Cards ①③

★★**Balladins** pl G-Crémieux,Quartier des
Epinettes ☎64972121 tx 649394
⇥✿28 P

★★**Ibis** 1 av du Lac,Parc Yertiare du Bois Briard
☎60777475 tx 601728
⇥✿135 P200 Lift
Credit Cards ①③

★★**Novotel Paris Évry** Parc Dubois Briard,3 r de
la Mare Neuve ☎60778270 tx 600685
⇥✿174 P250 Lift ▱
Credit Cards ①②③⑤

EYBENS
Isère

★★**Fimotel** 20 av J-Jaurès ☎76242312 tx 980371
⇥✿42 P35 Lift

ÉYZIES-DE-TAYAC, LES
Dordogne

★★★**Cro-Magnon** (MAP/BW) **DPn** ☎53069706 tx
570637
28 Apr-10 Oct
⇥✿24 A8rm P40 ▱
Credit Cards ①②③④⑤

★★**Centenaire** Ⓛ(Relais et Châteaux) **Pn**
☎53069718 tx 541921
Apr-Nov :Rest closed Tue midday
⇥✿26 A5rm ✿ P30 Lift ☾ ▱
Credit Cards ①③

★★**Centre** Ⓛ**E**Les Sireuils ☎53069713
Mar-Nov
⇥✿18
Credit Cards ①③

★★**Glycines** ☎53069707
mid Apr-3 Nov
⇥✿25 P60 ▱
Credit Cards ①②③

★**France- Auberge de Musée** Ⓛ**E**☎53069723
26 Mar-10 Nov
rm29(⇥✿22) A13rm P27 Mountain Lake
Credit Cards ①③

➽ **J C Dupuy** pl de la Port ☎ 53069732 **P** Ren

ÉZE
Alpes-Maritimes

★★★★**Cap Estel** **DPn** ☎93015044 tx 470305
Mar-Oct
⇥✿43 A6rm P50 Lift ☾ ▱ ⌂ Beach Sea
Credit Cards ①③

FALAISE
Calvados

★★**Normandie** 4 r Amiral Courbet ☎31901826
rm26(⇥✿16) ✿
Credit Cards ①③

★★**Poste** Ⓛ**E**Pn 38 r G-Clemenceau
☎31901314
rm19(⇥✿12) ✿ P8
Credit Cards ①②③

FAOUËT, LE
Morbihan

★**Croix d'Or** **DPn** 9 pl Bellanger ☎97230733
15 Jan-15 Dec :Rest closed Sat (out of season)
⇥✿12 ✿ P10
Credit Cards ①③

FARLÈDE, LA
See TOULON

FAVERGES
Haute-Savoie

★**Parc** rte d'Albertville ☎50445025
⇥✿12 Mountain
Credit Card ①

At DOUSSARD(7km NW)

★★**Marceau** Marceau Dessus ☎50443011 tx
309346
15 Jan-15 Dec :Rest closed Sun pm & Wed out of
season
⇥✿16 ✿ P30 ◑ Mountain Lake
Credit Cards ①②③⑤

FAVERGES-DE-LA-TOUR
See TOUR-DU-PIN, LA

FAYENCE
Var

★★★**Moulin de la Camandoule** **DPn** chemin N D
des Cypres ☎94760084
⇥✿11 P35 ▱ Mountain
Credit Cards ①③

➽ **G Difant** Quartier Prés-Gaudin ☎ 94760740 **P**

At TOURRETTES(1km W)

★**Grillon** N562 ☎94760296
⇥✿28 P30 ☾ ▱ Mountain
Credit Cards ①③

FÈRE, LA
Aisne

★**Tourelles** 51 r de la République (6km from A26)
(n.rest) ☎23563166
rm16(⇥✿8) ✿ P10
Credit Cards ①②③

FÈRE-EN-TARDENOIS
Aisne

★★★★**Château** (Relais et Châteaux) **DPn**
☎23822113 tx 145526
⇥✿23 P40 ▱
Credit Cards ①②③

FERTÉ-BERNARD, LA
Sarthe

★★**Climat** 43 bd Gl-de-Gaulle ☎43938470 tx
720435
⇥✿46 P40
Credit Cards ①②③

FERTÉ-ST-AUBIN, LA
Loiret

★★*Perron* (FAH) **Pn** 9 r du Gl-Leclerc
☎38765356 tx 782485
Closed 15-30 Jan
rm20(➔♠17) P40
Credit Cards ① ② ③ ⑤

FERTÉ-SOUS-JOUARRE, LA
Seine-et-Marne

🏩 *Parc* 10 av de Montmiral ☎ 60229000 Cit

FIGEAC
Lot

★★*Carmes* **LE**(FAH) enclos des Carmes
☎65342070 tx 520794
15 Jan-15 Dec
➔♠32 P35 Lift ⌂
Credit Cards ① ② ③ ⑤

FIRMINY
Loire

★★*Firm* 37 r J-Jaurès ☎77560899
:Rest closed Sun pm
➔♠20 (
Credit Cards ① ② ③ ④ ⑤

★★*Table du Pavillon* 4 av de la Gare
☎77560045
: Rest closed Sun evening & Mon
➔♠22 🅿 P15 Lift
Credit Cards ① ② ③ ⑤

FIXIN
Côte-d'Or

★★*Chez Jeannette* **LE**DPn ☎80524549
25 Jan-23 Dec :Rest closed Thu
rm11(♠9) P12
Credit Cards ① ② ③ ④ ⑤

FLEURAC
See **JARNAC**

FLEURANCE
Gers

★★*Fleurance* rte d'Agen ☎62061485
20 Jan-10 Dec :Rest closed Sun pm & Mon low season
➔♠24 P60
Credit Cards ① ② ③ ⑤

FLEURY-LES-AUBRAIS
Loiret

🏩 *Societé D.A.C.* 50 r de la Halte,Saran ☎
38734141 P

FLORAC
Lozère

★★*Parc* 47 av J-Monestier ☎66450305
15 Mar-1 Dec :Rest closed Sun eve & Mon low season
rm66(➔♠49) A26rm 🅿 P45 Mountain
Credit Cards ① ② ③ ④ ⑤

★*Gorges du Tarn* 48 r du Pêcher (n.rest)
☎66450063
May-Sep
rm31(➔13) A12rm 🅿 P20 Mountain

FLORENSAC
Hérault

★★*Leonce* **LE**2 pl de la République
☎67770305
Mar-20 Sep
rm14(➔♠10) Lift
Credit Cards ① ② ③ ⑤

FLOTTE, LA
See **RÉ, ILE DE**

FOIX
Ariège

★★★*Barbacane* 1 av de Lerida ☎61655044
Mar-Nov
➔♠22 🅿 P18 Mountain
Credit Card ③

★★★*Tourisme* 2 cours I-Cros ☎616549121 tx 530955
➔♠28 (
Credit Cards ① ② ③

FONTAINEBLEAU
Seine-et-Marne

★★★*Aigle Noir* (MAP/BW) 27 pl N-Bonaparte ☎64223265 tx 694080
➔♠57 P35 Lift (⊡
Credit Cards ① ② ③ ⑤

★★*Ibis Fontainbleau* 18 r de Ferrare
☎64234525 tx 692240
➔♠81 P25 Lift
Credit Cards ① ③

★★*Ile de France* **LE**(Inter) 128 r de France
☎64228515 tx 690358
➔♠25 P20 (
Credit Cards ① ② ③ ④ ⑤

★★*Londres* DPn 1 pl du Gl-de-Gaulle
☎64222021
Jan-20 Dec
rm22(➔♠7) P20
Credit Cards ① ② ③ ⑤

★★*Toulouse* 183 r Grande (n.rest) ☎64222273
20 Jan-20 Dec
rm18(➔♠15) (
Credit Cards ① ③

★*Forêt* 79 av Prés-Roosevelt ☎64223926
rm26(➔♠19) A9rm 🅿 P10 (
Credit Cards ① ③

🏩 *François 1er* 9 r de la Chancellerie ☎ 64222034 For

🏩 *St-Antoine* 111 r de France ☎ 64223188 AR

At **AVON**(2km S)

★★*Fimotel* 46 av F-Roosevelt ☎64223021 tx 693072
➔♠42 P Lift
Credit Cards ① ② ③ ⑤

At **URY**(6km SW on N51)

★★★*Novotel* rte Nationale 152 ☎64244825 tx 694153
➔♠127 P120 ℺ ⊃
Credit Cards ① ② ③ ⑤

FONTAINE-CHAALIS
Oise

★*Auberge de Fontaine* DPn Grande Rue ☎44542022
3 Mar-30 Jan :Rest closed Tue evening & Wed
➔8
Credit Card ①

FONTENAY-LE-COMTE
Vendée

★★*Rabelais* **LE**(Inter) rte Parthenay
☎51698620
➔♠45 🅿 P55 ⊃
Credit Cards ① ② ③ ⑤

🏩 *M Breton* 61 rte de Nantes P For

FONTENAY-SOUS-BOIS
Val-de-Marne

★★*Climat* r Rabelais ☎48762198 tx 629844
➔♠42 P30

★★*Fimotel* pl du Gl-de-Gaulle,av du Val-de-Fontenay ☎48766771 tx 232748
➔♠100 Lift
Credit Cards ① ② ③ ⑤

FONTEVRAUD-L'ABBAYE
Maine-et-Loire

★★*Croix Blanche* **LE**7 pl Plantagenets ☎41517111
Closed 13-19 Nov & 8 Jan-7 Feb
rm24(➔♠20) 🅿 P24 (
Credit Cards ① ③

FONT-ROMEU
Pyrénées-Orientales

★★★*Bellevue* av du Dr-Capelle ☎68300016
:Rest closed 15 Sep-15 Dec
rm65(➔30) P (Mountain

★★★*Carlit* ☎68300745 tx 375974
20 Dec-20 Apr & Jun-Oct
➔♠58 Lift ⊃ Mountain
Credit Cards ①

★★*Pyrénées* pl des Pyrénées ☎68300149
20 Dec-15 Apr & Jun-5 Nov
➔♠40 Lift ⊃ Mountain
Credit Cards ① ② ③ ⑤

FONVIALANE
See **ALBI**

FORBACH
Moselle

★★*Fimotel* r F-Barth ☎87870606 tx 861312
➔♠42 P200 Lift ⊃ Mountain

FORÊT-FOUESNANT, LA
Finistère

★★*Baie* **LE**☎98569735
➔♠24 ⊃ Sea
Credit Cards ① ② ③

★★*Esperance* **LE**☎98569658
Apr-Sep :Rest closed Wed
rm30(➔24) A18rm P8 Sea
Credit Cards ① ③

★*Beauséjour* 47 r de la Baie ☎98569718
17 Mar-15 Nov
rm26(➔♠17) P20 Sea
Credit Cards ① ③ ④

FOS-SUR-MER
Bouches-du-Rhône

★★★★*Altea Provence* La Bastidonne,rte d'Istres ☎42050057 tx 410812
:Rest closed Sat & Sun lunch in winter
➔♠66 🅿 P70 ℺ ⊃ Sea Lake
Credit Cards ① ② ③ ⑤

FOUESNANT
Finistère

★★*Pointe de Mousterlin* Pointe de Mousterlin ☎98560412
14 Apr-15 Oct
rm62(➔♠55) A20rm P70 Lift ℺ Sea
Credit Cards ① ③

★*Armorique* **LE**☎98560019
Mar-Oct
rm22(➔16) A12rm P15
Credit Cards ① ③

🏩 *J L Bourhis* rte de Quimper ☎ 98560265 P Ren

🏩 *Merrien* rte de Quimper ☎ 98560017 P Peu Tal

FOUGÈRES
Ille-et-Vilaine

★★*Mainotel* N12 ☎99998155 tx 730956
:Rest closed Sun dinner
➔♠50 P80 (℺
Credit Cards ① ③

★★*Voyageurs* 10 pl Gambetta ☎99990820 tx 730666
5 Jan-20 Dec :Rest closed Sat
➔♠37 A10rm Lift
Credit Cards ① ② ③ ④ ⑤

★*Moderne* **LE**15 r Tribunal ☎99990024
rm25(➔♠21) 🅿
Credit Cards ① ② ③ ④ ⑤

FOULAIN
Haute-Marne

★*Chalet* **LE**☎25311111
Oct-15 Sep :Rest closed Sun pm & Mon 15 Sep-15 Jun
rm12(➔♠5) P25 ℺
Credit Cards ② ③ ⑤

FOURAS
Charente-Maritime

★★**Grand Hotel des Bains DPn** 15 r Gl-Bruncher
☎46840344
25 Mar-11 Nov
rm36(➹♙35) ☎ P12
Credit Card ③

FOURMETOT
See PONT-AUDEMER

FOURMIES
Nord

★★**Ibis** Étangs des Moines (n.rest) ☎27602154 tx
810172
➹♙30 P50 Lake
Credit Cards ① ③

FOURNEAUX
See AUBUSSON

FRAYSSINET
Lot

★*Bonne Auberge* DPn ☎65310002
Apr-Oct
➹♙10 ☎ P15
Credit Cards ① ③

★*Escale* 𝐋𝐄☎65310001
15 Feb-Dec
➹♙8 P20
Credit Cards ① ③

➷ **Drianne** N 20 ☎ 65310017 **P** All makes

At PONT-DE-RHODES(1km N on N20)

★*Relais* ☎65310016
Etr-15 Nov
➹♙22 A13rm P20 ℺ ⌂
Credit Card ③

FRÉJUS
Var

★★★*St-Aygulf* 214 rte Nationale 98 ☎65310016
15 Mar-15 Nov
➹♙83 P Lift Sea Mountain
Credit Card ③

➷ **Satac** N 7 ☎ 94514061 Ren

➷ **Vagneur** 449 bd de la Mer ☎ 94513839 For

At COLOMBIER(3km W)

★★★*Residences du Colombier* rte de Bagnols
☎94514592 tx 470328
Apr-Oct
➹♙60 P120 ℂ ⌂ Mountain
Credit Cards ① ② ③ ④ ⑤

FRÉVENT
Pas-de-Calais

★*Amiens* 𝐋𝐄7 r Doullens ☎21036543
rm10(➹♙7) ☎ P Lift ℺ ☒
Credit Cards ① ② ③

At MONCHEL-SUR-CANCHE(7.5km NW D340)

★★*Vert Bocage* (n.rest) ☎21479675
➹♙10 P60 Mountain Lake
Credit Card ①

FRONTIGNAN
Hérault

★★*Balajan* DPn N112 ☎67481399
Closed Feb:Rest closed Sat lunch
rm21(➹♙19) ☎ P35 ⌂ Mountain
Credit Cards ① ③

FUMAY
Ardennes

★★*Roches* 393 av J-Jaurès ☎24411012
Apr-Nov
➹♙31 P30 Mountain
Credit Cards ① ③ ⑤

GACÉ
Orne

★★★*Champs* rte d'Alençon-Rouen ☎33390905
15 Feb-15 Nov
rm13(➹♙11) ☎ P15 ℺ ⌂
Credit Cards ① ③ ④ ⑤

★★*Morphée* 2 r de Lisieux (n.rest) ☎33355101 tx
771992
Closed Jan-15 Mar
➹♙10 P10
Credit Cards ① ② ③ ⑤

★*Etoile d'Or* 60 Grande r ☎33355003
Mar-Jan :Rest closed Sun evening & Mon
rm11(➹♙4) ☎ P6
Credit Cards ① ③

GAILLARD
Haute-Savoie
See also ANNEMASSE

★★★*Mercure* r des Jardins (exit Annemasse-
B41) ☎50920525 tx 385815
➹♙78 P Lift ⌂ Mountain
Credit Cards ① ② ③ ⑤

★★*Climat* r R-Cassin,ZAC de la Châtelaine
☎50371922 tx 309931
➹♙43 P45 Mountain
Credit Cards ① ② ③

GAILLON
Eure

➷ **Pourpardin** Côte-des-Sables ☎ 32530337 **P** All makes

GAP
Hautes-Alpes

★★*Fons Régina* 𝐋𝐄Quartier de Fontreyme
(N85) ☎92539899
rm20(➹♙16) ☎ P30 Mountain
Credit Cards ① ② ③ ⑤

★★*Grille* 2 pl F-Euzière ☎92538484 tx 405896
5 Jan-5 Dec :Rest closed Sun & Mon
➹♙30 ☎ P4 Lift
Credit Cards ① ② ③ ⑤

★★*Mokotel* Quartier Graffinel,rte de Marseille
(n.rest) ☎92515782
➹♙27 P27 Mountain
Credit Cards ① ② ③ ⑤

➷ **Europ'auto** rte de Briançon ☎ 92520546 **P**
For

➷ **Verdun** 4 r P-Bert ☎ 92512618 Rov LR

At PONT-SARRAZIN(4km NE on N94)

➷ **Berta** ☎ 92536730 **P** VW

GARDE, LA
See TOULON

GARDE-ST-CAST, LA
See ST-CAST-LE-GUILDO

GEISPOLSHEIM
See STRASBOURG

GÉMENOS
Bouches-du-Rhône

★★★★*Relais de la Magdeleine* rte d'Aix-en-
Provence ☎42822005
Mar-Oct
➹♙20 P40 ⌂ Mountain
Credit Cards ① ③

GENNES
Maine-et-Loire

★★*Loire* 𝐋𝐄Pn ☎41518103
10 Feb-28 Dec :Rest closed Mon evening & Tue
rm11(➹♙7) ☎ P12

★★*Naulets d'Anjou* r Croix-de-Mission
☎41518188
15 Mar-15 Nov :Rest closed Mon in high season
➹♙20 P℺
Credit Cards ① ③

GENNEVILLIERS
Hauts-de-Seine

★★*Fimotel* Ilot des Chevrins ☎42615014 tx
215269
➹♙60 P Lift
Credit Cards ① ② ③ ⑤

GENTILLY
SeePARIS

GÉRARDMER
Vosges

★★★★*Grand Bragard* pl du Tilleul ☎29630631
tx 960964
➹♙61 ☎ P60 Lift ℂ ⌂ Mountain
Credit Cards ① ② ③ ⑤

★★*Parc* 𝐋𝐅12-14 av de la Ville-de-Vichy
☎29633243 tx 961408
Etr-Oct & Feb
➹♙36 A14rm ☎ P20 Mountain Lake
Credit Cards ① ③

★★*Echo de Ramberchamp* (n.rest) ☎29630227
20 Dec-15 Nov
rm16(➹♙11) P30 Mountain Lake
Credit Card ③

At SAUT-DES-CUVES(3km NE N417)

★★★*Saut-des-Cuves* ☎29633046
➹♙27 ☎ Lift Mountain

GETS, LES
Haute-Savoie

★★★*Marmotte* 𝐋𝐄Pn☎50797539
Seasonal
➹♙45 Lift ℺ ☒ ⌂ Mountain
Credit Cards ① ② ③ ⑤

GEX
Ain

★*Bellevue* av de la Gare ☎50415540
Feb-15 Dec :Rest closed Sat evening & Sun
rm22(➹♙11) ☎ P6 Mountain Lake
Credit Cards ① ② ③

GIEN
Loiret

★★*Rivage* 𝐋𝐄DPn 1 quai de Nice ☎38672053
:Rest closed 5 Feb-1 Mar
➹♙22 P15
Credit Cards ① ② ③ ⑤

GIVORS
Rhône

★★*Balladins* Centre Commercial,de la Vallée-du-
Gier ☎72241516 tx 649394
➹♙28 ☎ P28
Credit Cards ① ② ③

GLACERIE, LA
See CHERBOURG

GLÉNIC
Creuse

★★*Moulin Noyé* Pn ☎55520911 tx 580064
Closed 15 Jan-15 Feb
rm32(➹♙14) ☎ P8 Beach
Credit Cards ② ③ ⑤

GLUGES
See MARTEL

GOLF LINKS
See TOUQUET-PARIS-PLAGE, LE

GONESSE
Val-d'Oise

★★*Campanile* ZA Economiques de la
Grande,Couture ☎39857999 tx 609021
➹♙50 P50
Credit Card ③

★★*Climat* La Croix-St-Benoît,r d'Aulnay (off
N370) ☎39874244 tx 609525
➹♙66
Credit Card ①

★★*Ibis* Patte d'Oie-de-Gonesse (N 2)
☎39872222 tx 609078
➹♙84 Lift ℺
Credit Cards ① ③

GONFREVILLE-L'ORCHER
See HAVRE, LE

GOUESNIÈRE, LA
See ST-MALO

GOUESNOU
See BREST

GOUMOIS
Doubs

★★**Taillard** LE☎81442075
Mar-Nov :Rest closed Wed Mar, Oct & Nov
⏷16 ☎ P20 ⌂ Mountain
Credit Cards 1 2 3 5

GOUVIEUX
See CHANTILLY

GRADIGNAN
See BORDEAUX

GRAMAT
Lot

★★**Centre** pl République ☎65387337
:Rest closed Sat low season
⏷14 ☎
Credit Cards 1 3

★**Lion d'Or** LEDPn pl République ☎65387318
15 Jan-15 Dec :Rest closed Mon lunch Mar
⏷15 ☎ P12 Lift
Credit Cards 1 3

At **RIGNAC**(4.5km NW)

★★★**Château de Roumégouse** (Relais et Châteaux) ☎65336381 tx 532592
Apr-2 Nov :Rest closed Tue
⏷14 P50 ⌂
Credit Cards 1 3 5

GRANDE-MOTTE, LA
Hérault

★★★★**Altea Grande-Motte** r du Port 140 ☎67569081 tx 480241
15 Mar-Nov
⏷135 P100 Lift ⌂ Sea
Credit Cards 1 2 3 4 5

GRANVILLE
Manche

★★**Bains** 19 r G-Clemenceau ☎33501731 tx 170600
Rest closed Mon in Winter
⏷56 Lift ℂ Sea
Credit Cards 1 2 3 5

🛏 **Poulain** av des Vendéens ☎ 33906499 Ren

GRASSE
Alpes-Maritimes
See also CHÂTEAUNEUF-DE-GRASSE

★★**Aromes** LEN85 ☎93704201
Feb-Nov :Rest closed Sat
⏷7 P30 Mountain
Credit Cards 1 3

★★**Ibis** r M-Carol,rte de Cannes (N85),Quartier St-Claude ☎93707070 tx 462682
⏷65 P70 Lift ⌂ ⌂ Mountain
Credit Cards 1 2 3

🛏 **Grasse Automobiles St-Christopher** 6 bd E-Zola ☎ 93363650 Peu Tal

🛏 **Montreal** av des Marronniers ☎ 93700093 P Alf

GRAVESON
Bouches-du-Rhône

★★**Mas des Amandiers** LErte d'Avignon (n.rest) ☎90958176
Mar-1 Nov
⏷26 ☎ P28 ℂ ⌂ Mountain
Credit Cards 1 2 3 5

GRAY
Haute-Saône

★★★**Château de Rigny** DPn ☎84652501 tx 362926
3 Feb-3 Jan
⏷24 P ℂ ⌂
Credit Cards 1 2 3 5

★★**Bellevue** LE1 av Carnot ☎84654776
Jan-Nov
rm15(⏷9) ☎ P8
Credit Cards 1 2 3 5

★★**Fer-a-Cheval** LE4 av Carnot (n.rest) ☎84653255
4 Jan-24 Dec
rm46(⏷45) ☎ P35 Sea
Credit Cards 1 2 3 5

GRENOBLE
Isère

★★★★**Mercure** 1 av d'Innsbruck ☎76095427 tx 980470
⏷100 ☎ P54 Lift ⌂ Mountain
Credit Cards 1 2 3 5

★★★★**Park** 10 pl P-Mistral ☎76872911 tx 320767
2 Jan-Jul & 21 Aug-24 Dec :Rest closed Sun midday
⏷59 ☎ Lift ℂ Mountain
Credit Cards 1 2 3 5

★★★**Angleterre** 5 pl V-Hugo (n.rest) ☎76873721 tx 320297
⏷70 Lift Mountain
Credit Cards 1 2 3 5

★★★**Grand** 5 r de la République ☎76444936 tx 980918
⏷72 Lift Mountain
Credit Cards 1 2 3 5

★★★**Terminus** 10 pl Gare (n.rest) ☎76872433 tx 320245
Closed Aug
⏷50 Lift

★★**Alpazur** 59 av Alsace-Lorraine (n.rest) ☎76464280 tx 980651
⏷30
Credit Cards 1 2 3

★★**Arcade Relais Grenoble** pl de la Gare,52 av Alsace-Lorraine ☎76460020 tx 320635
⏷110 ☎ P Lift Mountain
Credit Cards 1 3

★★**Climat** 15 r du Dr-Schweitzer ☎76217612 tx 308307
⏷45 P100 ⌂ Mountain
Credit Cards 1 2 3

★★**Fimotel** 20 av J-Jaurès,Eybens ☎76242312 tx 980371
⏷42 P38 Lift Mountain
Credit Cards 1 2 3

★★**Gallia** 7 bd MI-Joffre (n.rest) ☎76873921
Clo Aug
⏷23 ☎ Lift
Credit Cards 1 2 3 5

★★**Ibis** Centre Commerciale des Trois,Dauphins, 5 r Miribel ☎76474849 tx 320890
⏷71 Lift
Credit Cards 1 3

★★**Paris-Nice** 61 bd J-Vallier (n.rest) ☎76963618
rm29(⏷24) ☎ P29 ℂ
Credit Cards 1 2 3 5

At **CLAIX**(10.5km S)

★★★**Oiseaux** 8 r des Perouses ☎76980774 tx 308593
⏷20 ☎ P25 ⌂ Mountain
Credit Cards 1 3

At **MEYLAN**(3km NE on N90)

★**Climat** chemin du Vieux-Chêne,Zirst de Meylan ☎76907690 tx 305551
⏷38 P40 Mountain
Credit Cards 1 3

At **PONT-DE-CLAIX**(8km S on N75)

★★★**Villancourt** cours St-André ☎76981854 tx 308657
⏷33 ☎ P50 Lift ℂ Mountain
Credit Cards 1 2 3 5

At **ST-ÉGRÈVE**(10km NW)

★★**Campanile** av de l'Ille Brune ☎76755788 tx 980424
⏷42 P42

At **VOREPPE**(12km NW)

★★★**Novotel** Autoroute de Lyon ☎76508144 tx 320273
⏷114 P100 Lift ⌂ Mountain
Credit Cards 1 2 3 5

🛏 **Echaillon** 400 av de Juin 1940 ☎ 76502385 P Ren

GRÉOUX-LES-BAINS
Alpes-de-Haute-Provence

★★★**Villa Borghèse** (MAP/BW) av des Thermes ☎92780091 tx 401513
Mar-Nov
⏷70 ☎ P60 Lift ℂ ⌂ ⌂ Mountain
Credit Cards 1 2 3 5

GRIMAUD
Var

At **PORT-GRIMAUD**(5.5km E)

★★★**Port** pl du Marché ☎94563618 tx 460364
⏷20 P Lift Beach Sea
Credit Cards 1 2 3 5

GRISOLLES
Tarn-et-Garonne

★★**Relais des Garrigues** ☎63303159
Closed 4 Jan-10 Feb
rm27(⏷20) ☎ P40 ℂ
Credit Card 2

GUÉRANDE
Loire-Atlantique

🛏 **Cottais** rte de la Turballe ☎ 40249039 P Peu

GUÉRET
Creuse

★★**Auclair** LE19 av Senatorerie ☎55520126
8 Jan-Nov :Rest closed Sun pm & Mon midday
rm33(⏷24) A5rm ☎ P20
Credit Cards 1 2 3 5

GUÉTHARY
Pyrénées-Atlantiques

★★**Mariéna** av Mon-Mugabure (n.rest) ☎59265104
Jun-1 Oct
rm14(⏷5) P6 Sea

GUILLIERS
Morbihan

★★**Relais du Porhoët** pl de l'Église ☎97744017
⏷15 P15 ⌂
Credit Cards 1 2 3 5

GUILVINEC
Finistère

At **LECHIAGAT**(1km E)

★★**Port** (FAH) ☎98581010 tx 941200
6 Jan-20 Dec
⏷40 Sea
Credit Cards 1 2 3 5

HAGUENAU
Bas-Rhin

★★**Climat** rte de Bitche,chemin de Sandlach ☎88730666
⏷46 P60
Credit Cards 1 2 3

HAMBYE
Manche

★**Auberge de l'Abbaye** ☎33614219
:Rest closed Mon
rm7(⏷5) P30
Credit Cards 1 3

HAUCONCOURT
See METZ

HAUTE-GOULAINE
Loire-Atlantique

★★★**Lande St-Martin** rte de Poitiers ☎40062006 tx 700520
rm40(⏷33) ☎ P150 ℂ ⌂
Credit Cards 1 3

HAUTEVILLE-LÈS-DIJON
See DIJON

HAVRE, LE
Seine-Maritime
See Plan

★★★**Bordeaux** (Inter) 147 r L-Brindeau (n.rest)
☎35226944 tx 190428
⊷ℂ31 Lift ℂ Lake
Credit Cards ①②③⑤

★★★**Marly** (Inter) 121 r de Paris (n.rest)
☎35417248 tx 190369
⊷ℂ37 Lift ℂ
Credit Cards ①②③⑤

★★★**Mercure** chaussée d'Angoulême
☎35212345 tx 190749
⊷ℂ96 P Lift
Credit Cards ①②③④⑤

★★**Foch** 4 r Caligny (n.rest) ☎35425069 tx
190369
rm33(⊷ℂ29) P21 Lift
Credit Cards ①②③

★★**Grand Parisien** (Inter-Hotels) 1 cours de la
République (n.rest) ☎35252383 tx 190369
⊷ℂ22 P22 Lift ℂ Sea
Credit Cards ①②③⑤

★★**Ile de France** 104 r A-France (n.rest)
☎35424929
rm16(⊷ℂ8)
Credit Cards ①③

★★**Monaco** 16 r de Paris ☎35422101
Mar-15 Feb :Rest closed Mon ex Feb,Jul & Oct
rm10(⊷ℂ7) Sea
Credit Cards ①②③

★★**Petit Vatel** 86 r L-Brindeau (n.rest)
☎35417207
rm29(⊷ℂ27)
Credit Cards ①③

★★**Richelieu** 132 r de Paris (n.rest) ☎35423871
rm19(⊷ℂ12)
Credit Cards ①③

★**Barrière d'Or** 365 bd de Graville 33422
☎35240865
:Rest closed wknds
rm21(⊷ℂ2)
Credit Cards ①③

★**Voltaire** 14 r Voltaire (n.rest) ☎35413091
rm24(⊷ℂ16) P10
Credit Cards ①②③

At **GONFREVILLE-L'ORCHER**(10km E)

★★**Campanile** Zone d'Activities du Camp,Dolent
☎35514300 tx 771609
⊷ℂ49 P49

At **MONTIVILLIERS**(7km NE)

★★**Climat** ZAC de la Lézarde ☎35304139 tx
770346
⊷ℂ38 P40
Credit Cards ①②③

At **STE-ADRESSE**(4km NW)

★★**Phares** 29 r Gl-de-Gaulle ☎35463186
rm26(⊷ℂ23) 🅐 P10 ℂ
Credit Cards ①②③

HAYE-DU-PUITS, LA
Manche

★**Gare** LEDPn ☎33460422
Feb-Dec
rm12(ℂ5)
Credit Cards ①③

HÉDE
Ille-et-Villaine

★★★**Hostellerie du Vieux Moulin** LErte
Nationale 137 ☎99454570
Jan-20 Dec :Rest closed Sun evening & Mon
rm12(⊷ℂ11) 🅐 P20
Credit Cards ①③⑤

HENDAYE
Pyrénées-Atlantiques

★★★**Liliac** 2 r des Clématites (n.rest)
☎59200245
25 Mar-Sep
⊷ℂ23 Lift
Credit Cards ①②③⑤

★★★**Paris** Rond-Point (n.rest) ☎59200506
Whit-Oct
⊷ℂ39 P15 Lift
Credit Cards ①③⑤

HENIN-BEAUMONT
Pas-de-Calais

At **NOYELLES-GODAULT**(3km NE)

★★★**Novotel** Henin-Douai Autoroute A1
☎21751601 tx 110352
⊷ℂ81 P300 ♒
Credit Cards ①②③⑤

★★**Campanile** Zone Artisanale et
Commerciale,rte de Beaumont ☎21762626 tx
134109
⊷ℂ42 P42
Credit Card ③

HERBIGNAC
Loire-Atlantique

🆖 **Thudot** ☎40017107 P Cit

HERMIES
Pas-de-Calais

🆖 **Bachelet** 62 r d'Haurincourt ☎ 21074184 Peu

🆖 **Central Mourcia** 13 Grand-Pl ☎ 21074010 P
Ren

HÉROUVILLE-ST-CLAIR
See CAEN

HESDIN
Pas-de-Calais

★★★**Clery** Château d'Hesdin-l'Abbée
☎21831983 tx 135349
⊷ℂ19 A8rm P20 ⌕
Credit Cards ①②③

★**Flandres** LEDPn 22 r d'Arras ☎21868021
8 Jan-20 Dec
rm14(⊷ℂ12) 🅐 P10
Credit Cards ①②③

HONFLEUR
Calvados

★★★**Ferme St-Siméon et Son Manoir** (Relais et
Châteaux) r A-Marais ☎31892361 tx 171031
⊷ℂ38 P60 Lift ℂ ⌕ Sea
Credit Cards ①③

★★**Cheval Blanc** 2 quai des Passagers
☎31891349 tx 306022
Feb-Dec
⊷ℂ35 Sea
Credit Cards ①③

★★**Dauphin** 10 pl P-Berthelot (n.rest)
☎31891553
Feb-Dec
⊷ℂ30 A15rm ℂ
Credit Cards ①③

HOSSEGOR
Landes

★**Beauséjour** av Genêts par av Tour-du-Lac
☎58435107
10 May-15 Oct
⊷ℂ45 🅐 P8 Lift ℂ ♒ Lake
Credit Card ③

★★**Ermitage** LEallée des Pins Tranquilles
☎58435222
Jun-Sep
⊷ℂ14 P ⌕

HOUCHES, LES
Haute-Savoie

★★**Piste Bleue** rte les Chavants ☎50544066
20 Dec-1 May & 1 Jun-30 Sep
rm25(⊷ℂ19) P12 Mountain
Credit Card ③

HOUDAN
Yvelines

★**St-Christophe** LE6 pl du Gl-de-Gaulle
☎30596161 tx 78550
⊷ℂ9
Credit Card ③

HOUDEMONT
See NANCY

HOULGATE
Calvados

★★**Centre** 31 r des Bains (n.rest) ☎31911815
Apr-Sept
rm22(⊷ℂ19)
Credit Cards ①③

HUELGOAT
Finistère

★★**Triskel** 72 r des Cieux (n.rest) ☎98997185
Feb-15 Nov
⊷ℂ10 P14
Credit Card ③

HYÈRES
Var

🆖 **Fleschi** 7 rte de Toulon ☎ 94650283 P Fia

HYÈVRE-PAROISSE
See BAUME-LES-DAMES

IGÉ
Saône-et-Loire

★★★**Château d'Igé** (Relais et Châteaux)
☎85333399
15 Mar-5 Nov
⊷ℂ12 A1rm 🅐 P16
Credit Cards ①②③⑤

ILLKIRCH-GRAFFENSTADEN
See STRASBOURG

INOR
Meuse

★**Faisan Doré** LEr de l'Écluse ☎29803545
⊷ℂ13 P25
Credit Cards ①③

ISIGNY-SUR-MER
Calvados

★★**France** LEDPn 17 r Démagny ☎31220033
9 Jan-Nov :Rest closed Fri pm/Sat lunch low
season
rm19(⊷ℂ14) P20 ♒

🆖 **Etasse** 4 r de Littry ☎ 31220252 P Peu

ISLE-SUR-LE-DOUBS, L'
Doubs

🆖 **Marcoux** 64 r du Magny ☎ 81963154 P Ren

ISSOIRE
Puy-de-Dôme

★★**Le Pariou** LE18 av Kennedy ☎73892211 tx
393523
⊷ℂ33 🅐 P33 Lift ℂ Mountain
Credit Cards ①③⑤

ISSOUDUN
Indre

★★**France et Restaurant Les 3 Rois** LE(FAH) 3
r P-Brossolette ☎54210065 tx 751422
⊷ℂ24 🅐 P7
Credit Cards ①②③⑤

IVRY-LA-BATAILLE
Eure

★★**Grand St-Martin** LEDPn 9 r Ézy
☎32364739
Feb-Dec :Rest closed Mon
rm10(⊷ℂ8)
Credit Cards ①③

JARD-SUR-MER
Vendée

★★**Parc de la Grange** LE(FAH) rte du Payré
☎51334488
⊷ℂ60 A12rm P200 ℂ ⌕ ♒
Credit Cards ①②③⑤

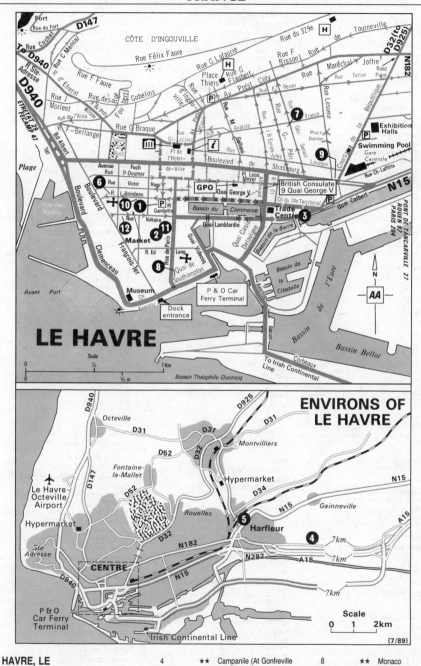

LE HAVRE

ENVIRONS OF
LE HAVRE

(7/89)

HAVRE, LE									
1	★★★	Bordeaux	4	★★	Campanile (At Gonfreville l'Orcher)	8	★★	Monaco	
2	★★★	Marly	5	★★	Climat (At Montivilliers)	9	★★	Grand Parisien	
3	★★★	Mercure	6	★★	Foch	10	★★	Petit Vatel	
			7	★★	Ile de France	11	★★	Richelieu	
						12	★	Voltaire	

JARNAC
Charente

At **FLEURAC**(10km NE)

★★*Domaine de Fleurac* (Inter-Hotels)
☎45817822
Closed Nov
↝⋔6 P40
Credit Cards ① ③ ⑤

JOIGNY
Yonne

★★★*Côte St-Jacques* (Relais et Châteaux) **Pn**
14 fbg de Paris ☎86620970 tx 801458
Closed 2 Jan-2 Feb
↝⋔30 A15rm ≋ P10 Lift ⊡
Credit Cards ① ② ③ ⑤

★★*Modern* Ⅼᴇ(MAP/BW) 17 av R-Petit
☎86621628 tx 801693
↝⋔21 ≋ P35 ⚲ ⊇
Credit Cards ① ② ③ ④ ⑤

JOINVILLE
Haute-Marne

★*Poste* Ⅼᴇ(FAH) pl Grêve ☎25941263
10 Feb-10 Jan
rm11(↝⋔8) ≋ P20
Credit Cards ① ② ③ ⑤

★*Soleil d'Or* Ⅼᴇ7 r des Capucins ☎25941566
Mar-7 Feb :Rest closed Mon
↝⋔11 ≋ P10
Credit Cards ① ② ③ ④ ⑤

JOSSELIN
Morbihan

★★*Château* Ⅼᴇ(Inter) 1 r Gl-de-Gaulle
☎97222011
rm36(↝⋔28)
Credit Cards ① ③

JOUÉ-LÈS-TOURS
Indre-et-Loire
See also TOURS

★★*Campanile* av du Lac, Les Bretonnières
☎47672489 tx 751683
↝⋔49 P49
Credit Card ③

★★*Château de Beaulieu* rte Villandry
☎47532026
↝⋔19 A10rm P80 ☾
Credit Cards ① ② ③ ⑤

★★*Parc* (Inter-Hotels) 17 bd Chinon (n.rest)
☎47251538
↝⋔30 ≋ P30 Lift
Credit Cards ① ② ③

JOUGNE
Doubs

★*Deux Saisons DPn* ☎81490004
Jun-Oct & 18 Dec-15 Apr
↝⋔21 ≋ P15 ☾ Mountain
Credit Cards ① ③ ⑤

JUAN-LES-PINS
Alpes-Maritimes

★★★★*Belles Rives* bd Littoral ☎93610279 tx 470984
end Mar-early Nov
↝⋔43 Lift ☾ Beach Sea
Credit Cards ① ② ③

★★★★*Juana* av G-Gallice,La Pinède ☎93610870 tx 470778
Apr-Oct
↝⋔50 P25 Lift ☾ ⊇ Beach Sea

★★★*Apparthotel Astor* 61 chemin F-Badine
☎93610738
↝⋔37 ≋ P15
Credit Cards ① ② ③ ④ ⑤

★★★*Helios* 3 av Daucheville ☎93615525 tx 970976
18 Apr-19 Oct
↝⋔70 ≋ P20 Lift ☾
Credit Cards ② ③ ⑤

★★*Alexandra* r Pauline ☎93610136
1Apr-15Oct
rm20(↝⋔17) ≋ Beach
Credit Cards ① ② ③

★★*Cyrano* (Inter-Hotels) av L-Gallet (n.rest)
☎93610483
Feb-15 Oct
↝⋔40 Lift ☾ Beach Sea

★★*Emeraude DPn* 11 av Saramartel ☎93610967
tx 470673
Feb-Nov
rm22(↝⋔20) ≋ P7 Lift Beach Mountain
Credit Cards ② ③ ⑤

★★*Noailles* av Gallice ☎93611170
15 Jun-end Sep
rm22(↝⋔9) ≋ P3 Sea

★★*Urbis Juan-Les-Pins* 95 bd R-Poincaré,N7
(n.rest) ☎93673967 tx 462722
↝⋔50 ≋ P6 Lift Sea
Credit Cards ① ③ ⑤

★*Midi* 93 bd R-Poincaré ☎93613516
4 Jan-20 Oct
rm23(↝⋔19) A8rm P8
Credit Card ③

KAYSERSBERG
See COLMAR

KREMLIN-BICÊTRE
See PARIS

LA
Each name preceded by 'La' is listed under the name that follows it.

LABASTIDE-MURAT
Lot

★★*Climat* ☎65211880
23 Jan-23 Dec
↝⋔20
Credit Cards ① ② ③ ④ ⑤

LABÈGE
See TOULOUSE

LABOUHEYRE
Landes

★★*Unic* rte de Bordeaux ☎58070055
Feb-19 Dec
↝⋔10 P
Credit Cards ① ② ③ ⑤

LADOIX-SERRIGNY
See BEAUNE

LAFFREY
Isère

★★*Grand Lac* Ⅼᴇ☎76731290
May-Sep
↝⋔27 A19rm Mountain Lake

LALINDE
Dordogne

★★*Château* Ⅼᴇ**DPn** r Verdun ☎53610182
10 Mar-15 Nov :Rest closed Fri
↝⋔8 Lake
Credit Cards ① ③ ⑤

★★*Résidence* 3 r Prof-Testut (n.rest) ☎53611081
May-Sep
↝⋔11

⬤ *Arbaudie* pl de l'Église ☎ 53610022 M/C **P** Peu Tal

LAMASTRE
Ardèche

★★★*Midi* pl Seignobos ☎75064150
Mar-15 Dec
rm18(↝⋔15) ≋ P6
Credit Cards ① ② ③ ⑤

⬤ *Rugani* av de la Gare ☎ 75064220 **P** Peu Tal

⬤ *Traversier* rte de Tournon ☎ 75064212 **P** Peu Tal

LAMBALLE
Côtes-du-Nord

★★*Angleterre* Ⅼᴇ(FAH/Inter-Hotels) 29 bd Jobert ☎96310016 tx 740994
↝⋔22 A13rm ≋ P10 Lift
Credit Cards ② ③ ⑤

★★*Auberge du Manoir des Portes* La Poterie
☎96311362
Mar-Jan :Rest closed Mon
↝⋔16 P20
Credit Cards ① ② ⑤

★★*Tour d'Argent* Ⅼᴇ2 r du Dr-Lavergne
☎96310137
:Rest closed Sat
rm31(↝⋔25) A16rm ≋ P6
Credit Cards ① ② ③ ⑤

LAMORLAYE
See CHANTILLY

LAMPAUL-GUIMILIAU
Finistère

★★*Enclos* Ⅼᴇ☎98687708 tx 29230
↝⋔36 P25
Credit Cards ① ② ③ ⑤

LANÇON-PROVENCE
See SALON-DE-PROVENCE

LANDERNEAU
Finistère

★★*Clos du Pontic* Ⅼᴇr du Pontic ☎98215091
tx 641155
:Rest closed Sat midday & Sun
rm38(↝⋔21) P60 ∪

★★*Ibis* BP 151 Mescoat ☎98213132 tx 940878
↝⋔42 P150 Lift
Credit Cards ① ③

LANDUJAN
See MONTAUBAN-DE-BRETAGNE

LANESTER
See LORIENT

LANGEAIS
Indre-et-Loire

★★*Hosten* Ⅼᴇ2 r Gambetta ☎47967063
↝⋔12
Credit Cards ① ② ③ ⑤

LANGRES
Haute-Marne

★★*Europe* Ⅼᴇ**DPn** 23 r Diderot ☎25871088
Closed 8-28 Oct :Rest closed Sun pm & Mon midday
rm28(↝⋔26) A9rm ≋ P20
Credit Cards ① ② ③ ⑤

★★*Lion d'Or* rte de Vesoul ☎25870330
Closed Jan
↝⋔14 ≋ P25 Lake
Credit Cards ① ② ③

★*Cheval Blanc* 4 r de l'Estres ☎25870700
4 Feb-4 Jan
rm23(↝⋔22) A8rm ≋ P12
Credit Cards ① ② ③ ⑤

LANNION
Côtes-du-Nord

★★*Climat* rte de Perros-Guirec ☎96487018 tx 741668
↝⋔47 P50
Credit Cards ① ② ③

⬤ *Corre* rte de Perros-Guirec ☎ 96484541 **P** For

LANSLEBOURG-MONT-CENIS
Savoie

★★★*Alpazur* Ⅼᴇ☎79059369 tx 980213
Jun-20 Sep & 20 Dec-20 Apr
↝⋔24 ≋ P10 Mountain
Credit Cards ① ② ⑤

★*Relais des Deux Cols* Ⅼᴇ73 Val Cenis
☎79059283
Seasonal
rm40(↝⋔22) A10rm ≋ P12 ☾ ⊇ Mountain
Credit Cards ① ② ③ ⑤

LANSLEVILLARD
Savoie

★★*Étoile des Neiges* ☎79059041 tx 309678
15 May-15 Sep & 15 Dec-15 Apr
➽♠24 ☎ P20 Mountain
Credit Cards [1] [3]

LANVOLLON
Côtes-du-Nord

At **PLEHEDEL**

★★★*Château de Coatguelen* (Relais et
Châteaux) ☎96223124 tx 741300
5 Apr-5 Jan :Rest closed Tue & Wed am
➽♠16 P40 ♀ ⌱ ♠♠ ∪ Lake
Credit Cards [1] [2] [3] [5]

LAON
Aisne

★★*Angleterre* (Inter-Hotels) 10 bd Lyon
☎23230462 tx 145580
rm30(➽♠15) ☎ P10 Lift ℂ
Credit Cards [1] [2] [3] [4] [5]

★★*Bannière de France* 11 r de F-Roosevelt
☎23232144
Closed 20 Dec-15 Jan & 1 May
rm19(➽♠13) ☎ P32
Credit Cards [1] [2] [3] [5]

★★*Fimotel* Zac Ile de France (N2) ☎23201811 tx
150531
➽♠40 P60 Lift
Credit Cards [1] [2] [3] [5]

★*Chevaliers* 3 r Serurier ☎23234378
Closed 15-28 Feb & 10-20 Aug :Rest closed for
dinner
rm15(➽♠10) P2
Credit Cards [1] [3]

➾ **S.I.C.B** 121 av de Belgique ☎ 23791408 M/C
P For

➾ *Tuppin* 132 av M-France ☎ 23235036 Peu Tal

LARAGNE-MONTEGLIN
Hautes-Alpes

★*Terrasses* 𝐋𝐄av Provence ☎92650854
May-Oct
rm17(➽♠6) P12 Mountain
Credit Cards [1] [2] [3] [4]

LAROQUE-DES-ARC
See **CAHORS**

LAUMES, LES
Côte-d'Or

★★*Lesprit* 𝐋𝐄☎80960046
➽♠24 ☎ P12
Credit Cards [1] [3]

LAURIS
Vaucluse

★★*Chaumière* 𝐋𝐄pl du Portail ☎90082025
15 Feb-15 Jan :Rest closed Tue & Wed lunch
➽♠15 P10 Mountain Lake
Credit Cards [1] [2] [3] [5]

LAVAL
Mayenne

★★*Campanile* bd Duguesclin ☎43690400 tx
722633
➽♠42 P42
Credit Card [3]

★★*Climat* bd des Trappistines ☎43028888
➽♠44 P45
Credit Cards [1] [2] [3]

★*Ibis* rte de Mayenne ☎43538182 tx 721094
:Rest closed Sun 15 Oct-15 Mar
➽♠51 P70 Lift
Credit Cards [1] [3]

LAVANDOU, LE
Var

★★★*Calanque* 62 av Gl-de-Gaulle (n.rest)
☎94710595
Etr-Oct
➽♠38 Lift Sea
Credit Cards [1] [2] [3] [4] [5]

★*Petite Bohème* **DP**n av F-Roosevelt
☎94711030
6 May-10 Oct
rm20(➽♠18) A4rm ☎ Sea
Credit Cards [1] [3]

LAVAUR
Tarn

At **ST-LIEUX-LES-LAVAUR**(11km NW)

★★*Château* ☎63416087
➽♠12 P10 ℂ

LAVERNAY
See **RECOLOGNE**

LAXOU
See **NANCY**

LE
Each name preceded by 'Le'is listed under the
name that follows it.

LECHIAGAT
See **GUILVINEC**

LECQUES, LES
Var

★★★*Grand* Les Lecques Plage ☎94262301 tx
400165
May- Oct
rm58(➽♠53) P50 Lift ♀ Sea
Credit Cards [1] [2] [3] [4] [5]

LECTOURE
Gers

★★*De Bastard* r Lagrange ☎62688244
1 Mar-31 Jan
➽♠29 ☎
Credit Cards [1] [2] [3] [5]

LENS
Pas-de-Calais

★★*Campanile* Zone d'Activités,rte de la Bassée
☎21288282 tx 134089
➽♠51 P51
Credit Card [3]

At **LIÉVIN**(4km W)

★★*Climat* r S-Goulet ☎21282222 tx 134430
➽♠26 P30
Credit Cards [1] [2] [3]

At **VENDIN-LE-VIEL**(6km NE)

★★*Lensotel* Centre Commercial Lens 11
☎21786453 tx 120324
➽♠70 P70 Lift ⌁
Credit Cards [1] [2] [3] [4] [5]

LES
Each name preceded by 'Les' is listed under the
name that follows it.

LESCAR
See **PAU**

LESQUIN
See **LILLE AIRPORT**

LEVROUX
Indre

★★*Cloche* 𝐋𝐄r Nationale ☎54357043
:Rest closed Mon evening & Tue
rm26(➽♠21) A14rm P5
Credit Cards [1] [3] [5]

LIBOURNE
Gironde

★★*Climat* Le Port du Noyer ☎57514141 tx
541707
➽♠42 P50
Credit Cards [1] [3]

★★*Loubat* 32 r Chanzy ☎57511758 tx 540436
rm25(➽♠23) P30 ℂ
Credit Cards [1] [2] [3]

➾ *Solica* Port du Noyer Arveyres ☎ 57513496 **P**
For

LIÉVIN
See **LENS**

LILLE
Nord

★★★*Bellevue* 5 r J-Roisin (n.rest) ☎20574564 tx
120790
➽♠80 P Lift
Credit Cards [1] [2] [3]

★★★*Carlton* (MAP/Inter-Hotels) 3 r de Paris
(n.rest) ☎20552411 tx 110400
rm65(➽♠60) P100 Lift ℂ
Credit Cards [1] [2] [3] [5]

★★★*Royal* (Inter-Hotels) 2 bd Carnot
☎20510511 tx 820575
rm102(➽♠98) P Lift
Credit Cards [1] [2] [3] [5]

★★*Campanile* r C-Borda ☎20533055 tx 136203
➽♠49 P49
Credit Card [3]

★*Ibis* Le Forum,av Charles,St Venant
☎20554444 tx 136950
➽♠151 P39 Lift
Credit Cards [1] [3]

★★*Urbis* 21 r Lepelletier (n.rest) ☎20062195 tx
136846
➽♠60 P15 Lift
Credit Cards [1] [3]

At **ENGLOS**(7.5km W)

★★★*Mercure* Autoroute Lille-Dunkerque
☎20923015 tx 820302
➽♠90 A20rm P200 ♀ ⌁
Credit Cards [1] [2] [3] [5]

★★★*Novotel Lille Lomme* Autoroute A25 (n.rest)
☎20070999 tx 132120
➽♠124 P ⌁
Credit Cards [1] [2] [3] [5]

At **MARCQ-EN-BAROEUL**(4.5km N)

★★★*Holiday Inn* bd de la Marne ☎20721730
tx 132785
➽♠125 P300 Lift ⌁
Credit Cards [1] [2] [3] [5]

➾ *Flandres Automobiles* 607 av de la
République ☎ 20550770 **P** For

LILLE AIRPORT

At **LESQUIN**(8km SE)

★★★★*Holiday Inn* 110 r J-Jaurès ☎20979202 tx
132051
➽♠213 P500 Lift ⌁
Credit Cards [1] [2] [3] [5]

★★★*Novotel Lille Aéroport* Autoroute A1
☎20979225 tx 820519
➽♠92 P100 ⌁
Credit Cards [1] [2] [3] [5]

LIMOGES
Haute-Vienne

★★★★*Royal Limousin* 1 pl de la République
☎55346530 tx 580771
➽♠75 P Lift
Credit Cards [1] [2] [3] [5]

★★★*Luk* 29 pl Jourdan ☎55334400 tx 580704
:Rest closed Sat lunch & Sun
➽♠55 Lift ℂ
Credit Cards [1] [2] [3] [5]

★★*Arcade* 14 r de Chinchauvaud ☎55798110 tx
590851
➽♠120 ☎ P Lift
Credit Cards [1] [3]

★★*Campanile* Le Moulin Pinard,r H-Giffard
☎55373562 tx 590909
➽♠42 P42
Credit Card [3]

★*Ibis Limoges* r F-Bastiat,ZAC Industrielle Nord
2 ☎55375014 tx 580009
➽♠76 P100 Lift
Credit Cards [1] [3]

★★Jourdan (Inter-Hotels) 2 av du Gl-de-Gaulle
☎55774962 tx 580121
rm41(⭲🛏40) Lift ℭ
Credit Cards ①②③⑤

★★Urbis 6 bd V-Hugo (n.rest) ☎55790330 tx
580731
⭲🛏68 Lift
Credit Cards ①③

★Relais Lamartine 10 r des Cooperateurs
(n.rest) ☎55775339
rm20(⭲🛏10) ☎

LINGOLSHEIM
Bas-Rhin
★★Campanile Parc des Tanneries,305 rte de
Schirmelic ☎88781010 tx 880454
⭲🛏50 P50
Credit Card ③

LION-D'ANGERS, LE
Maine-et-Loire
★Voyageurs DPn 2 r Gl-Leclerc ☎41953008
15 Feb-1 Oct & 1 Nov-15 Jan
rm13(⭲🛏5) ☎ P10
Credit Cards ①②③⑤

LISIEUX
Calvados
★★★Gardens rte de Paris (N13) ☎31611717 tx
170065
⭲🛏70 P150 ⌿
Credit Cards ①②③⑤

★★★Place (MAP/BW) 67 r H-Chéron (n.rest)
☎31311744 tx 171862
⭲🛏33 ☎ Lift
Credit Cards ①②③⑤

★★Lourdes 4 r au Char (n.rest) ☎31311948
rm33(⭲🛏32) ☎ Lift
Credit Cards ①③

★Coupe d'Or LE 49 r Pont-Mortain ☎31311684
tx 772163
rm18(⭲🛏14)
Credit Cards ①②③④⑤

🍴 **Lorant** 61 bd Ste-Anne ☎ 31310071 P Peu
Tal

🍴 **Pays d'Auge** 62 r du Gl-Leclerc ☎ 31311614
P Rov

LIVAROT
Calvados
★Vivier LE pl de la Mairie ☎31635029
rm11(⭲🛏7) P20
Credit Cards ①③

LIVRON-SUR-DRÔME
Drôme
🍴 **Gimenez** Elf Station (N7) ☎ 75616778 M/C P
All makes

LIVRY-GARGAN
See **PARIS**

LOCHES
Indre-et-Loire
★France Pn 6 r Picois ☎47590032 tx 750020
Feb-Dec
rm20(⭲🛏19) P20
Credit Cards ①③⑤
At **BRIDORÉ**(14km S)
★★★Barbe Bleue ☎47947269
⭲🛏10 P30 ℀
Credit Card ③

LOCRONAN
Finistère
★★Prieuré LEDPn 11 r de Prieuré
☎98917089
rm15(⭲🛏11) P25
Credit Cards ①③

LODÈVE
Hérault
★★Croix Blanche 6 av de Fumel ☎67441087
Apr-1 Dec
rm32(⭲🛏23) ☎ P15
Credit Cards ①③

LONDE, LA
See **ELBEUF**

LONGUYON
Meurthe-et-Moselle
★★Lorraine LE Face Gare ☎82265007 tx
861718
Feb-Dec :Rest closed Mon
rm15(⭲🛏12)
Credit Cards ①②③⑤

LONGWY
Meurthe-et-Moselle
★★Fimotel (N52) ☎82231419 tx 861270
⭲🛏42 P35 Lift
Credit Cards ①②⑤

LONS-LE-SAUNIER
Jura
★★Genève 19 pl XI Novembre ☎84241911
rm40(⭲🛏30) ☎ P12 Lift
Credit Cards ①②③⑤

🍴 **Lecourbe** 58 bis r Lecourbe ☎ 84472013 M/C
P For

🍴 **Thevenod** rte de Champagnole-Perrigny ☎
84244158

LORIENT
Morbihan
★★★Mercure 31 pl J-Ferry ☎97243573 tx
950810
⭲🛏58 Lift
Credit Cards ①②③⑤

🍴 **Service Auto Secours** 9 r J-Brel,ZI du
Plénéno ☎ 97370333 M/C P
At **LANESTER**(5km NE)
★★★Novotel Zone Commerciale de Bellevue
☎97760216 tx 950026
⭲🛏88 P80 ⌿
Credit Cards ①②③⑤

★★Climat ZA-Lann Sevelin ☎97764641
⭲🛏39 P50
Credit Cards ①③④

★★Ibis commerciale Kerpont-Bellevue (n.rest)
☎97764022
⭲🛏40 P50
Credit Cards ①③

LORMONT
See **BORDEAUX**

LOUDÉAC
Côtes-du-Nord
★Voyageurs LE 10 r Cadelac ☎96280047
15 Jan-20 Dec :Rest closed Sat
rm29(⭲🛏25) ☎ P26 Lift
Credit Cards ①②③⑤

LOUDUN
Vienne
★★★Mercure 40 av Leuze (n.rest) ☎49981922
⭲🛏29 Lift
Credit Cards ①②③⑤

LOUÉ
Sarthe
★★★Ricordeau (Relais et Châteaux) DPn 11 r
Libération ☎43884003 tx 722013
Closed Dec-3 Jan
rm22(⭲🛏19) A8rm ☎ P15 ⌷ ⌿
Credit Cards ①②③⑤

LOURDES
Hautes-Pyrénées
★★★Grotte (MAP/BW) 66 r de la Grotte
☎62945887 tx 531937
Etr-20 Oct
⭲🛏83 ☎ P40 Lift ℭ Mountain
Credit Cards ①②③⑤

★★Ibis chaussée Marensin ☎62943838 tx
521409
⭲🛏88 P20 Lift
Credit Cards ①③

★★Provençale (Inter-Hotels) 4 r Baron Duprat
☎62943134 tx 520257
⭲🛏46 Lift ℭ Mountain
Credit Cards ①②③④⑤

LOUVIERS
Eure
At **ST-PIERRE-DU-VAUVRAY**(8km E)
★★★Hostellerie de St-Pierre DPn ☎32599329
Mar-Dec :Rest closed Tue
⭲🛏14 P40 Lift ℀ Lake
Credit Cards ①③
At **VAL-DE-REUIL**(4km N A13)
★★★Altea Lieu dit les Clouets ☎32590909 tx
180540
⭲🛏58 P70 Lift ℭ ℀ ⌿
Credit Cards ①②③⑤
At **VIRONVAY**(4km SE)
★★Saisons ☎32400256
:Rest closed Sun evening
⭲🛏20 P80 ℀
Credit Cards ①②③

LOUVROIL
Nord
★★★Mercure rte d'Avesnes (N2) ☎27649373 tx
110696
:Rest closed Sat & Sun
⭲🛏59 P ⌿
Credit Cards ①②③⑤

LUC, LE
Var
★Hostellerie du Parc 1 r J-Jaurès ☎94607001
⭲🛏12 P20
Credit Cards ①②③⑤

LUCÉ
See **CHARTRES**

LUCHON
Haute-Garonne
★★★Poste & Golf 29 allées d'Etigny ☎61790040
tx 533354
Closed 21 Oct-19 Dec
rm63(⭲🛏60) P40 Lift ⌿ Mountain
Credit Cards ①③
★★Bains (Inter-Hotels) 75 allées d'Etigny
☎61790058 tx 521437
Feb-20 Oct
rm53(⭲🛏48) P15 Lift Mountain
Credit Cards ②③

LUÇON
Vendée
★★Grand Hotel du Croissant ☎51561115
Nov-Sep :Rest closed Sun in low season
rm40(⭲🛏33) ☎ P10

LUC-SUR-MER
Calvados
★★Grand Casino 3 r Guynemer ☎31973237 tx
170686
Apr-Sep
⭲🛏30 Lift ⌿ Sea
Credit Cards ①②③④⑤

LUDE, LE
Sarthe
★★Maine LEDPn 24 rte Saumur ☎43946054
⭲🛏24 ☎ P60
Credit Cards ①②⑤

LUDRES
See **NANCY**

LUNÉVILLE
Meurthe-et-Moselle
★★Europe 56 r d'Alsace (n.rest) ☎83741234
rm30(⭲🛏22) P15
Credit Cards ①③

LUS-LA-CROIX-HAUTE
Drôme

★**Chamousset LEDPn** ☎92585112
rm20(➤15) P15 Mountain
Credit Cards 2 3

★*Touring* 75 rte Nationale ☎92585001
:Rest closed Sun
rm10(➤5) Mountain

LUTTERBACH
Haut-Rhin

★★*Campanile* 10 r Pfastatt ☎89536655 tx
881432
➤53 P53
Credit Card 3

LUXEUIL-LES-BAINS
Haute-Saône

★★*Beau Site* LE18 r Thermes (n.rest)
☎84401467
Closed 24 Dec-2 Jan
➤39 A11rm ☎ P50
Credit Cards 1 3

LUYNES
Indre-et-Loire

★★★★*Domaine de Beauvois* DPn BP 27
☎47555011 tx 750204
10 Mar-10 Jan
➤38 A2rm P45 Lift (९ ⌣ Lake
Credit Cards 1 3

LYON
Rhône

Picturesquely set on the banks of
the rivers Saône and Rhône,
Lyon lies at the heart of some of
France's great vineyards. Her
neighbours include Mâcon and
St-Etienne, and the names of the
surrounding villages read like a
wine guide. The cliff-top
silhouette of Notre-Dame de
Fourvière is the city's most
striking symbol, while the
medieval Primatale St-Jean
Cathédral with its unusual 14th-
century astronomical clock is
worth visiting.
Lyon's old town, running north
of the cathedral along the west
bank of the Saône, brims with
historic medieval and
Renaissance buildings. Focal
point is Place Bellecour, one of
Europe's largest squares.
Of the city's museums, the most
interesting is the *Musée des
Beaus-Arts* (Museum of Fine
Arts), which contains sculpture,
classical relics and an extensive
collection of Old Masters and
Impressionists.

EATING OUT Lyon's restaurants
have an international reputation
for excellence, and are frequently
star-rated in top restaurant
guides. One of the best in town
is the *Léon de Lyon*, which offers
a selection of regional specialities

such as dumplings and hot
sausages, as well as *nouvelle
cuisine*. *Orsi*, in Place Kléber, has
a menu which provides excellent
value.
See also CHASSE-SUR-RHÔNE

LYON
Rhône

★★★★*Grand Concorde* 11 r Grôlée ☎78425621
tx 330244
➤140 ☎ P15 Lift (
Credit Cards 1 2 3 5

★★★★*Holiday Inn Crowne Plaza Lyon Atlas* r
de Bonnel 29 ☎72619090 tx 330703
➤156 P100 Lift (
Credit Cards 1 2 3 5

★★★★*Pullman Part-Dieu* 129 r Servient,Part
Dieu Nord ☎78629412 tx 380088
➤245 ☎ P Lift (
Credit Cards 1 2 3 5

★★★★*Royal* (MAP/BW) 20 pl Bellecour
☎78375731 tx 310785
➤90 ☎ P10 Lift (
Credit Cards 1 2 3 5

★★★★*Sofitel* 20 quai Gailleton ☎78427250 tx
330225
➤191 P100 Lift (
Credit Cards 1 2 3 4 5

★★★*Beaux-Arts* (MAP/BW) 75 r Prés-Herriot
(n.rest) ☎78380950 tx 330442
➤79 Lift
Credit Cards 1 2 3 5

★★★*Carlton* (MAP/BW) 4 r Jussieu (n.rest)
☎78425651 tx 310787
rm87(➤83) ☎ P6 Lift
Credit Cards 1 2 3 5

★★★*Grand Hotel de Bordeaux* (Inter-Hotels) 1 r
du Belier (n.rest) ☎78375873 tx 330355
➤80 Lift
Credit Cards 1 2 3 5

★★★*Terminus Lyon Perrache* 12 cours de
Verdun ☎78375811 tx 330500
➤124 ☎ P24 Lift (Mountain
Credit Cards 1 2 3 5

★★*Arcade* 78 r de Lyon ☎78629889 tx 37511
➤216 ☎ P Lift
Credit Cards 1 3

★★*Campaville* 17 pl Carnot ☎78374847 tx
305660
➤108 Lift
Credit Card 3

★★*Globe & Cecil* 21 r Gasparin (n.rest)
☎78425895 tx 305184
rm65(➤58) Lift
Credit Cards 1 2 3 5

★★*Ibis Lyon La Part-Dieu Sud* pl Renaudel
☎78954211 tx 310847
➤144 Lift
Credit Cards 1 3

★★*Ibis Lyon Gerland* Le Berg-du-Rhône,68 av
Gl-Leclerc ☎78583070 tx 305483
➤129 ☎ P46 Lift
Credit Cards 1 3

★★*Moderne* 15 r Dubois (n.rest) ☎78422183 tx
330949
rm31(➤26) P2 Lift (
Credit Cards 1 3

★★*Urbis* 51 r de l'Université (n.rest) ☎78727842
tx 340455
➤53 ☎ P10 Lift (
Credit Cards 1 2 3

✍ *Gallieni* 47 av Berthelot ☎ 78720227 For

At **BEYNOST**

★★*Ibis Lyon Est Beynost* Autoroute A42,Sortie
N5 ☎78554088 tx 305215
➤25
Credit Cards 1 3

At **BRON**(10km SE)

★★★*Novotel Lyon Bron* r L-Terray ☎78269748
tx 340781
➤191 P350 Lift ⌣
Credit Cards 1 2 3 5

★★*Campaville* quartier Rebufer,r Maryse-Bastie
☎78262540 tx 305160
➤50 P50

★★*Climat* Aéroport de Lyon ☎78265076 tx
375941
➤38 P30
Credit Cards 1 2 3

★★*Ibis Bron Montchat* 36 av de Doyen J-Lepine
☎78543134 tx 380694
➤140 P100 Lift (
Credit Cards 1 3

At **CHARBONNIÈRES-LES-BAINS**(8km NW on
N7)

★★★*Mercure* 78 bis rte de Paris (RN7)
☎78347279 tx 900972
➤60 ⌣
Credit Cards 1 2 3 4 5

At **DARDILLY**(10km on N6)

★★★★*Lyon-Nord* (MAP/BW) Porte de Lyon
☎78357020 tx 900006
➤205 P300 Lift ⌣ Mountain
Credit Cards 1 2 3 5

★★★*Mercure Lyon La Part-Dieu* 47 bd Vivier-
Merle ☎72341812 tx 306469
➤124 P Lift

★★★*Mercure Lyon Nord* Porte de Lyon (A6)
☎78352805 tx 330045
➤175 ☎ P200 ९ ⌣
Credit Cards 2 3 5

★★★*Novotel Lyon Nord* Porte de Lyon (A6)
☎78351341 tx 330962
➤107 P120 Lift ⌣
Credit Cards 1 2 3 5

★★*Campanile* Porte de Lyon Nord ☎78354844 tx
310155
➤43 P43
Credit Card 3

★★*Climat* Porte de Lyon Nord ☎78359847 tx
306156
➤38 P40
Credit Cards 1 3

★★*Ibis Lyon Nord* Porte de Lyon (A6)
☎78660220 tx 305520
➤47 ☎ P50
Credit Cards 1 2 3

At **ECULLY**(7.5km NW)

★★*Campanile* LEav de G-de-Collongue
☎78331693 tx 310154
➤50 P50
Credit Card 3

At **STE-FOY-LÈS-LYON**(6km SW)

★★*Campanile* chemin de ia Croix-Pivort
☎78593233 tx 305850
➤50 P50
Credit Card 3

★★*Provinces* LE10 pl St-Luc (n.rest)
☎78250155
➤14 P50 (

At **ST-GENIS-LAVAL**(10km SW)

★★*Climat* chemin de Chazelle ☎78566434 tx
602844
➤42 ९
Credit Cards 1 3

At **SATOLAS AIRPORT**(18km SW)

★★**Climat** Zone de Frêt ☎78409644 tx 306725
↝📞36 P50
Credit Cards ① ② ③

LYONS-LA-FORÊT
Eure

★★**Licorne** **LE**pl Benserade ☎32496202
25 Jan-15 Dec :Rest closed Sun evening & Mon
Oct-Apr
rm21(↝📞17) A2rm 🛋 P20
Credit Cards ① ② ③ ⑤

MÂCON
Saône-et-Loire

★★★★**Altea Mâcon** 26 r de Coubertin
☎85382806 tx 800830
↝📞63 P60 Lift ९ 🖵 🛋 Sea
Credit Cards ① ② ③ ⑤

★★★**Novotel Mâcon Nord** Autoroute A6
☎85360080 tx 800869F
↝📞115 P135 🛋
Credit Cards ① ② ③ ⑤

★★**Bellevue** (MAP/BW) 416-420 quai Lammartine
☎853870507 tx 800837
rm25(↝📞23) 🛋 P15 Lift ℂ
Credit Cards ① ② ③ ⑤

★★**Champs Elysées** (Inter) 6 r V-Hugo,2 pl de la
Barre ☎85383657 tx 351940
rm50(↝📞37) 🛋 Lift
Credit Cards ① ② ③ ⑤

★★**Europe et d'Angleterre** 92-109 quai J-Jaurès
(n.rest) ☎85382794 tx 800762
rm31(↝17) 🛋 P20
Credit Cards ① ② ③ ⑤

★★**Genève** (Inter) 1 r Bigonnet ☎85381810 tx
351934
rm63(↝📞51) 🛋 Lift
Credit Cards ① ② ⑤

★★**Terminus** **LE**(FAH) 91 r V-Hugo
☎85391711 tx 351938
↝📞48 🛋 P15 Lift ℂ 🛋
Credit Cards ① ② ③ ⑤

🍴 **Bois** 39 r Lacretelle ☎ 85386431 **P** Rov

🍴 **Chauvot** r J-Mermox,'Les Bruyères' ☎
85349898 **P** Ope Vol

🍴 **Corsin** 25 r de Lyon ☎ 85387333 For

🍴 **Duval** 53 rte de Lyon ☎ 85348000 **P** Fia Mer

🍴 **Mâcon Auto** 5 r du Concours ☎ 85389320 **P**
Dat

At **CHAINTRÉ-LA-CHAPELLE-DE-
GUINCHAY**(14km SW)

★★**Ibis Mâcon Sud** Les Bouchardes ☎85365160
tx 351926
↝📞62 🛋
Credit Cards ① ② ③

At **CRÈCHES-SUR-SAÔNE**(0.5km NW)

★★**Château de la Barge** ☎85371204
:Rest closed Sat & Sun (out of season)
rm24(↝📞22) P25 Lift
Credit Cards ① ② ③ ⑤

🍴 **Perrin** (N 6) ☎ 85371261 **P** Ren

🍴 **Romand** (N 6) ☎ 85371137 **P** Peu

At **ST-ALBAIN**(10km N)

★★★**Mercure** (A6) ☎85331900 tx 800881
↝📞100 🛋 Lift 🛋

At **SANCÉ-LES-MÂCON**(4km N)

★★★**Vielle Ferme** (N6) ☎85384693
↝📞32 🛋 🛋
Credit Cards ③ ⑤

★★**Balladins** ZAC des Platrières ☎05355575 tx
649394
rm38 P38
Credit Cards ① ② ③

★★**Climat** ZAC des Platières,r du 19 Mars 1962
☎85392133 tx 351076
↝📞42 P50
Credit Cards ① ③

MAGESCQ
Landes

★**Relais de la Poste** **LE**☎58477025 tx 371349
24 Dec-11 Nov :Rest closed Mon evening & Tue
↝📞12 🛋 P40 ९ 🛋
Credit Cards ① ② ③ ⑤

MAISONS-LAFFITTE
Yvelines

★★★**Climat** r de Paris ☎34460123 tx 692844
↝📞42 P

MALBUISSON
Doubs

★★★**Lac** ☎81693480 tx 360713
rm54(↝48) 🛋 P Lift Mountain Lake

MALÈNE, LA
Lozère

★★★**Manoir de Montesquiou** ☎66485112
Apr-Oct
↝📞12 P10 Mountain Lake
Credit Cards ③ ⑤

MANDELIEU
Alpes-Maritimes

★**Esterel** 1625 av de Fréjus (n.rest) ☎93499220
↝📞22 Mountain

★**Pavillon des Sports** rte de Fréjus (n.rest)
☎93495086
↝📞11 P20

MANOSQUE
Alpes-de-Haute-Provence

★★**Campanile** **LE**rte de Voix,(N96)
☎92875900 tx 405915
↝📞30 P30
Credit Card ③

🍴 **Renardat** 237 av F-Mistral ☎ 92878790 **P** Peu

MANS, LE
Sarthe

★★★★**Concorde** 16 av Gl-Leclerc ☎43241230 tx
720487
rm68(↝📞55) 🛋 P55 Lift
Credit Cards ① ② ③ ④ ⑤

★★★**Moderne** 14 r Bourg-Belé ☎43247920
↝📞32 A18rm 🛋 P20 ℂ
Credit Cards ① ② ③ ⑤

★★★**Novotel le Mans Est** ZAC les Sablons,bd R-
Schumann ☎43852680 tx 720706
↝📞94 P200 Lift 🛋
Credit Cards ① ② ⑤

★★**Arcade** 40 r de Vert Galant ☎43244724 tx
722967
↝📞95 🛋 P Lift
Credit Cards ① ③

★★**Chantecler** 50 r Pelouse ☎43245853 tx
722941
:Rest closed Sun (23 Dec-3 Jan)
rm35(↝📞30) P20 Lift
Credit Cards ① ③

★★**Climat** Les Grues Rogues ☎43213121
↝📞26 P40
Credit Cards ① ③

★★**Fimotel** 17 r de la Pointe,Rocade Sud
☎43722720 tx 722092
↝📞42 P50 Lift 🐾🐾
Credit Cards ① ② ③ ⑤

★★**Hotel Ibis** angle quai Ledru-Rollin,4 r des Ah
Ah ☎43231823 tx 722035
↝📞83 🛋 P Lift
Credit Cards ① ③

★★**Ibis** r C-Marot ☎43861414 tx 720651
↝📞49 P35
Credit Cards ① ③

At **ARNAGE**(9km S via N23)

★★**Balladins** Zone d'Activité de la Rivière,D 147
☎35355575 tx 649394
rm38 P38
Credit Cards ① ② ④ ⑤

★★**Campanile** La Gêmerie,bd P-le-Faucheux
☎43218121 tx 722803
↝📞42 P42
Credit Card ③

MANSLE
Charente

🍴 **Central** Grand rue ☎ 45222006 **P** Peu Tal

🍴 **Suire-Huguet** rte Nationale ☎ 45203031 **P**
Peu Tal

MANTES-LA-JOLIE
Yvelines

★★**Climat** r M-Tabu ☎30330370
↝📞41 P41 Lake

★**Ibis** allée des Martinets,ZAC des
Brosses,Magnanville ☎30926565 tx 695358
:Rest closed Sun
↝📞52
Credit Cards ① ③

MARCAY
See **CHINON**

MARCQ-EN-BAROEUL
See **LILLE**

MARGNY
See **COMPIÈGNE**

MARGUERITTES
See **NÎMES**

MARIGNANE
See **MARSEILLE AIRPORT**

MARLENHEIM
Bas-Rhin

★★**Cerf** 30 r du Gl-de-Gaulle ☎88877373
Closed Feb
↝📞17 P
Credit Cards ② ③

★★**Hostellerie Reeb** **LE**(N4) ☎88875270
↝📞35 🛋 P100
Credit Cards ① ② ③ ⑤

MARSANNAY-LA-CÔTE
Côte-d'Or

★★**Campanile** Zone d'Activités Acti-Sud
☎80526201 tx 351400
↝📞50 P50
Credit Card ③

MARSEILLE
Bouches-du-Rhône

In Marseille, dubbed 'the
meeting place of the entire world'
by Alexandre Dumas, the French
mix with North Africans,
gypsies, Indians and sailors from
all parts of the world. Centre of
the town is the Vieux Port,
flanked by two impregnable
fortresses and guarded on the
surrounding hills by the city's
old quarters. Running straight
out of the port is Marseille's
main artery, La Canebière, a
striking contrast to the narrow,
dusty streets of the nearby North
African quarter.
In Parc du Pharo stands a castle
built by Napoleon III for Empress

Eugénie; it offers excellent views of the harbour and city. The 19th-century Basilique de Notre-Dame-de-la-Garde, crowned with a gilded Virgin, and the Ancienne Cathédrale de la Major with its Romanesque altar reliquary from 1122 and a 15th-century altar dedicated to Lazarus are also worth visiting, as are the city's many specialised museums.

EATING OUT Marseille is the home of the fish stew cooked with wine, saffron and cayenne pepper, that is known as *bouillabaisse*. The restaurants on the Quai de Rive Neuve in the Vieux Port all serve their own versions of this. Mussels, eel and lobster are also widely available. One of the city's longest-established restaurants is *Maurice Brun*, in Quai Rive-Neuve, which serves good regional cuisine.

MARSEILLE
Bouches-du-Rhône

★★★★*Altea* Centre Bourse,r Neuve St-Martin 1 ☎91919129 tx 401886
➡ฅ200 P150 Lift
Credit Cards ①②③⑤

★★★★*Grand & Noailles* (MAP/BW) 66 Canebière (n.rest) ☎91549148 tx 430609
➡ฅ70 Lift
Credit Cards ①②③④⑤

★★★★*Sofitel Vieux-Port* 36 bd C-Livron ☎91529019 tx 401270
➡ฅ130 P160 Lift ℂ ⌫ Sea
Credit Cards ①②③⑤

★★★*St-Georges* 10 r du Cpt-Dessemond (n.rest) ☎91525692
➡ฅ27 Lift ℂ Sea
Credit Cards ①②③⑤

★★*Fimotel* 25 bd Rabatau ☎91256666 tx 402672
➡ฅ90 ☆ P70 Lift
Credit Cards ①②③⑤

★★*Ibis* angle av E-Triolet et,av J-Marlieu ☎91723434 tx 420845
➡ฅ88 ☆ P56 Lift ℀ ⌫ Sea
Credit Cards ①③

★★*Ibis Marseille Prado* 6 r de Cassis ☎91257373 tx 400362
➡ฅ118 ☆ P Lift
Credit Cards ①③

★★*Urbis* 46 r Sainte ☎91547373 tx 420808
➡ฅ141 ☆ P20 Lift ℂ
Credit Card ①

🚗 *Auto Diffusion* 36 bd National ☎ 91620805 For

🚗 *Ciotti* 11 r J-B-Astir ☎ 91497534 P

🚗 *Touchard* 151 av Montolivet ☎ 91661239 M/C P

At **PENNE-ST-MENET, LA**(10km E of A52)

★★★*Novotel Marseille Est* (A52) ☎91439060 tx 400667
➡ฅ131 P150 Lift ℀ ⌫
Credit Cards ①③⑤

MARSEILLE AIRPORT
At **MARIGNANE**(8km NW)

★★★★*Sofitel Marseille Aéroport* ☎42784278 tx 401980
➡ฅ180 P120 Lift ℂ ℀ ⌫
Credit Cards ①②③④⑤

★★*Ibis* av du 8 Mai 1945 ☎42883535 tx 440052
:Rest closed 6 July
➡ฅ36
Credit Cards ①③

At **VITROLLES**(8km N)

★★★*Novotel Marseille Aéroport* (A7) ☎42899044 tx 420670
➡ฅ163 ☆ P250 Lift ⌫
Credit Cards ①②③⑤

★★*Campanile* Le Griffon,rte d'Aix-en-Provence ☎42892511 tx 402722
➡ฅ44
Credit Card ③

★★*Climat* ZI de Couperigne,(CD20) ☎42752300
➡ฅ41 P100 ⌫
Credit Cards ①②③⑤

MARTEL
Lot

At **GLUGES**(5km SE N681)

★★*Falaises* DPn ☎65373359
Mar-Nov
rm15(➡ฅ13) P35
Credit Cards ①③

MARTIGUES
Bouches-du-Rhône

★★*Campanile* ZAC de Canto-Perdrix,bd de Tholon ☎42801400 tx 401378
➡ฅ42 P42
Credit Card ③

★★*Fimotel* Z I de Caronte,av Nobre ☎42818494 tx 441405
➡ฅ40 P60 Lift

MARVEJOLS
Lozère

★*Paix* LE2 av de Brazza ☎66321017
➡ฅ19 ☆ P6
Credit Cards ①③

MASSAT
Ariège

★★*Trois Seigneurs* av de St-Girons ☎61969589
Etr-Dec
➡ฅ25 A10rm P80 Mountain

MASSIAC
Cantal

★★*Poste* (FAH) 26 av Ch-de-Gaulle ☎71230201 tx 990989
20 Dec-10 Nov :Rest closed Wed
rm34(➡ฅ32) ☆ P25 Lift ⌫ Beach
Credit Cards ①②③⑤

MAULÉON-LICHARRE
Pyrénées-Atlantiques

★★*Bidegain* 13 r de la Navarre ☎59281605
15 Jan-15 Dec :Rest closed Fri & Sun pm & Sat lunch high season
rm30(➡ฅ15) ☆ P15 ℂ Mountain
Credit Cards ①②③⑤

MAYENNE
Mayenne

★★*Grand* LE(FAH) 2 r Ambroise-de-Loré ☎43009060 tx 722622
18 Jan-23 Dec
rm30(➡ฅ23) ☆ P40
Credit Cards ①③

★*Croix Couverte* LErte de Paris ☎43043248
Jan-23 Dec :Rest closed Sun evening (Oct-May)
➡ฅ13 ☆ P60
Credit Card ①

🚗 *P Legros* 15 r du Guesclin ☎ 43041627 For

MAZAMET
Tarn

★★★*Grand Balcon* sq G-Tournier ☎63610115 tx 530955
:Rest closed Sun evening
➡ฅ24 ☆ P20 Lift Mountain
Credit Cards ①②③⑤

MEAUX
Seine-et-Marne

★★*Climat* 32 av de la Victoire ☎64331547 tx 690020
➡ฅ60 P80
Credit Cards ①②③

★★*Sirène* 33 r Gl-Leclerc ☎64340780
rm19(➡ฅ14) P20

🚗 *Cornillon* 45 r Cornillon ☎ 64340558 Ren

MEGÈVE
Haute-Savoie

★★★★*Mont Blanc* (Inter) pl de l'Église ☎50212002 tx 385854
1 Dec-Oct
➡ฅ46 Lift ℂ ⌫ Mountain
Credit Cards ①②③⑤

★★★*Parc* r d'Arly (n.rest) ☎50210574
Xmas,Etr & end Jun-mid Sep
➡ฅ48 P40 Lift ℂ Mountain

MEHUN-SUR-YEVRE
Cher

★*Croix Blanche* Pn 164 r J-d'Arc ☎48573001
:Rest closed Sun evening & Mon
rm19(➡ฅ15) ☆ P24
Credit Cards ①③

MELUN
Seine-et-Marne
See also **PONTHIERRY**

★★★*Grand Monarque Concorde* rte Fontainebleau ☎64390440 tx 690140
➡ฅ50 ☆ P100 Lift ℂ ℀ ⌫
Credit Cards ①②③⑤

★★*Climat* 338 r R-Hervillard,Vaux-le-Penil ☎64527181 tx 693140
➡ฅ43 P50
Credit Cards ①②③

★★*Ibis* av de Meaux ☎60684245 tx 691779
➡ฅ74 Lift
Credit Cards ①③

At **DAMMARIE-LES-LYS**(5km SW)

★★*Campanile* 346 r C-de-Gaulle ☎64375151 tx 691621
➡ฅ50 P50
Credit Card ③

At **VERT-ST-DENIS**(NW on N6)

★*Balladins* av du Bois Vert ☎64416666
➡ฅ38
Credit Cards ①②③

MENDE
Lozère

★★*Lion d'Or* (MAP/BW) 12 bd Britexte ☎66491666 tx 480302
Mar-Nov :Rest closed Sun
➡ฅ40 P70 Lift ⌫ Mountain

★★*Paris* 2 bd du Soubeyran (n.rest) ☎66650003
25 Mar-15 Nov
rm45 ☆ P15 Lift Mountain

MENTON
Alpes-Maritimes

★★★*Aiglon* 7 av de la Madone (n.rest) ☎93575555
Dec-20 Oct
rm32(➡ฅ26) ☆ P16 Lift ℂ ⌫ Sea Mountain
Credit Cards ①②③⑤

★★★*Europ* 35 av de Verdun (n.rest) ☎93355992 tx 470673
➡ฅ33 ☆ P Lift
Credit Cards ①②③⑤

★★★**Méditerranée** 5 r de la République
☎93282525 tx 461361
⌂ℸ90 ☎ P40 Lift
Credit Cards ①②③⑤

★★★**Napoléon Pn** 29 Porte de France
☎93358950 tx 470312
Dec-Oct
⌂ℸ40 P Lift ⌘ ⌇ Sea Mountain
Credit Cards ①②③⑤

★★★**Parc** 11 av de Verdun ☎93576666 tx
470673
⌂ℸ72 ☎ P20 Lift ℂ
Credit Cards ①②③

★★★**Princess & Richmond** 617 prom du Soleil
(n.rest) ☎93358020
19 Dec-4 Nov
⌂ℸ45 ☎ Lift ℂ Sea
Credit Cards ①②③⑤

★★**El Paradiso** (Inter) 71 Porte de France
☎93357402
Jan-Oct
⌂ℸ42 P Lift ℂ

★★**Floréal DPn** Cours de Centenaire ☎93357581
10 Dec-10 Oct :Rest closed Sun
rm58(⌂ℸ36) P14 Lift Mountain
Credit Card ③

★★**Londres** 15 av Carnot ☎93357462
20 Dec-Oct :Rest closed Wed
rm26(⌂ℸ20) Lift
Credit Cards ①③

★★**Prince de Galles** 4 av Gl-de-Gaulle (n.rest)
☎93282121 tx 462540
⌂ℸ68 P10 Lift ℂ Sea
Credit Cards ①②③⑤

★★**Rives d'Azur** prom Ml-Joffre ☎93576760
20 Dec-Sep
⌂ℸ36 P6 Lift ℂ Sea Mountain
Credit Card ①

ﮩ **Ideal** 1 av Riviera ☎ 93357920 For

MÉRÉVILLE
Meurthe-et-Moselle

★★**Maison Carrée** LE☎83470923 tx 961052
⌂ℸ22 ☎ P150 ℺ ⌇
Credit Cards ①②③

MÉRIGNAC
See BORDEAUX

METZ
Moselle

★★★★**Altea St-Thiébault** 29 pl St-Thiébault
☎87361769 tx 930417
⌂ℸ112 P40 Lift
Credit Cards ①②③④⑤

★★★**Novotel Metz-Centre** Centre St-Jacques,pl
des Paraîges ☎87373839 tx 861815
⌂ℸ98 ☎ P42 Lift ⌇
Credit Cards ①②③⑤

★★★**Royal Concorde** 23 av Foch ☎87668111 tx
860425
rm73(⌂ℸ63) P8 Lift ℂ
Credit Cards ①②③④⑤

★★**Campanile** Parc d'Activités de Queuleu,bd de
la Défuse ☎87751311 tx 861597
⌂ℸ49 P49
Credit Card ③

★★**Ibis** r Chambière,Quartier du Pontiffroy
☎87310173 tx 930278
⌂ℸ79 P10 Lift
Credit Cards ①③

★★**Urbis** 3 bis r Vauban ☎87755343 tx 930281
⌂ℸ72 ☎ P2 Lift ℂ
Credit Cards ①③④

★**Lutèce** LE11 r de Paris ☎87302725
15 Jan-21 Dec :Rest closed Sat,Sun & holidays
rm20(⌂ℸ5) ☎
Credit Cards ①②③

ﮩ **Jacquot** 2 r P-Boileau ☎ 87325290 P Peu Tal

At HAUCONCOURT(9.5km N A31)

★★★**Novotel** (A31) ☎87804111 tx 860191
⌂ℸ132 P250 Lift ⌇
Credit Cards ①②③⑤

At TALANGÉ(5km N)

★★**Climat** La Ponte,r des Allies ☎87721311 tx
861731
⌂ℸ38 P
Credit Cards ①②③

At WOIPPY(5km NW)

★★★**Mercure** r du Port-Gambetta ☎87325279 tx
860891
⌂ℸ83 P120 Lift
Credit Cards ①②③⑤

MEULAN
Yvelines

★★★**Mercure** Lieu dit le Belle ☎34746363 tx
695295
⌂ℸ69 P100 Lift ℺ ⌘ ⌇
Credit Cards ①②③⑤

MEYLAN
See GRENOBLE

MEYRUEIS
Lozère

★★★**Château d'Ayres** (1.5km E via D57)
☎66456010
15 Apr-15 Oct
⌂ℸ24 P30 ℂ ℺ U Mountain
Credit Cards ①②③⑤

★★**Renaissance** (Inter) DPn ☎66456019
20 Mar-15 Nov
⌂ℸ20 Mountain

MÉZIÈRE-SUR-ISSOIRE
Haute-Vienne

ﮩ **A Boos** rte de Bellac ☎ 55683028 P For

MIGENNES
Yonne

★★**Gare et l'Escale** pl Laporte ☎86802099
rm12(⌂ℸ7) ☎ P15 ℂ
Credit Cards ①③

★★**Paris** LEDPn 57 av J-Jaurès ☎86802322
17 Jan-22 Jul & 22 Aug-Dec :Rest closed Fri pm
& Sat
⌂ℸ9 P4
Credit Cards ①③

MILLAU
Aveyron

★★★**International** 1 pl de la Tine ☎65602066 tx
520629
:Rest closed Sun evening & Mon (winter)
⌂ℸ110 ☎ P40 Lift ℂ Mountain
Credit Cards ①②③⑤

★★**Moderne** 11 av J-Jaurès ☎65605923 tx
520629
Apr-Oct
rm45(⌂ℸ42) ☎ P40 Lift ℂ Mountain
Credit Cards ①②③⑤

★**Causses** LE56 av J-Jaurès ☎65600319
:Rest closed Sat & Sun evening (winter)
rm22(⌂ℸ14) ☎ P4
Credit Card ①

★**Paris & Poste** 10 av A-Merle ☎65600052
3 Jan-15 Nov
rm22(⌂ℸ15) P14 Lift
Credit Cards ③⑤

ﮩ **G Alric** rte de Montpellier ☎ 65604144 P For

ﮩ **J Pineau** 161 av de Cates ☎ 65600855 P

ﮩ **H Pujol** 85 av J-Jaurès ☎ 65600921 P Peu
Tal

MILLES, LES
See AIX-EN-PROVENCE

MILLY
Indre-et-Loire

★**Château de Milly** rte de Richelieu-Châtellerault
☎47956456
Mar-Jan :Rest closed Thu (out of season)
rm15(⌂ℸ13) ☎ P ℧
Credit Cards ①②③⑤

MIMIZAN
Landes

ﮩ **J Poisson** 48 av de Bordeaux ☎ 58090873
Ren

At MIMIZAN-PLAGE

★★**Côte d'Argent Pn** 4 av M-Martin ☎58091522
20 May-Sep
rm73(⌂ℸ43) A33rm P60 Lift ℂ Sea
Credit Cards ①②③⑤

MIMIZAN-PLAGE
See MIMIZAN

MIRAIL, LE
See TOULOUSE

MIRAMBEAU
Charente-Maritime

★**Union** r Principale ☎46496164
rm9(⌂ℸ1) A2rm ☎ P10
Credit Cards ①③

ﮩ **Gauvin** 1 av C-Jourdain ☎ 46496185 P For

MIREPOIX
Ariège

★**Commerce** LEDPn cours du Dr-Chabaud
☎61681029
Feb-Dec
rm32(⌂ℸ28) A10rm ☎ P15
Credit Cards ①③⑤

MISSILLAC
Loire-Atlantique

★★★**Golf de la Bretesche DPn** (1km W via D2)
☎40883005 tx 701976
Mar-Jan
rm27(⌂ℸ23) P ℺ ⌇ ⋔ Lake
Credit Cards ①③

MOISSAC
Tarn-et-Garonne

★★★**Moulin** (MAP) 1 pl du Moulin ☎63040355 tx
521615
⌂ℸ57 P50 Lift ℂ Sea
Credit Cards ①②③

★★**Pont Napoléon** 2 allées Montebello
☎63040155
5 Feb-5 Jun & 25 Jun-5 Jan
rm14(⌂ℸ11) ☎ P12 Lake
Credit Cards ①③

MOLAY-LITTRY, LE
Calvados

★★★**Château de Molay** (MAP/BW) rte d'Isigny
☎31229082 tx 171912
Mar-Nov
⌂ℸ40 A8rm P60 Lift ℂ ℺ ⌇ Beach
Credit Cards ①②③④⑤

MONCHEL-SUR-CANCHE
See FRÉVENT

MONDEVILLE
See CAEN

MONTAGNY-LES-BEAUNE
See BEAUNE

MONTARGIS
Loiret

★**Tour d'Auvergne** LE20 r J-Jaurès
☎38850116
:Rest closed Fri
rm14(⌂ℸ12) ☎ P6
Credit Cards ①②③④⑤

At AMILLY(5km S)

★★**Climat** av d'Antibes ☎38982021
⌂ℸ41 P60
Credit Cards ①③

MONTAUBAN
Tarn-et-Garonne
★★**Midi** L€12 r Notre-Dame ☎63631723 tx
533548
rm62(➧♠59) A14rm Lift ☾
Credit Cards ①②③④⑤
★★**Orsay** (FAH) Face Gare,Villebourbon
☎63660666 tx 520362
:Rest closed Sun
➧♠20 P7 Lift
Credit Cards ①②③⑤
❧ **Denayrolles** 878 av J-Moulin ☎ 63036202 M/
C P AR Hon

At **MONTBETON**(3km W)
★★★**Coulandrières** Pn rte Castelsarrasin
☎63674747 tx 520200
➧♠21 P60 ☾ ⌣
Credit Cards ①②③⑤

MONTAUBAN-DE-BRETAGNE
Ille-et-Vilaine

At **LANDUJAN**(7km NE)
★★★**Château de Lauville** ☎99072114/99611010
tx 730800
Mar-Jan
➧♠6 P12 ⌣ ♨
Credit Cards ①③

MONTBARD
Côte-d'Or
★★**Gare** 10 r Ml-Foch,pl de la Gare (n.rest)
☎80920212
rm20(➧♠16) ☂ P12
Credit Cards ①③
★**Ecu** L€(FAH) 7 r A-Carré ☎80921166 tx
351102
rm25(➧♠24) ☂ P8
Credit Cards ①②③⑤

MONTBAZON
Indre-et-Loire
★★★★★**Château d'Artigny** (Relais et Châteaux)
(2km SW via D17) ☎47262424 tx 750900
11 Jan-Nov
➧♠53 A22rm P Lift ⚲ ⌣ ♘♞
Credit Card ③
★★★★**Domaine de la Tortinière** (1.5km N)
☎47260019 tx 752186
Mar-15 Nov :Rest closed Tue/Wed midday
➧♠21 A10rm P50 ⚲ ⌣
Credit Cards ①③

At **MONTS**(8km W)
★**Sporting** L€☎47267015
8 Mar-15 Sep & Oct-15 Feb
rm13(➧♠4) A5rm P40
Credit Cards ①③

MONTBÉLIARD
Doubs
★★**Ibis** r J-Foillet,ZAC du Pied d'Egouttes
☎81902158 tx 361555
➧♠42 Lift
Credit Cards ①③

At **BAVANS**(2.5km SW)
❧ **Esso** 85 Grande rue ☎ 81962659 P Peu

MONTBETON
See **MONTAUBAN**

MONTCABRIER
See **PUY-L'ÉVÊQUE**

MONTCHANIN
See **CREUSOT, LE**

MONT-DE-MARSAN
Landes
★★★**Richelieu** 3 r Wlerick ☎58061020 tx 550238
:Rest closed winter & Sat
rm70(➧♠50) ☂ P20 Lift ☾
Credit Cards ①②③⑤
❧ **Continental** 839 av de Ml-Foch ☎ 58063232
Rov

❧ **Hiroire Automobiles** bd d'Alingsas ☎
58753662 P For

MONT-DORE, LE
Puy-de-Dôme
★★★**Carlina** Les Pradets ☎7365042
➧♠50 ☂ P17 Lift ☾ Mountain
Credit Cards ①②③④⑤

At **PIED-DU-SANCY**(4km S on N683)
★★**Puy-Ferrand** L€☎73651899 tx 990332
Closed 15 Oct-20 Dec
➧♠42 P80 Lift Mountain
Credit Cards ①②③⑤

MONTE-CARLO BEACH
See **MONTE CARLO**

MONTÉLIMAR
Drôme
★★★**Relais de l'Empereur** pl M-Dormoy
☎75012900 tx 345537
22 Dec-11 Nov
rm40(➧♠34) A1rm ☂ P35 ☾
Credit Cards ①②③⑤
★★**Climat** 8 bd du Pêcher ☎75530770
➧♠44 P Lift
★★**Sphinx** 19 bd Desmarais (n.rest) ☎75018664
➧♠25 ☂ P18
Credit Cards ①②③
★**Beausoleil** L€14 bd Pêcher,pl d'Armes
(n.rest) ☎75011980
rm16(➧♠14) P14
Credit Cards ①③

At **SAUZET**(9km NE on D6)
❧ **M Chaix** ☎ 75467170 P Ren

MONTESSON
Yvelines
★★**Campanile** 9 r du Chant-des-Oiseaux
☎30716334 tx 698906
➧♠42 P42
Credit Card ③

MONTFAVET
See **AVIGNON**

MONTIGNAC
Dordogne
★★★**Château de Puy Robert** ☎53519213 tx
330616
11 May-15 Oct
➧♠38 A23rm P40 Lift ☾ ⌣ Mountain
Credit Cards ①②③⑤
★**Soleil d'Or** 16 r IV-Septembre ☎53518022
Closed Jan
➧♠38 P40 ⌣
Credit Cards ①②③

MONTIGNY-LA-RESLE
Yonne
★★**Soleil d'Or** L€Pn ☎86418121
1 Dec-30 Oct :Rest closed Mon
➧♠11 A4rm P15 ⚲
Credit Cards ①②③⑤

MONTIGNY-LE-ROI
Haute-Marne
★★**Moderne** av de Lierneux ☎25903018 tx
830349
➧♠25 ☂ P20
Credit Cards ①③
❧ **Flagez** N 74 ☎ 25903034 P Fia Peu Tal

MONTIVILLIERS
See **HAVRE, LE**

MONTLUCON
Allier
★★★**Terminus** 47 av M-Dormoy (n.rest)
☎70052893
rm42(➧♠36) Lift
Credit Cards ①②③⑤

★★**Château St-Jean** Parc St-Jean ☎70050465 tx
592339
➧♠19 P50 Lift ☐ Lake
Credit Cards ①②③⑤
❧ **Bourronnais** 10 r P-Sémard ☎ 70053437 P
Peu Tal

MONTMERLE-SUR-SAÔNE
Ain
★★**Rivage** L€12 r du Pont ☎74693392
:Rest closed Mon
➧♠21 A8rm ☂ P30
Credit Cards ①②③

MONTMIRAIL
Marne
★**Vert Galant** 2 pl Vert-Galant ☎26812017
rm12(♠3) P5
Credit Cards ①③

MONTMORENCY
Val-d'Oise
★★**Montmorency Etape Coqvert** 42 av de
Domont ☎34170002 tx 699886
➧♠42 P50 Lift
Credit Cards ①②③④

MONTMORILLON
Vienne
★★**France Mercier** 2 bd de Strasbourg
☎49910051
10 Feb-31 Dec :Rest closed Sun Dinner & Mon
rm29(➧♠19)
Credit Cards ①②③④⑤

MONTMORT
Marne
★★**Place** L€3 pl Berthelot ☎26591038
rm30(➧♠24) A5rm P15
Credit Cards ①③

MONTOIRE-SUR-LE-LOIR
Loire-et-Cher
★★**Cheval Rouge** L€DPn pl Ml-Foch
☎54850705
Mar-Jan :Rest closed Tue eve & Wed
rm17(➧♠12) ☂ P10
Credit Cards ①②③

MONTPELLIER
Hérault
★★★★**Altea Antigone** 218 r de Bastion-
Ventadour,Quartier le Polygone ☎67646566 tx
480362
:Rest closed Sat lunchtime & Sun
➧♠116 ☂ P10 Lift
Credit Cards ①②③⑤
★★★★**Métropole** (MAP/BW) 3 r C-René
☎67581122 tx 480410
rm92(➧♠90) ☂ Lift ☾
Credit Cards ①②③⑤
★★★★**Sofitel** Le Triangle (n.rest) ☎67584545 tx
480140
➧♠98 Lift ☾
Credit Cards ①②③⑤
★★★**Mercure Montpellier Est** 662 av de
Pompignane ☎67655024 tx 480656
➧♠122 P Lift ⌣
★★★**Novotel** 125 bis av de Palavas ☎67640404
tx 490433
➧♠97 P100 Lift ⌣ ♨
Credit Cards ①②③⑤
★★**Campanile** Lieudit "Terre du Mas
de,Sorrés",av du Mas-d'Argelliers ☎67587980 tx
485427
➧♠50 P50
Credit Card ③
★★**Hotel Campanile** ZAC du Millénaire,r H
Becquerel ☎67648585 tx 485659
➧♠84 P90 Lift
Credit Cards ①②③

★★*Climat* r de Caducée ☎67524333 tx 85693
⊶ℝ42 P80
Credit Cards [1][3][5]

★★*Ibis* rte de Palavas ☎67588230 tx 480578
⊶ℝ165 P150 Lift
Credit Cards [1][3]

⊷ *Imbert* rte de Sète,St-Jean-de-Vedars ☎
67424622 P For

MONTREUIL
See DREUX

MONTREUIL
Pas-de-Calais

★★★*Château de Montreuil* (Relais et Châteaux)
4 chaussée des Capucins ☎21815304 tx 135205
Feb - Mid Dec :Rest closed Thu Lunch
⊶ℝ15 A3rm ⌂ P7 ℂ
Credit Cards [1][3][4]

★*Central Pn* 7-9 r du Change ☎21861604
24 Jan-23 Dec
rm11(⊶ℝ5) A3rm ⌂
Credit Cards [1][2][3]

MONTREUIL-BELLAY
Maine-et-Loire

★*Splendid* LEPn r Dr-Gaudrez ☎41523021
:Rest closed 3-4 Jan
rm20(⊶ℝ19) A20rm P40 ⌐
Credit Cards [1][3]

MONTRICHARD
Loir-et-Cher

★★*Bellevue* LEquai du Cher ☎54320617 tx
751673
⊶ℝ29 P Lift ℃ ▭ ⌐
Credit Cards [1][2][3][5]

★★*Tête-Noire* rte de Tours ☎54320555
7 Feb-2 Jan :Rest closed Fri 15 Oct-15 Mar
rm38(⊶ℝ31) A9rm P10
Credit Cards [1][3]

At CHISSAY-EN-TOURAINE(6km W)

★★★*Château Menaudière* DPn rte Amboise
☎54320244 tx 751246
Mid Mar-Beg Dec
⊶ℝ25 A8rm ℃
Credit Cards [1][2][3][5]

MONTROUGE
See PARIS

MONTS
See MONTBAZON

MONT-ST-AIGNAN
See ROUEN

MONTSALVY
Cantal

★★*Nord* LEpl du Barry ☎71492003
1 Apr-31 Dec
rm26(⊶ℝ22) P15
Credit Cards [1][2][3][4][5]

MONTSOULT
Val-d'Oise

★★★*Novotel Château de Maffiers* ☎34739305
tx 695701
⊶ℝ80 P200 ℃ ⌐ U
Credit Cards [1][2][3][5]

MONT-ST-MICHEL, LE
Manche

★★*Digue* La Digue (2km S) ☎33601402 tx
170157
Apr-15 Nov
⊶ℝ35 P50 Sea
Credit Cards [1][2][3][5]

★★*K* LELa Digue (2km S on D976)
☎33601418 tx 170537
Etr-Nov
⊶ℝ60
Credit Card [2]

★★*Mère Poulard* LE(Inter) ☎33601401 tx
170197
⊶ℝ27 A14rm Sea
Credit Cards [1][2][3][5]

MORANGIS
See PARIS AIRPORTS under ORLY AIRPORT

MOREZ
Jura

★★*Central Modern* 106 r de la République
☎84330307
Closed 15 Jul-15 Aug
rm47(⊶ℝ18) A24rm ⌂ P Mountain
Credit Cards [1][3]

MORLAIX
Finistère

★★★*Grand Hotel d'Europe* (FAH) 1 r d'Aiguillon
☎98621199 tx 941676
rm67(⊶ℝ57) Lift
Credit Cards [1][2][3][4][5]

★★*Fontaine* rte de Lannion (n.rest) ☎98620955
20 Mar-12 Feb
⊶ℝ35 P50
Credit Cards [1][3]

MORTAGNE-AU-PERCHE
Orne

★*Tribunal* LE4 pl du Palais ☎33250477 tx
170841
rm19(⊶ℝ13) A9rm ⌂ P30
Credit Cards [1][3]

MORTAGNE-SUR-SÈVRE
Vendée

★★★*France* LE(FAH) 4 pl du Dr-Pichat
☎51650337 tx 711403
15 Aug-31 Jul
⊶ℝ25 P60 Lift ℃ ▭
Credit Cards [1][2][3][5]

MORTAIN
Manche

★*Cascades* 16 r du Bassin ☎33590003
3 Jan-20 Dec :Rest closed Sun dinner & Mon
rm13(⊶ℝ7)
Credit Cards [1][3]

MORZINE
Haute-Savoie

★★★*Carlina* DPn av J-Plane ☎50790103 tx
365596
15 Dec-15 Apr & Jul-Sep
rm20(⊶ℝ19) ⌂ P4 Mountain
Credit Cards [1][2][3][5]

★★★*Dahu* ☎50791112 tx 309514
15 Jun-15 Sep & 15 Dec-15 Apr
⊶ℝ26 P24 Lift ⌐ Mountain
Credit Cards [1][3]

MOULINS
Allier

★★★*Paris* (Relais et Châteaux) DPn 21 r de
Paris ☎70440058 tx 394853
⊶ℝ27 ⌂ P15 Lift ℃
Credit Cards [1][2][3][4][5]

★★*Ibis* Angle de la rte de Lyon(N7),bd Primaire
☎70467112 tx 090638
⊶ℝ43 P40 Lift
Credit Cards [1][3]

★★*Moderne* (Inter) 9 pl J-Moulin ☎70440506 tx
392968
⊶ℝ44 ⌂ P30 Lift ℃
Credit Cards [1][3]

★★*Parc* LE31 av Gl-Leclerc ☎70441225
⊶ℝ28 A5rm ⌂ P25 ℃
Credit Card [3]

At COULANDON(7km W)

★★*Chalet* ☎70445008
Feb-Oct :Rest closed lunch time
⊶ℝ25 A16rm P30
Credit Cards [1][2][3][5]

MOUSSY
See ÉPERNAY

MOUTHIER-HAUTE-PIERRE
Doubs

★★*Cascade* LEDPn ☎81609530
Feb-Nov
⊶ℝ23 ⌂ P20 Mountain
Credit Cards [1][3]

MOÛTIERS
Savoie

★★*Ibis* Colline de Champoulet ☎79242711 tx
980611
⊶ℝ62 P50 Lift
Credit Cards [1][3]

MULHOUSE
Haut-Rhin

★★★★*Altea de la Tour* 4 pl Gl-de-Gaulle
☎89460123 tx 881807
⊶ℝ96 P Lift
Credit Cards [1][2][3][4][5]

★★★★*Parc* 26 r de la Sinne ☎89661222 tx
881790
⊶ℝ76 ⌂ P30 Lift ℃
Credit Cards [1][2][3][4][5]

★★*Balladins* Z Industrielle,Ile Napoléon Ouest
☎05355575 tx 649394
rm38 P38
Credit Cards [1][2][3][4][5]

At RIXHEIM

⊷ *Ott et Wetzel* rte de Mulhouse 37 ☎
89440137 P AR DJ LR

At SAUSHEIM(6km NE D422)

★★★*Mercure* r de l'Ile Napoléon ☎89618787 tx
881757
⊶ℝ97 P150 Lift ℃ ⌐
Credit Cards [1][2][3][5]

★★★*Novotel* r de l'Ile Napoléon ☎89618484 tx
881673
⊶ℝ77 P100 ℃ ⌐ ▸▸
Credit Cards [1][2][3][5]

★★*Ibis* rte de Sausheim Est,Ille Napoléon
☎89618383 tx 881970
⊶ℝ76 P70 Lift
Credit Cards [1][3]

At WITTENHEIM(6km NW)

★★*Climat* r des Milleportuis ☎89535331 tx
881775
⊶ℝ43 ⌐ Mountain
Credit Cards [1][2][3]

MUREAUX, LES
Yvelines

★★*Climat* ZAC du Grand Ouest CD 43,r des
Pleiades ☎24747250 tx 399958
⊶ℝ42 P50
Credit Cards [1][3]

MURET
Haute-Garonne

⊷ *Ste-Clé Automobile* L'Escouplette (N117) ☎
61510330 P For

MUS
Gard

★★*Auberge de la Paillère* ☎66351333
:Rest closed Sun dinner & Mon
⊶ℝ8 P8
Credit Cards [1][2][3][5]

MUY, LE
Var

⊷ *St-Roch* ☎94451067 P CIT

NAJAC
Aveyron

★★*Belle Rive* LE☎65297390
Apr-Oct
⊶ℝ39 A12rm ⌂ P100 ⌐ Mountain
Credit Cards [1][2][3][5]

★★**Oustal del Barry** LEpl du Bourg
☎65297432
1 Apr-1 Nov
rm21(✒17) 🅰 P25 Lift ⚲ Mountain
Credit Cards ① ② ③

NAMPONT-ST-MARTIN
Somme

★★**Peupleraie** N1 ☎22299811
Closed 1-15 Jan
✒40 🅰 P

NANCY
Meurthe-et-Moselle

★★★★**Grand** (Relais et Châteaux) 2 pl Stanislas
☎83350301 tx 960367
✒51 Lift ℂ
Credit Cards ① ② ③ ⑤

★★★**Agora** 6 r Piroux ☎83355805 tx 960034
✒78 Lift ℂ
Credit Cards ① ② ③ ⑤

★★★**Altea Thiers** 11 r R-Poincaré,pl Thiers
☎83356101 tx 960034
✒112 P40 Lift

★★**Albert 1er/Astoria** 3 r Armée-Patton (n.rest)
☎83403124 tx 850895
rm123(✒103) P30 Lift
Credit Cards ① ② ③ ④ ⑤

★★**Central** 6 r R-Poincaré (n.rest) ☎83322124 tx
850895
rm68(✒60) Lift ℂ
Credit Cards ① ③ ④

★**Américain** 3 pl A-Maginot (n.rest) ☎83322853
tx 961052
✒51 Lift ℂ
Credit Cards ① ② ③ ④ ⑤

★**Poincaré** 81 r R-Poincaré (n.rest) ☎83402599
rm25(✒7)
Credit Cards ① ③

🍽 H Gras 11 r Lebrun ☎ 83365175 For

At **CHAUVIGNY**(4km SW)

★★**Balladins** Z I les Clairs Chénes,D974
☎83576363
✒28 P20
Credit Card ③

At **HOUDEMONT**(6km S)

★★★**Novotel Nancy Sud** rte d'Épinal,N57
☎83561025 tx 961124
✒86 ☐
Credit Cards ① ② ③ ④ ⑤

At **LAXOU**(3km SW)

★★★**Mercure** 2 r de la Saône ☎83964221 tx
850036
✒99 P Lift ☐

★★★**Novotel Nancy Ouest** N4 ☎83966746 tx
850988
✒119 P180 Lift ☐
Credit Cards ① ② ③ ⑤

🍽 Nancy Laxou Automobiles 21 av de la
Résistance ☎ 83984343 For

At **LUDRES**(8km S)

★★**Climat** ZI de Ludres ☎83261500 tx 961043
✒38 P20
Credit Cards ① ② ③

At **VANDOEUVRE-LES-NANCY**(4km S)

★★**Campanile** ZAC de Brabois,1 av de la Forêt-
de-Haye ☎83514151 tx 960604
✒42 P42
Credit Card ③

NANS-LES-PINS
Var

At **CHÂTEAUNEUF**(3.5km N)

★★★**Châteauneuf** (Relais et Châteaux)
☎94789006 tx 400747

Apr-Nov
✒32 🅰 P50 ⚲ ☐ 🐾 Mountain
Credit Cards ① ② ③ ⑤

NANTES
Loire-Atlantique

★★★★**Pullman Beaulieu** 3 r du Dr-Zamenhof
☎40471058 tx 711440
✒150 🅰 P70 Lift
Credit Cards ① ② ③ ⑤

★★★★**Sofitel** r A-Millerand ☎40476103 tx
710990
✒100 P150 Lift ⚲ ☐ Sea
Credit Cards ① ② ③ ⑤

★★★**Central** (MAP) 4 r du Couédic ☎40200935
tx 700666
✒120 Lift ℂ
Credit Cards ① ② ③ ⑤

★★★**Mercure** RN165 towards Vannes-La-Baule
☎40852317 tx 711823
✒54 P ⚲ ☐

★★★**Arcade** 19 r J-Jaurès ☎40353900 tx 701336
✒140 🅰 P Lift

★★**Astoria** 11 r Richebourg (n.rest) ☎40743990
tx 700615
✒45 🅰 P25 Lift ℂ
Credit Cards ① ③

★★**Bourgogne** 9 allée du Cdt-Charcot (n.rest)
☎40740334 tx 701405
Closed 20 days Xmas & 3-17 Jul
✒43 P3 Lift ℂ
Credit Cards ① ② ③ ⑤

★★**Graslin** (FAH) 1 r Piron (off pl Graslin) (n.rest)
☎40697291 tx 701619
✒47 Lift
Credit Cards ① ② ③

★★**Ibis** 3 allée Baco ☎40202120 tx 701382
✒104 🅰 P26 Lift
Credit Cards ① ③

🍽 Dao 14 r G-Clemenceau ☎ 40746666 P All
makes

At **CARQUEFOU**(4km NE)

★★★**Altea Carquefou** Le Petit Bel Air,La rte de
Paris (N23 exit A11) ☎40302924 tx 710962
✒79 P Lift ℂ ☐

★★★**Novotel Nantes Carquefou** allée des
Sapins ☎40526464 tx 711175
✒98 P200 ☐
Credit Cards ① ② ③ ⑤

★★**Balladins** CD 337,Petit Bel Air ☎05355575 tx
649394
rm38 P38
Credit Cards ① ② ③ ④ ⑤

★★**Campanile** bd des Pastureaux ☎40300182 tx
701393
✒77 P77
Credit Card ③

At **ST-HERBLAIN**(8km W)

★★**Balladins** rte de St Étienne-de-Montluc
☎40920410 tx 649394
✒38 P38
Credit Cards ① ② ③

★★**Campanile** rte de St Étienne-de-Montluc
☎40921533 tx 711063
✒50 P50
Credit Card ③

NANTIAT
See **CROUZILLE, LA**

NANTUA
Ain

★★★**France** DPn 44 r Dr-Mercier ☎74750055
20 Dec-Oct:Rest closed Tue Jan-Mar, Fri
May,Jun,Sep & Oct
✒19 🅰 Mountain
Credit Cards ① ② ③

NAPOULE-PLAGE, LA
Alpes-Maritimes

★★★★**Ermitage du Riou** (MAP/BW) av H-Clens
☎93499556 tx 470072
✒42 A5rm P25 Lift ℂ ☐ Sea Mountain
Credit Cards ① ② ③ ⑤

NARBONNE
Aude

★★★**Midi** LE4 av de Toulouse ☎68410462 tx
500401
: Rest closed Sun
rm46(✒36) 🅰 P32 Lift
Credit Cards ① ② ③ ⑤

★★★**Novotel Narbonne Sud** quartier
Plaisance,rte d'Espagne ☎68415952 tx 500480
✒96 P120 Lift ☐
Credit Cards ① ② ③ ⑤

★★**Climat** ZI de Plaisance,chemin de Tuileries
☎68410490 tx 505085
✒40
Credit Cards ① ② ③

★★**Ibis** quartier Plaisance ☎68411441 tx 550480
✒44 🅰 P Lift
Credit Cards ① ③

★★**Languedoc** (MAP/BW) 22 bd Gambetta
☎68651474 tx 605167
rm45(✒37) 🅰 P6 Lift ℂ
Credit Cards ① ② ③ ⑤

★★**Résidence** 6 r Premier-Mai (n.rest)
☎68321941 tx 500441
Closed 3 Jan-2 Feb
✒26 🅰
Credit Cards ① ③

★**Lion d'Or** LE39 av P-Sémard ☎68320692
:Rest closed Sun (in low season)
✒27 🅰 P4
Credit Cards ① ② ③ ⑤

🍽 G Delrieu 43 r P-L-Courier ☎ 68320838 Cit

🍽 Fraisse 33 av de Toulouse ☎ 68422915 Rov

🍽 Jansana r d'Aoste Razimbaud ☎ 68321869 P
Peu Tal

🍽 Lopez 180 av de Bordeaux ☎ 68421631 P All
makes

At **NARBONNE-PLAGE**(1.5km E)

★★★**Caravelle** LEDPn bd du Front-de-Mer
☎68498038
Etr-Oct
✒24 P20 Sea
Credit Cards ① ③

At **ORNAISONS**(14km W)

★★★**Relais Val d'Orbieu** DPn ☎68271027
✒15 A14rm P30 ⚲ ☐ 🐾 Mountain
Credit Cards ① ② ③ ④ ⑤

NARBONNE-PLAGE
See **NARBONNE**

NAVARRENX
Pyrénées-Atlantiques

★★**Commerce** (Inter) r Principale ☎59665016
Closed Jan:Rest closed Mon
✒29 A12rm 🅰 P30 Lift
Credit Cards ① ③

NEMOURS
Seine-et-Marne

★★★**Altea Darvault** L'Aire-de-Service (A6) (2km
SE on A6) (n.rest) ☎64281032 tx 690243
✒102 P80
Credit Cards ① ② ③ ⑤

★★★**Ecu de France** 3 r de Paris ☎64281154
rm28(✒22) 🅰 P
Credit Cards ① ③ ⑤

★★**Ibis** r des Moires,ZI de Nemours ☎64288800
tx 600212
✒42
Credit Cards ① ③

★**Roches** av d'Ormesson, St-Pierre ☎64280143
🛏🗗12 A6rm ☎ P8
Credit Cards 1 2 3 5

★**St-Pierre** 12 av Carnot (n.rest) ☎64280157
15 Mar-28 Feb
rm25(🛏🗗13) ☎ P25
Credit Cards 1 2 3

🍴 **Gambetta** 70 av Gambetta ☎ 64280546 P Fia
Lad VW-Aud

NEUF-BRISACH
Haut-Rhin

At **VOGELGRUN**(5km E on N415)

★★**Européan** ☎89725157 tx 880215
Closed Feb:Rest closed Sun dinner & Mon
🛏🗗23 ☎ P30
Credit Cards 1 2 3 5

NEUFCHÂTEL-EN-BRAY
Seine-Maritime

★★**Grand Cerf** Pn 9 Grande Rue ☎35930002
18 Jan-18 Dec :Rest closed Sun dinner & Mon
🛏🗗12 P5
Credit Cards 1 3

🍴 **Lechopier** 11 Grande Rue,St-Pierre ☎
35930082 P Ren

NEUILLY-SUR-SEINE
See **PARIS**

NEUVÉGLISE
Cantal

🍴 **Sauret** ☎ 71238090 P

NEUVILLE-LÈZ-BEAULIEU
Ardennes

★**Bois** LE RN43 ☎24543255
1 Feb-15 Dec :Rest closed Mon lunch
🛏🗗10 P
Credit Cards 1 2 3 5

NEVERS
Nièvre

★★★**Diane** (MAP/BW) 38 r du Midi ☎86572810
tx 801021
4 Jan-20 Dec
🛏🗗30 ☎ Lift ℂ
Credit Cards 1 2 3 4 5

★★★**Loire** quai Medine ☎86615092 tx 801112
:Rest closed 10 Dec-15 Jan
🛏🗗60 P Lift

★★**Climat** 35 bd V-Hugo ☎86214288 tx 800579
🛏🗗54 ☎ P53 Lift
Credit Cards 1 2 3

★★**Folie** LE rte des Saulaies ☎86570531
Closed 16 Dec-7 Jan
rm39(🛏🗗29) P100 ℂ ₅ ≘
Credit Cards 1 3

★★**Ibis** RN77 du Plateau de la Bonne Dame
☎86375600 tx 800221
🛏🗗56 P75 ℂ
Credit Cards 1 3

★★**Molière** LE 25 r Molière (n.rest) ☎86572996
rm18(🛏🗗15) P8
Credit Cards 1 3

★**Morvan** LE 28 r Mouësse ☎86611416
Closed 3 wks in Jan & Jul
rm11(🛏7) P12

★**Ste-Marie** 25 r Petit-Mouësse ☎86611002
Closed Feb:Rest closed Mon
rm17(🛏🗗8) A9rm ☎ P40
Credit Cards 1 3

At **VARENNES-VAUZELLES**(5km N)

★★**Etape Coqvert** ☎86380972 tx 801059
🛏🗗42 P50
Credit Card 3

NICE
Alpes-Maritimes

See plan

Nice comes nearest to being all things to all visitors with its beautiful setting, marvellous climate and successful blend of good, modern architecture with the narrow streets and alleys of the old town. It provides a good centre from which to tour the Riviera and is within easy reach of the perfume centre at Grasse.

EATING OUT Cooking in this part of France tends to be fairly rich, with plenty of full-flavoured, spicy dishes such as fish soup with garlic, rosemary and saffron (a speciality), and the vegetable stew known as *ratatouille*. Fish in this region is particularly original in its preparation and red mullet with rosemary and salt cod with garlic mayonnaise (aîoli) are especially delicious.
A pleasant accompaniment to meals is a bottle of one of the vigorous Provençal rosé or fresh red wines, excellent to drink with *banon*, a cheese made from cows', goats' or ewes' milk and wrapped in chestnut leaves. Try the popular local aniseed flavoured drink *pastis*, a golden-coloured liquid that turns milky when water is added.
One of the best places in town for seafood is *l'Ane Rouge*, a family-run restaurant in Quai des Deux-Emmanuels.

NICE
Alpes-Maritimes

★★★★★**Négresco** (SRS) 37 prom des Anglais
☎93883951 tx 460040
🛏🗗150 ☎ P30 Lift ℂ Beach Sea
Credit Cards 1 2 3 5

★★★★**Atlantic** 12 bd V-Hugo ☎93884015 tx
460840
🛏🗗123 Lift
Credit Cards 1 2 3 5

★★★★**Holiday Inn** 179 bd R-Cassin ☎93839192
tx 970202
🛏🗗151 ☎ P200 Lift ℂ ≘ Sea
Credit Cards 1 2 3 5

★★★★**Pullman Nice** 28 av Notre-Dame (n.rest)
☎93803024 tx 470662
🛏🗗201 P Lift ℂ ≘ Mountain
Credit Cards 1 2 3 5

★★★★**Sofitel Splendid** 50 bd V-Hugo
☎93886954 tx 460938
🛏🗗129 P40 Lift ℂ ≘ Sea Mountain Lake
Credit Cards 1 2 3 4 5

★★★★**Westminster Concorde** 27 prom des
Anglais ☎93882944 tx 460872
🛏🗗110 Lift ℂ Sea
Credit Cards 1 2 3 5

★★★**Altea Massena** 58 r Gioffredo (n.rest)
☎93854925 tx 470192
🛏🗗116 ☎ P15 Lift
Credit Cards 1 3 4 5

★★★**Bedford** 45 r du MI-Joffre ☎93822839 tx
970086
🛏🗗50 Lift

★★★**Brice** 44 r MI-Joffre ☎93881444 tx 470658
🛏🗗60 Lift ℂ
Credit Cards 1 3 5

★★★**Gounod** 3 r Gounod (n.rest) ☎93882620 tx
461705
🛏🗗50 ☎ P Lift ℂ ≘
Credit Cards 1 2 3 4 5

★★★**Locarno** 4 av des Baumettes (n.rest)
☎93962800 tx 970015
rm48(🛏🗗47) ☎ P12 Lift
Credit Cards 1 2 3 5

★★★**Malmaison** (MAP/BW) 48 bd V-Hugo
☎93876256 tx 470410
:Rest closed Sun evening
🛏🗗46 Lift
Credit Cards 1 2 3 4 5

★★★**Massenet** 11 r Massenet (n.rest)
☎93871131
🛏🗗46 ☎ P22 Lift ℂ
Credit Cards 1 3

★★★**Mercure** 2 r Halevy (n.rest) ☎93823088 tx
970656
🛏🗗124 Lift Sea
Credit Cards 1 2 3 4 5

★★★**Napoléon** 6 r Grimaldi (n.rest) ☎93877007
tx 460949
🛏🗗84 Lift
Credit Cards 1 2 3 5

★★★**Windsor** 11 r Dalpozzo ☎93885935 tx
970072
:Rest closed Sun
🛏🗗65 P3 Lift ℂ
Credit Cards 1 2 3 5

★★**Campanile** quartier de l'Aéroport,459-461
prom des Anglais ☎47571111 tx 610016
🛏🗗170 P Lift Sea
Credit Card 3

★★**Climat** 232 rte de Grenoble ☎93718080 tx
470673
🛏🗗72 ☎ P40 Lift
Credit Cards 1 2 3

★★**Fimotel** bd Pasteur ☎93807676 tx 460507
:Rest closed Sat evening & Sun pm
🛏🗗82 ☎ P25 Lift ℂ
Credit Cards 1 2 3 5

★★**Ibis** 350 bd C-Molinier ☎93833030 tx 461285
🛏🗗127 ☎ P80 Lift Sea
Credit Cards 1 2 3

🍴 **Albert-Ier** 5 r Cronstadt ☎ 93883935 Vol Toy

🍴 **Côte d'Azur** 370 rte de Grenoble ☎ 93298787
P

🍴 **Delfinauto** 49 bd GI-L-Delfino ☎ 93550452 M/
C Peu Tal

🍴 **D.T.A.** 297 rte de Grenoble ☎ 93298489 P All
makes

At **ST-LAURENT-DU-VAR**(7km SW off N7)

★★★**Novotel Nice Cap 3000** av de Verdun
☎93316115 tx 470643
🛏🗗103 P75 Lift ℂ
Credit Cards 1 2 3 4 5

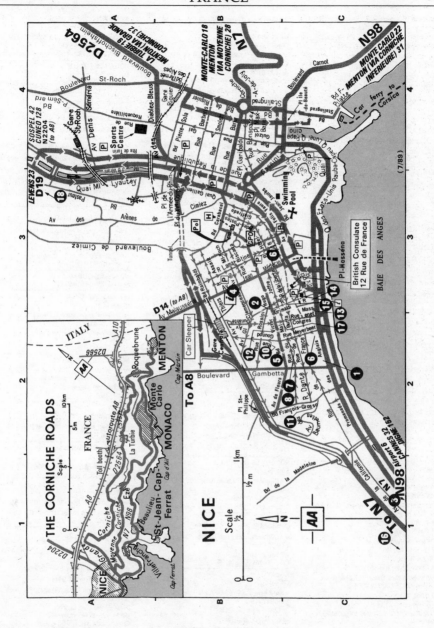

NICE

No.	Rating	Name
1	★★★★★	Négresco
2	★★★★	Atlantic
3	★★★★	Holiday Inn
4	★★★★	Pullman Nice
5	★★★★	Sofitel Splendid
6	★★★★	Westminster Concorde
6A	★★★	Altea Massena
7	★★★	Bedford
8	★★★	Brice
10	★★★	Gounod
11	★★★	Locarno
12	★★★	Malmaison
13	★★★	Massenet
14	★★★	Mercure
15	★★★	Napoléon
16	★★★	Novotel Nice Cap 3000 (At St-Laurent du Var)
17	★★★	Windsor
18	★★	Fimotel

NÎMES
Gard

Nîmes, like Rome, was built with Roman labour on seven hills, and 2,000 years later still competes with Arles for the title *la Rome français*. The well-presented Roman arena marks the centre of the city, and a good place to begin a visit is the Jardin de la Fontaine, containing fountains, pools and shady groves as well as the ruins of a Roman temple of Diana.

The most interesting of Nîmes' churches is the Cathédrale St-Castor, which has a spacious Romanesque nave and an elaborate façade depicting scenes from the Old Testament. Also of interest is the *Maison Carrée* (Square House), a Roman temple dedicated to the adopted sons of the Emperor Augustus. The temple has a Greek-style portico with fluted Corinthian columns. Inside the building is the *Musée des Antiquités* containing a display of superb Roman mosaics as well as statues of the Venus of Nîmes and Apollo.

EATING OUT Specialities of Nimes include *brandade de Morue* (puréed fish blended with olive oil and spices) and *herbes de Provence*, a mixture of herbs and olive oil.

NÎMES
Gard

★★★★**Imperator** quai de la Fontaine ☎66219030 tx 490635
:Rest closed Sat lunchtime
↩59 A3rm ☎ P18 Lift (⚘
Credit Cards 1 2 3 5

★★★**Cheval Blanc et des Arènes** (MAP/BW) ☎66672003 tx 480856
↩96 P120 ⌂
Credit Cards 1 2 5

★★★**Mercure Nîmes Ouest** Ville Active ☎66841455 tx 490746
↩100 Lift ⚘ ⌂
Credit Cards 1 2 3 4 5

★★★**Novotel Nîmes Ouest** 124 chemin de l'Hostellerie ☎66846020 tx 480675
↩96 P120 ⌂
Credit Cards 1 2 3 5

★★**Balladins** ZAC Ville Active ☎05355575 tx 649394
rm38 P38
Credit Cards 1 2 3 4 5

★★**Carrière** DPn 6 r Grizot ☎66672489 tx 490580
rm55(↩50) ☎ P10 Lift (
Credit Cards 2 3 5

★★**Climat** rte d'Arles, RN 113 ☎66842152 tx 485201
↩44 P50 ⌂
Credit Cards 1 2 3

★★**Ibis** Parc Hotelier,Ville Active ☎66380065 tx 490180
↩108 P108 Lift (
Credit Cards 1 3

★★**Louvre** 2 sq de la Couronne ☎66672275 tx 480218
↩33 P10 Lift (
Credit Cards 1 2 3 4 5

☞ **Fricon** 175 rte d'Alès ☎ 66291799 & M/C **P** All makes

At **CAISSARGUES-BOUILLARGUES**(4km S)

★★**Campanile** chemin de la Carréras ☎66842705 tx 480510
↩50 P50
Credit Card 3

At **MARGUERITTES**(7km NE)

★★**Marguerittes** rte d'Avignon ☎66260123
↩48 P

NIORT
Deux-Sèvres

★★★**Brèche** 8 av Bujault (n.rest) ☎49244178 tx 792343
rm50(↩44) Lift
Credit Cards 1 2 3 5

★★**Grand** 32 av Paris (n.rest) ☎49242221 tx 791502
↩40 ☎ P10 Lift (
Credit Cards 1 2 3 4 5

★★**Ibis** av de la Rochelle ☎49735454 tx 791635
↩68 P50 (
Credit Cards 1 3

★★**Terminus** LE(FAH) 82 r de la Gare ☎49240038
:Rest closed Sat
rm43(↩39) Lift (
Credit Cards 1 2 3 5

☞ **Genève** 117 av de Nantes ☎ 49734520 **P** For

NOEUX-LES-MINES
Pas-de-Calais

★★**Tourterelles** LE(FAH) 374 rte Nationale ☎21669075 tx 134338
:Rest closed Sat lunch & Sun
rm21(↩19) P35
Credit Cards 1 2 3 5

NOGENT-LE-ROTROU
Eure-et-Loir

★★**Dauphin** 39 r Villette-Gate ☎37521730
Mar-Nov
rm26(↩11) ☎ P6
Credit Cards 1 3

NOISIEL
Seine-et-Marne

★★**Climat** 50 cours des Roches ☎60061540 tx 693636
↩58 P20 Lift
Credit Cards 1 2 3 5

NOLAY
Côte-d'Or

★**Ste-Marie** LEDPn 36 r de la République ☎80217319
rm12(↩4) A5rm ☎ P12
Credit Cards 2 3 5

☞ **Fourrier Frères** rte de Beaune ☎ 80217219 Peu

NONANCOURT
Eure

★**Grand Cerf** LE 17 Grand Rue ☎32581527
↩6 ☎ P
Credit Cards 1 2 3 5

NONTRON
Dordogne

★★**Grand** LE 3 pl A-Agard ☎53561122
rm26(↩18) ☎ P35 Lift (
Credit Cards 1 3

NOUAN-LE-FUZELIER
Loir-et-Cher

★**Moulin de Villiers** Pn rte Chaon ☎54887227
20 Mar-Aug & 15 Sep-3 Jan :Rest closed Tue evening Wed & Nov-Dec
rm20(↩12) P30 Lake
Credit Cards 1 3

NOUVION-EN-THIÉRACHE, LE
Aisne

★**Paix** 37 r V-Vicary ☎23970455
15 Feb-14 Jul & Aug-20 Dec :Rest closed Sun evening
rm23(↩12) P10
Credit Cards 1 3

☞ **SARL Hannecart** 36 r V-Vicary ☎ 23970105 **P** Peu

NOVES
Bouches-du-Rhône

★★★**Auberge de Noves** DPn (2Km NW on D28) ☎90941921 tx 431312
Mar-Dec :Rest closed Wed Lunch
↩22 ☎ P50 Lift (⚘ ⌂ Mountain
Credit Cards 1 2 3 5

NOYELLES-GODAULT
See **HENIN-BEAUMONT**

NOYERS-SUR-CHER
Loir-et-Cher

★**Touraine et Sologne** LEDPn RN76/RN675 ☎54751523
20 Feb-4 Jan
rm14(↩12) P35
Credit Cards 1 2 3

NOYON
Oise

★**St-Eloi** 81 bd Carnot ☎44440149
rm30(↩26) A15rm P20
Credit Cards 1 3

NOZAY
Loire-Atlantique

★**Gergaud** LE 12 rte Nantes ☎40794754
rm8(↩6) P20

NUITS-ST-GEORGES
Côtes-d'Or

★★**Ibis** 1 av Chambolland ☎80611717 tx 350954
Rest closed Sat, Sun lunch & 15 Dec-15 Jan
↩52 P60
Credit Cards 1 3

☞ **Aubin** rte de Dijon ☎ 80610385 **P** Mer

☞ **Grands Crus** rte de Dijon ☎ 80610223 **P** Peu Tal

NYONS
Drôme

★★**Colombet** pl de la Libération ☎75260366
5 Jan-5 Nov
rm30(↩20) ☎ P12 Lift (Mountain

At **AUBRES**(3km NE D94)

★★**Auberge du Vieux Village** DPn rte de Gap ☎75261289
:Rest closed Wed Lunch
↩24 P25 ⌂ Mountain
Credit Cards 1 2 3 5

OBERNAI
Bas-Rhin

★★**Duc d'Alsace** LE 6 pl de la Gare (n.rest) ☎88955534 tx 880400
rm17(↩15)
Credit Cards 1 2 3 5

OBERSTEIGEN
Bas-Rhin
★★**Belle Vue DPn** 16 rte de Dabo ☎88873239
Closed 11 Jan-19 Feb
⊷♠40 A4rm ☜ P100 Lift ⌒ Mountain
Credit Cards ①③

OLÉRON, ILE D'
Charente-Maritime

REMIGEASSE, LA
★★★**Grand Large** (Relais et Châteaux) **DPn** pl
de la Remigeasse ☎46753789 tx 790395
Etr-Sep
⊷♠31 P31 ⊶ ☒ Beach Sea
Credit Card ③

ST-TROJAN-LES-BAINS
★★★**Novotel** Plage du Gatseau ☎4676246 tx
790910
⊷♠80 ☜ P100 Lift ⊂ ⊶ ☒ Sea
Credit Cards ①②③⑤

OLIVET
Loire
★★★★**Altea Reine Blanche** r de la Reine
Blanche ☎28664051 tx 760926
10 Jan-23 Dec :Rest closed Sat lunch
⊷♠65 P100 Lift ⊶
Credit Cards ①②⑤
★★**Climat** ZAC de la rte de Bourges ☎38692055
tx 692844
⊷♠42 P40
★★**Rivage DPn** 635 r de la Reine Blanche
☎38660293 tx 760926
⊷♠20 P40 ⊶
Credit Cards ①②③⑤

OLORON-STE-MARIE
Pyrénées-Atlantiques
★★**Darroze** 4 pl de la Mairie ☎59390099 tx
571865
⊷♠30 ☜ P6 Lift Mountain
Credit Cards ①②③⑤

ORANGE
Vaucluse
★★★**Altea** rte de Caderousse ☎96342410 tx
431550
⊷♠98 P ⌒
★★**Boscotel** rte de Caderousse ☎90344750 tx
431405
⊷♠57 P100
Credit Cards ①②③⑤
★★**Ibis** rte de Caderousse,Le Jonquier
☎90343535 tx 432752
⊷♠44 P44 ⌒
Credit Cards ①③
★★**Louvre & Terminus** 89 av F-Mistral
☎90341008 tx 431195
5 Jan-20 Dec
rm34(⊷♠32) ☜ P22 Lift ⊂
Credit Cards ①③
🛏 **Adiasse** 1 r Capty (rte de Camaret) ☎
90340387 All makes
🛏 **Amepper** 788 av Ml-Foch ☎ 90341234 **P** Ope
Vau
🛏 **Cretalles** Quartier de Condoulet ☎ 201345305
P Mer

ORGEVAL
Yvelines
★★★**Novotel** RN13/D113 ☎39759760 tx 697174
⊷♠119 P Lift ⊶ ⌒
Credit Cards ①②③⑤
★★**Moulin d'Orgeval** ☎39758574 tx 689036
⊷♠14 P ⊶ Lake
Credit Cards ①②③

ORLÉANS
Loiret

See also CHAPELLE-SAINT-MESMIN, LA
★★★★**Sofitel** 44-46 quai Barentin ☎38621739 tx
780073
⊷♠109 P90 Lift ⊂ ⌒
Credit Cards ①②③⑤
★★★**Cedres** 17 r du Ml-Foch (n.rest) ☎38622292
tx 782314
rm36(⊷♠32) ☜ P5 Lift ⊂
Credit Cards ①②③⑤
★★**Arcade** 4 r du Ml-Foch ☎28542311 tx
7806629
⊷♠125 ☜ P Lift
Credit Cards ①③
★★**Marguerite L̶E** 14 pl Vieux-Marché (n.rest)
☎385374321
rm25(⊷♠10) Lift
Credit Card ①
★★**Terminus** 40 r de la République (n.rest)
☎38532464 tx 782230
⊷♠50 ☜ P40 Lift
Credit Cards ①②③⑤
🛏 **Lion Fort** 51 r Porte St-Jean ☎ 38625829 **P**
AR LR
At **SARAN**(2km NW on A10)
★★**Campanile** 744 rte Nationale 20 ☎38736666
tx 783692
⊷♠50 P50
Credit Card ③
★★**Ibis** Chemin des Sablons ☎38733993 tx
760902
⊷♠104 P Lift
Credit Cards ①③
At **SOURCE, LA**(10km S)
★★★**Novotel Orléans La Source** 2 r H-de-
Balzac ☎38630428 tx 760619
⊷♠119 Lift ⊶ ⌒
Credit Cards ①②③⑤
★★**Campanile** 326 r Châteaubriand ☎38635820
tx 781228
⊷♠42 P42

ORLY AIRPORT
See PARIS AIRPORTS

ORNAISONS
See NARBONNE

ORSAY
Essonne
At **COURTABOEUF**(3km S on D35)
★★★**Mercure Paris Orsay** av du Parana,Z A
Courtaboeuf ☎69076396 tx 691247
⊷♠108 Lift ⌒
Credit Cards ①②③⑤

★★**Climat** av du Cap Horn,ZA de Courtboeuf
☎69281420 tx 692844
⊷♠26
Credit Cards ①③
At **SACLAY**(6km N)
★★★**Novotel** r C-Thomassin,Christ-de-Saclay
☎69418140 tx 601856
⊷♠134 P Lift ⊶ ⌒
Credit Cards ①②③⑤

ORTHEZ
Pyrénées-Atlantiques
★★**Climat** r du Soulor ☎(6)594460123 tx 692844
⊷♠24

OUISTREHAM-RIVA-BELLA
Calvados
★★**Broche d'Argent L̶E** pl du Gl-de-
Gaulle,Riva-Bella ☎31971216 tx 170352
⊷♠48 A10rm P35 Lift Sea
Credit Cards ①②③⑤
🛏 **Relais des Pommiers** rte de Caen,Riva-Bella
☎ 31961088 **P**

OYONNAX
Ain
★**Nouvel** 31 r R-Nicod (n.rest) ☎74772811
rm37(⊷♠24) ☜ P18 Lift
Credit Cards ①③

PACY-SUR-EURE
Eure
★★**Etape** 1 r Isambard ☎32369277
rm9(⊷♠5) ☜ P20
Credit Cards ①③
🛏 **Lepée** 92-102 r Isambard ☎ 32360673 **P** For

PALAISEAU
Essonne
★★★**Novotel** 18-20 r E-Baudot,Zone d'Activité de
Massy ☎69208491 tx 691595
⊷♠151 P200 Lift ⌒
Credit Cards ①②③⑤

PAMIERS
Ariège
★★**Parc L̶E** 12 r Picconnières ☎61670258
:Rest closed Mon
rm13(⊷♠12) ☜
Credit Cards ①③

PANTIN
SeePARIS

PARAMÉ
See ST-MALO

PARAY-LE-MONIAL
Saône-et-Loire
★★**Trois Pigeons** 2 r d'Argaud ☎85810377
Mar-Dec
rm47(⊷♠38) A29rm ☜
Credit Cards ①②③
★★**Vendanges de Bourgogne L̶E** 5 r D-Papin
☎85811343
23 Mar-15 Feb :Rest closed Sun pm & Mon lunch
rm14(⊷♠13) ☜ P60
Credit Cards ①②③

PARENTIS-EN-BORN
Landes
🛏 **Larrieu** av Ml-Foch ☎ 58784350 **P** Ren

PARIS

See plan pages 168–169
Population 9,878,500
Local Tourist Office 127 Avenue des Champs Élysées ☎47236172 (information only)
For information on making internal local calls, see page 118
The whole world knows Paris as THE romantic city, a metropolis with a magical atmosphere that has been working its spell on visitors for centuries. Nowhere else is the street life so entertaining, the cáfes so animated and the atmosphere so vibrant.
Newcomers to Paris are well advised to take a long, leisurely stroll, soak up the atmosphere, and perhaps take in a famous sight or two; a trip down the Seine on a *bateau mouche* is also rewarding. 'People-watching' on the Champs Elysees, one of the world's most glamorous thoroughfares, is still high on the list of most visitors' priorities - despite the exorbitant cost of a coffee at a pavement café - whilst art lovers delight in the sheer diversity of the paintings and sculptures in the *Louvre*
The most important thing is not to miss the magic of Paris - to open the senses to this captivating city and then visit the castles, royal cities and forests of the Ile-de-France.

EATING OUT Freshly baked *croissants*, savoury *crêpes*, tasty *patés* or succulent seafood - your only disappointment with French cuisine is likely to be that you just cannot eat everything. Eating is practically a national pastime in France, so the variety of food and wine is immense and the quality superb. Make sure you sample not only the main dishes such as *boeuf bourguignon* but also the tasty *hors d'oeuvres*, the delicious desserts and the cheeses - then round off the evening by lingering over coffee and brandy.
The choice of Paris restaurants is so wide, ranging from small side-street bistros and brasseries to well established restaurants with international reputations, that it is impossible to give specific recommendations. Two famous cafés well worth a visit are: *Le Dôme*, in Montparnasse, where vintage photographs of its bygone clientele adorn the wooden panelling of the dining alcoves - Picasso, Bonnard, Dufy, Gaugin and Modigliani among others, some depicted at work in their studios, gaunt and hungry-looking as artists should look; *La Coupole*, just along the boulevard, is the place to see, and be seen, among the literati and glitterati of the arts and media - and there is still a fair quota of larger-than-life personalities to focus on.
Many restaurants serve inexpensive and good quality meals which are excellent value for money. Look out for the *menu du jour* or *menu prix fixe*, often chalked up on a blackboard outside. For inexpensive restaurants, the 5th arrondissement, the student quarter, is a good hunting ground, but every quarter has its own restaurants, and provided you steer clear of the main tourist thoroughfares you should do very well.
See also **AULNAY-SOUS-BOIS,BOBIGNY, BUC, CHAMPS-SUR-MARNE, CHELLES, CONFLANS-STE-HONORINE, COURBEVOIE, ECOUEN, ÉPINAY-SUR-ORGE, ERMENONVILLE, ÉVRY, FONTENAY-SOUS-BOIS, GONESSE, LONGJUMEAU, MONTESSON, MONTMORENCY, MONTSOULT, NOISIEL, ORGEVAL, ORSAY, PALAISEAU, PLAISIR, PONTOISE, QUEUE-EN-BRIE (LA), RAMBOUILLET, ST GERMAIN-EN-LAYE, SANNOIS, SURESNES, SURVILLIERS-ST-WITZ, ULIS (LES), VERRIÈRES-LE-BUISSON,** and **VIRY-CHÂTILLON**
The distances shown after locations following the 18th Arrondissement are measured from the Place de la Concorde.

PARIS
1ST ARRONDISSEMENT
Opéra, Palais-Royal, Halles, Bourse
★★★★*Meurice* (Intercont) 228 r de Rivoli
☎42603860 tx 230673
⊷ℿ187 Lift (
Credit Cards ① ② ③ ④ ⑤
★★★★*Ritz* 15 pl Vendôme ☎42603830 tx 670112
⊷ℿ187 Lift (▣
Credit Cards ① ② ③ ④ ⑤
★★★★*Lotti* 7 r de Castiglione ☎42603734
⊷ℿ131 Lift (
Credit Cards ① ② ③ ④ ⑤
★★★★*Mayfair* 3 r R-de-l'Isle (n.rest) ☎42603814 tx 240037
⊷ℿ53 Lift
Credit Cards ① ② ③ ⑤
★★★*Cambon* 3 r Cambon (n.rest) ☎42603809 tx 240814
⊷ℿ44 Lift (
Credit Cards ① ② ③ ⑤

★★★*Castille* 37 r Cambon ☎42615520 tx 213505
⊷ℿ76 Lift (
Credit Cards ① ② ③ ④ ⑤
★★★*Duminy-Vendôme* 3 r Mont-Thabor (n.rest) ☎42603280 tx 213492
⊷ℿ79 Lift (
Credit Cards ① ② ③ ④ ⑤
★★★*France et Choiseul* 239 r St-Honoré,pl Vendôme (n.rest) ☎42615460 tx 680959
⊷ℿ120 Lift (
Credit Cards ① ② ③ ⑤
★★★*Louvre* pl A-Malraux ☎42615601 tx 220412
⊷ℿ200 Lift (
Credit Cards ① ② ③ ④ ⑤
★★★*Montana-Tuileries* 12 r St-Roch ☎42603510 tx 214404
⊷ℿ25 Lift (
Credit Cards ① ② ③ ⑤
★★*Family* 35 r Cambon (n.rest) ☎42615484
rm25(⊷ℿ22) Lift (

★★*Timhotel Louvre* 4 r Croix des Petit Champs (n.rest) ☎42603486 tx 216405
⊷ℿ56 Lift
Credit Cards ① ② ③ ④ ⑤
2ND ARRONDISSEMENT
Opéra, Palais-Royal, Halles, Bourse
★★★★*Westminster* 13 r de la Paix ☎42615746 tx 680035
:Rest closed Sat, Sun & Aug
⊷ℿ102 ☎ Lift
Credit Cards ① ② ③ ⑤
★★*France* 4 r du Caire (n.rest) ☎42333098
rm50(⊷ℿ40) Lift (
★★*Timhotel Bourse* 3 r de la Banque (n.rest) ☎42615390 tx 214488
⊷ℿ46 Lift
Credit Cards ① ② ③ ④ ⑤
5TH ARRONDISSEMENT
Quartier Latin, Luxembourg, Jardin-des-Plantes

★★Acacias Gobelins 18 av des Gobelins (n.rest) ☎45358012 tx 206856
⊷ℂ23 Lift
Credit Cards ①②③⑤

★★Collège de France 7 r Thénard ☎43267836
⊷ℂ29 Lift
Credit Card ②

6TH ARRONDISSEMENT
Quartier Latin, Luxembourg, Jardin-des-Plantes

★★★★Lutetia Concorde 45 bd Raspail (n.rest) ☎45443810 tx 270424
⊷ℂ293 P1000 Lift ℂ
Credit Cards ①②③④⑤

★★★Aramis St-Germain (BW) 124 r de Rennes (n.rest) ☎45480375 tx 205098
⊷ℂ42 Lift ℂ
Credit Cards ①②③⑤

★★★Madison 143 bd St-Germain (n.rest) ☎43297250 tx 201628
⊷ℂ55 Lift ℂ
Credit Cards ①②③

★★★Senat 22 r St-Sulpice (n.rest) ☎43254230 tx 206367
rm32(⊷ℂ28) Lift ℂ
Credit Cards ①②③⑤

★★★Victoria Palace 6 r Blaise-Desgoffe ☎45443816 tx 270557
⊷ℂ110 ☎ P17 Lift ℂ
Credit Cards ①②③⑤

★★Angleterre 44 r Jacob (n.rest) ☎42603472
⊷ℂ29 Lift ℂ
Credit Cards ①②③⑤

7TH ARRONDISSEMENT
Faubourg-St-Germain, Invalides, École Militaire

★★★★Pont-Royal (MAP/BW) 7 r Montalembert ☎45443827 tx 270113
:Rest closed Sun & Aug
⊷ℂ78 Lift ℂ
Credit Cards ①②③⑤

★★★★Sofitel Paris Invalides 32 r St-Dominique ☎45559180 tx 250019
⊷ℂ112 P15 Lift ℂ
Credit Cards ①②③⑤

★★★Bourdonnais 111-113 av Bourdonnais ☎47054542 tx 201416
⊷ℂ60 Lift ℂ
Credit Cards ①③⑤

★★★Bourgogne & Montana 3 r de Bourgogne ☎45512022 tx 270854
:Rest closed Sat & Sun
⊷ℂ35 Lift ℂ
Credit Cards ①②③⑤

★★★Cayré 4 bd Raspail (n.rest) ☎45443888 tx 270577
⊷ℂ130 Lift ℂ
Credit Cards ①②③④⑤

★★★Eiffel Park 17 bis r Amélie (n.rest) ☎45551001 tx 202950
⊷ℂ36 Lift
Credit Cards ①②③⑤

★★Splendid 29 av de Tourville (n.rest) ☎45512477 tx 206879
⊷ℂ45 Lift

8TH ARRONDISSEMENT
Champs-Élysées, St-Lazare, Madeleine

★★★★★Bristol (SRS) 112 fbg St-Honoré ☎42669145 tx 280961
⊷ℂ198 ☎ P220 Lift ℂ 🖵
Credit Cards ①②③④⑤

★★★★George V (THF) 31 av George V ☎47235400 tx 650082
⊷ℂ292 Lift ℂ
Credit Cards ①②③④⑤

★★★★Plaza-Athénée (THF) 25 av Montaigne ☎47237833 tx 650092
rm219(⊷ℂ177) Lift ℂ
Credit Cards ①②③④⑤

★★★★★Prince de Galles 33 av George V ☎47235511 tx 280627
⊷ℂ171 Lift ℂ
Credit Cards ①②③④⑤

★★★★★Royal Monceau (CIGA) 35 av Hoche ☎45619800 tx 650361
⊷ℂ220 ☎ P40 Lift ℂ ९ 🖵
Credit Cards ①②③④⑤

★★★★Bedford 17 r de l'Arcade ☎426622332 tx 290506
⊷ℂ147 Lift ℂ
Credit Cards ①③

★★★★Castiglione 40 r du fbg-St-Honoré ☎42650750 tx 240362
⊷ℂ114 Lift
Credit Cards ①②③⑤

★★★★Horset Astor 11 r d'Astorg ☎42665656 tx 642737
:Rest closed lunchtime in Feb
⊷ℂ128 Lift
Credit Cards ①②③⑤

★★★★Lancaster 7 r de Berri ☎43599043 tx 640991
⊷ℂ66 ☎ P10 Lift ℂ
Credit Cards ①②③⑤

★★★★Pullman Windsor 14 r Beaujon ☎45630404 tx 650902
:Rest closed Sat & Sun
⊷ℂ135 Lift ℂ
Credit Cards ①②③④⑤

★★★★Trémoille (THF) 14 r Trémoille ☎47233420 tx 640344
⊷ℂ111 ☎ P Lift ℂ
Credit Cards ①②③④⑤

★★★★Atala 10 r Châteaubriand ☎45620162 tx 640576
:Rest closed Sat & Sun
⊷ℂ50 Lift
Credit Cards ①②③⑤

★★★Élysées Marignan (BW) 12 r de Marignan ☎43595861 tx 6440188
⊷ℂ72 Lift ℂ
Credit Cards ①②③④⑤

★★★Élysées Ponthieu 24 r de Ponthieu (n.rest) ☎42256870 tx 640053
⊷ℂ62 Lift ℂ
Credit Cards ①②③④⑤

★★★Royal 33 av de Friedland (n.rest) ☎43590814 tx 280655
⊷ℂ57 Lift
Credit Cards ①②③④⑤

★★Brescia 16 r d'Edimbourg (n.rest) ☎45221431 tx 660714
⊷ℂ38 Lift
Credit Cards ①②③⑤

★★Élysée 12 r Saussaies (n.rest) ☎42652925 tx 281665
⊷ℂ32 Lift
Credit Cards ①②③⑤

★★Europe 15 r Constantinople (n.rest) ☎45228080 tx 280658
⊷ℂ57 P Lift
Credit Cards ①③

★★Ministère 31 r de Surène (n.rest) ☎42662143
rm32(⊷ℂ28) Lift ℂ
Credit Cards ①②③

★★Timotel 113 r St-Lazare (n.rest) ☎142962828 tx 215350
rm91 Lift
Credit Cards ①②③④⑤

9TH ARRONDISSEMENT
Opéra, Gare du Nord, Gare de l'Est, Grands Boulevards

★★★★Ambassador Concorde (GT) 16 bd Haussmann ☎42469263 tx 650912
⊷ℂ300 Lift ℂ

★★★★Grand (Intercont) 2 r Scribe ☎42681213 tx 220875
⊷ℂ515 Lift ℂ
Credit Cards ①②③④⑤

★★★Blanche Fontaine 34 r Fontaine (n.rest) ☎45267232 tx 660311
⊷ℂ49 ☎ P13 ℂ
Credit Cards ②③

★★★Caumartin 27 r Caumartin (n.rest) ☎47429595 tx 680702
⊷ℂ40 Lift ℂ
Credit Cards ①②③④⑤

★★★Excelsior Opéra 5 r La Fayette (n.rest) ☎48749930 tx 283312
⊷ℂ53 Lift
Credit Cards ①②③⑤

★★★Franklin (MAP/BW) 19 r Buffault ☎42802727 tx 640988
:Rest closed Sat & Sun
⊷ℂ64 Lift
Credit Cards ①②③④⑤

★★★Hélios 75 r de la Victoire (n.rest) ☎48742864 tx 283255
⊷ℂ50 Lift ℂ
Credit Cards ①②③⑤

★★Campaville B1 bd de Clichy (n.rest) ☎48740112 tx 643572
⊷ℂ78 Lift

★★Havane 44 r de Trevise (n.rest) ☎47707912 tx 283462
⊷ℂ53 Lift ℂ
Credit Cards ①②③⑤

★★Hotel Campaville 11 bis r P-Sémard (n.rest) ☎48782894 tx 643861
⊷ℂ47 Lift

★★Lorette 36 r Notre-Dame de Lorette (n.rest) ☎42851881 tx 283877
⊷ℂ84 Lift ℂ
Credit Cards ①②③⑤

★★Palmon 30 r Maubeuge (n.rest) ☎42850761 tx 641498
⊷ℂ38 ☎ Lift
Credit Cards ①②③⑤

★Laffon 25 r Buffault (n.rest) ☎48784991
25 Aug-25 Jul
rm45 Lift ℂ
Credit Cards ①③

10TH ARRONDISSEMENT
Opéra,Gare du Nord,Gare de l'Est,Grands Boulevards

★★★Horset Pavillon 38 r de l'Echiquier ☎42469275 tx 283905
⊷ℂ91 Lift
Credit Cards ①②③⑤

★★★Terminus Nord 12 bd Denain (n.rest) ☎42802000 tx 660615F
⊷ℂ220 Lift
Credit Cards ①②③⑤

★★Altona 166 r de fbg Poissonire (n.rest) ☎48786824 tx 281436
rm55(⊷ℂ50) Lift

★★Campaville 26 r de l'Aqueduc (n.rest) ☎42392626 tx 216200
⊷ℂ78 Lift

★★Campaville-Porte de Clichy 4 r Marcelin Berthelot (n.rest) ☎47375298 tx 616844
⊷ℂ55 Lift

★★Modern 'Est 91 bd de Strasbourg (n.rest) ☎40377720 tx 375974
⊷ℂ30 Lift ℂ
Credit Cards ①③

11TH ARRONDISSEMENT
Bastille, République, Hôtel-de-Ville

★★★★Holiday Inn 10 pl de la République ☎43554434 tx 210651
⊷ℂ321 Lift ℂ
Credit Cards ①②③④⑤

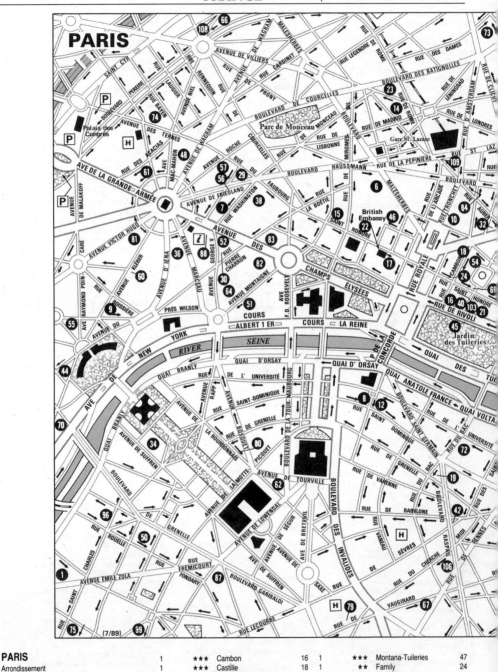

PARIS

PARIS					
Arrondissement		1	★★★ Cambon	16	1
		1	★★★ Castille	18	1
1 ★★★★★	Meurice	45	1 ★★★ Duminy-Vendôme	21	1
1 ★★★★★	Ritz	54	1 ★★★ Ladbroke France		2
1 ★★★★	Lotti	40	& Choiseul	69	2
1 ★★★★	Mayfair	103	1 ★★★ Louvre	41	2

★★★ Montana-Tuileries	47	
★★ Family	24	
★★ Timotel Louvre	104	
★★★★ Westminster	68	
★★ France	27	
★★ Timotel Bourse	105	

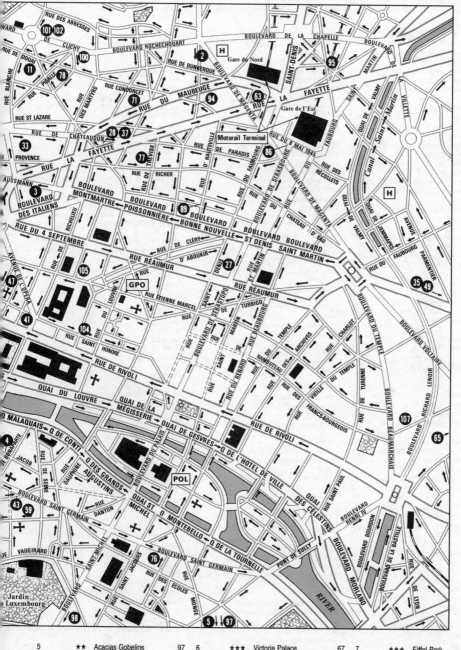

5	★★	Acacias Gobelins	97	6	★★★	Victoria Palace	67	7	★★★ Eiffel Park	1
5	★★	Collège de France	76	6	★★	Angleterre	4	7	★★★ Sofitel Paris Invalides	8
6	★★★★	Lutetia Concorde	42	7	★★★★	Pont Royal	72	7	★★ Splendid	62
6	★★★	Aramis St Germain	106	7	★★★	Bourdonnais	80	8	★★★★★ Bristol	15
6	★★★	Madison	43	7	★★★	Bourgogne & Montana	12	8	★★★★★ George-V	30
6	★★★	Senat	59	7	★★★	Cayré	19	8	★★★★★ Plaza-Athénée	51 →

PARIS continued

Arrondissement

8	★★★★★	Prince de Galles	52
8	★★★★★	Royal Monceau	57
8	★★★★	Bedford	10
8	★★★★	Castiglione	17
8	★★★★	Horset Astor	6
8	★★★★	Lancaster	38
8	★★★★	Pullman Windsor	29
8	★★★★	Trémoille	64
8	★★★	Atala	7
8	★★★	Élysées Marignan	82
8	★★★	Élysées Ponthieu	83
8	★★★	Royal	56
8	★★	Brescia	14
8	★★	Élysée	22
8	★★	Europe	23
8	★★	Ministère	46
8	★★	Timotel Saint-Lazare	109
9	★★★★	Ambassador-Concorde	3
9	★★★★	Grand	32
9	★★★	Blanche Fontaine	11
9	★★★	Caumartin	84
9	★★★	Franklin	28
9	★★★	Hélios	33
9	★★	Campaville	94
9	★★	Campaville	100
9	★★	Havane	77
9	★★	Lorette	78
9	★★	Palmon	71
9	★	Laffon	37
10	★★★	Horset Pavillon	89
10	★★★	Terminus Nord	63
10	★★	Altona	2
10	★★	Campaville	95
10	★★	Modern, Est	86
11	★★★★	Holiday Inn	90
11	★★	Arcade Bastille	65
11	★★	Campaville	107
13	★	Arts	5
14	★★★	Pullman St-Jacques	98
15	★★★★	Hilton	34
15	★★★★	Holiday Inn	91
15	★★★★	Sofitel Paris	75
15	★★★	Mercure Paris-Port de Versailles	99
15	★★	Arcade	87
15	★★	Arcade Montparnasse	79
15	★★	Campaville	96
15	★★	Pacific	50
15	★★	Timhotel Montparnasse	92
16	★★★★	Baltimore	9
16	★★★	Élysées Bassano	88
16	★★★	Frémiet	70
16	★★★	Massenet	44
16	★★★	Sevigné	60
16	★★	Bois	81
16	★★	Keppler	36
16	★★	Rond Point de Longchamp	55
17	★★★★	Regent's Garden	74
17	★★★★	Splendid Étoile	61
17	★★	Neuville	108
17	★★	Neva	48
17	★	Verniquet	66
18	★★★★	Terrass	73
18	★★★	Mercure Paris-Montmartre	101
18	★★	Ibis Paris-Montmartre	102
18	★★	Timhotel Montmartre	93
	★★★	Novotel Paris-Bagnolet (At Bagnolet)	49
	★★	Ibis (At Bagnolet)	35

★★***Arcade Paris Bastille*** Angle r Bregnet/ Froment ☎43386565 tx 216187
🛁305 ⌂ P Lift
Credit Cards [1] [3]

★★***Campaville*** 9 r du Chemin-Vert (n.rest) ☎43385808 tx 218019
🛁170 Lift
Credit Card [3]

12TH ARRONDISSEMENT
Gare de Lyon, Bois de Vincennes

★★***Campaville-Nation*** 54 r du Rendezvous (n.rest) ☎43430152 tx 215771
🛁32 Lift

➤ **Poniatowski** 57 bd Pontiatowski ☎ 43443732 **P** Ren

13TH ARRONDISSEMENT
Bastille, Gare d'Austerlitz, Place d'Italie

★★★**Mercure Hamac** 21 r de Tolbiac (n.rest) ☎45846161 tx 250822
🛁71 ⌂ Lift
Credit Cards [1] [2] [3] [5]

★★***Timhotel Italie*** 22 r Barrault (n.rest) ☎45806767 tx 205461
🛁73 Lift
Credit Cards [1] [2] [3] [4] [5]

★★**Timhotel Tolbiac** 35 r de Tolbiac (n.rest) ☎45837494 tx 201309
🛁54 Lift
Credit Cards [1] [2] [3] [4] [5]

★**Arts** 8 r Coypel (n.rest) ☎47077632
rm37(🛁29) Lift
Credit Cards [1] [3]

14TH ARRONDISSEMENT
Vaugirard, Gare Montparnasse, Grenelle, Denfert-Rochereau

★★★**Pullman St-Jacques** 17 bd St-Jacques ☎45898980 tx 270740
🛁798 ⌂ P50 Lift ☾
Credit Cards [1] [2] [3] [4] [5]

★★***Timotel*** 146 av du Maine (n.rest) ☎43355760 tx 205036
rm91 Lift
Credit Cards [1] [2] [3] [4] [5]

15TH ARRONDISSEMENT
Vaugirard, Gare Montparnasse, Grenelle, Denfert-Rochereau

★★★★**Hilton** 18 av Suffren ☎42739200 tx 200955
🛁489 Lift ☾
Credit Cards [1] [2] [3] [4] [5]

★★★★**Holiday Inn** 69 bd Victor ☎45337463 tx 260844
🛁90 ⌂ P50 Lift
Credit Cards [1] [2] [3] [5]

★★★★**Sofitel Paris** 8-12 r L-Armand ☎40603030 tx 201432
:Rest closed Sat & Sun
🛁635 ⌂ P300 Lift ☾ ▭
Credit Cards [1] [2] [3] [4] [5]

★★★***Mercure Paris-Porte de Versailles*** r du Moulin ☎46429322 tx 202195
🛁391 ⌂ P470 Lift
Credit Cards [1] [2] [3] [5]

★★**Arcade** 2 r Cambronne ☎45673520 tx 203842
🛁530 Lift
Credit Card [3]

★★***Arcade Paris Montparnasse*** 71 bd de Vaugirard N ☎43208912 tx 200864
🛁31 ⌂ P Lift
Credit Cards [1] [3]

★★***Campaville*** 30 r St-Charles (n.rest) ☎45786133 tx 203086
🛁76 Lift

★★***Pacific*** (Inter-Hotels) 11 r Fondary (n.rest) ☎45752049 tx 201346
rm66(🛁49) Lift
Credit Cards [1] [3]

★★***Timhotel Montparnasse*** 22 r de l'Arrivée (n.rest) ☎45489662 tx 270625
rm58
Credit Cards [1] [2] [3] [4] [5]

16th ARRONDISSEMENT
Passy,Auteuil,Bois de Boulogne,Chaillot,Porte Maillot

★★★★**Baltimore** 88 bis av Kléber ☎45538333 tx 611591
🛁119 Lift ☾
Credit Cards [1] [2] [3] [4] [5]

★★★**Élysées Bassano** 24 r de Bassano (n.rest) ☎47204903 tx 611559
🛁40 Lift ☾
Credit Cards [1] [2] [3] [4] [5]

★★★**Frémiet** (MAP/BW) 6 av Frémiet (n.rest) ☎45245206 tx 630329
🛁36 Lift ☾
Credit Cards [1] [2] [3] [5]

★★★**Horset St-Cloud** 21 r Gudin (n.rest) ☎46519922 tx 610929
🛁47 Lift
Credit Cards [1] [2] [3] [5]

★★★***Massenet*** (MAP/BW) 5 bis r Massenet (n.rest) ☎45244303 tx 620682
rm41(🛁37) Lift ☾
Credit Cards [1] [2] [3]

★★★***Sevigné*** 6 r de Belloy (n.rest) ☎47208890 tx 610219
🛁30 P5 Lift
Credit Cards [1] [2] [3] [5]

★★**Bois** 11 r du Dôme (n.rest) ☎45003196 tx 615453
🛁41 ☾
Credit Cards [1] [2] [3]

★★**Keppler** 12 r Keppler (n.rest) ☎47206505 tx 620440
🛁59 Lift ☾
Credit Cards [1] [2] [3]

★★***Murat*** 119 bis bd Murat (n.rest) ☎46511232 tx 648963
🛁28
Credit Cards [2] [3] [5]

★★**Rond Point de Longchamp** (Inter-Hotels) 86 r de Longchamp ☎45051363 tx 620653
:Rest closed Sat & Sun
🛁58 Lift ☾
Credit Cards [1] [2] [3] [5]

17th ARRONDISSEMENT
Clichy,Ternes,Wagram

★★★★**Regent's Garden** (MAP/BW) 6 r P-Demours (n.rest) ☎45740730 tx 640127
🛁40 P8 Lift ☾
Credit Cards [1] [2] [3] [5]

★★★★**Splendid Étoile** 1 bis av Carnot ☎43801456 tx 280773
:Rest closed Sat,Sun & Aug
🛁57 Lift ☾
Credit Cards [1] [3] [5]

★★**Neuville** 3 r Verniquet ☎43802630 tx 648822
🛁28 Lift ☾
Credit Cards [1] [2] [3] [5]

★★**Neva** 14 r Brey (n.rest) ☎43802826 tx 649041
🛁35 Lift
Credit Cards [1] [2] [3] [5]

➤ ***Sarca*** 53-55 av de St-Ouen ☎ 42283070 AR

18th ARRONDISSEMENT
Montmartre,La Villette,Belleville

★★★★**Terrass** (MAP/BW) 12 r J-de-Maistre ☎46067285 tx 280830
🛁104 Lift ☾
Credit Cards [1] [2] [3] [5]

★★★**Mercure Paris-Montmartre** 1-3 r Caulaincourt (n.rest) ☎42941717 tx 640605
🛁308 Lift
Credit Cards [1] [2] [3] [5]

★★Ibis Paris-Montmartre 5 r Caulaincourt
☎42941818 tx 640428
🛏326 ☎ P Lift
Credit Cards ①③

★★Pigalle Urbis Paris 100 bd Rochechouart
(n.rest) ☎46069917 tx 290416
🛏67 Lift
Credit Cards ①③

★★Timhotel Montmartre 11 pl E- Goudeau
(n.rest) ☎42557479 tx 650508
rm63 Lift
Credit Cards ①②③④⑤

At BAGNOLET(7km E)

★★★Novotel Paris-Bagnolet 1 av de la
République ☎43600210 tx 670216
🛏611 ☎ P160 Lift ⌷ ♒
Credit Cards ①②③⑤

★★Ibis r J-Jaurès ☎43600276
🛏414 Lift
Credit Cards ①③

At BOULOGNE-BILLANCOURT(7km W)

★★Campaville 5 r Carnot (n.rest) ☎48252251 tx
631863
🛏57 Lift

🍴 Parc Auto 6 r de la Ferme ☎ 46216602 P

At CACHAN(11km S)

★★Climat 2 r Mirabeau ☎45471800 tx 600609
🛏46 P50 Lift
Credit Cards ①②③

At CHESNAY, LE(16km W)

★★Urbis Versailles Ouest Parly II av du
Dutartre (n.rest) ☎39633793 tx 689188
🛏72 ☎ Lift ℂ
Credit Cards ①③

At CRÉTEIL(12km SE)

★★★Novotel rte de Choissy,N186 ☎42079102 tx
670396
🛏110 P50 Lift ⌷ Lake
Credit Cards ①②③⑤

★★Climat Quartier de la Brèche,r des Archives
☎49800800 tx 262190
🛏51 P50 Lift
Credit Cards ①②③

At DÉFENSE, LA(5km NW)

★★★★Sofitel Paris La Défense 34 cours
Michelet ☎47764443 tx 612189
🛏150 ☎ P Lift ℂ
Credit Cards ①②③⑤

At GENTILLY(6km S)

★★Ibis 13 r du Val-de-Marne ☎46641925 tx
250733
🛏296 Lift
Credit Cards ①③

At KREMLIN-BICÊTRE, LE(6km SE)

★★Campanile bd du Gl-de-Gaulle ☎46701186 tx
205026
🛏155 ☎ P40

At LIVRY-GARGAN(17km NE)

★★Climat 119 bd R-Schuman ☎43854141
🛏43 P70 Lift
Credit Cards ①②③

At MONTROUGE(6km S)

★★★Mercure Porte d'Orléans 13 r F-Ory
☎46571126 tx 202528
🛏192 ☎ P30 Lift
Credit Cards ①②③⑤

★★Ibis 33 r Barbès ☎47469595 tx 202527
🛏402 P350 Lift
Credit Cards ①③

At NEUILLY-SUR-SEINE(8km W)

★★Maillot 46 r de Sablonville (n.rest)
☎46242345
rm35(🛁34) ☎ P7 Lift ℂ

🍴 Reymond 18 bd Vital-Bouhot ☎ 47471919

At PANTIN(7km NE)

★★★Mercure-Paris 25 r Scandicci ☎48467066 tx
230742
:Rest closed Sat & Sun lunch
🛏138 ☎ Lift
Credit Cards ①②③⑤

★★Campanile av J-Lolive, ZAC "Ilôt 51"
☎45751111 tx 610016
🛏126 P Lift
Credit Card ③

At VILLENEUVE-LA-GARENNE(16km N)

★★Climat bd C-de-Gaulle ☎7995600 tx 692844
🛏37

PARIS AIRPORTS

BOURGET AIRPORT, LE

★★★Novotel-Paris Le Bourget r le Pont Yblon
(RN2) ☎48674888 tx 230115
🛏143 P250 Lift ⌷
Credit Cards ①②③⑤

CHARLES-DE-GAULLE AIRPORT

At ROISSY-EN-FRANCE(2km E)

★★★★Holiday Inn 1 allée du Verger ☎39880022
tx 695143
🛏240 P140 Lift
Credit Cards ①②③④⑤

★★★★Sofitel ☎48622323 tx 230166
🛏352 ☎ P250 Lift ℂ ⌷ 🖾
Credit Cards ①②③⑤

★★Arcade 10 r du Verseau ☎48624949 tx
212989
🛏356 P150 Lift
Credit Cards ①③

★★Ibis 2 av de la Raperie ☎34293434 tx 699083
🛏200 P210 Lift
Credit Cards ①③

ORLY AIRPORT

★★★★Hilton International 267 Orly Sud
☎46873388 tx 250621
🛏366 P200 Lift ℂ
Credit Cards ①②③④⑤

★★Arcade espl Aérogare Sud ☎46873350 tx
203121
🛏300 Lift
Credit Card ③

At ATHIS-MONS(2.5km SE)

🍴 Bidaud 59 rte de Fontainebleau ☎ 69388181
M/C P Peu

At MORANGIS(2.5km SW)

★★Campanile 34 av F-de-Lesseps ☎64486130
tx 600832
🛏50 P50

★★Climat 81 r Lavoisier,ZI des Sables
☎64483155 tx 603214
🛏38 P40
Credit Card ③

PARTHENAY

Deux-Sèvres

★★Grand 85 bd de la Meilleraie (n.rest)
☎49640016
rm26(🛁20) ☎ P15
Credit Cards ①②③④⑤

PASSENANS

See SELLIÈRES

PAU

Pyrénées-Atlantiques

★★★Continental (MAP/BW) 2 r Ml-Foch
☎59296931 tx 570906
🛏100 ☎ P35 Lift ℂ
Credit Cards ①②③④⑤

★★★Roncevaux (FAH) 25 r L-Barthou (n.rest)
☎59270844 tx 570849
rm44(🛁35) P10 Lift
Credit Cards ①②③④⑤

★★Bristol (Inter-Hotels) 3 r Gambetta (n.rest)
☎59277298 tx 570317
rm24(🛁22) P15 Lift ℂ
Credit Cards ①②③④⑤

★★Campanile bd de l'Aviation ☎59803233 tx
540208
🛏43 P43

★★Ibis 45 r F-Garcia-Lorca ☎59803233 tx
540208
🛏83 ☎ P20 Lift

★Central 15 r L-Daran (n.rest) ☎59277275
rm28(🛁15) ☎ P1 ℂ
Credit Cards ①②③⑤

At LESCAR(7.5km NW)

★★★Novotel (N 117) ☎59321732 tx 570939
🛏61 P80 ⌷ Mountain
Credit Cards ①②③④⑤

🍴 Morin Z.A.C. Monhauba ☎ 59811881 P Rov

PAYRAC

Lot

★★Hostellerie de la Paix 🄻🄴☎65379515 tx
521291
18 Feb-2 Jan
🛏50 P25 ⌷ Mountain
Credit Cards ①②③

PENNE-ST-MENET, LA

See MARSEILLE

PÉRIGUEUX

Dordogne

★★★Domino (Inter-Hotels) 21 pl Francheville
☎53082580 tx 570230
rm37(🛁31) P15 Lift ℂ
Credit Cards ①②③

★★Campanile ZI Carrefour,Boulazac ☎53090037
tx 572705
🛏42 P42
Credit Card ③

★★Climat "Le Breuil",Trelissac ☎53043636 tx
541707
🛏50 P92 ⌀
Credit Cards ①②③⑤

★★Ibis 8 bd Saumande ☎53536458 tx 550159
🛏89 ☎ P30 Lift ℂ
Credit Cards ①③

🍴 Laroumédie 182 rte de Bordeaux ☎
53080827 Maz Vol

PÉRONNE

Somme

★★St-Claude 🄻🄴42 pl L-Daudré ☎22844600 tx
145618
rm36(🛁22) ☎ P18
Credit Cards ①②③⑤

★Remparts 🄻🄴Pn 21 r Beaubois ☎22843821
rm17(🛁13) ☎ P7
Credit Cards ①②③⑤

At ASSEVILLERS(adj to A1)

★★★Mercure r Beaubois,A1 ☎22841276 tx
140943
🛏100 P50 Lift ⌷
Credit Cards ①②③⑤

PÉROUGES

Ain

★★Vieux Pérouges pl du Tilleul ☎74610088 tx
306898
🛏29 ☎ P15 Mountain
Credit Cards ①③

PERPIGNAN

Pyrénées-Orientales

★★★Mondial (MAP) 40 bd Clemenceau
☎68342345 tx 500920
🛏40 P6 Lift
Credit Cards ①②③⑤

★★★Windsor 8 bd Wilson (n.rest) ☎68511865 tx
500701
🛏57 Lift ℂ
Credit Cards ①③

★★*Campanile* r A-Levernan,Lottissement Porte d'Espagne ☎68567575 tx 505046
⇔ℿ43 P43

★★**Christina** 50 cours de Lassus (n.rest) ☎68352461
rm37(⇔ℿ32) ☎ P5 Lift
Credit Cards ①③

۩ Casadessus 4 bd St-Assiscle ☎ 68540396 AR LR

At **RIVESALTES**(5km NW by N9)

★★★*Novotel* N9 ☎68640222 tx 500851
⇔ℿ85 P83 ⊇ Mountain
Credit Cards ①②③⑤

۩ Guillouf Zone Artisanale,r de l'Alzin ☎ 68644097

PERRIGNY-LÈS-DIJON
See **DIJON**

PERROS-GUIREC
Côtes-du-Nord

★★★*Trestraou* Pn bd J-le-Bihan,Trestraou ☎96232405 tx 741261
rm68(⇔ℿ66) A2rm P Lift Sea
Credit Cards ①②③⑤

★★**Morgane** 46 av Casino,Plage de Trestraou ☎96232280 tx 740637
Mar-20 Oct
rm32(⇔ℿ30) A5rm P40 Lift ⊠ Sea
Credit Cards ①②③⑤

۩ Côte 39 r du MI-Joffre ☎ 96232207 **P** Peu Tal

At **PLOUMANACH**(6km NW)

★★★*Rochers* (FAH) Port de Ploumanach ☎96232302
Etr-Sep
⇔ℿ15 Sea
Credit Card ③

PESMES
Haute-Saône

★★*France* **LE**☎84312005
⇔ℿ10 P20 ℂ
Credit Cards ①②③

PETITE-PIERRE, LA
Bas-Rhin

★★*Vosges* **LE**Pn 30 r Principale ☎88704505
15 Dec-15 Nov :Rest closed Tue evening & Wed
rm30(⇔16) ☎ P25 Lift Mountain
Credit Cards ①③

PETIT-QUEVILLY, LE
See **ROUEN**

PEYREHORADE
Landes

★★**Central** pl A-Briand ☎58730322 tx 571310
15 Feb-15 Mar :Rest closed Mon
⇔ℿ17 P Lift Mountain
Credit Cards ①②③⑤

PIED-DU-SANCY
See **MONT-DORE, LE**

PIERRE-BUFFIÈRE
Haute-Vienne

★*Providence* 20 r Nationale ☎55006016
15 Mar-15 Nov
rm11(⇔ℿ8) ☎
Credit Card ②

۩ R Gauthier 17 av de Toulouse ☎ 55009034 **P** Cit

PIERRELATTE
Drôme

★★*Hostellerie Tom II* **LE**5 av GI-de-Gaulle (N7) ☎75004035
:Rest closed Mon
⇔ℿ15 ☎
Credit Cards ②③

۩ Mistral Z-I rte de St-Paul ☎ 75040158 All makes

PITHIVIERS
Loiret

★*Relais de la Poste* 10 Mail Quest ☎38304030
10 Jan-20 Dec :Rest closed Sun evening & Mon
⇔ℿ20 ☎ P5
Credit Cards ①②③④⑤

PLAISIR
Yvelines

★★*Campanile* ZI des Gâtines ☎30558150 tx 697578
⇔ℿ50 P50

★★*Climat* Lieudit le Hameau de la Chaine ☎30557737
rm38 P70
Credit Card ③

PLEHEDEL
See **LANVOLLON**

PLÉRIN
See **ST-BRIEUC**

PLESSIS-CHENET, LE
See **CORBEIL-ESSONNES**

PLOEREN
Morbihan

★★**Climat** ZI de Luscanen ☎97409191
⇔ℿ43 P40 Lift
Credit Card ②

PLOËRMEL
Morbihan

★★**Le Cobh** 10 r des Forges ☎97740049
:Rest closed Mon pm
rm13(⇔ℿ7) ☎ P2

★**Commerce** **LE**70 r de la Gare ☎97740532
rm19(⇔ℿ11) ☎ P10
Credit Cards ①③

PLOMBIÈRES-LES-BAINS
Vosges

★**Abbesses** 6 pl de l'Église ☎29660040
May-Sep
rm44(⇔20) Mountain

PLOUGASTEL-DAOULAS
See **BREST**

PLOUMANACH
See **PERROS-GUIREC**

POITIERS
Vienne

★★★*France* (MAP) 28 r Carnot ☎49413201 tx 790526
Closed 26 Dec-1 Jan
rm80(⇔ℿ71) A19rm ☎ P30 Lift ℂ
Credit Cards ①②③④⑤

★★★*Royal Poitou* rte de Paris (3km N on N10) ☎49017286
⇔ℿ32 P ℂ
Credit Cards ①②③⑤

★★*Balladins* r A-Haller,Lot de la République ☎49415500 tx 649394
⇔ℿ28 ☎ P28
Credit Cards ①③⑤

★★*Climat* Quartier de Beaulieu,3 r des Frères-Lumière ☎49613875 tx 792022
⇔ℿ70 P80
Credit Cards ①②③

★★*Europe* 39 r Carnot (n.rest) ☎49881200
rm50(⇔ℿ41) ☎ P35 ℂ
Credit Cards ①③

★★*Ibis* ZAC de Beaulieu,r du Bois Dousset ☎49611102 tx 790354
⇔ℿ47 ☎ P55
Credit Cards ①②③

★★*Ibis-Poitiers Sud* av du 8 Mai 1945 ☎49531313 tx 791556
⇔ℿ112 Lift
Credit Cards ①③

★★*Relais du Stade* 84-86 r J-Coeur (n.rest) ☎49462512
rm25(⇔ℿ22) A4rm ☎ P30 Lift
Credit Cards ①③

At **BIARD**(2km W)

۩ Barrault Z-I de Larnay ☎ 49583543 **P** Vol

At **CHASSENEUIL-DU-POITOU**(8km N by N10)

★★★*Novotel-Poitiers Nord* RN10 ☎49527878 tx 791944
⇔ℿ89 P100 Lift ⚲ ⊇
Credit Cards ①②③⑤

★★★*Relais de Poitiers* N10 ☎49529041 tx 790502
⇔ℿ97 P400 Lift ⚲ ⊠
Credit Cards ①②③⑤

★★*Campanile* ZI de Chasseneuil-de-Poitou,Voie Ouest ☎49528540 tx 791534
⇔ℿ42 P42

POIX-DE-PICARDIE
Somme

★★*Cardinal* pl de la République ☎22900823 tx 145379
⇔ℿ35
Credit Cards ①②③⑤

★*Poste* **LE**13 pl de la République ☎22900033
rm18(⇔ℿ15) P18
Credit Cards ①③

POLIGNY
Jura

★★*Hostellerie des Monts de Vaux* (Relais et Châteaux) DPn Monts de Vaux (4.5km SE) ☎84371250 tx 361493
Jan-Oct
⇔ℿ10 ☎ P15 ⚲
Credit Cards ①②③⑤

★★*Paris* **LE**7 r Travot ☎84371387
Feb-4 Nov
⇔ℿ25 ☎ P ⊠ Mountain

★★*Vallée Heureuse* **LE**rte de Genève ☎84371213
:Rest closed Thu lunch & Wed
⇔ℿ9 ☎ P22 Mountain
Credit Cards ①②③⑤

POLISOT
Aube

★*Seine* **LE**Pn ☎25385441
rm20(⇔ℿ9) ☎ P10
Credit Cards ①③

PONS
Charente-Maritime

★★*Auberge Pontoise* r Gambetta ☎46940099
Feb-20 Dec :Rest closed Sun pm & Mon in low season
⇔ℿ22
Credit Cards ①③④

PONT-A-MOUSSON
Meurthe-et-Moselle

★*Européen* 158 av Metz ☎838100757
:Rest closed Sun
rm30(⇔ℿ9) A6rm ☎ P40

★*Poste* DPn 42 bis r V-Hugo ☎83810116
:Rest closed Sun
rm25(⇔ℿ16) A8rm ☎ P8
Credit Cards ①③

PONTARLIER
Doubs

★★*Poste* 55 r de la République (n.rest) ☎81391812
rm21(⇔ℿ17) ☎ P10 Lift ℂ
Credit Cards ①③

۩ Beau Site 29 av de l'Armée de l'Est ☎ 81392395 **P** Peu Tal

FRANCE

PONTAUBAULT
Manche

★★★**13 Assiettes** Ⓛ(1km N on N175)
☎33581403 tx 772173
15 Mar-15 Nov :Rest closed Wed low season
rm36(⊷♠27) A24rm P40
Credit Cards ① ③

PONT-AUDEMER
Eure

★★★**Vieux Puits DPn** 6 r Notre-Dame-du-Pré
☎32410148
20 Jan-2 Jul & 11 Jul-20 Dec :Rest closed Mon
evening & Tue
rm12(⊷♠11) P10
Credit Cards ① ③

At **CORNEVILLE-SUR-RISLE**(6km SE)

★★★**Cloches de Corneville** rte de Rouen
☎32570104 tx 770581
⊷♠12 🅿 P10
At **FOURMETOT**(6km NE)

☜ **Bacheley** ☎ 32574069 **P** Ren

PONTCHARRA
Isère

★★**Climat** Lieudit "Le Gabion" RN90 ☎76719184
tx 320529
⊷♠24 P10 ⚲ Mountain
Credit Cards ① ② ③

PONT-D'AIN
Ain

★★**Alliés** Ⓛ☎74390009
20 Jan-20 Dec :Rest closed for dinner Mon
rm18(⊷♠14) 🅿 P10
Credit Cards ① ③

★★**Paris-Nice** 2 r du 1er Septembre 1944 (n.rest)
☎74390380
Closed Nov & Tue
rm20(⊷♠12) 🅿 P10

PONT-DE-CLAIX
See **GRENOBLE**

PONT-DE-L'ISÈRE
Drôme

★**Portes du Midi** RN 7 ☎75846026
Mar-Oct
rm18(♠11) P50 Mountain
Credit Cards ① ② ③ ⑤

PONT-DE-RHODES
See **FRAYSSINET**

PONT-DU-GARD
Gard

★★**Vieux Moulin** ☎66371435 tx 300121
10 Mar-11 Nov
rm17(⊷♠15) P100 Beach
Credit Cards ① ② ③ ⑤

At **REMOULINS**(4km E)

★★**Moderne DPn** pl des Grands-Jours
☎66372013
21 Nov-20 Oct :Rest closed Sat
rm24(⊷♠20) 🅿 P12
Credit Cards ① ③

PONTHIERRY
Seine-et-Marne

☜ **Tractaubat** 78 av de Fontainebleau ☎
60657039 Ren

☜ **Trois Sept** 62 av de Fontainebleau ☎
60657052 **P**

At **PRINGY**(2km SE)

★★**Ibis** 4 rte de Melun ☎60655928 tx 690723
⊷♠32 P

PONTIVY
Morbihan

★★**Porhoët** (Inter) 41 r du Gl-de-Gaulle (n.rest)
☎97253448
⊷♠28 P Lift
Credit Cards ① ②

☜ **Jouan** 25 et 29 r du Gl-Quiniv ☎ 97250265
For

PONT-L'ÉVÊQUE
Calvados

★★**Climat** Base de Loisirs ☎31646400 tx 772497
⊷♠42 P650 ⚲ ♠♠ ⚓ Beach Lake
Credit Cards ① ② ③

★★**Lion d'Or** Ⓛpl Calvaire ☎31650155
⊷♠25 🅿 P30 ☾
Credit Cards ① ② ③ ④ ⑤

PONTOISE
Val-d'Oise

★★**Campanile** r P-de-Coubertin ☎30385544 tx
698515
⊷♠50 P50
Credit Cards ① ② ③

At **CERGY**(4km SW)

★★★**Novotel** 3 av du Parc ☎30303947 tx
607264
⊷♠191 Lift ⚲
Credit Cards ① ② ③ ⑤

★★**Arcade** près Préfecture ☎30309393 tx
605470
:Rest closed Sat & Sun
rm140 Lift
Credit Card ①

★★**Balladins** 17 chaussée J-César ☎30321111
⊷♠28 P30
Credit Cards ① ② ③

★★**Climat** Sac d'Eragny,r des Pinsons
☎30378600 tx 696149
⊷♠50 P
Credit Card ④

At **ST-OUEN-L'AUMÔNE**(5km SE)

★★★**Cerf Hotel** 59 r Gl-Leclerc ☎34640313
7-22 Aug
⊷♠10
Credit Cards ② ③

PONTORSON
Manche

★★**Montgomery** Ⓛ(FAH) DPn 13 r Couesnon
☎33600009 tx 171332
18 Nov-18 Oct :Rest closed Sun pm & Wed winter
only
⊷♠32 🅿 P100
Credit Cards ① ② ③ ⑤

PONT-SARRAZIN
See **GAP**

PONTS-DE-CÉ, LES
Maine-et-Loire

★★**Campanile** chemin du Moulin-Marcille
☎41449244 tx 720959
⊷♠41 P47
Credit Card ③

PONT-SUR-YONNE
Yonne

★★**Ecu** 3 r Carnot ☎86670100
3 Mar-15 Jan :Rest closed Mon evening & Tue
rm8(⊷♠6) P5
Credit Cards ① ② ③ ⑤

PORNICHET
Loire-Atlantique

★★★**Sud-Bretagne** Ⓛ42 bd de la République
☎40610268 tx 701960
15 Mar-15 Jan
⊷♠30 🅿 P30 Lift ☾ ⚲ ⚓ ⚓
Credit Cards ① ② ③ ⑤

PORT-BLANC
Côtes-du-Nord

★**Grand** Ⓛ☎96926652
⊷♠26 P10 ⚲ Sea
Credit Cards ① ② ③ ⑤

PORTEL, LE
Pas-de-Calais
See also **BOULOGNE-SUR-MER**

★**Beau Rivage et Armada** pl Mons-Bourgain
☎21315982
rm10(⊷♠6) Sea
Credit Cards ① ② ③

PORT-GRIMAUD
See **GRIMAUD**

PORTICCIO
Corse-du-Sud
See **CORSE (CORSICA)**

PORT-LA-NOUVELLE
Aude

☜ **Pertil** bd Vals Francis ☎ 68480064 **P**

PORT-LOUIS
Morbihan

★★**Avel Vor** Ⓛ(FAH/Inter-Hotels) DPn 25 r de
Locmalo ☎97824759 tx 950826
⊷♠20 Lift Sea
Credit Cards ① ② ③ ⑤

PORTO-VECCHIO
Corse-du-Sud
See **CORSE (CORSICA)**

POUILLY-EN-AUXOIS
Côte-d'Or

☜ **Jean-Luc Omont** ☎ 80907321 **P** For

☜ **J J Jeannin** pl des Allies ☎ 80908211 **P** VW
Peu

☜ **P Orset** ☎ 80908045 **P** Ren

At **CHÂTEAUNEUF**(10km SE D18)

★★**Hostellerie du Château** ⓁDPn ☎80492200
Mar-12 Nov :Rest closed Mon evening & Tue in
season
⊷♠17 A6rm
Credit Cards ① ② ③

POUILLY-SUR-LOIRE
Nièvre

★★**Bouteille d'Or** ⓁPn 13 bis rte de Paris
☎86391384
15 Feb-10 Jan
rm29(⊷♠23) A10rm
Credit Card ③

★★**Relais Fleuri** Ⓛ(0.5km SE on N7)
☎86391299
15 Feb-15 Jan :Rest closed Sun evening & Mon
15Oct-Etr
⊷♠9 🅿 P20
Credit Cards ① ③

POULDU, LE
Finistère

★★**Armen** ☎98399044
28 Apr-25 Sep
⊷♠38 🅿 P45 Lift
Credit Cards ① ② ③ ⑤

★★**Castel Treaz** ☎98399111
10 Jun-10 Sep
⊷♠25 P19 Lift Sea

POUZAUGES
Vendée

★★**Auberge de la Bruyère** Ⓛ(FAH) r Dr-
Barbanneau ☎51919346 tx 701804
:Rest closed Mon 15 Sep-15 Jun
rm30(⊷♠26) P120 Lift ⚓ Beach
Credit Cards ① ② ③ ⑤

POUZIN, LE
Ardèche

☜ **M Pheby** N86 ☎ 75638016 **P** Cit

PRINGY
See **PONTHIERRY**

PROVINS
Seine-et-Marne

★★**Ibis** Lieu Dit 'Les Palis' ☎60676667 tx 691882
⊷♠51 P50
Credit Cards ① ③

PUILBOREAU
See **ROCHELLE, LA**

PUY, LE
Haute-Loire

★★★*Christel* 15 bd A-Clair ☎71022444
⊷♠29 P20 Lift ☾
Credit Cards ① ② ③

PUY-L'ÉVÊQUE
Lot

At **MONTCABRIER**(7km NW)
★★★*Relais de la Dolce* Pn rte de Villefranche
☎65365342
15 Apr-15 Oct
⊷♠12 P ⌐
Credit Cards ① ② ⑤

PYLA-SUR-MER
Gironde

★★★*Guitoune* 95 bd de l'Océan ☎56227010 tx
570503
⊷♠21 P30 ☾ Sea
Credit Cards ① ② ③ ④ ⑤

★★*Beau Rivage* 16 bd de l'Océan ☎56540182
Apr-Sep
rm22(⊷♠8) A4rm
Credit Cards ① ② ③

QUARRÉ-LES-TOMBES
Yonne

★*Nord et Poste* **LE**DPn pl de l'église
☎86322455
rm35(⊷♠10) A22rm P50
Credit Cards ① ③

QUÉTIGNY
See **DIJON**

QUETTREVILLE-SUR-SIENNE
Manche

★★*Château de la Tournée* ☎33476291
⊷♠10 ♠ P10
Credit Cards ① ③

QUEUE-EN-BRIE, LA
Val-de-Marne

★★*Climat* ☎45946161 tx 262209
⊷♠55 P60
Credit Cards ① ③

QUIBERON
Morbihan

★★★*Sofitel Thalassa* Pointe de Goulvas
☎97502000 tx 730712
⊷♠113 P150 Lift ☾ ⌐ Sea
Credit Cards ① ② ③ ⑤

★★*Ibis* av des Marroniers,Pointe de Goulvars
☎97304772 tx 951935
⊷♠96 P110 ♿ ⌐
Credit Cards ① ③

★★*Océan* DPn 7 quai de l'Océan ☎97500758
Etr-mid Nov
rm38(⊷♠26) P30 Lift Sea
Credit Cards ① ③

At **ST-PIERRE-QUIBERON**(4.5km N)
★★*Plage* **LE**DPn ☎97309210
Mid Mar-mid Oct
rm49(⊷♠48) P34 Lift Sea
Credit Cards ① ② ③

QUILLAN
Aude

★★*Chaumière* **LE**(Inter) bd Ch-de-Gaulle
☎68201790
rm38(⊷♠30) A21rm ♠ P Mountain
Credit Cards ① ③

★*Cartier* **LE**(FAH) 31 bd Ch-de-Gaulle
☎68200514
15 Mar-15 Dec
rm33(⊷♠27) Lift Mountain
Credit Cards ① ③

QUIMPER
Finistère

★★★*Griffon* (Inter) 131 rte de Bénodet
☎98903333 tx 940063
:Rest closed 20 Dec-20 Jan & Sat pm & Sun low
season
⊷♠50 P60 ▭
Credit Cards ① ② ③ ⑤

★★*Balladins* rte de Coray,Commune d'Ergue-
Gaberic ☎98595500 tx 649394
⊷♠38 P38
Credit Cards ① ② ③

★★*Gradlion* **LE**30 r Brest (n.rest) ☎98950439
⊷♠25
Credit Cards ① ② ③ ④ ⑤

★★*Ibis-Quimper* r G-Eiffel,ZI de
l'Hippodrôme,Secteur Ouest ☎98905380 tx
940007
⊷♠70 P65 Lift
Credit Cards ① ③

★★*Ibis-Quimper Nord* Le Gourvily,rte de Brest
☎98957764 tx 940749
⊷♠36 P50 ☾
Credit Cards ① ③

★★*Tour d'Auvergne* **LE**(FAH) 11-13 r des
Réguaires ☎98950870 tx 941100
:Rest closed Oct-Apr
rm43(⊷♠36) A2rm P30 Lift ☾
Credit Cards ① ② ③

🛨 *Auto Secours* 28 av A-de-Bretagne ☎
98902805

🛨 *Kemper Automobile* 13 av de la Libération ☎
98901849 AR

QUIMPERLÉ
Finistère

🛨 *Laita Automobiles S.A.* rte de Pont Scorff ☎
98960793 P For

QUINCY-VOISINS
Seine-et-Marne

★*Auberge Demi Lune* N36 ☎60041109
:Rest closed Wed
rm5 P Lift
Credit Card ①

RABOT, LE
Loir-et-Cher

★★★*Bruyères* N20 ☎54880570
⊷♠36 A12rm ♿ ⌐
Credit Cards ① ⑤

RAMBOUILLET
Yvelines

★★*Climat* Lieu dit La Louvière ☎34856262 tx
695645
rm77(⊷♠67) A23rm P68 ☾ ♿ ⌐
Credit Cards ① ② ③

★★*Ibis* Le Bel Air,N10 ☎30417850 tx 698429
⊷♠62 P80 ♿
Credit Cards ① ③

★*St-Charles* 15 r de Groussay (n.rest)
☎34830634
rm14(⊷♠12) A2rm ♠ P20

RANCOURT
Somme

★★*Prieuré* N17 ☎22850443
25 Jan-20 Dec :Rest closed Sun evening & Mon
⊷♠28 ♠ P50
Credit Cards ① ② ③

RAPHÈLE-LES-ARLES
See **ARLES**

RAYOL, LE
Var

★★★★*Bailli de Suffren* DPn Plage le Rayol
☎94056767 tx 420535
May-Oct
⊷♠46 P15 Lift ♿ Beach Sea
Credit Cards ① ② ③ ⑤

RÉ, ILE DE
Charente-Maritime

FLOTTE, LA

★★*Richelieu* DPn 44 av de la Plage ☎46096070
tx 791492
⊷♠30 P50 Sea
Credit Card ③

RECOLOGNE
Doubs

★*Escale* **LE**(n.rest) ☎81581213
Closed Oct
⊷♠11 ♠ P3
Credit Cards ② ③

At **LAVERNAY**(3.5km S)
🛨 *Pelot* ☎ 81581224 P Peu Tal

RECQUES-SUR-HEM
Pas-de-Calais

★★★*Château de Cocove*

REIMS
Marne

★★★★*Altea Champagne* 31 av P-Doumer
☎26885354 tx 830629
⊷♠125 ♠ Lift
Credit Cards ① ② ③ ⑤

★★★*Mercure-Reims Est* Zise Les Essillards,rte
de Châlons ☎26050008 tx 8302782
⊷♠98 P200 Lift ▭
Credit Cards ① ② ③ ④ ⑤

★★★*Paix* 9 r Buirette ☎26400408 tx 830914
⊷♠105 ♠ Lift ⌐
Credit Cards ② ③ ⑤

★★*Balladins* r M-Hollande (n.rest) ☎26827210 tx
649394
⊷♠34 P25
Credit Cards ① ② ③

★★*Campanile* av G-Pompidou ☎26366694 tx
830262
⊷♠41 P41
Credit Card ③

★★*Climat* (Inter-Hotels) r B-Russel,ZAC de la
Neuvilletts ☎26096273 tx 842639
⊷♠40 P50 ☾
Credit Cards ① ② ③

★★*Continental* 93 pl Drouet-d'Erlon (n.rest)
☎26403935 tx 830585
⊷♠60 Lift
Credit Cards ① ② ③ ④ ⑤

★★*Dom Pérignon* 14 r des Capucins
☎26473364
Closed Sun Nov-May
⊷♠10 P ☾
Credit Cards ① ② ③

★★*Europa* 8 bd Joffre (n.rest) ☎26403620 tx
840777
5 Jan-22 Dec
rm32(⊷♠23) Lift
Credit Cards ① ② ③ ④ ⑤

★★*Grand du Nord* 75 pl Drouet-d'Erlon (n.rest)
☎26473903 tx 842157
4 Jan-23 Dec
⊷♠50 Lift ☾
Credit Cards ① ② ③ ④ ⑤

★★*Touring* 17 ter bd Gl-Leclerc (n.rest)
☎26473815
⊷♠14
Credit Cards ① ② ③

★★*Univers* (Inter) 41 bd Foch ☎26886808 tx
842120
:Rest closed Sun pm
rm41(⊷♠36) Lift ☾
Credit Cards ① ② ③ ⑤

★★*Welcome* 29 r Buirette (n.rest) ☎26473939 tx
842145
5 Jan-20 Dec
rm68(⊷♠60) ♠ P6 Lift ☾
Credit Cards ① ② ③

At **TINQUEUX**(4km W off N31)

★★★*Novotel* rte de Soisson ☎26081161 tx 830234
🛏127 P150 ⌿
Credit Cards ①②③⑤

★★*Campanile* Zone de Camp Paveau,av S-Bernard ☎26040946 tx 842038
🛏50 P50
Credit Card ③

★★*ibis* A4 ☎26046070 tx 847116
🛏51 Lift
Credit Cards ①③

REMIGEASSE, LA
See OLÉRON, ILE D'

REMIREMONT
Vosges

At **ST-NABORD**(5km N on N57)

★★★*Montiroche* N57 (n.rest) ☎29620659
Apr-Oct
🛏14 P50 Mountain

REMOULINS
See PONT-DU-GARD

RENAISON
Loire

★*Jacques Coeur* LErte Vichy ☎77642534
Mar-Jan :Rest closed Sun pm Jul/Aug & Mon
🛏8 ⌿
Credit Cards ①②③⑤

RENNES
Ille-et-Vilaine

★★★*Altea* Parc du Colombier,r du Cpt-Maignan ☎99315454 tx 730905
🛏140 P Lift
Credit Cards ①②③⑤

★★★*Guesclin* 5 pl de la Gare (n.rest) ☎99314747 tx 740748
🛏68 Lift
Credit Cards ①②③⑤

★★★*Novotel-Rennes Alma* av du Canada ☎99506132 tx 740144
🛏98 ⌿
Credit Cards ①②③⑤

★★★*Président* 27 av Janvier (n.rest) ☎99654222
Closed 23 Dec-1 Jan
🛏34 Lift ☾
Credit Cards ①②③⑤

★★*Campanile* 120 r E-Pottier,ZAC de Cleunay ☎99304545 tx 741154
🛏45 P45
Credit Card ③

★★*Climat* ZAC de Beauregard Sud ☎99541203 tx 741544
🛏42 P35
Credit Cards ①②③④⑤

★★*Urbis* 1/3 bd Solferino (n.rest) ☎99673112 tx 730625
🛏60 Lift ☾
Credit Cards ①③

🚘 *Europe* 73-75 av du Mail ☎ 99590152 For

🚘 *J Huchet* 316 rte de St-Malo ☎ 99591122 P Rov BMW

At **CESSON-SÉVIGNÉ**(6km E)

★★*Ibis-Rennes* Centre Hotelier,La Perrière ☎99839393 tx 740321
🛏76 P150 Lift
Credit Cards ①③

★★*Ibis-Rennes Beaulieu* rte de Paris ☎99833172 tx 740378
🛏35 P35 ☾
Credit Cards ①③

RESSONS-SUR-MATZ
Oise

At **CUVILLY**(3km NW on N17)

🚘 *Brecqueville* r Planché (N 17) ☎ 44850016 P

RETHEL
Ardennes

★★*Moderne* LEpl de la Gare ☎24384454
rm25(🛏22) P10 ☾
Credit Cards ①②③④⑤

REZÉ-DE-NANTES
Loire-Atlantique

★★*Fimotel* Impasse Ordronneau ☎40042030 tx 700429
🛏42 P60
Credit Cards ①②③⑤

RIGNAC
See GRAMAT

RIVE-DE-GIER
Loire

★★*Hostellerie de la Renaissance* 41 r Marrel ☎77550431
:Rest closed Sun pm 15 Oct-15 Apr
🛏6 P25
Credit Cards ①②③⑤

RIVESALTES
See PERPIGNAN

RIXHEIM
See MULHOUSE

ROANNE
Loire

★★*France* 19 r A-Roche (n.rest) ☎77712117
rm46(🛏18)
Credit Cards ①②③

★★*Ibis* ZI du Côteau,53 bd Ch-de-Gaulle ☎77683622 tx 300610
🛏67 P70 Lift ☾ Mountain

★★*Troisgros* 22 cours de la République ☎77716697 tx 307507
Feb-4 Aug & 20 Aug-Dec :Rest closed Tue & Wed lunchtime
🛏24 ⌿ P20 Lift ☾
Credit Cards ①②③⑤

ROCAMADOUR
Lot

★★★*Beau Site & Notre Dame* (MAP/BW) Cité Medievale ☎65336308 tx 520421
7 Apr-11 Nov
rm55(🛏51) A5rm ⌿ P15 Lift Mountain
Credit Cards ①②③⑤

★★★*Château* LE(FAH) rte de Château ☎65336222 tx 521871
25 Mar-12 Nov
🛏58 A24rm P100 ⌿ ⌿
Credit Cards ①③

★★*Ste-Marie* r Grand Escalier,pl des Sehnal ☎65336307
Etr-10 Oct
rm22(🛏17) A5rm ⌿ P20 Mountain
Credit Cards ①③

★*Lion d'Or* LEPorte Figuier ☎65336204
Etr-1 Nov
rm32(🛏28) A6rm P14 Lift Mountain
Credit Cards ①③④

ROCHEFORT
Charente-Maritime

★★★*Remparts Fimotel* 43 r C-Pelletan ☎46871244 tx 290258
🛏73 P80 Lift
Credit Cards ①②③⑤

🚘 *Central* 31 av La Fayette ☎ 46990065 AR

🚘 *Zanker* 76 r Gambetta ☎ 46870755 For

ROCHELLE, LA
Charente-Maritime

★★★*Brises* chemin Digue Richelieu (n.rest) ☎46438937 tx 790754
15 Jan- 15 Dec
🛏46 ⌿ P Lift Sea
Credit Cards ①③

★★★*France et d'Angleterre* (MAP/BW) 22 r Gargoulleau ☎46413466 tx 790717
:Rest closed Sun & Mon midday
rm76(🛏67) P35 Lift ☾
Credit Cards ①②③⑤

★★★*Yachtman* 23 quai Valin ☎46412068 tx 790762
🛏40 P10 Lift ⌿
Credit Cards ①③⑤

★★*Campanile* rte de Paris,Fief des Ardennes Ouest ☎46340729 tx 791606
🛏32 P32

★★*Ibis* pl du Cdt-de-la-Motte-Rouge ☎46416022 tx 791431
🛏76 Lift
Credit Cards ①③

★★*St-Nicolas* (Inter) 13 r Sardinerie (n.rest) ☎46417155 tx 793075
🛏76 ⌿ P20 Lift
Credit Cards ①②③⑤

★★*Urbis* r Vieljeux et Chef-de-Ville (n.rest) ☎46506868 tx 791726
rm77(🛏67) Lift
Credit Cards ①③

★*Trianon et Plage* (FAH) 6 r de la Monnaie ☎46412135
Feb-23 Dec
🛏25 P20 ☾
Credit Cards ①②③⑤

At **PUILBOREAU**(4km NE)

★★*Climat* Zone Commerciale de Beaulieu,RN11 ☎46673737 tx 790398
🛏48 P50
Credit Cards ①③

🚘 *Depan Auto* Zone Commerciale de Beaulieu ☎ 46671616

ROCHE-POSAY, LA
Vienne

★*Parc* av Fontaines ☎49862002
May- Sep
rm80(🛏58) ⌿ P50 Lift ⌿

ROCHES-DE-CONDRIEU, LES
Isère

★★*Bellevue* Pn 1 quai du Rhône (n.rest) ☎74564142
:Rest closed Mon & Sun pm
rm18(🛏14) A3rm ⌿ P15 Lake
Credit Cards ①②③④⑤

ROCHE-SUR-YON, LA
Vendée

★★*Campanile* Les Bazinières,rte de Nantes ☎51372786 tx 701766
🛏42 P42
Credit Card ③

★★*Ibis* bd Arago ☎51362600 tx 700601
🛏63 P65
Credit Cards ①③

★*Ibis Nord* Z.I du Mouilleron-le-Captif,rte de Nantes ☎51378282 tx 701017
🛏90 P90
Credit Cards ①③

🚘 *Baudry* bd Lavoisier ☎ 51362235 For

ROCROI
Ardennes

★★*Commerce* pl A-Briand (n.rest) ☎24541115
10 Feb -5 Jan
🛏12 ⌿

RODEZ
Aveyron

★★★*Broussy* (MAP/BW) 1 av V-Hugo ☎6568187 tx 520198
🛏46 ⌿ P10 Lift
Credit Cards ①②③⑤

★★★*Tour Maje* bd Gally ☎65683468
rm48(🛏45) P Lift ☾
Credit Cards ①②③⑤

ROISSY-EN-FRANCE
See PARIS AIRPORTS under CHARLES-DE-GAULLE AIRPORT

ROMANS-SUR-ISÈRE
Drôme

★★*Terminus* (Inter) 48 av P-Sémard (n.rest)
☎75024688
Closed 5 Jan-22 Feb
rm32(♨18) Lift
Credit Card ①

ROMORANTIN-LANTHENAY
Loir-et-Cher

★★*Colombier* **LE** 18 pl Vieux Marché
☎54761276
15 Feb-15 Sep & 22 Sep-15 Jan
♨10 ☎ P10
Credit Cards ① ② ③ ④ ⑤

★★*Lion d'Or* (Relais et Châteaux) 69 r G-Clemenceau ☎54760028 tx 750990
Closed Jan-mid Feb
♨16 P16 Lift
Credit Cards ① ② ③ ⑤

ROQUEBRUNE-CAP-MARTIN
Alpes-Maritimes

★★★*Victoria & Plage* 7 prom du Cap (n.rest)
☎93356590
Feb-4 Nov
♨30 ☎ P7 ℂ Sea Mountain
Credit Cards ① ② ③ ④ ⑤

★★*Westminster* 14 av L-Laurens,quartier Bon-Voyage ☎93350068
10 Feb & 20 Oct
♨31 A4rm ☎ P15 Sea
Credit Cards ① ③

ROQUE-GAGEAC, LA
Dordogne

★*Belle Étoile* **LE** ☎53295144
Etr-15 Oct
rm17(♨16) ☎ Lake
Credit Cards ① ③

ROQUES-SUR-GARONNE
See TOULOUSE

ROSCOFF
Finistère

★★★*Gulf Stream* r Marquise-de-Kergariou
☎98697319
May-25 Nov
♨32 P30 Lift ℞ ☎ Sea
Credit Cards ① ② ③

★★*Talabardon* pl Église ☎98612495 tx 940711
15 Mar-15 Nov :Rest closed Sun evening
♨38 Lift Beach Sea
Credit Cards ① ③

★*Bains* pl Église ☎98612065
May-Oct
rm30(♨8) ☎ Lift Sea
Credit Cards ① ③

ROSIERS, LES
Maine-et-Loire

★★*Jeanne de Laval* (N152) ☎41518017
15 Feb-8 Dec
♨12 A7rm
Credit Cards ① ② ③ ④ ⑤
☎ *Ozil* ☎ 75395246 P Peu Tal

ROSPORDEN
Finistère

★★★*Bourhis* **LE** (FAH) 3 pl Gare ☎98592389
tx 914808
:Rest closed Mon & Sun evening
♨27 P15 Lift
Credit Cards ① ② ③ ⑤

ROUBAIX
Nord

★★★*Grand Altea* 22 av J-Lebas ☎20734000 tx
132301
♨92 Lift
Credit Cards ① ② ③ ⑤

★★*Ibis* Roubaix bd du Gl-Leclerc ☎20450000 tx
131471
♨94 ☎ P42 Lift ℂ
Credit Cards ① ③

At VILLENEUVE-D'ASCQ(6km S)

★★*Balladins* Quartier de l'Hôtel-de-Ville,angle bd
de Valmy,r Entre Deux Villes ☎20670720
♨38 P
Credit Cards ① ② ③

★★*Campanile* La Cousinerie,av de Canteleu
☎20918310 tx 133335
♨50 P50
Credit Cards ① ③

★★*Climat* Quartier de Triolo,r Trudaine
☎20050403 tx 692844
♨37
Credit Cards ① ③

★★*Ibis-Lille* Quartier de l'Hôtel-de-Ville,Rocade
Est ☎20918150 tx 160626
♨80 P80 Lift ℂ
Credit Cards ① ③

ROUEN
Seine-Maritime

★★★★*Pullman Albane* r Croix-de-Fer
☎35980698 tx 180949
♨125 P80 Lift ℂ
Credit Cards ① ② ③ ⑤

★★★*Dieppe* (MAP/BW) pl B-Tissot ☎35719600
tx 180413
♨42 Lift ℂ
Credit Cards ① ② ③ ④

★★*Arcade* 20 pl de l'Église St-Sever ☎35628182
tx 7706725
♨144 Lift
Credit Cards ① ③

★★*Cardinal* 1 pl de la Cathédrale (n.rest)
☎35702442
4 Jan-18 Dec
♨21 Lift
Credit Cards ① ③

★★*Cathédrale* 12 r St-Romaine (n.rest)
☎35715795
♨24 Lift
Credit Cards ① ③

★★*Europe* 87 r aux Ours,pl de la Pucelle (n.rest)
☎35708330 tx 172172
rm27(♨23) Lift ℂ
Credit Cards ① ② ③

★★*Gros Horloge* (Inter) 91 r Gros-Horloge
(n.rest) ☎35704141 tx 771938
♨62 Lift ℂ
Credit Cards ① ③

★★*Ibis Rouen Centre* 56 quai G-Boulet
☎35704818 tx 771393
♨88 P25 Lift
Credit Cards ① ③

★★*Normandie* (Inter) 19 & 21 r du Bec
☎35715577 tx 771350
♨23 Lift
Credit Cards ① ② ③ ⑤

★★*Paris* 12-14 r de la Champmeslé (off quai de
la Bourse) (n.rest) ☎35700926 tx 771979
rm24(♨23) ☎ P10 Lift
Credit Cards ① ② ③ ⑤

★★*Québec* 18-24 r Quebec (off r de la
République) (n.rest) ☎35700938 tx 771530
5 Jan -20 Dec
rm38(♨34) P4 Lift ℂ
Credit Cards ① ③

★★*Viking* (Inter) 21 quai du Havre (n.rest)
☎35703495 tx 770092
♨37 ☎ Lift Sea
Credit Cards ① ③

★*Arcades* 52 r des Carmes (n.rest) ☎35701030
rm16(♨5)
Credit Cards ② ③

★*Vieille Tour* 42 pl Haute Vieille Tour (n.rest)
☎35700327
rm23(♨14) Lift ℂ
Credit Cards ② ③
☎ *Guez* 135 r Lafayette ☎ 35727684 For

At BARENTIN(17km NW)

★★*Campanile* Lotissement de la Carbonnière
☎35926404 tx 741680
♨49 P ℂ

★★*Ibis* rte Nationale 15 ☎35910123 tx 180810
Rest closed Sun
♨40 P40
Credit Cards ② ③

At BOIS-GUILLAUME(5km NE)

★★*Climat* av de l'Europe ☎35616110 tx 172902
♨42 P42
Credit Cards ① ② ③ ④

At MONT-ST-AIGNAN(2km N)

★★*Campanile* ZAC de la Vatine,rte d'Hauppeville
☎35597500
♨41 P

At PETIT-QUEVILLY, LE

★★*Fimotel* 112 av J-Jaurès ☎35623850 tx
770132
♨40 Lift
Credit Cards ① ② ③ ⑤

At ST-ÉTIENNE-DU-ROUVRAY(2km S)

★★★*Novotel-Rouen Sud* Le Madrillet
☎35665850 tx 180215
♨135 P180 Lift ℞ ☎
Credit Cards ① ② ③ ⑤

★★*Campanile* r de la Mare aux Sangsues
☎35640416 tx 172145
♨49 P49
Credit Card ③

★★*Ibis-Rouen Sud* av Maryse-Bastie
☎35660363 tx 771014
♨108 P140
Credit Cards ① ③

At TOURVILLE-LA-RIVIÈRE(10km SE)

★★*Climat* Le Clos aux Antes ☎35784948 tx
771189
♨35 P300
Credit Cards ① ② ③

ROUFFACH
Haut-Rhin

At BOLLENBERG(6km SW)

★★*Bollenberg* **LE** ☎89496247 tx 880896
♨50 P50 Ʊ Mountain
Credit Cards ① ② ③ ⑤

ROUFFILLAC
See ST-JULIEN-DE-LAMPON

ROUSSILLON
Isère

★*Garrigon DPn* rte St-Saturnin-d'Apt ☎90056322
♨8 P30 ☎ Ʊ Mountain
Credit Cards ① ② ③ ⑤
☎ *Guilion* 133 rte de la Chapelle ☎ 74862436
M/C P Ope

At CHANAS(6km S on N7)
☎ *Modern* N7 ☎ 74842191 P Sko

ROYAN
Charente-Maritime

★★*Grand de Pontaillac* 195 av de Pontaillac
(n.rest) ☎46390044
Etr-Sep
rm55(♨50) A10rm ☎ P15 Lift ℂ Sea
Credit Cards ① ③
☎ *Richard* rte de Saintes Z C,38 r Lavoister ☎
46050355 Peu

At **CONCHE-DE-NAUZAN**(2.5km NW)

★★★**Résidence de Rohan** Parc des Fées (n.rest) ☎46390075
Etr-15 Nov
←♠41 A19rm P35 ℂ ℺ Sea
Credit Cards ②③

ROYAT
Puy-de-Dôme

★★★**Métropole** 4 bd Vaquez ☎73358018
May-Sep
rm76(←♠53) Lift ℂ Mountain
Credit Card ①

ROYE
Somme

✖ **Dallet** 5 pl de la République ☎ 22871089 **P**
For

RUFFEC
Charente

★**Toque Blanche** 16 r du Gl-Leclerc ☎45310016
←♠20 P25 ℂ
Credit Cards ①③

RUNGIS
Val-de-Marne
See also **ORLY AIRPORT** under **PARIS AIRPORTS**

★★★★**Holiday Inn** 4 av C-Lindbergh ☎46872666 tx 204679
←♠168 P200 Lift ℺ ≈
Credit Cards ①②③④⑤

★★★★**Pullman Paris Orly** 20 av C-Lindbergh ☎46873636 tx 260738
←♠206 ☎ P130 Lift ≈
Credit Cards ①②③⑤

★★**Campanile** angle r du Pont-des-Halles,r du Mondetours ☎46873529 tx 261163
←♠49 P49
Credit Card ③

★★**Ibis** 1 r Mondetour ☎46872245 tx 261173
←♠119 Lift
Credit Cards ①③

SABLES-D'OLONNE, LES
Vendée

★★**Residence** 36 prom Clemenceau (n.rest) ☎51320666
Mar-3 Nov
rm35(←♠30) ☎ P100 Sea
Credit Cards ①②③⑤

At **CHÂTEAU-D'OLONNE**(4km E on D36)

✖ **Tixier** La Mouzinère ☎ 51324104 VW Aud

SABLES-D'OR-LES-PINS
Côtes-du-Nord

★★★**Bon Accueil** allée des Acacias ☎96414219
Etr-Sep
rm39(←♠25) P15 Lift
Credit Cards ①③

★★**Ajoncs d'Or** allée des Acacias ☎96414212
15 May-Sep
rm75(←♠44) A40rm P30 Sea
Credit Card ③

★★**Diane** av Brouard ☎96414207
12 Apr-Sep
rm45(←♠40) A10rm ☎ P80 Sea Lake
Credit Cards ①③

★★**Dunes d'Armor et Mouettes** (n.rest) ☎96414206
May-Oct
←♠54 P30 Sea

★★**Manoir St-Michel** La Carquois,22240 Frehel (n.rest) ☎96414887
Etr-15 Nov
←♠20 P25 Sea
Credit Cards ①③⑤

★**Voile d'Or** r des Acacias ☎96414249
15 Mar-15 Nov
rm18(←♠16) A4rm P20 Sea
Credit Cards ①③

SABLÉ-SUR-SARTHE
Sarthe

★★**Campanile** 9 av Ch-de-Gaulle ☎43953053
←♠31 P31
Credit Card ③

★★**St-Martin** 3 r Haute St-Martin ☎43950003
Apr-Mar :Rest closed Fri pm,Sat lunch low season
rm10(←♠5) P8
Credit Card ③

At **SOLESMES**(3km NE on D22)

★★★**Grand** (FAH) ☎43954510 tx 722903
Closed Feb
←♠34 A2rm Lift
Credit Cards ①②③⑤

SACLAY
See **ORSAY**

ST-AFFRIQUE
Aveyron

★**Moderne** 54 av A-Pezet ☎65492044 tx 300121
15 Jan-15 Dec
rm39(←♠29) A11rm ☎ P4 Mountain
Credit Cards ①③

ST-AIGNAN
Loir-et-Cher

★★**St-Aignan** Ⅼ£7-9 quai J-J-Delorme ☎54751804
Apr-Oct :Rest closed Fri pm & Sun pm(winter)
rm23(←♠9) ☎ P12
Credit Cards ①②③

ST-ALBAIN
See **MÂCON**

ST-AMOUR
Jura

★★**Alliance** Ⅼ£rte Ste-Marie ☎84487494
Feb-Nov :Rest closed Mon & Sun evening
rm16(←♠8) P7
Credit Cards ①③⑤

★**Commerce** Ⅼ£pl Chevalerie ☎84487305
Feb-15 Dec :Rest closed Mon (out of season)
rm15(←♠7) ☎ P4 ℺ ≈ Mountain
Credit Card ③

ST-ANDRÉ-LES-ALPES
Alpes-de-Haute-Provence

✖ **Chabot** rte de Nice ☎ 92890001 **P** Cit

✖ **J Rouvier** rte Nationale 202 ☎ 92890302 M/C **P** Peu

ST-ANDRÉ-LES-VERGERS
See **TROYES**

ST-APOLLINAIRE
See **DIJON**

ST-AUBIN-SUR-MER
Calvados

★★**St-Aubin** Ⅼ£r de Verdun,Face Plage ☎31973039
Feb-Jan :Rest closed Sun evening & Mon (winter)
rm26(←♠20) P15 Sea
Credit Cards ①②③⑤

ST-AVOLD
Moselle

★★★**Novotel** RN33 ☎87922593
←♠61 P150 ≈
Credit Cards ①②③⑤

ST-BRIEUC
Côtes-du-Nord

★★★**Alexandre Ier** 19 pl du Guesclin ☎96337945
←♠43 P Lift
Credit Cards ①②③⑤

★★★**Griffon** (Inter) r de Guernsey ☎96945762 tx 950701
←♠48 ☎ P50 Lift ℺
Credit Cards ①②③⑤

At **PLÉRIN**(2km N via N12)

★★**Chêne Vert** Ⅼ£(FAH) 12 r de St-Laurent ☎96746320 tx 741323
:Rest closed Sun
←♠50 P80 ℺
Credit Cards ①②③⑤

At **YFFINIAC**(5km W)

★★**Fimotel de la Baie** Aire de Repos (N12) ☎96726410 tx 741107
←♠42 P60 Lift Sea
Credit Cards ①②⑤

ST-CAST-LE-GUILDO
Côtes-du-Nord

★**Angleterre et Panorama** Ⅼ£r Fosserole ☎96419144
rm40 P45 ℺ Sea
Credit Cards ①③

At **GARDE-ST-CAST, LA**(2 km SE)

★★★**Ar Vro** 10 bd de la Plage (n.rest) ☎96418501
5 Jun-6 Sep
rm47(←♠42) ☎ P40 Lift Sea
Credit Cards ①②③⑤

ST-CÉRÉ
Lot

★★**Coq Arlequin** DPn 1 bd du Dr-Roux ☎65380213
Mar-Dec
←♠32 ☎ P10 ℺ ≈ Beach
Credit Cards ①③

ST-CHAMANT
Corrèze

★**Roche de Vic** les quatre rtes d'Albussac ☎55281587
Mar-Dec
rm14(←♠8) ☎ P70 Lift
Credit Cards ①③

ST-CHÉLY-D'APCHER
Lozère

★**Lion d'Or** 132 r T-Roussel ☎66310014
Closed 1-20 Jan
rm30(←♠5) ☎

ST-CYPRIEN
Pyrénées-Orientales

★★**Ibis** Bassin Nord du Port ☎68213030 tx 500459
←♠34 P
Credit Cards ①③

ST-DENIS
Seine-St-Denis

★★**Climat** 212 av du Prés-Wilson ☎48099685 tx 230737
←♠57 ☎ P30 Lift
Credit Cards ①③

★★**Fimotel** 20 r J-Saulnier ☎48094810 tx 230046
←♠60 P5060 Lift ℂ
Credit Cards ①②⑤

ST-DENIS-SUR-SARTHON
Orne

★★**Faiencerie** rte Paris-Brest ☎33273016
Etr-Oct
←♠18 ☎ P50 Mountain
Credit Card ③

ST-DIZIER
Haute-Marne

★★★**Gambetta** (Inter) 62 r Gambetta ☎25565210 tx 842365
←♠63 ☎ P30 Lift ℂ
Credit Cards ①②③

★★**Champagne** 19 r P-Timbaud ☎25056754 tx 842385F
Rest closed Sun
←♠28 P30
Credit Card ③

★*Auberge la Bobotte* rte Nationale 4 (3km W on N4) ☎25562003
Etr-Dec
🚗f️🛏10 🅿 P6 ℂ

🚙 **Dynamic-Motors** rte de Bar-le-Duc ☎ 25560398 For

ST-DOULCHARD
See **BOURGES**

STE-ADRESSE
See **HAVRE, LE**

STE-ANNE-LA-PALUD
Finistère

★★★*Plage* (Relais et Châteaux) La Plage ☎98925012 tx 941377
Apr-Oct 12
🚗f️🛏30 A6rm P50 Lift ♀ ⌿ Sea
Credit Cards ①②③

STE-CATHÉRINE
See **BRIANÇON**

STE-FOY-LÈS-LYON
See **LYON**

ST-ÉGRÈVE
See **GRENOBLE**

ST-ÉLOY-LES-MINES
Puy-de-Dôme

★★*Ibis* r J-Jaurès ☎73852150 tx 392009
:Rest closed wknds in winter
🚗f️🛏29 P40
Credit Cards ① ③

STE-MAXIME
Var

See also BEAUVALLON

★★★*Beau Site* 6 bd des Cistes ☎94961963 tx 970080
11 Apr-Sep
🚗f️🛏36 Lift ♀ ⌿ Sea
Credit Cards ①②③⑤

ST-ÉMILION
Gironde

★★★*Hostellerie de la Plaisance* pl Clocher ☎57247232 tx 573032
Closed Jan
🚗f️🛏11
Credit Cards ①②③⑤

STE-ENIMIE
Lozère

★★*Commerce* (FAH) RN586 ☎66485001
Apr-Oct
rm20(🚗f️🛏13) A10rm 🅿 P8 ℂ ♀ Mountain Lake
Credit Cards ①②③

SAINTES
Charente-Maritime

★★★*Commerce Mancini* r des Messageries ☎46930561 tx 791012
rm39(🚗f️🛏32) P18 ℂ
Credit Cards ①②③⑤

★★★*Relais du Bois St-Georges* r de Royan ☎46935099 tx 790488
🚗f️🛏31 🅿 P60 ℂ ♀ ⌷ ⌿ Lake
Credit Cards ① ③

★★*Ibis* rte de Royan ☎46743634 tx 791394
🚗f️🛏71 P90 ℂ ⌷
Credit Cards ①②③

★★*Messageries* (Inter) r des Messageries (n.rest) ☎46936499 tx 793132
rm36(🚗f️🛏33) 🅿 P19 ℂ
Credit Cards ①②③⑤

★★*Terminus* espl de la Gare (n.rest) ☎46743503
10 Jan-15 Dec
🚗f️🛏30 🅿 ℂ
Credit Cards ①②③⑤

SAINTES-MARIES-DE-LA-MER
Bouches-du-Rhône

★★*Mirage* 14 r C-Pelletan (n.rest) ☎90978043
20 Mar-15 Oct
🚗f️🛏27
Credit Card ③

ST-ÉTIENNE
Loire

★★★★*Altea Parc de l'Europe* Rond Point,Parc de l'Europe,r de Wuppertal ☎77252275 tx 300050
🚗f️🛏120 P15 Lift
Credit Cards ①②③⑤

★★★*Grand* 10 av Libération ☎77329977 tx 300811
🚗f️🛏66

★★★*Terminus du Forez* (FAH) 31 av Denfert-Rochereau ☎77324847 tx 307191
:Rest closed Sun
🚗f️🛏66 🅿 P40 Lift ℂ
Credit Cards ①②③④⑤

★★*Ibis* 35 pl Massenet ☎77933187 tx 307340
🚗f️🛏85 🅿 P30 Lift ℂ Mountain
Credit Cards ① ③

ST-ÉTIENNE AIRPORT
Loire

At **ANDRÉZIEUX-BOUTHÉON**(2km W of N82)

★★★*Novotel* Centre de Ville (N82) ☎77365563 tx 900722
🚗f️🛏98 P150 Lift ⌿
Credit Cards ①②③⑤

ST-ÉTIENNE-DE-BAIGORRY
Pyrénées-Atlantiques

★★*Arcé* ☎59374014
15 Mar-11 Nov
🚗f️🛏20 A2rm 🅿 P30 ♀ ⌿ Mountain Lake
Credit Cards ① ③

ST-ÉTIENNE-DU-ROUVRAY
See **ROUEN**

ST-FLORENTIN
Yonne

★*Est* 7 r fbg St-Martin .13390 ☎86351035
🚗f️🛏22 A4rm 🅿 P30
Credit Cards ①②③⑤

At **VENIZY**(5.5km N)

★★*Moulin des Pommerats* ☎86350804
🚗f️🛏20 A18rm P30 ♀
Credit Cards ① ③⑤

ST-FLOUR
Cantal

★★★*Étape* 24 av de la République ☎71601303
🚗f️🛏34 A11rm Lift Mountain
Credit Cards ①②③④⑤

★★★*Europe* DPn 12-13 cours Spy-des-Ternes ☎71600364
1 Mar-30 Nov
rm45(🚗f️🛏41) 🅿 P100 Lift Sea Mountain
Credit Cards ① ③

★★*Nouvel Bonne Table* (MAP) 16 av de la République ☎71600586 tx 393160
Apr-Oct
rm48(🚗f️🛏47) 🅿 P60 Lift ♀ Mountain
Credit Cards ①②③④⑤

★★*St-Jacques* (FAH) 8 pl Liberté ☎71600920
15 Jan-11 Nov
🚗f️🛏28 🅿 P10 Lift ⌿ Mountain
Credit Cards ① ③④

★★*Voyageurs* DPn 25 r Collège ☎71603444
Apr-Nov
rm33(🚗f️🛏25) 🅿 P8 Lift Mountain
Credit Cards ①②③⑤

ST-GAUDENS
Haute-Garonne

★★*Ferrière & France* 1 r Gl-Leclerc (n.rest) ☎61891457
rm15(🚗f️🛏12) 🅿 P8
Credit Cards ①②③⑤

At **VILLENEUVE-DE-RIVIÈRE**(6km W on D117)

★★*Cèdres* ☎61893600
🚗f️🛏20 P40 ♀ ⌿ Mountain
Credit Cards ① ③

ST-GENIS-LAVAL
See **LYON**

ST-GENIS-POUILLY
Ain

★★*Climat* Lieudit le Marais ☎50420520
🚗f️🛏42 P58 Mountain
Credit Cards ①②③

ST-GERMAIN-DE-JOUX
Ain

★*Reygrobellet* ☎50598113
🚗f️🛏10 🅿 P10 Mountain
Credit Cards ③ ⑤

ST-GERMAIN-EN-LAYE
Yvelines

★★★*Ermitage des Loges* (MAP) 11 av des Loges ☎34518886 tx 697112
Rest closed Sun evening
🚗f️🛏34 P Lift
Credit Cards ①②③⑤

★★*Campanile* rte de Mantes,Maison Forestière ☎34515959 tx 697547
🚗f️🛏54 P54
Credit Card ③

At **CHAMBOURCY**(4km NW)

★★*Climat* r du Mur du Parc ☎30744261
🚗f️🛏46 P100 ⌷
Credit Cards ① ③

ST-GERVAIS-EN-VALLIÈRE
Saône-et-Loire

★★*Moulin d'Hauterive* DPn ☎85915556 tx 801391
Feb-15 Dec :Rest closed Mon & Sun evening
🚗f️🛏21 A2rm P50 ♀ ⌷ U
Credit Cards ① ③

ST-GERVAIS-LA-FORÊT
See **BLOIS**

ST-GERVAIS-LES-BAINS
Haute-Savoie

★★★*Splendid* (n.rest) ☎50782133
🚗f️🛏20 Lift Mountain

ST-GILLES
Gard

At **SALIERS**(4Km E on N572)

★★★*Cabanettes en Camargue* (MAP) ☎66873153 tx 480451
Closed 15 Jan-20 Feb
🚗f️🛏29 🅿 P50 ⌷
Credit Cards ①②③⑤

ST-GILLES-CROIX-DE-VIE
Vendée

★★*Embruns* 16 bd de la Mer (n.rest) ☎51551140
Rest closed Sat
🚗f️🛏17 🅿 Sea
Credit Cards ① ③

ST-GIRONS
Ariège

★★★*Eychenne* (MAP/BW) 8 av P-Laffont ☎61662055 tx 521273
Feb-22 Dec
rm48(🚗f️🛏43) 🅿 P15 ℂ ⌷ Mountain
Credit Cards ①②③⑤

★★★*Hostellerie la Truite Dorée* LE 28 av de la Résistance ☎61661689
Mar-Oct
🚗f️🛏15 🅿 P15 ℂ ⌷ Mountain Lake
Credit Cards ② ③⑤

ST-HERBLAIN
See **NANTES**

ST-HILAIRE-DU-HARCOUËT
Manche

★★**Cygne LE**67 r Waldeck-Rousseau
☎33491184 tx 171455
10 Jan-15 Dec
🍴45 A25rm ☎ P6 Lift
Credit Cards 1 2 3 5

★**Lion d'Or LE**120 r Avranches ☎33491082
rm20(🍴16) ☎ P25
Credit Cards 1 3

★**Relais de la Poste** 11 r de Mortain ☎33491031
:Rest closed Mon
rm12(🍴8)
Credit Card 1

ST-JEAN-CAP-FERRAT
Alpes-Maritimes

★★★★**Grand Cap Ferrat** bd Gl-de-Gaulle
☎93760021 tx 470184
Apr-Oct
🍴62 ☎ P40 Lift ୯ ⌇ ⌇ Sea Mountain
Credit Cards 1 2 3 5

ST-JEAN-DE-LUZ
Pyrénées-Atlantiques

★★★★**Chantaco** rte d'Ascain ☎59261476 tx
540016
Apr-Oct
🍴24 ☎ P60 ୯ ୯ ⌇ ⌇⌇ Mountain Lake
Credit Cards 1 2 3 5

★★★**Poste** 83 r Gambetta (n.rest) ☎59260453 tx
540140
rm34(🍴21) ୯
Credit Cards 1 2 3 5

★★**Paris** 1 bd Passicot (n.rest) ☎59260062
Feb-Dec
rm29(🍴14) Lift Mountain
Credit Cards 1 3

★**Continental** 15 av Verdun ☎59260123
🍴21 Lift Mountain
Credit Cards 1 2 3 5

At **CIBOURE**(1km SW)

★**Hostellerie de Ciboure** 10 av J-Jaurès
☎59470057
rm22(🍴16) P ⌇

ST-JEAN-DE-MAURIENNE
Savoie

★★**St-Georges** 334 r République (n.rest)
☎79640106
rm22(🍴20) P10 Mountain
Credit Cards 1 2

ST-JEAN-DE-MONTS
Vendée

★★**Plage** espl de la Mer ☎51580035
May-Sep
rm50(🍴48) P5 Lift ୯ Sea
Credit Cards 1 2 3

🏍 **G Vrignaud** rte de Challens ☎ 51582674 **P**
Ren

ST-JEAN-LE-THOMAS
Manche

★★**Bains** Face Post ☎33488420 tx 170380
15 Mar-10 Oct
rm29(🍴22) A8rm P50 ⌇
Credit Cards 1 2 3 5

ST-JEAN-PIED-DE-PORT
Pyrénées-Atlantiques

★★★**Continental** 3 av Rénaud (n.rest)
☎59370025
Etr-15 Nov
🍴22 P20 Lift Mountain
Credit Cards 1 2 3

★★**Central** (FAH) 1 pl Ch-de-Gaulle ☎59370022
5 Feb-23 Dec
rm14(🍴7) Mountain
Credit Cards 1 2 3 5

★★**Pyrénées** pl Marché ☎59370101 tx 570619
22 Dec-3 Jan & 20 Jan-20 Nov
🍴20 P6 Lift Mountain
Credit Cards 1 2 3

ST-JULIEN-DE-LAMPON
Dordogne

At **ROUFFILLAC**(N of river)

★★**Cayre DPn** (n.rest) ☎53297024
Closed Oct
🍴20 A12rm ☎ P50 ୯ ⌇ Mountain

ST-JULIEN-EN-BEAUCHÊNE
Hautes-Alpes

★★**Bermond-Gauthier** rte Nationale 75
☎92580352
Feb-20 Dec
rm20(🍴10) ☎ P20 ⌇ Mountain
Credit Cards 1 2 3 5

ST-JULIEN-EN-GENEVOIS
Haute-Savoie

★**Savoyarde DPn** 15 rte de Lyon ☎50492579
rm10(🍴1) P

ST-JUNIEN
Haute-Vienne

★★**Concorde LE**49 av H-Barbusse (n.rest)
☎55021708
15 Jan-15 Dec
🍴26 P18
Credit Cards 1 2 3

★**Relais de Comodoliac** (FAH) 22 av S-Carnot
☎55022726 tx 590336
🍴28 P40
Credit Cards 1 2 3 5

ST-LARY-SOULAN
Hautes-Pyrénées

★★**Terasse Fleurie** ☎62395148 tx 520360
15 Dec- 15 Apr & 15 Jun-15 Sep
rm28(🍴19) P20 Mountain
Credit Card 2

ST-LAURENT-DE-COGNAC
See **COGNAC**

ST-LAURENT-DU-VAR
See **NICE**

ST-LAURENT-SUR-SÈVRE
Vendée

At **TRIQUE, LA**(1km N)

★★★**Baumotel et la Chaumière DPn**
☎51678081 tx 701758
rm23(🍴21) A4rm ☎ P50 ⌇
Credit Cards 1 2 3 5

ST-LÉONARD-DES-BOIS
Sarthe

★★★**Touring** (MAP/BW) ☎43972803 tx 722006
15 Feb-15 Nov
🍴33 ☎ P30 Lift ⌇ Mountain
Credit Cards 1 2 3 5

ST-LIEUX-LES-LAVAUR
See **LAVAUR**

ST-LÔ
Manche

★★**Marignan** pl Gare ☎33051515
Closed Feb
rm18(🍴12) ☎ P60
Credit Cards 1 2 3 5

★★**Terminus** 3 av Briovère ☎33050860
15 Jan -15 Dec
rm15(🍴12) ☎ P4
Credit Cards 1 3

★**Univers** 1 av Briovère ☎33051084
rm24(🍴21) P20
Credit Cards 1 2 3 5

★★**Urbis St-Lô** L'Univers,1 av de Briovère
(n.rest) ☎33051084 tx 772504
🍴36 P35 Lift
Credit Cards 1 3

★**Armoric** 15 r de la Marne (n.rest) ☎335717447
20 Feb-26 Dec
rm21(🍴7) P Lift

★**Cremaillère DPn** 27 r du Belle,pl de la
Préfecture ☎33571468
🍴12 P15
Credit Cards 1 2 3

ST-MALO
Ille-et-Vilaine

★★★**Central** (MAP/BW) 6 Grande r ☎98408770
tx 740802
🍴46 ☎ Lift ୯
Credit Cards 1 2 3 5

★★★**Duguesclin** 8 pl Duguesclin (n.rest)
☎99560130 tx 740802
🍴22 P30 Lift Sea
Credit Cards 1 2 3

★★★**Mercure** chaussée du Sillon (n.rest)
☎99568484 tx 740583
🍴70 ☎ P27 Lift Sea
Credit Cards 1 2 3 5

★★**Ibis LE**r Gl-de-Gaulle,qtr de la Madelèine
☎99821010 tx 730626
🍴73 P60
Credit Cards 1 3

★**Louvre** 2-4 r de Marins (n.rest) ☎99408662 tx
740802
15 Feb-25 Nov
rm45(🍴40) Lift
Credit Cards 1 3 4

★**Noguette DPn** 9 r de la Fosse ☎99408357
Closed 11 Nov-17 Dec
🍴12 Lift
Credit Cards 1 3

At **GOUESNIÈRE, LA**(12km SE onD4)

★★**Gare** Gare de la Gouesnière ☎99891046 tx
740896
18 Jan-18 Dec :Rest closed Sun pm Oct & Etr
rm60(🍴57) A32rm ☎ P100 ୯ ⌇
Credit Cards 1 2 3 5

At **PARAMÉ**(1km E)

★★**Rochebonne** 15 bd Châteaubriand
☎99560172 tx 740802
rm38(🍴35) Lift
Credit Cards 1 2 3

ST-MARTIN-DE-BELLEVILLE
Savoie

★★★**Novotel Val Thorens** ☎79000404 tx
980230
Dec-Apr & Jul-Aug
🍴104 ☎ Lift ⌇ Mountain
Credit Cards 1 2 3 5

ST-MARTIN-EN-BRESSE
Saône-et-Loire

★★**Au Puits Enchanté** ☎85477196
Mar-Dec :Rest closed Sun evening & Tue
🍴15 P12 ୯
Credit Card 1

ST-MAURICE-SUR-MOSELLE
Vosges

★**Bonséjour LE**☎29251233
rm15(🍴2) P

ST-MAXIMIN-LA-STE-BAUME
Var

🏍 **Auto Real** Mont Fleury ☎ 94780358 **P** Fia

ST-MICHEL-DE-MAURIENNE
Savoie

★★**Savoy LE**25 r Gl-Ferrié ☎79565512
rm22(🍴20) ☎ P6 Mountain
Credit Cards 1 2 3

ST-MICHEL-SUR-ORGE
Essonne

★★★**Delfis-Bois-des-Roches** 17 r Berlioz
☎60154640 tx 692032
🍴80 Lift
Credit Cards 1 2 3 5

ST-NABORD
See **REMIREMONT**

ST-NAZAIRE
Loire-Atlantique

★★*Dauphin* 33 r J-Jaurès (n.rest) ☎40665961
rm20(👄📞16) ℂ
Credit Cards ①③

👄 *Hougard* 30 r J-B-Marcet ☎ 40901008 AR

ST-NICHOLAS
See **ARRAS**

ST-OMER
Pas-de-Calais

★★*Bretagne* (FAH) 2 pl Vainquai ☎21382578 tx
133390
👄📞43 P27 ℂ
Credit Cards ①②③⑤

★★*Frangins* LE5 r Carnot ☎21381247 tx
133436
👄📞20 Lift

★★*Ibis* r H-Dupuis ☎21931111 tx 135206
👄📞50 P27 Lift ℂ
Credit Cards ①③

★★*St-Louis* 25 r d'Arras ☎21383521
:Rest closed Sun
👄📞30 🏠 P10
Credit Cards ①③

At TILQUES(4km NW of N43)

★★★*Château Tilques* Tilques ☎21932899 tx
133360
5 Jan-mid Dec :Rest closed Sat lunch
👄📞30 A24rm P80 ९ Lake
Credit Cards ①②③⑤

★★*Château du Vert Mesnil* (FAH) Tilques
(1.5km E of N43) ☎21932899 tx 133360
👄📞61 A32rm P60 ९ ९ Lake
Credit Cards ①②③④⑤

ST-OUEN-L'AUMÔNE
See **PONTOISE**

ST-PALAIS-SUR-MER
Charente-Maritime

★★★*Courdouan* av Pontaillac ☎46231033
Apr-15 Oct
rm30 A7rm 🏠 P6 Sea
Credit Cards ①③

ST-PARDOUX-L'ORTIGIER
See **DONZENAC**

ST-PAUL
Alpes-Maritimes

★★★★*Mas d'Artigny* (Relais et Châteaux) rte de
la Colle ☎93328454 tx 470601
👄📞83 🏠 P120 Lift ℂ ९ 🔜 Sea Mountain
Credit Cards ①③

★★*Climat* rte de la Colle ☎93329424
rm19 P190 🔜 Sea

ST-PAUL-DE-LOUBRESSAC
Lot

★*Relais de la Madeleine* LE☎65219808
10 Jan-Nov :Rest closed Sat
rm16(👄📞8) P ९
Credit Card ③

ST-PÉE-SUR-NIVELLE
Pyrénées-Atlantiques

★★*Pyrénées Atlantiques* DPn (N618)
☎59540222
rm33(👄📞32) P30 ९ Mountain
Credit Card ②

ST-PIERRE-DE-CHARTREUSE
Isère

★★*Beau Site* LE☎76886134
👄📞33 🔜 Mountain
Credit Cards ①③⑤

ST-PIERRE-DU-VAUVRAY
See **LOUVIERS**

ST-PIERRE-QUIBERON
See **QUIBERON**

ST-POL-DE-LÉON
Finistère

👄 *E Charetteur* pl du Creisker ☎ 98690208 Ren

ST-POL-SUR-TERNOISE
Pas-de-Calais

★*Lion d'Or* 68 r Hesdin ☎21031293
Rest closed Sun
rm35(👄📞25) 🏠
Credit Cards ①②③⑤

ST-PONS
Hérault

★★*Château de Ponderach* rte de Narbonne
☎67970257
Apr-Oct
rm11(👄📞9) 🏠 P40 Mountain
Credit Cards ①②③⑤

★*Pastre* av Gare ☎67970054
Feb-Dec :Rest closed Sat Jan
rm20(👄📞8) Mountain
Credit Card ①

ST-POURÇAIN-SUR-SIOULE
Allier

★*Chêne Vert* (FAH) 35 bd Ledru-Rollin
☎70454065
rm30(👄📞25) A15rm P14
Credit Cards ①②③⑤

★*Deux Ponts* LE(FAH) Ilot de Tivoli
☎70454114
15 Dec-15 Nov
rm27(👄📞14) 🏠 P50 ℂ Beach Sea
Credit Cards ①③

ST-QUAY-PORTRIEUX
Côtes-du-Nord

★★*Gerbot d'Avoine* 2 bd Littoral ☎96704009 tx
950702
Rest closed Sun evening & Mon in season
rm26(👄📞17) P25
Credit Cards ①③

★*Bretagne* DPn 36 quai de la République (n.rest)
☎96704091
:Rest closed Tue
rm16(📞6) Sea

ST-QUENTIN
Aisne

★★★*Grand* 6 r Dachery ☎23626977 tx 140225
👄📞24 P14 Lift ℂ
Credit Cards ③⑤

★★*Campanile* ZAC de la Vallée,r C-Naudin
☎23092122 tx 150596
👄📞40 P40
Credit Card ③

★★*France et Angleterre* 28 r E-Zola (n.rest)
☎23621310 tx 140986
rm28(👄📞20)
Credit Cards ①②③

★★*Paix & Albert Ier* (Inter) 3 pl de Huit Octobre
☎23627762 tx 140225
rm82(👄64) P12 Lift
Credit Cards ①②③⑤

👄 *Auto* 418 rte de Paris ☎ 23623423 P Peu Tal

👄 *Moderne* r du Cdt-Raynal ☎ 23671490 For

ST-QUENTIN-EN-YVELINES
Yvelines

★★*Fimotel* ☎34605024 tx 699235
👄📞81 P60 Lift
Credit Cards ①②③⑤

ST-RAMBERT-D'ABLON
Drôme

★★*Ibis* 'La Champagnère',RN7 ☎75030400 tx
345958
👄📞46 Lift
Credit Cards ①③

ST-RAPHAËL
Var

★★★*Continental* prom du Prés-Coty (n.rest)
☎94950014 tx 970809
👄📞49 P Lift Sea

★★*Beau-Séjour* prom Prés-Coty ☎94950375
👄📞40 Lift Sea
Credit Cards ①③⑤

★★*Provençal* 197 r de la Garonne (n.rest)
☎94950152
👄📞28 ℂ Mountain
Credit Cards ①③

👄 *Agay* av Gratadis ☎ 94820616 Rov DJ

👄 *R Bacchi* 658 av de Verdun ☎ 94959851 Cit

ST-RÉMY-DE-PROVENCE
Bouches-du-Rhône

★★★*Antiques* 15 av Pasteur (n.rest) ☎90920302
Apr - Oct
👄📞27 A10rm P50 🔜
Credit Cards ①②③⑤

★★*Castelet des Alpilles* pl Mireille ☎90920721
20 Mar - 10 Nov
rm19(👄📞17) P30 ९ 🔜 ९९ ♡ Beach Mountain
Credit Cards ①②③⑤

ST-SATUR
Cher

★★*Laurier* LEr du Commerce ☎48541720
Dec-Jan & Mar- 15 Nov
rm9(👄📞6) P4
Credit Cards ①③

ST-SERNIN-SUR-RANCE
Aveyron

★★*Carayon* LEpl du Fort ☎65996026 tx
531917
rm40(👄📞38) 🏠 P15 Lift Mountain
Credit Cards ①②③⑤

ST-TROJAN-LES-BAINS
See **OLÉRON, ILE D'**

ST-TROPEZ
Var

★★★★*Byblos* av P-Signac ☎94970004 tx
470235
15 Mar-15 Oct
👄📞107 🏠 P30 Lift ℂ 🔜 Sea
Credit Cards ②③⑤

★★★*Ermitage* av P-Signac (n.rest) ☎94975233
rm30(👄📞7) P16 ℂ Sea Mountain
Credit Cards ②⑤

👄 *Fabbri* 6 r J-Mermoz ☎ 94970510 Rov

ST-VAAST-LA-HOUGUE
Manche

★★*France et des Fuchsias* LEDPn 18 r MI-
Foch ☎33544226
3 Jan-15 Feb :Rest closed Mon
rm33(👄📞29) A12rm P3
Credit Cards ①②③⑤

★★*Granitière* 64 bis r MI-Foch ☎33545899 tx
771992
Closed 15 Nov-15 Dec
rm9(👄📞7) 🏠 P7
Credit Cards ①③⑤

ST-VALERY-EN-CAUX
Seine-Maritime

★★★*Altea St-Valery* 14 av G-Clemenceau
☎35973548 tx 172308
👄📞157 P20 Lift Sea
Credit Cards ①②③⑤

ST-VIT
Doubs

👄 *S A Faivre-Nandot* 21 r de la Gare ☎
81551333 P Ren

SALBRIS
Loire-et-Cher

★★★*Mapotel du Parc* LE(MAP) DPn 10 av
d'Orléans ☎54971853 tx 751164

⇥♔27 ⋒ P30
Credit Cards [1] [2] [3] [5]
★**Dauphin LE**57 bd de la République
☎54970483
Feb-Dec :Rest closed Sun evening & Mon
⇥♔9 P15
Credit Cards [1] [3]

SALERS
Cantal
★**Beffroi** r du Beffroi ☎71407011
Apr-Oct
⇥♔10 P15 Mountain

SALIERS
See **ST-GILLES**

SALLANCHES
Haute-Savoie
★★**Ibis** av de Genève ☎50581442 tx 385754
:Rest closed Sun pm
⇥♔56 Lift
Credit Cards [1] [3]

SALON-DE-PROVENCE
Bouches-du-Rhône
★★**Ibis** rte d'Aix-Pelissanne,RN 572 ☎90422357
tx 441591
⇥♔48 P35 ⌖
Credit Cards [1] [2] [3]
❧ **Bagnis** 144 allée de Craponne ☎ 90534397 P
Col
❧ **Beaulieu Autos** bd du Roy René ☎ 90533537
P Rov
At **BARBEN, LA**(8km SE)
★**Touloubre** ☎90551685
15 Jan-15 Nov
⇥♔16 P100
Credit Cards [2] [3]
At **LANÇON-PROVENCE**(9km SE on A7)
★★★**Mercure** ☎90539070
:Rest closed Nov-Feb
⇥♔100 P20 Lift ⌖ Mountain
Credit Cards [1] [2] [3] [5]

SALSES
Pyrénées-Orientales
★★★**Relais Roussillon** ☎68386067
⇥♔56 P ⌖ Mountain

SANARY-SUR-MER
Var
★★**Tour** 24 quai de Gaulle ☎94741010
⇥♔28 P4 Sea
Credit Cards [1] [3] [5]

SANCÉ-LES-MÂCON
See **MÂCON**

SANCERRE
Cher
★★**Rempart LE**Rempart des Dames
☎48541018 tx 783541
⇥♔13 ⋒ P50
Credit Cards [1] [2] [3] [5]

SANNOIS
Val-d'Oise
★★**Campanile** ZUP d'Ermont Sannois,av de la
Sadernaude ☎34137957 tx 697841
⇥♔49 P49
Credit Card [3]

SARAN
See **ORLÉANS**

SARLAT-LA-CANÉDA
Dordogne
★★★**Hostellerie de Meysset** r des Éyzies
☎53590829
26 Apr-4 Oct
⇥♔26 P30
Credit Cards [1] [2] [3] [5]
★★★**Madeleine** 1 pl de la Petite-Rigaudie
☎53591041 tx 550689

15 Mar-5 Nov
⇥♔22 Lift
Credit Cards [1] [3]
★★★**Salamandre** r Abbé Surguier (n.rest)
☎53593598 tx 550059
⇥♔40 ⋒ P30 ⌖ Beach
Credit Cards [1] [2] [3] [5]
★**Lion d'Or** 48 av Gambetta ☎53593598
rm26(⇥♔20) A4rm
❧ **St-Michel** rte de Brive ☎ 53310888 M/C P
Rov Vol
❧ **Sarlat Autos** rte de Vitrac ☎ 53591064 Cit

SARREBOURG
Moselle
❧ **Deux Sarre** pl de la Gare ☎ 87033260 For

SARREGUEMINES
Moselle
❧ **Schwindt** 62 rte de Nancy ☎ 87982677 P Ren

SATOLAS AIRPORT
See **LYON**

SAULCE-SUR-RHÔNE
Drôme
★★**Ibis-Montélimar Nord** quartier Fraysse
(n.rest) ☎75630960 tx 345960
⇥♔29
Credit Cards [1] [3]
❧ **Central Garage Frey** RN 7 ☎ 75630038 P Cit

SAULIEU
Côte-d'Or
★★★**Poste LE**(Inter) 2 r Grillot ☎80640567 tx
350540
⇥♔48 P35 Lift ☾
Credit Cards [1] [2] [3] [4] [5]

SAUMUR
Maine-et-Loire
★★**Londres** 48 r Orléans (n.rest) ☎41512398
rm28(⇥♔27) P15
Credit Cards [1] [2] [3] [5]
★**Croix-Verte** 49 r de Rouen ☎41673931
2 Feb-20 Dec :Rest closed Sun & Mon evening
rm18(⇥♔5) P10
Credit Cards [1] [3] [5]
At **BAGNEUX**(1.5km SW)
★★**Campanile** Côte de Bournan ☎41501440 tx
722709
⇥♔43 P43
Credit Card [3]
At **CHÊNEHUTTE-LES-TUFFEAUX**(8km NW)
★★★**Prieuré** (Relais et Châteaux) ☎41679014 tx
720379
Closed 5 Jan-5 Mar
⇥♔35 A16rm P50 ☾ ⚲ ⌖
Credit Cards [1] [2] [3]

SAUSHEIM
See **MULHOUSE**

SAUT-DES-CUVES
See **GÉRARDMER**

SAUZET
See **MONTÉLIMAR**

SAVERNE
Bas-Rhin
★★**Geiswiller** 17 r Côte ☎88911851
⇥♔38 ⋒ P15 Lift
Credit Cards [1] [2] [3] [5]
★**Boeuf Noir** 22 Grand r ☎88911053 tx 890098
:Rest closed Tue
rm20(⇥♔5) ⋒ P10 Mountain
Credit Cards [1] [3]
★**Chez Jean DP**n 3 r de la Gare ☎88911019
10 Jan-22 Dec :Rest closed Sun eve & Mon ex
Jul & Aug
rm27(⇥♔24) P20 Lift Mountain
Credit Cards [1] [3] [5]

SAVIGNAC-LES-ÉGLISES
Dordogne
★★**Parc** ☎53050760 tx 573321
May-Oct :Rest closed for lunch all week & Tue
⇥♔11 P12 ⚲ ⌖
Credit Cards [1] [2] [3]

SAVONNIÈRES
See **TOURS**

SÉES
Orne
★**Cheval Blanc LEDP**n 1 pl St-Pierre
☎33278048
rm9(⇥♔8)
Credit Cards [1] [3]
★**Dauphin LE**31 pl Halls ☎33275515
⇥♔7
Credit Cards [1] [2] [3] [5]

SELLIÈRES
Jura
See also **POLIGNY**
At **PASSENANS**(6km SE)
★★**Domaine Touristique du Revermont
LE**☎844446102
Mar-Dec
⇥♔28 ⋒ P50 Lift ⚲ ⌖
Credit Cards [1] [3]

SEMUR-EN-AUXOIS
Côte-d'Or
★★**Lac** (3km S on D1036 at Lac-de-Pont)
☎80971111
Feb-15 Dec :Rest closed Sun pm & Mon (ex Jul &
Aug)
rm23(⇥♔20) ⋒ P29 Lake
Credit Cards [1] [3] [5]
★**Côte d'Or LEDP**n 3 pl G-Gaveau
☎80970313
18 Mar-10 Jan :Rest closed Wed
rm14(⇥♔13) ⋒ P3
Credit Cards [1] [2] [3] [4]
★**Gourmets LE** 4 r Varenne ☎80970313
15 Mar-15 Nov :Rest closed Wednesday
⇥♔15 ⋒ P8
Credit Cards [1] [2] [3]

SÉNAS
Bouches-du-Rhône
★**Luberon** 17 av A-Aune ☎90572010
:Rest closed Sun eve
rm7(⇥♔4) P15
Credit Cards [1] [3]
❧ **Testud** 31 av A-Aune ☎ 90590449 P

SENLIS
Oise
★★**Campanile** r E-Gazeau ☎44600507 tx 155028
⇥♔49 P49
Credit Card [3]
★★**Ibis** RN324 ☎44537050 tx 140101
⇥♔92 A42rm P90
Credit Cards [1] [3]
❧ **Delacharlery** 3-5 av Foch ☎ 44530818 Ren

SENNECEY-LE-DIJON
See **DIJON**

SENNECY-LE-GRAND
Saône-et-Loire
★**Lion d'Or DP**n r de la Gare ☎85448375
Dec-Oct
rm10(⇥♔8) P10

SENONCHES
Eure-et-Loir
★**Forêt LE**pl Champ de Foire ☎37377850
Closed Feb
rm17(⇥♔9) P30
Credit Cards [2] [3]

FRANCE

SENS
Yonne

★★★**Paris et Poste** (MAP/BW) 97 r de la République ☎86651743 tx 801831
⚞30 ☎ P20 ℂ
Credit Cards ①②③⑤

SEPT-SAULX
Marne

★★**Cheval Blanc DPn** r du Moulin ☎26039027 tx 830885
15 Feb-15 Jan
⚞22 P20 ℺
Credit Cards ①②③⑤

SERRES
Hautes-Alpes

★**Alpes DPn** av Grenoble ☎92670018
Apr-Nov
rm20(⚞9) P12 Mountain
Credit Cards ①②
🍴 **Gonsolin** 8 av M-Meyers ☎ 92670360 M/C **P** Peu

SÈTE
Hérault

★★★**Grand** 17 quai Ml-Lattre-de-Tassigny ☎67747177 tx 480225
⚞51 ☎ P25 Lift ℂ Sea
Credit Cards ①②③⑤
★★★**Imperial** (MAP/BW) pl E-Herriot ☎67532832 tx 480046
⚞44 ☎ P14 Lift Sea
Credit Cards ①②③⑤
🍴 **Port** 36 quai de Bosc ☎ 67744894 **P** For

SEVRAN
Seine-Maritime

★★**Campanile** 5 r A-Léonour ☎43846777 tx 233030
⚞58 P58
Credit Card ③
★★★**Climat** av R-Dautry,ZAC de Sevran ☎43834560 tx 233371
⚞43 ☎ P60 Lift
Credit Cards ①②③

SEVRIER
Haute-Savoie

★**Robinson** ☎50525411
Apr-Oct
rm12(⚞4) ☎ P20 ℺ Mountain Lake
Credit Cards ①②⑤

SEYSSEL
Ain

★★**Rhône** 𝐋𝐄☎50532030
15 Feb-15 Nov :Rest closed Oct-Jul
rm11(⚞10) Mountain
Credit Cards ①②③⑤

SÉZANNE
Marne

★★**Croix d'Or** 𝐋𝐄53 r Notre-Dame ☎26806110
Closed 31 Dec-15 Jan :Rest closed Mon
⚞13 ☎ P13
Credit Cards ①②③④⑤

SIGEAN
Aude

★**Ste-Anne** 𝐋𝐄☎68482438
rm12(⚞3) P28

SIORAC-EN-PÉRIGORD
Dordogne

★**Scholly** 𝐋𝐄r de la Poste ☎53316002 tx 550787
⚞33 P40
Credit Cards ①②③④⑤

SISTERON
Alpes-de-Haute-Provence

★★★**Grand du Cours** av de la Libération,pl de l'Église (n.rest) ☎92610451 tx 405923

---

1 Mar-10 Nov
⚞50 ☎ P20 Lift ℂ Mountain Lake
Credit Cards ①②③⑤

SOCHAUX
Doubs

★★**Campanile** r de Pontarlier ☎81952323 tx 361036
⚞42 P42
Credit Card ③

SOISSONS
Aisne

★★**Lions** rte de Reims ☎23732983 tx 140568
⚞28 P30
Credit Cards ①②③⑤
★★**Picardie** 6 r Neuve St-Martin ☎23532193
⚞33 P40 Lift
Credit Cards ①②③⑤
★**Rallye** 10 bd de Strasbourg (n.rest) ☎23530047
rm12(⚞6) ☎ P
Credit Cards ①③

SOLESMES
See **SABLÉ-SUR-SARTHE**

SOSPEL
Alpes-Maritimes

★★**Étrangers** 𝐋𝐄DPn 7 bd Verdun ☎93040009 tx 970439
rm40(⚞38) A5rm Lift ℺ ℺ Mountain
Credit Cards ①③

SOUILLAC
Lot

★★**Ambassadeurs** 𝐋𝐄7-12 av Gl-de-Gaulle ☎65327836
Nov-Sep :Rest closed Fri pm Sat ex Jul-Sep & BH
⚞28 A10rm ☎ P12 Mountain
Credit Cards ①③
★★**Auberge du Puits** 𝐋𝐄☎65378032
Closed Nov-Dec :Rest closed Sun pm & Mon
rm16(⚞9) P
Credit Cards ①③
★★**Périgord** 𝐋𝐄(FAH) 31 av Gl-de-Gaulle ☎65327828
1st May - 30 Sep
rm38(⚞35) A7rm ☎ P40 ℺
Credit Cards ①③
★★**Renaissance** (FAH) 2 av J-Jaurès ☎65327804
Apr-2 Nov
⚞21 ☎ P30 Lift ℺
Credit Cards ①③
★★**Roseraie** 𝐋𝐄42 av de Toulouse ☎65378269
15 Apr-15 Oct
⚞16 ☎ P10 Lift
Credit Card ③
★**Nouvel** 21 av Gl-de-Gaulle ☎65327958
rm28(⚞21) P30
Credit Cards ①③⑤

SOUPPES-SUR-LOING
Seine-et-Marne

🍴 **Cornut Osmin** 115 av Ml-Leclerc ☎ 64297032 **P** Ren

SOURCE, LA
See **ORLÉANS**

SOUSCEYRAC
Lot

★**Déjeuner de Sousceyrac** ☎65330056
Mar-15 Jan :Rest closed Mon in high season
rm10(⚞9) P30
Credit Cards ①③

SOUSTONS
Landes

★★**Bergerie** av du Lac ☎58411143
Apr-15 Nov
⚞30 A17rm P40
Credit Cards ①②

STRASBOURG
Bas-Rhin

★★★★**Grand** 12 pl de la Gare (n.rest) ☎88324690 tx 870011
rm90(⚞87) Lift ℂ
Credit Cards ①②③④⑤
★★★★**Hilton International** av Herrenschmidt ☎88371010 tx 890363
⚞246 P80 Lift
Credit Cards ①②③④⑤
★★★**Holiday Inn** 20 pl de Bordeaux ☎88357000 tx 890515
⚞170 P200 Lift ℺ ℺
Credit Cards ①②③④⑤
★★★★**Sofitel** pl St-Pierre-le-Jeune ☎88329930 tx 870894
⚞158 ☎ Lift ℂ
Credit Cards ①②③⑤
★★★**Altea de l'Europe** Parc du Rhin ☎88610323 tx 870833
⚞93 P ℺
Credit Cards ①②③⑤
★★★**France** 20 r du Jeu-des-Enfants (n.rest) ☎88323712 tx 890084
⚞70 ☎ Lift
Credit Cards ①②③⑤
★★★**Hannong** (FAH) 15 r du 22 Novembre ☎88321622 tx 890551
Closed 23-30 Dec :Rest closed Sat midday & Sun
⚞70 P18 Lift ℂ
Credit Cards ①②③⑤
★★★**Monopole-Métropole** 𝐋𝐄16 r Kuhn (n.rest) ☎88321194 tx 890366
Closed 24 Dec-2 Jan
⚞94 ☎ P20 Lift ℂ
Credit Cards ①②③④⑤
★★★**Novotel-Centre Halles** quai Kléber ☎88221099 tx 880700
⚞97 ☎ P Lift
Credit Cards ①②③⑤
★★★**Terminus-Gruber** (MAP/BW) 10 pl de la Gare ☎88328700 tx 870998
rm78(⚞70) Lift ℂ
Credit Cards ①②③④⑤
★★**Arcade** 7 r de Molsheim ☎88223000 tx 880147
⚞244 Lift
Credit Cards ①③
★★**Climat** pl A-Maurois,Maille Irène,ZUP Hautepierre ☎88263923
⚞38 P50
Credit Card ③
★★**Ibis** 1 r Sebastopol,quai Kléber ☎88221499 tx 880399
⚞97 Lift
Credit Cards ①③
★★**Vendôme** (Inter) 9 pl de la Gare ☎88324523 tx 890850
⚞48 Lift
Credit Cards ①②③⑤

At **GEISPOLSHEIM**(12km SE N83)
★★**Campanile** 20 r de l'Ill ☎88667477 tx 890797
⚞50 P50
Credit Card ③

At **ILLKIRCH-GRAFFENSTADEN**(7km S)
★★★**Mercure-Strasbourg Sud** r du 23 Novembre,Ostwald ☎88660300 tx 890277
⚞98 P50 ℺
Credit Cards ①②③⑤
★★★**Novotel-Strasbourg Sud** rte de Colmar (N83) ☎88662156 tx 890142
⚞76 P ℺
Credit Cards ①②③⑤

SULLY-SUR-LOIRE
Loiret

★★**Grand Sully** 𝐋𝐄10 bd Champ-de-Foire ☎38362756

---

15 Jan-15 Dec
rm11(➧9) ☎ P11
Credit Cards ① ② ③ ⑤
★★*Poste* (Inter) 11 r fbg St-Germain ☎38362622
Mar-25 Jan
rm27(➧26) A10rm P25
Credit Cards ① ② ③

SURESNES
Hauts-de-Seine
★★*Ibis* 6 r des Bourets ☎45064488 tx 614484
➧62 Lift
Credit Cards ① ③

SURVILLIERS-ST-WITZ
Val-d'Oise
★★★*Mercure-Paris-St-Witz* r J-Noulin
☎34682828 tx 695017
➧115 P200 Lift ⚲ ⌿
Credit Cards ① ② ③ ④ ⑤
★★★*Novotel-Paris Survilliers* Autoroute A1/D16
☎34686980 tx 695910
rm79 P ⌿

TAIN-L'HERMITAGE
Drôme
★★★*Mercure* 69 av J-Jaurès ☎75086500 tx
345573
➧50 P40 Lift ⚲ ⌿ Mountain
Credit Cards ① ② ③ ④ ⑤
✿ *Billon* 30 av de Prés-Roosevelt ☎ 75082810
P Peu Tal
✿ *45e Parallele* Pont-de-l'Isère ☎ 75846004 M/C
P Ope

TALANGÉ
See METZ

TALLOIRES
Haute-Savoie
★★★*Cottage* rte G-Bise ☎50607110 tx 309454
Apr-Oct
rm35(➧32) A14rm ☎ P30 Lift Mountain Lake
Credit Cards ① ② ③ ⑤
★★*Beau Site* ☎50607110 tx 309454
23 May-5 Oct
➧38 A28rm ☎ P40 ⚲ Mountain Lake
Credit Cards ① ② ③ ⑤
★★*Vivier* ☎50607054
Apr-Oct
➧30 ☎ P

TAMARISSIÈRE, LA
See AGDE

TAMNIÈS
Dordogne
★★*Laborderie* LE☎53296859
15 Mar-15 Nov
➧30 A15rm P50 ⌿
Credit Cards ① ③

TARARE
Rhône
★*Mère Paul* ☎74631457
:Rest closed 6 Sep
rm10(➧9) P10
Credit Cards ① ③

TARASCON
Bouches-du-Rhône
★★*Terminus* pl du Colonel-Berrurier ☎90911895
Closed 15 Jan-15 Feb
rm23(➧14)
Credit Cards ① ③
★*Provençal* 12 cours A-Briand (n.rest)
☎90911141
Mar-Oct
➧22 ☎ P10 ☾
Credit Cards ① ② ③ ④ ⑤

TARASCON-SUR-ARIÈGE
Ariège
★★*Poste* LEDPn 16 av V-Pilhès ☎61056041

rm30(➧20) Mountain
Credit Cards ① ② ③ ⑤

TARBES
Hautes-Pyrénées
★★★*Président* (MAP/BW) 1 r G-Faure
☎62939840 tx 530522
➧57 ☎ Lift ⌿ Mountain
Credit Cards ① ② ③ ④ ⑤
★★*Campanile* Lotissement Longchamp,rte de
Lourdes (4 km SW on N21) ☎62938320 tx
530571
➧42 P42
Credit Card ③
★★*Croix Blanche* pl Verdun (n.rest) ☎62441313
rm28(➧20)
Credit Cards ① ③
★*Henri-IV* (Inter-Hotels) 7 bd B-Barère (n.rest)
☎62340168
➧24 ☎ P10 Lift ☾
Credit Cards ① ② ③ ④ ⑤
✿ *Auto Selection* 2 bd du Juin ☎ 62936930 P
Toy

THÉOULE-SUR-MER
Alpes-Maritimes
★★*Guerguy La Galère* La Galère ☎93754454
Feb-Nov :Rest closed Wed
➧14 P30 Sea
★*Hermitage Jules César* 1 av C-Dahon
☎93499612
➧18 Lift Sea Mountain
Credit Cards ② ⑤

THIERS
Puy-de-Dôme
★★*Fimotel* rte de Clermont-Ferrand ☎73806440
tx 392000
➧40 P40 Lift
Credit Cards ① ② ③ ④ ⑤

THIONVILLE
Moselle
★★*Balladins* Forum 3000 Zone du Val
Marie,Face Zone Industrielle et,Commerciale du
Linkling ☎82348787 tx 861930
➧38 P40
Credit Cards ① ② ③
✿ *R Dillman* 18 rte de Garche ☎ 82532925 M/C
P Cit
✿ *Fort* r des Artisans ☎ 82561174 AR Lan

THOISSEY
Ain
★★★*Chapon Fin* (Relais et Châteaux) DPn r du
Champ de Foire ☎74040474 tx 305728
beg Feb - beg Jan :Rest closed Tues
➧25 ☎ P100 Lift
Credit Cards ① ③ ⑤
★*Beau-Rivage* DPn av Port ☎74040166
15 Mar-15 Oct :Rest closed Mon
➧10 P40 Mountain
Credit Cards ① ③

THONON-LES-BAINS
Haute-Savoie
★★*Ibis* av d'Evian ☎50712424 tx 309934
rm67 Lift Mountain Lake
Credit Cards ① ③

THURY-HARCOURT
Calvados
★*Relais de la Poste* rte Caen ☎31797212
Feb-20 Nov
➧11 P20
Credit Cards ① ② ③ ④ ⑤

TILQUES
See ST-OMER

TINQUEUX
See REIMS

TONNERRE
Yonne
★★★*Abbaye St-Michel* (Relais et Châteaux)
Montée St-Michel ☎86550599 tx 801356
Feb-20 Dec
➧11 P30
Credit Cards ② ③ ⑤

TORCY
See CREUSOT, LE

TOUL
Meurthe-et-Moselle
✿ *Dalier Fils* rte de Pont-a-Mousson ☎
83430613 For

TOULON
Var
★★★★*Altea Tour Blanche* bd Äml-Vence
☎94244157 tx 400347
➧92 P50 Lift ⚲ Sea
Credit Cards ① ② ③ ⑤
★★*América* 51 r J-Jaurès (n.rest) ☎94923219 tx
400479
➧30 Lift
Credit Cards ① ② ③ ⑤
✿ *Azur* av de l'Université ☎ 94210400 For
✿ *Soleil* 42 r A-Chenier Prolongée ☎ 94204090
P
At CAMP-ST-LAURENT(7.5km W)
★★★*Novotel Toulon* B52-Sortie Ollioules
☎94630950
➧86 P90 Lift ⌿
Credit Cards ① ② ③ ⑤
★★*Ibis* Autoroute (B52) ☎94632121 tx 400759
➧60 Lift
Credit Cards ① ③
At FARLÈDE, LA(8.5km NE)
★★*Climat* quartier de l'Auberte ☎94487427 tx
430541
➧39 P60
Credit Cards ① ② ③
At GARDE, LA(3Km W)
★★*Fimotel* (N98) ☎94632121 tx 400759
➧86 P90 Lift ⊡
Credit Cards ① ② ③ ⑤
At VALETTE-DU-VAR, LA(7km NE)
★★*Balladins* Zone d'Activité des Espaluns
☎05355575 tx 649394
rm38 P38
Credit Cards ① ② ③ ④ ⑤
★★*Campanile* ZA des Espaluns ☎94211301 tx
430978
➧50 P50
Credit Card ③

TOULOUSE
Haute-Garonne
★★★*Caravelle* (MAP/BW) 62 r Raymond-IV
(n.rest) ☎61627065 tx 530438
➧30 ☎ P10 Lift ☾
Credit Cards ① ② ③ ⑤
★★★*Compagnie du Midi* Gare Matabiau
☎61628493 tx 530171
➧65 Lift
Credit Cards ② ③
★★★*Concorde* 16 bd Bonrepos (n.rest)
☎61624860 tx 531686
➧97 P Lift ☾
★★★*Diane* 3 rte de St-Simon ☎61075952 tx
530518
➧35 P35 ⚲ ⌿
Credit Cards ① ② ③ ⑤
★★★*Mercure* r St-Jérome ☎61231177 tx 520760
➧170 Lift
Credit Cards ① ② ③ ⑤
★★*Arcade* 2 r C-Paulhac,pl J-d'Arc ☎61636163
tx 533802
➧176 ☎ P Lift
Credit Cards ① ③

★★**Ibis Toulouse** 27 bd des Minimes
☎61226060 tx 530437
◄♠130 Lift ① ③
Credit Cards ① ③

★★**Voyageurs** 11 bd Bonrepos (n.rest)
☎61628979 tx 532305
◄♠34 ☄ P6 Lift ℂ
Credit Cards ① ② ③ ④ ⑤

➔ **Lormand** 306 rte de Revel ☎ 61200916 **P**
Peu Tal

➔ **Vie** 57-59 allées C-de-Fitte ☎ 61429911 Peu

At **LABÈGE**(11km SE)

★★**Campanile** Fale carrefour ☎61340189 tx
532007
◄♠49 P
Credit Card ③

At **MIRAIL, LE**

★★**Climat** av du Mirail,2 r A-Coutét ☎61448644
tx 521980
◄♠43 P50
Credit Cards ① ③

★★**Ibis** r J-Babinet ☎61408686 tx 520805
◄♠89 P60 Lift
Credit Cards ① ③

At **ROQUES-SUR-GARONNE**(6km SW)

★★**Campanile** Le Chemin-des-Moines
☎61725151 tx 521426
◄♠50 P50
Credit Card ③

TOULOUSE AIRPORT

★★★★**Altea** 7 r de Labéda (n.rest) ☎61212175
tx 530550
◄♠95 ☄ Lift
Credit Cards ① ② ③ ④ ⑤

★★★**Novotel-Toulouse Purpan** 23 r de Maubec
☎61493410 tx 520640
◄♠123 P Lift ℂ ⌇
Credit Cards ① ② ③ ⑤

At **BLAGNAC**(7km NE)

★★**Balladins** ZAC du Grand Noble,Carrefour D-
Daurat ☎05355575 tx 649394
rm38 P38
Credit Cards ① ② ③ ④ ⑤

★★**Campanile** 3 av D-Daurat ☎61300340 tx
530915
◄♠42 P42
Credit Card ③

★★**Ibis Toulouse Blagnac** 80 av du Parc
☎61300100 tx 521062
◄♠88 P100 Lift
Credit Cards ① ③

TOUQUES
See **DEAUVILLE**

TOUQUET-PARIS-PLAGE, LE
Pas-de-Calais

★★★**Novotel-Thalamer** La Plage ☎21098500 tx
160480
rm104 P Lift ⌇ ⌇ Sea
Credit Cards ① ② ③ ④ ⑤

★★★**Westminster** (Inter-Hotels) av Verger
☎21054848 tx 160439
1 Mar-18 Nov
◄♠115 Lift ℂ ⌇
Credit Cards ① ② ③ ⑤

★★**Forêt** 73 r de Moscou (n.rest) ☎21050988
◄♠10
Credit Card ③

★★**Ibis** Front de Mer ☎21049700 tx 134273
◄♠90 P60 Lift Sea
Credit Cards ① ③

★★**Plage** 13 bd de la Mer (n.rest) ☎21050322
15 Mar-15 Nov
rm29(◄♠24) ℂ Sea
Credit Cards ① ③ ⑤

★★**Windsor-Artois** 7 r St-Georges (off r de la
Paix) ☎21050544
Apr-Sep
◄♠25 Lift

★**Chalet** 15 r de la Paix ☎21058765
15 Feb-15 Nov
rm36(◄♠27) A18rm Sea
Credit Cards ① ③

★**Robert's** 66 r de Londres ☎21051198
rm14(◄♠3)
Credit Card ③

★**Touquet** 17 r de Paris (n.rest) ☎21052254
rm16(◄♠10)

At **GOLF LINKS**(3km S)

★★★**Manoir** av du Golf Links ☎21052022 tx
135565
4 Mar-Jan
◄♠42 P ⌇ ⌇
Credit Cards ① ② ③

TOURCOING
Nord

★★★**Novotel Neuville** Autoroute Lille-Grand
☎20940770 tx 131656
◄♠118 P Lift ⌇

★**Fimotel** 320 bd Gambetta ☎20703800 tx
131234
◄♠40 ☄ P30 Lift
Credit Cards ① ③

★★**Ibis** Centre Gl-de-Gaulle,r Carnot ☎20248458
tx 132695
◄♠102 ☄ Lift
Credit Cards ① ③

TOUR-DU-PIN, LA
Isère

At **FAVERGES-DE-LA-TOUR**(10km NE)

★★★★**Château de Faverges** ☎74974252 tx
300372
May-Oct :Rest closed Mon
◄♠43 A23rm P100 Lift ℂ ⌇ ⌇ ⌇ ⌇ Mountain
Credit Cards ① ② ③

TOURNUS
Saône-et-Loire

★★★**Rempart** 2 & 4 av Gambetta ☎855110566
tx 351019
◄♠37 A8rm ☄ P60 Lift ℂ
Credit Cards ① ② ③ ⑤

★★★**Sauvage** (MAP/BW) pl du Champ-de-Mars
☎85511445 tx 800726
Jan-14 Nov & 16-31 Dec
◄♠30 ☄ P10 Lift ℂ
Credit Cards ① ② ③ ⑤

★**Terrasses** Ⅼ18 av du 23-Janvier
☎85510174
:Rest closed Sun & Mon
◄♠12 ☄ P
Credit Cards ① ③

➔ **Pageaud** 3 rte de Paris ☎ 85510705 **P** Ren

TOURRETTES
See **FAYENCE**

TOURS
Indre-et-Loire

See also **JOUÉ-LÈS-TOURS**

★★★**Alliance** 292 av de Grammont ☎47280080
tx 750922
◄♠125 P100 Lift ℂ ⌇ ⌇
Credit Cards ① ② ③ ④ ⑤

★★★**Bordeaux** Ⅼ3 pl du Ml-Leclerc
☎47054032 tx 750414
◄♠50 Lift ⌇ ⌇
Credit Cards ① ② ③ ⑤

★★★**Central** 21 r Berthelot (n.rest) ☎47054644 tx
751173
rm42(◄♠32) ☄ P10 Lift ℂ
Credit Cards ① ② ③ ⑤

★★★**Châteaux de Loire** 12 r Gambetta (n.rest)
☎47051005 tx 750008
5 Feb-22 Dec
rm32(◄♠30) P6 Lift ℂ
Credit Cards ① ② ③ ⑤

★★★**Royal** 65 av de Grammont (n.rest)
☎47647178 tx 752006
◄♠35 ☄ Lift
Credit Cards ① ② ③ ⑤

★★★**Univers** 5 bd Heurteloup ☎47053712 tx
751460
:Rest closed Sat
◄♠89 ☄ P20 Lift ℂ
Credit Cards ① ② ③ ⑤

★★**Arcade** 1 r G-Claude,angle r E-Vaillant
☎47614444 tx 751201
◄♠139 P28 Lift
Credit Cards ① ③

★★**Armor** Ⅼ26 bis bd Heurteloup (n.rest)
☎47052437 tx 752020
rm48(◄♠27) ☄ P9 Lift
Credit Cards ① ② ③ ⑤

★★**Balladins** La Petite Arche,av Maginot
☎5355575 tx 649394
rm38 P38
Credit Cards ① ② ③ ④ ⑤

★★**Climat** ZI Les Granges Galand (N76)
☎47277117 tx 752391
◄♠64 A26rm P40
Credit Cards ① ② ③

★★**Cygne** 6 r du Cygne (n.rest) ☎47666641
rm19(◄♠11) ☄
Credit Cards ① ③ ⑤

★★**Ibis** La Petite Arche,av A-Maginot ☎47543220
tx 751592
◄♠60 Lift
Credit Cards ① ③

★★**Mondial** Ⅼ3 pl de la Résistance (n.rest)
☎47056268
rm18(◄♠7)
Credit Cards ① ③ ⑤

★**Balzac** 47 r de la Scellerie (n.rest) ☎47054087
rm20(◄♠15) A8rm
Credit Cards ① ③

★**Choiseul** 12 r de la Rotisserie (n.rest)
☎47208576
◄♠16
Credit Cards ① ③

★**Colbert** 78 r Colbert (n.rest) ☎4766156
rm18(◄♠15)
Credit Cards ① ② ③ ⑤

★**Foch** 20 r Ml-Foch (n.rest) ☎47057059
rm15(◄♠12) A2rm
Credit Cards ① ② ③

➔ **Depannage-Auto-Touraine** 151 av A-Maginot
☎ 47411515 **P**

➔ **Pont** Z.A.C. La Vrillonnerie ☎ 47284222 For

At **CHAMBRAY-LES-TOURS**(6km S)

★★★**Novotel Tours Sud** ZAC de la Vrilloneric
☎47274138 tx 751206
◄♠125 Lift ⌇ ⌇
Credit Cards ① ② ③ ⑤

★★**Ibis** La Vrillonnerie,N10 ☎47282528 tx
751297
◄♠80 Lift
Credit Cards ① ③

At **SAVONNIÈRES**(10km W D7)

★**Faisan** ☎47500017
Mar-1 Nov
rm13(◄♠10) ☄ P50 ⌇
Credit Cards ① ③ ④

TOURVILLE-LA-RIVIÈRE
See **ROUEN**

TRANS-EN-PROVENCE
Var
★★**Climat** quartier de Cognet ☎94708211 tx
970625F
↩🛏34 P40 ⌂
Credit Cards ①②③

TRÉBEURDEN
Côtes-du-Nord
★★★**Manoir de Lan Kerellec** (Relais et
Châteaux) **Pn** allée de Lan Kerellec ☎96235009
tx 741172
15 Mar-15 Nov :Rest closed Mon lunch
↩🛏12 P20 ९ Sea
Credit Cards ①②③⑤
★★**Family** L̲E̲85 r des Plages ☎96235031 tx
741897F
:Rest closed Oct-Mar
rm25(↩🛏19) ☎ P12 Sea
Credit Cards ①②③
★★**Ker an Nod** L̲E̲2 r Pors-Termen
☎96235021
15 Mar-15 Nov
rm21(↩🛏14) Sea
Credit Cards ①②③

TRÉGASTEL-PLAGE
Côtes-du-Nord
★★★**Belle Vue** L̲E̲(FAH) **Pn** 20 r des Calculots
☎96238818
Etr-26 Sep
rm33(↩🛏31) P35 Sea
Credit Cards ①③
★★**Beau Séjour** L̲E̲DPn ☎96238802
10 Mar-10 Oct
rm18(↩🛏14) P12 Sea
Credit Cards ①②③⑤
★★**Mer et Plage** ☎96238803
May-Sep
rm40(↩🛏24) P12 Sea
Credit Cards ①③

TRÉGUIER
Côtes-du-Nord
★★**Kastell Dinec'h** L̲E̲(FAH) rte de Lannion
☎96924939
15 Mar-Dec
↩🛏15 P20 ⌂
Credit Cards ①③

TRÉPORT, LE
Seine-Maritime
★**Rex** 50 quai Francois-1er ☎35862655
rm17(↩🛏14) P Mountain

TRÉVOL
Allier
★★**Relais d'Avrilly** L̲E̲☎70426141 tx 392999
:Rest closed Sun pm
↩🛏42 P100 Lift ⌂
Credit Cards ①③

TRIGNAC
Loire-Atlantique
★★**Campanile** ZAC de la Fontaine au Brun
☎40904444 tx 701243
↩🛏48 P48
Credit Card ③
★★**Ibis** 5 r de la Fontaine au Brun ☎40903939 tx
701231
↩🛏45 Lift
Credit Cards ①③

TRIMOUILLE, LA
Vienne
★**Hostellerie de la Paix** r de la Liberté
☎49916050 tx 791316
rm12(↩🛏7)
Credit Cards ①②③⑤

TRINITÉ-SUR-MER, LA
Morbihan
★★**Rouzic** L̲E̲17 cours de Quais ☎97557206

Closed 15 Nov-15 Dec
↩🛏32 Lift Sea
Credit Cards ①②③⑤

TRIQUE, LA
See **ST-LAURENT-SUR-SÈVRE**

TROIS-ÉPIS, LES
Haut-Rhin
★★★★**Grand** (MAP/BW) ☎89498065 tx 880229
↩🛏50 P50 Lift ℂ ⌂ Mountain
Credit Cards ①②③⑤

TRONCHET, LE
Ille-et-Vilaine
★★**Hostellerie l'Abbatiale** ☎99589321 tx 741629
15 Feb-Dec
↩🛏72 P100 ९ ⌂ Lake
Credit Cards ①②③

TROUVILLE-SUR-MER
Calvados
★★★**Flaubert** r G-Flaubert (n.rest) ☎31883923
Mar-15 Nov
rm33(↩🛏26) Lift ℂ
Credit Cards ①②③⑤
★★**Reynita** 29 r Carnot ☎31881513
Closed Jan
rm26(↩🛏21) ☎ ℂ
Credit Cards ①②③⑤

TROYES
Aube
★★★**Grand** (Inter-Hotels) 4 av Ml-Joffre
☎25799090 tx 840582
↩🛏95 P Lift
Credit Cards ①②③⑤
★★**Fimotel** bd G-Pompidou ☎42615014 tx
215269
↩🛏42 P Lift
Credit Cards ①②③⑤
★★**Paris** (Inter) 54 r R-Salengro ☎25731170 tx
840216
rm27(↩🛏20) ☎ P10
Credit Cards ①③⑤
🍴 **Ets Belin (25)** 2 Mail des Charmilles ☎
25805419 P LR
At **BUCHÈRES**(6km SW)
★★**Campanile** Le Haut de Caurgerennes,(RN71)
☎25496767 tx 840840
↩🛏42 P42
Credit Card ③
At **ST-ANDRÉ-LES-VERGERS**
🍴 **Juszak** 37 rte d'Auxerre ☎ 25824655 P Rov
DJ

TROYES AIRPORT
At **BARBEREY**(6km NW on N19)
★★★**Novotel-Troyes Aéroport** RN19
☎25745995 tx 840759
↩🛏84 P100 ⌂
Credit Cards ①②③④⑤

TULLE
Corrèze
★★★**Limouzi** 19 quai République ☎55264200 tx
590140
Closed 1-7 Jan :Rest closed Sun pm
↩🛏50 ☎ Lift
Credit Cards ①②③④⑤
🍴 **Ets Carles** rte de Brive ☎ 55200805 P For

ULIS, LES
Essonne
★★**Campanile** ZA de Courtaboeuf ☎69286060 tx
603094
↩🛏50 P50
Credit Card ③
★★**Climat** av des Andes ☎64460506
↩🛏42

URY
See **FONTAINEBLEAU**

UZERCHE
Corrèze
★★**Ambroise** av de Paris ☎55731008 tx 590845
Dec-Oct :Rest closed Sat & Sun (ex. Jul & Aug)
↩🛏20 P20
Credit Cards ①②③
★★**Teyssier** r Pont-Turgot ☎55731005
Mar-10 Jan :Rest closed Wed
rm17(↩🛏10) ☎ P25
Credit Cards ①③
🚗 Renault rte de Limoges ☎ 55731333 P Ren

UZÈS
Gard
★**Provençale** 3 r Grande Bourgade ☎66221106
↩🛏10 Lift

VAISON-LA-ROMAINE
Vaucluse
★★**Beffroi** r de l'Evèche ☎90360471 tx 306022
15 Mar-15 Nov & 15 Dec-5 Jan :Rest closed Mon
& Tue lunchtime
rm22(↩🛏18) A10rm P11 Mountain
Credit Cards ①②③⑤

VAÏSSAC
Tarn-et-Garonne
★**Terrassier** ☎63309460
rm12(🛏4) ⌂

VAL-ANDRÉ, LE
Côtes-du-Nord
★**Bains** 7 pl Gl-de-Gaulle ☎96722011
20 May-20 Sep
rm26 P7 Sea

VALBONNE
Alpes-Maritimes
★★★**Novotel Sophia Antipolis** ☎93333800 tx
970914
↩🛏97 P Lift ९ ⌂ Mountain
★★**Ibis Sophia Antipolis** r A-Caquot ☎93653060
tx 461363
↩🛏99 Lift
Credit Cards ①③

VALDAHON
Doubs
★★**Relais de Franche Comté** L̲E̲☎81562318
15 Jan-20 Dec
↩🛏20 ☎ P100
Credit Cards ①②③⑤

VAL-DE-REUIL
See **LOUVIERS**

VAL D'ISÈRE
Savoie
★★★★**Sofitel** ☎79060830 tx 980558
Dec-5 May & Jul-25 Aug
↩🛏53 ☎ P Lift ℂ ⌂ Mountain
Credit Cards ①②③⑤
★★★**Aiglon** DPn ☎79060405
1 Dec-1 May
↩🛏21 Mountain
Credit Cards ①②③⑤
★★**Savoie** ☎79060630
rm36(↩🛏34) Lift Mountain
★**Vieux Village** L̲E̲☎79060379 tx 980077
Dec-5 May
↩🛏24 P10 Mountain
Credit Cards ①③

VALENÇAY
Indre
★★★**Espagne** (Relais et Châteaux) 8 r du
Château ☎5400002 tx 751675
Mar-Dec
↩🛏18 P18 ℂ ९ ⌂
Credit Cards ①③
★★**Lion d'Or** pl Marché ☎54000087
:Rest closed Mon
rm15(↩🛏8) ☎ P6
Credit Cards ①②③⑤

VALENCE
Drôme

★★★*Novotel Valence Sud* 217 av de Provence
(N7) ☎75422015 tx 345823
◀🏠107 P150 Lift ९ ⌂
Credit Cards ① ② ③ ④ ⑤

★★*Campanile* r du Dr-Abel ☎75569280 tx
346304
◀🏠42 P42
Credit Card ③

★★*Ibis* 355 av de Provence ☎75444254 tx
345384
◀🏠86 P86 Lift ℂ ⌂
Credit Cards ① ③

★★*Park* (Inter-Hotels) 22 r J-Bouin (n.rest)
☎75433706
Closed 24 Dec-8 Jan
◀🏠22 ☞ P22
Credit Cards ① ② ③ ⑤

★★*Pic* (Relais et Châteaux) 285 av V-Hugo
☎75441532
Closed Aug & Feb
◀🏠4 ☞ P24
Credit Cards ① ② ③ ⑤

๖ *Anayan* 170 r du Chateauvert ☎ 75441685 **P**
Cit

๖ *Bastien* 38-40 r G-Eiffel ☎ 75434268 **P** Peu
Tal

๖ *Brun Valence* 73-79 av de Verdun ☎
75556060 **P** Fia Hon Ope

๖ *Costechareyre* 31 av des Aureates ☎
75440109 **P**

๖ *J Jaurès* 410 av de Chabeuil ☎ 75421266 **P**

๖ *Minodier* rte de Benuvallon Z.I. ☎ 75443124 **P**
Cit

๖ *Molière* 164 av V-Hugo ☎ 75441137 **P** Por
Col

๖ *Vinson et Verde* 35 r de la Cartoucherie ☎
75430192 **P** Peu Tal

At BOURG-LÈS-VALENCE(1km N)

★★*Climat* rte de Châteauneuf-sur-Isère
☎75427746 tx 346565
◀🏠42 P50
Credit Cards ① ② ③

★★*Seyvet* 🄻(Inter-Hotels) 24 av M-Urtin
☎75432651 tx 346338
◀🏠34 A3rm ☞ P30 Lift ℂ Mountain
Credit Cards ① ② ③ ⑤

★★*Soleil d'Or* Montée du Long RN7 ☎75560229
tx 346710
◀🏠37 P40 Mountain
Credit Cards ① ③

VALENCE-D'AGEN
Tarn-et-Garonne

★*Tout-Va-Bien* 35-39 r de la République
☎63395483
Feb-Dec :Rest closed Mon
rm22(◀🏠20)
Credit Cards ① ③

VALENCE-SUR-BAÏSE
Gers

★★*Ferme du Flaran* ☎61285822
Feb-Dec :Rest closed Mon
◀🏠15 P30 Beach
Credit Cards ① ② ③

VALENCIENNES
Nord

★★★*Grand* (MAP/BW) 8 pl de la Gare
☎27463201 tx 110701
◀🏠96 Lift ℂ
Credit Cards ① ② ③ ⑤

★★★*Novotel Valenciennes-Ouest* DPn
Autoroute Paris-Bruxelles,N2 (n.rest) ☎27442080
tx 120970
◀🏠76 ⌂
Credit Cards ① ② ③ ④ ⑤

★★*Campanile* Valenciennes Aérodrome
☎27440123 tx 810288
◀🏠42 P42
Credit Card ③

★★*Ibis* A2,Sortie Valenciennes Ouest (n.rest)
☎27445566 tx 160737
◀🏠65 P70 Lift
Credit Cards ① ③

VALETTE-DU-VAR, LA
See TOULON

VALLOIRE
Savoie

★★*Grand de Valloire et Galibier* ☎79590095 tx
980553
15 Jun-15 Sep & 18 Dec-15 Apr
◀🏠43 P40 Lift Mountain
Credit Cards ② ④

VALOGNES
Manche

★★*Louvre* 28 r Réligieuses ☎33400007
4 Jan-Nov :Rest closed Sat
rm20(◀🏠9) ☞ P20

VALS-LES-BAINS
Ardèche

★★★*Vivarais* (MAP/BW) 5 r C-Expilly
☎75946585 tx 345866
:Rest closed 1 Feb-6 Mar
◀🏠40 P50 Lift ℂ ⌂ Beach Mountain
Credit Cards ① ② ③ ④ ⑤

★★*Europe* 🄻(FAH) 86 r J-Jaurès ☎75374394
tx 346256
10 Apr-10 Oct
rm33(◀🏠30) ☞ P6 Lift
Credit Cards ① ③

VAL-SUZON
Côte-d'Or

★★★*Val-Suzon* DPn ☎80356015 tx 351454
15 Jan-15 Nov :Rest closed Wed/Thus lunchtime
HS
◀🏠17 A10rm P50
Credit Cards ① ③

VANDOEUVRE-LES-NANCY
See NANCY

VANNES
Morbihan

★★★*Marebaudière* DPn 4 r A-Briand
☎97473429 tx 951975
6 Jan-18 Dec :Rest closed Etr
◀🏠41 P60 Lift
Credit Cards ① ② ③ ⑤

★★*Aquarium* Le Parc du Golfe ☎97404452 tx
850926
:Rest closed Sun evening
◀🏠48 ☞ P60 Lift Sea
Credit Cards ① ② ③ ⑤

★*Ibis Vannes* r E-Jourdan,ZI de Ménimur Est
☎97636111 tx 950521
◀🏠59 Lift
Credit Cards ① ③

★★*Image Ste-Anne* (FAH) 8 pl de la Libération
☎97632736 tx 950352
rm32(◀🏠28) P15
Credit Cards ① ③

★*Marée Bleue* DPn 8 pl Bir-Hakeim ☎97472429
tx 951975
6 Jan-18 Dec :Rest closed Etr
rm16(🏠8) P60
Credit Cards ① ② ③ ⑤

๖ *Autorep* 41 r du Vincin ☎ 97631035 **P** For

๖ *Poulichet* 126 bd de la Paix ☎ 97540325 Alf
Fia Toy

VARCES
Isère

★★*Escale* (Relais et Châteaux) pl de la
République (n.rest) ☎76728019
Closed Jan

◀🏠11 P10 ९ Mountain
Credit Cards ① ②

VARENGEVILLE-SUR-MER
Seine-Maritime

★★*Terrasse* 🄻DPn ☎35851254
15 Mar-15 Oct
◀🏠26 P20 ९ Sea
Credit Cards ① ③

VARENNES-VAUZELLES
See NEVERS

VARETZ
See BRIVE-LA-GAILLARDE

VAULX-EN-VELIN
Rhône

★★*Fimotel* 9 r N-Carmellino ☎78807226 tx
305964
◀🏠42 P20 Lift
Credit Cards ① ② ③ ⑤

VAUVENARGUES
Bouches-du-Rhône

★*Moulin de Provence* DPn ☎42660222 tx
410777
Mar-3 Jan :Rest closed Mon
rm12(◀🏠9) P22 Mountain
Credit Cards ① ③

VENCE
Alpes-Maritimes

★★★★*Domaine St-Martin* (Relais et Châteaux)
rte de Coursegoules ☎93580202 tx 470282
mid Mar-mid Nov
◀🏠25 A10rm ☞ P20 ℂ ९ ⌂ Sea
Credit Cards ① ② ③ ⑤

★★*Diana* av Poilus (n.rest) ☎93582856
◀🏠25 Lift ℂ Mountain
Credit Cards ① ② ③ ⑤

๖ *Simondi* 39 av Foch ☎ 93580121 **P** Peu Tal
Mer

VENDIN-LE-VIEL
See LENS

VENDÔME
Loir-et-Cher

★★*Vendôme* DPn 15 fbg Chartrain ☎54770288
tx 750383
5 Jan-19 Dec
◀🏠35 ☞ P8 Lift
Credit Cards ① ③

VENIZY
See ST-FLORENTIN

VERDUN
Meuse

๖ *M Rochette* r V-Schleiter ☎ 29865049 **P** For

At CHATTANCOURT(14km NW D38)

๖ *M Riboizi* ☎ 29843286 M/C **P** Ren

VERETZ
Indre-et-Loire

★*St-Honoré* 🄻☎47503006
Closed Jan :Rest closed Sun evening
rm9(◀🏠6)
Credit Cards ① ② ③ ⑤

VERNET-LES-BAINS
Pyrénées-Orientales

★★*Angleterre* 9 av de Burnay ☎68055058
2 May-26 Oct
rm20(◀🏠11) Mountain
Credit Cards ① ③

VERNEUIL-SUR-AVRE
Eure

★★★*Clos* (Relais et Châteaux) 98 r Ferte Vidame
☎32322181 tx 172770
Feb-Nov
◀🏠11 A3rm P30 ९
Credit Cards ① ② ③ ⑤

★★**Saumon** **LE**(FAH) 89 pl de la Madeleine
☎32320236 tx 172770
5 Jan-22 Dec
rm28(⇒24) A18rm
Credit Cards 1 3

🍴 **Martin** ☎ 32321327 **P** Peu Tal

VERRIÈRES-LE-BUISSON
Essonne

★★**Climat** ZAC des Prés Houts,av G-Pompidou
☎69307070
⇒38 P
Credit Cards 1 3

VERSAILLES
Yvelines

★★★**Trianon Palace** 1 bd de la Reine
☎39503412 tx 698863
⇒120 P200 Lift ℂ ⌖ ▱
Credit Cards 1 2 3 4 5

★★★**Cheval Rouge** 18 r A-Chenier ☎39500303
10 Jan-20 Dec
rm40(⇒22) P20

★★**Clagny** 6 Impasse Clagny (n.rest) ☎39501809
rm21(⇒18) ℂ

★★**St-Louis** 28 r St-Louis (n.rest) ☎39502355 tx
689793F
rm27(⇒25) ℂ
Credit Cards 1 3

VERT-ST-DENIS
See **MELUN**

VERVINS
Aisne

★★★**Tour du Roy** 45 r Gl-Leclerc ☎23980011 tx
155445
15 Feb-15 Jan
⇒15 A1rm P15 ⌖
Credit Cards 1 2 3 4 5

★**Cheval Noir** 33 r de la Liberté ☎23980415
Closed 25 Dec & 1 Jan
rm18(⇒12) ☎ P10
Credit Cards 1 2 3

VESOUL
Haute-Saône

★★**Nord** r Aigle Noir 7 ☎84750256
rm33(⇒30) Lift ℂ ℧ Beach Sea Mountain Lake
Credit Cards 1 3

★★**Relais N19** (Inter-Hotels) rte de Paris
☎84764242
12 Jan-22 Dec
⇒22 ☎ P32
Credit Cards 1 2 3 5

🍴 **Franche Comté** ZI Quest ☎ 84767210 **P** Rov

🍴 **Vesoul** av Pasteur,Echanoz la Meline ☎
84752801 **P** Dat

VEURDRE, LE
Allier

★★**Pont Neuf** **LE**(FAH) rte de Lurcy-Levis
☎70664012 tx 392978
rm35(⇒30) A10rm ☎ P30 ▱
Credit Cards 1 2 3 5

VEYRIER-DU-LAC
Haute-Savoie

★**Auberge du Colvert** ☎50601023
Apr-15 Nov
⇒10 P20 Mountain Lake
Credit Cards 1 3

VEYS, LES
See **CARENTAN**

VICHY
Allier

★★★**Pavillon Sévigné** (BW) 10 pl Sévigné
☎70321622 tx 392370
⇒40 P15 Lift ℂ Lake
Credit Cards 1 2 3 5

🍴 **Imperial** 59 av Thermale ☎ 70986771 **P** For

At BELLERIVE-SUR-ALLIER(2Km SW)

★★**Campanile** av de Vichy ☎70593223 tx
392985
⇒49 P49
Credit Card 3

🍴 **Vasseur** 93 av de Vichy ☎ 70320367 **P** Peu

VIC-SUR-CÉRE
Cantal

★★**Beauséjour** **LE**av A-Mercier ☎71475027
15 May-1 Oct :Rest closed 1 Oct-15 May
rm75(⇒65) A18rm P60 Lift Mountain
Credit Cards 1 3

At COL-DE-CUREBOURSE(6km SE on D54)

★**Auberge du Col** **LE**Curebourse ☎71475171
15 Jan-15 Oct :Rest closed 15 Oct-15 Jan
rm30(⇒27) A4rm P30 Mountain
Credit Card 1

VIENNE
Isère

★**Nord** (Inter-Hotels) 11 pl Miremont ☎74857711
⇒43 ☎ P22 Lift ℂ
Credit Cards 1 2 3 5

🍴 **Société du Central** 76 av du Gl-Leclerc ☎
74531344 For

At CHONAS-L'AMBALLAN(9km S on N7)

★★**Relais 500 de Vienne** ☎74580144 tx 380343
⇒44 ☎ P100 ▱
Credit Cards 1 2 3 5

VILLARS
Loire

★★**Campanile** r de l'Antisaneet ☎77935248 tx
307101
⇒42 P42
Credit Card 3

VILLEDIEU-LES-POÊLES
Manche

★★**St-Pierre et St-Michel** **LE**DPn 12 pl de la
République ☎33610011
:Rest closed Fri
rm23(⇒20) ☎ P10
Credit Cards 1 3

VILLEFRANCHE-DU-PÉRIGORD
Dordogne

★★**Bruyères** **LE**☎53299797
Closed 1st 2 wks Jan,Feb,Mar & Dec
⇒10 A4rm P20 ▱
Credit Cards 1 3

VILLEFRANCHE-SUR-MER
Alpes-Maritimes

★★★**Provençal** DPn 4 av Ml-Joffre ☎93017142
tx 970433
:Rest closed 1 Nov-20 Feb
rm45(⇒43) Lift ℂ Sea
Credit Cards 1 2 3 4 5

★★★**Welcome** (MAP/BW) 1 quai Courbet
☎93767693 tx 470281
15 Dec-15 Nov
rm32(⇒28) ☎ Lift Sea
Credit Cards 1 2 3 5

★★**Coq-Hardi** **LE**8 bd de la Corne d'Or
☎93017106
15 Dec-Oct
⇒20 P15 ▱ Sea

VILLEFRANCHE-SUR-SAÔNE
Rhône

★★★**Plaisance** (FAH) 96 av de la Libération
(n.rest) ☎74653352 tx 375746
2 Jan-24 Dec
⇒68 A6rm ☎ P20 Lift ℂ
Credit Cards 1 2 3 5

★★**Campanile** 210 r G-Mangin,La Ferme de
Poulet ☎74680758 tx 310208
⇒43 P43
Credit Card 3

★★**Climat** rte de Riotter le Peage ☎74629955 tx
300712
⇒43 P40
Credit Cards 1 2 3

★★**Ecu de France** 35 r d'Anse ☎74683448
⇒26 ☎ P
Credit Cards 1 2 3 5

★★**Ibis** Le Péage-Commune de Limas
☎74682273 tx 370777
⇒115 P110 Lift
Credit Cards 1 3

🍴 **Europe** r Ampère ☎ 74655059 **P**

VILLEFRANQUE
See **BAYONNE**

VILLENEUVE-D'ASCQ
See **ROUBAIX**

VILLENEUVE-DE-MARSAN
Landes

★**Europe** **LE**1 pl Foirail ☎58452008
⇒15 P15 ℂ ▱
Credit Cards 1 2 3 5

VILLENEUVE-DE-RIVIÈRE
See **ST-GAUDENS**

VILLENEUVE-LA-GARENNE
See**PARIS**

VILLENEUVE-LÈS-AVIGNON
Gard

★★★**Magnaneraie** 37 r Camp-de-Bataille
☎90251111 tx 432640
rm25(⇒20) ℂ ⌖ ▱
Credit Cards 1 2 3 5

★★★**Prieuré** 7 pl Chapître ☎90251820 tx 431042
15 Mar-15 Nov
⇒36 A24rm P60 Lift ℂ ⌖ ▱
Credit Cards 1 2 3 5

VILLENEUVE-LOUBET-PLAGE
See **CAGNES-SUR-MER**

VILLENEUVE-SUR-LOT
Lot-et-Garonne

★★★**Parc** (MAP/BW) 13 bd de la Marine
☎53700168 tx 550379
⇒40 Lift ℂ
Credit Cards 1 2 3 5

★**Prune d'Or** pl de la Gare ☎5390050
rm17(⇒11) ☎ P20

VILLENEUVE-SUR-YONNE
Yonne

★**Dauphin** DPn 14 r Carnot ☎86871855
Closed 1 Jan & 25 Dec
⇒11 ☎ P10

VILLERS-COTTERÉTS
Aisne

★★**Ibis** rte de Vivières ☎23962680 tx 145363
⇒62 P100 Lift
Credit Cards 1 3

VILLERS-LES-POTS
See **AUXONNE**

VILLERS-SEMEUSE
See **CHARLEVILLE-MÉZIÈRES**

VILLERS-SUR-MER
Calvados

★★★**Bonne Auberge** Pn 1 r du Ml-Leclerc
☎31870464
Mar-Jan
rm14(⇒11) A3rm Sea
Credit Cards 1 3

🍴 **Meridien** 13 r de Gl-Leclerc ☎ 31870213 Peu
Tal

VINAY
See **ÉPERNAY**

VINEUIL
See **BLOIS**

VIRONVAY
See **LOUVIERS**

VIRY-CHÂTILLON
Essonne
★★**Climat** r O-Longuet ☎69442121 tx 603478
⇥38 P Lake
Credit Cards ① ② ③

VITRAC
Dordogne
★*Plaisance* **LE**Au Port (N703) ☎53283304
1 Feb-20 Nov :Rest closed Fri
⇥38 A8rm P15 ⌇
Credit Cards ① ②

VITRÉ
Ille-et-Vilaine
★**Chêne Vert DP**n 2 pl du Gl-de-Gaulle
☎99750058
Jan-22 Sep & 22 Oct-Dec :Rest closed Sat
rm22(⇥8) ☎ P10
Credit Cards ① ③

VITROLLES
See **MARSEILLE AIRPORT**

VITRY-LE-FRANÇOIS
Marne
★**Bon Séjour** 4 fbg L-Bourgeois ☎26740236
Feb-Dec :Rest closed Sat
rm20(⇥12)
Credit Cards ① ③
★*Cloche* 34 r A-Briand ☎26740384
rm24(⇥19) ☎ P20
Credit Cards ① ② ③ ⑤
★*Nancy* 22 Grand r de Vaux ☎26740937
rm15(⇥7) ☎
Credit Cards ① ② ③

VIZILLE
Isère
★*Parc* 25 av A-Briand ☎76680301
rm24(⇥16) P4 Mountain
Credit Cards ② ③

VOGELGRUN
See **NEUF-BRISACH**

VOREPPE
See **GRENOBLE**

VOUILLÉ
Vienne
★★★*Château de Perigny* rte de Nantes
☎49518043 tx 791400
⇥40 P ⌇ ⇥

VOUVRAY
Indre-et-Loire
★**Grand Vatel LEDP**n av Brûle ☎47527032
16 Mar-14 Dec :Rest closed Sun evening & Mon
⇥7 P10
Credit Cards ① ② ③

WALHEIM
See **ALTKIRCH**

WAST, LE
Pas-de-Calais
★★**Château de Tourelles** ☎21333478
:Rest closed Mon lunchtime
⇥16 A6rm P40
Credit Cards ① ② ③ ⑤

WIMEREUX
Pas-de-Calais
★★**Atlantic** Digue de Mer ☎21324101
Apr-1 Oct
rm11(⇥10) ☎ P30 Lift Sea
Credit Cards ① ③ ⑤
★★**Paul et Virginie** 19 r Gl-de-Gaulle
☎21324212
20 Jan-15 Dec :Rest closed Sun pm
rm18(⇥16) P10
Credit Cards ① ② ③ ⑤
★*Centre* 78 r Carnot ☎21324108
20 Jan-20 Dec :Rest closed Mon
rm25(⇥18) ☎ P12
Credit Cards ① ③

WITTENHEIM
See **MULHOUSE**

WOIPPY
See **METZ**

YENNE
Savoie
★**Logis Savoyard** pl C-Dullin ☎79367038
:Rest closed Fri
rm13 A4rm P4

YFFINIAC
See **ST-BRIEUC**

MONACO

The principality of Monaco, which is 350 acres in extent, is an independent enclave inside France. It consists of three adjacent towns - Monaco, the capital, la Condamine, along the harbour and Monte-Carlo, along the coast immediately to the north.
Monte-Carlo is famous for its Casino, built in 1878, which has featured in many films and novels. In addition to its gambling tables it has a fine opera house and luxurious grounds. The harbour of la Condamine is a busy centre of colourful yachts and cabin-cruisers. The town is less pretentious and expensive than Monte-Carlo and contains the commercial quarter of the principality.

EATING OUT One of Monte-Carlo's institutions is the café, brasserie and drugstore *Café de Paris*, in Place du Casino. The restaurants *Dominique le Stanc*, in boulevard des Moulins, and *Rampoldi*, in avenue Spelugues, are both outstanding, the latter specialising in imaginative Italian cuisine.

MONTE CARLO
★★★★★**Paris** pl du Casino ☎93508080 tx 469925
⇥255 P170 Lift ℂ 🖴 Sea Mountain
Credit Cards ① ② ③ ⑤
★★★★*Hermitage* sq Beaumarchais ☎93506731 tx 479432
⇥260 P50 Lift ℂ 🖴 Sea
Credit Cards ① ② ③ ④ ⑤
★★★*Alexandra* 35 bd Princesse Charlotte (n.rest) ☎93506313 tx 489286
⇥55 Lift
Credit Cards ① ② ③ ⑤
📞 **British Motors** 15 bd Princesse Charlotte ☎93256484 Rov DJ RR

At **MONTE-CARLO BEACH**
★★★★**Beach** 22 av Princesse Grace ☎93309880 tx 479617
⇥320 Lift ℂ ➔ Beach Sea Mountain
Credit Cards ① ② ③ ⑤

Discover
FRANCE

A colourful gazetteer of more than 600 attractive towns and villages, with information on local customs and specialities. Interesting features on travelling, accommodation and eating out, plus a road atlas and a detailed street plan of Paris and the surrounding area.

Available at good bookshops and AA Centres

We're all you need to know.

GERMANY

Language
German

Local time
GMT + 1 (Summer GMT + 2)

Currency
Deutsche Mark, divided into 100
pfennige. At the time of going to press
£1 = DM3.11
US$1 = DM1.87

Emergency numbers
Fire ☎112
Police and Ambulance ☎110

Information in England
German National Tourist Office,
Nightingale House, 65 Curzon Street,
London W17 1PE
☎†01-495 3990/1
†071 from 6 May.

Information in the USA
German National Tourist Office, 747
Third Avenue, New York, NY 10017
☎212 308 3300

Germany is a land of mountains and plains, estuaries and inlets, forests and heaths, plus thriving modern cities and medieval country towns, fairytale castles and colourful traditions. The people are welcoming and encourage visitors to enjoy themselves. The people are welcoming and encourage visitors to enjoy themselves; the wines, beers and the food are not only good value, but are also hearty and satisfying.

Thanks to the superb German road network, the miles pass swiftly and easily, with motorways linking all the main areas, and delightful country lanes to travel in between. Most things in Germany are reasonably priced, and shopping – particularly in Hamburg and Berlin – is a delight.

Germany is a country of amazing variety, with a constantly changing pattern of scenery from the sea to the mountains, and from the lowlands to the forest-clad Bavarian Alps. Many small towns have preserved the aspect of past centuries, many cities have brought new life into their old town centres. The old imperial cities in the south have their splendid cathedrals, palaces and town halls, while beyond the towns there are great expanses of open countryside and countless health and holiday resorts.

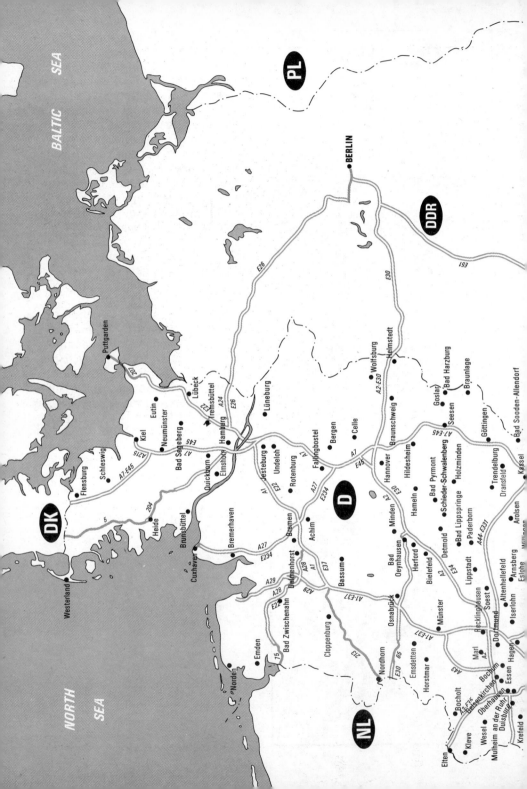

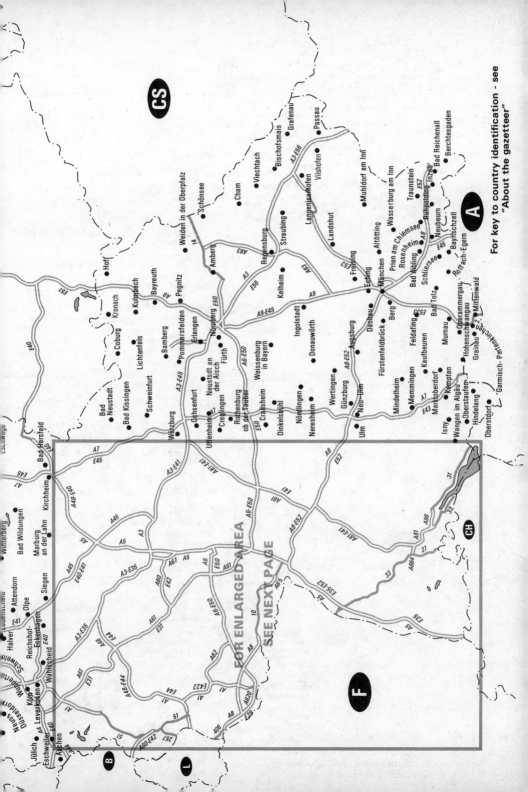

For key to country identification - see
"About the gazetteer"

FOR ENLARGED AREA
SEE NEXT PAGE

Düren
Siegburg
Betzdorf
Alsfeld
Hünfeld
Altenkirchen
BONN
Fulda
Königswinter
A48·E40
Rheinbach
Honnef am Rhein
Bad Marienberg
Giessen
Elfershausen
Simmerath
Remagen
Wetzlar
A61
Monschau
Ahrweiler
Bad Neuenahr
A3·E35
A5
Schleiden
Altenahr
Bad Breisig
E451
Blankenheim
Montabaur
Andernach
Neuwied
Limburg an der Lahn
B
E44
Bad Nauheim
Adenau
Maria
Koblenz
Bad Ems
Diez/Lahn
Laach
Lahnstein
Braubach
Bad Homburg
A48·E44
Kamp-Bornhofen
E451
A45
Daun
Brodenbach
Boppard
Manderscheid
Cochem
St Goarshausen
Königstein im Taunus
Kronberg im Taunus
Bad Bruckenau
Ediger-Eller
St Goar
Frankfurt-am-Main
A60
Oberwesel
Schlangenbad
Dreieich
Zell an der Mosel
Bacharach
Wiesbaden
Offenbach
Urzig/Mosel
Assmannshausen
Oestrich
A3·E42
Aschaffenburg
A3·E41
Marktheidenfeld
Traben-Trarbach
Rudesheim
Mainz
Bitburg
Lieser
Bingen
A60
Sinspelt
Bernkastel Kues
Nierstein
Gross-Gerau
Mülheim
an der Mosel
A67
Darmstadt
Wertheim
Trittenheim
Bad Kreuznach
A6
Trier
E31
Oppenheim
A5
267
Birkenfeld
E422
A41
Heppenheim
an der Bergstrasse
Worms
A6
406
Lampertheim
Weinheim
an der Bergstrasse
Bad
Mergentheim
A62
Viernheim
A1
Schriesheim
Eberbach am Neckar
A6·E50
Mannheim
A81·E41
Kaiserslautern
Bad
Ludwigshafen
Neckarsteinach
A620
Dürkheim
Heidelberg
Neckargemünd
A8
Homburg-Saar
Schwetzingen
Sinsheim
E29
A8
Speyer
Zweibrücken
10
Hockenheim
Walldorf
A6
Bad Wimpfen
A6
Landau
in der Pfalz
E50
Heilbronn
E50
Pirmasens
Germersheim
A5
Bad Bergzabern
Bruchsal
Schwäbisch
Hall
Rheinzabern
E35
Vaihingen
in der Enz
Murrhardt
Karlsruhe
A6·E52
Asperg
Kaisersbach
Ettlingen
Pforzheim
Ludwigsburg
Rastatt
Tiefenbronn
Korntal–Münchingen
Bad Herrenalb
Leonberg
Baden-Baden
Bad
Enzklösterle
Liebenzell
Stuttgart
Gernsbach
Bühl
Sindelfingen
Göppingen
Wildbad
im Schwarzwald
Böblingen
Achern
Sand
A8·E52
Schonmünzach
Herrenberg
F
Oberkirch
Nagold
Lossburg
Tübingen
Reutlingen
Offenburg
Klosterreichenbach
Lautenbach
Freudenstadt
Merklingen
Lahr
Alpirsbach
A81
E41
Wolfach
A5
Hornberg
33
St-Georgen
Rottweil
Biberach an der Riss
E35
Triberg
Königsfeld
im Schwarzwald
Sigmaringen
Villingen
Bad Dürrheim
Saulgau
Breisach
Glottertal
St-Märgen
Tuttlingen
Freiburg im Breisgau
Breitnau
Donaueschingen
Hinterzarten
Titisee Neustadt
27
A81·E41
A98
Stockach
Todtnau
Lenzkirch
Ravensburg
Feldberg im Schwarzwald
Überlingen
Sulzburg
Mülheim
Bonndorf
33
Meersburg
A5·E35
Badenweiler
Notschrei
Konstanz
Hagnau
Tettnang
Höchenschwand
Friedrichshafen
Haltingen
CH
Langenargen
Lörrach
Bad Säckingen
Lindau im Bodensee

**For key to country identification - see
"About the gazetteer"**

HOW TO GET THERE

If you use one of the short Channel crossings and travel via Belgium the Federal Republic of Germany is within a comfortable day's drive.

For northern Germany you could take one of the longer Channel crossings to the Netherlands, or take a direct ferry from **Harwich** to **Hamburg** (19½–21½hrs crossing time).

For southern Germany drive through northern France entering Germany near Strasbourg. This journey often requires an overnight stop. Or you could use the longer Channel crossings: Caen, Cherbourg, Dieppe or Le Havre to southern Germany.

Distance

From Calais to Köln (Cologne), 419km (260 miles). From Le Havre to Strasbourg is 685km (425 miles).

MONEYMATTERS

There are no restrictions on the amount of foreign or German currency that a bona fide tourist can import or export.

Banking hours

Monday–Friday 08.30–12.00hrs and 14.00–15.30hrs (17.30hrs on Thursdays).

Exchange offices of the Deutsche-Verehrs-Kredit-Bank are located at main railway stations, and road and rail frontier crossing points. Generally they are open from early morning until late at night.

Postcheques

may be cashed at all post offices up to a maximum of DM400 per cheque. Go to the counter marked Auskunft, Auszahlungen or Post giro checks.

MOTORING REGULATIONS AND GENERAL INFORMATION

The information given here is specific to Germany. It **must** be read in conjunction with the European ABC at the front of the book, which covers those regulations which are common to most countries.

Accidents*

You are generally required to call the police when individuals have been injured or considerable damage has been caused. Failure to give aid to anyone injured will render you liable to a fine. Callboxes with two luminous red stripes, installed alongside certain roads, contain an emergency telephone which can be used without inserting money. By lifting the receiver and pulling the emergency lever, you are automatically connected with fire or police. See also *Warning triangle* below.

Berlin

Documents required for travel through the German Democratic Republic (DDR) to West Berlin.

Be sure you have a valid standard passport (children over 16 years of age must have a separate passport), national driving licence and vehicle registration document. The Green Card is now accepted, but make sure that it covers you for the Democratic Republic before you depart from the United Kingdom. Third party insurance can be arranged at the border crossings. Transit visas for journeys to West Berlin can be obtained at the frontier crossings at a cost of DM5 per person (each way). Tourists travelling directly between the Federal Republic and West Berlin are exempt from paying road tax.

Customs crossings The main frontier Customs Houses between the Federal Republic and the Democratic Republic officially open for transit from the Federal Republic to West Berlin are listed below. The names printed in italics are within the DDR, the others outside it.

Frankfurt *Wartha*; Herleshausen
Hamburg *Zarrentin*; Gudow
Hanover *Marienborn*; Helmstedt
München *Hirschberg*; Saalebrücke; Rudolphstein

*Additional information will be found in the European ABC at the front of the book.

Hours Crossings are open day and night.

Entry to West Berlin is possible at Drewitz/ Dreilinden on the routes from Frankfurt, Hanover and München (Munich) and at Stolpe/ Heiligensee on the route from Hamburg.

Entry to East Berlin for day visits from West Berlin is at Kochstrasse ('Checkpoint Charlie') and Friedrichstrasse. There are no restrictions for tourists of non-German nationality who wish to make a day trip from West to East Berlin, but make sure that this is mentioned on the insurance policy. A minimum exchange of 25 marks of local currency is necessary. The cost of an entry visa for a day trip to East Berlin is DM5 per person.

A booklet entitled *Motoring in Eastern Europe* is available to AA members.

Breakdown*

If you car breaks down, try to move it to the side of the road so that it does not obstruct traffic flow. A warning triangle must be placed to the rear of the vehicle, and hazard warning lights, if fitted to the vehicle, must be used. See also *Warning triangle* below.

The German motoring club (ADAC) operates a breakdown service, similar to that run by the AA, called the *Strassenwacht*. Patrol cars operate on motorways, on the more important roads and in urban areas. On motorways, patrols are notified by the motorway authorities, whom you can contact by using the emergency telephones. The direction of the nearest telephone is indicated by the point of the black triangle on posts alongside the motorways.

In addition, the *Deutscher Touring Automobil Club* (DTC), with which the AA is allied, also has a patrol service. The *Automobil Club of Germany* (AvD) and the *Auto Club Europa* (ACE) operate patrol services, but the AA is not associated with these clubs and details are not available.

British Army of the Rhine (BAOR)

Service personnel posted to Germany should consult their Standing Orders or Commanding Officer before taking a car to Germany or using it there. Although enjoying some privileges, they will be regarded to some extent as residents in the country, and tourist regulations (as outlined in this section) may not apply. For example, a tourist can use a warning triangle not strictly to the German regulations, but

vice personnel will break local regulations unless theirs conform.

A leaflet entitled *Importation of Motor Vehicles into Germany by Members of the British Forces* is available to AA members.

British Embassy/Consulates*

The British Embassy is located at 5300 Bonn 1, Friedrich-Ebert-Allee 77 ☎(0228) 234061, but the Embassy has no consular section. There are British Consulates in Berlin, Dusseldorf, Frankfurt/Main, Hamburg and München (Munich); there are British Consulates with Honorary Consuls in Bremen, Frieburg, Hanover, Kiel, Nürnberg (Nurembourg) and Stuttgart.

Children in cars

Children under 12 are not permitted to travel in a vehicle as front or rear-seat passengers unless they are using special seats or safety belts suitable for children.

Dimensions and weight restrictions

Private **cars** and **trailers** or **caravans** are restricted to the following dimensions – height, 4 metres; width, 2.50 metres; length, 12 metres. The maximum permitted overall length of vehicle/trailer or caravan combinations is 18 metres.

A fully-laden trailer without an adequate braking system must not weigh more than 37.5kg plus 50% of the weight of the towing vehicle. A fully-laden trailer with an adequate braking system must not weigh more than the towing vehicle.

Driving licence*

The minimum age at which a visitor may use a temporarily imported car or motorcycle is 17 years.

Emergency messages to tourists*

Emergency messages to tourists are broadcast daily on German radio.

Deutschlandfunk transmitting on 396.8 metres medium wave broadcasts these messages in German after the news at 16.00 and 23.00hrs between May and September.

*Additional information will be found in the European ABC at the front of the book.

Saarländischer Rundfunk transmitting on 211 metres medium wave broadcasts the messages in German at 05.00 and 01.00hrs throughout the year.

Emergency messages are also broadcast by a variety of regional radio stations transmitting on ultra-short wavelengths.

Lights*

Driving on sidelights only is prohibited. When fog, falling snow or rain substantially affect driving conditions, dipped headlights or fog lamps should be used even during daylight. The use of two fog lamps together with dipped headlamps in such conditions is required by law. However, rear fog lights only may be used when visibility is less than 50 metres (55yds).

Motoring clubs*

 The principal German motoring clubs are the **Allgemeiner Deutscher Automobil Club** (ADAC) which has its headquarters at 8000 München 70, Am Westpark 8, ☎(089) 76760 and the **Deutscher Touring Automobil Club** (DTC) whose headquarters are at 8000 München 60, Amalienburgstrasse 23 ☎(089) 8111048. Both clubs have offices in the larger towns, and office hours are 08.00–17.00hrs Mon–Fri. The ADAC also has offices at major frontier crossings. See the *Town Plan of Central München* within the gazetteer.

Motorways

A comprehensive motorway (*Autobahn*) network dominates the road system and takes most of the long-distance traffic. It is considered negligent to run out of petrol on a motorway, and the police can fine offending motorists up to *DM75*.

Orange badge scheme for disabled drivers*

In the Federal Republic, special parking places reserved for disabled drivers are indicated by a parking sign (white letter on blue panel) with the international disabled symbol added. Provided no other parking facilities are available within the immediate vicinity, badge holders may:

a. park for a maximum of three hours where

a parking prohibited sign (red rign and bars on blue background) is displayed. The time of arrival must be shown on the parking disc;

b. park beyond the permitted time where a limited duration zone sign (white panel, red ring and diagonal bar on blue background) is displayed;

c. park beyond the permitted time where a parking sign (white letter on blue panel) is displayed with an additional panel restricting parking time;

d. park during the permitted periods for loading and unloading in pedestrian zones;

e. park without charge or time limit at parking meters.

Parking*

Make sure you park in the direction of the traffic flow. Parking is forbidden in the following places: on a main road or one carrying fast-moving traffic; on or near tram lines; within 15 metres (50ft) of a bus or tram stop; above man-hole covers; on the left-hand side of the road (unless the road is one-way). A vehicle is considered to be parked if the driver has left it so that it cannot be immediately removed if required, or if it is stopped for more 3 minutes. When stopping is prohibited under all circumstances, this is indicated by an international sign. Parking meters, and special areas where parking discs are used, are indicated by signs which also show the permitted duration of parking. Disabled drivers may be granted special parking concessions; application should be made to the local traffic authority. Spending the night in a vehicle is tolerated for one night, provided there are no signs to the contrary and the vehicle is lit and parked in a lay-by. The sign showing an eagle in a green triangle (wild-life reserve) prohibits parking outside parking lots.

Petrol*

Credit cards Generally the major credit cards are accepted at all company owned filling stations.

Duty-free petrol In addition to the petrol in the vehicle tank, up to 10 litres in a can may be imported free of customs duty and tax.

Petrol (leaded) Super benzin (98 octane) grade.

Petrol (unleaded) is sold in Germany as Normal benzin (91 octane) and Super benzin

*Additional information will be found in the European ABC at the front of the book.

(95 and 98 octane) grades. These octane ratings are not indicated on the pumps, but in most cases the pumps dispensing unleaded petrol are marked *bleifrei* (lead-free).

Post information

Mail Postcards DM0.60; letters up to 20gm DM1.00.
Post offices There are 15,000 post offices in the Federal Republic. Opening hours are from 08.00–18.00hrs Monday to Friday and 08.00–12.00hrs Saturday. In some large towns, the Head Post Office is open 24hrs a day. Some small offices close for a break at noon.

Priority*

On pedestrian crossings (zebra crossings), pedestrians have the right of way over all vehicles except trams. Buses have priority when leaving public bus stops, and other vehicles must give way to a bus driver who has signalled an intention to leave the kerb.

Public holidays*

Official Public holidays in the Federal Republic for 1990 are given below. Epiphany, Corpus Christi, Assumption and All Saints' Day are not holidays throughout the Federal Republic.

January 1 (New Year's Day)
January 6†† (Epiphany)
April 13 (Good Friday)
April 16 (Easter Monday)
May 1 (May Day)
May 24 (Ascension Day)
June 4 (Whit Monday)
June 14 (Corpus Christi)
June 17† (Berlin Day)
August 15 (Assumption)
November 1 (All Saints' Day)
November 21 (Repentance Day)
December 25 (Christmas Day)
December 26 (Second day of Christmas)

††Saturday   †Sunday

Roads, including holiday traffic

The *Bundesstrassen* – or state roads – vary in quality. In the north and west and in the touring areas of the Rhine Valley, Black Forest and Bavaria, the roads are good and well-graded.
    Traffic at weekends increases considerably during the school holidays, which are from July to mid-September. In order to ease congestion, heavy lorries are prohibited on all roads at weekends from approximately mid-June to the end of August, and generally on all Sundays and Public holidays. See also *Road conditions* in the European ABC.

Road signs*

A blue rectangular sign with, for example, '70/110km' in white – indicates a recommended speed range.
    A blue rectangular sign with a white arrow pointing upwards and 'U' and a figure in white – indicates a diversion for motorway traffic.

Shopping hours

Generally, these are: *food shops* – from Monday to Friday 08.00–13.00 and 14.00–18.30hrs, Saturdays 07.00–13.00hrs; *department stores* – from Monday to Friday 09.00–18.00hrs, Saturday 09.00–14.00hrs. Some shops close for lunch between 13.00 and 15.00hrs.

Speed limits*

The speed limit in *built-up areas* is 50kph (31mph), unless otherwise indicated by signs. The beginning of a built-up area is indicated by the placename sign. *Outside built-up areas*, the limit for private cars is 100kph (62mph), unless otherwise signposted. Motorways (*Autobahnen*), dual-carriageways and roads with at least two marked lanes in each direction which are not specifically signposted, have a recommended speed limit at 130kph (81mph). Vehicles towing a caravan or trailer are limited to 80kph (49mph). All lower limits must be adhered to. Where indicated by a sign (circular, with white figures against a blue background) vehicles may **not** travel at a speed **lower** than that displayed.

Note Outside built-up areas, motor vehicles to which a special speed limit applies, as well as vehicles with trailers with a combined length of more than 7 metres (23ft), must keep sufficient distance from the preceding vehicle so that an overtaking vehicle may pull in.

Spiked or studded tyres

The use of *tyres* is not permitted on German registered vehicles. However, foreign registered vehicles may use them in a restricted zone near

*Additional information will be found in the European ABC at the front of the book.

the German/Austrian border on ordinary roads, not motorways.

Telephone*

Insert coin **after** lifting the receiver; the dialling tone is a continuous tone. When making calls to subscribers within the Federal Republic, precede the number with the relevant area code (shown in parentheses before the hotel/garage enquiry number in the gazetteer). Use three 10 **pfennig** coins for local calls and *DM*1 (Dial) or *DM*5 (Push-button) coins for national and international calls.
International callboxes have payphones marked 'International'.
Charges are based on units of time, 1 unit – 10.667 seconds, the cost is *DM*0.23. Many hotels and garages provide, as a service, direct line telephones, but charges are likely to be over double the public rate.

Telephone codes

UK to Germany	010 49
Germany to UK	00 44
Germany to Republic of Ireland	00 353
Germany to the USA	001

Traffic lights*

At some interesections with several lanes going in different directions, there are lights for each lane; watch the light arrow for your lane.

Warning triangle*

The use of a warning triangle is compulsory in the event of accident or breakdown. The triangle must be placed on the road behind the vehicle to warn following traffic of any obstruction: 100 metres (110yds) on ordinary roads and 200 metres (220yds) on motorways. Vehicles over 2,800kg must also carry a yellow flashing light.

Wheel chains

These must not be used on snow-free roads. In winter months, the ADAC hires out chains for cars and caravans. Chains can only be returned to ADAC offices, and then only during opening hours. On production of a valid AA membership card, chains may be hired at the following reduced charges.

Deposit	members (DM)	non-members (DM)
Matic brand	100	100

Hire charge per day (days of collection and return are both counted as whole days)

	members (DM)	non-members (DM)
Matic brand	5.00	7.00

If the chains are used, a fee of *DM*10.00 (members) and *DM*20.00 (non-members) is payable. If chains are lost or damaged, or their wear exceeds the normal, the full selling price is charged. If the deposit receipt is lost, the chains can be returned only to the station from which they were hired.

Chains are considered to have been used if the seal on the packaging has been removed. In this case, the hire charge is calculated on the basis of the fees for used chains for the whole period of hire, irrespective of the actual number of days in use. The maximum period of hire is 60 days. Reservations are not possible, and the ADAC does not dispatch the chains by post. Chains are made in several sizes, but as foreign-made tyres may be different, it is not guaranteed that the appropriate size will be available; in this case, alternative arrangements must be made. Further details may be obtained from the ADAC Head Office, Department 'Strassendienste Schneekettenverleih', Am Westpark 8, 8000 München 70 ☎(089) 76760. (No wheel chains are actually hired out from head office.) Speed must be restricted to 50kph (31mph) when using chains. See also *Cold-weather touring* in the European ABC.

*Additional information will be found in the European ABC at the front of the book.

ACCOMMODATION

The prices shown below are an average for each classification. Accommodation is likely to be more expensive in larger towns and some of the more popular tourist areas.

At the time of going to press, £1 *Sterling = DM3.11 and US$1 = DM1.87* but you should check the rate of exchange before your departure.

AVERAGE PRICES

	Single Room	Double Room	Breakfast	Lunch/Dinner
★★★★★	DM210–382	DM272–560	from DM18	from DM49
★★★★	DM158–213	DM213–303	DM18–24	DM25–61
★★★	DM143–162	DM168–231	DM15–17	DM21–51
★★	DM64–135	DM115–160	DM12–15	DM20–40
★	DM52–82	DM86–127	DM12–13	DM16–41

Abbreviations
pl   platz   str   strasse

AACHEN
Nordrhein-Westfalen
★★★★*Quellenhof* (SRS) Monheimsalle 52 ☎(0241)152081 tx 832864
⊷♨200 ☎ P50 Lift (⊡
Credit Cards ① ② ③ ⑤
★★★*Novotel* Am Europapl ☎(0241)1687-0 tx 832435
⊷♨119 P170 Lift (⊇
Credit Cards ① ② ③ ⑤
★★*Benelux* Franzstr 21-23 ☎(0241)22343
⊷♨33 ☎ P12 Lift (
Credit Cards ① ② ③ ④ ⑤
★★*Brabant* Stolberger Str 42 ☎(0241)500025
⊷♨24 ☎ P15 Lift.(
★★*Marschiertor* Wallstr 1-7 (n.rest)
☎(0241)31941
4 Jan-23 Dec
⊷♨50 Lift (
Credit Cards ① ② ③ ④ ⑤
★★*Stadt Koblenz* Leydelstr 2 (n.rest)
☎(0241)22241 & tx 832761
10 Jan-20 Dec
⊷♨16 ☎
Credit Cards ① ② ③ ⑤
★*Braun* Lütticher Str 517 ☎(0241)74535
:Rest closed Sat
rm13(♨5) ☎ P15
Credit Card ①
★*Lousberg* Saarstr 108 (n.rest) ☎(0241)20331
rm25(♨10) ☎ P5 Lift
Credit Cards ① ② ③ ⑤
⊷ *Kuckartz* Dresdner Str 20 ☎(0241) 503083 **P** Ren

ACHERN
Baden-Württemberg
★★★*Götz Sonne-Eintracht* Hauptstr 112 ☎(07841)6450 tx 752277
⊷♨55 ☎ P50 Lift (⊡ Mountain
Credit Cards ① ② ③ ⑤
★★★*Seehotel* ☎(07841)3011 tx 752240
Jan-Oct
⊷♨58 ☎ P80 Lift (⊇ Lake
Credit Cards ① ② ③ ④ ⑤

ACHIM
Niedersachsen
At ACHIM-UPHUSEN(5.5km NW)
★★★*Novotel* Bremer Kreuz Zum Klumoor ☎(04202)6086 tx 249440
⊷♨116 P130 Lift (⊇
Credit Cards ① ② ③ ⑤

ACHIM-UPHUSEN
See ACHIM

ADENAU
Rheinland-Pfalz
⊷ *H Gebauer* Im Bröl ☎(02691) 1889 **P** For

AHRWEILER
Rheinland-Pfalz
★*Stern* Marktpl 9 ☎(02641)34738
:Rest closed Mon
rm16(♨3) ☎

AIBLING, BAD
Bayern
★★*Lindner* Marienpl 5 ☎(08061)4050
rm32(⊷♨22) ☎ P18
Credit Cards ① ② ③ ⑤
★★*Schuhbräu* Rosenheimer Str 6-8 ☎(08061)2029
rm45(⊷♨42) P32 Lift ⊡ Mountain
Credit Cards ① ② ③ ⑤

ALPIRSBACH
Baden-Württemberg
⊷ *Karl Jautz* Hauptstr 29 ☎(07444) 2345 **P** For
At EHLENBOGEN(4km N)
★★*Adler* Hauptstr 1 ☎(07444)2215
Feb-Dec :Rest closed Wed
rm16(⊷♨11) ☎ P32 ∪ Mountain
Credit Cards ① ② ⑤

ALSFELD
Hessen
★*Schwalbennest* Pfarrwiesenweg 14 ☎(06631)5061
⊷♨31 ☎ P
⊷ *Hartman* Hersfelder Str 81 ☎(06631) 4044 Ope
⊷ *W Klöss* Grünberger Str 72-74 ☎(06631) 3005 **P** For

ALTENAHR
Rheinland-Pfalz
★★*Post* Brückenstr 2 ☎(02643)2098 tx 172643911
20 Dec-20 Nov
⊷♨55 A8rm P30 Lift ⊡ Mountain
Credit Cards ① ② ③ ⑤
At MAYSCHOSS(2km NE)
★★*Lochmühle* (BW) Bundesstr 62 ☎(02643)8080 tx 8651766
rm64(⊷♨62) ☎ P100 Lift (⊡
Credit Cards ① ② ③ ⑤

ALTENHELLEFELD
Nordrhein-Westfalen
★★★*Gut Funkenhof* ☎(02934)1012 tx 84277
⊷♨71 ☎ P55 (♘ ⊡ Mountain
Credit Cards ① ② ③ ⑤

ALTENKIRCHEN
Rheinland-Pfalz
⊷ *J Odenthal KG* Kölner Str 72-76 ☎(02681) 2611 **P** For

ALTÖTTING
Bayern
★★★*Post* (ROM) Kapellpl 2 ☎(08671)5040 tx 56962
⊷♨90 A28rm P10 Lift ⊡
Credit Cards ① ② ③ ④ ⑤

AMBERG
Bayern
★*Goldenes Lamm* Rathaus Str 6 ☎(09621)21041
:Rest closed Sat
rm24(♨5) ☎ P10
Credit Cards ① ② ③ ⑤
⊷ *Weiss* Bayreuther Str 26 ☎(09621) 62081 **P** For

ANDERNACH
Rheinland-Pfalz
★★*Rhein* Rheinpromenade ☎(02632)42240
Apr-Oct
rm26(♨25) ☎ P100 Lift
Credit Cards ① ② ③ ⑤
★*Anker* K-Adenauer Allee 21 ☎(02632)42907
Mar-Nov
rm27(♨26) P Lake
Credit Cards ① ② ③
⊷ *R Heinemann* Koblenzer Str 56 ☎(02632) 43016 **P** For
⊷ *E Kirsch* Fullscheuerweg 36 ☎(02632) 492401 **P** Ren
⊷ *Loehr* Koblenzer Str 77 ☎(02632) 43008 VW Aud

ARNSBERG
Nordrhein-Westfalen
★★★*Dorint-Sauerland* DPn Zu Den Drei Banken ☎(02932)
⊷♨165 ☎ P210 Lift (⊡
Credit Cards ① ② ③ ⑤

AROLSEN
Hessen
★★★*Dorint Schlosshotel Arolsen* Grosse Allee 1 ☎(05691)3091 tx 994521
⊷♨56 ☎ P50 Lift (⊡
Credit Cards ① ② ③ ⑤

ASCHAFFENBURG
Bayern
★★★*Aschaffenburger Hof* Frohsinnstr 11 ☎(06021)21441 tx 188736
⊷♨63 ☎ P60 Lift (
Credit Cards ① ② ③ ⑤

GERMANY

★★★*Romantik Hotel-Post* Goldbacherstr 19
☎(06021)21333 tx 4188736
⇴75 ⌂ P Lift ⌂
✎ Amberg Würzburger Str 67 ☎(06021) 91018 **P**
Fia Lan Alf DJ AR
✎ K Grundhoefer Würzburger Str 101 ☎(06021)
91028 Col
✎ P Thomas Würzburger Str 97 ☎(06021)
91021 **P** For

ASENDORF
See **JESTEBURG**

ASPERG
Baden-Württemberg
★★★**Adler** Stuttgarter Str 2 ☎(07141)63001 tx
7264603
⇴65 ⌂ P60 Lift ⌂ ⌂
Credit Cards ①②③④⑤

ASSMANNSHAUSEN
Hessen
See also RÜDESHEIM
★★**Anker** Rheinstr 5 ☎(06722)2912 tx 42179
15 Mar-15 Nov
⇴50 A20rm ⌂ P27 Lift
Credit Cards ①③⑤
★★**Café Post** Rheinufer Str 2A ☎(06722)2326
Mar-Nov
rm16(⇴10) ⌂ P10
Credit Cards ①②③④⑤
★★**Krone** Rheinuferstr 10 ☎(06722)2036 tx
413576
25 Mar-15 Nov
⇴53 ⌂ P40 Lift ⌂ ⌂ Mountain
Credit Cards ①③④⑤

ATTENDORN
Nordrhein-Westfalen
★★**Burg Schnellenberg** (GS) ☎(02722)6940 tx
876732
Closed Xmas & 3 wks Jan
⇴42 P96 ⌂ Mountain
Credit Cards ①②③⑤

AUGSBURG
Bayern
★★★★**Holiday Inn Turmhotel** Wittelsbacher Park
☎(0821)577087 tx 533225
⇴185 ⌂ P20 Lift ⌂ ⌂
Credit Cards ①②③④⑤
★★★**Drei Mohren** (SRS) Maximilianstr 40
☎(0821)510031 tx 53710
⇴107 ⌂ P45 Lift ⌂
Credit Cards ①②③⑤
★★**Ost** Fuggerstr 4-6 (n.rest) ☎(0821)33088 tx
533576
Closed 25 Dec-5 Jan
rm50(⇴46) Lift ⌂
Credit Cards ①②③⑤
★**Post** Fuggerstr 7 ☎(0821)36044
⇴50 ⌂ P6 ⌂ ⌂
Credit Cards ①②③④
✎ R Esst Meringer Str 58 ☎(0821) 63003 **P** For
✎ Listle Kriegshaberstr 58 ☎(0821) 403055 **P**
Ren

BACHARACH
Rheinland-Pfalz
★★**Altkölnischer Hof** Blucherstr 2 ☎(06743)1339
Apr-1 Nov
rm20(⇴19) ⌂ P9 Lift
Credit Cards ②③⑤

BAD
Each place preceded by 'Bad' is listed under the
name that follows it.

BADEN-BADEN
Baden-Württemberg
★★★★★**Brenner's Park** Schillerst 6
☎(07221)3530 tx 781261
⇴100 ⌂ P35 Lift ⌂ ⌂
Credit Cards ①②⑤
★★★**Badischer Hof** (SRS) Lange Str 47
☎(07221)22827 tx 781121
⇴140 ⌂ Lift ⌂ ⌂ ⌂
Credit Cards ①②③④⑤
★★★★**Europäischer Hof** (SRS) Kaiserallee 2
☎(07221)23561 tx 781188
⇴140 ⌂ P30 Lift ⌂
Credit Cards ①②③④⑤
★★★★**Holiday Inn Sporthotel** Falkenstr 2
☎(07221)2190 tx 781255
⇴121 ⌂ P70 Lift ⌂ ⌂ Mountain
Credit Cards ①②③④⑤
★★★**Golf** Fremersbergstr 113 ☎(07221)23691 tx
781174
Apr-Oct
⇴85 ⌂ P45 Lift ⌂ ⌂ ⌂ Mountain
Credit Cards ①②③④⑤
★★★**Hirsch** Hirschstr 1 ☎(07221)23896 tx
781193
rm59(⇴58) ⌂ Lift ⌂
Credit Cards ①②③④⑤
★★★**Waldhotel Fischkultur** Gaisbach 91
☎(07221)71025
Mar-10 Dec
rm30(⇴25) A14rm ⌂ P20 Lift Mountain
Credit Cards ①②
★★**Allee-Hotel-Bären** Hauptstr 36
☎(07221)7020-0 tx 781291
⇴81 ⌂ P41 Lift ⌂
Credit Cards ①②③⑤
★★**Markt** Marktpl 17 ☎(07221)22747
:Rest closed Sun & Wed
rm26(⇴12) P5 Lift
Credit Cards ①②③⑤
★**Bischoff** Römerpl 2 (n.rest) ☎(07221)22378
Feb-15 Dec
⇴21 ⌂ P2 Lift
Credit Cards ①②③④⑤
★**Römerhof** Sofienstr 25 (n.rest) ☎(07221)23415
Feb-15 Dec
⇴27 Lift
Credit Cards ①②③④⑤
✎ H Bürkle Malschbacher Str 4-6 ☎(07221)
7418 **P** For Tal
✎ H P Nagel Lange Str 104 ☎(07221) 22672 AR
Dat
✎ E Scheibel Hubertustr 19 ☎(07221) 62005 For
At **MUMMELSEE**(29km S)
★★**Berghotel Kandel** ☎(07221)6001
20 Dec-10 Nov
rm37(⇴35) A23rm P
Credit Cards ①②③

BADENWEILER
Baden-Württemberg
★★★★**Römerbad** Schlosspl 1 ☎(07632)700 tx
772933
⇴107 ⌂ P50 Lift ⌂ ⌂ ⌂ Mountain
Credit Cards ②③
★★★**Park** (BW) E-Eisenlohrstr 6
☎(07632)7763210
Mar-15 Nov
rm75(⇴73) A25rm ⌂ P40 Lift ⌂ ⌂ ⌂
Credit Cards ①②③
★★★**Sonne** (ROM) Moltkestr 4 ☎(07632)7508-0
Feb-Nov :Rest closed Wed
⇴43 ⌂ P17
Credit Cards ①②③⑤

BAMBERG
Bayern
★★★**Bamberger Hof-Bellevue** Schonleinspl 4
☎(0951)22216 tx 662867
:Rest closed Sun pm
⇴48 P Lift ⌂
Credit Cards ①②③⑤
★★★**National** Luitpoldstr 37 ☎(0951)24112 tx
662916
⇴41 ⌂ P5 Lift ⌂
Credit Cards ①②③④⑤
★★**Messerschmitt** (ROM) Langestr 41
☎(0951)27866
⇴14 ⌂ P4
Credit Cards ①②③⑤
★**Straub** Ludwigstr 31 (n.rest) ☎(0951)25171
rm38(⇴14) ⌂ P14 ⌂
At **BUG**(4km S)
★★**Buger Hof** Am Regnitzufer 1 ☎(0951)56054
rm32(⇴14) ⌂ P

BASSUM
Niedersachsen
✎ H Holtorf Bremer Str 47 ☎(04241) 2356 M/C
P For

BAYREUTH
Bayern
★★★**Bayerischer Hof** Bahnhofstr 14
☎(0921)22081 tx 642737
:Rest closed Sun & 1-21 Jan
⇴61 ⌂ P32 Lift ⌂ ⌂
Credit Cards ①②③⑤

BAYRISCHZELL
Bayern
★★**Alpenrose** Schlierseestr 100 ☎(08023)620
Dec-5 Nov
⇴50 A10rm ⌂ P200 ⌂ Mountain

BERCHTESGADEN
Bayern
★★★**Geiger** (Relais et Châteaux) Stanggasse
☎(08652)5055 tx 56222
⇴49 ⌂ P Lift ⌂ ⌂ Mountain
Credit Cards ①②③⑤
★★**Königliche Villa** (GS) Kalbersteinstr 4
☎(08652)5097
⇴20 P20 Mountain
Credit Cards ①②③④⑤
✎ H Buchwinkler Bahnhofstr 21 ☎(08652) 4087
P Aud Por VW
✎ G Köppl Hindenburg Allee 1 ☎(08652) 2615
M/C **P** Aud VW

BERG
Bayern
At **LEONI**(1km S)
★★★**Dorint Starnberger See** Assenbucher Str 44
☎(08151)5060 tx 526483
⇴71 P40 Lift ⌂ ⌂ Beach Lake
Credit Cards ①②③⑤

BERGEN
Niedersachsen
★**Kohlmann** Lukenstr 6 ☎(05051)3014
:Rest closed Mon lunch
rm14(⇴13) ⌂ P50
Credit Cards ①②③⑤

BERGZABERN, BAD
Rheinland-Pfalz
★★★**Park** Kurtalstr 83 ☎(06343)2415
Closed 15 Jan-20 Feb
⇴40 ⌂ P60 Lift ⌂ ⌂ Mountain
Credit Cards ①③⑤

BERLIN

Berlin is one of the most exciting places to visit in Europe. There is a buzz in the air which no one can ignore, a vibrant energy which stems as much from the city as the people themselves. Berlin is a big city of contrasts in every sense of the word. One third of it has peaceful havens of parks, forests and lakes, but the Kürfurstendamm packs no fewer than 1,000 shops, boutiques, restaurants and galleries into an elegant half-mile. Museums and art galleries cater for every interest and taste, and there are palaces and playgounds, a circus and a world-famous zoo.

Following the exciting and historic events of 1989, that brought down the barriers which once divided the city, visiting East Berlin is easier than ever. It provides yet another contrast, for here you can gain an impression of 'old' Berlin by strolling along the Unter den Linden. You can enjoy a coffee in Alexanderplatz and visit the fascinating Pergamon Museum.

Back in the West the nightlife stays open as long as you can stay up. Entertainment goes on round the clock and offers opera and theatres, cinemas and cabarets and nightclubs ranging from the cosy to the erotic.

EATING OUT One of West Berlin's most popular mid-priced restaurants is *Hecker's Deele*, close to the lively Kürfurstendamm in Grolmannstrasse. Here you can dine on hearty Westphalian dishes such as knuckle of pork. For vegetarian cuisine the *Thurnagel*, in Gneisenaustrasse, is reliable and fun.

BERLIN

★★★★★*Bristol Kempinski Berlin* Kurfürstendamm 27 ☎(030)881091 tx 1853553
✦♠334 ☎ P150 Lift ☒
Credit Cards ①②③④⑤

★★★★★*Inter-Continental Berlin* Budapester Str 2 ☎(030)26020 tx 184380
✦♠600 ☎ P300 Lift ☒
Credit Cards ①②③④⑤

★★★★*Ambassador* Bayreuther Str 42/43 ☎(030)21902 tx 184259
✦♠199 Lift ☾ ☒
Credit Cards ①②③④⑤

★★★★*Berlin* Lützowplatz 17 ☎(030)26050 tx 184332
✦♠537 ☎ P170 Lift ☾
Credit Cards ①②③④⑤

★★★★*Berlin Plaza* Knesebeckstr 63 ☎(030)884130 tx 184181
✦♠131 ☎ P60 Lift ☾
Credit Cards ①②③⑤

★★★★*Franke* A-Achilles Str 57 ☎(030)8921097 tx 184857
rm69(✦♠65) ☎ P15 Lift ☾ ☒
Credit Cards ①②③⑤

★★★★*Ibis* Messendamm 10 ☎(030)302011 tx 182882
✦♠191 P100 Lift ☾
Credit Cards ①②③⑤

★★★★*Savoy* (BW) Fasanenstr 9-10,Charlottenburg ☎(030)311030 tx 184292
✦♠132 ☎ P200 Lift ☾
Credit Cards ①②③④⑤

★★★★*Schweizerhof Berlin* Budapester Str 21-31 ☎(030)26960 tx 185501
✦♠430 P60 Lift ☾
Credit Cards ①②③④⑤

★★★*Alsterhof* Augsburger Str 5 ☎(030)219960 tx 183484
✦♠144 ☎ P20 Lift ☾ ☒
Credit Cards ①②③⑤

★★★*Arosa* Lietzenburgerstr 79-81 ☎(030)880050 tx 183397
✦♠90 P24 Lift ☾ ☒
Credit Cards ①②③⑤

★★★*Hamburg* Landgrafen Str 4 ☎(030)269161 tx 184974
✦♠240 ☎ P40 Lift ☾
Credit Cards ①②③⑤

★★★*Lichtburg* Paderbornerstr 10 ☎(030)8918041 tx 184208

✦♠63 P7 Lift
Credit Cards ①②③⑤

★★★*Novotel* Ohmctr 4-6 ☎(030)381061 tx 181415
✦♠119 P80 Lift ☾
Credit Cards ①②③④⑤

★★★*Queens* ADAC Haus,Guntzelstr 14 (n.rest) ☎(030)870241 tx 182948
✦♠108 ☎ P Lift ☾
Credit Cards ①②③④⑤

★★★*Zoo* Kurfürstendamm 25 (n.rest) ☎(030)883091 tx 183835
✦♠138 ☎ P40 Lift ☾
Credit Cards ①②③⑤

★★*Astrid* Bleibtreustr 20,Charlottenburg ☎(030)8815959
rm11(♠6) Lift

★★*Charlottenburger Hof* Stuttgarter Pl 14˙ ☎(030)3244819
rm45(✦♠15) P30 ☾

✦❀ *Butenuth* Forckenbeckstr 94,Wilmersdorf ☎(030) 33090840 For

✦❀ *W Hinz* Naumannstr 79 ☎(030) 7843051 Hon Lan Rov

BERNKASTEL-KUES
Rheinland-Pfalz

★★*Burg-Landshut* Gestade 11,Bernkastel ☎(06531)3019 tx 4721565
1 Mar-15 Dec & 27 Dec :Rest closed Jan & Feb
rm30(✦♠28) ☎ P200 Mountain
Credit Cards ①②③⑤

★*Drei Könige* Bahnofstr 1,Bernkastel (n.rest) ☎(06531)2035
Apr-Dec
✦♠35 ☎ P18 Lift Mountain Lake
Credit Cards ①②③⑤

★*Post* Gestade 17,Bernkastel ☎(06531)2022 tx 4721569
:Rest closed 4-28 Jan
✦♠42 ☎ P12 Lift Mountain
Credit Cards ①②③⑤

★*Sonnenlay* Hauptstr 47,Wehlen (4km NW) ☎(06531)6496
✦♠11 P12

★*Graacher Tor* ☎(06531)2566
Apr-Oct
rm33(✦♠24) A12rm P

BETZDORF
Rheinland-Pfalz

✦❀ *F Grab* Kölner Str ☎(02741) 23040 **P** For

BIBERACH AN DER RISS
Baden-Württemberg

★★★*Reith* Ulmer Str ☎(07351)7828
5 Jan-19 Dec
rm37(✦♠32) ☎ P28 Lift ☾
Credit Cards ②⑤

✦❀ *Schwaben* Steigmuhlstr 34 ☎(07351) 7878 **P** For Hon

BIELEFELD
Nordrhein-Westfalen

★★★*Novotel* Am Johannisberg 5 ☎(0521)124051 tx 932991
✦♠119 P100 Lift ☾ ☒
Credit Cards ①②③⑤

★★*Waldhotel Brand's Busch* Furtwangler Str 52 ☎(0521)24093 tx 532835
✦♠60 ☎ P Lift
Credit Cards ①②③⑤

✦❀ *S Tiekotter* Detmolder Str 661 ☎(0521) 80158 **P** For

BIERSDORF
See **BITBURG**

BIESSENHOFEN
See **KAUFBEUREN**

BINGEN
Rheinland-Pfalz

★★★*Rheinhotel Starkenburger Hof* Rheinkai 1-2 ☎(06721)14341
Feb-1 Dec
rm30(✦♠24) ☎ P ☾
Credit Cards ①②③④⑤

✦❀ *Pieroth* Mainzerstr 439

BIRKENFELD
Baden-Württemberg

✦❀ *P Wiegand* Wasserschieder Str 24 ☎(06782) 1846 **P** For

BISCHOFSMAIS
Bayern

★★★*Wastlsäge* (BW) Lina-Mueller-Weg 3,Wastlsäge ☎(09920)216 tx 69158
15 Dec-Oct
✦♠90 Lift ☾ ☒

BITBURG
Rheinland-Pfalz

★*Mosella* Karenweg 11 ☎(06561)3147
rm16(✦♠6) ☎ P5

✦❀ *Auto Jegen* Saarstr 46 ☎(06561) 1054 Maz

✦❀ *C Metzger* Mötscherstr 49 ☎(06561) 7004 Alf

At BIERSDORF(12km NW)

★★★**Dorint Sporthotel Südeifel** Am Stausee
Bitburg ☎(06569)841 tx 4729607
⊷⋔159 A59rm P200 Lift ℂ ℴ ⊡ Lake
Credit Cards ①②③⑤

BLANKENHEIM
Nordrhein-Westfalen

★★**Schlossblick** Nonnenbacher Weg 2-4
☎(02449)238 tx 833631
22 Dec-1 Nov :Rest closed Wed
rm33(⋔23) P Lift ⊡
Credit Cards ①②③⑤

BÖBLINGEN
Baden-Württemberg

★★★**Novotel** O-Lilienthal Str 18 ☎(07031)23071
tx 7265438
⊷⋔118 Lift ℂ ⊐
Credit Cards ①②③④⑤

BOCHOLT
Nordrhein-Westfalen

☙ **Tepasse & Co** Dinxperloerstr 285 ☎(02871)
43989 M/C P Nis

BOCHUM
Nordrhein-Westfalen

★★★**Novotel** am Stadionsring 22 ☎(0234)594041
tx 825429
⊷⋔118 P70 Lift ℂ ⊐
Credit Cards ①②③④⑤

★★**Arcade** Universitatstr 3 ☎(0234)33311 tx
825447
⊷⋔157 P60 Lift ℂ
Credit Cards ①③

BONN *Nordrhein-Westfalen*

See Plan page 202 *Population*286,000 *Local Tourist Office*Rathaus Bonn-Bad Godesberg, Kurfürstenstr 2-3
☎(0228) 773927

Bonn, federal capital of West Germany, is situated in North Rhineland-Westphalia, 16 miles south-south-east of Cologne, on the left bank of the Rhine. The archbishops of Cologne resided here from 1265 to 1794 and the town's beautiful minster (*Münster*), dating from the 11th century, contrasts with extensive modern buildings of the federal parliament and ministries.

The University of Bonn was re-established here in 1818 and is housed in the former electoral palace; in 1934 the agricultural college of Bonn-Poppelsdorf was incorporated with it.

Beethoven was born in this city in 1770, at Bonngasse 20, now a museum, and Schumann spent his last years in Sebastianstrasse. Among Bonn's other attractions are the Baroque Jesu Church, 13th-century Remigius Church, the 18th-century castle, *Poppelsdorfer Schloss*, and the *Alter Zoll*, a bastion overlooking the Rhine.

EATING OUT Bonn has a variety of restaurants serving Chinese, French and German specialities. There are also numerous cafés and wine-bars, notably the *Weinkrüger*, a historic wine-bar in Mauspfad. Located in the heart of Bonn's old town district, the *Schaarschmidt*, in Brüdergasse, serves excellent German cuisine. *Zum Kapellchen*, in the same street, is an atmospheric wine tavern.

BONN
Nordrhein-Westfalen

★★★★**Bristol** Prinz-Albert-Str 2 ☎(0228)26980 tx
8869661
⊷⋔116 ☎ P10 Lift ℂ ⊡ Mountain
Credit Cards ①②③⑤

★★★★**Pullman Königshof** Adenauerallee 9
☎(0228)26010 tx 886535
⊷⋔137 P150 Lift ℂ
Credit Cards ①②③④⑤

★★★**Novotel Bonn Hardtberg** Konrad-Adenauer-Damm,Max-Habermann Str 2 ☎(0228)52010 tx
886743
⊷⋔142 ☎ P100 Lift ℂ ⊐
Credit Cards ①②③④⑤

★★**Beethoven** Rheingasse 26 ☎(0228)631411 tx
886467
:Rest closed Sat
rm60(⊷⋔54) ☎ P10 Lift ℂ
Credit Cards ①②③⑤

★★**Bergischer Hof** Munsterpl 23 ☎(0228)633441
rm28(⊷⋔25) Lift

★★**Mozart** Mozartstr 1 ☎(0228)659071
rm42(⊷⋔25) P Lift ℂ
Credit Cards ①②⑤

Auto-Kumpel Bonner Talweg 319-325 ☎(0228)
232061 P AR Dat DJ LR

☙ **Auto-Mahlberg** K-Frowein Str 2 ☎0228
636656 All makes

At GODESBERG, BAD(7km SW road 9)

★★★*Godesberg* Godesberg 5 ☎(0228)31607 tx
885503
⊷⋔22 P ℂ
Credit Cards ①②③⑤

★★★**Insel** Theaterpl 5-7 ☎(0228)364082 tx
885592
⊷⋔66 P32 Lift ℂ
Credit Cards ①②③④⑤

★★★*Park* am Kurpark 1 ☎(0228)363081 tx
885463
6 Jan-22 Dec :Rest closed Wed
rm52(⊷⋔46) ☎ P20 Lift ℂ
Credit Card ①

★★★**Rheinhotel Dressen** Rheinstr 45-49
☎(0228)82020 tx 885417
⊷⋔68 ☎ P310 Lift ℂ Mountain
Credit Cards ①②③⑤

★★**Rheinland** Rheinalle 17 ☎(0228)353087
rm45(⊷⋔40) P50 ℂ
Credit Cards ①②③⑤

At RÖTTGEN(7km S on 257)

★★★*Bonn* Reichsstr 1 ☎(0228)251021 tx
8869505
⊷⋔43 ☎ P150
Credit Cards ①②③⑤

BONNDORF
Baden-Württemberg

★★**Schwarzwald** Rothausstr 7 ☎(07703)421
15 Dec-15 Nov
⊷⋔67 A27rm ☎ P36 Lift ⊡
Credit Cards ①②③④⑤

★**Germania** Martinstr 66 ☎(07703)281
:Rest closed Mon
rm8(⊷⋔4) P20

BOPPARD
Rheinland-Pfalz

★★★**Bellevue** (BW) Rheinallee 41-42
☎(06742)1020 tx 426310
⊷⋔95 Lift ℂ ℴ ⊡ Sea
Credit Cards ①②③⑤

★★★**Klostergut Jakobsberg** (12km N via B9 to
Spay) ☎(06742)3061 tx 426323
⊷⋔110 P200 Lift ℂ ℴ ℴ
Credit Cards ①②③⑤

★★**Ebertor** Heerstr (B9) ☎(06742)1020 tx
426310

Apr-Oct
⊷⋔66 ☎ P54 ℂ ℴ
Credit Cards ①②③⑤

★★**Europe** Mainzer Str 4 ☎(06742)5088
⊷⋔84 ☎ P45 Lift Mountain

★★*Günther* Rheinallee 40 (n.rest) ☎(06742)2335
15 Jan-16 Dec
rm19(⊷⋔18) P Lift

★★*Rheinlust* Rheinallee 27-30 ☎(06742)3001 tx
426319
15 Apr-Oct
rm91(⊷⋔76) A38rm ☎ P20 Lift ℂ
Credit Cards ①②③⑤

★**Hunsrücker Hof** Steinstr 26 ☎(06742)2433
⊷⋔23 A2rm
Credit Card ①

BRAUBACH
Rheinland-Pfalz

★**Hammer** Untermarktstr 15 ☎(02627)336
Closed Jan-15 Feb:Rest closed Thurs
⊷⋔10 ☎ P5
Credit Cards ①②⑤

BRAUNLAGE
Niedersachsen

★★★★**Maritim Berghotel** am Pfaffensteig
☎(05520)3051 tx 96261
⊷⋔300 ☎ P400 Lift ℂ ℴ ℴ ⊐ Mountain
Credit Cards ①②③⑤

★★**Tanne** (ROM) Herzog-Wilhelm Str 8
☎(05520)1034
⊷⋔13 A10rm ☎ P25 Mountain
Credit Cards ①②③④⑤

BRAUNSCHWEIG (BRUNSWICK)
Niedersachsen

★★★★**Mercure Atrium** Berliner Pl 3
☎(0531)70080 tx 952576
⊷⋔130 ☎ P250 Lift ℂ
Credit Cards ①②③

BONN

1	★★★★	Bristol
2	★★★★	Pullman Königshof
3	★★★	Bonn (At Röttgen)
4	★★★	Godesberg (At Godesberg, Bad)
5	★★★	Insel (At Godesberg, Bad)
6	★★★	Novotel Bonn Hardtberg
7	★★★	Park (At Godesberg, Bad)
8	★★★	Rheinhotel Dressen (At Godesberg, Bad)
10	★★	Beethoven
11	★★	Bergischer Hof
12	★★	Mozart
13	★★	Rheinland (At Godesberg, Bad)

★★★**Forsthaus** Hamburgerstr 72 ☎(0531)32801
rm50(⊷♠29) ☎ P30 Lift 《
Credit Cards ①②③⑤

★★**Mövenpick** (Mövenpick) Welfenhof
☎(0531)48170 tx 952777
⊷♠22 ☎ P Lift 《
Credit Cards ①②③⑤

★★**Frühlings** Bankpl 7 ☎(0531)49317
⊷♠65 Lift 《
Credit Cards ①②③⑤

✎ Opel Dürkop Helmstedter Str 60 ☎(0531)
703-0 Ope

BREISACH
Baden-Württemberg

★★★**Münster** Münsterbergstr 23 ☎(07667)7071
tx 772687
Closed 6-21 Jan
⊷♠42 ☎ P Lift 《 ⊡
Credit Cards ①②③⑤

BREISIG, BAD
Rheinland-Pfalz

★**Vater & Sohn** Zehnerstr 78 ☎(02633)9148
rm7(⊷♠3) P50
Credit Cards ①②③⑤

BREITNAU
Baden-Württemberg

★★★**Kreuz** Dorfstr 1 ☎(07652)1388
20 Dec-2 Nov
⊷♠17 ☎ P

BREITSCHEID
See **DÜSSELDORF**

BREMEN
Bremen

★★★★**Bremen Park** im Bürgerpark
☎(0421)34080 tx 244343
⊷♠150 A52rm ☎ P Lift 《 Lake
Credit Cards ①②③⑤

★★★★**Mercure Columbus** Bahnhofspl 5-7
☎(0421)14161 tx 244688
rm152(⊷♠147) ☎ Lift 《
Credit Cards ①②③⑤

★★★**Überseehotel** am Markt-Wachtstr 27-29
☎(0421)36010 tx 246501
⊷♠126 Lift 《
Credit Cards ①②③④⑤

★★★**Queens Moat House** (QM) A-Bebel Allee 4
☎(0421)23870 tx 244560
⊷♠144 P150 Lift 《
Credit Cards ①②③⑤

✎ *Auto Handelshaus* Stresemannstr 9 ☎(0421)
499040 P For

At **BRINKUM**(4km S)

★★**Atlas** G-Daimler-Str 3,2805 Gtuhr I
☎(0421)874037
⊷♠30 ☎ P50
Credit Cards ①②③④⑤

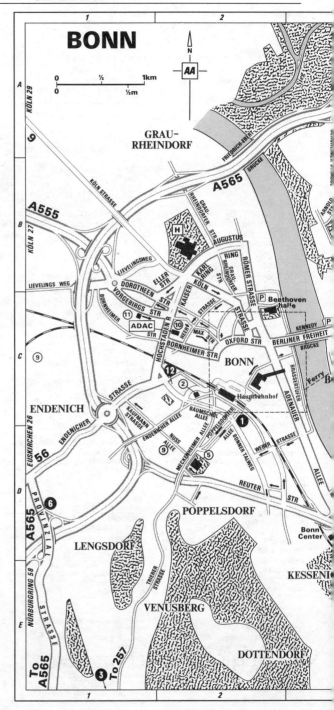

BONN

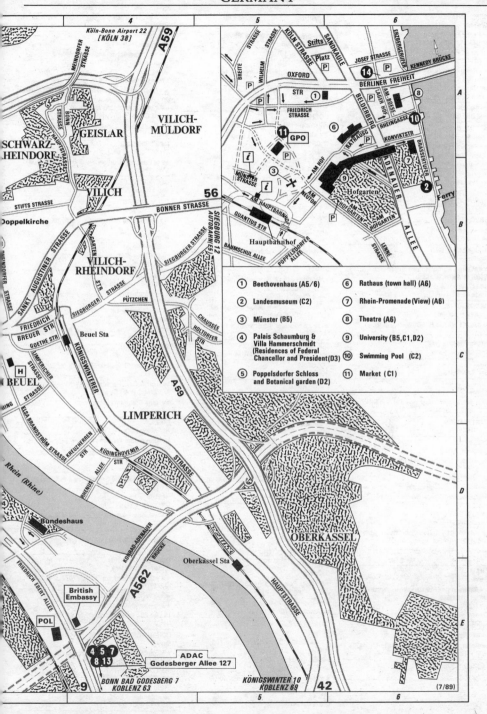

1. Beethovenhaus (A5/6)
2. Landesmuseum (C2)
3. Münster (B5)
4. Palais Schaumburg & Villa Hammerschmidt (Residences of Federal Chancellor and President)(D3)
5. Poppelsdorfer Schloss and Botanical garden (D2)
6. Rathaus (town hall) (A6)
7. Rhein-Promenade (View) (A6)
8. Theatre (A6)
9. University (B5,C1,D2)
10. Swimming Pool (C2)
11. Market (C1)

Köln-Bonn Airport 22 [KÖLN 38]

VILICH-MÜLDORF

GEISLAR

SCHWARZ-HEINDORF

VILICH

Doppelkirche

STIFTS STRASSE

MEINDORFER STRASSE

BONN STRASSE

HAUPTSTRASSE

BONNER STRASSE

56

SIEGBURG 12 AUTOBAHN E51

SIEGBURGER STRASSE

VILICH-RHEINDORF

SANKT AUGUSTINER STRASSE

WENDORFER STRASSE

SIEGBURGER STR

PÜTZCHEN

CHAUSSEE

HOLTORFER STR

FRIEDRICH BREUER STR

GOETHE STR

Beul Sta

KÖNIGSWINTERER

LIMPRICHER STRASSE

H

BEUEL

KÖNIGSWINTERER

A 59

ELSA BRANDSTRÖM STRASSE

KREUZHERREN STR

KÜDINGHOVENER STR

RHENUS ALLEE

LIMPERICH

STRASSE

Rhein (Rhine)

Bundeshaus

KONRAD-ADENAUER BRÜCKE

A 562

Oberkassel Sta

OBERKASSEL

HAUPTSTRASSE

FRIEDRICH EBERT ALLEE

British Embassy

POL

4 5 7 8 13

ADAC
Godesberger Allee 127

9

BONN BAD GODESBERG 7
KOBLENZ 63

KÖNIGSWINTER 10
KOBLENZ 69

42

Stifts Platz

KÖLN STRASSE

STRASSE

SANDKAULE

ERZBERGERUFER

KENNEDY BRÜCKE

BREITE

WILHELM

OXFORD

STR

JOSEF STRASSE

BERLINER FREIHEIT

FRIEDRICH STRASSE

GPO 11

AM BASEL

ADENAUER HOF

BELDERBERG

RHEINGASSE

8

10

A

MÜNSTER STRASSE

i

3

i

AM HOF

RATHAUS

6

7

BRASSERUFER

KONVIKTSTR

2

Ferry

AM NEDTON

9

University

Hofgarten

AM HAUPTBAHNHOF

QUANTIUS STR

Hauptbahnhof

BAHNMSCHUL ALLEE

POPPELSDORFER ALLEE

AM HOFGARTEN

AM HOFGARTEN

ADENAUER ALLEE

LENNE STRASSE

B

C

D

E

14

(7/89)

BREMERHAVEN
Bremen

★★★**Nordsee-Hotel-Naber** Theodor-Heuss-Pl
☎(0471)48770 tx 238881
⛽99 🏠 P30 Lift ℂ
Credit Cards 1 2 3 4 5

★★**Haverkamp** Prager Str 34 ☎(0471)48330 tx
238679
⛽108 🏠 P49 Lift ℂ 🖃
Credit Cards 1 2 3 5

BRINKUM
See **BREMEN**

BRODENBACH
Rheinland-Pfalz

★★**Peifer** Moselstr 69 ☎(02605)756
Closed 20-30 Dec
rm29 P100 Lift 🖃 Mountain
Credit Cards 1 2 5

★★*Post* Rhein-Mosel-Str 21 ☎(02605)3048
Apr-11 Nov
rm30(⛽16) A10rm 🏠 P30 Mountain Lake
Credit Cards 1 2 3 5

BRUCHSAL
Baden-Württemberg

☎ *Hetzel* Murgstr 12 ☎(07251) 2283 **P** AR

BRÜCKENAU, BAD
Bayern

★★★**Dorint Kurhotel** Heinrich-von-Bibra-Str 13
☎(09741)850 tx 9741810
⛽147 A31rm 🏠 P200 Lift ℂ 🔍 🖃
Credit Cards 1 2 3 5

BRUNSBÜTTEL
Schleswig-Holstein

At **SANKT MICHAELISDONN**(13km N)

★★★**Ringhotel Brünsbüttel** Westerstr 15-19
☎(04852)566 tx 28625
rm93(⛽75) 🏠 P110 ℂ 🖃

BUG
See **BAMBERG**

BÜHL
Baden-Württemberg

☎ **H Schwoerer** Industriege biet Sud,R-Bosch-Str
7 ☎(07223) 25444 **P** DJ LR Rov

CARTHAUSEN
See **HALVER**

CELLE
Niedersachsen

★★★**Celler Hof** Stechbahn 11 ☎(05141)28061 tx
925117
rm61(⛽58) 🏠 Lift ℂ
Credit Cards 1 2 3 5

★★**Hannover** Wittinger Str 56 ☎(05141)35014 tx
925117
⛽13 🏠 P15
Credit Card 1

☎ *Von Maltzan & Trebeljahr* Stadtausgang B3
☎(05141) 3921 For

☎ *W Friedrich* Wiesenstr 22 ☎(05141) 1057 M/C
P AR Col

CHAM
Bayern

★★★**Randsberger Hof** Randsbergerhofstr 15
☎(09971)126669
rm84(⛽66) 🏠 P120 Lift ℂ 🗻
Credit Cards 1 2 5

CLOPPENBURG
Niedersachsen

☎ *Eggers* Industrierign-Emstekerfeld ☎(04471)
6674 **P** For

COBBENRODE
See **ESLOHE**

COBURG
Bayern

★★**Blankenburg** Rosenauer Str 30
☎(09561)75005
⛽36 🏠 P37 Lift ℂ 🖃 🗻
Credit Cards 1 2 3 5

★★*Goldener Anker* Rosengasse 14
☎(09561)95027
:Rest closed on Sun
⛽60 🏠 P20 Lift 🖃
Credit Cards 1 2 3 5

COCHEM
Rheinland-Pfalz

★★**Alte Thorschenke** (GT) Brückenstr 3
☎(02671)7059
15 Mar-5 Jan
rm45(⛽35) 🏠 P8 Lift ℂ
Credit Cards 1 2 3 5

★★**Brixiade** Uferstr 13 ☎(02671)3015
⛽40 🏠 P10 Lift
Credit Card 2

★★**Germania** Moselpromenade 1 ☎(02671)261 tx
869422
Feb-Dec :Rest closed Wed in winter
⛽15 🏠 P8 Lift
Credit Cards 1 2 3 5

★★**Hafen** Uferstr & Zehnthaustr ☎(02671)8474
rm31(⛽30) A15rm 🏠 P15
Credit Cards 1 2 5

☎ *Hendriks* Jahnstr 8 (n.rest) ☎(02671)7361
⛽12 P Mountain
Credit Cards 1 2 5

☎ *Autohof Cochem* Sehler Anlagen 53
☎(02671) 8426 Ope

☎ *M J Schneider* Industriegebiet ☎(02671) 4078
M/C **P** For

CÖLBE
See **MARBURG AN DER LAHN**

COLOGNE
See **KÖLN**

CONSTANCE
See **KONSTANZ**

CRAILSHEIM
Baden-Württemberg

★★**Post-Faber** Langestr 2-4 ☎(07951)8038 tx
74318
⛽75 A8rm 🏠 P28 Lift ℂ
Credit Cards 1 2 3 4 5

CREGLINGEN
Baden-Württemberg

★★**Gasthof Krone** Hauptstr 12 ☎(07933)558
Feb-15 Dec :Rest closed Mon
rm25(⛽14) A17rm 🏠 P10

CUXHAVEN
Niedersachsen

★★★**Donners** Seedeich 2 ☎(04721)5090 tx
232152
⛽86 🏠 P100 Lift ℂ 🖃 Sea
Credit Cards 1 2 3 5

DACHAU
Bayern

★★★**Götz** Pollnstr 6 ☎(08131)21061
⛽38 🏠 P20 Lift 🖃
Credit Cards 1 2

☎ *Autohaus Till* ☎(08131) 1644 For

DARMSTADT
Hessen

★★★★**Maritim Darmstadt** Rheinstr 105
☎(06151)878-0 tx 419625
⛽352 P150 Lift ℂ 🖃
Credit Cards 1 2 3 4 5

★★**Weinmichel** Schleiermacherstr 10/12
☎(06151)26822 tx 419275
⛽74 P15 Lift ℂ
Credit Cards 1 2 3 4 5

☎ *J Wiest* Riedstr 5 ☎(06151) 8640 VW Audi
Porsche

DAUN
Rheinland-Pfalz

★★★**Kurfürstliches Amtshaus** (BW) Auf dem
Burgberg ☎(06592)3031 tx 4729310
⛽42 P40 Lift 🖃 Mountain
Credit Cards 1 2 3 5

★★**Hommes** Wirichstr 9 ☎(06592)568 tx 4729301
20 Dec-15 Nov
⛽42 P45 Lift 🖃 Mountain
Credit Cards 1 2 3 5

★★**Stadt Daun** Leopoldstr 14 ☎(06592)3555 tx
4729311
⛽27 P30 Lift 🖃
Credit Cards 1 2 3 5

☎ *M Gessner* Bitburger Str ☎(06592) 691 Aud
VW

DECHSENDORF
See **ERLANGEN**

DELMENHORST
Niedersachsen

★★**Annenriede** Annenheider Damm 129
☎(04221)6871 tx 249514
⛽60 P100 ℂ
Credit Cards 1 2 3 5

☎ *O Fünke* Wildeshauser Str 19 ☎(04221)
81300 **P** Nis

DETMOLD
Nordrhein-Westfalen

★★**Detmolder Hof** Langestr 19 ☎(05231)28244
tx 935850
⛽39 A18rm 🏠 Lift ℂ 🔍
Credit Cards 1 2 3 5

★**Friedrichshöhe** Paderbornestr 6,Heiligenkirchen
☎(05231)47053
:Rest closed Mon
⛽16 P15 Mountain

☎ *Bergmann* Lagesche Str 19-23 ☎(05231)
25396 For

☎ *British Cars* Paderborner Str 52 ☎(05231)
47556 M/C **P** AR DJ MG

☎ *Hans Stein* Am Gelskamp 23 ☎(05231) 66880
P Peu Tal

DIEZ
Rheinland-Pfalz

☎ *Auto-Müller* Wilhelmstr 44 ☎(06432) 2622 **P**
All makes

DINKELSBÜHL
Bayern

★★**Goldene Kanne** Segringerstr 8 ☎(09851)6011
tx 61107
⛽26 🏠 P10
Credit Cards 1 2 3 4 5

★★**Goldene Rose** Marktpl 4 ☎(09851)831 tx
61123
Feb-6 Jan
⛽34 A14rm 🏠 P20
Credit Cards 1 2 3 4 5

DONAUESCHINGEN
Baden-Württemberg

★★★**Oschberghof** Am Golfpl ☎(0771)841 tx
792717
⛽53 🏠 P Lift ℂ 🔍 🐾
Credit Cards

★★*Sonne* ☎(0771)3144
15 Dec-20 Jan :Rest closed Sun & Mon
⛽20 🏠 P5

DONAUWÖRTH
Bayern

★★**Traube** Badische Weinstube,Kapellstr 14
☎(0906)6096 tx 51331
:Rest closed Wed
⛽43 A26rm 🏠 P29 Lift
Credit Cards 1 2 3 5

☎ *Autohaus J Schlicker* Berger Allee 11
☎(0906) 3001 **P** For

DORTMUND
Nordrhein-Westfalen

• *Eickmann Leegeweg 8 ☎(0231) 516333 **P** All models

• *H Peters Juchostr 25 ☎(0231) 596021 M/C **P** For

• *Tremonia-Auto Eisenstr 50 ☎(0231) 818811 **P** Peu Tal

At **OESPEL**(6km W)

★★★★**Novotel Dortmund-West** Brennaborstr 2 ☎(0231)65485 tx 8227007
🛏104 P130 Lift (⌐
Credit Cards ① ② ③ ⑤

DRANSFELD
Niedersachsen

• *Röhlig Lange Str 7 ☎(1839) 3581 **P** For

DREIEICH
Hessen

★★★**Dorint Kongress Frankfurt** Eisenbahnstr 200,Sprendlingen ☎(06103)6060 tx 417954
🛏94 P100 Lift (⌐
Credit Cards ① ② ③ ⑤

DUISBURG
Nordrhein-Westfalen

★★★**Duisburger Hof** (SRS) Neckarstr 2,König-Heinrich-Pl ☎(0203)331021 tx 855750
🛏111 ⩟ P1800 Lift (
Credit Cards ① ② ③ ④ ⑤

★★**Ibis** Hercator Str 15 ☎(0203)300050 tx 855872
🛏95 P Lift

DÜREN
Nordrhein-Westfalen

★★★**Germania** J Schregel-Str 20 ☎(02421)15000
rm50(🛏49) Lift (
Credit Cards ① ③ ⑤

★**Nachtwächter** Kölner Landstr 12 ☎(02421)75081
5 Jan-20 Dec
rm36(🛏32) A11rm P20
Credit Card ①

At **MARIAWEILER**(3km NW)

★★**Mariaweiler Hof** An Gut Nazareth 45 ☎(02421)87900 & 81005
rm17(🛏13) ⩟ P40
Credit Cards ① ②

DÜRKHEIM, BAD
Rheinland-Pfalz

★★★**Crest** Kurbrunnenstr ☎(06322)601 tx 45694
🛏101 P Lift (
Credit Cards ① ② ③ ④ ⑤

★★★**KurParkhotel Bad Dürkheim** (BW) Schlosspl 1-4 ☎(06322)7970 tx 454818
🛏109 ⩟ P80 Lift (⚬ ⌐ Mountain
Credit Cards ① ② ③ ⑤

DÜRRHEIM, BAD
Baden-Württemberg

★★★**Waldeck** Waldstr 18 ☎(07726) 63100 tx 7921315
🛏65 A18rm ⩟ P70 Lift (⌐
Credit Cards ① ② ③ ⑤

DÜSSELDORF
Nordrhein-Westfalen

Düsseldorf is an attractive city on the east bank of the Rhine, its nucleus a compact semi-circle centred on the original 12th-century settlement. The city contains many interesting public buildings. Of about 40 churches, the two most imposing are those of St Andrew, completed in 1629, and St Lambert, dating from the 13th and 14th centuries. The *Wilhelm-Marx-Haus* (1924) is Germany's oldest skyscraper. The reconstructed mile-long Königsallee, the main shopping street, has many impressive buildings in modern styles. Düsseldorf is an important cultural centre; Heine, Brahms, Schumann and Goethe all lived here, the last is honoured by the *Goethe-Museum*. The Museum of Art (*Kunstmuseum*) displays collections of paintings, sculpture, medieval arts and crafts and 200 years of ceramics.

EATING OUT The *Orangerie*, in Bilkerstrasse, offers both atmosphere and good food, and also usually reliable is Robert's Restaurant, in Oberkasseler Strasse. *Frankenheim*, in Wielandstrasse, specialises in hearty local dishes.

DÜSSELDORF
Nordrhein-Westfalen

★★★★★**Park** (SRS) Corneliuspl 1 ☎(0211)8651 tx 8582331
🛏160 P40 Lift (
Credit Cards ① ② ③ ④ ⑤

★★★★**Hilton International** G-Glock-Str 20 ☎(0211)43770 tx 8584376
🛏374 P273 Lift (⌐
Credit Cards ① ② ③ ④ ⑤

★★★★**Holiday Inn** (QM) Graf-Adolf-Pl 10 ☎(0211)38730 tx 8586359
🛏177 P40 Lift (⌐
Credit Cards ① ② ③ ④ ⑤

★★★**Börsen** Kreuzstr 19A (n.rest) ☎(0211)363071 tx 8587323
🛏75 Lift (
Credit Cards ① ② ③ ⑤

★★★**Novotel** Am Schonenkamp 9 ☎(0211)741092 tx 8584374
🛏120 P100 Lift (⌐
Credit Cards ① ② ③ ⑤

★★★**Ramada** Am Seestern 16 ☎(0211)591047 tx 8585575
🛏222 P100 Lift (⌐
Credit Cards ① ② ③ ④ ⑤

At **BREITSCHEID**(12km N on A52)

★★★**Novotel Breitscheider Kreuz** Lintorfer Weg 75 ☎(02102)17621 tx 8585272
🛏120 P180 Lift (⚬ ⌐
Credit Cards ① ② ③ ⑤

At **RATINGEN**(5km N on A52)

★★★**Crest** Briochofstr 3 ☎(02102)46046 tx 8585235
🛏200 P200 (⌐ ⌐
Credit Cards ① ② ③ ④ ⑤

EBERBACH
Baden-Württemberg

★★**Krone-Post** Hauptstr 1 ☎(06271)2013
rm46(🛏33) P20 Lift
Credit Cards ① ② ③ ⑤

ECHING
Bayern

★★**Olymp** Wielandstr 3 ☎(089)3190910 tx 5214960
🛏62 ⩟ P58 Lift ⌐
Credit Cards ① ② ③ ⑤

EDIGER-ELLER
Rheinland-Pfalz

★★**Weinhaus Oster** Moselweinstr 61 ☎(02675)232
15 Mar-15 Nov
rm15(🛏11) A3rm ⩟ P12 Mountain Lake
Credit Cards ① ② ⑤

EHLENBOGEN
See **ALPIRSBACH**

EICHERSCHEID
See **SIMMERATH**

ELFERSHAUSEN
Bayern

★★★**Ullrich** A-Ullrich 42 ☎(09704)281 tx 672807
rm71(🛏67) ⩟ P90 Lift ⌐
Credit Cards ① ② ⑤

ELMSHORN
Schleswig-Holstein

• *Braun Ramskamp 43 ☎(04121) 72081 **P** For Vol

ELTEN
Nordrhein-Westfalen

★★**Wald** Lindenallee 34 ☎(02828)2091 tx 8125286
:Rest closed 2-13 Jan
🛏21 P40 Lift ⌐
Credit Cards ① ② ⑤

EMDEN
Niedersachsen

★**Goldener Adler** Neutorstr 5 ☎(04921)24055
:Rest closed Sun & Mon
🛏16 P12 (Lake
Credit Cards ① ② ③ ⑤

• *Westermann Auricher Str 227 ☎(04921) 42051 **P** For

EMS, BAD
Rheinland-Pfalz

★★★**Staatliches Kurhaus** (BW) Rmerstr 1-3 13911 ☎(02603)7990 tx 869017
🛏105 P Lift (⌐
Credit Cards ① ② ③ ⑤

★★**Russischer Hof** Römerstr 23 ☎(02603)4462
rm23(🛏16) P Lift Mountain
Credit Cards ① ② ③ ④ ⑤

• *Gebr Ebert Lahn Str 63-65 ☎(02603) 3028 M/C **P** For

EMSDETTEN
Nordrhein-Westfalen

• *F Maltezen Borghorster Str 64 ☎(02572) 2405 **P** For

ENZKLÖSTERLE
Baden-Württemberg

★★**Parkhotel Hetschelhof** ☎(07085)273
Dec-Oct
rm18(🛏16) ⩟ P

ERFTTAL
See **NEUSS**

ERLANGEN
Bayern

★★★★**Transmar Kongress** (GT) Beethoven Str 3 ☎(09131)8040 tx 629750
🛏138 ⩟ P37 Lift (⌐
Credit Cards ① ② ③ ⑤

★★★**Grille** Bunsenstr 35 ☎(09131)6136 tx 629839
🛏62 ⩟ P35 Lift (
Credit Cards ① ② ③ ④ ⑤

★★**Luise** Sophienstr 10 (n.rest) ☎(09131)1220 tx 9131812
◗♠75 ☎ P30 Lift 〔 ⌷
Credit Cards ①③⑤

◗◗ *Auto Winter* Resenscheckstr 10 ☎(09131) 38888 Peu Tal

At DECHSENDORF(5km NW)

★*Rasthaus am Heusteg* Heusteg 13 ☎(09131)41225
6 Jan-23 Dec :Rest closed Sat
rm20(♠3) ☎ P50
Credit Card ①

At TENNENLOHE(3km S)

★★★*Transmar Motor* (GT) Wetterkreuzstr 7 ☎(09131)6080 tx 629912
◗♠126 P110 Lift 〔 ⌷
Credit Cards ①②③⑤

◗◗ **Konrad** P-Gossen Str 116 ☎(09131) 12090 For.

ESCHBORN
See FRANKFURT AM MAIN

ESCHWEGE
Hessen

◗◗ **König** Hessenring 34 ☎(05651) 8755 P For

ESCHWEILER
Nordrhein-Westfalen

★*Schwan* ☎(02403)26810
rm11(◗2) P10 Mountain

◗◗ *H Adenau* Tulpenweg 6 ☎(02403) 4162 P AR Maz

ESLOHE
Nordrhein-Westfalen

At COBBENRODE(7km S)

★★*Hennemann* Olperstr ☎(02970)236
:Rest closed 10-30 Apr
◗♠25 ☎ P30 Lift ♒ ∪ Mountain
Credit Card ②

ESPENAU
See KASSEL

ESSEN
Nordrhein-Westfalen

★★★*Handelshof Essen* (Mövenpick) am Hauptbahnhof 2 ☎(0201)17080 tx 857562
◗♠196 ☎ P Lift 〔
Credit Cards ①②③⑤

★★*Arcade* Hollestr 50 ☎(0201)24280 tx 8571133
:Rest closed Sat & Sun
◗♠144 P70 Lift 〔
Credit Cards ①③

At ESSEN-BREDENEY(7km S on 224)

★★★*Scandic Crown Essen-Bredeney* T-Althoff Str 5 ☎(0201)7690 tx 0857597
◗♠297 ☎ P180 Lift 〔
Credit Cards ①②③④⑤

At ESSEN-RÜTTENSCHEID

★★*Arosa* Rüttenscheider Str 149 ☎(0201)72280 tx 857354
◗♠68 P55 Lift 〔
Credit Cards ①②③④⑤

ESSEN-BREDENEY
See ESSEN

ESSEN-RÜTTENSCHEID
See ESSEN

ETTLINGEN
Baden-Württemberg

★★★*Erbprinz* (Relais et Châteaux) Rheinstr 1 ☎(07243)12071 tx 782848
◗♠48 ☎ P120 Lift 〔
Credit Cards ①②⑤

EUTIN
Schleswig-Holstein

★*Wittler* Bahnhofstr 28 ☎(04521)2347
rm29(◗17) A8rm ☎ P20
Credit Cards ①②⑤

◗◗ **Dunkelmann** Industriestr 8 ☎(04521) 1768 P For

FALLINGBOSTEL
Niedersachsen

★★*Berlin* Düshorner Str 7 ☎(05162)3066
◗♠22 ☎ P30 Lake
Credit Cards ①②⑤

FELDAFING
Bayern

★★★*Kaiserin Elisabeth* Tutzinger Str 2 ☎(08157)1013 tx 5-26408
rm67(◗♠48) A17rm Lift 〔 ♒ Mountain Lake
Credit Cards ①②③⑤

FELDBERG IM SCHWARZWALD
Baden-Württemberg

★★★*Dorint Feldberger Hof* Seebück 12 ☎(07676)311 tx 7721124
◗♠70 ☎ P100 Lift 〔 ⌷ Mountain
Credit Cards ①②③⑤

FINTHEN
See MAINZ

FLENSBURG
Schleswig-Holstein

★★*Europa* Rathausstr 1-5 ☎(0461)17522
rm71(◗♠35) P 〔
Credit Cards ①②③⑤

★★*Flensburger Hof* Süderhofenden 38 ☎(0461)17320 tx 22594
:Rest closed Sat
rm28(◗♠27) ☎ P22 Lift 〔
Credit Cards ①②③⑤

◗◗ *C Christiansen* Nordstr ☎(0461) 6031 P Peu Tal

At HARRISLEE(5km N)

★★*Grenze* 2391 Kupfermühle ☎(0461)7020 tx 461108
◗♠300 P700 Lift 〔 ♒ ⌷ ⌷ Sea Lake
Credit Cards ①②③⑤

FRANKFURT AM MAIN
Hessen

Electronic room reservation facilities are available at the airport, the main railway station and the ADAC Service Centre, autobahn exit 'Frankfurt West'. These facilities are not operative during trade fairs.
Frankfurt represents the largest settlement in a chain of towns and cities stretching over 35 miles along the middle Rhine above and below the Main confluence, and its position in relation to natural routes make it a leading railway hub.
Frankfurt, the birthplace of Goethe, is a cultural centre of considerable significance. It has several theatres (for both operas and plays) and picture galleries - such as the Städel Art Institute (*Städelsches Kinstinstitut*). St Bartholemew's Cathedral dates from the 13th century, as do the Leonhardskirch and the Nikolaikirche. Other important churches are the 14th-century Liebrauenkirche and the

Paulskirche, where the first German National Assembly met in 1848-49.

EATING OUT Frankfurt residents are closely attached to traditional, regional food, such as sausages - including the famed *frankfurter* - and game, especially venison and boar. One of the city's longest established and most atmospheric cellar restaurants is the up-market *Weinhaus Brückenkeller*, in Schüzenstrasse, where specialities include a version of pot roast known as *tafelspitz*. The moderately-priced *Bistro 77* in Ziegelhuttenweg serves Alsatian specialities, while those on a budget should seek out *Zum Gemalten Haus*, in Schweizer Strasse, a traditional wine tavern which has a courtyard for summer dining.

FRANKFURT AM MAIN
Hessen

★★★★*Frankfurt Intercontinental* W-Leuschnerstr 43 ☎(069)230561 tx 413639
◗♠798 P500 Lift 〔 ⌷
Credit Cards ①②③④⑤

★★★★*Crest* Isenburger Schneise 40 ☎(069)67840 tx 416717
◗♠289 P Lift 〔
Credit Cards ①②③④⑤

★★★★*Frankfurter Hof* (SRS) Am Kaiserpl ☎(069)21502 tx 411806
rm360(◗♠356) Lift 〔
Credit Cards ①②③④⑤

★★★★*Hessischer Hof* F-Ebert-Anlage 40 ☎(069)75400 tx 411776
◗♠121 ☎ P120 Lift 〔
Credit Cards ①②③④⑤

★★★★*Holiday Inn* (QM) Mailander Str 1 ☎(069)68020 tx 411805
◗♠404 ☎ P400 Lift 〔
Credit Cards ①②③④⑤

★★★★*Parkhotel Frankfurt* (Mövenpick) Wiesenhüttenpl 28-38 ☎(069)26970 tx 412808
◗♠299 P80 Lift 〔
Credit Cards ①②③④⑤

★★★★*Pullman Hotel Savigny* Savignystr 14-16 ☎(069)75330 tx 412061
◗♠124 Lift 〔
Credit Cards ①②③⑤

★★★*Excelsior Monopol* Mannheimerstr 7-13 ☎(069)256080 tx 413061
◗♠300 ☎ P40 Lift 〔
Credit Cards ①②③④⑤

★★★*National* (BW) Baseler Str 50 ☎(069)234841 tx 412570
◗♠75 P10 Lift 〔
Credit Cards ①②③④⑤

★★★*Ramada Caravelle* Oserstr 180 ☎(069)39050 tx 416812
◗♠236 ☎ P50 Lift 〔 ⌷
Credit Cards ①②③④⑤

◗◗ *British Car Service* Sulzbacher Str 10-14 ☎(069) 731084 P AR Jag MG

◗◗ *B Kneifel* Praunheimer Landstr 21 ☎(069) 780925 P DJ LR Nis Rov

At ESCHBORN(12km NW)

★★★**Novotel Frankfurt Eschborn** P-Helfman Str 10 ☎(06196)42812 tx 4072842
⊷🏠227 P250 Lift ℂ ⌂
Credit Cards ①②③⑤

At SULZBACH(14km W A648)

★★★★**Holiday Inn** am Main Taunus Zentrum 1 ☎(06196)7878 tx 4072536
⊷🏠291 ☎ P300 Lift ℂ
Credit Cards ①②③④⑤

FRANKFURT AM MAIN AIRPORT
Hessen

★★★**Novotel** am Weiner 20 ☎(06107)75050 tx 4170101
⊷🏠151 P150 Lift ℂ ⌂ Lake
Credit Cards ①②③⑤

FREIBURG IM BREISGAU
Baden-Württemberg

★★★★**Colombi** (SRS) Rotteckring 16 ☎(0761)31415 tx 772750
⊷🏠101 ☎ P50 Lift ℂ
Credit Cards ①②③⑤

★★★**Novotel** am Karlspl 1 ☎(0761)31295 tx 772774
⊷🏠115 Lift ℂ Mountain
Credit Cards ①②③⑤

★★★**Rappen** Münsterpl 13 ☎(0761)31353
rm20(⊷🏠13) Lift
Credit Cards ①②③④⑤

★★★**Victoria** Eisenbahnstr 54 ☎(0761)31881 tx 761103
⊷🏠65 ☎ P15 Lift ℂ
Credit Cards ①②③⑤

★★**Roten Bären** Oberlinden 12,am Schwabentor ☎(0761)36913 tx 7721574
⊷🏠25 P8 Lift ℂ
Credit Cards ①②③⑤

🐾 **Buhri** Egonstr 79-83 ☎(0761) 272061 P For

FREISING
Bayern

★★**Bayerischer Hof** Untere Hauptstr 3 ☎(08161)3037
rm70(⊷🏠69) ☎ P25 Lift

FREUDENSTADT
Baden-Württemberg

★★★**Schwarzwald Hof** Hohenrieder Str 74 ☎(07441)7421 tx 764371
⊷🏠40 ☎ P21 Lift ⌂
Credit Cards ①②③⑤

★★★**Sonne Am Kurpark** Turnhalle Str 63 ☎(07441)6044 tx 764388
Closed 10-25 Dec
⊷🏠45 ☎ P20 Lift ℂ ⌂ ∪
Credit Cards ①②③⑤

★★★**Steigenberger** (SRS) K-Von-Hahe Str 129 ☎(07441)81071 tx 64266
⊷🏠136 P120 Lift ℂ ⌂
Credit Cards ①②③⑤

★**Krone** Marktpl 29 ☎(07441)2007
rm25(🏠7) ☎ P

★★**Kurhotel Eden** Am Golfpl ☎(07441)70379 tx 764270
⊷🏠92 A30rm ☎ P80 Lift ℂ ⌂
Credit Cards ①②③⑤

★★**Württemberger Hof** Lauterbadstr 10 ☎(07441)6047 tx 764388
16 Dec-Nov
rm22(⊷🏠13) ☎ P20 Lift ⌂ ∪
Credit Cards ①②③⑤

★**See** Forststr 15-17 ☎(07441)2688
15 Dec-15 Nov :Rest closed Wed
rm13(🏠10) A9rm ☎ P11

🐾 **Hornberger U Schilling** Jetzt Deutzstr 2 ☎(07441) 7084 M/C P All makes

🐾 **Katz & Co** Wittlensweiler Str 1 ☎(07441) 4085 P Ren

🐾 **Oberndorfer & Hiller** Alte Poststr 3 ☎(07441) 2278 For

At LAUTERBAD(3km SE)

★★**Gruner Wald** Kinzigtalstr 23 ☎(07441)2427
rm40(⊷🏠35) ☎ P55 ⌂ ∪ Mountain
Credit Card ①

FRIEDRICHSDORF
See HOMBURG, BAD

FRIEDRICHSHAFEN
Baden-Württemberg

★★**Buchhorner Hof** Friedrichstr 33 ☎(07541)2050 tx 734210
10 Jan-22 Dec
⊷🏠65 ☎ Lift ℂ Lake
Credit Cards ①②③④⑤

FULDA
Hessen

★★★**Lenz** Leipzigerstr 122 ☎(0661)601041 tx 49733
Closed 25-31 Dec
rm47(⊷🏠24) A23rm P50 Lift ℂ
Credit Cards ①②③⑤

🐾 **W Fahr** Langebrücke Andreasberg 4 ☎(0661) 83030 Ope

🐾 **E Sorg** Kreuzbergstr 44 ☎(0661) 49500 P For

FÜRSTENFELDBRÜCK
Bayern

★★**Post** Hauptstr 7 ☎(08141)24074
7 Jan-23 Dec :Rest closed Sat & Sun evening
⊷🏠45 ☎ P30 Lift
Credit Cards ①②③④⑤

FÜRTH
Bayern

★★★**Novotel Fürth** Laubenweg 6 ☎(0911)791010 tx 622214
⊷🏠131 P100 Lift ℂ ⌂
Credit Cards ①②③⑤

GAIMERSHEIM
See INGOLSTADT

GARMISCH-PARTENKIRCHEN
Bayern

★★★★**Residence** (QM) Mittenwalderstr 2 ☎(08821)7561 tx 592415
⊷🏠117 ☎ P86 Lift ℂ ∝ ⌂ Mountain
Credit Cards ①②③⑤

★★★**Dorint** Mittenwalderstr 59 ☎(08821)7060
⊷🏠156 ☎ P150 Lift ℂ ⌂ Mountain
Credit Cards ①②③⑤

★★★**Grand Sonnenbichl** Burgstr 97 ☎(08821)7020 tx 59632
⊷🏠90 P80 Lift ℂ ⌂ Mountain
Credit Cards ①②③⑤

★★★**Wittelsbach** Von Brugstr 24 ☎(08821)53096 tx 59668
20 Dec-20 Oct
⊷🏠60 ☎ P30 Lift ℂ ⌂ Mountain
Credit Cards ①②③⑤

★★**Garmischer Hof** Bahnhofstr 51 (n.rest) ☎(08821)51091
⊷🏠43 P25 Lift ℂ Mountain
Credit Cards ①②③⑤

★★**Partenkirchner-Hof** Bahnhofstr 15 ☎(08821)58025 tx 592412
15 Dec-15 Nov
⊷🏠80 ☎ P20 Lift ℂ ⌂ Mountain
Credit Cards ①②③④⑤

🐾 **Maier** Unterfeldstr 17 ☎(08821) 50141 Fia Lan

GELSENKIRCHEN
Nordrhein-Westfalen

★★★**Maritim** Am Stadtgarten 1 ☎(0209)15951 tx 824636
:Rest closed Jul-Aug
⊷🏠223 ☎ P200 Lift ℂ ⌂
Credit Cards ①②③⑤

★★**Ibis** Bahnofsvorpl 12 ☎(0209)17020 tx 824705
⊷🏠104 P Lift ℂ
Credit Cards ①②③④⑤

🐾 **A Stork** Ringstr 50-56 ☎(0209) 21941 P For Mit

GERMERSHEIM
Rheinland-Pfalz

🐾 **Deutschler** Hockenheimer Str 2 ☎(07274) 20021 P For

GERNSBACH
Baden-Württemberg

★**Ratsstuben** Hauptstr 34 ☎(07224)2141
rm21 P15 Mountain

GIESSEN
Hessen

★★★**Kübel** Bahnhofstr 47 ☎(0641)77070 tx 4821754
:Rest closed Sun midday & hols
rm45(⊷🏠43) ☎ P20 ℂ
Credit Cards ①②③⑤

★**Lahn** Lahnstr 21 (n.rest) ☎(0641)73516
⊷🏠15 ☎

★**Krahn** Frankfurter Str 82-149 ☎(0641) 2003-0 P For

GLOTTERTAL
Baden-Württemberg

★★**Hirschen** Rathausweg 2 (n.rest) ☎(07684)810 tx 772349
:Rest closed Mon
⊷🏠43 P Lift ∝ Mountain
Credit Card ①

GODESBERG, BAD
See BONN

GÖGGLINGEN
See ULM

GÖPPINGEN
Baden-Württemberg

★★**Hohenstaufen** Freihofstr 64 ☎(07161)70077 tx 727619
:Rest closed Fri
⊷🏠50 A24rm ☎ P15
Credit Cards ①②③④⑤

GOSLAR
Niedersachsen

At GRAUHOF BRUNNEN(4km NE)

★★**Landhaus Grauhof** ☎(05321)84001 tx 953855
rm31(🏠21) ☎ P3 Lift
Credit Cards ①②③⑤

At HAHNENKLEE(15km SW)

★★★**Dorint Harzhotel Kreuzeck** Am Kreuzeck ☎(05325)741 tx 953721
⊷🏠105 ☎ P50 Lift ℂ ∝ ⌂ 👣 Lake
Credit Cards ①②③⑤

GÖTTINGEN
Niedersachsen

★★★**Sonne** Paulinerstr 10-12 ☎(0551)56738 tx 96787
5 Jan-20 Dec
⊷🏠41 ☎ P20 Lift ℂ
Credit Cards ①③⑤

GRAFENAU
Bayern

★★★**Sonnenhof** (SRS) Sonnenstr 12 ☎(08552)2033 tx 57413
⊷🏠196 ☎ P100 Lift ℂ ∝ ⌂
Credit Cards ①②③⑤

GRAINAU
Bayern

★★★**Alpenhotel Waxenstein** Eibseestr 16 ☎(08821)8001 tx 59663
⊷🏠49 ☎ P30 Lift ⌂ Mountain
Credit Cards ①②③⑤

★★**Post** Postgasse 10 (n.rest) ☎(08821)8853
20 Dec-8 Jan & May-1 Oct
⊷ℝ25 ☎ P20 Mountain
Credit Cards ①②③⑤

GRAUHOF BRUNNEN
See GOSLAR

GRIMLINGHAUSEN
See NEUSS

GROSS-GERAU
Hessen

★★**Adler** Frankfurter Str 11 ☎(06152)8090
rm68(⊷ℝ59) A13rm ☎ P64 Lift
Credit Cards ①②③

GÜNZBURG
Bayern

★★**Goldene Traube** Marktpl 22 ☎(08221)5510
rm34(⊷ℝ27) ☎ P14
Credit Cards ①②③⑤

★★**Hirsch** Marktpl 18 ☎(08221)5610
⊷ℝ14 A12rm ☎ P10
Credit Card ②

HAGEN
Nordrhein-Westfalen

★★★**Crest** Wasserloses Tal 4 ☎(02331)3910 tx 823441
⊷ℝ148 P Lift (🖾
Credit Cards ①②③④⑤

★★**Deutsches Haus** Bahnhofstr 35 ☎(02331)3910 tx 823441
⊷ℝ148 P250 Lift (🖾
Credit Cards ①②③④⑤

HAGNAU
Baden-Württemberg

★**Landhaus Messmer** Meersburgerstr 12 (n.rest) ☎(07532)6227
Mar-5 Nov
⊷ℝ14 ☎ P10 Beach Mountain Lake

HAHNENKLEE
See GOSLAR

HALTINGEN
Baden-Württemberg

★**Rebstock** Grosse Gasse 30 ☎(07621)62257
rm19(ℝ10) A4rm ☎ P (

HALVER
Nordrhein-Westfalen

At CARTHAUSEN(4km NE)

★★★**Frommann** ☎(02353)611 tx 8263658
:Rest closed 23-25 Dec
⊷ℝ22 ☎ P50 ⌖ 🖾
Credit Cards ①②③⑤

HAMBURG
Hamburg

Hamburg is a bustling, thriving port city, known for its love of the arts. It also has vast shopping centres, more than 2,000 restaurants appealing to every kind of taste, and the colourful St Pauli district.
Sightseeing possibilities include an exploration of the harbour and attractive Alster Lakes; a visit to the *Planten un Blomen* park the Botanical Garden built around the city's old ramparts, Hagenbeck's Zoo, the old townhouses on Deichstrasse, and the many museums and art galleries.

Hamburg is also a great place for shopping; prices are reasonable, and many historic buildings have been converted into exclusive covered arcades.
Hamburg is renowned for its lively nightlife. There are around 30 theatres, the Ballet Company and the Hamburg State Opera.

EATING OUT One of Hamburg's most popular local delicacies is *aalsuppe* (eel soup), virtually a meal in itself, made from fresh eel with leeks, carrots, dumplings, apricots, prunes and apples, served in a heavily seasoned ham broth. Good traditional German cuisine can be enjoyed at *Peter Lembke*, in Holzdamm, where eel soup can usually be found on the menu together with more conventional dishes such as steaks. *Il Giardino*, in Ulmenstrasse, has an attractive courtyard garden and serves excellent Italian cuisine, while for an inexpensive meal there is the popular *Avocado*, in Kanalstrasse.

HAMBURG

★★★★★**Vier Jahreszeiten** Neuer Jungfernstieg 9-14 ☎(040)34940 tx 211629
⊷ℝ170 ☎ P140 Lift (Lake
Credit Cards ①②③⑤

★★★★**Atlantic Kempinski Hamburg** an der Alster 72 ☎(040)28880 tx 2163297
⊷ℝ256,Lift (🖾 Lake
Credit Cards ①②③④⑤

★★★★**Berlin** Borgfelderstr 1-9 ☎(040)251640 tx 213939
⊷ℝ96 ☎ P62 Lift (
Credit Cards ①②③⑤

★★★★**Holiday Inn Hamburg** Graumannsweg 10 ☎(040)228060 tx 2165287
⊷ℝ290 ☎ P170 Lift (🖾 Lake
Credit Cards ①②③④⑤

★★★★**SAS Plaza Hamburg** Marseiller Str 2 ☎(040)35020 tx 214400
⊷ℝ570 ☎ Lift (🖾 Lake
Credit Cards ①②③④⑤

★★★**Europäischer Hof** (GT) Kirchenalle 45 (n.rest) ☎(040)6305051 tx 2174155
⊷ℝ185 P200 Lift (
Credit Cards ①②③④⑤

★★★**Novotel Hamburg Nord** Oldesloer Str 166 ☎(040)5502073 tx 212923
⊷ℝ120 P178 Lift (🖾
Credit Cards ①②③⑤

★★★**Oper** Drehbahn 15 ☎(040)35601 tx 212475
⊷ℝ112 P200 Lift (
Credit Cards ①②③⑤

★★★**Queens** Mexikoring 1,City Nord ☎(040)6305051 tx 2174155
⊷ℝ185 ☎ P Lift (
Credit Cards ①②③④⑤

★★★**Reichshof** (SRS) Kirchenalle 34-36 ☎(040)248330 tx 2163396
⊷ℝ300 ☎ P120 Lift (
Credit Cards ①②③⑤

★★★**Smolka** Iserstr 98 Harvestehüde ☎(040)475057 tx 215275
:Rest closed Sun
⊷ℝ40 ☎ P12 Lift (
Credit Cards ①②③⑤

★★**Ibis** Wandsbeker Zollstr 25-29 ☎(040)6829021 tx 2164929
⊷ℝ144 ☎ P Lift (⌖
Credit Cards ①②③⑤

★★**Pacific** Neuer Pferdemarkt 30 (n.rest) ☎(040)4395094
⊷ℝ60 P30 Lift (

★**City Inter** Halskestr 72 ☎(040)789691 tx 2161936
⊷ℝ175 P140 Lift (

★**Hamburg** Hoheluftchaussee 119 (n.rest) ☎(040)4204141
2 Jan-20 Dec
rm36(⊷ℝ17) ☎ P12 (
Credit Cards ①②③⑤

🅖 **Dethlefs Automobile** Neuländer Str 6 ☎(040) 774775 P AR Dai LR

🅖 **Nemeth** Koppel 65 ☎(040) 244849 DJ Peu Rov RR

🅖 **P Nitzschke** Möllin -Landstr 76 ☎(040) 7128459 P Rov

🅖 **Vidal** Angerstr 20-22 ☎(040) 257900 P DJ LR Mer

HAMELN
Niedersachsen

★★★**Dorint Hameln** 164er Ring 3 ☎(05151)7920 tx 924716
⊷ℝ103 P13 Lift (🖾
Credit Cards ①②③⑤

★★**Zur Börse** Oster Str 41A ☎(05151)7080
Closed Xmas-New Year
⊷ℝ34 ☎ P6 Lift
Credit Cards ①②⑤

🅖 **Autozentrale** Ruthrnstr 7 ☎(05151) 7461 For

🅖 **Hild & Comp** ☎(05151) 23055 P Aud Por VW

HANNOVER
Niedersachsen

★★★**Kastens Luisenhof** (SRS) Luisenstr 1-3 ☎(0511)12440 tx 922325
⊷ℝ160 ☎ P60 Lift (
Credit Cards ①②③⑤

★★★**Parkhotel Kronsberg** (BW) Messeschnellweg ☎(0511)861086 tx 923448
⊷ℝ144 ☎ P400 Lift (
Credit Cards ①②③④⑤

★★★**Queens Moat House** (QM) Tiergartenstr 117 ☎(0511)5103-0 tx 922748
⊷ℝ108 ☎ P210 Lift (
Credit Cards ①②③④⑤

★★**Central Kaiserhof** E-August-Pl 4 ☎(0511)36830 tx 922810
⊷ℝ81 P20 Lift (
Credit Cards ①②③④⑤

★★**Föhrenhof** (BW) Kirchhorster Str 22 ☎(0511)61721 tx 923448
⊷ℝ78 P150 Lift (
Credit Cards ①②③④⑤

🅖 **British Cars** Constantin Str 90C ☎(0511) 691150 P Rov DJ

🅖 **Deisterstrasse** Deisterstr 33-37 ☎(0511) 444016 For

HANNOVER AIRPORT

★★★★**Holiday Inn** (QM) Petzelstr 60 ☎(0511)7707-0 tx 924030
⊷ℝ145 P140 Lift (🖾
Credit Cards ①②③④⑤

HARRISLEE
See FLENSBURG

HARZBURG, BAD
Niedersachsen

★★★*Bodes* Stadtpark 48 (n.rest) ☎(05322)2041 tx 957630
⇔↑80 A45rm ⚐ P20 Lift ℂ Mountain
Credit Cards ①②③⑤

★★*Braunschweiger Hof* Herzog Wilhelm Str 52-56 ☎(05322)7880 tx 957821
⇔↑78 ⚐ P70 Lift ℂ ⌸ Mountain
Credit Cards ①②③⑤

HEIDELBERG
Baden-Württemberg

See also WALLDORF

★★★*Alt Heidelberg* Rohrbacher Str 29 ☎(06221)9150 tx 461897
⇔↑80 A24rm ⚐ P18 Lift ℂ
Credit Cards ①②③⑤

★★★*Anlage* F-Ebert Anlage 32 ☎(06221)26425
Closed Feb
⇔↑20 P8 Lift ℂ
Credit Cards ①②③⑤

★★★*Europäische Hof* (SRS) F-Ebert Anlage 1 ☎(06221)515-0 tx 461840
⇔↑150 Lift ℂ
Credit Cards ①②③⑤

★★★*Queens Moat House* (QM) Pleikartsforsterstr 101 ☎(06221)71021 tx 461650
⇔↑113 ⚐ P140 ℂ
Credit Cards ①②③⑤

★★★*Ritter* (ROM) Hauptstr 178 ☎(06221)20203 tx 461506
:Rest closed 24 Dec
rm30(⇔↑26) P Lift ℂ
Credit Cards ①②③⑤

★★*Central* (n.rest) ☎(06221)20672 tx 461566
⇔↑52 P10 Lift ℂ
Credit Cards ①②③

★*Kohler* Goethestr 2 (n.rest) ☎(06221)24360
10 Jan-16 Dec
rm43(⇔↑36) Lift ℂ
Credit Cards ①③

★*Vier Jahreszeiten* Haspelgasse 2,an der Alten Brücke ☎(06221)24164
rm22(⇔↑15) ⚐ P8 ℂ Mountain
Credit Cards ①②③④⑤

✆ *Auto Bähr* in der Neckarhelle 41 ☎(06221) 800181 P Peu Tal

✆ *Auto-Kunz* Pleikartzsforster Str 13 ☎(06224) 71055 M/C P BMW Hon Peu Tal

✆ *L Fath* Trippmacher K-Benz Str 2 ☎(6221) 22171

✆ *Raichle & Baur* Hebelstr 12 ☎(06221) 24954 P Rov DJ

HEILBRONN
Baden-Württemberg

★★★*Insel* F-Ebert Brücke ☎(07131)6300 tx 72877
⇔↑120 ⚐ P30 Lift ℂ ⌸
Credit Cards ①②③④⑤

★★*Kronprinz* Bahnhofstr 29 ☎(07131)83941 tx 728561
⇔↑35 ⚐ P6 Lift

✆ *ASG Auto-Service* Grundäckerstr 2 ☎(07131) 21333 P AR DJ LR

HEILIGENROTH
See **MONTABAUR**

HELMSTEDT
Niedersachsen

★★*Petzold* Schöninger Str 1 ☎(05351)6001
:Rest closed Sun evenings
rm28(⇔↑23) ⚐ P34 ℂ

✆ *Wagner* K-Adenauer Pl 3 ☎(05351) 31007 P Aud VW

HEPPENHEIM AN DER BERGSTRASSE
Hessen

★*Goldenen Engel* Grosser Markt 2 ☎(06252)2563
rm35(⇔↑34) ⚐ P10 Mountain

HERFORD
Nordrhein-Westfalen

✆ *P Wiegers* Waltgeriststr 71 ☎(05221) 2086 Hon AR DJ

HERRENALB, BAD
Baden-Württemberg

★★★★*Mönchs Posthotel* (Relais et Châteaux) Dobler Str 2 ☎(07083)7440 tx 7245123
⇔↑50 Lift ℂ ⌲ ♙ Mountain
Credit Cards ①②⑤

HERRENBERG
Baden-Württemberg

★*Neue Post* Wilhelmstr 48 ☎(07032)5156
19 Jan-20 Dec
rm6(↑4) P12

HERSFELD, BAD
Hessen

★★*Parkhotel Rose* Am Kurpark 9 ☎(06221)15656 tx 493279
⇔↑20 ⚐ P10 Lift Mountain
Credit Cards ①②③⑤

★★*Stern* (ROM) Lingg Pl 11 ☎(06621)72007
:Rest closed Fri lunchtime
⇔↑49 A19rm ⚐ P35 Lift ⌸
Credit Cards ①②③④⑤

HILDESHEIM
Niedersachsen

✆ *Felske Automobile* Porchester 2 ☎(05121) 575077 P AR DJ

HINDELANG
Bayern

★★★*Prinz-Luitpold-Bad* Bad Oberdorf ☎(08324)8901
⇔↑115 ⚐ P80 Lift ℂ ♙ ⌸ ⌲ Mountain

HINTERZARTEN
Baden-Württemberg

★★★★*Parkhotel Adler* Adlepl ☎(07652)1270 tx 765212
rm74(⇔↑73) A15rm ⚐ P200 Lift ℂ ♙ ⌸
Mountain
Credit Cards ①②③④⑤

HÖCHENSCHWAND
Baden-Württemberg

★★★*Kurhaus* Kurhauspl 1 ☎(07672)4110 tx 7721212
⇔↑50 ⚐ P60 Lift ℂ ⌸ Mountain
Credit Cards ①②③⑤

HÖCHSTADT AN DER AISCH
Bayern

★★*Kapuzinerbräu* Hauptstr 28 ☎(09193)8327
⇔↑46 ⚐ P25 Lift

HOCKENHEIM
Baden-Württemberg

★★*Luxhof* an der Speyerer Brücke ☎(06205)3581
⇔↑46 A9rm ⚐ P
Credit Cards ①②③⑤

HOF
Bayern

✆ *Autoveri* C-Benz Str 4 ☎(09281) 9067 P For

HOHENSCHWANGAU
Bayern

★*Lisl Und Jägerhaus* Neuschwansteinstr 1 ☎(08362)81006 tx 541332
20 Mar-4 Jan
rm56(⇔↑45) A20rm P50 Lift ℂ Beach Mountain
Credit Cards ①②③⑤

HOHR-GRENZHAUSEN
Rheinland-Pfalz

✆ *Lohr* Auf der Haide ☎(02624) 4033 P VW & Aud

HOLZMINDEN
Niedersachsen

✆ *H Friedrich* Bulte 3 ☎(05531) 7820 P AR Cit

HOMBURG, BAD
Hessen

At FRIEDRICHSDORF(5km NE on 455)

★★★*Queens Moat House* (QM) Im Dammwald 1 ☎(06172)7390 tx 415892
⇔↑127 ⚐ P52 Lift ℂ ⌸
Credit Cards ①②③⑤

HOMBURG SAAR
Saarland

★★★*Stadt Homburg* Ringstr 80 ☎(06841)1331 tx 44683
⇔↑42 A3rm P50 Lift ℂ ⌸
Credit Cards ①②③⑤

HONNEF AM RHEIN, BAD
Nordrhein-Westfalen

At **WINDHAGEN-REDERSCHEID**(8km SE)

★★★*Waldbrunnen* Brunnenstr 7 ☎(02645)150 tx 863020
⇔↑116 ⚐ P150 Lift ℂ ♙ ⌸ ⌲ ∪
Credit Cards ①②③

HORNBERG
Baden-Württemberg

★★*Schloss Hornberg* Auf dem Schlossberg 1 ☎(07833)6841
Feb-20 Dec
⇔↑39 P50 Mountain
Credit Cards ①②③⑤

HORSTMAR
Nordrhein-Westfalen

★*Crins* Münsterstr 11 ☎(02558)7370
:Rest closed Fri
rm10 ⚐
Credit Card ①

HÜNFELD
Hessen

✆ *K Sorg* Indstriegebiet ☎(06652) 3656 P For

INGOLSTADT
Bayern

★★★★*Ambassador* Geothestr 153 ☎(0841)5030 tx 55710
⇔↑123 P120 Lift ℂ ⌸
Credit Cards ①②③④⑤

★★*Rappensberger* Harderstr 3 ☎(0841)3140 tx 55834
3 Jan-24 Dec :Rest closed Sat, Sun evening
rm90(⇔↑80) ⚐ Lift ℂ
Credit Cards ①②③⑤

★*Adler* Theresienstr 22 ☎(0841)35107
rm45(⇔↑40) P15 ℂ

✆ *Bacher* Goethestr 56 ☎(0841) 2261 P For

✆ *E Willner* Goethestr 61 ☎(0841) 2205 P Ope

✆ *Leyland-Service Ingoldstadt* Esplanade 3 ☎(0841) 32603 P AR

At GAIMERSHEIM(8km NW)

★★*Heidehof* Ingolstadter Str 121 ☎(08458)640 tx 55688
⇔↑76 ⚐ P96 Lift ⌸
Credit Cards ①②③④⑤

INZELL
Bayern

★★★*Chiemgauer Hof* Larchenstr 5 ☎(08665)6700 tx 866580
⇔↑216 P Lift ℂ ⌸ Mountain
Credit Cards ①②③⑤

ISERLOHN
Nordrhein-Westfalen

➨ **Auto-Will** Baarstr 125-127 ☎(02371) 4991 **P**
For

➨ **Sportcar Centre** Baarstr 119 ☎(02371) 40048
P Alf Rov

ISNY
Baden-Württemberg

★★**Hohe Linde** Lindauerstr 75 ☎(07562)2066
:Rest closed Fri
⇔♫26 ☎ P30 ⌂ Mountain
Credit Cards ① ② ③ ⑤

JESTEBURG
Niedersachsen

At **ASENDORF**(4.5km SE)
★★**Heidschnucke** Zum Auetal 14 ☎(04183)2094
tx 2189781
⇔♫50 P150 Lift ⌂
Credit Cards ① ② ③ ⑤

KAISERSBACH
Baden-Württemberg

At **KAISERSBACH-EBNI**(3km SW)
★★★**Schassbergers DPn** ☎(07184)2920 tx
7246726
⇔♫52 ☎ P104 Lift ⌖ ⌂ ⌄ Beach Sea
Credit Cards ① ② ③ ④ ⑤

KAISERSBACH-EBNI
See **KAISERSBACH**

KAISERSLAUTERN
Rheinland-Pfalz

★★★**Dorint Pfalzerwald** St Quentin Ring 1
☎(0631)20150 tx 45614
⇔♫153 ☎ P150 Lift ⌖ ⌂ ⌄
Credit Cards ① ② ③ ⑤
➨ **Schicht** Kaiserstr 74 ☎(0631) 54060 **P** BMW

KAMP-BORNHOFEN
Rheinland-Pfalz

★ **Anker** Rheinuferstr 46 ☎(06773)215
Apr-Oct
⇔♫16 ☎ P4 Mountain
Credit Card ①

KARLSRUHE
Baden-Württemberg

★★★**Berliner Hof** Douglasstr 7 (n.rest)
☎(0721)23981 tx 7825889
rm55(⇔♫53) ☎ P20 Lift ⌖
Credit Cards ① ② ③ ④ ⑤
★★★**Kaiserhof** Am Marktpl ☎(0721)26615-16 tx
7825600
rm40(⇔36) Lift ⌖
Credit Cards ① ② ③ ④ ⑤
★★★**Park** (Mövenpick) Ettlingerstr 23
☎(0721)37270 tx 7825443
⇔♫147 P160 Lift ⌖
Credit Cards ① ② ③ ④ ⑤
★★★**Ramada Renaissance** Mendelsohnpl
☎(0721)37170 tx 7825699
⇔♫215 ☎ P107 Lift ⌖
Credit Cards ① ② ③ ④ ⑤
★★★**Schloss** Bahnhofpl 2 ☎(0721)3540 tx
7826746
⇔♫96 P48 Lift ⌖
Credit Cards ① ② ③ ④ ⑤
★★**Eden** Bahnhofstr 17-19 ☎(0721)18180
⇔♫68 ☎ P38 Lift ⌖
Credit Cards ① ② ③ ⑤
★★**Hasen** Gerwigstr 47 ☎(0721)615076
:Rest closed Sun & Mon
rm37(⇔♫35) ☎ Lift ⌖
Credit Cards ① ② ③
★★**Markt** Kaiserstr 76 (n.rest) ☎(0721)20921
rm31(⇔28) Lift ⌖
Credit Cards ① ② ③ ④ ⑤
➨ **Autohaus Jurgen** Kussmaulstr 15 ☎(0721)
751099 **P** Rov DJ Mit

➨ **Böhler** Ottostr 6 ☎(0721) 409090 **P** Vol

➨ **Fritz Opel** H-Billing Str 8-12 ☎(0721) 1301
Ope

➨ **Vollmer & Sack** Gottesauerstr 37 ☎(0721)
66200 For

➨ **Zentral** Blumenstr 4 ☎(0721) 27141 Peu Tal

KASSEL
Hessen

★★★★**Kassel Moat House** Helligenroederstr 61
☎(0561)52050 tx 99814
⇔♫142 P150 Lift ⌂
Credit Cards ① ② ③ ⑤
★★★**Dorint Reiss** W-Hilpert Str 24
☎(0561)78830 tx 99740
rm100(⇔78) ☎ P100 Lift ⌖
Credit Cards ① ② ③ ⑤
At **ESPENAU**(10km NW)
★★**Waldhotel Schäferberg** Wilhelmsthaler Str 14
☎(05673)7951 tx 991814
rm95(⇔94) ☎ P120 Lift ⌖
Credit Cards ① ② ③ ④ ⑤

KAUFBEUREN
Bayern

➨ **Langer** Neugablonzer Str 88 ☎(08341) 8448
For

At **BIESSENHOFEN**(6.5km S)
★★**Neue Post** Fussener Str 17 ☎(08341)8525
⇔♫20 ☎ P Lift ⌖
Credit Cards ① ② ③ ⑤

KELHEIM
Bayern

★★**Ehrnthaller** Donaustr 22 ☎(09441)3333
Closed 1 wk Xmas
rm60(⇔46) ☎ P50 Lift
Credit Cards ① ② ③ ⑤

KEMPTEN (ALLGÄU)
Bayern

★★★**Fürstenhof** (BW) Rathauspl 8
☎(0831)25360 tx 541535
⇔♫76 A21rm ☎ P20 Lift ⌖
Credit Cards ① ② ③ ④ ⑤
★★★**Peterhof** Salzstr 1 ☎(0831)25525 tx 541585
⇔♫51 ☎ P35 Lift ⌖
Credit Cards ① ② ③ ④ ⑤

KIEL
Schleswig-Holstein

★★★**Conti-Hansa** (BW) Schlossgarten 7
☎(0431)51150 tx 292813
⇔♫164 ☎ P70 Lift ⌖ Lake
Credit Cards ① ③ ⑤

KIRCHHEIM
Hessen

★★★**Motel Center** (1.5km S near Autobahn exit)
☎(06625)1080 tx 493337
⇔♫140 ☎ P140 ⌖ ⌂ ⌄ Mountain
Credit Cards ① ② ③ ⑤

KISSINGEN, BAD
Bayern

★★★**Bristol** Bismarckstr 8-10 ☎(0971)4031
Mar-Oct
⇔♫101 ☎ P20 Lift ⌖ ⌂
★★★**Rixen Bad Kissingen** Frühlingstr 1
☎(0971)8230 tx 672910
⇔♫94 P45 Lift ⌖
Credit Cards ① ② ③ ⑤
★★**Fürst Bismarck** Euerdorferstr 4 ☎(0971)1277
Feb-Nov
rm32(⇔31) A2rm ☎ P30 Lift ⌖ ⌂ Mountain
Credit Cards ① ② ③ ⑤
➨ **Karl Heinz Fursch** Kapellenstr 35 ☎809719
61413 AR

KLEVE
Nordrhein-Westfalen

➨ **Autohaus Hörbelt** Kalkarer Str 41 ☎02821
24045 **P** For

KLOSTERREICHENBACH
Baden-Württemberg

★★**Sonne-Post** Mürgtalstr 167,Baiersbronn 6
☎(07442)2277
Closed 2-21 Dec
rm28(⇔♫19) ☎ P25 Mountain

KOBLENZ
Rheinland-Pfalz

★★★**Diehl's Rheinterrasse** Ehrenbreitstein
☎(0261)72010 tx 862663
⇔♫65 ☎ P50 Lift ⌖ ⌂ Sea
Credit Cards ① ② ③ ⑤
★★★**Kleiner Riesen** Rheinanlagen 18 (n.rest)
☎(0261)32077 tx 862442
⇔♫30 ☎ P4 Lift ⌖
Credit Cards ① ② ③ ④ ⑤
★★★**Scandic Crown** J-Wegeler Str ☎(0261)1360
tx 862338
⇔♫167 ☎ P Lift ⌖
Credit Cards ① ② ③ ⑤
★★**Scholz** Moselweisser Str 121 ☎(0261)408021
tx 862648
:Rest closed Sun & 20 Dec-7 Jan
⇔♫62 ☎ P30 Lift
Credit Cards ① ② ③ ⑤
➨ **G Schilling** Andernacher Str 232 ☎(0261)
85002 Ren
➨ **P Wirtz** Andernacher Str 201 ☎(0261) 80720
Ope Alf

KÖLN (COLOGNE)
Nordrhein-Westfalen

See Plan page 212
Köln is one of the largest cities in West Germany and the most important in Rhineland. It stands on the left bank where the Rhine is a quarter of a mile wide, and is 120ft above sea level in a fertile plain. The city's long-standing importance in religious, economic and political affairs is reflected in its buildings. All are dominated by the magnificent cathedral, one of the finest Gothic structures in Europe.
Much of Köln, including many fine old churches - notably those of St Andrew, St Maria im Kapitol and St Peter, was destroyed during the Second World War, but many buildings have been reconstructed or restored. The *Wallraf-Richartz Museum* has an important collection of paintings.

EATING OUT Germans have hearty appetites, and restaurateurs in Köln go out of their way to satisfy them. Pork dishes come in a variety of forms, from local ham to spicy *würst* sausages. Other regional specialities include sweet-and-sour red cabbage with apples, raisins and white vinegar; potato pancakes; and potato salad laced with onions and bacon.

KÖLN (COLOGNE)
Nordrhein-Westfalen

★★★★★**Excelsior Hotel-Ernst** (SRS) Dompl
☎(0221)2701 tx 8882645
↝♠165 Lift ℂ
Credit Cards ①②⑤

★★★★**Holiday Inn Crowne Plaza**
Habsburgerring 9-13 ☎(0221)20950 tx 8886618
↝♠300 P405 Lift ℂ ⌇
Credit Cards ①②③④⑤

★★★**Augustinerplatz** Hohestr 30 (n.rest)
☎(0221)236717 tx 17221
↝♠57 ☙ P Lift ℂ
Credit Cards ①②③⑤

★★★**Haus Lyskirchen** Filzengraben 26/32
☎(0221)234891 tx 8885449
2 Jan-23 Dec :Rest closed Sun, Fri & Sat midday
↝♠95 ☙ P40 Lift ℂ ⌇
Credit Cards ①②③④⑤

★★★*Rheingold* Engelbertstr 33 (n.rest)
☎(0221)236531 tx 8882923
↝♠52 ☙ P4 Lift ℂ
Credit Cards ①②③⑤

★★**Ariane** Hohe Pforte 19-21 (n.rest)
☎(0221)236033 tx 8881991
↝♠40 P5 Lift ℂ

★★*Berlin* Domstr 10 ☎(0221)123051 tx 8885123
rm78(↝♠76) ☙ P14 Lift ℂ
Credit Cards ①②③④⑤

★★**Conti** Brüsseler Str 42 ☎(0221)219262 tx
8881644
5 Jan-19 Dec
↝♠43 ☙ Lift ℂ
Credit Cards ①②③

★★**Intercity Ibis** Bahnhofvorpl (n.rest)
☎(0221)132051 tx 8881002
↝♠66 Lift ℂ
Credit Cards ①②③⑤

★★**Panorama** Siegburgstr 33-37 (n.rest)
☎(0221)884041-43 tx 887754
2 Jan-22 Dec
↝♠30 ☙ P2 Lift ℂ Mountain
Credit Card ①

At KÖLN-BONN AIRPORT(17km SE)

★★★**Holiday Inn** (QM) Waldstr 255
☎(02203)5610 tx 8874665
↝♠113 P120 Lift ℂ ⌇ ⬠
Credit Cards ①②③④⑤

At KÖLN-LINDENTHAL

★★★*Queens* Dürenerstr 287 ☎(0221)463001 tx
8882516
↝♠154 ☙ P Lift ℂ Lake
Credit Cards ①②③④⑤

★★**Bremer** Dürenerstr 225 ☎(0221)405013 tx
8882063
5 Jan-22 Dec
rm69(↝♠58) A16rm ☙ P2 Lift ℂ ⬠
Credit Cards ①②③⑤

At KÖLN-MARSDORF

★★★**Novotel** Horbeller Str 1 ☎(02234)5140 tx
8886365
↝♠199 P200 Lift ⬠ ⌇
Credit Cards ①②③④⑤

At KÖLN-MÜLHEIM

★★★**Kaiser** Genovevastr 10-14 ☎(0221)623057
tx 8873546
rm51(↝♠47) ☙ P50 Lift ℂ ⬠
Credit Cards ①②③⑤

KÖLN-BONN AIRPORT
See **KÖLN (COLOGNE)**

KÖLN-LINDENTHAL
See **KÖLN (COLOGNE)**

KÖLN-MARSDORF
See **KÖLN (COLOGNE)**

KÖLN-MÜLHEIM
See **KÖLN (COLOGNE)**

KÖNIGSFELD IM SCHWARZWALD
Baden-Württemberg

★★★**Schwarzwald** H-Voland Str 10
☎(07725)7093 tx 792426
rm56(↝♠47) ☙ P32 Lift ⌇ ⬠
Credit Cards ①②③⑤

KÖNIGSTEIN IM TAUNUS
Hessen

★★★**Sonnenhof** Falkensteinerstr 9
☎(06174)29080 tx 410636
rm44(↝♠41) A26rm ☙ P83 ℂ ⌇ ⬠ Mountain
Credit Cards ①②③⑤

★★**Parkhotel Bender** Frankfurterstr 1
☎(06174)1005
↝♠36 ☙ P10
Credit Cards ①②⑤

☙ P **Ohlenschlager** Forellenweg 1 ☎(06174)
1299 For

KÖNIGSWINTER
Nordrhein-Westfalen

★**Siebengebirge** Hauptstr 342 ☎(02223)21359
1 Feb-15 Dec :Rest closed Wed
rm10(♠5) ☙ P6
Credit Cards ①②③⑤

☙ *Vogt* Oberkasseler Str ☎(02223) 23001 P Colt
For

KONSTANZ (CONSTANCE)
Baden-Württemberg

★★★**Insel** (SRS) Auf der Insel 1 ☎(07531)25011
tx 733276
↝♠100 P80 Lift ℂ ⌒ Lake
Credit Cards ①②③④⑤

★★**Deutsches Haus** Marktstätte 15 (n.rest)
☎(07531)27065
rm42(↝♠34) P Lift ℂ
Credit Cards ①②③⑤

KORNTAL-MÜNCHINGEN
Baden-Württemberg

★★★**Mercure** Siemensstr 50 ☎(07150)130 tx
723589
↝♠210 ☙ P300 Lift ℂ ⬠
Credit Cards ①②③⑤

KREFELD
Nordrhein-Westfalen

★★★**Parkhotel Krefelder Hof** (BW) Uerdinger Str
245 ☎(02151)5840 tx 853748
:Rest closed 24-25 Dec
↝♠147 A63rm Lift ℂ ⬠
Credit Cards ①②③⑤

☙ *Preckel* Virchowstr 140/146 ☎(02151) 37110
Ren

KREUZNACH, BAD
Rheinland-Pfalz

☙ *E Holzhauser* Mannheimer Str 183-185
☎(0671) 30031 For

KREUZWERTHEIM
See **WERTHEIM**

KRONACH
Bayern

☙ *Eisenträger* Siechenangerstr 27-29 ☎(09261)
734 P For

KRONBERG IM TAUNUS
Hessen

★★★**Schloss** Hainstr 25 ☎(06173)701-01 tx
415424
↝♠57 P90 Lift ℂ ♍♍
Credit Cards ①②③④⑤

KULMBACH
Bayern

★★★*Hansa-Hotel-Hönsch* Weltrichstr 2A (n.rest)
☎(09221)7995
↝♠28 ☙ P Lift
Credit Cards ①②③④⑤

LAHNSTEIN
Rheinland-Pfalz

★★★**Rhein-Lahn** Im Kurzentrum,Zu den Thermen
1 ☎(02621)151 tx 869827
↝♠220 ☙ P300 Lift ℂ ⌇ ⬠ ⌒ Mountain
Credit Cards ①②③⑤

LAHR
Baden-Württemberg

★★**Schulz** Alte-Bahnhofstr 6 ☎(07821)26097
:Rest closed Sun
rm48(↝♠41) ☙ P5 Lift
Credit Cards ①②③⑤

LAMPERTHEIM
Hessen

★★★**Deutsches Haus** Kaiserstr 47
☎(06206)2022 tx 466902
6 Jan-22 Dec
↝♠27 P8 Lift
Credit Cards ②③⑤

LANDAU IN DER PFALZ
Rheinland-Pfalz

★★**Körber** Reiterstr 11 ☎(06341)4050
15 Jan-20 Dec :Rest closed Fri
rm40(↝♠32) ☙ P ℂ
Credit Cards ①②

☙ *Autohaus Nesper* Wieslauterstr 61 ☎(06341)
80066 P Col Tal

LANDSHUT
Bayern

☙ *K Meusel* Ottostr 15 ☎(0871) 72048 For

LANGENARGEN
Baden-Württemberg

★★**Schiff** Marktpl 1 ☎(07543)2407
Apr-Oct
rm42(↝♠37) Lift Lake
Credit Card ①

LANGENISARHOFEN
Bayern

★**Buhmann** Kreuzstr 1 ☎(09938)277
↝♠10 ☙ P22 ⌒ Mountain
Credit Cards ①②⑤

LAUTENBACH
Baden-Württemberg

★**Sternen** Hauptstr 47 ☎(07802)3538
mid Dec-mid Nov :Rest closed Mon
rm40(↝♠38) ☙ P42 Lift Mountain
Credit Cards ①③⑤

LAUTERBAD
See **FREUDENSTADT**

LENGFELD
See **WÜRZBURG**

LENZKIRCH
Baden-Württemberg

★★**Ursee** Grabenstr 18 ☎(07653)781
15 Dec-3 Nov
rm54(↝♠51) ☙ P30 Lift
Credit Cards ①②③⑤

LEONBERG
Baden-Württemberg

★★★**Eiss** Neue Ramtelstr 28 ☎(07152)20041 tx
724141
rm100(↝♠75) A20rm ☙ P130 Lift ℂ
Credit Cards ①②③⑤

★★**Sonne** Stuttgarterstr 1 ☎(07152)27626
rm37(↝♠28) A17rm ☙ P40 ℂ

LEONI
See **BERG**

LEVERKUSEN
Nordrhein-Westfalen

★★★**Ramada** Am Büchelter Hof 11 ☎(0214)3830
tx 8510238
↝♠202 ☙ P150 Lift ℂ ⬠
Credit Cards ①②③④⑤

KÖLN (COLOGNE)

1	★★★★	Excelsior Hotel-Ernst
2	★★★★	Holiday Inn Crowne Plaza
3	★★★	Augustinerplatz
4	★★★	Crest (At Köln-Lindenthal)
5	★★★	Haus Lyskirchen
6	★★★	Novotel (At Köln-Marsdorf)
7	★★★	Kaiser (At Köln-Mülheim)
9	★★★	Rheingold
10	★★	Ariane
11	★★	Berlin
12	★★	Bremer (At Köln-Lindenthal)
13	★★	Conti
14	★★	Intercity Ibis
15	★★	Panorama

At **OPLADEN**(2km NW)

W Werlich Kopernikusstr 25-29 ☎(02171)
48401 P For

LICHTENFELS
Bayern

Szymansky Bamberg Str 125 ☎(09571) 3654
M/C P AR

LIEBENZELL, BAD
Baden-Württemberg

★★★**Kronen** Badweg 7 ☎(07052)2081
➤60 A17rm ➯ P24 Lift ⚘ 🖼 Mountain
Credit Cards 1 4

LIESER
Rheinland-Pfalz

★★**Mehn** Moselstr 2 ☎(06531)6019
Feb-15 Dec
rm24(➤7) ➯ P25 Mountain
Credit Cards 1 3

LIMBURG AN DER LAHN
Hessen

★★**Dom** Grabenstr 57 ☎(06431)24077
7 Jan-20 Dec
rm59(➤51) ➯ P20 Lift ℂ
Credit Cards 1 2 3 5

★★**Zimmermann** Blumenröderstr 1
☎(06431)4611 tx 484782
➤26 A5rm ➯ P15
Credit Cards 1 2 3 5

★**Huss** Bahnhofpl 3 ☎(06431)25087
rm34(➤24) ➯ P14 Lift ℂ
Credit Cards 1 2 3 5

Tritsch Industriestr ☎(06431) 4601 P For

Unterfeld Westerwaldstr 82 ☎(06431) 25277
P Maz

LINDAU IM BODENSEE
Bayern

★★★**Bayrischer Hof** Seepromenade
☎(08382)5055 tx 54340
Etr-Oct
➤195 ➯ P60 Lift ℂ ⌂ Mountain Lake
Credit Cards 1 3

★★★**Reutemann** Seepromenade ☎(08382)5055
tx 54340
➤37 ➯ P Lift ℂ ⌂ Mountain Lake
Credit Cards 1 3

★★**Kellner** Alwindstr 7 (n.rest) ☎(08382)5686
Mid Apr-Mid Sep
rm11(➤7) P7

★★**Lindauer Hof** Seehafen ☎(08382)4064 tx
541813
Mar-Dec
➤23 Lift 🖼 Mountain Lake
Credit Cards 1 2 3

★★**Seegarten** Seepromenade ☎(08382)5055 tx
54340
Mar-Nov
rm27(➤26) ➯ P Lift ℂ ⌂ Mountain Lake
Credit Cards 1 3

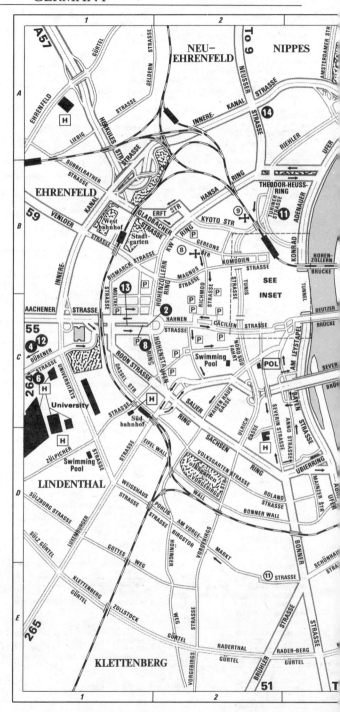

KÖLN
(COLOGNE)

① Botanical gardens & Flora Park (A3)

② Dom (cathedral) (D6)

③ Gürzenich (Festival Hall) (E6)

④ Messegelände (Exhibition Halls) (B3)

⑤ Rathaus (town hall) (D/E6)

⑥ Römisch–Germanisches Museum (D6)

⑦ Schnütgen Museum (E5)

⑧ St. Gereon Church (B2)

⑨ St.Ursula Church (B2)

⑩ Wallraf–Richartz Museum (D5)

⑪ Market (E2)

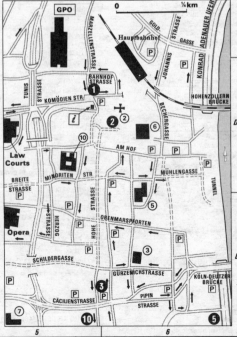

213

GERMANY

๑ *Stöver* Bregenzer Str 121 ☎(08382) 7106 P For

LIPPSPRINGE, BAD
Nordrhein-Westfalen

★★★*Bad Lippspringe* Postfach 1280
☎(05252)2010 tx 936933
◀📶75 P105 Lift ℃ ९ ◻
Credit Cards 1 2 3 5

LIPPSTADT
Nordrhein-Westfalen

๑ *Mertens* Planckstr 12 ☎(02941) 14041 P For

LÖRRACH
Baden-Württemberg

★★★*Binoth Am Markt* Baslerstr 169
☎(07621)3018
:Rest closed Tue pm & Wed
rm22(◀📶18) ☆ P8 Lift ℃
Credit Cards 1 2 3 4 5

LOSSBURG
Baden-Württemberg

At SCHÖMBERG

★★*Waldhufen* Ortsstr 8 ☎(07446)1746
Closed Nov-20 Dec:Rest closed Mon
◀📶9 ☆ P9

LÜBECK
Schleswig-Holstein

★★★*Lysia* (Mövenpick) Auf der Wallhalbinsel
☎(0451)1504 tx 26707
◀📶197 ☆ P Lift ℃
Credit Cards 1 2 3 5

★★*Kaiserhof* Kronsförder Allee 13
☎(0451)791011 tx 26603
:Rest closed Sat & Sun
◀📶73 A16rm ☆ P30 Lift ℃ ◻
Credit Cards 1 2 3 5

★★*Lindenhof* Lindenstr 1A ☎(0451)84015 tx
26621
:Rest closed Sun
◀📶51 P15 Lift ℃
Credit Cards 1 3 4 5

๑ *Jäckel* Travemünder Allee 15-17 ☎(0451)
33088 Ren

๑ *N Köster* Heiligen Geist-Kamp 6-8 ☎(0451)
32032 Cit

LÜDENSCHEID
Nordrhein-Westfalen

★★★*Queens Moat House* (QM) Parkstr 66
☎(02351)1560 tx 826644
◀📶174 P120 Lift ℃ ◻ Mountain
Credit Cards 1 2 3 4 5

๑ *Märkischer Automobile* Nottebohm Str 2
☎(02351) 45066 For

LUDWIGSBURG
Baden-Württemberg

At MONREPOS (SCHLOSS)(5km NW)

★★★★*Schlosshotel Monrepos* (BW)
☎(07141)3020 tx 7264720
8 Jan-22 Dec
◀📶81 P1500 Lift ℃ ◻ Lake
Credit Cards 1 2 3 5

LUDWIGSHAFEN
Rheinland-Pfalz

★★★*City Europa* Ludwigspl 5-6 ☎(0621)519011
tx 464701
:Rest closed Sat
◀📶91 ☆ P100 Lift ℃ ◻
Credit Cards 1 2 3 4 5

★★★*Excelsior* (BW) Lorientalle 16 ☎(0621)5985-
0 tx 464647
◀📶160 ☆ P30 Lift ℃ ◻
Credit Cards 1 2 3 5

LÜNEBURG
Niedersachsen

★★*Landwehr* Hamburgerstr 15 ☎(04131)121024

---

29 Jan-23 Dec :Rest closed Sun
◀📶35 ☆ P40 ℃ ९ ◻ ♓ ♒
Credit Cards 1 3 5

MAINZ
Rheinland-Pfalz

★★★★*Hilton International* Rheinstr 68
☎(06131)2450 tx 4187570
◀📶433 ☆ P20 Lift ℃
Credit Cards 1 2 3 4 5

★★★*Central* Bahnhofspl 8 ☎(06131)674001 tx
4187794
4 Jan-23 Dec :Rest closed Sun
◀📶61 ☆ Lift ℃
Credit Cards 1 2 3 4 5

★★★*Europa* Kaiserstr 7 ☎(06131)6350 tx
4187702
rm93(◀📶89) P100 Lift ℃
Credit Cards 1 2 3 5

★★★*Mainzer Hof* Kaiserstr 98 ☎(06131)233771
tx 4187787
◀📶99 Lift ℃
Credit Cards 1 2 3 5

★★★*Novotel Mainz Süd* Essenheimer Str 200
☎(06131)361054 tx 4187236
◀📶121 P Lift ℃ ◻
Credit Cards 1 2 3 5

๑ *Heinz* Bismarckpl ☎(06131) 676011-15 For

At FINTHEN(7kw W)

★★*Kurmainz* Flugplatzstr 44 ☎(06131)4910 tx
4187001
5 Jan-21 Dec
◀📶84 ☆ P52 Lift ℃ ९ ◻
Credit Cards 1 2 3 5

MANDERSCHEID
Rheinland-Pfalz

★★*Zens* Kurfürstenstr 35 ☎(06572)769
2 Dec-1 Jan
◀📶200 P200 Lift ℃ ◻
Credit Cards 1 2 3 5

MANNHEIM
Baden-Württemberg

★★★★*Mannheimer Hof* (SRS) Augusta Anlage
4-8 ☎(0621)45021 tx 462245
◀📶170 P Lift ℃
Credit Cards 1 2 3 5

★★★*Augusta* (BW) Augusta Anlage 43-45
☎(0621)418001 tx 462395
◀📶106 ☆ P15 Lift ℃
Credit Cards 1 2 3 4 5

★★★*Novotel* auf dem Friedenspl 1
☎(0621)417001 tx 463694
◀📶180 P160 Lift ℃ ◻
Credit Cards 1 2 3 5

★★*Intercity Mannheim* Hauptbahnhof
☎(0621)1595-0 tx 463604
rm48(◀📶47) P10 Lift ℃
Credit Cards 1 2 3 5

★*Kaiserring* Kaiserring 18 (n.rest)
☎(0621)23931
rm62(◀📶50) Lift ℃
Credit Cards 1 2 3 5

★★*Mack* Mozartstr 14 ☎(0621)23888 tx 462116
7 Jan-7 Aug & 26 Aug-19 Dec
rm54(◀📶35) A6rm ☆ P8 Lift ℃
Credit Cards 1 2 3 5

๑ *H Kohlhoff* Obere Riedstr 117-119 ☎(0621)
737005 P For

At SANDHOFEN(10km N)

★★*Weber* Frankenthaler Str 85 ☎(0621)77010 tx
463537
:Rest closed Sat & end Dec-mid Jan
◀📶100 ☆ P80 Lift ℃
Credit Cards 1 2 3 5

MARBURG AN DER LAHN
Hessen

★★*Europäischer Hof* Elisabethstr 12
☎(06421)64044 tx 482636

:Rest closed 30 Jul-21 Aug
◀📶100 A50rm ☆ P20 Lift ℃
Credit Cards 1 2 3 5

At CÖLBE(7km N)

๑ *M Feeser* Erlenring 9 ☎(06421) 23038 For

MARIA LAACH
Rheinland-Pfalz

★★*Seehotel* ☎(02652)5840
rm67(◀📶63) ☆ P50 Lift ℃ ◻ Lake
Credit Cards 1 2

MARIAWEILER
See DÜREN

MARIENBERG, BAD
Rheinland-Pfalz

★★★*Kneipp-Kurhotel Wildpark* Kurallee 1 (1km
W) ☎(02661)7069
20 Dec-15 Nov
rm45(◀📶40) ☆ P Lift ◻ Mountain

MARKTHEIDENFELD
Bayern

★★*Schöne Aussicht* Brückenstr 8
☎(09391)3455
rm48(◀📶43) ☆ P34 Lift

★*Anker* Obertorstr 6-8 ☎(09391)4041 tx 689608
◀📶38 A25rm ☆ P31 Lift ℃ Mountain
Credit Cards 1 2

MARKTOBERDORF
Bayern

★★*Sepp* Bahnhofstr 13 ☎(08342)2048
◀📶55 ☆ P50 ℃ Mountain
Credit Cards 1 5

MARL
Nordrhein-Westfalen

★★★*Novotel* E-Weitsch Weg 2 ☎(02365)1020 tx
829916
◀📶96 P50 Lift ℃ ◻ Lake
Credit Cards 1 2 3 5

๑ *E Herzig* Victoria Str 174 ☎(02365) 45057 P
For

MAYSCHOSS
See ALTENAHR

MEERSBURG
Baden-Württemberg

★★*Bären* Marktpl 11 ☎(07532)6044
◀📶16 P15

★★*3 Stuben* Winzergasse 1 ☎(07532)6019
:Rest closed Nov-Feb
◀📶20 ☆ P4

★★*Weinstube-Löwen* Marktpl 2 ☎(07532)6013
◀📶14 ☆ P12

MEMMINGEN
Bayern

★★★*Adler* Maximilianstr 3 ☎(08331)87015
rm51(◀📶30) A4rm ☆ P10 Lift ℃
Credit Cards 1 2 3 5

๑ *C Schenk* Donaustr 29 ☎(08331) 86048 Ope

MERGENTHEIM, BAD
Baden-Württemberg

★★★★*Victoria* Poststr 2-4 ☎(07931)5930 tx
74224
◀📶85 ☆ P40 Lift ℃ ◻ ◻
Credit Cards 1 2 3 4 5

MERKLINGEN
Baden-Württemberg

★*Ochsen* Hauptstr 12 ☎(07337)283
Dec-Oct :Rest closed Sun
rm19(📶12) ☆ P20
Credit Cards 1 2

MINDELHEIM
Bayern

๑ *Krumm & Schragl* Kanzelwandstr 5 ☎(08261)
99140 Aud VW

214

MINDEN
Nordrhein-Westfalen

★★**Kruses Park** Marienstr 108 ☎(0571)46033 tx 97986
rm34(♨32) 🏠 P40
Credit Cards ①②③⑤

★★**Silke** Fischerglacis 21 (n.rest) ☎(0571)23736
♨21 🏠 P10 ⌣

🍴 **Gössling & Boger** Ringstr 11 ☎(0571) 27037
P For

MITTENWALD
Bayern

★★*Post* Obermarkt 9 ☎(08823)1094
rm96(♨68) 🏠 P Lift ℂ ⌣ Mountain

★**Zerhoch** H-Barth-Weg 7 (n.rest) ☎(08823)1508
20 Dec-Oct
♨15 🏠 P8 Mountain

MÖNCHENGLADBACH
Nordrhein-Westfalen

★★★★**Ambassador** (BW) am Geropl
☎(02161)3070 tx 852363
♨127 P200 Lift ℂ ⌣
Credit Cards ①②③④⑤

★★★★**Dorint Mönchengladbach** Hohenzollernstr 5 ☎(02161)86060 tx 852656
♨102 P40 Lift ℂ ⌣
Credit Cards ①②③⑤

🍴 **Autohaus W Coenen** Monschauerstr 36
☎(02161) 31166 M/C P For

At **RHEYDT**(4km S)

★★★**Besch Parkhotel** H-Junkers Str 2
☎(02166)44011 tx 8529143
♨33 🏠 P5 Lift ℂ
Credit Cards ①②③④⑤

★★**Coenen** Giesenkirchener Str 41-45
☎(02166)10088 tx 8529237
♨47 Lift
Credit Cards ①②③④⑤

MONREPOS (SCHLOSS)
See **LUDWIGSBURG**

MONSCHAU
Nordrhein-Westfalen

★★**Aquarium** Heidgen 34 ☎(02472)693
♨13 A3rm 🏠 P16 Mountain
Credit Card ⑤

★★**Horchem** Rurstr 14 ☎(02472)420
15 Mar-15 Feb
rm14(♨13) 🏠 P5 Mountain
Credit Cards ①②③⑤

★★**Lindenhof** Laufenstr 77 ☎(02472)686
rm12(♨9) A4rm P10 ℂ Mountain
Credit Cards ①②③⑤

★**Burgau** St-Vitherstr 16 ☎(02472)2120
Feb-Dec :Rest closed Tue
rm13(♨7) 🏠 P8 Mountain
Credit Cards ①②

★*Haus Herrlichkeit* Haagweg 3A (n.rest)
☎(02472)3190
♨6 🏠 P10 Mountain

MONTABAUR
Rheinland-Pfalz

★*Post* Bahnhofstr 30 ☎(02602)3361
rm22(♨13) 🏠 P Lift
Credit Cards ①②

★**Schlemmer** Kirchstr 18 ☎(02602)5022
10 Jan-22 Dec :Rest closed Sun
rm30(♨20) 🏠 P16

🍴 **Zakowski** Alleestr 6-8 ☎(02602) 4058 P For

At **HEILIGENROTH**

★★**Heiligenroth** ☎(02602)504445 tx 869675
♨28 🏠 P40 Lift ℂ
Credit Cards ①②③⑤

MÜHLDORF AM INN
Bayern

★*Jägerhof* Stadtpl 3 ☎(08631)4004
rm27(♨20) P20
Credit Cards ①②③⑤

MÜLHEIM
Rheinland-Pfalz

★★*Moselhaus Selzer* Moselstr 7 ☎(06534)707
15 Mar-15 Nov
♨18 🏠 P30 Sea

MÜLHEIM AN DER RUHR
Nordrhein-Westfalen

★★★**Noy** Schlossstr 28-30 ☎(0208)4505-0 tx 1720835
:Rest closed Sun
♨60 🏠 P30 Lift ℂ
Credit Cards ①②③④⑤

🍴 **Deterding** Oberhausener Str 85-95 ☎(0208) 402041 P For

🍴 **Krumey & Gilles** Cacilienstr 2-8 ☎(0208) 422045 DJ Mit Rov

MÜLLHEIM
Baden-Württemberg

★★★*Euro-Hotel Alte Post* An Der Bundesstr 3 ☎(07631)5522
rm57(♨48) A42rm 🏠 P50 ℂ
Credit Cards ①②③⑤

MUMMELSEE
See **BADEN-BADEN**

MÜNCHEN (MUNICH)
Bayern

See plan page 216

München is the capital of Bavaria and one of the most beautiful cities in Europe; its heritage includes the ornate buildings of the Mareinplatz, a fine cathedral, several Baroque churches and a major art collection.
Contemporary München features the 1972 Olympic Park, the BMW Automobile Museum, where exhibits are displayed in parallel with political and social events, and the celebrated *Hofbräuhaus*, where you can sample the product at long tables in the courtyard.
München has some of Germany's, most fashionable shops; tailoring here is among the best in the world, so suits and jackets in the traditional wool Loden cloth are good investments.

EATING OUT Start the day with a hearty breakfast which often includes ham, salami, cheeses and pumpernickel. Veal and pork are popular main dishes, accompanied by excellent potato salads or *sauerkraut* (cabbage cooked with white wine, cloves and caraway seeds). Among the most popular, and tempting, desserts, are *apfelstrudel*, plum cake and cherry gâteau. Between meals try a fresh pretzel, and to accompany your meals there is an excellent choice of Mosel and Rhine wines.
One of München's finest restaurants is the *Walterspiel* at the Hotel Vier Jahreszeiten in Maximilianstrasse, while for those on a budget there is an excellent choice of moderately priced restaurants in Schwabing, the attractive old part of the city.

MÜNCHEN (MUNICH)
Bayern

★★★★★**Vier Jahreszeiten** (Intercont) Mazimilianstr 17 ☎(089)230390 tx 523859
♨340 🏠 Lift ℂ ⌣
Credit Cards ①②③⑤

★★★**Bayerischer Hof** (SRS) Promenadepl 2-6 ☎(089)21200 tx 523409
♨440 🏠 P120 Lift ℂ ⌣
Credit Cards ①②③④⑤

★★★**Excelsior** Schützenstr 11 ☎(089)551370 tx 522419
♨115 🏠 P Lift ℂ
Credit Cards ①②③⑤

★★★★**Holiday Inn - München Sud** Kistlerhofstr 142 ☎(089)780020 tx 5218645
♨320 🏠 P200 Lift ℂ ⌣
Credit Cards ①②③⑤

★★★**Park Hilton München** Am Tucherpark 7 ☎(089)38450 tx 5215740
♨477 P300 Lift ℂ
Credit Cards ①②③④⑤

★★★**Austrotel** Arnulfstr 2 ☎(089)53860 tx 522650
♨174 P25 Lift ℂ
Credit Cards ①②③⑤

★★★*Park* Zschokkestr 55 ☎(089)579360 tx 5218609
♨71 🏠 P30 Lift ℂ
Credit Cards ①②③④⑤

★★★*Penta* (Forum) Hochstr 3 ☎(089)4485555 tx 529046
♨583 P500 Lift ℂ ⌣
Credit Cards ①②③④⑤

★★★*Queens* Effnerstr 99 ☎(089)982541 tx 524757
♨154 🏠 P Lift ℂ
Credit Cards ①②③④⑤

★★**Daniel** Sonnenstr 5 (n.rest) ☎(089)554945 tx 523863
rm76(♨72) Lift ℂ
Credit Cards ①②③⑤

★★**Drei Löwen** (BW) Schillerstr 8 ☎(089)55104-0 tx 523867
♨130 🏠 P25 Lift ℂ
Credit Cards ①②③④⑤

★★**Leopold** Leopoldstr 119 ☎(089)367061 tx 5215160
:Rest closed Sat
rm82(♨69) A52rm 🏠 P25 Lift ℂ
Credit Cards ①②③④⑤

★★**Platzl** Platzl 1 ☎(089)237030 tx 522910
:Rest closed Sun
♨170 P80 Lift ℂ
Credit Cards ①②③

🍴 **Auto-Frühling** Klarastr 20 ☎(089) 187081 AR DJ Maz

🍴 *Wolf* Müllerstr 50 ☎089 265488 P AR Dai

MÜNCHEN (MUNICH)

1	★★★★	Vier Jahres
2	★★★★	Bayerischer Hof
3	★★★★	Excelsior
4	★★★★	Hilton International
5	★★★	Austrotel
6	★★★	Crest
7	★★★	Penta
8	★★	Daniel
9	★★	Drei Löwen
10	★★	Leopold
11	★★	Platzl

MÜNSTER
Nordrhein-Westfalen

★★★**Kaiserhof** Bahnhofstr 14/16 (n.rest)
☎(0251)40059 tx 892141
➡♠109 P40 Lift ☾
Credit Cards [1] [2] [3] [5]

★★★**Mövenpick** (Mövenpick) Kardinal-Von-Galen
Ring 65 ☎(0251)89020 tx 1725110
➡♠120 P100 Lift ☾
Credit Cards [1] [2] [3] [5]

★★★**Schloss Wilkinghege** (GS) Steinfürterstr
374 ☎(0251)213045
➡♠37 A18rm ♠ P ☾ ⚲ ﹩﹩

★★**Conti** Berlinerpl 2A ☎(0251)40444 tx 892113
➡♠57 Lift ☾
Credit Cards [1] [2] [3] [4] [5]

❧ **Hartmann** Alberloher Weg 668 ☎(0251)
616003 P Peu Tal

❧ **Ing W Brandes** Altenbergerstr 32 ☎(0251)
02533 P Alf Rov DJ

❧ **Lich** ☎(0251) 230613 P Dat

❧ **Müller** Kohienbissener Str 40-42 ☎(0251)
4499 P AR

MURNAU
Bayern

★★★**Alpenhof Murnau** Ramsachstr 8
☎(08841)1045
➡♠48 ♠ P55 Lift ☾ ◺ Mountain

MURRHARDT
Baden-Württemberg

★★**Sonne Post** Karlstr 6-9 ☎(07192)8083/4/5 tx
7245929
➡♠37 ♠ P20 Lift ▱
Credit Cards [1] [2] [3] [4] [5]

NAGOLD
Baden-Württemberg

★★**Post** (ROM) Bahnhofstr 3-4 ☎(07452)4048
:Rest closed Sat until 5pm
➡♠23 A7rm P11 Lift ☾
Credit Cards [1] [2] [3] [4] [5]

NAUHEIM, BAD
Hessen

★★★**Parkhotel am Kurhaus** Nördlicher Park 16
☎(06032)3030 tx 415514
➡♠99 ♠ P150 Lift ☾ ▱
Credit Cards [1] [2] [3] [4] [5]

NECKARGEMüND
Baden-Württemberg

★★**Ritter** (GT) Neckarstr 40 ☎(06223)7035 tx
461837
➡♠40 ♠ P4 ☾ Lake
Credit Cards [1] [2] [3] [4]

NECKARSTEINACH
Hessen

★★**Schiff** Neckargemünderstr 2 ☎(06229)324
Jan-Nov :Rest closed Mon
➡♠22 P15 Lift Mountain

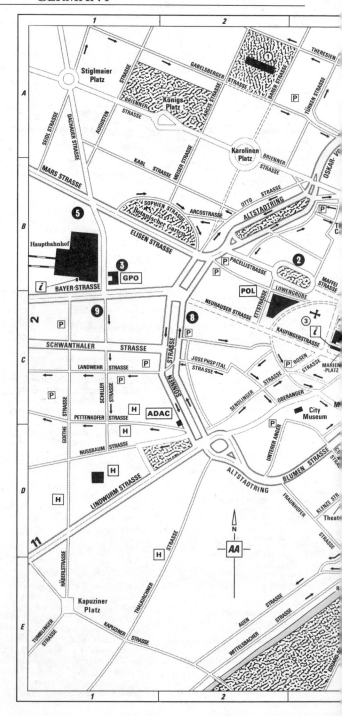

MÜNCHEN (MUNICH) CENTRAL

Englischer Garten

State Gallery of Modern Art

National Museum

Hof Garten

Ethnological Museum

Maximilian Brücke

Max Joseph Brücke

Prinzregenten Brücke

Ludwigs Brücke

Bosche Brücke

Cornelius Brücke

ISAR

Car Sleeper

Ostbahnhof

To A8

A94

304

| 0 | | ½km |
| 0 | | ½m |

ALTSTADTRING
(RING ROAD)

(7/89)

NERESHEIM
Baden-Württemberg

★**Klosterhospiz** ☎(07326)6282
:Rest closed 15 Jan-28 Feb
rm53(↔28) P80 Lift

NEUASTENBERG
See **WINTERBERG**

NEUBEURN
Bayern

★★**Burg** Marktpl 23 ☎(08035)2456
↔13 ☚ P19 Lift Mountain
Credit Cards ①②③⑤

NEUENAHR, BAD
Rheinland-Pfalz

★★★**Dorint** Am Dahliengarten ☎(02641)8950 tx
861805
↔180 ☚ P120 Lift ℂ 🖃
Credit Cards ①②③⑤

★★★**Kurhotel** (SRS) Kurgartestr 1
☎(02641)2291 tx 861812
↔244 P40 Lift ℂ 🖃
Credit Cards ①②③④⑤

★★**Giffels Goldener Anker** Mittelstr 14
☎(02641)8040 tx 861768
rm120(↔86) ☚ P58 Lift
Credit Cards ①②③④⑤

★★**Hamburger Hof** Jesuitenstr 11 (n.rest)
☎(02641)26017
rm36(↔27) ☚ P ℂ

NEUMÜNSTER
Schleswig-Holstein

★★**Lenz** Gasstr 11-12 (n.rest) ☎(04321)450720
↔19 P300

💀 **Fröhling** Kieler Str 239-245 ☎(04321) 32031
For

NEUSS
Nordrhein-Westfalen

At **ERFTTAL**(5km SE)

★★★**Novotel Neuss** Am Derikumer Hof 1
☎(02101)17081 tx 8517634
↔116 ☚ P150 Lift ⌐
Credit Cards ①②③④⑤

At **GRIMLINGHAUSEN**(4.5km SE)

★★**Landhaus** Husenstr 17 ☎(02101)37030 tx
8517891
↔30 ☚ P15 Lift
Credit Card ①

NEUSTADT
See **TITISEE-NEUSTADT**

NEUSTADT AN DER AISCH
Bayern

★★**Römerhof** R-Wagnerstr 15 ☎(09161)3011
↔23 ☚ P4
Credit Cards ①②③⑤

NEUSTADT AN DER SAALE, BAD
Bayern

★★★**Schwan & Post** Am Hohntor ☎(09771)9107
rm33(↔3) ☚ P25 🖃
Credit Cards ①②③⑤

NEU-ULM
Bayern

★★★**Mövenpick** (Mövenpick) Silcherstr 40
☎(0731)80110 tx 721539
↔109 A26rm P250 Lift ℂ 🖃
Credit Cards ①②③④⑤

💀 **Schwabengarage** M-Eyth-Str 45 ☎(0731)
78071 **P** For

NEUWIED
Rheinland-Pfalz

💀 **Sportwagen Service** Konigsberger Str 12
☎(02631) 53018 M/C **P** All makes

NIEFERN-ÖSCHELBRONN
See **PFORZHEIM**

NIERSTEIN
Rheinland-Pfalz

★★**Alter Vater Rhein** ☎(06133)5628
20 Jan-2 Aug & 24 Aug-15 Dec :Rest closed Sun
rm11(↔10) P5

★**Rheinhotel** Mainzerstr 16 ☎(06133)5161 tx
4187784
10 Jan-10 Dec
↔15 ☚ P8 Sea
Credit Cards ①②③⑤

NORDEN
Niedersachsen

★★**Deutsches Haus** Neuer Weg 26
☎(04931)4271
↔40 ☚ P30 Lift
Credit Cards ①②③⑤

NORDHORN
Niedersachsen

★**Euregio** Denekamperstr 43 ☎(05921)5077
rm26(↔24) ☚ P18 ℂ
Credit Cards ①②③⑤

NÖRDLINGEN
Bayern

★★**Sonne** Markpl 3 ☎(09081)5067 tx 51749
:Rest closed Fri
rm40(↔30) ☚ P16
Credit Cards ①②

💀 **Bachmair** Augsburger Str 42 ☎(09081) 3096
For

NOTSCHREI
Baden-Württemberg

★★**Waldhotel am Notschrei** ☎(07602)219
rm36(↔32) ☚ P100 Lift 🖃 Mountain
Credit Cards ①⑤

NÜRNBERG (NUREMBERG)
Bayern

★★★★★**Grand** (THF) Bahnhofstr 1
☎(0911)203621 tx 622010
↔185 Lift ℂ
Credit Cards ①②③④⑤

★★★★**Carlton** (BW) Eilgutstr 13 ☎(0911)20030
tx 622329
↔130 P6050 Lift ℂ
Credit Cards ①②③④⑤

★★★★**Queens Hotel Nürnberg** (QM) Münchener
Str 283 ☎(0911)49441 tx 622930
↔141 P100 Lift ℂ
Credit Cards ①②③⑤

★★★**Atrium** (BW) Münchenerstr 25
☎(0911)47480 tx 626167
↔200 ☚ P280 Lift ℂ 🖃
Credit Cards ①②③④⑤

★★★**Bayerischer Hof** Gleissbühlstr 15 (n.rest)
☎(0911)2321-0 tx 626547
↔80 ☚ P2 Lift ℂ
Credit Cards ①②③⑤

★★★**Novotel Nürnberg Süd** Münchenerstr 340
☎(0911)81260 tx 626449
↔117 P120 Lift ℂ ⌐
Credit Cards ①②③④⑤

★★★**Sterntor** Tafelhofstr 8-14 ☎(0911)23581 tx
622632
↔116 Lift ℂ
Credit Cards ①②③⑤

★★★**Victoria** Königstr 80 ☎(0911)203801 tx
626923
7 Jan-23 Dec
rm64(↔59) P750 Lift ℂ
Credit Cards ①②⑤

★★**Drei Linden** Aussere Sulzbacherstr 1
☎(0911)533233 tx 626455
↔28 P20 ℂ
Credit Cards ①②③⑤

💀 **Kaiser** H-Kolb Str 35 ☎(0911) 831001 **P** Saa

💀 **Motus** Cuxhavenerstr 2 ☎(0911) 34915 **P** Jag
LR Vol

💀 **Pieper** Eibacher Haupstr 34 ☎(0911) 643042
P Vol

💀 **Wuestner** Leyher Str-23 ☎(0911) 327211 **P**
Dat

OBERAMMERGAU
Bayern

★★**Alte Post** Dorfstr 19 ☎(08822)6691
mid Dec-Oct
rm32(↔25) A5rm ☚ P20 Mountain
Credit Cards ①②③

★★**Böld** König-Ludwigstr 10 ☎(08822)520 tx
592406
rm57 ☚ P Mountain
Credit Cards ①③⑤

★★**Friedenshöhe** König-Ludwigstr 31
☎(08822)598
20 Dec-25 Oct
↔11 ☚ P50 Mountain
Credit Cards ①②③⑤

★★**Schilcherhof** Bahnhofstr 17 ☎(08822)4740
Closed Dec-9 Jan
rm17(↔12) A10rm ☚ P Mountain

OBERHAUSEN
Nordrhein-Westfalen

★★★**Ruhrland** Berlinerpl 2 ☎(0208)805031 tx
856900
rm60(↔45) ☚ P20 Lift ℂ
Credit Cards ①②③⑤

💀 **Gerstmann** Wehrstr 17-33 ☎(0208) 865020
M/C For

OBERKIRCH
Baden-Württemberg

★★★**Obere Linde** (ROM) Hauptstr 25-27
☎(07802)8020 tx 752640
rm45(↔35) A20rm ☚ P75 Lift ⚲
Credit Cards ①②③⑤

At **ÖDSBACH**(3km S)

★★★**Grüner Baum** Almstr 33 ☎(07802)2801 tx
752627
↔60 ☚ P100 Lift ℂ 🖃 Mountain
Credit Cards ①②③④⑤

OBERSTAUFEN
Bayern

★★**Kurhotel Hirsch** Kalzhoferstr 4 (n.rest)
☎(08386)2032
rm27(↔21) ☚ P150 Mountain

OBERSTDORF
Bayern

★★★**Wittelsbacher Hof** Prinzenstr 24
☎(08322)1018 tx 541905
17 Dec-16 Apr & 15 May-20 Oct
↔90 ☚ P50 Lift ℂ 🖃 Mountain
Credit Cards ①②③⑤

OBERWESEL
Rheinland-Pfalz

★★**Auf Schönburg** (GS) Schönburg
☎(06744)7027 tx 42321
Mar-Nov :Rest closed Mon
rm21(↔20) P20 Lift
Credit Cards ①②③⑤

★★**Römerkrug** (GS) Marktpl 1 ☎(06744)8176
Feb-20 Dec
↔7 P7
Credit Cards ①③

★**Goldner Pfropfenzieher** ☎(06744)207
:Rest closed Nov-20 Mar
↔17 ☚ P10
Credit Card ②

OCHSENFURT
Bayern

★**Bären** Hauptstr 74 ☎(09331)2282
6 Mar-15 Jan :Rest closed Mon
rm28(↔14) ☚ P22
Credit Cards ①⑤

ÖDSBACH
See **OBERKIRCH**

OESPEL
See **DORTMUND**

OESTRICH
Hessen

★★★**Schwan** (ROM) Rheinallee 5-7
☎(06723)3001 tx 42146
Mar-Nov
◄ᐪ63 A20rm ☎ P24 Lift ℂ
Credit Cards ①②③④⑤

OEYNHAUSEN, BAD
Nordrhein-Westfalen

★★**Hahnenkamp** Alte Reichsstr 4 (2.5km NE)
☎(05731)5041
◄ᐪ23 A4rm P50
Credit Cards ①②③⑤

OFFENBACH
Hessen

★★★**Novotel** Strahlenbergerstr 12 ☎(069)818011
tx 413047
◄ᐪ122 P200 Lift ℂ ⌂
Credit Cards ①②③⑤

★★**Graf** Berlinerstr/Ecke Schlosstr (n.rest)
☎(069)811702 tx 416213
◄ᐪ32 ☎ P12
Credit Cards ①②③⑤

🍽 **Odenwaldring** Odenwaldring 40 ☎(069)
832031 P For

OFFENBURG
Baden-Württemberg

★★★**Dorint** Messepl ☎(0781)5050 tx 752889
◄ᐪ132 Lift ℂ ⌂
Credit Cards ①②③⑤

★★★**Palmengarten** Okenstr 15-17 ☎(0781)2080
tx 752744
◄ᐪ63 ☎ P43 Lift ℂ
Credit Cards ①②③⑤

★**Sonne** Hauptstr 94 ☎(0781)71039
:Rest closed Sat in Apr
rm37(◄ᐪ20) A16rm ☎ P5
Credit Cards ①②③

🍽 **Linck** Freiburgstr 26 ☎(0781) 25005 Ope

At **ORTENBERG**(4km SE)

★**Glattfelder** Kinzigtalstr 20 ☎(0781)31219
:Rest closed Sun
◄ᐪ14 P30
Credit Cards ①②③⑤

OLPE
Nordrhein-Westfalen

★★**Tillmanns** Kölnerstr 15 ☎(02761)26071
:Rest closed Fri evening
rm15(◄ᐪ12) P20
Credit Card ②

OPLADEN
See **LEVERKUSEN**

OPPENHEIM
Rheinland-Pfalz

★★**Kurpfalz** Wormserstr 2 ☎(06133)2291 tx
4187784
11 Jan-9 Dec
rm20(◄ᐪ12) ☎ P5
Credit Cards ①②③⑤

★**Oppenheimer Hof** F-Ebertstr 84 ☎(06133)2495
:Rest closed Sun
◄ᐪ25 P20
Credit Cards ①②③⑤

🍽 **Heinz** Gartenstr 15-19 ☎(06133) 2055 P For

ORTENBERG
See **OFFENBURG**

OSNABRÜCK
Niedersachsen

★★★★*Parkhotel* Edinghausen 1 ☎(0541)46083
tx 94939

◄ᐪ90 ☎ P150 Lift ℂ ⌂
Credit Cards ①②③

★★★*Hohenzollern* H-Heinestr 17 ☎(0541)33170
tx 094776
rm105(◄ᐪ95) P56 Lift ℂ ⌂
Credit Cards ①②③④⑤

★★**Ibis** Blumenheller Weg 152 ☎(0541)40490 tx
94831
◄ᐪ96 P70 Lift ℂ Sea
Credit Cards ①②③④⑤

🍽 **Beinke** Schuetzenstr 27 ☎(0541) 73520

🍽 **Meierrose** Pagenstecherstr 74 ☎(0541)
691110 M/C P BMW

PADERBORN
Nordrhein-Westfalen

★★**Arosa** (BW) Westernmauer 38 ☎(05251)2000
tx 936798
◄ᐪ100 P100 Lift ℂ ⌂
Credit Cards ①②③⑤

★★**Ibis** Am Paderwall 1-5 ☎(05251)25031 tx
936972
◄ᐪ90 ☎ P20 Lift ℂ
Credit Cards ①②③④⑤

🍽 **Kleine** Rathenaustr 79-83 ☎(05251) 2080 For

PASSAU
Bayern

★★**Weisser Hase** Ludwigstr 23 ☎(0851)34066 tx
57960
rm117(◄ᐪ95) P30 Lift ℂ
Credit Cards ①②③⑤

🍽 **Hofbauer** Neuburgerstr 141 ☎(0851) 70070
Ope

PEGNITZ
Bayern

★★★★*Pflaum's Posthotel* (Relais et Châteaux)
Nürnbergerstr 14 ☎(09241)7250 tx 642433
◄ᐪ50 ☎ P74 Lift ℂ ⌇ ⌂ ☉
Credit Cards ①②③⑤

PFORZHEIM
Baden-Württemberg

★★★**Ruf am Schlossberg** Am Schlossberg
☎(07231)16011 tx 783843
◄ᐪ51 ☎ P10 Lift ℂ
Credit Cards ①②③⑤

🍽 **Schweickert** Karlsrühe Str 40 ☎(07231)
16364 AR DR LR Vol

At **NIEFERN-ÖSCHELBRONN**(6km E)

★★★**Queens Moat House** (QM) Pforzheimer Str
☎(07233)1211 tx 783905
◄ᐪ71 ☎ P4 Lift ℂ Mountain
Credit Cards ①②③⑤

PIRMASENS
Rheinland-Pfalz

🍽 **Hoch** Im Erienteich 59 ☎(06331) 76037 P For

POMMERSFELDEN
Bayern

★★**Schloss** ☎(09548)487
rm66(◄ᐪ64) ☎ P100 ℂ ⌇ ⌂

PRIEN AM CHIEMSEE
Bayern

★★**Bayerischer Hof** Bernauerstr 3
☎(08051)1095
◄ᐪ48 ☎ P45 Lift Mountain
Credit Card ①

PUTTGARDEN
Schleswig-Holstein

★★**Dänia** Am Fahrbahnhof ☎(04371)3016 tx
29814
◄ᐪ72 P100 Lift ℂ Sea
Credit Cards ①②③

PYRMONT, BAD
Niedersachsen

★★**Kurhaus** Heiligenangerstr 4 ☎(05281)151 tx
931636

Mar-6 Jan
rm103(◄ᐪ86) P100 Lift ℂ
Credit Cards ①②③⑤

QUICKBORN
Schleswig-Holstein

★★★**Jagdhaus Waldfrieden** (ROM) Kieler Str 1
(On B4 3km N) ☎(04106)3771
◄ᐪ15 P
Credit Cards ①②③⑤

RASTATT
Baden-Württemberg

★*Katzenberger's Adler* Josefstr 7
☎(07222)32103
Closed July
rm6 ☎ P

RATINGEN
See **DÜSSELDORF**

RAVENSBURG
Bayern

★★**Waldhorn** Marienpl 15 ☎(0751)16021 tx
732311
Closed 24-25 Dec:Rest closed 6pm Sun
◄ᐪ40 A25rm ☎ Lift
Credit Cards ①②③⑤

RECKLINGHAUSEN
Nordrhein-Westfalen

🍽 **Mohag** Hertener Str 100 ☎(02361) 58040 M/C
P For

🍽 **VEFA** Bochumer Str 222-224 ☎(02361)
651919 P Hon

REGENSBURG
Bayern

★★★**Avia** Frankenstr 1-3 ☎(0941)4300 tx 65703
◄ᐪ80 ☎ P100 Lift ℂ
Credit Cards ①②③④⑤

★★**Karmeliten** Dachaupl 1 ☎(0941)54308 tx
65170
20 Jan-20 Dec :Rest closed Sun
rm72(◄ᐪ63) P20 Lift ℂ
Credit Cards ①②③⑤

★★*Straubinger Hof* A-Schmetzerstr 33
☎(0941)798355 tx 990099
rm64(ᐪ38) ☎ P22 Lift ℂ Mountain
Credit Cards ①②③⑤

★*Wiendl* Universitätstr 9 ☎(0941)90416 & 96322
:Rest closed Sat
rm33(◄ᐪ28) ☎ P45

🍽 *Bindig* Vilsstr 28 ☎(0941) 47015 P Cit Peu
Tal

🍽 **Kellnberger** Kirchmeierstr 24 ☎(0941) 37850
M/C P Ren

🍽 *Seitz* Alte Straubinger Str 19 ☎(0941) 794031
AR LR

REICHENHALL, BAD
Bayern

★★★**Axelmannstein** (SRS) Salzburgerstr 2-6
☎(08651)4001 tx 56112
◄ᐪ151 ☎ P100 Lift ℂ ⌇ ⌂ Mountain
Credit Cards ①②③⑤

★★★**Kurhotel Luisenbad** Ludwigstr 33
☎(08651)5011 tx 56131
20 Dec-Oct
◄ᐪ88 ☎ P30 Lift ℂ ⌂ Mountain
Credit Cards ①③⑤

★★**Panorama** Baderstr 6 ☎(08651)61001 tx
56194
◄ᐪ83 P50 Lift ℂ ⌂ Mountain
Credit Cards ①②③⑤

REICHSHOF-ECKENHAGEN
Nordrhein-Westfalen

★★★**Haus Leyer** Am Aggerberg 33
☎(02265)9021
◄ᐪ16 P30 ⌂ Mountain
Credit Cards ①②⑤

REMAGEN
Rheinland-Pfalz

★★*Fürstenberg* Rheinprom 41 ☎(02642)23020
rm14(₩🛏12) P
Credit Cards ① ② ③ ⑤

★*Fassbender* Marktstr 78 ☎(02642)23472
rm36(🛏5) 🏖 P5

REUTLINGEN
Baden-Württemberg

★★*Ernst* Leonhardspl ☎(07121)4880 tx 729898
rm67(₩🛏63) A52rm 🏖 P4 Lift 🖾
Credit Cards ① ② ③ ⑤

RHEINBACH
Nordrhein-Westfalen

★★★*Ratskeller* vor dem Voigttor ☎(02226)4978
₩🛏26 P10
Credit Cards ① ② ③ ⑤

RHEINZABERN
Rheinland-Pfalz

★*Goldenes Lamm* Hauptstr 53 ☎(07272)2377
10 Jan-20 Dec
rm11(🛏4) 🏖 P15

RHEYDT
See **MÖNCHENGLADBACH**

ROSENHEIM
Bayern

★★★*Goldener Hirsch* Münchnerstr 40
☎(08031)12029
:Rest closed 24 Dec
rm34(₩🛏33) P8 Lift ℂ
Credit Cards ① ② ③ ⑤

🍴 *Rupp* Innstr 34 ☎(08031) 13970 P AR

ROTENBURG (WÜMME)
Niedersachsen

★*Deutsches Haus* Grossestr 51 ☎(04261)3300
rm8 P20

🍴 *Bassen* Industriestr 15 ☎(04261) 5050 P Toy

ROTHENBURG OB DER TAUBER
Bayern

★★★★*Eisenhut* (SRS/Relais et Châteaux)
Herrngasse 3 ☎(09861)7050 tx 61367
₩🛏80 🏖 P20 Lift ℂ
Credit Cards ① ② ③ ⑤

★★*Burg* Klostergasse 1 (n.rest) ☎(09861)5037
tx 61315
₩🛏15 🏖 P10
Credit Cards ① ② ③ ⑤

★★★*Goldener Hirsch* Untere Schmiedgasse 16
☎(09861)7080 tx 61372
Feb-15 Dec
rm80(₩🛏66) A20rm 🏖 P50 Lift ℂ
Credit Cards ① ② ③ ⑤

★★*Glocke* Plönlein 1 ☎(09861)3025 tx 61318
:Rest closed Sun
rm26(₩🛏21) 🏖 P16 Lift
Credit Cards ① ② ③ ⑤

★★*Markusturm* (ROM) Rödergasse 1
☎(09861)2370 tx 986180
₩🛏25 🏖 P50
Credit Cards ① ② ⑤

★★*Merian* Ansbacher Str 42 (n.rest)
☎(09861)3096 tx 61357
Apr-20 Dec
₩🛏32 P15 Lift
Credit Cards ① ② ③ ④ ⑤

★★*Reichsküchenmeister* Kirchpl 8
☎(09861)2046 tx 61370
:Rest closed Tue
rm34(₩🛏33) A4rm 🏖 P12 Lift
Credit Cards ① ② ③ ④ ⑤

★★*Tilman Riemenschneider* Georgengasse 11-
13 ☎(09861)2086 tx 61384
₩🛏65 🏖 P6 Lift ℂ
Credit Cards ① ② ③ ⑤

🍴 **Central** Schutzenstr 11 ☎(09861) 3088 P DJ
Mer

🍴 **Döhler** Ansbacherstr 38-40 ☎(09861) 0284 P
Ope

ROTTACH-EGERN
Bayern

★★★★*Bachmair am See* DPn Seestr 47
☎(08022)2720 tx 526920
₩🛏263 🏖 P Lift ℂ ☢ 🖾 ⌂ 🏊🏊 Beach Mountain
Lake
Credit Cards ② ⑤

RÖTTGEN
See **BONN**

ROTTWEIL
Baden-Württemberg

★★*Johanniterbad* Johannsergasse 12
☎(0741)6083 tx 762705
17 Jan-Dec :Rest closed Sun evening
rm27(₩🛏26) P5 Lift
Credit Cards ① ② ③ ⑤

RUDESHEIM
Hessen
See also **ASSMANNSHAUSEN**

★★★*Jagdschloss Niederwald* (GS)
☎(06722)1004 tx 42152
Closed Jan-14 Feb
₩🛏52 A25rm 🏖 P Lift ℂ ☢ 🖾
Credit Cards ① ③ ⑤

RUHPOLDING
Bayern

★*Sporthotel am Westernberg* Am
Wundergraben 4 ☎(08663)1674
15 Dec-Oct
₩🛏36 A10rm P45 ☢ 🖾 ⌂ Mountain
Credit Cards ① ② ③ ④ ⑤

SAARBRÜCKEN
Saarland

★★★★*Residence* Faktoreistr 2 ☎(0681)33030 tx
4421409
:Rest closed Sat lunch & Sun
₩🛏74 🏖 P20 Lift ℂ
Credit Cards ① ③ ④ ⑤

★★★*Novotel* Zinzingerstr 9 ☎(0681)58630 tx
4428836
₩🛏99 P120 Lift ℂ ⌂
Credit Cards ① ② ③ ⑤

★★★*Pullman Kongress* Hafenstr 8
☎(0681)30691 tx 4428942
₩🛏150 🏖 P12 Lift ℂ 🖾
Credit Cards ① ② ③ ④ ⑤

★★*Christine* Gersweilerstr 39 ☎(0681)55081 tx
4428736
Closed 23 Dec-27 Dec
rm75(₩🛏70) 🏖 P Lift ℂ 🖾
Credit Cards ① ② ③ ④ ⑤

★★*Wien* Gütenbergstr 29 (n.rest) ☎(0681)55088
6 Jan-20 Dec
₩🛏27 🏖 P10 Lift ℂ

🍴 *Müller* Kaiserstr 32/Hammerweg ☎(0681)
811118 P AR DJ

SÄCKINGEN, BAD
Baden-Württemberg

★*Kater Hiddigeigei* Tanzenpl 1 ☎(07761)4055
:Rest closed Sat
rm15(₩🛏12) P6
Credit Cards ① ③ ⑤

ST-GEORGEN
Baden-Württemberg

★★*Hirsch* Bahnhofstr 70 ☎(07724)7125
:Rest closed Sat
₩🛏22 🏖 P10
Credit Cards ① ② ③ ⑤

ST-GOAR
Rheinland-Pfalz

★★*Goldenen Löwen* Heerstr 82 ☎(06741)1674
15 Mar-Oct
₩🛏12 P20

★★*Schneider* am Markt 1 ☎(06747)1689
Mar-Nov
rm18(₩🛏10) P Mountain

★*Hauser* Heerstr 77 ☎(06741)333
Closed 15 Dec-1 Feb
rm15(₩🛏12) 🏖 Mountain
Credit Cards ① ② ③ ⑤

ST-GOARSHAUSEN
Rheinland-Pfalz

★★*Erholung* Nastätterstr 161 ☎(06771)2684
:Rest closed 15 Nov-15 Mar
₩🛏104 🏖 P50 Mountain

ST-MÄRGEN
Baden-Württemberg

★★*Hirschen* Feldberg Str 9 ☎(07669)787
₩🛏42 A22rm 🏖 P67 Lift Mountain
Credit Cards ① ② ③ ⑤

SAND
Baden-Württemberg

★★*Plättig-Hotel Bühlerhöhe*
Schwarzwaldhochstr 1 (1.5km N) ☎(07226)55300
tx 17722610
₩🛏57 P80 Lift ℂ ☢ 🖾 Mountain
Credit Cards ① ② ③ ④ ⑤

SANDHOFEN
See **MANNHEIM**

SANKT MICHAELISDONN
See **BRUNSBÜTTEL**

SAULGAU
Baden-Württemberg

★★*Kleber-Post* Hauptstr 100 ☎(07581)3051 tx
732284
Feb-Dec
₩🛏43 A8rm 🏖 P ℂ
Credit Cards ① ② ③ ⑤

SCHACKENDORF
See **SEGEBERG, BAD**

SCHIEDER-SCHWALENBERG
Nordrhein-Westfalen

★★*Burghotel Schwalenberg* (GS)
☎(05284)5167
₩🛏15 🏖 P100 ℂ Mountain
Credit Cards ① ③ ⑤

SCHLANGENBAD
Hessen

★★★*Staatliches Kurhaus* Rheingauerstr 47
☎(06129)420 tx 4186468
rm96(₩🛏94) 🏖 P50 Lift ℂ 🖾 ⌂ Mountain
Credit Cards ① ② ⑤

SCHLEIDEN
Nordrhein-Westfalen

★*Schleidener Hof* Gemünderstr 1 ☎(02445)216
:Rest closed Mon
rm15(₩🛏11) P ⌂ Mountain
Credit Card ①

SCHLESWIG
Schleswig-Holstein

★★*Strandhalle* am Jachthafen ☎(04621)22021
₩🛏27 🏖 P27 🖾 ⌂ Lake
Credit Cards ① ② ③ ⑤

★*Weissen Schwan* Gottorfstr 1 ☎(04621)32712
rm17(₩🛏10) A4rm 🏖 P20 ⌂

🍴 *Wriedt* Flensburger Str 88 ☎(04621) 25087 P
Ren

SCHLIERSEE
Bayern

★★★*Arabella Schliersee* Kirchbichlweg 18
☎(08026)4086 tx 526947
₩🛏100 🏖 P60 Lift ℂ 🖾 Mountain
Credit Cards ① ② ③ ⑤

SCHÖMBERG
See **LOSSBURG**

SCHÖNMÜNZACH
Baden-Württemberg

★★**Kurhotel Schwarzwald** Murgtalstr 655
☎(07447)1088
15 Dec-15 Nov
➥✿26 ☎ P20 Lift Mountain

SCHÖNSEE
Bayern

★★**St-Hubertus** am Lauberberg ☎(09674)415 tx
631825
rm92(➥✿81) ☎ P150 Lift ♥ ⌂
Credit Cards ②⑤

SCHRIESHEIM
Baden-Württemberg

★★**Luisenhöhe** Eichenweg 10 ☎(06203)65617
➥✿23 Mountain
Credit Card ②

SCHWÄBISCH HALL
Baden-Württemberg

★★★**Hohenlohe** Weilertor 14 ☎(0791)7587 tx
74870
➥✿98 ☎ P80 Lift ℂ ⌂ Lake
Credit Cards ①②③⑤

★★**Goldener Adler** am Markt 11 ☎(0791)6168
➥✿20 ☎
Credit Card ①

SCHWEINFURT
Bayern

★★★**Dorint Panorama** Am Oberen Marienbach 1
(n.rest) ☎(09721)1481 tx 673358
➥✿77 ☎ P100 Lift ℂ
Credit Cards ①②③⑤

★★**Central** Zehntstr 20 (n.rest) ☎(09721)2009-0
tx 673349
➥✿35 ☎ Lift
Credit Cards ①②③⑤

➥ **A Saalmüller** R-Diesel-Str 14 ☎(09721) 65040
P For

SCHWELM
Nordrhein-Westfalen

★★**Prinz Von Preussen** Altmarkt 8
☎(02336)13444
➥✿15 P18
Credit Card ⑤

SCHWETZINGEN
Baden-Württemberg

★★**Adler Post** Schlossstr 3 ☎(06202)10036 tx
1762029
:Rest closed Mon, 2 wks Jan & 3 wks Jul
➥✿29 ☎ P8
Credit Cards ①②③⑤

SEESEN
Niedersachsen

★★**Goldener Löwe** Jacobsonstr 20
☎(05381)1201/02/03
rm37(➥✿28) A9rm ☎ P Lift ℂ
Credit Cards ①②⑤

➥ **Hoffmann** Autobahnizubringerstr ☎(05381)
1215 **P** For

SEGEBERG, BAD
Schleswig-Holstein

At **SCHACKENDORF**(5km NW B404)

★★**Hotel B404 & Haus Stefanie** ☎(04551)3600
rm36(➥✿22) A17rm ☎ P100
Credit Cards ①②③⑤

SIEGBURG
Nordrhein-Westfalen

➥ **M Bässgen** Frankfurterstr 1-5 ☎(02241)
66001 **P** Ope

SIEGEN
Nordrhein-Westfalen

★★★**Johanneshöhe** Wallhausenstr 1
☎(0271)310008
➥✿26 ☎ P25 Mountain
Credit Cards ①②③⑤

★★★**Queens Moat House** (QM) Kampenstr 83
☎(0271)54072 tx 872734
➥✿94 ☎ P50 Lift ℂ ⌂
Credit Cards ①②③⑤

➥ **F Grab** Sieghüttr Hauptweg 97 ☎(0271) 40940
P For

SIGMARINGEN
Baden-Württemberg

➥ **J Zimmermann** In der Burgwiesen 18
☎(07571) 1696 Ope

SIMMERATH
Nordrhein-Westfalen

At **EICHERSCHEID**(4km S)

★**Haus Gertrud** Bachstr 4 ☎(02473)1310
➥✿8 A3rm P20 ♥ Mountain

SINDELFINGEN
Baden-Württemberg

★★★★**Holiday Inn** (QM) Schwertstr 65
☎(07031)61960 tx 7265569
➥✿185 ☎ P200 Lift ℂ
Credit Cards ①②③④⑤

★★★★**Queens Moat House** (QM) W-Haspel-Str
101 ☎(07031)6150 tx 7265778
➥✿146 P80 Lift ℂ
Credit Cards ①②③⑤

➥ **Schwabengarage** Böblinger Str 66 ☎(07031)
69000 M/C **P** For Hon

SINSHEIM
Baden-Württemberg

➥ **Kraichgau Bohland** Neulandstr 20 ☎(07261)
724 **P** For

SINSPELT
Rheinland-Pfalz

★★**Altringer** Neuenburgerstr 4 ☎(06522)712
➥✿20 P40 ♥ Mountain
Credit Card ①

SOEST
Nordrhein-Westfalen

★★**Andernach Zur Börse** Thomastr 31
☎(02921)4010
rm16(✿10) ☎ P70
Credit Cards ①②⑤

★★**Historiches Hotel & Restaurant** Jakobistr 75
☎(02921)1828
➥✿6 ☎ P6
Credit Cards ①②③⑤

➥ **H Siedler** Riga Ring 15 ☎(02921) 70138 M/C
P All makes

SOODEN-ALLENDORF, BAD
Hessen

★★**Kurhaus Kurparkhotel** ☎(05652)3031
rm40(➥✿20) P Lift ⌂
Credit Cards ①②③④⑤

SPEYER
Rheinland-Pfalz

★★**Goldener Engel** Mühlturmstr 1A
☎(06232)76732
Closed 23 Dec-2 Jan
➥✿43 ☎ P Lift
Credit Cards ①②③⑤

STAMMHEIM
See **STUTTGART**

STOCKACH
Baden-Württemberg

★★**Linde** Goethestr 23 ☎(07771)2226
rm30(➥18) P100 Lift
Credit Cards ①②③⑤

STRAUBING
Bayern

★★**Seethaler** Theresienpl 25 ☎(09421)12022
:Rest closed Mon
➥✿23 P20 Lift
Credit Cards ①②

★★**Wittelsbach** Stadtgraben 25 ☎(09421)1517
➥✿37 ☎ P20 Lift
Credit Cards ①②③⑤

STUTTGART
Baden-Württemberg

★★★★**Graf Zeppelin** (SRS) A-Klett-Pl 7
☎(0711)299881 tx 722418
➥✿280 ☎ P410 Lift ℂ ⌂
Credit Cards ①②③⑤

★★★★**Schlossgarten** Schillerstr 23
☎(0711)299911 tx 722936
➥✿126 P40 Lift ℂ
Credit Cards ①②③⑤

★★★**Europe** (BW) Siemensstr 26-38
☎(0711)815091 tx 723650
➥✿150 ☎ P220 Lift ℂ
Credit Cards ①②③④⑤

★★★**Intercity** A-Klett-Pl 2 ☎(0711)299801 tx
723543
➥✿105 P Lift ℂ
Credit Cards ①②③④⑤

★★★**Parkhotel** Villastr 21 ☎(0711)280161 tx
723405
➥✿80 P20 Lift ℂ
Credit Cards ①②③④⑤

★★★**Rieker** Friedrichstr 3 (n.rest)
☎(0711)221311
➥✿63 ☎ Lift

★★★**Waldhotel Degerloch** Guts-Muths-Weg 18
☎(0711)765017 tx 7255728
➥✿50 ☎ P30 Lift ℂ ♥
Credit Cards ①②③⑤

★★**Ketterer** Marienstr 3 ☎(0711)20390 tx 722340
:Rest closed Fri & Sat
➥✿105 P Lift ℂ
Credit Cards ①②③⑤

➥ **A V G Auto-Verkaufs** Chemnitzer Str
7,Degerloch ☎(0711) 722094 DJ Mit Rov

At **STAMMHEIM**(8km N)

★★★**Novotel Stuttgart Nord** Korntaler Str 207
☎(0711)801065 tx 7252137
➥✿117 P90 Lift ℂ
Credit Cards ①②③④⑤

STUTTGART AIRPORT

★★★**Movenpick** (Mövenpick) Flüghafen,Randstr
☎(0711)79070 tx 7245677
➥✿230 P250 Lift ℂ
Credit Cards ①②③④⑤

SULZBACH
See **FRANKFURT AM MAIN**

SULZBURG
Baden-Württemberg

★★**Waldhotel Bad Sulzburg** Badstr 67
☎(07634)8270
1 Feb-8 Jan
➥✿38 A22rm ☎ P80 Lift ♥ ⌂ Mountain
Credit Cards ①⑤

TENNENLOHE
See **ERLANGEN**

TETTNANG
Baden-Württemberg

★★**Rad** Lindauerstr 2 ☎(07542)6001 tx 734245
➥✿72 ☎ P60 Lift
Credit Cards ①②③④⑤

TIEFENBRONN
Baden-Württemberg

★★**Ochsen Post** F-J-Gall Str 13 ☎(07234)8030
Closed 3 wks Jan:Rest closed Sun & Mon
➥✿19 Sea
Credit Cards ①②③⑤

TITISEE
See **TITISEE-NEUSTADT**

TITISEE-NEUSTADT
Baden-Württemberg

At NEUSTADT

★★★**Adler Post** (ROM) Hauptstr 16
☎(07651)5066
⊷♠30 ♠ P32 ⌂ Mountain
Credit Cards ①②③⑤

At TITISEE

★★★**Brugger** Strandbadstr 14 ☎(07651)8010 tx
7722332
⊷♠68 ♠ P80 Lift ℂ ℚ ▤ Beach Lake
Credit Cards ①②③④⑤

★★★**Schwarzwaldhotel Am See** Seestr 12
☎(07651)8111 tx 7722341
20 Dec-Oct
rm86(⊷♠83) ♠ P100 Lift ℂ ℚ ▤ ⌂ Mountain
Lake
Credit Cards ①②③④

★★**Rauchfang** Bärenhofweg 2 ☎(07651)8255
⊷♠17 ♠ P20 ℚ ▤ Mountain
Credit Cards ①③⑤

★★**Seehof Am See** Seestr 47 (n.rest)
☎(07651)8314
23 Dec-Oct
⊷♠24 ♠ P20 Lift Mountain Lake
Credit Cards ①②③⑤

★**Seerose** Seestr 21 (n.rest) ☎(07651)8274
20 Dec-Oct
rm11(⊷♠2) P10
Credit Cards ①②③⑤

TODTNAU
Baden-Württemberg

★★**Waldeck** Poche 6 (Near B317) ☎(07671)216
15 Dec-15 Nov :Rest closed Tue
⊷♠14 ♠ P30 ℚ ⌂ Mountain
Credit Cards ①②③⑤

TÖLZ, BAD
Bayern

★★★**Post Hotel Kolberbräu** Marktstr 29
☎(08041)9158
⊷♠42 ♠ P40 Lift ℂ
Credit Cards ①②③⑤

★★**Gaissacher Haus** An Der Umgehungsstr
☎(08041)9583
Dec-Oct :Rest closed Wed
rm45(⊷♠20) A10rm ♠ P80 Mountain
Credit Cards ①②⑤

⊷ **A Spagl** Demmeljochstr 9 ☎(08041) 6385 **P**
For

TRABEN-TRARBACH
Rheinland-Pfalz

★★**Krone** an der Mosel 93 ☎(06541)6363 & 6004
⊷♠22 ♠ P15
Credit Cards ①③⑤

★★**Rema-Hotel Bellevue** Moselufer
☎(06541)6431 tx 4729227
⊷♠55 P30 Lift ℂ ▤ Mountain
Credit Cards ①②③⑤

TRAUNSTEIN
Bayern

★★**Parkhotel Traunsteiner Hof** Bahnhofstr 11
☎(0861)69041
rm60(⊷♠58) ♠ P10 Lift ℂ
Credit Cards ①②③⑤

⊷ **K Schaffler** Wasserburger Str 64-66 ☎(0861)
3003 For

TREMSBÜTTEL
Schleswig-Holstein

★★★**Schloss** (GS) ☎(04532)6544
Closed 12 Jan-10 Feb
rm20(⊷♠16) ♠ P300 ℂ ℚ
Credit Cards ①②⑤

TRENDELBURG
Hessen

★★**Burg** (GS) ☎(05676)1021

Closed Jan
⊷♠22 P60 ℚ ∪ Mountain
Credit Cards ①②③④

TRIBERG
Baden-Württemberg

★★★★**Parkhotel Wehrle** (ROM/Relais et
Châteaux) Gartenstr 24 ☎(07722)86020 tx
17772215
rm57(⊷♠54) A27rm ♠ P20 Lift ℂ ▤ ⌂
Credit Cards ①②③⑤

⊷ **E Harle** Nussbacherstr 82 ☎(07722) 6011 **P**
AR Col

TRIER
Rheinland-Pfalz

★★★**Dorint Porta Nigra** Porta Nigra Pl 1
☎(0651)27010 tx 472895
⊷♠106 ♠ P400 Lift ℂ
Credit Cards ①②③

★★★**Scandic Crown** Zurmaiener str 164
☎(0651)1430 tx 472808
⊷♠217 P300 Lift ℂ ▤
Credit Cards ①②③④⑤

★★**Hügel** Bernhardstr 14 ☎(0651)33066
⊷♠25 ♠ P15
Credit Cards ①②③

★★**Petrisberg** Sickingenstr 11 (n.rest)
☎(0651)41181
⊷♠30 A14rm ♠ P30

⊷ **D Daewel** Im Siebenborn ☎(0651) 87063 **P** DJ
LR Rov

⊷ **J Arweiler** Am Verteilerring ☎(0651) 20080
Ope

TRITTENHEIM
Rheinland-Pfalz

★**Moselperle** Moselweinstr 42 ☎(06507)2221
6 Jan-22 Dec :Rest closed Mon
rm14(⊷♠11) ♠ P11 ▤

TÜBINGEN
Baden-Württemberg

★★★**Bad** Am Freibad 2 ☎(07071)73071
10 Jan-20 Dec
⊷♠35 ♠ P35 ℚ ⌂
Credit Cards ①②③④

★**Stadt Tübingen** Stuttgarterstr 97
☎(07071)31071
:Rest closed Sun
⊷♠56 ♠ P80
Credit Card ②

TUTTLINGEN
Baden-Württemberg

★★**Schlack** Bahnhofstr 59 ☎(07461)72081 tx
762577
:Rest closed Sat evening
⊷♠31 A9rm ♠ P50
Credit Cards ①②③⑤

★**Ritter** Königstr 12 ☎(07461)8855 & 79027
:Rest closed Sat
rm19(⊷♠13) ♠ P6
Credit Card ①

ÜBERLINGEN
Baden-Württemberg

★★★**Parkhotel St-Leonhard** Obere St-
Leonhardstr 83 ☎(07551)8080 tx 733983
⊷♠145 A4rm ♠ P200 Lift ℂ ℚ ▤ Lake
Credit Card ②

★★**Alpenblick** Nussdorferstra 35 ☎(07551)4559
10 Jan-24 Dec :Rest closed Wed pm
rm25(⊷♠23) ♠ P20 ⌂ Lake

★★**Bad** Christophstr 2 ☎(07551)61055 tx 733909
⊷♠50 P30 Lift ℂ Lake
Credit Cards ①②③⑤

★★**Hecht** Münster Str 8 ☎(07551)63333
:Rest closed Mon
⊷♠14 ♠ P4 ℂ
Credit Cards ①②③④⑤

★★**Seegarten** Seepromenade 7 ☎(07551)63498
15 Feb-Nov
⊷♠21 Lift Mountain Lake
Credit Card ①

⊷ **L Kutsche** Oberriedweg 11 ☎(07551) 5222 **P**
For

UFFENHEIM
Bayern

★**Traube** Am Marktpl 3 ☎(09842)8288
Feb-20 Dec
rm16(⊷♠8) ♠ P10 ⌂
Credit Cards ①②

ULM
Baden-Württemberg

★★**Goldenes Rad** Neue Str 65 ☎(0731)61221 tx
712871
rm111(⊷♠92) P120 Lift ℂ
Credit Cards ①②③④⑤

★★**Ibis** Neutorstr 12 ☎(0731)619001 tx 712927
:Rest closed wknds
⊷♠90 ♠ P40 Lift ℂ
Credit Cards ①②③⑤

★★**Intercity Ulm** Bahnhofspl 1 ☎(0731)61221 tx
712871
⊷♠92 Lift ℂ
Credit Cards ①②③④⑤

★★**Neutor Hospiz** Neuer Graben 23
☎(0731)15160 tx 712401
rm92(⊷♠85) ♠ P25 Lift ℂ
Credit Cards ①②③⑤

★★**Roter Löwe** Ulmer Gasse 8 ☎(0731)62031
rm30(⊷♠24) ♠ P10 Lift ℂ

★★**Stern** Sterngasse 17 ☎(0731)63091 tx
712923
⊷♠62 ♠ P10 Lift ℂ
Credit Cards ①②③⑤

⊷ **Schwabengarage** Marchtaler Str 23 ☎(0731)
1621 M/C **P** For Hon

At GÖGGLINGEN(8km SW)

★★**Gasthof Ritter** ☎(07305)7365
:Rest closed Wed
rm15(⊷♠12) ♠ P64
Credit Card ⑤

UNDELOH
Niedersachsen

★**Witte's** In der Nordheide ☎(04189)200 tx
2189799
Mar-Nov
⊷♠22 P100
Credit Card ①

ÜRZIG-MOSEL
Rheinland-Pfalz

★**Moselschild** Hauptstr 12-14 ☎(06532)3001 tx
4721542
:Rest closed 10-31 Jan
⊷♠14 ♠ P24 Beach
Credit Cards ①②③⑤

★**Rotschwänzchen** Moselufer 18 ☎(06532)2183
Apr-15 Dec
rm11 A4rm P4 Mountain
Credit Cards ①②

VAIHINGEN AN DER ENZ
Baden-Württemberg

✦★**Post** Franckstr 23 ☎(07042)4071
rm21(⊷♠12) ♠ P4 Lift
Credit Cards ①②③④⑤

VIECHTACH
Bayern

★★**Sporthotel Schmaus** Stadtpl 5 ☎(09942)1627
tx 69441
Feb-9 Jan
⊷♠42 ♠ P22 Lift ▤
Credit Cards ①②③⑤

⊷ **Krah & Blümi** Schmidstr 21 ☎(09942) 1022 **P**
For

VIERNHEIM
Hessen
★★★★*Holiday Inn* Bürgermeister Neff Str 12
☎(06204)5036
⊷♁121 P200 Lift 《 ⌂
Credit Cards 1 2 3 4 5

VILLINGEN
Baden-Württemberg
★★*Ketterer* Brigachstr 1 ☎(07721)22095 tx
792554
:Rest closed Sat & Sun
⊷♁36 P25 Lift 《
Credit Cards 1 2 3 5

VILSHOFEN
Bayern
☙ K Bachhuber Ortenburger Str 64 ☎(08541)
5424 For

WAHLSCHEID
Nordrhein-Westfalen
★★★*Schloss Auel* (GS) 5204 Lohmar 21 (1.5km
NE) ☎(02206)2041 tx 887510
rm23(⊷♁21) P80 ९ ⌂ ◡ Mountain
Credit Cards 1 2 5

WALLDORF
Baden-Württemberg

See also HEIDELBERG
★★★★*Holiday Inn* Roterstr ☎(06227)360 tx
466009
⊷♁158 ♨ P150 Lift 《 ९ ⌂ ⌂
Credit Cards 1 2 3 4 5
★★*Vorfelder* Bahnhofstr ☎(06227)2085 tx
466016
:Rest closed 2 wks Jul
rm36(⊷♁28) P30 Lift 《
Credit Cards 1 2 3 5

WANGEN IM ALLGÄU
Baden-Württemberg
★★*Alte Post* (ROM) Postpl 2 ☎(07522)4014 tx
732774
:Rest closed Mon & Tue evening
⊷♁19 ♨ P6
Credit Cards 1 2 3 5

WASSERBURG AM INN
Bayern
★★*Fletzinger* Fletzingergasse 1 ☎(08071)8010
20 Jun-10 Dec :Rest closed Sat in winter
⊷♁40 ♨ P5 Lift
Credit Cards 1 2 3 5
☙ Lemke & Martl Brunhuber Str 41 ☎(08071)
8041 P For

WEIDEN IN DER OBERPFALZ
Bayern
☙ G Zwack Regensburger Str 81-89 ☎(0961)
43001 P For
☙ Stegmann Obere Bauscherstr 16 ☎(0961)
4040 Aud

WEINHEIM AN DER BERGSTRASSE
Baden-Württemberg
★★*Fuchs'Sche Mühle* Birkenauer Talstr 10
☎(06201)61031
⊷♁21 ♨ P50 Lift ⌂
Credit Card 1

WEISSENBURG IN BAYERN
Bayern
★★*Rose* (ROM) Rosenstr 6 ☎(09141)2096 &
2691 tx 624687
:Rest closed Sat lunchtime
rm29(⊷♁28) ♨ P4
Credit Cards 1 2 3 5

WERTHEIM
Baden-Württemberg
★★*Schwan* Mainpl 8 ☎(09342)1278
15 Jan-22 Dec
rm33(⊷♁28) A10rm ♨ P5
Credit Cards 1 2 3 5

At **KREUZWERTHEIM**
★*Herrnwiesen* Herrnwiesen 4 ☎(09342)37031
⊷♁22 ♨ P14

WERTINGEN
Bayern
★*Hirsch* Schulstr 7 ☎(08272)2055
:Rest closed Sat
rm29(⊷♁24) ♨ P30
Credit Cards 1 2

WESEL
Nordrhein-Westfalen
★★★*Kaiserhof* Kaiserring 1 ☎(0281)21972
⊷♁37 ♨ P40 Lift
Credit Cards 1 2 3 5
☙ Huying Schermbecker Landstr 18-20 ☎(0281)
5405 For

WESTERLAND (Island of Sylt)
Schleswig-Holstein No road connection exists
between the mainland and the Island of Sylt;
however there is a rail connection between Niebül
and Westerland. Cars are loaded on-to trains by
ramps.
★★★*Stadt Hamburg* (Relais et Châteaux)
Strandstr 2 ☎(04651)8580 tx 221223
⊷♁68 P40 Lift 《

WETZLAR
Hessen
★★★*Mercure* Bergstr 41 ☎(06441)48031 tx
483739
⊷♁144 P90 Lift 《 ⌂
Credit Cards 1 2 3 5
★★★*Euler-Haus* Buderuspl 1 (n.rest)
☎(06441)47016 tx 483763
rm24(⊷♁15) P6 Lift
Credit Cards 1 2 3 5
☙ Pohl Wetzlar B 277 ☎(06441) 33066 P For

WIESBADEN
Hessen
★★★★*Nassauer Hof* (SRS) Kaiser Friedrich-Pl
3-4 ☎(06121)1330 tx 4186847
⊷♁206 A52rm P80 Lift 《 ⌂
★★★*Forum* A-Lincoln-Str 17 ☎(06121)7970 tx
4186369
⊷♁157 P100 Lift 《 ⌂
Credit Cards 1 2 3 4 5
★★★*Fürstenhof-Esplanade* Sonnenbergerstr 32
☎(06121)52209 tx 4186447
rm74(⊷♁52) ♨ P10 Lift 《
Credit Cards 1 2 3 5
★★★*Schwarzer Bock* Kranzpl 12 ☎(06121)1550
tx 4186640
⊷♁150 P10 Lift 《 ⌂
Credit Cards 1 2 3 4 5
★★*Central* Bahnhofstr 65 (n.rest)
☎(06441)372001 tx 4186604
rm70(⊷♁45) ♨ P10 Lift 《
Credit Cards 1 2 3 5
★*Oranien* Platterstr 2 ☎(06121)525025 tx
4186217
:Rest closed Fri, Sat & Sun
⊷♁85 ♨ P70 Lift 《
Credit Cards 1 2 3 5
☙ Heine Mainzerstr 141 ☎(06121) 19780 P Alf
Peu
☙ Wink Flachstr 7-9 ☎(01621) 701026 For

WILDBAD IM SCHWARZWALD
Baden-Württemberg
★★★★*Sommerberg* Heermannsweg 5
☎(07081)1740 tx 724015
⊷♁100 ♨ P Lift 《 ९ ⌂ Mountain

WILDUNGEN, BAD
Hessen
★★★*Staatliches Badehotel* Dr-Marc Str 4
☎(04421)860 tx 994612

Apr-30 Oct
⊷♁70 ♨ P Lift 《 ⌂
Credit Cards 1 5

WILLINGEN
Hessen
★★*Waldhotel Willingen* am Köhlerhagen 3
☎(05632)6016 tx 991174
⊷♁39 P40 ९ ⌂ Mountain
Credit Cards 1 5

WIMPFEN, BAD
Baden-Württemberg
★★*Blauer Turm* Burgviertel 5 ☎(07063)225 &
7884
:Rest closed Mon
rm22(♁13) P50 Lake
Credit Cards 1 3 5
★★*Weinmann* Marktpl 3 ☎(07063)8582
Mar-Oct
⊷♁10 ♨ P Lift

WINDHAGEN-REDERSCHEID
See HONNEF AM RHEIN, BAD

WINTERBERG
Nordrhein-Westfalen
At **NEUASTENBERG**(6km SW)
★★★*Dorint Ferienpark* ☎(02981)2033 tx 84539
⊷♁142 P150 ९ ⌂ Lake
Credit Cards 1 2 3 5
At **WINTERBERG-HOHELEYE**(10km SE)
★★★*Hochsauerland* ☎(02758)313 tx 875629
⊷♁90 P50 Lift ९ ⌂ Mountain

WINTERBERG-HOHELEYE
See WINTERBERG

WOLFACH
Baden-Württemberg
★★*Krone* Marktpl 33 ☎(07834)350
rm23(⊷♁14) A9rm ♨ P4 Mountain

WOLFSBURG
Niedersachsen
★★★★*Holiday Inn* (QM) Rathausstr 1
☎(05361)2070 tx 958475
⊷♁207 ♨ Lift 《 ⌂
Credit Cards 1 2 3 4 5

WORMS
Rheinland-Pfalz
★★★*Dom* Obermarkt 10 ☎(06241)6913 tx
467846
Closed 24 Dec:Rest closed Sun
⊷♁60 ♨ P40 Lift 《
Credit Cards 1 2 3 5
☙ Betriebe Berkenkamp Speyerer Str 88
☎(06241) 6343 P For

WUPPERTAL
Nordrhein-Westfalen
At **WUPPERTAL I-ELBERFELD**
★★★★*Kaiserhof* Döppersberg 50
☎(0202)459081 tx 8591405
⊷♁127 P250 Lift 《
Credit Cards 1 2 3 5
★★*Rathaus* Wilhelmstr 7 (n.rest) ☎(0202)450148
tx 8592424
⊷♁32 ♨ P8 Lift 《
Credit Cards 1 2 3
★★*Zur Post* Poststr 4 (n.rest) ☎(0202)450131
rm55(⊷♁51) Lift 《
Credit Cards 1 2 3 5
At **WUPPERTAL II-BARMEN**
☙ H Wilke Kohlenstr 19 ☎(0202) 606052 AR Lan
Saa
At **WUPPERTAL XXII-LANGERFELD**
★*Neuenhof* Schwelmerstr 246-248
☎(0202)602536
⊷♁25 ♨ P25

At **WUPPERTAL XXI-RONSDORF**

🚗 **Automobile Vosberg** Remscheider Str 192
☎(0202) 4698066 **P** Rov Hon LR

WUPPERTAL I-ELBERFELD
See **WUPPERTAL**

WUPPERTAL II-BARMEN
See **WUPPERTAL**

WUPPERTAL XXII-LANGERFELD
See **WUPPERTAL**

WUPPERTAL XXI-RONSDORF
See **WUPPERTAL**

WÜRZBURG
Bayern

★★★**Bahnhofhotel Excelsior** Haugerring 2-3 (n.rest) ☎(0931)50484 tx 68435
🛁🚿54 Lift ☾ Mountain
Credit Cards [1] [2] [3] [4] [5]

★★★**Rebstock** (BW) Neubaustr 7 ☎(0931)30930 tx 68684
Closed 2-14 Jan:Rest closed Fri & Sun pm
🛁🚿81 P300 Lift ☾
Credit Cards [1] [2] [3] [5]

★★**Central** Köllikerstr 1 (n.rest) ☎(0931)56952
15 Jan-15 Dec
rm23(🚿20) 🏠 Lift ☾
Credit Cards [1] [2] [3] [5]

★★**Franziskaner** Franziskanerpl 2 ☎(0931)15001
rm47(🛁🚿32) P Lift ☾
Credit Cards [1] [2] [3] [5]

★★***Walfisch*** Am Pleidenturm 5 ☎(0931)50055 tx 68499
🛁🚿40 🏠 P Lift ☾
Credit Cards [1] [2] [3] [5]

At **LENGFELD**(4km NE on 19)

🚗 **Autohaus Stoy** Industriestr 1 ☎(0931) 27646 **P** Nis

ZELL AN DER MOSEL
Rheinland-Pfalz

★★***Post*** Schlossstr 25 ☎(06542)4217
:Rest closed Mon
🛁🚿16 P18 Lift
Credit Cards [1] [2] [5]

ZWEIBRÜCKEN
Rheinland-Pfalz

★★★**Fasanerie** (ROM) Fasaneriestr ☎(06332)44074 tx 451182
🛁🚿50 🏠 P100 Lift ☾ 📺
Credit Cards [1] [2] [3] [5]

★★***Rosen*** Von-Rosenstr 2 (n.rest) ☎(06332)6014
rm40(🛁🚿35) Lift
Credit Cards [1] [2] [3] [5]

🚗 **Carbon** Zweibrückerstr 4 ☎(06332) 6048 **P** For

ZWISCHENAHN, BAD
Niedersachsen

★***Ferien-Motel*** am Schlart 1 (2km E) ☎(04403)2005 tx 254713
rm30(🛁🚿26) A4rm P 🏊

🚗 ***Mengers*** Mühlenstr 2 ☎(04403) 3378 **P**

AA Road Map – Benelux and Germany

Featuring:

- **Up-to-date road information**
- **Scenic routes and viewpoints**
- **Contours and gradients**
- **Distances between towns**
- **Full colour, 16 miles to 1 inch**

An ideal map for route-planning and touring — available at good bookshops and AA Centres

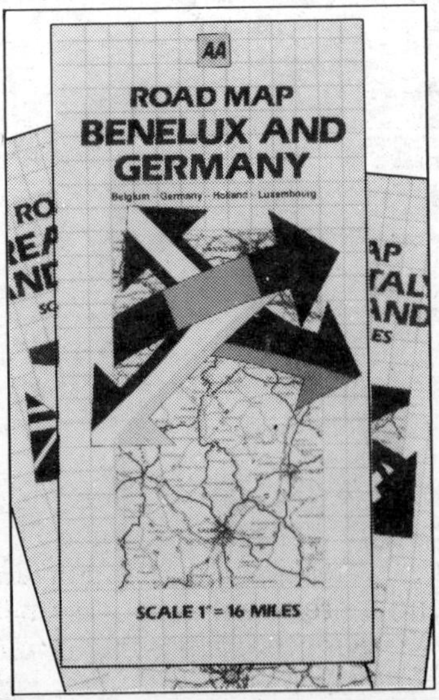
AA
ROAD MAP
BENELUX AND GERMANY
Belgium · Germany · Holland · Luxembourg
SCALE 1" = 16 MILES

Don't leave the country without one

Gibraltar lies at the western entrance to the Mediterranean on the southern tip of the Iberian peninsula. A rocky promontory surrounded by sandy and rocky beaches, 'The Rock' rises to a height of almost 1,400 feet at its highest point.

Gibraltar has witnessed a turbulent history and is a melting pot of Moorish, Spanish and British culture. Here you can soak up the sun at Sandy Beach, or watch the Changing of the Guard at the Governor's Residence. No visit would be complete without a cable car ride to the top of the Rock to see the Atlantic and the Mediterranean, Africa and Europe. Stop off to see the apes, too – legend has it that the British will leave Gibraltar if the apes ever go. You can even explore inside the Rock as there is a maze of tunnels under the surface.

The Rock is of great strategic importance in time of war, and the galleries tunnelled through the rock face from 1782 onwards so that cannon could be positioned for its defence are a fascinating place to visit. They also played their part in World War Two, when the Royal Engineers added another thirty miles. A natural underground phenomenon is St Michael's Cave. Legend has it that it conceals an underground link with Africa, the route by which the original Barbary apes arrived. Prepared as a hospital during the war, the caverns, with their stalactites, stalagmites and lake make an atmospheric venue for concerts. Other attractions include sailing, deep-sea angling or relaxing in the beautiful Alameda Gardens.

The bazaars and shops of Main Street make a happy hunting ground for watches, electrical goods, perfumes, jewellery and cigarettes, and there's easy access to Spain and Africa for those looking for more unusual souvenirs.

GIBRALTAR

Language
English

Local time
GMT + 1 (Summer GMT + 2)

Currency
Gibraltar pound, which is at par with the pound Sterling. The legal tender is Gibraltar Government and British notes and coins. At the time of going to press US$1 = £0.60

Emergency numbers
Fire ☎190   Police and ambulance ☎199

Information in England
The Gibraltar Information Bureau, Arundel Great Court, 179 The Strand, London WC2R 1EH
☎†01-836 0777/8
†071 from 6 May

Information in Gibraltar
Gibraltar Tourism Agency, Cathedral Square, and at the frontier.

HOW TO GET THERE

Gibraltar is normally approached overland through France and Spain via the Bayonne-San Sebastian route at the western end of the Pyrenees. The promontory itself is entered via the La Linea customs post and is open to pedestrian and vehicular traffic of all nationalities.

Distance

From Calais to Gibraltar is 2,285km (1,420 miles) and would normally require three or four overnight stops.

MONEYMATTERS

There is no restriction on the amount of currency which may be imported, but large amounts which are subsequently to be re-exported should be declared on entry.

Banking hours

Monday–Friday 09.00–15.30hrs, and 16.30–18.00hrs also on Friday.

Postcheques

may be cashed at the General Post Office up to a maximum of £100 per cheque. Go to the counter with the *Postcheque* window sticker.

MOTORING REGULATIONS AND GENERAL INFORMATION

The information given here is specific to Gibraltar. It **must** be read in conjunction with the European ABC at the front of the book, which covers those regulations which are common to many countries.

AA Port Agent

Gibraltar J Lucas Imossi & Sons Ltd, 1–5 Irish Town, PO Box 167 ☎73525/79435. See also *AA Service* in the European ABC.

Accidents

There are no firm rules of procedure after an accident; you are advised to follow the recommendations under *Accidents* in the European ABC.

Accommodation

The Tourism Agency produces a complete list of hotels which details facilities offered. Hotels provide an international cuisine; fish and seafoods are predominant, but there are restaurants offering continental food as well as Chinese, Italian, Spanish and Indian dishes. There are a number of establishments providing the atmosphere of an English pub which sell familiar beers.

Breakdown*

If your car breaks down, try to move it to the side of the road so that it obstructs the traffic flow as little as possible, and contact a local garage for assistance. See also *Warning triangle* below.

British/Embassy Consulate*
(See also page 8)

There is no Embassy or Consulate in Gibraltar; as a Crown Colony, the Governor is the British representative.

Caravans and luggage trailers*

The temporary importation of trailer caravans into Gibraltar is restricted, and an import

*Additional information will be found in the European ABC at the front of the book.

licence is necessary; luggage trailers, however, do not require an import licence. Overnight camping is prohibited.

Children in cars*

There are no restrictions on the ages of front-seat passengers, but it is recommended that children travel in the back.

Dimensions and weight restrictions

On some specified roads, vehicles must not exceed – height, 4.22 metres; width, 2.51 metres; length, 15.54 metres. In the city and Upper Rock, vehicles must not exceed – height, 3.66 metres; width, 2.13 metres; length, 15.54 metres. The combined weight of car/caravan combinations must not exceed 3.500kg. See also *Caravan and luggage trailers* above.

Driving licence*

A valid UK or Republic of Ireland licence is acceptable in Gibraltar. The minimum age at which a visitor may use a temporarily imported car or motorcycle is 18 years.

Emergency messages to tourists*

Emergency messages to tourists are broadcast by the *Gibraltar Broadcasting Corporation* (GBC) throughout the year. The messages are transmitted once only as soon as air time is available on 1458KHz medium wave, 91.3MHz and 100.5MHz VHF.

Horn, use of

Use of the car horn is not permitted within the city limits.

Lights

Sidelights should be used in badly-lit areas and when visibility is poor. Dipped headlights should be used during the hours of darkness; the use of full headlights is prohibited.

Parking*

It is prohibited to park by a bus stop, loading/unloading bay, taxi stand, traffic sign or in any position which is likely to cause unnecessary obstruction.

Petrol

Credit cards Petrol stations do not accept credit cards.
Duty-free petrol The petrol in the vehicle tank may be imported free of customs duty and tax.
Petrol cans Petrol may only be imported in a purpose-made steel container. Duty will be charged; the lead content of the petrol must be 0.15 grammes.
Petrol (leaded) Super (98 octane) grade only.
Petrol (unleaded) is not sold in Gibraltar.

Postal information

Mail Postcards 19p; letters up to 20gm 22p.
Post offices The General Post Office is located at 104 Main Street. There are also two sub-post offices, one in the North District and one in the South District. Opening hours are 09.00–17.00hrs Monday to Friday, and 10.00–13.00hrs on Saturday.

Public holidays*

Official Public holidays in Gibraltar for 1990 are given below.
January 1 (New Year's Day Holiday)
March 12 (Commonwealth Day)
April 13 (Good Friday)
April 16 (Easter Monday)
May 1 (May Day)
May 28 (Spring Bank Holiday)
June 18 (Queen's Birthday)
August 27 (Summer Bank Holiday)
December 25 (Christmas Day)
December 26 (Boxing Day)

Roads

Generally, the roads are in good condition, although most tend to be very narrow. Those on the Rock are steep, while in the town there are sharp bends.

Shopping hours

Shops are open Monday to Friday, 09.00–13.00hrs and 15.00–19.30hrs, and 09.00–13.00hrs on Saturday.

*Additional information will be found in the European ABC at the front of the book.

GIBRALTAR

Speed limits*

The standard legal limit for cars and
motorcycles within Gibraltar City is 32kph
(20mph) and 48kph (30mph) outside; car/
caravan combinations are restricted to 32kph
(20mph) in and out of the city.

Telephone*

Insert coin **after** lifting the receiver
(instructions in English in all callboxes). Use 5p
coins for local calls and 20p or 50p coins for
international calls.
All coinboxes within the town area have
International Direct Dial (IDD) facilities.
A telephone call to the UK costs 70p per
minute. Cheap rate calls costing 60p per minute
may be made from 24.0hrs on Friday to
12.00hrs on Saturday and from 24.00hrs on
Saturday to 12.00hrs on Sunday.

Telephone codes
UK to Gibraltar	010 350
Gibraltar to UK	00 44
Gibraltar to Republic of Ireland	00 353
Gibraltar to the USA	00 1

Visitor's registration*

British subjects in transit or staying in Gibraltar
as temporary visitors are automatically issued
with a permit enabling them to stay for one
month; if necessary the permit can be renewed.

Warning triangle*

The use of a warning triangle is not
compulsory, but is strongly recommended in
the event of accident or breakdown.

***Additional information will be found in the
European ABC at the front of the book.**

ACCOMMODATION

The prices shown below are an average for each
classification. At the time of going to press
US$1 = £0.60.

AVERAGE PRICES

	Single Room	Double Room	Breakfast	Lunch/Dinner
★★★★	£50–67	£63–75	from £5	£10–12
★★★	£25–29	£34–42	from £2	£7–9

Abbreviations
Pde Parade   St Street
Rd Road

★★★★**Caleta Palace** Catalan Bay ☎76501 tx 2345
170 A80rm P20 Lift ℂ ⌐ Sea
Credit Cards [1][2][3][5]
★★★★**Holiday Inn** 2 Governor's Pde ☎70500 tx 2242

112 P20 Lift ℂ ⌐ Sea Mountain
Credit Cards [1][2][3][5]
★★★★**Rock** 3 Europa Rd ☎73000 tx 2238
150 P1 Lift ℂ ⌐ Sea
Credit Cards [1][2][3][4][5]
★★★**Montarik** Main St ☎77065 tx 2226
70 Lift ℂ
Credit Cards [1][2][3]

★★★**Queen's** Boyd St ☎74000 & 74025 tx 2269
rm62(47) Lift ℂ Sea Mountain
Credit Cards [1][2][3]
Central 20 Line Wall Rd ☎ 74813 M/C Dai Mer Rov
J Lucas Imossi Waterport Circle ☎ 75627
North Garage Corral Rd, West Place of Arms
☎ 77159 M/C Peu Tal

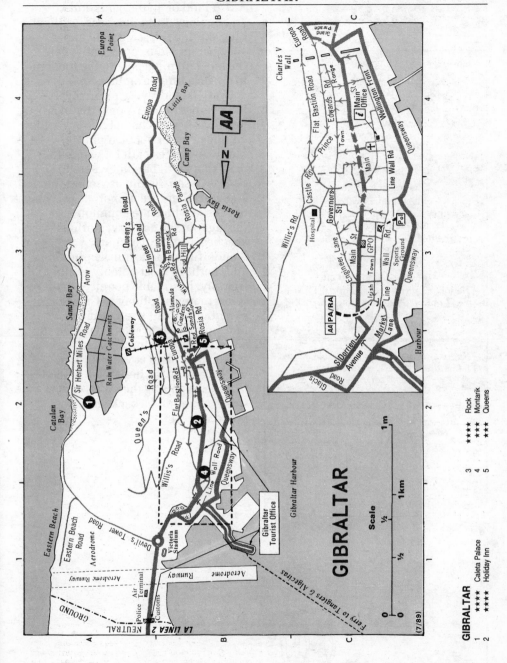

GIBRALTAR

Scale

0 ½ 1km

0 ½ 1m

GIBRALTAR

1 ★★★★ Caleta Palace
2 ★★★★ Holiday Inn

3 ★★★★ Rock
4 ★★★ Montarik
5 ★★★ Queens

(7/89)

GREECE

Language
Greek

Local time
GMT + 2 (Summer GMT + 3)

Currency
Greek *drachma* divided into 100 *lepta*.
At the time of going to press.
£1 = Dr269
US$1 = Dr162

Emergency numbers
In Athínai: Fire ☎199
Police ☎100 (as in most big cities)
Ambulance ☎166
In other cities: consult telephone
directory.
Tourist police ☎171

Information in England
National Tourist Organisation of Greece,
4 Conduit Street, London W1R 0DJ
☎†01-734 5997
†071 from 6 May

Information in the USA
National Tourist Organisation of Greece,
645 Fifth Avenue, Olympic Tower, New
York
☎212 421 5777

Greece is a country of many facets. A land of myths, gods and archaeology, turquoise seas, brilliant blue skies, irridescent light and spectacular landscapes, and where the ancient mingles with the modern to create a unique ambiance.

Every island, every resort, every town and city has its own distinct personality and character. So whether your taste is for hectic nightlife, secluded shores or delving into the past, there will be somewhere in Greece to satisfy. But as well as the contrasts there are numerous aspects of Greece which are common throughout the country: glorious beaches, beautiful scenery, a wonderful climate, quirky plumbing and, perhaps most notably of all, friendly, hospitable people.

For many, a holiday in Greece is essentially about stretching out on fine, golden sand, soaking up the sun and the relaxed atmosphere, perhaps trying their hand at windsurfing, whiling away the hours in a sea-side taverna or joining the locals over a Greek coffee and a backgammon board.

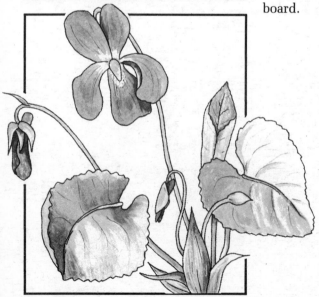

HOW TO GET THERE

The most direct road route is through Belgium, Federal Republic of Germany (Köln/Cologne and München/Munich), Austria (Salzburg) and Yugoslavia (Beograd/Belgrade).

The alternative road route is via France or Switzerland, Italy (Milano/Milan and Trieste), and Yugoslavia.

The third way is to drive to southern Italy and use the direct ferry services.

Distance

To Athínai (Athens) is about 3,220km (2,000 miles) using the most direct route and would normally require four or five overnight stops.

Car-sleeper trains operate during the summer from Brussels and 's-Hertogenbosch to Ljubljana; from Boulogne, Brussels, Paris and 's-Hertogenbosch to Milan; and on from Milan to Bari and Brindisi to connect with the ferry service to Greece.

MONEYMATTERS

The maximum amount of Greek currency which may be taken into Greece is Dr100,000, but no more than Dr20,000 may be exported. It is not permitted to import or export Dr5,000 banknotes. There are no restrictions on the import or export of foreign currency up to the equivalent of US$1,000. Amounts in excess of this must be declared to the Currency Control Authorities on arrival.

Banking hours

Monday–Friday 08.00–14.00hrs. Some foreign exchange offices are open in the afternoon.

Postcheques

may be cashed at all post offices up to a maximum of Dr25,000 per cheque in multiples of Dr1,000 per cheque. Go to the counter marked *Mandats* or *Orders*, or with the Greek letters ΕΠΙΤΑΓΕΧ

MOTORING REGULATIONS AND GENERAL INFORMATION

The information given here is specific to Greece. It **must** be read in conjunction with the European ABC at the front of the book, which covers those regulations which are common to many countries.

Accidents*

In the case of accidents in which private property is damaged or persons injured, the police should be called. They should also be called to minor incidents that cannot be settled amicably on the spot. Your own insurance company should be informed as well as the *Motor Insurers Bureau* in Athínai. The Motoring Club (ELPA) should also be informed, preferably at their Head Office (see under *Motoring club* for address). See also *Warning triangle* below.

Breakdown*

The *Automobile and Touring Club of Greece* (ELPA) provides a breakdown service in most big cities, and assistance can be obtained by dialling 104. See also *Warning triangle* below.

British Embassy/Consulates*

The British Embassy is located at 10675 Athínai, 1 Ploutarchou Street ☎(01) 7236211. There is a British Consulate with Honorary Consul in Thessaloníki (Salonica); there are British Vice-Consulates in Kríti (Crete) and Kérkira (Corfu); British Vice-Consulates with Honorary Consuls in Pátrai (Patras), Rodhos (Rhodes), Samos, Syros and Volos. See also the *Town Plan of Athínai* in gazetteer below.

Children in cars*

Children under 10 are not permitted to travel in a vehicle as front-seat passengers.

Dimensions and weight restrictions

Private **cars** and towed **trailers** or **caravans** are restricted to the following dimensions – height, 4 metres; width, 2.50 metres; length (including any coupling device), up to 2,500kg – 8 metres,

*Additional information will be found in the European ABC at the front of the book.

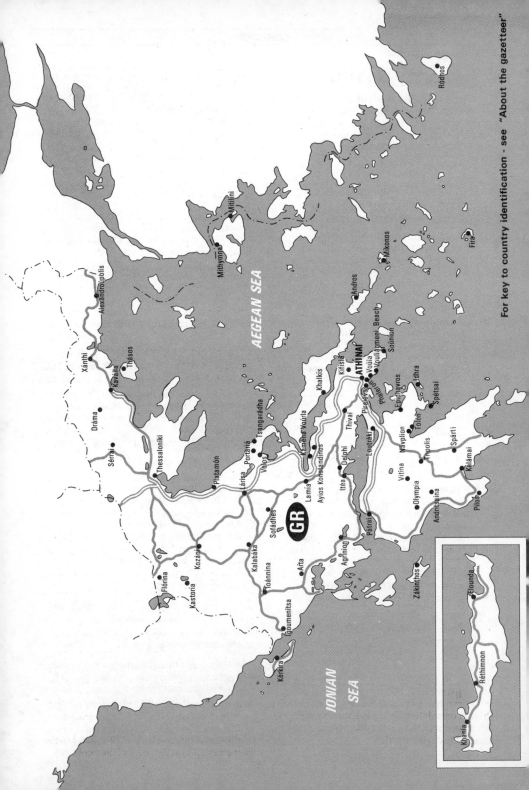

For key to country identification - see "About the gazetteer"

AEGEAN SEA

IONIAN SEA

GR

Ródhos

Mitilíni

Fíra

Míkonos

Mithymna

Andros

Alexándroúpolis

Voulagmeni Beach

Soúnion

ATHÍNAI

Voúla

Kifisiá

Pireévs

Fáliron

Khalkís

Eridhavros

Idhra

Spétsai

Xánthi

Thásos

Kaválla

Kaména Voúrla

Toloń

Dráma

Tsangarádha

Pórtariá

Thívai

Návplion

Argolis

Spárti

Sérrai

Platamón

Vólos

Delphi

Loutráki

Thessaloniki

Lárisa

Itéa

Vítina

Kalámai

Lamía

Ayios Konstandimos

Pátrai

Olympia

Andrítsaina

Pílos

Sofádhes

Agrínion

Kalabáka

Árta

Zákinthos

Kozáni

Ioánnina

Flórina

Kastoría

Igoumenítsa

Kérkira

Elounda

Khaniá

Réthimnon

over 2,500kg – 10 metres. The maximum permitted overall length of vehicle/trailer or caravan combinations is 18 metres.

Trailers without brakes may have a total weight of up to 50% of the unladen weight of the towing vehicle and of the driver (whose weight is considered equal to 70kg). The total weight of trailer and towing vehicle must not exceed 3,500kg.

Driving licence*

A valid UK licence is acceptable in Greece. The minimum age at which a visitor may use a temporarily imported car, or motorcycle (over 50cc), is 17 years. However, an International Driving Permit is required by the holder of a licence issued in the Republic of Ireland – compulsory if a red three-year licence and recommended if a pink EC type licence. See under *Driving licence* and *International Driving Permit* page 00 for further information.

Emergency messages to tourists

Emergency messages to tourists are broadcast daily by the *National Broadcasting Institute of Greece.*

ET1, transmitting on 411 metres medium wave, broadcasts these messages in English, French, German and Arabic at 07.40hrs daily throughout the year.

ET2, transmitting on 305 metres medium wave, broadcasts the messages in English and French at 14.25 and 21.15hrs daily throughout the year.

Fire extinguisher*

It is compulsory for all vehicles to be equipped with a fire extinguisher.

First-aid kit*

It is compulsory for all vehicles to be equipped with a first-aid kit.

Lights*

Driving on sidelights only is not permitted. It is recommended that *motorcycles* use dipped headlights during the day.

Motoring club*

 The **Automobile and Touring Club of Greece** (ELPA) has its head office at 11527 Athínai, 2 Messogion Street ☎(1) 779 1615 (located on the town plan of Athínai within the gazetteer). Branch offices are maintained in major towns throughout the country, and on Kérkira (Corfu) and Kríti (Crete). Office hours are 08.30–19.30hrs Monday to Friday; Saturday 08.30–13.30hrs. The club is able to provide general touring information and this may be obtained on ☎174 in Athínai and ☎(01) 777 7452 throughout the country, Monday to Saturday 08.30–/15.00hrs.

Motorways

The motorways are usually only single carriageway, with some dual-carriageway sections. Tolls are charged on most sections. Thessaloníki (Salonica)–Athínai (Athens) Dr450; Athínai–Pátrai (Patras) Dr200.

Parking*

According to Greek law, parking is prohibited within 5 metres (16½ft) of an intersection; within 15 metres (50ft) of a bus stop or a level crossing; within 3 metres (10ft) of a fire hydrant; and where there is a continuous central white line, unless there are two lanes in each direction.

Parking in Athínai can be difficult, and some garages charge high rates. It is forbidden to park in the *Green Zone* except where parking meters have been installed. *Warning*: the police in Athínai are empowered to confiscate and detain the *number plates* from visitors' cars which are illegally parked. A heavy fine will also be imposed upon offenders, and visitors are reminded that it is illegal to drive a vehicle without number plates.

Petrol*

Credit cards Acceptance of them for petrol purchases is limited.
Duty-free petrol The petrol in the vehicle tank may be imported free of customs duty and tax.
Petrol cans It is forbidden to carry petrol in cans in a vehicle.
Petrol (leaded) Venzini Apli (91–92 octane) and Venzini Super (96–98 octane) grades.

*Additional information will be found in the European ABC at the front of the book.

Petrol (unleaded) is sold in Greece as Super (95 octane). Stations selling unleaded petrol will display a special sign.

Postal information

Mail Postcards Dr60, letters up to 20gm Dr60. *Post offices* There are 850 post offices in Greece. Opening hours are 07.30–20.30hrs Monday to Friday in large towns, and 07.30–15.00hrs Monday to Friday in small ones. Post offices in central Athínai are located in Syntagma Square, Omonia Square and at Eolou Street 100.

Priority*

At crossroads outside cities, traffic on a main road has priority.

Public holidays*

Official Public holidays in Greece for 1990 are given below.

January 1 (New Year's Day)
January 6†† (Epiphany)
February 26 (First Day of Lent)
March 25† (National Holiday)
April 13 (Good Friday)
April 15 (Easter Sunday)
May 1 (May Day)
June 4 (Whit Monday)
August 15 (Assumption)
October 28† (National Holiday)
December 25 (Christmas Day)
December 26 (Boxing Day)

††Saturday   †Sunday

Roads

Although the road system is reasonably comprehensive, surfaces vary and secondary roads may be poor. On long drives, a good average speed is 48–64kph (30–40mph). The islands are best visited by sea or air. Only the large islands – Kríti (Crete), Kérkira (Corfu) and Rodhos (Rhodes) – have reasonably comprehensive road systems. Roads on the smaller islands are generally narrow, and surfaces vary from fairly good to rather poor.

Road signs*

The signposting is fairly good, and both Greek and English are used.

Shopping hours

Generally, between June and September, shops and stores are open on Monday 13.30–20.30hrs (foodstores 08.00–15.00hrs); on Tuesday, Thursday and Friday 08.00–14.00hrs and 17.30–20.30hrs; on Wednesday and Saturday 08.00–15.00hrs. During the winter, they open on Monday and Wednesday 09.00–17.00hrs; on Tuesday and Thursday 10.00–19.00hrs; on Saturday 08.30–15.30hrs.

Speed limits*

Unless otherwise indicated by signs, private cars with or without trailers are subject to the following restrictions; 50kph (31mph) in *built-up areas*; 80kph (49mph) *outside built-up areas*; 100kph (62mph) on *motorways*.

Spiked or studded tyres

There are no special regulations regarding the use of *spiked tyres*.

Telephone*

Insert coin **after** lifting the receiver; the dialling tone is the same as the UK. When making calls to subscribers within Greece, precede the number with the relevant area code (shown in parentheses before the hotel/garage enquiry number in the gazetteer). Use Dr5coin for local calls (*blue/grey callbox*) and Dr10 or Dr20 coins for national and international calls (all coins must be dated 1976 or later).
For international and out-of-town national calls use a callbox with an orange sign round the top. The cost of a call between Athínai and London is Dr55 per minute.
Telephone codes

UK to Greece	010 30
Greece to UK	00 44
Greece to Republic of Ireland	00 353
Greece to the USA	00 1

Tourist police

On duty in all resorts and at major frontier crossings. They all speak English and their job is to assist tourists in any way they can.

*Additional information will be found in the European ABC at the front of the book.

GREECE

Warning triangle*

The use of a warning triangle is compulsory in the event of accident or breakdown. The triangle must be placed 20 metres (22yds)

behind the vehicle in built-up areas, and 50 metres (55yds) outside built-up areas.

*Additional information will be found in the European ABC at the front of the book.

ACCOMMODATION

Hotel prices are controlled by the National Greek Tourist Office and should be exhibited in rooms. ATV, stamp duty and local taxes are not included in quoted rates, and additional charges are sometimes made for air conditioning.

The prices shown below are an average for

each classification. Accommodation is likely to be more expensive in Athens and some of the more popular areas.

At the time of going to press £1 Sterling = Dr269 and US$1 = Dr162 but you should check the rate of exchange before your departure.

AVERAGE PRICES

	Single Room	Double Room	Breakfast	Lunch/Dinner
★★★★★	—	—	Dr1592	Dr3392
★★★★	Dr14000	Dr15500	Dr1000	Dr2100
★★★	Dr3850–5500	Dr5000–7250	from Dr550	from Dr1600
★★	—	—	—	—
★	—	—	Dr510–530	Dr1270–1430

Abbreviations:
Av   Avenue
Pl   Place
Sq   Square
St   Street

AGRÍNION
Central Greece
★★**Soumelis** 3 Ethniki Odos ☎(0641)23473
rm20(⊷4) P

ALEXANDROÚPOLIS
Thrace

★★**Astir** 280 av Komotinis ☎(0551)26448
⊷♠53 P30 Lift ℂ ⌐ Beach Sea
Credit Cards ① ② ③ ⑤
★★**Egnatia** ☎(0551)28661
⊷♠96 ⋒ P ⋍ Beach Sea

ANDRÍTSAINA
Peloponnese
★**Theoxenia** (n.rest) ☎(0626)22219
15 Mar-Oct
rm40(⊷♠9)

ANDROS
Island of Andros
★★**Xenia** (n.rest) ☎(0282)22270
Apr-Oct
⊷♠26 P

ÁRTA
Epirus
★★**Xenia** DPn Frourion ☎(0681)27413
⊷♠22 ⋒ P22 ℂ Mountain
Credit Cards ① ② ③ ⑤

ATHÍNAI *(ATHENS)*

Attica
See Plan page 238 *Population* 3,027,331 *Local Tourist Office* 2 Karayeoryi Servias ☎(01)3222545
Encircled by hills and only four miles from the sea, Athínai is Europe's southernmost capital, and with its modern buildings and bustling streets standing side by side with ancient monuments - reminders of one of the world's oldest civilisations - is a delight to visit. But where to begin? Probably with the Acropolis, Greece's most famous landmark and the great symbol of classical civilisation. It dominates the city by day, the marble pillars of the Parthenon gleaming in the sun, and by night is brilliantly lit against a velvety black sky.
At the foot of the Acropolis is the oldest part of the city, Plaka, a district formed after Greece's independence, with a mass of narrow streets bursting with life, especially at night when the hundreds of bars, tavernas and clubs offer something to suit practically every taste and pocket. During the day Plaka is a marvellous place to browse among the countless craft shops, while not far away is the famous flea market, Monastiraki, where it is possible to pick up bargains, especially leather goods. But in the midst of the cosmopolitan streets you are just as likely to come across something as typically Greek as a tiny kiosk masquerading as a general store in miniature, or a little man selling pistachio nuts or lottery tickets. Broadly speaking, the main shopping areas are around Sintagma Square, Kolonaki, Omonia Square, Monastiraki, Patission Street and Kipseli.
If you want to get away from the pace and excitement of the capital, whether for relaxing or sightseeing, a short drive or bus or taxi ride will take you to the Athenian Riviera with its attractive resorts and long beaches.

235

EATING OUT The Greeks eat out frequently and consequently Athínai has a wide choice of restaurants where Greek food can be enjoyed. In some tavernas it is not unusual to walk straight into the kitchen to choose a speciality such as *dolmades* - vine leaves stuffed with lamb, accompanied by the tangy local wine, retsina. For inexpensive Greek and international food the popular and usually crowded *Delphi*, in Nikis, is recommended, as is *O Platanos*, located in the Plaka. At the upper end of the price bracket, *Dionysos*, in Robertou Gali, offers diners a wonderful view of the Acropolis. Right in the centre of town, *Floca's* and *Zonar's*, both in Venizelou Avenue, are the leading café restaurants.

ATHÍNAI (ATHENS)

★★★★★***Acropole Palace*** 51 28th Octovriou
☎(01)5223851 tx 15909
✦♠107

★★★★★***Astir Palace*** Syntagma Sq
☎(01)3643112 tx 222380
✦♠77 P2 Lift ℂ
Credit Cards ①②③④⑤

★★★★★***Athénée Palace*** 1 Kolokotroni
☎(01)3230791 tx 6188
✦♠150 ♠ P Lift ℂ
Credit Cards ②⑤

★★★★★***Athens Hilton*** 46 Vassilissis Sofias Av
☎(01)7220201 tx 215808
✦♠453 ♠ P240 Lift ℂ ➔ Sea
Credit Cards ①②③④⑤

★★★★★***Grande Bretagne*** Platia Syntagmatos
☎(01)3230251 tx 219615
✦♠384 Lift ℂ
Credit Cards ①②③④⑤

★★★★★***King George*** Constitution Sq
☎(01)3230651 tx 215296
✦♠140 ♠ P Lift ℂ
Credit Cards ①②③④⑤

★★★★★***St George Lycabettus*** Kleomenous 2
☎(01)7290711 tx 214253
✦♠150 └╴ ℂ ➔ Sea Mountain
Credit Cards ①②③④⑤

★★★★***Amalia*** 10 Amalias Av ☎(01)3237301 tx 215161
✦♠97 Lift ℂ
Credit Cards ①②③⑤

★★★★***Esperia Palace*** 22 Stadiou Str
☎(01)3238001 tx 5773
✦♠185 Lift ℂ
Credit Cards ①②③④⑤

★★★★***Holiday Inn*** 50 Michalakopoulou,Ilissia
☎(01)7248322 tx 218870
✦♠191 ♠ P25 Lift ➔ Mountain
Credit Cards ①②③④⑤

★★★★***King Minos*** 1 Pireos ☎(01)5231111 tx 215339
✦♠175 Lift ℂ
Credit Cards ①②③⑤

★★★★***Olympic Palace*** 16 Philellinon
☎(01)3237611 tx 215178
✦♠90 P Lift

★★★***Adrian*** 74 Andrianou Pl (n.rest)
☎(01)3221553
20 Mar-15 Nov
✦♠22 Lift

★★★***Asty*** 2 Pireos (n.rest) ☎(01)5230424 tx 224721
rm128(✦♠127) Lift
Credit Cards ①②③④⑤

★★★***El Greco*** 65 Athinas ☎(01)3244553
✦♠100 ♠ P30 Lift

★★★***Omonia*** 4 Platia Omonias ☎(01)5237210
✦♠275 Lift

★★★***Stadion*** 38 Vassileos Konstantinou
☎(01)7226054 tx 215838
rm70(✦♠56) Lift ℂ Mountain
Credit Cards ②⑤

★★★***Stanley*** 1-5 Odysseos St ☎(01)5241611 tx 216550

✦♠395 ♠ P120 Lift ℂ ➔
Credit Cards ①②③

★★***Diomia*** 5 Diomias St,Constitution Sq
☎(01)3238034 tx 214265
✦♠71 Lift ℂ
Credit Cards ①②③④⑤

★★***Imperial*** 46 Mitropoleos St (n.rest)
☎(01)3227617
rm45(✦♠20) ♠ P10 Lift ℂ
Credit Cards ①③

★★***Kronos*** 18 Aghiou Dimitriou (n.rest)
☎(01)3211601
rm56(✦♠29) ♠ P5 Lift Mountain

✎ ***G Maglaras*** Velvendous 127 ☎(01) 8624891
Toy

✎ ***J E Condellis*** Piracus St 165,Argyroymonis
☎(01) 3425031 For

✎ ***Tzen*** 101 Syngrou Av ☎(01) 9221870 **P** Saa

At GLIFÁDHA(17km S)

★★★***Astir*** 58 Vassileos Georgiou B
☎(01)8946461 tx 215925
16 May-Sep
✦♠128 P ℂ ℚ ➔ Beach Sea
Credit Cards ①②③④⑤

★★★***Florida*** 33 L-Metaxa ☎(01)8945254
rm86(✦♠27) P Lift

AYIOS KONSTANDÍNOS
Central Greece

★★***Levendi*** ☎(0235)31806 tx 61489
✦♠68 P70 ℂ ℚ ➔ Beach Sea
Credit Cards ②③⑤

CHALKIS
SeeKHALKIS

CRETE
SeeKRÍTI

DELPHI
Central Greece

★★★***Amalia*** Apollonos ☎(0265)82101 tx 215161
✦♠185 Lift ℂ ▣ ➔ Sea Mountain
Credit Cards ①②③⑤

★★★***Delphi-Xenia*** ☎(0265)82151
✦♠45 P30 Sea Mountain
Credit Cards ②⑤

★★★***Europa*** ☎(0265)82353
✦♠46 P Sea

✎ ***Dionyssos*** 34 Vassileos Pavlou,& Frideriks (n.rest) ☎(0265)82257
Apr-Sep
rm12 Sea

DRÁMA
Macedonia

★★***Xenia*** 10 Ethnikis Amynis ☎(0521)23195
rm32(✦♠20) P

ELOUNDA
See KRÍTI (CRETE)

EPÍDHAVROS (EPIDAURUS)
Peloponnese

★★***Xenia*** ☎(0753)22003
rm24(♠12) ℂ Mountain

FALERON
SeePHALERON

FIRA
See THÍRA (SANTORINI)

FLÓRINA
Macedonia

★★★***King Alexander*** 68 Leoforos Nikis
☎(0385)23501
✦♠59 P50 Lift ℂ Mountain

★★★***Tottis*** ☎(0385)22645
rm32 P

GLIFÁDHA
See ATHÍNAI (ATHENS)

IDHRA (HYDRA)
Island of Hydra

★★***Hydroussa*** (n.rest) ☎(0298)52217 tx 219338
May-Oct
✦♠36 ℂ Sea
Credit Cards ①②③④⑤

★★***Miramare*** Mandraki ☎(0298)52300
Etr-Oct
✦♠28 Beach Sea
Credit Card ①

IGOUMENITSA
Epirus

★***Xenia*** 2 Vassileous Pavlou (n.rest)
☎(0665)22282
Apr-Oct
✦♠72 ♠ P36 ℂ Beach Sea
Credit Cards ①②③④⑤

IOÁNNINA (JANINA)
Epirus

★★★***Palladion*** 1 Pan Scoumbourdi,28th
Octovriou ☎(0651)25856 tx 322212
rm135(✦♠119) P Lift ℂ Mountain Lake
Credit Cards ①②③⑤

★★***Acropole*** 3 Vassileos Georgiou A (n.rest)
☎(0651)26560
rm33(✦♠20) Lift ℂ Lake

★★***Xenia DPn*** 33 Vassileos Georgiou B
☎(0651)25087
✦♠60 P Lift ℂ Mountain Lake

ITÉA
Central Greece

★***Xenia*** ☎(0265)32263
Apr-Oct
✦♠18 P Beach

JANINA
SeeIOÁNNINA

KALABÁKA
Thessaly

★***Xenia*** ☎(0432)22327 tx 295345
Apr-Oct
✦♠22 P ℂ Mountain
Credit Card ⑤

KALÁMAI (KALAMATA)
Peloponnese

★★★***Rex*** 26 Aristomenous ☎(0721)22334
rm51(✦♠30) Lift

KAMÉNA VOÚRLA
Central Greece

★★★★***Astir Galini DPn*** ☎(0235)22327 tx 296140
✦♠131 P50 Lift ℂ ℚ ➔ Beach Sea Mountain
Credit Cards ①②③④⑤

KASTORÍA
Macedonia

★★*Xenia du Lac* pl Dexamenis ☎(0467)22565
🍴26 ☂ P

KAVÁLLA
Macedonia

★★*Galaxy* 51 El Venizelou ☎(051)224605 tx 452207
🍴149 A33rm P20 Lift ℂ Sea Mountain
Credit Cards ①②③⑤

★*Panorama* 32C El Venizelou (n.rest)
☎(051)224205
rm52(🍴18) P2 Lift ℂ Sea Mountain
Credit Card ③

🍴 *D Hionis-G Vardavoulaias* E Venizelou 77 St
☎(051) 25058 P AR Maz Mer

KÉRKIRA (CORFU)

KÉRKIRA

★★★★Corfu Palace L-Democratias
☎(0661)39485 tx 332126
Apr- Oct
🍴115 P40 Lift ℂ ▱ ⌿ Sea Mountain
Credit Cards ①③④⑤

KOMENO BAY

★★★★Astir Palace DPn ☎(0661)91490 tx 332169
11 Apr-Oct
🍴308 P10 Lift ℂ ९ ⌿ Beach Sea
Credit Cards ①②③④⑤

KHALKIS (CHALKIS)
Euboea

★★★*Lucy* 10 L-Voudouri ☎(0221)23831
rm92(🍴80) P Lift Beach Sea

KHANIÁ
See KRÍTI (CRETE)

KIFISÍA
Attica

★★★*Cecil* 7 Xenias,Kefalari (n.rest)
☎(01)8013836
Apr-Oct
🍴85 P100 Lift ℂ Mountain
Credit Cards ②③

KOMENO BAY
See KÉRKIRA (CORFU)

KOZÁNI
Macedonia

★★*Hermionion* 7 Platia Nikis ☎(0461)36007
rm20(🍴8)

KRÍTI (CRETE)

ELOUNDA

★★★★Astir Palace DPn ☎(0841)41580 tx 262215
11 Apr-Oct
🍴300 P Lift ℂ ९ ▱ ⌿ Beach Sea Mountain
Credit Cards ①②③④⑤

KHANIÁ

★★★*Kydon* Platia Agoras ☎(0821)26190 tx 291146
🍴114 P40 Lift Sea Mountain
Credit Cards ①②③④⑤

★★*Xenia* Theotokopoulou ☎(0821)24561
🍴44 P

RÉTHIMNON

★★*Xenia* N Psarrou 30 ☎(0831)29111
🍴25 P ℂ ९ Beach Sea

LAMÍA
Central Greece

★★*Apollonion* 25 Hatzopoulou (n.rest)
☎(0231)22668
rm36(🍴24) P Lift

LÁRISA
Thessaly

★*Xenia* 135 Fassalon ☎(041)239002
🍴130 ☂ ℂ

LESBOS

MITHYMNA

★★*Delphinia 1* ☎(0253)71315 tx 297116
:Rest closed Nov-Mar
🍴122 P ℂ ९ ⌿ Beach Sea
Credit Cards ②⑤

MITILÍNI

★★★*Xenia* ☎(0251)22713 tx 297113
Apr-Dec
🍴74 P6 Lift ℂ ▱▱ Sea
Credit Cards ①②③

🍴 *Vamvakoula* A-Gianareli 50 ☎(0251) 27091 P
Toy

LOUTRÁKI
Attica

★★★*Karelion* 23 G-Lekka ☎(0741)42347
🍴40 P ▱ Beach

MÍKONOS
Island of Míkonos

★★★*Leto* ☎(0289)22207 tx 293201
🍴25 Sea
Credit Cards ①②③

★★★*Theoxenia* (n.rest) ☎(0289)22230 tx 239201
Apr-Oct
rm57(🍴33) ℂ Sea
Credit Cards ①②③

MITHYMNA
See LESBOS

MITILÍNI
See LESBOS

NÁVPLION (NAUPLIA)
Peloponnese

★★★★*Amphityron* Akti Miaouli ☎(0752)27366
🍴48 P30 Lift ℂ ▱ Sea
Credit Cards ①④⑤

★★★*Amalia* 93 Argous ☎(0752)24400 tx 215161
🍴172 P200 Lift ℂ ▱ Sea
Credit Cards ①②③④⑤

★★*Park* 1 Dervenakion ☎(0752)27428
🍴70 Lift ℂ

★★*Xenia* Acronafplia ☎(0752)28981
🍴58 P Lift Beach Sea

OLYMPIA
Peloponnese

★★★*Amalia* ☎(0624)22190 tx 215161
🍴147 Lift ℂ Mountain
Credit Cards ①②③⑤

★★★*Spap* ☎(0624)23101
🍴61 P Lift ℂ Mountain
Credit Cards ①②③④⑤

★★*Xenia* (n.rest) ☎(0624)22510
Apr-Oct
🍴36 P ℂ Mountain

PÁTRAI (PATRAS)
Peloponnese

★★*Méditerranée* 18 Aghiou Nicolaou
☎(061)279602
🍴100 Lift Sea
Credit Cards ②③⑤

PHALERON (FALERON)
Attica

★★★*Coral* 35 Possidonos Av ☎(01)9816441 tx 210879
🍴89 P Lift ▱
Credit Cards ①②③④⑤

PÍLOS
Peloponnese

★★*Miramare* 3 Tsamadou ☎(0723)22226

🍴20 P ℂ Beach Sea
Credit Cards ①②③④⑤

PIRAIÉVS (PIRAEUS)
Attica

★★*Arion* 109 Vassileos Pavlou,Kastella (n.rest)
☎(01)4121425
rm36(🍴2) P Lift Sea

★★*Phedias* 189 Koundourioti,Passalimani (n.rest)
☎(01)4170552
rm26 ☂ P Lift ℂ

PLATAMÓN
Macedonia

★*Olympos* 18 Frouriou (n.rest) ☎(0352)41380
Jul-Sep
rm23 P Beach Sea

PORTARIA
Thessaly

★★*Xenia DPn* ☎(0421)99158 tx 223334
🍴76 A9rm P Lift Sea Mountain
Credit Cards ①③

RÉTHIMNON
See KRÍTI (CRETE)

RÓDHOS (RHODES)
Island of Rhodes

★★★★Grand Astir Palace DPn Akti Miaouli
☎(0241)26284 tx 292121
🍴377 P3 Lift ℂ ९ ▱ ⌿ Sea
Credit Cards ①②③④⑤

★★★★*Ibiscus* 17 Nissyrou ☎(0241)24421 tx 292131
Mar-Nov
🍴207 Lift Sea
Credit Cards ①②⑤

★★★*Elafos & Elafina (Astir)* Mount Profitis Elias
☎(0246)21221 tx 292121
Apr-Oct
🍴68 Lift Sea Mountain
Credit Cards ①②③④⑤

★★★*Mediterranean* 35-37 Ko ☎(0241)24661 tx 292108
🍴154 Lift ℂ Sea

★★★*Park* 12 Riga Ferreou ☎(0241)24611 tx 292137
Apr-Oct
🍴92 P Lift ℂ ▱

★★★*Spartalis* 2 N-Plastira (n.rest)
☎(0241)24371
🍴79 Lift
Credit Cards ①②③⑤

★★*Arion* 17 Ethnarhou Makariou (n.rest)
☎(0241)20004
May-Oct
🍴48 ℂ

★★*Soleil* 2 Democratias ☎(0241)24190
Jul- 20 Sep
rm90(🍴41) P Lift
Credit Card ②

★*Achillion* 14 Platia Vassileos Pavlou (n.rest)
☎(0241)24604
Mar-Oct
🍴50 Lift

🍴 *Zuvalas* Afstralias 10 ☎(0241) 23281 Ope

SALONICA
See THESSALONÍKI

SANTORINI
See THÍRA

SÉRRAI
Macedonia

★★*Xenia* 1 Aghias Sophias ☎(0321)22931
rm32 P

SOFÁDHES
Thessaly

🍴 *G Popotas* 7 St-George's ☎(0443) 22341 M/C
P

SOÚNION
Attica

★★**Aegalon** ☎(0292)39200
⊶44 P Lift Beach Sea

★**Mount Belevedere Park** ☎(0292)39102 tx 223914
May-Oct
⊶90 P30 ℂ ⚲ ⌣ Sea

SPÁRTI (SPARTA)
Peloponnese

★★★**Lida** Atreidon-Ananiou ☎(0731)23601
15 Mar-Oct
⊶42 P Lift Mountain
Credit Cards ①⑤

★★★**Xenia** Lofos Dioskouron ☎(0731)26524
⊶33 P

★★**Dioskuri** 94 Lykourgou-Atreidon
☎(0731)28484
⊶34 Lift Mountain

SPÉTSAI
Island of Spétsai

★★★**Kastell** ☎(0298)72311 tx 214531
15 Mar-15 Dec
⊶90 P ℂ ⚲ ♁♁ ∪ Beach Sea
Credit Cards ②⑤

THÁSOS
Island of Thásos

★★**Xenia** ☎(0593)22105
May-Sep
⊶24 A10rm P ℂ Beach Sea Mountain
Credit Card ①

THEBES
SeeTHÍVAI

ATHÍNAI (ATHENS)

1	Acropole Palace	★★★★★
2	Astir Palace	★★★★★
3	Athenée Palace	★★★★★
4	Athens Hilton	★★★★★
5	Grande Bretagne	★★★★★
6	King George	★★★★★
7	Amalia	★★★★
8	Esperia Palace	★★★★
9	Holiday Inn	★★★★
10	King Minos	★★★★
11	Olympic Palace	★★★★
13	Adrian	★★★
14	Astir (At Glifádha)	★★★
15	Asty	★★★
18	El Greco	★★★
19	Florida (At Glifádha)	★★★
20	Omonia	★★★
21	Stadion	★★★
22	Stanley	★★★
23	Diomia	★★
24	Imperial	★★
25	Kronos	★★

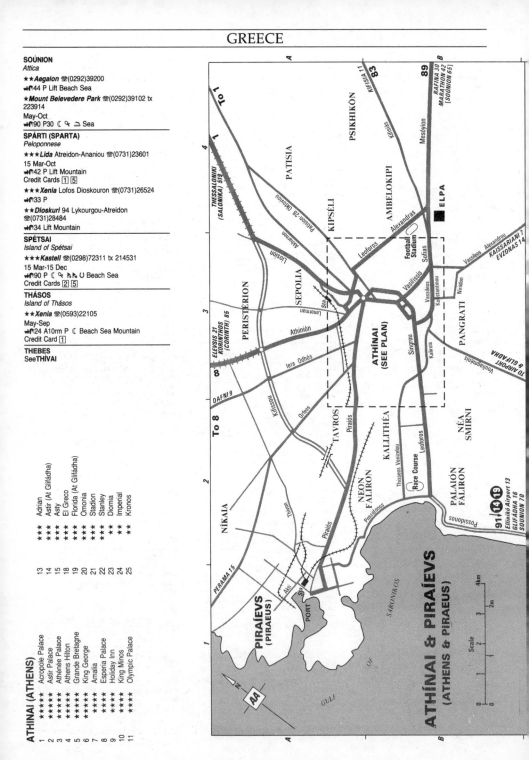

ATHÍNAI & PIRAÍEVS
(ATHENS & PIRAEUS)

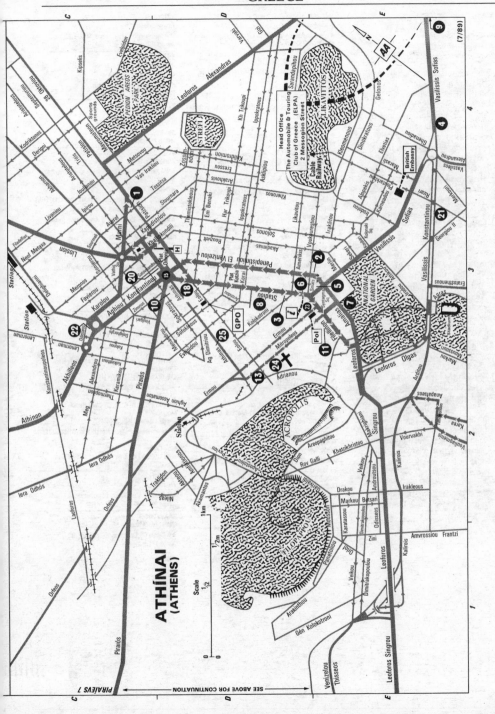

ATHÍNAI (ATHENS)

Scale

1km

½

½m

0

The Automobile & Touring Club of Greece (ELPA)
Head Office
2 Messogion Street

(7/89)

AA

N

SEE ABOVE FOR CONTINUATION
PIRAÍEVS 7

239

THESSALONÍKI (SALONICA)
Macedonia

Greece's second largest city and the birthplace of Aristotle, Thessaloníki is not particularly old by Greek standards, having been founded as recently as BC315. The historic nucleus of narrow winding lanes, with picturesque wooded houses with overhanging balconies, though largely engulfed by modern apartment blocks, is nonetheless well worth exploring, as are the numerous Byzantine churches. A Venetian tower and Turkish mosques and baths remain from subsequent occupations. Among the other visitor sights are the White Tower, including the Citadel of the Seven Towers, facing the Monastery of Vlatadon; the Rotunda and the Arch of Galerius; the Archaeological Museum, containing impressive gold treasures; and the Museum of Popular Art.

EATING OUT Food, on the whole, is cheaper and better value here than in Athens. Local specialities include *midia tiganita* (fried mussels), usually accompanied by the local white Corona wine. Also popular is meat baked with yoghurt. The best fish restaurants are to be found in the suburb of Aretsou. Winter visitors may find wild boar or hare on the menu, usually casseroled. The restaurants *Stratis*, in Nikis, and *Ta Nissia*, in Koromila, are both recommended, the latter for seafood.

THESSALONÍKI (SALONICA)
Macedonia

★★★★**Makedonia Palace** L-Megalou Alexandrou ☎(031)837520 tx 412162
◖♠287 P Lift ☾ Sea
Credit Cards ①②③④⑤

★★★**Capsis** 28 Monastiriou ☎(031)521321 tx 412206
◖♠428 Lift ☾ ➔
Credit Cards ①②③④⑤

★★★**City** 11 Komninon ☎(031)269421 tx 412208
rm104(◖100) Lift ☾
Credit Cards ②⑤

★★★**Olympic** DPn 25 Egnatia (n.rest) ☎(031)522131
rm52(◖♠39) P20 Lift

★★★**Rotonda** 97 Monastiriou ☎(031)517121 tx 412322
◖♠79 ☒ P Lift ☾ Mountain

★★★**Victoria** 13 Langada ☎(031)522421 tx 412145
◖♠68 P Lift ☾
Credit Card ②

●● **ETEA** Grammou-Bitsi 142,Phoenix ☎(031)417421 P Aud VW

●● **G Anastassiades** 2-4 Vassileos Georgiou ☎(031) 515209 For

●● **Ioannidis** 136-138 Queen Olga ☎ 844412 P

●● **Saracakis** 5 Kilom Monastiriou Str ☎(031) 764802 P Hon Vol

●● **Sinis** 18 Grammou Vitsi ☎(031) 417127 Ope

●● **Tasta** 7th Km Thessveria,Diavata ☎(031) 7636236 Mer

THÍRA (SANTORINI)
Island of Thíra

FIRA

★★**Atlantis** (n.rest) ☎(0286)22232 tx 293113
Apr-Oct
◖♠27 ☾ Sea
Credit Cards ①②③⑤

THÍVAI (THEBES)
Attica

★★**Dionyssion Melathron** 71 Metaxa & Kadmou ☎(0262)27855
rm30(◖4) ☒ ☾

TOLÓN
Peloponnese

★★**Minoa** 56 Aktis ☎(0752)59207 tx 0298157
15 Mar-Oct
◖♠62 A18rm Lift Beach Sea
Credit Cards ①②③④⑤

★**Solon** DPn ☎(0752)59204
15 Mar-Oct
◖♠28 P ☾ Beach Sea Mountain
Credit Cards ①②③④

TRÍPOLIS
Peloponnese

★★★**Menalon** Platia Areos ☎(071)222450
◖♠40 P Lift

TSANGARÁDHA
Thessaly

★★**Xenia** ☎(0423)49205
rm46(◖42) ☾ Sea Mountain
Credit Cards ①②③⑤

VITÍNA
Peloponnese

★★**Xenia** ☎(0795)21218
Apr-Sep
◖♠20 P ☾ Mountain

VÓLOS
Thessaly

★★★**Xenia** 1N Plastira,Aghios Konstantinos ☎(0421)24825
◖♠48 Lift Beach

★★**Aegli** 17A Argonafton (n.rest) ☎(0421)25691
rm40(◖14) P Lift Sea

★★**Pallas** 44 Lassonos & Argonafton (n.rest) ☎(0421)23510
rm50(◖12) P Lift Sea

VOÚLA
Attica

★★★**Atlantis** 6 Aphroditis ☎(01)8958443
◖♠15 P

★**Miramare** 4 Vassileos Pavlou (n.rest) ☎(01)8958446
rm20 P

VOULIAGMENI BEACH
Attica

★★★★★**Astir Palace Aphrodite** ☎(01)8960211 tx 223046
2 May-1 Oct
◖♠169 P20 Lift ☾ ✆ ⊟ ➔ ∪ Beach Sea Mountain
Credit Cards ①②③④⑤

★★★★★**Astir Palace Arion** ☎(01)8960211 tx 215013
◖♠208 P50 Lift ☾ ✆ ⊟ ➔ ∪ Beach Sea Mountain
Credit Cards ①②③④⑤

★★★★★**Astir Palace Nafsika** ☎(01)8960211 tx 210712
May-Oct
◖♠172 P50 Lift ☾ ✆ ⊟ ➔ ∪ Beach Sea
Credit Cards ①②③④⑤

XÁNTHI
Thrace

★★**Xenia** 9 Vassilissis Sophias ☎(0541)24135
◖♠24 P

ZÁKINTHOS
Island of Zákinthos

★★**Xenia** 66 D-Roma ☎(0695)22232
◖♠39 P Lift Beach

IRELAND

Language
Irish, English

Local time
GMT (Summer GMT + 1)

Currency (Republic)
Irish pound or punt, divided into 100 pence. At the time of going to press
£1 = IR£1.16
US$1 = IR£0.70

Emergency numbers
Fire, Police, Ambulance ☎999

Information in England
Irish Tourist Board, 150 New Bond Street, London W1Y 0AQ
☎†01-493 3201

Northern Ireland Tourist Board, 11 Berkeley Street, London W1
☎†01-493 0601
†code changes to 071 on 6 May

Sean Taaffe, 38 High Street, Sutton Coldfield, West Midlands
☎021-354 1431

Information in the USA
Irish Tourist Board, 757 Third Avenue, New York, NY10017
☎212 418 0800

Information in Northern Ireland
Irish Tourist Board, 53 Castle Street, Belfast BT1 1GH
☎(0232) 372888

40 Foyle Street, Londonderry BT48 6AR
☎(0504) 369501

Northern Ireland Tourist Board, 48 High Street, Belfast BT1 2DS
☎(0232) 231221
(for tourist information 246609)

Information in Republic of Ireland
Irish Tourist Board, Baggot Street Bridge, Dublin
☎(01) 765871

Tourist Information at 14 Upper O'Connell Street, Dublin 1
☎(01) 747733

Northern Ireland Tourist Board at Clery's Department Store, O'Connell Street, Dublin
☎(01) 786055

Politically, Ireland consists of the Republic, which is a sovereign independent state, and Northern Ireland which forms part of the UK. To assist visitors to the island, we have included both Northern Ireland and the Republic in this section of the book. However, in Northern Ireland motoring conditions and regulations are virtually the same as in Britain, so the general information which follows applies only to the Republic.

Ireland is a place to linger. Whether you decide to explore the lush green valleys and cobalt lakes of the Wicklow mountains, the stunning coastlines of the Ring of Kerry, the stone-walled and whitewashed cottage landscape of Connemara or the near-deserted sandy beaches of the west coast, you will find enchantment and a warm welcome.

If you decide to take shelter in a local pub – and there are plenty of them – get yourself a drink, breathe in the delightful aroma of a peat fire, and listen to the rain of conversation. For whichever part of Ireland you choose to visit you will encounter drinking companions with a thousand tales to tell, hospitable hosts and a people of great charm.

A wide variety of sporting opportunities is available – from angling and sailing to golf and horse-riding. Those who prefer quieter pursuits will find an abundance of history and culture in the form of castles, museums and stately homes.

Once the home of saints and scholars of early Christian Europe, Ireland is a country rich in prehistoric remains, distinctive Celtic high crosses, Romanesque monasteries, castles, and handsome mansions. It also offers an abundance of lakes, rivers and seas teeming with fish, and some of the most exhilarating walking country to be found anywhere.

ATLANTIC OCEAN

NORTH CHANNEL

Malin
Ballyliffen
Moville
Rosapenna
Dunfanaghy
Portrush
Portballintrae
Ballycastle
Red Castle
Gortahork
Port-na-Blagh
Rathmullan
Eglington
Coleraine
Ballymoney
Cushendall
Dungloe
Letterkenny
Londonderry
Limavady
Cullybackey
Carnlough
Raphoe
Swatragh
Ballymena
Ballygally
Convoy
Strabane
Maghera
Larne
Ballybofey
Doagh
Carrickfergus
Carrick
Moneymore
Antrim
Glengormley
Newtownabbey
Donegal
Omagh
Cookstown
Holywood
Bangor
Crawfordsburn
Newtowna
Rossnowlagh
Ederney
Carrickmore
Dunmurry
Moneyreagh
Ballyshannon
Kesh
Six Mile
Dungannon
Lisburn
Killinchy
Irvinestown
Cross
Moy
Craigavon
Saintfield
Clou
Garrison
Derrygonelly
Fintona
Portadown
Killyleagh
Clogher
Aughnacloy
Ballynahinch
Rosses Point
Enniskillen
Caledon
Armagh
Banbridge
Downpatrick
Loughbrickland
Sligo
Lisnaskea
Tassagh
Newcastle
Drumkeeran
Kinawley
Monaghan
Castleblayney
Newry
Bangor-Erris
Belturbet
Cootehill
Crossmaglen
Kilkeel
Crossmolina
Ballina
Cavan
Carrickmacross
Ravensdale
Dundalk
Foxford
Boyle
Carrick-on-Shannon
Ardee
Drogheda
Newport
Charlestown
Slane
Laytown
IRISH SEA
Castlebar
Strokestown
Longford
Navan
Julianstown
Westport
Castlerea
Edgeworthstown
Ashbourne
Donabate
Louisburgh
Claremorris
Roscommon
Ballymahon
Malahide
Ballinrobe
Mullingar
Howth
Renvyle
Athlone
Moate
Kilcock
Clifden
Headford
Ballinasloe
Edenderry
DUBLIN
Ballynahinch
Oughterard
Rosscahill
Ferbane
Prosperous
Dun Laoghaire
Cashel
Spiddal
Galway
Naas
Blackrock
Killiney
Roundstone
Furbo
Craughwell
Kildare
Blessington
Bray
Rosmuc
Kinvarra
Portumna
Birr
Emo
Monasterevin
Ashford
Kilmacanogue
Ballyvaughn
Lisdoonvarna
Mountrath
Port Laoise
Glendalough
Glen of the Downs
Liscannor
Kilfenora
Roscrea
Castledermot
Aughrim
Rathnew
Milltown
Ennis
Borris in
Carlow
Woodenbridge
Wicklow
Malbay
Newmarket-
Nenagh
Ossory
Shillelagh
Coolgreany
Kilkee
on-Fergus
Lissycasey
Gorey
Kilrush
Bunratty
Limerick
Thurles
Kilkenny
Courtown Harbour
Adare
Dundrum
Callan
Ballycanew
Ballybunion
Listowel
Newcastle West
Tipperary
Cashel
Enniscorthy
Lixnaw
Abbeyfeale
Aherlow
Cahir
New Ross
Wexford
Tralee
Rath Luirc
Clonmel
Waterford
Rosslare
(Charleville)
Killinick
Rosslare Harbour
ST GEORGE'S CHANNEL
Mitchelstown
Dunmore East
Killarney
Fermoy
Ballyduff
Lismore
Lemybrien
Mallow
Knockanore
Ballinskelligs
Blarney
Killeagh
Ardmore
Waterville
Kenmare
Macroom
Cork
Kinsalebeg
Sneem
Gougane
Inchigeelagh
Little
Midleton
Youghal
Parknasilla
Barra
Island
Garryvoe
Caherdaniel
Ballylickey
Kinsale
Ballycotton
Bantry
Drimoleague
Ballinspittle
Castletownbere
Clonakilty
Garrettstown
Skibbereen
Courtmacsherry
Baltimore

**For key to country identification - see
"About the gazetteer"**

HOW TO GET THERE

Car-carrying ferry services operate from Britain to both the Republic and Northern Ireland countries.

To the Republic
from Pembroke to Rosslare takes 3¾hrs
from Fishguard to Rosslare takes 3½hrs
from Holyhead to Dublin takes 3½–4¾hrs
from Holyhead to Dun Laoghaire
takes 3½hrs

To the North
from Liverpool to Belfast takes 9hrs
from Stranraer to Larne
takes 2hrs 20mins
from Cairnryan to Larne takes 2¾hrs

There are also services to and from France: Cherbourg and Le Havre and Rosslare; Roscoff and Le Havre (summer only) to Cork.

MONEYMATTERS

There is no restriction on the amount of foreign and Irish currency or travellers' cheques which may be imported into the Republic, but large amounts which are to be re-exported should be declared on entry. Visitors and residents leaving the Irish Republic may only export up to IR£150 in Irish currency and up to IR£1,200 in foreign currency, together with the imported amount declared on entry.

Banking hours
Monday–Friday 10.00–12.30hrs and 13.30–15.00hrs (17.00hrs on Thursdays in Dublin). Other late opening days vary from town to town.

Postcheques
may be cashed at sub-post offices displaying a *Postcheque* sticker and at all main post offices up to a maximum of IR£100 per cheque. Go to the counter marked *Money orders*.

MOTORING REGULATIONS AND GENERAL INFORMATION

The information given here is specific to Ireland. It **must** be read in conjunction with the European ABC at the front the book, which covers those regulations which are common to many countries.

Accidents

If you are involved in an accident you must stop immediately and exchange particulars with the other party. If this is not possible you must report the accident to a member of the *Garda Siochana* or at the nearest *Garda Station*. See also *Warning triangle* below.

Breakdown*

If your car breaks down, try to move it to the side of the road so that it obstructs the traffic flow as little as possible. The AA's Breakdown Service is available to members, on terms similar to those in Britain. Patrols operate throughout the country, and their services are complemented by garages. See also *Warning triangle* below.

British Embassy/Consulate*

The British Embassy together with its consular section is located at 31–33 Merrion Road, Dublin 4 ☎(01) 695211.

Children in cars*

Children under 12 are not permitted to travel in a vehicle as front seat passengers, unless they are using special seats or safety belts suitable for children.

Dimensions and weight restrictions

Private **cars** and towed **trailers** or **caravans** are restricted to the following dimensions – height, no restriction; width, 2.50 metres; length, 12 metres. The maximum permitted overall length of vehicle/trailer or caravan combinations is 18 metres.
    Trailers without brakes may weigh up to 762kg or may have a total weight of up to 50% of the towing vehicle.

*Additional information will be found in the European ABC at the front of the book.

Driving licence*

A valid UK licence is acceptable in the Republic of Ireland. The minimum age at which a vistor may use a temporarily imported motorcycle (exceeding 150cc) or car is 17 years.

Emergency messages to tourists*

Emergency messages to tourists are broadcast on Irish radio (RTE). These messages are transmitted in English on 529 metres medium wave at 08.00–09.00, 13.30 and 18.30hrs.

Horn, use of

On roads where a permanent speed limit is in force, the use of a horn is prohibited from 23.30 to 07.00hrs.

Insurance*

Short-term third-party insurance cover cannot be arranged at the frontier, or point of entry.

Lights*

As the rule of the road in the Republic is to drive on the left, the general advice regarding adjustment of headlights for driving on the right should be ignored.

Motoring club*

The Automobile Association has its regional headquarters in the **Republic of Ireland** at 23 Rock Hill, Blackrock, Co Dublin ☎(01) 833555, and an AA Centre at 12 Emmet Place, Cork ☎(021) 276922. In **Northern Ireland**, there is an AA Centre at 108–110 Great Victoria Street, Belfast ☎(0232) 244538. The offices are open Monday to Friday 09.00–17.00hrs and 09.00–12.30hrs on Saturday (09.30–13.00hrs in Belfast). The AA Centre in Cork closes for lunch between 13.00 and 14.00hrs.

Motorways

The Republic has two stretches of motorway; the 5 miles which bypass the town of Naas on the N7 and the 3 miles north of Dublin in the N1.

Northern Ireland has various stretches of motorway:
M1 (38 miles) Belfast – south west to join A29 south of Dungannon.

M2 (18.5 miles) Belfast – north west to join M22 north of Antrim.
M5 (1.5 miles) Belfast–Larne coastal route linking M2 to A2.
M12 (1 mile) North of Portadown linking M1 and A3.
M22 (5 miles) south of Randalstown linking M2 to A6.

Orange badge scheme for disabled drivers*

In the Republic of Ireland, badge holders may park without payment of fees at parking meters and in areas where parking discs are in operation. They are not entitled to park on single or double yellow lines, or in areas where they are likely to cause an obstruction.

Parking

Parking is prohibited where there are yellow lines on the roadway, and within the boundary of a bus stop as defined by roadway markings. The offence of dangerous parking carries heavy penalties, particularly if committed in the hours of darkness.

Parking meters are in use in the central zones of Dublin, and operate Monday to Friday 08.00–18.30hrs. Disc parking operates in some parts of Dublin City and in Carlow, Cork City, Drogheda, Dungarvan, Enniscorthy, Galway City, Killarney, Limerick City, Mullinger, Naas, Tralee, Waterford City and Wexford.

Petrol

Credit cards Petrol stations generally accept recognised credit cards
Duty-free petrol The petrol in a vehicle tank may be imported free of customs duty and tax. Up to 10 litres in a can may also be imported duty and tax-free, if crossing into the Republic from Northern Ireland.
Petrol (leaded) Regular (90 octane) and Premium (99 octane) grades.
Petrol (unleaded) is sold in the Republic of Ireland. It has an octane rating of 95.

Post information

Mail Postcards 24p; letters up to 20gm 28p.
Post offices There are some 250 main and sub-post offices in the Republic; opening hours are from 09.00–17.30hrs Monday to Friday.

*Additional information will be found in the European ABC at the front of the book.

IRELAND

Priority*

At uncontrolled road junctions where both roads are principal roads, or alternatively, where neither road is a principal road, drivers must give way to vehicles approaching from the right. Principal roads are indicated by authorised signs at uncontrolled road junctions.

Public holidays*

Official Public holidays in the Republic of Ireland for 1990 are given below.
January 1 (New Year's Day)
March 17†† (St Patrick's Day)
April 13† (Good Friday)
April 16 (Easter Monday)
June 4 (Whit Monday)
August 6 (Bank Holiday)
October 29 (Public holiday)
December 25 (Christmas Day)
December 26 (St Stephen's Day)
††Saturday
†Not official Public holidays, but banks, government offices and most businesses close.

Roads

The road numbering system in the Republic of Ireland has been changed, and new direction signs are gradually being brought into use. These are National Primary, National Secondary and Regional. The National Primary roads have the prefix 'N' and a number between 1 and 25. National Secondary roads also have the prefix 'N', but a number above 50. Regional roads have the prefix 'R'

Shopping hours

Generally, shops are open 09.00–17.30hrs Monday to Saturday, with some supermarkets open until 21.00hrs on Thursday or Friday. Most shops have one early closing day each week, and this is usually 13.00hrs on Wednesday and Saturday.

Speed limits*

In built-up areas, 48kph (30mph); *outside built-up areas*, 88kph (55mph). Vehicle/trailer combinations 56kph (35mph).

Telephone*

Insert coin **after** lifting the receiver; the dialling tone is the same as the UK. When making calls within the Republic, precede the number with the relevant area code as necessary (shown in parentheses before the hotel/garage enquiry number in the gazetteer where applicable). Use 5p and 10p coins for local calls, and 5p, 10p and 50p coins for national and international calls.
International calls can be made from Payphone or Telefón callboxes.
A direct call to the UK from a payphone between 08.00 and 18.00hrs costs 60p per minute.
Telephone codes
UK to Irish Republic   010 353
            except Dublin 0001
Irish Republic to UK   Direct to all
                              exchanges except
                              from old-style coin-
                              box telephones
Irish Republic to the USA   010 3531
            except Dublin 0001 1

Traffic lights*

Traffic lights are used in most large towns, and go in sequence from red, straight to green; when changing back they go to amber, then red.

Warning triangle*

In the event of accident or breakdown, the use of a warning triangle is only compulsory in respect of vehicles with an unladen weight of 1524kg (1½ tons).

*Additional information will be found in the European ABC at the front of the book.

ACCOMMODATION

There is excellent accommodation of all types available, from first-class luxury hotels to more modest but nevertheless comfortable hotels. Guesthouse, Farmhouse and Town and Country Home accommodation is widely available, and fuller information on this type of accommodation can be found in the AA Guide *Bed & Breakfast in Europe*, or the *AA Handbook Ireland*.

In the Ireland gazetteer hotels are graded by star classification as in Britain. The AA's full-time, highly qualified team of inspectors regularly visit all listed establishments in Ireland.

The prices shown below are an average for each classification. Accommodation is likely to be more expensive in main towns and some of more popular tourist areas.

At the time of going to press, £1 *Sterling = IR£1.16* and *US$1 = IR£0.70* but you should check the rate of exchange before your departure.

AVERAGE PRICES

	Single Room	Double Room	Breakfast	Lunch/Dinner
★★★★	£71–£84	£78–£115	£4.25–£6	£12–£17
★★★	£25–£43	£53–£65	£4–£5	£9–£15
★★	£26–£33	£41–£50	£3	£7–£13
★	£13–£19	£26–£37	from £2	from £10

The counties of Northern Ireland are: Co Antrim, Co Armagh, Co Down, Co Fermanagh, Co Londonderry, Co Tyrone and City of Belfast.
According to our information garages with no specific service will handle any make of car.

Abbreviations

Av	Avenues	Sq	Square
Pl	Place	St	Street
Rd	Road	m	mile

ABBEYFEALE
Co Limerick
★*Leen's* ☎(068)31121
Closed 24-31 Dec
rm14(♠3) P
Credit Cards [1] [3]
⏳ O'Leary's Convent Rd ☎(068) 31137

ACHILL ISLAND
Co Mayo
★*McDowell's* Slievemore Rd ☎(098)43148
Etr-Sep :Rest closed Sun
rm10(♠4) P12 Sea Mountain Lake
⏳ E T Sweeney & Sons Achill Sound ☎(098) 45243
⏳ Henry's Achill Sound ☎(098) 45246

ADARE
Co Limerick
★★★*Dunraven Arms* ☎(061)86209 tx 70202
♠24 P22 ℂ
Credit Cards [1] [2] [3] [5]

AHERLOW
Co Tipperary
★★★*Glen* ☎(062)56146
rm24(♠22) P200
Credit Cards [1] [2] [3]

ANTRIM
Co Antrim
⏳ Hugh Tipping 23 Crosskennan Rd ☎(08494) 62225

ARDEE
Co Louth
⏳ McCabes Castle St ☎(041) 53291 Toy

ARDMORE
Co Waterford
★*Cliff House* ☎(024)94106

May-Sep
rm21(♠13) P40
Credit Cards [2] [3] [5]

ARMAGH
Co Armagh
⏳ H Corr & Sons Killylea Rd
⏳ *Mallview S/Sta* Mail View ☎(0861) 523415

ASHBOURNE
Co Meath
⏳ Ashbourne S/Sta ☎(01) 351121

ASHFORD
Co Wicklow
★★*Cullenmore DPn* ☎(0404)40187
Closed 25 & 26 Dec & 4-18 Jan
♠13 P160
Credit Cards [1] [2] [3] [5]

ATHLONE
Co Westmeath
★★★*Prince of Wales* ☎(0902)72626 tx 53068
Closed 25-27 Dec
♠42 P35 ℂ
Credit Cards [1] [2] [3] [4] [5]
★★*Royal Hoey* ☎(0902)72924
Closed 25-28 Dec
rm57(♠30) P50 Lift ℂ
Credit Cards [1] [2] [3] [5]
⏳ B.C.R. Garage Ballymahon Rd ☎(0902) 72560
⏳ Kenna Motors Dublin Rd ☎(0902) 72726 BL
⏳ Kenny & O'Brien Cornafulla ☎(0902) 37103
⏳ Kilmartin Dublin Rd ☎(0902) 75426 For

AUGHNACLOY
Co Tyrone
⏳ Watson & Haddon 138 Moore St ☎ 281

AUGHRIM
Co Wicklow
⏳ Aughrim Motor Factors ☎(0402) 36257

BALLINA
Co Mayo
★★★*Downhill* (Inter) ☎(096)21033 tx 40796
Closed 22-25 Dec
♠54 P300 ℂ ⏳ ⛳
Credit Cards [1] [2] [3] [5]
⏳ Finmax Dublin Rd ☎(096) 21288 For
⏳ Judges Auto Svcs Sligo Rd ☎(096) 21864

BALLINASLOE
Co Galway
★★★*Hayden's* Dunloe St ☎(0905)42347
Closed 25 Dec
rm52(♠47) P Lift ℂ
Credit Cards [1] [2] [3] [5]
⏳ Fred Kilmartin Athlone Rd ☎(0905) 42517 For
⏳ Louis Bannerton Galway Rd ☎(0905) 42420

BALLINROBE
Co Mayo
★*Lakelands* ☎(092)41020 tx 53703
Closed 24 Dec
rm18(♠5) P40
Credit Cards [3] [5]

BALLINSPITTLE
Co Cork
⏳ J O Regan ☎(021) 778120

BALLYBOFEY
Co Donegal
★★★*Kee's* Stranorlar ☎(074)31018
Closed 25 & 26 Dec
♠27 P80 Mountain
Credit Cards [1] [2] [3] [5]

BALLYBUNION
Co Kerry
★★*Marine* ☎(068)27139
16 Mar-Oct
♠10 P15 ℂ Sea
Credit Cards [1] [2] [3]

BALLYCANEW
Co Wexford
⏳ Kinsella's ☎(055) 27108

BALLYCASTLE
Co Antrim
⏳ Colgan Mtrs 47 Glentasie Rd ☎ 62242

BALLYCOTTON
Co Cork
★*Bay View* ☎(021)646746
rm20(♠5) ⏳ P40
Credit Cards [2] [3]

BALLYLICKEY
Co Cork
★★*Sea View* ☎(027)50462
Apr-Oct
rm12(♠10) A2rm ⏳ P40

BALLYLIFFEN
Co Donegal
★★**Strand** ☎(077)76107
Closed 24-26 Dec
⊶🏠19 A7rm P20 ℂ
Credit Cards ①③

BALLYMAHON
Co Longford
🏮 *Finnegan's* ☎(0902) 32229

BALLYMENA
Co Antrim
★★★**Adair Arms** Ballymoney Rd ☎(0266)653674
Closed 25 Dec
⊶🏠41 P50 ℂ
Credit Cards ①②③⑤
🏮 *R G Mcburney & Sons* 1-21 Railway St
☎(0266) 46014 Aud VW

BALLYMONEY
Co Antrim
🏮 *Curragh F/Sta* Frocess Rd ☎(02656) 62071
🏮 *GMG* 4 Portrush Rd ☎(02656) 64761 Col
🏮 *Lexie Kerr* 45 Rd ☎(02656) 62343

BALLYNAHINCH
Co Down
🏮 *R Gibb & Sons* 41 Main St ☎(0238) 562519
For

BALLYNAHINCH
Co Galway
★★★**Ballynahinch Castle** ☎(095)31006 tx 50809
⊶🏠28 P40 ⌖
Credit Cards ①②③⑤

BALLYSHANNON
Co Donegal
★★**Dorrian's Imperial** ☎(072)51147
Closed 25-31 Dec
⊶🏠26 P20 ℂ Mountain
Credit Cards ①③
🏮 *Abbey* Donegal Rd ☎(072) 51246

BALLYVAUGHAN
Co Clare
★★★**Gregans Castle** ☎(065)77005
Etr-Oct
⊶🏠16 P18 Sea Mountain
Credit Card ③
★★*Hyland's* ☎(065)77037
Etr-Sep
rm12(⊶🏠9) P50
Credit Cards ①③⑤

BALTIMORE
Co Cork
★**Baltimore House** ☎(028)20164
May-Sep
⊶🏠10 P15 Sea
Credit Cards ①②③⑤

BANBRIDGE
Co Down
🏮 *Banbridge Mtr Co* Dramore Rd ☎ 23411

BANGOR
Co Down
★★**Winston** 19-23 Queens Pde ☎(0247)454575
rm46(⊶🏠28) P6 ℂ
Credit Cards ①②③⑤
🏮 *Ballyrobert Cars* 402 Belfast Rd ☎(0247)
852262 Ope Vau
🏮 *Bangor Auto Recovery* 32-34 Belfast Rd
☎(0247) 457428
🏮 *D & G Car Sales* 12 Crosby St
🏮 *P W Gethin & Sons* 16 Belfast Rd ☎(0247)
465881 Sko
🏮 *S Mellon & Sons* 40 Bingham St ☎(0247)
457525 Maz

BANGOR-ERRIS
Co Mayo
🏮 *Daly's* ☎(097) 83463

BANTRY
Co Cork
★★★**Westlodge** ☎(027)50360 tx 75880
⊶🏠100 P400 ℂ ⌖ 🖃
Credit Cards ①②③④⑤
🏮 *Hurley* Bridge St ☎(027) 50092
🏮 *O'Learys* ☎(027) 50127

BELFAST

Belfast, capital of Northern Ireland, straddles the winding River Lagan. To the south it is surrounded by lush green hills, and to the south-west the River Lagan runs along a steep-sided wooded valley. The 18th and 19th-century city is centred around Castle Place and Cornmarket, on the west bank of the river. But many of Belfast's principal visitor attractions are on the outskirts, including the zoo; Belfast Castle, a Scottish Baronial-style pile built in 1870 and standing in the shadow of Cave Hill; the Ulster Folk Museum, a 20-minute drive away near Holywood in County Down; and Stormont Castle. Principal shopping streets are centred around Castle Junction and include Donegal Place, Howard Street, Fountain Street, Castle Lane and Cornmarket. Many shops sell craft products - wood carvings, stone and metal artefacts and Irish jewellery. Irish craft work is a rapidly expanding cottage industry.

EATING OUT Belfast is not noted for its culinary traditions, but standards have improved enormously in recent years, with more emphasis on the use of fresh ingredients and the avoidance of the Irish habit of overcooking. The Strand, in Strandmills Road, enjoys a good reputation, as does Thompson's, in Arthur Street. Truffles, in Donegal Square West, is also popular, especially at lunchtime. For traditional oysters and Guinness in an atmospheric pub setting, try Robinson's, opposite the Forum Hotel.

BELFAST
★★★★*Belfast Europa* Great Victoria St
☎(0232)230091 tx 74491
⊶🏠199 P20 Lift ℂ
Credit Cards ①②③④⑤
★★★*Stormont* 587 Upper Newtonards Rd
☎(0232)658621 tx 748198
⊶🏠67 P600 Lift ℂ
Credit Cards ①②③⑤
🏮 *A S Baird* Boucher Rd ☎(0232) 661811 Peu
Tal
🏮 *Castle Mtrs* 18-20 Parkgate Av
🏮 *Charles Hurst Mtr Cycles* 201-207
Castlereagh Rd ☎(0232) 732393 M/C
🏮 *DIY Auto Engineering Works* 47-51 Duncrue
Crescent
🏮 *Finaghy (W G Creighton)* 87-89 Upper
Lisburn Rd ☎(0232) 626711
🏮 *GMC Mtrs (G McKeown)* 2a Ardmore
Av,Finaghy Rd North ☎(0232) 622063
🏮 *GMG (City Cars)* 182-184 Shore Rd ☎(0232)
772054 Col Sko

🏮 *G Wright Mtrs* 73-77 Ravenhill Rd ☎(0232)
56697
🏮 *J E Coulter* 58-82 Antrim Rd ☎(0232) 744744
For
🏮 *Noel Orr Mtr Cycles* 78-80 Castlereagh Rd
☎(0232) 58622 M/C
🏮 *Phillips* 28 Adelaide St
🏮 *Sydney Pentland* 17-29 Ravenhill Rd ☎(0232)
51422 Ope Vau
🏮 *SMW Volvo (Stanley Mtr Wks)* 59-75 Latas
Dr ☎(0232) 703666 Vol
🏮 *T H Clarke & Co* 441A Beersbridge Rd
☎(0232) 650328
🏮 *Ulster* Boucher Rd ☎(0232) 681721 Ren

BELTURBET
Co Cavan
🏮 *O'Reilly* ☎(049) 22104

BIRR
Co Offaly
★★*County Arms* ☎(0509)20791
⊶🏠18 P100 ℂ
Credit Cards ①②③⑤

🏮 *P L Dolan & Sons* Main St ☎(0509) 20006

BLACKROCK
Co Dublin
🏮 *Appleyard Mtrs* Stillorgan Ind Est ☎(01)
953933 Peu
🏮 *Carroll & Kinsella* Rock Rd ☎(01) 888624 Dai
Sko Toy

BLARNEY
Co Cork
★★★*Hotel Blarney* ☎(021)385281 tx 75022
⊶🏠74 P150 ℂ ⌖ 🖃
Credit Cards ①②③④

BLESSINGTON
Co Wicklow
★★★*Downshire House* ☎(045)65199
Closed mid Dec-mid Jan
⊶🏠18 A7rm ℂ ⌖
🏮 *Blessington Mtr Co* ☎(045) 65555 BL

BORRIS-IN-OSSORY
Co Laois
★★*Leix County* ☎(0505)41213

Closed 25 Dec
→♯19 P ℃
Credit Cards [1] [2] [3]

BOYLE
Co Roscommon

★★**Royal** ☎(079)62016
Closed 25-26 Dec
→♯16 P100
Credit Cards [1] [2] [3] [5]

🐝 **Carty's** ☎(079) 62318

BRAY
Co Wicklow

★★**Royal** Main St ☎(01)862935 tx 33502
→♯70 P120 Lift ℃
Credit Cards [1] [2] [3] [5]

BUNRATTY
Co Clare

★★★**Fitzpatrick's Shannon Shamrock**
☎(061)361177 tx 72114
Closed 25 Dec
→♯105 P ℃ ⌂
Credit Cards [1] [2] [3] [4] [5]

BUSHMILLS
Co Antrim

🐝 *J C Halliday & Sons* 206 Straid Rd ☎(02657)
31452 Cit

CAHERDANIEL
Co Kerry

★★**Derrynane** (BW) ☎(0667)5136
May-Sep
→♯75 P100 ℃ ❄ ⌂
Credit Cards [2] [3] [5]

CAHIR
Co Tipperary

★★**Kilcoran Lodge** ☎(052)41288
rm21(→♯18) A4rm P60 ℃
Credit Cards [1] [2] [3] [5]

CALEDON
Co Tyrone

🐝 *Donnelly Bros* Armagh Rd ☎(0861) 568235

CALLAN
Co Kilkenny

🐝 **Hennessy's** Lower Bridge St ☎(056) 25149

CARLOW
Co Carlow

★★★**Royal** ☎(0503)31621
Closed 25-27 Dec
rm25(→♯23) ❄ P40 ℃
Credit Cards [1] [2] [3] [5]

🐝 **Deepark S/Sta** Dublin Rd ☎(0503) 31414
🐝 **Statham Sheridan** Court Pl ☎(0503) 31694
For

CARNLOUGH
Co Antrim

★★**Londonderry Arms** ☎(0574)85255
→♯14 P18 Sea
Credit Cards [1] [2] [3] [5]

CARRICK
Co Donegal

🐝 **McLoughlin's** ☎(074) 39018

CARRICKFERGUS
Co Antrim

★★**Coast Road** 28 South Quarter
☎(09603)51021
Closed 25 & 26 Dec
rm20(→♯15) ℃
Credit Cards [3] [5]

★**Dobbins Inn** 6-8 High St ☎(09603)51905
Closed 25 & 26 Dec
→♯13 ℃
Credit Cards [1] [2] [3] [5]

🐝 *H Wilson & Sons* 85 Belfast Rd

CARRICKMACROSS
Co Monaghan

🐝 **Meegan's** 3 Kings Court Rd ☎(042) 61608

CARRICKMORE
Co Tyrone

🐝 *Rockview S/Sta* 351 Drumnakilly Rd
☎(066273) 244

CARRICK-ON-SHANNON
Co Leitrim

★★**Bush** ☎(078)20014 tx 40394
3 Mar-18 Oct
rm25(→♯20) P25 ℃
Credit Cards [1] [2] [3] [5]

★★**County** ☎(078)20042
→♯18 ℃
Credit Cards [1] [2] [3]

🐝 **W Cox & Sons** Main St ☎(078) 20217

CASHEL
Co Galway

★★★**Cashel House** (Relais et Châteaux)
☎(095)31001 tx 50812
Closed 15 Nov-20 Dec & 15 Jan-15 Feb
→♯32 P40 ❄ ∪ Beach Sea Mountain
Credit Cards [1] [2] [3] [4] [5]

★★★**Zetland House** ☎(095)31111 tx 50853
15 Apr-30 Oct
→♯19 ☎ P20 Sea
Credit Cards [1] [2] [3]

CASHEL
Co Tipperary

★★★★**Cashel Palace** ☎(062)614111 tx 70638
→♯20 P50 ℃
Credit Cards [1] [2] [3] [5]

CASTLEBAR
Co Mayo

★★★**Breaffy House** (BW) ☎(094)22033 tx 53790
Feb-20 Dec
→♯40 P200 Lift ℃
Credit Cards [1] [2] [3] [5]

★**Welcome Inn** ☎(094)22054
Closed 24-26 Dec
rm26(→♯16) P10 ℃
Credit Cards [1] [2] [3]

CASTLEBLAYNEY
Co Monaghan

🐝 **Trunk Road** Dublin Rd ☎(042) 40041

CASTLEDERMOT
Co Kildare

🐝 **M Hennessay & Sons** ☎(0503) 44114 Cit

CASTLEREA
Co Roscommon

🐝 **Lavin's** The Demesne ☎(0907) 20096

CASTLETOWNBERE
Co Cork

🐝 **Hanley's** Oakmount ☎(027) 70264

CAVAN
Co Cavan

🐝 **Brady's** Dublin Rd ☎(049) 31833 Col Ren
🐝 **Jackson's** Farnham St ☎(049) 31700 For

CHARLESTOWN
Co Mayo

🐝 **Walsh's Auto Svc** Bellaghy ☎(094) 54131

CLAREMORRIS
Co Mayo

🐝 **Duggan's** Convent Rd ☎(094) 71610

CLIFDEN
Co Galway

★★★**Abbeyglen Castle** ☎(095)21201 tx 50866
Closed 10 Jan-10 Feb
→♯40 P40 ❄ ⌂ ♁♁
Credit Cards [1] [2] [3] [5]

★★★**Ardagh** Bally Conneely Rd ☎(095)21384
Etr-Oct
→♯21 P45 ℃ Sea Mountain
Credit Cards [1] [2] [3] [5]

★★★**Rock Glen** ☎(095)21035 tx 50915
mid Mar-Oct
→♯30 P60 ❄ Sea Lake
Credit Cards [1] [2] [3] [5]

🐝 **Brian Walsh Mtrs** Galway Rd ☎(095) 21037

CLOGHER
Co Tyrone

🐝 *R Armstrong* Augher Rd ☎(06625) 48661

CLONAKILTY
Co Cork

🐝 **Western** Western Rd ☎(023) 33327

CLONMEL
Co Tipperary

★★★**Clonmel Arms** ☎(052)21233 tx 80263
rm35(→♯25) Lift ℃
Credit Cards [1] [2] [3] [4] [5]

★★★**Minella** ☎(052)22388
→♯30 P ℃ Mountain
Credit Cards [1] [2] [3] [4] [5]

🐝 **Blue Star** Cashel Rd ☎(052) 21177 Toy
🐝 **Central** Dungarvan Rd ☎(052) 21071 Dat Ope
🐝 **Clonmel S/Sta** Jackson's Cross ☎(052) 22905

CLOUGHEY
Co Down

★★**Roadhouse** 204-208 Main Rd ☎(02477)71500
Closed 25 Dec
→♯8 P30
Credit Cards [1] [3]

COLERAINE
Co Londonderry

🐝 *Coleraine* 2 Castlerock Rd ☎(0265) 51311
🐝 *JKC Specialist Cars* 7-9 Millburn Rd ☎(0265)
55222 BMW
🐝 *Macfarlane Mtrs* Gateside Rd,,Loughanmill Ind
Est ☎(0265) 3153

CONVOY
Co Donegal

🐝 **McGlinchey's** ☎(074) 47174

COOKSTOWN
Co Tyrone

🐝 *R A Patrick* 21-23 Orritor Rd ☎(06487) 63601
🐝 *R Turkington* 45 Killmoon St ☎(06487) 62675
Ren

COOTEHILL
Co Cavan

★★**White Horse DPn** ☎(049)52124
rm30(→♯24) P ℃
Credit Cards [1] [2] [3]

CORK
Co Cork

★★★★**Jury's** Western Rd ☎(021)276622 tx
76073
Closed 24-26 Dec
→♯190 P400 Lift ℃ ⌂ ⌂
Credit Cards [1] [2] [3] [4] [5]

★★★**Fitzpatrick Silver Springs** Lower Glanmire
Rd ☎(021)507533 tx 26111
Closed 23 Dec-3 Jan
→♯72 P300 Lift ℃
Credit Cards [1] [2] [3] [5]

★★**Moore's** Morrison Island ☎(021)271291
Closed 25-26 Dec
rm38(→♯34) ℃
Credit Cards [1] [3]

🐝 **Lee** Model Farm Rd ☎(021) 42933 Fia Lan

COURTMACSHERRY
Co Cork

★★**Courtmacsherry** ☎(023)46198

Etr-Sep
rm15(✦9) ⚲ ∪
Credit Card ③

COURTOWN HARBOUR
Co Wexford

★★*Bay View* ☎(055)25307
17 Mar-Sep
rm19(✦3) P ⚲
Credit Cards ①③

★★*Courtown* ☎(055)25108
Apr-Oct
rm28(✦♪26) ⚫ ⌂
Credit Cards ①②③⑤

🐝 Doyle's Askingarrow ☎(055) 27318

CRAIGAVON
Co Armagh

🐝 *Irish Rd Mtrs* Highfield Heights,Highfield Rd
☎(0762) 42424 For

CRAUGHWELL
Co Galway

🐝 Craughwell Mtrs ☎(091) 46018

CRAWFORDSBURN
Co Down

★★★*Old Inn* 15 Main St ☎(0247)853255
Closed 25 & 26 Dec
✦♪21 P50 ⚫
Credit Cards ①②③⑤

CROSSMAGLEN
Co Armagh

🐝 *Donaghy Bros* Newry St ☎(0693) 861228

CROSSMOLINA
Co Mayo

🐝 *J Connor Mtrs* Erris Rd ☎(096) 31377

🐝 Park Erris Rd ☎(096) 31331

CULLYBACKEY
Co Antrim

🐝 *Albert Wylie* 46 Craigs Rd ☎(0266) 880554

CUSHENDALL
Co Antrim

★★*Thornlea* 6 Coast Rd ☎(02667)71223
rm13(✦♪9) P25
Credit Cards ①②③⑤

DERRYGONELLY
Co Fermanagh

🐝 *Derrygonelly Autos* Main St ☎(036564) 217

DOAGH
Co Antrim

🐝 *Agnew* 49 Station Rd ☎(09603) 40462

DONABATE
Co Dublin

🐝 *Matt Halpin Mtrs* Beaverstown ☎(01) 436580

DONEGAL
Co Donegal

★★★*Abbey* The Diamond ☎(073)21014

Closed 25-27 Dec
✦♪51 Lift ⚫ Sea Mountain
Credit Cards ①②③④⑤

★★★Hyland's Central (BW) DPn The Diamond
☎(073)21027 tx 40522
Closed 24-27 Dec
✦♪62 P14 Lift ⚫
Credit Cards ①②③

🐝 *R E Johnston Mtrs* Quay St ☎(073) 21039
BL LR

🐝 *J Owen Car Sales* Derry Rd ☎(073) 21791

DOWNPATRICK
Co Down

🐝 *C Keown Mtrs* 9A Ballynagross Rd ☎(0396)
3755 Ren

DRIMOLEAGUE
Co Cork

🐝 S Collins ☎(028) 31206

DROGHEDA
Co Louth

★★★*Boyne Valley* ☎(041)37737 tx 91880
✦♪21 P ⚫
Credit Cards ①②③⑤

🐝 *N Smith & Sons* North Rd ☎(041) 31106 For

🐝 *TFK Autos* North Rd ☎(041) 38566 Dat

DRUMKEERAN
Co Leitrim

🐝 Bohans ☎(078) 48001

DUBLIN
Co Dublin

See Plan page 250 *Population 915,115 Irish Tourist Board* 14 Upper O'Connell Street ☎(01)747733
Dublin, capital of the Republic of Ireland, is a delightful city of low-profile buildings, many of them
outstanding examples of 18th-century architecture. Birthplace and inspiration of many great authors,
its contrasts are apparent everywhere: sweeping avenues and intimate sidestreets, chic shopping and
smokey pubs, distinguished museums and colleges and fascinating shops. History is at your elbow at
every turn. Long streets of stately Georgian houses and spacious, peaceful squares and parks take you
back into the 19th century.
A good place to begin a tour of this compact city is O'Connell Bridge, which leads to the city's main
shopping area, O'Connell Street. The best buys are local products such as Irish linen and lace,
homespun tweeds and knitwear. The top fashion houses of Dublin are now world-famous and make
special provision for tourists. The quality and design of contemporary jewellery and handicrafts are
especially good. Waterford crystal glassware is another popular gift item, while for old glass and silver
Dublin offers fascinating antique shops where bargains can still be found.
City attractions include Parnell Square, one of Dublin's earliest and most attractive squares of
handsome, brick-faced Georgian houses; Charlemont House, which contains the Hugh Lane Municipal
Gallery of Modern Art; St Mary's Pro-Cathedral; Nassau Street, with its bookstores; Merrion Square,
containing a house once occupied by Oscar Wilde's parents; the National Gallery, housing more than
2,000 works; the National Museum, containing a fascinating collection of Irish treasures; the Civic
Museum and Trinity College Library.
St Patrick's and Christ Church cathedrals are also worth visiting, while a tourist 'must' is Dublin
Castle, guided tours of whose splendid state apartments are offered every half hour. Visitors can also
attend a 30-minute film show at the Guinness Brewery, and later sample the famous beverage.

EATING OUT Prime beef, locally raised lamb and pork, free-range poultry and abundant seafood are
widely available in Dublin restaurants, together with traditional Irish dishes such as boiled bacon and
cabbage and Irish stew. Another speciality is *colcannon* - cooked potatoes diced and fried with onions
and cabbage or leeks and covered with cream. Other specialities include shellfish such as lobster,
Dublin Bay prawns, and oysters. *Le Coq Hardi*, in Pembroke Road, and Ernie's in Mulberry Gardens,
are both excellent, if expensive, restaurants. More moderately priced, Rudyard's in Crown Alley, is
justly popular. Dublin also has a wide selection of pubs which, with their relaxed atmosphere, have
been likened to the cafés of Paris.

DUBLIN

1	★★★★	Burlington
2	★★★★	Jury's
3	★★★★	Shelbourne
4	★★★	Ashling
5	★★★	Blooms
6	★★★	Dublin International
7	★★★	Green Isle
8	★★★	Marine
9	★★★	Montrose
12	★★★	Skylon
13	★★★	Tara Tower

DUBLIN

★★★★*Burlington* Lesson St ☎(01)605222 tx 93815
◣450 ☻ P400 Lift ℂ
Credit Cards ①②③④⑤

★★★★*Jurys* Ballsbridge ☎(01)605000 tx 93723
◣300 P320 Lift ℂ ▭ ▭
Credit Cards ①②③④

★★★★*Shelbourne* St Stephen's Green
☎(01)766471 tx 93653
◣167 ☻ P40 Lift ℂ
Credit Cards ①②③⑤

★★★*Ashling* Parkgate St ☎(01)772324 tx 32802
Closed Xmas
◣56 ☻ P70 Lift ℂ
Credit Cards ①②③④⑤

★★★*Blooms* Anglesea St ☎(01)715622 tx 31688
Closed 24-25 Dec
◣86 P20 Lift ℂ
Credit Cards ①②③④⑤

★★★*Dublin International* (THF) Dublin Airport
(6m N on N1) ☎(01)379211 tx 32849
◣195 P200 ℂ
Credit Cards ①②③⑤

★★★*Green Isle* Clondalkin (6m S on N7)
☎(01)593476 tx 90280
◣84 A34rm P400 ℂ
Credit Cards ①②③⑤

★★★*Marine* Sutton (8m N on coast rd R106)
☎(01)322613 tx 93567
Closed 25 Dec
◣27 P100 ℂ
Credit Cards ①②③⑤

★★★*Montrose* Stillorgan Rd ☎(01)693311 tx 91207
◣190 P150 Lift ℂ
Credit Cards ①②③④⑤

★★★*Skylon* Drumcondra ☎(01)379121
◣88 P150 Lift ℂ
Credit Cards ①②③④⑤

★★★*Tara Tower* Merrion Rd ☎(01)694666 tx 93815
◣82 P300 Lift ℂ
Credit Cards ①②③④⑤

🛥 **Alasta Auto Engineering** 7-9 South Lotts Rd
☎(01) 603982

🛥 **Ashley Motor Co** 305 North Circular Rd
☎(01) 309911 For

🛥 **Bagenal Fagan & Sons** 8/12 Terenure Pl
☎(01) 901840 Cit Dat

🛥 **Ballsbridge Mtrs** 162 Shelbourne
Rd,Ballsbridge ☎(01) 689651 Aud Maz Mer VW

🛥 **Cahill Mtrs** Howth Rd,Raheny ☎(01) 3140066
Dat

🛥 **Callow Gilmore Mtrs** Bluebell Av ☎(01)
516877 Dat

🛥 **Carroll & Kinsella** Upper Churchtown Rd
☎(01) 983166 Toy

🛥 **Carroll & Kinsells Mtrs** 164 Walkinstown Rd
☎(01) 508142 Toy

🛥 **Clonskeagh Mtrs** Clonskeagh Rd ☎(01)
694142

🛥 **Dublin Automotive Svcs** Kilbarrack Ind
Est,,Kilbarrack Rd ☎(01) 392811

🛥 **J Duffy Mtrs** Ballygall Rd ☎(01) 342577 BMW
Col

🛥 **D B Motors** 52 Curlew Rd ☎(01) 556839

🛥 **Esmonde Mtrs** Stillorgan ☎(01) 886821 For

🛥 **Gowan Mtrs** Merrion Rd ☎(01) 696222 Peu
Tal

🛥 **Huet Motors** 78-84 Townsend St ☎(01)
779177 Lot RR Vol

🛥 **T Kane Mtrs** 17A Rear Fairview Av,Fairview
☎(01) 338143

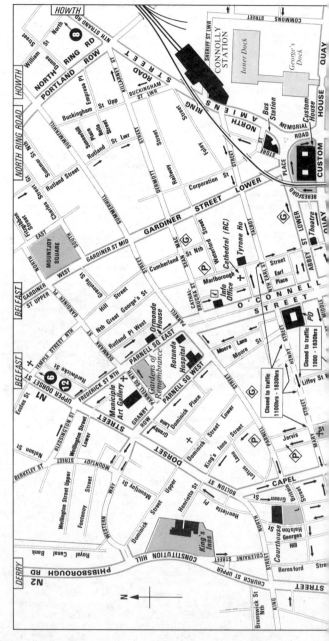

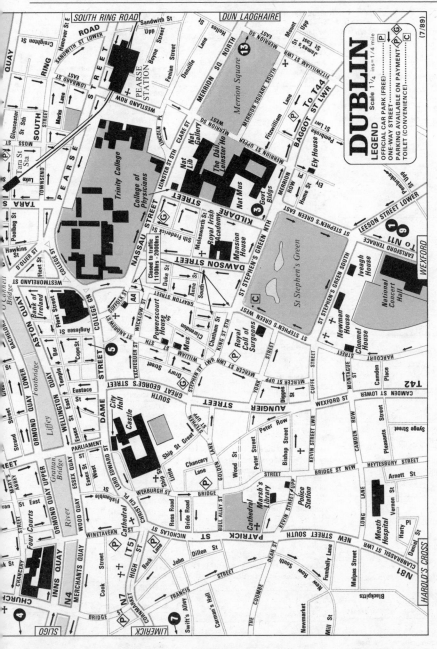

🐝 **G Kellett** 44 South Dock Rd,Ringsend ☎(01) 689177

🐝 **Linders of Smithfield** Smithfield ☎(01) 721222 Toy

🐝 **McCarville Mtrs** 5 Old Bawn Rd,Tallaght ☎(01) 516685

🐝 **E P Mooney & Co** Long Mile Rd ☎(01) 552416 Dat

🐝 **Murphy & Gunn** Rathgar Rd ☎(01) 979456 BMW Toy

🐝 **Park Mtrs** 218 North Cicruclar Rd ☎(01) 387211 Aud Maz Mer VW

🐝 **Ross Mtrs** 49A Dorset Ln ☎(01) 364479

🐝 **Sweeney & Forte** 54 Howth Rd ☎(01) 332301 Fia Lan

🐝 **Walden Motor Co** 171 Parnell St ☎(01) 730400

DUNDALK
Co Louth
★★★**Ballymascanlon House** (BW) ☎(042)71124 tx 43735
Closed 25 Dec
₩36 P300 🏌 ᐟ ◱ ⋔
Credit Cards 1 2 3 5

★★★*Imperial* (Inter-Hotels) ☎(042)32241 tx 43735
Closed 25 Dec
₩50 P100 Lift ℂ
Credit Cards 1 2 3 5

🏍 **Nursey Garage** Mullaharlin Rd ☎(042) 35088

DUNDRUM
Co Tipperary
★★★*Dundrum House* ☎(062)71116 tx 70255
Closed Xmas
₩18 A38rm P300 Lift ℂ ⋏
Credit Cards 1 2 3 4 5

★★*Rectory House* ☎(062)71115
Apr-mid Nov
₩11
Credit Cards 1 2 3 5

DUNFANAGHY
Co Donegal
★★**Arnold's** ☎(074)36208
Apr-Sep
rm36(₩26) P40 ⋏ Sea
Credit Cards 1 2 3 5

★★**Carrig Rua** ☎(074)36133
Etr-Oct
₩22 P20 Sea Mountain
Credit Cards 2 3

DUNGANNON
Co Tyrone
🏍 *Donnelly Bros* 14-18 Georges St ☎(08687) 22887

🏍 *Park Rd S/Sta (H Corrigan)* 1-7 Park Rd ☎(08687) 24929

DUNGLOE
Co Donegal
★★*Ostan Na Rosann* ☎(075)21088
May-Oct
₩48 P80 ℂ ◱ Sea
Credit Cards 1 2 3 5

DUN LAOGHAIRE
Co Dublin
★★★*Victor* (BW) Rochestown Av ☎(01)853555 tx 93366
₩58 ☎ P200 Lift ℂ
Credit Cards 1 2 3 4 5

🏍 **JPS Mtrs** Ashgrove Ind Est, Kill Av ☎(01) 805727 BMW Cit Vol

DUNMORE EAST
Co Waterford
★★**Haven** ☎(051)83150 & 83540
Mar-Oct
₩14 P40 ℂ Sea
Credit Cards 1 2 3

DUNMURRY
Co Antrim
★★★★*Conway* (Trusthouse Forte) Kingsway ☎(0232)612101
rm78(₩76) ☎ P200 Lift ℂ
Credit Cards 1 2 3 4 5

🏍 **Saville Mtrs** 101 Kingsway ☎(0232) 614211

EDENDERRY
Co Offaly
🏍 *B McNelis* Rathangan Rd ☎(0405) 31480

EDERNEY
Co Fermanagh
🏍 *McEhills* Market St ☎(03656) 31294

EDGEWORTHSTOWN
Co Longford
🏍 **Kane's** ☎(043) 71032

EGLINTON
Co Londonderry
★★*Glen House* 9 Main St ☎(0504)810527
rm16(₩15) P ℂ
Credit Cards 1 2 3 5

EMO
Co Laois
★★★*Montague* (BW) ☎(0502)26154 tx 60036
₩78 P600 ℂ
Credit Cards 1 2 3 4 5

ENNIS
Co Clare
★★★*Auburn Lodge* Galway Rd ☎(065)21247
Closed 25 Dec
₩43 P200
Credit Cards 1 2 3 4 5

★★★*Old Ground* (THF) ☎(065)28127 tx 28103
₩60 P150 ℂ
Credit Cards 1 2 3 4 5

★★★*West County Inn* (BW) ☎(065)70794 tx 28294
₩110 P Lift ℂ
Credit Cards 1 2 3 5

★★*Queen's* Abbey St ☎(065)28963
Closed 25 Dec
₩30 Lift
Credit Cards 1 2 3 5

ENNISCORTHY
Co Wexford
★★**Murphy-Floods** Main St,Town Centre ☎(054)33413
Closed 25 Dec
₩22 ℂ
Credit Cards 1 2 3 5

ENNISKILLEN
Co Fermanagh
★★★*Kyllyhevlin* ☎(0365)23481
Closed Xmas day
rm22(₩21) P200 ℂ
Credit Cards 1 2 3 5

★*Railway* ☎(0365)22084
Closed 25-28 Dec
rm19(₩18) ℂ
Credit Card 3

🏍 *Erne Eng Co* Queens St ☎(0365) 3721 For

🏍 *L McGory & Sons* Tempo Rd ☎(0365) 24351

🏍 *P McNulty & Sons Motorcycles* 24-26 Belmore St ☎(0365) 22423 M/C

🏍 *Modern Mtrs* 74 Forthill St ☎(054) 22974 Aud VW

FERBANE
Co Offaly
🏍 *Vaugh Car Sales* Ballycumber Rd ☎(0902) 54202

FERMOY
Co Cork
🏍 *Cavanagh's* Ashe Quay ☎(025) 31211 For

🏍 *H O'Sullivan* 41-43 McCurtain St ☎(025) 31797 Aud VW

FINTONA
Co Tyrone
🏍 *Irwins* 12-14 King St ☎(0662) 841208

FOXFORD
Co Mayo
🏍 *Reape's Auto Svc* ☎(094) 56119

FURBO
Co Galway
★★★*Connemara Coast* ☎(091)92108 tx 50905
₩84 P300 ◱ Sea
Credit Cards 1 2 3 5

GALWAY
Co Galway
★★★★*Great Southern* Eyre Sq ☎(091)64041 tx 50164
₩120 Lift ℂ ◱
Credit Cards 1 2 3 5

★★★*Ardilaun House* (Inter-Hotels) Taylor's Hill ☎(091)21433 tx 50013
Closed 20-30 Dec
₩85 P150 Lift ℂ
Credit Cards 1 2 3 5

★★★*Corrib Great Southern* Dublin Rd ☎(091)55281 tx 50044
₩115 P250 Lift ℂ ◱ Mountain
Credit Cards 1 2 3 5

★★**Anno Santo** Threadneedle Rd,Salthill ☎(091)23650
Closed 20 Dec-1 Jan:Rest closed Sun pm
₩13 P9
Credit Cards 1 2 3 5

★★*Galway Ryan* Dublin Rd ☎(091)53181 tx 50149
Closed 24 & 25 Dec
₩96 P120 Lift ℂ
Credit Cards 1 2 3 4 5

★★*Lochlurgain* 22 Monksfield,Upper Salthill ☎(091)22122
Closed Jan-13 Mar & Nov-Dec
rm14(₩7) P8
Credit Cards 1 2 3

★*Atlanta* ☎(091)62241
rm20 P30

🏍 **Bradley Mtr Works** Prospect Hill ☎(091) 63694

🏍 **J J Fleming** Tuam Rd ☎(091) 55451 Hon Ope

🏍 **Higgin's** Headford Rd ☎(091) 61263 For

🏍 **J Kelleher** Salthill ☎(091) 22463 Vol

GARRETTSTOWN
Co Cork
★★*Coakley's Atlantic* ☎(021)778215
Closed Xmas
₩22 P60 ℂ
Credit Cards 1 2 3

GARRISON
Co Fermanagh
🏍 *Melvin (A & S Rasdale)* ☎(036586) 246

GARRYVOE
Co Cork
★★**Garryvoe** ☎(021)646718
Closed 25 Dec
rm21(₩15) P30 ⋏ Sea
Credit Cards 1 2 3 5

GLENDALOUGH
Co Wicklow
★★*Royal* ☎(0404)5135
14 Mar-Oct
₩13 P20 Lift
Credit Cards 1 2 3

GLENGORMLEY
Co Antrim
🏍 *Dencourt Mtrs* Rush Pk,,Mallusk Rd ☎(02313) 48221 Vau

GLEN OF THE DOWNS
Co Wicklow
🏍 *Glen* ☎(01) 874932

GLOUNTHAUNE
Co Cork
★★*Ashbourne House* ☎(021)353319
rm26(₩24) P ⋏ ⌒
Credit Cards 1 2 3 5

GOREY
Co Wexford
★★★*Marlfield House* ☎(055)21124 tx 80757
Closed 15 Nov-15 Dec
₩12 P Lift ℂ ⋏

O'Sullivans Scarnagh,Coolgreany ☎(042) 7127

GORTAHORK
Co Donegal

★★**McFadden's** ☎(074)35267
Closed 25 Dec
rm20(➥♠18) P20
Credit Cards ① ② ③ ⑤

GOUGANE BARRA
Co Cork

★★**Gougane Barra** ☎(026)47069
Apr-Sep
rm32(➥♠18) P30
Credit Cards ① ③

HEADFORD
Co Galway

★**Angler's Rest** ☎(093)35528
5 Jan-20 Dec
rm14(➥♠8) P40
Credit Cards ① ② ③

HOLYWOOD
Co Down

★★★★**Culloden** (HG) ☎(02317)52223 tx 74617
➥♠91 P500 Lift ℂ ℺ Sea
Credit Cards ① ② ③ ⑤
R Henderson & Sons New Rd,Redburn Sq ☎(02317) 3795

HOWTH
Co Dublin

★★★**Howth Lodge** (BW) ☎(01)390228
Closed 25-26 Dec
➥♠17 P175 ℂ Sea Mountain
Credit Cards ① ② ③ ④ ⑤

INCHIGEELAGH
Co Cork

★**Creedon's** ☎(026)49012
rm16(➥♠14) P3
Credit Cards ① ② ③ ④ ⑤

★**Lake** ☎(026)49010
rm15(➥♠1) ☎ P10 ℺
Credit Card ③

IRVINESTOWN
Co Fermanagh

★★**Mahons** ☎(03656)21656
Closed 25 Dec
➥♠18 ☎ P20
Credit Cards ① ③
Killadess S/Sta Drummall,Lisnarick ☎(03656) 21530

JULIANSTOWN
Co Meath

★★**Glenside** Smithstown ☎(041)29049
Closed 18-31 Dec
➥♠14 P70
Credit Cards ① ② ③ ⑤

KENMARE
Co Kerry

★★★★**Park** (Relais et Châteaux) **DPn**
☎(064)41200 tx 73905
Closed 2 Jan-Etr
➥♠48 P60 Lift ℂ ℺ ⏤⏤
Credit Cards ① ② ③ ④ ⑤

★★★**Kenmare Bay** (BW) ☎(064)41300 tx 73880
Mar-Oct
➥♠100 P150 ℂ
Credit Cards ① ② ③ ④ ⑤

★**Lansdowne Arms** ☎(064)41368
Closed 4 Jan-15 Mar
rm23(➥♠10) ☎ P10
Credit Cards ① ③

Randle Bros Shelbourne St ☎(064) 41355 Dat

KESH
Co Fermanagh

★★**Lough Erne** Main St ☎(03656)31275
Closed 25 Dec
➥♠12 P100
Credit Cards ① ② ③ ⑤

KILCOCK
Co Kildare

Dermot Kelly Dublin Rd ☎ 287311 For
McGeeney's Church St ☎ 287375

KILDARE
Co Kildare

T & A Boyle Cherryville ☎(045) 21898

KILFENORA
Co Clare

Connole's ☎(065) 88008

KILKEE
Co Clare

★**Halpin's** Erin St ☎(065)56032
rm11(➥♠10) ℂ Sea
Credit Cards ① ② ③ ⑤

KILKEEL
Co Down

★★**Kilmorey Arms** ☎(06937)62220
rm17(➥♠16) P ℂ

KILKENNY
Co Kilkenny

★★★**Kilkenny** College Rd ☎(056)62000
➥♠60 P200 ℂ ℺ ⏤⏤
Credit Cards ① ② ③

★★★**Newpark** ☎(056)22122 tx 80080
rm60(➥♠59) P250 ℂ ℺ ⏤⏤
Credit Cards ① ② ③ ④ ⑤

Kilkenny S/Sta Carlow Rd ☎(056) 22528
W Tallis 1 Johns Quay ☎(056) 65384

KILLARNEY
Co Kerry

★★★★**Great Southern** ☎(064)31262 tx 73998
Mar-Dec
➥♠180 Lift ℂ ℺ ⏤⏤ Mountain
Credit Cards ① ② ③ ④ ⑤

★★★**Aghadoe Heights** ☎(064)31766
21 Jan-20 Dec
➥♠60 P150 ℂ ℺ Mountain Lake
Credit Cards ① ② ③ ⑤

★★★**Cahernane** Muckross Rd ☎(064)31895 tx 73823
Closed Nov-19 Dec & 7 Jan-Etr
➥♠52 A36rm P40 ℂ ℺ ♙♙ Mountain Lake
Credit Cards ① ② ③ ④ ⑤

★★★**Gleneagle** ☎(064)31870 tx 73923
Closed 25 Dec
➥♠96 P200 Lift ℂ ℺ ♙♙ Mountain
Credit Cards ① ② ③ ⑤

★★★**International** (BW) Kenmare Place
☎(064)31816 tx 73825
Mar-Oct
➥♠88 Lift ℂ
Credit Cards ① ② ③ ④ ⑤

★★★**Torc Great Southern** ☎(064)31611 tx 73807
25 Apr-12 Oct
➥♠96 ℂ ℺ ⏤⏤
Credit Cards ① ② ③ ⑤

★★**Arbutus** ☎(064)30137 & 31261
24 Dec-10 Jan
➥♠35 ℂ Mountain
Credit Cards ① ③ ⑤

★★**Castlerosse** (BW) ☎(064)31144 tx 73910
Closed Nov-Apr
➥♠67 P ℂ ℺ Mountain Lake
Credit Cards ① ② ③ ④ ⑤

★★★**Killarney Ryan** ☎(064)31555 tx 73950
Apr-Oct
➥♠168 P Lift ℂ ℺
Credit Cards ① ② ③ ④ ⑤

★★**Lake** Muckross Rd,On Lake Shore ☎(064)31035
Mar-Nov
➥♠65 ☎ P150 ℂ ℺ Beach Mountain Lake
Credit Cards ① ② ③ ⑤

P Murphy Clohane Iron Mills,Cork Rd ☎(064) 54006
Randles Muckross Rd ☎(064) 31237

KILLEAGH
Co Cork

T E Fitzgibbon ☎(024) 95113

KILLINCHY
Co Down

H A McBriar 64 Comber Rd ☎(0238) 541261 Toy

KILLINEY
Co Dublin

★★★**Court** ☎(01)851622 tx 33244
Closed 25 Dec
➥♠36 P120 Lift ℂ Sea
Credit Cards ① ② ③ ⑤

★★★**Fitzpatrick's Castle** ☎(01)851533 tx 30353
➥♠92 P300 Lift ℂ ℺ ⏤⏤ Sea
Credit Cards ① ② ③ ⑤

KILLINICK
Co Wexford

Home Svcs ☎(053) 58965

KILLYLEAGH
Co Down

T M Martin & Sons 6-8 Cross St ☎(0396) 828203

KILMACANOGUE
Co Wicklow

Conroy Mtrs ☎(01) 861141

KILMEADEN
Co Waterford

Henessy's ☎(051) 84129

KILRUSH
Co Clare

★★**Inis Cathaig** ☎(065)51036
➥♠16 P15
Credit Cards ① ③
Kilrush Motor Co Ennis Rd ☎(065) 51048

KINAWLEY
Co Fermanagh

V G Brennan Enniskillen Rd ☎(036574) 314

KINSALE
Co Cork

★★★**Acton's** (THF) ☎(021)772135 tx 75443
➥♠57 P60 Lift ℂ ⏤⏤ Sea
Credit Cards ① ② ③ ⑤

KINSALEBEG
Co Waterford

D McGrath ☎(024) 92588

KINVARRA
Co Galway

P O Loughlin ☎(091) 37135

KNOCKANORE
Co Waterford

Nugent's ☎(024) 97642

LARNE
Co Antrim

★★★**Magheramorne House** 59 Shore Rd (3m Son A2) ☎(0574)79444
➥♠23 P50 Lift ℂ
Credit Cards ① ② ③ ⑤
GMG 96-98 Glenarm Rd ☎(08494) 77328 Col Dat

Rock Mtr Wks 52 Ballymena Rd ☎(0574) 73122

LAYTOWN
Co Meath
Clarke's ☎(041) 27278

LEMYBRIEN
Co Waterford
J N Kirwan ☎(051) 91121

LETTERKENNY
Co Donegal
★★**Gallagher's** ☎(074)22066
Closed 25-31 Dec
⊶27 P25 ℂ
Credit Cards ①②③⑤
P Doherty & Sons Pluck ☎(074) 57116

LIMAVADY
Co Londonderry
T A Kerr Rascahan ☎(05047) 64903

LIMERICK
Co Limerick
★★★★**Limerick Inn** Ennis Rd ☎(061)51544 tx 70621
Closed 25 Dec
⊶153 P600 Lift ℂ ⚲ ⛰ Mountain
Credit Cards ①②③④⑤
★★★**Jury's** Ennis Rd ☎(061)55266 tx 70766
Closed 25-26 Dec
⊶95 P ℂ
Credit Cards ①②③④⑤
★★★**Limerick Ryan** Ennis Rd ☎(061)53922 tx 26920
⊶184 P150 Lift ℂ
Credit Cards ①②③④⑤
★★★**New Green Hills** Caherdavin ☎(061)53033 tx 70246
⊶55 P500 ℂ
Credit Cards ①②③④⑤
★★★**Two Mile Inn** (BW) Ennis Rd ☎(061)53122 tx 70157
Closed 24-25 Dec
⊶125 P200 ℂ
Credit Cards ①②③④⑤
★★**Royal George** O'Connell St ☎(061)44566
Closed 25-26 Dec
⊶58 P200 Lift ℂ
Credit Cards ①②③④⑤
Gleeson Bros Ellen St ☎(061) 45567
F Hogan Dublin Rd ☎(061) 460000 Maz Mer Por VW
P Keogh Castle St ☎(061) 43133 BMW Dat

LISBURN
Co Antrim
J Hanna Mtrs 1 Queens Rd ☎(08462) 72416 Hon

LISCANNOR
Co Clare
★★**Liscannor Golf** ☎(065)81186
Apr-Nov
⊶26 P120 ℂ
Credit Cards ①②③⑤

LISDOONVARNA
Co Clare
★★**Keane's** ☎(065)74011
May-Sep
rm11(⊶7) P8
Credit Cards ①②
★★**Lynch's** ☎(065)74010
Jun-5 Oct
⊶16 P10 ℂ
Credit Cards ①③
★★**Spa View** ☎(065)74026
2 Apr-Sep
⊶11 P40 ⚲
Credit Cards ①③⑤

LISMORE
Co Waterford
★★**Ballyrafter House** ☎(058)54002
Apr-Sep
rm12(⊶8) ⚲ P20

LISNASKEA
Co Fermanagh
★★**Ortine** ☎(03657)21206
Closed 25 Dec
⊶17 ⚲ P ℂ
Credit Cards ①③
Monaghan Bros Drumhaw ☎(03657) 21354

LISSYCASEY
Co Clare
Clancy's ☎(065) 34262

LITTLE ISLAND
Co Cork
D O'Brien Rockgrove ☎(021) 353226

LIXNAW
Co Kerry
O'Keeffes ☎(066) 32702

LONDONDERRY
Co Londonderry
★★★**Everglades** Prehan Rd ☎(0504)46722 tx 748005
Closed 24-25 Dec
⊶56 ⚲ P200 Lift ℂ Sea Mountain Lake
Credit Cards ①②③④⑤
Desmond Mtrs 173 Strand Rd ☎(0504) 267613 For
Eakin Bros Maydown Rd ☎(0504) 860601 Vau
Stewart & Irwin 31c Abercorn Rd
Tullyally Car Breakers Tulyally Rd,Ardmore ☎(0504) 49395

LONGFORD
Co Longford
Longford Auto Svc Little Water St ☎(043) 41046

LOUGHBRICKLAND
Co Down
F McGrath Main St ☎(08206) 22396

LOUISBURGH
Co Mayo
Harney's ☎(098) 66051

MACROOM
Co Cork
★★**Castle** ☎(026)41074
⊶16 ⚲ P4
Credit Cards ①②③④⑤
★**Victoria** ☎(026)41082
rm22(⊶4)
Credit Cards ①②③⑤
Kellhers Lower Main St ☎(026) 41029 For

MAGHERA
Co Londonderry
D Otterson Fairhill ☎(0648) 42651

MALAHIDE
Co Dublin
★★★**Grand** ☎(01)450633 tx 31446
⊶48 P600 Lift ℂ Sea
Credit Cards ①②③⑤
Heely Motors Main St ☎(01) 452044 For

MALIN
Co Donegal
★**Malin** ☎(077)760606
rm12(⊶2)
Credit Cards ①③⑤

MALLOW
Co Cork
Lynch's Ballydaheen ☎(022) 21436

MIDLETON
Co Cork
Lee Broderick St ☎(021) 631306 Fia

MILLTOWN MALBAY
Co Clare
McCarthy's Flag Rd ☎(065) 84039

MITCHELSTOWN
Co Cork
Murphy's Church St ☎(025) 246110

MOATE
Co Westmeath
Keenan Bros Ferboy ☎(0902) 81375

MONAGHAN
Co Monaghan
★★**Hilgrove** ☎(047)81288
rm46(⊶35) P700 ℂ ⚲
Credit Cards ①③⑤
G Mullin North Rd ☎(047) 81396

MONASTEREVIN
Co Kildare
M A Finlay & Sons ☎(045) 25331 Fia Lan

MONEYMORE
Co Londonderry
T J Boyce 43 Lawford St ☎(06487) 48257

MONEYREAGH
Co Down
Todd's Miligan Cross ☎(023123) 576

MOUNTRATH
Co Laois
Dooley's Motors Dublin Rd ☎(0502) 32221

MOVILLE
Co Donegal
★★**McNamara's** ☎(077)82010
Closed 24-26 Dec
⊶15 P
Credit Cards ①③
★**Foyle** ☎(077)82025
rm20 ⚲ Sea
Credit Cards ①②③⑤

MOY
Co Tyrone
McMullan Bros 17 Dungannon St ☎(08687) 84252

MULLINGAR
Co Westmeath
Mullingar Autos Dublin Bridge ☎(044) 41164 Aud Maz VW
Westmeath Motors Dublin Rd ☎(044) 48806 Fia Lan

NAAS
Co Kildare
T Hennessy Sallins Rd ☎(045) 79251 Aud Maz Mer VW

NAVAN
Co Meath
Mac Rel Commons Rd ☎(046) 29040

NENAGH
Co Tipperary
Cleary's Limerick Rd ☎(067) 31310

NEWCASTLE
Co Down
★★★**Slieve Donard** (HG) ☎(03967)23681
rm120(⊶110) P500 Lift ℂ ⚲ ⛰ Sea Mountain
Credit Cards ①②③⑤
★★**Enniskeen** Bryansford Rd ☎(03967)22392
Mar-Oct
⊶12
Credit Cards ①③
Mourne Svc 8 Bryansford Av

NEWCASTLE WEST
Co Limerick
★**River Room Motel** ☎(069)62244
:Rest closed Good Fri & Xmas Day
→⌐15 ⌂ ⚲
Credit Cards [1] [2] [3] [5]

NEWMARKET-ON-FERGUS
Co Clare
★★★★***Dromoland Castle*** (Relais et Châteaux) ☎(061)71144 tx 70654
Apr-Oct
→⌐67 P100 ☾
Credit Cards [1] [2] [3] [4] [5]
★★★***Clare Inn*** ☎(061)71161 tx 72085
Mar-Dec
→⌐121 P Lift ☾ ⚲ ⛳
Credit Cards [1] [2] [3] [4] [5]

NEWPORT
Co Mayo
★★★***Newport House*** ☎(098)41222 tx 53740
20 Mar-Sep
→⌐12 A8rm P30 ☾
Credit Cards [2] [3] [5]

NEW ROSS
Co Wexford
⊳ **Priory Lane** Priory Ln ☎(051) 21844
⊳ **D P Sycs** The Rookery,Stokestown ☎(051) 22114

NEWRY
Co Down
⊳ ***N Kehoe*** 18 Patrick St ☎(3193) 4644

NEWTOWNABBEY
Co Antrim
★★★**Chimney Corner** 630 Antrim Rd ☎(02313)44925 tx 748158
Closed Xmas wk & 12-13 Jul
→⌐63 P320 ☾ ⚲
Credit Cards [1] [2] [3] [5]
⊳ ***Adair Smith Motors*** 581 Doagh Rd,Mossley ☎(02313) 49401 Dat

NEWTOWNARDS
Co Down
⊳ ***M Ferguson*** Regent House,Regent St ☎(0247) 812626 For

OMAGH
Co Tyrone
★★**Royal Arms** 51 High St ☎(0662)3262
Closed 25 Dec
rm21(→⌐20) P200 ☾
Credit Cards [1] [3]
⊳ ***Duncan*** ☎(0662) 44161
⊳ ***Johnston King Motors*** 82 Derry Rd ☎(0662) 41520 For

OUGHTERARD
Co Galway
★★★**Connemara Gateway** ☎(091)82328 tx 50905
→⌐62 P80 ⚲ ▭ ⌂ Mountain
Credit Cards [1] [2] [3] [4] [5]
★★**Corrib DPn** ☎(091)82329
→⌐26 A8rm P60
Credit Cards [1] [2] [3]
★★***Egan's Lake*** ☎(091)82205
Closed Xmas
rm24(→16) P

PARKNASILLA
Co Kerry
★★★★**Great Southern** ☎(064)45122 tx 73899
Apr-Oct
→⌐57 A33rm P ☾ ⚲ ▭ ⛳ U Sea Mountain
Credit Cards [1] [2] [3] [5]

PORTADOWN
Co Armagh
⊳ ***T A Bryans*** 111 Harford St ☎(0762) 336347

PORTBALLINTRAE
Co Antrim
★★**Bayview** 2 Bayhead Rd ☎(02657)31453
→⌐16 P40 ☾ Sea
Credit Cards [1] [3]
★★**Beach** ☎(02657)31214
rm28(→25) P40 ☾ Sea
Credit Cards [1] [3]

PORTLAOISE
Co Laois
★★★***Killeshin*** Dublin Rd ☎(0502)21663 tx 60036
→⌐44 P3000 ☾
Credit Cards [1] [2] [3] [4] [5]
⊳ ***Portlaoise S/Sta*** Dublin Rd ☎(0502) 22048

PORT-NA-BLAGH
Co Donegal
★★★**Port-Na-Blagh** ☎(074)36129 & 36280
Etr-Sep
→⌐49 P70 ☾ ⚲ ⛳ Sea Mountain

PORTUMNA
Co Galway
★★**Westpark** ☎(0509)41121
Apr-Sep
→⌐29 P100 ☾ ⚲
Credit Cards [1] [2] [3] [5]
⊳ **G A Claffey Motors** Clonfert Ave ☎(0509) 41009

PROSPEROUS
Co Kildare
★★**Curryhills House** ☎(045)68150
Closed 23-30 Dec:Rest closed Sun
→⌐10 P
Credit Cards [1] [2] [3] [5]

RAPHOE
Co Donegal
★**Central** ☎(074)45126
Closed 23-30 Dec
rm10(→⌐6) ⌂ P5

RATH LUIRC (CHARLEVILLE)
Co Cork
⊳ **Park Motors** Smiths Rd ☎(063) 81367

RATHMULLAN
Co Donegal
★***Pier*** ☎(074)58178
2 Mar-Sep
rm16(→⌐11)

RATHNEW
Co Wicklow
★★★**Tinakilly House** ☎(0404)69274
→⌐14 P100 ⚲ Sea Lake
Credit Cards [1] [2] [3] [4] [5]
★★**Hunter's** ☎(0404)40106
:Rest closed 25 Dec
rm18(→⌐10) P50
Credit Cards [1] [2] [3] [5]

RAVENSDALE
Co Louth
⊳ **Dromad Vehicle Repairs** ☎(052) 71822

RENVYLE
Co Galway
★★★***Renvyle House*** Tully Cross ☎(095)43444 tx 50896
16 Mar-Oct & 21-31 Dec
→⌐70 P75 ☾ ⚲ ⛳ U
Credit Cards [1] [3]

ROSAPENNA
Co Donegal
★★★**Rosapenna Golf** ☎(074)55301
Apr-Oct
→⌐40 ☾ ⚲ ⛳ Mountain Lake
Credit Cards [1] [2] [3] [5]

ROSCOMMON
Co Roscommon
★★★**Abbey** ☎(0903)26505
Closed 25-26 Dec
→⌐20 P30 ☾
Credit Cards [1] [2] [3] [5]
⊳ **P Casey & Sons** Athlone Rd ☎(0903) 26101 For

ROSCREA
Co Tipperary
★★***Racket Hall*** ☎(0505)21748
Closed 25-27 Dec
→⌐10 P50
Credit Cards [1] [2] [3] [5]
★**Pathe** ☎(0505)21102
Closed 25-26 Dec
rm20(→9) P8
Credit Cards [1] [2] [3] [5]
⊳ **Spooners** Glebe View ☎(0505) 21063 Aud VW

ROSMUCK
Co Galway
⊳ **Manion's** ☎(091) 74113

ROSSCAHILL
Co Galway
★★***Ross Lake House*** ☎(091)80109
→⌐12 P100 ⚲
Credit Cards [1] [2] [3]

ROSSES POINT
Co Sligo
★★**Yeats Country Ryan** ☎(071)77211 tx 40403
Apr-Oct
→⌐79 Lift ☾ ⚲ Sea Mountain
Credit Cards [1] [2] [3] [4] [5]

ROSSLARE
Co Wexford
★★★**Kelly's Strand** ☎(053)32114 tx 80111
26 Feb-5 Dec
→⌐89 P100 Lift ☾ ⚲ ⌂
★***Golf*** ☎(053)32179
Mar-4 Nov
rm25 P20 ⚲
Credit Cards [1] [2] [3]

ROSSLARE HARBOUR
Co Wexford
★★★***Great Southern*** ☎(053)33233 tx 80788
May-30 Oct
→⌐98 P150 ☾ ⚲ ▭
Credit Cards [1] [2] [3] [4] [5]
★★★**Rosslare** ☎(053)33110 tx 80772
Closed 25 Dec
rm25(→⌐22) ☾ Sea
Credit Cards [1] [2] [3]

ROSSNOWLAGH
Co Donegal
★★★***Sand House*** (Inter-Hotels) ☎(072)51777 tx 40460
Etr-4 Oct
→⌐40 P60 ⚲
Credit Cards [1] [2] [5]

ROUNDSTONE
Co Galway
⊳ **Toombeola S/Sta** ☎(095) 31116

SAINTFIELD
Co Down
Lakeview Car Sales 139 Belfast Rd

SHILLELAGH
Co Wicklow
⊳ **Shillelagh Mtrs** ☎(055) 29127 Fia

SIX MILE CROSS
Co Tyrone
⊳ ***R Alcorn*** 17 Drumlister Rd ☎ 451

SKIBBEREEN
Co Cork
🛏 **Hurley Bros** Ilen St ☎(028) 21143

SLANE
Co Meath
★**Conyngham Arms** ☎(041)24155 tx 91297
Closed 25 Dec
rm12(🚿11) P10
Credit Cards 1 2 3 5

SLIGO
Co Sligo
★★★**Ballincar House** Rosses Point Rd
☎(071)45361
Closed 23 Dec-14 Jan
🚿20 P50
Credit Cards 1 2 3 5
★★★**Sligo Park** Cornageeha ☎(071)60291 tx
40397
🚿60 P300 ℂ
Credit Cards 1 2 3 5
★★**Silver Swan** ☎(071)43231
Closed 25-26 Dec
rm24(🚿13) P40 ℂ
Credit Cards 1 2 3 5
🛏 **Henderson Mtrs** Bundoran Rd ☎(071) 42610
For

SNEEM
Co Kerry
🛏 **Sneem Motorworks** ☎(064) 45101

SPIDDAL
Co Galway
★★**Bridge House** ☎(091)83118
6 Jan-23 Dec
🚿14 P20 ℂ
Credit Cards 1 3
★★**Park Lodge** ☎(091)83159
Jun-Sep
🚿23 P50 Sea
Credit Cards 1 2 3 5

STRABANE
Co Tyrone
★★★**Fir Trees Lodge** Melmount Rd
☎(0504)382382
🚿26 P200 ℂ
Credit Cards 1 2 3 5
🛏 **J Sayers Mtrs** 107 Melmount Rd,Sion Mills
☎(0504) 58232
🛏 **R A Wallace & Sons** 85 Fyfin Rd,Victoria
Bridge ☎(0504) 58334 Ren

STROKESTOWN
Co Longford
🛏 **Green's Sales** 'Tiernan House',Elphin St
☎(078) 21044

SWATRAGH
Co Londonderry
🛏 **T McGulgahan** Main St

TASSAGH
Co Armagh
🛏 **J O'Hare** 39 Dundrum Rd ☎ 531269

THURLES
Co Tipperary
🛏 **E Hayden** Loughbeg ☎(0504) 22403

TIPPERARY
Co Tipperary
★**Royal** Bridge St ☎(062)51204
Closed 25 Dec & Good Friday
🚿16 P200
Credit Cards 1 2 3
🛏 **Galtee S/Stn** Limerick Rd ☎(062) 51689

TRALEE
Co Kerry
★★★**Earl of Desmond** Killainey Rd ☎(066)21299
tx 73064
🚿52 P300 ℂ ⚲ Mountain
Credit Cards 1 2 3 5
★★★**Mount Brandon** ☎(066)23333 tx 71303
🚿160 P500 Lift ℂ
Credit Cards 1 2 3 4 5
🛏 **McEllott's** Oak Park ☎(066) 23011 Fia Lan
🛏 **Ruane's** 13 Prince's St ☎(066) 21838

WATERFORD
Co Waterford
★★★**Ardree** ☎(051)32111 tx 80684
Closed 25-26 Dec
🚿100 P250 Lift ℂ ⚲
Credit Cards 1 2 3 4 5
★★★**Granville** (BW) The Quay ☎(051)55111 tx
80188
Closed 25-26 Dec
🚿76 Lift ℂ
Credit Cards 1 2 3 5
★★★**Tower** The Mall ☎(051)75801 tx 80699
Closed 25-28 Dec
🚿83 P60 Lift ℂ
Credit Cards 1 2 3 4 5
★★**Bridge** The Quay ☎(051)77222 tx 80141
🚿67 Lift ℂ
Credit Cards 1 2 3 4 5
★★**Dooley's** 30 The Quay ☎(051)73531 tx 91880
Closed 25-27 Dec
rm37(🚿34)
Credit Cards 1 2 3 5
🛏 **C J Deevy & Co** 48 Parnell St ☎(051) 55719
🛏 **McConnell Bros** William St ☎(051) 74037 Toy

🛏 **T Murphy** Morgan St ☎(051) 76614 Aud Maz
Mer VW
🛏 **Sheridan's** Cork Rd ☎(051) 72891 For

WATERVILLE
Co Kerry
🛏 **Concannon's** ☎(0667) 4121

WESTPORT
Co Mayo
★★**Clew Bay** ☎(098)25438
rm28(🚿25)
Credit Cards 1 2 3 5
★★**Olde Railway** The Mall ☎(098)25166
🚿20 ⚲ P30 ℂ
Credit Cards 1 2 3 5
★★**Westport** ☎(098)25122 tx 53974
🚿49 P150 ℂ
Credit Cards 1 2 3 5
★★**Westport Ryan** ☎(098)25811 tx 53757
Closed 20 Dec-31 Jan
🚿57 P100 ℂ
Credit Cards 1 2 3 4 5
🛏 **Duffy's** Mill St ☎(098) 25942

WEXFORD
Co Wexford
★★★**Ferrycarrig** Ferrycarrig ☎(053)22999 tx
80147
🚿30 P50 Lift ℂ ⚲
Credit Cards 1 2 3 5
★★★**Talbot** Trinity St ☎(053)22566 tx 80658
🚿103 ⚲ P60 Lift ℂ ▱
Credit Cards 1 2 3 4 5
★★★**White's** (BW) George's St ☎(053)22311 tx
80630
Closed 24-25 Dec
🚿75 P100 Lift ℂ
Credit Cards 1 2 3 4 5
🛏 **Ferrybank Motors** Ferrybank ☎(053) 22107
Ope

WICKLOW
Co Wicklow
🛏 **Vartry Svc** New St ☎(0404) 68127 VW

WOODENBRIDGE
Co Wicklow
★★**Woodenbridge** ☎(0402)5146 & 5219
🚿12 P50 Mountain
Credit Cards 1 3 5

YOUGHAL
Co Cork
★★**Devonshire Arms** Pearse Sq ☎(024)92827
2 Jan-13 Dec
🚿10 P20
Credit Cards 1 2 3 5

Opening doors to the World of books

Book Tokens can be bought and exchanged at most bookshops

*I*magine a land with a superb climate, set in a sparkling sea, almost surrounded by thousands of miles of beaches and a spectacular, rugged coastline. Fill it with artistic, architectural and historic treasures; introduce a superb musical tradition; add breathtaking mountains and tranquil lakes, enchanting offshore islands, orange and lemon groves, vineyards, great cities, spas and resorts – plus good hotels, fine cuisine, splendid wines, and a unique atmosphere created by a combination of the country's myriad attractions and the character of its people.

Italy is a land of striking contrasts, hardly surprising, perhaps, since it stretches from snow-peaked mountains in the north to the warm and sunny waters far south in the Mediterranean. It is also a land of dramatic history and great civilisations, of art treasures and of unforgettable historical architectural achievements standing in the midst of the busy, bustling life of cities and towns where the modern style of Italy harmonises happily with its wonderful past.

Italian cities, towns and its very landscape reflect its rich and diverse history, but above all the wonders of Italy and the unparalleled genius of its artistic giants are to be found in almost unbelievable profusion in the art galleries, museums and palaces where the Italians proudly display their artistic heritage.

ITALY

Language
Italian

Local time
GMT + 1 (Summer GMT + 2)

Currency
Italian *lira*. At the time of going to press
£1 = Lit2,235
US$1 = Lit1,346

Emergency numbers
Fire, Police, Ambulance ☎113

Information in England
Italian State Tourist Office (ENIT), 1 Princes Street, London W1R 8AY
☎01-408 125
†071 from 6 May

Information in the USA
Italian Government Travel Office, 630 Fifth Avenue, Suite 1565, New York, NY10111
☎

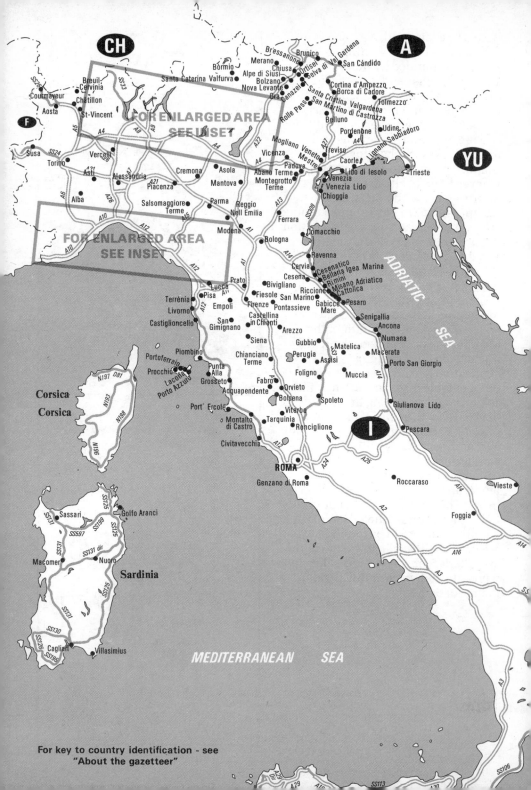

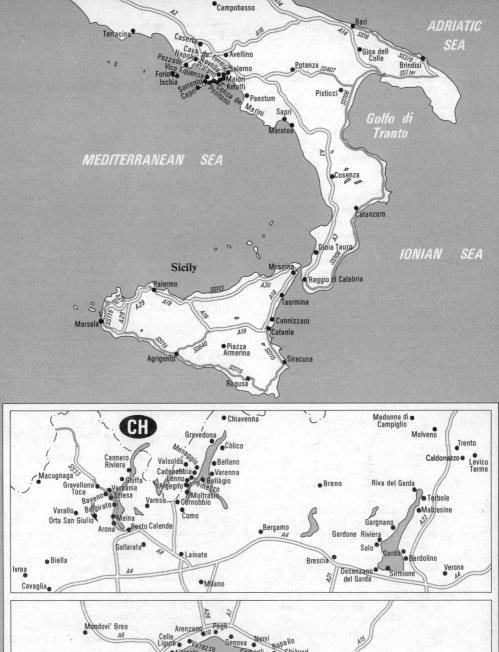

ADRIATIC SEA

Campobasso

Bari

A14

A2

A16

Terracina

Caserta

SS16

Cava de' Tirreni

Avellino

Gioa dell Colle

Napoli

Pozzuoli

Ravello

Salerno

Potenza

SS379

Brindisi

SS7 ter

Vico Equense

Praiano

Maiori

Forio

Amalfi

Ischia

Sorrento

Conca dei

Capri

Positano

Marini

Pisticci

SS407

SS106

Paestum

Sapri

GOLFO di TRANTO

MEDITERRANEAN SEA

Maratea

A3

Cosenza

Catanzaro

Sicily

Gioia Tauro

SS106

A3

IONIAN SEA

Palermo

SS113

Messina

Reggio di Calabria

A20

Marsala

A29

A19

A29

A19

A19

Taormina

SS115

A19

Cannizzaro

Catania

SS115

SS640

Piazza Armerina

SS115

Siracusa

Agrigento

SS115

Ragusa

CH

Chiavenna

Madonna di Campiglio

Molveno

Gravedona

Trento

Menaggio

Còlico

Caldonazzo

Cannero Riviera

Valsolda

Bellano

Levico Terme

Ghiffa

Cadenabbia

Varenna

Macugnaga

SS33

Lenno

Bellàgio

Gravellona Toce

Verbània

Tremezzo

Breno

Riva del Garda

Bàveno

Stresa

Argegno

Moltràsio

Torbole

Varallo

Belgirate

Varese

Cernòbbio

Gargnano

Malcèsine

Orta San Giulio

Meina

Como

Gardone Riviera

Arona

Sesto Calende

Bergamo

Salo

Garda

Bardolino

Gallarate

A8

Lainate

A4

Brescia

Desenzano del Garda

Sirmione

Verona

Ivrea

Biella

A4

A21

A4

Cavaglià

Milano

A22

F

Mondovì Breo

A26

A7

Pegll

A6

Arenzano

Celle Ligure

A10

Varazze

Genova

Nervi

Rapallo

A15

Albisola Marina

Camogli

Chiàvari

Savona

Santa Margherita Ligure

Lavagna

Spotorno

Portofino

Sestri Levante

Finale Ligure

Pietra Ligure

Loano

Levanto

Laigueglia

Alassio

La Spezia

Sarzana

San Bartolomeo al Mare

Lerici

Marina di Carrara

A10

Diano Marina

Marina di Massa

Forte dei Marmi

Ventimiglia

Imperia

Marina di Pietrasanta

Montecatini Terme

Bordighera

San Remo

Lido di Camaiore

Viareggio

Ospedaletti

Golfo di Genova

HOW TO GET THERE

Although there are several ways of getting to Italy, entry will probably be by way of France and Switzerland. The major passes, which are closed in winter, are served by road or rail-tunnels.

Distance

From the Channel ports Milano (Milan) is about 1,050–1,130km (650–700 miles), requiring one or two overnight stops. Roma (Rome) is 580km (360 miles) further south.

Car-sleeper services

operate during the summer from Boulogne, Brussels, 's-Hertogenbosch or Paris to Milano; Boulogne to Bologna, and Paris to Rimini.

MONEYMATTERS

Visitors may import an unlimited amount of Italian and foreign currency and export up to Lit1,000,000 and up to Lit5,000,000 in foreign currency. However, if you wish to export amounts in excess of the above you must declare the amount on entry using the form V2 obtainable at frontier customs posts. You must then show the form to customs when leaving Italy.

Banking hours

Monday–Friday 08.30–13.00hrs and 15.30–16.30hrs.

Postcheques

may be cashed at all post offices up to a maximum of Lit3,000,000 per cheque. Go to the counter with the *Postcheque* window sticker.

MOTORING REGULATIONS AND GENERAL INFORMATION

The information given here is specific to Italy. It **must** be read in conjunction with the European ABC at the front of the book, which covers those regulations which are common to many countries.

Accidents*

No particular procedure is required following an accident, excepting that a report must be made to the insurance company. If the accident involves personal injury, medical assistance must be sought for the injured party, and the incident reported to the police. On some *autostrade*, there are emergency telephones as well as emergency push-button call boxes. See also *Warning triangle* below.

Boats

Boat registration and a Helmsman's Overseas Certificate of Competence are required. Third-party insurance is compulsory in Italian waters for craft with engines of more than 3hp, and an Italian translation of the insurance certificate should be carried.

Breakdown*

Try to move the car to the side of the road, and place a warning triangle to warn following traffic of the obstruction. The Italian motoring club, *Automobile Club d'Italia* (ACI), provides a breakdown service operated by the *Breakdown Service Company* of the ACI, using its own staff on motorways and authorised repair garages on ordinary roads. The service can be used by any visiting motorist driving a foreign registered vehicle. It provides free towage from the breakdown location to the nearest ACI affiliated garage, but a charge is made if the vehicle is towed elsewhere. Assistance can be obtained by using the little telephone columns placed along motorways (every 2km) or on ☎116 from any part of the country on ordinary roads. Any additional services must be paid for. See also *Warning triangle* below.

*Additional information will be found in the European ABC at the front of the book.

British Embassy/Consulates*

The British Embassy together with its consular section is located at 00187 Roma, Via XX Settembre 80A ☏(06) 4755441 and 4755551. There are British Consulates in Firenze (Florence), Genova (Genoa), Milano (Milan), Napoli (Naples), Turin and Venezia (Venice); there are British Consulates with Honorary Consuls in Cagliari and Trieste. See also the *Town Plan of Roma* within the gazetteer.

Children in Cars*

Children under 10 are not permitted to travel in a vehicle as front or rear-seat passengers unless wearing a seat belt. From 26 April 1990 all children between 4 and 10 seated in the front or rear must use a restraint system.

Dimensions and weight restrictions

Private cars and towed trailers or caravans are restricted to the following dimensions – **car** height, 4 metres; width, 2.50 metres; length, with one axle 6 metres, with two or more axles 12 metres. **Trailer/caravan** height, 4 metres; width, 2.30 metres; length, with one axle 6 metres, with two axles 7.50 metres. The maximum permitted overall length of vehicle/trailer or caravan combinations is 12 metres.

Trailers with an unladen weight of over 750kg or 50% of the weight of the towing vehicle must have service brakes on all wheels.

Driving licence*

A valid red three-year Republic of Ireland† or green UK† licence is acceptable in Italy if accompanied by an official Italian translation which may be obtained free from the AA. The minimum age at which a visitor may use a temporarily imported car is 18 years. The minimum age for using a temporarily imported motorcycle of up to 125cc, not transporting a passenger, is 16 years; to carry a passenger, or use a motorcycle over 125cc, the minimum age is 18 years.

†The translation is not required by the holder of a pink EC type Republic of Ireland or UK licence. The respective licensing authorities cannot exchange a licence purely to facilitate continental travel.

Emergency messages to tourists*

Emergency messages to tourists are broadcast by the ACI through the Italian radio-television network (RAI) as follows:

RAI first channel transmitting on medium wave broadcasts these messages in English and Italian at 06.56, 07.57, 09.57, 11.57, 12.56, 14.57, 16.57, 18.56, 20.57, 22.57 and 00.20hrs daily throughout the year. Emergency messages are also broadcast in English, French, Spanish and German at 13.56hrs in the programme *Green Wave-Euroradio*.

Fiscal receipt

In Italy, the law provides for a special numbered fiscal receipt (*ricevuta fiscale*) to be issued after paying for a wide range of goods and services, including meals and accommodation. This receipt indicates the cost of various goods and services obtained, and the total charge after adding VAT. Tourists should ensure that this receipt is issued, as spot checks are made by the authorities, and both the proprietor and consumer are liable to an on-the-spot fine if the receipt cannot be produced.

Horn, use of

In *built-up* areas, the use of the horn is prohibited except in cases of immediate danger. At night, flashing headlights may be used instead of the horn. *Outside built-up areas*, it is compulsory to use the horn when warning of approach is necessary.

Lights*

Full-beam headlights can be used only outside cities and towns. Dipped headlights are compulsory when passing through tunnels, even if they are well lit. Fog lamps must be used in pairs, and only in fog or snow when visibility is restricted.

Motoring clubs*

There are two motoring organisations in Italy: the **Touring Club Italiano** (TCI), which has its head office at 20122 Milano, 10 Corso Italia ☏(02) 85261, and the **Automobile Club d'Italia** (ACI), whose head office is at 00185 Roma, 8 Via Marsala ☏(06) 49981. Both clubs have branch offices in most leading cities and towns. See also the

*Additional information will be found in the European ABC at the front of the book.

Town Plan of Roma within the gazetteer.

The TCI usually open between 09.00 and 19.00hrs, although some open earlier and close later. A few are closed all day on Mondays or Saturdays. However, all close for three hours for lunch between 12.00 and 16.00hrs.

The ACI offices and those of the provincial Automobile Clubs open between 08.30 and 13.30hrs Monday to Saturday. The head office in Roma opens between 08.00 and 14.00hrs Monday to Saturday, and 15.00 and 19.00hrs Tuesday to Friday; a 24-hour information service is in operation on ☎(06) 4212.

Motorways

A comprehensive motorway (*autostrada*) system reaching most parts of the country is available. To join a motorway, follow the green signposts. Tolls are charged on most sections, eg Milan to Rome is *Lit*9,500 for a small car, rising to *Lit*42,500 for a large car. The methods of calculating tolls are based either on the wheel-base or the cubic capacity of the vehicle, and the distance covered.

On the majority of toll-motorways, a travel ticket is issued on entry and the toll is paid on leaving the motorway. The travel ticket gives all relevant information about toll charges, including the toll category of the vehicle. At the exit point, the ticket is handed in. On some motorways, notably A8, A9, A11, A14 (Pescara–Lanciano) and A12 (Roma–Civitavecchia), a toll is paid at intermediate toll stations for each section of the motorway used. However, on a few motorways, the destination must be declared and the toll paid on entering the motorway. There is no refund on a broken journey.

A leaflet entitled *Motorways in Italy* is available to AA members.

Orange badge scheme for disabled drivers*

In Italy, public transport is given priority in town centres, and private cars may be banned. However, the local authorities are required to take special measures to allow badge holders to take their vehicles into social, cultural and recreational areas. Reserved parking bays may be provided in some areas, and these will be indicated by signs featuring the international disabled symbol.

Parking*

Parking is forbidden on a main road or one carrying fast moving traffic, on or near tram lines, opposite another stationary vehicle, on or within 12 metres (39½ft) of a bus or tram stop, and at times in some cities. Violators of parking regulations are subject to heavy fines. In Milano (Milan) and Roma (Rome) wheel clamps are used on illegally parked vehicles.

Blue zone (*zona disco*) Areas in most cities where parked vehicles must display a disc on the windscreen. Discs are obtainable from petrol stations and automobile organisations. They are set at the time of parking and show when the parking time expires according to the limits of the area concerned. Disc parking operates 08.00–20.00hrs on working days.

Green zones (*zona verde*) Areas where parking is absolutely prohibited between 08.00–09.30hrs and 14.30–16.00hrs. Vehicles will be towed away at the owner's expense, even when they are not causing an obstruction.

Petrol*

Credit cards are rarely accepted at petrol stations.

Duty-free patrol The petrol in the vehicle tank may be imported free of customs and duty tax.

Petrol cans It is forbidden to carry petrol in cans in a vehicle.

Petrol coupons At the time of going to press, a concessionary package of Italian petrol coupons and motorway toll vouchers may be purchased from the AA. An additional benefit of the package is free breakdown and replacement car concession, but see also *Breakdown* page 00 for details of the *AA 5-Star Service*. The package is available to personal callers only, and a passport and vehicle registration document must be produced at the time of application. Further information may be obtained from any AA Centre. The package **cannot** be purchased inside Italy, but may be obtained from ACI offices at main crossing points, and also many ACI offices in port areas, if arriving by ship.

Petrol (leaded) Benzina Normale (85–88 octane) and Benzina Super (98–100 octane) grades.

Petrol (unleaded) is sold in Italy as Super Senza Piombo (95 octane). Pumps dispensing unleaded petrol are marked in English, 'Super Unleaded'.

*****Additional information will be found in the European ABC at the front of the book.**

Postal information

Mail Postcards *Lit*500 (max 5 words), letters first 20gm *Lit*650. Express surcharge *Lit*2,500.
Post offices There are 14,000 post offices in Italy. Opening hours are 08.15–13.00hrs Monday to Friday and 08.15–12.00hrs Saturday. On the last day of the month, offices close at 12.00hrs.

Priority*

Traffic on state highways (*Strade Statali*), which are all numbered and indicated by signs, has right of way, as do public service vehicles and, on postal routes, buses belonging to the service. These bus routes are indicated by a special sign.

If two vehicles are travelling in opposite directions and the drivers of each vehicle want to turn left, they must pass in front of each other (not drive round as the in UK).

Public holidays*

Official Public holidays in Italy for 1990 are given below. Many towns have local holidays on the Feast Day of their patron saint.

January 1 (New Year's Day)
January 6† (Epiphany)
April 16 (Easter Monday)
April 25 (Liberation Day)
May 1 (Labour Day)
August 15 (Assumption)
November 1 (All Saints' Day)
December 8† (Immaculate Conception)
December 25 (Christmas Day)
December 26 (Boxing Day)
†Saturday

Roads

Main and secondary roads are generally good, and there are an exceptional number of by-passes. Mountain roads are usually well engineered; for details of mountain passes and road conditions refer to the European ABC.

Shopping hours

Generally, *food shops* are open Monday to Saturday between 08.00–13.00hrs and 16.00–20.00hrs, but close at 13.00hrs on Thursday. Most *other shops* are open Monday to Saturday between 09.00–13.00hrs and 16.00–19.30hrs, but only open at 16.00hrs Monday.

Speed limits*

In *built-up areas* 50kph (31mph); *outside built-up areas* 90kph (56mph). For cars towing a caravan or trailer the speed limits are 50kph (31mph), 80kph (49mph) and 100kph (62mph) respectively; *on motorways* 130kph (81mph) for vehicles over 1100cc and motorcycles over 350cc. For vehicles up to 1099cc and motorcycles between 150cc and 349cc the speed limit is 110kph (68mph). Motorcycles under 150cc are not allowed on motorways.

Spiked or studded tyres

May be used provided that:
a they are used between 15 November and 15 March;
b the vehicle does not exceed a total weight of 3,500kg;
c they are fitted to all wheels, including those of a trailer (if any).

Additionally, visiting motorists are advised to have mud flaps fitted behind the rear wheels. Spiked tyres may be used on roads where wheel chains are compulsory, provided they are used on all four wheels. See also Cold-weather touring in the European ABC.

Telephone*

Insert coins **before** lifting the receiver; the dialling tone is short and long tones. When making calls to subscribers *within* Italy, precede the number with the relevant area code (shown in parentheses before the hotel/garage enquiry number in the gazetteer). Use *Lit*200 *gettoni* tokens, available at bars, tobacconists and slot machines, or *Lit*100, 200 or 500 coins in new payphones.
International calls can be made from callboxes with a yellow or red sign showing a telephone dial and receiver.
The cost of a call to the UK if dialled direct is twelve tokens per minute.

Telephone codes

UK to Italy	010 39
Italy to UK	00 44
Italy to Republic of Ireland	00 353
Italy to the USA	00 1

*Additional information will be found in the European ABC at the front of the book.

Warning triangle

The use of a warning triangle is compulsory in the event of accident or breakdown. It should be used to give advance warning of a stationary vehicle which is parked on a road in fog, near a bed, on a hill or at night when the rear lights have failed. The triangle must be placed on the road not less than 50 metres (55yds) behind the vehicle. Motorists who fail to do this are liable to an administrative fine of between Lit25,000 and Lit100,000.

Wheel chains

Roads where these are compulsory are marked by a national sign. Chains cannot be hired in Italy, but can be purchased at garages or vehicle accessory shops everywhere. Approximate prices per pair are as follows: iron Lit10,000–30,000, steel/iron, Lit20,000–40,000. Drivers of vehicles proceeding without wheel chains on roads where they are compulsory are liable to prosecution. See also Cold-weather touring *in the European ABC.*

Winter conditions*

It is possible to approach northern Italy, Milano (Milan) and Torino (Turin) by road or train tunnel.

From Switzerland via Simplon rail tunnel; via the Grand St Bernard road tunnel; via the St Gotthard road tunnel; via the San Bernardino road tunnel; also via the Julier and Maloja passes.

From France via the Mont Blanc road tunnel; via the Fréjus road tunnel; in favourable weather, via the Lautaret and Montgenèvre passes; also via the French Riviera coast, entering at Ventimiglia.

From Austria via the Resia and Brenner passes; wheel chains may be necessary in severe weather. The Plöcken pass is occasionally closed in winter, but the roads entering Italy at Dobbiaco and Tarvisio are normally free from obstruction.

Roads within the country, apart from those in the Dolomites, are not seriously affected in winter, although during January and February certain highways across the Apennines may be obstructed. Touring in the Dolomites is generally confined to the period from early May to mid October.

SAN MARINO

A small Republic, 23 square miles in area, situated in the hills of Italy near Rimini. The official information office in the UK is the Italian State Tourist Office at 1 Princes Street, London W1R 8AY. The chief attraction is the city of San Marino on the slopes of Monte Titano. Its laws, motoring regulations and emergency telephone number are the same as for Italy.

*Additional information will be found in the European ABC at the front of the book.

ACCOMMODATION

Hotels are officially classified from five-star (luxury or, if satisfying special requirements, de luxe or *lusso*) to one-star (formerly pensions). All charges must be agreed by the Provincial Tourist Board (*Ente provinciali per il Tuismo*).

The prices shown below are an average for each classification. Accommodation is likely to be more expensive in Roma (Rome), other large cities and some of the more popular tourist areas.

At the time of going to press, £1 Sterling = Lit2,235 and US$1 = Lit1,346 but you should check the rate of exchange before your departure.

AVERAGE PRICES

	Single Room	Double Room	Breakfast	Lunch/Dinner
★★★★★	Lit234,400–286,700	Lit333,800–433,250	Lit18,600–18,700	Lit50,000–66,250
★★★★	Lit149,500–179,100	Lit228,320–293,100	Lit17,460–19,625	Lit45,700–55,750
★★★	Lit77,850–98,100	Lit110,580–158,200	Lit10,780–11,010	Lit29,975–40,250
★★	Lit44,350–63,180	Lit73,750–94,800	Lit8,300–9,250	Lit24,650–33,850
★	Lit41,000–54,750	Lit66,125–90,360	Lit9,250–18,750	Lit26,500–26,750

Abbreviations
Gl Generale   pza piazza

ABANO TERME
Padova
★★★★**Grand Hotel Trieste & Victoria** (SRS) via
Pietro d'Abano ☎(049)669101 tx 430250
Mar-Nov
⌂102 P80 Lift ℂ ℀ ▱ ⌓
Credit Cards ①②③⑤
★★★**Bristol Buja** via Monteortone 2
☎(049)669390 tx 430210
⌂129 ☜ P92 Lift ℂ ℀ ▱ ⌓
Credit Cards ①②③⑤
★★★**Terme Milano** viale delle Terme 169
☎(049)669444 tx 431878
9 Mar-6 Jan
rm90(⌂80) P80 Lift ℂ ℀ ▱ ⌓
Credit Cards ①②③⑤

ACQUAPENDENTE
Viterbo
★**Roma** viale dei Fiore 13 ☎(0763)74016
rm26(⌂20) ☜ ℀

AGRIGENTO
Agrigento
See SICILIA, ISOLA (SICILY)

ALASSIO
Savona
★★★★**Diana** via Garibaldi 110 ☎(0182)42701 tx
270655
Closed Dec & Jan
⌂77 P40 Lift ℂ ▱ Beach Sea
Credit Cards ①②③⑤
★★★★**Spiaggia** via Roma 78 ☎(0182)430403 tx
271617
⌂83 ☜ Lift Beach Sea
Credit Cards ①③
★★★**Flora** Lungomare Cadorna 22
☎(0182)40336
15 Mar-10 Jan :Rest closed Thu
⌂39 Lift ℂ Beach Sea
Credit Cards ①②③④⑤
★★★**Majestic** via Leonardo da Vinci 300
☎(0182)42721 tx 272032
Etr-Sep
⌂77 ☜ Lift ℂ Beach
★★★**Méditerranée** via Roma 63 ☎(0182)42564
Apr-Oct
rm80(⌂79) A24rm ☜ Lift ℂ Beach Sea
Credit Cards ①②③
★★**Mare** via Boselli 24 ☎(0182)40657
rm49(⌂48) Lift Beach Sea
Credit Cards ①③
★★**Toscana** via Leonardo da Vinci
☎(0182)40657 tx 335215
Closed 20 Oct-20 Dec:Rest closed Mon
⌂65 P15 Lift ℂ ▱ Beach
Credit Cards ②③⑤
★★**Villa Carlotta** via Adelasia 11 ☎(0182)40463
Apr-Oct
rm16(⌂8) Beach Sea Mountain

ALBA
Cuneo
★★**Savona** pza Savona ☎(0173)42381
⌂103 ☜ P18 Lift ℂ
Credit Cards ①②③④⑤

ALBISOLA MARINA
Savona
★★★**Corallo** via M-Repetto 116 ☎(0182)41784
20 Mar-Nov :Rest closed Mon
rm22(⌂20) ☜ P8 ℂ Sea
Credit Cards ①②③⑤

ALESSANDRIA
Alessandria
★★**Europa** via Palestro ☎(0131)446226
⌂33 P10 Lift ℂ
Credit Cards ①②③④⑤

ALPE DI SIUSI
Bolzano
★★★**Eurotel** DPn ☎(0471)72928 tx 400181
Dec-Apr & Jul-mid Sep
⌂84 ☜ P92 ℂ Mountain
Credit Cards ②⑤

AMALFI
Salerno
★★★**Aurora** pza dei Prontontini 7 ☎(089)871209
Apr-15 Oct
⌂30 ☜ P ℂ Beach Sea
Credit Cards ①②③⑤
★★★**Luna Convento** Via P Comite 19
☎(089)871002 tx 770161
⌂45 ☜ P Lift ℂ ▱ Beach Sea
Credit Cards ①②③④⑤
★★★**Miramalfi** ☎(089)871588 tx 720325
:Rest closed Tue
⌂48 Lift ℂ ▱ Beach Sea
★★★**Santa Caterina** via Statale ☎(089)871012 tx
770093
⌂70 A9rm ☜ P30 Lift ℂ ▱ ⌓ Beach Sea
Credit Cards ①②③⑤
★★**Bellevue** via Nazionale 163 ☎(089)831349
Apr-Sep
⌂23 P10 ℂ Sea
★★**Marina Riviera** via F- Gioia 22 ☎(089)871104
15 Mar-Oct
rm18(⌂16) ☜ P3 Lift Beach Sea
At LONE(2.5Km W)
★★★**Caleidoscopio** via P-Leone X 6
☎(089)871220
Apr-10 Oct
⌂24 A7rm P35 ▱ Beach Sea
At MINORI(3Km E)
★★**Caporal** DPn ☎(0131)877408
⌂36 A14rm P10 ℂ Beach Sea
Credit Cards ①②③⑤
★★**Santa Lucia** via Nazionale 44 ☎(089)877142
Mar-Oct
rm29(⌂27) Lift
Credit Cards ②③

ANACAPRI
See CAPRI, ISOLA DI under CAPRI

ANCONA
Ancona
★★★**AGIP** Palombina Nuova ☎(071)888241 tx
611627
⌂50 P Lift ℂ
★★★**Jolly** Rupi di via XX1X Settembre 14
☎(071)201171 tx 560343
⌂89 P Lift ℂ
Credit Cards ①②③④⑤
At PORTONOVO(14Km SE)
★★**Fortino Napoleonico** DPn via Poggio
☎(021)801124 & 801314
⌂30 P100 ℂ Beach Sea Mountain
Credit Cards ①②③⑤
Samet ☎(071) 82903 For

AOSTA
Aosta
★★★**Ambassador** via Duca Degli Abruzzi
☎(0165)42230
rm43(⌂40) ☜ P Lift ℂ Mountain
★★★**Motelalp** Saint Christophe (n.rest)
☎(0165)40007 tx 214256
⌂52 ☜ P63 ℂ Mountain
Credit Cards ①②③
★★★**Valle d'Aosta** corso Ivrea 146 (n.rest)
☎(0165)41845 tx 212472
⌂104 ☜ P85 Lift ℂ Mountain
Credit Cards ①②③④⑤
★★**Gran Paradiso** via L'Binel 12 ☎(0165)40654
⌂33 P Mountain
★★**Mignon** viale Gran San Bernardo 7
☎(0165)40980 tx 215013
⌂22 ☜ P30 ℂ Mountain
Credit Cards ①②③④⑤
★★**Rayon de Soleil** viale Gran St Bernardo
☎(0165)362247
Mar-15 Oct
⌂45 ☜ P40 Lift ℂ ⌓ Mountain
Credit Cards ①②③⑤
★★**Turin** via Torino 14 ☎(0165)44593
20 Dec-15 Nov
⌂51 ☜ P157 Lift ℂ Mountain
Credit Cards ①②③⑤
Gai ☎(0165) 32088

ARENZANO
Genova
★★★**Miramare** rm42(⌂35) ☜ Lift ℂ ☎(010)9127325
Credit Cards ①②⑤
★**Europa** (n.rest) ☎(010)9127384
May-Sep
rm15(⌂7) P15 Sea
Credit Cards ②⑤

AREZZO
Arezzo
★★★**Continentale** pza G-Monaco 7
☎(0575)20251
⌂80 Lift ℂ
Credit Cards ①②③④⑤
Magi Ezlo di Piero & Corrado Magi M-Perennio
24 ☎(0575) 21264 AR

ARGEGNO
Como

★**Belvedere** Lake Como ☎(031)821116
Apr-Oct
rm17(❤11) P15 Lake
Credit Cards ⅓⅓⅝

ARONA
Novara

★★★**Antares** via Gramsci 9 (n.rest) ☎(0322)3438
❤51 ⇌ P25 Lift ℂ Lake
Credit Cards ①②③⑤

ASOLO
Treviso

★★★★**Villa Cipriani** (CIGA/Relais et Châteaux)
☎(0423)55444 tx 411060
❤31 ⇌ P60 Lift ℂ Mountain
Credit Cards ①②③⑤

ASSISI
Perugia

★★★**Giotto** via Fontebella 41 ☎(075)812209 tx
563259
15 Mar-15 Nov
rm70(❤63) ⇌ P40 ℂ
Credit Cards ①②③⑤

★★★**Subasio** via Frate Elia 2 ☎(075)812206 tx
662029
❤70 ⇌ P10 Lift ℂ Mountain
Credit Cards ①②③④⑤

★★★**Windsor Savoia** porta San Francesco 1
☎(075)812210 tx 564074
❤34 ⇌ Lift ℂ Mountain
Credit Cards ①②③⑤

★★**Umbra** via degli Archi 2 ☎(075)812240
15 Mar-15 Jan :Rest closed Tue
rm28(❤26) ℂ Mountain
Credit Cards ②⑤

ASTI
Asti

★★★**Salera** via M-Marello 19 ☎(0141)211815
❤54 Lift ℂ

Asti Elettromeccanica Ticino 1 ☎(0141) 55016
M/c

AVELLINO
Avellino

★★★**Jolly** via Tuoro Cappuccini 97a
☎(0825)25922 tx 722584
❤72 P Lift ℂ
Credit Cards ①②③④⑤

BADIA, LA
See **ORVIETO**

BARBARANO
See **GARDONE RIVIERA**

BARDOLINO
Verona

★★★**Vela d'Or** 22 Cisano ☎(045)7210067
15 Apr-Sep
❤50 P30 ℂ ⇌ Lake

A Tortella Marconi 26 ☎(045) 7210053

BARI
Bari

★★★★**Grand Ambasciatori** via Omodeo 51
☎(080)410077 tx 810405
:Rest closed Sun (Aug)
❤177 ⇌ P Lift ℂ ⇌ Sea
Credit Cards ①②③⑤

★★★★**Palace** via Lombardi 13 ☎(080)216551
due to change 5216551 tx 810111
❤203 ⇌ P80 Lift ℂ
Credit Cards ①②③④⑤

★★★**Boston** via Casella Postale 508
☎(080)216633 tx 810435
❤70 ⇌ P18 Lift ℂ
Credit Cards ①②③⑤

★★★**Jolly** via G.Petroni 15 ☎(080)364366 tx
810274
❤164 ⇌ Lift ℂ
Credit Cards ①②③④⑤

Losito Clinia 36 ☎ (080) **P** For

At **TORRE A MARE**(12km E)

★★★**AGIP** SS 16 Km 816 ☎(080)300001 tx
611627
❤95 P Lift ℂ

BAVENO
Novara

★★★**Lido Palace** (BW) Strada Statale Sempione
30 ☎(0323)24444 tx 200697
Mar-Nov
❤104 ⇌ P80 Lift ℂ ℀ ⇌ Beach Lake
Credit Cards ①②③④⑤

★★**Beau Rivage** viale della Vittoria 36
☎(0323)24534
Apr-Oct
❤80 A6rm ⇌ Lift ℂ Mountain Lake
Credit Cards ①②③④⑤

★★**Simplon** via Garibaldi 52 ☎(0323)924112 tx
200217
30 Mar-Oct
❤100 ⇌ P156 Lift ℂ ℀ ⇌ Beach Lake

★★**Splendid** via Sempione 12 ☎(0323)924583 tx
200217
Apr-Oct
❤105 ⇌ P100 Lift ℂ ℀ ⇌ Beach Lake

At **FERIOLO**(3km NW)

★★**Carillon** Strada Nazional del Sempione 2
☎(0323)28115
Apr-Sep :Rest closed wknds
❤26 P Lake
Credit Cards ①②③④⑤

BELGIRATE
Novara

★★★**Milano** (BW) via Sempione 2 ☎(0322)76525
tx 200490
❤50 ⇌ P50 Lift ℂ ℀ ⇌ Beach Lake
Credit Cards ①②③⑤

★★★**Villa Carlotta** (BW) via Sempione 119
☎(0322)76461 tx 200490
❤115 ⇌ P100 Lift ℂ ℀ ⇌ Beach Lake
Credit Cards ①②③⑤

BELLAGIO
Como

★★★★**Villa Serbelloni** via Roma 1
☎(031)950216 tx 380330
15 Apr-15 Oct
❤82 ⇌ P100 Lift ℂ ℀ ⇌ Lake
Credit Cards ①②③⑤

★★★**Ambassadeur Metropole** pza Mazzini 1
☎(031)950409 tx 380861
Mar-3 Jan
❤44 Lift ℂ ⇌ Sea Lake
Credit Card ②

★★★**Lac** pza Mazzini 32 ☎(031)950320 tx
326299
18 Apr-14 Oct
❤48 ⇌ P3 Lift ℂ Lake
Credit Cards ①②③

★★**Belvedere** via Valassina 33 ☎(031)950410
Apr-10 Oct
rm50(❤45) ⇌ P30 Lift ℂ Mountain Lake
Credit Cards ②③

★★**Florence** pza Mazzini ☎(031)950342
15 Apr-20 Oct
rm40(❤31) Lift ℂ Lake
Credit Cards ①②③⑤

BELLANO
Como

★★**Meridiana** via C-Alberto 19 ☎(0341)821126
❤35 A4rm P60 Lift Beach Sea Lake
Credit Cards ①②③⑤

BELLARIA IGEA MARINA
Forlì

At **IGEA MARINA**

★★★**Touring Spiaggia** via la Pinzoni 217
☎(0541)631619
16 May-20 Sep
❤39 P20 Lift ℂ ⇌ Beach Sea
Credit Card ②

BELLUNO
Belluno

B Mortti T-Veccellio 117 ☎(0437) 30790 Alf

BERGAMO
Bergamo

★★★**Excelsior San Marco** pza Repubblica 6
☎(035)232132 tx 301295
:Rest closed Sun
❤151 Lift ℂ
Credit Cards ①②③⑤

★★**Agnello d'Oro** via Gombito 22 ☎(035)249883
:Rest closed Sun pm & all day Mon
❤20 Lift
Credit Cards ①②③⑤

BIELLA
Vercelli

★★★**Astoria** viale Roma 9 (n.rest) ☎(015)20545
tx 214083
❤50 P4 Lift ℂ Mountain
Credit Cards ①②③⑤

BIVIGLIANO
Firenze

★★**Giotto Park** ☎(055)406608 tx 580051
:Rest closed Tue & 15-30 Nov & 1-15 Feb
rm38(❤32) A19rm P40 ℂ ℀ Mountain
Credit Cards ①②⑤

BOLOGNA
Bologna

Bologna is the capital of Emilia-Romagna, a region bordered by the River Po, the Adriatic and the Apennine mountains. The old centre is distinctively built in sturdy brick; its leaning towers - two out of several hundred that were built in the city as a type of medieval status symbol by the great ruling families - are of special interest. From the top of the Asinelli Tower (320ft) there is a magnificent bird's-eye view over the terracotta rooftops and slender church spires.
The old city revolves around the two adjacent squares, Piazza del Nettuno and the Piazza Maggiore. In the first is Giovanni Bologna's splendid bronze statue of Neptune and the opulent *Palazzo di Re Enzo*, in the second the immense Basilica of San Petronio and the Renaissance-style *Palazzo del Podesta*. The university, the oldest in Europe, is a notable seat of learning and the *Pinacoteca Nazionale*, beyond it, offers a comprehensive view of Bolognese art. Definitely not to be missed is the sanctuary of the Madonna di San Luca, linked to

ITALY

the city gate by a portico of arches, over two miles long and commanding views across Bologna to the Apennines beyond.

EATING OUT Bologna is noted for its restaurants, for its pasta sauces, *mortadella* sausages, *tortellini* and the *tagliatelle* reputedly invented for the wedding of Lucrezia Borgia. Regional wines are sparkling Lambrusco, red Sangiovese and the whites, Albana and Trebbiano.

BOLOGNA

★★★★★*Royal Carlton* (SRS) via Montebello 8 ☎(051)55141 tx 510356
↩ℳ250 ☂ P400 Lift ℂ
Credit Cards ②③

★★★★*Jolly* pza 20 Settembre 2 ☎(051)248921 tx 510076
↩ℳ176 Lift ℂ
Credit Cards ①②③④⑤

★★★*AGIP* via EM Lepido 203/4 ☎(051)401130
↩ℳ60 P Lift ℂ

★★★*Crest* pza della Costituzione ☎(051)372172 tx 510676
↩ℳ163 ☂ P Lift ℂ ⌇
Credit Cards ①②③④⑤

★★★*Garden* via Lame 109 ☎(051)522222
↩ℳ83 ☂ P Lift ℂ

Automassina Po 2A ☎(051) 492552 Ren Lan
Cisa via A-d-Vincenzo 6 ☎(051) 370434 AR

BOLSENA
Viterbo

★★*Columbus* viale Colesanti 27 ☎(0761)799009 tx 612457
 Mar-Nov
↩ℳ38 A4rm ☂ P30 ℂ ℴ Beach Lake
Credit Cards ①③

BOLZANO-BOZEN
Bolzano

★★★★*Alpi* via Alto Adige 35 ☎(0471)970535 tx 400156
:Rest closed Sun
↩ℳ110
Credit Cards ①②③④⑤

★★★*Grifone* pza Walther 7 ☎(0471)977056 tx 400081
↩ℳ132 P100 Lift ℂ ⌇ Mountain
Credit Cards ①②③④⑤

★★*Luna* via Piave 15 ☎(0471)975642 tx 400309
↩ℳ75 ☂ P30 Lift ℂ
Credit Cards ①②③④⑤

★*Citta di Bolzano* pza Walther 21 ☎(0471)975221 tx 401434
:Rest closed Sun
↩ℳ102 ☂ P110 Lift ℂ Mountain
Credit Cards ①②③⑤

★*Scala* via Brennero 11 ☎(0471)976222
↩ℳ60 ☂ P25 Lift ℂ ⌇ Mountain
Credit Cards ①②③⑤

Mich G-Galilei 6 ☎(0471) 932419 P AR DJ Hon
1000 Miglia Macello 13 ☎(0471) 972000 Ope Vau
Motor Macello ☎(0471) 971617 BMW

BORCA DI CADORE
Belluno

At **CORTE DI CADORE**(2km E)

★★★*Boite* Corte di Cadore ☎(0435)82001 tx 440072
20 Jun-20 Sep & 20 Dec-31 Mar
↩ℳ84 P84 Lift ℂ ℴ Mountain
Credit Cards ①②③⑤

BORDIGHERA
Imperia

★★★★*Grand del Mare* Portico della Punta 34 ☎(0184)262201 tx 270535
24 Dec-Oct
↩ℳ113 A34rm ☂ P75 Lift ℂ ℴ ℴ Beach Sea
Credit Cards ②③

★★*Excelsior* Via GI-Biamonti 30 ☎(0184)262979
20 Dec-Oct
rm43(↩ℳ37) ☂ P45 Lift ℂ Sea Mountain

★★*Villa Elisa* via Romana 70 ☎(0184)261313 tx 272540
20 Dec-20 Oct
↩ℳ32 P20 Lift ℂ ℴ Beach Sea
Credit Cards ①②③④

BORMIO
Sondrio

★★*Posta* via Roma 66 ☎(0342)904753 tx 321425
Dec-Apr & Jun-Sep :Rest closed Mon
↩ℳ55 ☂ Lift ℂ Mountain
Credit Cards ①②③⑤

BRENO
Brescia

★★*Giardino* ☎(0364)22376
↩ℳ40 ☂ P40 Lift ℂ Mountain
Credit Card ②

BRESCIA
Brescia

★★★*AGIP* viale Bornata 42 (SS 11km 236) ☎(030)361654
↩ℳ42 P ℂ

Autolombarda L-Appollonio 17A ☎(030) 50051 AR Lan

BRESSANONE-BRIXEN
Bolzano

★★★*Elefante* Rio Bianco 4 ☎(0472)22288 tx 401277
Mar-Nov
↩ℳ44 A14rm ☂ P40 ℂ ℴ Beach Mountain

★★★*Gasser* via Giardini 19 ☎(0472)36105
Etr-end Oct
↩ℳ30 ☂ P30 Lift ℂ Mountain
Credit Cards ①②③④⑤

★★*Corona d'Oro-Goldene Krone* via Fienili 4 ☎(0472)35154
:Rest closed Tue
↩ℳ38 ☂ P16 Lift Mountain
Credit Cards ①③

F I Lanz Stazion 32 ☎(0472) 33326 P Aud VW
A Pecora V-Veneto 57 ☎(0472) 23277

BREUIL-CERVINIA
Aosta

★★*Valdotain* Lac Bleu ☎(166)949428 tx 211822
Dec-Apr & Jun-Sep
↩ℳ35 ☂ P40 Lift ℂ Mountain Lake
Credit Cards ①②③

BRINDISI
Brindisi

★★★*Internazionale* Lungomare Regina Margherita ☎(0831)23475
↩ℳ87 ☂ P Lift ℂ Sea

T Marino E-Fermi,Zone Indusriale ☎(0831) 473124 P For

BRUNICO-BRUNECK
Bolzano

★★★*Posta* Groben 9 ☎(0474)85127 tx 400350

:Rest closed Mon & Nov-20 Dec
rm60(↩ℳ44) P40 ℂ

CADENABBIA
Como

★*Beau-Rivage* via Regina 87 ☎(0344)40426
Apr-Oct :Rest closed Wed
rm20(↩ℳ9) P20 Lake
Credit Cards ①②

CAGLIARI
Cagliari
See SARDEGNA, ISOLA (SARDINIA)

CALDONAZZO
Trento

★★*Albergo Gilda* Via Brenta 22 ☎(0461) 723446
May-Sep
rm28(↩ℳ20) P30 ℴ

CAMAIORE, LIDO DI
Lucca

L Galletti del Termine 2 ☎(0584) 90024 DJ Vol

CAMOGLI
Genova

★★★★*Cenobio del Dogi* via Cuneo 34 ☎(0185)770041 tx 281116
Mar-3 Jan :Rest closed 3 Jan-28 Feb
↩ℳ89 P100 Lift ℂ ⌇ ℴ Beach Sea Mountain
Credit Cards ①②③

★★*Casmona* via Garibaldi 103 ☎(0185)770015
rm34(↩ℳ24) ℂ Sea
Credit Cards ①③⑤

CAMPOBASSO
Campobasso

P Vitale XX1V Maggio 95 ☎(0874) 61069 Aud Mer Por VW

CANAZEI
Trento

★★*Croce Bianca* via Roma 3 ☎(0462)61111
15 Jun-10 Oct
↩ℳ41 P35 Lift ℂ Mountain
Credit Cards ①②③⑤

CANDELI
See FIRENZE (FLORENCE)

CÀNNERO RIVIERA
Novara

★★★*Cànnero* Lungo Lago 2 ☎(0323)788046 tx 200285
10 Mar-6 Nov
↩ℳ36 ☂ P20 Lift ℴ Mountain Lake
Credit Cards ①②③⑤

CANNIZZARO
Catania
See SICILIA, ISOLA (SICILY)

CAORLE
Venezia

★★*Excelsior* viale Vespucci 11 ☎(0421)81515
14 May-24 Sep
↩ℳ55 P45 Lift ℂ Beach Sea
Credit Card ②

G Cecotto Strada Nuova 64 ☎(0421) 81315

CAPRI
See CAPRI, ISOLA DI

CAPRI, ISOLA DI
Napoli

CAPRI

★★★★*Grand Quisisana* (CIGA) via Camerelle 2 ☎(081)8370788 tx 710520
Apr-Oct
↩ℳ150 Lift ℂ ℴ Sea
Credit Cards ①②③④⑤

At **ANACAPRI**(3.6km W)

★★★*San Michele* via G-Orlandi 1 ☎(081)8371427
25 Mar-Oct
↩ℳ60 ☂ P25 Lift ℂ ℴ ℴ Sea
Credit Cards ①②③⑤

267

CARRARA, MARINA DI
Massa Carrara
★★*Mediterraneo* via Genova 2 Bis
☎(0585)635222
rm50(✦♠48) P30 Lift ℂ Sea

CASERTA
Caserta
★★★*Jolly* viale V-Veneto 9 ☎(0823)325222 tx
710548
✦♠89 P Lift ℂ
Credit Cards ①②③④⑤
Colombo Colombo 56 ☎(0823) 325268 Cit Lan
Mer Ren

CASTELLINA IN CHIANTI
Siena
★★*Villa Casalecchi* ☎(0577)740240
Apr-Oct
✦♠19 A3rm P30 ⌁ Mountain
Credit Cards ②③⑤
At RICAVO(4km N)
★★★Tenuta di Ricavo DPn Ricavo
☎(0577)740221
Apr-22 Oct
✦♠25 A17rm ⚜ P33 ⌁

CASTIGLIONCELLO
Livorno
★★★*Miramare* via Marconi 8 ☎(0586)752435
Apr-Sept :Rest closed Thur
rm64(✦♠60) A6rm P45 Lift ℂ Sea
Credit Cards ②③
★★*Guerrini* via Roma 12 ☎(0586)752047
Closed Nov & public hols
rm22(✦12) P2 Sea
Credit Cards ②③⑤

CATANIA
Catania
See SICILIA, ISOLA (SICILY)

CATANZARO
Catanzaro
★★★*AGIP* Ustica Strada due Mari ☎(0961)51791
✦♠76 P Lift ℂ

CATTOLICA
Forli
★★★★*Victoria Palace* via Carducci 24
☎(0541)962921 tx 550459
15 May-28 Sep
✦♠98 P45 Lift ℂ Beach Sea
Credit Cards ①②③⑤
★★★*Europa-Monetti* via Curiel 33
☎(0541)961468
10 May-25 Sep
✦♠77 ⚜ P16 Lift ℂ ⌁ Beach
★★★*Gambrinus* via Carducci 86 ☎(0541)961347
May-Oct
rm42(♠33) P Lift Beach Sea
★★★*Grand Diplomat* via del Turismo 9
☎(0541)967442
May-Sep
✦♠89 P40 Lift ℂ ℚ ⌁ Beach Sea
Credit Cards ①②
★★★*Maxim* via Facchini 7 ☎(0541)962137 tx
551084
May-Sep
✦♠66 P22 Lift ℂ Sea
★★★*Moderno-Majestic* viale D'Annunzio 15
☎(0541)954169
21 May-20 Sep
✦♠60 P40 Lift ℂ Beach Sea
Credit Card ②
★★★*Rosa* via Carducci 80 ☎(0541)963275
15 May-Sep
✦♠53 P40 Lift ℂ Sea
Credit Card ②
★★*Senior* viale Del Prete (n.rest) ☎(0541)963443
2 May-Sep
✦♠43 P12 Lift ℂ ⌁ Beach Sea
Credit Cards ①②③

★*Bellariva* via Fiume 10 ☎(0541)961609
20 May-20 Sep
rm22(✦♠20) P12 ℂ
Credit Card ②

CAVA DE TIRRENI
Salerno
★★*Victoria* Corso Mazzini 4 ☎(089)464022
✦♠61 ⚜ P40 Lift ℂ ℚ Mountain
Credit Cards ②③⑤
At CORPO DI CAVA(4km SW)
★★*Scapolatiello* Corpo di Cava ☎(089)463911
:Rest closed Tue
✦♠52 ⚜ P14 Lift ℂ ⌁ Mountain
Credit Cards ②③⑤

CAVAGLIA
Vercelli
★★*Prateria* ☎(0161)96115
Mar-Nov
✦♠32 ⚜ P Mountain

CAVI
See LAVAGNA

CELLE LIGURE
Savona
★★★*San Michele* via Monte Tabor 26
☎(019)990017
Jun-Sep :Rest closed Mon
✦♠50 P30 Lift ℂ ⌁ Sea

CERNOBBIO
Como
★★★★★*Villa d'Este* via Regina 40 ☎(031)51147
tx 380025
Apr-Oct
✦♠180 A40rm ⚜ P Lift ℂ ℚ ⟐ ⌁ Mountain
Lake
★★★*Regina Olga* via Regina 18 ☎(031)510171
tx 380821
✦♠83 ⚜ P40 Lift ℂ ⌁ Mountain Lake
Credit Cards ①②③⑤
★*Asnigo* pza San Stefano ☎(031)510062
✦♠30 ⚜ P40 Lift ℂ ℚ Mountain Lake
Credit Cards ①②③⑤

CERVIA
Ravenna
★★*Buenos Aires* Lungomare G-Deledda 130
☎(0544)973174 tx 550394
Apr-Oct
✦♠62 ⚜ P38 Lift ℂ Beach Sea
Opel-Cervia Oriani ☎(0544) 991390 Ope

CERVINIA-BREUIL
See BREUIL-CERVINIA

CESENA
Forli
★★★*Casali* via Benedetto Croce 81
☎(0547)22745 tx 550480
✦♠48 ⚜ P100 Lift ℂ
Credit Cards ①②③④⑤

CESENATICO
Forli
★★★*Britannia* viale Carducci 129 ☎(0547)80041
tx 550036
21 Apr-16 Sep :Rest closed 21 Apr-25 May & 10-
16 Sep
✦♠44 ⚜ P20 Lift ℂ ⌁ Beach Sea
Credit Cards ①②③④⑤
★★*Internazionale* via Ferrara 7 ☎(0547)80231
Jun-Sep
✦♠51 P50 Lift ℂ ℚ ⌁ Beach Sea
★★★*Torino* viale Carducci 55 (n.rest)
☎(0547)80044
20 May-Sep
✦♠45 P50 Lift ⌁ Beach Sea
Credit Cards ②③⑤
Luciano A-Saffi 91 ☎(0547) 81347 BMW Mer

CHATILLON
Aosta
★★*Marisa* via Pellissier 10 ☎(0166)61845
16 Nov-Oct :Rest closed Thu
✦♠28 ⚜ P16 Lift ℂ Mountain
Credit Cards ①②③⑤

CHIANCIANO TERME
Siena
★★★*Grand Capitol* viale della Libertà 492
☎(0578)64681
Apr-Oct
✦♠68 ⚜ P40 Lift ℂ ⌁ Lake
Credit Cards ②③⑤

CHIAVARI
Genova
★★*Santa Maria* via T-Groppo ☎(0185)309621
:Rest closed Nov
✦♠36 ⚜ P20 Lift ℂ Sea
Credit Cards ①②③④⑤
Cantero corso Dante 90 ☎(0185) 307018 P
G Ughini Nazario Sauro 13-15 ☎(0185) 308278
Aud Mer VW

CHIAVENNA
Sondrio
★★★*Conradi* pza Verdi 10 ☎(0343)32300
:Rest closed Mon
rm38(✦♠26) ⚜ P15 Lift Mountain
Credit Cards ②③⑤

CHIOGGIA
Venezia
★★*Grande Italia* pza Vigo (n.rest) ☎(0343)32300
:Rest closed Tue
rm50(✦♠40)

CIVITAVECCHIA
Roma
SAC Garibaldi 42 ☎(0766) 21830 AR

CÒLICO
Como
★★*Risa* Lungo L-Polti 1
Mar-Oct
✦♠45 P20 Lift
★*Gigi* ☎(0341)940268
:Rest closed Nov-Apr
rm15(♠10) ⚜ P4
Credit Cards ①③

COLLE DI VAL D'ELSA
See SIENA

COMACCHIO
Ferrara
At LIDO DEGLI ESTENSI(7km SE)
★★*Conca del Lido* viale G-Pascoli 42
☎(0533)327459 tx 216149
15 Apr-Sep
rm63(♠59) P30 Lift ℂ ⌁ Sea
Credit Cards ①②③⑤

COMO
Como
★★★*Albergo Firenze* Piazza Volta 16 (n.rest)
☎(031)300333 tx 300101
✦♠25 Lift ℂ Sea Mountain
Credit Cards ②③⑤
★★★*Barchetta Excelsior* pza Cavour 1
☎(031)266531 tx 380435
:Rest closed Sun
✦♠69 ⚜ P10 Lift ℂ ℚ Lake
Credit Cards ①②③⑤
★★★*Como* via Mentana 28 ☎(031)266173
✦♠72 ⚜ P25 Lift ℂ ⌁ Mountain Lake
Credit Cards ①②③⑤
★★★*Flori* via Per Cernobbio 12 ☎(031)557642
✦♠49 ⚜ P10 Lift ℂ Mountain Lake
Credit Cards ①②③④⑤
★★★*Metropole Suisse* pza Cavour 19
☎(031)269444 tx 350426
✦♠72 ⚜ Lift ℂ Lake
Credit Cards ①②③④⑤

★★Engadina viale Rosselli 22 (n.rest)
☎(031)550415
Mar-10 Nov
◀🚗21 P6 Lift ☾

★★Park viale Rosselli 20 (n.rest) ☎(031)556782
Mar-Oct
◀🚗40 P40 Lift ☾ Lake
Credit Cards 1 2 5

★★San Gottardo pza Volta ☎(031)263531
◀🚗60 ☎ P4 Lift ☾ Mountain

Autoimessa Dante via Dante 59 ☎(031) 272545
P Ren

Grassi & Airoldi via Napoleona 50 ☎(031)
266027 AR

CONCA DEI MARINI
Salerno

★★★Belvedere SS 163 ☎(089)831282 tx 770184
Apr-Oct
◀🚗40 ☎ P25 Lift ☾ ⌣ Beach Sea
Credit Cards 1 2 3

CORPO DI CAVA
See **CAVA DE TIRRENI**

CORTE DI CADORE
See **BORCA DI CADORE**

CORTINA D'AMPEZZO
Belluno

★★★★Corona corso C-Battisti (n.rest)
☎(0436)3251 tx 440004
20 Dec-Mar & Jul-15 Sep
rm57(◀🚗46) A11rm ☎ P30 Lift ☾ Mountain
Credit Cards 2 3 5

★★★★Grand Savoia via Roma 62 ☎(0436)3201
tx 440811
20 Dec-4 Apr & 12 Jul-13 Sep
rm142(◀🚗139) ☎ P100 Lift ☾ Mountain

★★★Ancora (ROM) corso Italia 62 ☎(0436)3261
tx 440221
22 Dec-15 Apr & Jul-15 Sep
◀🚗71 ☎ P20 Lift ☾ Mountain
Credit Cards 1 2 3 4 5

★★★AGIP via Roma 70 (SS 51Km 102)
☎(0436)61400
◀🚗28 Lift

★★★Concordia Parc corso Italia 28
☎(0436)4251 tx 440004
22 Dec-25 Mar & 9 Jul-31 Aug
◀🚗60 ☎ P30 Lift ☾ Mountain
Credit Cards 1 2 3

★★★Cortina corso Italia 94 ☎(0436)4221 tx
328507
19 Dec-10 Apr & 25 Jun-15 Sep
◀🚗50 ☎ P20 Lift ☾ Mountain
Credit Cards 1 2 3 4 5

★★★Cristallo (CIGA) via R-Menardi 42
☎(0436)4281 tx 440090
25 Jun-15 Sep & 20 Dec-Mar
◀🚗102 ☎ P Lift ☾ ⌣ ⌣ 🏊🏊 Mountain

★★★Europa corso Italia 207 ☎(0436)3221 tx
440043
◀🚗52 P40 Lift ☾ Mountain
Credit Cards 1 2 3 4 5

★★★Poste pza Roma 14 ☎(0436)4271 tx
440044
20 Dec-10 Oct
◀🚗81 ☎ P55 Lift ☾ ⍩ 🏊 Mountain
Credit Card 2

★★Alpes via La Verra 2 ☎(0436)862021 tx
440066
20 Dec-Etr & Jul-Sep :Rest closed Wed
rm30(◀🚗21) P30 Mountain

★★San Marco pza Roma 6 ☎(0436)866941 tx
440066
20 Jun-10 Oct & 20 Dec-10 Apr
rm25(◀🚗22) P14 ☾ Mountain
Credit Cards 1 2 3 5

Dolomiti corsa Italia ☎(0436) 861077 **P** Fia Lan

COSENZA
Cosenza

At **RENDE**(6km NW)

★★★AGIP ☎(0984)839101
◀🚗65 P Lift ☾

COURMAYEUR
Aosta

★★★★Royal & Golf via Roma 87
☎(0165)843621 tx 214312
Dec-Apr & Jul-Aug
◀🚗100 A4rm ☎ P30 Lift ☾ ⌣ Mountain
Credit Cards 2 3

★★★★Palace Bron Verso Plan Gorret (2km E)
☎(0165)842545 tx 211085
Dec-Apr & Jul-Sep
◀🚗27 P30 Lift ☾ Mountain
Credit Cards 2 3 5

★★★★Pavillon Strada Regionale 60
☎(0165)842420 tx 210541
3 Dec-20 Apr & 20 Jun-20 Sep
◀🚗40 ☎ P15 Lift ☾ ⌣ Mountain
Credit Cards 1 2 3 5

CREMONA
Cremona

General Cars Catelleone 77-79 ☎(0372) 20343
Ope Vau

At **SAN FELICE**(5km E)

★★★AGIP San Felice ☎(0372)43101
◀🚗77 P Lift ☾

DESENZANO DEL GARDA
Brescia

★★★Mayer & Splendid pza del Porto
☎(030)9141409
15 Mar-15 Nov
rm55(◀🚗54) ☎ P15 Lift Lake
Credit Cards 1 2 3 5

★★★Ramazzotti viale Dal Molin 78 (n.rest)
☎(030)9141808 tx 300395
Apr-Sep
rm22(◀🚗10) ☎ P

★★Europa ☎(030)9142333
Mar-Oct
rm37(◀🚗31) ☎ P Lift Lake

★★Vittorio Portovecchio 4 ☎(030)9108117
◀🚗40 P15 Lift ☾ Lake
Credit Cards 1 3 5

DIANO MARINA
Imperia

★★★★Diana Majestic via Degli Oleandri 15
☎(0183)495445 tx 271025
Apr-15 Oct
rm82(◀🚗78) A22rm ☎ P50 Lift ☾ ⌣ Beach Sea

★★★Bellevue & Mediterranée via GI-Ardoino 2
☎(0183)495089
rm71(◀🚗64) ☎ P60 Lift ☾ ⌣ Beach Sea
Credit Cards 2 3 4 5

ELBA, ISOLA D'
Livorno

LACONA

★★★Capo Sud ☎(0565)964021
May-Sep
◀🚗39 ☎ P40 ☾ ⍩ Beach Sea
Credit Card 5

PORTO AZZURRO

★★★Elba International ☎968611 tx 590669
Apr-Sep
◀🚗242 Lift ☾ ⍩ Beach Sea

★★Belmare DPn ☎(0565)95012 tx 590276
:Rest closed Fri Nov-Dec
◀🚗27 P ☾ Sea
Credit Cards 1 2 3 5

PORTOFERRAIO

★★★Hermitage ☎(0565)969932 tx 500219
May-Sep
◀🚗100 P100 Lift ☾ ⍩ Beach Sea
Credit Card 2

PROCCHIO

★★★★Golfo Lido Di Procchio ☎(0565)907565 tx
290690
22 May-26 Sep
◀🚗98 ☎ P180 ☾ ⍩ Beach Sea
Credit Cards 1 2 3

At **SPARTAIA**

★★★Desirée ☎(0565)907311 tx 590649
15 Apr-15 Oct
◀🚗69 P60 ☾ ⍩ Beach Sea
Credit Cards 1 2 3 5

EMPOLI
Firenze

★★Tazza d'Oro via del Papa 46 ☎(0571)72129
tx 530378
:Rest closed Sun
rm56(◀🚗51) Lift ☾
Credit Cards 1 2 3 5

FABRO
Umbria

★★Fabro Contrada della Stazione 70
☎(0763)82063
rm15(◀🚗10) P30 ☾

FERIOLO
See **BAVENO**

FERRARA
Ferrara

★★★Astra viale Cavour 55 ☎(0532)26234 tx
226150
:Rest closed Sun in Aug
◀🚗82 ☎ Lift ☾
Credit Cards 1 2 3 5

SIRA ☎(0532) 93275 For

FIESOLE
Firenze

★★★★Villa San Michele (Relais et Châteaux)
DPn via Doccia 4 ☎(055)59451 tx 570643
Mar-Nov
◀🚗27 P20 ☾ ⍩
Credit Cards 1 2 3 5

★★Villa Bonelli DPn via F-Poeti 1 ☎(055)59513
:Rest closed Nov-Mar
rm23(◀🚗14) ☎ P8 Lift ☾ Mountain
Credit Cards 1 2 3 5

FINALE LIGURE
Savona

At **VARIGOTTI**(6km SE)

★★★Nik-Mehari via Aurelia 104 ☎(019)698030
◀🚗40 ☎ P Lift ☾ Beach Sea

FIRENZE (FLORENCE)
Firenze

See Plan page 271
Firenze, spread along both banks
of the timeless River Arno, is an
exquisite treasure chest of
paintings, sculptures and
terracotta-domed buildings, a
tribute to artists such as Da
Vinci, Botticelli and Michelangelo
from a glorious golden age which
lasted three centuries. Places of
interest are all within walking
distance of each other, and now
that more of the historic centre
has been closed to coaches and
visiting vehicles, sightseeing is a
more leisurely affair.
If any one building could be said
to epitomise the entire city, then

it must surely be the *Duomo* (Cathedral), created by the architect Brunelleschi,whose marvellous dome is proof of Renaissance ingenuity. In front of the cathedral is Giotto's handsome campanile, and Ghiberti's famous gilded bronze doors.

Other architectural gems worth exploring include the pretty churches of San Miniato, across the river; Santa Maria Novella, near the station, with its many famous works of art; and Santa Croce, containing the tombs of Michelangelo, Machiavelli and Galileo.

Renowned galleries include the world-famous *Uffizi*; the grand *Palazzo Veccio*, the *Palazzo Pitti*, with paintings by Titian, Rubens and Raphael; the *Accademia*, housing some of Michelangelo's most powerful statues, including the impressive *David*, originally on the Piazza della Signoria; and other museums like the *Bargello* and *San Marco*.

Shoppers will delight in the Via Tornabuoni, one of the most elegant streets in the world, and the Ponte Vecchio, the world-famous bridge lined with goldsmiths' and jewellers' shops. The biggest market is in the Piazza San Lorenzo (Tuesday to Sunday). The remarkable Straw Market, the *Logge Mercato Nuovo*, near Piazza della Signoria, sells everything from baskets to men's ties made from straw.

EATING OUT *Enoteca Pinchiorri*, in Via Ghebellina, enjoys a reputation as one of the best restaurants in Florence. Much less expensive but with a high reputation for its regional specialities is the atmospheric *Angiolino*, in Via Santo Spirito. Firenze specilities include *bistecca alla fiorentina*, a huge steak usually charcoal-grilled; *fegatelli*, slices of liver rolled in chopped fennel flowers; *bruschetta*, a type of garlic bread with olive oil; or *baccala*, a robust cod stew. For starters, look out for delicious *prosciutto crudo con fichi*, raw ham with fresh figs.

Moderately priced restaurants are to be found near Piazza Santa Croce, Borgo San Lorenzo or San Jacopo.

FIRENZE (FLORENCE)

★★★★★*Excelsior Italia* (CIGA) pza Ognissanti 3
☎(055)264201 tx 570022
⫩205 ⌂ P20 Lift ℂ
Credit Cards ①②③④⑤

★★★★★*Savoy* pza della Repubblica 7
☎(055)283313 tx 570220
⫩101 Lift ℂ
Credit Cards ①②③⑤

★★★★★*Villa Medici* (SRS) via il Prato 42
☎(055)261331 tx 570179
⫩108 P Lift ℂ ⌿
Credit Cards ①②③⑤

★★★★*Grandhotel Baglioni* (BW) pza Unita Italiana 6 ☎(055)218441 tx 570225
⫩195 P Lift ℂ
Credit Cards ①②③⑤

★★★★*Jolly* pza V-Veneto 4a ☎(055)2770 tx 570191
⫩167 P Lift ℂ ⌿
Credit Cards ①②③④⑤

★★★★*Londra* (GT) via Jacopo da Diacceto 16-20 ☎(055)262791 tx 571152
⫩107 ⌂ P35 Lift ℂ
Credit Cards ①②③④⑤

★★★★*Minerva* pza Santa Maria Novella 16
☎(055)284555 tx 570414
⫩107 ⌂ P6 Lift ℂ ⌿
Credit Cards ①②③⑤

★★★*Adriatico* via Maso Finiguerra 9
☎(055)261781 tx 572265
⫩114 P30 Lift ℂ
Credit Cards ①②③⑤

★★★*AGIP* Autostrada del Sole,Raccordo Firenze-Mare ☎(055)44081 tx 570263
⫩156 P Lift ℂ

★★★*Crest* viale Europa 205 ☎(055)686841 tx 570376
⫩92 P Lift ℂ
Credit Cards ①②③④⑤

★★★*Croce di Malta* (BW) via della Scala 7
☎(055)211740 tx 570540
:Rest Sun & Mon lunch
⫩98 ⌂ Lift ℂ ⌿
Credit Cards ①②③⑤

★★★*Pierre* via Lamberti 5 (n.rest) ☎(055)216218 tx 573175
⫩39 ⌂ Lift ℂ
Credit Cards ②③⑤

★★★*Regency* (Relais et Châteaux) pza d'Azeglio 3 ☎(055)245247 tx 571058
:Rest closed Sun
⫩38 ⌂ P40 Lift ℂ
Credit Cards ①②③⑤

★★★*Roma* pza Santa Maria Novella 8 (n.rest)
☎(055)210366 tx 575831
⫩66 ⌂ P20 Lift ℂ
Credit Cards ②③⑤

★★★*Villa Belvedere* Via Benedetto Castelli 3 (n.rest) ☎(055)222501 tx 575648
Mar-Nov
⫩27 P30 Lift ℂ ⌿
Credit Cards ①②③

★★*Basilea* via Guelfa 41 ☎(055)214587 tx 571689
⫩59 ⌂ P6 Lift ℂ
Credit Cards ①②③④⑤

★★*Liana* via Vittorio Alfieri 18 (n.rest)
☎(055)245303
rm22(⫩14) P17 ℂ
Credit Cards ②③

★★*Rapallo* via S Caterina d'Alessandria 7
☎(055)472412 tx 574251
rm30(⫩20) ⌂ P3 Lift ℂ
Credit Cards ①②③④⑤

Europa ☎(055) 219817 **P** Ope Vol

M Ronchi ☎(055) 489855 For

FIRENZE (FLORENCE)

1	★★★★★	Excelsior Italia
3	★★★★★	Savoy
4	★★★★★	Villa Medici
5	★★★★	Grandhotel Baglioni
6	★★★★	Jolly
7	★★★★	Londra
8	★★★★	Minerva
9	★★★★	Villa Massa (At Candeli)
10	★★★	Adriatico
11	★★★	AGIP
13	★★★	Crest
14	★★★	Croce di Malta
17	★★★	Pierre
18	★★★	Regency
19	★★★	Roma
20	★★★	Villa Belvedere
23	★★	Basilea
27	★★	Liana
28	★★	Rapallo
30	★★	Villa Villoresi (At Sesto Florentino)

Zaniratti ☎(055) 357661 AR Vol

At **CANDELI**(6km SE)

★★★★*Villa Massa* ☎(055)630051 tx 573555
:Rest closed Mon Nov-Mar
⫩40 A13rm P200 Lift ℂ ⌿ ⌂ Mountain
Credit Cards ①②③⑤

At **SESTO FIORENTINO**(9km NW)

★★*Villa Villoresi* ☎(055)4489032
⫩30 P ⌿

FOGGIA
Foggia

★★★*Cicolella* viale 24 Maggio 60 ☎(0881)3890 tx 810273
:Rest closed Sat, Sun & 1-20 Aug 24 Dec-6 Jan
⫩125 ⌂ P Lift ℂ
Credit Cards ①②③⑤

FOLIGNO
Perugia

★★★*Umbria* via C-Battisti 3 ☎(0742)52821
⫩47 P25 Lift ℂ Mountain
Credit Cards ①②③④⑤

FORIO
See **ISCHIA, ISOLA D'**

FORTE DEI MARMI
Lucca

★★★★*Augustus* DPn viale Morin 169
☎(0584)80202 tx 590673
15 May-Sep
⫩70 A27rm P81 Lift ℂ ⌿ ⌂ Beach
Credit Cards ①②③⑤

★★★*Alcione* viale Morin 137 ☎(0584)89952
Jun-Sep
rm45(⫩40) P30 Lift ℂ
Credit Cards ②③④⑤

★★★*Astoria Garden* via Leonardo-da-Vinci 10
☎(0584)80754 tx 501383
15 May-30 Sep
⫩40 ⌂ P20 Lift ℂ Beach Sea
Credit Cards ①②③⑤

★★★*Byron* viale Morin 46 ☎(0584)80087
May-Oct
⫩40 A5rm P30 Lift ℂ ⌿
Credit Cards ①②③④⑤

★★★*Raffaelli Park* (BW) DPn via Mazzini 37
☎(0584)81494 tx 590239
⫩28 A6rm P50 Lift ℂ ⌿ ⌷ Beach
Credit Cards ①②③⑤

★★★*Raffaelli Villa Angela* via G-Mazzini 64
☎(0584)80652 tx 590239
May-10 Oct
⫩33 A15rm P50 Lift ℂ ⌿ ⌂ Beach
Credit Cards ①③⑤

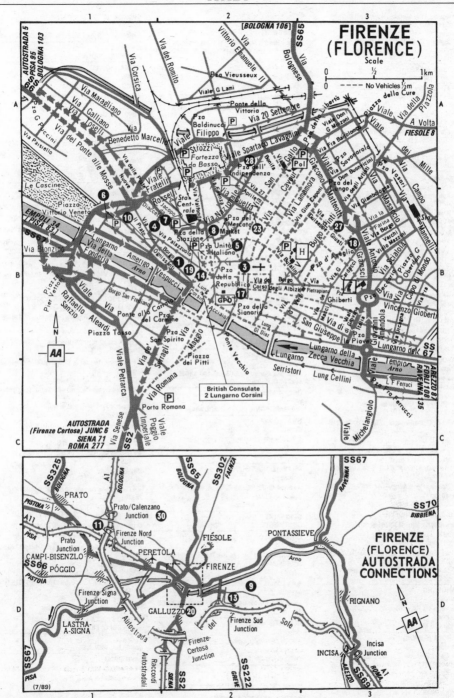

FIRENZE (FLORENCE)

Scale

0 ½ 1km
0 ½m — No Vehicles

[BOLOGNA 106]

British Consulate
2 Lungarno Corsini

AUTOSTRADA
(Firenze Certosa) JUNC 6
SIENA 71
ROMA 277

FIRENZE (FLORENCE) AUTOSTRADA CONNECTIONS

(7/89)

★★**Adams Villa Maria** Lungomare 110
☎(0584)80901 tx 83666
Apr-Sep
➜⋔38 A2rm ⌘ P50 Lift ℂ ⌒ Beach Sea
Mountain
Credit Cards ① ② ③ ⑤

GABBICE MARE
Pesaro & Urbino

★★★**Alexander** via Panoramica 35
☎(0541)954166 tx 550535
May-Sep
➜⋔50 P50 Lift ℂ ⌒ Sea
Credit Cards ② ⑤

★★**Club de Bona** via Panoramica 33
☎(0775)962622 tx 550535
May-Sep
➜⋔50 ⌘ P24 Lift ℂ ⌒ Beach Sea
Credit Cards ② ③ ⑤

GALLARATE
Varese

★★**Astoria** pza Risorgimento 9A (n.rest)
☎(0331)791043 tx 351005
➜⋔50 ⌘ P Lift ℂ
Credit Cards ① ② ③ ⑤

GARDA
Verona

★★★★**Eurotel** via Gardesana 18 ☎(045)7255107
tx 431299
Apr-20 Oct
➜⋔143 ⌘ P Lift ℂ ℃ ⌒ Lake
Credit Cards ① ② ③ ⑤

★★★**Regina Adelaide Palace** via 20 Settembre
☎(045)7255013 tx 341078
➜⋔56 A4rm P Lift ℂ Lake
Credit Cards ① ② ③

★★**Tre Corone** via Lungolago 44 ☎(045)7255033
Mar-Oct
➜⋔26 P8 Lift Lake

GARDONE RIVIERA
Brescia

★★★★**Grand** via Zanardelli 72 ☎(0365)20261 tx
300254
Apr-Oct
➜⋔180 P20 Lift ℂ ⌒ Beach Lake
Credit Cards ① ② ③ ⑤

★★★**Lac** Corso Repubblica 58 ☎(0365)20124
Apr-15 Oct
rm30(➜⋔17) Lift Lake

★★★**Monte Baldo** ☎(0365)20951
25 Apr-Sep :Rest closed Thur
rm46(➜⋔40) A15rm P38 Lift ℂ ⌒ Lake
Credit Cards ② ③

★★**Bellevue** via Zanardelli 44 ☎(0365)20235
Apr-10 Oct
➜⋔33 ⌘ P30 Lift Lake

At **BARBARANO**(1km W)

★★★**Astoria** ☎(0365)20761 tx 301088
➜⋔90 ⌘ P50 Lift ℂ ⌒ Lake
Credit Cards ① ② ③ ⑤

★★★**Spiaggia d'Oro** (BW) ☎(0365)20764 tx
301088
➜⋔42 ⌘ P30 Lift ℂ ℃ ⌒ Beach Lake
Credit Cards ① ② ③ ⑤

GARGNANO
Brescia

★**Europa** via Repubblica 40 ☎(0365)71191
Apr-Oct
➜⋔20 P20 Mountain Lake

GENOVA (GENOA)
Genova

★★★★★**Colombia** (CIGA) via Balbi 40
☎(010)261841 tx 270423
rm172 P15 Lift ℂ
Credit Cards ① ② ③ ⑤

★★★★**Plaza** via M-Piaggio 11 ☎(010)893641 tx
283142

:Rest closed Sat & Sun
➜⋔97 ⌘ P20 Lift ℂ
Credit Cards ① ② ③ ⑤

★★★★**Savoia Majestic** (SRS) via Arsenale di
Terra 5,Stazione Centrale Principe ☎(010)261641
tx 270426
➜⋔120 A54rm ⌘ P150 Lift ℂ
Credit Cards ① ② ③ ⑤

ARA via Marsillio de Padova ☎(010) 317388

Dilia C-E-Mello Rosselli 18 ☎(010) 300430 For

B Koelliker corso Europa 810 ☎(010) 3993241
AR

Oram via G-Bandi 10 Quarto ☎(010) 384653 DJ
Vol

XX-Settembre ☎(010) 511941 **P** Cit

GENZANO DI ROMA
Roma

★★**Villa Robinia** viale Frattelli Rosselli 19
☎(06)9396409
➜⋔30 P30 Lift ℂ

GHIFFA
Novara

★★★**Ghiffa** via Belvedere 88-90 ☎(0323)59285 tx
200285
Apr-Sep
rm24(➜⋔19) ⌘ P30 Lift ℂ Lake
Credit Cards ① ② ③ ④

GIOIA DEL COLLE
Bari

Carrozzeria via Santeramo 120 ☎(080) 830417 **P**
Ren

GIOIA TAURO
Reggio di Calabria

★★★**Mediterraneo** via Nazionale ☎(0966)51854
➜⋔55 ⌘ P Lift ℂ
Credit Cards ① ② ③ ⑤

GIULIANOVA LIDO
Teramo

Ubaldo & Forlini via G-Galilei 180 ☎(085)
862771 Ope Vau

GOLFO ARANCI
Sassari
See **SARDEGNA, ISOLA (SARDINIA)**

GRAVEDONA
Como

★**Turismo** ☎(0344)85227
Mar-Nov :Rest closed Thu
rm12(➜7) ⌘ P20 Mountain Lake

GRAVELLONA TOCE
Novara

★**Helios** ☎(0323)848096
:Rest closed Mon
rm19(➜⋔11) P15 Mountain

GRIGNANO
See **TRIESTE**

GROSSETO
Grosseto

★★★**AGIP** SS 1 km 179 exit Roma
☎(0564)24100
➜⋔32 P

★★★**Lorena** via Trieste 3 ☎(0564)25501
➜⋔66 ⌘ P Lift ℂ

Morelli via Privata dei Curiazi 13 ☎(0564) 23000
AR Vol

GUBBIO
Perugia

★★**Tre Ceri** via Benamati 6 ☎(075)9273304
➜⋔38 P10 Lift ℂ
Credit Cards ② ③ ④

IESOLO
See **JESOLO, LIDO DI**

IGEA MARINA
See **BELLARIA IGEA MARINA**

IMPERIA
Imperia

Riviera Motori viale Matteotti ☎(0183) 20297 AR

ISCHIA
See **ISCHIA, ISOLA D'**

ISCHIA, ISOLA D'
Napoli

FORIO

★★**Splendid** (1km N) ☎(081)987374
Apr-Oct
➜⋔40 P15 ℂ ⌒ Sea
Credit Cards ① ② ③ ⑤

ISCHIA

★★★★**Jolly** via A.De Luca 42 ☎(081)991744 tx
710267
Mar-Oct
➜⋔208 P Lift ℂ ⌒ ⌒
Credit Cards ① ② ③ ④ ⑤

IVREA
Torino

★★**Eden** corso Massimo d'Azeglio 67 (n.rest)
☎(0125)49190
rm40(➜⋔36) ⌘ P23 Lift ℂ Mountain
Credit Card ③

M Peroni via S-Lorenzo 10 ☎(0125) 422022 VW

JESOLO, LIDO DI
Venezia

★★★★**Las Vegas** via Mascagni 2 (n.rest)
☎(0421)971515 tx 223535
6 May-24 Sep
➜⋔104 P70 Lift ℂ ⌒ Beach Sea
Credit Cards ① ② ③ ⑤

★★★**Anthony** via Padova 25 ☎(0421)971711 tx
420142
Apr-Oct
➜⋔68 P Lift ℂ ℃ ⌒ Beach Sea
Credit Cards ② ⑤

★★★**Cesare Augustus** ☎(0421)90971 tx 410423
May-Sep
➜⋔120 P Lift ℂ ⌒ Beach Sea

★★★**London** via Dalmazia 64 ☎(0421)90988
May-Sep
rm84(➜⋔82) P Lift ℂ Beach Sea
Credit Card ②

★★★**Ritz** via Zanella 2 ☎(0421)90861
May-25 Sep
➜⋔48 P30 Lift ℂ ⌒ Beach Sea

★★**Regina** via Bafile 115 ☎(0421)380383 tx
410433
May-Sep
➜⋔50 Lift ℂ Beach Sea

★★**Termini** via Altinate 32 ☎(0421)962312 tx
223491
20 Apr-4 Oct
➜⋔45 P50 Lift ℂ ℃ ⌒ ⌒ U Beach Sea

Brusa pza Mazzini ☎(0421) 972314 For

At **JESOLO PINETA**(6km E)

★★★**Bellevue** via Oriente 100 ☎(0421)961233 tx
410433
15 May-15 Sep
➜⋔64 P Lift ℂ ℃ Beach Sea

★★**Danmark** Via Airone 1/3 ☎(0421)961013 tx
410433
May-Sep
rm58(➜⋔50) P48 ℂ ⌒ Beach Sea

JESOLO PINETA
See **JESOLO, LIDO DI**

LACONA
See **ELBA, ISOLA D'**

LAIGUEGLIA
Savona

★★★**Aquilia** via Asti 1 ☎(0182)49040
Apr-Oct
➜⋔40 ⌘ P25 Lift Beach Sea

★★***Mariolina*** via Concezione 15 ☎(0182)49024
Apr-Sep
→⌐22 Beach Sea
Credit Card [1]

★★***Splendid*** pza Badaro 4 ☎(0182)49325
Etr-Sep
→⌐50 P30 Beach Sea
Credit Cards [2] [3] [5]

★★***Windsor*** pza 25 Aprile 7 ☎(0182)49000
→⌐53 Lift Beach Sea
Credit Card [2]

LAINATE
Milano

★**Golf** via Manzoni 45 ☎(02)9370869 & 9374401 tx 324354
→⌐34 P50 ☾ ⚲ ⌓
Credit Cards [1] [2] [3] [4] [5]

LAVAGNA
Genova

★★**Tigullio** via Matteotti 3 ☎(0185)392965
Apr-Oct :Rest closed Mon
rm40(→⌐32) ⌂ P4 Lift Sea

At **CAVI**(3km SE)

★**Scogliera** (n.rest) ☎(0185)390072
Jun-10 Sep
→⌐22 P20 Beach Sea

LEGHORN
See **LIVORNO**

LENNO
Como

★★**San Giorgio** via Regina 81 (n.rest) ☎(0344)40415
Apr-Sep
rm29(→⌐27) ⌂ P30 Lift ☾ ⚲ Mountain Lake
Credit Cards [1] [3]

LERICI
la Spezia

★★★**Doria** via A-Doria (n.rest) ☎(0187)967124
rm42(→31) P60 Lift ☾ Sea
Credit Cards [1] [2] [3] [5]

★★***Italia*** ☎(0187)967108
→⌐16 P Sea

LEVANTO
la Spezia

★★★***Crystal*** via Vallesanta ☎(0187)808261
15 Jun-Sep
rm16(→⌐14) A9rm P ☾ Sea

★★***Carla*** via M-della-Liberta 28 ☎(0187)808275
3 Jan-4 Nov
→⌐36 P20 Lift Sea
Credit Cards [1] [3]

★**Garden** corso Italia 6 ☎(0187)808173
Apr-Sep
rm18 Lift Sea
Credit Cards [1] [2] [3] [4] [5]

LEVICO TERME
Trento

★★★**Grand Bellavista** via V-Emanuele 7 ☎(0461)706136
May-15 Oct
→⌐78 P50 Lift ☾ ⌓ Mountain Lake
Credit Cards [1] [3]

LIDO DEGLI ESTENSI
See **COMACCHIO**

LIDO DI CAMAIORE
See**CAMAIORE, LIDO DI**

LIGNANO PINETA
See **LIGNANO SABBIADORO**

LIGNANO RIVIERA
See **LIGNANO SABBIADORO**

LIGNANO SABBIADORO
Udine

At **LIGNANO PINETA**(5km SW)

★★★**Medusa Splendid DPn** Arco dello Scirocco 13 ☎(0431)422211 & 422251
15 May-15 Sep
→⌐56 P50 Lift ☾ ⌓ Beach Sea
Credit Cards [1] [2] [3] [5]

At **LIGNANO RIVIERA**(7km SW)

★★★***Eurotel*** calle Mendelssohn 13 ☎(0431)428992 tx 450211
14 May-26 Sep
→⌐60 P Lift ☾ ⌓ Beach Sea
Credit Cards [1] [2] [3] [5]

LIVORNO (LEGHORN)
Livorno

★★★***Giappone*** via Grande 65 ☎(0586)880241
→⌐60 ⌂
Credit Cards [1] [2] [3] [5]

At **STAGNO**(5km N on SS1)

★★★***AGIP*** (SS1 Km320) ☎(0586)943067 tx 611627
→⌐50 P Lift ☾

LOANO
Savona

★★★***Garden Lido*** Lungomare N-Sauro 9 ☎(019)669666 tx 213178
→⌐95 ⌂ P Lift ⌓ Beach Sea
Credit Cards [1] [2] [3] [5]

LONE
See **AMALFI**

LUCCA
Lucca

At **MASSA PISANA**(4.5km S)

★★★***Villa la Principessa*** (Relais et Châteaux) ☎(0583)370037 tx 590068
21 Feb-Nov
→⌐44 P50 Lift ☾ ⌓
Credit Cards [1] [2] [3] [5]

MACERATA
Macerata

★★★***AGIP*** via Roma 149B,SS 77 Km 89 ☎(0733)34248 tx 11627
→⌐51 P Lift ☾

MACOMER
Nuoro
See **SARDEGNA, ISOLA (SARDINIA)**

MACUGNAGA
Novara

★★***Cristallo*** Franzione Pecetto ☎(0324)65139
Jun-Sep & Dec-Apr
rm21(→17) ⌂ P25 Mountain
Credit Cards [1] [2] [3] [5]

MADONNA DI CAMPIGLIO
Trento

★★★**Savoia** ☎(0465)41004 tx 400882
Dec-10 Apr
→⌐57 ⌂ P25 Lift ☾
Credit Cards [2] [5]

★★**Golf** ☎(0465)41003 tx 400882
20 Dec-5 Apr & 16 Jul-25 Aug
→⌐124 P120 Lift ☾ ⛳ Mountain
Credit Cards [1] [2] [3] [5]

MAIORI
Salerno

★★★**San Francesco** via S-Tecla 54 ☎(089)877070
15 Mar-15 Oct
→⌐44 Lift ☾ Beach Sea
Credit Cards [1] [2]

MALCESINE
Verona

★★★**Lac** via Gardesana 18 ☎(045)7400156 tx 430567
Apr-Oct
→⌐40 ⌂ P35 Lift ☾ ⌓ Lake

★★**Vega DPn** via Roma 10 ☎(045)7400151 tx 480448
Apr-Oct
→⌐19 P15 Lift Beach Mountain Lake
Credit Cards [1] [2] [3] [5]

MANTOVA
Mantova

★★***Apollo*** pza Don Leoni 17 (n.rest) ☎(0376)350522
→⌐35 ⌂ P20 Lift ☾
Credit Cards [1] [2] [3] [4] [5]

★★**Broletto** via Accademia 1 (n.rest) ☎(0376)326784
Closed 24-31 Dec
→⌐16 Lift ☾
Credit Cards [1] [2] [3] [4] [5]

Filipini via Curtatone & Montanara 58 ☎(0376) 329696 Aud Por VW

MARATEA
Potenza

★★★★**Santavenere** ☎(0973)876910
Apr-Oct
rm44(→⌐42) A5rm P35 ☾ ⚲ ⌓ Beach Sea Mountain
Credit Cards [1] [2] [3] [5]

MARGHERA
See **MESTRE**

MARINA DI CARRARA
See **CARRARA, MARINA DI**

MARINA DI MASSA
See**MASSA, MARINA DI**

MARINA DI PIETRASANTA
See**PIETRASANTA, MARINA DI**

MARSALA
Trapani
See **SICILIA, ISOLA (SICILY)**

MASSA, MARINA DI
Massa Carrara

★★★**Marina** viale Magliano 3 ☎(0585)245261
15 May-Sep
→⌐30 P16 ☾ Beach Mountain

MASSA PISANA
See **LUCCA**

MATELICA
Macerata

★★★***AGIP*** SS 256 Muccese Km 29 ☎(0737)82381 tx 611627
→⌐16 P

MAZZARÒ
See **SICILIA, ISOLA (SICILY)** under **TAORMINA**

MEINA
Novara

★***Bel Sit*** via Sempione 76 ☎03226483
Mar-Oct
→⌐12 ⌂ P10 Lake
Credit Cards [1] [2] [3] [5]

MENAGGIO
Como

★★★***Bella Vista*** via IV Novembre 9 ☎(0344)32136
Apr-15 Oct
→⌐40 ⌂ P15 Lift Mountain Lake
Credit Cards [1] [2] [3] [5]

★★**Loveno** via N-Sauro M37 ☎(0344)32110
Apr-Oct
rm13(→10) A5rm ⌂ P8 Mountain Lake
Credit Cards [1] [3]

At **NOBIALLO**(1km N)

★★***Miralago*** via Diaz 26 ☎(0344)32363
Apr-Oct
rm28(→23) ⌂ P Lake

MERANO-MERAN
Bolzano

★★★★***Grand Bristol*** via O-Huber 14 ☎(0473)49500 tx 400662
15 Mar-Oct
→⌐146 ⌂ P40 Lift ☾ ⌓ Mountain
Credit Cards [1] [2] [3] [5]

★★★*Adria* via Gilm 2 ☎(0473)36610 tx 401011
28 Mar-Oct
⇝51 A9rm P25 Lift ☾ ▣ ⌓ Mountain

★★★**Augusta** via O-Huber 2 ☎(0473)49570 & 49119 tx 400632
Apr-Oct
⇝26 ⌂ P15 Lift ☾ Mountain
Credit Cards [1] [3]

★★★*Eurotel Merano* via Garibaldi 5 ☎(0473)34900 tx 400471
Mar-Oct
⇝125 ⌂ Lift ☾ Mountain
Credit Cards [1] [2] [3] [4] [5]

★★★*Mirabella* via Garibaldi 35 ☎(0473)36512
23 Mar-3 Nov
⇝30 ⌂ Lift ☾ ▣ ⌓ Mountain

★★★*Palace* via Cavour 2 ☎(0473)400256
Mar-Nov & Xmas
⇝120 P80 Lift ☾ ▣ ⌓ Mountain
Credit Cards [1] [2] [3] [5]

★★**Irma** via Belvedere 17 ☎(0473)30124 tx 401089
Mar-Nov
⇝50 A2rm P30 Lift ☾ ⚲ ▣ ⌓ Mountain

★★*Regina* via Cavour 101 (n.rest) ☎(0473)33432 tx 401595
15 Mar-Oct
⇝80 ⌂ P15 Lift ☾ ⌓ Mountain
Credit Cards [1] [2] [3] [5]

★**Westend** ☎(0473)47654 tx 401606
15 Mar-10 Nov
⇝22 P8 Lift ☾ Mountain
Credit Cards [1] [2] [3] [5]

MESSINA
Messina
See **SICILIA, ISOLA (SICILY)**

MESTRE
Venezia
See also VENEZIA (VENICE)

★★★**Ambasciatori** corso del Popolo 221 ☎(041)5310699 tx 410445
⇝97 ⌂ P60 Lift ☾
Credit Cards [1] [2] [3] [4] [5]

★★★**Bologna & Stazione** pza Stazione,via Piave 214 ☎(041)931000 tx 410678
⇝132 P50 Lift ☾
Credit Cards [1] [2] [3] [5]

★★★**Plaza** pza Stazione 36 ☎(041)929388 tx 410490
⇝226 ⌂ P30 Lift ☾
Credit Cards [1] [2] [3] [5]

★★★**President** via Forte Marghera 99 (n.rest) ☎(041)985655
⇝51 ⌂ P15 Lift ☾
Credit Cards [1] [2] [3] [5]

★★★*Sirio* via Circonvallazione 109 ☎(041)949194 tx 410626
⇝100 ⌂ P40 Lift ☾
Credit Cards [1] [2] [3] [5]

★★★**Tritone** pza Stazione 16 (n.rest) ☎(041)930955 tx 411188
⇝67 P Lift ☾
Credit Cards [1] [2] [3] [5]

★★**Aurora** pza G Bruno 15 (n.rest) ☎(041)989832
⇝28 P10 Lift ☾
Credit Card [3]

★★**Venezia** pza XXVII Ottobre ☎(041)985533 tx 410693
⇝100 ⌂ P60 Lift ☾
Credit Cards [1] [2] [3] [5]

Autolambro SAS ☎(041) 5311322 For

Caldera via Piave 182 ☎(041) 929611 Fia

Crivellari via le Stazione 34 ☎(041) 929225 **P** Fia

Damiami & Giorgio ☎(041) 5310844 For

S Lorenzo via Giustizia 27 ☎(041) 926722 **P** Ope Vau

At **MARGHERA**(1km S)

★★**Lugano** via Rizzardi 11 ☎(041)936777 & 920111 tx 411155
⇝62 P16 Lift ☾ ⌓
Credit Cards [1] [2] [3] [4] [5]

MILANO (MILAN)
Milano

See Plan page 276

Rapidly rivalling Paris as Europe's fashion capital, Milano beckons life's connoisseurs. Elegant shops along the Corso Venezia and Corso Vitorio Emanuele rarely fail to inspire a spending spree, while enjoying an aperitif in one of the many cafés of the elaborate Galleria can be just as memorable. Tourist highlights revolve round the Piazza del Duomo and the white marbled cathedral, third largest in the world, where only the voices of *La Scala* opera house rise higher. You can gaze in awe at Leonardo da Vinci's *Last Supper* in Santa Maria delle Grazie.

EATING OUT Delicious starters to look out for in Milano's many and varied restaurants include *antipasto misto*, which usually comprises salami, olives, radishes, fennel and pickled mushrooms; and minestrone soup, made from mixed vegetables and tomatoes and served with a sprinkling of grated Parmesan cheese. Other local specialities are lake perch and trout and seafood fried in batter. Milan is famous for its ice creams, which make delicious desserts. Regional cheeses include *gorgonzola, mascarpone* and *Bel Paese*.
The oldest restaurant in Milano is *Boeucc*, in Piazza Belgioso, near *La Scala* opera house, which specialises in traditional Milanese cuisine. In the moderately priced category *Antica Brasera Meneghina*, in Via Circo, has a lovely garden for *al fresco* dining in summer.

MILANO (MILAN)

★★★★★**Diána Majestic** (CIGA) viale Piáve 42 (n.rest) ☎(02)203404 & 202122 tx 333047
⇝94 P20 Lift ☾
Credit Cards [1] [2] [3] [4] [5]

★★★★★**Excelsior-Gallia** (SRS) pza Duca d'Aosta 9 ☎(02)6277 tx 311160
⇝266 Lift ☾
Credit Cards [1] [2] [3] [5]

★★★★★*Palace* (CIGA) pza della Repubblica 20 ☎(02)6336 tx 311026
⇝199 ⌂ P Lift ☾

★★★★ **Principe di Savoia** (CIGA) pza della Repubblica 17 ☎(02)6230 tx 310052
⇝285 ⌂ P20 Lift ☾
Credit Cards [1] [2] [3] [4] [5]

★★★★**Duomo** via San Raffaele 1 ☎(02)8833 tx 312086
⇝160 P6 Lift ☾
Credit Cards [1] [3] [4]

★★★★**Hilton International** via Galvani 12 ☎(02)69831 tx 330433
⇝332 ⌂ Lift ☾
Credit Cards [1] [2] [3] [4] [5]

★★★★**Jolly President** Largo Augusto 10 ☎(02)7746 tx 312054
⇝220 ⌂ Lift ☾
Credit Cards [1] [2] [3] [4] [5]

★★★★**Jolly Touring** via U.Tarchetti 2 ☎(02)6335 tx 320118
⇝270 ⌂ Lift ☾
Credit Cards [1] [2] [3] [4] [5]

★★★★*Select* via Baracchini 12 (n.rest) ☎(02)8843 tx 312256
⇝140 ⌂ Lift ☾
Credit Cards [1] [2] [3] [4]

★★★*AGIP* Milano Tangenziale Ovest (14km SW) ☎(02)8843 tx 312256
⇝222 P Lift ⌓

★★★**Concorde** (BW) viale Monza 132 (n.rest) ☎(02)2895853 tx 315805
⇝90 ⌂ Lift ☾
Credit Cards [1] [2] [3] [5]

★★★**Ibis** via Finocchiaro Aprile 2 ☎(02)6315 tx 332109
⇝425 ⌂ P80 Lift ☾
Credit Cards [1] [2] [3] [4] [5]

★★★**Manin** via Manin 7 ☎(02)6596511 tx 320385
:Rest closed Sun
⇝110 Lift ☾
Credit Cards [1] [2] [3] [4] [5]

★★*Eur* via L-da-Vinci 36a (n.rest) ☎(02)4451951
⇝39 ⌂ P30 Lift ☾
Credit Cards [1] [2] [3] [5]

★★*Fini* via Del Mare 93 (n.rest) ☎(02)8464041 rm98(⇝72) ⌂ P Lift ☾

★★*Gamma* via Valvassori Peroni 85 ☎(02)2141116
⇝55 ⌂ Lift ☾

Forlanini ☎(02) 5062660 Fia

At **SAN DONATO MILANESE**(8km SE on N9)

★★★*AGIP* Ingresso Autostrada del Sole ☎(02)512941 tx 320132
⇝270 P Lift ☾

At **SEGRATE**(6km E)

★★★★**Jolly Milano 2** via Flli Cervi ☎(02)2175 tx 321266
⇝149 P Lift ☾
Credit Cards [1] [2] [3] [4] [5]

MINORI
See **AMALFI**

MISANO ADRIATICO
Forli

★★**Gala** via Pascoli 8 ☎(0541)615109
Apr-Sep
⇝27 P30 Lift ☾ Sea
Credit Cards [1] [2] [3] [5]

MODENA
Modena

★★★★**Fini** via Emilia Est 441 ☎(059)238091 tx 510286
Closed 29 Jul-20 Aug :Rest closed Mon & Tue
⇝93 ⌂ Lift ☾
Credit Cards [1] [2] [3] [4] [5]

★★★**AGIP** SS 9 via Tremolmi,Autosole Raccordo Brennero ☎(059)518221 tx 611627
➤♠184 P Lift ℂ
Bellei E-Est 1127 ☎(059) 366271 For

MOGLIANO VENETO
Treviso

★★★★**Villa Condulmer** via Zermanese 1 (n.rest) ☎(041)457100
➤♠54 P ℂ ℀ ⌂ ♁♁ ∪

MOLTRASIO
Como

★★**Caramazza** via Besana 50 ☎(031)290050
Mar-Dec
➤♠20 ♠ P10 Lift Mountain Lake
Credit Cards ①③

MOLVENO
Trento

★★**Cima Tosa** via Scuole 5 (n.rest) ☎(0461)586928
20 May-Sep
➤♠36 P30 Lift Mountain Lake
Credit Cards ②③⑤

★★**Miralago** pza Scuole ☎(0461)586935
20 May-Sep & Dec-20 Mar
➤♠35 P28 Lift ⌂ Mountain Lake
Credit Cards ②③⑤

MONDOVI
Cuneo

F **Govone** Piava 4 ☎(0174) 40355 P Cit Fia

MONTALTO DI CASTRO
Viterbo

★★★**AGIP** via Aurelia (SS 1 Km 108) ☎(0572)75871 tx 574041
➤♠115 P30 Lift ℂ ℀ ⌂
Credit Cards ①②③

MONTECATINI TERME
Pistoia

★★★★**Croce di Malta** (SRS) via IV-Novembre 18 ☎(0572)75871 tx 574041
➤♠115 P30 Lift ℂ ℀ ⌂
Credit Cards ①②③

★★★**Astoria** viale Fedeli 1 ☎(0572)71191
Apr-Oct
rm65(➤♠62) A10rm P50 Lift ℂ ⌂ Mountain
Credit Card ②

★★**Lido Palace Risorgimento** via IV-Novembre 14 ☎(0572)70731
Apr-Oct
➤♠52 Lift ℂ

MONTEGROTTO TERME
Padova

★★★**International Bertha** Largo Traiano ☎(049)793100 tx 430277
➤♠126 ♠ P80 Lift ℂ ℀ ⌂ ♁♁ Mountain
Credit Cards ①②③④⑤

MONTESILVANO MARINA
See PESCARA

MUCCIA
Macerata

★★★**AGIP** Bivio Maddalena (SS 77 Km 44) ☎(0737)43138
➤♠37 P Lift ℂ

NAPOLI (NAPLES)
Napoli

★★★★★**Excelsior** (CIGA) via Partenope 48 ☎(081)417111 tx 710043
➤♠136 ♠ P100 Lift ℂ Sea
Credit Cards ①②③④⑤

★★★★**Vesuvio** (SRS) via Partenope 45 ☎(081)416000 tx 720335
➤♠178 ♠ Lift ℂ Sea
Credit Cards ①②③④⑤

★★★**Jolly** via Medina 70 ☎(081)416000 tx 720335
rm280(➤♠252) ♠ Lift ℂ
Credit Cards ①②③④⑤

★★★**Royal** via Partenope 38 ☎(081)400244 tx 710167
➤♠287 ♠ P Lift ℂ ⌂ Sea
Credit Cards ①②③⑤

S **Luigi** ☎(081) 455724 Ren
SVAI ☎(081) 611122 For
At **SECONDIGLIANO**(8km N)
★★★**AGIP** (SS7 bis km24) ☎(081)7540560
➤♠57 P Lift ℂ

NERVI
Genova

★★★**Giardino Riviera** Passeggiata a Mare ☎(010)328581
rm30(➤♠25) P20 Lift ℂ Sea
Credit Card ②

★★**Milano** via Somma Donato 39 ☎(010)328292
rm50(➤♠37) ♠ P Lift ℂ Sea
Credit Card ①

NOBIALLO
See MENAGGIO

NOVA LEVANTE-WELSCHNOFEN
Bolzano

★★★**Posta Cavallino Bianco** via Carezza 30,Strada Dolomiti ☎(0471)613113
20 Dec-10 Apr & 28 May-3 Nov
➤♠46 ♠ P70 Lift ℂ ℀ ⊠ ⌂ Mountain
Credit Cards ①②③⑤

NUMANA
Ancona

★★★**Numana Palace** via Litoranea 10 ☎(071)930155
May-Dec
➤♠78 P50 Lift ℂ ℀ ⌂ Sea

NUORO
Nuoro
See SARDEGNA, ISOLA (SARDINIA)

ORA-AUER
Bolzano

★★**Elefant** pza Principale 45 ☎(0471)810129
➤♠54 ♠ P120 Lift ⊠ Mountain

ORTA SAN GIULIO
Novara

★★★**San Rocco** via Gippini de Verona 11 ☎(0322)90222 tx 223342
➤♠74 ♠ Lift ℂ ℀ ⌂ Mountain Lake
Credit Cards ①②③⑤

ORTISEI-ST ULRICH
Bolzano

★★★**Adler** via Rezia 7 ☎(0471)76203 tx 400305
15 Jun-10 Oct & 20 Dec-15 Apr
rm85(➤♠80) ♠ P100 Lift ℂ ℀ ⊠ Mountain
Credit Cards ①②③⑤

ORVIETO
Terni

★★★**Maitani** via L-Maitani 5 ☎(0763)42011 tx 564021
➤♠40 ♠ P Lift ℂ
Credit Cards ①②③⑤

At **BADIA, LA**(5km S)
★★★**Badia** Badia ☎(0763)90359
Mar- Dec
➤♠22 ♠ P200 ℂ ℀ ⌂
Credit Cards ①②③

OSPEDALETTI
Imperia

★★★**Floreal** corso R-Margherita 83 ☎(0184)59638
Closed Nov
➤♠26 ♠ P2 Lift ℂ Sea
Credit Cards ②③⑤

★★★**Rocce del Capo** Lungomare C-Colombo 102 ☎(0184)59733
➤♠23 A3rm ♠ P15 Lift ℂ ⌂ Beach Sea
Credit Cards ①②③⑤

★★**Petit Royal** via Regina Margherita 86 ☎(0184)59026
15 Dec-25 Sep
➤♠33 P18 Lift ℂ
Credit Cards ①②

PADOVA (PADUA)
Padova

★★★★**Park Villa Altichiero** (6km N on SS47) ☎(049)615111
➤♠70 P Lift ℂ ⌂

PAESTUM
Salerno

★★**Calypso** via Molina Mare 63,Zona Pinesta ☎(0828)811031
➤♠50 A10rm ♠ P110 ℂ Beach Sea Mountain
Credit Cards ②③⑤

PALERMO
Palermo
See SICILIA, ISOLA (SICILY)

PALLANZA
See VERBANIA

PARMA
Parma

★★★**Palace Maria Luigia** viale Mentana 140 ☎(0521)281032 tx 531008
➤♠102 ♠ P10 Lift ℂ
Credit Cards ①②③⑤

★★**Button** via S-Vitale 7 (n.rest) ☎(0521)208039
Closed Jul
➤♠41 ♠ P15 Lift ℂ
Credit Cards ①②③④⑤

★★**Milano** viale Ponte Bottego 9/A ☎(0521)773031
rm47(➤♠32) ♠ P25 Lift ℂ
Credit Cards ①②③⑤

PASSO DI ROLLE
SeeROLLE

PEGLI
Genova

★★★**Mediterranée** Lungomare 69 ☎(010)683041
➤♠77 P80 Lift ℂ Sea
Credit Cards ①②③

PERUGIA
Perugia

★★★**Rosetta** pza Italia 19 ☎(075)20841 tx 563271
rm97(➤♠89) ♠ P Lift ℂ Mountain
Credit Cards ①②③④⑤

Negri & Ricci ☎(075) 395044 BMW

PESARO
Pesaro & Urbino

★★★**Mediterraneo Ricci** viale Trieste 199 (n.rest) ☎(0721)31556 & 34148 tx 560062
➤♠42 Lift ℂ Beach Sea
Credit Cards ①②③④⑤

★★★**Savoy** viale Repubblica ☎(0721)67440 & 67449 tx 561624
:Rest closed Sun in winter
➤♠54 ♠ Lift ℂ ⌂
Credit Cards ①②③④⑤

★★★**Vittoria** pza della Libertá 2 ☎(0721)34343 tx 561624
:Rest closed Sun in winter
➤♠36 ♠ P20 Lift ℂ ℀ ⌂ Sea
Credit Cards ①②③④⑤

★★**Atlantic** viale Trieste 365 ☎(0721)61911 & 61861 tx 560062
15 May-25 Sep
➤♠43 ♠ Lift ℂ Sea

A Gabellini ☎(0721) 279325 Aud Por VW
Paolo del Monte via Porta Rimini ☎(0721) 32919 AR

MILANO (MILAN)

1	★★★★★	Excelsior-Gallia
2	★★★★★	Palace
3	★★★★★	Principe di Savoia
4	★★★★	Diána Majestic
5	★★★★	Duomo
6	★★★★	Hilton International
7	★★★★	Jolly President
8	★★★★	Select
9	★★★★	Jolly Touring
10	★★★	AGIP
11	★★★	AGIP (At San Donato Milanese)
12	★★★	Ibis
13	★★★	Concorde
14	★★★	Manin
15	★★	Fini
16	★★	Gamma

PESCARA
Pescara

★★★**AGIP** Autostrada Adriatica Casello,Pescara Nord (SS 16) ☎(085)95321
◄╫╲85 P Lift ☾

★★★**Carlton** viale Riviera 35 ☎(085)373125 tx 564123
◄╫╲71 P15 Lift ☾ Beach Sea
Credit Cards ① ② ③ ④ ⑤

At **MONTESILVANO MARINA**(8km NW SS16)

★★★★**Grand Montesilvano** via Riviera 28 ☎(085)838251 tx 600118
◄╫╲140 ☎ P200 Lift ☾ Beach Sea Mountain
Credit Cards ② ⑤

★★★**Serena Majestic** viale Kennedy ☎(085)835412 tx 600186
15 May-15 Oct
◄╫╲210 P100 Lift ☾ ⚲ ⌒ Beach Sea

PIACENZA
Piacenza

★★★**Grand Albergo Roma** via Cittadella 14 ☎(0523)23201 tx 530874
◄╫╲84 ☎ P20 Lift ☾
Credit Cards ① ② ③ ⑤

Agosti & Lunardi ☎(0523) 60333 AR

Mirani & Toscani via E-Parmense 6 ☎(0523) 62721 For

PIETRA LIGURE
Savona

★★★★**Royal** via Don Bado 129 ☎(0523)647192
18 Dec-15 Oct
◄╫╲102 ☎ P10 Lift ☾ Beach Sea
Credit Cards ① ② ③ ④

PIETRASANTA, MARINA DI
Lucca

★★★**Battelli** viale Versilia 189,Motrone ☎(0584)20010 tx 590403
15 May-Sep
◄╫╲38 P30 Lift ☾ ⚲ Beach Sea

★★★**Palazzo della Spiaggia** Lungomare Roma Focette ☎(0584)21195 tx 501383
May-Sep
◄╫╲47 P20 Lift ☾ ⌒ Beach Sea Mountain
Credit Cards ① ② ③ ⑤

★★**Esplanade** viale Roma 235,Tonfano ☎(019)21151 tx 590403
Mar-Oct
◄╫╲30 Lift ☾ Sea
Credit Cards ① ②

PIOMBINO
Livorno

★★**Centrale** pza Verdi 2 ☎(0565)36466
:Rest closed Sat & Sun 20 Dec-7 Jan
rm38(◄╫╲34) ☎ Lift ☾
Credit Card ⑤

E Blanchetti pza Constituzione 54 ☎(0565) 33017 For

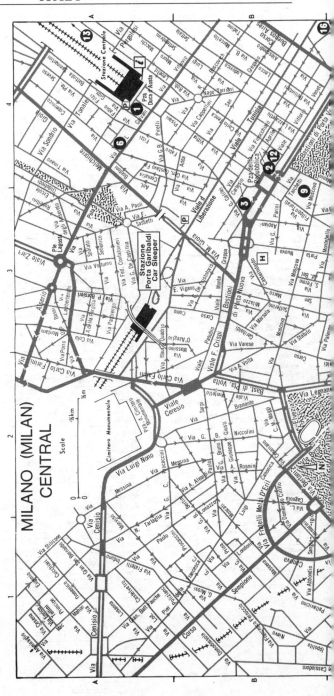

MILANO (MILAN)
CENTRAL

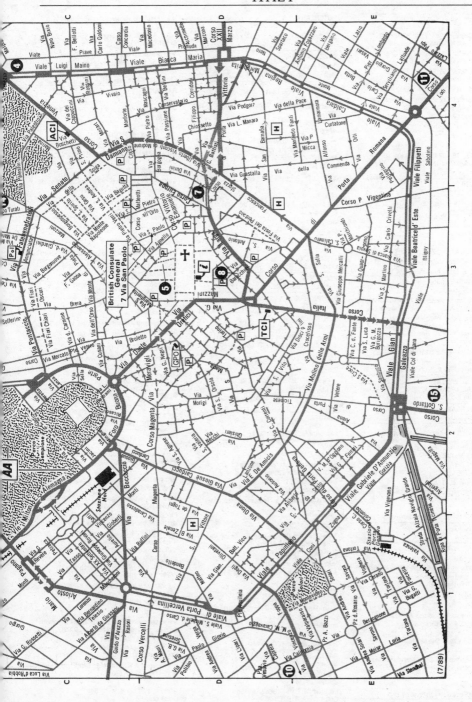

British Consulate
General
7 Via San Paolo

ITALY

PISA
Pisa

★★★★**Cavalieri** (CIGA) pza Stazione 2
☎(050)43290 tx 590663
↔♠100 ☆ P30 Lift ℂ
Credit Cards ①②③⑤

★★**Arno** ☎(050)501820
↔♠33 Lift ℂ
Credit Cards ①②③⑤

★★**California Park** via Aurelia (4km NW on
SS67) ☎(050)890726 tx 502161
↔♠74 P100 Lift ℂ ⌒
Credit Cards ①②③⑤

PISTICCI
Matera

★★★**AGIP** (SS 407 Basentana Km 137)
☎(0835)462007 tx 611627
↔♠64 P ℂ

PONTASSIEVE
Firenze

★★★**Moderno** (n.rest) ☎(055)8315541 tx 574381
↔♠120 ☆ P30 Lift ℂ
Credit Cards ②③⑤

PORDENONE
Pordenone

Automobile via Grigoletti ☎(0434) 32591 AR

Cossetti & Vatta via Venezia ☎(0434) 31474
Ren

PORT'ERCOLE
Grosseto

★★★★**Pelicano** (Relais et Châteaux) **DPn** Cala
dei Santi (4.5km SW on Strada Panoramica)
☎(0564)833914 & 833801 tx 500131
14 Apr-Oct
↔♠34 A16rm ℂ ℚ ⌒ Beach Sea
Credit Cards ①②③⑤

★**Don Pedro** via Panoramica ☎(0564)833914
Apr-Oct
↔♠34 A16rm P60 ℂ ℚ ⌒ Beach Sea
Credit Cards ②③⑤

PORTO AZZURRO
See **ELBA, ISOLA D'**

PORTOFERRAIO
See **ELBA, ISOLA D'**

PORTOFINO
Genova

★★★★**Splendido** (Relais et Châteaux) **DPn** viale
Baratta 13 ☎(0185)269551 tx 281057
24 Mar-27 Oct
↔♠65 ☆ P40 Lift ℂ ℚ ⌒ Sea
Credit Cards ①②③⑤

★★**Piccolo** via Duca degli Abruzzi 31
☎(0185)69015
Mar-2 Nov
rm27(↔♠25) ☆ P ℂ Beach Sea

PORTONOVO
See **ANCONA**

PORTO SAN GIORGIO
Ascoli Piceno

★★**Terrazza** via Castelfidardo 2 ☎(0734)676005
May-Sep :Rest closed Mon
↔♠32 ☆ P25 Lift Beach

POSITANO
Salerno

★★★**Savoia** via C-Colombo 73 (n.rest)
☎(089)875003 & 811518
Apr-7 Oct
rm44(↔♠43) Lift ℂ Sea Mountain
Credit Card ③

★★**Buca di Bacco & Buca Résidence** via
Rampa Teglia 8 ☎(089)875699 tx 722574
Apr-Oct
↔♠54 Lift ℂ Sea
Credit Cards ①②③⑤

POTENZA
Potenza

L Olita via del Gallitello ☎(0971) 52041 **P** Ope
Vau

POZZUOLI
Napoli

Pelli via E-Scarfoglio ☎(081) 7605322 Ope Vau

PRAIANO
Salerno

★★★**Grand Tritone** via Campo 1 ☎(089)874333 tx
770025
Apr-21 Oct :Rest closed Nov-Mar
↔♠60 P50 Lift ℂ ⌒ Beach Sea
Credit Cards ①②③⑤

★★★**Tramonto d'Oro** via G-Capriglione 119
☎(089)874008 tx 720397
↔♠33 ☆ P35 Lift ℂ ⌒ Sea
Credit Cards ①②③④⑤

PRATO
Firenze

★★★**President** via Simintendi 20 ☎(0574)30251
tx 571587
↔♠78 ☆ P30 Lift ℂ
Credit Cards ①②③④⑤

★★**Flora** via Cairoli 31 (n.rest) ☎(0574)20021 tx
571358
↔♠31 ☆ Lift
Credit Cards ①②③④⑤

PROCCHIO
See **ELBA, ISOLA D'**

PUGNOCHIUSO
See **VIESTE**

PUNTA ALA
Grosseto

★★★★**Gallia Palace** (Relais et Châteaux) via
delle Sughere ☎(0564)922022 tx 590454
15 May-Sep
↔♠98 P80 Lift ℂ ℚ ⌒ Beach Sea
Credit Card ②

★★★★**Golf DPn** ☎(0564)922026 tx 590538
23 May-8 Oct
↔♠180 P130 Lift ℂ ℚ ⌒ ♄ ♄ Beach Sea
Credit Cards ①②③⑤

RAGUSA
Ragusa
See **SICILIA, ISOLA (SICILY)**

RAPALLO
Genova

★★★**Eurotel** via Aurelia Ponente 22
☎(0185)60982 tx 283851
↔♠65 ☆ P100 Lift ℂ ⌒ Sea
Credit Cards ①②③⑤

★★★**Grande Italia & Lido** Lungomare Castello 1
☎(0185)50492
↔♠52 ☆ P10 Lift ℂ Beach Sea
Credit Cards ①③⑤

★★★**Miramare DPn** Lungomare Vittorio Veneto
27 ☎(0185)50293 & 51270
rm31(↔♠25) Lift Sea
Credit Cards ①②③⑤

★★★**Riviera** pza IV Novembre 2 ☎(0185)50248
20 Dec-6 Nov
↔♠20 Lift ℂ Sea
Credit Cards ①②③④

★**Bandoni** via Marsala 24 ☎(0185)50423
Dec-Oct :Rest closed Nov
rm16(↔♠5) Lift ℂ Sea
Credit Card ①

E Massa ☎(0185) 50689 AR

RAVELLO
Salerno

★★★**Caruso Belvedere DPn** via Toro 52
☎(089)857111
rm24(↔♠23) P10 ℂ Sea Mountain
Credit Cards ①②③⑤

★★★**Palumbo** via Toro 28 ☎(089)857244 tx
770101
↔♠21 A7rm ☆ P ℂ Sea
Credit Cards ①②③⑤

★★**Parsifal** via d'Anna 5 ☎(089)857144
20 Apr-10 Oct :Rest closed Mon
↔♠19 ☆ ℂ Sea
Credit Cards ①②③④⑤

RAVENNA
Ravenna

★★★★**Jolly** pza Mameli 1 ☎(0544)35762 tx
550575
↔♠75 Lift ℂ
Credit Cards ①②③④⑤

★★★**Bisanzio** via Salara 30 (n.rest)
☎(0544)27111 tx 551070
↔♠36 Lift ℂ
Credit Cards ①②③⑤

★★**Centrale Byron** via IV Novembre 14 (n.rest) ·
☎(0544)22225 & 33479 tx 551070
rm57(↔♠54) Lift ℂ
Credit Cards ①②③⑤

★**Romea** via Romea 1 (2.5km S on SS16)
☎(0544)61247
↔♠39 P100 Lift ℂ
Credit Cards ①②③⑤

Pasini via M-Perilli 40 ☎(0544) 421579 **P** Fia Ren

REGGIO DI CALABRIA
Reggio di Calabria

Automotor Reggina via San Caterina 12
☎(0965) 48600 Aud Por VW

REGGIO NELL'EMILIA
Reggio Nell'Emilia

★★★★**Grand Astoria** via L-Nobili 4
☎(0522)35245 tx 530534
↔♠112 P50
Credit Cards ①②③④⑤

★★★**Posta** pza C-Battisti 4 (n.rest)
☎(0522)32944 tx 530036
↔♠58 A15rm ☆ P Lift ℂ
Credit Cards ①②③⑤

RENDE
See **COSENZA**

RICAVO
See **CASTELLINA IN CHIANTI**

RICCIONE
Forli

★★★**Atlantic** Lungomare Della Liberta 15
☎(0541)601155 tx 550192
Apr-Oct
↔♠74 ☆ P40 Lift ℂ ⌒ Beach Sea
Credit Cards ①②③④⑤

★★★★**Savioli Spiaggia** via G-D'Annunzio 2-6
☎(0541)43252 tx 551038
Etr-Sep & 26 Dec-3 Jan
↔♠100 P5040 Lift ℂ ⌒ Beach Sea
Credit Cards ①②③⑤

★★★**Abner's** Lungomare Repubblica 7
☎(0541)600601 tx 550153
10 May-Sep
↔♠60 P12 Lift ℂ ℚ ⌒ Beach Sea
Credit Cards ②⑤

★★★**Arizona** via G-D'Annunzio 22 ☎(0541)48520
10 May-Sep
↔♠68 P25 Lift ℂ Beach Sea
Credit Card ②

★★★**Lungomare** viale Milano 7,via Lungomare
della Liberta 7 ☎(0541)41601 tx 550561
:Rest closed 1 Nov-25 Jan
↔♠58 ☆ P30 Lift ℂ Beach Sea
Credit Cards ①②③⑤

★★★**Vienna & Touring** viale Mirano 78c
☎(0541)601700 tx 550153
May-Sep
↔♠85 P20 Lift ℂ ℚ ⌒ Sea
Credit Card ②

★★Alexandra Plaza viale Torino 61
☎(0541)610344 tx 550330
Apr-Sep
⬩⬩60 P60 Lift 〔 ⊇ Beach Sea
Credit Cards ① ② ③

★★Nevada via Milano 54 ☎(0541)601254 tx
551245
25 May-20 Sep
⬩⬩50 ☎ P45 Lift 〔 Beach Sea

RIMINI
Forlì

★★★Ambasciatori viale Vespucci 22
☎(0541)55561 tx 550132
:Rest closed Sep-May
⬩⬩66 ☎ P20 Lift 〔 ⊇ Beach Sea
Credit Cards ① ② ③ ⑤

★★★President via Tripoli 270 ☎(0541)25741 tx
550340
10 May-Sep
⬩⬩50 Lift 〔
Credit Cards ① ② ③ ⑤

★★Alpen viale Regina Elena 205 ☎(0541)80662
May-Sep
⬩⬩53 P20 Lift 〔 Sea

🐦Grattacielo viale Regina Margherita 46
☎(0541) 24610 P Ope

At **RIVAZZURRA**(4km SE)

★★★Grand Meeting viale Regina Margherita 46
☎(0541)372123
May-Sep
⬩⬩50 P30 Lift 〔 Sea
Credit Card ⑤

★★★Little via Gubbio 16 ☎(0541)373258
Apr-Sep
⬩⬩50 P15 Lift 〔 Mountain Lake
Credit Cards ③ ⑤

RIVA DEL GARDA
Trento

★★★★Lac & Parc (BW) **DPn** viale Rovereto 44
☎(0464)520202 tx 400258

Apr-20 Oct :Rest closed Mon
⬩⬩177 ☎ P150 Lift 〔 ዓ ⊠ ⊇ Beach Mountain
Lake
Credit Cards ① ② ③ ⑤

RIVAZZURRA
See **RIMINI**

ROCCARASO
L'Aquila

★★★AGIP Roccaraso (SS 17 dell'
Appennino,l'Abruzzese Km 136) ☎(0864)62443
⬩⬩57 P 〔 Mountain

ROLLE, PASSO DI
Trento

★Passo Rolle ☎(0439)68216
Closed 15 Apr-30 Jun :Rest closed Thu 15 Sep-
30 Nov
rm27(⬩⬩16) Mountain

ROMA (ROME)

See Plan page 280 *Population 3,000,000 Local Tourist Office* Via Parigi 5 ☎(06)461851

Roma is one of the world's greatest cultural centres, with evidence of the glory that was ancient Roma to be found everywhere. The Forum contains the ruins of the centre of the Empire's administration, and the heart of its cultural and political life; close by are Trajan's Column, magnificent with its pictorial spiral illustrating the city's earliest history, and the awe-inspiring Coliseum where the people came to be entertained by the feats of the gladiators.

A short drive away is the Vatican City, the smallest sovereign state in the world. This contains not only the residence of the Pope but also the world's largest church and St Peter's Square, an immense masterpiece designed and completed in less than 12 years, and an incomparable achievement in symmetry. The 1st-century Egyptian obelisk in the centre was once the goal post of Nero's Circus. The treasures of St Peter's Basilica include Michelangelo's *Pieta* and a 13th-century bronze statue of St Peter by Arnolfo do Cambio, its foot worn smooth by the kisses of millions of pilgrims. Climb to the top of the Basilica for a magnificent view of Roma and the Vatican City.

In addition to its wide range of museums, art galleries and churches, the city offers delightful city parks and gardens to stroll in, especially the beautiful *Villa Borghese* and the *Giardini degli Aranci*. Markets abound - the best known are the Sunday market at Porta Portese and the daily market at Piazza Vittorio Emanuele, while Roma's best known stores are found close to the Spanish Steps and in Via del Corso, where designer labels include Valentino and Gucci.

EATING OUT You need not spend a fortune to eat in Roma. In traditional areas such as Trastevere you will find small, family-run *trattorie* serving Roman cooking at its best. No visit to Roma would be complete without having tried an appetising pizza or a dish of homemade pasta, such as *spaghetti carbonara*, made with a creamy sauce of beaten egg with smoked bacon. The meat dishes are delicious, too, especially the *saltimbocca*, veal with sage and ham in Marsala wine. You will find daily menus (*piatto del giono*) in inexpensive *trattorie* where a carafe of *vino della casa* provides a palatable accompaniment to your meal. For some local flavour try the excellent Frascati and Marino wines which are produced from the vineyards on the hills surrounding the city.

Try cafés in the elegant Via Condotti for *capuccino* coffee and sweet pastries such as *maritozze*, a kind of brioche roll with sweet custard filling: or, if you feel like splashing out, the stylish *Café de Paris* in Via Veneto, the original *dolce vita* café.

Among the city's best restaurants are *Andrea* in Via Sardegna, and *Alberta Ciarla*, in Piazza San Cosimato, which specialises in seafood.

ROMA (ROME)

★★★★★Cavaleri Hilton via Cadlolo 101
☎(06)31511 tx 625337
⬩⬩373 ☎ P700 Lift 〔 ዓ ⊇
Credit Cards ① ② ③ ④ ⑤

★★★★★Excelsior (CIGA) via Vittorio Veneto 125
☎(06)3151 tx 610296
⬩⬩394 ☎ P Lift 〔

★★★★★Grand (CIGA) via V-E-Orlando 3
☎(06)4709 tx 610210
⬩⬩171 ☎ P Lift 〔
Credit Cards ① ② ③

★★★★★Grand Flora via V-Veneto 191 (n.rest)
☎(06)497821 tx 22256
⬩⬩176 ☎ Lift 〔
Credit Cards ② ③ ⑤

★★★★★Hassler pza Trinitá dei Monti 6
☎(06)6782651 tx 610208
⬩⬩100 ☎ P5 Lift 〔
Credit Card ②

★★★★★Jolly-Leonardo da Vinci via dei Gracchi
324 ☎(06)39680 tx 611182
⬩⬩256 ☎ Lift 〔
Credit Cards ① ② ③ ④ ⑤

★★★★★Jolly V-Veneto Corso Italia 1 ☎(06)8495
tx 612293
⬩⬩203 ☎ Lift 〔
Credit Cards ① ② ③ ④ ⑤

★★★★Eliseo (BW) via di Porta Pinciana 30
☎(06)460056 tx 610693
⬩⬩53 ☎ Lift 〔
Credit Cards ① ② ③ ⑤

★★★★Holiday Inn Eur Parco dei Medici viale
Castello della,Magliana 65 (10km W of autostrada
to Fiumicino Airport) ☎(06)5475 tx 613302
⬩⬩308 P150 Lift 〔 ዓ ⊇
Credit Cards ① ② ③ ④ ⑤

★★★★*Holiday Inn St Peter's* via Aurelia Fintica 415 ☎(06)5872 tx 625434
⊷🛏334 P400 Lift ◖ ९ ⌐
Credit Cards ①②③⑤

★★★★*Quirinale* (SRS) via Nazionale 7 ☎(06)4707 tx 610332
⊷🛏200 ⌂ Lift ◖
Credit Cards ①②③⑤

★★★★*Sheraton* viale del Pattinaggio ☎(06)5453 tx 614223
⊷🛏621 ⌂ P300 Lift ◖ ९ ⌐
Credit Cards ①②③④⑤

★★★★*Ville* (Forum) via Sistina 69 ☎(06)6733 tx 620836
⊷🛏195 ⌂ P40 Lift ◖
Credit Cards ①②③④⑤

★★★*AGIP* via Aurelia (SS 1) ☎(06)6379001 tx 613699
⊷🛏222 P Lift ◖ ⌐

★★★*Bernini-Bristol* (SRS) pza Barberini 23 ☎(06)463051 tx 610554
⊷🛏125 ⌂ P100 Lift ◖
Credit Cards ①②③⑤

★★★*Britannia* via Napoli 64 (n.rest) ☎(06)463153 tx 611292
⊷🛏32 P7 Lift ◖
Credit Cards ①②③⑤

★★★*Columbus* via della Concilazione 33 ☎(06)5565436 tx 620096
rm107(⊷70) ⌂ P20 Lift ◖
Credit Cards ①②③④⑤

★★★*Commodore* via Torino 1 ☎(06)4754112 tx 612170
⊷🛏65 ⌂ Lift ◖
Credit Cards ①②⑤

★★*Lord Byron* (Relais et Châteaux) via G-de-Notaris 5 ☎(06)3609541 tx 611217
:Rest closed Sun
⊷🛏50 ⌂ P Lift ◖
Credit Cards ①②③④⑤

ROMA (ROME)

★★★★★	Cavalieri Hilton
★★★★★	Excelsior
★★★★★	Grand
★★★★★	Grand Flora
★★★★★	Hassler
★★★★★	Jolly-Leonardo da Vinci
★★★★★	Jolly V-Veneto
★★★★	Eliseo
★★★★	Holiday Inn Eur Parco dei Medici
★★★★	Quirinale
★★★★	Holiday Inn St Peter's
★★★★	Sheraton

13	★★★★	Ville
14	★★★	AGIP (6km W on SS1)
15	★★★	Bernini-Bristol
16	★★★	Britannia
17	★★★	Columbus
18	★★★	Commodore
19	★★★	Lord Byron
20	★★★	Nord-Nuova Roma
21	★★★	Pullman Boston
22	★★★	Regina-Carlton
23	★★★	Rivoli
24	★★★	Savoy
25	★	Bela (At La Storta)
26	★	Scalinata di Spagna

ROMA (ROME)

ITALY

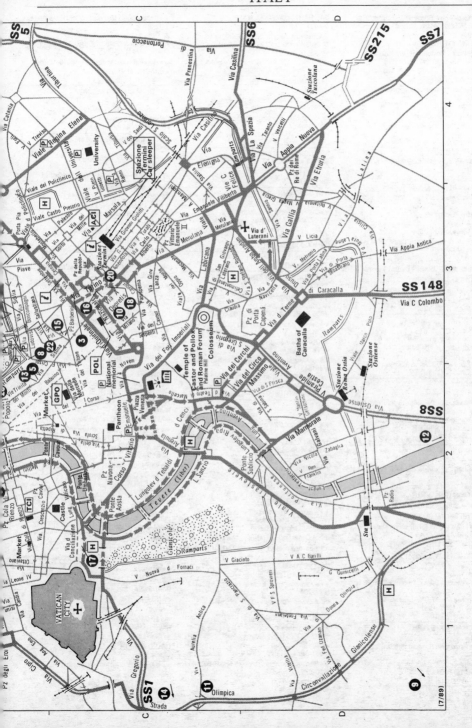

(7/89)

★★★**Nord-Nuova Roma** via G-Amendola 3
(n.rest) ☎(06)465441 tx 610556
◢♠159 ♿ Lift ℂ ① ② ③ ⑤
Credit Cards ① ② ③ ⑤

★★★**Pullman Boston** via Lombardia 47
☎(06)473951 tx 622247
◢♠127 ♿ P Lift ℂ
Credit Cards ① ② ③ ⑤

★★★**Regina-Carlton** via V-Veneto 72
☎(06)476851 tx 620863
◢♠132 ♿ Lift ℂ
Credit Cards ① ② ③ ⑤

★★★**Rivoli** via Torquato Taramelli 7
☎(06)476851 tx 620863
◢♠55 Lift ℂ
Credit Cards ① ② ③ ⑤

★★★**Savoy** via Ludovisi 15 ☎(06)4744141 tx
611339
◢♠115 Lift ℂ
Credit Cards ① ② ③ ④ ⑤

★★**Hiberia** via 24 Maggio 7 ☎(06)6782662 tx
621399
:Rest closed Mon
◢♠21 Lift ℂ
Credit Cards ① ② ③ ⑤

★**Scalinata di Spagna** pza Trinita dei Monti 17
☎(06)6793006
◢♠14 ℂ

Primauto ☎(06) 3599693 DJ Sko Toy VW

At **STORTA, LA**(16km NW)

★**Bela** via Cassia 1801 ☎(06)3790232
◢♠44 P44 ℂ ♒ ⌒
Credit Cards ① ② ③ ⑤

RONCIGLIONE
Viterbo

★★★**Rio Vicano** via Cassia Cimina (Km19)
☎(0761)612336 tx 616083
:Rest closed Tue
◢♠46 A2rm ♿ P120 ℂ ⌒ Mountain Lake
Credit Cards ① ② ③ ④ ⑤

ST VINCENT
Aosta

★★★★**Billia** viale Piemonte 18 ☎(0166)3446 tx
212144
◢♠250 ♿ P800 Lift ℂ ♒ ⌒ Mountain
Credit Cards ① ② ③ ④ ⑤

Walther pza Zerbion ☎(0166) 3113 P Cit

SALERNO
Salerno

★★★★**Jolly** Lungomare Trieste 1 ☎(089)225222
tx 770050
rm105(◢♠102) P Lift ℂ Sea
Credit Cards ① ② ③ ④ ⑤

Jannone ☎(089) 331522 AR DJ

At **VIETRI SUL MARE**(3km W)

★★★★**Lloyd's Baia** (SRS) via de Marinis
☎(089)210145 tx 770043
◢♠120 ♿ P100 Lift ℂ ⌒ Beach Sea
Credit Cards ① ② ③ ④ ⑤

SALÓ
Brescia

★★★**Duomo** via Duomo 18 ☎(0365)21026 tx
303028
:Rest closed Mon, Tue
◢♠22 ♿ P Lift ℂ Lake
Credit Cards ② ③ ⑤

SALSOMAGGIORE TERME
Parma

★★★★**Porro** viale Porro 10 ☎(0524)78221 tx
530639
8 Mar-Dec
rm85(◢♠79) P100 Lift ℂ ⊟
Credit Cards ① ② ⑤

SAN BARTOLOMEO AL MARE
Imperia

★★★**Mayola** Lungomare Delle Nazioni 56
☎(0183)400739 tx 271620
15 Mar-15 Oct
◢♠80 P20 Lift ℂ ⌒ Beach Sea Mountain
Credit Cards ① ② ③ ④ ⑤

SAN CÁNDIDO-INNICHEN
Bolzano

★★**Park Sole Paradiso** via Sesto 11
☎(0474)73120 tx 400329
28 May-8 Oct, 22 Dec-2 Apr :Rest closed Thu
(low season)
◢♠44 ♿ P50 Lift ♒ Mountain
Credit Cards ② ⑤

SAN DONATO MILANESE
See **MILANO (MILAN)**

SAN FELICE
See **CREMONA**

SAN GIMIGNANO
Siena

★★**Cisterna** pza della Cisterna 23
☎(0577)940328 tx 575152
10 Mar-10 Nov :Rest closed Tue, Wed lunchtime
◢♠50 P Lift ℂ Mountain
Credit Cards ① ② ③ ⑤

SAN MAMETE
See **VALSOLDA**

SAN MARTINO DI CASTROZZA
Trento

★★★**San Martino** ☎(0439)680011 tx 401543
20 Dec-30 Mar & Jul-15 Dec
◢♠36 ♿ P30 Lift ℂ ♒ ⊟ Mountain

★★**Savoia** via Passo Rolle 233 ☎(0439)68094 tx
401543
20 Dec-30 Mar & Jul-30 Aug
◢♠68 P50 Lift ♒ ⊟ ⌒

★**Belvedere** via Passo Rolle 247 ☎(0439)68000
tx 401543
Jan-4 Apr & 25 Jun-10 Sep
◢♠47 Lift Mountain
Credit Cards ① ② ③

SAN REMO
Imperia

★★★★★**Royal DPn** corso Imperatrice 80
☎(0184)79991 tx 270511
17 Dec-17 Sep
◢♠138 ♿ P58 Lift ℂ ♒ ⊟ Sea
Credit Cards ① ② ③ ④ ⑤

★★★★**Miramare** corso Matuzia 9
☎(0184)882381 tx 275566
20 Dec-Sep :Rest closed Mon
◢♠59 P60 Lift ℂ ⌒ Sea
Credit Cards ① ② ③ ⑤

★★★**Astoria West End** corso Matuzia 8
☎(0814)70791 tx 283834
◢♠120 ♿ P37 Lift ℂ ⌒
Credit Cards ① ② ③ ④ ⑤

★★★**Europa** corso Imperatrice 27 ☎(0184)70605
tx 272024
rm75(◢♠61) Lift ℂ Sea
Credit Cards ① ② ③ ⑤

★★★**Paradiso** corso Imperatrice ☎(0184)85112
tx 272264
:Rest closed Mon
◢♠41 ♿ P14 Lift ℂ Beach Sea
Credit Cards ① ② ③ ④ ⑤

★★★**Residence Principe** via Asquasciati 48
☎(0184)83565 tx 270620
◢♠50 Lift ℂ ⌒ Sea
Credit Cards ① ② ③

★★**Beaurivage** corso Trieste 49 ☎(0184)85146 tx
270620
:Rest closed Nov
◢♠29 Lift ℂ Sea
Credit Card ⑤

★★**Bobby** Corso Marconi 208 ☎(0184)60255 tx
271249
22 Dec-20 Oct
◢♠75 A10rm ♿ P60 Lift ℂ Beach Sea
Credit Cards ① ② ③ ⑤

★★**Morandi** corso Matuzia 51 ☎(0184)73686
◢♠32 P18 Lift ℂ Sea
Credit Cards ① ② ③ ⑤

SANTA CATERINA VALFURVA
Sondrio

★★**Sobretta** ☎(0342)935510
Dec-Apr & Jul-10 Sep
rm26(◢♠20) ♿ P25 Mountain

SANTA CRISTINA IN VALGARDENA
Bolzano

★★**Posta** ☎(0471)796678
May & Nov
◢♠59 A16rm ♿ P50 Lift ℂ ♒ ⌒ Mountain

SANTA MARGHERITA LIGURE
Genova

★★★★★**Imperial Palace** via Pagana 19
☎(0185)288991 tx 271398
10 Apr-Oct
◢♠106 P100 Lift ℂ ⌒ Beach Sea
Credit Cards ① ② ③ ④ ⑤

★★★★**Miramare** (SRS) via Milite Ignoto 30
☎(0185)287013 tx 270437
◢♠81 ♿ P25 Lift ℂ ⌒ Beach Sea Mountain
Credit Cards ① ②

★★★**Continental** via Pagana 8 ☎(0185)286512
tx 271601
◢♠76 ♿ P50 Lift ℂ Beach Sea
Credit Cards ① ② ③ ⑤

★★★**Laurin** corso Marconi 3 (n.rest)
☎(0185)289971 tx 275043
◢♠45 Lift ℂ Sea
Credit Cards ① ② ③ ⑤

★★★**Metropole DPn** via Pagana 2
☎(0185)286134 tx 272022
20 Dec-Oct
◢♠50 A20rm ♿ P50 Lift ℂ Beach Sea
Credit Cards ① ② ③ ⑤

★★★**Park Suisse** via Favale 31 ☎(0185)289571
tx 271549
◢♠85 ♿ P85 Lift ℂ ⌒ Sea

★★★**Regina Elena** Lungomare Milite Ignoto 44
☎(0185)287003 tx 271563
◢♠94 A22rm P60 Lift ℂ Beach Sea
Credit Cards ① ② ③ ④ ⑤

★★**Villa Anita** viale Minerva ☎(0185)286543
20 Dec-20 Oct :Rest closed Mon
rm15(◢♠14) ♿ P6
Credit Cards ① ③

★**Europa** via Trento 5 ☎(0185)287187
Mar-10 Jan
rm18(◢♠11) ♿ P7
Credit Cards ① ③ ⑤

SAPRI
Salerno

Comisso via Pisacane 22 ☎(0973) 391370 P For

SARDAGNA
See **TRENTO**

SARDEGNA, ISOLA (SARDINIA)

CAGLIARI
Cagliari

★★★**AGIP** Circonvallazione Nuova
☎(070)561645 tx 611627
◢♠57 P Lift ℂ

GOLFO ARANCI
Sassari

★★**Margherita** ☎(0789)46906
:Rest closed Oct-Mar
rm26(◢♠24) P20 Lift ℂ Sea
Credit Cards ① ② ③ ④ ⑤

MACOMER
Nuoro
★★★*AGIP* corso Umberto 1 ☎(0785)71066 tx
611627
⌿ñ96 P Lift ℂ

NUORO
Nuoro
★★★*Motel AGIP* via Trieste ☎(0784)34071
⌿ñ51 P Lift ℂ

SASSARI
Sassari
★★★*AGIP* Serra Secca ☎(079)271440
⌿ñ57 P Lift ℂ

VILLASIMIUS
Cagliari
★★★*Timi-Ama* ☎(070)791228
Jun-20 Sep
⌿ñ65 P ℂ ℚ Beach

SARZANA
La Spezia
★★★*AGIP* Circonvallazione Aurelia 32
☎(0187)621491 tx 611627
⌿ñ51 P Lift ℂ

SASSARI
Sassari
See SARDEGNA, ISOLA (SARDINIA)

SAVONA
Savona
★★★*AGIP* via Nizza,Zinola ☎(019)621491 tx
611627
⌿ñ60 ☎ Lift ℂ
★★★*Riviera-Suisse* via Paleocapa 24 (n.rest)
☎(019)820683 tx 272421
rm70(⌿ñ65) P20 Lift ℂ
Credit Cards ①②③④⑤
M Spirto ☎(019) 806869

SECONDIGLIANO
See NAPOLI (NAPLES)

SEGRATE
See MILANO (MILAN)

SELVA DI VAL GARDENA
Bolzano
★★*Solaia* via Centro 142 ☎(0471)75104 tx
400359
1 Dec-10 Apr & 15 Jun-30 Sep
⌿ñ28 ☎ P30 ℂ ℚ Mountain

SENIGALLIA
Ancona
★★★*City* Lungomare Dante Alighieri 12
☎(071)63464
⌿ñ60 P20 Lift ℂ Beach Sea
Credit Cards ①②③④⑤
★★★*Ritz* Lungomare Dante Alighieri 142
☎(071)63563 tx 560044
21 May-18 Sep
⌿ñ150 P100 Lift ℂ ℚ ☎ Beach Sea
Credit Cards ①②③⑤
G E Luzi ☎(071) 7924633 P Aud Por VW

SESTO CALENDE
Varese
★★*Tre Re* pza Garibaldi 25 ☎(0331)924229
Mar 5-Dec
⌿ñ35 ☎ P6 Lift ℂ Lake
Credit Card ②

SESTO FIORENTINO
See FIRENZE (FLORENCE)

SESTRI LEVANTE
Genova
★★★★*Villa Balbi* viale Rimembranze 1
☎(0185)42941
7Apr-23Oct
⌿ñ100 P45 Lift ℂ ☎ Beach
Credit Cards ①②③⑤

★★★*Vis à Vis DPn* via della Chiusa 28
☎(0185)42661 tx 272443
⌿ñ50 P50 Lift ℂ ☎ Sea Mountain
Credit Cards ①②③⑤
★★*Due Mari* Vico Del Coro 18 ☎(0185)42695
23 Dec-1 Nov
⌿ñ26 P15 Lift ℂ Sea
★★*Helvetia* via Cappuccini 17 ☎(0185)41175 tx
272003
25 Mar-25 Oct :Rest closed Mon
⌿ñ28 ☎ P11 Lift ℂ Beach Sea Mountain

SETTIMO
See TORINO (TURIN)

SICILIA, ISOLA (SICILY)

AGRIGENTO
Agrigento
★★★*Jolly dei Templi* Parco Angeli,Villaggio
Mose ☎(0922)606144 tx 910086
⌿ñ146 P Lift ℂ ☎
Credit Cards ①②③④⑤

CANNIZZARO
Catania
★★★*Grand Baia Verde* (BW) via della Scogliera
8-10 ☎(095)491522 tx 970285
⌿ñ127 ☎ P100 Lift ℂ ℚ ☎ Beach Sea
Credit Cards ①②③④⑤

CATANIA
Catania
★★★*AGIP* Ognina (SS 114 Km 92) (n.rest)
☎(095)492233 tx 611627
⌿ñ56 ☎ Lift ℂ
★★★*Jolly* pza Trento 13 ☎(095)316933 tx
970080
⌿ñ159 P Lift ℂ
Credit Cards ①②③④⑤

MARSALA
Trapani
★★★*AGIP* Uscita per Mazara del Vallo,(SS 115
Km 31) ☎(0923)43401 tx 980074
⌿ñ32 ☎ Lift ℂ

MESSINA
Messina
★★★★*Jolly* via Garibaldi 126 ☎(090)43401 tx
980074
⌿ñ99 Lift ℂ
Credit Cards ①②③④⑤

PALERMO
Palermo
★★★★*Jolly* Foro Italico ☎(091)6165090 tx
910076
⌿ñ290 P Lift ℂ ☎
Credit Cards ①②③④⑤
★★★*AGIP* via della Regione Siciliana
☎(091)552033 tx 611627
⌿ñ100 P Lift ℂ

RAGUSA
Ragusa
CAI via R-Morandi ☎(0932) 24047 Cit

SIRACUSA (SYRACUSE)
Siracusa
★★★★*Grand Villa Politi* via M-Politi Laudlen 3
☎(0931)32100 tx 970205
⌿ñ93 P100 Lift ☎ Sea
Credit Cards ①②③⑤
★★★*AGIP* viale Teracati 30/32 ☎(0931)66944 tx
611627
⌿ñ76 P Lift ℂ
★★★*Jolly* corso Gelone 43 ☎(0931)64744 tx
970108
⌿ñ100 P Lift
Credit Cards ①②③④⑤

TAORMINA
★★★*Jolly* via Bagnoli Croce 75 ☎(0942)23312 tx
980028
⌿ñ103 P Lift ℂ ☎ Sea
Credit Cards ①②③④⑤

★★*Villa Paradiso* via Roma 2 ☎(0942)23921
20 Dec-4 Nov
⌿ñ33 Lift ℂ ℚ ☎ Beach Sea Mountain
Credit Cards ①②③⑤
At MAZZARÒ(4.5km NE)
★★★★*Mazzarò Sea Palace* (SRS) via Nazionale
16 ☎(0942)24004 tx 980041
6 Apr-Oct
⌿ñ81 ☎ P100 Lift ℂ ☎ Beach Sea
Credit Cards ①②③④⑤
★★★★*Villa Sant'Andrea* via Nazionale 137
☎(0942)23125 tx 980077
25 Mar-Oct
⌿ñ48 A2rm P30 ℂ Beach Sea
Credit Cards ①②③⑤

SIENA
Siena

Siena stands proudly 1,000ft up
in the Tuscan hills at the meeting
point of three ridges. One of
Italy's great art centres,
abounding with buildings of
fascinating historic and
architectural merit, it also ranks
among its best preserved
medieval towns and is a splendid
example of successful early town
planning with an abundance of
fascinating twisting lanes and
alleys that rise and dip as they
follow the land's hilly contours.
Siena's main square - the
Campo - is a superb vista of
marble and red brick paving in
the pattern of a gigantic fan
dominated by the tower of the
Gothic town hall (1297 - 1310).
The old Roman forum,
surrounded by ancient palaces,
shops and restaurants, is very
much the focal point of the city.
A first glimpse quickly explains
how the colour known as burnt
seinna obtained its name: the
pigment comes from this area,
and its hue is imprinted on many
of the fine buildings.

EATING OUT *Tullio ai Tre Cristi*,
in Vicolo Provenzano, is a long-
time favourite of both residents
and visitors. *Al Mangia*, in
Piazzao del Campo, has outdoor
tables on one of the world's most
beautiful piazzas.

SIENA
★★★★*Jolly Excelsior* pza la Lizza
☎(0577)288448 tx 573345
⌿ñ126 Lift ℂ
Credit Cards ①②③④⑤
★★★★*Park* (CIGA) via Marciano 16
☎(0577)44803 tx 571005
⌿ñ69 P150 Lift ℂ ℚ ☎ Mountain
Credit Cards ①②③④⑤
★★★*Palazzo Ravizza DPn* Piano dei Mantellini
34 ☎(0577)280462 tx 575304
rm30(⌿ñ21) ☎ P50 Lift ℂ Mountain
Credit Cards ①②③⑤

★★★*Villa Scacciapensieri* via Scacciapensieri 10 ☎(0577)41441 tx 573390
15 Mar-1 Nov :Rest closed Wed
⊶ℍ29 ☎ P25 Lift ℂ ᖰ ᗐ
Credit Cards ①②③⑤

★★Santa Caterina E.S.Piccolomini 7 (n.rest)
☎(0577)221105 tx 575304
Mar-Nov
⊶ℍ19 ☎ P5 ℂ
Credit Cards ①②③⑤

At COLLE DI VAL D'ELSA(22km NW)

★★*Arnolfo* via F-Campana 8 ☎(0577)922020
:Rest closed Tue
⊶ℍ32 Lift ℂ
Credit Cards ②⑤

★★Villa Belvedere ☎(0577)920966 tx 575304
⊶ℍ15 P60 ℂ Mountain
Credit Cards ①②③⑤

SIRACUSA (SYRACUSE)
Siracusa
See SICILIA, ISOLA (SICILY)

SIRMIONE
Brescia

★★★*Florida Pn* via Colombare ☎(030)919018 tx 300395
10 Mar-30 Oct
⊶ℍ28 ☎ P30 ℂ ᗐ Lake
Credit Cards ①③

★★★Grand Terme DPn viale Marconi 7
☎(030)916261 tx 305573
16 Apr-Oct
⊶ℍ59 P60 Lift ℂ ᗐ Mountain Lake
Credit Cards ①②③④⑤

★★★*Sirmione* pza Castello ☎(030)916331 tx 300395
Apr-6 Nov
rm76(⊶ℍ71) A24rm Lift ℂ Lake

★★Lac DPn via XXV Aprile 60 ☎(030)916026
25 Mar-26 Oct
rm34(⊶ℍ32) A6rm P30 ᗐ Beach Lake
Credit Card ③

SORRENTO
Napoli

★★★★Excelsior Vittoria pza Tasso 34
☎(081)8071044 tx 720368
⊶ℍ115 P50 Lift ℂ ᗐ Sea
Credit Cards ①②③⑤

★★★★Imperial Tramontano via V-Veneto 1
☎(081)8781940 & tx 722424
Mar-Dec
⊶ℍ115 P20 Lift ℂ ᗐ Beach Sea
Credit Cards ②③

★★★Aminta Grand via Nastro Verde 7
☎(081)8781821
Apr-Oct
⊶ℍ73 ☎ P30 ℂ ᗐ Sea
Credit Card ⑤

★★★Cocumella via Cocumella 7 ☎(081)8782933 tx 720370
⊶ℍ52 P30 Lift ℂ ᖰ ᗐ Beach Sea
Credit Cards ①②⑤

★★★Eden via Correale 25 ☎(081)8781909
Apr-Oct
⊶ℍ60 P Lift Beach Sea

★★★Grand Ambasciatori via Califano 18
☎(081)8782025 tx 710645
⊶ℍ103 P20 Lift ℂ ᗐ Beach Sea
Credit Cards ②③

★★★Grand Capodimonte via del Capo 14
☎(081)8784076 tx 721210
Apr-Oct
⊶ℍ131 P80 Lift ℂ ᗐ Sea
Credit Cards ②③

SPARTAIA
See ELBA, ISOLA D' under PROCCHIO

SPEZIA, LA
La Spezia

★★★★*Jolly* via XX Settembre 2 ☎(0187)27200 tx 281047
⊶ℍ110 Lift
Credit Cards ①②③④⑤

Cozzani & Rossi pza Caduti per La Liberta 6
☎(1087) 25386 AR

SPOLETO
Perugia

★★★AGIP Uscita per Foligno,(SS3 Km127)
☎(0743)49340 tx 611627
⊶ℍ57 P Lift ℂ

SPOTORNO
Savona

★★★Royal Lungomare Kennedy ☎(019)745074 tx 283867
18 May-Sep
⊶ℍ100 P50 Lift ℂ ᗐ Beach Sea
Credit Cards ①②③⑤

★★Ligure Pn pza della Vittoria ☎(019)745118/9
May-Nov
rm37(⊶ℍ36) P10 Lift ℂ Sea
Credit Card ②

★ Villa Teresina via Imperia ☎(019)745160
Apr-Sep
⊶ℍ20 P12

STAGNO
See LIVORNO (LEGHORN)

STORTA, LA
See ROMA (ROME)

STRESA
Novara

★★★★★Grand et des Iles Borromées (CIGA)
Lungolago Umberto 1 er 63 ☎(0323)30431 tx 200377
⊶ℍ164 ☎ P Lift ℂ ᖰ ᗐ Mountain Lake
Credit Cards ①②③⑤

★★★★Bristol via Nazionale del Sempione 73
☎(0323)32601 tx 200212
15 Mar-15 Nov
⊶ℍ255 P150 Lift ℂ ᖰ ▱ ᗐ ∪ Beach Mountain Lake

★★★★Regina Palace Lungolago Umberto 1er 27
☎(0323)30171 tx 200381
⊶ℍ176 ☎ P80 Lift ℂ ᖰ ᗐ Mountain Lake
Credit Cards ①②③④⑤

★★★Astoria Lungolago Umberto 1er 31
☎(0323)32566 tx 200085
End Mar-Oct
rm106(⊶ℍ98) A9rm ☎ P70 Lift ℂ ᗐ Lake
Credit Cards ①②③④⑤

★★★Palma Lungolago Umberto 1er
☎(0323)32401 tx 200541
Mar-Nov
⊶ℍ128 ☎ P40 Lift ℂ ᗐ Beach Mountain Lake
Credit Cards ①②③④⑤

★★Italia & Svizzera pza G Marconi 1
☎(0323)30540
15 Mar-20 Nov
⊶ℍ32 P Lift ℂ Lake
Credit Cards ①②③⑤

★★Lido la Perla Nera pza Stazione Funivia
☎(0323)30384
Apr-10 Oct
rm27(⊶ℍ24) P10 Mountain Lake
Credit Cards ①②③⑤

★★Milan & Speranza au Lac pza Imbarcadero
☎(0323)31178 & 31190 tx 200113
Mar-Nov
⊶ℍ170 ☎ P Lift ℂ ᗐ Mountain Lake
Credit Cards ①②③④⑤

★★Parc via Gignous 1 ☎(0323)30335/6
Apr-Oct
⊶ℍ22 A16rm P Lift Lake
Credit Cards ①②③

★★Royal DPn via Nazionale del Sempione
☎(0323)32777 tx 200396
Etr-Oct
⊶ℍ45 P30 Lift ℂ Mountain Lake
Credit Card ③

Jolly Car ☎(0323) 32161 AR

SUSA
Torino

★★Napoleon via Mazzini 44 ☎(0122)2704
:Rest closed Jan & Sat
⊶ℍ43 ☎ P20 Lift Mountain
Credit Cards ①③

SYRACUSE
SeeSIRACUSAunderSICILIA (SICILY)

TAORMINA
Messina
See SICILIA, ISOLA (SICILY)

TARQUINIA
Viterbo

★★*Tarconte* via Tuscia 19 ☎(0766)856585 tx 612172
⊶ℍ53 P25 Lift ℂ
Credit Cards ②⑤

TERRACINA
Latina

★★*Palace* Lungomare Matteotti 2
☎(0773)752585
⊶ℍ73 ☎ P60 Lift ℂ Beach Sea
Credit Cards ②③④⑤

TIRRENIA
Pisa

★★★Golf via dell Edera 29 ☎(050)37545
⊶ℍ77 ☎ P15 Lift ℂ ᖰ ᛉ ᛉ Beach Sea

TOLMEZZO
Udine

Automezzi Tolmezzo Paluzza 3 ☎(0433) 2151 Fia

TORBOLE
Trento

★★★Lago di Garda Via Lungolago Verona
☎(0464)505111 tx 401530
Mar-Oct
⊶ℍ36 P5 Lift ℂ Mountain Lake
Credit Cards ①②③⑤

TORINO (TURIN)
Torino

Torino's grace and charm surprise many visitors. For this delightful city bears a mantle of French influence, characterised by the wide, formal avenues, elegant squares and gardens. Torino is the capital of the Piemonte region, an important centre for trade and industry and a place of learning and culture. It has many fine art collections and the world-famous treasure, the Holy Shroud of Turin, is housed in the vast cathedral.
The Via Roma is lined with smart boutiques boasting top names in Italian fashion. For antiques and books, look in the Piazza San Carlo and Via Po. The Balon flea market is held every Saturday morning in the Piazza della Republica.

EATING OUT Local specialities include *agnolotti* - ravioli stuffed with truffles, spinach, lamb or veal; white truffles from Alba; *bolliti con salsa verde* - boiled meats with a green herb sauce; *gianduia* - chocolate pudding; *zabaglione* - whipped egg yolks and Marsala; and *grissini* - thin breadsticks. Regional wines include the red Barolo and the sparkling white Asti Spumante. Vermouth is made in Turin using a blend of wines flavoured with Alpine herbs.

TORINO (TURIN)
★★★★★**Jolly Principi di Piemonte** via P-Gobetti 15 ☎(011)519693 tx 221120
◀♠107 Lift ℂ
Credit Cards ①②③④⑤

★★★★**Jolly Ambasciatori** corso V-Emanuele 104 ☎(011)5752 tx 221296
◀♠197 ☎ Lift ℂ
Credit Cards ①②③④⑤

★★★★**Jolly-Ligure** pza C-Felice 85 ☎(011)55641 tx 220167
◀♠156 P Lift ℂ
Credit Cards ①②③④⑤

★★★★**Turin Palace** (SRS) via Sacchi 8 ☎(011)515511 tx 221411
◀♠123 ☎ P10 Lift ℂ
Credit Cards ①②③④⑤

★★★**Patria** via Cernaia 42 ☎(011)519903
rm108(◀♠86) ☎ Lift ℂ

★★**Alexandra** Lungo Dora Napoli 14 (n.rest) ☎(011)858327 tx 221562
◀♠55 ☎ Lift ℂ
Credit Cards ①②③④⑤

B Koellker Barletta 133-135 ☎(011) 353632 AR DJ

At **SETTIMO**(8km NE on A4)
★★★*AGIP* ☎(011)800185 tx 611627
◀♠100

TORRE A MARE
See BARI

TREMEZZO
Como
★★★**Bazzoni** via Regina ☎(0344)26335
rm80(◀♠75) ☎ P Lift ℂ

★★★**Grand Tremezzo** (BW) via Regina 8 ☎(0344)40446 tx 320810
◀♠102 P25 Lift ℂ ⚘ ⊇ Mountain Lake
Credit Cards ①②③⑤

TRENTO
Trento
★★**Venezia** pza Duomo 45 ☎(0461)34114 & 34559
:Rest closed Sep-Jun
rm45(◀♠31) A15rm P10 Lift ℂ
Credit Cards ②③⑤

Franceschi ☎(0461) 822110 Ope Vau

At **SARDAGNA**(4km W)
★★★*AGIP* via Brennero, 168 Uscita per,Bolzano ☎(0461)981117 tx 611627
◀♠45 P Lift ℂ

TREVISO
Treviso
★★★**Continental** via Roma 16 (n.rest) ☎(39422)57216 tx 420385
◀♠82 Lift ℂ
Credit Cards ①②③④⑤

Bobbo della Repubblica ☎(0422) 62396 AR DJ
Sile Motori della Repubblica 278 ☎(0422) 62743 AR
SOCAART della Repubblica 19 ☎(0422) 63725 For

Trevisauto ☎(0422) 63265 Ope Vau

TRIESTE
Trieste
★★★★**Duchi d'Aosta** (CIGA) Piazza Unita'd'Italia 2 ☎(040)62081 tx 460358
◀♠50 Lift ℂ Sea
Credit Cards ①②③⑤

★★★**Jolly** corso Cavour 7 ☎(040)7694 tx 460359
◀♠170 P Lift ℂ
Credit Cards ①②③④⑤

★★★*AGIP* Duino Service Area,(On Autostrada A42) ☎(040)208273
◀♠80 P Lift ℂ

Antonucci ☎(040) 420426 Peu
Filotecnica Guilliana F-Severo 42-48 ☎(040) 569121 AR Vol
Grandi Flavia 120 ☎(040) 281166 Fia
Regina ☎(040) 725345 **P** BMW Ope Vau

GRIGNANO
★★★★**Adriatico Palace** ☎(040)224241 tx 460449
Apr-12 Oct
◀♠102 ☎ P200 Lift ℂ ⚘ ⊇
Credit Cards ①②③④⑤

TURIN
SeeTORINO

UDINE
Udine
★★★**Astoria Italia** pza XX Settembre 24 ☎(0432)505091 tx 45012
◀♠80 ☎ Lift ℂ
Credit Cards ①②③④⑤

★★★**Cristallo** pza G-d'Annunzio 43 ☎(0432)501919
◀♠81 ☎ P5 Lift ℂ
Credit Cards ①②③⑤

Autofriulana Europa Unita 33 ☎(0432) 504330 **P** AR

Edera ☎(0432) 33502
Furgiuele & Baldelli ☎(0432) 32168 **P** For

VALSOLDA
Como
At **SAN MAMETE**
★★★**Stella d'Italia** ☎(0344)68139
Apr-Oct
◀♠36 ☎ P14 Lift Beach Mountain Lake
Credit Cards ①②③⑤

VARALLO
Vercelli
★★★*AGIP* (SS 299 d'Alagna, Km26) (SS299 d'Alagna-km26) ☎(0163)52447
◀♠38 P Lift ℂ Mountain

VARAZZE
Savona
★★**Delfino** via Colombo 48 ☎(019)97073
:Rest closed Fri
rm40(◀♠26) A14rm ☎ P14 Lift ℂ Beach Sea Mountain
Credit Cards ①②③⑤

VARENNA
Como
★★**Olivedo** ☎(0341)830115
Closed Nov
rm15(◀♠12) A4rm P Mountain Lake

VARESE
Varese
★★★**Palace** via L-Manara 11 ☎(0332)312600 tx 380163

◀♠108 P300 Lift ℂ ⚘ Mountain Lake
Credit Cards ①②③④⑤
VARIGOTTI
See FINALE LIGURE

VENEZIA (VENICE)
Venezia

Situated over a sprawling archipelago, 4 kilometers from the Italian mainland and split by more than 150 canals, Venice is unique among European cities. No road communications exist in the city. Vehicles may be left in garages in Piazzale Roma or at the island end of the causeway or at open parking places on the mainland approaches. Garages will not accept advance bookings. Transport to hotels is by waterbus, etc, for which there are fixed charges for fares and porterage. Hotel rooms overlooking the Grand Canal normally have a surcharge. Venezia is built on more than 100 islands with at least as many canals spanned by over 400 bridges. Use the *vaporetto*, the fast, cheap waterbus, for travel on the canals; water taxis or gondolas are very expensive. The imposing *Palazza Ducale* (Duke's Palace), stands at the heart of the city near St Mark's Square, a superb ensemble dominated by the Basilica of St Mark. Like Venice itself, the Basilica is a magnificent blend of Eastern and Western artistic styles, combining marble, mosaics and glittering gold. Venezia offers a wealth of great palaces, churches, museums and galleries to visit, notably the *Accademia*, with its definitive collection of Venetian paintings. You can combine a visit here with a wander round the Zattere, the stone-flagged quay that borders the Giudecca Canal and leads round to the Baroque Church of Santa Maria della Salute.
Among the islands to visit are San Giorgia Maggiore, with its marvellous Palladian church; Muran, famous for glass-making; Burano, noted for its lace; and Torcello, which boasts a magnificent cathedral. The Venice Lido is still one of Europe's most fashionable beach resorts. Excellent shops are to be found

around St Mark's Square, particularly impressive are those in the Mercerie. For budget-priced clothes the best place is around the Rialto where there is also an excellent daily food market with tantalising fruit, vegetables and fish.

EATING OUT Traditional Venetian cooking is largely based on seafood. Lobster, crab, scampi and a tasty white fish locally known as *San Pietro* are popular. Specialities include *brodetto do pesce* (fish soup); *soppressa* (Venetian sausages) and *fegato alla veneziana* - thinly sliced calves' liver cooked with onions. For a treat, stop at *Fiorian's* or *Quadri's* in St Mark's Square for a coffee or ice cream.

Venetian restaurants tend to be expensive even by Italian standards, especially those in the centre, but if cost is not a problem then the terrace restaurants of the Danieli, overlooking the lagoon, and its sister hotel the Gritti Palace, overlooking the Grand Canal, are outstanding. In the moderately priced category, *Fiaschetteria Toscane*, in Campo San Giovanni Cristomo, is deservedly popular with Venetians as well as visitors.

See also MESTRE

VENEZIA (VENICE)

★★★★★**Daniell** (CIGA) Riva degli Schiavoni 4196 ☎(041)5226480 tx 41007
↝↟231 Lift ℂ Sea
Credit Cards ① ② ③ ④ ⑤

★★★★★**Gritti Palace** (CIGA) Campo Santa Maria del Giglio 2467 ☎(041)
↝↟99 Lift ℂ ℺ ≙ ⵉⵉ Beach
Credit Cards ① ② ③ ④ ⑤

★★★★**Europa & Regina** (CIGA) Canal Grande-San Marco 2159 ☎(0332)5200477 tx 410123
↝↟188 Lift ℂ ℺ ≙ ⵉⵉ Ʊ Beach Sea
Credit Cards ① ② ③ ④ ⑤

★★★**Cavalletto** calle del Cavalletto 1107,pza San Marco ☎(041)5200955 tx 410684
↝↟79 Lift ℂ
Credit Cards ① ② ③ ⑤

★★★**Concordia** (GT) calle Larga-San Marco 367 (n.rest) ☎(041)5206886 tx 411069
↝↟55 Lift ℂ
Credit Cards ① ② ③

★★★**Gabrielli-Sandwirth** (BW) Riva degli Schiavoni 4110 ☎(041)5231580 tx 410228
18 Mar-10 Nov
rm111(↝↟89) Lift ℂ Sea
Credit Cards ① ② ③ ⑤

★★★**Metropole** Riva degli Schiavoni 4149 (n.rest) ☎(041)5205044 tx 410340
↝↟64 Lift ℂ
Credit Cards ① ② ③ ⑤

★★★**Saturnia & International** via XXIII Marzo San Marco 2399 ☎(041)5208377 tx 410355
↝↟95 Lift ① ② ③ ⑤

★★**Flora** via XXII Marzo 2283A (n.rest) ☎(0332)5205844 tx 410401
Feb-15 Nov
↝↟44 Lift ℂ
Credit Cards ① ② ③ ⑤

★★**Giorgione** Santa Apostoli 4587 ☎(0332)5225810
↝↟56 Lift ℂ
Credit Cards ① ② ③ ④

★★**Panada** (GT) calle Larga San Marco 656 ☎(041)709088 tx 410153
↝↟46 Lift ℂ
Credit Cards ① ② ③ ⑤

★**Basilea** S Croce-Rio Marin 817 (n.rest) ☎(041)718477 tx 420320
↝↟45 A15rm ℂ
Credit Cards ② ③

VENEZIA LIDO
Venezia
There is a car ferry service from Venice (piazzale Roma).

★★★★★**Excelsior** (CIGA) Lungomare Marconi 41 ☎(0041)5260201 tx 410023
Mar-Nov
↝↟230 ≉ P50 Lift ℂ ℺ ≙ ⵉⵉ Beach
Credit Cards ① ② ③ ④ ⑤

★★★★**Bains** (CIGA) Lungomare Marconi 17 ☎(041)765921 tx 410142
15 Apr-30 Oct
↝↟193 P150 Lift ℂ ℺ ≙ ⵉⵉ Beach Sea
Credit Cards ① ② ③ ④ ⑤

★★★**Adria-Urania & Villa Nora & Ada** viale Dandolo 24,27 & 29 ☎(041)5260120 tx 410666
1 Apr-30 Oct
↝↟88 A17rm P15 Lift ℂ
Credit Cards ① ② ③ ④ ⑤

VENTIMIGLIA
Imperia

★★**Posta** Sottoconvento 15 (n.rest) ☎(0184)351218
Mar-Dec
↝↟18 Lift ℂ
Credit Cards ① ③

Revelli ☎(0184) 292784 BMW Saa

VERBANIA
Novara

At **PALLANZA**(1km SW)

★★★**Majestic** via V-Veneto 32 ☎(0323)504305 tx 223339
Mar-Oct
↝↟119 P50 Lift ℂ ℺ ⛱ Beach Mountain Lake
Credit Cards ① ② ③ ⑤

★★**Belvedere** pza IV-Novembre 10 ☎(0323)503202 tx 200269
Mar-30 Oct
↝↟56 Lift ℂ Lake
Credit Cards ① ② ③ ⑤

★★**San Gottardo** viale delle Magnolie 4 ☎(0323)503202 tx 200269
Mar-30 Oct
↝↟40 Lift ℂ Lake
Credit Cards ① ② ③ ⑤

VERCELLI
Vercelli

★★★**Viotti** via Marsala 7 ☎(061)61602
↝↟161 P10 Lift ℂ
Credit Cards ① ② ③ ⑤

VERONA
Verona

Readers of Shakespeare are familiar with Verona, most obviously through *The Two Gentlemen of Verona*, but also as the setting for *Romeo and Juliet*, and a stroll along Via delle Arche Scaligere will reveal the alleged site of *Casa di Romeo* and, at 23 Via Cappello, Juliet's house, complete, of course, with balcony.

But Verona has much more to offer the visitor than its links with Shakespeare. It became a Roman town in BC49 and contains many reminders of those times. Perhaps most impressive is the Arena, the 3rd-century amphitheatre seating 22,000; unlike Rome's Colosseum it is still in use as an opera house and theatre.

Standing on the banks of the River Adige in a setting of cypress-covered hills, Verona has been described as one of the country's most prosperous and elegant cities. The Basilica of San Zeno Maggiore is arguably the noblest Romanesque church in northern Italy, and the *Loggia del Consiglio*, the old town hall, one of the most beautiful of all early Renaissance buildings.

EATING OUT Verona is as well known for its wines as for its food. Some of Italy's best-known wines are produced in the area and names such as Soave, Bardolino and Valpolicella have gained international renown. To complement the wines try one of the many local pasta and seafood dishes.

VERONA

★★★★**Colomba d'Oro** via C-Cattaneo 10 ☎(045)595300 tx 480872
↝↟52 ≉ P Lift ℂ
Credit Cards ① ② ③ ⑤

★★★★**Due Torri** (SRS) pza Sant'Anastasia 4 ☎(0457)595044 tx 480524
↝↟100 ≉ P Lift ℂ
Credit Cards ① ② ③ ⑤

★★★**Accademia** via Scala 12 ☎(045)596222 tx 480874
↝↟100 ≉ P75 Lift ℂ
Credit Cards ① ② ③ ⑤

★★★**AGIP** via Unita d'Italia 346 (SS1 1km 307) ☎(045)972033 tx 611627
↝↟68 P Lift ℂ

★★★**San Pietro** via Santa Teresa 1 ☎(045)582600 tx 480523
↝↟57 ≉ P8 Lift ℂ
Credit Cards ① ③

★★Capuleti via del Pontiere 26 (n.rest)
☎(045)8000154 tx 351609
10 Jan-24 Dec
⚑36 🏊 P Lift ℂ
Credit Cards ① ② ⑤

★★Italia via G-Mameli 54 (n.rest) ☎(045)918088
tx 431064
⚑53 🏊 P20 Lift ℂ
Credit Cards ① ② ③ ⑤

Auto Motor ☎(045) 509361 Aud Por VW

SVAE ☎(045) 508088 For

VIAREGGIO
Lucca

★★★★Palace via F-Gioia 2 ☎(0584)46134 tx
501044
⚑68 🏊 P Lift ℂ Beach Sea
Credit Cards ① ② ③ ⑤

★★★Plaza & de Russie Lungomare Manin 1
(n.rest) ☎(0584)46546 tx 501383
⚑50 🏊 P15 Lift ℂ Beach Sea
Credit Cards ① ② ③ ④ ⑤

★★★Garden DPn via Ugo Foscolo 70
☎(0584)44025 tx 590403
⚑41 🏊 Lift ℂ
Credit Cards ① ② ③ ④ ⑤

Fazioli Buonarroti 67 ☎(0584) 47580 Ope Vau

Pecchia ☎(0584) 393967 Cit

VICENZA
Vicenza

★★★AGIP via Degli Scaligeri,Fiera
☎(0444)56471 tx 611627
⚑123 P Lift ℂ

Americana San Lazzaro 15 ☎(0444) 563118 Ope
Vau

Sabema della Pace 50 ☎(0444) 500348 P BMW

VICO EQUENSE
Napoli

★★Oriente via Napoli ☎(081)8798143 tx 721051
⚑80 🏊 P350 ℂ Sea
Credit Cards ① ③ ⑤

VIESTE
Foggia

★★★★Pizzomunno Vieste Palace
☎(0884)78741 tx 810267
Apr-Oct
⚑224 A41rm 🏊 P100 Lift ℂ ⚓ ⚒ ⋃ Beach Sea
Credit Cards ① ② ③ ⑤

At **PUGNOCHIUSO**(22km S)

★★★Ulivi Pugnochiuso ☎(0884)79061 tx 810122
⚑202 P Lift ⚒ ⚓ Beach

VIETRI SUL MARE
See **SALERNO**

VILLASIMIUS
Cagliari
See **SARDEGNA, ISOLA (SARDINIA)**

VITERBO
Viterbo

★★Leon d'Oro via della Cava 36 (n.rest)
☎(0761)344444
rm44(⚑36) P9 Lift ℂ
Credit Cards ① ② ③ ⑤

Ferri Antonio L-Garbini ☎(0761) 342109 For

SAN MARINO

San Marino is an independent republic situated between the Italian provinces of Forlì and Pesaro e Urbino, about seven miles south-west of Rimini on the Adriatic coast. The city of San Marino is built on the western slopes of the most northerly peak of Monte Titano, which is crowned by a fortress overlooking the precipice. A new suburb has grown up on the south, near the former railway station, but the chief suburb, Borgo Maggiore, lies to the north-east on a lower shoulder below the cliff-face. Otherwise, apart from the township of Serravalle, there are only small villages and hamlets in the republic.

SAN MARINO

★★★Grand via Antonio Onofri 31
☎(0549)992400 tx 0505555
1 Mar-Nov
⚑56 🏊 P15 Lift ℂ Mountain
Credit Cards ① ② ③ ⑤

★★★Titano Contrada del Collegio 21
☎(0549)991007 tx 505444
15 Mar-15 Nov
⚑50 A50rm 🏊 P30 Lift ℂ Mountain
Credit Cards ① ② ③ ④ ⑤

★★Excelsior via J-Istriani ☎(0541)991163
⚑25 🏊 P25 Lift ℂ Mountain

★Tre Penne via Lapidici Marini ☎(0541)992437
⚑12 Lift Mountain
Credit Cards ① ② ③ ⑤

MOTORING IN EUROPE?

IF SO YOU NEED AA 5-STAR SERVICE

If you are taking a European motoring holiday let AA 5-Star Service give you the added peace of mind of knowing that you, your family and your car are well cared for by the world's No. 1 motoring organisation.

AA 5-Star Service gives you roadside assistance, vehicle recovery, medical expenses and lots more besides — no wonder over 300,000 cars and over 800,000 people were covered last year.

So why not contact your local AA Centre or phone 021-550 7648 and ask for details now.

Have the Best — Don't Hope for The Best

AA

DIRECTORY

Getting the most from your motoring

Ring us for practical advice about running your car. Compiled by our experienced technical, engineering and research staff, the topics are based on questions our members frequently ask.

Anti-lock brakes	**0836-401-501**
Anti-theft devices	**0836-401-502**
Automatic transmission for smaller cars: what's available?	**0836-401-503**
Auctions: how they work	**0836-401-504**
Checks before you start, planning your route, safe motorway driving	**0836-401-505**
Child seats and harnesses	**0836-401-506**
Costs of motoring: AA's latest calculations	**0836-401-507**
Disabled drivers: motability, conversions	**0836-401-509**
Diesel cars: pros and cons	**0836-401-510**
Disputes with garages and car makers	**0836-401-511**
Fire extinguishers	**0836-401-512**
Four-wheel driver: utility to luxury	**0836-401-513**
Fuel economy devices: do they work?	**0836-401-514**
Fuel injection and turbo charging: what are the benefits?	**0836-401-515**
Laying up your car	**0836-401-517**
Lead-free petrol: pros and cons	**0836-401-525**
Motorway breakdowns	**0836-401-526**
Roof racks	**0836-401-518**
Sell privately — or trade in?	**0836-401-519**
Spare fuel cans	**0836-401-521**
Towing: matching the vehicle to the load	**0836-401-522**
Seasonal motoring and protecting your car	**0836-401-523**

For your free copy of the complete AA Directory, call

0256 491648

Messages last from about 1 up to 7 minutes and are charged at 25p per minute cheap rate, 38p per minute at other times (including VAT); callers pay only for the time they use. Prices for mobile calls can vary — see your service provider.

We're all you need to know.

LUXEMBOURG

Language
French, but German and the
Luxembourgeois patois are also spoken

Local Time
GMT + 1 hour (Summer GMT + 2 hours)

Currency
Luxembourg franc, divided into 100
centimes. At the time of going to press,
£1 = LFr65.05
US$1 = LFr39.18

Emergency numbers
Fire ☎012 – Civil Defence emergency
services (Secours d'urgence)

Information in Britain
Luxembourg National Tourist Office,
36–37 Picadilly (entrance Swallow
Street), London W1V 9PA
☎01-434 2800 (071-434 2800 from 6th
May 1990)

Information in the USA
Luxembourg National Tourist Office, 801
Second Avenue, New York NY10017
☎212 370 7367

The Grand Duchy of Luxembourg is a small independent state, 998 sq miles in area, situated between France, Germany and Belgium. It comprises parts of the Ardenne uplands and the Lorraine scarplands. Luxembourg, the capital, is an attractive and historic town founded on a natural defensive site. Under successive occupations by the Spaniards, Austrians and French, its fortifications were so elaborated that it came to be considered the strongest inland fortress in Europe – the Gibraltar of the continent. The fortifications, dismantled in accordance with the treaty of London, have been largely replaced by parks and gardens, although many relics, including the Casemates – the network of underground fortifications – remain. Notable buildings include the grand-ducal palace (1572), cathedral (1618) and town hall. The main shopping areas are to be found in the south of the city, around the Place de la Gare.

Apart from Luxembourg, the chief towns are Esch-sur-Alzette, Dudelange, Ettelbruck, Diekirch, Echternach and Wiltz. The Luxembourgeois patois (mainly Germanic) and French are official languages, but side by side with these the German language is freely used.

As a destination for walkers, Luxembourg has few equals, while those interested in history and culture have a choice of no fewer than one hundred and thirty castles at which to marvel.

HOW TO GET THERE

The usual Continental Channel ports for this journey are Boulogne, Calais or Dunkerque (Dunkirk) in France, and Oostende (Ostende) or Zeebrugge in Belgium.

Distance

Luxembourg City is just over 320km (200 miles) from the Belgian ports, or about 420km (260 miles) from the French ports, and is, therefore, within a day's drive of the Channel coast.

MONEYMATTERS

There are no restrictions on the amount of foreign or local currency which you can take into or out of Luxembourg, but because of the limited market for Luxembourg notes in other countries, it is advisable to change them into Belgian or other foreign notes.

Banking hours

Monday–Friday 08.30/09.00–12.00 hours and 13.30/14.00–16.30/17.00 hours.

Postcheques

may be cashed at all post offices up to a maximum of LFr7,000 per cheque. Go to a counter position which displays the word **Chèques** or **Postchèques**.

MOTORING REGULATIONS AND GENERAL INFORMATION

The information given here is specific to Luxembourg. It **must** be read in conjunction with the European ABC at the front of the book, which covers those regulations which are common to many countries.

Accidents*

There are no firm rules to adopt following an accident. However, anyone requested to give assistance must do so. See also *Warning triangle* below.

Boats*

When temporarily importing boats into Luxembourg, documentation, in addition to the *Customs regulations* referred to below.

Breakdown*

The Automobile Club du Grand Duché de Luxembourg (ACL) operates a 24-hour road assistance service throughout the whole country. The vehicles of the ACL are yellow in colour and bear a black inscription '*Automobile Club Service Routier*'. This service should not be confused with the '*Dépannages Secours Automobiles*' (DSA), which is a commercial enterprise not connected with the AA or any other organisation. See also *Warning triangle* below.

British Embassy/Consulate*

The British Embassy together with its consular section is located at Luxembourg Ville, 14 Boulevard Roosevelt ☎29864/66.

Children in cars

Children under 10 years are not permitted to travel in a vehicle as front-seat passengers when rear seating is available.

Customs regulations*

A *Customs Carnet de Passages en Douane* is required for all temporarily imported boats, unless entering and leaving by water.

*Additional information will be found in the European ABC at the front of the book.

Dimensions and weight restrictions

Private **cars** and towed **trailers** or **caravans** are restricted to the following dimensions – height, 4 metres; width, 2.50 metres; length, 12 metres. The maximum permitted overall length of vehicle/trailer or caravan combinations is 18 metres.

The weight of a caravan must not exceed 75% of the weight of the towing vehicle.

Driving licence*

A valid UK or Republic of Ireland licence is acceptable in Luxembourg. The minimum age at which a visitor may use a temporarily imported car or motorcycle is 17 years.

Emergency messages to tourists*

Emergency messages to tourists are broadcast during the summer on the German *RTL* programme. These messages are transmitted on 208 metres medium wave, and may be given at any time between 06.00 and 01.00hrs.

Horn, use of

In built-up areas, it is prohibited to use the horn except to avoid an accident. *Outside built-up areas*, use the horn instead of lights only, during a day, to warn of approach.

Lights*

It is prohibited to drive on sidelights only. At night, and also during the day when necessary, vehicles parked on a public road must have their sidelights on if the public lighting does not enable them to be seen from a sufficient distance. Vehicles equipped with a side parking light may use this instead of sidelights. Should fog or snow reduce visibility to less than 100 metres (110yds), vehicles stopped or parked outside a built-up area must be illuminated by dipped headlights or fog lamps. Two fog lamps may be used at the same time as dipped headlights, but full headlights together with fog or spot lights may not be used at the same time. At night, it is compulsory to flash your headlights before overtaking another vehicle at places where visibility is restricted, and whenever road safety requires it. It is compulsory for *motorcyclists* to use dipped headlights during the day.

Motoring club*

The **Automobile Club du Grand-Duché de Luxembourg** (ACL) has its head office at 8007 Bertrange (Luxembourg), 13 route de Longwy ☎450045. ACL office hours are 08.30–12.00hrs and 13.30–18.00hrs from Monday to Friday; closed Saturday and Sunday.

Motorways

Only short sections totalling 64km (40 miles) are at present open, but an eventual network of 160km (100 miles) is planned.

Orange badge scheme for disabled drivers*

In Luxembourg, parking places reserved for disabled drivers are indicated by a parking sign (white letter on a blue panel) or a parking prohibited sign (red ring and bars with blue background), both with the international disabled symbol added. However, badge holders are not permitted to exceed the parking time limit.

Overtaking*

Outside built-up areas at night, it is compulsory to flash your headlight's before overtaking another vehicle. During the day, use the horn instead of lights.

Parking*

Park on the right-hand side of the road in the direction of the traffic flow, unless parking is prohibited on this side. Spending the night in a vehicle or trailer on the roadside is prohibited. In towns, parking is controlled by parking discs, parking meters and persons who issue tickets. Discs are available from the ACL, petrol companies and principal banks. Discs must be displayed on the windscreen; they are set at the time of parking and show when parking time expires. Wheel clamps are used on illegally parked vehicles throughout the country.

Petrol*

Credit cards Many petrol stations will accept Visa.

*Additional information will be found in the European ABC at the front of the book.

Duty-free petrol In addition to the petrol in the vehicle tank, up to 10 litres in a can may be imported free of customs duty and tax.
Petrol (leaded) Super (98 octane) grade.
Petrol (unleaded) is sold in Luxembourg as Normal (91 octane) and Super (95 octane) grades. Pumps dispensing unleaded petrol are marked *2085* and *essence sans plomb* (lead-free petrol).

Post information

Mail Postcards LFr12, letters up to 20gm LFr12.
Post offices There are 100 post offices in Luxembourg. Opening hours are 08.00–12.00hrs and 14.00–17.00hrs. Monday to Friday. The post office at Luxembourg station is open every day 06.00–22.00hrs, and the airport post office every day 07.00–21.30hrs. The Esch-sur-Alzette office is open on Saturdays. Small offices are open for shorter hours; these are shown at the entrance to each post office.

Priority*

All road users must yield right of way to other road users when entering a public road, starting from the kerb or reversing.

Public holidays*

Official Public holidays in Luxembourg for 1990 are given below.
    January 1 (New Year's Day)
    April 16 (Easter Monday)
    May 1 (Labour Day)
    May 24 (Ascension Day)
    June 4 (Whit Monday)
    June 23† (National Day)
    August 15 (Assumption)
    November 1 (All Saints' Day)
    December 25 (Christmas Day)
    December 26 (Boxing Day)
†Saturday

Roads

There is a comprehensive system of good main and secondary roads.

Shopping hours

Some shops close on Monday mornings, but the usual hours of opening for *food shops* are from Monday to Saturday 08.00–12.00hrs and 14.00–18.00hrs. However, *supermarkets* open from 09.00 to 20.00hrs but close at 18.00hrs on Saturdays.

Speed limits*

The placename indicates the beginning and the end of a built-up area. The following speed limits for cars are in force if there are no special signs: *built-up areas*, 60kph (37mph); *main roads*, 90kph (56mph); Motorways, 120kph (74mph) (lower limits apply to caravans). All lower signposted speed limits must be adhered to.

Spiked or studded tyres

Spiked tyres may be used between December and March; however, they must be fitted to all four wheels, and speeds must not exceed 60kph (37mph) on ordinary roads and 90kph (56mph) on motorways. Vehicles registered in Luxembourg and equipped with spiked tyres must display a disc bearing the figure '60' in black; foreign-registered vehicles only need to comply if obligatory in country of registration.

Telephone*

Insert coin **after** lifting the receiver; the dialling tone is the same as in the UK. Use LFr5 coins for local calls and LFr5 or LFr20 for national and international calls. Belgian coins may also be used.
International callbox identification Roadside callboxes.
Telephone rates A telephone call to the UK costs LFr75 for three minutes and LFr25 for each additional minute.
Telephone codes

UK to Luxembourg	010 352
Luxembourg to UK	00 44
Luxembourg to Republic of Ireland	00 353
Luxembourg to the USA	00 1

Warning triangle*

The use of a warning triangle is compulsory in the event of accident or breakdown. The triangle must be placed on the road about 100 metres (110yds) behind the vehicle to warn following traffic of any obstruction.

*Additional information will be found in the European ABC at the front of the book.

ACCOMMODATION

The prices shown below are an average for each classification. At the time of going to press, £1 = LFr65.05 and US$1 = LFr39.18, but you should check the rate of exchange before your departure.

AVERAGE PRICES

	Single Room	Double Room	Breakfast	Lunch/Dinner
★★★★	—	—	—	—
★★★	LFr2500–3500	LFr3500–5000	—	LFr1400–2200
★★	LFr1200–1900	LFr1150–2150	LFr200	LFr475–700
★	LFr900–1700	LFr1300–2350	LFr250	from LFr650

See French section for abbreviations

BEAUFORT

★★*Meyer* Grand r 120 ☎86262 tx 1524
Closed 16 Jan-19 Mar
⤙ℝ40 ☎ P Lift ⚲ ∪

BERDORF

★★*Ermitage* rte du Gundhof 44 ☎79184
Apr-Sep
⤙ℝ16 ☎ P

CLERVAUX

★★*Abbaye* Principale 80 ☎91049 tx 1522
24 Mar-30 Oct & 20-31 Dec
rm50(⤙ℝ35) ☎ P Lift

★★*Claravallis* r de la Gare 3 ☎91034 tx 3134
Mar-Jan
⤙ℝ28 P40 Lift ☾ Mountain
Credit Cards ①②③⑤

🍴 *E Wagener* Grand r 52 ☎ 91080 Toy

DIEKIRCH

★*Beau Séjour* Esplanade 10-12 ☎803403
Closed 11-23 Oct
⤙ℝ28 Lift

DOMMELDANGE

★★★*Parc* rte d'Echternach 120 ☎435643 tx 1418
⤙ℝ221 P400 Lift ☾ ⚲ ⊐ ⋔⋔ ∪ Beach
Credit Cards ①②③⑤

ECHTERNACH

★★★*Bel Air* (Relais et Châteaux) rte Berdorf 1
☎729383 tx 2640
Closed 3 Jan-14 Feb :Rest closed 15-25 Nov
⤙ℝ34 ☎ P50 Lift ⚲ Mountain
Credit Cards ①②③⑤

★★*Commerce* pl du Marché 16 ☎72301
Mar-15 Nov & 20 Dec-1 Jan
rm56(⤙ℝ52) ☎ P Lift

★★*Parc* r de l'Hôpital 9 ☎729481 tx 60455
25 Mar-15 Nov
⤙ℝ27 P ▣

★*Universel Cheval Blanc* r de Luxembourg 40
☎352729991
Apr- 1 Nov
rm35(⤙ℝ30) P20 Lift
Credit Card ③

🍴 *Schneiders* r de Luxembourg 17 ☎ 729045
Ren

EHNEN

★*Bamberg's* 131 route du Vin ☎76717
17 Jan-Nov
⤙ℝ18 ☎ P6 Lift Sea Mountain
Credit Cards ①②③

ESCH-SUR-ALZETTE

🍴 *Euro-Motor Esch* bd Kennedy 108 ☎ 540134
For

🍴 *Muller Esch* bd Kennedy 122-4 ☎ 544844
Ope

🍴 *C Reding* r de Belvaux 109 ☎ 552323 Peu Tal

ETTELBRUCK

🍴 *Grand Garage P Wengler* av des Alliés 32-36
☎ 82157 For

FINDEL

See LUXEMBOURG

GREVENMACHER

★*Poste* 26 r de Tréve ☎75136
rm12(⤙1) ☎ P

GRUNDHOF

★★*Brimer* ☎86251 tx 1308
15 Feb-15 Nov :Rest closed Tue
⤙ℝ25 P100 Lift Mountain
Credit Cards ① ③

★*Ferring* rte Beaufort 4 ☎86015
26 Mar-15 Nov
rm27(⤙ℝ25) ☎ P Lift

HALLER

★*Hallerbach* r des Romains 2 ☎86151
Closed 11 Jan-Feb & Dec
⤙ℝ18 P Lift ⚲ ▣

HEINERSCHEID

★*Wagener* r de Stavelot 29 ☎98503
rm10 ☎ P

KAUTENBACH

★*Hatz* ☎958561
15 Feb-Dec
rm17(⤙ℝ12) ☎ P

KIRCHBERG

See LUXEMBOURG

LAROCHETTE

★★*Residence* r de Medernach 14 ☎87391 tx
60529
Feb-Nov
⤙ℝ22 P40 Beach
Credit Cards ①②③⑤

LUXEMBOURG
Luxembourg

See Plan page 294
Population 78,000 *Local Tourist Office* Cercle, Place d'Armes
☎22809
The old city of Luxembourg was for centuries one of the most powerful fortresses in the world - the 'Gibraltar of the North'. Today this capital of the Grand

Duchy of Luxembourg is a natural tourist centre. It has a wide selection of restaurants providing good food. The cuisine is largely French, but local specialities include *quenelles* (liver dumplings) and *treipen* (black pudding). The main shopping areas are in the south of the city, around the Place de la Gare. Interesting sights include the Cathedral of Notre Dame, with its magnificent sculptures, and Casemates (the network of underground fortifications), and the impressive span of the Pont Adolphe.

EATING OUT Cuisine in Luxembourg is a happy blend of French, Belgian and German, with its own special flair. Crayfish, pike and trout from the rivers form the basis of some tempting dishes. Other regional specialities are treipen (black pudding), sausages served with creamed potatoes and horseradish and Quenelles (liver dumplings). Ardennes ham is particularly delicious as a starter.

LUXEMBOURG

★★★★*Intercontinental* r J-Engling 4 ☎43781 tx
3754
⤙ℝ346 ☎ P100 Lift ⚲ ▣
Credit Cards ①②③④⑤

★★★★*Kons* pl de la Gare 24 ☎486021 tx 2306
⤙ℝ141 Lift

★★★*Central Molitor* (GT) av de la Liberté 28
☎489911 tx 2613
⤙ℝ36 ☎ Lift ☾
Credit Cards ①②③⑤

★★★*Cravat* bd Roosevelt 29 ☎21975 tx 2846
⤙ℝ60 Lift ☾
Credit Cards ①②③⑤

★*Francais* pl d'Armes 14 ☎474534 tx 60591
rm26(⤙ℝ23) Lift

🍴 *Grand Garage de la Pétrusse* r des Jardiniers
13-15 ☎ 442324 AR DJ

🍴 *P Lentz* rte d'Arlon 257 ☎ 444545 Dat

LUXEMBOURG

1	★★★★	Aerogolf Sheraton (At Findel)
2	★★★★	Holiday Inn (At Kirchberg)
3	★★★★	Intercontinental
4	★★★★	Kons
5	★★★	Central Molitor
6	★★★	Cravat
7	★★	Dany (At Strassen)
8	★	Francais

M Losch rte de Thionville ☎ 488121 Aud Por VW

At **FINDEL**(8km NW)

★★★★**Aerogolf Sheraton** rte de Treves ☎34571 tx 2662
150 P250 Lift ℂ
Credit Cards ① ② ③ ⑤

At **KIRCHBERG**

★★★★**Pullman** European Centre ☎437761 tx 2751
260 P300 Lift ⌫
Credit Cards ① ② ③ ⑤

Euro-Motor Autosonte, Neudorf exit ☎ 433030 For

At **STRASSEN**(2km W on N9)

★★**Dany** rte d'Arlon 72 ☎450881-83/84 tx 60517
18 A2rm ☎ P30 ∪

MERSCH

★**Marisca** pl de l'Étoile 1 ☎328456
Closed 21 Aug-14 Sep
rm20(8) ☎ P

MONDORF-LES-BAINS

★★★**Grand Chef** av des Bains 36 ☎681222 tx 1840
23 Apr-20 Oct
46 ☎ P Lift

STRASSEN
See **LUXEMBOURG**

VIANDEN

★★**Collette** Grande r 68-70 ☎84004
Apr-Oct
rm30(28) Mountain

★★**Heintz** Grand r 55 ☎84155
28 Mar-12 Nov :Rest closed Wed low season
rm30(25) ☎ P18 Lift Mountain
Credit Cards ① ② ③ ④ ⑤

★**Oranienburg** Grand r 126 ☎84153
Closed Jan-14 Feb:Rest closed Mon
rm34(28) Lift
Credit Cards ① ② ③ ⑤

ENVIRONS OF LUXEMBOURG

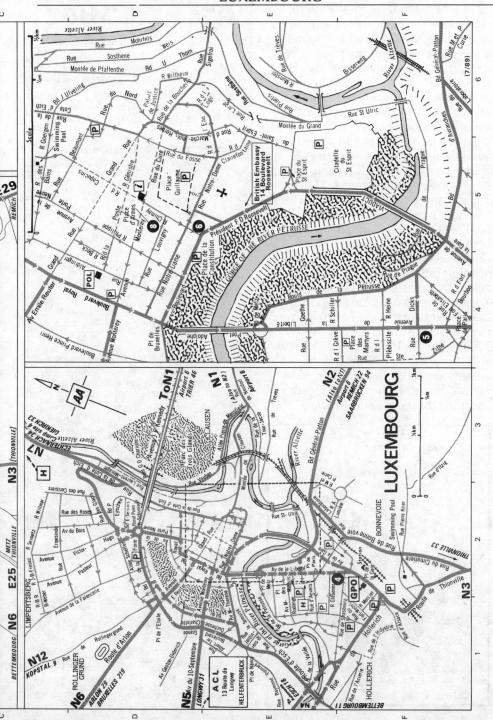

The Netherlands is a small country, a great advantage for the visitor since there are so many attractions from which to choose within a small area. Amsterdam, for instance, is less than an hour from the sea, while The Hague is almost on the seashore. With so many areas of water, Holland is an ideal country for watersports, with countless opportunities to participate.

The country's many and varied attractions include leisure parks, theme parks and wildlife parks, plus a huge selection of museums. There are a staggering 500 of these, ranging from great and famous museums such as the *Rijksmuseum* (National Museum) or the *Rijksmuseum Vincent Van Gogh* in Amsterdam to the unique open-air museums *Nederlands Openluchtmuseum* in Arnhem, the *Zaanse Schans* near Amsterdam, or the *Zuiderzee Museum* in Enkhuizen. Even a walk through the old part of Amsterdam, Delft, Gronigen or Gouda will reveal a fascinating array of artistic wealth, with unbroken rows of 16th, 17th and 18th-century façades adorning the canals and streets.

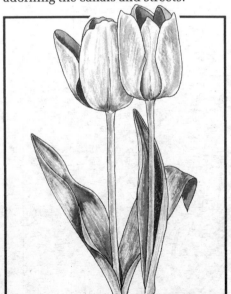

NETHERLANDS

Language
Dutch, with a tendency to use local dialect in Friesland

Local Time
GMT + 1 hour (Summer GMT + 2 hours)

Currency
Dutch guilder or *florin* (Fls), divided into 100 *cents*. At the time of going to press
£1 = Fls3.50
US$1 = Fls2.10

Emergency numbers
Fire: Amsterdam ☎212121
Den Haag ☎3222333
Rotterdam ☎4292929

Police: Amsterdam ☎222222
Den Haag ☎3222222
Rotterdam ☎4141414

Ambulance: Amsterdam ☎5555555
Den Haag ☎3222111
Rotterdam ☎4333300

Numbers for other towns are in the front of the local directories. If necessary, contact the **State Police Emergency Centre** ☎(03438) 14321

Information in Britain
Netherlands Board of Tourism, 25–28 Buckingham Gate, London SW1E 6LD ☎01–630 0451 (071–630 0451 from 6th May 1990)

Information in the USA
Netherlands Board of Tourism, 355 Lexington Avenue, New York, NY10017 ☎212 370 7367

NORTH

SEA

NL

D

B

For key to country identification - see
"About the gazetteer"

Groningen
Leeuwarden
Eernewoude
Drachten
Haren
Veendam
De Koog
Sneek
Assen
Beetsterzwaag
Heerenveen
Emmen
Den Helder
Dwingeloo
Hoogeveen
Giethoorn
Ommen
Enkhuizen
Emmeloord
Bergen
Hoorn
Lelystad
Kampen
Bergen-aan-Zee
Alkmaar
Zwolle
Heiloo
Dronten
Egmond-aan-Zee
Edam
Nijverdal
Ootmarsum
Beverwijk
Volendam
Raalte
Almelo
Bloemendaal
Haderwijk
Deventer
Hengelo
Oldenzaal
Overveen
Katwoude
Holten
Delden
De Lutte
Zandvoort
Amsterdam
Vierhouten
Enschede
Haarlem
Heemstede
Laren
Leuvenum
Apeldoorn
Lochem
Boekelo
Noordwijk-aan-Zee
Sassenheim
Bussum
Baarn
Putten
Zutphen
Warnsveld
Katwijk
Aalsmeer
Hilversum
Leusden
Lunteren
Wassenaar
Leiden
Woerden
Zeist
Ede
Doetinchem
Boskoop
DEN HAAG
Zoetermeer
Utrecht
Maarsbergen
Arnhem
Zeddam
Delft
Gouda
Scherpenzeel
Oosterbeek
Rotterdam
Wageningen
Heusden
Schiedam
Heelsum
Nijmegen
Papendrecht
Gorinchem
Oss
Berg-en-Dal
Noordgouwe
Middelharnis
Dordrecht
Nuland
Groesbeek
Zierikzee
's-Hertogenbosch
Mook-en-Middelaar
Domburg
Roosendaal
Oisterwijk
Venray
Veere
Breda
Middelburg
Goes
Gilze-Rijen
Tilburg
Helmond
Arcen en Velden
Vlissingen
Bergen-op-Zoom
Eindhoven
Breskens
Venlo
Cadzand
Hoogerheide
Tegelen
Sluis
Roermond
Born
Beek
Heerlen
Maastricht
Valkenburg
Epen

HOW TO GET THERE

There are direct ferry services to the
Netherlands:
Harwich to the Hoek van (Hook of)
Holland
(6¾hrs day, 8hrs night)
Hull to Rotterdam-Europoort
(14 hours)
Sheerness to Vlissingen/Flushing
(7hrs day, 8½hrs night)

Alternatively, take one of the Short
Channel crossings and drive through
France and Belgium.

Distance
from Calais to Den Haag (The Hague) is
just over 320km (200 miles) (within a
day's drive)

MONEYMATTERS

There are no restrictions on the amount
of currency you make take into the
Netherlands. Any currency taken in may
be freely taken out, as may also any
currency obtained in the Netherlands by
exchange or by withdrawal from an
account.

Banking hours
Monday–Friday 09.00–16.00hrs

At all ANWB offices, money can be
exchanged:
Monday–Friday 08.45–16.45 hrs,
and Saturday 08.45–12.00hrs.

There are also exchanges at the principal
railways stations (eg Amsterdam,
Arnhem, Eindhoven, Den Haag, Hoek
van Holland, Maastricht, Rosendaal,
Rotterdam, Utrecht and Venlo).

Postcheques
may be cashed at all post offices up to a
maximum of Fls300 per cheque. Go up to
a counter position which displays the
words **Alle Geldhandelingen** or
Postbank.

MOTORING REGULATIONS AND GENERAL INFORMATION

The information given here is specific to
the Netherlands. It **must** be read in conjunction with the European ABC at the
front of the book, which covers those
regulations which are common to many
countries.

Accidents*

If you have a serious or complicated accident,
especially if anyone is injured, the police
should be called before the vehicles are
removed. See also Warning triangle below.

Breakdowns*

If your car breaks down, try to move it to the
verge of the road so that it obstructs the traffic
flow as little as possible, and place a warning
triangle behind the vehicle to warn following
traffic of the obstruction. The Royal Dutch
Touring Club (ANWB) maintain a 24-hour road
patrol service (Wegenwacht), which operates
throughout the country. See also Warning
triangle below.

British Embassy/Consulate*

The British Embassy is located at 2514 ED Den
Haag, Lange Voorhout 10 ☎(070) 3645800, but
the Embassy has no consular section. The
British Consulate is located at 1075 AE
Amsterdam, Koningslaan 44 ☎(020) 764343.

Children in Cars

Children under 12 are not permitted to travel in
a vehicle as front-seat passengers, with the
exception of children under 4 sitting in a
special baby seat and children over 4 using a
safety belt which does not cross the chest.

Dimensions and weight restrictions

Private **cars** and towed **trailers** or **caravans** are
restricted to the following dimensions – height,
4 metres; width, on 'A' roads† 2.55 metres, on
'B' roads† 2.20 metres; length‡ with 2 axles 12
metres. The maximum permitted overall length

***Additional information will be found in the
European ABC at the front of the book.**

of vehicle/trailer or caravan combinations is 18 metres.

The maximum weight of caravan/luggage trailers will be determined by the instructions of the manufacturer of the towing vehicle and/or the manufacturer of the caravan/luggage trailer.

†'A' roads are main roads; 'B' roads are secondary roads. 'B' roads are indicated by signs bearing the capital letter 'B'; roads which do not have these signs may be considered 'A' roads.

‡Trailers with single axle and manufactured *before* 1967 – 10 metres; *after* 1967 – 8 metres.

Driving licence*

A valid UK or Republic of Ireland licence is acceptable in the Netherlands. The minimum age at which a visitor may use a temporarily imported car or motorcycle is 18 years.

Emergency messages to tourists*

Emergency messages to tourists are broadcast daily on *Radio Hilversum 1*. The messages are transmitted in Dutch on 1008Khz medium wave at 17.55hrs. Between 1 June–1 October these messages are repeated every day on the same wavelength at 23.02hrs.

Firearms

The Dutch laws concerning the possession of firearms are the most stringent in Europe. Any person crossing the frontier with any type of firearm will be arrested. The law applies also to any object which, on superficial inspection, shows resemblance to real firearms (eg plastic imitations). If you wish to carry firearms, real or imitation, of any description into the Netherlands, seek the advice of the Netherlands Consulate.

Lights*

Driving on sidelights only is prohibited. Dipped headlights must be used at all times in built-up areas. In fog or falling snow, fog lamps may be used in pairs in conjunction with sidelights only. Headlights should be flashed as a warning of approach at night, provided that they do not inconvenience other traffic. All vehicles parked on a public road must have their sidelights on if not within 30 metres (33yds) of a street lamp.

Motoring club*

 The **Koninklijke Nederlandse Toeristenbond** (ANWB) has its headquarters at 2596 EC Den Haag, Wassenaarseweg 220, and offices in numerous provincial towns. They will assist motoring tourists generally, and supply road and touring information. Offices are usually open between 08.45 and 16.45hrs Monday to Friday, and 08.45 and 12.00hrs on Saturdays. Traffic information can be obtained from the ANWB, ☎(070) 3313131 (24-hour service).

Motorways

There is a network of Motorways (*Autosnelweg*) carrying most inter-city and long-distance traffic. Nearly all motorways are part of the European international network, and carry an 'E' number (green and white sign with the prefix 'E'), as well as the national number (red and white sign with the prefix 'A').

In 1986, a new numbering system of the European international network was introduced. Below is a list of the old and new 'E' numbers.

Old No	Route	New No
E3	Belgian Frontier – Eindhoven – Venlo	E34
E8	Hoek van Holland – Den Haag – Utrecht – Oldenzaal	E30
E9	Utrecht – Eindhoven – Maastricht	E25
E9	Amsterdam – Utrecht	E35
E10	Amsterdam – Rotterdam – Breda	E19
E10	Amsterdam – Groningen	E22
E35	Amsterdam – Amersfoort	E23
E35	Amersfort – Groningen	E232
E35	Groningen – German Frontier	E22
E36	Hoek van Holland – Rotterdam – Utrecht	E25
E36	Utrecht – Arnhem – German Frontier	E35
E37	Breda – Utrecht	E311
E38	Vlissingen – Breda – Eindhoven	E312
	Rotterdam – Nijmegen	E31

*Additional information will be found in the European ABC at the front of the book.

Orange badge scheme for disabled drivers*

In the Netherlands, badge holders may:

a park in special car parks set aside for the handicapped where there is no time limit;

b park for an indefinite period in blue zones;

c park for an indefinite period where a parking sign (white letter on blue panel with additional panel stating parking times) is displayed;

d park for a maximum of three hours where parking is prohibited (red driving and bars on blue background), or alternative parking (red ring and bars on blue background with the white upright 'line' symbol) signs appear. A handicapped person's parking disc must be used. However, this concession does not apply when other parking facilities are to be found within a reasonable distance.

Parking*

You can stop, provided that you keep to the extreme right of the road and do not interfere with other traffic. You are allowed to stop to let passengers in and out at bus stops.
Spending the night in a vehicle or trailer on the roadside is **not** permitted.

Parking meters and/or parking discs are used in many towns. Discs can be obtained from police stations, ANWB offices and many tobacco shops and must be displayed on the windscreen. They must be set at the time of parking, and show when parking time lapses according to the limit in the area concerned. Failure to observe zonal regulations could result in a fine and/or the vehicle being towed away or wheel clamped.

Petrol*

Credit cards Some recognised credit cards accepted at petrol stations.
Duty-free petrol In addition to the petrol in the vehicle tank, up to 10 litres in a can may be imported free of customs duty and tax.
Petrol (leaded) Super Benzine (98 octane) grade.
Petrol (unleaded) is sold in the Netherlands as Normal Benzine (91 octane) and Eurosuper (95 octane) grades. All petrol stations sell Eurosuper but only 300 sell Normal Benzine. The octane rating is not indicated on pumps, but those dispensing Super Benzine are coloured green.

Postal information

Mail Postcards Fls0.55; letters up to 20gm Fls0.75.
Post offices There are 2,600 post offices in the Netherlands. Opening hours of main post offices are 08.30–17.00hrs Monday to Friday and 09.00–12.00hrs Saturday. Smaller offices are open 08.30–17.00hrs Monday to Friday.

Priority*

Regulations in the Netherlands take account of the very large numbers of cyclists, for whom special tracks are provided on a number of roads. Motor vehicles generally have priority over the slower moving traffic, except when this is altered by the appropriate road signs. However, cyclists proceeding straight ahead at intersections have priority over all turning traffic. Visitors should be extremely alert.

Public holidays*

Official Public holidays in the Netherlands for 1990 are given below.

January 1 (New Year's Day)
April 13 (Good Friday)
April 16 (Easter Monday)
April 30 (The Queen's Birthday)
May 24 (Ascension Day)
May 5† (Liberation Day)
June 4 (Whit Monday)
December 25 (Christmas Day)
December 26 (Boxing Day)
†Saturday

Religious services*

The Intercontinental Church Society welcomes visitors from any denomination to English language services in the following centres:
1011 HW Amsterdam The Rev Canon John Wheatley Price, Christ Church, Groenburgwal 42 ☎(020) 248877. Chaplain's residence, 373 Tobias Asserlaan, 1111 KB Diemen ☎(020) 952705.
2585 HA Den Haag 2 Riouwstraat ☎(070) 3555359.
6525 XG Nijmegen Schepenenstraat 63 ☎(080) 560875 (East Netherlands Chaplaincy serving Arnhem, Nijmegen and Twente)
3024 Rotterdam The Rev Michael Fulljames, 113 Pieter de Hoochweg ☎(010) 4765025.

*Additional information will be found in the European ABC at the front of the book.

Utrecht The Rev Douglas Beukes, Holy Trinity Church, Van Hogendorpstraat 26 ☏(030) 513424.

Roads

Main roads usually have only two lanes, but they are well-surfaced. The best way to see the countryside is to tour along minor roads (often alongside canals).

Road signs*

Signposting is good; in some places, there are special by-way tours signposted by the ANWB. In residential areas, the sign '*woonerven*' indicates that speed control ramps have been installed across the road. When leaving a '*woonerf*' priority must be given to traffic on the normal road.

Shopping hours

Generally, *food shops* are open 08.00–18.00hrs Monday–Saturday. Most food shops close for one half-day per week, but this varies according to location. Most *other shops* including department stores open 13.00–17.30hrs on Monday, 09.00–17.30hrs Tuesday–Friday, and 09.00–16.00hrs on Saturday.

Speed Limits*

The placename indicates the beginning and end of a built-up area. the following speed limits for cars and motorcycles are in force if there are no special signs. *Built-up areas*, 50kph (31mph). *Outside built-up areas*, 80kph (49mph) and, on motorways, 120kph (74mph). Vehicles towing a single axle caravan or trailer are limited to 80kph (49mph).

Spiked or studded tyres*

Although residents are not permitted to use *spiked tyres*, visitors may do so provided that they do not exceed 80kph (49mph), and only if spikes are allowed in their home country.

Telephone*

Insert coin **after** lifting the receiver (instructions appear in English in all public callboxes). When making calls to subscribers *within* the Netherlands, precede the number with the relevant area code (shown in parentheses before the hotel/garage enquiry number in the gazetteer). Use 25 *cent* coins or *Fls*1.00 coins.
International callbox identification All payphones. Cardphones.
Telephone rates The cost of a call to the UK is *Fls*0.95 for each minute. Local calls cost 25 cents. The cheap rate operates from 18.00–07.00hrs on Saturday and Sunday; the charge is *Fls*0.70 per minute for calls to the UK.
Telephone Codes

UK to Netherlands	010 31
Netherlands to UK	09†44
Netherlands to Republic of Ireland	09†353
Netherlands to the USA	09†1

†Wait for second dialling tone

Toll bridges and tunnels

Toll bridges: Zeeland (Oosterschelde) bridge – cars *Fls*4.00; car/caravan *Fls*6.00. *Waalbrug* (near Tiel) – car *Fls*2.90; car/caravan *Fls*3.50.
Toll tunnels: Kiltunnel ('s-Gravendeel-Dordrecht) – car *Fls*3.50; car/caravan *Fls*10.

Warning Triangle*

In the event of accident or breakdown a motorist may use either a warning triangle or hazard warning lights. However, it is compulsory to carry a warning triangle outside built-up areas as hazard warning lights may be damaged or inoperative.

*Additional information will be found in the European ABC at the front of the book.

ACCOMMODATION

Hotels are officially classified, and the category is exhibited outside each. Room prices must, by law, be indicated in hotel receptions and in each bedroom, but they are not subject to official control. The service charge amounts to 15%, and it is usual for this to be included in the charges as well as Value Added Tax.

The **National Reservation Centre** (NRC) is open 08.00–20.00hrs Monday to Saturday, and will secure accommodation free of charge. Applications may be made direct by post, telephone or telex to NRC, PO Box 404, 2260 AK Leidschendam ☎(070) 3202500 (if calling this number from the UK refer to your telephone dialling code book) or telex 33755. For those already in the Netherlands, the VVV offices in larger towns and cities will book a room for a small charge.

When dining out, typical Dutch restaurants can be recognised by the sign of **Neerlands Dis** – the red, white and blue soup dish. A list of these restaurants is available from the Netherlands Board of Tourism or local VVV or ANWB offices.

The prices shown below are an average for each classification. Accommodation is likely to be more expensive in Amsterdam and some of the more popular tourist areas. At the time of going to press, *£1 Sterling = Fls3.50* and *US$1 = Fls2.10*, but you should check the rate of exchange before your departure.

AVERAGE PRICES

	Single Room	Double Room	Breakfast	Lunch/Dinner
★★★★★	Fls245–324	Fls308–398	Fls21–23	Fls49–90
★★★★	Fls169–360	Fls235–289	Fls20–21	Fls37–83
★★★	Fls114–140	Fls151–184	Fls14–16	Fls22–79
★★	Fls78–112	Fls110–151	Fls12–15	Fls19–60
★	Fls55–85	Fls85–124	from Fls11	Fls15–75

Abbreviations
pl   plein   st   straat

AALSMEER
Noord-Holland
🛏 *Boom* Oosteindeweg 220 ☎(02977) 25667 P AR

ALKMAAR
Noord-Holland
🛏 *Klaver* Helderseweg 29-30 ☎(072) 127033 P AR

🛏 *N Schmidt* Nassaupl 1 ☎(072) 113545 P For

ALMELO
Overijssel
★★★*Postiljon* (BW) Aalderinkssingel 2 ☎(05490)26655 tx 44817
🛏🍴50 P
Credit Card [1]

🛏 *Autobedrijf* Wierdensestr 107 ☎(05490) 12472 Mit

🛏 *Konink* H-R-Holst Laan 1 ☎(05490) 11064 Aud Por VW

🛏 *Schiphorst* Sluiskade 22-37 ☎(05490) 17069 For

AMERSFOORT
Utrecht
★★*Berghotel* Utrechtseweg 225 ☎(033)620444 tx 79213
🛏🍴52 P Lift ⚲ ➤➤
Credit Cards [1] [2] [3] [5]
🛏 *Stan Amersfoort* Kapelweg 12 ☎(033) 635104 Ren

AMSTERDAM *(NOORD-HOLLAND)*

See Plan page 304 *Population 679,000 Local Tourist Office* Stationsplein ☎(020) 266444

Amsterdam is a fascinating city of contradictions. As one of the world's greatest diamond markets, it is undeniably rich, yet the most popular drinking places are 'brown bars', loved for the very sparseness of their décor. The daytime peace and calm of the shady canals belies the vibrant neon-lit nightlife of this cosmopolitan city.

Attractions range from the *Rijksmuseum*, containing some of the finest works of Hals, Rembrandt and Vermeer, to the *Rijksmuseum Vincent Van Gogh*; the Royal Palace and the Rembrandt House. The Anne Frank House in Prinseengracht, the hiding place of the Frank family during World War II, is now a museum. Lovers of horticulture might care to visit the hothouses of the Botanical Garden, or browse through the famous floating Singel Flower Market.

When it comes to nightlife, Amsterdam has everything from lively discos and sophisticated nightclubs to a more sedate evening listening to the *Concertgebouw Orchestra* or taking in an opera or ballet.

The main shopping streets are Haarlemmerdijk, Nieuwendijk, Kakverstraat, Damrak, Rokin, Regulierbreestraat, Heilgeweg and Leidsestraat. Popular souvenirs include clogs, tea, spices, bottles, candles and locally made cigars, renowned throughout the world for their aroma, and the city has an international reputation for cutting and polishing diamonds.

EATING OUT Dutch food is hearty and uncomplicated. Specialities include pea soup, red kidney bean soup, potato and vegetable hash with Dutch sausage, and fresh sea fish. Dutch apple tart is made with apples, sultanas and cinnamon. Pancakes are also firm favourites with the Dutch, and the *Pannekoekenhuisje* in Damrak, specialises in them. For good value try the *eetcafes* in the Jordaan area. There are numerous international restaurants in the streets around Leidseplein; Indonesian cooking is particularly popular with the Dutch and generally good value. Bakeries provide tasty and inexpensive snacks, and there are several 'English-style' establishments offering quick meals, one such is Shorts of London in Rembrandtsplein.

At the upper end of the restaurant price range, *Dikkeren Thijs*, in Prinsengracht, has a picturesque canalside setting and specialises in Dutch cuisine. A restaurant which oozes charm and character is *d'Vijff Vlieghen*, located in five converted old houses in Spuistraat. For Indonesian cuisine at its best, *Bali*, in Leidsestraat, is renowned for its wide-ranging menu and generous portions.

AMSTERDAM (NOORD-HOLLAND)

★★★★★**American** (Forum) Leidsekade 97
☎(020)245322 tx 12545
✸ⁿ188 P10 Lift ℂ
Credit Cards ①②③⑤

★★★★★**Amstel** (Intercont) Prof-Tulppl 1
☎(020)226060 tx 11004
✸ⁿ111 ☎ P160 Lift ℂ
Credit Cards ①②③④⑤

★★★★★*Amsterdam Hilton* Apollolaan 138
☎(020)780780 tx 11025
✸ⁿ274 P Lift
Credit Cards ①②③④⑤

★★★★★**Apollo** (THF) Apollolaan 2
☎(020)735922 tx 14084
✸ⁿ219 P110 Lift ℂ
Credit Cards ①②③⑤

★★★★★**Europe** (Relais et Châteaux) Nieuwe
Doelenstraat 2-8 ☎(020)234836 tx 12081
✸ⁿ114 ☎ P40 Lift ℂ ⊟
Credit Cards ①②③④⑤

★★★★**Amsterdam Marriott** Stadhouderskade
19-21 ☎(020)835151 tx 15087
✸ⁿ395 ☎ P40 Lift ℂ
Credit Cards ①②③④⑤

★★★★*Caransa* Rembrandtspl 19 ☎(020)229455
tx 13342
✸ⁿ66 Lift ℂ
Credit Cards ①②③④⑤

★★★★**Carlton** Vijzelstr 2-18 (n.rest)
☎(020)222266 tx 11670
✸ⁿ157 ☎ Lift ℂ
Credit Cards ①②③④⑤

★★★★**Crest** 2 de Boelelaan,Europa bd
☎(020)462300 tx 13647
✸ⁿ261 Lift ℂ
Credit Cards ①②③④⑤

★★★★**Crowne Plaza (Holiday Inns)** Nieuwezijds
Voorburgwal 5 ☎(020)200500 tx 15183
✸ⁿ270 P40 Lift ℂ ⊟
Credit Cards ①②③⑤

★★★★**Doelen** Nieuwe Doelenstr 24
☎(020)220722 tx 14399
✸ⁿ86 Lift ℂ
Credit Cards ①②③④⑤

★★★★*Memphis* de Lairessestr 87 ☎(020)733141
tx 12450
✸ⁿ81 Lift
Credit Cards ①②③⑤

★★★★**Port van Cleve** Voorburgwal 178
☎(020)244860 tx 13129
✸ⁿ103 Lift ℂ
Credit Cards ①②③⑤

★★★★**Pulitzer** (GT) Prinsengracht 315-331
☎(020)228333 tx 16508
✸ⁿ241 ☎ P25 Lift ℂ
Credit Cards ①②③⑤

★★★★**Victoria** Damrak 1-6 ☎(020)234255 tx
16625

✸ⁿ169 Lift ℂ
Credit Cards ①②③④⑤

★★★**Altea Amsterdam** Joan Muyskenweg 10
☎(020)6658181 tx 13382
✸ⁿ180 A180rm ☎ P125 Lift
Credit Cards ①②③⑤

★★★*Apollofirst* Apollolaan 123-125
☎(020)730333 tx 13446
✸ⁿ32 Lift

★★★*Barbizon Centre* (GT) Stadhouderskade 7
☎(020)851351 tx 12601
✸ⁿ242 ☎ P Lift
Credit Cards ①②③⑤

★★★**Delphi** Apollolaan 101-105 (n.rest)
☎(020)795152 tx 16659
✸ⁿ50 Lift ℂ
Credit Cards ①②③⑤

★★★**Grand Krasnapolsky** (SRS) Dam 9
☎(020)5549111 tx 12262
✸ⁿ300 ☎ P150 Lift ℂ
Credit Cards ①②③④⑤

★★★**Jan Luyken** J-Luykenstr 58 (n.rest)
☎(020)764111 tx 16254
✸ⁿ63 Lift

★★★**Novotel** Europa boulevard 10
☎(020)5411123 tx 13375
✸ⁿ600 P Lift ℂ
Credit Cards ②③⑤

★★★**Pullman Schiphol DPn** Oude Haagseweg
20 ☎(020)179005 tx 15524
✸ⁿ151 P300 Lift ℂ
Credit Cards ①②③⑤

★★★**Rembrant (Crest)** Herengracht 255 (n.rest)
☎(020)221727 tx 15424
✸ⁿ111 Lift ℂ
Credit Cards ①②③④⑤

★★★**Schiller (Crest)** Rembrantspl 26-36
☎(020)231660 tx 14058
✸ⁿ96 Lift ℂ
Credit Cards ①②③④⑤

★★**Ams Hotel Terdam** (BW) Tesselschadestr 23-
29 ☎(020)831811 tx 14275
✸ⁿ52 Lift
Credit Card ②

★★**Cordial** Rokin 62-64 ☎(020)264411 tx 15621
✸ⁿ44 Lift
Credit Cards ①②③

★★**Hoksbergen** Singel 301 (n.rest)
☎(020)266043 tx 33756
✸ⁿ14 ℂ
Credit Cards ①②③④⑤

★★*Piet Hein* Vossiusstr 53 (n.rest)
☎(020)628375 tx 10869
rm27(✸ⁿ19)

★★*Sander* J-Obrechstr 69 (n.rest)
☎(020)6627574 tx 18456
Feb-Nov
✸ⁿ16 P6 Lift ℂ
Credit Cards ①②③⑤

★★**Wilhelmina** 169 Koninginneweg (n.rest)
☎(020)6625467 tx 10873
rm18(✸ⁿ13)
Credit Cards ①②③⑤

★**Asterisk** Den Texstr 14-16 (n.rest)
☎(020)262396
rm19(✸ⁿ14)
Credit Cards ①③

★**City Amsterdam** Prins Hendrikkade 130
☎(020)230836
rm18(✸ⁿ7) ℂ Sea
Credit Cards ①②⑤

★**Sphinx** Weteringschans 82 (n.rest)
☎(020)273680
rm17(✸ⁿ8)
Credit Cards ①②③⑤

★●*Asmoco* J-Rebelstr ☎(020) 195444 P BMW

AMSTERDAM AIRPORT
At SCHIPHOL(10km SW)

★★★★*Barbizon Schiphol* (GT) Kruisweg 495
☎(02503)64422 tx 74546
✸ⁿ244 P400 Lift ℂ
Credit Cards ①②③⑤

★★*Ibis* Schipholweg 181 ☎(02968)91234 tx
16491
✸ⁿ508 P350 Lift ℂ
Credit Cards ①②③④⑤

APELDOORN
Gelderland

★★★*Bloemink* Loolaan 56 ☎(055)214141 tx
49253
rm86(✸ⁿ80) P Lift ⊟
Credit Cards ①②③⑤

★★★*Cantharel* Van Golsteinlaan 20
☎(055)414455 tx 49550
✸ⁿ48 P Lift

★★★**Keizerskroon** (QM) Koningstr 7
☎(055)217744 tx 49221
✸ⁿ103 A3rm ☎ P100 Lift ℂ ⊟
Credit Cards ①②③⑤

★**Berg en Bos** Aquamarijnstr 58 ☎(055)552352
✸ⁿ17

★●*Bakker* Gazellestr 21 ☎(055) 214208 P Ren

★●*Nefkens-Apeldoorn* Wagenhakershoek
2,Edisonlaan 270 ☎(055) 414222 Peu

ARCEN
Limburg

★*Maas* Schans 18 ☎(04703)1556
6 Mar-1Dec
✸ⁿ13 ☎ P ⊇

ARNHEM
Gelderland

★★★*Haarhuis* (BW) Stationspl 1 ☎(085)427441
tx 45357
✸ⁿ96 P Lift
Credit Card ②

★★★**Postiljon** (BW) Europaweg 25
☎(085)573333 tx 45028
⊷♪30 P
Credit Card ②

❧ **J Reymes** Amsterdamseweg 5A ☎(085)
423204 P

❧ **Reymes/Elderveld** Hollandweg/Petterstraat 4
☎(085) 811133 Mit

❧ **Rosler & Meijer** Boulevard Houvelink 5a
☎(085) 435984 For

At **VELP**(2km NE)

★★★★**Velp** (QM) Pres-Kennedylaan 102
☎(085)649849 tx 45527
⊷♪74 A2rm P80 ℂ ▨
Credit Cards ① ② ③ ④ ⑤

ASSEN
Drenthe

★★★**Overcingel** Stationspl 10 ☎(05920)11333
rm36(⊷♪32) P Lift

❧ **AZA** Europaweg ☎(05920) 55944 P Mer

BAARN
Utrecht

★**Prom** Amalialaan 1 ☎(02154)12913
⊷♪43

❧ **M Kooy** Eemnesser 57a ☎(02154) 12619 All
makes

❧ **Splinter Eemland** Eemnesserweg 16-22
☎(02154) 155555 P For

BEATRIXHAVEN
See **MAASTRICHT**

BEEK
Limburg

★★★**Altea Limburg** Vliegveldweg 19
☎(043)642131 tx 56059
⊷♪64 P

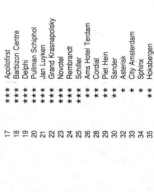

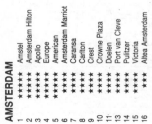

AMSTERDAM

1	★★★★★	Amstel
2	★★★★★	Amsterdam Hilton
3	★★★★★	Apollo
4	★★★★★	Europe
5	★★★★★	American
6	★★★★	Amsterdam Marriott
7	★★★★	Caransa
8	★★★★	Carlton
9	★★★★	Crest
10	★★★★	Crowne Plaza
11	★★★★	Doelen
13	★★★★	Port van Cleve
14	★★★★	Pulitzer
15	★★★★	Victoria
16	★★★	Altea Amsterdam
17	★★★	Apollofirst
18	★★★	Barbizon Centre
19	★★★	Delphi
20	★★★	Pullman Schiphol
21	★★★	Jan Luyken
22	★★★	Grand Krasnapolsky
23	★★★	Novotel
24	★★★	Rembrandt
25	★★★	Schiller
26	★★	Ams Hotel Terdam
28	★★	Cordial
29	★★	Piet Hein
30	★★	Sander
32	★	Asterisk
33	★	City Amsterdam
34	★	Sphinx
35	★★	Hoksbergen

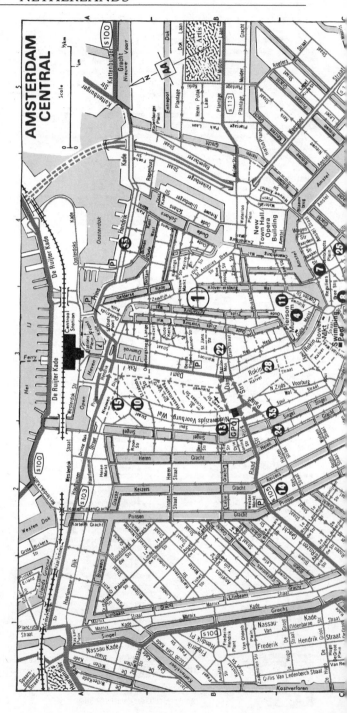

AMSTERDAM CENTRAL

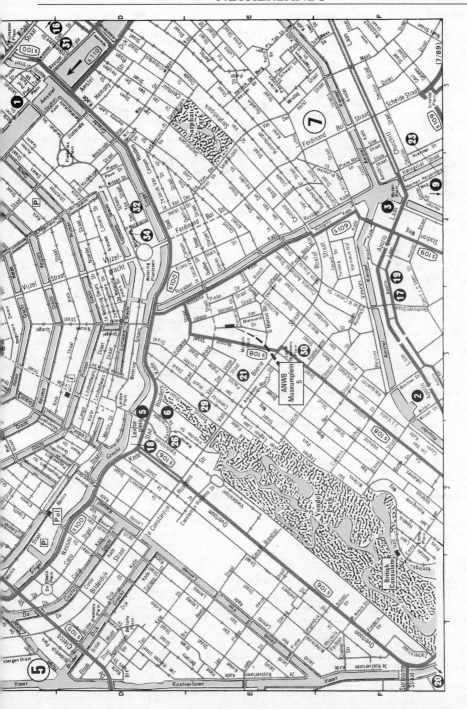

BEETSTERZWAAG
Friesland
★★★★**Lauswolt** (Relais et Châteaux) **DPn** Van Harinxmaweg 10 ☎(05126)1245 tx 46241
◆↱54 ☈ P152 Lift ⒞ ℺ ▱ ◺ ♫♫
Credit Cards ① ② ③ ⑤

BERGEN
Noord-Holland
★**Park** Breelaan 19 ☎(02208)12223
◆↱31 P

BERGEN-AAN-ZEE
Noord-Holland
★★★**Nassau Bergen** van der Wyckpl 4 ☎(02208)97541
5 Jan-22 Dec
rm42(◆↱41) P50 ◺ Sea
★**Prins Maurits** van Hasseltstr 7 ☎(02208)12364
Apr-oct
rm24(↱22) ☈ P26

BERG EN DAL
Gelderland
★★★**Val Monte** (GT) Oude Holleweg 5 ☎(08895)41704 tx 48428
◆↱106 P150 Lift ⒞ ℺ ▱
Credit Cards ① ② ③ ⑤

BERGEN-OP-ZOOM
Noord-Brabant
★★★**Gouden Leeuw** Fortuinstr 14 (n.rest) ☎(01640)35000 tx 78265
◆↱29 Lift
Credit Cards ① ② ③ ⑤
★**Draak** Grote Markt 37-38 ☎(01640)33661
◆↱32 Lift ⒞
Credit Cards ① ② ③ ⑤
☜ **Difoga** Bredasestr 25 ☎(01640) 50200 For
☜ **Swagemakers** Moerstraatsebahn 50 ☎(01640) 36285 P Alf
☜ **Vos** Ravelstr 10-12 ☎(01640) 42050 Cit

BEST
Noord-Brabant
★★**Climat** De Maas 2 ☎(04998)90100 tx 59073
◆↱70 P70 Lift ⒞ ▱
Credit Cards ① ② ③

BEVERWIJK
Noord-Holland
☜ **Admiraal & Zn** Laan der Nederlanden 1 ☎(02510) 360510 P Cit
☜ **Wijkeroog** Bulklerlaan 6 ☎(02510) 41664 P AR

BLOEMENDAAL
Noord-Holland
★★**Iepenhove** Hartenlustlaan 4 ☎(023)258301 tx 71241
rm38(◆↱35) P Lift
☜ **Van Loon's** Korte Kleverlaan 30-34 ☎(023) 259311 P Lan Ren Saa

BOEKELO
Overijssel
★★★★**Crest Boekelo** Oude Deldenerweg 203 ☎(05428)1444 tx 44301
◆↱78 P ℺ ▱ ◺ ♫♫

BORN
Limburg
★★★**Born** (QM) Langereweg 21 ☎(04498)51666 tx 36048
◆↱49 P150 ⒞
Credit Cards ① ② ③ ④ ⑤

BOSKOOP
Zuid-Holland
★★**Neuf** Barendstr 10 ☎(01727)2031
◆↱12 P
☜ **Eerste Boskoops** Plankier 2-6 ☎(01727) 2110 P Mer Ope

BREDA
Noord-Brabant
★★★**Brabant** Heerbaan 4-6 ☎(076)224666 tx 54263
◆↱60 P150 Lift ▱
Credit Cards ① ② ③ ⑤
★★★**Novotel** Dr-Batenburglaan 74 ☎(076)659220 tx 74016
◆↱105 P Lift ⒞ ℺ ◺
Credit Cards ① ② ③ ⑤
★★**Breda** Roskam 20 ☎(076)222177 tx 54126
◆↱98 P100 Lift ⒞
Credit Cards ① ② ③ ⑤
☜ **Jongerius** Loevesteinstr 20 ☎(076) 659211 P Peu
☜ **Tigchelaar** Boeimeersingel 6 ☎(076) 224400 P For
☜ **Valkenberg** Spinveld 74 ☎(076) 222371 Cit
☜ **Van Nunen** Haagweg 442-444 ☎(076) 224940 P AR
At **GINNEKEN**(2km S)
★★★**Mastbosch** (GT) Burg-Kerstenslaan 20 ☎(076)650050 tx 54406
◆↱37 Lift ⒞
Credit Cards ① ② ③ ⑤

BRESKENS
Zeeland
★★**Wapen van Breskens** Grote Kade 33 ☎(01172)1401
rm20(↱6) P Lift
☜ **Van De Ree** Mercurivsstr 11-13 ☎(01172) 1729 P For

BUNNIK
See **UTRECHT**

BUSSUM
Noord-Holland
★**Goolland** Stationsweg 16-22 ☎(02159)43724
◆↱12
☜ **Hogguer Bussum** Vlietlaan 58-66 ☎(02159) 18651 For
☜ **Van Meurs** Huizerweg 84-86 ☎(02159) 34047 Ope
☜ **Garage Van Meurs** Noorderweg 2 ☎(02159) 30024 P Ren

CADZAND
Zeeland
★★★**Scheide DPn** Scheldestr 1 ☎(01179)1720
:Rest closed 1 Jan
◆↱24 ⒞ ▱ Sea

DELDEN
Overijssel
★★**Zwaan DPn** Langestr 2 ☎(05407)61206
◆↱9 ☈ P64 ⒞
Credit Cards ① ② ③ ⑤

DELFT
Zuid-Holland
★★**Leeuwenbrug** Koornmarkt 16 (n.rest) ☎(015)147741 tx 33756
rm32(◆↱6) P150 Lift
Credit Cards ① ② ③ ⑤
★**Central** Wynhaven 6-8 ☎(015)123442 tx 38302
rm38(◆↱27) ⒞
Credit Cards ① ② ③
☜ **Kinesis** Vulcenesweg 281 ☎(015) 616464 For

DEN BOSCH
See **'S-HERTOGENBOSCH**

DENEKAMP
Overijssel
★★★**Dinkeloord** Denekamperstr 48 ☎(05413)1387
◆↱40 P120 Lift ⒞ ℺ ▱
Credit Cards ① ② ③ ⑤

DEN HAAG
See **HAAG, DEN (HAGUE, THE)**

DEN HELDER
See **HELDER, DEN**

DEVENTER
Overijssel
★★★**Postiljon** (BW) Deventerweg 121 ☎(05700)24022 tx 49028
◆↱103 P Lift
Credit Card ②

DOETINCHEM
Gelderland
☜ **Martens** Edison Str 1 ☎(08340) 33250 P For

DOMBURG
Zeeland
★★**Duinheuvel** Badhuisweg 2 ☎(01188)1282
◆↱20 P

DORDRECHT
Zuid-Holland
★★★**Bellevue Groothoofdspoort** Boomstr 37 ☎(078)137900
◆↱19 P
★★★**Postiljon** Rijksstraatweg 30 ☎(078)184444 tx 20478
◆↱96 P Lift ⒞
☜ **Dubbelsteyn** Vyuerlaan 9 ☎(078) 16155 P BMW
☜ **Kern's** Copernicusweg 1 ☎(078) 139751 Ren
☜ **J Van den Berg** Blekersdijk 96 ☎(078) 143088 For
☜ **H W Van Gorp & Zonnen** A-Cuypsingel 296 ☎(078) 142044 Peu

DRACHTEN
Friesland
★★★**Drachten** (QM) **DPn** Zonnedauw 1 ☎(05120)20705 tx 46693
◆↱48 P120 Lift ⒞
Credit Cards ① ② ③ ④ ⑤
☜ **Garage Siton** de Knobben 25 ☎(05120) 14455 Ope

DRONTEN
Gelderland
☜ **Visser** de Ketting 1 ☎(03210) 13114 Ope Vau

DWINGELOO
Drenthe
At **LHEE**(1.5km SE)
★★**Borken** ☎(05219)7200
Closed 31 Dec & 1 Jan
◆↱24 ☈ P ♫♫

EDAM
Noord-Holland
★**Dam** Keizersgracht ☎(02993)71766
Apr-Sep
rm12(↱8)
☜ **Evodam** D-Porschlaan ☎(02993) 65551 Ren

EDE
Gelderland
☜ **Van Der Kolk** Klaphekweg 30 ☎(083380) 30201 For
☜ **Van Silthout** Proodgweg 1-5 ☎(083380) 36710 Ren
At **VEENENDAAL**(8km W)
★★**Ibis DPn** Vendelier 8 ☎(08385)22222 tx 37210
:Rest closed Sat & Sun lunchtime
◆↱41 P100 Lift
Credit Cards ① ② ③ ⑤

EEMNES
See **LAREN**

EERNEWOUDE
Friesland
★★★**Princenhof** P-Miedemaweg 15 ☎(05117)9206
◆↱45 P

EGMOND-AAN-ZEE
Noord-Holland

★★★**Bellevue** Boulevard Noord (A7)
☎(02206)1025 tx 57565
◀🛏48 Lift ℂ Sea
Credit Cards ①②③⑤
◥● *J A Karels* Trompstr 17 ☎(02206) 1250 AR

EINDHOVEN
Noord-Brabant

★★★★★**Cocagne** (SRS) Vestdijk 47
☎(040)444755 tx 51245
◀🛏203 ☒ P100 Lift ℂ
Credit Cards ①②③④⑤
★★★★**Holiday Inn** Veldmaarschalk
Montgomerylaan,1 ☎(040)433222 tx 51775
◀🛏200 P Lift ☒
★★★**Eindhoven** Aalsterweg 322 ☎(040)123435
◀🛏180 P300 Lift ℂ ॰ ☒
Credit Cards ①②
◥● *Driessen* Pieterbergweg 31 ☎(040) 313701
Saa
◥● *L Lang* Pisanostr 49 ☎(040) 433887 Fia Lan
◥● *OBAM* Aalsterweg 135 ☎(040) 16441
◥● *Van Laarhoven's Auto* Hondsruglaan 99
☎(040) 413615 P AR

EMMELOORD
Overijssel

◥● *Gorter* Kampwai 50 ☎(05270) 3541 AR Ope
Vau

EMMEN
Drenthe

◥● *Jong* Statenweg 5-7 ☎(05910) 22330 Cit
◥● *Misker* Odoornerweg 4 ☎(05910) 18288 AR

ENKHUIZEN
Noord-Holland

★★**Wapen van Enkhuizen** Breedstr 59
☎(02280)13434
rm27(◀🛏11) P
◥● *Watses* Westerstr 273-275 ☎(02280) 12708
For

ENSCHEDE
Overijssel

★★★**Memphis** M-H-Tromplaan 55 ☎(053)318244
tx 44702
◀🛏37 P Lift
◥● *Auto Fischer* Oldenzaalsestr ☎(053) 354555
For
◥● *Oldenhof* Europalaan 23 ☎(053) 310961 BMW
◥● *Ruinemans* de Reulver 30
☎(053) 770077 Hon

EPEN
Limburg

★**Gerardushoeve** Julianastr 23 ☎(04455)1793
2 Jan-Nov
◀🛏6 P Lift

FLUSHING
See VLISSINGEN

GIETHOORN
Overijssel

★★★**Giethoorn** Beulakerweg 128 ☎(05216)1216
◀🛏20 P

GILZE-RYEN
Noord-Brabant

★★★**Gilze Rijen** Klein Zwitserland 8
☎(01615)2051 tx 54800
◀🛏138 P Lift ॰ ☒ ⌂ ♒

GINNEKEN
See BREDA

GOES
Zeeland

★**Ockenburgh** van de Spiegelstr 104
☎(01100)16303
Closed Sunday
◀🛏7 P

◥● *Adria* West Havendyk 150 ☎(01100) 20440 P
For
◥● *B Oeveren* A-Plasmanweg 2 ☎(01100) 12730
Mer
◥● *Van Frassen* Voorstad 79 ☎(01100) 27353 M/
C P Cit
◥● *Van Strien* Van de Spiegelstr ☎(01100) 01830
P Aud VW

GORINCHEM
Zuid-Holland

★★★**Gorinchem** Van Hogendorpstr 8-10
☎(01830)22400
◀🛏18 P120
◥● *Auto Centre Gorkum* Hogendorpweg 6
☎(01830) 32622

GOUDA
Zuid-Holland

◥● *J L Hulleman* Burg Jamessingel 2 ☎(01820)
12977 P For

GROESBEEK
Gelderland

★★**Wolfsberg** Mooksebaan 12 ☎(08891)71327
rm20(◀🛏16) P50

GRONINGEN
Groningen

★★★**Altea Groningen** Expositielaan 7
☎(050)258400 tx 53795
◀🛏159 Lift ☒
Credit Cards ①②③⑤
★★★**Enter Groningen** DPn Donderslaan 156
☎(050)252040 tx 53394
◀🛏59 ℂ
Credit Cards ①②③④⑤
◥● *A-Z* Friesestraatweg 22 ☎(050) 120012 P Hon
◥● *Gronam* Rijksstraatweg 130,Oosterhoogeburg
☎(050) For
◥● *B Oosterhuis* Prontonstr ☎(050) 182223 Toy

HAAG, DEN (HAGUE, THE)
Zuid-Holland

Though not the official capital of the Netherlands, Den Haag is the seat of government, host to more than 60 foreign embassies, home of the International Court of Justice and home to Queen Beatrix who chose to live here following her inauguration; wide tree-lined avenues, spacious boulevards and parks all contribute to a royal grandeur. Den Haag invites discovery with its charming little oriental shops, pedestrian precincts crowded with boutiques, and the antique market at the Lange Voorhout. This is a vital, cosmopolitan city with some of the most interesting attractions in Holland.

EATING OUT The most luxurious restaurant in Den Haag is the Royal, housed in an elegant, 16th-century mansion in Lange Voorhout. Locally caught seafood is a speciality of the *Auberge de Kieviet*, just outside the city in Wassenaar.

HAAG, DEN (HAGUE, THE)
Zuid-Holland

★★★★★**Promenade** Van Stolkweg 1
☎(070)3525161 tx 31162
◀🛏100 P Lift
★★★★**Bel Air** (GT) J-de-Wittlaan 30
☎(070)3502021 tx 31444
◀🛏350 P250 Lift ℂ ☒
Credit Cards ①②③④⑤
★★★★**Indes** (Crest) Lange Voorhout 54-56
☎(O7O)3469553 tx 31196
◀🛏77 Lift ℂ
Credit Cards ①②③④⑤
★★★★**Sofitel** Koningin Julianapl 35
☎(070)3814901 tx 34001
◀🛏144 P450 Lift ℂ ॰
Credit Cards ①②③⑤
★★★**Corona** Buitenhof 39-42 ☎(070)3637930 tx
31418
◀🛏26 ☒ P5 Lift ℂ
Credit Cards ①②③⑤
★★★**Parkhotel de Zalm** Molenstr 53
☎(070)3624371 tx 33005
◀🛏115 ☒ Lift
★**Esquire** Van Aerssenstr 59-61 ☎(070)3522341
tx 32112
rm26(◀🛏20)
◥● *Auto Haag* Calanpl 2 ☎(070) 889255 Ren
◥● *Case* Pletterijstr 6 ☎(070) 858780
◥● *Central Auto Bedrijf* Prinses Megrietplantsoen
10 ☎(070) 814131 For
◥● *National Automobiel Bedrijf* Scheldestr 2
☎(070) 47617 Hon
◥● *Zoet* Meteorstr 87-89 ☎(070) 880855

At RIJSWIJK

★★★**Hoornwick** J-Thijssenweg 1 ☎(070)3903130
tx 32538
◀🛏70 P

At SCHEVENINGEN

★★★★**Europa** (QM) Zwolsestr 2 ☎(070)512651
tx 33138
◀🛏174 ☒ P65 Lift ℂ ☒ Sea
Credit Cards ①②③⑤
★★★**Badhotel** Gevers Deynootweg 15
☎(070)3512221 tx 31592
◀🛏96 P30 Lift ℂ Sea
Credit Cards ①②③⑤
★★★**Flora Beach** Gevers Deynootweg 63
☎(070)543300 tx 32123
◀🛏88 P40 Lift ℂ
Credit Cards ①②③⑤
★★**Aquarius** Zeekant 107-110 ☎(070)543543 tx
31490
◀🛏23 P
★★**Bali** Badhuisweg 1 ☎(070)502434
rm34(◀🛏8) P

HAARLEM
Noord-Holland

★★★**Lion d'Or** (GT) Kruisweg 34-36
☎(023)321750 tx 71101
◀🛏36 Lift ℂ
Credit Cards ①②③⑤
◥● *Kimman* Zijlweg 35 ☎(023) 330969 M/C P AR
DJ

HAGUE, THE
See HAAG, DEN

HARDERWIJK
Gelderland

★★**Baars** Smeepoortstr 52 ☎(03410)12007
◀🛏17 P
◥● *Gelderse Auto Service* Handelsweg 4
☎(03410) 17374 For

HAREN
Groningen

★★★**Postiljon** Emmalaan 33 ☎(050)347041 tx 53688
➼♠97 P350 Lift ℂ
Credit Cards ①②③⑤

HEELSUM
Gelderland

★★★**Klein Zwitserland** (QM) Klein Zwitserlandlaan 5 ☎(08373)19104 tx 45627
➼♠61 P140 Lift ℂ ℚ ▭
Credit Cards ①②③⑤

HEEMSTEDE
Noord-Holland

➼● *Barnhoorn* Roemer Visscherspl 21 ☎(023) 242250 Toy

HEERENVEEN
Friesland

★★★**Postiljon** (BW) Schans 65 ☎(05130)24041 tx 46591
➼♠61 P Lift
Credit Card ②

HEERLEN
Limburg

★★★**Grand** Groene Board 23 ☎(045)713846 tx 56920
➼♠105 P65 Lift ℂ ℚ
Credit Cards ①②③⑤
★★★**Heerlen** Terworm 10 ☎(045)719450 tx 56759
➼♠78 P Lift
➼● *Canton-Reiss* Valkenburgerweg 34 ☎(045) 718040 AR
➼● *Hiljnen Heeren* Frankenlaan 1 ☎(045) 713600 Ren
➼● *Sondagh* ☎(045) 223300 P Cit
➼● *Van Haaren* Schandelerboord 25 ☎(045) 271152 For
➼● *Vencken* Heesbergstr 60-64 ☎(045) 412641 P Aud VW

HEILOO
Noord-Holland

★★★**Heiloo** Kennemerstraatweg 425 ☎(02205)2244
➼♠22 P ▭

HELDER, DEN
Noord-Holland

➼● *Ceres* Baljuwstr 139 ☎(02230) 30000 Peu
At **NIEUW DEN HELDER**(2km SW)
★★**Den Helder** Marsdiepstr 2 ☎(02230)22333
➼♠75 P

HELMOND
Noord-Brabant

★★★**West Ende** Steenweg 1 ☎(04920)24151 tx 51376
rm35(➼♠33) P Lift
➼● *Alards* Gerwenseweg 31 ☎(04920) 42645 P AR
➼● *J Gorp* Englesweg 220 ☎(04920) 39670 Cit

HENGELO
Overijssel

★★★*t'Lansink* C-T-Storkstr 14-18 ☎(074)910066
➼♠24 P
★★**Ten Hoopen** Burg Jansenpl 20 ☎(074)910265
rm25(♠23)
Credit Cards ①②③
➼● *W Noordegraf* Oldenzaalsestr 19-23 ☎(074) 914444 M/C For
➼● *G Ter Haar* Braemarsweg 140 ☎(074) 913901 AR

'S-HERTOGENBOSCH
Noord-Brabant

★★★**Eurohotel** (BW) Hinthamerstr 63 ☎(073)13777 tx 50014

➼♠47 ☆ Lift
Credit Card ②
➼● *Rietvelden* Rietwelderweg 34 ☎(073) 211355 Fia

HILVERSUM
Noord-Holland

★★**Hilfertsom** Koninginneweg 28-30 ☎(035)232444 tx 73030
rm37(➼♠28) P30 ℂ
Credit Cards ①②③⑤
★★**Hof van Holland** (BW) Kerkbrink 1-7 ☎(035)46141 tx 43399
➼♠59 P Lift
Credit Card ②
➼● *H Koster* Langestr ☎(035) 41156 BMW
➼● *J K Poll* Zoverijnstr 2 ☎(035) 47841 For

HOLTEN
Overijssel

★★**Hoog Holten** Forthaarsweg 7 ☎(05483)61306
rm20(➼♠18) P25 ℂ ℚ
Credit Cards ①②③⑤
★**Losse Hoes** Holterbergweg 14 ☎(05483)61353
rm28(➼♠16) P120 ♠♠ ℧ Mountain
Credit Cards ①②③⑤

HOOGERHEIDE
Noord-Brabant

★★**Pannenhuis** Antwerpsestraatweg 100 ☎(01646)14552
Closed 25 Dec-1 Jan
rm31(♠22) A10rm ☆ P52

HOOGEVEEN
Drenthe

★★★**Hoogeveen** Mathijsenstr 1 ☎(05280)63303
➼♠39 P
Credit Cards ①②③⑤
➼● *Europagarage* van Limburg Stirumstr ☎(05280) 66666 P For

HOORN
Noord-Holland

★**Kelzerskroon** Breed 31-33 ☎(02290)12717
➼♠20
➼● *Koopmans* Dampten 5 ☎(02290) 17644 P Hon
➼● *Van der Linden & Van Sprankhulzen* Berkhouterweg 11 ☎(02290) 36464 P Ope Vau Vol

KAMPEN
Overijssel

★★**Van Dijk** IJsselkade 30-31 ☎(05202)14925
➼♠19
➼● *J H R Van Noort* Nijverheidsstr 35 ☎(05202) 12241 For

KATWIJK AAN ZEE
Zuid-Holland

★★**Noordzee** Boulevard 72 ☎(01718)13450
Closed 2 Dec-Feb:Rest closed Nov-Mar
➼♠42 Lift
➼● *Rijnland West* Kon Wilhelminastr 16 ☎(01718) 72743 For

KATWOUDE
Noord-Holland

★★★**Katwoude** Wagenweg ☎(02993)65656 tx 16025
➼♠86 P500 Lift ℂ ℚ ▭
Credit Cards ①②③

KOOG, DE
Texel

★★★**Opduin** Ruyslaan 22 ☎(02220)17445 tx 57555
Mar-17 Nov & 17 Dec-1 Jan
rm82(➼♠73) ☆ P80 Lift ℂ ℚ ▭ Beach Sea
Credit Cards ①②③⑤

LAREN
Noord-Holland

At **EEMNES**(2km E)
★★★**Witte Bergen** Rijksweg A1 ☎(02153)86754 tx 73041
➼♠62 P300 ℂ
Credit Cards ①②③④

LEEUWARDEN
Friesland

★★★**Oranje** (GT) Stationsweg 4 ☎(058)126241 tx 46528
Closed 25-26 Dec
➼♠78 ☆ P21 Lift ℂ
Credit Cards ①②③⑤
★★**Eurohotel** Europapl 20 ☎(058)131113 tx 46674
Closed Xmas & New Year
rm56(➼♠46) P Lift
➼● *Molenaar* Keidam 2 ☎(058) 661115 P Toy
➼● *Nagelhout* Brandmeer 2 ☎(058) 663633 Dai Dat
➼● *Zeeuw* Valerinsstr 2-11 ☎(058) 131444 M/C P For

LEIDEN
Zuid-Holland

★★★★**Holiday Inn** (GT) Haagse Schouwweg 10 ☎(071)355555 tx 39213
➼♠192 P400 Lift ℂ ℚ
Credit Cards ①②③⑤
➼● *Br Automobeil* Bedr Oldenbamereldstr 37 ☎(071) 172679 AR
➼● *Rijnland* Vijf Meilaan 7 ☎(071) 310031 For
At **LEIDERDORP**(2km SE)
★**Ibis Leiderdorp** Elisabethhof 4 (Exit Hoogmade off motorway) ☎(071)414141 tx 30251
:Rest closed Sat & Sun lunchtime
➼♠70 P75 Lift ℂ
Credit Cards ①②③④⑤

LEIDERDORP
See **LEIDEN**

LELYSTAD
Flevoland

★★★**Congres Centrum Lelystad** Agoraweg 11 ☎(03200)42444 tx 70311
➼♠86 ☆ P400 Lift ℂ
Credit Cards ①②③⑤

LEUSDEN
Utrecht

★★**Hulze den Treek DPn** Treekerweg 23 ☎(03498)1425
Closed Xmas-3 Jan
rm18(➼♠14) ☆ P1510 Lift Lake
Credit Cards ①②⑤

LEUVENUM
Gelderland

★★**Roode Koper** Jhr-Sandbergweg 82 ☎(05770)7393 tx 49633
➼♠25 P ℚ ▭

LHEE
See **DWINGELOO**

LISSE
Zuid-Holland

★★★★**Nachtegaal van Lisse** Heereweg 10 ☎(02521)14447 tx 41122
➼♠148 P150 Lift ℂ ℚ ▭
Credit Cards ①②③⑤

LOCHEM
Gelderland

★★**Lochemse Berg** Lochemseweg 42 ☎(05730)1377
Etr-Oct & 20-31 Dec
➼♠15 P Lift
➼● *Van de Staat* Tramstr 36 ☎(05730) 1652 M/C P AR

LUNTEREN
Gelderland

★★★**Lunterse Boer DPn** Boslaan 87
☎(08388)3657
✦♠16 P Lift ℂ
Credit Cards ①②③⑤

★★**Wormshoef** Dorpsstr 192 ☎(08388)4241
✦♠32 P

LUTTE, DE
Overijssel

★★★**Bloemenbeek** Beuningerstr 6
☎(05415)1224
✦♠55 ☒ P100 Lift ℂ ℃ ⊡
Credit Cards ②③⑤

MAARSBERGEN
Utrecht

★★**Maarsbergen** Woudenbergseweg 44
☎(03433)1341 tx 47986
✦♠36 P250 ℂ
Credit Cards ①②③⑤

MAASTRICHT
Limburg (NI)

★★★★★**Maastricht** (GT) De Ruiterij 1
☎(043)254171 tx 56822
✦♠111 P Lift ℂ Mountain
Credit Cards ①②③④⑤

★★★**Casque** Helmster 14 ☎(043)214343 tx
56657
rm43(✦♠38) ☒ P4 Lift ℂ
Credit Cards ①②③⑤

➥ **Straten** via Regia 170 ☎(043) 434500 Aud
VW
At BEATRIXHAVEN(4km N)

➥ **Feyts Autos** Korvetweg 20-22 ☎(043) 632555
P For

MIDDELBURG
Zeeland

★★★**Commerce** Loskade 1 ☎(01180)36051 tx
36217
:Rest closed Sun
rm53(✦♠52) P15 Lift ℂ
Credit Cards ①②③④⑤

★★★**Nieuwe Doelen** Loskade 3-7
☎(01180)12121
rm28(♠13) Lift

★**Huifkar** Markt 19 ☎(01180)12998
Closed Sun Nov-Apr
✦♠4

➥ **Louisse** Kalverstr 1 ☎(01180) 25841 Ope

MIDDLEHARNIS
Zuid-Holland

➥ **Auto Service** Kastanjelaan 41-43 ☎(01870)
2222

➥ **Knöps** Langeweg 113 ☎(01870) 2222 Ope
Vau

MOOK EN MIDDELAAR
Limburg

★★★**Plasmolen** Rijksweg 170 ☎(08896)1444
rm29(✦♠27) P ℃

NIEUW DEN HELDER
See **HELDER, DEN**

NIJMEGEN
Gelderland

★★★**Altea Nijmegen** Stationspl 29
☎(080)238888 tx 48670
✦♠100 P Lift ℂ
Credit Cards ①②③⑤

➥ **Jansen & Ederveen** Winkelsteegseweg 150
☎(080) 563664 Ren

➥ **W Peeters** Kronenbergersingel 207 ☎(080)
239300

NIJVERDAL
Overijssel

➥ **Blokken** Bergleidingweg 27 ☎(05486) 12959
AR

NOORDGOUWE
Zeeland

➥ **Akkerdaas** Klooserweg 2 ☎(01112) 1347 P
Ope Vau

NOORDWIJK AAN ZEE
Zuid-Holland

★★★**Noordwyk DPn** Parallelboulevard 7
☎(01719)19231 tx 39116
✦♠36 Lift ℂ Sea
Credit Cards ②③⑤

★★**Alwine** Jan van Henegouwenweg 7
☎(01719)12213-19354
✦♠28 ☒ Lift ℂ ℃ ⊡
Credit Card ①

★★**Clarenwijck** Kon-Astrid Boulevard 46
☎(01719)12727
15 Jan-20 Dec
✦♠25 P

★**Duinlust** Koepelweg 1 ☎(01719)12916
Mar-Oct
rm16(♠4) P6 ℂ
Credit Cards ②⑤

➥ **Beuk** Golfweg 19 ☎(01719) 19213 fia Lan

➥ **Rijnland West** Beeklaan 5 ☎(01719) 14300
For

NULAND
Noord-Brabant

★★★**Nuland** Rijksweg 25 ☎(04102)2231 tx
50448
✦♠95 P350 Lift ℂ ℃ ⊡
Credit Card ①

ODOORN
Drenthe

★★★**Oringer Marke** Hoofdstr 9 ☎(05919)12888
rm42(✦♠38) A4rm P150
Credit Cards ①②③⑤

OISTERWIJK
Noord-Brabant

★★★**Swaen** de Lind 47 ☎(04242)19006 tx 52617
Closed 10-24 Jul: Rest closed Mar
✦♠18 P6 Lift ℂ
Credit Cards ①②③⑤

➥ **Spoormakers** Sprintlingstr 10 ☎(04242)
83568

OLDENZAAL
Overijssel

➥ **Munsterhuis** Oliemolenstr 4 ☎(05410) 15661
Ren

➥ **Olde Monnikhof** Vos de Waelstr 20
☎(05410) 14451 Ope

OMMEN
Overijssel

★★**Zon DPn** Voorbrug 1 ☎(05291)1141
Closed 1-3 Jan
✦♠25 P50 Lift ℂ
Credit Cards ①②③⑤

OOSTERBEEK
Gelderland

★★★**Bilderberg** (QM) Utrechtseweg 261
☎(085)340843 tx 45484
✦♠146 Lift ℃ ℂ

★★**Strijland** Stationsweg 6 & 8 ☎(085)343034
:Rest closed Sun Nov-Apr
✦♠30 P35 Lift ℂ
Credit Cards ①②③⑤

★**Dreyeroord** Gr-van-Rechterenweg 12
☎(085)333169
rm28(✦♠25) P Lift

OOTMARSUM
Overijssel

★★★★★**Wiemsel** (Relais et Châteaux) **DPn**
Winhofflaan 2 ☎(05419)2155 tx 44667
✦♠47 P ℂ ℃ ⊡ ∪
Credit Cards ①②③④⑤

★★**Wapen van Ootmarsum** Almelosestr 20
☎(05419)1500
Feb-4 Jan
✦♠20 P25
Credit Cards ①②③

OSS
Noord-Brabant

★**Alem** Molenstr 81 ☎(04120)22114
rm12(✦♠11) P60
Credit Cards ①②③⑤

➥ **Autobedrijt Caros** Abel Tasmanstr 16
☎(04120) 37090

OVERVEEN
Noord-Holland

★★**Rosendaal** Bloemendaalseweg 260
☎(023)277457
✦♠12 P

PAPENDRECHT
Zuid-Holland

★★★**Papendrecht** (QM) Lange Tiendweg 2
☎(078)152099 tx 29331
✦♠83 A33rm P160 Lift ℂ
Credit Cards ①②③④⑤

➥ **Autodrecht** Noordhoek 51 ☎(078) 157300
Toy

➥ **Hoog en Laag** Hoeklandsstr,Patten ☎(078)
334757

PUTTEN
Gelderland

★★★**Postiljon** Strandboulevard 3
☎(03418)56464 tx 47687
✦♠38 P Lift

RAALTE
Overijssel

★★★**Zwaan DPn** Kerkstr 2 ☎(05720)53122
rm20(✦♠16) P30 ⊡
Credit Cards ①②③⑤

RIJSWIJK
See **HAAG, DEN (HAGUE, THE)**

ROERMOND
Limburg

➥ **Nedam** Orajelaan 802 ☎(04750) 23351 P Ope
Vau

➥ **Opheij** II Singel 29-31 ☎(04750) 32125 AR
Hon

ROOSENDAAL
Noord-Brabant

★★**Central** Stationspl 9 ☎(01650)35657 tx 78192
rm20(✦♠17)

➥ **Parkgarage** A-Lonchestrl ☎(01650) 36924 For

➥ **Rob Levis** Hoogstrsst 177 ☎(01650) 36566
AR

ROTTERDAM
Zuid-Holland

Rotterdam rose out of the ashes of the Second World War like a phoenix, superbly planned and beautifully constructed to cater for every taste - sports, music, shops, theatres, outdoor parks covering over 10,000 acres, 12 museums and numerous galleries. A stroll from the centre, however, will take you to the 17th century preserved and reconstructed in the city's western quarter of Delfshaven. In its old town hall is the Stolk Atlas, one of the best known

collections of old maps and sea charts. An interesting visit can also be paid to the *Oude Kerk*, built in 1416, where the Pilgrim Fathers prayed before departing for the New World. By contrast, a boat trip round the port - the largest in the world - is impressive, as is the view you get if you go up the Euromast in the revolving space tower - offering a view of 33 miles on a clear day.

EATING OUT Rotterdam's restaurants are mostly in the centre of the city, especially in Lijnbaan, Coolsingel, Schouwburgplein, Stadhuisplein, Schouwburgplein and Meent. The Old Dutch, in Rocherssenstraat, is one of the city's best restaurants for atmosphere and Dutch cuisine. **See also SCHIEDAM**

ROTTERDAM
Zuid-Holland

★★★★**Hilton International** Weena 10
☎(010)4144044 tx 22666
🛏248 ☎ P Lift ℂ
Credit Cards ① ② ③ ④ ⑤

★★★★**Atlanta** (GT) Aert van Nesstr 4
☎(010)4110420 tx 21595
🛏169 ☎ P50 Lift ℂ
Credit Cards ① ② ③ ⑤

★★★★**Central** Kruiskade 12 ☎(010)4140744 tx 24040
🛏64 Lift ℂ
Credit Cards ① ② ③ ⑤

★★★★**Park** (BW) Westersingel 70
☎(010)4363611 tx 22020
🛏157 P60 Lift ℂ
Credit Cards ① ② ③ ④ ⑤

★★★★**Rijn** (QM) Schouwburgpl 1
☎(010)4333800 tx 21640
🛏100 Lift ℂ
Credit Cards ① ② ③ ⑤

★★★**Savoy** (GT) Hoogstr 81 ☎(010)4139280 tx 21525
🛏94 ☎ P10 Lift ℂ
Credit Cards ① ② ③ ⑤

★★**Baan** Rochussenstr 345 (n.rest)
☎(010)4770555
15 Jan-15 Dec
rm14(🛏9)

★★**Pax** Schiekade 658 (n.rest) ☎(010)4663344
🛏57 A8rm P10 Lift ℂ
Credit Cards ① ② ③ ⑤

★★**Walsum** Mathenesserlaan 199
☎(010)4363275 tx 20010
Jan 2-Dec 20
🛏26 P12 Lift ℂ
Credit Cards ① ② ③ ④ ⑤

★**Holland** Provenierssingel 7 (n.rest)
☎(010)4653100
rm28(🛏4) ℂ
Credit Cards ① ② ③ ⑤

👄 **Dunant** Dunanstr 22-40 ☎(010) 760166 Toy

👄 **Gam Rotterdam** Smirnoffweg 21-23 ☎(010) 298844 Aud VW

👄 **Hoogenboom** Geissendorfferweg 5-15 ☎(010) 298844 P Aud VW

👄 **Vliet** Kleiweg 35 ☎(010) 225029 AR

At **VLAARDINGEN**

★★★★**Delta** (QM) Massboulevard 15
☎(010)4345477 tx 23154
🛏78 A4rm P100 Lift ℂ ⌷
Credit Cards ① ② ③ ⑤

SASSENHEIM
Zuid-Holland

★★★**Sassenheim** Warmonderweg 8
☎(02522)19019 tx 41688
🛏57 P Lift ℂ
Credit Card ①

SCHEVENINGEN
See **HAAG, DEN (HAGUE, THE)**

SCHIEDAM
Zuid-Holland

See also ROTTERDAM

★★★**Novotel** Hargalaan 2 ☎(010)4713322 tx 22582
🛏138 P Lift ⌷
Credit Cards ① ③ ⑤

SCHIPHOL
See **AMSTERDAM AIRPORT**

SLUIS
Zeeland

★**Sanders de Pauw** Kade 42 ☎(01178)1224
rm10(🛏5) P12
Credit Cards ① ② ③ ⑤

SNEEK
Friesland

★★**Wijnberg** Markstr 23 ☎(05150)12421
rm21(🛏19) P ⌷
Credit Cards ① ② ③ ⑤

★**Bonnema** Stationsstr 62-66 ☎(05150)13175
Closed 1 Jan:Rest closed Sun
rm14(🛏10) P25
Credit Cards ① ② ③ ⑤

👄 **Deinum** Edisonstr 1 ☎(05150) 22055 M/C Oud Vau

👄 **F Ozinga's** Akkerwinde ☎(05150) 13344 For

👄 **H de Vries** Oosterkade 28 ☎(05150) 13291 P Ren

TEGELEN
Limburg

👄 **Linssen** Roermondseweg 139 ☎(077) 731421 M/C P Fia

TILBURG
Noord-Brabant

★★★**Altea Heuvelpoort** Heuvelpoort 300
☎(013)354675 tx 52722
🛏63 ☎ Lift ℂ
Credit Cards ① ② ③ ⑤

★★**Postelse Hoeve** Deelenlaan 10
☎(013)636335 tx 52788
🛏22 P

👄 **Bink** Winkler Prinsstraat 24 ☎(013) 421043

UTRECHT
Utrecht

Founded by the Romans, Utrecht was already established when the Netherlands were in their infancy, and became the country's foremost cultural centre in the Middle Ages. Reminders of its long history that have survived include the *Domkerk* with its 367ft-high tower, the former Bishop's Palace, the *Rijksmuseum Het*

Catharijneconvent, the *Academiegebouw* of the University, many churches, and picturesque *hofjes* - the courtyards of almshouses. The city has a wealth of museums, spanning such interests as historic trains, musical boxes, barrel organs and an old-fashioned grocer's shop. Visitors can also stroll alongside the canals and perhaps visit one of the terraces which have been built over the old wharfs, right on the waterfront, or the environs of the city that include woods, heaths and the attractive lakeland area around Loosdrecht, Maarseveen and Vinkeveen. Hoog Catharijne, one of the largest covered shopping complexes in the Netherlands is located between the Centraal Station and the old central area of the city.

EATING OUT There are many kinds of restaurants offering meals in various price ranges. Most are on the Oude Gracht, often in old buildings that have been skilfully restored, or in waterside cellars. Other restaurants can be found in Hoog Catharijne and Vredenburg.

UTRECHT

★★★★**Holiday Inn** Jaarbeurspl 24 ☎(030)910555 tx 47745
🛏280 Lift ⌷
Credit Cards ① ② ③ ⑤

★★★**Pays Bas** (GT) Janskerkhof 10 (n.rest)
☎(030)333321 tx 47485
🛏47 ☎ P18 Lift ℂ
Credit Cards ① ② ③ ⑤

★★★**Smits DPn** Vredenburg 14 ☎(030)331232 tx 47557
🛏84 Lift ℂ
Credit Cards ① ② ③ ⑤

★★**Malie Hers** Maliestr 2 (n.rest) ☎(030)316424 tx 70870
🛏30 Lift ℂ
Credit Cards ① ② ③ ⑤

👄 **Stichtse** Leidseweg 128 ☎(030) 931744 For

👄 **Van Meeuwen's** Weerdsingel 42-44 ☎(030) 719111 Alf Hon Vau

At **BUNNIK**(7km SE)

★★★**Postiljon** (BW) Kosterijland 8
☎(03405)69222 tx 70298
🛏84 P300 Lift ℂ
Credit Cards ① ② ③ ⑤

VALKENBURG
Limburg

★★★★**Prinses Juliana** (Relais et Châteaux) DPn Broekhem 11 ☎(04406)12244 tx 56351
Rest closed Sat lunchtime
🛏27 A10rm ☎ P58 Lift ℂ
Credit Cards ① ② ③ ④ ⑤

★★★**Atlanta** Neerhem 20 ☎(04406)12193
rm35(⇆32) P Lift

★★**Apollo** Nieuweweg 7 ☎(04406)15341
⇆32 P
Credit Cards 1 2 3 4 5

★★**Tourotel** Wilhelminlaan 28-34 ☎(04406)13998
tx 56714
15 Feb-15 Nov & 19 Dec-2 Jan
rm42(⇆31) ☎ P
Credit Cards 1 2 3 5

◗◗ **Auto-Caubo** Neerham 25 ☎(04406) 15041

◗◗ **Nerum** Neerham 25 ☎(04406) 15041 P Aud VW

VEENDAM
Groningen

◗◗ **Bakker** Dr-Bossaan 21 ☎(05987) 12288 P Alf

VEENENDAAL
See **EDE**

VEERE
Zeeland

★**Campveerse Toren** Kade 2 ☎(01181)1291
rm17(⇆13) A11rm Lake

VELP
See **ARNHEM**

VENLO
Limburg

★★★★**Bovenste Molen** (QM) Bovenste
Molenweg 12 ☎(077)541045 tx 58393
⇆62 P100 Lift ℂ ⚓ ⬛ ♪♪
Credit Cards 1 2 3 4 5

★★★**Novotel** Nijmeegseweg 90 ☎(077)544141 tx
58229
⇆88 P150 Lift ⌐
Credit Cards 1 2 3 5

★★**Wilhelmina** Kaldenkerkerweg 1
☎(077)516251
Closed 25 Dec
⇆34 P30 Lift ℂ
Credit Cards 1 2 3 5

★**Grolsch Quelle** Eindhovensestr 3-8
☎(077)13560
rm20

◗◗ **AML** Wezelseweg 53E Vit ☎(077) 829999 P
Mer

◗◗ **Van Gorp** Ferd Bolstr 10 ☎(077) 16752 Cit

◗◗ **L Van den Hombergh** Straelseweg 18 ☎(077)
11441 For

◗◗ **Kok** Burg Bloemartsstr 30 ☎(077) 54354 Vol

◗◗ **J B Nefkens & Zonen** Staelseweg 52 ☎(077)
12474 Peu

VENRAY
Limburg

◗◗ **J V Gorp** Horsterweg 10a ☎(04780) 86825 Cit

◗◗ **Van Haren** Raadhuisstr 38 ☎(04780) 85300 P
For

VIERHOUTEN
Gelderland

★★★**Mallejan** Nunspeterweg 70 ☎(05771)241
Closed 5 Dec
⇆42 ☎ P Lift ९

VLAARDINGEN
See **ROTTERDAM**

VLISSINGEN (FLUSHING)
Zeeland

★★★**Strand** (GT) bd Eversten 4 ☎(01184)12297
tx 37878
:Rest closed Sun pm
⇆40 P20 Lift ℂ Sea
Credit Cards 1 2 3 5

◗◗ **Dýkwel Vlissingen** Pres-Rosseveltlaan 745
☎(01184) 12008 Peu

VOLENDAM
Noord-Holland

★★**Van Diepen** Haven 35 ☎(02993)63705 tx
13141
16 Mar-2 Nov
rm18(⇆11) P

WAGENINGEN
Gelderland

◗◗ **Van der Kolk** Station Str NR 21 ☎(08373)
19055 For

WARNSVELD
Gelderland

★**Het Jachthuis** Vordenseweg 2 ☎(05750)23328
rm8(⇆6) P ९

WASSENAAR
Zuid-Holland

★★**Duinoord** Wassenaarseslag 26
☎(01751)19332) tx 34383
⇆20 P

◗◗ **A Blankespoor** Oostdorperweg 29-31
☎(01751) 12405 AR DJ

◗◗ **Jansen** Rijstraatweg 773 ☎(01751) 79941 Aud
VW

WOERDEN
Zuid-Holland

★★★**Baron Woerden** (GT) Utrechtsestraatweg 33
☎(03480)12515 tx 76151
⇆66 ☎ P26 ℂ
Credit Cards 1 2 3 5

ZAANDAM
Noord-Holland

◗◗ **Verenigde** Zeemanstr 43 ☎(075) 172751 For

ZANDVOORT
Noord-Holland

★★★**Palace** Burg van Fenemapl 2
☎(02507)12911 tx 41812
⇆43 P Lift

★★**Hoogland** Westerparkstr 5 ☎(02507)15541 tx
71222
Mar-Oct
⇆25
Credit Cards 1 2 3 5

ZEDDAM
Gelderland

★★**Aaldering's** Heerenbergseweg 1
☎(08345)1273
rm24(⇆14) P ▱

ZEIST
Utrecht

★★★**Hermitage** Het Rond 7 ☎(03404)24414
Closed 1 Jan
⇆14 P Lift

◗◗ **J Molenarr's** 2e Hogeweg 109 ☎(03404)
18041 P Alf

◗◗ **A F Phillippo** Laan Van Cattenbroek 23
☎(03404) 14529 Toy

ZIERIKZEE
Zeeland

★★**Mondragon** DPn Havenpark 21
☎(01110)13051
16 Jan-14 Dec :Rest closed Sun lunch
⇆9
Credit Cards 1 2 3 5

ZOETERMEER
Zuid-Holland

★★★**Baron Zoetermeer** Boerhaavelaan
☎(079)219228 tx 36726
⇆60 P Lift ℂ
Credit Cards 1 2 3 5

ZUTPHEN
Gelderland

★★**Inntel Zutphen** De Stoven 14 ☎(05750)25555
tx 49701
⇆65 P Lift ९ ℂ

◗◗ **N Nijendijk** Splittaalstr 32-34 ☎(05750) 15257
AR

◗◗ **Welmers** H-Dunentweg 2 ☎(05750) 12537 P
Fia

ZWOLLE
Overijssel

★★★**Postiljon** Hertsenbergweg 1 ☎(038)216031
tx 42180
⇆72 P300 Lift ℂ
Credit Cards 1 2 3 5

★★★**Wientjes** (GT) Stationsweg 7 ☎(038)254254
tx 42640
⇆57 P45 Lift ℂ
Credit Cards 1 2 3 5

HIRE SERVICE
Ultrasonic Car Alarm

The alarm combines the security of
ultrasonics with the convenience of
remote control. Placed on the
dashboard or rear parcel-shelf it is a
highly visible deterrent. Available for
all cars fitted with cigarette lighters.

Contact AA Hire Service, Snargate
Street, Dover, Kent CT17 9XA
Telephone: Dover (0304) 203655

Don't leave the country without one

There is little doubt that if the Scandinavian countries were judged on scenery alone Norway would come very high up the list. Few can fail to be impressed by the unfolding panorama of mountains, fjords, lakes, waterfalls and rivers – and delightful cities and towns. The west coast region is particularly attractive. Its three splendid but quite different fjords – Sogne, Hardanger and Nord – embrace a vast region of delightful villages offering much to do and see as well as excellent accommodation. Even the 'gateway' town of Bergen deserves some time, whether you are arriving by air or sea.

Norway's coast is steep, fringed with islands and deeply cut by fjords. The highest mountains are the Jotunheimen in the south. Barren plateaux, lakes and ice fields separate the mountain ranges.

In addition to Oslo, the capital, and Bergen, the second biggest city, other cities of interest include Trondheim and Tromso, both being pleasant places for a visit and located close to glorious countryside.

NORWAY

Language
Norwegian (Bokmôl and Landsmôl) and Lappish

Local Time
GMT + 1 hour (Summer GMT + 2 hours)

Currency
Norwegian krone, divided into 100 ore.
At the time of going to press
£1 = NOK11.41
US$1 = NOK6.87

Emergency numbers
In Oslo:
Fire ☎001   Police ☎002
Ambulance ☎003
For other towns, see inside front cover of the local telephone directory.

Information in Britain
Norwegian Tourist Board, 5–11 Charles House,
Lower Regent Street, London SW1Y 4LR
☎01-839 6255 (071-839 6255 from 6 May 1990)
(recorded message service between 09.00–11.00hrs and 14.00–17.00hrs)

Information in the USA
Scandinavian National Tourist Office,
655 Third Avenue, New York, NY 10017
☎212 949 2333

HOW TO GET THERE

Direct Ferry Services are available:
Newcastle to *Bergen* and *Stavanger* (via
the Bergen sailing)
and (via Hirtshals (Denmark)) to *Oslo*
Crossing times vary between
approximately 17 and 36 hours.

You may use one of the Short Channel
Crossings to *France* or *Belgium*, driving
through the *Netherlands*, *Northern
Germany* and *Denmark*; then either take
the direct ferry link to Southern Norway,
or travel via Sweden.

The driving distance may be shortened
by crossing to *Germany*:
Harwich to Hamburg (19½–21½hrs), and
then driving through Germany and
Denmark.

Distance

from the Channel ports to Oslo, via
Sweden, is about 1600km (1000 miles),
requiring three overnight stops.

MONEYMATTERS

There are no restrictions on the amounts
of foreign or Norwegian currency you
may take into the country, but you are
advised to declare any large amounts on
arrival in case you wish to take them out
again when you leave. No more than
NOK5,000 in notes not higher than
NOK100 may be taken out of Norway.

Banking hours

Monday–Friday 08.30–15.00hrs

Currency may usually be exchanged at
railway stations and airports. These are
normally open: Monday–Friday 08.00–
21.00hrs, and Sunday 08.00–14.00hrs,
but these times may vary.

At Bogstad Camping (a well-equipped
NAF site near Oslo), there is an exchange
office, open weekdays June–August. The
opening hours are as for ordinary banks,
and it is closed Saturday and Sunday.

Postcheques

may be cashed at all post offices up to a
maximum of NOK1,000 per cheque. Go
to a counter position which displays the
words **Postgiro** or **Inn-og Utbetalinger**.

MOTORING REGULATIONS AND GENERAL INFORMATION

The information given here is specific to
Norway. It **must** be read in conjunction
with the European ABC at the front of the
book, which covers those regulations
which are common to many countries.

Accidents*

There are no firm rules of procedure, except
when personal injuries are sustained, in which
case the police must be called. Under such
circumstances, you should obtain medical
assistance for the injured person. It is also
obligatory to place a warning triangle on the
road to notify following traffic of the
obstruction. See also *Warning triangle* below.

Breakdown*

The Norwegian Motoring Club (NAF) operates a
limited road patrol service between 20 June and
1 September. The service operates from 10.00 to
19.00hrs daily, but in view of its limitations, a
local garage may offer help more quickly. See
also *Warning triangle* below.

British Embassy/Consulates

The British Embassy together with its consular
section is located at 0264 Oslo 2, Thomas
Heftyesgate 8 ☎552400. There are British
Consulates with Honorary Consuls in Ålesund,
Bergen, Harstad, Haugesund, Kristianand (S),
Kristiansund (N), Stavanger, Tromsø and
Trondheim. See also *Town Plan of Oslo* in
gazetteer below.

Children in Cars

Children under 12 years are not permitted to
travel in a vehicle as front-seat passengers.

Dimensions*

Private cars and towed trailers or caravans are
restricted to the following dimensions – **car**
height, no restriction; width, 2.35† metres;
length, 10 metres. **Trailer/caravan** height, no
restriction; width, 2.30†† metres; length, 10
metres. The maximum permitted overall

***Additional information will be found in the
European ABC at the front of the book.**

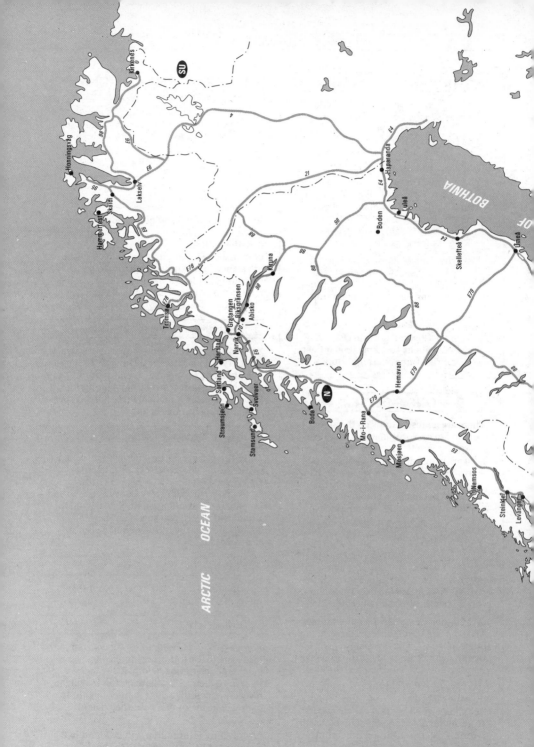

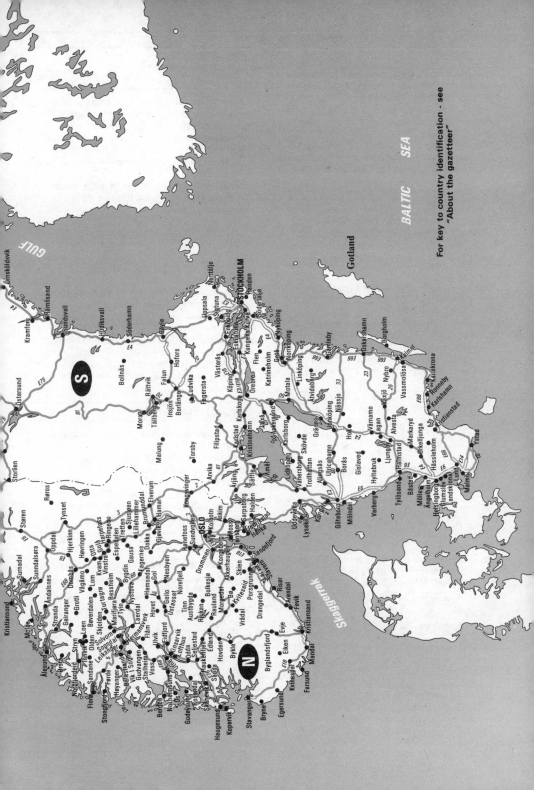

GULF

BALTIC

SEA

Gotland

For key to country identification - see
"About the gazetteer"

S (Sweden)

N (Norway)

Skagerrak

Örnsköldsvik
Härnösand
Kramfors
Sundsvall
Hudiksvall
Söderhamn
Gävle
Uppsala
Sigtuna
Enköping
STOCKHOLM
Kungens Kurva
Södertälje
Norrtälje
Handen

Östersund
Storlien
Sundsvall

Bollnäs
Falun
Hofors
Rättvik
Ludvika
Insjön
Borlänge
Mora
Tällberg
Hagersta
Västerås
Köping
Eskilstuna
Flen
Katrineholm
Örebro
Nyköping
Norrköping
Linköping

Oskarshamn
Borgholm
Gamleby
Kalmar

Röros
Tynset
Oppdal
Hjerkinn
Høvringen

Malung
Torsby
Arvika
Kongsvinger
Elverum

Filipstad
Karlstad
Kristinehamn
Karlskoga
Laxå
Askersund
Motala
Atvidaberg
Jönköping
Nässjö
Gränna
Hok
Vetlanda
Nybro
Vassmolösa
Ronneby
Karlshamn
Kristianstad

Nyköping
Säffle
Arjäng
Åmål
Vänersborg
Trollhättan
Alingsås
Borås
Ulricehamn
Värnamo
Lagan
Alvesta
Växjö
Markaryd
Hässleholm
Ljungby
Gislaved
Hyltebruk
Halmstad
Ängelholm
Helsingborg
Landskrona
Malmö
Lund

Ystad

Varberg
Tylösand
Båstad
Mölle

Göteborg
Mölndal
Kungälv

Uddevalla
Lysekil

Halden
Fredrikstad
Sarpsborg
Moss

OSLO
Kolbotn
Askim
Drammen
Kongsberg
Hokksund
Åkerhaugen
Skien
Porsgrunn
Larvik
Sandefjord
Tønsberg
Horten

Hamar
Lillehammer
Brumunddal
Gjøvik
Dokka
Gausa
Hønefoss
Sundvollen
Haneftoss
Elverum

Risør
Tvedestrand
Arendal
Fevik
Kristiansand
Mandal

Sumadal
Sunndalsøra
Andalsnes
Stranda
Geiranger
Kristiansund
Molde
Loen
Olden
Grotli
Lom
Bøverdalen
Skjolden
Vinstra
Ringebu
Otta
Vågåmo
Kvam
Gol
Fagernes
Nystøva
Espedalen
Sjusjøen
Tretten

Ålesund
Norddjupet
Flåm
Sandane
Førde
Stryn

Byglandsfjord
Eiken
Evje
Bykle
Hovden
Edland
Rauland
Austbygda
Rjukan
Seljestad
Morgedal
Vrådal
Dalen
Drangedal
Bø
Notodden
Kviteseid
Tinn
Nesbyen
Ål
Hemsedal
Hovet
Bygdin
Tyin

Haukeligrend
Røldal
Sauda
Odda
Kinsarvik
Ulvik
Eidfjord
Geilo
Finse

Lærdal
Årdal
Gudvangen
Leikanger
Vik, Sogn
Balestrand
Høyanger
Vadheim

Stavanger
Bryne
Egersund
Farsund

Haugesund
Kopervik

Bergen
Os
Norheimsund
Godøysund
Skånevik

Florø
Stongfjord
Måløy
Nordfjordeid

Kristiansund
Surnadal

E75
E4
18
70
50
40
60
61
7
45
3
E3
E18
E6
33
23
25
993
66
9
E14
813
15
2
20
27
5
E39
E136
55
51
13

length of vehicle/trailer or caravan combinations is 18 metres (15 metres on some roads).

Trailers without brakes may have a total weight of up to 50% of the towing vehicle with a maximum of 750kg.

†Caravans over 2.30 metres, but not exceeding 2.50 metres in width, are permitted only when the towing vehicle is of at least the same width.

Driving licence*

A valid UK or Republic of Ireland licence is acceptable in Norway. The minimum age at which a visitor may use a temporarily imported car or motorcycle is 17 years.

Emergency messages to tourists*

Emergency messages to tourists are broadcast in English by Norwegian State Radio (NRK) in the programme *Reiseradio* ('Travel Radio'). The messages are transmitted on medium wave on 228 metres and 1376 metres at 09.00hrs Monday to Friday.

Lights*

It is compulsory for all motorists and motorcyclists to keep their dipped headlights on during the day.

Motoring club

The **Norges Automobil – Forbund** (NAF) which has its headquarters at 0155 Oslo 1, Storgaten 2 ☎(02) 429400, located on the Oslo town plan within the gazetteer. It also has offices or agents in main towns. Office hours are generally 08.30–16.00hrs Monday to Friday. The NAF Travel Agency is open on Saturday, 09.00–13.00hrs.

Motorways

Several main roads incorporate stretches of motorway (*motorvei*), mainly around Oslo, with short stretches at Bergen, Stavanger, and Moss. Motorways are divided into two classes – *Motorvei Klasse* and *Motorvei Klasse B*. The first is the usual two-lane dual-carriageway and the second is a two-lane road from 20–25 feet wide with limited access points.

Parking*

Parking places and no parking areas in towns are clearly marked with the appropriate international signs. Do not park by signs bearing the inscription *All stans forbudt*, which means 'stopping prohibited'. Spending the night in a vehicle or trailer on the roadside is **not** permitted.

Parking meters are in use in main towns. The free use of unexpired time on meters is authorised.

Petrol*

Credit cards The use of credit cards to obtain petrol is common, but should be checked.
Duty-free petrol In addition to the petrol in the vehicle tank, up to 15 litres in a can may be imported free of custom duty and tax.
Petrol (leaded) Super Benzin (98 octane grade).
Petrol (low lead) is sold as 97 octane grade.
Petrol (unleaded) is sold throughout Norway and has an octane rating of 95. Pumps dispensing unleaded petrol in *Norol* stations are green; in *Esso* stations they are marked with a green sign.

Postal information

Mail Postcards NOK4.00; letters 5–20gm NOK4.00.
Post offices There are 2,700 post offices in Norway. Opening hours are 09.00–16.00hrs Monday to Friday and 09.00–13.00hrs Saturday. Oslo Sentrum post office is open 08.00–20.00hrs Monday to Friday and 09.00–15.00hrs on Saturday.

Priority*

In Norway trams always have right of way.

Public holidays*

Official Public holidays in Norway for 1990 are given below.
January 1 (New Year's Day)
April 12 (Maundy Thursday)
April 13 (Good Friday)
April 16 (Easter Monday)
May 1 (Labour Day)
May 17 (National Day)

*Additional information will be found in the European ABC at the front of the book.

May 24 (Ascension Day)
December 25 (Christmas Day)
December 26 (Boxing Day)

Roads

In southern and eastern Norway, the most important routes have modern surfaces. In the west and north, some road surfaces are oil-bound (partly water-bound) grit. Vehicles with a high ground clearance are more suitable on mountain roads than those with low ground clearance. As a courtesy to other road users, you should fit mudguard flaps. The roads sometimes have soft edges – a great inconvenience to motorcyclists. Watch for the warning signs *Løse Veikanter* and *Svake Kanter*. In the fjord district and often in other areas, careful and confident driving is necessary, although gradients are seldom excessive and hairpin bends can usually be easily negotiated. The region is mainly unsuitable for large vehicles or caravans. There are sometimes ferry crossings, and a reasonable touring maximum is 100–150 miles a day.

Bergen tollring experiment A pay-and-display toll system has been introduced by the local authorities to help finance improvements to the roads of Bergen. All motorists entering Bergen must now pay NOK5.00 (approximately 50p). However, visiting motorists coming by ferry from Britain to the Skoltegrunnskaien pier will not have to pay any toll on arrival.

Shopping hours

Monday to Friday 08.30/09.00–17.00hrs (09.00–19.00hrs Thursdays), Saturday 08.30/09.00–14.00hrs. During the month of July, some shops restrict their opening times to 09.00–16.00hrs.

Speed limits*

In *built-up areas*, all vehicles are restricted to 50kph (31mph), unless there are signs to the contrary. *Outside built-up areas*, private vehicles are restricted to 80kph (49mph), and on certain *motorways*, the speed limit is 90kph (56mph). Vehicles towing caravans are limited to 80kph (49mph) if the trailer is equipped with a braking system, and 60kph (37mph) if not.

Spiked or studded tyres*

These may be used from 1 November to the end of the week following Easter Day. If *spiked tyres* are used, they must be fitted to all four wheels. No special speed limits apply. See also *Winter conditions*, below.

Telephone*

Insert coins **after** lifting the receiver (instructions appear in English in international callboxes). When making calls to subscribers *within* Norway, precede the number with the relevant area code (shown in parentheses before the hotel/garage enquiry number in the gazetteer). Use NOK2.00 coins for local calls and NOK1, 5 or 10 coins for national and international calls.
International callbox identification Most callboxes.
Telephone rates The cost of a direct dialled call to the UK is NOK1 for 10.4 seconds. An operator assisted call costs NOK17.70 for 3 minutes and NOK5.90 for each additional minute. An extra charge of NOK14 is made for a personal call. Local calls cost NOK2.00
Telephone codes

UK to Norway	010 47
Norway to UK	095 44
Norway to Republic of Ireland	095 353
Norway to the USA	095 1

Trams*

Stationary trams may be overtaken on the right at moderate speed, or on the left where there is no room on the right. Moving trams may normally be overtaken only on the right, but overtaking is permitted on the left in oneway streets, or where there is no room on the right. See also *Priority*, above.

Warning triangle*

The use of a warning triangle is advisable in the event of accident or breakdown.

Wheel chains*

Chains may be necessary if tyre equipment is not adequate for driving under winter conditions. See also *Winter conditions*, below.

Winter conditions

Roads to the Swedish frontier (leading to Stockholm and Göteborg (Gothenburg)) are kept

*Additional information will be found in the European ABC at the front of the book.

clear. The western fjord district is generally unsuitable for motoring between mid-October and late May, and in places until mid-June. During this period, the road from Bergen to Oslo via Haukeli remains open, but the road via Eidfjord and Geilo is obstructed. It is possible to take cars by train between Voss and Ål (see below), or to motor via Voss, Gudvangen (ferry to Revsnes), Laerdal, and Fagernes. On this stretch, it is necessary to use spiked tyres or chains during the winter.

The road from Stavanger to Oslo and the Oslo–Trondheim–Mo-i-Rana road is always open. The possibility of motoring further north depends on the weather. Ålesund and Kristiansund (N) can be approached from Dombås and Oppdal. A map showing roads passable in winter can be obtained from the Norwegian Tourist Board in London. Information may also be obtained from the 24-hour NAF Emergency Centre in Oslo ☎(02) 429400.

In winter only, cars may be conveyed by the Bergen railway between Voss and Ål, provided space is booked at least 24 hours in advance. Cars must be at the station at least three hours before departure. Vehicle rates are calculated at time of booking.

ACCOMMODATION

There is no official classification of hotels, but all establishments offering overnight accommodation must be officially authorised. Such establishments must be easily recognisable as hotels, and must have adequate amenities.

Establishments mainly catering for international tourist traffic, which must satisfy the more rigorous requirements, may qualify for the description of 'tourist' and 'mountain' hotels (turist and høyfjells-hoteller). At these establishments, wine and spirits are available between 13.00 and 23.45hrs. On Sundays and National holidays, only beer and wine are available.

In most towns of any size, there is a range of hotels from the simple to the more luxurious. Higher standards are required of these hotels than is generally the case with country hotels.

Pensionater and hospitser are too small to be classified as hotels, but they provide electricity, modern sanitation and, frequently, hot and cold water in bedrooms. Turiststasjoner (tourist stations) and fjellstuer (mountain inns) provide comfortable rooms, but often there is no electricity or modern sanitation. Nevertheless, they are scrupulously clean.

The prices shown below are an average for each classification. Accommodation is likely to be more expensive in Oslo and some of the more popular tourist areas. At the time of going to press, £1 Sterling = NOK11.41 and US$1 = NOK6.87, but you should check the rate of exchange before your departure.

AVERAGE PRICES

	Single Room	Double Room	Breakfast	Lunch/Dinner
★★★★	NOK974–1105	NOK1155–1424	—	NOK115–250
★★★	NOK472–670	NOK597–867	NOK47–51	NOK124–137
★★	NOK400–594	NOK550–718	NOK51–53	NOK93–147
★	NOK275–513	NOK400–638	NOK40–60	NOK60–119

In Norwegian Ø is the equivalent to oe. The Norwegian alphabet differs from the English one in that the last letters after Z are Æ,Ø,Å; this must be borne in mind when using Norwegian reference books.
According to our information, garages with no specific service agencies will handle any make of car.
Abbreviations:
gt   gaten   pl   plads

AKKERHAUGEN
Telemark
★★*Norsj Turisthotel* ☎(036)958211
⊶↿50 P60 Lift ℂ Beach Mountain Lake
Credit Cards ① ③

ÅL
Buskerud
★★★Bergjøstølen ☎(067)84618

Feb-Apr & 20 Jun-20 Oct
rm35(↿25) Sea Mountain Lake
Credit Card ③
★★*Sundre* (n.rest) ☎(067)81100
rm26(⊶16) P25 ℂ Mountain
Credit Cards ① ③
ÅLESUND
Mre-og-Romsdal
★★*Noreg* Kongensgate 27 ☎(071)22938 tx 40440
⊶↿107 ﹫ P10 Lift ℂ 🖭
Credit Cards ① ② ③ ⑤
⤙ *Ødegårds Karrosserifabrikk* ☎(071) 42079
⤙ *Holens Bilverksted* ☎(071) 22658

ÅNDALSNES
Mre-og-Romsdal
⤙ *Isylte* ☎(072) 21477

ARENDAL
Aust-Agder
★★★*Phönix* Tyholmen ☎(041)25160 tx 21374
:Rest closed Sun
⊶↿83 Lift ℂ
Credit Cards ① ② ③ ④ ⑤
⤙ *Josephsens Auto* ☎(041) 26200

ASKIM
Østfold
⤙ *Martiniussen Bilservice* ☎(02) 887776

BALESTRAND
Sogn-og-Fjordane
★★★*Kvikne's* (BW) Balholm ☎(056)91101 tx 42858
May-Sep
rm210(⊶185) P Lift ℂ Beach Sea Mountain
Credit Cards ① ② ③ ⑤

★★*Kringsjå* ☎(056)91303
5 Jan-28 Aug
rm30(➔17) P Sea

★★*Midtnes Pensionat* (n.rest) ☎(056)91133
Jan-Nov
rm35(➔30) Lift Beach Sea

★*Balestrand Pensionat* ☎(056)91138
rm28(➔20) A8rm P30 Lift Beach Sea
Credit Cards ③ ⑤

BERGEN
Hordaland

Norway's second largest city offers everything necessary for an enjoyable and memorable visit. Surrounded by sea and mountains, its location is impressive, and a fine panoramic view rewards those taking the funicular up Mount Floyen. Many attractive museums and other places of interest, such as the Aquarium, King Haakon's Hall, Bryggen Wharf and Fantoft Stave Church are well worth exploring, as are the old merchant houses and the imposing 13th-century cathedral. A good programme of excursions, some by fjord steam, is available, and public transport can also be used for independent sightseeing.
The fish market and the adjoining flower and vegetable market near the city centre are fascinating sights, and so are the 17th-century warehouses and the Bergenhus fortress. St Mary's Church is the oldest edifice in Bergen, built in the 12th century. Edward Grieg was born in Bergen and his mansion, located 8km from the city, is now a museum.

EATING OUT Of the many noteworthy fish restaurants in this city, *Bryggen Tracteursted*, in Bryggestredet, enjoys a particularly high reputation for the freshness of its fish from the adjacent market.

BERGEN
Hordaland

★★★★*Bergen Airport* Kokstadvelen 3,N-Kokstad
☎(05)229200 tx 40148
➔264 P Lift (⚲
Credit Cards ① ② ③ ⑤

★★★★*SAS Royal* Bryggen ☎(05)318000 tx 40640
➔270 ☼ P4033 Lift (⌂
Credit Cards ① ② ③ ⑤

★★★*Admiral* C Sundtsgt 9-13 ☎(05)475324730
tx 40614
➔107 P Lift (Sea
Credit Cards ① ② ③ ④ ⑤

★★★*Grand Terminus* Kong Oscarsgt 71
☎(05)311655 tx 42262
➔130 ☼ Lift (
Credit Cards ① ② ③ ④ ⑤

★★★*Norge* Ole Bulls Plass 4 ☎(05)210100 tx 42129
➔348 ☼ P20 Lift (⌂ Mountain
Credit Cards ① ② ③ ④ ⑤

★★★*Orion* Bradbenken 3 ☎(05)318080 tx 42442
➔75 P5 Lift (Sea
Credit Cards ① ② ③ ⑤

★★★*Scandic* Kokstadflaten 2,Kokstad
☎(05)227150 tx 40890
2 Jan - 22 Dec
rm201 Lift (⌂
Credit Cards ① ② ③ ⑤

★★*Hanseaten* Sandbroogt 3 ☎(05)316155
Closed 22 Dec-5 Jan
rm31(➔23) Lift (Sea
Credit Cards ① ② ③ ⑤

★★*Hordaheimer* c Sundtsgt 18 ☎(05)232320 tx 40926
➔69 P6 Lift (
Credit Cards ① ② ③ ⑤

★★*Neptun* Walckendorffsgt 8 ☎(05)326000 tx 40040
➔122 ☼ P15 Lift (
Credit Cards ① ② ③ ④ ⑤

★★*Rosenkrantz* Rosenkrantzgatan 7
☎(05)318080
➔118 Lift (Sea
Credit Cards ① ② ③ ⑤

★*Park* H-Harfagresgt 35 (n.rest) ☎(05)320960 tx 40365
Closed Etr-Jul
➔20 (Mountain

🛏 *NAF-Sentralen* ☎(05) 292462 AR Cit DJ

BESSHEIM
Oppland

★*Fjellstue* ☎(062)38913
20 Feb-5 May & 1 Jun-29 Sep
rm35(➔13) P50 Sea Mountain
Credit Cards ① ③

BØ
Telemark

★★*Bø*(BW) ☎(036)95011
➔64 P120 Lift (⌂ Mountain
Credit Cards ① ② ③ ⑤

★★*Lifjell Turist* ☎(950011)953300 tx 21119
rm74(➔70) A5rm P40 (⚲ ⌂ ⌂ Mountain Lake
Credit Cards ① ② ③ ⑤

BODØ
Nordland

★★★*Grand* ℒ Storgt 3 ☎(081)20000
➔48 P (
Credit Cards ① ② ③ ⑤

★★★*SAS Royal* Storgaten 2 ☎(081)24100 tx 64031
:Rest closed 25 Dec
➔184 P10 Lift (Sea Mountain
Credit Cards ① ② ③ ④ ⑤

BOLKESJØ
Telemark

★★★*Bolkesjø* ☎(036)18600 tx 21007
➔123 P Lift (⌂ Sea

BØVERDALEN
Oppland

★*Jotunheimen Fjellstue* DPn ☎(062)14700
15Feb-Sep
rm39(➔24) A7rm P50 Mountain Lake
Credit Card ①

At ELVESETER(4km SW)
★★★*Elveseter Turist* ☎(062)12000
1 Jun-20 Sep
➔100 P ⌂ Mountain

BRUMUNDDAL
Hedmark

★★★*Hedemarken* ☎(065)40011
➔57 (
Credit Cards ① ③ ⑤

BRYNE
Rogaland

★★*Jæren Turist Rica* ☎(04)482488
rm51 (⌂
Credit Cards ① ② ③ ⑤

BYGDIN
Oppland

★★*Bygdin Hoyfjellshotell* ☎(061)41213
25 Jun-15 Sep
➔22 P100 (Mountain

BYGLANDSFJORD
Aust-Agder

★★*Revsnes Turisthotell* (BW) (n.rest)
☎(043)34105
➔53 P40 (Beach Mountain lake
Credit Cards ① ② ③ ⑤

BYKLE
Aust-Agder

★*Bykle* ☎(043)38120
rm15 A10rm Lift Mountain

DOKKA
Oppland

★★★*Spatind Hoyfjellshotell* ☎(061)19506 tx 721976
Closed 6-20 May
➔84 A33rm P100 (⚲ ⌂ ⌂ Mountain Lake
Credit Cards ① ③

DOMBÅS
Oppland

★★★*Dombås* DPn ☎(062)71001
➔100 A24rm P Lift (Mountain
Credit Cards ① ② ③ ⑤

★★★*Dovrefjell* ☎(062)41005 tx 19959
➔100 A24rm P60 Lift (⌂ Mountain
Credit Cards ① ② ③ ⑤

🛏 *Garage Storrusten* ☎(062) 411009

DRAMMEN
Buskerud

★★★★*Park* Gamle Kirkpl 3 ☎(03)838280 tx 74278
➔103 P70 Lift (
Credit Cards ① ② ③ ⑤

🛏 *Bilberging* ☎(03) 824930

DRANGEDAL
Telemark

★★★*Gautefall* ☎(03)996600 tx 21756
:Rest closed Sun
➔106 A30rm P100 Lift (⚲ ⌂ ⌂ ⋔ ⋔ Mountain
Credit Cards ① ② ③ ⑤

🛏 *Lia Bil* ☎(03) 996060

EDLAND
Telemark

★★*Vågslid* ☎(036)70585 tx 21441
15 May-15 Oct
➔48 P80 (Beach Mountain lake
Credit Cards ① ② ③ ⑤

EGERSUND
Rogaland

★★*Elger* J-Feyers gt 3 ☎(04)49181
➔28 Lift (
Credit Cards ① ③ ⑤

EIDFJORD
Hordaland

★★*Voringfose* ☎(054)65184
rm54(➔44) A27rm P35 (Beach Sea Mountain
Credit Cards ① ② ③ ④ ⑤

EIKEN
Vest-Agder

★★★**Eiken Feriesenter** ☎(043)48200
⊷🛏48 P50 Beach Sea Mountain Lake
Credit Cards 1 3

ELVERUM
Hedmark

🛏 *Kristiansen* ☎(064) 11827

ELVESETER
See **BØVERDALEN**

ESPEDALEN
Oppland

★★**Dalseter Hyfjellshotell Pn** Svatsun
☎(062)99910
Jun-1 Oct & 26 Dec-1 May
rm88(⊷🛏79) 🍴 P70 Lift 🤸 ⅅ Mountain Lake
Credit Card 1

★*Espedalen Fjellstue* (n.rest) ☎(062)99912
Jun-20 Apr
⊷🛏30 P30 Mountain Lake

EVJE
Aust-Agder

★★**Grenaderen** ☎(043)30400
⊷🛏30 P200 🤸 ⅅ Mountain
Credit Cards 1 2 3 5

🛏 *Lanz Auto* ☎(043) 30301

FAGERNES
Oppland

★★★*Hotel Fagernes* ☎(061)31100 tx 76562
⊷🛏110 P100 ⅅ Lake
Credit Cards 1 2 3 5

★★★**Sanderstolen** Tisleidalen (28km SW on road
to Gol) ☎(063)64000 tx 19061
⊷🛏100 🍴 P150 🤸 ⅅ Mountain
Credit Cards 1 2 3 5

★*Fagerlund* ☎(061)30600
rm25(⊷🛏6) A8rm P 🤸 Mountain Lake

🛏 *Autoservice* ☎(061) 32266

FARSUND
Vest-Agder

★★★*Fjordhotel* ☎(043)91022
⊷🛏63 P80 Lift 🤸 Beach Sea
Credit Cards 1 2 5

🛏 *Kjell Ore & Oljesenter* ☎(043) 93111

FEVIK
Aust-Agder

★★*Strand* ☎(041)47322 tx 21854
⊷🛏40 P150 🤸 Beach Sea
Credit Cards 1 2 3 5

FLÅM
Sogn-og-Fjordane

★★★*Fretheim* ☎(056)32200 tx 40428
1 May-1 Oct
rm85(⊷🛏60) A14rm 🍴 P30 🤸 ⅅ Sea
Credit Cards 1 2

FLORØ
Sogn-og-Fjordane

★★*Victoria* ☎(057)41033
rm91(⊷🛏81) P50 Lift 🤸 Sea Mountain
Credit Cards 1 2 3 4 5

FØRDE
Sogn-og-Fjordane

★★*Sunnifjord* ☎(057)21622 tx 42217
⊷🛏161 P Lift 🤸 ⅅ

🛏 *Autoservice* ☎(057) 25311 Fia

FREDRIKSTAD
Østfold

★★★*City* ☎(032)17750 tx 17072
⊷🛏104 🍴 P Lift 🤸

🛏 *Fredrikstad Automobil-Forr* Mosseveien 3
☎(032) 11260

GAUSA
Oppland

★★★*Gausdal Højfjellshotell* Højfjellshotel
☎(062)28500 tx 71805
⊷🛏115 🍴 P100 🤸 🌡 U Mountain
Credit Cards 1 2 3 5

★★★**Skeikampen Høyfjellshotell** ☎(062)28505
⊷🛏80 P45 Lift 🤸 🌡 🛏🛏 U Mountain
Credit Cards 1 2 3 5

GEILO
Buskerud

★★★★**Bardløa** ☎(067)85400 tx 78771
⊷🛏102 A2rm 🍴 P100 Lift 🤸 🌡 ⅅ Mountain
Credit Cards 1 2 3 5

★★★★**Highland** ☎(067)85600 tx 78401
⊷🛏126 P Lift 🤸 🌡 Mountain
Credit Cards 1 2 3

★★★**Vestlia Høyfjellshotell & Sportell**
☎(067)85611 tx 19874
⊷🛏76 A35rm P100 🤸 🌡 🌡 Mountain Lake
Credit Cards 1 2 3 5

★★*Alpin* (n.rest) ☎(067)85544
Closed May: Rest closed Mon
⊷🛏27 P30 Mountain Lake
Credit Cards 1 2 3 5

★★*Geilo* (BW) ☎(067)85511 tx 74919
⊷🛏73 P50 🤸 Mountain Lake
Credit Cards 1 2 3 5

★★*Haugen* (n.rest) ☎(067)85644
rm50(⊷🛏35) P35 🤸 Mountain
Credit Cards 2 3

🛏 *Geilo Auto* ☎(067) 85790 For

GEIRANGER
Mre-og-Romsdal

★★★*Geiranger* (BW) ☎(071)63005 tx 40670
1 May-1 Oct
⊷🛏69 P20 Lift 🤸 ⅅ Sea
Credit Cards 1 2 3 5

★★★*Union* ☎(071)63000 tx 42339
Mar-Dec
⊷🛏140 P Lift 🤸 🌡 ⅅ Sea
Credit Cards 1 2 3 4 5

★★*Grande Fjord* ☎(071)63067
May-Sep
rm15(⊷🛏10) P Beach Sea Mountain

★★*Meroks Fjord* ☎(071)63002 tx 40670
May-Sep
⊷🛏55 P Lift 🤸 Sea
Credit Cards 1 2 3 5

GJØVIK
Oppland

★★★*Strand Rica* ☎(061)72120 tx 71610
rm87(⊷🛏73) Lift 🤸 🌡 Lake
Credit Cards 1 2 3 5

★★*Norton Grand* Jernbanegt 5 ☎(061)72180
⊷🛏70 P40 Lift 🤸
Credit Cards 1 2 3 5

GODØYSUND
Hordaland

★★*Godøysund Fjord* ☎(054)31404
⊷🛏45 🌡 Sea
Credit Cards 1 2 3 5

GOL
Buskerud

★★★*Oset Høyfjellshotell* (BW) ☎(067)77920
Closed 15-19 May
⊷🛏105 🤸 🌡 🌡 Beach Mountain Lake
Credit Cards 1 3

★★★*Pers* ☎(067)74500 tx 78472
⊷🛏203 A53rm 🍴 P70 Lift 🤸 🌡 Mountain
Credit Cards 1 3 5

★★*Eidsgard* ☎(067)75644
⊷🛏32 A8rm P 🤸 Mountain
Credit Cards 1 2 3

★★*Storefjell Høyfjellshotell* (n.rest)
☎(067)77930

★*Thorstens* (n.rest) ☎(067)74062
⊷🛏26 P

GOLÅ
Oppland

★★★*Golå Høifjellshotell* Gudbrandsdalen
☎(062)98109 tx 78601
⊷🛏37 P60 🌡 ⅅ Beach Sea Mountain
Credit Cards 1 3 5

GRATANGEN
Troms

★*Gratangen* ☎(082)20255
Mar-Oct
⊷🛏20 P Mountain Lake

GROTLI
Oppland

★★*Grotli Høyfjellshotell* (BW) ☎(062)13912 tx
72149
Mar-10 Oct
rm55(⊷🛏52) P200 Lift Mountain
Credit Cards 1 2 3 5

GUDVANGEN
Sogn-og-Fjordane

★★*Gudvangen* (n.rest) ☎(05)531929
⊷🛏7 🍴 P20 Sea Mountain

HALDEN
Østfold

🛏 *Thanstrm* ☎(031) 81122

HAMAR
Hedmark

★★★*Rica Olrud* P.B 3025 Stavsberg
☎(065)50100 tx 72834
⊷🛏176 P Lift 🤸 🌡 ⅅ
Credit Cards 1 2 3 5

★★★*Victoria* Strandgt 21 ☎(065)30500 tx 78568
rm118(⊷🛏116) P Lift 🤸 Lake
Credit Cards 1 2 3

🛏 *Furnes Bil* ☎(065) 50300

HAMMERFEST
Finnmark

★★*Rica Hammerfest* ☎(084)11333 tx 65814
⊷🛏100 🤸 Sea
Credit Cards 1 2 3 4 5

HANKØ
Østfold

★★*Hankø Nye Fjord* ☎(032)32105 tx 74950
Mar-20 Dec
⊷🛏67 🍴 P Lift 🤸 ⅅ Beach

HARPEFOSS
Oppland

★★★*Wadahl Høyfjellshotell* (5km S of railway
station) ☎(062)98300 tx 72534
Seasonal
⊷🛏95 🍴 P170 Lift 🤸 🌡 ⅅ 🌡 U Mountain Lake
Credit Cards 1 3 4

HARSTAD
Troms

★★★*Grand Nordic* ☎(082)62170 tx 64152
★★★*Viking Nordic* ☎(082)64080 tx 64322
⊷🛏100 A5rm P20 Lift 🤸 🌡 Sea Mountain
Credit Cards 1 2 3 5

HAUGESUND
Rogaland

★★★*Maritim* Asbygt 3 ☎(047)711100 tx 42691
⊷🛏247 P110 Lift 🤸 Sea
Credit Cards 1 2 3 5

★★★*Saga* Skippegt 11 ☎(047)11100 tx 42691
rm90(⊷🛏85) 🍴 P25 Lift 🤸
Credit Cards 1 2 3 5

★★*Haugaland* Rutebilstasjonen (n.rest)
☎(047)13466 tx 42691
rm22(⊷🛏16) P 🤸

★★Imi Strandgaten 192 ☎(04)723699
rm22(♜18) P12 ☾ Sea
Credit Cards ①②③⑤
★★Park ☎(047)712000 tx 42921
⬩♜114 ☎ Lift ☾ ▭ Sea
Credit Cards ①②③⑤
⬩⬩ Geims Bilhjelp ☎(047) 831000

HAUKELIFJELL
Telemark
★Haukeliseter Fjellstue (n.rest) ☎(036)70515
rm45(♜14) P50 Mountain Lake

HEMSEDAL
Buskerud
★★Hemsedal ☎(067)74500 tx 78472
⬩♜135 Lift ☾ ▭ ◿ Mountain
Credit Cards ①②③④⑤
★★Skogstad ☎(067)78333
⬩♜80 Lift ☾ Mountain Lake
Credit Cards ①②③⑤

HERMANSVERK
Sogn-og-Fjordane
★★Sognefjord Turist ☎(056)53444
⬩♜45 P50 Lift ☾ ▭ Beach Sea
Credit Cards ①②③⑤

HJERKINN
Oppland
★Hjerkinn Fjellstue ☎(062)42927
Jun-Sep
rm34(♜8) A20rm P50 ◡ Mountain Lake
Credit Cards ①②③

HØNEFOSS
Buskerud
★★Grand (n.rest) ☎(067)22722
rm46(⬩♜35) A7rm ☎ P30 ☾
Credit Cards ①③
At **KLEKKEN**(3km E)
★★★Klaekken ☎(067)32200 tx 78838
⬩♜112 P100 Lift ☾ ☜ ▭ Mountain
Credit Cards ①②③⑤

HONNINGSVÅG (MAGERØYA ISLAND)
Finnmark
(Access by ferry from KÅFJORD)
★★★SAS Nordkapp ☎(084)72333
rm174(⬩158) Lift Sea
Credit Cards ①②③⑤

HOVDEN
Aust-Agder
★★★Hovdestøylen (BW) ☎(043)39552 tx 21257
⬩♜76 P200 Lift ☾ ☜ Mountain Lake
Credit Cards ①②③⑤
★★Hovden Høyfjellshotell ☎(043)39600 tx 21968
⬩♜76 P200 Lift ☾ ▭ ◡ Mountain
Credit Cards ①②③⑤

HOVET
Buskerud
★★★Hallingskarvet ☎(067)88525
15 Jun-Apr
rm34(⬩32) ☾ ☜ ♟ ◡ Mountain Lake
Credit Cards ①②③⑤

HØVIK
See OSLO

HØVRINGEN
Oppland
★★Brekkeseter Fjellstue ☎(062)33711 tx 11954
15 Feb-20 Apr & 20 Jun-Sep
rm75(⬩60) ☎ P ☾ Mountain
★★Hovringen Høyfjellshotell (n.rest) ☎(062)33722
end Jan-end Apr & Jun-Sep
rm65(⬩♜47) A4rm P100 ☾ Mountain

HØYANGER
Sogn-og-Fjordane
★★Øren (n.rest) ☎(057)12606
A3rm

INNVIK
Sogn-og-Fjordane
★★Misjonsheimen ☎(057)74252
rm26(⬩14) P20 Lift ☾ ◿ Sea

KINSARVIK
Hordaland
★★★Kinsarvik Fjord (BW) ☎(054)63100 tx 42292
Closed 21 Dec-Jan
rm75(⬩62) P50 Lift ☾ ◡ Sea Mountain
Credit Cards ①②③⑤

KIRKENES
Finnmark
★★★Rica Kirkenes ☎(085)91491
rm42 Lift ☾ ☭ Sea Mountain
Credit Cards ①②③⑤

KLEKKEN
See HØNEFOSS

KOLBOTN
Oslo
★★★Müller Lienga 1 ☎(02)807500 tx 74260
⬩♜145 P200 Lift ☾
Credit Cards ①②③⑤

KONGSBERG
Buskerud
★★★Grand Kristian Ausgustsgt 2 ☎(03)732029 tx 72991
⬩♜94 P45 Lift ☾ ☭ ▭ Mountain
Credit Cards ①②③⑤
★★★Gyldenløve ☎(03)731744 tx 74908
⬩♜61 ☎ P32 Lift ☾ Mountain
Credit Cards ①②③⑤

KONGSVINGER
Hedmark
★★Vinger ☎(066)17222
Closed Etr
⬩♜63 A11rm P100 Lift ☾ ▭
Credit Cards ①②③⑤
⬩⬩ Kristiansen Bilberging ☎(066) 15180

KOPERVIK
Rogaland
★★★Karmøy ☎(084)61377
⬩♜55 P Lift ☾ Sea
Credit Cards ①②③

KRISTIANSAND
Vest-Agder
★★★Caledonien V-Strandgt 7 ☎(042)29100 tx 21222
⬩♜205 ☎ P400 Lift ☾ Sea
Credit Cards ①②③⑤
★★★Christian Quart (BW) ☎(042)22210 tx 21126
Apr-23 Dec
⬩♜111 P ☾
Credit Cards ①②③⑤
★★★Ernst Park Rådhusgt 2 ☎(042)21104 tx 21104
⬩♜115 Lift ☾ Sea
Credit Cards ①②③④⑤
★★★Norge Dronningensgt 5-9 ☎(042)20000 tx 21369
⬩♜115 ☎ P Lift ☾
Credit Cards ①②③④⑤
★★★Rica Fregatten Dronningensgt 66 ☎(042)21500 tx 21792
⬩♜50 Lift ☾
Credit Cards ①②③⑤
⬩⬩ NAF-Sentralen ☎(042) 99099

KRISTIANSUND
Mre-og-Romsdal
★★★Grand Bernstorffstredetl ☎(073)73011
⬩♜126 P60 Lift ☾
Credit Cards ①②③⑤
⬩⬩ Mobilstasjonen ☎(073) 74680

KVAM
Oppland
★★Vertshuset Sinclair ☎(062)94024
⬩♜16 P100 Mountain
Credit Cards ①②③⑤

KVINESDAL
Vest-Agder
★★★Utsikten Turist (n.rest) ☎(043)50444
★★Rafoss (n.rest) ☎(043)50388
Closed Xmas & Etr
rm19(⬩♜17) P12 Lake
Credit Card ②

KVITESEID
Telemark
★★Kviteseid ☎(036)53222
rm32(⬩♜16) A7rm P25 Sea Mountain Lake
Credit Cards ①③

LAERDAL
Sogn-og-Fjordane
★★★Lindstrm Turisthotell (BW) ☎(056)66202 tx 40689
May-Sep
⬩♜86 A33rm P50 Lift ☾ Sea Mountain
Credit Cards ①②③⑤

LAKSELV
Finnmark
★★Porsangerfjord ☎(084)61377
⬩♜42 P100 Lift ☾ Sea Mountain Lake
Credit Cards ①②③⑤
⬩⬩ Lakselv Bilberging ☎(084) 61744

LARVIK
Vestfold
★★★Grand Storgt 38-40 ☎(034)87800 tx 21024
⬩♜108 P100 Lift ☾
Credit Cards ①②③⑤
⬩⬩ Larvik Auto ☎(034) 81212 For

LEIKANGER
Sogn-og-Fjordane
★★Leikanger Fjord ☎(056)53622
Mar-20 Dec
⬩♜42 P30 Beach Sea Mountain
Credit Cards ①③

LEVANGER
Nord-Trøndelag
★★Backlund Kirkegt 41 ☎(076)81600
⬩♜65 Lift ☾
Credit Cards ①②③⑤
⬩⬩ Nilsen Bilberging ☎(076) 82522

LILLEHAMMER
Oppland
★★★Lillehammer ☎(062)54800 tx 19592
⬩♜166 P Lift ☾ ◿
Credit Cards ①②③⑤
★★★Oppland (BW) ☎(062)58500 tx 74869
⬩♜75 A8rm P75 Lift ☾ ▭ Mountain Lake
Credit Cards ①②③⑤
★★★Rica Victoria Storgt 82 ☎(062)50049 tx 19806
⬩♜94 Lift ☾
★★Ersgaard ☎(062)50684
rm29(♜16) A9rm ☾ Lake
Credit Card ②
★Breiseth Jerbanegt 5 ☎(062)50060 tx 16384
rm34(⬩♜2) ☎ P25 ☾
⬩⬩ Furnes Bil & Karosseriverkstad ☎(062) 51016

At **NORDSETER**(14km NE)

★★★*Nevra* ☎(062)64001 tx 19598
↔🏠70 P20 ℂ ℃ ⌂ Mountain Lake
Credit Cards ①②③⑤

★★★**Nordseter Høyfjellshotell** ☎(062)64004 tx 19706
↔🏠46 P50 ℂ ⌂ Mountain
Credit Cards ①②③⑤

LOEN
Sogn-og-Fjordane

★★★★**Alexandra** ☎(057)77660 tx 42665
20 Jan-Dec
↔🏠200 🏊 P160 Lift ℂ ℃ ⌂ ⋔⋔ Beach Sea Mountain
Credit Cards ①②③⑤

★★**Richards** ☎(057)77657 tx 42665
May-Sep
↔🏠25 P30 ℂ ⌂ Sea Mountain
Credit Cards ①②③⑤

★*Rake* (n.rest) ☎(057)1534

LOFTHUS
Hordaland

★★★**Ullensvang** ☎(054)61100 tx 42659
↔🏠131 A1rm 🏊 P115 Lift ℂ ℃ ⌂ Sea Mountain
Credit Cards ①②③⑤

LOM
Oppland

★★**Fossberg Turiststasjon** ☎(062)11073
rm42(🏠30) A17rm P30 ℂ Mountain
Credit Cards ①②③⑤

★★**Fossheim** ☎(062)11205
15 Mar-15 Dec
rm48(↔45) A16rm P60 Mountain
Credit Cards ①②③⑤

🚗 *Skaansar* ☎(062) 11041

MANDAL
Vest-Agder

★★★**Solborg Turisthotell** Neseveien 1,P.O Box 4 ☎(043)61311 tx 21922
↔🏠66 P50 Lift ℂ ⌂ Sea Mountain
Credit Cards ①②③⑤

★*Bondehelmen* Elvegt 23A (n.rest) ☎(043)61422

🚗 *Viking Bilservice* ☎(043) 65005

MARIFJØRA
Sogn-og-Fjordane

★★**Tørvis** ☎(056)87200 tx 40654
rm50(↔43) A7rm P Beach Sea Mountain
Credit Cards ①②③⑤

MO-I-RANA
Nordland

★★★**Meyergården** ☎(087)50555 tx 55649
↔🏠160 P100 Lift ℂ Sea Mountain Lake
Credit Cards ①②⑤

🚗 *Rana Bilopphvggeri* ☎(087) 30083

MOLDE
Mre-og-Romsdal

★★★**Alexandra** Storgt 1-7 ☎(072)51133 tx 42847
rm150(↔140) 🏊 P30 Lift ℂ ⌂ Sea Mountain
Credit Cards ①②③⑤

★*Knausen* Noisornhedsun 12 ☎(072)51577
↔🏠68 A18rm P Lift ℂ ℃ ⋔⋔ Sea Mountain
Credit Cards ①②③⑤

🚗 *Bj-Rdseth* ☎(072) 56755

MORGEDAL
Telemark

★★**Morgedal** ☎(036)54144 tx 21772
↔🏠70 P Lift ℂ ℃ ⌂ Mountain Lake
Credit Cards ①②③⑤

MOSJØEN
Nordland

★★**Fru Haugans** ☎(087)70477
rm54(↔🏠40) A26rm P Lift ℂ Beach Sea Mountain
Credit Cards ①③⑤

★★**Lyngengården** ☎(087)74800
rm29(🏠20) P ℂ Mountain
Credit Cards ①③⑤

🚗 *Sparby Bilberging* ☎(087) 71023

MOSS
Østfold

★★★**Refsnes-Gods** Godset 5 - Jeløy
☎(09)270411 tx 74353
Closed Xmas & Etr
↔🏠60 P60 Lift ℂ ⌂ Beach Sea
Credit Cards ①②③⑤

🚗 *Moss Bilberging* ☎(032) 55433

NAMSOS
Nord-Trøndelag

★★*Grand Bondehelmen* Kirkegt 7-9
☎(077)73155
rm48(🏠12)

🚗 *Snippen Bilservice* ☎(077) 72485

NARVIK
Nordland

★★★*Grand Royal* Kongensgt 64 ☎(082)41500 tx 64032
↔🏠112 P60 Lift ℂ Mountain
Credit Cards ①②③⑤

🚗 *A Olsen Bill & Kranservice* ☎(082) 44208

NESBYEN
Buskerud

★★★*Østenford Turisthotell* (BW) ☎(067)71530 tx 78398
↔🏠63 P50 Lift ℂ ⌂ Mountain Lake
Credit Cards ①②⑤

★★*Ranten Fjelistue Mykingstlen* ☎(067)73445
Closed May
↔🏠34 Mountain Lake
Credit Cards ①③⑤

★★*Smedsgarden Pensonat* ☎(067)73125
5 May-Sep
rm40(↔20) A2rm Beach Sea Mountain

★★*Svenkerud* ☎(067)71260
↔🏠51 P40 Lift ℂ Mountain

🚗 *Nesbyen Auto* ☎(067) 71066 Aud VW

NORDFJORDEID
Sogn-og-Fjordane

★★★*Nordfjord Turist* ☎(057)60433
↔🏠55 P50 ℂ ℃ Sea Mountain
Credit Cards ①②③⑤

NORDSETER
See LILLEHAMMER

NOREFJELL
Buskerud

★★*Fjellhvil* ☎(067)46174
rm50(↔32) ℂ

★*Sandumseter* (n.rest) ☎(067)46155
15 Nov-Apr
rm26 A16rm P150 Mountain Lake

NORHEIMSUND
Hordaland

★★★*Norheimsund Fjord* ☎(05)551522 tx 42757
Feb-20 Dec
↔🏠36 P50 Beach Sea
Credit Cards ①②③⑤

★★*Sandven* ☎(05)551911
15 Jan-15 Dec
↔🏠46 P200 ℂ Sea Mountain Lake
Credit Cards ①②③⑤

NYSTOVA
Oppland
(European Highway E68/5)

★★★*Nystuen Fjellhotell* ☎(061)37710
rm50 A22rm P75 ℂ Beach Sea Mountain Lake
Credit Cards ①②③

ODDA
Hordaland

★★★*Hardanger* ☎(54)42133
↔🏠50 P10 Lift ℂ Sea Mountain
Credit Cards ①②③⑤

🚗 *Moe Motor* ☎(054) 42364 Fia
🚗 *Nå Auto* ☎(054) 42700

OLDEN
Sogn-og-Fjordane

★★★*Yris Turisthotell* ☎(057)73240
May-Sep
rm39(↔34) ℂ ⌂ Sea Mountain

★★*Olden Fjord* (BW) ☎(057)73235 tx 40560
Apr-Oct
↔🏠40 P40 ℂ Beach Sea Mountain
Credit Cards ①②③⑤

★*Olden Krotell* ☎(057)73296
↔🏠13 ℃ Sea
Credit Cards ①②③

OPPDAL
Sør-Trøndelag

★★*Müllerhotell Oppdal* ☎(074)21611
rm52(↔50) P ℂ Mountain

★★*Oppdal Turisthotell* ☎(074)21111 tx 65726
Jan-20 Dec
↔🏠75 P100 Lift ℂ Mountain
Credit Cards ①②③⑤

★*Fagerhaug* ☎(074)23601
↔🏠16 P200 Mountain
Credit Card ⑤

🚗 *Oppdal Bilberging* ☎(074) 23486 Peu

ØRSTA
Mre-og-Romsdal

★★*Viking Fjord* ☎(070)66800 tx 40790
rm40(↔🏠38) P35 Lift ℂ ⋔⋔ Sea Mountain
Credit Cards ①②③⑤

🚗 *Mur Bil* ☎(070) 66514

OS
Hordaland

★★★*Solstrand* ☎(05)300099 tx 42050
↔🏠132 P Lift ℂ ℃ ⌂ ⋔⋔ Beach Sea Mountain
Credit Cards ①②③⑤

OSLO (*OSLO*)

See Plan pages 324 and 325 *Population* 460,000 *Local tourist office* Town Hall (Entrance seaside)
☎(02) 427170 (open 15 May-15 Sept 0830-1900hrs Mon-Sat, 0900-1700hrs Sun; in winter, 0830-1430/
1600hrs, closed on Sun)

Oslo is justly proud of her Viking ancestry and seafaring heritage, and extends a warm welcome to
visitors. The city's history is reflected in her cathedral, parliament buildings and town hall, from where
38 bells peal out every hour - and you can also look inside at the engravings, carvings and artwork
recounting Norwegian legends and myths. Lovers of the past should explore the Bergfjerdingen, Oslo's
old city, and for a glimpse of something contemporary, pay a visit to the Holmenkollen ski-jump,
which has wonderful views.

There is a fascinating site at Bygdog, easily reached by ferry, which includes the Viking Ships Museum
containing three of these proud vessels, ultimately the graves of their rulers on their final journey to
Valhalla; the Kon Tiki - Thor Heyerdahl's balsa raft on which he made his perilous voyage from Peru
to Polynesia in 1947 - and the Ra II, his reconstruction of an Egyptian papyrus boat in which he
crossed the Atlantic; and an open-air site where homes, farms and churches brought from all parts of
the country have been rebuilt using the original material.

Frogner Park is the setting for the sculptures of Gustav Vigeland. The collection is unique and
controversial, and revolves round the monolith of bodies entitled *The Wheel of Life*.

Once a royal fortress, later a political prison, the Akerhus Castle now contains the Resistance Museum,
a reminder of Nazi occupation and a monument to the patriots who fell defending their country.
Norwegian crafts reflect the country's legends and striking scenery in beautiful wood carvings,
jewellery and glassware, while their skill in design is evident in the furniture and knitwear. Karl
Johans Gate, the main boulevard, provides a wealth of shops, street stalls, cafés, restaurants and
department stores.

EATING OUT Breakfast consists not only of rolls and coffee but fish, cold meats and cheeses too - a
delicious start to the day. Dinner is the most substantial meal, and, as one would expect with
Norway's coastline, fish is a great speciality. Trout, salmon, sole and plaice are widely available and
always fresh. Norwegian fish and shellfish are specialities of the Grand Hotel's rooftop restaurant,
Etoile, while Oslo's oldest restaurant is the *Gamle Radhus*, housed in a 17th-century building in Nedre
Slottsgate. For inexpensive meals and snacks the *Café Frooich*, in Drammensvn, is popular, especially
with students and musicians.

OSLO

★★★★**Bristol** PO Box 6764 St Olavs Pl
☎(02)415840 tx 71668
➜ℳ141 Lift ℂ ⌂
Credit Cards ① ② ③ ⑤

★★★★**Continental** Stortingsgt 24 ☎(02)419060
tx 71012
➜ℳ170 ⌂ P40 Lift ℂ
Credit Cards ① ② ③ ⑤

★★★★**Grand** K-Johansgt 31 ☎(02)429390 tx
71683
➜ℳ308 ⌂ Lift ℂ ⌷
Credit Cards ① ② ③ ④ ⑤

★★★★*KNA* Parkveien 68 ☎(02)446970 tx 71763
➜ℳ151 P13 Lift ℂ Sea
Credit Cards ① ② ③ ⑤

★★★★*Sas Scandinavia* Holbergsgt 30
☎(02)113000
➜ℳ491 ⌂ P Lift ℂ ⌷
Credit Cards ① ② ③ ④ ⑤

★★★**Ambassadeur** C-Colletsvej 15 ☎(02)441835
tx 71446
Closed Xmas & Etr
➜ℳ42 Lift ℂ ⌷
Credit Cards ① ② ③ ⑤

★★★*Astoria* Akersgt 21 ☎(02)426900 tx 18754
rm99(➜ℳ91) Lift ℂ

★★★*Gyldenløve* Bogstadveien 20 (n.rest)
☎(02)601090 tx 79058
rm160(➜ℳ90) Lift ℂ
Credit Cards ① ② ③ ⑤

★★★**Rica Carlton** Parkveien 78 ☎(02)696170 tx
17902
➜ℳ50 Lift ℂ
Credit Cards ① ② ③ ⑤

★★★**Smestad** Sorkedalsveien 93 ☎(02)146490
➜ℳ31 A2rm P30 ℂ
Credit Cards ① ② ③ ⑤

★★★**SAS Park Royal** Fornebuparken,PO Box
185 ☎(02)120220 tx 78745
➜ℳ254 P150 Lift ℂ ⌣ Beach Sea
Credit Cards ① ② ③ ④ ⑤

★★★*Triangel* Holbergsplass 1 (n.rest)
☎(02)208855 tx 19413
➜ℳ144 Lift ℂ
Credit Cards ① ② ③ ⑤

★★★**Voksenåsen** (SARA) Ullveien 4
☎(02)143090 tx 77450
Closed 22 Dec-2 Jan
➜ℳ72 P80 ℂ ⌂ Sea
Credit Cards ① ② ③ ⑤

★★*Forbunds* Holbergs Plass 1 ☎(02)208855 tx
19413
rm107(➜ℳ100) ⌂ P Lift ℂ

★★**IMI** Staffeldtsgt 4 ☎(02)205330 tx 78142
rm66 ⌂ P10 Lift ℂ
Credit Cards ① ② ③ ⑤

★★*Nye Helsfyr* Strmsveien 108 ☎(02)654110 tx
76776
Closed Jul & Etr
➜ℳ115 P120 Lift ℂ
Credit Cards ① ② ③ ⑤

★★*Pan Kurs og Konferansenter* Sognsveien
218 ☎(02)237640 tx 78432
➜ℳ90 P90 Lift ℂ
Credit Cards ① ② ③ ⑤

★★**Sara Christiania** (SARA) Bishop Gunnerusgt
3 ☎(02)429410 tx 71342
➜ℳ456 Lift ℂ ⌷ Sea Mountain
Credit Cards ① ② ③ ④ ⑤

★★**Stefan** Rosenkrantzgt 1 ☎(02)429250 tx
19809
Closed Xmas & Etr
➜ℳ130 ⌂ Lift ℂ
Credit Cards ① ② ③ ⑤

★**Ansgar** Mllergtn 26 (n.rest) ☎(02)204735 tx
19602
rm58(➜ℳ18) ⌂ Lift ℂ
Credit Cards ① ② ③ ④ ⑤

At **HØVIK**(10km W)

★★★**Scandic** Drammensveien 507,1322 Hovik
☎(02)121740 tx 72430
2 Jan-22 Dec
rm103 ℂ ⌷
Credit Cards ① ② ③ ⑤

OTTA
Oppland

★★★**Otta Turist** ☎(062)30033
➜ℳ85 ⌂ P Lift ℂ ⌂

🖙 *Otta Auto* ☎(062) 30111

PORSGRUNN
Telemark

★★*Vic* Skelegtn 1 ☎(035)55580 tx 21450
➜ℳ100 P40 Lift ℂ
Credit Cards ① ② ③ ⑤

🖙 *Goberg* ☎(035) 97499

RANDABERG
See **STAVANGER**

RAULAND
Telemark

★★★**Rauland Hyfjellshotell** DPn ☎(036)73222
tx 21580

Closed 1-22 May
◄🛏115 ℂ ⛰ Mountain
Credit Cards ① ② ③ ⑤

★**Austbø** ☎(036)73425
Jun-Sep
rm33(➜23) ℂ Mountain
Credit Cards ① ② ⑤

⋊ø Rauland Servicesenter ☎(036) 73103

RINGEBU
Oppland

★★**Venabu Fjellhotell** ☎(062)84055
◄🛏56 P150 Lift ∪ Sea Mountain Lake
Credit Cards ① ② ③ ⑤

RISØR
Aust-Agder

★★★**Risør** ☎(041)50700
◄🛏31 P18 ℂ ℺ Sea
Credit Cards ① ② ③ ⑤

RJUKAN
Telemark

★★★**Gaustablikk Høyfjellshotell** (BW)
☎(036)91422 tx 21677
◄🛏90 P100 ℂ ℺ ⛰ Mountain Lake
Credit Cards ① ② ③ ④ ⑤

★★★**Skinnarbu Høyfjellshotell** ☎(041)95461 tx
21633
rm60(➜50) ⍪ Mountain Lake

★**Rjukan Fjellstue** ☎(036)95162
rm46 A35rm P70 Mountain

⋊ø Berge Bilforretning ☎(036) 94422

RØROS
Sør-Trøndelag

★★★**Bergstadens Turisthotell** (BW)
☎(074)11111 tx 55617
◄🛏65 P50 ℂ ⛰ Mountain
Credit Cards ① ② ③ ⑤

OSLO

1	★★★★	Bristol	
2	★★★★	Continental	
3	★★★★	Grand	
4	★★★	KNA	
5	★★★	Astoria	
6	★★★	Carlton Rica	
7	★★★	Glydenløve	
8	★★★	SAS Park Royal	
9	★★★	Smestad	
10	★★★	Triangel	
11	★★★	Voksenåsen	
12	★★	Forbunds	
13	★★	Nye Helsfyr	
14	★★	IMI	
15	★★	Panorama	
16	★★	Stefan	
17	★★	Sara Oslo	
18	★	Ansgar	

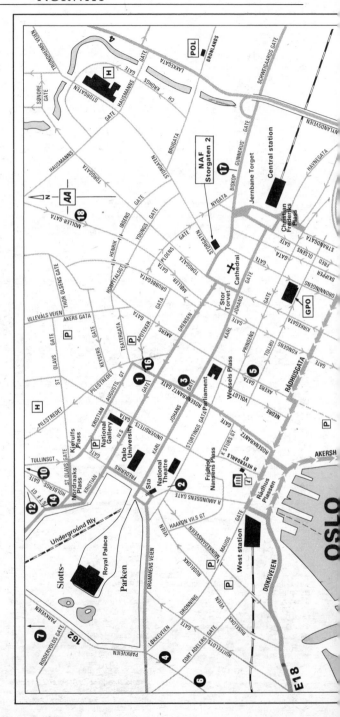

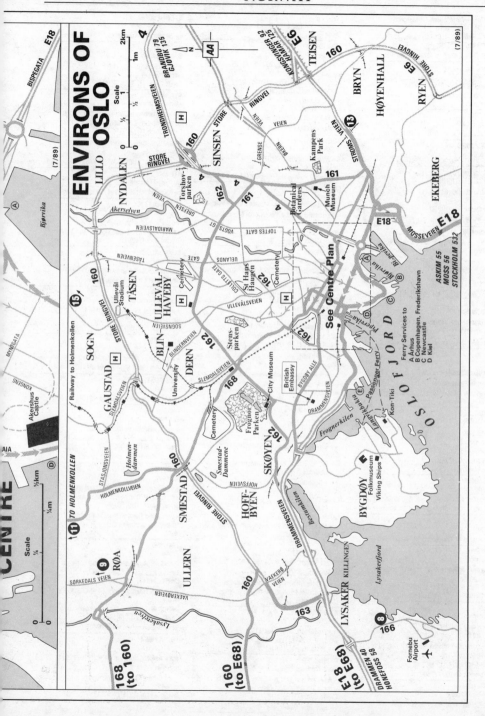

NORWAY

★★★**Røros Turisthotell** An-Margrittsv
☎(074)11011 tx 55570
rm118 A10rm Lift ⚲ ⌂ Mountain
Credit Cards ①②③④⑤
९ Nye Røros Auto ☎(074) 11855 For

ROSENDAL
Hordaland
★★**Fjord** ☎(054)81511
⚙ᐟ56 P200 Lift ⌕ ∪ Lake
Credit Cards ①②③⑤

SANDANE
Sogn-og-Fjordane
★**Firdaheimen** ☎(057)66177

SANDEFJORD
Vestfold
★★★★**Park** ☎(034)65550 tx 21055
⚙ᐟ160 ☼ P105 Lift ⌕ ⌂ Sea
Credit Cards ①②③⑤
★★**Kong Carl** ☎(034)63117
☼ P ⌕
Credit Cards ①②③⑤
९ Kjell's Bilhejlp ☎(4734) 75792

SARPSBORG
Østfold
★★★**Saga** Sannesundsveien 1 ☎(09)154044 tx
78544
Closed Xmas & New Year
⚙ᐟ70 ☼ P5 Lift ⌕
Credit Cards ①②③⑤
★★**St-Olav** Glengsgate 29 ☎(09)152055 tx 78744
rm74(⚙64) ☼ Lift ⌕
Credit Cards ①②③⑤
★**Victoria** ☎(09)154500
rm18(⚙16) P
९ Jansen Bilberging ☎(09) 151500

SAUDA
Rogaland
At **SAUDASJØEN**(5km SW)
★★**Sauda Fjord** ☎(04)781211
rm38(⚙30) A9rm P40 ⌕ ⚲ Sea Mountain
Credit Cards ①②③⑤

SAUDASJØEN
See **SAUDA**

SELJESTAD
Hordaland
★★**Seljestad** ☎(054)45155
⚙ᐟ43 P100 ⌕ Mountain
Credit Cards ①③⑤

SJUSJØEN
Oppland
★★**Rustad Fjellstue** (n.rest) ☎(065)63408
rm50(⚙30) A20rm P20 Beach Sea Mountain Lake

SKAIDI
Finnmark
९ Holmgrens Transport ☎(084) 16145

SKÅNEVIK
Hordaland
★★**Skånevik Fjord** (BW) ☎(04)755500
Closed 20 Dec-6 Jan
⚙ᐟ52 P50 ⌕ Sea Mountain
Credit Cards ①②③⑤

SKIEN
Telemark
★★★**Høyer** ☎(035)205470
rm73 P Lift ⌕
★★★**Ibsen** Kuerndalen 10 ☎(035)24990 tx 21136
⚙ᐟ118 P Lift ⌕ ⌂
Credit Cards ①②③⑤
९ Goberg ☎(035) 97500

SKJOLDEN
Sogn-og-Fjordane
★★**Skjolden** ☎(056)86606 tx 40654

May-Sep
rm54(⚙50) P Lift ⌕ ⚲ Beach Mountain Lake
Credit Card ③

SOGNDAL
Sogn-og-Fjordane
★★★**Sogndal** ☎(056)72311 tx 42727
5 Jan-22 Dec
⚙ᐟ110 P70 Lift ⌕ ⌂ Mountain
Credit Cards ①②③⑤
★★**Hofslund Fjord** Sogn og Fjordane (n.rest)
☎(056)71022
⚙ᐟ47 P30 ⌕ ⌀ Beach Sea Mountain
९ SMS Maskin ☎(056) 72230

SOLVORN
Sogn-og-Fjordane
★★**Walaker** ☎(056)84207
10 May-30 Sep 89
rm25(⚙21) A10rm ☼ P21 Beach Sea Mountain

SORTLAND
Nordland
No road connection: rail services from HARSTAD
★★**Sortland Nordic** Vesterålsgt 59 ☎(088)21833
tx 75845
⚙ᐟ65 P Lift ⌕ Sea Mountain
Credit Cards ①②③⑤

STALHEIM
Hordaland
★★★★**Stalheim** ☎(475)520122 tx 40536
May-1 Oct
⚙ᐟ130 P80 Lift ⌕ ∪ Mountain
Credit Cards ①②③⑤

STAMSUND
Nordland
★★★**Lofoten** ☎(088)597022 tx 73694
⚙ᐟ53 A20rm P200 ⌕ ⚲ Beach Sea
Credit Cards ①②③⑤

STAVANGER
Rogaland
★★★★**Atlantic** Jernbaneveien 1 ☎(04)527520 tx
534869
⚙ᐟ360 ☼ P100 Lift ⌕ Sea Mountain Lake
Credit Cards ①②③④⑤
★★★**Grand** Klubbgt 3 (n.rest) ☎(04)533020 tx
73646
⚙ᐟ92 P5 Lift ⌕
Credit Cards ①②③④⑤
★★★**KNA** Lagårdsvegen 61 ☎(04)528500 tx
33385
⚙ᐟ190 ☼ P130 Lift ⌕ Sea Mountain
Credit Cards ①②③⑤
★★★**Scandic** Eiganesveien 181 ☎(04)4526500 tx
33177
Closed Xmas
rm153 ⌕ ⌂
Credit Cards ①②③⑤
★★**Alstor** (BW) 31 Tjensvollveien ☎(04)527020
tx 30756
⚙ᐟ79 P130 ⌕ ⌂ Sea Mountain Lake
Credit Cards ①②③⑤
९ NAF-Sentralen ☎(04) 582500
At **RANDABERG**(8.5km NW)
★★★**Viste Strand** ☎(04)417022 tx 73694
⚙ᐟ53 A20rm P200 ⌕ ⚲ Beach Sea
Credit Cards ①②③⑤

STAVERN
Vestfold
★★**Wassilioff** ☎(034)98311
⚙ᐟ47 P ⌕ ⚲ ∪ Sea
Credit Cards ①②③⑤

STEINKJER
Nord-Trndelag
★★**Grand** Kongensgt 37 ☎(077)64700 tx 55111
⚙ᐟ114 P6 Lift ⌕ Mountain
Credit Cards ①②③⑤
९ Steinkjer Bilberging ☎(077) 63458

STONGFJORD
Sogn-og-Fjordane
९ Stongfjord Auto ☎(057) 31675 Hon

STØREN
Sør-Trøndelag
★★★**Stren** ☎(074)31118
⚙ᐟ32 P40 Lift ⌕
Credit Cards ①②③④⑤

STRANDA
Møre-og-Romsdal
★★★**Müllerhotell Stranda** ☎(071)60000
⚙ᐟ70 P40 Lift ⌕ ⚲ Sea Mountain
Credit Cards ①②③⑤

STRAUMSJØEN
Nordland
९ Strømme ☎(088) 38259 Vau

STRYN
Sogn-og-Fjordane
९ Karstad ☎(057) 71011 Maz

SUNDVOLLEN
Buskerud
★★**Sundvolden** ☎(067)39140
⚙ᐟ135 P300 Lift ⌕ ⌂ Lake
Credit Cards ①③

SUNNDALSØRA
Møre-og-Romsdal
★★**Müllerhotell Sunndalen** ☎(073)91655
⚙ᐟ65 ☼ P Lift ⌕ ⚲ Mountain

SURNADAL
Møre-og-Romsdal
★★**Surnadal** (BW) ☎(073)61544
⚙ᐟ74 Lift ⌕ Beach
Credit Cards ①②③⑤

SVOLVÆR
Nordland
★★★**Lofoten Nordic** ☎(088)71200 tx 64451
rm68(⚙63) Lift ⌕ Sea Mountain

TINN AUSTBYGDA
Telemark
९ Marumsrud Bilverksted ☎(036) 97166

TØNSBERG
Vestfold
★★**Grand** (BW) ☎(033)12203
⚙ᐟ64 ☼ P35 Lift ⌕
Credit Cards ①②③⑤
९ NAF-Sentralen ☎(033) 13560

TRETTEN
Oppland
★★★**Gausdal** ☎(033)28500 tx 71805
⚙ᐟ115 ☼ P70 ⌕ ⚲ ⌂ ∪ Mountain
Credit Cards ①②③⑤
★**Glomstad Gard** (n.rest) ☎(062)76257
16 Dec-Apr & Jun-10 Oct
rm27

TROMSØ
Troms
★★★**SAS Royal** ☎(083)56000 tx 64260
⚙ᐟ193 P25 Lift ⌕ Sea Mountain
Credit Cards ①②③④⑤
★★**Grand Nordic** Storgt 44 ☎(083)85500 tx
64204
⚙ᐟ103 ☼ P5 Lift ⌕ Sea Mountain
Credit Cards ①②③⑤
९ NAF-Sentralen ☎(083) 70700

TRONDHEIM
Sør-Trøndelag
★★★**Astoria** Nordregt 24 ☎(07)529550 tx 55154
rm52(⚙48) Lift ⌕
★★★**Britannia** Dronningengate 5 ☎(07)530040
tx 55451
rm120(⚙112) P Lift ⌕

326

★★★**Prinsen** Kongensgt 30 ☎(07)530650 tx 55324
⇛65 P35 Lift ℂ
Credit Cards [1] [2] [3] [5]
★★★**Royal Garden** Kjoepmannsgate 73 ☎(07)521100 tx 55060
⇛297 ☎ P40 Lift ℂ
Credit Cards [1] [2] [3] [4] [5]
★★★**Scandic** Brsetveien 186 ☎(07)7939500 tx 55420
Closed 23 Dec-2 Jan
rm153 ℂ
Credit Cards [1] [2] [3] [5]
★★**Larssens** T-Angellsgt 106 ☎(07)528851
⇛30 P4 Lift ℂ
Credit Cards [1] [2] [3] [5]
⅊ *NAF-Sentralen* ☎(07) 966288

TURTAGRØ
Sogn-og-Fjordane
★★*Turtagrø* ☎(056)86116
20 Jun-1 Sep
rm27(⇛4) A8rm P20 Lift Mountain

TYIN
Oppland
★★★*Tyin Høyfjellshotell* (BW) ☎(061)37712
Jan-Oct
⇛100 Lift ℂ ⌂ Mountain Lake

TYNSET
Hedmark
★★*Tynset* ☎(064)80600
rm44(⇛32) A10rm P120 ℂ
Credit Cards [1] [2] [3] [5]

ULVIK
Hordaland
★★★*Brakanes* ☎(05)526105 tx 42955

Mar-20 Dec
⇛105 ☎ P100 Lift ℂ ⌂ ⅌⅌ Beach Sea
Credit Cards [1] [2] [3] [5]
★★*Strand* (BW) ☎(05)526305
May-Oct
⇛57 A11rm P30 ℂ ⌂ Beach Sea
Credit Cards [1] [2] [3] [5]
★★*Ulvik* ☎(05)526200 tx 40680
⇛57 P15 Lift ℂ Beach Sea
Credit Cards [1] [2] [3] [5]
★*Bjotveit* (n.rest) ☎(05)26300
Sea

USTAOSET
Buskerud
★*Ustaoset Fjellstue* ☎(067)87123
15 Jun-Sep
rm26(⇛7) A8rm P Mountain

UTNE
Hordaland
★★*Utne* ☎(054)66983
rm23(⇛19) A7rm P15
Credit Cards [1] [2] [3] [5]

VÅGÅMO
Oppland
★★★*Villa* ☎(062)37071 tx 78876
⇛60 P40 ℂ ⌂ Mountain
Credit Cards [1] [2] [3] [5]

VIKI I SOGN
Sogn-og-Fjordane
★★*Hopstock* ☎(056)95102 tx 42071
⇛32 ☎ P46 Lift ℂ ⌂ Mountain
Credit Cards [1] [2] [3] [5]

VINSTRA
Oppland
★★★*Fefor Høyfjellshotell* ☎(062)90099 tx 78039

⇛128 P Lift ℂ ⌂ ⌂ ⌂ ∪ Beach Sea Mountain Lake
Credit Cards [1] [2] [3] [5]
★★*Sødorp Gjestgivengård* ☎(062)91000 tx 18601
rm27 A12rm P100 Mountain
Credit Cards [1] [2] [3] [5]
★★*Vinstra* ☎(062)90199

VOSS
Hordaland
★★★*Fleischer's* ☎(05)511155 tx 40470
⇛71 Lift ℂ ⌂ ⌂
Credit Cards [1] [2] [3] [5]
★★★*Park Voss* ☎(05)511322
⇛48 ☎ P Lift ℂ Mountain Lake
★★★*Voss* Skulestadmo ☎(05)512006 tx 42748
⇛20 P30 Mountain
Credit Cards [1] [3] [5]
★★*Jarl* ☎(05)511933 tx 42748
⇛80 P Lift ℂ ⌂ Mountain Lake
Credit Cards [1] [2] [3] [5]
★*Nøring Pensjonat* ☎(05)511211
⇛23 P Mountain Lake
⅊ *Voss Bilberging* ☎(05) 515300

VRÅDAL
Telemark
★★★*Straand* 09 Konferansesenter ☎(036)56100 tx 21762
⇛125 P Lift ℂ ⌂ ∪ Beach Sea
Credit Cards [1] [2] [3] [5]
★★*Hyttepark* ☎(036)56127 tx 21471
rm60(⇛54) P Lift ℂ ⌂ ⌂ ∪ Beach Mountain Lake
Credit Cards [1] [2] [3] [5]

AA **Big Road Atlas Europe**

This comprehensive giant atlas covers 26 European countries, and includes useful through-route plans of 16 major cities. The maps are produced in full colour at scales of between 16 and 24 miles to 1 inch.

Available at good bookshops and AA Centres

Don't leave the country without one

Portugal's great charm lies in its infinite variety, with spectacular scenery ranging from tranquil mountainside villages to bustling cities; from forests and vineyards to harsh, rocky landscapes; and from peaceful sandy coves to magnificent, craggy cliffs. The most popular of the holiday area is undoubtedly the Algarve, whose glorious sandy beaches stretch the length of Portugal's southern coastline. It offers a choice of resorts, and is particularly popular with golfers, having half a dozen or so courses of top international standard.

To the west of Lisbon, the Estoril coast is quieter and more sedate. Bordering the sandy beaches are elegant tree-lined streets with beautiful villas and fine Victorian-style houses.

Madeira, the tiny and enchanting Portuguese island off the north-west coast of Africa, has soil so fertile that almost everything grows, making it a blaze of colour throughout the year. The island's capital, Funchal, makes an ideal base for exploring the rest of the picturesque island.

Portugal boasts so many attractive and picturesque cities, towns and villages that the visitor is spoilt for choice. There's Lisbon, offering an excellent range of hotels to suit most budgets and tastes, a host of visitor attractions and splendid restaurants. Not far from Lisbon lies Sintra, noted for both its setting and its wealth of palaces and museums.

On the Costa Verde (Green Coast), the enchanting whitewashed town of Ponte de Lima is attracting an ever-increasing number of visitors; so, too, are Amarante and Viseu in the country's mountainous region, Coimbra, seat of one of the oldest universities in the world, and the museum town of Evora.

PORTUGAL

Language
Portuguese

Local Time
GMT (Summer GMT + 1 hour)

Currency
Escudo, divided into 100 centavos. It is sometimes written with a dollar sign, eg 1$50 (one escudo, fifty centavos). One thousand escudos are known as 1 conto. At the time of going to press
£1 = Esc295.80
US$1 = Esc156.50

Emergency numbers
Fire, Police and Ambulance – Public Emergency Service ☎115

Information in Britain
Portuguese National Tourist Office, New Bond Street (above National Westminster bank, entrance in Burlington Gardens opposite Burlington Arcade), London W1Y 0NP
☎01-493 3873 (071-493 3873 from 6 May 1990)

Information in the USA
Portuguese National Tourist Office, 548 Fifth Avenue, New York, NY 10036
☎212 354 4403

HOW TO GET THERE

You can ship your vehicle to *Spain*, using the Plymouth to *Santander* car ferry, and then travel onwards by road.

Distance

from Santander to Lisboa is about 1,050km (550 miles), normally requiring one or two overnight stops. Using the Channel ports, driving through *France* and *Spain* (enter Spain on the *Biarritz* to *San Sebastian* road at the western end of the Pyrenees).

Distance

from the Channel ports to Lisboa (Lisbon) is about 2,100km (1,300 miles). This will require 3 or 4 overnight stops.

Car sleeper trains

Services are available: Boulogne or Paris to *Biarritz*, or Paris to *Madrid*

Freight trains

Cars may be sent from Paris to Lisboa (50 hours). Passengers travel by '**Sud Express**' Paris–Lisboa.

MONEYMATTERS

Visitors may import up to *ESc*100,000 in Portuguese currency and unlimited foreign currency, but amounts of foreign currency greater than *ESc*100,000 must be declared on arrival. However, visitors entering Portugal must possess at least *ESc*10,000 of Portuguese or the equivalent in foreign currency, plus *ESc*2,000 for each day of their stay. Any amount of foreign currency may be taken out as long as it was declared on entry, but no more than *ESc*100,000 in Portuguese currency may be taken out of the country.

Banking hours

Monday–Friday 08.30–15.00hrs
During the summer, currency exchange facilities are usually provided throughout the day in main resorts, frontier posts, airports and some hotels.

Postcheques

may be cashed at all post offices up to a maximum of *ESc*25,000 per cheque. Go to a counter position with the **Postcheque** sign.

MOTORING REGULATIONS AND GENERAL INFORMATION

The information given here is specific to Portugal. It **must** be read in conjunction with the European ABC at the front of the book, which covers those regulations which are common to many countries.

Accidents*

There are no firm rules of procedure after an accident. See *Warning triangle* below.

Breakdown*

The Portuguese motoring club, *Automóvel Club de Portugal* (ACP), operates a breakdown service, and assistance may be obtained on ☎(02) 316732 (Porto) in the north and ☎(01) 736121 (Lisboa) in the south. See also *Warning triangle* below.

Should you break down or need assistance on the Ponte 25 de Abril (on the southern approach to Lisboa), keep the vehicle as near to the right-hand side of the bridge as possible, remain the in the vehicle and hang a white handkerchief out of the window. You must wait inside the vehicle until the road patrol arrives. Vehicles must not be towed, except by purpose-built towing vehicles, or pushed by hand on the bridge. If you run out of petrol on the bridge you will be fined *ESc*600 and have to buy 10 litres (2gals, 1½pts) of petrol from the bridge authorities at the official price.

British Embassy/Consulates*

The British Embassy together with its consular section is located at 1296 Lisboa Cedex, 35–37 Rua de São Domingos à Lapa ☎661122, located on the Lisboa town plan within the gazetteer. There is a British Consulate in Oporto, and one with an Honorary Consul in Portimão.

Children in Cars

Children under 12 are not permitted in front seats unless the seats are fitted with a child restraint system.

Dimensions and weight restrictions

Private **cars** and towed **trailers** or **caravans** are restricted to the following dimensions – height,

***Additional information will be found in the European ABC at the front of the book.**

4 metres; width, 2.50 metres; length, 12 metres. The maximum permitted overall length of vehicle/trailer or caravan combinations is 18 metres.

There are no weight restrictions governing the temporary importation of trailers into Portugal. However, it is recommended that the following be adhered to – weight (unladen), up to 750kg if the towing vehicle's engine is 2,500cc or less; up to 1,500kg if the towing vehicle's engine is between 2,500cc and 3,500cc; up to 2,500kg if the towing vehicle's engine is more than 3,500cc.

Driving licence*

A valid UK or Republic of Ireland licence is acceptable in Portugal. The minimum age at which a visitor may use a temporarily imported motorcycle (over 50cc) or car is 17years†. See also *Speed limits* below.
†Visiting UK or Republic of Ireland driving licence holders under 18 may encounter local difficulties in some areas as the official minimum age to hold a driving licence in Portugal is 18 years.

Emergency messages to tourists*

Emergency messages to tourists are broadcast all year by Portuguese Radio.

Radiodifusão Portuguesa (RDP1) transmitting on 383 metres and 451 metres medium wave broadcasts these messages in English, French, German, Italian, Portuguese and Spanish every hour during the news, Monday to Saturday.

Radiodifusão Portuguesa (RDP2) transmitting on 290 metres and 397 metres medium wave broadcasts the messages as RDP1 above.

Lights*

The use of full headlights is prohibited in built-up areas.

Motoring Club*

The **Automovel Club de Portugal** (ACP) which has its headquarters at Lisboa 1200, rua Rosa Araújo 24 ☎563931, located on the Lisboa town plan within the gazetteer. It also has offices in a number of provincial towns. They will assist motoring tourists generally and supply information on touring and other matters. ACP offices are normally open 09.00–16.45hrs, Monday to Friday; English and French are spoken. Offices are closed on Saturday and Sunday.

Motorways

About 140 miles of motorway (*Auto-Estrada*) are open, and more stretches are under construction. A 200-mile network is planned. Tolls are charged on most sections. A leaflet entitled *Motorways in Spain and Portugal* is available to AA members.

Orange badge scheme for disabled drivers*

In Portugal, parking places reserved for disabled drivers are indicated by signs displaying the international disabled symbol. However, badge holders are not allowed to park in places where parking is otherwise prohibited.

Overtaking*

Vehicles more than 2 metres wide must stop, if need be, to facilitate passing.

Parking*

Parking is forbidden, except where parking signs are displayed, as well as on a main road outside a built-up area, and on a road carrying fast-moving traffic. At night, parking is prohibited on all roads outside built-up areas. Always park in the direction of the traffic flow, except where regulations decree otherwise, or where parking is allowed on only one side of the road. Parking lights must be used in badly-lit areas, and when visibility is poor. Spending the night in a vehicle by the roadside is not advisable.

Petrol*

Credit cards Petrol stations accept credit cards. A tax of ESc100 is added to the cost of petrol when paid for in this way.
Duty-free petrol In addition to the petrol in the vehicle tank, an unlimited quantity in cans may be imported free of customs, duty and tax.
Petrol (leaded) Gasolina Normal (85 Octane) and Gasolina Super (98 octane) grades.

*Additional information will be found in the European ABC at the front of the book.

Petrol (unleaded) is sold in Portugal as Gasolina Super (95 Octane) grade.

Postal information

Mail Postcards ESc60.00; letters 5-220gm ESc60.00
Post offices There are 1,045 post offices in Portugal. Opening hours are from 08.30–18.30hrs Monday to Friday, with the smaller offices closing 12.30–14.30hrs. Larger offices open on Saturdays from 09.00–12.30hrs.

Priority*

Vehicles on motorways have right of way over all vehicles approaching from the respective slip roads.

Public holidays*

Official Public holidays in Portugal for 1990 are given below.
January 1 (New Year's Day)
February 27 (Carnival Day)
April 13 (Good Friday)
April 25 (Revolution Day)
May 1 (Labour Day)
June 10 (Portugal Day)
June 14 (Corpus Christi)
August 15 (Assumption)
October 5 (Republic Day)
November 1 (All Saints' Day)
December 1 (Independence Day)
December 8† (Immaculate Conception)
December 24 (Christmas Eve)
December 25 (Christmas Day)
†Saturday

Registration document*

If the vehicle is not registered in your name, a special certificate is required authorising you to use it. This certificate is available free from the AA.

Roads

Main roads and most of the important secondary roads are good, as are the mountain roads of the north-east.

Shopping hours

Shops are usually open Monday to Friday 09.00–13.00hrs and 15.00–19.00hrs, and Saturdays 09.00–13.00hrs.

Speed limits*

The beginning of a built-up area is marked by a sign bearing the placename; there are no signs showing the end – the only identification is the sign for the beginning of the area (on the other side of the road) for motorists coming from the other direction. In *built-up areas*, the limit is 60kph (37mph), or 50kph (31mph) for vehicles towing trailers. *Outside built-up areas*, private vehicles must not exceed 120kph (74mph) on *motorways* and 90kph (56mph) *on other roads*; *private vehicles towing trailers* must not exceed 90kph (56mph) on *motorways* and 70kph (43mph) on *other roads*. There is a *minimum* speed limit of 40kph (24mph) on *motorways*, except where otherwise signposted.
  Visiting motorists who have held a full driving licence for less than one year are restricted to driving at top speed of 90kph (56mph). They must also display a yellow disc bearing the figure '90' at the rear of their vehicle (obtainable from any vehicle accessory shop in Portugal). Leaflets giving details in English are handed to visitors at entry points.

Spiked or studded tyres*

The use of *spiked tyres* is prohibited in Portugal.

Telephone*

Insert coin **after** lifting the receiver; the dialling tone is the same as in the UK. When making calls to subscribers *within* Portugal, precede the number with the relevant area code as necessary (shown in parentheses before the hotel/garage enquiry number in the gazetteer). Use ESc5 or ESc10 coins for local calls, and ESc25 for national and international calls.
International callbox identification
Payphones with notice in English.
Cardphones
Telephone rates Calls to the UK cost ESc7.80 per 2.8 seconds. Local calls cost ESc7.80.
Telephone codes

UK to Portugal	010 351
Portugal to UK†	00 44
Portugal to Republic of Ireland†	00 353
Portugal to the USA†	00 1
†or see local instructions	

*Additional information will be found in the European ABC at the front of the book.

Toll bridges

Lisbon Tagus Bridge	ESc
Cars	80
Cars with caravans/trailers	130–350
Motorcycles over 50cc	40

Pedestrians, bicycles, and motorcycles with auxiliary motors of less than 50cc, are prohibited.

Drivers must maintain a speed of 40–70kph (24–43mph) on the bridge. Speed is checked by radar. Heavy vehicles must keep at least 20 metres (66ft) behind the preceding vehicle. **Toll payable in one direction only** – when travelling from Lisbon to the south. There are no charges for vehicles travelling northbound into Lisbon.

Visitors' registration*

Visitors wishing to stay in Portugal for more than 60 days must apply in person for an extension to the Servio de Estrangeiros (Foreigner's Registration Service), 1200 Lisboa, Av Antonio Augusto de Agular 20 ☎7141027/ 7141179. Applications must be made before expiry of the authorised period of stay. The cost is ESc1,500.

Warning triangle*

The use of a warning triangle is compulsory in the event of accident or breakdown. The triangle must be placed on the road 30 metres (33yds) behind the vehicle and must be clearly visible from 100 metres (110yds). See also *Warning triangle*.

Wheel chains

The use of wheel chains is permitted when weather conditions make them necessary.

*Additional information will be found in the European ABC at the front of the book.

ACCOMMODATION

Hotels are officially approved and classified by the Office of the Secretary of State for Information and Tourism. Details of officially authorised charges and the classification of the hotel must be exhibited in every bedroom. The cost of meals served in bedrooms, other than breakfast, is subject to an increase of 10%.

Children under eight years of age are granted a discount of 50% on prices of meals.

While commendations and complaints about hotels are an important source of information to us, members may also like to know that an official complaint book, which must be kept in all establishments, enables guests to record their comments.

Complaints may also be made to local Tourism Delegations and Boards, or to the State Tourism Department, Palácio Foz, Praça dos Restauradores, Lisboa. The Government has encouraged the building of well-equipped hotels, particularly in the Algarve region. Tourist inns known as **pousadas** and **estalagens** are controlled by the **Direcçao General de Turismo**, the official Portuguese tourist organisation; details of most of these are included in the gazetteer.

Pousadas are Government-owned by privately run. They have been specially built or converted, and are often located in the more remote touring areas where there is a lack of other hotels. Visitors may not usually stay more than five nights.

Estalagens are small, well-equipped wayside inns (although there are some in towns), which are privately owned and run, and normally in the one- or two-star category.

The prices shown below are an average for each classification. Accommodation is likely to be more expensive in Porto and some of the more popular tourist areas.

At the time of going to press, £1 *Sterling = ESc259.80* and *US$1 = Esc156.50*, but you should check the rate of exchange before your departure.

AVERAGE PRICES

	Single Room	Double Room	Breakfast	Lunch/Dinner
★★★★★	ESc18,475–25,625	ESc21,600–29,500	—	ESc3,480
★★★★	ESc8,550–12,205	ESc10,500–15,750	ESc675–800	ESc2,500–2,770
★★★	ESc4,850–7,790	ESc6,450–9,450	ESc410–460	ESc1,500–2,090
★★	ESc4,620–6,780	ESc5,997–8,644	ESc425–585	ESc1,750–2,200
★	ESc3,150–4,360	ESc5,080–7,260	ESc250	—

Abbreviations
av avenida Gen General
Capt Capitão r rua
esp esplanada

ABRANTES
Ribatejo
★★★**Turismo** (BW) Largo de Santo Antonio
☎(041)21261 tx 43626
♨♟42 P30 Lift ℂ ℛ ⌖ Mountain
Credit Cards ①②③④⑤
◔ *Mercar* av das Forcas Armadas 2 ☎(041)
21474 Ren
◔ **Sosepor** Largo do Chafariz ☎(041) 22127 Cit

AGUEDA
Costa de Prata
At **SEREM**(11km N)
★★*Pousada San Antonio* Mourisca do Vouga
☎(034)521230 tx 37150
♨♟13 A1rm ⌖ P18 ⬚ Mountain
Credit Cards ①②③⑤

ALBERGARIA A VELHA
Beira Litoral
◔ *Alameda* Estrada Naciónal N1 ☎(034)521402
:Rest closed 25 Dec
A15rm ⌖ P20 ℂ Mountain
Credit Card ③

ALBUFEIRA
Algarve
★★★★*Balaia* (SRS) Praia Maria-Luisa
☎(089)52681 tx 56278
♨♟193 P150 Lift ℂ ℛ ⌖ U Beach Sea
★★★*Sol e Mar* r J-Bernardino de Sousa
☎(089)52121 tx 56217
:Rest closed lunchtime
♨74 A8rm Lift ℂ ℛ ⌖
Credit Cards ①②③④⑤
★★**Estalagem do Cerro** r B-Cerro da Piedade
☎(089)52191 tx 56211
♨♟83 Lift
★★**Estalagem Mar á Vista** Cerro de Piedade
☎(089)52154
♨♟29 Lift

ALCÁCER DO SAL
Baixo Alentejo
★★*Estalagem da Barrosinha* Estrada Naciónal 5
☎(065)62363
♨♟10 ⌖ P Mountain

ALCOBAÇA
Estremadura
◔ *Assessor* Qinta da Roda ☎(044) 41032 Ren

ALPEDRINHA
Beira Baize
★*Estalagem São Jorge* ☎(052)57154
Closed Oct
rm12(♨♟10) A4rm ℂ
Credit Cards ①②③⑤

AMARANTE
Douro Litoral
★★★*Navarras* r A-Carneiro ☎(055)424036 tx
28270

♨♟61 ⌂ P30 Lift ℂ ⬚ Mountain
Credit Cards ①②③⑤
At **SERRA DO MARÃO**(25km E on N15)
★*Pousada de São Gonçalo* ☎(055)461123/4 tx
26321
♨♟15 ⌂ P30 ℂ Mountain
Credit Cards ①②③④⑤

ARMAÇÃO DE PÉRA
Algarve
★★★*Estalagem Algar* av Beira-Mar
☎(082)32353
Mar-Oct
♨♟19
★★★**Garbe** av Marginal ☎(082)312187 & 312194
tx 57485
♨♟109 P70 Lift ℂ ⌖ Sea
Credit Cards ① ③

AVEIRO
Beira Litoral
★★*Arcada* r Viana do Castelo 4 (n.rest)
☎(034)23001 tx 37460
♨♟52 Lift ℂ
Credit Cards ①②③④⑤
◔ **Garage Auto-Variante,Lda** Quinta do Simão
☎(034) 312738 For

AZEITÃO
Estremadura
★*Estalagem Quintas das Torres* Quinta das
Torres ☎2080001
♨♟12 P40 Mountain

BEJA
Baixo Alentejo
◔ *Candido Chicharo* Terreiro Valentes 3 ☎(084)
22090 P Toy
◔ *Jose Pinto Caeiro* av Fialho de Almeida la 7
☎(084) 23031 P Fia Lan

BRAGA
Minho
◔ *J M Costa* av da Liberdada 618 ☎(053) 24105
AR
◔ **F Mota** Extremo de Sequeira ☎(053) 74715
M/C P Cit Hon Peu Alf

BRAGANÇA
Tras-Os-Montes Alto Douro
★★*Pousada de São Bartolomeu* Estrada de
Turismo (n.rest) ☎(0503)22493
⌂ P Mountain

CALDAS DA RAINHA
Estremadura
★*Central* Largo do Dr J-Barbosa 22 ☎(062)22078
rm40(♨♟18) P ℂ
◔ **Adazil** Edificio Adazil,Estrada Caldas/Obidos
☎(062) 95889 Toy

CANAS DE SENHORIM
Beira Atla
At **URGEIRIÇA**(1km NE N234)
★★★*Urgeiriça* ☎(032)67267 tx 53535
♨♟53 P200 ℂ ℛ ⌖ Mountain
Credit Cards ①②③⑤

CANIÇADA
Minho
★★**Pousada de São Bento** Cerdeirinhas-
Soengas ☎(053)647190 & 647317 tx 32339
♨♟18 A8rm ℂ Mountain Lake
Credit Cards ①②③④⑤

CARCAVELOS
Estremadura
★★★*Praia-Mar* r do Guru 16 ☎(01)2473131 tx
42283
♨♟158 P9 Lift ℂ ℛ ⌖ Sea Mountain
Credit Cards ①②③⑤

CASCAIS
Estremadura
★★★★*Estoril Sol* Estrada Marginal ☎(01)282831
tx 15102
:Rest closed daytime
♨♟317 ⌂ P35 Lift ℂ ⬚ ⌖ U Beach
Credit Cards ①②③④⑤
★★★*Albatroz* r F-Arouca 100 ☎(01)282821 tx
16052
♨♟40 ⌂ P10 Lift ℂ ⌖ Sea
Credit Cards ①②③④⑤
★★★**Baia DPn** Estrada Marginal ☎(01)281033 tx
43468
♨♟87 P12 Lift ℂ ⌖ Sea Mountain
Credit Cards ①②③④⑤
★★★**Nau** r Dr-Iracy Doyle Lote 14 ☎(01)282861/
4 tx 42289
♨♟56 ⌂ P Lift ℂ ⌖ Sea Mountain
Credit Cards ①②③⑤
★★**Solar do Carlos** r Latino Coelho 8 (n.rest)
☎(01)2868463
♨♟18 A5rm P ℂ Mountain
Credit Cards ①②③⑤
At **PRAIA DO GUINCHO**(4km W)
★★★★*Guincho* ☎(01)2850491 tx 43138
♨♟36 P Lift ℂ ℏℏ Mountain
Credit Cards ①②③④⑤

CASTELO DO BODE
See **TOMAR**

CHAVES
Tras-Os-Montes Alto Douro
★★*Estalagem Santiago* r do Olival (n.rest)
☎(0506)22545
♨♟31

COIMBRA
Beira Litoral
◔ *Auto-Garagem de Coimbra* Ponte de Eiras-
Ademia P For
◔ *Barreiros & Vilas* Estrada de Coselhas
☎(039) 23331 Cit
◔ *S Caetano* Comercio de Automoveis SA,Estrada
de Eirus ☎(039) 25534 M/C P BMW Toy
◔ *Carvelho & Sobrinho* r M-Alemida e Sousa
☎(039) 27071 P Ren
◔ *Ramalda-Mario Ramalho* av Fernao de
Magalhaes 557-581 ☎(039) 28006 P Dai Maz
Saa

COLARES
Estremadura

★*Estalagem do Conde* Quinta do Conde
☎(01)2991652
Closed Nov-Dec
🍴10 P20 Mountain
Credit Cards ① ③ ④

At **PRAIA DAS MAÇÃS**(4km NW N375)

★★★**Miramonte** ☎(01)9291230 tx 13221
🍴89 P10 ℂ ➘ Mountain

COSTA DA CAPARICA
Estremadura

★★*Estalagem Colobri* ☎(01)2900776
🍴25 P10 Lift ℂ
Credit Cards ① ②

CURIA
Beira Litoral

★★★**Palace** (BW) ☎(031)52131 tx 42589
20 Mar-15 Oct
🍴125 P70 Lift ℂ ℂ ➘
Credit Cards ② ③ ⑤

ELVAS
Alto Alentejo

★★*Estalagem D Sancho II* Praa da Sancho II 20
☎(068)62684
🍴26 Lift ℂ
Credit Cards ① ② ③ ④ ⑤

★*Pousada De Santa Luzia* (outside town on
Borba-Badajoz rd) ☎(068)62128 tx 12469
🍴10 P ℂ
Credit Cards ① ② ③ ⑤

ERICEIRA
Estremadura

★★*Estalagem Morais* r M-Bombarda 3 (n.rest)
☎(061)62611 & 62643 tx 44938
Dec-Oct
🍴40 Lift ℂ ℂ ➘ Sea
Credit Cards ① ② ③ ④ ⑤

ESPINHO
Douro Litoral

★★★**Praialgolfe** ☎(02)720630 tx 23727
🍴139 A6rm ☎ P50 Lift ℂ ℂ ▭ ➘ 🐾 Sea
Lake
Credit Cards ① ② ③ ④ ⑤

ESPOSENDE
Minho

★★*Suave-Mar* av E-Duarto Pacheco
☎(053)961445 tx 32362
🍴59 ☎ P ℂ ℂ ➘ Sea
Credit Cards ① ③

ESTORIL
Estremadura

★★★★**Palacio Estoril** Parque Estoril
☎(01)2680400 tx 12757
🍴165 P150 Lift ℂ ➘ 🐾 Sea
Credit Cards ① ② ③ ④ ⑤

★★★★**Estoril Anka** Estrada Marginal
☎(01)2681811 tx 16007
🍴91 Lift ℂ ➘ Sea
Credit Cards ① ② ③ ④ ⑤

★★*Founder's Inn (Estalagen do Fundador)* r D-
A-Henriques 161 ☎(01)2682221 & 2682346
:Rest closed Wed
🍴9 P6 ℂ ➘ Sea Mountain
Credit Cards ① ② ③ ⑤

ESTREMOZ
Alto Alentejo

★★★*Pousada da Rainha Santa Isabel* Castelo
de Estremoz ☎(068)22618 tx 43885
🍴23 P Lift ℂ
Credit Cards ① ② ③ ④ ⑤

ÉVORA
Alto Alentejo

Évora, located in Portugal's vast,
rolling plains, is a delightful
museum town, built on a hill that
rises out of the surrounding
Alentejo; almost completely
surrounded by a perfectly
preserved 14th-century wall, it
has many monuments testifying
to its 1,000 years of history,
enhanced by picturesque
whitewashed houses and villas.
Here the dissident Roman
general Sertorius had a base,
while Julius Caesar conferred
upon the town the title of
Liberalitas Julia. The beautiful
granite and marble Temple of
Diana - perhaps the most famous
of the town's monuments, was
built by another Roman Emperor,
possibly Hadrian.
Among Évora's many places of
interest are the 12th to 13th-
century Romanesque-Gothic
cathedral, containing religious art
treasures, Cadaval Palace, a
private museum, a regional
museum containing
archaeological finds and Roman
art, Calvario convent and church,
Santa Clara convent and church,
and the palace of Dom Manuel, a
16th-century example of Moorish,
Manueline and Renaissance
architecture.

EATING OUT Regional
specialities are served in the
restaurant of the attractive
Pousada dos Loios, which
occupies part of the former
monastery of dos Loios, built in
the 15th century.

ÉVORA
Alto Alentejo

★★★★*Pousada dos Loios* Largo Conde de Vila
Flor ☎(066)24051 tx 43288
🍴31 ℂ
Credit Cards ① ② ③ ⑤

★★★*Planicie* (BW) r M-Bombarda 40
☎(066)24026 tx 13500
🍴33 P Lift ℂ
Credit Cards ① ② ③ ④ ⑤

FARO
Algarve

The district capital of the
southern region of Portugal
known as the Algarve is also one
of the area's most popular and
lively resorts. A prehistoric
fishing village and later a
Phoenician and Greek trading
post, Faro knew splendor under
the Romans who named it
Ossonoba and turned it into an
important port and
administrative centre.
Places of interest include the
cathedral, a Romanesque-Gothic
edifice built in 1251 and
containing a Renaissance altar-
piece and several 17th-century
statues; majestic 17th-century
Bishop's Palace noted for its
lovely panels of decorative tiles;
stretches of the former city walls;
Prince Henry Archaeological
Museum, housed in a former
convent; and a museum
dedicated to St Anthony
containing a collection of statues
and engravings as well as books
on the saint.

EATING OUT Portuguese
cuisine is a feature of
the *Alfagher* in rua Tenente
Valadim, which has a pleasant
terrace. One of the most highly
regarded restaurants in the
Algarve is *Cidade Velha* near the
cathedral.

FARO
Algarve

★★★★*Eva Dom Pedro* av da República
☎(089)24054 tx 56524
🍴150 P20 Lift ℂ ➘ Beach Sea
Credit Cards ① ② ③ ⑤

★★★*Faro* Praça D-F-Gomes 2 ☎(089)22076 tx
56108
🍴52 Lift ℂ Lake
Credit Cards ① ② ③ ⑤

★★*Albacor* r Brites de Almeida 25 (n.rest)
☎(089)22093 tx 56778
🍴38 P15 Lift ℂ
Credit Cards ① ② ③ ⑤

At **PRAIA DE FARO**(8km SW)

★★*Estalagem Aeromar* ☎(089)23542
Feb-Nov
🍴20

FÁTIMA
Beira Litoral

★★★*Fátima* (BW) Joao Paulo II ☎(049)52351 tx
43750
🍴118 P20 Lift ℂ
Credit Cards ① ② ③ ⑤

★★*Trés Pastorinhos* Cova da Iria ☎(049)52429
🍴92 P50 Lift ℂ Mountain
Credit Cards ① ② ③ ④ ⑤

FIGUEIRA DA FOZ
Beira Litoral

★★★★*Figueira* av 25 de Abril ☎(033)22146 &
22147 tx 53086
🍴91 Lift ℂ ➘ Sea
Credit Cards ① ② ③ ④ ⑤

GUARDA
Beira Alta

★★★*Turismo* (BW) Largo de Sao Francisco
☎(071)22206 tx 18760
🍴105 ☎ P Lift ℂ
Credit Cards ② ③

★★Aliança r V-da-Gama ☎(071)22135 tx 52516 rm31(➔ᵔ24) ☂ P20 ℂ Mountain
Credit Cards ①②③④⑤

★★Filipe r V-da-Gama 9 ☎(071)22658 tx 53746 rm40(➔ᵔ36) ℂ ℺ Mountain
Credit Cards ①②③④⑤

✿❀ Morgado & Raimundo av Dr-Afonso Costa ☎(071) 22766 P Toy

GUIMARAES
Costa Verde

★★★Fundactor Dom Pedro ☎(53)413781 tx 32866
➔ᵔ63 ☂ P40 Lift ℂ Mountain

★★Pousada Sta Maria Oliveira Largo da Oliveira ☎(53)412157 tx 32875
➔ᵔ16 P10 Lift ℂ
Credit Cards ①②③⑤

LAGOS
Algarve

★★★Meia Praia Meia Praia (4km NE) ☎(082)62001 tx 57497
Apr-Oct
➔ᵔ66 P Lift ℂ ℺ Sea
Credit Cards ①②③④⑤

★★Pensão Dona Ana Praia de Dona Ana ☎(082)62322
Apr-Oct
rm11(➔5)

★★Residential Mar Azul r 25 de Abril 13 (n.rest) ☎(082)62181
➔ᵔ18 ℂ Sea

LECA DO BALIO
Douro Litoral

★★★Estalagem via Norte Estrada via Norte ☎9480294 tx 26617
➔ᵔ12 ☂ P20 ℂ ⌣
Credit Cards ①②③④⑤

LEIRA
Beira Litoral

★★★Eurosol Jardim r D-J-Alves da Silva ☎(044)24101 tx 42031
➔ᵔ92 ☂ P70 Lift ℂ ⌣ Mountain
Credit Cards ①②③④⑤

LISBOA *(LISBON)*

Estremadura **See Plan pages 336 and 337** *Population* 820,000 *Local tourist office* Rua das Portas de Sto Antao 141 (01) 327058

Lisboa, the capital city of Portugal lies on seven low hills at the estuary of the river Tagus (Tejo). The attractions of the city lie in the magnificent vistas from its many belvederes, its shady tree-lined avenues and squares with decorated pavements, the freshness of its public gardens, flower-filled balconies, patterned wall-tiles and its wealth of monuments, churches and museums.

The architectural intrigue of the city bears witness to a brilliant historical past. Its origins are shrouded in legend, its mythical founders including Elisha and Ulysses. It was occupied successively by Phoenicians, Greeks, Carthiginians, Romans, Visigoths and Moors and finally conquered in 1147 by Portugal's first king, Afonso Henriques, with the aid of the English Crusaders. But it was at the time of the Great Discoveries that Lisboa really came into its own as capital of the Portuguese Empire and the world centre for trade in spices, silks, jewels and gold. Relics of their fabulous wealth are to be seen everywhere in the Manueline architecture of Lisboa's churches, monasteries and palaces.

Among the chief places of interest is Alfama, a charming ancient Moorish quarter with narrow, winding streets and picturesque white-washed houses, crowned by St George's Castle, which dominates the city. Together with Bairro Alto, Alfama is also the centre of *fado*, the traditional haunting folk song of Portugal.

Other places of interest include Praça do Comércio, a magnificent square with a superb triumphal arch, the city's range of fascinating churches and museums and Belém, from where the ships of Vasco da Gama and other famous explorers set sail, with its graceful tower and Hieronimite Monastery - two of the finest examples of the Manueline style of architecture.

EATING OUT As befits a great seafaring nation the Portuguese cook fish to perfection. Meat lovers, on the other hand, can find tasty pork and lamb dishes, while local specialities include *Bacalhau a Gomes de Sa* - dried cod baked with potatoes, onions and olives; and baked kid served with potaoes and rice. The cafés of Chiado (an area damaged by fire in 1988), Alfama and Bairro Alto are worth a visit and a simple but satisfying meal can be enjoyed at a very reasonable price. *Gambrinus*, in Rua Portas S. Antao, is one of Lisbon's longest established restaurants, and specialises in fish and shellfish.

Also long-established is *Anarquistas* in Largo de Trindade, which serves traditional Portuguese dishes. For less expensive local cuisine the *Atinel Bar*, in Cais dos Carilheiros, is recommended not only for its food but also its setting by the river Tagus.

LISBOA (LISBON)
★★★★★Lisboa Sheraton & Towers r Latino Coelho 1 ☎(01)575757 tx 12774
➔ᵔ385 ☂ Lift ℂ ⌣
Credit Cards ①②③④⑤

★★★★★Ritz (Intercont) r R-da-Fonseca 88A ☎(01)692020 tx 12589
➔ᵔ304 ☂ P50 Lift ℂ
Credit Cards ①②③④⑤

★★★★Avenida Palace r 1 de Dezembro 123 ☎(01)360151 tx 12815
➔ᵔ93 A93rm P20 Lift ℂ
Credit Cards ①②③④⑤

★★★★Eduardo VII (BW) av Fontes Pereira de Mello 5 ☎(01)530141 tx 18340
➔ᵔ130 ☂ P Lift ℂ
Credit Cards ①②③⑤

★★★★Fénix Praça Marques do Pombal 8 ☎(01)535121 tx 12270
➔ᵔ122 Lift ℂ
Credit Cards ①②③④⑤

★★★★Florida r Duque de Palmela 32 (n.rest) ☎(01)576145 tx 12256
➔ᵔ112 Lift ℂ
Credit Cards ①②③④⑤

HOTEL LISBOA PLAZA ★★★★

Style and imagination in the heart of Lisbon

Av. Liberdade / Tv. Salitre · 1200 Lisboa - Portugal
Tel. 34 63 92 2 · Telex 16 402 P · Fax 37 16 30

LISBOA (LISBON)

1	★★★★★	Lisboa Sheraton & Towers
2	★★★★★	Ritz
3	★★★★	Avenida Palace
4	★★★★	Eduardo VII
5	★★★★	Fénix
6	★★★★	Florida
7	★★★★	Mundial
8	★★★★	Plaza
9	★★★★	Tivoli
10	★★★	Flamingo
11	★★★	Miráparque
12	★★★	Torre
13	★★	Borges
14	★★	Jorge V
15	★★	Principe

★★★★**Mundial** r D-Duarte 4 ☎(01)863101 tx 12308
⇜147 P Lift ℂ
Credit Cards ① ② ③ ④ ⑤

★★★★**Novotel Lisboa** av J-Malhoa 1642
☎(01)7266022 tx 40114
⇜246 ⋒ P58 Lift ℂ ⌓
Credit Cards ① ② ③ ④ ⑤

★★★★**Plaza** (BW) Travessa do Salitre 7,(off av de Liberdade) ☎(01)3463922 tx 16402
⇜93 P120 Lift ℂ
Credit Cards ① ② ③ ④ ⑤

★★★★**Tivoli** (SRS) av da Liberdade 185
☎(01)530181 tx 12588
⇜342 ⋒ P200 Lift ℂ ⚲ ⌓
Credit Cards ① ② ③ ⑤

★★★**Flamingo** (GT/BW) r Castilho 41
☎(01)5832191 tx 14736
rm39 P Lift ℂ
Credit Cards ① ② ③ ⑤

★★★**Miraparque** av Sidonio Pais 12
☎(01)578070 tx 16745
⇜108 A7rm Lift ℂ

★★★**Torre** r dos Jeronimos 8 ☎(01)630161
⇜50 P Lift ℂ
Credit Cards ① ② ③ ④ ⑤

★★**Borges** r Garrett 108 ☎(01)3461951 tx 15825
⇜100 P10 Lift ℂ
Credit Cards ① ② ③

★★**Jorge V** r Mouzinho da Silveira 3 (n.rest)
☎(01)562525 tx 18454
⇜52 P6 Lift ℂ
Credit Cards ① ② ③ ④ ⑤

★★**Principe** av Duque d'Avila 201 ☎(01)536151 tx 43565
⇜68 P25 Lift ℂ
Credit Cards ① ② ③ ④ ⑤

� **Gilauto** r Cidade da Beira 48 Km ☎(01) 31765 Ren

🚗 **Jol** Pecas Oficinas Lda,R Antonio Patricio 11 ☎ 767094/7 P AR

🚗 **Melisauto-Mercado Lisbonense** r Pinheiro Chagas 101-B ☎(01) 705215 TOYOTA

🚗 **J Mendes Coelho** r S-Sebastião da Pedeira 122 ☎(01) 539807 M/C Ford

🚗 **Rall** r C-Mardel 12 ☎(01) 562061 For Vau

🚗 **Retic** r A-Redol 15-C ☎(01) 730436 Ren

🚗 **Sociedade Portugesa** r Escola Politecnica 261 ☎(01) 690378 Ren

🚗 **Sociedade Comercial Guerin** r J-Saraiva 1 ☎(01) 883840 Aud VW

🚗 **Strand Moderno** r J-Sariva 15 ☎(01) 891065 M/C P For

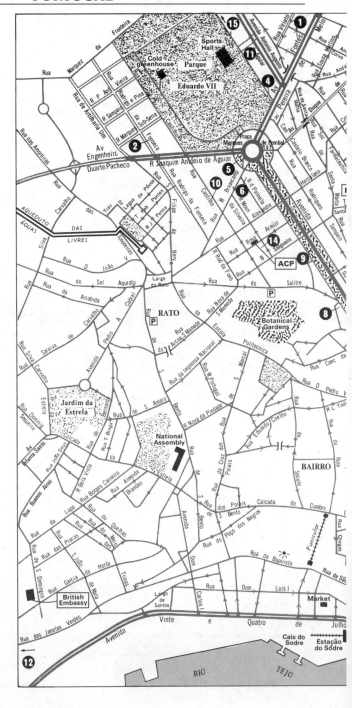

LISBOA
(LISBON)
CENTRAL

Scale

CASTELO
DE
SÃO
JORGE

ALFAMA

BAIXA

Estacão
de Santa
Apolonia
Car
Sleeper

Praça do
Comercio

GPO

Car Ferries
to Cacilhas

Praça Duque
de Terceira

Avenida Ribeira das Naus

Theatre

POL

Estação
do Rossio

Praça Dom
Pedro IV

Praça José
Fontana

Market

Market

Market

Market

(RIVER TAGUS)

0   ½ km
0   ¼ m

(7/89)

LUSO
Beira Litoral
★★★★**Termas** (BW) r dos Banhos ☎(031)93450 tx 53342
🍴🛏173 P100 Lift ℂ ♀ ⌂⌐ Mountain
Credit Cards ① ② ③ ④ ⑤

MACEDO DE CAVALAIEROS
Tras-Os-Montes Alto Douro
★**Estalagem Caçador** Largo Pinto de Azevedo ☎(35178)42354/56
🍴🛏25 Lift ℂ ⌐

MANGUALDE
Beira Alta
★★**Estalagem Cruz de Mata** Estrada Nacional ☎(032)62556
🍴🛏13

MANTEIGAS
Beira Alta
★★**Pousada de São Laurenco** (13km N on the road to Gouveia) ☎(075)98150 tx 53992
🍴🛏12 A3rm ⋦ P20 Mountain
Credit Cards ① ② ③ ④ ⑤

MIRANDA DO DOURO
Tras-Os-Montes Alto Douro
★★**Pousada De Santa Catarina** ☎(0503)42255
🍴🛏12 ⋦ P

MONTE GORDO
Algarve
★★★**Das Caravelas** r Diogo Cão ☎(081)44458 tx 56020
Apr-Oct
🍴🛏86 Lift ℂ
Credit Cards ① ② ③ ⑤
★★★**Dos Navegadores** r Gancalso Velho ☎(081)42490 tx 56054
🍴🛏400 ⋦ P50 Lift ℂ ⌐ Beach Sea
Credit Cards ① ② ③ ④ ⑤
★★★**Vasco da Gama** av Infante D-Henrique ☎(081)44321 tx 56020
🍴🛏180 A20rm P50 Lift ℂ ♀ ⌐ Beach Sea
Credit Cards ① ② ③ ④ ⑤

MONTES DE ALVOR
See **PORTIMÃO**

NAZARÉ
Estremadura
★★★**Dom Fuas** ☎(062)51351 tx 13889
Apr-Oct
🍴🛏35 P30 Lift ℂ Sea Mountain
Credit Cards ① ② ③ ④ ⑤
★★★**Nazaré** Largo A-Zuquete ☎(062)51311 & 51348 tx 16116
🍴🛏52 P Lift ℂ
Credit Cards ① ② ③ ⑤
★★★**Praia** av V-Guimaraes 39 (n.rest) ☎(062)51423 tx 16329
Closed 29 Nov-29 Dec
🍴🛏41 ⋦ Lift ℂ Sea Mountain
Credit Cards ① ② ③ ④ ⑤
🍴 **Auto Coelho** Estrada Do Pinhal ☎ 51048 P Ren

ÓBIDOS
Estremadura
★★**Estalagem do Convento** r Dr-J-de-Ornelas ☎(062)95217/4 tx 44906
🍴🛏30 P40 ℂ
Credit Cards ① ② ③ ⑤
★**Pousada Do Castelo** (on the Caldas da R-Vedras-Lisbon road) ☎(062)95105 tx 15540
🍴🛏9 P10 ℂ
Credit Cards ① ② ③ ⑤

OFIR
Minho
★★★**Estalagem do Parque do Rio** ☎(0351)053/961521-4 tx 32066

Apr-Oct
🍴🛏36 P50 Lift ℂ ♀ ⌐
Credit Cards ① ② ③ ④ ⑤
★★★**Pinhal** (BW) Estrada do Mar ☎(0351)961473 tx 32857
🍴🛏90 Lift ♀ ⌐

OLHÃO
Algarve
★**Ria-Sol** r Gl-Humberto Delgado 37 (n.rest) ☎(351)72167/8 tx 56923
🍴🛏52 P10 Lift ℂ
Credit Cards ① ③

OLIVEIRA DO HOSPITAL
Beira Alta
At **POVOA DAS QUARTAS**(7km E on N17)
★★**Pousada Santa Bárbara** ☎(038)52252 tx 53794
🍴🛏16 ⋦ P50 ℂ ♀ ⌐ Mountain
Credit Cards ① ② ③ ④ ⑤

OPORTO
See**PORTO**

PORTALEGRE
Alto Alentejo
★**Alto Alentejo** r 19 de Junho 59 (n.rest) ☎(045)22290
🍴🛏16 ℂ Mountain
Credit Cards ① ② ③ ⑤

PORTIMÃO
Algarve
★★★★**Alvor Praia** Praia dos Tres Irmaos ☎(082)24021 tx 57611
🍴🛏223 P Lift ⌐ Sea
Credit Cards ① ② ③ ④ ⑤
★★**Miradoiro** r Machado dos Santos 13 (n.rest) ☎(082)23011
🍴🛏26
★**Estalagem Mira-Foia** r V-Vaz das Vacas 33 ☎(082)22011
🍴🛏23 Lift
🍴 **Forportil** Serro Ruivo-Estrada de Alvor ☎(082)26091 P For
At **MONTES DE ALVOR**(5km W N125)
★★★★**Penina Golf** ☎(082)22051 tx 57307
🍴🛏198 P200 Lift ℂ ♀ ⌐ ⋔⋔ Mountain
Credit Cards ① ② ③ ⑤

PORTO (OPORTO)
Douro Litoral

Capital of northern Portugal and the country's second largest city, Porto is big and bustling with elegant hotels, homely pensions, an abundance of excellent restaurants, rich museums, fine theatres and cinemas and no shortage of sporting opportunities.
Many monuments scattered around the city provide rich examples of Romanesque, Gothic, Baroque, Roccoco and neo-classical architecture, while the fine Clerigos Tower, the city landmark, majestically overlooks the old part of the the city. Being at the centre of the Port wine industry, many visitors take the opportunity to visit one of the ancient Port wine lodges at

Vila Nova de Gaia, on the left bank of the Douro.

EATING OUT The best places to eat in Porto are the interesting *tascas* in the medieval part of the city, among whose specialities is a dish for which the city is famous - tripe. Indeed the inhabitants of Porto are often affectionately known as the *tripeiros*(tripe-eaters), a curious epithet gained in 1415 from having given away all the meat they had to the early navigators, keeping only the entrails for themselves. One restaurant specialising in tripe is the appropriately-named *Tripeiro* in Rua Passos Manuel.
Apart from tripe, other regional dishes to look out for include *caldo verde* - finely shreded kale broth - and *cabrito* - roast kid. Desserts include a range of quaintly named egg, almond and sugared cakes such as *Barrigas de Feira* - nun's tummies

PORTO (OPORTO)
Douro Litoral
★★★★**Infante de Sagres** (BW) Praa Filipa de Lencastre 62 ☎(02)28101 tx 26880
🍴🛏84 P20 Lift ℂ
Credit Cards ① ② ③ ④ ⑤
★★★**Dom Henrique** r Guedes de Azevedo 179 ☎(02)25755 tx 22554
🍴🛏112 Lift
Credit Cards ① ② ③ ⑤
★★★**Grande da Batalha** Praça da Batalha 116 ☎(02)20571 tx 25131
🍴🛏142 ⋦ Lift ℂ
Credit Cards ① ② ③ ⑤
★★★**Grande do Porto** r de Santa Catarina 197 ☎(02)28176 & 25741 tx 22553
🍴🛏100 Lift ℂ
Credit Cards ① ② ③ ⑤
★★★**Império** Praça da Batalha 130 (off r Sao Lidesfosa) ☎(02)26861 tx 26060
🍴🛏95
🍴 **Batalha** r A-Herculano 385 ☎(02) 23024 P Vol
🍴 **Gomes da Costa** r Tander 1280 ☎(02) 683971 P Ren
🍴 **Filinto Mota** 546 r Pinto Bessa ☎(02) 562202 P Cit
Mota 180 av dos Aliados ☎(02) 564455 P Cit
🍴 **Ouro** 71 r F-Tomas ☎(02) 579008 Aud VW
🍴 **Strand Autolisporto** r 5 de Outubro 400 ☎(02) 699798 Aud VW

POVOA DAS QUARTAS
See **OLIVEIRA DO HOSPITAL**

PRAIA DA ROCHA
Algarve
★★★★**Algarve** av T-Cabreira ☎(082)24001/9 tx 57347
🍴🛏220 P50 Lift ℂ ♀ ⌐ Sea Mountain
Credit Cards ① ② ③ ⑤
★★★**Estalagem Mira Sol** r E-F-Bivar ☎(082)24046
rm38

338

★★*Belavista* av T-Cabriera ☎(082)24055 tx 57347

♨♒27 A10rm P ℂ Sea

★★*Estalagem Alcala* av Tomas Cabreira ☎(082)24062 tx 57352

♨♒61 P40 Lift ℂ Sea

★★*Estalagem São José* r A-de-Albuguerique ☎(082)24037

♨♒25 A14rm P ℂ Sea

PRAIA DA SALEMA
Algarve

★★*Estalagem Infante Do Mar* ☎(082)65137 & 65443 tx 57451

Mar-Oct

♨♒30 P40 ℂ ⌿ Sea

PRAIA DAS MAÇÃS
See COLARES

PRAIA DE FARO
See FARO

PRAIA DE SANTA CRUZ
Estremadura

★★*Santa Cruz* r J-P-Lopes ☎(063)97148 tx 42509

♨♒32 P5 Lift ℂ

Credit Cards ①②③⑤

PRAIA DO GUINCHO
See CASCAIS

QUARTEIRA
Algarve

At VILAMOURA(2.5km NW)

★★★★*Atlantis Vilamoura* ☎(089)32535 tx 56838

♨♒305 Lift ℂ ⌿⌿ Sea

Credit Cards ①②③⑤

★★★*Dom Pedro Golf* ☎(089)889650 tx 56149

♨♒261 P100 Lift ℂ ↻ ⌿ Sea

Credit Cards ①②③④⑤

SAGRES
Algarve

★★★*Baleeira* ☎(082)64212 tx 57467

♨♒118 P80 ℂ ↻ ⌿ Sea

Credit Cards ①②③⑤

★★*Pousada do Infante* Ponta da Atalaia ☎(082)64222 tx 57491

♨♒23 ☆ P50 ℂ ↻ ⌿ Sea

Credit Cards ①②③④⑤

SANTA CLARA-A-VELHA
Baixo Alentejo

★★*Pousada De Santa Clara* Barragem de Santa Clara ☎(083)52250

♨♒6 P ⌿ Mountain Lake

SANTA LUZIA
See VIANA DO CASTELO

SANTARÉM
Ribatejo

★★*Abidis* r Guilherme de Azevedo 4 ☎(043)22017

rm28(♨6) ☆ ℂ

♨ *Alpial* Praceta Alves Redol 19-21 ☎(043)27865 P Toy

SANTIAGO DO CACÉM
Baxio Alentejo

★*Pousada De São Tiago* Estrada National ☎(069)22459 tx 16166

♨♒107 A3rm P15 ⌿

Credit Cards ①②③④⑤

SÃO BRAS DE ALPORTEL
Algarve

★*Pousada de São Bras* (5km N on main road) ☎(089)42305 tx 56945

♨♒25 A8rm P30 Lift ℂ ⌿ Mountain

Credit Cards ①②③⑤

SEREM
See AGUEDA

SERPA
Baixo Alentejo

★★*Pousada de São Gens* Alto de So Gens ☎(084)90327 tx 43651

♨♒18 P8 ℂ ⌿ Mountain

Credit Cards ①②③④⑤

SERRA DO MARÃO
See AMARANTE

SESIMBRA
Estremadura

★★★★*Do Mar* ☎(01)2233326 tx 13883

♨♒119 P60 Lift ℂ ↻ ⌿ Sea

Credit Cards ①②③⑤

★★★★*Espadarte* Esp do Atlantico ☎(01)2233189 tx 14699

♨♒80 P Lift ℂ Sea

Credit Cards ①②③⑤

SETÚBAL
Estremadura

★★★★*Esperança* av L-Todi 220 ☎(065)25151/2/3 tx 17158

♨♒76 Lift ℂ

Credit Cards ①②③⑤

★★*Pousada de São Filipe* ☎(065)23844 tx 44655

♨♒14 P30 ℂ ↻ ♒♒ Sea Mountain

Credit Cards ①②③④⑤

♨ Setubauto av Combatentes Grande Guerra,89-91 ☎(065) 23131 For

SINES
Baixo Alentejo

★★★*Malhada* av 25 de Abril ☎(069)62105

♨♒27

SINTRA
Estremadura

Sintra is undoubtedly one of the most attractive small towns in Portugal and a popular excursion venue for holidaymakers staying in Estoril, neighbouring Cascais or Lisbon. Set amidst luxuriant vegetation on the range of hills of the same name, it combines natural scenic attractions with the delights of numerous palaces and museums, the oldest building in Sintra being the Moorish Castle, which dates back to Hispano-Arab times. The Royal Palace, once the summer residence of Portuguese monarchs, was constructed on the site of the old palace of the Moorish kings, mainly commissioned by Dom Joao I (1385-1433), Dom Manuel I (1495-1521) adding the right wing. Situated at a greater height even than the Moorish castle is the impressive Pena Palace, built by Dom Fernando II between 1840 and 1850 adjacent to the monastery which Dom Manuel I had built between 1503 and 1511. Also worth visiting are the churches of Santa Maria (12th century), Sao Pedro (16th century) and Sao Martinho (12th century origins); and the Museum Library, containing a fascinating collection of prints and paintings of the town district.

EATING OUT The *Cantinho de Sao Pedro*, in Largo de Feira, near the centre of Sintra, is one of the most popular restaurants in town. Specialities include fresh soups, raspberry tart, and tempting stews of veal and pork. The restaurant *O Regional*, opposite the Town Hall, is also recommended.

SINTRA
Estremadura

★★★★*Palàcio De Seteais* r Barbosa do Bogage 8 ☎(01)9233200 tx 14410

♨♒18 P60 Lift ℂ ↻ ⌿ Sea Mountain

Credit Cards ①②③④⑤

C Augusto dos Santo av Bombeiros Voluntarios ☎(02) 9291078 P Ren

♨ *Lopes Pereira* av 29 de Acosta 283 ☎(01)9277037 M/C P Ren

TAVIRA
Algarve

★★★*Eurotel-Tavira* Quinta das Oliveiras ☎(081)22041 & 23071 tx 56218

♨♒80 P50 Lift ℂ ↻ ⌿ Sea Mountain

Credit Cards ①②③④⑤

TOMAR
Ribatejo

♨ *Pinto* r Coimbra 36-40 ☎(049) 32098 P Toy

At CASTELO DO BODE(14km SE)

★★*Pousada de São Pedro* Castelo do Bode ☎(049)38159

♨♒15 A7rm P Mountain Lake

TORRES VEDRAS
Estremadura

♨ *Tecauto-Techica* de Automovies Lda,av Gen-Humberto Delgado ☎(061) 25075 Rov Aud Mer

♨ *Toltorres-Sociedade* Edificio Toitorres EN8 Km 439 ☎ 25171-25646 M/C P Toy BMW Hon

URGEIRIÇA
See CANAS DE SENHORIM

VALE DO LOBO
Algarve

★★★★*Dona Filipa* (THF) ☎(089)94141 tx 56848

♨♒135 ☆ P150 Lift ℂ ⌿ ⌿

Credit Cards ①②③⑤

VALENÇA DO MINHO
Minho

★★*Pousada de São Teotónio* ☎(051)22242/52 tx 32837

♨♒15 A3rm P ℂ Mountain Lake

Credit Cards ①②③④⑤

VIANA DO CASTELO
Minho

★★★★*Parque* Praca da Galiza ☎(058)24151 tx 32511

♨♒124 ☆ P90 Lift ℂ ↻ ⌿ U Sea Mountain Lake

Credit Cards ①②③④⑤

★★★*Afonso III* (BW) av Afonso 494 ☎(058)24123 tx 32599

♨♒89 P50 Lift ℂ ⌿ Sea Mountain Lake

Credit Cards ①②③④⑤

★★*Alianca* av dos Combatentes da Grande,Guerra ☎(058)23001

rm29(♨15) P ℂ Sea

★★*Rali* av Alfonso 3 (n.rest) ☎(058)22176
₩ſ39 P Lift 《 ⌂ Mountain
Credit Cards ①③
At **SANTA LUZIA**(2km NW)
★★★★*Santa Luzia* ☎(058)22192 tx 32420
₩ſ47 P50 Lift 《 ⌂⌐ Sea Mountain
Credit Cards ①②③⑤

VILA DO CONDE
Douro Litoral
★★*Estalagem do Brasào* r J-M-de-Melo
☎(052)632016/28
₩ſ28 P30 《
Credit Cards ①②⑤
ﻝ **J Felix & Filhos** r 5 de Outubro 57 ☎(052)
631050 AR

VILAMOURA
See **QUARTEIRA**

VILA REAL
Tras-Os-Montes Alto Douro
★★*Tocalo* av Carvalho Araujo 45 ☎(059)23106
₩ſ52 ☇ Lift 《 Mountain

VILA REAL DE SANTO ANTÓNIO
Algarve
★★★*Eurotel* Praia da Altura ☎(081)95450 tx
56068
Apr-Oct
₩ſ135 P70 Lift 《 ⌂ ⌐⌐ Beach Sea
Credit Cards ①②③④⑤

VISEU
Beira Alta

Well served by roads winding through lovely countryside, Viseu is one of the most beautiful towns in Portugal, with a distinctly medieval flavour. Historic mansions perch on the edge of rocks; street vendors sell their wares in ancient, flagstoned streets in front of great houses bearing coats of arms; and the cloisters and lofty towers of the cathedral dominate the skyline. According to history, Roderico, the last Visigoth king, established his court in Viseu during the resistance against Arab invasion, and in the 8th century Viseu was capital of 'Portucale'.
Among the many sights are the 13th-century Romanesque cathedral; The *Grao Vasco* Museum, containing valuable paintings; an historical museum housed in the 18th-century *Casa do Cimo da Vila*; and numerous fascinating churches of the 17th and 18th centuries.

EATING OUT Viseau's two best-known and most respected restaurants are *Herminios*, in Estrada National, and *Infante*, in Avenida Dom Henriques, both of which offer regional specialities.

VISEU
Beira Alta
★★★*Grào Vasco* (BW) r G-Barreiros
☎(032)23511 tx 53608
₩ſ88 P80 Lift 《 ⌐ Mountain
Credit Cards ①②③⑤
ﻝ **Lopes & Figueiredo** av da Belgica 52 ☎(032)
41151 P Rov Mer Maz
ﻝ **Tevisauto** r Nova do Hospital ☎(032) 26002
Toy

AA Road Map – Spain and Portugal

Featuring:

- **Up-to-date road information**
- **Scenic routes and viewpoints**
- **Contours and gradients**
- **Distances between towns**
- **Full colour, 16 miles to 1 inch**

An ideal map for route-planning and touring — available at good bookshops and AA Centres

Don't leave the country without one

An ancient, sundrenched land whose soil has known numerous civilizations, Spain has been dubbed a 'miniature continent', and the contrasts among its various regions and peoples, language and customs certainly merit the label. The Iberian Peninsula – Spain and Portugal – takes the form of a pentagon bound by rocky coasts. There is an insular Spain, made up of the Canaries and the Balearics, and an African Spain, consisting of the cities of Ceuta and Melilla. With a total area of 300,000 square miles it is the third largest country in Europe, ranks seventh in population, and is the most mountainous country after Switzerland. The distinctive feature of Spanish geography is the great cultural plateau with an area of 120,000 square miles and an average altitude of more than 2,000 feet. Flanking this central plateau are great mountain ranges and the lateral depressions formed by the Ebro and Guadalquivir valleys.

Spain is a great museum displaying every facet of artistic endeavour from the pre-historic paintings of the Altamira Caves to Picasso's modern-day abstracts. The world-famous Prado Museum in Madrid contains masterpieces by Valazquez, El Greco, Zurbaran, Ribera and Murillo, and especially Goya, the influence of whose genius is still felt in art today.

The varied landscapes of Spain is literally covered with castles, palaces, monasteries and cathedrals housing precious collections of sculptures, paintings, jewels and tapestries. Toledo is arguably the most complete complex of Spanish art, and boasts one of the finest gothic cathedrals, whilel Catalonia and the eastern regions have imposed a peculiarly personal style on their gothic buildings.

SPAIN

Language
Spanish is the main language; Catalan and Basque are both spoken regionally. In Andorra, French and Spanish are both spoken.

Local Time
GMT + 1 hour (Summer GMT + 2 hours)

Currency
Spanish peseta, divided into 100 *centimos*. At the time of going to press
£1 = Ptas195.15
US$1 = Ptas117.56

Emergency numbers
Fire: in Madrid and Barcelona ☎080
in other towns call the operator.

Police: in all cities ☎091
in other towns call the operator

Ambulance: on main roads, ask for **auxillio en carretera** (road assistance). See **Accidents** below

Information in Britain
Spanish National Tourist Office, Metro House, 57–58 St James's Street, London SW1A 1LD
☎01-449 0901 (071-449 0901 from 6 May 1990)

Information in the USA
National Tourist Office of Spain, 665 Fifth Avenue, New York NY 10022
☎212 759 5944

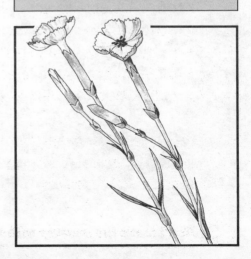

BAY OF BISCAY

Ferrol Ribadeo Luarca Gijón Ribadesella Llanes San Vicente de la Barquera Comillas Suances Playa Santillana Santander Laredo Zarauz

A8 N632 N634 Oviedo Mieres Arenas de Cabrales Fuente Dé Reinosa N634 Bilbao A8 Cestona N240 Alsa

La Coruña NVI Villalba N634 A66 Cervera de Pisuerga N611 Pancorbo A1 Vitoria Argomaniz

Santiago de Compostela Lugo Puerto de Pajares Léon Burgos Logroño Calah A68

Portomarín Villafranca del Bierzo Ponferrada Astorga N630 N620 Santo Domingo de la Calzada

Cambados A9 Orense Puebla de Sanabria N525 Benavente C620 Palencia Covarrubias Soria

Isla de la Toja Pontevedra Baiona Tui Valença do Minho Verín Chaves Bragança Zamora Valladolid N620 Aranda de Duero

Viana do Castelo Caniçada N2 Macedo de Cavaleiros Miranda do Douro Tordesillas Santa Maria de Huerta XII C.

Esposende Ofir Braga Guiaraes Vila Real Amarante N620 Salamanca Medinaceli Sigüenza

Vila do Conde Leca do Baliò Porto Espinho Segovia Rascafria La Cabrera El Molar Guadalajara

Albergaria a Velha Mangualde Viseu Guarda Ciudad Rodrigo Ávila San Lorenzo de el Escorial A2 A3 MADRID Chinchon

Aveiro Agueda Canas de Senhorim Manteigas Béjar Gredos NV Toledo

Curia Luso Oliveira do Hospital El Barco de Ávila

Figueira da Foz Coimbra Alpedrinha Plasencia Jarandilla de la Vera Talavera de la Reina Oropesa E

Nazaré Leiria Fátima P Navalmoral de la Mata Alarcón

Alcobaça Tomar Abrantes N30 Cáceres Guadalupe N301

Caldas da Rainha Santarém Portalegre Manzanares

Obidos Praia de Santa Cruz Torres Vedras Ericeira Estremoz Elvas NV Mérida Almagro Valdepeñas

Sintra LISBOA N4 E4 Badajoz Santa Cruz de Mudela

Azeitão Évora Zafra Almuradiel

Sesimbra Setúbal Alcácer do Sal N630 La Carolina

Santiago do Cacém N259 N21 Bailén Ubeda

Sines N262 E52 Beja N260-E52 Serpa Córdoba Cazorla

Santa Clara a Velha N264 N2 Jaén N342

São Brás de Alportel N431 N449 Carmona Granada

Praia da Salema N125 Huelva Sevilla N342

Portimão Albufeira Faro Tavira Monte Gordo Mazagón Antequera N221 Almi

Segres Lagos Praia da Rocha Quarteira Vilamoura Vale do Lobo Vila Real de San Antonio Jerez de la Frontera Ronda Málaga N340 Salobreña El Ejido Motril

Golfo de Cadiz Puerto de Santa Maria Arcos de la Frontera Ojén Mijas Nerja San Pedro de Alcántara Marbella Estepona N340 Torremolinos Benalmádena Fuengirola

1 Colares Cádiz N340 Gibraltar Algeciras
2 Cascais Tarifa
3 Estoril
4 Carcavelos
5 Costa da Caparica

F

Hendaría
Irun
San Sebastián
Lecumberri
Pamplona
415
Viella
Arties
Soldeu
Jaca
Bielsa
Andorra la Vella
Les Escaldes
Sabiñánigo
Sant Julià
de Lòria
Olite
Sos del Rey Católico
Huesca
rra
N152
A7
Tudela
Balaguer
C1313
FOR ENLARGED AREA
SEE INSET
Zaragoza
A2
Lleida
A2
A7
latayud
A7
Reus
Coma-ruga
Nuévalos
N330
Alcañiz
Tarragona
Salou
Tortosa
MEDITERRANEAN   SEA
Albarracin
Teruel
N234
Alcanar
Vinaroz
Benicarlo
Peñiscola
Mahón
uenca
Pollensa
Formentor
Benicasim
Castellón de la Plana
Cala Ratjada
Burriana
Puzol
Andraitx
Palma
Paguera
Montilla del Palancar
Magaluf
Valencia
ISLANDS
Albacete
Cullera
Gandía
San Antonio
A7
Denia
Javea
BALEARIC
Calpe
N301
Benidorm
Villajoyosa
Elche
N340
Alicante
A7
N340
Murcia
N301
Puerto
Lumbreras
Cartagena
N340
Mojácar
ria

For key to country
identification - see
"About the gazetteer"

Inset (F)

Puigcerdá
La Seu d'Urgell
La Jonquera
Ribes de Freser
Portbou
Llançà
Figueres
Cadaqués
Olot
Roses
N152
L'Escala
Girona
L'Estartit
Cardona
Vic
A7
Riudellots
de la Selva
Begur
Palafrugell
Santa Cristina d'Aro
Palamós
La Platja d'Aro
S'Agaró
Sant Feliu de Guíxols
Tossa de Mar
Igualada
Lloret de Mar
Blanes
Malgrat de Mar
Pineda de Mar
Calella de la Costa
Sant Pol de Mar
Arenys de Mar
Caldes d'Estrac
Vilafranca
del Penedès
Mataró
Premià de Mar
Barcelona
Calafell
Castelldefels
Sitges
Vilanova i la Geltrú
MEDITERRANEAN   SEA

HOW TO GET THERE

You can ship your vehicle direct to Spain on the Plymouth to *Santander* car ferry (taking about 24 hours)
Using the Channel ports, approach Spain through *France*; pass either end of the Pyrenean mountains: *For central and southern Spain* take the Biarritz to San Sebastian–Donostia road at the western end; *For the Costa Brava, and beyond* take the Perpignan to Barcelona road, or motorway, at the eastern end of the mountains. *For Andorra* from France via the Pas de la Casa (6851ft) then over the Envalira Pass (7897ft). Between November and April the roads may sometimes be closed. From Spain, the approach via La Seu d'Urgell is always open. Weather information on the Envalira Pass is available on ✆21166 or 21055. Wheel chains must be used on the Pass whenever conditions require them.

Distance

from Calais to Madrid is about 1,900km (990 miles), usually requiring two or three overnight stops.

Car sleeper trains

Boulogne, Calais or Paris to *Narbonne*
Boulogne or Paris to *Biarritz*
Paris to *Madrid*

MONEYMATTERS

You may take in unlimited amounts of Spanish and foreign currency, but you must declare on arrival amounts over *Ptas*100,000 (Spanish) and *Ptas*500,000 (foreign currency).
No more than *Ptas*100,000 (Spanish) and *Ptas*500,000 (foreign currency) may be taken out of the country.

Banking hours

In summer: Monday–Friday 08.30–13.00hrs, Saturday 08.30–12.30hrs (times may vary)

There are also exchange offices at travel agents: open Monday–Friday 09.00–13.00hrs, and 16.00–19.00hrs; Saturday 09.00–13.00hrs.

Postcheques

may be cashed up to *Ptas*25,000 per cheque in multiples of *Ptas*1,000. Go to a counter which displays the words **Caja Postal de Ahorros** or **Reintegros**.

MOTORING INFORMATION AND GENERAL INFORMATION

The information given here is specific to Spain. It **must** be read in conjunction with the European ABC at the front of the book, which covers those regulations which are common to many countries.

AA Port agent*

Santander Viajes Ecuador SA, Calle Lealtad 21 ✆(942) 215708, located on the *town plan of Santander* within the gazetteer.

Accidents*

There are no firm rules of procedure after an accident. See *Warning triangles* below.
    There is an assistance service for victims of traffic accidents which is run by the Central Traffic Department. The service operates day and night on every main road in Spain.
    There is an SOS telephone network on these roads; motorists in need of help should ask for *auxillio en carretera* (road assistance). The special ambulances used are in radio contact with the hospitals participating in the scheme.

Bail Bond

An accident in Spain can have very serious consequences, including the impounding of the car, and property, and the detention of the driver, pending bail. A Bail Bond can often facilitate release of person and property, and you are advised to obtain one of these from your insurer, for a nominal premium, together with your Green Card. A Bail Bond is a written guarantee that a cash deposit of usually up to £1,500 will be paid to the Spanish Court as surety for bail, and as security for any fine which may be imposed, although in such an event you have to reimburse any amount paid on your behalf. In very serious cases, the Court will not allow bail, and it has been known for a minor Spanish court to refuse Bail Bonds, and to insist on cash being paid by the driver. Nevertheless, motorists are strongly advised to obtain a Bail Bond, and to ensure that documentary evidence of this (in Spanish) is attached to the Green Card.

*Additional information will be found in the European ABC at the front of the book.

Breakdown*

If you car breaks down, try to move it to the verge of the road so that it obstructs the traffic flow as little as possible, and place a warning triangle 30 metres behind the vehicle to warn following traffic. A 24-hour breakdown service is run by the Spanish Motoring Club (RACE). To obtain assistance in the Madrid area or elsewhere in Spain, call the *Real Automovil Club de España* (RACE) national breakdown centre in Madrid, ☎(91) 5933333, which provides an English-speaking service. In Andorra, the Automobile Club d'Andorra will give assistance, but motorists are asked to go to the garage and personally accompany the mechanic to the ear. See also *Warning triangle* below.

British Embassy/Consulates

The British Embassy, located on the town plan of Madrid within the gazetteer, is at Madrid 4, Calle de Fernando el Santo 16 ☎(91) 4190200, but the Embassy has no consular section. However, there is a Consulate-General in Madrid at Centro Colón, Marqués de la Ensenada 16-2° ☎(91) 5325217. There are British Consulates in Alicante, Barcelona, Bilbao, Malaga, Seville and Palma (Majorca); there are British Consulates with Honorary Consuls in Santander, Tarragona and Vigo. There is a British Vice-Consulate in Algericas and Ibiza, and a British Vice-Consulate with Honorary Consul in Menorca. The British Consul General at Barcelona also deals with Andorra.

Children in Cars

It is recommended that children do not travel in a vehicle as front-seat passengers. In Andorra, children under 10 years are not permitted as front-seat passengers.

Customs regulations*

A television set, radio, pocket calculator, tape recorder, video camera or video recorder may be temporarily imported, but only against a deposit of duty and a permit valid for three months issued by the Spanish Customs.

Dimensions and weight restrictions

Private **cars** and towed **trailers** and **caravans** are restricted to the following dimensions –

height, 4 metres; width, 2.50 metres; length, 12 metres. In Andorra the maximum height for vehicles going through tunnels is 3.5 metres.

The maximum permitted overall length of vehicle/trailer or caravan combinations is 18 metres.

Trailers with an unladen weight exceeding 750kg must have an independent braking system.

Driving licence*

The minimum age at which a visitor may use a temporarily imported motorcycle (over 75cc) or car is 18 years. An International Driving Permit (IDP) is compulsory for the holder of a red three-year Republic of Ireland or green UK driving licence, unless the licence is accompanied by an official Spanish translation stamped by a Spanish Consulate. The IDP is not compulsory for the holder of a pink EC type Republic of Ireland* or UK* driving licence but, as local difficulties may arise over its acceptance, an IDP is recommended.
*The respective licensing authorities cannot exchange a licence purely to facilitate continental travel.

Emergency messages to tourists*

Emergency messages to tourists are broadcast daily throughout the year by *Radio Nacional de España*. The messages are transmitted in Spanish, French and occasionally English and German on 513 metres medium wave at 5 minutes past the hour beginning at 05.05hrs and ending at 00.05hrs.

Garages

Garages are officially classified. *Blue signs* displayed outside garages indicate the classification *I* to *III* as well as the type of work that can be dealt with, by means of symbols. There must be set prices for common repair jobs, and these must be available to customers so that they may authorise repairs. They are also required by law to keep and produce complaint forms on request by a customer. If you are unable to obtain one, they are available from Tourist Information Offices, or write to the Delegado de Turismo in the capital of the province concerned, or to the Dirección General de Servicios, Sección de Inspección y

*Additional information will be found in the European ABC at the front of the book.

Reclamaciones enclosing all factual evidence. This should be done as soon as possible whilst still in Spain.

Lights*

Passing lights (dipped headlights) are compulsory on motorways and fast dual-carriageways even if they are well-lit. The use of full headlights in built-up areas is prohibited – use sidelights, or dipped headlights, depending on how well-lit the road is. Visiting motorists must equip their vehicle with a set of replacement bulbs. It is also compulsory for *motorcyclists* to use dipped headlights during the day.

Motoring club*

 The **Real Automovil Club de España** (RACE), has its headquarters at 28003 Madrid, Calle José Abascal 10 ☎(01) 4473200, located on the town plan of Madrid within the gazetteer. It is associated with local clubs in a number of provincial towns. Motoring club offices are normally open 09.00–14.00hrs Monday to Friday, and are closed on Sundays and Public holidays. Some, including Madrid, are closed on Saturdays.

The *Automobil Club d'Andorra* has its head office at Andorra la Vella, Carrer Barbot Camp 4 ☎(078) 20890.

Motorways

There are approximately 1,230 miles of motorway (*Autopista*) open, and more are projected.

Apart from a few stretches of motorway in the Madrid and Barcelona areas, tolls are charged on most of the motorways eg La Jonquera (French–Spanish border) to Valencia is *Ptas*4,070 for a car (with or without caravan).

The majority of toll motorways issue a travel ticket on entry, and the toll is paid on leaving the motorway. The travel ticket gives all relevant information about the toll charges, including the toll category of the vehicle. The ticket is handed in at the exit point and the toll paid. On some toll motorways, the toll collection is automatic; have the correct amount ready to throw into the collecting basket. If change is required, use the separate lane marked accordingly.

A leaflet entitled *Motorways in Spain and Portugal* is available to AA members.

Orange badge scheme for disabled drivers*

There is no national system of parking concessions in operation. However, many large cities and towns operate their own individual schemes, and it is understood that consideration is shown to badge holders from other countries.

Overtaking*

Both at night and during the day, drivers who are about to be overtaken must operate their right-hand indicator to show the driver following that their intention to overtake has been understood. Outside built-up areas, drivers about to overtake must sound their horn during the day and flash their lights at night. Stationary trams must not be overtaken whilst passengers are boarding or alighting.

Parking*

Parking is **forbidden** in the following places: within 5 metres (16½ft) of cross-roads or an intersection; near a level crossing; within 5 metres of the entrance to a public building; on a main road or one carrying fast-moving traffic; on or near tram lines; within 7 metres (23ft) of a tram or bus stop. You must not park on a two-way road if it is not wide enough for three vehicles. In one-way streets, vehicles are parked alongside buildings with even numbers on even dates and on the opposite side on odd dates; any alteration to this system is announced by signs or notices in the press. Drivers may stop their vehicles alongside another parked vehicle if there is no space free nearby and the flow of traffic is not obstructed, but only long enough to let passengers in or out or to load or unload goods.

A special parking zone has been established in the centre of Madrid, and motorists wishing to park in this zone may obtain tickets from tobacconists. The tickets must be displayed on the windscreen and cost *Ptas*25 for ½hr, *Ptas*50 for 1hr and *Ptas*75 for 1½hrs.

*Additional information will be found in the European ABC at the front of the book.

Petrol*

Credit cards The use of credit cards to obtain petrol is not widespread but some petrol stations will accept them.
Duty-free petrol In addition to the petrol in the vehicle tank, up to 10 litres, in a can, may be imported free of customs duty and tax.
Petrol (leaded) Gasolina Normal (92 octane) and Gasolina Super (97 octane) grades.
Petrol (unleaded) is sold in Spain as Gasoline Super (95 octane) grade.

Postal information

Mail Postcards Ptas45, letters up to 20gm Ptas45.
Post offices There are 1,550 post offices in Spain. Opening hours are from 08.00–14.00hrs, Monday to Saturday.

Priority*

Drivers on secondary roads must give way to vehicles in both directions when entering a main road.

Public holidays*

Official Public holidays in Spain for 1990 are given below. In addition, there are many local and regional holidays throughout mainland Spain.
January 1 (New Year's Day)
January 6† (Epiphany)
March 19 (Saint Joseph)
April 12 (Maunday Thursday)
April 13 (Good Friday)
May 1 (May Day)
May 24 (Ascension Day)
June 14 (Corpus Christi)
July 25 (St James the Apostle)
August 15 (Assumption)
October 12 (Day of our Lady of El Pilar)
November 1 (All Saint's Day)
December 8† (Immaculate Conception)
December 25 (Christmas Day)
†Saturday

Religious services*

The Intercontinental Church Society welcomes visitors from any denomination to English language services in the following centres:
Barcelona 08022 The Rev Robin Sewell, San Joan de la Salle 41, Horaci 38 ☎4178867;

Ibiza 07820 The Rev Joe Yates-Round, Aptdo 6, San Antonio Abad, Ibiza, Baleares ☎343383.

Roads, including holiday traffic

The surfaces of the main roads vary, but on the whole are good. The roads are winding in many places, and at times it is not advisable to exceed 30–35mph. Secondary roads are often rough, winding, and encumbered by slow, horse-drawn traffic.
Holiday traffic, particularly on the coast road to Barcelona and Tarragona and in the San Sebastián–Donostia area, cause congestion which may be severe at weekends.
In Andorra the three main roads are prefixed 'N' and numbered; side roads are prefixed 'V'.

Road signs*

All main roads are prefixed 'N'; six of those radiating from Madrid are numbered in Roman numerals. Secondary roads are prefixed 'C'.
In the Basque area, local versions of some placenames appear on signposts together with the national version used in current AA gazetteers and maps. Some local names differ considerably from the national spelling – eg San Sebastián = Donostia. In the Catalonia area, some local spellings are used exclusively on signposts, but most of these are recognisable against the national version – eg Gerona = Girona, Lérida = Lleida.

Shopping hours

Generally, shops are open Monday to Saturday, 09.00–14.00hrs and 15.00–20.00hrs, with a two-hour break for lunch; department stores may open at 10.00hrs and close at 20.00hrs.

Speed limits*

In built-up areas, all vehicles are limited to 60kph (37mph), except where signs indicate a lower limit. Outside built-up areas, cars are limited to 120kph (74mph) on motorways and *90kph (56mph) or **100kph (62mph) on other roads. Vehicles towing a caravan or trailer are limited to 80kph (49mph) on motorways and *70kph (43mph) or **80kph (49mph) on other roads.
In Andorra cars with or without caravans are limited to 40kph (25mph) in built-up areas; on

*Additional information will be found in the European ABC at the front of the book.

other roads 70kph (43mph). Some villages have a speed limit of 20kph (12mph).
*On ordinary roads.
**On roads with more than one lane in each direction, a special lane for slow-moving vehicles or wide lanes.

Spiked or studded tyres*

Spikes on tyres must be 10mm in diameter and not more than 2mm in length.

Telephone*

Insert coin **before** lifting the receiver. Do **not** press the button to the left of the dial or you may lose your money. When making calls to subscribers within Spain, precede the number with the relevant area code (shown in parentheses before the hotel/garage enquiry number in the gazetteer). Use Ptas5, 25 or 100 coins or local calls (Min 2 × Ptas5) and Ptas100 for national and international calls. The international telephone system connects all principal towns, but long delays on trunk calls are not unusual.
International callbox identification Any payphone with sign 'Telefono . . . Internacional' or 'Locutarios Telefonos'.
Telephone rates A call to the UK costs Ptas261 for the first 3 minutes and Ptas97 for each additional minute. The cost of local calls is determined by the distance (within the town limits) and the time taken. Hotels, restaurants etc., usually make an additional charge.
Telephone Codes

UK to Spain	010 34
Spain to UK	07†44
Spain to Republic of Ireland	07†353
Spain to the USA	07†1

†Wait for second dialling tone.

Traffic lights*

In some cases, the green light remains on with the amber light when changing from green to red. Two red lights, one above the other, mean '**no entry**'. Usually, lights on each side of crossroads operate independently, and must be obeyed independently. A policeman with a whistle may over-ride the traffic lights, and he must be obeyed.

Turning

Unless there is a 'turning permitted' sign, three-point turns and reversing into side streets are prohibited in towns.

Warning triangles*

In the event of accident or breakdown, the use of two warning triangles is compulsory for vehicles weighing more than 3,500kg (3tons, 8cwt, 100lbs) and passenger vehicles with more than nine seats (including the driver's). The triangles must be placed on the road in front of and behind the vehicle at a distance of 30 metres (33yds) and be visible from at least 100 metres (110yds). In Andorra, the use of one warning triangle in the event of accident or breakdown is compulsory.

Winter conditions*

Most roads across the Pyrenees are either closed or affected by winter weather, but the roads or motorways to Biarritz and Perpignan in France avoid the mountains. The main routes in Portugal are unaffected. Within the country, motoring is not severely restricted, although certain roads may be temporarily blocked, particularly in January and February. The most important roads likely to be affected are San Sebastián (Donostia)–Burgos–Madrid; Madrid–Granada; Zaragoza–Teruel, and Granada–Murcia, but these are swept immediately there is a snowfall. On the Villacastin–Madrid road, there is a tunnel under the Guadarrama Pass. Roads likely to be affected by heavy snowfall are:

Pass	Road
Pajares	León–Gijon
Reinosa	Santander–Palencia
Escudo	Santander–Burgos
Somosierra	Burgos–Madrid
Orduña	Bilbao (Bilbo)–Burgos
Barazar	Bilbao (Bilbo)–Vitoria (Gasteiz)
Piqueras	Logroño–Madrid
Navacerrada	Madrid–Le Granja

The Real Automóvil Club de España will give you up-to-date information about road conditions.

*Additional information will be found in the European ABC at the front of the book.

ANDORRA

Andorra, an independent Principality, is situated high in the Pyrenees between France and Spain, and jointly administered by the two co-princes (the president of France, the Bishop of La Seu d'Urgell) and the Andorrans. French and Spanish are both spoken, and the currency of either country is accepted. General regulations for France and Spain apply to Andorra unless specific details for Andorra are given under the appropriate headings.

Motoring club*

The *Automobil Club d'Andorra* has its head office at Andorra la Vella, Carrer Barbot Camp 4 ☎(078) 20890.

*Additional information will be found in the European ABC at the front of the book.

ACCOMMODATION

Spain has some of the most attractively furnished hotels in Europe – especially luxury hotels converted from former monasteries or palaces. Provincial hotels are pleasantly old-fashioned; usually, the plumbing and lavatories are just about adequate, and do not compare with those in modern hotels in coastal resorts. Hotels are officially classified, and the category exhibited outside each. Establishments are now permitted to charge for breakfast, whether taken or not.

While commendations or complaints about hotels are an important source of information to us, AA members may also like to know that Spanish hotels must keep official complaint forms. If these are unobtainable at the hotel, they are available from Tourist Information Offices.

Paradores are fully-appointed tourist hotels,

usually on the outskirts of towns or in the country. Some are newly built, but others are converted country houses, palaces or Moorish castles. They offer very good value for money. A stay must normally be limited to ten days. Bookings for Paradores should be addressed to: Madrid 1, Central de Reservas de los Paradores del Esta do Apartado de Correos 50043, ☎(91) 4359700 (if calling this number from the UK refer to your Telephone Dialling Codes booklet) or telex 46865. Alternatively, you may contact their London Office on ☎01-402 8182. (071-402 8182 from 6 May 1990).

The prices shown below are an average for each classification. Accommodation is likely to be more expensive in Madrid and some of the more popular tourist areas. At the time of going to press, *£1 Sterling = Ptas195.15* and *US$1 = Ptas117.56*, but you should check the rate of exchange before your departure.

AVERAGE PRICES

	Single Room	Double Room	Breakfast	Lunch/Dinner
★★★★★	*Ptas*6,650–23,440	*Ptas*16,209–25,094	*Ptas*1,158–1,290	*Ptas*3,656–3,773
★★★★	*Ptas*6,650–8,870	*Ptas*9,885–11,914	from *Ptas*803	*Ptas*3,492
★★★	*Ptas*4,560–5,600	*Ptas*6,855–8,305	*Ptas*570–615	*Ptas*2,062–2,125
★★	*Ptas*3,460–4,008	*Ptas*5,080–5,970	*Ptas*500–502	*Ptas*1,700–1,775
★	*Ptas*2,315–3,223	*Ptas*4,090–5,475	*Ptas*385–540	*Ptas*2,787–2,950

Abbreviations

av	avenida	ctra	carretera
c	calle	Gl	Generalisimo
Cdt	Commandant	pl	plaza
Cpt	Capitán	ps	paseo

AIGUA BLAVA
See BEGUR

ALARCÓN
Cuenca
★★**Parador del Marques de Villena** ☎(966)331350
🛏13 P Lift ℂ Lake
Credit Cards ① ② ③ ⑤

ALBACETE
Albacete
★★★**Parador Nacional de la Mancha** ☎(967)229450
🛏70 P Lift ℂ ℚ ⌣

ALBARRACIN
Teruel
★★★**Albarracin** Azgara ☎(974)710011 tx 62614
🛏36 P ℂ ⌣ Mountain
Credit Cards ① ② ③ ⑤

ALCANAR
Tarragona
★★**Biarritz** (n.rest) ☎(977)737025

15 Jun - 15 Sep
🛏24 P25 ℂ ℚ ⌣ Beach Sea
Credit Cards ② ⑤

ALCAÑIZ
Teruel
★★★**Parador Nacional de la Concordia** ☎(J74)830400
1 Feb - 16 Dec
🛏12 Lift ℂ Mountain
Credit Cards ① ② ③ ⑤
🍴 **Agullo** Rondas de Castelseras 4 ☎(974) 830777 Fia Lan

ALGECIRAS
Cádiz

★★★★**Reina Cristina** (THF) ps de las
Conferencias ☎(956)602622 tx 78057
⊷📶140 P250 Lift ℂ ℺ ⌂ Sea
Credit Cards ①②③④⑤

★★★*Alarde* Alfonso X1-4 ☎(956)660408 tx
78009
⊷📶70 ⌑ P12 Lift ℂ
Credit Cards ①②③⑤

Baltanas ctra Cádiz-Málaga 23 ☎(956) 660950
LR

❧ *Villalobos* ctra N340 ☎(956) 656550 All makes

ALICANTE
Alicante

★★★*Meliá Alicante* Playa de el Postiguet
☎(96)205000 tx 66131
rm545 ⌑ P Lift ℂ ⌂ Beach Sea
Credit Cards ①②③④⑤

★★★**Palas** Cervantes 5 ☎(96)5209211
Closed Nov
⊷📶49 ⌑ P1 Lift ℂ Sea
Credit Cards ①②③⑤

★★**Husa Gran Sol** Méndez Núñez 3 (n.rest)
☎(96)5203000
⊷📶150 Lift ℂ Sea
Credit Cards ①②③④⑤

Nuevo C/Thomas Aznar Domenech 7 ☎(96)
5283932 All makes

ALMAGRO
Ciudad Real

★★★*Parador Nacional* Ronda de San Francisco
☎(926)860100
⊷📶55 P40 Lift ℂ ⌂ Sea
Credit Cards ①②③④⑤

ALMERÍA
Almeria

★★★★**Gran** av Reina Regente 4 (n.rest)
☎(951)238011 tx 75343
⊷📶117 ⌑ P24 Lift ℂ ⌂ Sea
Credit Cards ①②③④⑤

★★★**Costasol** ps de Almeria 58 (n.rest)
☎(951)234011
⊷📶55 P50 Lift
Credit Cards ①②③④⑤

★★★**Perla** pl del Carmen 1 ☎(951)238877
⊷📶44 P4 ℂ
Credit Cards ②③⑤

Automecanica Almeriense Paraje los
Callejones,N340 Km 117.4 ☎(951) 237033 M/C **P**
For

ALMURADIEL
Ciudad Real

★★★*Podencos* ctra N1V-Km 232 ☎(926)339000
⊷📶64 ⌑ P150 ℂ ⌂ Mountain
Credit Cards ①③④

ALSASUA
Navarra

★★*Alaska* ctra Madrid-Irún Km 402
☎(948)562802
⊷📶30 ⌑ P50 ℂ ⌂ Mountain
Credit Cards ①②③

❧ *P Calaya Urrestarazu* ctra GI-Irún-Madrid
☎(948) 560233 Vol

ANTEQUERA
Málaga

★★**Parador Nacional** Parque M-Christina
☎(952)840901
⊷📶55 ⌑ P60 ℂ ⌂ Mountain
Credit Cards ①②③④⑤

ARANDA DE DUERO
Burgos

★★★*Bronces* ctra Madrid-Irún Km 161
☎(947)500850
⊷📶29 ⌑ P18 ℂ
Credit Cards ①②③④⑤

★★★*Montehermoso* ctra Madrid-Irún Km 163
☎(947)501550
rm54(⊷50) ⌑ P100 Lift ℂ Mountain
Credit Cards ①②③⑤

★★**Area Tudanca** N.I. Km. 153 ☎(947)506011
⊷📶20 ⌑ P100 Mountain
Credit Cards ①②③⑤

★★*Tres Condes* ☎(947)502400 tx 39451
:Rest closed Sun pm
⊷📶35 ⌑ P Lift ℂ ⌂ ⌂ ♮♮ ∪ Beach Sea
Mountain Lake
Credit Cards ②③

Electro-Sanz av Castilla 49 ☎(947) 501134 AR

ARCOS DE LA FRONTERA
Cádiz

★★★*Parador Nacional Casa del Corregidor* pl
d'España ☎(956)700500
⊷📶24 Lift ℂ Mountain
Credit Cards ①②③④⑤

ARENAS DE CABRALES
Asturias

★*Naranjo de Bulnes* ctra General ☎(985)845119
⊷📶38 A18rm Mountain

ARENYS DE MAR
Barcelona

★★★**Raymond** ps Xifré ☎(93)7921700
⊷📶33 ⌑ P Lift ℂ Sea

★★*Floris* Playa Cassá 78 ☎(93)7920384
Mar-Oct
⊷📶30 Lift ℂ Sea
Credit Cards ①②③⑤

★*Impala* Apartado 20 (n.rest) ☎(93)7921504
⊷📶52 P Sea

ARGOMANIZ
Alava

★★★*Parador Nacional de Argomaniz* Apartado
N601 ☎(945)282200
⊷📶48 P50 Lift ℂ Mountain
Credit Cards ①②③⑤

ARTIES
Lleida

★★★*Parador Turismo Don Gaspar de Portola*
☎(973)640801 tx 641001
⊷📶40 ⌑ P40 Lift ℂ Mountain
Credit Cards ①②③④⑤

ASTORGA
León

❧ *Meichor* ctra Madrid-Coruña 186 ☎(987)
615259 **P** For LR

ÁVILA
A'vila

★★★★**Palacio Valderrabanos** pl Catedral 9
☎(918)211023 tx 23539
⊷📶73 P Lift ℂ
Credit Cards ①②③⑤

★★★*Parador Nacional Raimundo de Borgona*
Marques de Canales de Chozas,16
☎(918)211340
⊷📶62 ⌑ P Lift

★★*Cuatro Postes* ctra Salamanca 23
☎(918)220000
⊷📶36 ⌑ P Lift ℂ
Credit Cards ①②③④⑤

AYAMONTE
Huelva

★★★*Parador Nacional Costá de la Luz*
☎(955)320700
Closed 15 Jan-Feb
⊷📶20 P ⌂
Credit Cards ①②⑤

BADAJOZ
Badajoz

★★★*Gran Zurbaran* ps Castelar ☎(924)223741
tx 28818

⊷📶215 ⌑ P100 Lift ℺ ⌂
Credit Cards ①②③④⑤

BAGUR
SeeBEGUR

BAILEN
Jaén

★★★*Don Lope de Sosa* ctra Madrid-Cádiz Km
295 ☎(953)670058 tx 28311
⊷📶27 P50 ℂ Mountain
Credit Cards ①②③④⑤

★★★*Parador Nacional* (1km S on N1)
☎(953)670100
⊷📶86 P90 ℂ ⌂
Credit Cards ①②③⑤

BAIONA
Pontevedra

★★★*Parador Nacional Conde de Gondomar*
☎(986)355000 tx 83424
⊷📶128 ⌑ P300 ℂ ⌂ Beach Sea Mountain
Credit Cards ①②③⑤

BALAGUER
Llerida

★★★*Parador Colaborador Conde Jaime de
Urgel* c Urgel 2 ☎(973)445604
⊷📶60 ⌑ P Lift ℂ ⌂

BALEARES, ISLAS DE

IBIZA

SAN ANTONIO

★★★*Tanit* Cala Gracio ☎(971)341300 tx 69221
Apr-Oct
⊷📶386 P Lift ℂ ⌂ Sea

MALLORCA (MAJORCA)

CALA RATJADA

★★★**Son Moli** c Triton 25 ☎(971)563100
Apr-Oct
⊷📶118 Lift ℂ ⌂ Sea Mountain
Credit Cards ③⑤

FORMENTOR

★★★★★*Formentor* ☎(971)531300 tx 68523
12 Mar-Oct
⊷📶127 P100 Lift ℂ ℺ ⌂ ∪ Beach Sea Mountain
Credit Cards ①②③⑤

MAGALUF

★★★★*Magaluf Playa Sol* ☎(971)680700 tx
69175
⊷📶317 P40 Lift ℂ ℺ ⌂ Sea
Credit Cards ①②③④⑤

PAGUERA

★★★★**Villamil** (THF) ☎(971)686050 tx 68841
⊷📶125 P17 Lift ℂ ℺ ⌂ Sea Mountain
Credit Cards ①②③④⑤

PALMA DE MALLORCA

★★★★★**Son Vida Sheraton** ☎(971)790000 tx
69300
⊷📶165 P60 Lift ℂ ℺ ⌂ ⌂ ♮♮ Sea Mountain
Credit Cards ①②③④⑤

★★★★*Victoria-Sol* av J-Miró 21 ☎(971)234342
tx 68558
⊷📶167 P20 Lift ℂ ⌂ Sea
Credit Cards ①②③⑤

★★★★*Maricel* C'as Catala Beach ☎(971)402712
⊷📶55 A8rm P20 Lift ℂ ⌂ Sea Mountain
Credit Cards ①②③④⑤

★★★★*Meliá Mallorca* c de Monseñor Palmer 2
☎(971)205000 tx 68538
⊷📶240 P Lift ⌂ Sea

★★★*Nixe-Palace* av J-Miró 269 ☎(971)403811 tx
68569
⊷📶130 ⌑ P35 Lift ℂ ⌂ Beach Sea Mountain
Credit Cards ①②③④⑤

★★★*El Paso* Alvaro de Bazán 3 ☎(971)232740
tx 68652

:Rest closed wknds 15 Jul-15 Aug
rm210 A45rm P8 Lift ℂ ⊑ ⊐
Credit Cards ① ③ ⑤

T Minaco Gran via Asima 11 ☎(971) 200111
Cit LR

Taller Grand Prix Tenient Lizasoain ☎(971)
281666 All Makes

At PLAYA DE PALMA

★★**Oasis** B-Riutort 25 ☎(971)260150 tx 69103
23 Dec-11 Nov
♨110 ☎ P5 Lift ℂ ⊐ Sea
Credit Cards ① ② ③ ④ ⑤

At PLAYA DE PALMA NOVA(16km SW)

★★★**Hawaii** ☎(971)681150 tx 68670
May-Oct
♨230 Lift ℂ ⊐ Sea

POLLENSA

At CALA SAN VINCENTE

★★★★**Molins** ☎(971)530200
Apr-Nov
♨100 P22 Lift ℂ ℀ ⊐ Sea
Credit Cards ① ② ③

At PUERTO DE POLLENSA(6km NE)

★★★**Miramar** ps de Anglada Camarasa 39
☎(974)531400
Apr-30 Oct
♨69 Lift ℂ Sea
Credit Cards ① ② ③ ⑤

SON SERVERA

At COSTA DE LOS PINOS(7.5km NE)

★★★★**Eurotel Golf Punta Rotja DPn**
☎(971)567600 tx 68666
Apr-Oct
♨212 P100 Lift ℂ ℀ ⊐ ♨♨ Beach Sea
Credit Cards ① ② ③ ⑤

MENORCA (MINORCA)

MAHÓN

At VILLACARLOS(3km W)

★★★★**Agamenon** Fontanillas ☎(971)362150
May-Nov
rm75(♨51) ☎ P40 Lift ℂ ⊐ Sea
Credit Cards ① ② ③ ④ ⑤

BARAJAS
See **MADRID**

BARCELONA
Barcelona

See plan pages 352 and 353
Barcelona, capital of Catalonia
and of the province of Barcelona,
stretches from the Mediterranean
to the foot of the mountain of
Tibidabo, across a great plain
dotted with hills, such as Taber,
on which the magnificent
cathedral stands. The city is
flanked to the north by the river
Besos and to the south by the
Llobregat.
Spain's second city rivals Madrid
in size, sophistication and sheer
entertainment value; the Picasso
Museum houses one of Europe's
finest collections and no visit
would be complete without a
stroll along the wide traffic-free
Ramblas where bird and flower
markets alternate with
restaurants and shops.

EATING OUT Simple
straightforward ingredients fresh
from the sea and the farm are the
mainstay of Catalan cuisine, with
the emphasis on fish and
shellfish, especially sole, sea bass,
red mullet, squid, prawns and
lobster. One of the regional
specialities is *zaizuela*, a mixture
of seafood in a wine sauce.
Quo Vadis, just off the *Ramblas*,
enjoys an excellent reputation
with locals and visitors, as does
Can Culleretes, in Quitana, one of
Barcelona's most atmospheric
restaurants. Another established
favourite is *Sete Portes*, in Passeig
Isabel II, near the waterfront,
while in the inexpensive
category, *Agut*, in Gignas, has
been popular since its opening in
the mid 1920s.

BARCELONA

★★★★★**Avenida Palace** av Gran via des les
Corts,Catalones 605-607 ☎(93)3019600 tx 54734
♨229 Lift ℂ
Credit Cards ① ② ③ ④ ⑤

★★★★★**Ritz** av Gran via de les Corts,Catalones
668 ☎(93)3185200 tx 52739
♨161 ☎ P10 Lift ℂ
Credit Cards ① ② ③ ④ ⑤

★★★★**Condado** Aribau 201 ☎(93)2002311 tx
54546
:Rest closed Sat & Sun
♨88 Lift
Credit Cards ① ② ③ ④ ⑤

★★★★**Diplomatic** (GT) carrer de Pau Claris
☎(93)3173100 tx 54701
♨215 ☎ P80 Lift ℂ ⊐
Credit Cards ① ② ③ ④ ⑤

★★★★**Majestic** (BW) ps de Gracia 70
☎(93)2154512 tx 52211
rm355 P Lift ℂ ⊐

★★★★**Presidente** av Diagonal 570
☎(93)2002111 tx 52180
♨161 P10 Lift ℂ ⊐
Credit Cards ① ② ③ ④ ⑤

★★★★**Princesa Sofia** pl del Papa Pius X11
☎(93)3307111 tx 51032
♨505 ☎ P400 ℂ ⊟ ⊐
Credit Cards ① ② ③ ④ ⑤

★★★★**Regente** Rambla de Cataluña 76
☎(93)2152570 tx 51939
♨78 Lift ℂ ⊐
Credit Cards ① ② ③ ⑤

★★★**Arenas** Capitan Arenas 20 (n.rest)
☎(93)2040300 tx 54990
♨59 ☎ P6 Lift ℂ
Credit Cards ① ② ③ ⑤

★★★**Astoria** (BW) c de Paris 203 (n.rest)
☎(93)2098311 tx 97429
♨114 Lift ℂ
Credit Cards ① ② ③ ④ ⑤

★★★**Calderón** (BW) Rambla de Cataluña 26
☎(93)3010000 tx 51549
♨244 P80 Lift ℂ ⊐
Credit Cards ① ② ③ ④ ⑤

★★★**Cristal** Diputación 257 ☎(93)3016600 tx
54560
♨148 ☎ P40 Lift ℂ Mountain
Credit Cards ① ② ③ ⑤

★★★**Dante** c Mallorca 181 ☎(93)3232254 tx
52588
♨81 ☎ P25 Lift ℂ
Credit Cards ① ② ③ ④ ⑤

★★★**Derby** (BW) c de Loreto 21 (n.rest)
☎(93)3223215 tx 97429
♨116 A40rm ☎ P200 Lift ℂ
Credit Cards ① ② ③ ④ ⑤

★★★**Expo** (GT) c Mallorca 1 ☎(93)3251212 tx
54147
♨432 P Lift ⊐ Lake
Credit Cards ① ② ③ ④ ⑤

★★★**Gaudi** c Nou de la Rambla 12
☎(93)3179032 tx 98974
♨71 Lift ℂ
Credit Cards ① ② ③ ④ ⑤

★★★**Regina** (BW) c Vergara 4 ☎(93)3013232 tx
59380
♨102 Lift
Credit Cards ① ② ③ ④ ⑤

★★★**Wilson** av Diagonal 568 ☎(93)2092511 tx
52180
♨52 ☎ Lift ℂ
Credit Cards ② ③ ⑤

★★**Park** av Marques Argentera II ☎(93)3196000
♨95 ☎ P Lift
Credit Cards ② ③ ⑤

Auto-Layetana c Infanta Carlota 2 ☎(93)
3216150 For

British Motors Florida Blanca 133 ☎(93)
4230882 RR

F Roca Duplitación 43 ☎(93) 3251550 AR DJ
RR

Romagosa C Bolivia 243-245 ☎(93) 3072710
LR

Ryvesa Aragon 179 ☎(93) 2531600 Mer

BARCO DE ÁVILA, EL
Ávila

★★★**Manila** ctra de Plasencia Km 69
☎(918)340845
♨50 ☎ P85 Lift ℂ Mountain
Credit Cards ② ③ ⑤

BEGUR
Girona

★★★**Bagur** De Comay Ros 8 ☎(972)622207
Feb-15 Dec
♨35 A5rm P Lift ℂ Mountain
Credit Card ③

★★**Sa Riera** Playa de Sa Riera ☎(972)623000 tx
57077
15 Mar - 15 Oct
♨41 P55 Lift ℂ ⊐ Sea Mountain
Credit Card ③

At AIGUA BLAVA(3.5km SE)

★★★**Aigua-Blava** Playa de Fornells
☎(72)622058 tx 56000
25 Mar - 24 Oct
rm90(♨83) ☎ P126 ℂ ℀ ⊐ Sea
Credit Cards ① ② ③

★★★**Parador Nacional Costa Brava**
☎(972)622162 tx 56275
♨87 A10rm P50 Lift ℂ ⊐ Beach Sea
Credit Cards ① ② ③ ④ ⑤

BÉJAR
Salamanca

★★★**Colón** c Colón 42 ☎(923)400650 tx 26809
♨54 P Lift ℂ Mountain
Credit Cards ① ② ③ ⑤

BENALMÁDENA
Málaga

★★★★**Riviera** ctra Cádiz-Málaga Km 288
☎(952)441240 tx 77041
♨189 P50 Lift ℂ ℀ ⊐ Sea
Credit Cards ① ② ③ ⑤

BARCELONA

1	★★★★★	Avenida Palace
2	★★★★★	Ritz
4	★★★★	Condado
6	★★★★	Diplomatic
7	★★★★	Majestic
8	★★★★	Presidente
9	★★★★	Princesa Sofia
10	★★★★	Regente
11	★★★	Arenas
12	★★★	Astoria
13	★★★	Calderón
14	★★★	Cristal
15	★★★	Dante
16	★★★	Derby
17	★★★	Expo
19	★★★	Regina
20	★★★	Wilson
21	★★	Park

★★★**Siroco** av A-Machado 28 ☎(952)443040 tx 77135
➡ ♠261 P30 Lift ℂ ९ ⌑ Sea
Credit Cards ① ② ③ ④ ⑤

★**Puerto Benalmádena** ctra de Cádiz Km 229 ☎(952)441640 tx 77330
➡ ♠78 P14 Lift ℂ ⌑ Sea

BENAVENTE
Zamora

★★★**Parador Nacional** ☎(988)630304
➡ ♠30 P20
Credit Cards ② ③ ④ ⑤

BENICARLO
Castellón

★★★**Parador Costa del Azahar** av del Papa Luna 5 ☎(964)470100
➡ ♠108 ♠ P ℂ ९ ⌑ Beach Sea
Credit Cards ① ② ③ ⑤

★★**Sol** av Magallanes 90 ☎(954)471349
➡ ♠22 ♠ P50 Lift Sea Mountain

BENICASIM
Castellón

★★★★**Azor** ps Maritimo ☎(964)300350 tx 65626
Mar-Oct
➡ ♠88 P50 Lift ℂ ९ ⌑ Sea
Credit Cards ① ③ ④ ⑤

★★★**Voramar** ps Coloma 1 ☎(964)300150
25 Mar 13 Oct
➡ ♠55 ♠ P16 Lift ℂ ९ Beach Sea Mountain
Credit Cards ① ③

★★**Bonaire** ps Maritimo ☎(964)300800 tx 65503
Apr-Oct
➡ ♠88 P50 ℂ ९ ⌑ Sea Mountain
Credit Cards ① ③ ④ ⑤

BENIDORM
Alicante

★★★★**Gran Delfin** Playa de Poniente ☎(96)853400
22 Mar-Sep
➡ ♠99 P37 Lift ℂ ९ ⌑ Sea
Credit Cards ① ② ③ ⑤

★★**Presidente** av Filipinas ☎(96)853950
➡ ♠228 Lift ℂ ९ ⌑ Mountain
Credit Cards ② ③ ⑤

🛥 *Autonautica* ctra Alicante-Valencia ☎(96) 5853562 For

BIELSA
Huesca

At **VALLE DE PINETA**(14km NW)

★★★**Parador Nacional Monte Perdido** ☎(974)501011
➡ ♠16 P Lift ℂ Mountain

BARCELONA

Scale

SPAIN

BILBAO (BILBO)
Vizcaya

★★★★★**Villa de Bilbao** Gran Via 87
☎(94)4416000 tx 32364
⊷📞142 Lift ℂ

★★★★**Aránzazu** Rodriguez Arias 66
☎(94)4413100 tx 32164
⊷📞172 ♨ P Lift ℂ
Credit Cards ① ② ③ ⑤

★★★★**Avenida** av Zumalacarregui 40
☎(94)41243000 tx 31040
rm116 P Mountain
Credit Cards ① ② ③ ⑤

★★★★**Carlton** pl F-Moyua 2 ☎(94)4162200 tx
32233
⊷📞144 Lift ℂ
Credit Cards ① ② ③ ⑤

★★★★**Ercilla** (GT) Ercilla 37 ☎(94)4438800 tx
32449
⊷📞346 ♨ P80 Lift ℂ
Credit Cards ① ② ③ ④ ⑤

BLANES
Girona

★★★★**Park** ☎(972)330250 tx 54136
May-Oct
⊷📞131 P200 Lift ℂ ℃ ➨ Beach Sea
Credit Cards ① ② ③ ⑤

★★**Horitzo** ps Maritimo 11 ☎(972)330400
20 Mar-15 Oct
⊷📞122 Lift ℂ
Credit Card ③

★★**San Antonio** ps del Mar 63 (n.rest)
☎(972)331150
May-Oct
⊷📞156 ♨ P20 Lift ℂ Sea Mountain

★★**San Francisco** ps del Mar 72 ☎(972)330477
Apr-Oct
⊷📞32 ♨ P32 Lift ℂ Sea Mountain

BURGOS
Burgos

★★★★**Almiranté Bonifaz** Vitoria 22-24 (n.rest)
☎(947)206943 tx 39430
7 Jan - 24 Dec
⊷📞79 ♨ P2 Lift ℂ
Credit Cards ① ② ③ ⑤

★★★★**Landa Palace** (Relais et Châteaux) ctra de
Madrid-Irún Km 236 (2km S on N1)
☎(947)206343 tx 39534
⊷📞42 ♨ P Lift ℂ ▱ ➨
Credit Cards ① ③

★★★**Asubio** Carmen 6 (n.rest) ☎(947)203445
⊷📞30 P10 Lift
Credit Cards ① ③

✎ **Barrios** c de Vitoria 109 ☎(947) 224900 Fia
Lan

✎ **Mecanico** San Agustin 5-7 ☎(947) 202364 P
Aud VW

✎ **Pedro** ctra Madrid-Irún Km247 ☎(947) 224528
P Peu Tal

BURRIANA
Castellón

★★★**Aloha** av Mediterraneo 75 (2.5km E)
☎(964)510104
Mar-Oct
rm30 A30rm P27 Lift ℂ ➨ Sea Mountain
Credit Cards ① ② ③

CABRERA, LA
Madrid

★★**Mavi** ctra de Madrid-Irún 58 ☎(91)8688000
⊷📞43 P30 ℂ Mountain
Credit Cards ① ③

CÁCERES
Cáceres

★★★**Alcántara** av Virgen de Guadalupe 14
☎(927)228900
⊷📞67 Lift ℂ
Credit Cards ① ② ③ ⑤

★★**Alvarez** Moret 20 ☎(927)246400
⊷📞37 P4 Lift ℂ
Credit Cards ② ③ ⑤

CADAQUES
Girona

★★★**Playa-Sol** (n.rest) ☎(972)258100
Closed 8 Jan-Feb
⊷📞50 ♨ P50 Lift ℂ ℃ ➨ Sea Mountain Lake
Credit Cards ① ② ③ ⑤

CÁDIZ
Cádiz

★★★**Atlantico** Parque Genovés 9 ☎(956)226905
tx 76316
rm173(⊷153) A73rm ♨ P80 Lift ℂ ➨ Sea
Credit Cards ① ② ③ ④ ⑤

✎ **Salna** Ronda del Puente s/n ☎(956) 253285
Ren

CALAFELL
Tarragona

★★★**Kursaal** av San J-de-Dios 119
☎(977)692300
Closed one week from 16 Oct
⊷📞39 ♨ P15 Lift ℂ Sea Lake
Credit Cards ① ② ③ ⑤

★★★**Miramar** Rambla Costa Dorada 1
☎(977)690700 tx 56547
22 Mar-29 Oct
⊷📞200 ♨ P30 Lift ℂ ➨ Sea Mountain
Credit Cards ① ② ③ ④ ⑤

CALAHORRA
Rioja

★★★**Parador Nacional Marco Fabio Quintiliano**
av Generalisimo ☎(941)130358
⊷📞61 P Lift ℂ
Credit Cards ① ② ③ ⑤

CALA RATJADA
See BALEARES, ISLAS DE under MALLORCA
(MAJORCA)

CALA SAN VINCENTE
See BALEARES, ISLAS DE under POLLENSA

CALATAYUD
Zaragoza

★★**Calatayud** (2km NE on N11 at Km 237)
☎(976)881323
⊷📞63 ♨ P16 ℂ
Credit Cards ② ③

CALDES D'ESTRAC
Barcelona

★★★★**Colón** ps 16 ☎(93)7910400
10 Apr-Oct
⊷📞82 ♨ P Lift ℂ ➨ Sea Mountain

CALELLA DE LA COSTA
Barcelona

★★★★**Las Vegas Pn** ctra de Francia
☎(93)7690850 tx 98407
May - Nov
⊷📞95 P25 Lift ℂ ➨ Sea Mountain
Credit Cards ① ② ③ ⑤

★★★★**Mont-Rosa** ps de las Rocas s/n
☎(93)7690508
Mid May - End Oct
⊷📞120 P15 Lift ℂ ➨ Sea

★★**Fragata** ps de las Rocas (n.rest)
☎(93)7692112
15 May - 15 Oct
⊷📞73 Lift ℂ ℃
Credit Cards ① ② ③ ⑤

CALELLA DE PALAFRUGELL
See PALAFRUGELL

CALPE
Alicante

★★★**Paradero Ifach** Explanada del Puerto 50
(n.rest) ☎(96)5830300
Mar-Nov
⊷📞29 P100 ℂ ℃ Sea

★★**Venta la Chata** (4km N) ☎(96)5830308
:Rest closed 15 Nov-Dec
⊷📞17 ♨ P30 ℂ ℃ Sea Mountain
Credit Cards ① ② ③ ⑤

✎ **Autocrats** av Diputación ☎(96) 5832803 Toy

CAMBADOS
Pontevedra

★★★**Parador Nacional del Albariño** ps de
Cervantes ☎(986)542250
⊷📞63 P70 Lift ℂ ℃ Sea
Credit Cards ① ② ③ ④ ⑤

CARDONA
Barcelona

★★★**Parador Nacional Duques de Cardona**
☎(93)8691275
⊷📞61 P Lift Mountain
Credit Cards ① ② ③ ⑤

CARMONA
Sevilla

★★★★**Parador Nacional Alcázar Rey Don
Pedro** ☎(954)141010 tx 72992
⊷📞59 P100 Lift ℂ ℃
Credit Cards ① ② ③ ④ ⑤

CAROLINA, LA
Jaén

★★★**Perdiz** ctra N1V ☎(953)660300 tx 28315
⊷📞87 ♨ P ➨ Mountain
Credit Cards ① ② ③

CARTAGENA
Murcia

★★★**Cartagonova** Marcos Redondo 3 (n.rest)
☎(968)504200
⊷📞126 ♨ P100 Lift ℂ
Credit Cards ① ② ③ ⑤

CASTELLCIUTAT
See SEU D'URGELL, LA

CASTELLDEFELS
Barcelona

★★★**Neptuno** ps Garbi 74 ☎(93)6651450
⊷📞42 P Lift ℂ ℃ ➨

★★★**Rancho** ps de la Marina 212 ☎(93)6651900
tx 57638
⊷📞60 Lift ℂ ℃ ➨ Mountain
Credit Cards ③ ⑤

CASTELLÓN DE LA PLANA
Castellón

★★★**Mindoro** Moyano 4 ☎(64)222300 tx 65413
⊷📞114 ♨ P60 Lift ℂ
Credit Cards ① ② ③ ④ ⑤

✎ **Tagerbaf** Hños Vilafana 13 ☎(964) 216653 P
All makes

At GRAO DE CASTELLÓN(5km E)

★★★★**Golf** Playa del Pinar ☎(964)221950
Mar-Oct
⊷📞127 ♨ P Lift ℂ ℃ ➨ ♙♙ Beach Sea
Credit Cards ① ③ ⑤

CASTILLO DE SANTA CATALINA
See JAÉN

CAZORLA
Jaén

★★**Parador Nacional el Adelantado** (25km SE)
☎(953)721075
Closed 25 Jan-Mar
⊷📞33 P ℂ Mountain
Credit Cards ① ② ③ ⑤

CERVERA DE PISUERGA
Palencia

★★★**Parador Nacional de Fuentes Carrionas**
☎(988)870075
25 Dec-2 Nov
⊷📞80 ♨ P Lift ℂ Mountain Lake

CESTONA
Guipúzcoa

★★★★**Arocena** ☎(943)867040

354

SPAIN

:Rest closed Mon,Tue & Wed
★↟109 ☎ P60 Lift ℂ ℀ ⌫ Mountain
Credit Cards ① ② ③ ⑤

CHINCHÓN
Madrid

★★★**Parador Nacional** av Generalísimo 1
☎(91)8940836 tx 49398
★↟38 ☎ P48 ℂ ⌫
Credit Cards ① ② ③ ④ ⑤

CIUDAD RODRIGO
Salamanca

★★★**Parador Nacional Enrique II** pl del Castillo
1 ☎(923)460150
★↟27 P30 Lift ℂ
Credit Cards ① ② ④ ⑤

🍴 *Vicente* crta de Salamanca, km 320 ☎(923)
461426 All makes

COMA-RUGA
Tarragona

★★★**Gran Europa** av Palfurina ☎(977)680411 tx
56681
Apr-Nov
★↟160 ☎ P70 Lift ℂ ⌫ Beach Sea
Credit Cards ① ③ ⑤

COMILLAS
Cantabria

★★★**Casal del Castro** San Jeronimo
☎(942)720036
Apr-Oct
★↟45 P60 Lift ℂ ℀ Sea Mountain
Credit Card ②

CÓRDOBA
Córdoba

★★★★**Gran Capitan** av America 3-5
☎(957)470250 tx 76662
★↟96 ☎ P40 Lift ℂ
Credit Cards ① ② ③ ④

★★★★**Meliá Córdoba** Jàrdines de la Victoria
☎(957)298066 tx 76591
rm105 P Lift ℂ ⌫
Credit Cards ① ② ③ ④ ⑤

★★★★**Parador Nacional de la Arruzafa** av de la
Arruzafa ☎(957)275900 tx 76695
★↟94 ℂ ℀ ⌫ Mountain
Credit Cards ① ② ③ ⑤

★★**Marisa** Cardenal Herrero 6 (n.rest)
☎(957)2173142
★↟28 P15 ℂ
Credit Cards ① ② ③ ⑤

★*Brillante* av del Brillante 97 ☎(957)275800
rm28(★↟25) ℂ
Credit Cards ① ③

CORUÑA, LA (CORUÑA A)
La Coruña

★★★★**Finisterre** ps del Parrote 2
☎(981)2505400 tx 84086
★↟127 P200 Lift ℂ ℀ ⌫ Beach Sea
Credit Cards ① ② ③ ④ ⑤

COSTA DE LOS PINOS
See BALEARES, ISLAS DE under SON
SERVERA

COVARRUBIAS
Burgos

★★★**Arlanza** pl de Doña Urraca ☎(947)403025
15 Mar - 15 Dec
★↟40 Lift ℂ Mountain
Credit Cards ① ② ③ ④ ⑤

CUENCA
Cuenca

★★★**Cueva del Fraile** (BW) ctra Cuenca a
Buenache ☎(966)211571
Mar-10 Jan
★↟54 P100 ℂ ⌫ Mountain
Credit Cards ① ② ③ ⑤

★★★**Torremangana** San Ignacio de Loyola 9
☎(966)223351 tx 23400

★↟117 ☎ P75 Lift ℂ
Credit Cards ① ② ③ ⑤

CULLERA
Valencia

★★★*Sicania* ctra el Faro,Playa del Raco
☎(96)1520143 tx 64774
★↟117 ☎ P Lift ℂ Beach Sea

DENIA
Alicante

At PLAYA DE LES MARINAS(1km N)
★★*Los Angeles* ☎(96)5780458
Apr-Oct
★↟55 P50 ℂ ℀ Sea Mountain
Credit Cards ① ② ③ ⑤

EJIDO, EL
Almeria

★★★★**Golf Almerimar** Almerimar ☎(951)480950
tx 78933
★↟149 P Lift ℂ ℀ ⌫ ♣♣ ♌ Sea
Credit Cards ① ② ③ ④ ⑤

EL
Each name preceded by 'El' is listed under the
name that follows it.

ELCHE
Alicante

★★★*Huerto del Cura* F-G-Sanchíz 14
☎(965)458040 tx 66814
★↟70 ☎ P35 ℂ ℀ ⌫
Credit Cards ① ② ③ ⑤

ESCALA, L'
Girona

★★★*Barca* E-Serra 25 ☎(972)770162
Jun-Sep
★↟26 ℂ Sea

ESCORIAL, EL
See SAN LORENZO DE EL ESCORIAL

ESTARTIT, L'
Girona

★★*Amer* ☎(972)757212
May-Oct
★↟54 A11rm ℂ ⌫

★*Vila* Santa Ana 34 ☎(972)758113
Jun-Sep
★↟58 A20rm ℂ

ESTEPONA
Málaga

★★★★*Atalaya Park* (SRS) ☎(952)781300 tx
77210
★↟448 P1 Lift ℂ ℀ ▱ ♣♣ Sea
Credit Cards ① ② ③ ④ ⑤

★*Buenavista* ps Maritimo ☎(952)800137
:Rest closed Sun pm
★↟38 ☎ Lift ℂ Sea
Credit Cards ① ③

FERROL
La Coruña

🍴 *Castelos* ctra a la Gándara 11/17 ☎(981)
313365 For

FIGUERES
Girona

★★★★*President* ctra Madrid-Francia
☎(972)501700
★↟77 ☎ P40 Lift ℂ
Credit Cards ① ② ③ ④ ⑤

★★★*Ampurdan* ctra Madrid-Francia
☎(972)500562 tx 57032
★↟42 ☎ P90 Lift ℂ Mountain
Credit Cards ① ② ③ ⑤

★★★*Durán* c Lasuaca 5 ☎(972)501250
★↟63 ☎ P30 Lift ℂ
Credit Cards ① ② ③ ⑤

★★*Muriscot* ☎(972)505151
★↟20 ☎ P40 Lift ℂ Mountain
Credit Cards ① ② ③

🍴 *Central* Carrer Nou s/n, Zona Rally Sud
☎(972) 500667 For

Victoria ctra de Rosas ☎(972) 500293 LR

FORMENTOR
See BALEARES, ISLAS DE under MALLORCA
(MAJORCA)

FORNELLS DE LA SELVA
See GIRONA (GERONA)

FUENGIROLA
Málaga

★★★★*Mare Nostrum* ctra de Cádiz
☎(952)471100 tx 27578
Jul-15 Oct
★↟242 ☎ P100 Lift ℀ ⌫ Sea
Credit Cards ① ② ③ ④

★★★★*Palmeras* ps Maritimo ☎(952)472700 tx
77202
★↟428 ☎ P Lift ℀ ⌫ Sea Mountain
Credit Card ②

★★★★*Piramides* ps Maritimo ☎(952)470600 tx
77315
★↟320 ☎ P50 Lift ℂ ⌫ Sea Mountain
Credit Cards ① ② ③ ④ ⑤

★★★*Florida* Playa Florida ☎(952)476100 tx
77791
★↟116 Lift ℂ ⌫ Beach Sea
Credit Cards ① ② ③ ⑤

FUENTE DÉ
Cantabria

★★*Parador Nacional del Rio Deva*
☎(942)730001
Closed Nov-15 Dec
★↟78 P ℂ Mountain

FUENTERRABIA (HONDARRIBIA)
Guipúzcoa

★★*Guadalupe* Punta de España (n.rest)
☎(943)641650
1 Jun - 30 Sep
★↟35 P22 ℂ ⌫ Lake
Credit Card ③

★★*Parador Nacional el Emperador* pl de Armas
del Castillo (n.rest) ☎(943)642140
★↟16 ℂ Sea
Credit Cards ① ② ③ ④ ⑤

At JAIZKÍBEL(8km SW)
★★★*Jaizkibel* ☎(943)641100
★↟13

GANDÍA
Valencia

★★*Ernesto* ctra de Valencia 40 ☎(96)2864011
★↟85 P Lift ℂ
Credit Cards ③ ④ ⑤

GERONA
See GIRONA

GIJÓN
Asturias

★★★★*Robledo* A-Truan 2 (n.rest) ☎(985)355940
★↟138 ℂ
Credit Cards ① ② ③ ⑤

★★*Parador Nacional Molino Viejo* Parque de
Isable la Catolica,19 ☎(985)370511
★↟40 P Lift ℂ
Credit Cards ① ② ③ ⑤

GIRONA (GERONA)
Girona

★★*Europa* J-Garreta 23 (n.rest) ☎(972)202750
★↟26 P Lift ℂ

At FORNELLS DE LA SELVA(5km S off N11)
★★★*Fornells Park* ctra Nacional 11 Km 711
☎(972)476716
★↟41 P150 Lift ℂ ⌫ Mountain
Credit Cards ① ② ③ ⑤

🍴 *Blanch* ctra N11 Km 710 ☎(972) 476028 Ope

GRANADA
Granada

Granada - capital of the Andalusian province of the same name - is situated at the foot of the mighty Sierra Nevada and is dominated by the magnificent pink-gold palace of the *Alhambra*, the most beautiful of Andalusia's Moorish monuments.
Also of interest are the nearby *Generalife*, one time summer palace of the emirs, the flamboyant Royal Chapel and the huge cathedral, commissioned in 1521 by Charles V.
The Plaza de Bib-Ramblas is a pleasant square, animated by outdoor cafés in the summer, while shoppers will find plenty of interest in the streets of Alcaiceria, especially handicrafts inspired by Granada's Moorish heritage.

EATING OUT There are several atmospheric restaurants serving regional and international cuisine in the area of the *Alhambra*, and also in the Alcaiceria, where the *Sevilla*, which has an excellent tapas bar also has an attractive restaurant.

GRANADA

★★★★**Alhambra Palace** Peña Partida 2
☎(958)221466 tx 78400
⊷145 P Lift ℂ Mountain
Credit Cards ① ② ③ ④ ⑤

★★★★**Brasilia** Recogidas 7 (n.rest)
☎(958)258450
⊷68 ☎ P Lift ℂ
Credit Cards ① ③ ④ ⑤

★★★★**Carmen** Acera del Darro 62
☎(958)258300 tx 78408
⊷205 P25 Lift ℂ
Credit Cards ① ② ③ ④ ⑤

★★★★**Meliá Granada** Aganivet 7 ☎(958)227400
tx 78429
rm221 ☎ P Lift ℂ

★★★**Guadalupe** av de los Alijares ☎(958)223423
tx 78755
⊷43 P Lift ℂ Mountain
Credit Cards ① ② ③ ⑤

★★★**Kenia** Molinos 65 (n.rest) ☎(958)227507
⊷19 ☎ P15 ℂ
Credit Cards ① ② ③ ⑤

★★★**Parador Nacional de San Francisco**
Alhambra ☎(958)221462
⊷32 P ℂ Mountain

★★**Inglaterra** Cetti Merien 4 (n.rest)
☎(958)221559
⊷45 A4rm ☎ P Lift ℂ ⊷⊷
Credit Cards ② ③ ⑤

★**América** Real Alhambra 53 ☎(958)227471
Mar-Oct
⊷14 ℂ ⊷ ◻ Mountain

◗◗ **Audisa** av Andalucia, Km 3 ☎(958) 280104
Aud VW

◗◗ **Autiberia** av Andalucia, Km 3 ☎(958) 205602
Ope

At **SIERRA NEVADA**(40km SE)

★★★★**Meliá Sierra Nevada** Prodollano-Sierra
Nevada ☎(958)480400 tx 78507
1 Dec - 15 May
rm221 ☎ P Lift ℂ ◻ Mountain
Credit Cards ① ② ③ ④ ⑤

★★★**Meliá Sol y Nieve** Pradollano Sierra Nevada
☎(958)480300 tx 78507
1 Dec - 15 May
rm180 ☎ P Lift ℂ Mountain
Credit Cards ① ② ③ ④ ⑤

★★★**Parador Nacional Sierra Nevada**
☎(958)480200
Closed Nov
⊷32 ☎ P ℂ ⊶ Mountain

GRAO DE CASTELLÓN
See **CASTELLÓN DE LA PLANA**

GREDOS
Avila

★★★**Parador Nacional de Gredos**
☎(918)348048
⊷77 ☎ P70 Lift ℂ ⊶ ∪ Mountain
Credit Cards ① ② ⑤

GUADALAJARA
Guadalajara

★★★**Pax** ctra Madrid-Barcelona Km57
☎(911)221800 tx 27521
⊷61 P100 Lift ℂ ⊶ ◻ Mountain
Credit Cards ① ② ③ ⑤

◗◗ **R Aguilera** Ingenieri Marino no. 44 ☎(911)
220029 All makes

GUADALUPE
Cáceres

Hospederiá del Real Monasterio pl J-Carlos 1
(Monastry where accomm. is provided by monks)
☎(927)367000
18 Feb - 31 Dec
⊷40 P30 Lift ℂ Mountain
Credit Cards ① ③

★★**Parador Nacional de Zurbarán** Marques de
la Romana 10 ☎(927)367075
⊷40 ☎ P Lift ℂ ⊶ ◻ Mountain
Credit Cards ① ② ③ ⑤

HUELVA
Huelva

★★★★**Luz Huelva** av Sundheim 26 (n.rest)
☎(955)25011 tx 75527
⊷105 ☎ P16 Lift ℂ ⊶ ⊶⊶
Credit Cards ① ② ③ ⑤

★★★**Tartessos** av M-A-Pinzon 13-15
☎(955)245611
⊷112 Lift ℂ
Credit Cards ① ② ③ ⑤

HUESCA
Huesca

★★★**Pedro I de Aragón** av del Parque 34
☎(974)220300 tx 58626
⊷120 ☎ P30 Lift ℂ ◻
Credit Cards ① ② ③ ⑤

◗◗ **Tumasa** ctra Zaragoza ☎(974) 243294 LR
Peu Tal

IBIZA
See **BALEARES, ISLAS DE**

IGUALADA
Barcelona

★★★**América** ctra N11 Km 553 ☎(93)8031000
Closed 25 Dec
⊷52 P40 Lift ◻ Mountain
Credit Cards ① ② ③ ⑤

IRÚN
Guipúzcoa

★★★**Alcázar** av Iparralde 11 ☎(943)620900
⊷48 P40 Lift ℂ
Credit Cards ① ② ③

★★**Lizaso** Marires de Guadalupe 5 (n.rest)
☎(943)611600
⊷20 ℂ

★**Paris** ps de Colón 94-96 ☎(943)616545
rm22(⊷14)

JACA
Huesca

★★★**Gran** ps del Gl-Franco 1 ☎(974)360900
Closed Nov
⊷170 P25 Lift ℂ ◻ Mountain
Credit Cards ① ② ③ ⑤

★★**Conde Aznar** Gl-Franco 3 ☎(974)361050
⊷23 ℂ
Credit Cards ① ② ③

JAÉN
Jaén

◗◗ **Lopez** Sta Tomás 2 ☎(953) 228501 Sko

At **CASTILLO DE SANTA CATALINA**(4km W)

★★★★**Parador Nacional** ☎(953)264411
⊷43 Lift ℂ ◻ Mountain
Credit Cards ① ② ③ ⑤

JAIZKÍBEL
See **FUENTERRABÍA (HONDARRIBIA)**

JÁVEA
Alicante

★★★**Parador Nactional Costa Blanca** Playa del
Arenal No 2 ☎(96)5790200 tx 66914
⊷65 ☎ P57 Lift ℂ ◻ Sea
Credit Cards ① ② ③ ⑤

◗◗ **Auto Jávea** av de Ondara 11 ☎(96) 5790178
For All makes

JEREZ DE LA FRONTERA
Cádiz

★★★★**Jerez** (CIGA) av A-Domecq 35
☎(956)300600 tx 75059
⊷121 P Lift ℂ ⊶ ◻
Credit Cards ① ② ③ ⑤

★★**Aloha** (On western bypass) ☎(956)332500
⊷30 ☎ P ◻

JONQUERA, LA
Girona

★★★**Porta Catalana** A17 (2km SW on A17
service area) ☎(972)540640
⊷81 P81 Lift ℂ Mountain
Credit Cards ① ② ③ ⑤

★★★**Puerta de España** ctra Nacional 11
☎(972)540120
⊷26 P ℂ Mountain

LA
Each name preceded by 'La' is listed under the
name that follows it.

LAREDO
Cantabria

★★★**Cosmopol** av de la Victoria ☎(942)605400
15 Jun-15 Sep
⊷60 P50 Lift ℂ ◻ Sea
Credit Cards ① ② ③ ⑤

★**Ramona** av J-Antonio 4 ☎(942)607189
rm13 P35 ℂ

LECUMBERRI
Navarra

★★**Ayestaran** ctra San Juan 64 ☎(948)504127
⊷120 A94rm ☎ P Lift ◻ Mountain Lake

LEÓN
León

★★★★**Conde Luna** Indepencia 7 (n.rest)
☎(987)206512 tx 89888
⊷150 ☎ P18 Lift ℂ ◻
Credit Cards ① ② ③ ④ ⑤

★★★★**San Marcos** pl San Marcos
☎(987)237300 tx 89809
⊷258 P70 Lift ℂ
Credit Cards ① ② ③ ⑤

★★★**Riosol** av de Palancia 3 ☎(987)216650 tx 89693
⊷🛏141 Lift ℂ Mountain
Credit Cards ①②③④⑤

★★**Quindos** av J-Antonio 24 ☎(987)236200
:Rest closed Sun
⊷🛏96 P Lift ℂ
Credit Cards ①②③④⑤

LÉRIDA
SeeLLEIDA

LLAFRANC
See PALAFRUGELL

LLANÇÁ
Girona

At PUERTO DE LLANÇÁ(2km NE)

★★★*Mendisol* Playa de Grifeu ☎(972)380100
Jun-Sep
⊷🛏35 P100 ℂ Sea Mountain
Credit Cards ③⑤

★★**Berna DPn** ps Maritimo 13 ☎(972)380150
15 May-31 Sep
⊷🛏38 A38rm P51 ℂ Beach Sea

★*Miramar* ps Maritimo 23 ☎(972)380132
Apr-Sep
rm31

LLANES
Asturias

★★**Peñablanca** Pidal 1 (n.rest) ☎(985)400166
Jun-Sep
⊷🛏31 ℂ Sea Mountain
Credit Cards ①③

LLANSA
SeeLLANÇÁ

LLEIDA (LÉRIDA)
Lleida

★★★**Condes de Urgel** av de Barcelona 17-27 ☎(973)202300 tx 57703
⊷🛏105 ☆ P150 Lift ℂ
Credit Cards ①②③⑤

🍴 *Dalmau* av Ejercito 44 ☎(973) 261611 Aud VW

LLORET DE MAR
Girona

★★★★**Monterrey** ctra de Tossa ☎(972)364050 tx 57374
Mar-Oct
⊷🛏228 P200 Lift ℂ ℚ 🖭 ⌿ Sea
Credit Cards ①②③⑤

★★★★**Rigat Park** Playa de Fanals ☎(972)365200 tx 57015
Feb-Oct
⊷🛏108 ☆ P100 Lift ℂ ℚ ⌿ Sea Mountain
Credit Cards ①②③⑤

★★★★**Santa Marta** (Relais et Châteaux) Playa de Santa Cristina ☎(972)364904 tx 57394
20 Jan-15 Dec
⊷🛏78 A18rm ☆ P200 Lift ℂ ℚ ⌿ Sea Mountain
Credit Cards ①②③⑤

★★★**Anabel** Feliciá Serra 10 ☎(972)366200 tx 57380
26 Mar-5 Nov
⊷🛏230 ☆ P20 Lift ℂ 🖭 ⌿ Sea Mountain
Credit Cards ①③④

★★**Excelsior** ps M-J-Verdaguer 16 ☎(972)364137 tx 97061
Mar-Oct
⊷🛏45 Lift ℂ Sea
Credit Cards ①②③⑤

★★**Fanals** ctra de Blanes ☎(972)364112 tx 57362
Apr-Oct
⊷🛏80 ☆ P100 Lift ℂ ℚ 🖭 ⌿ Mountain
Credit Cards ①③⑤

🍴 *Celler* av Vidreras 22-26 ☎(972) 365397 Peu Tal

LOGROÑO
Rioja

★★★★**Carlton Rioja** av Rey-J-Carlos 5 ☎(941)242100 tx 37295
:Rest closed Sun
⊷🛏120 ☆ P22 Lift ℂ
Credit Cards ②③④⑤

★★*El Cortijo* ctra del Cortijo Km2 ☎(941)225050
⊷🛏40 P ℂ ⌿ Mountain

LOS
Each name preceded by 'Los' is listed under the name that follows it.

LUARCA
Asturias

★*Gayoso* ps de Gómez 4 ☎(985)640050
:Rest closed Oct-Apr
⊷🛏28 P Lift ℂ
Credit Cards ①③⑤

LUGO
Lugo

★★**Méndez Nuñez** Reina 1 (n.rest) ☎(982)230711
⊷🛏90 Lift ℂ

HOTEL SANTA MARTA ★ ★ ★ ★
PLAYA DE SANTA CRISTINA,
E-17310 LLORET DE MAR (Gerona/COSTA BRAVA)
Phone: (972) 36.49.04. or 36.45.12. Telex: 57394 HSM
Excellent situation in an 8Ha park. Swimming pool — tennis
— private beach with bar and restaurant — conference rooms.
Member of "Relais et Châteaux"
— Cable: SANTAMARTA

HOTEL R. LLEIDA
**Autopista A-2 *Lleida (Lérida)*
Tel. (010-34-73) 11 60 23
P.O. Box 502, E-25001 LLEIDA, Spain**

Situated on the Lleida-Zaragoza autopista, 6 km from Lleida
(Lérida). Comfortable, modern (1981) hotel with 75 double
rooms all with bath, background music, automatic direct
dialling system and air conditioning. Completely sound-
proof. Television room. Bar. Conference rooms. Large
parking area. Cafeteria, restaurant and shops on the same
grounds. Open throughout the year. English spoken.
    This Hotel is a Member of Hesperia Hotel Chain.

MADRID

See plan pages 360 and 361
Population 3,655,000 *Local tourist office* Plaza Mayor 3 (91) 2664874
This exciting modern capital combines Castillian traditions with a marvellous live-for-today
atmosphere, the numerous *tapas* bars seemingly never shut and the art in the Prado including many of
the world's great masterpieces. Shopping on and near the Gran Via, especially for leather goods, can
produce some real bargains, whilst the most elegant shopping areas are Calle de Serrano and Calle
Goya.
Madrid stands in the the centre of the Iberian peninsula and is the highest capital city in Europe at
about 2,170 ft; because of its height and exposed position the climate shows great extremes, although
sunshine is abundant throughout the year.
Originally growing up on the north bank of the Manzares river, there are still vestiges of Old Madrid
in the south-west and around the Plaza Mayor, while the newer areas of the centre and north have
wider boulevards constructed in 1868 on the site of the old city wall. The centre has now moved from
Plaza Mayor - the hub of life in bygone days - to the Puerto del Sol.
Buildings of note include the former royal palace with its gardens and famous armoury, the palace of
justice, parliamentary buildings, national library, opera house, the 18th-century church of S Francisco
el Grande and the unfinished cathedral of Nuestra Senora de la Almudena, begun in 1881.

EATING OUT Spanish cooking is hearty and wholesome, with specialities including *Cocido Madrileno*,
a tasty hot pot, *sopa Castellana*, a baked garlic soup served with a poached egg, and stewed tripe,
known as *Callos a la Madrilena*. Restaurants are officially graded one to five and meal times are
generally much later than in other European countries. Most of the popular establishments are to be
found in the old centre of the city. In addition, *tapas* are available in most cafés and bars.
La Dorada, located in Orense, near the Holiday Inn, has an enthusiastic following for its fish dishes,
while for a good choice of *paellas*, *La Barraca* in Reina is recommended. *La Quinta del Sordo*, in
Sacramento, is noted for its inexpensive cuisine, especially baked chicken and roasts.

MADRID

★★★★★**Meliá Madrid** c de la Princesa 27
☎(91)2418200 tx 22537
◄►ℝ265 ⋒ P200 Lift ℂ
Credit Cards ① ② ③ ⑤

★★★★★**Palace** pl de las Cortes 7 ☎(91)4297551
tx 22272
◄►ℝ500 ⋒ Lift ℂ
Credit Cards ① ② ③ ⑤

★★★★★**Princesa Plaza** (SRS) Serrano Jover 3
☎(91)5422100 tx 44377
◄►ℝ406 ⋒ P51 Lift ℂ
Credit Cards ① ② ③ ④ ⑤

★★★★★**Ritz** (THF) pl de la Lealtad 5
☎(91)5212857 tx 43986
◄►ℝ156 P Lift ℂ
Credit Cards ① ② ③ ⑤

★★★★★**Villa Magna** ps de la Castellana 22
☎(91)2614900 tx 22914
◄►ℝ194 ⋒ P200 Lift ℂ
Credit Cards ① ② ③ ⑤

★★★★**Alcalá** (BW) c Alcala 66 ☎(91)4351060 tx
48094
◄►ℝ153 ⋒ P1 Lift ℂ
Credit Cards ① ② ③ ⑤

★★★★**Castellana Inter-Continental** ps de la
Castellana 49 ☎(91)4100200 tx 27686
◄►ℝ305 P80 Lift ℂ
Credit Cards ① ② ③ ⑤

★★★★**Emperador** Gran Via 53 ☎(91)2472800 tx
46261
◄►ℝ232 Lift ℂ ⊐
Credit Cards ② ③ ④ ⑤

★★★★**Emperatriz** López de Hoyos 4
☎(91)5638088 tx 43640
◄►ℝ170 ⋒ P Lift ℂ
Credit Cards ① ② ③ ④ ⑤

★★★★**Meliá Castilla** Cpt Haya 43 ☎(91)5712211
tx 23142
rm907 ⋒ P Lift ℂ ⊐
Credit Cards ① ② ③ ④ ⑤

★★★★**Plaza** (SRS) pl de España ☎(91)2471200
tx 27383
◄►ℝ306 Lift ℂ ⊐
Credit Cards ① ② ③ ④ ⑤

★★★★**Sanvy** c de Goya 3 ☎(91)2760800 tx
44994
◄►ℝ141 ⋒ Lift ℂ ⊐
Credit Cards ① ② ③ ⑤

★★★★**Tryp Velázquez** Velazquez 62
☎(91)2752800 tx 22779
◄►ℝ145 A28rm ⋒ P12 Lift ℂ
Credit Cards ① ② ③ ⑤

★★★**Atlántico** Gran Via 38 ☎(91)5226480 tx
43142
◄►ℝ62 Lift ℂ
Credit Cards ① ② ③ ④ ⑤

★★★**Carlos-V** c Maestro Vitoria 5 (n.rest)
☎(91)2314100 tx 48547
◄►ℝ67 Lift ℂ
Credit Cards ① ② ③ ④ ⑤

★★★**Carlton** ps de las Delicias 28 ☎(91)2297100
tx 44571
◄►ℝ133 P75 Lift ℂ
Credit Cards ① ② ③ ⑤

★★★**Centro Norte** M-Ravel 10 ☎(91)7333400 tx
42598
◄►ℝ179 P140 Lift ℂ ⊐
Credit Cards ② ③ ⑤

★★★**Gran Via** Gran Via 25 (n.rest)
☎(91)2221121 tx 44173
◄►ℝ162 Lift

★★★**Miguel Angel** c de M-Angel 31
☎(91)4420022 tx 44235
◄►ℝ300 ⋒ P ℂ ⊠
Credit Cards ① ② ③ ④ ⑤

★★★**Novotel** Albacete 1 (esquinia av Badajoz)
☎(91)4054600 tx 41862
◄►ℝ236 ⋒ P20 Lift ⊐ Mountain
Credit Cards ① ② ③ ⑤

★★★**Principe Pio** ps de Onesimo Redondo 16
☎(92)2470800 tx 42183
◄►ℝ157 A60rm ⋒ P200 Lift ℂ
Credit Cards ① ② ③

★★★**Residenciá Madrid** Carretas 10 (Off Puerto
del Sol) ☎(91)2216520
Closed 2 weeks Dec
◄►ℝ71 Lift ℂ
Credit Cards ① ② ③ ④ ⑤

★★★**Tirol** Marques de Urquijo 4 (n.rest)
☎(91)2481900
◄►ℝ97 ⋒ Lift ℂ
Credit Cards ① ③

★★**Mercator** c de Atocha 123 (n.rest)
☎(91)4290500 tx 46129
◄►ℝ90 ⋒ P38 Lift ℂ Sea
Credit Cards ① ② ③ ④ ⑤

At **BARAJAS**(15km N on N1)

★★★★★**Barajas** (GT) av Logrono 305
☎(91)7477700 tx 22255
◄►ℝ230 P Lift ℂ ⋒ ⊠ ⊐ ⋔⋔ ∪
Credit Cards ① ② ③ ④ ⑤

★★★**Aeropuerto Diana** Galéon 27
☎(91)7471355 tx 45688
◄►ℝ271 Lift ℂ
Credit Cards ① ② ③ ⑤

MAGALUF
See **BALEARES, ISLAS DE** under **MALLORCA**
(MAJORCA)

MAHÓN
See **BALEARES, ISLAS DE** under **MENORCA**
(MINORCA)

MÁLAGA
Málaga

★★★★**Málaga Palacio** av Cortina del Muelle 1
(n.rest) ☎(52)215185 tx 77021

⚙223 Lift ⌐ Sea
Credit Cards ①②③④⑤

★★★**Las Vegas** ps de Sancha 22 ☎(952)217712
⚙73 Lift ⌐ Sea
Credit Cards ①②③⑤

★★★**Naranjos** ps de Sancha 35 ☎(952)224317
tx 77030
⚙41 ☎ P Lift ☾ Sea

★★**Parador Nacional de Gibralfaro**
☎(952)221902
⚙12 P ☾ Sea
Credit Cards ①②③⑤

MALLORCA (MAJORCA)
See BALEARES, ISLAS DE

MANZANARES
Ciudad Real

★★**Cruce** ctra Madrid-Cádiz Km 173
☎(926)611900
⚙37 P ⌐
Credit Card ③

★★**Parador Nacional** (2km S) ☎(926)610400
⚙50 Lift ⌐
Credit Cards ①②③④⑤

Serrano-Calvillo ctra Madrid-Cádiz ☎(926)
611315 Ope

MARBELLA
Málaga

★★★★★**Meliá Don Pepe** ctra de Cádiz-Málaga
Km 186 ☎(952)770300 tx 77055
rm210 P Lift ☾ ⌐ ⌐ Beach Sea Mountain
Credit Cards ①②③④⑤

★★★★**Monteros** ctra de Cádiz ☎(952)771700
tx 77059
⚙169 P200 Lift ☾ ⌐ ⌐ ⌐ ☾ ∪ Beach Sea
Credit Cards ①②③④⑤

★★★★**Chapas** ctra de Cádiz ☎(952)831375 tx
77057
⚙117 P Lift ☾ ⌐ Sea Mountain

★★★★**Guadalpin** ctra Cádiz-Málaga Km 186
☎(952)771100
⚙110 P49 ☾ ⌐
Credit Cards ①②③⑤

★★★**Artola** (SRS) ctra de Cádiz ☎(952)831390
tx 79678
⚙31 ☎ P50 Lift ☾ ⌐ ⌐ ☾ ☾ Sea Mountain
Credit Cards ①②③

★★★**Estrella del Mar** ctra Cádiz-Málaga Km
191.5 ☎(952)831275 tx 79669
Mar-Nov
⚙98 P40 Lift ☾ ⌐ ⌐ Beach Sea Mountain
Credit Cards ①②③

★★★**Fuerte** av El Fuerte ☎(952)771500
⚙262 ☎ P65 Lift ☾ ⌐ ⌐ ⌐ Sea Mountain
Credit Cards ①②③④⑤

MATARÓ
Barcelona

★★★**Castell de Mata** N 11 ☎(093)7905807
⚙52 P150 Lift ☾ ⌐ ⌐ Beach Sea Mountain
Credit Cards ①②③④⑤

MAZAGÓN
Huelva

★★★**Parador Nacional Cristóbal Colón**
☎(955)376000
⚙23 P ☾ ⌐ Sea
Credit Cards ①②③⑤

MEDINACELI
Soria

★★★**Duque de Medinaceli** rte N11 ☎(975)326111
rm12(**⚙6**) Mountain
Credit Cards ①②③⑤

★★**Nico** ctra General Km 151 ☎(976)326011
⚙22 Lift ☾ ⌐ Mountain
Credit Cards ①②③⑤

MENORCA (MINORCA)
See BALEARES, ISLAS DE

MÉRIDA
Badajoz

★★★**Emperatriz** pl España 19 ☎(924)313111
⚙41 ☾
Credit Cards ②③

★★★**Parador Nacional 'Via la Plata'** pl de La
Constitucion 3 ☎(924)313800
⚙82 ☎ P30 Lift ☾
Credit Cards ①②③⑤

★★**Zeus** ctra de Madrid Km 341 ☎(924)318111
⚙44 P80 Lift ☾
Credit Cards ②③⑤

MIERES
Asturias

Talleres Mieres Poligono Industrial ☎(985)
463323 Peu Tal

MIJAS
Málaga

★★★**Mijas** (BW) Tamisa ☎(952)485800 tx 77393
⚙90 A10rm P60 Lift ☾ ⌐ ⌐ Sea Mountain
Credit Cards ①②③⑤

MOJÁCAR
Almeria

★★★**Moresco** ☎(951)478025
⚙147 Lift ⌐
Credit Cards ①②③⑤

★★★**Parador Nacional Reyes Catolicos**
☎(951)478250
⚙98 P100 ☾ ⌐ Sea
Credit Cards ①②③④⑤

MOLAR, EL
Madrid

Sato ctra Burgos Km42.3 ☎(91) 8410081 P
Ren

MONTILLA DEL PALANCAR
Cuenca

★★★**Sol** ctra Madrid-Valencia 11 ☎(966)331025
⚙37 ☎ P20 ☾ Mountain
Credit Cards ①②③④⑤

MOTRIL
Granada

Litoral ctra de Almeria Km1.4 ☎(958) 601950
Peu Tal

MURCIA
Murcia

★★★**7 Coronas Meliá** Ronda de Garay 3
☎(968)217772 tx 67067
rm120 ☎ P Lift

T Gullén ctra de Alicante 119 ☎(968) 241212
P Peu Tal

NAVALMORAL DE LA MATA
Cáceres

★**Moya** Apartado 110 ☎(927)530500
rm40(**⚙24**) Lift ☾ Mountain
Credit Cards ①②③⑤

NERJA
Málaga

★★★★**Parador de Turismo** ☎(952)520050
⚙60 P40 Lift ☾ ⌐ ⌐ Sea
Credit Cards ①②③⑤

NUÉVALOS
Zaragoza

★★★**Monasterio de Piedra** ☎(976)849011
⚙61 P ⌐ Mountain
Credit Cards ①②③⑤

OJÉN
Málaga

★**Refugio de Juanar** Sierra Blanca
☎(952)881000-1
⚙23 P50 ☾ ⌐ Mountain
Credit Cards ①②③④⑤

OLOT
Girona

A Noguer ctra San Juan de la Mer,Abadesas
☎(972) 269273 All makes

ORENSE (OURENSE)
Orense

★★**Barcelona** av Pontevedra 13 ☎(988)220800
rm40(**⚙18**) Lift ☾
Credit Cards ①③⑤

OROPESA
Toledo

★★★**Parador Nacional de Virrey Toledo** pl del
Palacio 1 ☎(925)430000
⚙44 P Lift ☾ Mountain
Credit Cards ①②③⑤

HR ●●●

HOTEL GARBI

(Girona, Costa Brava, Spain). Tel: 010 34 72 300100. Fax: 010 34 72 611803

Far from main tourism, in the most beautiful part of the unspoilt Costa Brava, in a lovely Catalan village. Lovely family hotel, situated in a magnificent pine-tree forest. Only 40 rooms with complete bathroom and all overlooking the sea. Convention rooms. Swimming pool. Well-kept garden. Children's playground. Excellent restaurant. Cafeteria-Bar. Climatized swimming pool with Bar. Open from 15th March to 30th October.

Reservations: Hotel Garbi, Avda, Costa Dorada 20 E. 17210, CALELLA DE PALAFRUGELL

OVIEDO
Asturias

★★★★★**Reconquista** Gil de Jaz 16
☎(985)241100 tx 84328
⇤141 🅟 P80 Lift
Credit Cards 1 2 3 4 5

★★★**Gruta** Alto de Buenavista ☎(985)232450
:Rest closed Mon
⇤55 P300 Lift ℂ Mountain
Credit Cards 1 2 3 5

★★**Principado** San Francisco 6 ☎(985)217792 tx
84003
⇤60 Lift ℂ
Credit Cards 1 2 3 4 5

PAGUERA
See **BALEARES, ISLAS DE** under **MALLORCA**
(MAJORCA)

PAJARES (PUERTO DE)
Asturias

★★**Parador Nacional Puerto de Pajares**
☎(985)496023 tx 84003
⇤34 P30 ℂ Mountain
Credit Cards 1 2 3 5

PALAFRUGELL
Girona

🛥 *Commercial Autonautica* Bagur 45 ☎(972)
300248 Cit

Masca Motor c Luna 51 ☎(972) 301530 Ope &
All makes

At **CALELLA DE PALAFRUGELL**(5km SE)

★★★★**Alga** ☎(972)300058 tx 507077
25 Mar - 25 Oct :Rest closed Mar & Apr
⇤54 P70 Lift ℂ ♀ ⌒ Sea Mountain
Credit Cards 1 3

★★★**Garbi** av Costa Dorada 20 ☎(972)300100
Apr-15 Oct
⇤30 A6rm P80 Lift ℂ ⌒ Sea
Credit Cards 1 3

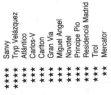

MADRID			
2	★★★★★	Meliá Madrid	13	★★★★	Sanvy
3	★★★★★	Palace	14	★★★★	Tryp Velázquez
4	★★★★★	Princesa Plaza	15	★★★	Atlántico
5	★★★★★	Ritz	16	★★★	Carlos-V
6	★★★★★	Villa Magna	17	★★★	Carlton
7	★★★★	Alcalá	18	★★★	Gran Vía
8	★★★★	Castellana Inter-Continental	19	★★★	Miguel Angel
9	★★★★	Emperador	20	★★★	Novotel
10	★★★★	Emperatriz	21	★★★	Príncipe Pío
11	★★★★	Meliá Castilla	22	★★★	Residencia Madrid
12	★★★★	Plaza	23	★★★	Tirol
			24	★★	Mercator

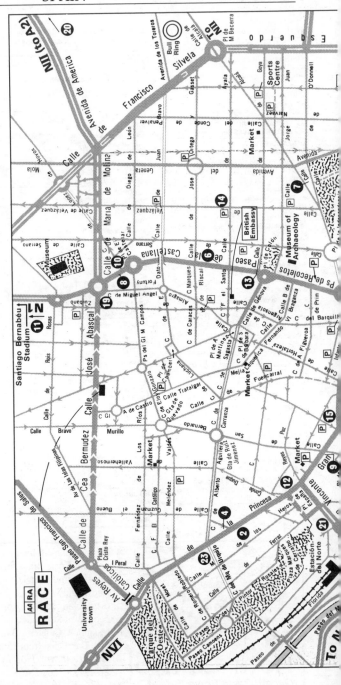

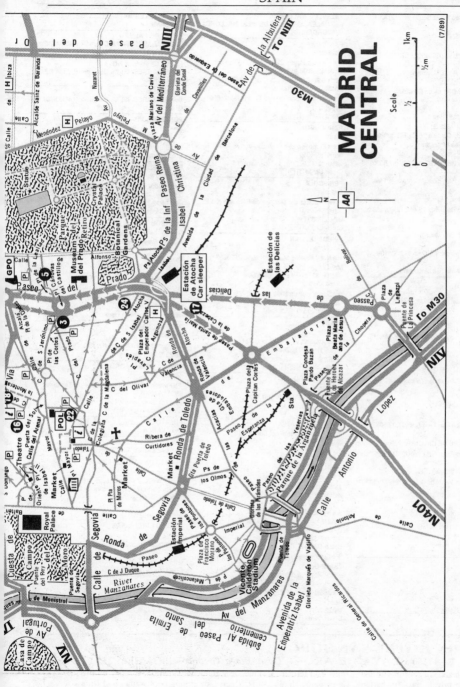

MADRID
CENTRAL

Scale

★★**Mediterráneo** Playa Baños ☎(972)300150
15 May-Sep
←🏠38 P40 ℂ ९ Sea

At LLAFRANC

★★★**Paraiso** ☎(972)300450 tx 57077
15 Apr-10 Oct
←🏠55 P Lift ℂ ९ ⌂ Mountain
Credit Cards 1 2 3 5

★★★**Terramar DPn** ps de Cypsele 1
☎(972)300200 tx 57077
May-30 Oct
←🏠56 ⌂ P7 Lift ℂ Sea
Credit Cards 1 2 3 4 5

★★**Llafranch** ps Cypsele 16 ☎(972)300208
rm28(←24) P Sea Mountain
Credit Cards 1 3 5

★**Llevant** Francisco de Blanes 5 ☎(972)300366
tx 57077
15 Dec-23 Oct :Rest closed Sun pm Jan-Mar
←🏠20 Sea

At TAMARIU(4km SE)

★★★**Hostalillo** Bellavista 22 ☎(972)300158 tx
54136
Jun-20 Sep
←🏠71 ⌂ Lift ℂ Sea Mountain
Credit Cards 3 5

★★★**Tamariu** ps del Mar 3 ☎(972)300108
15 May-Sep
←🏠46 A22rm ⌂ ℂ Sea Mountain

PALAMÓS
Girona

★★★**Trias** ps del Mar ☎(972)314100
7 Apr-15 Oct
←🏠80 ⌂ P30 Lift ℂ ⌂ Beach Sea
Credit Cards 1 2 3 5

★★**Marina** av 11 de Septembre 48
☎(972)314250
Closed 22 Dec-30 Jan
←🏠62 Lift ℂ Sea
Credit Cards 1 2 3 4 5

★★**San Juan DPn** av de la Victoria
☎(972)314208
Apr-Sep
←🏠31 ⌂ P6 ℂ ⌂ Sea
Credit Cards 1 3

🚗 **Central** ctra a San Feliú 6 ☎(972) 650635 Aud
VW

At SANT ANTONI DE CALONGE(2.5km S)

★★★**Lys** ctra de San Feliú ☎(972)314150
Jun-Sep
←🏠70 ⌂ P Lift ℂ Beach Sea

★★★**Rosa dels Vents** ps del Mar ☎(972)651311
tx 57077
10 Mar-Sep
←🏠70 ⌂ P200 Lift ℂ ९ Beach Sea
Credit Cards 1 3 4 5

★★★**Rosamar** ps del Mar 33 ☎(972)650548
May-15 Oct
←🏠64 ⌂ P40 Lift ℂ Sea
Credit Cards 2 4

PALENCIA
Palencia

★★★**Rey Sancho** av Ponce Leon s/n
☎(988)725300
←🏠100 ⌂ P100 Lift ℂ ९ ⌂
Credit Cards 1 2 3 4 5

PALMA DE MALLORCA
See **BALEARES, ISLAS DE** under **MALLORCA
(MAJORCA)**

PAMPLONA
Navarra

★★★★**Tres Reyes** Jardines de la Taconera
☎(948)226600 tx 37720
←🏠180 ⌂ P20 Lift ℂ ⌂
Credit Cards 1 2 3 5

★★★**Yoldi** av San Ignacio 11 ☎(948)224800
←🏠46 ⌂ P30 Lift ℂ
Credit Cards 1 3 4 5

PANCORBO
Burgos

★★★**El Molino** ctra G-Madrid-Irún Km 306
☎(947)354050
←🏠48 ⌂ P50 ℂ ९ ⌂ Mountain
Credit Cards 1 2 3 5

PÉNISCOLA
Castellón

★★★**Hosteria del Mar** ctra de Benicarló Km 6
☎(964)480600
←🏠85 P100 Lift ℂ ९ ⌂ Beach Sea
Credit Cards 1 2 3 4 5

PINEDA DE MAR
Barcelona

★★**Mont Palau** c Mayor 21 ☎(93)7623387
Mar-Oct
←🏠109 A17rm P14 Lift ℂ ⌂ Sea
Credit Card 3

★★**Sorrabona** ps Maritimo 10 ☎(93)7623250
May-Oct
←🏠100 P20 Lift ℂ ⌂ Sea

PLASENCIA
Cáceres

★★★**Alfonso V111** c Alfonso V111 32
☎(927)410250 tx 28960
←🏠57 ⌂ Lift ℂ Mountain
Credit Cards 1 2 3 5

PLATJA D'ARO, LA
Girona

★★★**Cliper DPn** ☎(972)817000
Closed 15 Nov-15 Apr
←🏠40 P ℂ Sea
Credit Cards 1 2 5

★★★**Miramar** Verge del Carme N12
☎(972)817150
Apr-Oct
←🏠48 ⌂ P9 Lift ℂ Sea
Credit Cards 1 3

★★★**Rosamar** pl Mayor ☎(972)817304
15 May-15 Oct
←🏠60 ⌂ Lift ℂ Mountain
Credit Card 3

★★★**Xaloc** Cala de Rovira ☎(972)817300 tx
94421
Closed Nov-Feb
←🏠50 P Lift ℂ Sea
Credit Cards 1 3

★★**Els Pins** ☎(972)817219
22 Mar-Oct
←🏠70 ⌂ Lift ℂ Sea
Credit Cards 1 2 3 4 5

★★**Japet** ctra de Palamós 20 ☎(972)817366
Jan-Oct
←🏠22 ⌂ ℂ
Credit Cards 1 2 3

PLAYA DE LES MARINAS
See **DENIA**

PLAYA DE PALMA
See **BALEARES, ISLAS DE** under **PALMA DE
MALLORCA**

PLAYA DE PALMA NOVA
See **BALEARES, ISLAS DE** under **PALMA DE
MALLORCA**

POLLENSA
See **BALEARES, ISLAS DE** under **MALLORCA
(MAJORCA)**

PONFERRADA
Léon

★★**Madrid** 50 Av La Puebla 44 ☎(987)411550
←🏠55 Lift ℂ
Credit Cards 1 3 4

PONTEVEDRA
Pontevedra

★★**Parador Nacional Casa del Barón** Maceda
S/n ☎(986)855800
←🏠47 P12 Lift ℂ
Credit Cards 1 2 3 4 5

PORTBOU
Girona

★**Costa Brava** Cerbere 20-26 ☎(972)390003
Jun-Sep
rm30(←6)
Credit Cards 1 3

PORTOMARÍN
Lugo

★★★**Parador Nacional de Puertomarin**
☎(982)545025
←🏠10 P ℂ Mountain Lake

PREMIÁ DE MAR
Barcelona

★★**Premiá** c San Miguel 46 ☎(93)7510336
←🏠23 ℂ Sea Mountain

PUEBLA DE SANABRIA
Zamora

★★**Parador Nacional de Puebla de Sanabria**
☎(988)620001
←🏠44 ⌂ P30 Lift
Credit Cards 1 2 3 4 5

PUERTO DE LLANÇÁ
See **LLANÇÁ**

PUERTO DE POLLENSA
See **BALEARES, ISLAS DE** under **POLLENSA**

PUERTO DE SANTA MARIA, EL
Cádiz

★★★★**Meliá el Caballo Blanco** Playa de
Valdelagrana (2.5km S on ctra de Cádiz)
☎(956)863745 tx 76070
rm94 ℂ ९ Beach
Credit Cards 1 2 3 4 5

PUERTO LUMBRERAS
Murcia

★★**Parador Nacional de Puerto Lumbreras**
☎(968)402025
←🏠60 ⌂ P30 Lift ℂ ⌂ Mountain
Credit Cards 1 2 3 4 5

PUIGCERDÁ
Girona

★★**Maria Victoria** Florenza 9 ☎(972)972880
←🏠50 ⌂ Lift ℂ Mountain
Credit Cards 1 2 3 5

PARK HOTEL SAN JORGE ★ ★ ★ ★

E—17250 PLAYA DE ARO — *Costa Brava/Gerona* Tel. (34-72) 65.23.11

180 beds. All rooms with bath, toilet and terrace. Unique, very romantic situation, directly by the sea
with private bays for bathing. Large park, tennis courts. Heated swimming pool, sauna and fitness-
centre. Air-conditioning. Covered parking. Restaurant with good cuisine.

SPAIN

★★**Martinez** ctra de Llivia ☎(972)880250
⊷15 ℂ ⌂ Mountain

PUZOL
Valencia

★★★★**Monte Picayo** Paraje Denominado Monte Picayo (Autoroute 7, exit 6) ☎(96)1420100 tx 62087
⊷82 P50 Lift ℂ ℴ ∪ Sea Mountain
Credit Cards 1 2 3 5

RASCAFRIA
Madrid

★★★★**Santa Maria de el Paular** (CIGA)
☎(91)8693200 tx 23222
⊷58 P30 ℂ ℴ ⌂ ∪ Mountain
Credit Cards 2 3 5

REINOSA
Cantabria

★★★**Vejo** av Cantabria 15 ☎(942)751700
⊷71 ☂ P Lift ℂ Mountain
Credit Cards 2 3 5

★★**Fontibre-Iberia** Nestares ☎(942)750450
⊷51 ☂ P Lift ℂ Mountain

⊷ **Partes** av Cantabria 26 ☎(942) 750334 Aud VW

REUS
Tarragona

★★**Gaudi** Arrabal Robuster 49 ☎(977)305545
⊷73 Lift ℂ Sea
Credit Cards 1 3 5

RIBADEO
Lugo

★★**Eo** av de Asturias 5 (n.rest) ☎(982)110750
10 Apr-Sep
⊷24 ℂ ⌂ Sea
Credit Cards 1 2 3 5

★★**Parador Naciónal** ☎(982)110825
⊷47 ☂ P Lift ℂ Sea
Credit Cards 1 2 3 5

RIBADESELLA
Asturias

★★★**Gran del Sella DPn** La Playa
☎(985)860150
Apr-Sep
⊷82 P45 Lift ℂ ℴ ⌂ Sea Mountain
Credit Cards 1 2 3 5

RIBES DE FRESER
Girona

★★**Prats** San Quintin 20 ☎(972)727001
⊷30 P30 ℂ ⌂ Mountain
Credit Cards 1 2 3 4 5

★★**Terralta** El Baiell ☎(972)727350
24 Jun-Sep
⊷22 P ⌂ Mountain

RIUDELLOTS DE LA SELVA
Girona

★★★**Novotel Gerona** Autopista A17,Salida No 8
☎(972)477100 tx 57238
⊷81 P150 ℂ ℴ ⌂ Mountain
Credit Cards 1 2 3 5

RONDA
Málaga

★★★**Reina Victoria** c Jerez 39 ☎(952)871240
⊷88 P Lift ℂ ⌂ Mountain
Credit Cards 1 2 3 5

ROSES
Girona

★★★★**Almadraba Park** Playa de Almadraba
☎(972)256550 tx 57032
⊷70 ☂ P90 Lift ℂ ℴ ⌂ Beach Sea
Credit Cards 1 2 3 4 5

★★★**Coral Playa** ctra Playa S/N ☎(972)256250
tx 57191
Apr-Oct
⊷133 P68 Lift ℂ Sea Mountain
Credit Cards 1 2 3

★★★**Vistabella** Cañyelles Petites ☎(972)256200
Apr-Oct
⊷46 ☂ P50 ℂ ℴ ⊟ Beach Sea Mountain
Credit Cards 1 2 3 5

★★★**Terraza** Playa ☎(972)256154
Mar-Nov
⊷110 ☂ P Lift ℂ ℴ Sea

SABIÑANIGO
Huesca

★★**Pardina** ☎(974)780975
⊷64 P50 Lift ⌂ Mountain Lake
Credit Cards 1 3 5

S'AGARÓ
Girona

★★★★★**Gavina** (Relais et Châteaux)
☎(972)321100 tx 57132
Apr-Oct
⊷74 ☂ P112 Lift ℂ ℴ ⌂ ℏℏ Sea
Credit Cards 1 2 3 4 5

★★★**Caleta Park** Platja de Sant Pol
☎(972)320012 tx 57366
26 Mar-2O Oct
⊷105 ☂ P75 Lift ℂ ℴ ⌂ Sea Mountain
Credit Cards 1 2 3 4 5

SALAMANCA
Salamanca

★★★**Monterrey** Azafranal 21 ☎(923)214400 tx 26809
⊷89 ☂ Lift ℂ
Credit Cards 1 2 3 5

★★★**Parador Nacional** ☎(923)228700 tx 23585
⊷108 ☂ P150 Lift ℂ ℴ ⌂
Credit Cards 1 2 3 4 5

⊷ **Vicente Snachez Marcos** av de las Comuneros 30 ☎(923) 222450 Cit

At **SANTA MARTA DE TORMES**(4km E)

★★★**Jardin Regio** ☎(923)200250 tx 22895
⊷118 ☂ P200 Lift ℂ ℴ ⌂ Mountain
Credit Cards 1 2 3 5

SALER, EL
See **VALENCIA**

SALOBREÑA
Granada

★**Salambina** (1km W) ☎(958)610037
⊷14 P14 ℂ Sea
Credit Cards 1 2 3 5

SALOU
Tarragona

★★★**Calaviña** ctra Tarragona-Salou Km10
☎(977)380848 tx 56501
15 May-15 Oct
⊷70 P Lift ℂ ⌂ Sea

★★★**Picnic** ctra Salou-Reus Km1 ☎(977)380158
⊷45 P ℂ ⌂ Sea

★★★**Salou Park** Bruselas 35, Cala Copellons
☎(977)380208
⊷102 ☂ P Lift ℂ ⌂ Sea
Credit Cards 1 2 3 4 5

★★**Planas** pl Bonet 2 ☎(977)380108
Apr-Oct
⊷100 Lift ℂ Sea

⊷ **Internaciónal** c P-Martel ☎(977) 380614 P All makes

SAN ANTONIO
See **BALEARES, ISLAS DE** under **IBIZA**

SAN LORENZO DE EL ESCORIAL
Madrid

★★★★**Victoria Palace** J-de-Toledo 4
☎(91)8901511
⊷85 P14 Lift ⌂ Mountain
Credit Cards 1 2 3 5

SAN PEDRO DE ALCÁNTARA
Málaga

★★★★**Golf Guadalmina** ☎(952)781400 tx 77058

⊷80 P40 ℂ ℴ ⌂ ℏℏ Beach Sea
Credit Cards 1 2 3 5

SAN SEBASTIÁN (DONOSTIA)
Guipúzcoa

★★★★**Costa Vasca** av Pio Baroja 9
☎(943)211011 tx 36551
⊷203 ☂ P125 Lift ℂ ℴ ⌂
Credit Cards 1 2 3 5

★★★**Gudamendi** (4km W) ☎(943)214000
⊷20 P300 Sea Mountain
Credit Cards 1 2 3 4 5

★★★**Monte Igueldo** ☎(943)210211 tx 58096
⊷125 P40 Lift ℂ ⌂ Sea
Credit Cards 1 2 3 4 5

⊷ **Gruas España** av Isabel 11 15 ☎(943) 458352 P

⊷ **Ingels** av A-Elosegui 108 ☎(943) 396516 Ope

SANTA CRISTINA D'ARO
Girona

★★★★★**Costa Brava Golf** ☎(972)837052 tx 57252
Apr-15 Oct
⊷91 P80 Lift ℂ ℴ ⌂ ℏℏ Mountain
Credit Cards 1 2 3 5

SANTA CRUZ DE MUDELA
Ciudad Real

⊷ **Izquierdo** ctra Madrid-Cádiz Km 217 ☎(926) 342072 P All makes

SANTA MARIA DE HUERTA
Soria

★★★**Parador Nacional de Santa Maria de Huerta** ☎(975)327011
⊷40 ☂ P26 ℂ
Credit Cards 1 2 3 4 5

SANTA MARTA DE TORMES
See **SALAMANCA**

SANTANDER
Cantabria
See plan page 364

★★★★**Bahia** av de Alfonso XIII 6 ☎(942)221700 tx 35859
⊷179 Lift ℂ Sea
Credit Cards 1 2 3 5

★★**Colón** pl de las Brisas 1 (n.rest)
☎(942)272300
Jul-Sep
rm31(⊷30) ℂ ℴ Sea

Sancho Motor c Castilla 62 ☎(942) 370017 For

At **SARDINERO, EL**(3.5km NE)

★★★**Rhin** Reina Victoria 153 ☎(942)274300
⊷95 ☂ Lift ℂ Sea
Credit Cards 1 2 3 4 5

★★★**Santemar** J-Costa 28 ☎(942)272900 tx 35963
⊷350 ☂ Lift ℴ
Credit Cards 1 2

★★★**Sardinero** pl Italia 1 ☎(942)271100 tx 35795
⊷112 Lift ℂ Sea
Credit Cards 1 2 3 4 5

SANT ANTONI DE CALONGE
See **PALAMÓS**

SANT FELIÚ DE GUIXOLS
Girona

★★★★**Murlá Park** Paseig dels Guixols 22
☎(972)320450 tx 57364
:Rest closed Nov-Feb
⊷86 P25 Lift ℂ Sea
Credit Cards 1 2 3

★★★**Montecarlo** San Elmo ☎(972)320000
Jun-Sep
⊷61 P Lift ℂ Sea

★★★**Montjoi** San Elmo ☎(972)320300 tx 80433
12 May-15 Oct
⊷64 P35 Lift ℂ ⌂ Sea Mountain
Credit Cards 1 2 3 5

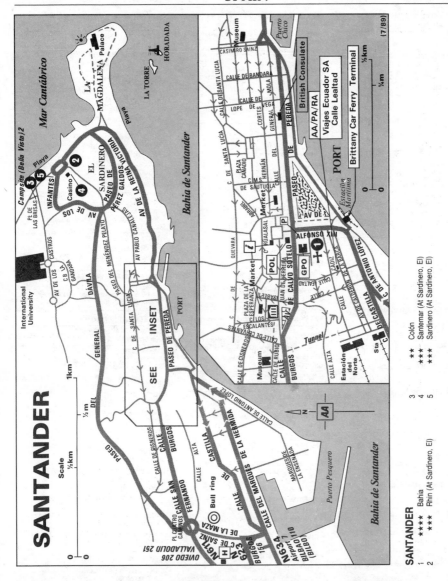

SANTANDER

Scale
0 — — 0
0 ¼km ½m 1km

(7/89)

SANTANDER

★★★★ Bahia
★★★ Rhin (At Sardinero, El)

1
2

3 ★★ Colón
4 ★★★ Santemar (At Sardinero, El)
5 ★★★ Sardinero (At Sardinero, El)

★★★**Rex** Rambla Portalet 16 (n.rest)
☎(972)320312
10 Jun-20 Sep
🛏25 Lift ℂ Sea
Credit Cards ①②③④⑤

★★**Noies** Rambla J-Antonio 10 (n.rest)
☎(972)320400 tx 57159
Apr-Nov
🛏55 ☎ P20 Lift ℂ
Credit Cards ①②③⑤

★★**Turist Pn** San Ramón 39 ☎(972)320841
15 May-5 Oct
🛏23 A11rm ☎ Lift ℂ Mountain
Credit Cards ①②③④⑤

🚲 **Metropol Comercial** ctra Gerona 7 ☎(972)
325100 Ren

SANTIAGO DE COMPOSTELA
la Coruña

★★★★★**Los Reyes Catolicos** pl de España 1
☎(981)582200 tx 86004
🛏157 P50 Lift ℂ Mountain
Credit Cards ①②③④⑤

★★★**Peregrino** av Rosalia de Castro
☎(981)591850 tx 82352
🛏148 P50 Lift ℂ ⌂
Credit Cards ①②③⑤

SANTILLANA DEL MAR
Cantabria

★★★**Los Infantes** av le Dorat 1 ☎(942)818100
🛏30 P30 ℂ
Credit Cards ①②③④⑤

★★★**Parador de Gil Blas** ☎(942)818000
🛏28 ℂ
Credit Cards ①②③⑤

★★**Altamira** Cantn 1 ☎(942)818025
🛏60 P18 ℂ Mountain
Credit Cards ①②③④⑤

SANTO DOMINGO DE LA CALZADA
Rioja
★★**Parador Nacional** ☎(941)340300
⊷♠27 P30 ℂ
Credit Cards ①②③④⑤

SANT POL DE MAR
Barcelona
★★★**Gran Sol Pn** ctra de Francia Km670
☎(93)7600051
⊷♠44 P40 Lift ℂ ℀ ➔ Sea
Credit Cards ①②③⑤

SAN VINCENTE DE LA BARQUERA
Cantabria
★★**Miramar** ☎(942)710075
Mar-15 Dec
⊷♠15 A15rm P150 ℂ Sea Mountain
Credit Cards ②③

SARDINERO, EL
See SANTANDER

SEGOVIA
Segovia
★★★**Linajes** Dr-Velasco 9 ☎(911)431712
⊷♠55 ♠ Lift ℂ Mountain
Credit Cards ①②③⑤

★★★**Parador Nacional de Segovia**
☎(911)430362 tx 47913
⊷♠80 ♠ P150 Lift ℂ ➔ Mountain
Credit Cards ①②③④⑤

★★★**Puerta de Segovia** ctra de Soria
☎(911)437161 tx 22336
⊷♠116 P Lift ℂ ℀ ➔
Credit Cards ②③⑤

★★★**R Las Sirenas** J-Bravo 30 (n.rest)
☎(911)434011
⊷♠39 P6 Lift ℂ Mountain
Credit Cards ①②③④⑤

SEU D'URGELL, LA
Lleida
★★**Parador Nacional** Santo Domingo
☎(973)352000
⊷♠79 ♠ Lift ℂ ➔ Mountain
Credit Cards ①②③④⑤
★**Avenida** av Gl-Franco 18 ☎(973)350104
:Rest closed Sat
rm40(⊷♠33) Lift ℂ Mountain
Credit Cards ①③⑤
At CASTELLCIUTAT(1km SE)
★★★**Castell** (Relais et Châteaux) ctra C1313
☎(973)350704 tx 93610
:Rest closed 15 Jan-15 Feb
⊷♠40 P ℂ ➔ Mountain
Credit Cards ①②③⑤

SEVILLA (SEVILLE)
Sevilla

Sevilla is the spiritual capital of Andalusia and its most famous city, with a wealth of interesting monuments to explore and a unique ambience. The cathedral - the largest in Spain and reputedly the largest Gothic building in the world - houses the remains of St Ferdinand, Sevilla's liberator, and of Christopher Columbus. Also worth discovering are the city's old Jewish quarter, Santa Cruz, with its twisting alleys where old houses mingle with secondhand shoe stalls and antique shops, the

Maria Luisa Park - arguably the prettiest in Spain, the Plaza de España with its elaborate tile decorations and the Fine Arts Museum.

EATING OUT The diner in Sevilla is faced with a huge choice of restaurants and tempting regional cuisine. This includes *Ajo blanco,* cold garlic soup with almonds and raisins, *frituro mixta,* a selection of fried fish, and *huevos a la flamenca,* eggs baked with tomato onion and ham and garnished with asparagus and spicy sausages. Mouth-watering desserts include traditional almond cakes.
Egana Oriza, in San Ferdando, offers Basque specialities such as white fish in clam sauce. Also recommended is *Meson Dom Raimundo,* near the cathedral.

SEVILLA (SEVILLE)
Sevilla
★★★★★**Alfonso XIII** (CIGA) San Fernando 2
☎(954)222850 tx 72725
⊷♠149 ♠ P60 Lift ℂ ➔
Credit Cards ①②③④⑤

★★★**Colón** J-Canalejas 1 ☎(954)222900 tx 72726
rm268 Lift ℂ

★★★**Inglaterra** (BW) pl Nueva 7 ☎(954)224970 tx 72244
⊷♠120 ♠ P40 Lift ℂ
Credit Cards ①②③⑤

★★★**Becquer** (BW) Reyes Catolicos 4 (n.rest)
☎(954)228900 tx 72884
⊷♠126 ♠ Lift ℂ
Credit Cards ①②③⑤

★★**Doña Maria** Don Remondo 19 (n.rest)
☎(954)224990
⊷♠61 ♠ P Lift ➔
Credit Cards ②③⑤

SIERRA NEVADA
See GRANADA

SIGÜENZA
Guadalajara
★★★**Parador Nacional Castillo de Sigüenza**
☎(911)390100 tx 22517
⊷♠77 P Lift ℂ Mountain
Credit Cards ①②③⑤

SITGES
Barcelona
★★★★**Terramar** ps Calvo Sotelo ☎(93)8940050 tx 53186
May-Oct
⊷♠209 Lift ℂ ℀ ➔ ♣♣ Sea
Credit Cards ①②③④⑤

★★★**Antemare** av Nuestra Señora de,Montserrat 48/50 ☎(93)8940600 tx 52692
⊷♠72 ♠ P30 Lift ℂ ➔ Sea Mountain
Credit Cards ①②③④⑤

★★★**Platjador** ps Ribera 35 ☎(93)8945054
May-Oct
⊷♠60 Lift ℂ Sea

★★★**Arcadia** c Socias 22-24 (n.rest)
☎(93)8940900 tx 52692

Apr-Oct
⊷♠37 P30 Lift ℂ ➔ Sea Mountain
Credit Cards ①②③④⑤

★★★**Luna Playa** Puerto Alegre 51-53 (n.rest)
☎(93)8940430
⊷♠13 P15 Lift ℂ Sea
Credit Cards ①②③

★★**Sitges Residencia** San Gaudencio 5 (n.rest)
☎(93)8940072 tx 52962
Jun-Sep
rm52(⊷♠28) Lift ℂ

★**Romantic** San Isidre 33 (n.rest) ☎(93)8940643 tx 52962
15 Apr-15 Oct
rm71(⊷♠65) A16rm ℂ
Credit Cards ①②③

SON SERVERA
See BALEARES, ISLAS DE under MALLORCA
(MAJORCA)

SORIA
Soria
★★★**Caballero** E-Saavedra 4 ☎(975)220100
⊷♠84 P100 Lift ℂ
Credit Cards ①②③⑤

★★★**Mesón Leonor** ps del Mirón ☎(975)220250
⊷♠32 ♠ P Lift ℂ
Credit Cards ①②③⑤

★★**Les Heras** pl R-Cajal 5 ☎(975)213346
⊷♠24 P ℂ

★★★**Parador Nacional Antonio Machado** Parque del Castillo ☎(975)213445
⊷♠34 P60 ℂ Mountain
Credit Cards ①②③④⑤

SOS DEL REY CATÓLICO
Zaragoza
★★★**Parador Nacional Fernando de Aragón**
☎(948)888011
⊷♠66 ♠ P Lift ℂ Mountain

SUANCES-PLAYA
Cantabria
★**Lumar** ctra de Tagle ☎(942)810214
Jun-15 Sep
⊷♠29 P Sea Mountain

TALAVERA DE LA REINA
Toledo
★★**Auto-Estacion** av Toledo 1 ☎(925)800300
⊷♠40 ♠ ℂ
Credit Cards ①②③⑤

TAMARIU
See PALAFRUGELL

TARIFA
Cádiz
★★★**Mesón de Sancho** ctra Cádiz-Málaga
☎(956)684900
⊷♠50 A30rm ♠ P40 ℂ ℀ ➔ Sea Mountain
Credit Cards ①②③④⑤

★★**Balcón de España DPn** ctra Cádiz
☎(956)684326
Apr-Oct
⊷♠38 P34 ℂ ℀ ➔ Mountain
Credit Cards ②③

★★**Dos Mares** ctra Cádiz-Málaga Km 78
☎(956)684035
Mar-15 Jan
⊷♠19 ℂ ℀ ➔ U Beach Sea
Credit Cards ①②③

TARRAGONA
Tarragona
★★★★**Imperial Terraco** Rambla Vela 2
☎(977)233040 tx 56441
⊷♠170 Lift ℂ ➔ Sea
Credit Cards ①②③⑤

★★★**Astari** via Augusta 95 ☎(977)238106
May-30 Oct
rm83(⊷♠74) ♠ P80 Lift ℂ ➔ Sea
Credit Cards ①②③⑤

★★★**Lauria** Lauria 4 (n.rest) ☎(977)236712
⊷72 ☎ P15 Lift ℂ ⌒ Sea
Credit Cards ① ② ③ ⑤
★★**Nuria** via Augusta 217 ☎(977)23501107
Apr-Sep
⊷61 Lift ℂ Sea
Credit Cards ① ③
⬥ **Minicar Pons** Gasometro 40-42 ☎(977)
216169 All makes
⬥ **Tarrauto** ctra de Valencia ☎(977) 540870 Pue
Tal

TARTER, EL
See **SOLDEU**

TERUEL
Teruel
★★★**Parador Nacional** ☎(974)601800
⊷60 P60 Lift ℂ ℺ ⌒
Credit Cards ① ② ③ ④ ⑤
⬥ **Zuriaga Perruca** ctra Sagunto-Burgos Km 121
☎(974) 601061 For

TOJA, ISLA DE LA
Pontevedra
★★★★★**Gran DPn** ☎(986)730025 tx 88042
⊷200 Lift ℺ ℟ ℟ Beach Sea
Credit Cards ① ② ③ ⑤

TOLEDO
Toledo
★★★**Parador Conde de Orgaz** ☎(925)221850 tx
47998
⊷77 P Lift ℂ ⌒
Credit Cards ① ② ③ ⑤
★★**Maravilla** Barrio Rey 5-7 ☎(925)223300
⊷18 Lift ℂ
Credit Cards ① ② ③ ⑤

TORDESILLAS
Valladolid
★★★**Montico** ctra N122 Km145 ☎(983)770551 tx
26575
⊷55 ☎ P100 ℂ ℺
Credit Cards ① ② ③ ④ ⑤
★★★**Parador Nacional de Tordesillas** ctra N620
Km153 ☎(983)770051
⊷73 ☎ P50 Lift ℂ ⌒
Credit Cards ① ② ③ ⑤

TORREMOLINOS
Málaga
★★★★**Meliá Torremolinos** av de C-Alessandri
109 ☎(952)380500 tx 77060
1 Mar - 31 Oct
rm281 ☎ P Lift ℂ ℺ ⌒
Credit Cards ① ② ③ ④ ⑤
★★★★**Parador Nacional del Golf** ☎(952)381255
⊷40 P ℂ ℺ ⌒ ℟ ℟ Beach Sea
★★★★**Pez Espada** via Imperial ☎(952)380300 tx
77655
Apr-Oct

⊷149 P50 Lift ℂ ℺ ⌒ Beach Sea
Credit Cards ① ② ③ ⑤
★★★**Isabel** ps Maritimo 97,Playa del Lido
☎(952)381744
Mar-Nov
⊷40 ☎ P Lift ℂ ⌒ Beach Sea
Credit Cards ① ② ③ ⑤
★★★**Meliá Costa del Sol** ps Maritimo,Playa de
Bajondillo ☎(952)386677 tx 77362
rm540 P Lift ℂ ⌒ Sea
Credit Cards ① ② ③ ④ ⑤
★★★**Tropicana** Tropico 2 ☎(952)386600 tx
77107
⊷86 Lift ℂ ⌒ Sea
Credit Cards ① ② ③ ⑤
⬥ **Salamanca** av C-Allessandri 27 ☎(952)
381151 AR DJ LR

TORTOSA
Tarragona
★★★**Parador Nacional Castillo de la Zuda**
☎(977)444450
⊷82 A82rm Lift ℂ ⌒ Mountain
Credit Cards ① ② ③ ⑤

TOSSA DE MAR
Girona
★★★★**Gran Reymar DPn** Playa de Mar Menuda
☎(972)340312 tx 57094
May-Oct
⊷130 ☎ P50 Lift ℂ ℺ ⌒ Sea Mountain
Credit Cards ① ② ③ ⑤
★★★**Ancora** av de la Palma 4 ☎(972)340299
Jun-Sep
⊷60 ☎ ℂ ℺ Sea
★★★**Florida** av de Palma 21 ☎(972)340308
Apr-Oct
⊷45 P22 Lift ℂ
Credit Cards ① ② ③ ⑤
★★★**Mar Menuda** Playa de Mar Menuda
☎(972)341000
⊷45 A5rm ☎ P50 Lift ℂ ℺ ⌒ Beach Sea
Mountain
Credit Cards ① ② ③ ⑤
★★**Corisco** ps del Mar (n.rest) ☎(972)340174 tx
56317
Apr-15 Oct
⊷28 Lift ℂ Sea
Credit Cards ① ② ③ ⑤
⬥ **Nautica** ctra San Feliú ☎(972) 341021 Aud
VW & All makes

TUDELA
Navarra
★★**Morase** ps de Invierno 2 ☎(948)821700
:Rest closed Aug
⊷11 ☎ P ℂ
Credit Cards ① ② ③ ④ ⑤

★**Tudela** ctra de Zaragoza ☎(948)820558
⊷16 P13 ℂ
Credit Cards ① ③

TUI
Pontevedra
★★★**Parador Nacional San Telmo**
☎(986)600300
⊷22 ☎ P30 ℂ ⌒ Mountain
Credit Cards ① ② ③ ④ ⑤

ÚBEDA
Jaén
★★★**Parador Nacional Condestable-Dávalos** pl
Váquez de Molina 1 ☎(953)750345
⊷31 ℂ
Credit Cards ① ② ③ ④ ⑤

VALDEPEAS
Ciudad Real
★★★**Meliá el Hidalgo** ctra Andalucia
☎(926)323254 tx 48136
rm54 ⌒
Credit Cards ① ② ③ ④ ⑤

VALENCIA
Valencia
★★★★**Reina Victoria** c de las Barcas 4
☎(96)3520487 tx 64755
⊷100 P Lift ℂ
Credit Cards ① ② ③ ④ ⑤
★★★★**Rey Don Jaime** av Baleares 2
☎(96)3607300 tx 64252
⊷320 P Lift ℂ ⌒
Credit Cards ① ② ③ ⑤
★★★**Dimar** Gran via Marqués del Turia 80
☎(96)3341807 tx 62952
⊷95 ☎ P120 Lift ℂ
Credit Cards ① ② ③ ④ ⑤
★★★**Excelsior** Barcelonina 5 ☎(96)3514612
⊷65 Lift ℂ
Credit Cards ② ③ ⑤
★★**Bristol** Abadia de San Martin 3 (n.rest)
☎(96)3521176
15 Jan-1 Dec
⊷40 Lift ℂ
Credit Cards ① ② ③ ⑤
⬥ **J V Arnau** E-Bosca 22 ☎(96) 3627707 All
makes
⬥ **Auto Montalt** c San Vicente 118 ☎(96)
3703150 For
At **SALER, EL**(12km S)
★★★**Parador Nacional Luis Vives**
☎(96)1611186
⊷58 P60 Lift ℂ ℺ ⌒ ℟ ℟ Beach Sea Mountain
Credit Cards ① ② ③ ⑤

GRAN HOTEL REYMAR

Telegrammes: REYMAR — Tossa.
Tel.: (010-34-72) 34.03.12 & 34.02.74
Telex: 570 94 — 1st Cat.

E-17320 Tossa de Mar (Girona/Costa Brava)

Situated in one of the most beautiful spots of the Costa Brava, in
the residential area of Tossa, 8 yards from the beach. All 130 rooms
have bath, are modern and comfortable, terrace and view onto sea.
Some rooms with private garden. Several suites. Large, 800 sq m
terrace, swimming-pool, solarium, tennis court, dining room facing
the sea, snack-bar, tea room, restaurant, conference room. Parking.

VALLADOLID
Valladolid

★★★★*Olid Mellá* pl San Miguel 10
☎(983)357200 tx 26312
rm240 🅰 P Lift ℂ
Credit Cards ①②③④⑤

★★★*Conde Ansurez* Maria de Molina 9 (n.rest)
☎(96)3521176
🍴40 Lift ℂ
Credit Cards ①②③⑤

★★★*Mellá Parque* J-G-Morato 17 ☎(983)470100
tx 26355
rm300 🅰 P Lift ℂ
Credit Cards ①②③④⑤

VALLE DE PINETA
See **BIELSA**

VERÍN
Orense

★★*Parador Nacional de Monterrey*
☎(988)410075
🍴23 P ℂ ⌲ Mountain
Credit Cards ①②③④⑤

VIC
Barcelona

★★★*Parador Nacional* (15km NE)
☎(93)8887211
🍴36 🅰 P80 Lift ℂ ९ ⌲ Lake
Credit Cards ①②③⑤

★★*Colón* Rambla ps 1 ☎(93)8860220
🍴40 🅰 P ℂ

VIELLA
Lleida

★★★*Parador Nacional Valle de Ara'n* Estación
de la Túca ☎(973)640100
🍴135 🅰 P Lift ℂ

VILANOVA I LA GELTRÚ
Barcelona

★*Solvi 70 DPn* ps Ribes Roges 1 ☎(93)8151245
Nov-Sep
rm30(🍴28) 🅰 Lift ∪ Sea

VILLACARLOS
See **BALEARES, ISLAS DE** under **MAHÓN**

VILLAFRANCA DEL BIERZO
León

★★★*Parador Nacional Villafranca del Bierzo*
☎(987)540175
🍴40 🅰 P ℂ Mountain
Credit Cards ①②③⑤

VILLAJOYOSA
Alicante

★★★★*Montiboli* (Relais et Châteaux) ctra N332
Km 108.6 ☎(96)5890250 tx 68288
🍴49 🅰 P30 Lift ℂ ९ ⌲ Sea
Credit Cards ①②③⑤

VILLALBA
Lugo

★★*Parador Nacional Condes de Villalba*
☎(982)510011
🍴6 P6 Lift ℂ Mountain
Credit Cards ①②③⑤

VINAROZ
Castellón

★★*Duc de Vendôme* ctra N340 Km144
☎(964)450944
🍴12 ℂ
Credit Cards ①②③④⑤

★★*Roca* ctra Valencia-Barcelona Km140
☎(964)450350
🍴36 🅰 P150 ℂ ९ Sea

🍴*Automecanica López* Convento 29 ☎(964)
451022 All makes

VITORIA (GASTEIZ)
Alava

★★★★*Canciller Ayala* Ramón y Cajal 5
☎(945)130000 tx 35441
🍴185 P60 Lift ℂ
Credit Cards ①②③④⑤

★★★*General Álava* av de Gasteiz 79
☎(945)222200 tx 35468
🍴112 Lift
Credit Cards ①②④⑤

★★★*Parador Nacional* Apartado 601
☎(945)282200 tx 4686
🍴53 P75 Lift ℂ Mountain
Credit Cards ①②③⑤

ZAFRA
Badajoz

★★★*Parador Nacional Hernán Contés* pl de
Maria Cristina S/N ☎(924)550200
16 Dec-Oct
🍴28 ℂ ⌲

At **N432 Badajoz road** (16km NW)
🍴*Alvarez Ruiz* ctra Badajoz-Granada ☎(924)
551160 P Cit

ZAMORA
Zamora

★★*Cuatro Naciones* av Alfonso 1X 7
☎(988)532275
🍴40 Lift ℂ
Credit Cards ②③⑤

★★*Parador Nacional Condes de Albe & Aliste*
pl de Cánovas 1 ☎(988)514497
🍴19 🅰 P ℂ ⌲

ZARAGOZA
Zaragoza

★★★*Goya* Cinco de Marzo 5 (off ps de la
Independencia) ☎(976)229331 tx 58680
🍴150 Lift ℂ
Credit Cards ①②③⑤

★★*Conde Blanco* Predicadores 84 (n.rest)
☎(976)441411
🍴83 🅰 P40 Lift ℂ

At **N11 Madrid road** (8km SW)
★★*Cisne* ctra Madrid ☎(976)332000
🍴51 P ℂ ⌲ Mountain
Credit Cards ①②③⑤

ZARAUZ (ZARAUTZ)
Guipúzcoa

★★★*Zarauz* av de Navarra 4 ☎(943)830200
15 Jan-15 Dec
🍴82 P Lift ℂ Sea Mountain
Credit Card ③

★★*Alameda* Travesia Alameda ☎(943)830143
Apr-20 Sep
rm26(🍴4) P20 ℂ Mountain
Credit Cards ①③④

ANDORRA

Andorra is a semi-independent principality in a cluster of valleys in the eastern Pyrenées between France and Spain, and consists of deep glaciated valleys interrupted by gorges. There are several small villages, some with skiing facilities, and the attractive capital, Andorra La Vella plays host to numerous summer visitors as well, drawn by its delightful scenery and facilities. Known as 'the garden of the Pyrenées' it boasts a sunny, dry climate, scores of lush green valleys, sparkling mountain streams that abound with trout, and an incredible display of wild flowers.
Sporting attractions range from trout fishing, stimulating hiking, as well as skiing in winter. Entertainment facilities include excellent restaurants, nightclubs and bars and a bull-fight arena. The *festes* held each summer are particularly colourful and lively.

EATING OUT Andorran cuisine is a blend of French, Spanish and Catalan influences, with pork, ham and fish figuring prominently in many dishes. A particular speciality is *roster amb mel*, ham prepared with honey. The restaurant *Chez Jaques* in Andorra La Vella is popular with locals and visitors alike, while for atmosphere, *Moli del Fanals* is housed in an old windmill.

ANDORRA LA VELLA

★★★*Andorra Center* ctra Dr-Nequi 12 ☎24999
🍴150 🅰 P75 Lift ℂ ९ ▱ Mountain
Credit Cards ①②③④⑤

★★★*Andorra Palace* Prat de la Creu ☎21072 tx
208
🍴140 🅰 P180 Lift ℂ ९ ▱ Mountain
Credit Cards ①②③⑤

★★★*Andorra Park* (MAP) ☎20979
🍴40 P Lift ℂ ९ ⌲ Mountain
Credit Cards ①②③④⑤

★★★*Mercure* av Méritxell 58 ☎20773 tx 208
🍴70 🅰 P180 Lift ℂ ९ ▱ Mountain
Credit Cards ①②③⑤

HOTEL ROC BLANC ★ ★ ★
ANDORRA — 5, Placa Coprinceps
Phone: (33-628) 21486 Telex: 224 AND
240 rooms - sauna - thermal swimming pool - restaurant - cafeteria - piano bar - garage - garden.
The newest, best equipped and most exclusive hotel of Andorra. *Open all the year round.*
Reservations London: (01) 636 52 42.

★★★**Sasplugas** av del Princep Iglesias ☎20311
:Rest closed Sun
⏪26 ☄ P14 Lift ☾ Mountain
Credit Cards [1] [2] [3]

★★**Internacional** ctra Mossen Tremosa 2
☎21422
⏪50 Lift

★★**Pyrénées DPn** av Princep Benlloch 20
☎20508 tx 421
⏪74 ☄ P30 Lift ☾ ℘ ⌐ Mountain
Credit Cards [1] [3] [5]

🞔 **CIMEX** av Dr-Mitjavila 5 ☎ 23190 Fia

ESCALDES, LES

★★★**Roc Blanc** (MAP) **DPn** pl dels Co-Princeps
5 ☎21486 tx 224
⏪240 ☄ P145 Lift ☾ ℘ ▱ ⌐ Mountain
Credit Cards [1] [2] [3] [5]

★★**Pia** (n.rest) ☎21432
Jul-25 Aug
rm32(⏪15) Lift Mountain

SANT JULIÁ DE LÓRIA

★★★**Co-Princeps** ctra de Hué 1 ☎41002
Apr-Oct
⏪80 P Lift ☾ Mountain

★★**Sardana** pl Major 2-4 ☎41018
Apr-Sep
⏪25 Mountain

SOLDEU

At **TARTER, EL**(3km W)

★★★**Tarter DPn** ☎51165
Dec-15 Oct
⏪38 ☄ P20 Lift ☾ Mountain
Credit Cards [1] [3] [5]

HIRE SERVICE

The Motoring Emergency Pack contains the following:

Booster Cable • Fire Extinguisher
First-aid Outfit • Reflective Belt • Tool Kit
Tow Rope • Warning Triangle • Spare Bulbs
Disposable Gloves

Contact AA Hire Service, Snargate Street, Dover, Kent CT17 9XA
Telephone: Dover (0304) 203655

Don't leave the country without one

The days are long and the nights short during the summer months in Sweden, a popular destination for activity-filled family holidays or tranquil get-away-from-it-all breaks. The scenery is fascinating and wonderfully varied as well as being easy to explore since the roads are good and in many places virtually traffic free. Elk and deer roam the forests, birds and wildflowers abound, for watersports and fishing enthusiasts there are around 96,000 lakes to try, and there's a jagged coastline with countless archipelagoes, as well as forests, mountains and rushing rivers.

Sweden is divided into three geographical regions: Norrland, the northern sixty per cent including Lapland, mountainous except for a narrow coastal plain; Svealand, the central lake plain; and Gotaland, the fertile southern plateau and plain including Scania, the chief agricultural district, in the far south.

Each of Sweden's major cities has its own particular atmosphere and character. Stockholm enjoys a wonderful lakeside setting, while Gothenburg is a pleasant and green city noted for its spacious avenues and attractive parks.

SWEDEN

Language
Swedish, with Finnish and Lappish spoken in parts

Local Time
GMT + 1 hour (Summer GMT + 2 hours)

Currency
Swedish krona, divided into 100 öre. At the time of going to press
£1 = SKr10.63
US$1 = SKr6.40

Emergency numbers
Fire, Police and Ambulance ☎90000. The emergency telephone number should only be used in the case of personal injury or illness.

Information in Britain
Swedish National Tourist Office, 3 Cork Street, London W1X 1HA ☎01-437 5816 (071-437 5816 from 6 May 1990)

Information in the USA
Swedish Tourist Board, Scandinavian National Tourist Office, 655 Third Avenue, New York, NY 10017 ☎212 949 2333

SWEDEN

HOW TO GET THERE

Ferries run from Harwich or Newcastle (Summer only) to Göteborg (Gothenberg), taking 22½ to 27 hours.

You may use one of the Short Channel crossings to *France* or *Belgium*, driving through the *Netherlands*, *Northern Germany* and *Denmark*; then one of the ferry connections to Sweden:
Puttgarden to Rødbyhavn
Helsingør to Helsingborg

The driving distance may be shorted by crossing to *Germany*: Harwich to Hamburg (19½ to 21½ hours), or to *Denmark*: Harwich or Newcastle (Summer only) to Esbjerg (19–22 hours)

Distance
from Calais to Stockholm is about 1,600km (1,000 miles), normally requiring three overnight stops.

MONEYMATTERS

There are no restrictions on the amount of foreign or Swedish currency that a bona fide tourist may take into the country. No more than SKr6,000 in local currency may be taken out, including bank notes with a value more than SKr1,000. There are no restrictions on the amount of foreign currency which may be taken out, as long as it was obtained outside Sweden.

Banking hours
In towns: generally 09.30–15.00hrs (but some may be open until 18.00hrs Monday–Thursday)
In the country: usually Monday–Friday 10.00–14.00hrs.

Postcheques
may be cashed up to a maximum of SKr1,200 per cheque at all post offices except those in smaller villages. You may go to any counter position.

MOTORING REGULATIONS AND GENERAL INFORMATION

The information given here is specific to Sweden. It **must** be read in conjunction with the European ABC at the front of the book, which covers those regulations which are common to many countries.

Accidents*

In the case of an accident you do not have to call the police, but you have to give information regarding name and address to other persons concerned. You are not allowed to leave the scene of the accident before this is done, no matter how slight the damage. If you go away, you may be sentenced to imprisonment, or be fined. However, as a general rule, report the matter to the police in your own interests.

Breakdown*

The Swedish motoring organisation *Motormännens Riksförbund* (M) operates a road service on main roads (E-roads) during the summer months. There are also alarm centres organised by *Larmtjanst AB* (Alarm Services Ltd), or garages which are open day and night to help motorists in difficulties. The service is restricted to breakdowns and accidents and is not free. See also *Warning triangle* below.

British Embassy/Consulates*

The British Embassy together with its consular section is located at 11527 Stockholm, Skarpögatan 6–8 ☎(08) 6670140, located on the town plan of Stockholm within the gazetteer. There are British Consulates with Honorary Consuls in Gävle, Göteborg and Malmö.

Children in Cars

A child of 7 or under is not permitted to travel in a vehicle unless seated in a special child restraint or special seat enabling the child to use the normal seat belts.

Dimensions and weight restrictions*

Private **cars** and towed **trailers** or **caravans** are restricted to the following dimensions – height,

*Additional information will be found in the European ABC at the front of the book.

370

no restriction; width, 2.60 metres; length, 24 metres (which is also the maximum permitted overall length of vehicle/trailer or caravan combinations).

Trailers without brakes must not exceed twice the maximum weight of the towing vehicle.

Driving licence*

A valid UK or Republic of Ireland licence is acceptable in Sweden. The minimum age at which a visitor may use a temporarily imported car is 18 years and a temporarily imported motorcycle 17 years.

Emergency messages to tourists*

Emergency messages to tourists are broadcast daily throughout the year by Swedish Radio. *Sveriges Radio* (Programme 1) transmitting on medium wave 245 metres, 255 metres, 306 metres, 388 metres, 417 metres and 506 metres broadcasts these messages in English, French, German and Swedish at 08.10, 13.10, 16.45 and 21.50hrs. *Sveriges Radio* (Programme 3) transmitting as above, broadcasts messages at 11.55 and 19.02hrs.

Lights*

It is compulsory for all motorists and motor cyclists to keep their dipped headlights on during the day.

Motoring clubs*

The **Motormännens Riksförbund** (M) has its headquarters at 10248 Stockholm, Sturegaten 32 ☎(08) 7823800, located on the town plan of Stockholm within the gazetteer, and the **Svenska Turistföreningen** (STF) at 10120 Stockholm, Drottninggatan 31-33 ☎(08) 7903100. Both have branch offices and agents in main towns.

Motorways

Several main roads (mainly E3, E4, E6 and E18) incorporate stretches of motorway (*motorväg*) and semi-motorway (*motortrafikled*). There are 875 miles open in all, and further sections are under construction or in the planning stage. No tolls are charged.

Orange badge scheme for disabled drivers*

Foreign badge holders are granted parking concessions, provided their badge features the international disabled symbol. A visitor whose badge does not feature this symbol can apply to the local authorities for a Swedish parking permit.

Generally badge or permit holders may park as follows:

a for up to 3 hours in a parking place where parking is not normally permitted or permitted for less than 3 hours. For 24 hours in places where parking is permitted for a period of 3–24 hours;

b free in a parking place where a charge is normally made.

Further parking concessions may be available on application to local authorities. However, disabled drivers must observe all other traffic regulations and respect the parking rules in parking places reserved for disabled drivers, especially when they conflict with *a* above.

Overtaking*

On roads where the hard shoulder is separated from the driving lane(s) with a continuous white line, it is strongly recommended not to use it other than in the case of emergency. In other cases, the hard shoulder may also be used by vehicles travelling at not more than 30kph (18mph) to facilitate overtaking and traffic flow. However, priority must be given to all other traffic when leaving the hard shoulder. These hard shoulders may also be used by cyclists and vehicles with a maximum speed of 30kph.

Parking*

In Stockholm and most of the larger towns, there are parking restrictions which are connected with road cleaning and are decided locally. A sign (blue disc with red border and red diagonal) is placed under the street name and gives the day and times when parking is prohibited. The restriction applies only to the side of the street on which the sign is displayed.

Petrol*

The majority of petrol stations are equipped with 24-hour filling stations where payment is

*Additional information will be found in the European ABC at the front of the book.

made with 10, 50 or 100 kroner bank notes.
Credit cards International credit cards are widely accepted at petrol stations.
Duty-free petrol The petrol in the vehicle tank may be imported free of custom duty and tax.
Petrol cans It is permitted to import petrol in cans, but only on payment of duty.
Petrol (leaded) is sold as the 98 octane grade.
Petrol (low lead) is sold as the 96 octane grade.
Petrol (unleaded) is sold in Sweden. It has an octane rating of 95 and pumps dispensing unleaded petrol are marked *Blyfri 95*.

Postal information

Mail Postcards and letters up to 20gm SKr3.30.
Post offices There are 2,500 post offices in Sweden. Opening hours of the larger offices are 09.00–18.00hrs Monday to Friday and 09.00–13.00hrs Saturday. Smaller offices open 10.00–16.00hrs Monday to Friday and 10.00–13.00hrs Saturday. In Stockholm, the Head Post Office is open 08.00–21.00hrs (11.00–13.00hrs on Sunday). The Central Station post office is open 07.00–22.00hrs on weekdays.

Priority*

Buses giving a signal have priority when leaving bus stops in areas where speed is restricted to 50kph (32mph).

Public holidays*

Official Public holidays in Sweden for 1990 are given below.

    January 1 (New Year's Day)
    January 6† (Epiphany)
    April 13 (Good Friday)
    April 15 (Easter Sunday)
    April 16 (Easter Monday)
    May 1 (May Day)
    May 24 (Ascension Day)
    June 3 (Whit Sunday)
    June 4 (Whit Monday)
    June 23† (Midsummer Day)
    November 1 (All Saints' Day)
    December 25 (Christmas Day)
    December 26 (Boxing Day)
†Saturday

Roads

There is a comprehensive network of numbered, well-signposted highways, but minor roads are not numbered. Although many roads in the south are being improved,

others – particularly in central and northern Sweden – are surfaced with loose gravel.

In various parts, chiefly along the Baltic coast, there are restricted areas where only certain roads are open to motorists, and in these areas, visitors may stay only at certain places and for a limited time. The two areas likely to concern visitors are around Boden and Kalix in the provinces of Norrbotten. Warning notices are displayed in English and other languages on the boundaries of these areas.

Shopping hours

Shopping hours vary, especially in large cities, but most are open 09.00–18.00hrs Monday to Friday, and 09.00–14.00hrs or 16.00hrs on Saturday.

Speed limits*

There are maximum speed limits indicated by signs on all roads in Sweden. *In built-up areas*, 50kph (31mph); on *all minor roads* and roads *with a high traffic density*, 70kph (43mph); on *all other roads*, 90kph (56mph), and 110kph (68mph) on *motorways*. Cars towing caravans fitted with brakes 70kph (43mph); without brakes 40kph (24mph).

Spiked or studded tyres*

Spiked tyres are permitted from 1 November until Sunday in the week after Easter Monday. They may be used during the rest of the year if the authorities announce that weather conditions require their use. When spiked tyres are used, they must be fitted on all wheels. If a vehicle with spiked tyres tows a trailer, the trailer must be fitted with spiked tyres.

Telephone*

Insert coin **after** lifting the receiver (instructions appear in English in all callboxes). When making calls to subscribers *within* Sweden, precede the number with the relevant area code (shown in parentheses before the hotel/garage enquiry number in the gazetteer). Use a SKr1 coin for local calls and SKr1 or 5 coins for national and international calls.
International callbox identification Callboxes with 1/3 slots.
Telephone rates A call to the UK costs SKr5.65 per minute. Local calls cost a minimum of SKr1.

*Additional information will be found in the European ABC at the front of the book.

Telephone Codes

UK to Sweden	010 46
Sweden to UK	009†44
Sweden to Republic of Ireland	009†353
Sweden to the USA	009†1

†Waiting for second dialling tone

Trams*

Trams should be overtaken on the right if the position of the tracks permits this. If there is no refuge at a tram stop, drivers should stop and give way to passengers alighting from and boarding the tram. All road users must give way to trams.

Warning triangle*

The use of a warning triangle is advisable in the event of accident or breakdown.

Wheel chains*

There are no special regulations governing the use of wheel chains. They may be used whenever the need arises.

Winter conditions

During winter, there is usually no difficulty in driving to Stockholm from Göteburg, Oslo or Denmark. Farther north, motoring is also possible subject to prevailing conditions, as the main roads are cleared as quickly as possible. Generally, however, the touring season is from May to September.

*Additional information will be found in the European ABC at the front of the book.

ACCOMMODATION

Swedish hotels have a particularly good reputation for cleanliness. A full list is published by the Swedish Tourist Board, but there is no official classification. Many local tourist offices ('Turistbyrå') offer a booking service for accommodation. The Swedish equivalent of VAT is included in all prices, as is the service charge. In many places, summer chalets can be rented. In the South, it is possible to holiday on a farm or as a paying guest at a manor house. The Swedish Touring Club (**Svenska Turistforeningen**) has over fifty lodges at which families can be accommodated. They provide from 4 to 6 beds, hot and cold water, and showers.

The prices shown below are an average for each classification. Accommodation is likely to be more expensive in Stockholm and some of the more popular tourist areas. At the time of going to press, £1 = SKr10.63 and US$1 = SKr6.40, but you should check the rate of exchange before your departure.

AVERAGE PRICES

	Single Room	Double Room	Breakfast	Lunch/Dinner
★★★★★	SKr1,113–1,568	SKr1,475–1,978	SKr90–155	—
★★★★	SKr656–962	SKr838–1,099	from SKr65	SKr67–200
★★★	SKr661–835	SKr831–1,032	SKr48–59	SKr61–229
★★	SKr415–642	SKr556–772	SKr43–47	SKr49–155
★	SKr323–585	SKr430–710	SKr35–45	from SKr43

Abbreviations
gt   gatan

ABISKO
Lappland

★★**Abisko Turistation** ☎(0980)40000
Mar-15 Sep
rm100(➜2) A35rm P50 Mountain Lake
Credit Cards ①②③

ALINGSÅS
Västergötland

★★★**Scandic** Bankgt 1 ☎(0322)14000 tx 21535
2 Jan-22 Dec
➜67 P Lift (
Credit Cards ①②③⑤
Allbärgning Ölandsgt 15 ☎(0322) 36300

ALVESTA
Småland

★★★**Scandic** Centralgt 2 ☎(0472)11350
2 Jan-23 Dec
➜48 ➔ P Lift (
Credit Cards ①②③⑤

ÅMÅL
Dalsland

★★**Stadshotellet** Kungsgt 9 ☎(0532)12020
➜49 A12rm ➔ P Lift ⊕ ⌂

ÄNGELHOLM
Skåne

★**Erikslunds** N Varalov 2137 ☎(0431)22114
rm15(➜14) ➔ P30 Lift
Credit Cards ①②

ÅRE
Jämtland

★★**Diplomat Åre-Aregarden** ☎(0647)50265 tx 44050
➜85 P50 ⚲ ⌂ Mountain Lake
Credit Cards ①②③⑤

ÅRJÄNG
Värmland

★★★**Scandic** Arikvagen ☎(0573)11070 tx 12636
➜40 P (⌂

ARLÖV
See **MALMÖ**

ARVIKA
Värmland

★★★**Bristol Arvika** Kyrkogt 25 (n.rest)
☎(46570)13280
15 Jan-17 Dec
⏷♨37 ♨ P70 Lift
Credit Cards ①②③⑤
★★**Oscar Statt** Torggt 9 ☎(0570)19750
⏷♨73 P60 Lift (
Credit Cards ①②③⑤

ASKERSUND
Närke

★★★**Scandic** Marieborg Sundsbrgt
☎(0583)12010 tx 73403
Jan-22 Dec
⏷♨64 P (
Credit Cards ①②③⑤
★★**Vättern** Torgparken 3 ☎(0583)11155
rm24(⏷♨18) P25
Credit Card ①

ÅTVIDABERG
Östergötland

★★★**Stallet** Östantorpsvägen 2 ☎(0120)11940 tx
5586
⏷♨68 P50 (⌂
Credit Cards ①②③⑤

BÅSTAD
Skåne

★★**Enehall** Stationsterrassen 10 ☎(0431)75015
tx 72955
rm60(♨45) A50rm P50
Credit Cards ①②③⑤
★★**Hallandsås** ☎(0430)24270
⏷♨19 P20 ♿
Credit Cards ①②③⑤

BODEN
Norrbotten

★★★**Bodensia** (Inter S) Medborgarplatsen
☎(0921)17710
⏷♨99 P10 Lift (
Credit Cards ①②③⑤

BOLLNÄS
Hälsingland

★★**Frimurarehotellet** Stationsgt 15
☎(0278)13220 tx 17930
⏷♨67 ♨ Lift

BORÅS
Västergötland

★★★**Grand** (SARA) Hallbergsgt 14
☎(033)108200 tx 36182
⏷♨163 ♨ P Lift (
Credit Cards ①②③⑤
★★★**Scandic** Hultasjogt 7 ☎(033)157000 tx
36906
2 Jan-22 Dec
⏷♨101 P Lift (⌂ Lake
Credit Cards ①②③⑤

BORGHOLM
Öland

☞ **Lundgren** Långgt ☎(0485) 10068 Dat

BORLÄNGE
Dalarna

★★★**Galaxen** Jussi Bjorlings Vag 25
☎(0243)80010 tx 74270
⏷♨129 ♨ P36 Lift (Mountain
Credit Cards ①②③⑤
★★★**Scandic** Stationsgt 21-23 ☎(0243)28120 tx
74138
2 Jan-23 Dec
⏷♨116 ♨ P Lift (⌂
Credit Cards ①②③⑤
★★**Brage** Stationsgt 1-3 ☎(0243)24150
⏷♨96 ♨ P32 Lift (
Credit Cards ①②③⑤

ENKÖPING
Uppland

★★**Stadshotellet** Stora Torget ☎(0171)20010
rm67(♨63) P Lift (⌂

ESKILSTUNA
Södermanland

★★★**Eskilstuna** (SARA) Hamngt 11
☎(016)137225 tx 46046
⏷♨228 P400 Lift (⌂ ♿
Credit Cards ①②③④⑤

FAGERSTA
Västmanland

★★★**Scandic** Blomstervagen ☎(0223)17060 tx
40977
2 Jan-22 Dec
⏷♨49 P (⌂
Credit Cards ①②③⑤

FALUN
Dalarna

★★★**Grand** (SARA) Trotzgt 9-11 ☎(46)02318700
tx 74141
Closed Xmas
⏷♨183 ♨ P95 Lift (⌂
Credit Cards ①②③⑤
★★★**Scandic** Norslund ☎(023)22160 tx 74137
2 Jan-22 Dec
⏷♨107 P Lift (⌂
Credit Cards ①②③⑤
☞ **Borlänge Bilbägning** H-Hedstrossvag ☎(023)
19630

FILIPSTAD
Värmland

★★★**Scandic** Lasarettsgt 2 ☎(0590)12530 tx
66362
⏷♨47 P (⌂
Credit Cards ①②③⑤

FLEN
Södermanland

★★★**Scandic** Brogt 5 ☎(0157)13940
2 Jan-23 Dec
⏷♨48 P (
Credit Cards ①②③⑤

FLENINGE
See **HELSINGBORG**

GAMLEBY
Småland

★**Tjust** ☎(0493)11550
rm17(♨7) P100 (Lake
Credit Cards ①②③⑤

GÄVLE
Gästrikland

★★★**Scandic** Hemmlingby ☎(026)188060 tx
47355
2 Jan-23 Dec
⏷♨210 P Lift (⌂
Credit Cards ①②③⑤

GETÅ
Östergötland

★★**Getå** ☎(011)62050
⏷♨50 ♨ P50 (♿ ⌂ Beach Sea Mountain
Credit Cards ①②③⑤

GISLAVED
Småland

★★★**Scandic** Riksvag 26 ☎(0371)11540 tx
70918
:Rest closed Jul
⏷♨54 Lift (
Credit Cards ①②⑤

GLUMSLÖV
Skåne

★★★**Örenäs Slott** ☎(0418)70250 tx 72759
⏷♨128 A11rm P150 Lift (♿ ⌂ Sea
Credit Cards ①②③⑤

GÖTEBORG (GOTHENBURG)
Bohuslän

The old city was built by the
Dutch with a formal grid of
canals and encircling moat; be
sure to see the *Antikhallarna*,
Scandinavia's largest antiques
and collectors' centre, and the
17th-century Queen Kristina's
Hunting Lodge where you can
stop for coffee and delicious
waffles. The 'new' city has wide
tree-lined avenues, elegant
houses and large parks, the
Liseberg Amusement Park -
claimed to be the largest leisure
complex in Scandinavia -
combining the fun of a
traditional fair with a stroll
through magnificent gardens.
Other attractions include the
Botanical Garden, the Slottskogen
Park and zoo, the bronze statue
of Poseidon and the Gotaplatsen
cultural centre and art gallery. If
you are an early riser, wander
down to the fish harbour and
watch the weekday auctions.
Being Sweden's largest port,
Göteborg has many maritime
attractions, including the four-
masted schooner *Viking*, which
you can board and tour.
Swedish design is legendary, and
you can find many beautiful
products in the city's two miles
of car-free streets.

EATING OUT One of Göteborg's
most popular restaurants is
Rakan, in Lorensbergsgatan,
where the house speciality is
shrimp. If expense is not a
problem, *Johann*, in Sodra
Hamngatan, has built up a
reputation as one of the best
restaurants in Sweden.

GÖTEBORG (GOTHENBURG)
Bohuslän

★★★★★**Park Avenue** (SRS) Kungsports Aveyn
36-38 ☎(031)176520 tx 2320
⏷♨320 ♨ P15 Lift (⌂
Credit Cards ①②③⑤
★★★★**Europa** (SARA) Kopmansgt 38
☎(031)801280 tx 21374
⏷♨480 ♨ P Lift (
Credit Cards ①②③⑤
★★★★**Opalen** Engelbrektsgt 73 ☎(031)810300 tx
2215
⏷♨237 P20 Lift (
★★★**Eggers** Drottningtorget 1,Box 323
☎(031)806070 tx 27223
⏷♨77 ♨ P Lift (
Credit Cards ①②③⑤

SWEDEN

★★★**Ekoxen** (Inter S/BW) Norra Hamngatan 38
(n.rest) ☎(031)805080 tx 21993
🛏75 P Lift ℂ
Credit Cards ① ② ③ ④ ⑤

★★★**Gothia** (SARA) Mässans Gata 24
☎(031)409300 tx 21941
🛏300 P1500 Lift ℂ ⌂ Mountain
Credit Cards ① ② ③ ⑤

★★★**Novotel** Klippan 1 ☎(031)149000 tx 28181
🛏150 P150 Lift ℂ Sea
Credit Cards ① ② ③ ④ ⑤

★★★**Rubinen** Kungsports Avengn 24
☎(031)810800 tx 20837
🛏185 ☎ P Lift ℂ
Credit Cards ① ② ③ ⑤

★★★**Scandic** Bäckebolsvägen ☎(031)520060 tx
27767
2 Jan-22 Dec
🛏232 ☎ P Lift ℂ ⌂
Credit Cards ① ② ③ ⑤

★★★**Scandinavia** (SARA) Kustgt 10,Postbox
12123 ☎(031)427000 tx 21522
🛏323 ☎ P150 Lift ℂ ⌂ Sea
Credit Cards ① ② ③ ⑤

★★★**Windsor** Kungsportsavenyn 6
☎(031)176540 tx 21014
🛏83 ☎ P Lift ℂ

★★**Örgryte** Danska Vagen 68 ☎(031)197620 tx
27565
🛏71 ☎ P70 Lift ℂ
Credit Cards ① ② ③ ⑤

★★**Ritz** Burggrevegat 25 ☎(031)800080 tx 21283
Closed 24 Dec-4 Jan
🛏107 P Lift ℂ
Credit Cards ① ② ③ ⑤

★**Liseberg Heden** Sten Sturegatan
☎(031)200280 tx 27450
🛏160 P25 Lift ℂ

★**Örnen** Lorensbergsgt 6,(Off Vasagatan)
☎(031)182380
rm30 Lift
Credit Cards ① ② ③

🖘 **Motorverken** Frofastegt 68 ☎(031) 289560
For

GRÄNNA
Småland

★★★**Scandic Gyllene Uttern** ☎(0390)10800 tx
70856
2 Jan-22 Dec
🛏53 P ℂ Sea Lake
Credit Cards ① ② ③ ⑤

HÄGERSTEN
See **STOCKHOLM**

HALMSTAD
Halland

★★★★**Hallandia** Radhusgatan 2 ☎(035)118800
tx 38030
🛏132 ☎ P20 Lift ℂ Sea
Credit Cards ① ② ③ ④ ⑤

★★★**Grand** (Inter/BW) Stationsgt 44 15885
☎(035)119140 tx 38260
🛏120 P240 Lift ℂ
Credit Cards ① ② ③ ⑤

★★★**Mårtenson** Storgatan 52 ☎(035)118070 tx
38210
🛏102 ☎ P15 Lift ℂ
Credit Cards ① ② ③ ⑤

★★★**St-Kristoffer** Strandvallen 3 ☎(035)104300
tx 38279
🛏117 P200 Lift ⅋ ⌂
Credit Cards ① ② ③ ⑤

HANDEN
Stockholm

★★★**Najaden** Rudsjoterrassen 3 ☎(0874)57400
tx 19594

🛏72 ☎ P20 Lift ℂ Beach Lake
Credit Cards ① ② ③ ④ ⑤

HAPARANDA
Norrbotten

★★**Stadshotellet** Torget 7 ☎(0922)11490
🛏40 ☎ P Lift ℂ

HÄRNÖSAND
Ångermanland

★★★**Scandic** Ådalsvägen ☎(0611)19560
2 Jan-23 Dec
🛏59 P ℂ
Credit Cards ① ② ③ ⑤

HÄSSLEHOLM
Skåne

★★**Göingehof** Frykholmsgt 23 ☎(0451)14330
rm42(🛏39) P Lift ℂ
Credit Cards ① ② ③ ⑤

HELSINGBORG
Skåne

★★★**Grand** (Inter S) Stortorget 8-12
☎(042)120170 tx 72271
🛏120 ☎ P60 Lift ℂ ⅋ Sea
Credit Cards ① ② ③ ⑤

★★★**Horisont** Gustaf Adolfs Gata 47
☎(042)149260 tx 72739
🛏171 P130 Lift ℂ ⌂ Sea
Credit Cards ① ② ③ ⑤

★★★**Scandic** Florettgt 41 ☎(042)151560 tx 72149
2 Jan-23 Dec
🛏181 P ℂ ⌂
Credit Cards ① ② ③ ⑤

★★**Kronan** Ängelholmsvagen 35 ☎(042)127965
rm60(🛏50) A50rm P60 Mountain
Credit Cards ① ② ③ ⑤

★★**Mollberg** Stortorget 18 ☎(042)120270 tx
72234
🛏115 ☎ P60 Lift ℂ
Credit Cards ① ② ③ ④ ⑤

🖘 **Scania** Muskötgt 1 ☎(042) 170000 VW
At **FLENINGE**(10km NE)

★★**Fleninge** ☎(042)205155
🛏27 P50
Credit Cards ① ③

HEMAVAN
Lappland

★★★**Hemavane** ☎(0954)30150 tx 8807
Seasonal
rm68(🛏10) A8rm P110 ℂ Mountain Lake
Credit Cards ① ② ③ ⑤

HOFORS
Gästrikland

★★★**Scandic** Skolgt 11 ☎(0290)23010
🛏40 P40 Lift ℂ
Credit Cards ① ② ③ ⑤

HOK
Småland

★★★**Hook Manor** (Relais et Châteaux)
☎(393)21080 tx 70419
🛏90 P100 ⅋ ⌂ 🏌 Mountain Lake
Credit Cards ① ② ③ ④ ⑤

HUDIKSVALL
Hälsingland

★★★**Stadshotellet** (Inter S) Storgt 36
☎(0650)15060 tx 71534
🛏144 ☎ P Lift ℂ ⌂
Credit Cards ① ② ③ ⑤

HYLTEBRUK
Småland

🖘 **Hylte Bilverstad** Gamia Nissastigen ☎(0345)
10206 Ope

INSJÖN
Dalarna

★★★**Insjön** Hotellvagen ☎(0277)41050
🛏25 ⅋
Credit Cards ① ② ③ ⑤

JÖNKÖPING
Småland

★★★★**Portalen** Västra Storgt 9,Box 413
☎(036)118200 tx 70037
rm207(🛏206) ☎ P155 Lift ℂ ⌂ Mountain Lake
Credit Cards ① ② ③ ④ ⑤

★★★**City** Västra Storgt 25 ☎(036)119280 tx
70611
:Rest closed Sun & Mon
🛏70 Lift ℂ Lake

★★★**Savoy** Brunnsgt 15 ☎(936)119480
:Rest closed Sat & Sun
rm53(🛏41) P50 Lift ℂ
Credit Cards ① ② ③ ⑤

★★★**Scandic** Rosenlund ☎(036)112160 tx 70820
2 Jan-23 Dec
🛏220 P Lift ℂ ⌂
Credit Cards ① ② ③ ⑤

★★★**Stora** (Inter S) ☎(036)119300 tx 70057
:Rest closed Sun
🛏111 ☎ P200 Lift ℂ Sea Mountain Lake
Credit Cards ① ② ③ ⑤

★★**Grand** Hovrattstorget ☎(036)119600
rm60(🛏16) ☎ P Lift Mountain Lake

🖘 **Atteviks** J-Bauersgt 1 ☎(044) 169100 Aud Por
VW

🖘 **Autolarm Börje Linden** Ö Stradt 5 ☎(036)
114048 All makes

KALMAR
Småland

★★★**Scandic** Dragonvagen 7 ☎(0480)22360 tx
43007
2 Jan-23 Dec
🛏152 P Lift ℂ ⌂
Credit Cards ① ② ③ ⑤

★★★**Stads** (Inter S) Stortorget 14 ☎(0480)15180
tx 43109
:Rest closed Sun
🛏139 ☎ P25 Lift ℂ
Credit Cards ① ② ③ ⑤

★★★**Witt** (SARA) Södra Langgt 42
☎(0480)15250 tx 43133
🛏112 ☎ P Lift ℂ ⌂
Credit Cards ① ② ③ ⑤

KARLSBORG
Västergötland

★★★**Kanalhotellet** Storgt 94 ☎(0505)12130
rm22(🛏19) A19rm P30 Lake
Credit Cards ① ② ③ ⑤

KARLSHAMN
Blekinge

★★★**Scandic** Strömmavägen ☎(0454)16660 tx
4596
2 Jan-23 Dec
🛏100 P Lift ℂ ⌂
Credit Cards ① ② ③ ⑤

KARLSKOGA
Värmland

★★★**Scandic** Hyttåsen ☎(0586)50460 tx 73392
2 Jan-23 Dec
🛏100 Lift ℂ ⌂
Credit Cards ① ② ③ ⑤

KARLSKRONA
Blekinge

★★★**Statt** (Inter S) Ronneebygt 37
☎(0455)19250 tx 43187
Closed 21 Dec-1 May:Rest closed Sun
🛏105 ☎ P40 Lift ℂ
Credit Cards ① ② ③ ⑤

KARLSTAD
Värmland

★★★**Gustav Froding** Höjdgt 3 ☎(054)831000 tx
66083
🛏165 Lift ℂ ⌂
Credit Cards ① ② ③ ④ ⑤

★★★Scandic Sandbäcksgt 6 (n.rest)
☎(054)187120 tx 66379
2 Jan-23 Dec
◄⋔146 P Lift ℂ 🖵 Lake
Credit Cards ① ② ③ ⑤

★★★Stads (Inter S) Kungsgt 22 ☎(054)115220 tx 66024
◄⋔143 ♠ P40 Lift ℂ Lake
Credit Cards ① ② ③ ⑤

★★★Winn (SARA) Norra Strandgt 9-11
☎(054)102220 tx 66120
:Rest closed Sun
◄⋔177 ♠ Lift ℂ
Credit Cards ① ② ③ ⑤

★★Gösta Berling DPn Drottninggt 1
☎(054)150190 tx 66144
◄⋔75 ♠ P10 Lift ℂ
Credit Cards ① ② ③ ④ ⑤

★★Ritz Vastra Torggt 20 ☎(054)11540
◄⋔54 ♠ P25 Lift ℂ
Credit Cards ① ② ③ ④ ⑤

★Drott Järnvägsgt 1 ☎(054)115635 tx 66329
rm38(◄⋔12) Lift

KATRINEHOLM
Södermanland

★★★Stads (Inter S) Storgt 20 ☎(0150)50440 tx 64055
◄⋔92 Lift ℂ

KIRUNA
Lappland

★★★Ferrum Lars Janssongt 15 ☎(0980)18600 tx 8746
◄⋔170 ♠ P50 Lift ℂ Mountain
Credit Cards ① ② ③ ⑤

KÖPING
Västmanland

★★★Scheele Hultgrensgt 10 ☎(0221)18120 tx 40423
◄⋔112 P112 Lift ℂ
Credit Cards ① ② ③ ⑤

KRAMFORS
Ångermanland

★★★Kramm Torgt 14 ☎(0612)13160 tx 71325
:Rest closed Sun
◄⋔109 ♠ P3 Lift ℂ
Credit Cards ① ② ③ ⑤

KRISTIANSTAD
Skåne

★★Grand (Inter/BW) V Storgt 15 ☎(044)103600 tx 48234
◄⋔147 ♠ P25 Lift ℂ
Credit Cards ① ② ③ ⑤

🝙 Kristianstads Bilcentrum Blekringevägen 2 ☎(044) 115890 Aud VW

KRISTINEHAMN
Värmland

🝙 Andersson Bil & Maskin 1a Indstrigt 3 ☎(0550) 15540 BMW For RR

KUNGÄLV
Bohuslän

★★★Fars Hatt ☎(0303)10970 tx 2415
◄⋔123 A28rm P350 Lift ℂ 🖵 Mountain
Credit Cards ① ② ③ ④ ⑤

KUNGENS KURVA
Stockholm

★★★Scandic Ekgardsvägen 2 ☎(08)7100460 tx 13830
2 Jan-22 Dec
rm266 P Lift ℂ 🖵
Credit Cards ① ② ③ ⑤

LAGAN
Småland

★★★Scandic Laganland ☎(0372)35200
◄⋔32 P100
Credit Cards ① ② ③ ⑤

LANDSKRONA
Skåne

★★★Öresund Kungsgt 15 ☎(0418)29000 tx 72327
◄⋔140 P100 Lift ℂ ⌕ 🖵 ⌴
Credit Cards ① ② ③ ④ ⑤

LAXA
Närke

★★★Scandic Vägkrog ☎(0587)11540
2 Jan-23 Dec
◄⋔42 ℂ
Credit Cards ① ② ③ ⑤

LIDKÖPING
Västergötland

🝙 Bjöstig Wennerbergsvägen 33 ☎(0510) 22480 Por

🝙 Per Bengtsson Wennerbergsvägen 27 ☎(0510) 22470 Hon Ope Vau

LINKÖPING
Östergötland

★★★Ekoxen (Inter/BW) Klostergt 68
☎(013)146070 tx 50142
◄⋔194 ♠ P105 Lift ℂ 🖵
Credit Cards ① ② ③ ④ ⑤

★★★Frimurarehotellet St Larsgt 14
☎(013)129180 tx 50053
◄⋔208 P80 Lift
Credit Cards ① ② ③ ⑤

★★★Rally Storgt 72 ☎(013)130200 tx 50055
2 Jan-23 Dec
◄⋔135 ♠ P28 Lift ℂ
Credit Cards ① ② ③ ⑤

★★★Scandic Rydsvagen ☎(013)171060 tx 50934
2 Jan-22 Dec
◄⋔119 P ℂ 🖵
Credit Cards ① ② ③ ⑤

★★★Stora Stora Torget 9 ☎(013)129630 tx 50937
Closed 23-30 Dec
◄⋔94 P20 Lift ℂ
Credit Cards ① ② ③ ⑤

LJUNGBY
Småland

★★★Terraza (Inter S) Stora Torget 1
☎(0372)13560 tx 52046
Mar-4 Jul & 10 Aug-7 Jul :Rest closed Sun
◄⋔95 ♠ P30 Lift ℂ
Credit Cards ① ② ③ ⑤

LUDVIKA
Dalarna

★★★Grand (Inter S) Eriksgt 6 ☎(0240)18220 tx 74023
Closed 3 Jul-6 Aug
◄⋔103 ♠ P Lift ℂ Lake
Credit Cards ① ② ③ ⑤

LULEÅ
Norrbotten

★★★★SAS Luleå Storgt 17 ☎(0920)94000 tx 80406
◄⋔211 ♠ P50 Lift ℂ 🖵 Sea
Credit Cards ① ② ③ ⑤

★★★Luleå Stads (Inter S) DPn Storgt 15
☎(0920)10410 tx 80413
:Rest closed Sun
◄⋔135 ♠ P15 Lift ℂ Sea
Credit Cards ① ② ③ ⑤

★★★Scandic Mjolkudden (n.rest) ☎(0920)28360 tx 80235
2 Jan-22 Dec
rm158 P Lift ℂ ⌕
Credit Cards ① ② ③ ⑤

LUND
Skåne

★★★Grand (Inter S) Bantorget 1 ☎(046)117010 tx 33484
◄⋔87 ♠ P Lift ℂ
Credit Cards ① ② ③

★★★Lundia (Inter S) DPn Knut den Stores Gata 2 ☎(046)124140 tx 32761
:Rest closed Sun & holidays
◄⋔97 ♠ P200 Lift ℂ
Credit Cards ① ② ③ ④ ⑤

LYSEKIL
Bohuslän

★★Lysekil Rosvikstorgt 1 ☎(0523)11860
◄⋔50 P60 Lift ℂ Sea
Credit Cards ① ② ③ ⑤

🝙 Winthers Landsvägsgt 50 ☎(0523) 15050 VW

MALMÖ
Skåne

★★★★Savoy (Inter S) N Vallgt 62 ☎(040)70230 tx 32383
◄⋔108 ♠ P40 Lift ℂ
Credit Cards ① ② ③ ⑤

★★★★Scandinavia (Inter S) Drottninggt 1F
☎(040)936700 tx 32235
◄⋔215 ♠ P Lift ℂ

★★★Kramer Stortorget 7 ☎(040)70120 tx 32159
◄⋔65 P Lift ℂ
Credit Cards ① ② ③ ④ ⑤

★★★St-Jörgen St Nygt 35 ☎(040)7730 tx 32404
◄⋔285 ♠ P100 Lift ℂ
Credit Cards ① ② ③ ④ ⑤

★★Tunneln Adelgt 4 ☎(040)101930 tx 238978
rm49(◄⋔35) ♠ P15 Lift ℂ
Credit Cards ① ② ③ ⑤

★★Winn (SARA) Jorgen Knocksgt 3 (n.rest)
☎(040)101800 tx 33295
◄⋔101 ♠ P Lift ℂ Sea
Credit Cards ① ② ③ ⑤

At ARLÖV(7km NW)

★★★Scandic Kronetorpsvagen ☎(040)433620 tx 32994
2 Jan-22 Dec
◄⋔72 P ℂ ⌕ 🖵
Credit Cards ① ② ③ ⑤

At SEGEVÅNG(5km E)

★★★Scandic Segesvängen ☎(040)80120 tx 33478
2 Jan-22 Dec
◄⋔158 P ℂ 🖵 ⌴
Credit Cards ① ② ③ ⑤

MALUNG
Dalarna

★Nya Skinnargården Grönlandsvägan ☎(0280)11750
◄⋔51 P60 Mountain
Credit Cards ① ② ③

MARKARYD
Småland

★★Stora ☎(0433)10730
◄⋔44 A20rm P

MÖLLE
Skåne

★Grand Bökebolsv 11 ☎(031)47280
Etr-Sep
rm50(◄⋔30) P ℂ Sea Mountain

MÖLNDAL
Västergötland

★★★Scandic Abro ☎(031)275060 tx 21801
2 Jan-22 Dec
◄⋔214 P Lift ℂ 🖵
Credit Cards ① ② ③ ⑤

🝙 Bilexa Mölndalsvägen ☎(031) 813560 Maz Ope Vau

MORA
Dalarna

★★★Mora (Inter S) Strandgt 12 ☎(0250)11750 tx 12636
:Rest closed Sun Nov-May
rm92(◄⋔87) ♠ Lift ℂ ⌴ Lake
Credit Cards ① ② ③ ⑤

★★★**Scandic** Kristinebergsgt ☎(0250)15070 tx 74248
2 Jan-22Dec
⚞79 A32rm P Lift ℂ 🖃
Credit Cards ① ② ③ ⑤

MOTALA
Östergötland

★★★**Stads** (Inter S) Stora Torget ☎(0141)16400 tx 64900
:Rest closed Sun
⚞79 P7 Lift ℂ Lake
Credit Cards ① ② ③ ⑤

🚗 *Jansen Motor* Vadstenavagen 30-34 ☎(0141)16230 For

🚗 *Wahistedts* ☎(0141) 16030 VW

NÄSSJÖ
Småland

★★★**Högland** (SARA) Esplanaden 4 ☎(0380)13100 tx 35289
⚞105 ☎ P Lift ℂ

🚗 *Höre Bil* Höregt 12 ☎(0380) 11005 AR

NORRKÖPING
Östergötland

★★★**Scandic** Järngt ☎(011)100380 tx 64115
2 Jan-22 Dec
⚞150 P Lift ℂ 🖃
Credit Cards ① ② ③ ⑤

★★★**Standard** (SARA) Slottsgt 99 ☎(011)129220 tx 64171
2 Jan-23 Dec & 27-31 Dec
rm176(⚞164) ☎ P40 Lift ℂ
Credit Cards ① ② ③ ④ ⑤

NORRTÄLJE
Uppland

🚗 *Norrtälje Bilcentral* Trädgårdsgt 3 ☎(0176) 12510 For

NYBRO
Småland

★★**Stora** Stadshusplan ☎(0481)11935
⚞37 P40 Lift
Credit Cards ① ② ③ ⑤

NYKÖPING
Södermanland

★★★**Scandic** Gumsbacken ☎(01551)89000 tx 64162
2 Jan-22 Dec
⚞96 P Lift ℂ 🖃
Credit Cards ① ② ③ ⑤

ÖREBRO
Närke

★★★**Grand** Fabriksgt 21-25 ☎(019)150200 tx 73362
⚞227 ☎ P80 Lift ℂ 🖃 Mountain
Credit Cards ① ② ③ ⑤

★★★**Grev Rosen** Södra Grev Rosengt 2 ☎(019)130240 tx 735575
rm73(⚞70) ☎ P Lift ℂ
Credit Cards ① ② ③ ⑤

★★★**Scandic** Västhagagt 1 ☎(019)130480 tx 73581
2 Jan-23 Dec
⚞204 P Lift ℂ 🖃
Credit Cards ① ② ③ ⑤

★★★**Stora** (Inter/BW) Drottningt 1 ☎(019)124360 tx 73230
⚞97 ☎ P97 Lift ℂ Lake
Credit Cards ① ② ③ ④ ⑤

★★**Bergsmannen** Drottningt 42 ☎(019)130320
Closed Jul
rm66(⚞36) ☎ P Lift ℂ

ÖRKELLJUNGA
Skåne

★★★**Scandic** Naum ☎(0435)51442
⚞29 P60
Credit Cards ① ② ③ ④ ⑤

ÖRNSKÖLDSVIK
Ångermanland

★★★**Scandic** Hastmarksvagen 4 ☎(0660)82870 tx 71962
2 Jan-22 Dec
⚞103 P Lift ℂ 🖃
Credit Cards ① ② ③ ⑤

★**Örnsköldsvik** (SARA) Lasarettsgt 2 ☎(0660)10110 tx 6000
⚞115 P80 Lift ℂ Sea Mountain
Credit Cards ① ② ③ ⑤

OSKARSHAMN
Småland

🚗 *Ekelunds* Ringplatsen 11 ☎(0491) 14330 AR Fia Vau

ÖSTERSUND
Jämtland

★★★**Östersund** (Inter S) Kyrkgt 70 ☎(063)117640 tx 44065
⚞129 ☎ P55 Lift ℂ Mountain Lake
Credit Cards ① ② ③ ⑤

★★★**Scandic** Krondikesvagen 97 ☎(063)127560 tx 44022
2 Jan-22 Dec
⚞127 P Lift ℂ 🖃
Credit Cards ① ② ③ ⑤

★★**Winn** (SARA) Prästgt 16 ☎(063)127740 tx 44038
Closed Xmas
⚞198 ☎ Lift 🖃 Sea Mountain Lake
Credit Cards ① ② ③ ⑤

RÄTTVIK
Dalarna

★★**Rättvikshästen** Nyåkersvägen ☎(0248)11015
rm40(⚞20) A40rm P40 ℀ 🖃 🐾 Mountain
Credit Cards ① ④ ⑤

RIKSGRÄNSEN
Lappland

★★★**Riksgränsen** ☎(0980)40080 tx 8767
15 Feb-15 Dec
⚞144 Lift Mountain Lake
Credit Cards ① ② ③ ⑤

★*Lapplandia Sporthotel* ☎(0980)43120
⚞95 A9rm Lake

RONNEBY
Blekinge

★★★**Ronneby Brunn** ☎(0457)12750 tx 43505
⚞301 A34rm Lift ℂ ℀ 🖃
Credit Cards ① ② ③

SÄFFLE
Värmland

★★★**Scandic** O-Tratjagt 2 ☎(0533)2660 tx 66092
2 Jan-22 Dec
⚞65 P Lift ℂ 🖃
Credit Cards ① ② ③ ⑤

SALTSJÖBADEN
See **STOCKHOLM**

SEGEVÅNG
See **MALMÖ**

SIGTUNA
Uppland

★★**Stads** St Nygt 3 ☎(0760)50100
⚞26 P26 ℂ Lake
Credit Cards ① ② ③ ⑤

SKELLEFTEÅ
Västerbotten

★★★**Malmia** (Inter S) Torget 2 ☎(0910)77300 tx 65201
⚞140 ☎ P Lift ℂ
Credit Cards ① ② ③

★★**Statt** (SARA) Stationsgt 8-10 ☎(0910)141
⚞110 ☎ P Lift ℂ

SKÖVDE
Västergötland

★★★**Billingehus** (SARA) Alphyddevagen ☎(0500)83000 tx 67006
⚞240 P1000 Lift ℂ ℀ 🖃 🖃
Credit Cards ① ② ③ ⑤

★★**Billingen** Trädgårdsgt 10 ☎(0500)10790
⚞92 ☎ P5 Lift ℂ
Credit Cards ① ② ③ ⑤

SÖDERHAMN
Hälsingland

★★★**Scandic** Montorsbacken ☎(0270)18020 tx 47910
2 Jan-22 Dec
⚞87 P ℂ 🖃
Credit Cards ① ② ③ ⑤

SÖDERTÄLJE
Södermanland

★★★**Scandic** Verkstadsvagen ☎(0755)34260 tx 16682
2 Jan-22 Dec
⚞125 P Lift ℂ 🖃
Credit Cards ① ② ③ ⑤

★★★**Skogshöjd** (Inter S) Tappgt 15 ☎(0755)32670 tx 13672
⚞230 ☎ P70 Lift ℂ 🖃 Mountain
Credit Cards ① ② ③ ⑤

SOLNA
See **STOCKHOLM**

STOCKHOLM

See Plan pages 380 and 381 *Population* 1,420,000 (with suburbs) *Local tourist office* Hamngatan 27 *(08) 7892000

Stockholm, capital of Sweden, lies on several islands and on the adjacent mainland, in a situation that is widely regarded as one of the most picturesque in Europe. The nucleus of the city is an island in mid-channel called the old town, on which stand the imposing Royal Palace (1697 - 1754), the principal church (St Nicholas), the House of the Nobles (1648 - 70) in which they held periodic meetings, and the Ministries of the Kingdom. Immediately west of the central island lies the Knights' Island, containing the old Franciscan church in which all the later sovereigns of Sweden have been buried.

The districts of Norrmalm and Ostermalm lie to the north of these two islands, separated by a narrow channel in which there is an islet containing the houses of parliament. The largest buildings and institutions in Norrmalm and Ostermalm are the National Museum, with valuable collections of coins, paintings and sculptures; most of the theatres; the Academy of Fine Arts; Humlegarden, a magnificent park; and the Academy of Sciences with natural history collections.

East of the old town lies Djurgarden, a beautiful island once a hunting-ground of Gustavus Vasa. Situated there are the Northern Museum, the Biological Museum and a great open-air park and museum (*Skansen*). Immediately south of the old town island is the extensive district of Sodermalm, the houses of which climb up the steep slopes that rise from the water's edge. An archipelago east of the city forms a large recreational ground popular with residents and visitors alike.

EATING OUT If it is traditional Swedish fare you are after look for *Husmanskost* (home cooking), or the special dishes of the day. If it is fish you fancy, go to Ostermalmshaller, a market area where fishmongers' stalls have grown into seafood bars and restaurants. Treat yourself to *gravadlax* (salmon with dill in mustard sauce), or *Jansonns frestele*, a casserole of potatoes, anchovies, onion and cream. Wash down your meal with *snaps* - served ice cold in small glasses to be drunk in one gulp. Food is substantial and nourishing, but eating out is expensive. A good idea is to look for establishments displaying the sign *Dagens ratt* (today's special) which usually represents good value. One of Stockholm's best known restaurants is *Aurora in Munkbron*. Housed in a 17th-century building, it offers both Swedish and international specialities. Excellent harbour views can be enjoyed at the Quarter Deck, located on the waterfront in the old town, and salmon is a speciality of *Glada Laxen*, centrally located in Regeringsgatan.

STOCKHOLM

★★★★★**Grand** Södra Blasieholmshamnen 8 ☎(08)221020 tx 19500
◗ｲ319 P Lift Sea

★★★★★**Strand** (BW) Nybrokajen 9 ☎(08)22900 tx 10504
◗ｲ134 ☎ P Lift (Sea
Credit Cards ①②③⑤

★★★★**Mornington** (Inter S) Nybrogatan 53 ☎(08)6631240 tx 10145
◗ｲ140 ☎ Lift (
Credit Cards ①②③④⑤

★★★**Amaranten** (THF) Kungsholmsgt 31 ☎(08)541060 tx 17498
◗ｲ410 ☎ P Lift (🖾
Credit Cards ①②③④⑤

★★★**Bromma** Brommaplan 1 ☎(08)252920 tx 13125
2 Jan-23 Dec
◗ｲ141 P50 Lift (
Credit Cards ①②③⑤

★★★**Continental** Vasagt ☎(08)244020 tx 10100
◗ｲ250 ☎ Lift (
Credit Cards ①②③⑤

★★★**Diplomat** Strandvägen 7C ☎(08)6635800 tx 17119
Closed Xmas:Rest closed Sun
◗ｲ130 P Lift (Sea
Credit Cards ①②③④⑤

★★★**Malmen** Götgt 49-51 ☎(08)226080 tx 19489
◗ｲ280 ☎ P100 Lift (
Credit Cards ①②③④⑤

★★★**Palace** St-Eriksgt 115 ☎(08)241220 tx 19877
Closed Xmas & New Year
◗ｲ214 ☎ P65 Lift (
Credit Cards ①②③④⑤

★★★**Reisen** (THF) Skeppsbron 12-14 ☎(08)223260 tx 17494
Closed 23 Dec-2 Jan
◗ｲ113 P Lift (🖾 Sea
Credit Cards ①②③⑤

★★★**Sjöfartshotellet** Kataringavagen 26 ☎(08)226960 tx 19020
◗ｲ184 ☎ Lift
Credit Cards ①②③⑤

★★★**Terminus** (Inter S) Vasagt 20 ☎(08)222640 tx 11749
Closed Xmas
◗ｲ155 ☎ P20 Lift (
Credit Cards ①②③⑤

★★★**Wellington** (Inter S) Storgt 6 ☎(08)6670910 tx 17963
◗ｲ51 Lift (
Credit Cards ①②③④⑤

★★**Adlon** Vasagt 42 (n.rest) ☎(08)245400 tx 11543
◗ｲ62 Lift
Credit Cards ①②③⑤

★★**City** ☎(08)222240 tx 12487
◗ｲ300 P Lift (
Credit Cards ①②③⑤

★★**Eden Terrace** Sturegt 10 ☎(08)223160 tx 10570
:Rest closed Sun
rm69(◗ｲ60) ☎ P30 Lift
Credit Cards ①②③④⑤

★**Kung Carl** Birger Jarlsgt 23 (n.rest) ☎(08)221240 tx 12262
27 Dec-23 Dec
◗ｲ90 A34rm ☎ P25 Lift (
Credit Cards ①②③⑤

✆◗ **Kindwall** Roslagsgt 4,Järfalla ☎(08) 970820
All makes

✆◗ **Phillipsons Norr** Regeringsgt 109 ☎(08) 340000 Mer

At HÄGERSTEN(5km SW on E3)

★★★**Attaché** Cedergrensvagen 16 ☎(08)181185 tx 16726
◗ｲ59 P15 Lift (
Credit Cards ①②③⑤

At SALTSJÖBADEN(20km SE)

★★★★**Grand** ☎(08)7170020 tx 10210
◗ｲ103 P50 Lift (℃ Sea
Credit Cards ①②③⑤

At SOLNA(5km N)

★★★**Flamingo** Hotellgt 11 ☎(08)830800 tx 10060
◗ｲ130 P Lift (
Credit Cards ①②③⑤

★★★**Scandic** Jarva Krog,Uppsalav Ulriksdale ☎(08)850360 tx 13767
◗ｲ204 ☎ P Lift (🖾
Credit Cards ①②③⑤

At TÄBY(15km N)

★★★**Scandic** ☎(08)7680580 tx 16630
2 Jan-22 Dec
◗ｲ118 P Lift (🖾
Credit Cards ①②③⑤

STORLIEN
Jämtland

★★**Storliens Högfjällshotellet** ☎(0647)70170 tx 44051
7 Feb-5 Jan
rm191(◗ｲ150) P100 Lift (℃ 🖾 Beach Mountain Lake
Credit Cards ①②③

SUNDSVALL
Medelpad

★★★**Bore** (Inter S) Tradgardsgt 31-33 ☎(060)150600 tx 71280
:Rest closed Sun
◗ｲ145 ☎ P15 Lift (⌐
Credit Cards ①②③⑤

★★★**Scandic** Vardshusbacken 6 ☎(060)566860 tx 71092
2 Jan-22 Dec
◗ｲ150 P Lift (🖾
Credit Cards ①②③⑤

★★★**Strand** (SARA) Strandgt 10 ☎(060)121800 tx 71340
28 Dec-23 Dec :Rest closed Sun
◗ｲ203 ☎ P Lift (🖾
Credit Cards ①②③⑤

★★★**Sundsvall** Esplanaden 29 ☎(060)171600 tx 71254
◗ｲ201 ☎ P50 Lift (Mountain Lake
Credit Cards ①②③④⑤

TÄBY
See STOCKHOLM

TÄLLBERG
Dalarna

★★★**Green** ☎(0247)50250 tx 74188
◗ｲ100 P50 🖾 ⌐ ♟♟ Mountain Lake
Credit Cards ①③

★★**Dalecarlia** ☎(0247)50255
◗ｲ53 P100 ℃ 🖾 ⌐ Lake
Credit Cards ①②③

★★**Långbers** ☎(0247)50290
◗ｲ55 P Lift Mountain Lake
Credit Cards ①②③⑤

★★*Siljansgården* ☎(0247)50040 tx 74088
22 Dec-Sep
rm25(◄12) A18rm ⌂ P ♀ Lake

TORSBY
Värmland

★★*Björnidet* Kyrkogt 2 ☎(0560)13820
◄⋔28 P20 ➤
Credit Cards 1 2 3 5

TROLLHÄTTAN
Västergötland

★★★*Swania* (Inter S) Storgt 49 ☎(0520)12570
tx 42225
◄⋔56 Lift ➤

TYLÖSAND
Halland

★★*Tylösands* ☎(035)30500 tx 38209
◄⋔230 P190 Lift ℂ ♀ ➤ Beach Sea
Credit Cards 1 2 3 4 5

UDDEVALLA
Bohuslän

★★★*Carlia* Norra Drottningt 20-22 ☎(0522)14140
tx 42224
Closed Xmas & New Year:Rest closed Sun
◄⋔64 ⌂ Lift ℂ
Credit Cards 1 2 3 5

★*Viking* Strömstadsvägen 25 (n.rest)
☎(0522)14550
rm20(◄⋔6) P10 ℂ
Credit Cards 1 2 3 5

ULRICEHAMN
Västergötland

★★★*Scandic* Nyboholm ☎(0321)12040
2 Jan-22 Dec
◄⋔58 P ℂ
Credit Cards 1 2 3 5

UMEÅ
Västerbotten

★★★*Blå Aveny* (Inter S) Rådhusesplanaden 14
☎(090)132300 tx 54010
◄⋔165 ⌂ P80 Lift ℂ
Credit Cards 1 2 3 5

★★★*Scandic* Yrkesvägen 8 ☎(090)135250 tx
54012
2 Jan-22 Dec
◄⋔159 P Lift ℂ ➤
Credit Cards 1 2 3 5

★★★*Strand* V-Strandgtn 11 (n.rest)
☎(090)129020
Closed Xmas & New Year
◄⋔44 Lift

★★★*Winn* (SARA) Skolgt 64 ☎(090)122020 tx
54118
◄⋔165 ⌂ P Lift ℂ
Credit Cards 1 2 3 5

UPPSALA
Uppland

★★★★*Uplandia* (Inter S) Dragarbrunnsgt 32,Box
1023 ☎(018)102160 tx 76125
◄⋔133 ⌂ P33 Lift ℂ
Credit Cards 1 2 3 4 5

★★*Gillet* (SARA) Dragarbrunnsgt 23
☎(018)155360 tx 76028
◄⋔169 ⌂ P250 Lift ℂ
Credit Cards 1 2 3 5

VÄNERSBORG
Västergötland

★★★*Scandic* Nabbensberg ☎(0521)62120 tx
42901
2 Jan-22 Dec
◄⋔119 P Lift ℂ ➤
Credit Cards 1 2 3 5

VARBERG
Halland

★★*Statt* Kungsgt 24-26 ☎(0340)16100 tx 3481
◄⋔126 Lift ℂ Sea
Credit Cards 1 2 3 5

VÄRNAMO
Småland

★★★*Värnamo* (SARA) Storgatsbacken 20
☎(0370)11530 tx 70885
:Rest closed Sun
◄⋔125 P100 Lift ℂ
Credit Cards 1 2 3 4 5

VASSMOLÖSA
Småland

★*Wassmolösa Gästgiveri* ☎(0480)32065 Jan-22
Dec
rm9
Credit Cards 1 2 3 5

VÄSTERÅS
Västmanland

★★★*Park* (Inter S) Gunnilbogt 2 ☎(021)110120
tx 40477
◄⋔141 Lift
Credit Cards 1 2 3 5

★★★*Scandic* Pilgt ☎021180280 tx 40765
2 Jan - 22 Dec
rm175 P Lift ℂ ➤
Credit Cards 1 2 3 5

VÄXJÖ
Småland

★★★*Österleden* Sandviksvägen 1 ☎(0470)29050
tx 52277
:Rest closed Fri pm/Sun & wknds summer
◄⋔147 P100 Lift ➤
Credit Cards 1 2 3 5

★★★*Scandic* Hejaregt 15 ☎(0470)22070 tx
52150
2 Jan - 22 Dec
◄⋔106 P Lift ℂ ➤
Credit Cards 1 2 3 5

★★★*Statt* (SARA) Kungsgt 6 ☎(0470)13400 tx
52139
◄⋔130 P130 Lift ℂ
Credit Cards 1 2 3 4 5

YSTAD
Skåne

★★★*Ystads Saltsjöbad* ☎(0411)13630 tx 32342
◄⋔109 P500 ℂ ➤ Beach Sea
Credit Cards 1 2 3 5

Opening doors to the World of books

Book Tokens can be bought and exchanged at most bookshops

STOCKHOLM

2	★★★★★	Grand
3	★★★★★	Strand
4	★★★★	Grand (At Saltsjöbaden)
5	★★★★	Mornington
7	★★★	Amaranten
8	★★★	Bromma
9	★★★	Continental
10	★★★	Diplomat
11	★★★	Flamingo (At Solna)
12	★★★	Malmen
13	★★★	Palace
14	★★★	Reisen
15	★★★	Scandic (At Täby)
16	★★★	Sjöfartshotellet
17	★★★	Terminus
18	★★★	Wellington
19	★★	Adlon
20	★★	City
21	★★	Eden Terrace
22	★★★	Attaché (At Hägersten)
24	★	Kung Carl

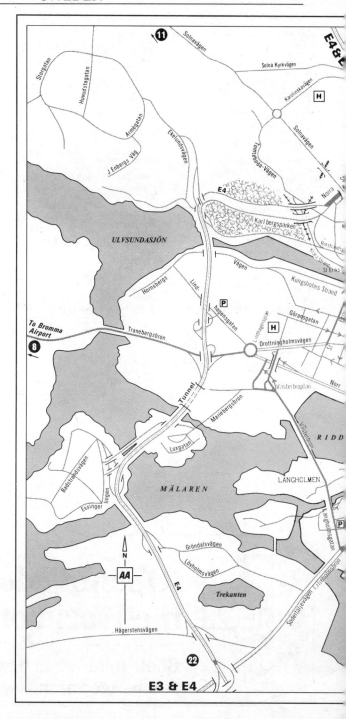

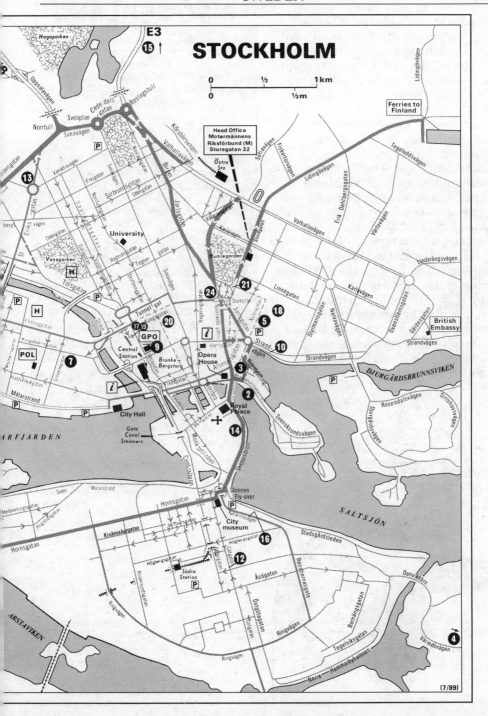

STOCKHOLM

With breathtaking mountain scenery, some of the world's most luxurious and stylish hotels, winter sports resorts that are without equal, a transportation system that is the envy of the world and picturesque villages and towns, Switzerland is a magnet for visitors at any time of the year.

Landlocked in the middle of Europe and conditioned by its historic evolution, Switzerland has four natural languages. The German-speaking area north of the Alps is by far the largest, whereas Swiss-German is only a spoken dialect with the added flavour of local versions. In the French-speaking regions of the south-west there is a marked French touch, while south of the Alps the waving palms of the Ticino herald the Italia tongue and way of life. In the small mountainous area of south-east Switzerland, the Grisons, an ancient Latin tongue, Rhaeto-Romanic (Romansch), has survived right through the centuries.

SWITZERLAND

Language
Switzerland has German, French and Italian regions, with Romansch as a local minority language.

Local Time
GMT + 1 hour (Summer GMT + 2 hours)

Currency
Swiss franc, divided into 100 *centimes* or *rappen*. At the time of going to press
£1 = SFr2.67
US$1 = SFr1.60

Emergency numbers
Fire ☎118
Police and Ambulance ☎117
(144 for Ambulance if the area code of the number of the telephone from which you are making the call is 01, 022, 030, 031, 032, 033, 042, 043, 052, 056, 057, 061, 062, 063 or 064)

Information Britain
Swiss National Tourist Office, 1 New Coventry Street, London W1V 8EE
☎01-734 1921 (071-734 1921 from 6 May 1990)

Information in the USA
Swiss National Tourist Office, 608 Fifth Avenue, New York, NY 10020
☎212 757 5944

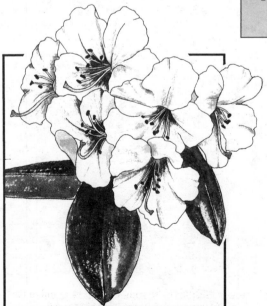

HOW TO GET THERE

From Britain, Switzerland is usually approached via *France*.

Distance

from the Channel ports to Bern is approximately 1,000km (530 miles), a distance which will normally require only one overnight stop.

If you intend to use Swiss motorways, you will be liable for a tax of *SFr30* – see 'Motorways' below for full details.

MONEYMATTERS

There are no restrictions on the amounts of foreign or Swiss currency that you may take into or out of the country.

Banking hours

Monday–Friday:

Basel	08.15–17.300hrs (Wednesday or Friday 18.30hrs);
Bern	08.00–16.30hrs (Thursday 18.00hrs);
Genève	08.30–16.30/17.30hrs;
Lausanne	08.30–12.00hrs and 13.30–16.30hrs (Friday 17.00hrs);
Lugano	09.00–12.00/12.30hrs and 13.00/13.30–16.00hrs;
Zurich	08.15/09.00–16.30/17.00hrs (Thursday 18.00hrs).

There are exchange offices in nearly all **Touring Club Suisse** offices, open during office hours.

At railway stations in large towns, and at airports, exchange offices are open 08.00–20.00hrs (times may vary slightly from place to place).

Postcheques

may be cashed at all post offices up to a maximum of *SFr300* per cheque in multiples of *SFr10*. Go to a counter position which displays the words **Paiements/Auszahlungen/Pagamenti**.

MOTORING REGULATIONS AND GENERAL INFORMATION

The information given here is specific to Switzerland. It **must** be read in conjunction with the European ABC at the front of the book, which covers those regulations which are common to many countries.

Accidents*

The most important principle is that all persons involved in an accident should ensure, as far as possible, that the traffic flow is maintained. Should anyone have been injured, the police must be called immediately. Those injured should be assisted by the persons at the scene of the accident until the arrival of medical help. It is not necessary to call the police if the accident has only caused material damage, although the driver(s) concerned should immediately report the incident to the owner of the damaged property and exchange particulars. If this is not possible, the police must be informed. See *Warning triangle* below.

Boats*

Third party insurance is compulsory for craft used on the Swiss lakes. Boat registration is also required.

Breakdown*

The major motoring club, *Touring Club Suisse* (TCS), operates a patrol service and a day and night breakdown service, but is is likely that you will be charged for any service. The service (*Secours routier*) operates from several centres throughout the country and can be summoned by telephone. When calling, give the operator the password *Touring Secours*, *Touring Club Suisse*, and state your location and if possible the nature of the trouble. The operator will state within a short time whether it will be a black and yellow patrol car or garage assistance, and how soon help can be expected. See also *Motorways* and *Warning triangle* below.

British Embassy/Consulates*

The British Embassy together with its consular section is located at 3000 Berne 15, Thunstrasse

*Additional information will be found in the European ABC at the front of the book.

For key to country identification - see "About the gazetteer"

A

FL

I

D

CH VORARLBERG AREA SEE INSET

BERN

F

Mustair, Santa Maria, Bad Scuol, Vulpera, Zernez, Poschiavo, Zuoz, St-Moritz, Pontresina, Celerina, Samedan, Sils-Maria, Silvaplana, Maloja, Bivio, Klosters, Davos, Arosa, Lenzerheide, Tiefencastel, Parpan, Chur, Thusis, Laax, Ilanz, Bad Ragaz, Sargans, Vaduz, Triesenberg, Schaan, N13, Flims-Waldhaus, Brigels, Disentis, Bellinzona, Biasca, Faido, Minusio, Bissone, Lugano, Morcote, Chiasso, Ascona, Brissago, Porto Ronco, Wassen, Göschenen, Göschenen, Furka Pass, Fiesch, Simplon-Kulm, Simplon-Dorf, Gabi, Saas-Fee, Brig, Visp, Grächen, Bürchen, Zermatt, Münster, Evolène, Arolla, Sierre, Montana-Vermala, St-Luc, Crans-sur-Sierra, Verbier, Sion, Gsteig, Gstaad, Villars-sur-Ollon, Bex, Leysin, Aigle, Champéry, Morgins, Martigny, Orsières, Bourg St-Pierre, Andermatt, Airolo, Gütnellen

Schaffhausen, Neuhausen, Steckborn, Gottlieben, Kreuzlingen, Romanshorn, Arbon, Rorschach, Teufen, St-Gallen, Appenzell, Wil, Mettendorf, Berlingen, Unterwasser, Buchs, Altstätten, Wildhaus, Nesslau, N3, Näfels, Glarus, Schwanden, Bollingen, Lachen, Rapperswil, Niederurnen, Winterthur, Zürich, Thalwil, Wädenswil, Feusisberg, Baden, Dietikon, Brugg, Aarau, Sursee, Frick, Rheinfelden, Olten, Basel, Arlesheim, Mariastein, Liestal, Langenbruck, Balsthal, Seckingen, Solothurn, Fraubrunnen, Burgdorf, Biel, Nyss, Thielle, Neuenegg, Delémont, Porrentruy, Tafers, Fribourg, Kandersteg, Schönried, Lenk, Adelboden, Gruyères, Bulle, Zweisimmen, Chateau d'Oex, Chexbres, Vevey, Montreux, Lausanne, Morges, Rolle, Nyon, Geneve, Colonge-Bellerive, Coppet, Etoy-Buchillon, Vallorbe, Fleurier, Travers, Neuchâtel, St-Blaise, Murten, Avenches, Estavayer, Verdon, Sevion, La Chaux-de-Fonds

Saanenmoser Pass, Handegg

Inset

Chur, Baar, Zug, Unterägeri, Steinen, Immensee, Einsiedeln, Meggen, Küssnacht, Weggis, Vitznau, Gersau, Beckenried, Sisikon, Flüelen, Altdorf, Amsteg, Luzern, Horw, Stans, Sachseln, Engelberg, Goldswil, Alpnachstad, Samen, Giswil, Lungern, Sarnen, Sarnen, Bönigen, Brienz, Meiringen, Grindelwald, Wengen, Interlaken, Ebligen, Wilderswil, Mürren, Lauterbrunnen, Sigriswil, Oberhofen, Gunten, Merlingen, Thun, Spiez, Gwatt

1 Aeschi
2 Frutigen
3 Krattigen
4 Leissigen
5 Beatenberg

6 Hergiswil
7 Stanstad
8 Greppen
9 Fürigen
10 Hertenstein 11 Bürgenstock

Entlebuch

50 ☎(031) 445021/6. There are British Consulates in Genève and Zürich, a British Consulate with Honorary Consul in Lugano and a British Vice-Consulate with Honorary Vice-Consul in Montreaux.

Children in Cars

Children under 12 are not permitted to travel in a vehicle as front seat passengers unless the seat is fitted with child restraints.

Dimensions and weight restrictions

Private cars and towed trailers or caravans are restricted to the following dimensions – **car** height, 4 metres; width, 2.30 metres; length, up to 3,500kg 8 metres, over 3,500kg 12 metres. **Trailer/caravan** height, 4 metres; width†, 2.10 metres; length†, 6 metres (including tow bar). The maximum permitted overall length of vehicle/trailer or caravan combinations is 18 metres.

Note It is dangerous to use a vehicle towing a trailer or caravan on some mountain roads; motorists should ensure that roads on which they are about to travel are suitable for the conveyance of vehicle/trailer or caravan combinations.

The fully-laden weight of trailers which do not have an independent braking system should not exceed 50% of the unladen weight of the towing vehicle, but trailers which have an independent braking system can weigh up to 100% of the unladen weight of the towing vehicle.

†The Swiss Customs authorities can authorise slightly larger limits for foreign caravans for direct journeys to their destination and back, ie caravans up to 2.20 metres (7ft 2in) in width and up to either 6.50 metres (21ft 4in) or 7 metres (23ft) in length, depending on whether Alpine passes are used. A charge is made for these special authorisations. Caravans up to 2.50 metres (8ft 2in) in width may enter Switzerland if towed by a four-wheel-drive vehicle or one exceeding 3.5 tonnes; no special authorisation is then required.

Driving licence*

A valid UK or Republic of Ireland licence is acceptable in Switzerland. The minimum age at which a visitor may use a temporarily imported car is 18 years and a temporarily imported motorcycle (exceeding 125cc) 20 years.

Emergency messages to tourists*

Emergency messages to tourists are broadcast daily throughout the year by Swiss Radio. Any messages broadcast in English will be grouped together after the last news bulletin.

Radio Suisse Romande transmitting on 392 metres medium wave broadcasts these messages in French at 12.25 and 18.25hrs.

Radio der deutschen und rätoromanischen Schweiz transmitting on 567.1 metres medium wave broadcasts these messages in German at 12.25 and 18.25hrs.

Radio della Svizzera Italiana transmitting on 538 metres medium wave broadcasts the messages in Italian at 12.25 and 18.50hrs.

Radio Suisse Internationale transmitting on short wave broadcasts the messages in French at 12.35 and 20.35hrs on 31.46 metres, in German at 13.05hrs on 24.94 metres and in Italian at 20.05hrs on 75.28 metres.

Lights*

Driving on sidelights only is prohibited. Spotlights are forbidden. Fog lamps can be used only in pairs of identical shape, brilliance and colour; dipped headlights must be used in cities and towns. Dipped headlights must be used at all times in tunnels, whether they are lit or not, and failure to observe this regulation can lead to a fine. Switzerland has a 'tunnel' road sign (a red triangle showing a tunnel entrance in the centre), which serves to remind drivers to turn on their dipped headlights. In open country, headlights must be dipped as follows: at least 200 metres (220yds) in front of any pedestrian or oncoming vehicle (including trains parallel to the road); when requested to do so by the driver of an oncoming vehicle flashing lights; or when reversing, travelling in lines of traffic or stopping. Dipped headlights must be used when waiting at level crossings, or near roadworks. They must also be used in badly-lit areas when visibility is poor. It is recommended that *motorcyclists* use dipped headlights during the day.

*Additional information will be found in the European ABC at the front of the book.

Motoring club*

 The **Touring Club Suisse** (TCS) has branch offices in all important towns, and has its head office at 1211 Genève, 3 rue Pierre-Fatio 9 ☎(022) 7371212 located on the town plan of Genève within the gazetteer. The TCS will extend a courtesy service to all motorists but their major services will have to be paid for. TCS offices are usually open from 08.30 to 12.00hrs and 13.30 to 17.00hrs and between 08.00 and 11.30hrs on Saturday mornings (summer only). They are not open on Sunday.

Motorways

There are approximately 928 miles of motorways (*Autobahn* or *Autoroute*) and more are under construction. A network of 1,067 miles is planned.

Motorways are numbered 'N' (national road) and are divided into classes 1, 2 and 3; they vary from the usual two-lane (sometimes three) dual-carriageway to 25ft-wide, two-lane roads with limited access points. To join a motorway, follow the green and white signposts, or signposts with the motorway symbol.

Motorway telephones are placed 2km (1¼m) apart along all motorways, and give an automatic connection with the motorway control police. Ask for TCS patrol assistance. A patrol will normally be sent, but if one is not available, help will be sent from a TCS affiliated office.

Motorway tax The Swiss authorities levy an annual motorway tax. A vehicle sticker, costing SFr30 for vehicles up to 3.5 tonnes (unladen) and known locally as a *vignette*, must be displayed by vehicles using Swiss motorways including motorcycles, trailers and caravans. Motorists may purchase the stickers from AA or at the Swiss frontier. Vehicles over 3.5 tonnes (unladen) are taxed on all roads in Switzerland; a licence for one day, 10 days, one month and one year periods can be obtained. There are no stickers, and the tax must be paid at the Swiss frontier.

Orange badge scheme for disabled drivers*

Parking places reserved for drivers displaying the disabled drivers badge are specially marked. A disabled person (unless obviously disabled) must be able to produce a letter from the issuing authority as proof of having the badge on the windscreen.

Parking*

Parking restrictions are indicated by international signs, or by broken yellow lines or crosses at the side of the road, or yellow markings on pavements or poles. Parking is forbidden where it would obstruct traffic or view on a main road or one carrying fast-moving traffic, and on or within 1.5 metres (5ft) of tram lines. Stopping is forbidden, even for passengers to get in or out of a vehicle, for unloading goods, in places marked by a continuous yellow line at the side of the road or red markings on pavements or poles. When parked on a slope or incline, use the handbrake and place chocks or wedges under the wheels. If you have to stop in a tunnel, you must immediately switch off your engine. Spending the night in a vehicle or trailer on the roadside may be tolerated in some Cantons, but make sure you do not contravene local regulations. In some towns wheel clamps are used on illegally parked vehicles.

In some large towns, there are short-term parking areas known as *blue zones*. In these areas, parked vehicles must display a disc on the windscreens; discs are set at the time of parking, and show when parking times expire. Restrictions apply 08.00–19.00hrs on weekdays throughout the year. Discs can be obtained from the TCS, the police, some large shops and tobacconists, in petrol stations, garages and some restaurants. Failure to observe zonal regulations could result in a fine or the vehicle being towed away.

In Lausanne, a *red zone* system is in operation; for this, adjustable discs entitling up to 15 hours' parking are available from the local TCS office or the tourist information office. These discs may be used for either *red* or *blue* zones (one side of the disc to be used for the *blue* zone and the other side for the *red* zone). Failure to observe zonal regulations could result in a fine, or in the vehicle being towed away.

Petrol*

Credit cards Acceptance of credit cards for petrol purchases is mainly limited to Access/ Eurocard/Mastercard.

*Additional information will be found in the European ABC at the front of the book.

Duty-free petrol In addition to the petrol in the vehicle tank, up to 25 litres in a can may be imported free of custom duty and tax.
Petrol (leaded) Super (98–99 octane) grade.
Petrol (unleaded) is sold in Switzerland as the medium (95 octane) grade. Pumps dispensing unleaded petrol should be identified with either the colour green or the words 'Sans plomb', 'Bleifrei' or 'senza plombo' (according to the area).

Postal information

Mail Postcards SFr0.80; letters 5–20gm SFr1.10.
Post offices There are 4,000 post offices in Switzerland. Open hours are from 07.30–12.00hrs and 13.30–18.00hrs Monday to Friday and 07.30–11.00hrs Saturday.

Priority*

When the road is too narrow for two vehicles to pass, vehicles towing trailers have priority over other vehicles and heavy vehicles over light vehicles. If two vehicles of the same category cannot pass, the vehicle nearest to the most convenient stopping point or lay-by must reverse. On mountain roads, if there is no room to pass, the descending vehicle must manoevre to give way to the ascending vehicle – unless the ascending vehicle is obviously near a lay-by. If two vehicles are travelling in opposite directions and the driver of each vehicle wants to turn left, they must pass in front of each other (not drive round). Drivers turning left may pass in front of traffic islands in the centre of an intersection.

Lanes reserved for buses have been introduced; these are marked with either a continuous or broken yellow line and the word 'Bus'. Bus lanes may be supplemented with the sign 'Bus lane only'– *Voie réservée aux bus'* (a circular blue sign with the white silhouette of a bus superimposed on it). Only the broken yellow line may be crossed, either at a junction when turning or to enter the premises of a company.

Public holidays*

Official Public holidays throughout Switzerland for 1990 are given below. There are other official Public holidays such as Epiphany, Corpus Christi and All Saints' Day, but they vary from Canton to Canton.

January 1 (New Year's Day)
April 13 (Good Friday)
April 16 (Easter Monday)
May 24 (Ascension Day)
June 4 (Whit Monday)
December 25 (Christmas Day)

Religious services*

The Intercontinental Church Society welcomes visitors from any denomination to English language services in the following centres:
4051 Basel The Revd Canon Tom Roberts, Chaplain's Flat, Henric Petri Strasse 26 ☎(061) 235761
1807 Blonay (near Vevey) The Revd David Ritchie, Chemin de Champsavaux 1 ☎(021) 9432239.

Roads, including holiday traffic

The road surfaces are generally good, but some main roads are narrow in places. Traffic congestion may be severe at the beginning and end of the German school holidays (see this section under *Germany*).

On any stretch of mountain road, the driver of a private car may be asked by the driver of a postal bus, which is painted yellow, to reverse, or otherwise manoeuvre to allow the postal bus to pass. Postal bus drivers often sound a distinctive three note horn; no other vehicles may use this type of horn in Switzerland.

Shopping hours

Generally, shops are open 08.00/09.00–18.30/18.45hrs Monday to Friday and 08.00/09.00–16.00/17.00hrs on Saturday. In large towns, some shops close on Monday morning; in suburban areas and small towns, shops normally close on Wednesday or Thursday afternoons.

Speed limits*

Because the country is mountainous with many narrow and twisting roads, it is not safe to maintain a high speed. *Built-up areas* are indicated by signs bearing the placename, and in these areas, the speed limit is 50kph (31mph) for all vehicles.

Outside built-up areas, there is a limit of 80kph (49mph), except on motorways where vehicles are subject to a limit of 120kph

*Additional information will be found in the European ABC at the front of the book.

(74mph). Car/caravan or luggage trailer combinations are restricted to 80kph† (49mph) on all roads outside built-up areas. These limits do not apply if another limit is indicated by signs, or if the vehicle is subject to a lower general speed limit.

†If the weight of the caravan or luggage trailer exceeds 1,000kg, a speed limit of 60kph (37mph) applies on roads outside built-up areas, but 80kph (49mph) is still permissible on motorways.

Spiked or studded tyres*

Spiked or studded tyres may be used on light vehicles, and on trailers drawn by such vehicles, from 1 November to 31 March, provided they are fitted to all four wheels and a speed of 80kph (49mph) is not exceeded. They are prohibited on motorways and semi-motorways, with the exception of the N13 between Thusis and Mesocco (San Bernardino road tunnel), and between Göschenen and Airolo on the N2 (St Gothard road tunnel). Spiked or studded tyres may not be substituted for wheel chains when these are compulsory. On-the-spot fines of SFr30 are imposed for use of spiked or studded tyres after 31 March.

Telephone*

Insert coin after lifting the receiver; the dialling tone is a continuous tone. When making calls to subscribers within Switzerland, precede the number with the relevant area code (shown in parentheses before the hotel/garage enquiry number in the gazetteer). Use coins to the value of 40 centimes for local calls and SFr1 or SFr5 coins for national and international calls.
International callbox identification All phones, including cardphones.
Telephone rates A direct dial call to the UK costs SFr1.40 per minute. Local calls and calls to other European countries are cheaper from 21.00–08.00hrs Monday to Friday and at weekends.
Telephone Codes

UK to Switzerland	010 41
Switzerland to UK	00 44
Switzerland to Republic of Ireland	00 353
Switzerland to the USA	00 1

Warning triangle/Hazard warning lights*

The use of a warning triangle is compulsory in the event of accident or breakdown. The triangle must be placed on the road at least 50 metres (55yds) behind the vehicle on ordinary roads, and at least 150 metres (164yds) on motorways. If the vehicle is in an emergency lane, the triangle must be placed on the right of the emergency lane. Hazard warning lights may be used in conjunction with the triangle on ordinary roads, but on motorways and semi-motorways they must be switched off as soon as the warning triangle is erected. If this is not done, the police may impose an on-the-spot fine.

Weather services

The Touring Club Suisse operates a weather service to give up-to-the-minute conditions of mountain passes. The information appears on notices placed at strategic points along the roads leading up to the passes. When the weather is exceptional, special bulletins are issued by the TCS through the press and broadcasting services. You can also get road/weather reports in French, German or Italian, according to the Canton from which the call is made, on the national telephone system by dialling 162 (weather) or 163 (road conditions).

Wheel chains*

These are generally necessary on journeys to places at high altitudes. Roads with a sign 'chains compulsory' (a tyre with chains on it drawn on a white board, which also includes the name of the road) are closed to cars without wheel chains. It is a punishable offence to drive without this equipment.

Winter conditions*

Entry from France and Germany: the main entries are seldom affected, but minor routes through the Jura, Vosges, and Black Forest may be obstructed. The Faucille Pass on the Dijon–Geneva road may be temporarily obstructed, but the approach to Switzerland, via the A40, Macon–Geneva motorway is always open.

To Italy: from western Switzerland – during the winter months, this is via the Grand St Bernard road tunnel† or the Simplon rail tunnel† or, from Genève via France and the Mont Blanc road tunnel†; wheel chains are sometimes necessary on the approach to the Grand St Bernard road tunnel. From central Switzerland,

*Additional information will be found in the European ABC at the front of the book.

use the St Gotthard road tunnel. From eastern *Switzerland*, the San Bernardino tunnel or the Julier or Maloja passes can be used.
†see Major Road Tunnels and Major Rail Tunnels within the Route Planning section of the book.

To Austria: the route across northern Switzerland via Liechtenstein is open all the year.

Within the country: the main highways linking Basel, Zürich, Luzern, Bern, Lausanne, and Genève are unaffected. The high passes are usually closed in the winter months, but it is generally possible to drive within reasonable distance of all winter sports resorts. According to weather conditions, wheel chains may be compulsory.

LIECHTENSTEIN

The principality of Liechtenstein although an independent state, is represented in diplomatic and other matters by Switzerland. Vaduz is the capital.
Traffic regulations, insurance laws, and the monetary unit are the same as for Switzerland, and prices are adjusted to match those in the major country.

ACCOMMODATION

Hotel classifications are indicated in the **Guide to Swiss Hotels**, published annually by the Swiss Hotel Association. The Guide, which also contain details of spas and facilities for sports, is available from the Swiss National Tourist Office in London (see Tourist **Information** above); local tourist offices issue tourist guides on a regional basis.

Prices generally include continental breakfast, all services and taxes. Some hotels offer reduced prices for children not requiring separate rooms.

The Swiss Hotel Association operates a service for dealing with complaints – these should be addressed to 3001 Berne, PO Box 2657, and marked **Complaints Service**.

The prices shown below are an average for each classification. Accommodation is likely to be more expensive in main towns and in some of the more popular tourist areas. At the time of going to press, *£1 Sterling = SFr2.67* and *US$1 = SFr1.60*, but you should check the rate of exchange before your departure.

AVERAGE PRICES

	Single Room	Double Room	Breakfast	Lunch/Dinner
★★★★★	SFr206–272	SFr314–404	SFr15–24	SFr42–90
★★★★	SFr127–189	SFr205–297	SFr14–16	SFr30–62
★★★	SFr89–132	SFr145–220	SFr11–13	SFr22–46
★★	SFr59–98	SFr99–148	SFr9–11	SFr17–38
★	SFr47–70	SFr83–119	SFr9–11	SFr13–38

Abbreviations
pl place, platz
pza piazza
r rue
rte route
str strasse

AARAU
Aargau
🏩 *Brack* Buchserstr 17-25 ☎(064) 221851 **P** For
🏩 *Glaus* Entfelderstr 8 ☎(064) 221332 Dat

ADELBODEN
Bern
★★★★Nevada Palace ☎(033)732131 tx 922184
15 Dec-14 Apr & 15 Jun-15 Sep
rm70(♨47) P100 Lift ☾ ♋ ⛰ Mountain
★★Parkhotel Bellevue DPn ☎(033)731621
Dec-Apr & Jun-Oct
♨60 P30 Lift ⛰ Mountain

★*Alpenrose* ☎(033)731161
18 Dec-Etr & 14 Jun-20 Sep
rm26(♨11) ♋ P12 Mountain
Credit Cards ①③⑤
★*Bären* ☎(033)732151
rm12

ADLISWIL
See ZÜRICH

AESCHI
Bern
★★*Baumgarten* ☎(033)544121
rm23(♨5) A14rm ♋ P20 Mountain
Credit Cards ①②③⑤

AIGLE
Vaud
★★*Nord* r Colomb 4 ☎(025)261055
♨19 P10 Lift Mountain
Credit Cards ①②③⑤

AIROLO
Ticino
🏩 *Airolo* ☎(094) 881765 Alf Cit
🏩 *Gottardo* ☎(094) 881177 **P** Toy
🏩 *Wolfisberg* via San Gottardo ☎(094) 881055 AR Vol

ALPNACHSTAD
Obwalden
★★Rössli ☎(041)961181
10 Feb-10 Dec
♨45 P50 ⛵ Mountain Lake
Credit Cards ①②③⑤

ALTDORF
Uri
★*Schwarzer Löwen* Gotthardstr ☎(044)21007
rm19(♨5) ♋ Lift Mountain
Musch Bruno Gothardstr 54 ☎(044) 21120 **P** Cit
Dat Vol

AMSTEG
Uri

★★★**Stern & Post** (ROM) Gotthardstr
☎(044)64440 tx 866385
Closed Tue & Wed in winter
rm40(➔20) 🅿 P50 Lift Mountain
Credit Cards ①②③⑤

ANDERMATT
Uri

★★★**Badus** ☎(044)67286
Closed 10 May-10 Jun & 25 Oct-1 Dec
➔♠23 🅿 P24 Lift Mountain
Credit Cards ①②③⑤

★★**Helvetia** ☎(044)61515 tx 868608
rm35(➔28) A1rm 🅿 P20 Lift Mountain
Credit Cards ①②③

★★**Ideal Krone** ☎(044)67206 tx 868605
rm50(➔40) A1rm 🅿 P20 Lift
Credit Cards ①②③⑤

★★**Monopol Metropol** ☎(044)67575 tx 868606
15 Dec-30 Apr & Jun-15 Oct
➔♠31 🅿 P20 Lift 🖪 Mountain
Credit Cards ①②③⑤

✖ *Loretz* ☎(044) 67243 P Ren

APPENZELL
Appenzell

★★★**Hecht** (Amb) Hauptgasse 9 ☎(071)871026
tx 719267
Closed 23 Nov-23 Dec
➔♠41 P Lift
Credit Cards ①②③⑤

★★**Mettlen** ☎(071)871246
rm44(♠29) A15rm P Mountain

★★**Santis** (ROM) ☎(071)878722 tx 883733
Closed 7 Jan-14 Feb
➔♠33 P15 Lift Mountain
Credit Cards ①②③⑤

✖ *Baumann* Weissbadstr 11 ☎(071) 871466 Cit
Dat Peu

ARBON
Thurgau

★★★**Metropol** (Amb) Bahnhofstr 49
☎(071)463535 tx 881747
➔♠42 P100 Lift 🅒 🅪 Lake
Credit Cards ①②③⑤

★**Rotes Kreuz** ☎(071)461914
20 Jan-20 Dec :Rest closed Sun
rm18(➔14) P6 Lake
Credit Card ③

ARLESHEIM
Basel

★**Ochsen** ☎(061)725225
rm26(➔14) 🅿 P20
Credit Cards ①②③④⑤

AROLLA
Valais

★★**Grand Hotel & Kurhaus** ☎(027)831161
Jul-Aug & 20 Dec-20 Apr
➔♠72 P80 Lift Mountain
Credit Cards ①②③⑤

AROSA
Graubünden

★★★★**Kulm** ☎(081)310131 tx 851679
Dec-Apr & Jul-Sep
➔♠146 🅿 P100 Lift 🅒 🕿 🖪 Mountain
Credit Cards ①②③⑤

★★★**Alexandra-Palace** ☎(081)310111
5 Dec-20 Apr & 20 Jun-Sep
➔♠125 🅿 P75 Lift 🅒 🖪 Mountain
Credit Cards ①②③⑤

★★★**Cristallo** ☎(081)312261 tx 851670
Closed 26 Apr-17 Jun & 3 Oct-Nov
rm40(➔36) 🅿 P5 Lift Mountain Lake
Credit Cards ①②③

★★★**Sporthotel Valsana** (Amb) ☎(081)310275 tx
851632
25 Jun-25 Sep & 10 Dec-9 Apr
➔♠86 🅿 P40 Lift 🅒 🕿 🖪 🖪 Mountain
Credit Cards ①②③④⑤

★★**Seehof** ☎(081)311541 tx 851677
Dec-Apr
➔♠40 🅿 P45 Lift Mountain
Credit Cards ①②③⑤

✖ *Grand Dosch* Seebodenpl ☎(081) 312222 M/
C P Alf Mer Ope Vau

ASCONA
Ticino

★★★★**Acapulco au Lac** Lago di Maggiore
☎(093)354521 tx 846135
4 Mar-5 Nov
➔♠44 P44 Lift 🅒 🖪 Beach Lake
Credit Cards ①②③⑤

★★★★**Eden Roc** via Albarelle ☎(093)350171 tx
846164
18 Mar-14 Nov
➔♠55 🅿 P60 Lift 🅒 🖪 🖪 Beach Lake
Credit Cards ①②③⑤

★★★**Ascona** (Amb) via Collina ☎(093)351135 tx
846035
Mar-Dec
➔♠75 P50 Lift 🅒 🖪 Mountain Lake
Credit Cards ①②③⑤

★★★**Schweizerhof** via Locarno ☎(093)351214 tx
846217
18 Mar-19 Nov
➔♠44 P18 Lift 🖪
Credit Cards ①②③⑤

★★★**Tamaro au Lac** (ROM) ☎(093)350282 tx
846132
12 Mar-15 Nov
rm51(➔43) A7rm 🅿 P5 Lift 🅒 🖪 Lake
Credit Cards ①②③

★**Piazza au Lac** ☎(093)351181
Mar-Nov
rm24(➔21) A4rm Lift 🅒 Mountain Lake
Credit Cards ①②③④⑤

✖ *Buzzini* via Locarno 124 ☎(093) 352414 Aud
VW

✖ *Cristallina* via Circonvallazione ☎(093)
351320 P Alf AR Maz

✖ *Storelli* via Cantonale ☎(093) 352196 Mer Toy

AVENCHES
Vaud

✖ *Divorne* rte de Berne ☎(037) 751263 P Ope

BAAR
Zug

★★**Lindenhof** Dorfstr ☎(042)311220
Closed 3 wks Jul
➔♠5 P25 Lift
Credit Cards ①②③⑤

BAD
Each name preceded by 'Bad' is listed under the
name that follows it.

BADEN
Aargau

★★★**Parc** (Amb) Römerstr 24 ☎(056)201311 tx
825013
Closed 24 Dec-3 Jan
➔♠71 🅿 P50 Lift 🅒
Credit Cards ①②③④⑤

★★★**Verenahof** Kurpl ☎(056)225251 tx 828278
rm111(➔84) P280 Lift 🅒 🖪 🖪
Credit Cards ①②③⑤

✖ *Müller J Kappelerhof* ☎(056) 227326 P Aud
VW

BÂLE
See **BASEL**

BASEL (BÂLE)

1	★★★★★	Drei Könige
2	★★★★★	Euler
3	★★★★★	Basel Hilton
4	★★★★	International
5	★★★★	Schweizerhof
6	★★★	Admiral
7	★★★	Bernina Basel
9	★★★	Drachen
10	★★★	Europe
12	★★★	Merian am Rhein
13	★★★	Victoria am Bahnhof
14	★★	Greub
16	★★	Krafft am Rhein
17	★★	Rochat
18	★★	St-Gotthard-Terminus
19	★	Bristol

BALSTHAL
Solothurn

★★★**Kreuz** Hauptstr ☎(062)713412
rm70(➔67) P50
Credit Cards ①②③⑤

★**Rössli** ☎(062)715858
➔♠6 P

BASEL (BÂLE)
Basel
See Plan

★★★★★**Basel Hilton** Aaeschengraben 31
☎(061)226622 tx 965555
➔♠217 🅿 P100 Lift 🅒 🖪
Credit Cards ①②③④⑤

★★★★★**Drei Könige** Blumenrain 8
☎(061)255252 tx 962937
➔♠80 🅿 P Lift 🅒
Credit Cards ①②③⑤

★★★★★**Euler** Centralbahnpl 14 ☎(061)234500 tx
962215
➔♠64 🅿 P17 Lift 🅒
Credit Cards ①②③④⑤

★★★★**International** (Amb) Steinentorstr 25
☎(061)221870 tx 962370
➔♠212 🅿 P40 Lift 🅒 🖪
Credit Cards ①②③④⑤

★★★★**Schweizerhof** Centralbahnpl 1
☎(061)222833 tx 962373
➔♠75 P15 Lift 🅒 Mountain
Credit Cards ①②③⑤

★★★**Admiral** (Amb) Rosentalstr 5
☎(061)6917777 tx 963444
rm130(➔125) 🅿 P5 Lift 🅒 🖪
Credit Cards ①②③④⑤

★★★**Bernina Basel** Innere Margarethenstr 14
(n.rest) ☎(061)237300 tx 963813
➔♠35 P1500 Lift 🅒
Credit Cards ①②③④⑤

★★★**Drachen** Aeschenvorstadt 24 ☎(061)239090
tx 62346
➔♠38 🅿 P Lift 🅒

★★★**Europe** Clarastr 43 ☎(061)6918080 tx
964103
➔♠170 A34rm 🅿 P130 Lift 🅒
Credit Cards ①②③④⑤

★★★**Merian am Rhein** Rheingasse 2
☎(061)6810000 tx 963537
➔♠63 🅿 P20 Lift 🅒
Credit Cards ①②③④⑤

★★★**Victoria am Bahnhof** Centralbahnpl 3-4
☎(061)225566 tx 962362
➔♠115 🅿 P24 Lift 🅒
Credit Cards ①②③④⑤

★★**Greub** Centralbahnstr 11 ☎(061)231840
rm56(➔30) Lift
Credit Cards ①②③⑤

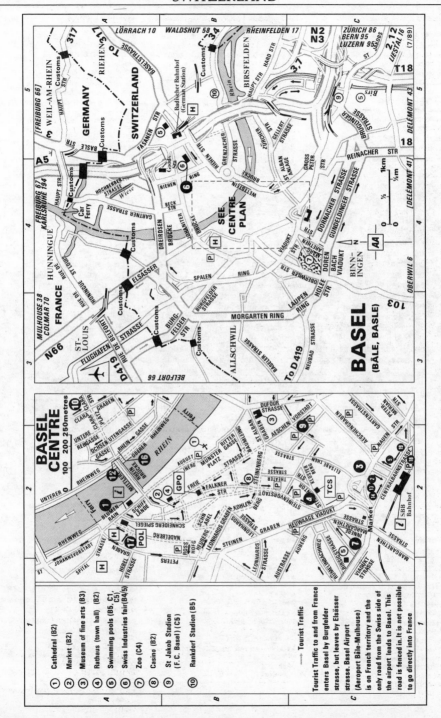

★★**Krafft am Rhein** Rheingasse 12
☎(061)9618877 tx 964360
rm52(✦♠45) ☎ P8 Lift ℂ Lake
Credit Cards ① ② ③ ④ ⑤

★★**Rochat** Petersgraben 23 ☎(061)258140
✦♠48 P10 Lift ℂ

★★**St-Gotthard-Basel** Centralbahnstr 13
☎(061)225250
✦♠60 A36rm P Lift ℂ
Credit Cards ① ② ③ ④ ⑤

★**Bristol** Centralbahnstr 15 ☎(061)223822
rm30(✦♠6) P10 Lift ℂ
Credit Cards ① ② ③ ④ ⑤

✎ Autavia Hardstr ☎(061) 427878 For

✎ Dufour Dufourstr 36 ☎(061) 231214

✎ Grosspeter Grosspeterstr 12 ☎(061) 507000
P Ope

✎ Scheidegger Viadukstr 45 ☎(061) 222220
BMW

✎ Schlotterbeck Viadukstr 40 ☎(061) 220050
AR Cit

✎ Settelen Turkheimerstr 17 ☎(061) 383800 AR
Cit

✎ Uecker Nafelserstr ☎(061) 385076

BEATENBERG
Bern

★**Jungfraublick & Beauregard** ☎(036)411581 tx
923290
rm29(✦♠23) P20 Mountain Lake
Credit Cards ① ② ③ ⑤

BECKENRIED
Nidwalden

★★**Edelweiss** ☎(041)641252
rm24(✦♠17) ☎ P25 Mountain Lake
Credit Cards ① ② ③ ⑤

★**Mond** ☎(041)641204
15 Mar-15 Feb
rm30(♠23) P25 Lift ☐ Mountain Lake
Credit Cards ① ② ③ ⑤

★**Sonne** ☎(041)641205
Feb-Dec
rm28 P20 Mountain Lake

BELLINZONA
Ticino

★★★**Unione** via G-Guisan 1 ☎(092)255577 tx
846277
20 Jan-20 Dec
✦♠33 Lift ℂ Mountain
Credit Cards ① ② ③ ⑤

BERLINGEN
Thurgau

★**Seestern** ☎(054)611404
rm9(✦4) ☎ P50 Lake

BERN *(BERNE)*

See Plan pages 394-395 *Population* 290,000 *Local tourist office* Bahnof (station) ☎(031)221212
By European standards, Bern, the capital of Switzerland, is not a big city. It has only 290,000
inhabitants, but it is very Swiss and certainly picturesque. In the past 50 years there has been
enormous expansion and wide bridges span the Aare to link the old town with its new suburbs. While
retaining its medieval appearance, the old city has developed into an important business centre, with
ancient rows of houses lining broad streets and magnificent fountains seemingly untouched by time.
The principal features of many of these streets are the arcades which are let into the façades of
buildings; no new or renovated building can be built without one.
High above the roofs of Bern towers the cathedral, one of the finest ecclesiastical buildings in
Switzerland. Like most of the city it dates from the 15th century; the greater part of old Bern was
reduced to ashes in 1405 in a gigantic fire. Also of special note is the clock tower or *Zytglogge* as it is
called, which dates from the 12th century. In 1530 the artistic astronomical or calendar clock showing
the position of the sun, moon, stars and planets as well as the month and day of the week, was
constructed; and at the same time the delightful mechanical figure-play was made.
The *Gerechtigkeltsgasse* has many elegant shops and the *Marketgasse* and the *Spitalgasse* are both
pedestrian precincts.

EATING OUT Typical Swiss cuisine includes cheese *fondue* - bread dipped in a bubbling mixture of
cheese and wine, and *raclette*, which is sliced melted cheese served with potato. *Berne Platte* is a dish
of local meat, sausages, *sauerkraut* and potatoes. Among the many delicious pastries are *Zuger
Kirschtorte*, a cake made with kirsch brandy.
Rablus, in *Zeughausgasse*, is one of Bern's most distinguished restaurants. For moderately priced Swiss
food, the *Kornhauskellar* in Kornhausplatz, is recommended, as is the *Taverne Valaisanne*, in
Neuengasse.

BERN (BERNE)

★★★★★**Bellevue Palace** Kochergasse 3-5
☎(031)224581 tx 911524
✦♠166 Lift ℂ Mountain
Credit Cards ① ② ③ ⑤

★★★★★**Schweizerhof** (Amb) Bahnhofpl 11
☎(031)224501 tx 911783
✦♠94 P Lift ℂ
Credit Cards ① ② ③ ④ ⑤

★★★★**City Mövenpick** (Mövenpick) Bubenbergpl
7 ☎(069)26970 tx 412808
✦♠306 P40 Lift ℂ
Credit Cards ① ② ③ ④ ⑤

★★★**Astor Touring** Eigerpl/Zieglerstr 66
☎(031)458666 tx 912834
✦♠63 P Lift ℂ
Credit Cards ① ② ③ ⑤

★★★**Bären** (Amb) Schauplatzgasse 4
☎(031)223367 tx 912819
✦♠57 Lift ℂ
Credit Cards ① ② ③ ④ ⑤

★★★**Bern** Zeughausgasse 9 ☎(031)211021 tx
911555
✦♠100 P Lift ℂ
Credit Cards ① ② ③ ⑤

★★★**Bristol** Schauplatzgasse 10 (Off Barenpl)
☎(031)220101 tx 2912819
✦♠92 Lift ℂ
Credit Cards ① ② ③ ④ ⑤

★★★**Savoy** Neuengasse 26 (n.rest)
☎(031)224405 tx 911863
✦♠56 Lift ℂ
Credit Cards ① ② ③ ④ ⑤

★★★**Wächter** (Mövenpick) Neuengasse 44
☎(031)220866 tx 912230
rm44(✦♠35) Lift ℂ
Credit Cards ① ② ③ ④ ⑤

★★**Continental** Zeughausgasse 27 (n.rest)
☎(031)222626 tx 912222
✦♠37 Lift ℂ
Credit Cards ① ② ③ ④ ⑤

★**Goldener Schlüssel** Rathausgasse 72
☎(031)220216
rm29(✦21) Lift
Credit Cards ① ③ ⑤

✎ Auto Marti Eigerpl 2 ☎(031) 451515 BMW

✎ Citroën (Suisse) Freibergstr 447 ☎(031)
553311 P Cit

✎ Egghölzil Eghölzllstr ☎(031) 446336 P Hon
Peu Vau

✎ Schultheiss Hofweg 5 ☎(031) 427742 P For

✎ Willy Freibergstr 443 ☎(031) 552511 P Fia

At **LYSSACH**

★★**Lyssach** ☎(031)471601 tx 914245
✦♠37 ☎ P40 Lift Mountain
Credit Cards ① ② ③ ④ ⑤

At **MURI**(3km SE on N6)

★**Krone** ☎(031)521666
✦♠14 ☎ P22
Credit Cards ① ② ③

At **WABERN**(2km S)

≈⊗ Waeny Seftigenstr 198 ☎(031) 542622 **P** AR Maz

BEX-LES-BAINS
Vaud

★**St-Christophe** ☎(0041)025652977
16 Jan-21 Dec
rm12(→10) P60 Mountain
Credit Cards ① ③

≈⊗ Rallye r Servannaz ☎(025) 631225 Saa Toy

BIASCA
Ticino

★★**Poste** via Stazione ☎(092)722121
rm11(→10) ⌂ P36 Lift ☾
Credit Cards ① ② ③ ④ ⑤

≈⊗ Maggetti via San Gottardo ☎(092) 721266

BIEL (BIENNE)
Bern

★★★★**Élite** pl Gl-Guisan ☎(032)225441 tx 934101
→⋔67 Lift ☾
Credit Cards ① ② ③ ④ ⑤

★★★**Continental** (Amb) r d'Aarberg 29 ☎(032)223255 tx 934440
→⋔80 P50 Lift ☾
Credit Cards ① ② ③ ④ ⑤

BISSONE
Ticino

★★★**Lago di Lugano** ☎(041)91688591 tx 844698
Closed 2 Jan-18 Mar :Rest closed Tue & Wed am
→⋔80 P50 Lift ☾ ⊒ Lake
Credit Cards ① ② ③ ④ ⑤

BIVIO
Graubünden

★★★**Post** Julierstr ☎(081)751275
rm21(→19) A19rm ⌂ P35 ☾ Mountain
Credit Cards ① ② ③ ④ ⑤

BOLLINGEN
St-Gallen

★★**Schiff** am Oberen Zürichsee ☎(055)283888
→⋔10 ⌂ P ☾ Mountain Lake

BÖNIGEN
Bern

★★★**Seiler au Lac** (Amb) ☎(036)223021 tx 923164
Dec-20 Oct :Rest closed Tue in winter
→⋔48 ⌂ P30 Lift ☾ Mountain Lake
Credit Cards ① ② ③ ④ ⑤

BOURG-ST-PIERRE
Valais

≈⊗ Tunnel du Grand St-Bernard ☎(026) 49124

BRÈ
See **LUGANO**

BRIENZ
Bern

★★**Bären** ☎(036)512412
Mar-Dec
rm35(→10) ⌂ P19 Lift ⊒ Mountain Lake ,
Credit Cards ① ③ ⑤

★★**Schönegg** (n.rest) ☎(036)511113
Jan-15 Nov
rm17(→8) P10 Mountain Lake

BRIG (BRIGUE)
Valais

★★★**Viktoria** (Amb) Bahnhofstr 2 ☎(028)231503 tx 473861
Closed Nov
rm39(→37) ⌂ P5 Lift ☾ Mountain
Credit Cards ① ③ ⑤

★★**Brigerhof** Rhonesandstr 18 (n.rest) ☎(028)231607
Feb-Oct
→⋔29 ⌂ P16 Lift ☾ Mountain
Credit Cards ① ② ③ ⑤

★★**Sporting** (n.rest) ☎(028)232363
→⋔33 ⌂ P20 Lift Mountain
Credit Cards ① ② ③ ⑤

BRIGELS
Graubünden

★★★**Residenza La Val** ☎(086)41252 tx 856177
25 Jun-15 Oct & 4 Dec-Mar
rm46(→45) ⌂ P40 Lift ⊒ Mountain
Credit Cards ① ② ③ ⑤

BRISSAGO
Ticino

★★**Mirto au Lac** ☎(093)651328
Mar-Nov
rm26(→24) ⌂ P10 Lift Lake
Credit Card ③

BRUGG
Aargau

★★★**Rotes Haus** Hauptstr 7 ☎(056)411479 tx 825105
→⋔24 P200 Lift ☾
Credit Cards ① ② ③ ⑤

BRUNNEN
Schwyz

★★★**Metropole au Lac** Vierwaldstrattersee ☎(043)311039
Mar-Nov
→⋔21 ⌂ Lift Lake

★★★**Waldstätterhof** (Amb) ☎(043)331133 tx 866007
→⋔100 ⌂ P100 Lift ☾ ⊒ Mountain Lake
Credit Cards ① ② ③ ④ ⑤

★★★**Weisses-Rössell** ☎(043)311023
rm30(→13) P
Credit Cards ① ② ③ ④ ⑤

★★**Bellevue** Vierwaldstrattersee ☎(043)311318 tx 866022
Apr-Oct
→⋔50 ⌂ P28 Lift ☾ ⊒ Mountain Lake
Credit Cards ① ② ③ ⑤

★★**Élite & Aurora** ☎(043)311024 tx 866104
16 Feb-15 Nov
→⋔60 A15rm ⌂ P6 Lift ☾ Mountain Lake
Credit Cards ① ② ③ ⑤

★★**Schmid** ☎(043)311882
Apr-Oct
rm11(→8) ⌂ P1 Lift Mountain Lake
Credit Cards ① ② ③ ⑤

★**Alpina** ☎(043)311813
Feb-Nov
rm20(→17) ⌂ P20 ☾ Mountain
Credit Cards ① ② ③ ⑤

≈⊗ Inderbitzin Gersauerstr 17 ☎(043) 311313 Aud VW

BUCHS
St-Gallen

≈⊗ Sulser St-Gallerstr 19 ☎(085) 61414 Ope Vau

BULLE
Fribourg

★★**Rallye** rte de Riaz 8 ☎(029)21313
→⋔21 ⌂ P20 Lift Mountain
Credit Cards ① ② ③ ④ ⑤

BÜRCHEN
Valais

★★★**Bürchnerhof** ☎(028)442434
mid Dec-mid Apr & Jun-Nov
→⋔19 P20 Mountain

BURGDORF
Bern

≈⊗ Central Gotthelfstr 21 ☎(034) 288288 **P** Cit Vau

BÜRGENSTOCK
Nidwalden

★★**Waldheim** ☎(041)632383
rm55(→48) P Lift ⊒ Mountain
Credit Cards ① ② ③ ⑤

BUSSIGNY
See **LAUSANNE**

CASSARATE
See **LUGANO**

CASTAGNOLA
See **LUGANO**

CELERINA
Graubünden

★★★**Cresta Palace** (Amb) ☎(082)33564 tx 852261
25 Jun-20 Sep & 18 Dec-Mar
→⋔100 ⌂ P50 Lift ☾ ☾ ⊒ Mountain
Credit Cards ① ② ③ ⑤

★★**Cresta Kulm** (n.rest) ☎(082)33373
2 Jul-8 Oct
rm43 Lift ⊒ Mountain
Credit Cards ① ② ③ ⑤

CHAM
Zug

≈⊗ Ettmüller Steinhauserstr ☎(042) 416666 **P** Cit

CHAMPÉRY
Valais

★★**Alpes** ☎(025)791222
15 Dec-15 Apr & Jun-20 Sep
→⋔23 P12 Mountain
Credit Cards ① ② ③ ⑤

★★**Beau-Séjour** ☎(025)791701
Dec-15 Apr & Jun-Sep
→⋔20 P12 Lift Mountain
Credit Cards ① ② ③ ④ ⑤

★★**Parc** ☎(025)791313
Seasonal
rm30(→24) Mountain

CHÂTEAU-D'OEX
Vaud

★★★**Beau-Séjour** ☎(029)47423
Closed Oct
rm41(→32) P10 Lift ☾ Mountain
Credit Cards ① ② ③

★★★**Hostellerie du Bon Accueil** ☎(029)46320 tx 940022
20 Dec-20 Oct :Rest closed Tue
→⋔19 A18rm P30 Mountain
Credit Cards ① ② ③ ⑤

≈⊗ Pont Petit Pré ☎(029) 46173 M/C **P** Ope Vau

≈⊗ Yersin ☎(029) 47539 **P** Cit Toy Vol

CHÂTELET, LE
See **GSTEIG**

CHAUX-DE-FONDS, LA
Neuchâtel

★★★**Club** r du Parc 71 ☎(039)235300 tx 952190
→⋔40 P100 Lift Mountain
Credit Cards ① ② ③ ⑤

≈⊗ E Frey r F-Courvoisier 68 ☎(039) 286677

≈⊗ Migrol du Locie 69 ☎(039) 265926 Alf AR DJ For

≈⊗ Trois Rois bd des Eplatures 8 ☎(039) 268181 For Lan

CHERNEX
See **MONTREUX**

CHEXBRES
Vaud

★★★**Bellevue** ☎(021)9461481
Mar-Jan
→⋔23 P35 Lift ☾ Mountain Lake
Credit Cards ① ② ③ ④ ⑤

★★★**Signal** ☎(021)9462525 tx 452212
Apr-Oct
→⋔82 ⌂ P65 Lift ☾ ☾ ⊒ U Mountain Lake
Credit Cards ① ③

★★**Cécil** ☎(021)9461292
rm23(→17) P50 Lift ⊒ Mountain Lake
Credit Cards ① ② ③ ⑤

BERN (BERNE)

1	★★★★★	Bellevue Palace
2	★★★★★	Schweizerhof
3	★★★★	City Mövenpick
4	★★★	Astor Touring
5	★★★	Bären
6	★★★	Bern
7	★★★	Bristol
8	★★★	Savoy
9	★★★	Wächter
10	★★	Continental
11	★★	Krone (At Muri)
12	★★	Lyssach (At Lyssach)
13	★	Goldener Schlüssel

CHIASSO
Ticino

★★★**Touring Mövenpick** (Mövenpick) pza
Indipendenza ☎(091)445331 tx 842493
◢ฅ60 Lift ☾
Credit Cards ① ② ③ ⑤

CHUR (COIRE)
Graubünden

★★★**Duc de Rohan** (Amb) Masanserstr 44
☎(081)221022 tx 74161
◢ฅ35 ☎ P35 Lift ☾ ☒ Mountain
Credit Cards ① ② ③ ⑤

★★**A B C** Bahnhofpl (n.rest) ☎(081)226033 tx
851340
◢ฅ33 Lift ☾ Mountain
Credit Cards ① ② ③ ⑤

★★**Drei Könige** Reichsgasse 18 ☎(081)221725
rm38(◢ฅ28) ☎ P Lift Mountain
Credit Cards ① ② ③ ④ ⑤

★★**Sommerau** Emserstr ☎(081)225545 tx 74172
◢ฅ88 P200 Mountain
Credit Cards ① ② ③ ④ ⑤

★★**Stern** (ROM) Reichsgasse 11 ☎(081)223555
tx 851298
◢ฅ55 ☎ P15 Lift ☾ Mountain
Credit Cards ① ② ③ ⑤

☙ **Auto Center Triboillet** Rossbodenstr 14
☎(081) 221212 AR For Toy

☙ **Calanda** Kasernenstr 30 ☎(081) 221414 Peu
Tal

☙ **Comminot** Rossbodenstr 24 ☎(081) 223737 **P**
AR Maz

☙ **Grand Garage Dosch** Kasernenstr 128
☎(081) 215171 Ope Vau

☙ **Lidoc** St-Margrethenstr 9 ☎(081) 221313 **P** Alf
Mer Vau

COLLONGE-BELLERIVE
Genève

★★**Bellerive** ☎(022)521282
Feb-15 Dec
rm7(◢ฅ6) P50 Mountain Lake

COPPET
Vaud

☙ **Port** rte de Suisse ☎(022) 761212 AR Maz

CORNAREDO
See **LUGANO**

CRANS-SUR-SIERRE
Valais

★★★★**Alpina & Savoy** ☎(027)412142 tx 473134
15 Dec-Etr & 20 Jun-15 Sep
rm60(◢ฅ45) ☎ P30 Lift ☾ ☒ Mountain
Credit Cards ① ② ③ ④ ⑤

★★★**Élite** ☎(027)414301
Jun-Oct & 15 Dec-10 Apr
◢ฅ25 P30 Lift ☒ Mountain
Credit Cards ① ② ③ ⑤

★★★**Robinson** ☎(027)441353
15 Jun-15 Apr
◢ฅ16 P16 Lift
Credit Cards ① ② ③ ⑤

★★★**Royal** ☎(027)413931 tx 473227
Seasonal
◢ฅ70 P40 Lift ☾ Mountain
Credit Cards ① ② ③ ④ ⑤

★★★**Splendide DPn** ☎(027)412056
15 Dec-Apr & 20 Jun-20 Sep
◢ฅ30 ☎ P25 Lift Mountain Lake
Credit Cards ① ② ③ ⑤

CULLY
See **LAUSANNE**

DAVOS
Graubünden

At **DAVOS DORF**

★★★**Alpes** Promenade 136 ☎(083)61261 tx
74341
◢ฅ57 ☎ P19 Lift ☾ Mountain Lake
Credit Cards ① ② ③ ⑤

★★★**Meierhof** Promenade ☎(083)61285 tx
853263
Dec-Apr & Jun-Oct
◢ฅ80 ☎ P40 Lift ☾ ⚘ ☒ Mountain
Credit Cards ① ② ③ ⑤

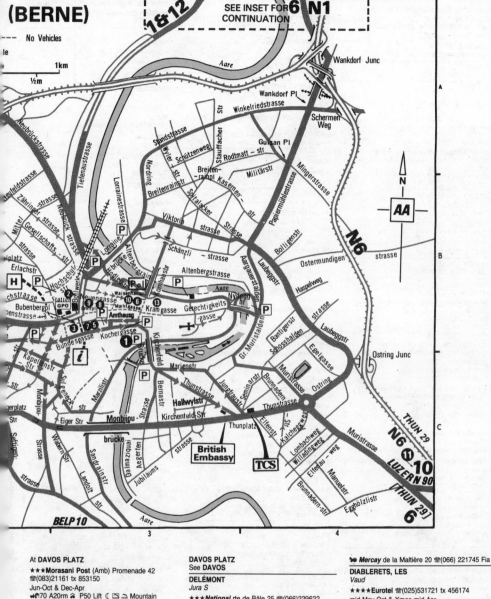

(BERNE)

- - - No Vehicles

1km
½m

At DAVOS PLATZ

★★★**Morasani Post** (Amb) Promenade 42 ☎(083)21161 tx 853150
Jun-Oct & Dec-Apr
↱70 A20rm ⌂ P50 Lift ℂ ⊑ ⌂ Mountain
Credit Cards [1][2][3][5]

★★★**Schweizerhof** (Amb) Promenade 50 ☎(083)21151 due to change tx 853124
27 May-1 Oct
↱93 ℂ P Lift ℂ ⊑ Mountain
Credit Cards [1][2][3][4][5]

DAVOS DORF
See **DAVOS**

DAVOS PLATZ
See **DAVOS**

DELÉMONT
Jura S

★★★**National** rte de Bâle 25 ☎(066)229622
↱27 ⌂ Lift
Credit Cards [1][2][3][5]

★**Bonne Auberge** r du 23 Juin 32 ☎(066)221758
Closed Feb
↱9 P20 ℂ
Credit Cards [1][2][3][5]

☞ *Gare Williemin* rte de Moutier 65 ☎(066) 222461 **P** Ren Vol

☞ *Mercay* de la Maltière 20 ☎(066) 221745 Fia

DIABLERETS, LES
Vaud

★★★★**Eurotel** ☎(025)531721 tx 456174
mid May-Oct & Xmas-mid Apr
↱106 ⌂ P40 Lift ℂ ⊑ Mountain
Credit Cards [1][2][3][5]

DIETIKON
Zürich

★★**Krone** (ROM) Limmatquai 88 ☎(01)2514222
rm25(↱2) Lift
Credit Cards [1][2][3][5]

DISENTIS-MUSTER
Graubünden
★★★★*Park Baur* ☎(086)74545 tx 74585
Closed Nov
◖ℳ54 ☎ P100 Lift ℂ ♋ ◰ Mountain
Credit Cards ①②③⑤

DÜRRENAST
See **THUN (THOUNE)**

EBIKON
See **LUZERN (LUCERNE)**

EBLIGEN
Bern
★*Hirschen* ☎(036)511551
◖ℳ14 P30 ➦ Mountain Lake

EGERKINGEN
Solothurn
See also **OLTEN**
★★★*Mövenpick* (Mövenpick) (Autobahn
crossroads N1/N2) ☎(062)626211 tx 982936
◖ℳ140 Lift Mountain
Credit Cards ①②③④⑤
★★*AGIP* (Autobahn crossroads N1/N2)
☎(062)612121 tx 984856
◖ℳ68 P160 ℂ
Credit Cards ①②③④⑤

EINSIEDELN
Schwyz
★★★*Drei Könige* ☎(055)532441 tx 875293
◖ℳ52 ☎ P Lift Mountain

EMMENBRÜCKE
See **LUZERN (LUCERNE)**

ENGELBERG
Obwalden
★★★*Bellevue Terminus* ☎(041)941213 tx
866220
Dec-Apr May-Oct
rm63(◖ℳ39) P20 Lift ℂ ♋ Mountain
Credit Cards ①③⑤
★★★*Dorint Regina Titlis* Dorfstr 33
☎(041)942828 tx 866272
Closed Nov
◖ℳ128 P54 Lift ℂ ◰ Mountain
Credit Cards ①②③⑤
★★★*Europäischer Hof* (Amb) Postfach 272
(n.rest) ☎(041)941263 tx 866461
Dec-Apr May-Oct
rm80(◖ℳ55) P10 Lift
Credit Cards ①②③⑤
★★*Hess* ☎(041)941366 tx 866270
Closed Nov
◖ℳ58 P Lift Mountain
★*Engelberg* Dorfstr 14 ☎(041)941168 tx 866183
Dec-Oct
◖ℳ21 A13rm P Lift Mountain
Credit Cards ①②③④⑤

ENTLEBUCH
Luzern
★★*Drei Könige* ☎(041)721227
:Rest closed Mon
rm14(◖ℳ10) P2 ♋ ➦ Mountain
Credit Cards ①②③⑤

ESTAVAYER-LE-LAC
Fribourg
★*Lac* ☎(037)631343
◖ℳ18 P12 Mountain Lake
Credit Cards ①②⑤

ETOY-BUCHILLON
Vaud
★★*Pêchers-Etoy* rte du Lac Genève-Lausanne
☎(021)8073277
◖ℳ14 ☎ P ℂ ➦ Mountain Lake

EVOLÈNE
Valais
★★*Hermitage* ☎(027)831232
Jun-Sep & Dec-Apr
rm22(◖ℳ12) ☎

★*Eden* ☎(027)831112
Closed Nov
rm18 ☎

FAIDO
Ticino
★★*Milan* ☎(094)381307
20 Apr-Oct
rm39(◖ℳ26) ☎ P30 Lift Mountain
Credit Cards ①②③⑤

FERNEY VOLTAIRE (France)
See **GENÈVE AIRPORT**

FEUSISBERG
Zürich
★★★*Panorama* Tagungszentrum ☎(01)7842464
tx 875825
◖ℳ72 P200 Lift ℂ Mountain Lake
Credit Cards ①②③⑤

FIESCH
Valais
★*Glacier & Poste* ☎(028)711301
rm40(◖ℳ25) ☎ P ♋ ◰ Mountain

FILZBACH
Glarus
★*Seeblick* ☎(058)321455
15 Dec-Oct :Rest closed Tue
rm10 P Mountain Lake

FLEURIER
Neuchâtel
◖◖ *Duthe* r de Temple ☎(038) 611637 P Aud Tal
◖◖ *Holz* r de l'Industrie ☎(038) 612922 Cit Peu
Tal

FLIMS-WALDHAUS
Graubünden
★★★★*Park-Hotels Waldaus* ☎(081)390181 tx
74125
Dec-Mar & Apr-Oct
◖ℳ160 ☎ P Lift ℂ ♋ ➦ ◰ Mountain
Credit Cards ①②③④
★★★*Alpes* Hauptstr ☎(081)330101 tx 851965
21 May-27 Oct & 15 Dec-14 Apr
◖ℳ80 ☎ P70 Lift ℂ ◰ Mountain
Credit Cards ①②③④⑤
★★★*Schloss* ☎(081)391245
Dec-mid Apr & May-Oct
◖ℳ41 A19rm ☎ P Lift Mountain
★★★*Segnes* ☎(081)391281 tx 851981
15 Dec-15 Apr & 16 Jun-10 Oct
◖ℳ30 P30 Lift ♋ ∪ Mountain
Credit Cards ①②③⑤
★★*Guardaval* (n.rest) ☎(081)391119
Jun-Sep & Dec-Apr
rm10(◖ℳ7) ☎ P8 Mountain
Credit Cards ①②③
★★*National* ☎(081)391224 tx 851977
Jun-Oct & Dec-Apr
rm26(◖ℳ25) P Lift ℂ Mountain
Credit Cards ①②③⑤

FLÜELEN
Uri
★*Weisses Kreuz* ☎(044)21717
rm62(◖ℳ23) P ➦ Mountain Lake
Credit Cards ②⑤
◖◖ *Sigrist* Axenstr 30 ☎(044) 21260 P Ren

FRAUBRUNNEN
Bern
★★*Löwen* ☎(031)967219
rm6(◖ℳ4) A1rm ☎ ∪
Credit Cards ①②③⑤

FRIBOURG
Fribourg
★★★*Eurotel* Grand-Places 14 ☎(037)813131 tx
942459
◖ℳ130 ☎ P250 Lift ℂ ◰ Mountain
Credit Cards ①②③④⑤

◖◖ *Central* r de l'Industrie 7 ☎(037) 243530 For
◖◖ *Gendre* rte de Villars ☎(037) 240331 Aud VW
◖◖ *Piller* r Guillimann 24-26 ☎(037) 223092 Cit
Lan

FRICK
Aargau
★*Engel* ☎(064)615454
:Rest closed Mon
rm20(◖ℳ15) P70 ℂ ♋
Credit Cards ①②③⑤

FRUTIGEN
Bern
★*Simplon* ☎(033)711041
:Rest closed Tue
rm15(◖ℳ4) P30 Mountain

FÜRIGEN
Nidwalden
★★★*Fürigen* ☎(041)632222 tx 66257
◖ℳ90 Lift ℂ ♋ Mountain Lake
Credit Cards ①②③④⑤

FURKA PASS
Uri
★*Furkablick* ☎(044)67297
25 Jun-30 Sep
rm20 P100 Mountain

GABI
Valais
★★*Weissmies* Simplonstr ☎(028)291116
rm20(◖ℳ8) ☎ P24 Mountain
Credit Cards ①③⑤

GENÈVE *(GENEVA)*
Genève

See Plan page 398
Framed by the Alps and the Jura
mountains and located on the
shores of the largest of the
Alpine lakes, Genève is a major
hub of European cultural life, an
important venue for international
meetings, a popular centre for
conventions and exhibitions, and
a major financial, commercial and
industrial city. Yet, thanks to a
lovely, cosmopolitan atmosphere,
a wealth of museums, parks,
excellent hotels and restaurants,
Genève also attracts more visitors
each year than any other Swiss
city - and has refined the art of
looking after them to a high
degree.

EATING OUT Every country is
represented by restaurants here,
from Mexican to Russian, from
formal to informal. As well as
traditional Swiss specialities such
as the *fondue* and the *raclette*,
diners are likely to encounter
fresh fish from the lakes,
especially trout, perch and pike.
Many restaurants also offer hare,
venison, and game birds in
season, usually cooked in rich
wine sauces. Regional specialities
also include *saucisson vaudois*, a

spicy smoked sausage. Pastries are particularly irresistible. The *Brasserie Lipp*, at the Confederation Centre, has a cosmopolitan atmosphere, and the *Café Valaisanne et Chalet Suisse* serves excellent Swiss dishes, including *fondue*. *raclette* and *assiette valaisanne*. In the less expensive category, *Chez Bouby*, in Rue Grenus, has its devotees.

GENÈVE (GENEVA)

★★★★★**Bergues** (THF) quai des Bergues 33 ☎(022)7315050 tx 23383
➡📶123 ♨ P8 Lift ℂ Mountain Lake
Credit Cards 1 2 3 5

★★★★★**Noga Hilton International** quai du Mont-Blanc 19 ☎(022)7319811 tx 289704
➡📶413 ♨ P400 Lift ℂ 🖵 Mountain Lake
Credit Cards 1 2 3 4 5

★★★★★**Président** 47 quai Wilson ☎(022)7311000 tx 22780
➡📶180 ♨ P80 Lift ℂ Mountain Lake
Credit Cards 1 2 3 4 5

★★★★**Rhône** quai Turrettini 1 ☎(022)7319831 tx 22213
rm281(➡📶280) ♨ P120 Lift ℂ Mountain Lake
Credit Cards 1 2 3 5

★★★★★**Richemond** (Relais et Châteaux) Jardin Brunswick ☎(022)7311400 tx 22598
➡📶101 ♨ Lift ℂ Mountain Lake
Credit Cards 1 2 3 4 5

★★★**Beau Rivage** (Amb) quai du Mont-Blanc 13 ☎(022)7310221 tx 23362
:Rest closed Sat & Sun
➡📶115 ♨ P14 Lift ℂ Mountain Lake
Credit Cards 1 2 3 5

★★★**Paix** quai du Mont-Blanc 11 ☎(022)7326150 tx 22552
➡📶100 ♨ P10 Lift ℂ Sea Mountain Lake
Credit Cards 1 2 3 5

★★★**Ambassador** quai des Bergues 21,pl Chevelu ☎(022)7317200 tx 23231
➡📶86 ♨ P10 Lift ℂ
Credit Cards 1 2 3 5

★★★**Angleterre** quai du Mont-Blanc 17 ☎(022)7328180 tx 22668
➡📶60 ♨ P Lift ℂ Mountain Lake
Credit Cards 1 2 3 5

★★★**Berne** r de Berne 26 ☎(02241)7316000 tx 22764
➡📶89 Lift ℂ
Credit Cards 1 2 3 4 5

★★★**Century** (Amb) av de Frontenex 24 (n.rest) ☎(022)7368095 tx 413246
➡📶139 P20 Lift ℂ
Credit Cards 1 2 3 5

★★★**Cornavin** bd J-Fazy 33 (n.rest) ☎(022)7322100 tx 22853
rm125(➡📶65) Lift ℂ
Credit Cards 1 2 3 4 5

★★★**Cristal** 4 r Pradier (n.rest) ☎(022)7313400 tx 289926
➡📶79 Lift ℂ
Credit Cards 1 2 3 4 5

★★★**Eden** r de Lausanne 135 ☎(022)7326540 tx 23962
➡📶54 Lift ℂ Lake
Credit Cards 1 2 3 4 5

★★★**Grand Pré** r du Grand-Pré 35 (n.rest) ☎(022)7339150 tx 23284
➡📶80 ♨ P20 Lift ℂ
Credit Cards 1 2 3 5

★★★**Lutetia** r de Carouge 12 ☎(022)204222 tx 28845
➡📶42 Lift

★★★**Warwick** (Amb) r de Lausanne 14 ☎(022)7316250 tx 23630
:Rest closed Sat & Sun
➡📶169 P Lift Mountain Lake
Credit Cards 1 2 3 4 5

★★**Montbrillant** r de Montbrillant 2 ☎(022)7337784 tx 412155
➡📶55 ♨ P10 Lift
Credit Cards 1 2 3 4 5

★★**Touring-Balance** (Amb) pl Longemalle 13 ☎(022)287122 tx 427634
➡📶56 Lift ℂ Lake
Credit Cards 1 2 3 4 5

★**Adris** r Gevray 6-8 ☎(022)7315225
➡📶22 Lift
Credit Cards 1 2 3 5

🖪 **Acacias Motors** Boissonnas 11 ☎(022) 433600

🖪 **Athénée** rte de Meyrin 122 ☎(022) 7960044 P BMW Mer VW

🖪 **Auto Import** Vigett 1 Acacias ☎(022) 425824 P BMW

🖪 **Autohall Metropole** rte du Pont Butin ☎(022) 7921322 For

🖪 **Bouchet** rte de Meyrin 54-56 ☎(022) 7968900 P AR Peu

🖪 **Frey** r des Acacias ☎(022) 421010 AR Mer Toy

🖪 **Nouveau** Pré-Jérome 21-23 ☎(022) 202111 M/C BMW

At **MIES**(10km N on N1)

★**Buna** ☎(022)7551535
➡📶6 P Mountain

At **VÉSENAZ**(6km NE)

★★**Tourelle** rte d'Hermance 26 (n.rest) ☎(022)7521628
6 Feb-26 Dec
➡📶22 A2rm P30 Mountain Lake
Credit Cards 1 3 5

GENÈVE AIRPORT
(7km N)

At **FERNEY VOLTAIRE (France)**(4km NW)

★★★**Novotel Genève Aéroport** rte de Meyrin ☎(50)408523 tx 385046
➡📶79 P100 🗬 🖵 Mountain
Credit Cards 1 2 3 5

★★**Campanile** chemin de la Plache Brulée ☎50407479 tx 380957
➡📶42 ♨ P42
Credit Card 3

GERSAU
Schwyz

★★★**Beau-Rivage** ☎(041)841223
May-End Sep
rm34(➡📶28) ♨ P14 Lift 🖵 ♪♪ Mountain
Credit Card 1

★★★**Seehof du Lac** ☎(041)841245 tx 862489
Mar-Oct
➡📶18 P25 Lift 🖵 Beach Mountain Lake
Credit Cards 1 2 3 5

★**Bellevue** ☎(041)841120
15 May-Sep
rm8(➡📶4) P6 🖵 Sea Lake

GISWIL
Obwalden

★**Krone** Brünigstr ☎(041)682424 tx 866467
rm100(📶60) ♨ P Lift ℂ 🗬 Mountain
Credit Cards 1 2 3 5

GLARUS
Glarus

★★**Glarnerhof** Bahnhofstr 2 ☎(058)631191 tx 895533

➡📶31 Lift Mountain
Credit Cards 1 2 3 5

🖪 **Autocentre** Buchholzstr ☎(058) 611834 M/C P BMW

🖪 **Enz** Schweizerholstr 7 ☎(058) 611770 P Cit

GLATTBRUGG
See ZÜRICH AIRPORT

GLION
See MONTREUX

GOLDSWIL
Bern

★**Park** ☎(036)222942
rm55(➡2) A7rm P Mountain

🖪 **Bergseeli** Brienzerseestr ☎(036) 221043 Saa Toy

GÖSCHENEN
Uri

★**St-Gotthard** ☎(044)65263
rm25(➡📶8) ♨ P

GOTTLIEBEN
Thurgau

★★★**Krone** (ROM) ☎(072)692323
20 Feb-Dec
➡📶22 P10 Lift
Credit Cards 1 2 3 5

GRÄCHEN
Valais

★★**Beausite** ☎(028)562656
Dec-Apr & Jun-Oct
rm42(➡📶18) ♨ Lift 🖵

★**Grächerhof & Schönegg** (Amb) ☎(028)562515
Closed May & Nov
rm35

GREPPEN
Luzern

★**St-Wendelin** (n.rest) ☎(041)811016
➡📶8 ♨ P40 🖵 Mountain Lake
Credit Cards 1 2 3 5

GRINDELWALD
Bern

★★★★**Grand Regina** ☎(036)545455 tx 923263
mid Dec-mid Oct
➡📶98 ♨ P65 Lift ℂ 🗬 🖵 🖵 Mountain
Credit Card 3

★★★**Belvédère** DPn ☎(036)545434 tx 923244
17 Dec-22 Oct
rm55(📶4) P45 Lift 🖵 Mountain
Credit Cards 1 2 3 4 5

★★★**Gletschergarten** ☎(036)531721
20 Dec-15 Apr & 30 May-10 Oct :Rest closed Mon
➡📶28 P22 Lift Mountain

★★★**Parkhotel Schöenegg** DPn ☎(036)531853 tx 923245
Closed May & Nov
➡📶48 ♨ P25 Lift ℂ 🖵 Mountain
Credit Cards 1 2 3

★★★**Schweizerhof** ☎(036)532202 tx 923254
20 Dec-10 Apr & 28 Jun-6 Oct
➡📶51 P40 Lift ℂ 🖵 Mountain
Credit Cards 2 3

★★★**Sunstar & Adler** ☎(036)545417 tx 923230
19 Dec-10 Apr & 28 May-9 Oct
➡📶200 P Lift ℂ 🖵 Mountain
Credit Cards 1 2 3 5

★★**Derby** ☎(036)545461 tx 923277
Seasonal
rm74(➡📶72) ♨ P30 Lift ℂ Mountain
Credit Cards 1 2 3 5

★★**Grindelwald** ☎(036)532131
Jun-Sep & Dec-Apr
➡📶20 ♨ P20 Mountain
Credit Card 3

★★**Hirschen** ☎(036)532777
➡📶30 A12rm ♨ P16 Lift Mountain
Credit Cards 1 3 5

SWITZERLAND

GENÈVE (GENEVA)

1	★★★★★	Bergues
2	★★★★★	Noga Hilton International
3	★★★★★	Président
4	★★★★★	Rhône
5	★★★★★	Richemond
6	★★★★	Beau Rivage
7	★★★★	Paix
8	★★★	Ambassador
9	★★★	Angleterre
10	★★★	Berne
11	★★★	Century
12	★★★	Cornavin
13	★★★	Cristal
14	★★★	Eden
15	★★★	Grande Pré
16	★★★	Lutetia
17	★★★	Warwick
18	★★★	Novotel Genève Aéroport (At Ferney Voltaire, GENÈVE AIRPORT)
19	★★	Campanile (At Ferney Voltaire, GENÈVE AIRPORT)
20	★★	Montbrillant
21	★★	Touring-Balance
22	★	Adris
23	★	Buna (At Mies)
24	★★	Tourelle (At Vésenaz)

★Alpenblick ☎(036)531105 tx 923287
rm16 P20 Mountain
Credit Cards 1 2 3 5

★ Rothenegg Rothenegg ☎(036) 531507 Aud
VW

GRUYÈRES
Fribourg

★★★Hostellerie des Chevaliers ☎(029)61933 tx
940175
19 Feb-10 Jan :Rest closed Wed
⇥♠34 ☎ P15 Lift Mountain
Credit Cards 1 2 3 4 5

★★Hostellerie St-Georges ☎(029)62246 tx
940096
⇥♠14 Mountain
Credit Cards 1 2 3 5

GSTAAD
Bern

★★★Bellevue Grand (Amb) ☎(030)83171 tx
922232
15 Dec-10 Apr & Jun-Sep
rm55(⇥♠52) ☎ P34 Lift ℂ Mountain
Credit Cards 1 2 3 5

★★National-Rialto Hauptstr ☎(030)43474
⇥♠33 ☎ P Lift ℂ Mountain

★★Olden ☎(030)43444
2 Jun-Apr :Rest closed Wed in summer
⇥♠15 ☎ P10 Mountain
Credit Cards 1 2 3 5

★★Rössli ☎(030)43412 tx 922299
Closed mid May-mid Jun
rm22(⇥♠19) ☎ Mountain
Credit Cards 1 2 3 5

GSTEIG (LE CHÂTELET)
Bern

★Viktoria ☎(030)51034
:Rest closed Tue & Wed
⇥♠20 ☎ P20 ℂ Mountain
Credit Cards 1 2 3 5

GUNTEN
Bern

★★★Hirschen am See (Amb) ☎(033)512244 tx
922100
May-Oct

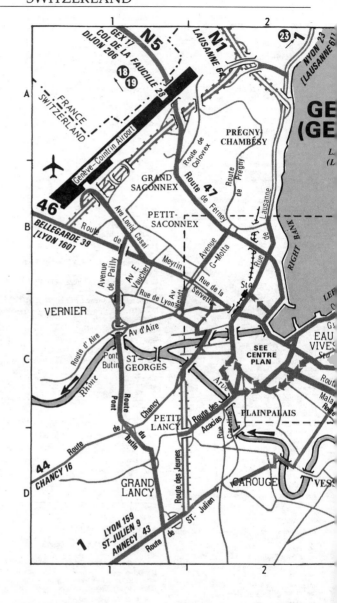

⇥♠68 ☎ P60 Lift Mountain Lake
Credit Cards 1 2 3 5

★Bellevue ☎(033)511121
Mar-Oct
rm22(♠11) P50 Mountain Lake

GURTNELLEN
Uri

★Gotthard ☎(044)65110
:Rest closed Tue
rm11(⇥♠7) ☎ P30 Mountain
Credit Cards 1 2 3 5

GWATT
Bern

★Lamm ☎(033)362233
:Rest closed Mon
⇥♠11 ☎ P30

HANDEGG
Bern

★★Handeck ☎(036)731131 tx 923257
May-Oct
rm29(⇥♠19) P50 Mountain
Credit Cards 1 2 5

398

GENÈVE (GENEVA) CENTRE

British Consulate General

AA

Scale ½km ½m

LAC LÉMAN (Lake Geneva)

RIGHT BANK

LEFT BANK

AA RA TCS
9 Rue Pierre Fatio

PARK

(7/89)

HERGISWIL
Nidwalden

★★★*Belvédère* (Amb) ☎(041)950101 tx 866160
🛏️50 A12rm P60 Lift ℂ ⌄ Mountain Lake
Credit Cards ①②③⑤

★★★*Piltaus* ☎(041)951555 tx 866159
🛏️70 P60 Lift ℂ ⌄ Mountain Lake
Credit Cards ①②③⑤

HERTENSTEIN
Luzern

★★★*Hertenstein* ☎(041)931444 tx 862984

15 Nov-Feb
rm63(🛏️55) ⩫ P300 Lift ℂ ⌄ Mountain Lake
Credit Cards ①②③⑤

HORW
Luzern

★★*Waldhaus* (Relais et Châteaux)
☎(041)471754
🛏️17 A12rm P ⌄ Mountain Lake
Credit Cards ①②③⑤

HÜNIBACH
See THUN (THOUNE)

ILANZ
Graubünden

★*Casutt* ☎(086)21131
Aug-Jun
🛏️15 P25 Mountain

🚲 *Spescha* via S-Clan Suta ☎(086) 21424 P Cit
For

399

SWITZERLAND

IMMENSEE AM ZUGERSEE
Schwyz

★★*Rigi-Royal* ☎(041)813131/32
rm44(➔🛁35) A12rm ⓐ P45 ℂ 🔺 Sea Mountain
Lake
Credit Cards ①②③④⑤

INTERLAKEN
Bern

★★★★**Beau Rivage** (Amb) Höheweg 211
☎(036)216272 tx 923122
Mid Dec-Mid Nov
➔🛁99 ⓐ P66 Lift ℂ 🖾 Mountain
Credit Cards ①②③⑤

★★★★**Metropole** (Amb) Höheweg 37
☎(036)212151 tx 923122
➔🛁100 A15rm ⓐ P30 Lift ℂ 🖾 Mountain Lake
Credit Cards ①②③⑤

★★★★*Victoria-Jungfrau* Höheweg 41
☎(036)212171 tx 923121
mid Dec-mid Nov
➔🛁228 ⓐ P284 Lift ℂ ⚲ 🖾 Mountain
Credit Cards ①②③④⑤

★★★**Bellevue Garden** Marktgasse 59
☎(036)224431 tx 923102
Seasonal
rm60(➔🛁55) ⓐ P12 ℂ Mountain
Credit Cards ①③⑤

★★★**Bernerhof** (Amb) Bahnhofstr 16
☎(036)223131 tx 923138
➔🛁36 ⓐ P6 Lift Mountain
Credit Cards ①②③⑤

★★★**Carlton** Höheweg 92 ☎(036)223821 tx
923155
Apr-Oct
rm50(➔🛁36) ⓐ P20 Lift Mountain
Credit Cards ①②③⑤

★★★*Crystal* Rugenparkstr 13 ☎(036)226233 tx
923362
21 Dec-Oct
➔🛁38 P16 Lift Mountain
Credit Cards ①②③⑤

★★★**Eden-Nova** Bahnhofpl 45 ☎(036)228812 tx
923143
Dec-Oct :Rest closed Mon
➔🛁48 P22 Lift Mountain
Credit Cards ①②③④⑤

★★★**Goldey** Goldey 85 Unterseen ☎(036)224445
tx 923114
Closed Nov-15 Dec
➔🛁40 P20 Lift Mountain Lake
Credit Cards ①②③⑤

★★★*Interlaken* Höheweg 74 ☎(036)212211 tx
923120
:Rest closed Tue
➔🛁63 P Lift ℂ Mountain
Credit Cards ①②③⑤

★★★**Krebs** Bahnhofstr 4 ☎(036)227161 tx
923150
May-20Oct
➔🛁51 ⓐ P21 Lift ℂ Mountain
Credit Cards ①②③④⑤

★★★*Lac* (Amb) Höheweg 225 ☎(036)222922 tx
923100
mid Feb-mid Jan :Rest closed Wed winter
rm30(➔🛁25) P20 Lift ℂ Mountain Lake
Credit Cards ①②③⑤

★★★**Merkur** ☎(036)226655 tx 923153
➔🛁36 P7 Lift ℂ Mountain
Credit Cards ①②③⑤

★★★*Royal St-Georges* Höheweg 139
☎(036)227575 tx 923175
15 Apr-Oct
➔🛁115 ⓐ P60 Lift ℂ Mountain
Credit Cards ①②③⑤

★★**Beau Site** Seestr 16 ☎(036)228181 tx 923131
15 Dec-15 Oct
rm50(➔🛁36) ⓐ P25 Lift ℂ Mountain

★★**Marti** Brienzstr 38 ☎(036)222602 tx 923199
rm29(🛁21) P35 Mountain Lake
Credit Cards ①②③④⑤

★★**National** Jungfraustr 46 ☎(036)223621 tx
923187
➔🛁45 ⓐ P15 Lift ℂ Mountain
Credit Cards ①②③④⑤

★★**Nord** Höheweg 70 ☎(036)222631 tx 923101
15 Dec-Oct
➔🛁52 P14 Lift ℂ Mountain
Credit Cards ①②③④⑤

★★**Oberland** Postgasse 1 ☎(036)216221 tx
223136
➔🛁58 A28rm P12 Lift ℂ Mountain
Credit Cards ①②③⑤

★★**Splendid** Höheweg 33 ☎(036)227012 tx
923189
Dec-Oct
➔🛁35 P10 Lift Mountain
Credit Cards ①②③④

★★*Strand-Hotel Neuhaus* Seestr 121
☎(036)228282 tx 923196
15 Dec-20 Oct
➔🛁57 A40rm P 🔺 Beach Mountain Lake
Credit Cards ①②③⑤

★★**Weisses Kreuz DPn** Höheweg ☎(036)225951
tx 923166
Dec-Oct :Rest closed Wed winter
rm56(➔🛁51) P4 Lift

★**Harder-Minerva** Harderstr 15 ☎(036)232313 tx
923361
15 Dec-15 Nov :Rest closed Sun
➔🛁34 ⓐ P60 Lift ℂ Mountain
Credit Cards ①②③④⑤

🛢 *Bohren & Urfer* Rugenparktr 34 ☎(036)
223231 P Cit

🛢 *Garage National* Weldeggstr 34a ☎(036)
222143 P

🛢 *Hilbergarage* Harderstr 25 ☎(036) 223651
Mer Vau

🛢 *Waldegg* Waldeggstr 34a ☎(036) 221939 P
AR

🛢 *Zimmermann* Seestr 109 Unterseen ☎(036)
221515 Toy Vol

JONGNY
See **VEVEY**

KANDERSTEG
Bern

★★★★★**Royal Bellevue** ☎(033)337512 tx
922192
18 Dec-Mar & 28 May-Sep
➔🛁35 ⓐ P46 Lift ⚲ 🖾 🔺 U Mountain

★★★**Parkhotel Gemmi** ☎(033)751117
Dec-Apr & Jun-Oct
➔🛁42 ⓐ P50 Lift 🖾 Mountain
Credit Cards ①③

★★★**Schweizerhof** ☎(033)751919 tx 922118
Apr-May & Nov-15 Dec
➔🛁24 ⓐ P40 Lift ⚲ 🖾 Mountain
Credit Cards ①②③⑤

★★**Adler** ☎(033)751121
➔🛁21 ⓐ P20 Lift Mountain
Credit Cards ①②③④⑤

★★**Alpenrose** ☎(033)751170
Closed Apr-May & Oct-Nov:Rest closed Tue
rm35(➔🛁10) A17rm P12 Mountain
Credit Cards ①②③⑤

★**Doldenhorn** ☎(033)751818 tx 922110
10 Dec-21 Apr
➔🛁24 A5rm ⓐ P42 Lift Mountain
Credit Cards ①②③⑤

KERZERS
Fribourg

★*Löwen* ☎(031)955117
➔🛁16 Mountain

KLOSTERS
Graubünden

★★★**Grand Vereina** ☎(083)691161 tx 853359
15 Dec-2 Apr
rm100(➔🛁80) ⓐ P26 Lift ℂ 🖾 Mountain
Credit Cards ①②③

★★*Sport Ferienzentrum* ☎(083)42921
Jun-Oct & Dec-Apr
➔🛁65 ⓐ P60 Lift ⚲ 🖾 Mountain
Credit Cards ①③

★**Walserhof** ☎(083)44242 tx 853348
Closed Jun & Nov
➔🛁11 ⓐ P22 Lift Mountain
Credit Cards ①②③⑤

KRATTIGEN BEI SPIEZ
Bern

★★**Bellevue-Bären** ☎(033)556144
➔🛁23 A3rm ⓐ P14 Lift Mountain Lake
Credit Cards ①②③⑤

KREUZLINGEN
Thurgau

🛢 *Amag* Haupstr 99 ☎(072) 722424 Aud VW

KRIENS
See **LUZERN (LUCERNE)**

KÜSSNACHT AM RIGI
Schwyz

★★**Hirschen** ☎(041)811027
3 Jan-19 Dec
➔🛁25 P50 Lift Mountain
Credit Cards ①②③④⑤

🛢 *Aebi* Hürtelstr ☎(041) 811050 Aud VW

LA
Each place preceded by 'La' is listed under the
name that follows it.

LAAX
Graubünden

★★★*Sporthotel Laax* ☎(086)30281 tx 56121
mid Dec-mid Oct
➔🛁81 P78 Lift ℂ Mountain
Credit Cards ①②③⑤

LACHEN
Schwyz

★★**Bären** ☎(055)631602
rm16(➔🛁11) P12 Lift
Credit Cards ①②③⑤

LANGENBRÜCK
Basel

★**Bären** ☎(062)601414
➔🛁17 A6rm ⓐ P105 Mountain
Credit Cards ①②③⑤

LAUSANNE
Vaud

Lausanne, which lies about half
way along the right bank of Lake
Geneva (Lac Leman), has a
strongly individual charm, from
Ouchy on the lakeside at 1,240ft
to La Sallaz, about 770ft above.
At Ouchy, the Lake Geneva
steamers come alongside and
sailing boats can be hired; a
mile-long railway runs up to the
city centre. Here, a covered
wooden stairway, the *Escalier du
Marché* leads to the *Palace de la
Palud*, where a colourful market
is held every Wednesday and
Saturday morning. Many first-
class stores are to be found along

the rue St François and the rue de Borg.

Lausanne is the headquarters of the Federal Court and the International Committee for the Olympic Games, while the Palais de Beaulieu is the venue for exhibitions and other events. The beautiful *Château de Chillon* stands on a rock promontory in the lake near Montreux.

EATING OUT *Le Wellingtonia* at the Hotel Beau Rivage has a deservedly high reputation as one of the best restaurants in Switzerland. Also good are *La Grappe d'Or, Le Relais*, at the Lausanne Palace Hotel and *La Voile d'Or*. For delicious pastries try the *Café Manuel* in Place St François.

LAUSANNE
Vaud

★★★★★**Palace** r du Grand Chêne 7-9 ☎(021)203711 tx 454171
◂♠164 P Lift ℂ Lake
Credit Cards ①②③④⑤

★★★★**Continental** pl de la Gare 2 ☎(021)201551 tx 454500
◂♠120 ☆ Lift ℂ Mountain Lake
Credit Cards ①②③④⑤

★★★**Agora** av du Rond Point 9 ☎(021)271211 tx 455300
:Rest closed Mon & Sat lunch & Sun
◂♠83 ☆ P36 Lift ℂ
Credit Cards ①②③⑤

★★★**Alpha** r du Petit Chêne 34 ☎(021)230131 tx 454999
◂♠133 ☆ P125 Lift ℂ Mountain Lake
Credit Cards ①②③⑤

★★★**Carlton** (Amb) av de Cour 4 ☎(021)263235 tx 454800
◂♠48 P25 Lift ℂ Mountain Lake
Credit Cards ①②③④⑤

★★★**City** r Caroline 5 ☎(021)202141 tx 454400
◂♠58 Lift ℂ
Credit Cards ①②③⑤

★★★**Jan** av de Beaulieu 8 ☎(021)361161 tx 455744
◂♠60 P15 Lift ℂ Mountain Lake
Credit Cards ①②③⑤

★★★**Mirabeau** av de la Gare 31 ☎(021)206231 tx 455030
◂♠64 P6 Lift ℂ Mountain Lake
Credit Cards ①②③④⑤

★★★**Paix** av de B-Constant 5 ☎(021)207171 tx 454080
◂♠116 ☆ Lift ℂ Mountain Lake
Credit Cards ①②③⑤

★★★**Victoria** av de la Gare 46 ☎(021)205771 tx 450644
rm60(◂♠48) ☆ P14 Lift ℂ Mountain Lake
Credit Cards ①②③④⑤

At BUSSIGNY(7km NW)
★★★**Novotel** r des Condémines ☎(021)7012871 tx 459531
◂♠100 P200 Lift ☐ Mountain

At CULLY(8.5km SE)
★★**Intereurop** ☎(021)7992091 tx 455973
Mar-Dec

◂♠61 P50 Lift ℂ Mountain Lake
Credit Cards ①②③⑤

At OUCHY
★★★★**Beau-Rivage Palace** pl Gl-Guisan ☎(021)263831/9171717 tx 454341
◂♠203 P Lift ℂ ℚ ☐ ☌ Mountain Lake
Credit Cards ①②③④⑤

★★★★**Royal Savoy** av d'Ouchy 40 ☎(021)264201 tx 454640
◂♠107 ☆ P220 Lift ☌ Mountain Lake
Credit Cards ①②③⑤

★★★**Aulac** pl de la Navigation 4 ☎(021)271451 tx 25823
◂♠69 P Lift Lake

★★**Angleterre** pl du Port 9 ☎(021)264145
Closed Jan
rm35(◂♠19) P30 ℂ Mountain Lake
Credit Cards ①②③⑤

✍ **City** rte de Genève 60 ☎(021) 242600 AR
✍ **Edelweiss** av de Morges 139 ☎(021) 253131 Vau
✍ **Frey** chemin du Martinet ☎(021) 363721
✍ **Gare** av de la Gare 45 ☎(021) 203761 P AR BMW
✍ **Occidental** av de Morges 7 ☎(021) 258225
✍ **Tivoli** av Tivoli 3 ☎(021) 203071 AR BMW DJ

At PULLY(2km SE)
★★★**Montillier** av de Lavaux 35 ☎(021)287585 tx 25747
rm45(◂♠30) ☆ P Lift ℂ Mountain Lake

At RENENS(5km NW)
✍ **Étole** rte de Cossonay ☎(021) 351521 Fia Lan Mer

At ST SULPICE(7km SW)
★**Pierrettes** ☎(021)254215
:Rest closed Mon mid-day
◂♠21 P35 ☌ Mountain Lake
Credit Cards ①②③⑤

LAUTERBRUNNEN
Bern

★★**Jungfrau** ☎(036)553434 tx 923240
15 May-15 Oct & 15 Dec-15 May
◂♠20 ☆ P20 Mountain
Credit Cards ①②③⑤

★★**Silberhorn** ☎(036)551471
15 Dec-Oct
◂♠50 A10rm P40 Mountain
Credit Cards ①②③⑤

★★**Staubbach** DPn ☎(036)551381 tx 923255
20 Dec-22 Oct
◂♠25 A5rm ☆ P30 Lift Mountain
Credit Cards ①②③④⑤

✎**Oberland** ☎(036)551241 tx 923285
Dec-Oct
rm26(◂♠22) A2rm P20 Mountain
Credit Cards ①②③④⑤

LE
Each name preceded by 'Le' is listed under the name that follows it.

LEISSIGEN
Bern

★★**Kreuz** ☎(036)471231
◂♠30 ☆ P40 Lift ☌ Beach Mountain Lake
Credit Cards ①②③⑤

LENK
Bern

★★★**Parkhotel Bellevue** ☎(030)31761 tx 922246
11 Jun-Sep 20 Dec-Mar
rm50(◂♠46) P Lift ☐ Mountain
Credit Cards ①②③⑤

★★★**Wildstrubel** ☎(030)63111 tx 922258
28 May-2 Oct
◂♠46 P20 Lift Mountain
Credit Cards ①②③⑤

LENZERHEIDE
Graubünden

★★★**Palanca** ☎(081)343131
14 Dec-14 Apr & 2 Jun-19 Oct
◂♠35 ☆ P Lift ℂ Mountain

LEYSIN
Vaud

★★★**Central Residence** (Amb) ☎(025)341211 tx 822518
12 Dec-17 Apr & 21 May-16 Oct
◂♠89 P60 Lift ℂ ℚ ☐ Mountain

✎**Mont-Riant** (n.rest) ☎(025)341235 tx 456166
5 Jun-21 Sep & 19 Dec-10 Apr
rm20(◂♠7) P10 Lift Mountain
Credit Cards ①②③⑤

LIESTAL
Basel

★★★**Engel** (Amb) Kasernenstr 10 ☎(061)912511 tx 966040
2 Jan-23 Dec
◂♠35 P35 ℂ
Credit Cards ①②③⑤

★★**Radackerhof** Rheinstr 93 ☎(061)943222
◂♠27 ☆ P Lift

✍ **Peter Auto** Gasstr 11 ☎(061) 919140 M/C P For
✍ **Rheingarage Buser** Rheinstr 95 ☎(061) 945025 P Cit Vol

LOCARNO
Ticino
See also MINÚSIO

★★★★★**Palma au Lac** via Verbano 29 ☎(093)330171 tx 846124
◂♠64 P15 Lift ℂ ☌ Mountain Lake
Credit Cards ①②③⑤

★★★**Lac** pza Grande (n.rest) ☎(093)312921
Mar-15 Nov
◂♠32 Lift ℂ Mountain Lake
Credit Cards ②④⑤

★★★**Quisisana** via del Sole 17 ☎(093)330141
rm75 P15 Lift ℂ ℚ ☌ Mountain Lake
Credit Cards ①②③⑤

★★★**Reber au Lac** DPn via Verbano ☎(093)330202 tx 846074
◂♠94 A17rm ☆ P40 Lift ℂ ℚ ☌ Mountain Lake
Credit Cards ①②③⑤

★★**Montaldi** pza Stazione ☎(004193)330222
5 Mar-10 Jan
rm70(◂♠45) A7rm P15 Lift ℂ Mountain Lake
Credit Cards ①②③④⑤

✍ **Alfa Romeo** pza 5 Vie ☎(093) 311616 Cit
Autocentro Leoni via Ciceri 19 ☎(093) 314880 Cit Fia

At MURALTO(1km W)
✍ **Autostar** via Sempione 12 ☎(093) 333355 Chy
✍ **Starnini** via Sempione ☎(093) 333355 AR

LUCERNE
See LUZERN

LUGANO
Ticino

★★★★**Excelsior** riva V-Vela 4 ☎(091)228661 tx 844187
◂♠81 Lift ℂ Lake
Credit Cards ①②③⑤

★★★**Splendide Royal** riva A-Caccia 7 ☎(091)542001 tx 844273
◂♠114 ☆ P80 Lift ℂ ☐ Mountain Lake
Credit Cards ①②③⑤

★★★**Arizona** via S-Gottardo 58 ☎(091)229343 tx 79087
rm56(◂♠50) ☆ Lift ℂ ☌ Mountain Lake

★★★**Bellevue au Lac** riva A-Caccia 10
☎(091)543333 tx 844348
Apr-Oct
╍🄵70 P50 Lift ℂ ⌴ Mountain Lake
Credit Cards ①②③

★★★**Gotthard-Terminus** via Gl-Maraini 1
☎(091)227777 tx 843271
11 Mar-27 Oct
╍🄵42 🄰 P10 Lift Mountain Lake
Credit Cards ①②③⑤

★★★**Holiday Select** via Zoppi 4 (n.rest)
☎(091)236172
Apr-Oct
╍🄵42 🄰 P Lift Mountain Lake
Credit Cards ②③

★★★**International au Lac** via Nassa 68
☎(091)227541 tx 840017
18 Mar-Oct
╍🄵80 Lift ℂ Mountain Lake
Credit Cards ①②③⑤

★★★**Ticino** (ROM) pza Cioccaro 1
☎(091)227772 tx 841324
╍🄵23 🄰 P8 Lift ℂ
Credit Cards ①②③④

★★**Continental Beauregard** Basilea 28-30
☎(091)561112 tx 844444
16 Feb-14 Nov
╍🄵135 P20 Lift ℂ Mountain Lake
Credit Cards ①②

★★**Everest** via Ginevra 7 (n.rest) ☎(041)229555
tx 840057
rm45(╍🄵30) Lift ℂ Lake
Credit Cards ①②③

🆖 **Cencini** via Ceresio ☎(091) 512826 **P** BMW
DJ

🆖 **Centro Mercedes** via Cantonate 24 ☎(091)
220732 Mer

🆖 **Lugano-Sud SA** via A-Riva 6 ☎(091) 543651
Ope

At BRÈ(5km E)

★**Brè Paese** ☎(091)514761
Closed Nov-Mar
rm18(╍🄵14) P20 Mountain Lake

At CASSARATE

★★★★**Villa Castagnola au Lac** ☎(091)512213 tx
841200
╍🄵100 🄰 P70 Lift ℂ ⌴ ⌴ Lake
Credit Cards ①②③⑤

★**Atlantico** via Concordia 12 (n.rest)
☎(091)512921
15 Feb-Nov
rm17(╍🄵13) Lift ℂ
Credit Cards ③⑤

★**Hotel Atlantico** via Concordia 12 (n.rest)
☎(091)512921
15 Feb-Nov
rm17(╍🄵13) Lift ℂ
Credit Cards ③⑤

🆖 **Vismara** via Concordia 2 ☎(091) 512614 For

At CASTAGNOLA(2km E)

★★**Carlton Villa Moritz** via Cortivo 9
☎(091)513812 tx 840003
Mar-Oct
╍🄵60 🄰 P10 Lift ℂ ⌴ Mountain Lake
Credit Cards ①②③

At CORNAREDO

🆖 **Camenisch** Pista del Ghiaccio ☎(091) 519725
M/C AR Maz

At MELIDE(6km S)

★★**Riviera** ☎(091)687912
Apr-Oct
╍🄵25 P Lift ⌴ Lake
Credit Cards ①③⑤

At PARADISO(2Km S)

★★★★**Admiral** (QM) via Geretta 15
☎(091)542324 tx 844281

╍🄵92 🄰 P Lift ℂ ⌴ ⌴ Mountain
Credit Cards ①②③④⑤

★★★**Conca d'Oro** Riva Paradiso 7
☎(091)543131
May-Oct
rm35(╍🄵18) P ⌴ Mountain Lake

★★★**Grand Eden** Riva Paradiso 7
☎(091)1550121 tx 844330
╍🄵126 🄰 P80 Lift ℂ ⌴ Mountain Lake
Credit Cards ①②③

★★★**Lac Seehof** ☎(091)541921 tx 844355
24 Mar-4 Jan
╍🄵53 P50 Lift ℂ ⌴ Mountain Lake
Credit Cards ①②③⑤

★★★**Meister** viale San Salvatore 11
☎(091)541412 tx 79365
Apr-Oct
╍🄵130 P Lift ⌴
Credit Cards ①②③④⑤

🆖 **Mazzuchelli-Auto** riva Paradiso 26 ☎(041)
543412 P Lan RR

At VEZIA(3km NW)

★★**Vezia** via S Gottardo 32 ☎(091)563631
Mar-Nov
rm60(╍🄵45) 🄰 P74 ⌴ Mountain
Credit Cards ①②③④⑤

LUNGERN
Obwalden

★**Rössli** ☎(041)691171
mid Oct-mid Nov :Rest closed Wed
╍🄵15 A12rm P26 Mountain Lake
Credit Cards ①②③⑤

LUZERN (LUCERNE)
Luzern

See Plan. Luzern, for many the
most delightful of Swiss cities,
stands in a magnificent setting
bordering the lake of the same
name, in the foothills of the St
Gotthard Pass. Lake excursions
are high on the list of visitors'
priorities, the Lake Lucerne
Navigation Company providing a
wide selection of half-day or full-
day excursions.
The sights of Luzern, best
enjoyed on foot, include the
Chapel Bridge, built in 1333, with
its numerous gable paintings and
sturdy water tower. Nearby are
quaint alleys that will intrigue
and fascinate, while in the city's
arcades you can enjoy the hustle
and bustle of the market crowds.

EATING OUT Luzern's favourite
soup is *brotsuppe* (bread soup),
and another popular starter is
bundnerfleisch, thin slices of dried
beef. Pork and veal sausages are
widely available, as are *rosti*,
grated fried potatoes.
Among the best restaurants in
town are *Chez Marianne*, the Old
Swiss House and the *Barbatti*,
which is located in a fine 19th-
century building.

LUZERN (LUCERNE)

★★★★**Carlton-Tivoli** (Amb) Haldenstr 57
☎(041)513051 tx 868119
Apr-Oct
╍🄵98 🄰 P106 Lift ℂ ᛜ Mountain Lake
Credit Cards ①②③④⑤

★★★★**Grand National** (SRS) Haldenstr 4
☎(041)501111 tx 868135
╍🄵79 🄰 P200 Lift ℂ ⌴ Mountain Lake
Credit Cards ①②③④⑤

★★★★**Palace** Haldenstr 10 ☎(041)502222 tx
865222
╍🄵152 🄰 P24 Lift ℂ Mountain Lake
Credit Cards ①②③⑤

★★★★**Astoria** Pilatusstr 29 ☎(041)244466 tx
865720
╍🄵140 Lift ℂ
Credit Cards ①②③⑤

★★★★**Balances** (Amb) Weinmarkt 5
☎(041)511851 tx 868148
╍🄵64 Lift ℂ Mountain Lake
Credit Cards ①②③④⑤

★★★★**Montana** Adligenswilerstr 22
☎(041)516565 tx 862820
Apr-Oct
╍🄵70 P17 Lift ℂ Mountain Lake
Credit Cards ①②③④⑤

★★★**Baslertor** ☎(041)220918 tx 862876
rm40(╍🄵35) A5rm Lift ℂ ⌴
Credit Cards ①②③④⑤

★★★**Château Gütsch** (GS) Kanonenstr
☎(041)220272 tx 868699
╍🄵40 🄰 P80 Lift ℂ ⌴ Mountain Lake
Credit Cards ①②③⑤

★★★**Drei Könige** Bruchstr 35/Klosterstr 10
☎(041)228833 tx 865511
rm74(╍🄵67) P6 Lift ℂ Mountain
Credit Cards ①②③⑤

★★★**Jägerhof** Baselstr 57 ☎(041)224751
╍🄵54 P25 Lift ℂ
Credit Card ②

★★★**Luzernerhof** Alpenstr 3 ☎(041)514646 tx
868116
rm85(╍🄵75) A22rm 🄰 P Lift ℂ
Credit Cards ①②③⑤

★★★**Monopol & Métropole** Pilatusstr 1
☎(041)230866 tx 865692
╍🄵108 Lift ℂ Mountain Lake
Credit Cards ①②③⑤

★★★**Park** Morgartenstr 4/13 ☎(041)239232 tx
78553
╍🄵70 Lift ℂ
Credit Cards ①②③⑤

★★★**Royal** Rigistr 22 ☎(041)511233 tx 862795
Apr-Oct
╍🄵50 P Lift Mountain Lake
Credit Cards ①③⑤

★★★**Schiller** Sempacherstr 4 ☎(041)235155 tx
865721
╍🄵72 Lift ℂ
Credit Cards ①②③⑤

★★★**Schweizerhof** Schweizerhof quai 3
☎(041)502211 tx 868157
╍🄵120 P40 Lift ℂ Mountain Lake
Credit Cards ①②③⑤

★★★**Union** Löwenstr 16 ☎(041)513651 tx
868142
╍🄵80 Lift ℂ
Credit Cards ①②③

★★★**Wilden Mann** Bahnhofstr 30 ☎(041)231666
tx 868260
╍🄵50 Lift ℂ
Credit Cards ①②③④⑤

★★**Alpes** Rathausquai 5 ☎(041)515825 tx
868221
Closed Jan
╍🄵41 Lift ℂ Mountain Lake
Credit Cards ①②③⑤

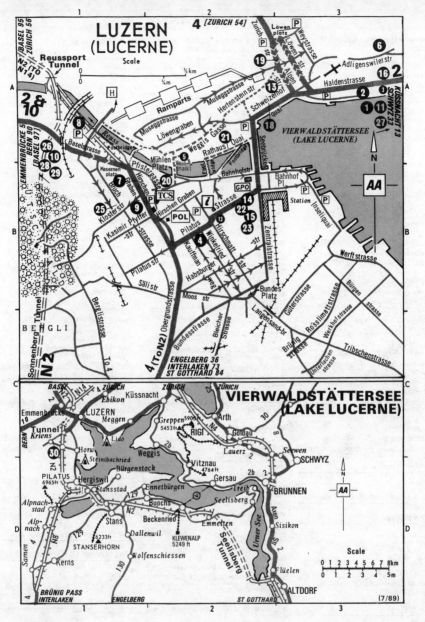

LUZERN (LUCERNE)

1	★★★★★	Carlton-Tivoli	10	★★★	Jägerhof	21	★★	Alpes
2	★★★★★	Grand National	11	★★★	Hermitage (At Seeburg)	22	★★	Continental Park
3	★★★★★	Palace	13	★★★	Luzernerhof	23	★★	Diana
4	★★★★	Astoria	14	★★★	Monopol & Métropole	25	★★	Rothaus
5	★★★★	Balances	15	★★★	Park	26	★★	St Christoph (At Emmenbrücke)
6	★★★★	Montana	16	★★★	Royal	27	★★	Seeburg
7	★★★	Baslertor	17	★★★	Schiller	28	★	Emmenbaum (At
8	★★★	Château Gütsch	18	★★★	Schweizerhof			Emmenbrücke)
9	★★★	Drei Könige	19	★★★	Union	29	★★	Landhaus (At Emmenbrücke)
			20	★★★	Wilden Mann	30	★	Pilatusblick (At Kriens)

★★**Continental** Morgartenstr 4/13 ☎(041)237566 tx 865639
⇜🛏68 Lift ℂ
Credit Cards 1 2 3 5

★★*Diana* Sempacherstr 16 (n.rest)
☎(041)232623 tx 868298
⇜🛏39 Lift ℂ Mountain Lake
Credit Cards 1 2 3 5

★★**Rothaus** Klosterstr 4 ☎(041)224522 tx 865504
⇜🛏54 P9 Lift ℂ
Credit Cards 1 2 3 5

★★**Seeburg** ☎(041)311922 tx 865770
rm102(⇜🛏88) 🅿 P40 Lift ℂ Mountain Lake
Credit Cards 1 2 3 5

🍴 *Epper Luzern* Horwerstr 81 ☎(041) 411122 DJ Peu

🍴 *Macchi* Maihofstr 61 ☎(041) 363334 AR Maz Saa

🍴 *Ottiger* Spitalstr 8 ☎(041) 365555 Fia Mer Por

🍴 *Schwerzmann* Wyssmatt, Kriens ☎(041) 414361 AR

🍴 *Willy* Obergrundstr 109 ☎(041) 402222 For

At **EBIKON**(4.5km NE)
🍴 *Windlin* Luzernerstr 57 ☎(041) 367500 Dat Mer

At **EMMENBRÜCKE**(1km N)
★★*Landhaus* ☎(041)531737 tx 862741
⇜🛏30 🅿 P40 Lift Mountain
Credit Cards 2 3 5

★★*St-Christoph* Rothenburgstr 45
☎(041)538636/37
16 Jan-21 Dec
rm21(⇜🛏12) P50 Lift
Credit Cards 1 2 3 5

★*Emmenbaum* Gerliswilstr 8 ☎(041)552960
⇜🛏10 🅿 P25
Credit Cards 2 3

At **KRIENS**(5Km SW)
★*Pilatusblick* Autobahn Luzern-Süd
☎(041)413546 tx 862905
⇜🛏40 P ℂ ⌇ Mountain
Credit Cards 1 2 3

At **SEEBURG**(2km E)
★★★*Hermitage* Seeburgstr 72 ☎(041)313737 tx 862709
⇜🛏33 A24rm P Lift Mountain Lake

LYSS
Bern
🍴 *Aebi* Bernstr 38-40 ☎(032) 844944 M/C P Cit

LYSSACH
See **BERN (BERNE)**

MALOJA
Graubünden
★★*Maloja-Kulm* ☎(082)43105
15 Dec-20 Oct
rm28(⇜🛏24) Lift Mountain
Credit Cards 1 2 3 5

★*Sporthotel Maloja* ☎(082)43126
May-Oct & Dec-Apr
rm32(⇜🛏8) P20 Mountain
Credit Card 1

MARTIGNY
Valais
★★★*Central* pl Centrale ☎(026)21184 tx 473841
rm30(⇜22) P Lift ℂ Mountain

★★★*Durhône* (Amb) 11 av du Grand St-Bernard
☎(026)221717 tx 473341
Closed Nov:Rest closed Sun
⇜🛏54 🅿 P30 Lift ℂ Mountain
Credit Cards 1 2 3 4 5

★★★*Forclaz* av du Léman 15 ☎(026)227013 tx 473591
rm36(⇜22) 🅿 Lift

★★★*Porte d'Octodure* ☎(026)227121 tx 473721
Closed 7-24 Jan:Rest closed Mon
⇜🛏56 🅿 P100 Lift ℂ ⍭ Mountain
Credit Cards 1 2 3 5

★★★*Poste* ☎(026)21444
⇜🛏32 P Lift ℂ Mountain

★★*Kluser* ☎(026)22641 tx 473641
Dec-Oct
rm48(⇜🛏40) 🅿 P ℂ Mountain
Credit Cards 1 2 3 4 5

🍴 *Mont-Blanc* av du Grand St-Bernard ☎(026) 21181 P Ren

MEGGEN
Luzern
★★*Balm* ☎(041)371135
20 Jan-20 Dec :Rest closed Mon
rm21(⇜🛏12) 🅿 P43 Mountain Lake
Credit Cards 1 2 3 5

MEIRINGEN
Bern
★★*Löwen* ☎(036)711407
rm20(⇜🛏12) P Mountain
Credit Cards 1 2 3 4 5

★★*Weisses Kreuz* ☎(036)714971 tx 923264
⇜🛏35 P Lift Mountain
Credit Cards 1 3

🍴 *E Boss* Alpbachstr ☎(036) 711631 P For Mer

MELIDE
See **LUGANO**

MERLIGEN
Bern
★★★★*Beatus* ☎(033)512121 tx 922147
31 Mar-8 Nov
⇜🛏75 🅿 P65 Lift ℂ ⍭ ⍭ 🖧 Mountain Lake
Credit Cards 1 2 3 5

★★*Mon Abri* ☎(033)511380
:Rest closed Wed Nov-Mar
rm21(⇜🛏19) 🅿 P43 Mountain

🍴 *K Wittwer* Hauptstr ☎(033) 512222 Cit Saa

METTENDORF
Thurgau
🍴 *W Debrunner* Hauptstr 90 ☎(054) 651119 P Toy

MEYRIEZ
See **MURTEN (MORAT)**

MIES
See **GENÈVE (GENEVA)**

MINÚSIO
Ticino
See also **LOCARNO**
★★★★*Esplanade* via Delle Vigne ☎(093)332121 tx 846146
rm84(⇜🛏52) 🅿 P40 Lift ℂ ⌇ Mountain Lake
Credit Cards 1 2 3 5

★★*Remorino* (n.rest) ☎(093)331033
Mar-Apr
⇜🛏26 🅿 P28 Lift ℂ ⌇ Mountain Lake

🍴 *Rivaplana* via R-Simen ☎(93) 334056 BMW

MONTANA-VERMALA
Valais
★★★*Mirabeau* (Amb) (n.rest) ☎(027)413912 tx 473365
Closed Nov
rm54(⇜🛏46) P Lift ℂ Mountain

★★★*St-Georges* ☎(027)412414 tx 473854
Closed May & Nov
⇜🛏45 🅿 P20 Lift ℂ ⌇ Mountain
Credit Cards 1 2 3 4 5

★★*Eldorado* ☎(027)411333 tx 473203
⇜🛏36 P36 Lift ℂ ⍭ Mountain
Credit Cards 1 2 3 5

🍴 *Lac* ☎(027) 411818 P Alf For

MONTREUX
Vaud
★★★★*Bonivard* 1 r Bonivard ☎(021)9634341 tx 453301
⇜🛏75 🅿 P Lift 🖃

★★★★*Eurotel Riviera* Grand Rue 81
☎(021)9634951 tx 453120
⇜🛏175 🅿 P55 Lift ℂ ⍭ 🖃 Mountain Lake
Credit Cards 1 2 4 5

★★★★*Palace* (SRS) Grande Rue 100
☎(021)9635373 tx 453101
⇜🛏226 🅿 P100 Lift ℂ ⍭ ⌇ Mountain Lake
Credit Cards 1 2 3 5

★★★*Eden au Lac* (Amb) r du Théâtre 11
☎(021)9635551 tx 453151
⇜🛏105 Lift ℂ ⌇ Mountain Lake
Credit Cards 1 2 3 5

★★★*Excelsior* r Bon Port 21 ☎(021)963323 tx 453133
⇜🛏80 🅿 P25 Lift ℂ 🖃 ⌇ Sea
Credit Cards 1 2 3 5

★★★*Golf* r Bon Port 35 ☎(021)9634631 tx 453255
⇜🛏60 🅿 P10 Lift ℂ Mountain Lake
Credit Cards 1 2 3 4 5

★★★*Suisse & Majestic* av des Alpes 43
☎(027)9635181 tx 453126
⇜🛏150 Lift ℂ Mountain Lake
Credit Cards 1 2 3 4 5

★★*Bon Accueil* Grande Rue 80 ☎(021)630551 tx 453126
⇜🛏39 🅿 Lift ℂ Mountain Lake

★★*Europe* av des Alpes 15 (n.rest)
☎(021)9637404 tx 453261
⇜🛏97 P6 Lift ℂ Mountain Lake
Credit Cards 1 2 3 5

★★*Parc et Lac* Grande Rue 38 ☎(021)633738
Mar-Nov
⇜🛏44 Lift ℂ
Credit Cards 1 2 3 5

★★*Terminus* r de la Gare 22 ☎(021)9631071 tx 453155
⇜🛏51 P15 Lift Mountain Lake
Credit Cards 1 2 3 5

🍴 *Central* Grand Rue 106 ☎(021) 633491 Vau

🍴 *Kursaal* av du Théâtre 7 ☎(021) 633491 DJ For

At **CHERNEX**(2Km NE)
★*Les Iris* ☎(021)9644252
Closed Nov
rm23(🛏6) P10 Mountain Lake
Credit Cards 1 2 3

At **GLION**(3km E)
★★★*Victoria* ☎633131 tx 453102
⇜🛏55 🅿 P Lift ℂ Mountain Lake

MORAT
See **MURTEN**

MORCOTE
Ticino
★*Rivabella* ☎(091)691314
Apr-Oct
rm15(⇜🛏10) A6rm P Mountain Lake

MORGES
Vaud
★★★*Fleur du Lac* (Amb) DPn rte de Lausanne 70 ☎(021)8024311 tx 458147
⇜🛏31 P51 Lift ℂ Mountain Lake
Credit Cards 1 2 3 5

MORGINS
Valais
★*Beau-Site* ☎(025)771138
rm15 P

MÜNSTER
Valais
🍴 *Grimsel* ☎(028) 731350 M/C P For

MURALTO
See **LOCARNO**

MURI
See **BERN (BERNE)**

MÜRREN
Bern
No road connections: take funicular from
LAUTERBRUNNEN or **STECHELBERG**
★★★*Eiger* ☎(036)551331 tx 923262
11 Jun-18 Sep & Xmas-Etr
⊷ৰ44 Lift ⊡ Mountain
Credit Cards ① ② ③ ⑤

MURTEN (MORAT)
Fribourg
★★*Bâteau Schiff* ☎(037)712701
Mar-20 Nov
⊷ৰ15 P50 Lake
Credit Cards ① ② ③ ⑤

★★*Weisses Kreuz* Rathausgasse 31
☎(037)712641
Mar-16 Dec :Rest closed Mon Nov-Dec & Mar-Apr
⊷ৰ26 Lift ℂ Mountain Lake
Credit Cards ① ③ ⑤

✎ *P Morier* Ryffstr 66 ☎(037) 731350 M/C **P** For
At MEYRIEZ(1km S)
★★★★*Vieux Manoir au Lac* ☎(037)711283 tx
942026
20 Feb-15 Dec
⊷ৰ23 P50 Lift ⊐ Lake
Credit Cards ① ② ③ ⑤

MUSTAIR
Graubünden
★★*Münsterhof* ☎(082)85541
rm19(⊷ৰ12) ☎ P2 Mountain
Credit Cards ① ② ③ ⑤

NÄFELS
Glarus
★★*Schwert* ☎(58)343373
Closed 2 wks Jul; Rest closed Mon
rm8(⊷ৰ7) P5 Lift Mountain
Credit Cards ① ② ③ ⑤

✎ *J Felber* Hauptstr ☎(058) 343440 For

NEIDERURNEN
Glarus
★★*Mineralbad* Badstr 43 ☎(058)211703
:Rest closed Mon & Tue lunch
⊷ৰ7 ☎ P40 ℀ Mountain

NEUCHÂTEL
Neuchâtel
★★★★*Eurotel* av de la Gare 15-17
☎(038)212121 tx 952588
⊷ৰ107 ☎ P60 Lift ℂ ⊡ Lake
Credit Cards ① ② ③ ⑤

★★★*Beaulac* (Amb) quai L-Robert 2
☎(038)258822 tx 952531
⊷ৰ46 A5rm P14 Lift ℂ Lake
Credit Cards ① ② ③ ⑤

★★★*Touring* ☎(038)255501
rm42(⊷ৰ38) P15 Lift ℂ Lake
Credit Cards ① ② ③ ⑤

★★*City* pl Piaget 12 ☎(038)255412 tx 952598
⊷ৰ35 Lift ℂ Mountain Lake
Credit Cards ① ② ③ ⑤

✎ *M Facchinetti* av Portes Rouges 1-3 ☎(038)
242133 Fia

✎ *Trois Rois* pl A-Mazel 11 ☎(038) 268301 For
Lan
At PESEUX(3km W)
✎ *Waser* r de Neuchâtel 15 ☎(038) 317573 AR

NEUHAUSEN AM RHEINFALL
Schaffhausen
★★★*Bellevue* ☎(053)222121
25 Jan-23 Dec
⊷ৰ10 Lift ℂ ⊐
Credit Cards ① ② ③ ⑤

NYON
Vaud
★★★*Clos de Sadex* rte de Lausanne
☎(022)612831
Closed mid Jan-mid Feb
rm18(⊷ৰ14) A5rm P50 Mountain Lake
Credit Cards ① ② ③ ⑤

★★★*Nyon* r de Rive 15 ☎(022)611931 tx 23591
Closed Nov
⊷ৰ40 P Lift Mountain Lake

✎ *L Jacques* rte de Lausanne 114 ☎(022)
612902 Alf Fia Lan

✎ *Quai* quai des Alpes ☎(022) 614133 Lan

OBERHOFEN
Bern
★★★*Moy* Schneckenbühlstr 9 (n.rest)
☎(033)431514
15 May-Sep
⊷ৰ25 P20 ⊡ Mountain Lake
Credit Cards ① ③ ⑤

★★*Kreuz* ☎(033)431448
:Rest closed Thu
rm19(⊷ৰ12) P Lift Mountain Lake
Credit Cards ① ③ ④ ⑤

OERLIKON
See **ZÜRICH**

OLTEN
Solothurn
See also **EGERKINGEN**
★★★*Schweizerhof* Bahnhofquai 18
☎(062)264646
rm60(⊷ৰ10) P Lift ℀
At STARRKIRCH(2km)
✎ *Pilloud* Aarauerstr 235 ☎(062) 353232 For

ORSIÈRES
Valais
★★*Catogne* ☎(026)831230
Closed Nov:Rest closed Mon
rm30(⊷ৰ25) P50 Mountain
Credit Card ③

OUCHY
See **LAUSANNE**

PARADISO
See **LUGANO**

PARPAN
Graubünden
★*Alpina* Hauptstr ☎(081)351184
15 May-15 Oct & 15 Dec-15 Apr
⊷ৰ45 ☎ P35 Lift ℂ Mountain
Credit Cards ① ② ③

PESEUX
See **NEUCHÂTEL**

PFÄFFIKON
Schwyz
★★*Sternen* ☎(055)481291
:Rest closed Thu
⊷ৰ25 P25

PONTRESINA
Graubünden
★★★*Grand Kronenhof* ☎(082)60111 tx 852500
mid Dec-mid Apr & mid Jun-mid Sep
rm125(⊷ৰ96) ☎ P82 Lift ℂ ℀ ⊡ ⊐ Mountain
Credit Cards ① ② ③ ⑤

★★★*Müller* ☎(082)66341
12 Apr-6 Oct
rm46(⊷ৰ39) A11rm ☎ P25 Lift ⊐ Mountain
Credit Cards ② ③ ⑤

★★★*Palü* ☎(082)66688
15 Jun-15 Oct & 20 Dec-15 Apr
⊷ৰ70 ☎ P50 Lift ℀ Mountain
Credit Cards ① ② ③ ⑤

★★★*Schweizerhof* (Amb) Berninastr
☎(082)60131 tx 852542
Jun-18 Oct & 18 Dec-10 Apr

⊷ৰ81 P40 Lift ℂ Mountain
Credit Cards ① ② ③ ⑤

PORRENTRUY
Jura
✎ *J Montavron* Cuenin 21 ☎(066) 661206 **P**
Ren

✎ *Ponts* rte de Courgenay ☎(066) 661206 **P**
Ope

✎ *L Vallat* ☎(066) 661913 M/C **P** For

PORTO-RONCHO
Ticino
★*Eden* (n.rest) ☎(093)355142
Mar-Oct
rm14(⊷ৰ2) P Mountain Lake

POSCHIAVO
Graubünden
At PRESE, LE(4.5km S)
★★★*Prese* ☎(082)50393
15 May-15 Oct
rm29(⊷ৰ27) P25 Lift ℀ ⊐ Mountain Lake

PRESE, LE
See **POSCHIAVO**

PULLY
See **LAUSANNE**

RAGAZ, BAD
St-Gallen
★★★*Quellenhof* ☎(085)90111 tx 855897
rm132(⊷ৰ129) ☎ P80 Lift ℂ ℀ ⊡ ♣♣ Mountain
Credit Cards ① ② ③ ⑤

★★*Park* ☎(085)92244 tx 855808
Mar-Nov
rm65(⊷ৰ39) A20rm ☎ P42 Lift ℂ Mountain
Credit Cards ① ② ③ ⑤

★★*TM Schloss Ragaz* 3 ☎(085)92355
Closed 20 Nov-20 Dec
rm62(⊷ৰ45) P100 Lift ⊐ Mountain
Credit Cards ① ② ③ ⑤

REGENSDORF
See **ZÜRICH**

RENENS
See **LAUSANNE**

RHEINFELDEN
Aargau
★★*Schwanen* Kaiserstr 8 ☎(061)875344
rm65(⊷ৰ41) ☎ P34 Lift ℂ ⊡
Credit Cards ① ② ③ ⑤

★*Ochsen* ☎(061)875101
:Rest closed Tue
⊷ৰ6 ☎ P35
Credit Cards ① ② ③ ④ ⑤

✎ *Grell* Kaiserstr 30 ☎(061) 875051 **P** For

ROLLE
Vaud
★★★*Tête Noire* ☎(021)752251
rm20(⊷ৰ15) Lake

ROMANSHORN
Thurgau
★★*Bodan* ☎(071)631502
⊷ৰ15 P50 Lift
Credit Cards ① ② ③ ⑤

RORSCHACH
St-Gallen
★★★*Anker* Hauptstr 71 ☎(071)414243
⊷ৰ33 P Lift Lake
Credit Cards ② ⑤

SAANENMOSER PASS
Bern
★★★*Hauts de Gstaad* ☎(030)83232 tx 922220
15 Jun-Sep & 20 Dec-15 Apr
⊷ৰ30 ☎ P50 Lift ℂ ℀ Mountain
Credit Cards ① ② ③ ④ ⑤

SAAS-FEE
Valais

★★*Bergfreude* ☎(028)572137
Feb-May & Aug-Oct
rm24(☀️🛁16) ℂ

SACHSELN
Obwalden

★★★*Kreuz* ☎(041)661466 tx 866411
rm50(☀️🛁48) A24rm P50 Lift ℂ Mountain
Credit Cards ① ② ③ ⑤

ST BLAISE
Neuchâtel

★★*Cheval Blanc* ☎(038)333007
Feb-Dec :Rest closed Mon
☀️🛁12 P Mountain Lake
Credit Cards ① ② ③ ⑤

ST GALLEN
St-Gallen

★★★*Einstein Mövenpick* Berneggstr 2
☎(071)200033 tx 77478
☀️🛁65 P100 Lift ℂ
Credit Cards ① ② ③ ④ ⑤

★★★*Walhalla* (Amb) Bahnhofpl ☎(071)222922
tx 77160
☀️🛁55 🚗 P Lift ℂ
Credit Cards ① ② ③ ⑤

★★★*Im Portner* Bankgasse 12 ☎(071)229744
☀️🛁25 🚗 Lift

🍴 *Capitol* Rorscherstr ☎(071) 315444 Ope

🍴 *Citroën St-Gallen* Fürstenlandstr 25 ☎(071)
282121 Cit

🍴 *City* Zürcherstr 162 ☎(071) 291131 P Aud Por
VW

🍴 *H Erb* Fürstenlandstr 149 ☎(071) 273333

ST LUC
Valais

★★*Bella-Tola & St-Luc* ☎(027)651444 tx 472094
Jun-Sep & Xmas-Etr
☀️🛁33 🚗 P45 Lift Mountain

ST MORITZ
Graubünden

★★★★★*Kulm* ☎(082)21151 tx 852172
3 Dec-9 Apr & 25 Jun-11 Sep
☀️🛁210 🚗 P110 Lift ℂ 🔍 🚇 Mountain Lake
Credit Cards ① ② ③

★★★★*Carlton* (SRS) ☎(082)21141 tx 852154
Dec-Apr & Jun-Sep
☀️🛁105 🚗 P Lift ℂ 🚇 Mountain Lake
Credit Cards ① ② ③ ⑤

★★★★*Crystal* ☎(082)21165 tx 852149
Dec-Etr & Jun-Oct
☀️🛁100 Lift ℂ Mountain
Credit Cards ① ② ③ ⑤

★★★★*Suvretta House* ☎(082)21121 tx 852191
Dec-Apr & Jun-Sep
☀️🛁230 🚗 P80 Lift ℂ 🔍 🚇 Mountain Lake

★★★*Bellevue* via dal Bagn 18 ☎(082)22161 tx
852128
☀️🛁40 🚗 P Lift ℂ Mountain Lake
Credit Cards ① ② ③ ④ ⑤

★★★*Belvédère* via dal Bagn 18 ☎(082)33906 tx
852135
15 Dec-15 Apr & 15 Jun-15 Oct
☀️🛁70 🚗 P50 Lift ℂ 🚇 Mountain Lake

★★★*Neues Posthotel* ☎(082)22121 tx 852130
rm83(☀️🛁76) Lift ℂ Mountain
Credit Cards ① ② ③

★★*Baren* Hauptstr ☎(082)33656 tx 74509
May-Nov
☀️🛁65 P Lift 🚇 Mountain

★★*Margna* Bahnhofstr ☎(082)22141 tx 852104
Jun-mid Oct & mid Dec-mid Apr
☀️🛁64 🚗 P50 Lift ℂ Mountain Lake
Credit Cards ② ③

🍴 *Dosch* via Maistr 46 ☎(082) 33333 P Alf Mer
Ope

At **ST MORITZ BAD**(1km S)

★*National* ☎(082)33274
15 Jun-Sep & Dec-Apr
☀️🛁18 A8rm 🚗 P10 Lift 🚇 Mountain Lake
Credit Cards ③

At **ST MORITZ CHAMPFÉR**(3km SW)

★★★★*Europa* ☎(082)21175 tx 74458
11 Jun-29 Nov
☀️🛁119 🚗 P100 Lift ℂ 🔍 🚇 Mountain
Credit Cards ① ② ③ ⑤

ST MORITZ BAD
See **ST MORITZ**

ST MORITZ CHAMPFÉR
See **ST MORITZ**

ST SULPICE
See **LAUSANNE**

SAMEDAN
Graubünden

★★★*Bernina* (Amb) Hauptstr ☎(082)65421 tx
74486
16 Jun-Oct
rm59(☀️🛁56) 🚗 P50 Lift ℂ Mountain
Credit Cards ① ② ③ ⑤

🍴 *Gebrüder Pilster* ☎(082) 65666 Toy Vol

SANTA MARIA
Graubünden

★★*Schweizerhof* Hauptstr ☎(082)85124
15 May-Oct
rm38(☀️🛁37) A12rm 🚗 P39 Lift Mountain
Credit Cards ① ② ③ ⑤

SARGANS
St-Gallen

★★*Post* ☎(085)21214
rm15(☀️🛁11) 🚗 P21 Mountain

SARNEN
Obwalden

At **WILEN**(2km SW)

★★*Wilerbad* ☎(041)660015 tx 866420
rm54(☀️🛁41) A4rm 🚗 Lift 🏊 ♨️ Mountain Lake
Credit Cards ① ② ③ ⑤

SCHAFFHAUSEN
Schaffhausen

★★*Bahnhof* Bahnhofstr 46 ☎(053)241924 tx
896399
☀️🛁44 🚗 P10 Lift ℂ
Credit Cards ① ② ③ ⑤

★★*Kronenhof* Kirchhofpl 7,(off Vordergasse)
☎(053)897068
☀️🛁33 P Lift
Credit Cards ① ② ③ ④ ⑤

★★*Parkvilla* Parkstr 18 ☎(053)252737
rm20(☀️🛁17) P Lift
Credit Cards ① ② ③ ⑤

🍴 *Auto-Ernst* Schweizerbildstr 61 ☎(053) 33322
P BMW

SCHÖNRIED
Bern

★★★*Ermitage & Golf* ☎(030)42727 tx 922213
Dec-Apr & May-Oct
☀️🛁71 A25rm 🚗 P84 Lift ℂ 🔍 🚇 🏊 Mountain
Credit Cards ① ② ③ ⑤

SCHWANDEN
Glarus

★*Adler* ☎(058)811171
2 Jan-18 Jul & 10 Aug-Dec :Rest closed Mon &
Tue
☀️🛁9 P20
Credit Cards ② ③ ④ ⑤

SCUOL, BAD
Graubünden

★★★*Kurhotel Belvedere* ☎(084)91041
Jun-Oct & Dec-Apr

rm60(☀️🛁50) P50 Lift ℂ Mountain
Credit Cards ① ③ ⑤

SEEBURG
See **LUZERN (LUCERNE)**

SERVION
Vaud

★★*Fleurs* ☎(021)9032054
rm32(☀️🛁14)
Credit Cards ① ② ③ ⑤

SIERRE (SIDERS)
Valais

★*Victoria-Jardin* rte de Sion 5 ☎(027)551007
rm16(☀️🛁14) 🚗 P
Credit Cards ① ② ③ ④ ⑤

🍴 *International* rte de Noës ☎(027) 551436 P
Pau Tal

🍴 *Rawylav* M-Huber 18 ☎(027) 550308 P For

SIGRISWIL
Bern

★*Adler* ☎(033)512424
rm28(☀️🛁21) P30 Lift Mountain Lake
Credit Cards ① ③ ⑤

SILS-BASEGLIA
See **SILS-MARIA**

SILS-MARIA
Graubünden

★★★*Waldhaus* ☎(082)45331 tx 852244
mid Dec-mid Apr & Jun-mid Oct
☀️🛁150 🚗 P80 Lift ℂ 🔍 🚇 Mountain Lake
Credit Cards ① ③

★*Privata* ☎(033)45247
Dec-Apr & Jun-Oct
rm20

At **SILS-BASEGLIA**

★★★*Margna* ☎(082)45306 tx 852296
Dec-Apr & Jun-Oct
☀️🛁72 🚗 P55 Lift ℂ 🔍 Mountain Lake

SILVAPLANA
Graubünden

★★*Sonne* ☎(082)48152 tx 74649
Closed 25 May-Jun
rm50(☀️🛁34) P40 Lift Mountain
Credit Cards ① ② ③ ⑤

★*Corvatsch* ☎(082)48162
rm16 P20 Mountain Lake

SIMPLON-DORF
Valais

★*Poste* ☎(028)292111
rm14(☀️🛁8) 🚗 P Mountain
Credit Cards ① ② ③

SIMPLON-KULM
Valais

★★*Bellevue* Simplon Pass ☎(028)291331
Mar-Oct
rm45(☀️🛁20) 🚗 P105 Lift Mountain
Credit Cards ① ② ③ ④ ⑤

SION (SITTEN)
Valais

★★★*Rhône* (Amb) r du Sex 10 ☎(027)228291 tx
472504
☀️🛁44 P400 Lift Mountain
Credit Cards ① ② ③ ⑤

★★*Continental* r de Lausanne 116
☎(027)224641
☀️🛁24 ℂ Mountain
Credit Cards ① ② ③ ⑤

★★*Touring* av de la Gare 6 ☎(027)231551
:Rest closed Sat
rm28(☀️🛁24) 🚗 P10 Lift Mountain
Credit Cards ① ② ③ ⑤

🍴 *Aviation* ave Mce-Troillet 84 ☎(027) 223924
Maz Vol

🍴 *Hediger* Batasse ☎(027) 220131 Mer

🍴 *Kasper* du Tunnel 22 ☎(027) 221271 For

Nord av Ritz 35 ☎(027) 223413 Ren

Tourbillon av de Tourbillon 23 ☎(027) 222077
P Maz

SISIKON
Uri

★★★**Tellsplatte** ☎(044)121612 tx 866337
rm50(🚿46) 🏊 P54 Lift ℂ ⊒ Mountain Lake
Credit Cards ① ② ③ ④ ⑤

SOLOTHURN (SOLEURE)
Solothurn

★★★**Krone** (Amb) Hauptgasse 64 ☎(065)224412
tx 934678
🚿42 🏊 P6 Lift ℂ
Credit Cards ① ② ③ ⑤

SPIEZ
Bern

★★★**Eden** Seestr 58 ☎(033)541154 tx 955181
May-Oct
rm56(🚿47) 🏊 P39 Lift ℀ ⊒ Mountain Lake
★★**Alpes** Seestr 38 ☎(033)543354 tx 911513
:Rest closed Mon
🚿45 🏊 P22 Lift ℀ Mountain Lake
★★**Terminus** Bahnhofpl ☎(033)543121
rm65(🚿30) P Lift Mountain Lake

STANS
Nidwalden

★★**Stanserehof** Stansstaderstr 20 ☎(041)614122
:Rest closed Sun & Mon
🚿32 🏊 P20 Lift ℂ Mountain

STANSSTAD
Nidwalden

★★★**Freienhof** ☎(041)613531
rm50(🚿35) 🏊 P40 Lift ⊒ Mountain Lake
Credit Cards ① ② ③ ④
★★★**Schützen** (Amb) Stanserstr 23
☎(041)611355 tx 866256
Mar-Jan
rm38(🚿28) P65 Lift Mountain
Credit Cards ① ② ③ ⑤

STARRKIRCH
See OLTEN

STECKBORN
Thurgau

Bürgl's Erben Seestr 143 ☎(054) 611251 P
Dat Saa

SURSEE
Luzern

★★**Hirschen** Oberstadt 10 ☎(045)211048
rm10(🚿7) P300 Lift
Credit Cards ① ② ③ ⑤
★**Bellevue** Mariazell ☎(045)21188
rm15(🚿2) A1rm P Mountain Lake

TAFERS
Fribourg

Schweingruber Mariahilfstr 283 ☎(037)
441750 M/C Ope

TARASP
See VULPERA

TEUFEN
Appenzell

★**Ochsen** ☎(071)332188
rm13(🚿2) P Mountain

THALWIL
Zürich

★★**Thalwilerhof** Bahnhofstr 16 ☎(01)7200603
rm25(🚿16) P Lift Lake
Credit Cards ① ② ③

THIELLE
Neuchâtel

★★★**Novotel-Neuchâtel Est** rte de Berne
☎(038)335757 tx 952799
🚿60 P150 ⊒
Credit Cards ① ② ③ ⑤

THUN (THOUNE)
Bern

★★★★**Elite** Bernstr 1-3 ☎(033)232823 tx 921214
🚿39 🏊 P7 Lift ℂ Mountain
Credit Cards ① ② ③ ④ ⑤
★★★**Beau Rivage** ☎(033)222236
May-20 Oct :Rest closed Mon
rm30(🚿25) 🏊 P15 Lift ⊒ Mountain Lake
Credit Cards ① ② ③ ⑤
★★★**Freienhof** (Amb) Freienhofgasse 3
☎(033)215511 tx 921190
🚿63 Lift ℂ ⊒ Mountain Lake
Credit Cards ① ② ③ ⑤
★**Metzgern** Rathauspl ☎(033)222141
Closed 1-24 Oct :Rest closed Thu
rm8 Mountain
Credit Cards ① ③
City Kyburgstr ☎(033) 229578 Cit Maz
Touring Industriestr 5 ☎(033) 224455
At DÜRRENAST(2km S)
★★★**Holiday** Gwattstr 1 ☎(033)365757 tx
921357
🚿57 🏊 P40 Lift ℂ Mountain Lake
Credit Cards ① ② ③ ⑤
At HÜNIBACH(1km SE)
K Schick Staatsstr 134 ☎(033) 433131 BMW
Ren

THUSIS
Graubünden

Central ☎(081) 811154 P For
Viamala Hauptstr ☎(081) 811822 P For Ope
Vau

TIEFENCASTEL
Graubünden

★★**Posthotel Julier** Julierstr ☎(081)771415
Closed 20 Oct-20 Dec
rm46(🚿43) 🏊 P35 Lift Mountain
Credit Cards ① ② ③ ⑤
★**Albula** ☎(081)711121
🚿43 🏊 P28 Lift Mountain
Credit Cards ① ② ③ ⑤

TRAVERS
Neuchâtel

★**Crêt** ☎(038)631178
5 Jan-20 Dec :Rest closed Mon
🚿6 ℀ Mountain
Credit Card ②

UNTERÄGERI
Zug

★★★**Seefeld** Seestr 8 ☎(042)722727 tx 864981
rm37(🚿34) P Lift Mountain Lake
Credit Cards ② ③ ⑤

UNTERWASSER
St-Gallen

★★★**Sternen** ☎(074)52424 tx 884148
15 Dec-Oct
🚿55 P70 Lift Mountain
Credit Cards ① ② ③ ⑤

VALLORBE
Vaud

★**Jurats** ☎(021)8431991
🚿16 P Mountain
Credit Card ③
Moderne de l'Ancien Poste 61 ☎(021) 831156
P Aud VW

VERBIER
Valais

★★★**Farinet** ☎(026)76626 tx 473334
rm15(🚿14) P20 Lift Mountain
Credit Cards ① ② ③ ⑤
★★★**Grand Combin DPn** ☎(026)75515 tx
473795
Jan-May & Jul-Sep
🚿26 P20 Lift Mountain
Credit Cards ① ② ③ ⑤

★★★**Rhodania** (Amb) ☎(026)316121 tx 473392
Xmas-Etr & Jun-Sep
🚿44 🏊 P14 Lift ℂ Mountain
Credit Cards ① ② ③ ④ ⑤
Verbier ☎(026) 76666

VÉSENAZ
See GENÈVE (GENEVA)

VEVEY
Vaud

★★★**Lac** (Amb) r d'Italie 1 ☎(021)9211041 tx
451161
rm56(🚿53) 🏊 P18 Lift ℂ ⊒ Mountain Lake
Credit Cards ① ② ③ ⑤
★★**Famille** ☎(021)9213931 tx 451181
rm63(🚿59) P12 Lift ℀ ⊒
Credit Cards ① ② ③ ⑤
At JONGNY(3Km N)
★★★**Léman** ☎(021)9210544 tx 451198
🚿60 A29rm 🏊 P30 Lift ℂ Mountain
Credit Cards ① ② ③

VEZIA
See LUGANO

VILLARS-SUR-OLLON
Vaud

★★★★**Eurotel** ☎(025)353131 tx 456206
19 Dec-15 Oct
🚿170 🏊 P15 Lift ℂ ℀ ⊒ ⊒ ♪♬ ∪ Mountain
Credit Cards ① ② ③ ⑤
★★**Montesano et Regina** ☎(025)352551 tx
456206
15 Dec-Etr & Jul-Aug
rm45(🚿20) 🏊 P10 Lift ℂ ℀ Mountain
Credit Cards ① ② ③ ④ ⑤

VISP
Valais

Moderne ☎(028) 464333 P Fia Mer
Touring Kantonstr ☎(028) 461040 P Aud Por
VW

VITZNAU
Luzern

★★★**Park** ☎(041)831322 tx 862482
Apr 20-Oct 22
🚿98 🏊 P80 Lift ℂ ℀ ⊒ ⊒ Mountain Lake
Credit Cards ② ③
★★★**Vitznauerhof** (Relais et Châteaux)
☎(041)831315 tx 862485
Jan-27 Oct & 2 Dec-Dec :Rest closed Tue (Winter
Season)
🚿60 P50 Lift ℂ ℀ Mountain Lake
Credit Cards ① ② ③ ⑤
★★**Terrasse Am See** ☎(041)831033
May-15 Oct
rm28(🚿22) P8 Lift ℂ ⊒ Mountain Lake

VULPERA (TARASP)
Graubünden

★★★**Schweizerhof** ☎(084)91331 tx 74427
Jun-Sep & Dec-Apr
rm116(🚿101) 🏊 P100 Lift ℂ ℀ ⊒ ♪♬
Mountain
Credit Cards ① ② ③ ⑤

WABERN
See BERN (BERNE)

WÄDENSWIL
Zürich

★★★**Lac** Seestr 100 ☎(01)7800031
rm24(🚿14) P Lift Lake
Credit Cards ① ② ③ ⑤
Zentrum Seestr 114 ☎(01) 7808080

WASSEN
Uri

★**Alpes** ☎(044)65233
🚿12 🏊 P Lift Mountain
Credit Card ②

WEGGIS
Luzern

★★★*Albana* (Relais et Châteaux) ☎(041)932141 tx 862463
Apr-16 Oct
⇥♠70 ♨ P50 Lift ९ ⌒ Mountain Lake
Credit Cards ① ② ③ ⑤

★★★Alexander ☎(041)932222 tx 862465
Mar-Nov
⇥♠55 Lift (९ ⌒ Mountain Lake
Credit Cards ① ② ③ ④ ⑤

★★★*Park* ☎(041)931313 tx 868822
May-10 Oct
⇥♠62 ♨ P30 Lift (९ Mountain Lake
Credit Cards ① ② ③ ⑤

★★★*Waldstätten* ☎(041)931341 tx 862988
⇥♠42 ♨ P25 Lift ⧓ Mountain Lake
Credit Cards ① ② ③ ④ ⑤

★★Beau Rivage Gotthardstr ☎(041)931422 tx 862982
Apr-15 Oct
⇥♠44 ♨ P25 Lift (⌒ Mountain Lake
Credit Cards ① ② ③ ⑤

★★*Central Am See* ☎(041)931252
15 Mar-Nov
rm50(⇥♠40) ♨ P Lift ⌒ Mountain Lake
Credit Cards ① ② ③ ⑤

★★*Rigi* Seestr ☎(041)932157
May-Oct
rm55(⇥♠29) A35rm P20 ⌒ Mountain Lake
Credit Card ⑤

★★Rössli Seestr ☎(041)931106 tx 862931
20 Mar-20 Oct
⇥♠50 ♨ P17 Lift Mountain Lake
Credit Cards ② ③ ⑤

★★Seehof Hotel du Lac ☎(041)931151
Mar-Nov
rm25(⇥♠23) P15 Lift Mountain Lake
Credit Cards ① ② ③ ④ ⑤

★*Frohburg* (n.rest) ☎(041)931022
Apr-15 Oct
⇥♠20 P30 ⌒ Mountain Lake
Credit Cards ① ② ③ ⑤

WENGEN
Bern

★★★*Silberhorn* ☎(036)565131 tx 923222
Apr-Oct
rm71(⇥♠63) Lift (
Credit Cards ① ② ③ ⑤

★★★Victoria-Lauberhorn ☎(036)565151 tx 923232
Jun-24 Sep & 15 Dec-15 Apr
rm71(⇥♠62) Lift Mountain
Credit Cards ① ② ③ ④ ⑤

★★★Wengener Hof (n.rest) ☎(036)552855 tx 923240
15 May-Sep & 15 Dec-15 Apr
⇥♠40 Lift (Mountain
Credit Cards ① ② ③ ⑤

WIL
St-Gallen

♠ *Bahnhof* Untere Bahnhofstr 9 ☎(073) 221112 AR Ren

WILDERSWIL
Bern

★★Bären ☎(036)223521 tx 923137
⇥♠43 A7rm P45 (Mountain
Credit Cards ① ② ③ ④ ⑤

★★Luna ☎(036)228414
⇥♠10 A6rm ♨ P31 ⌒ Mountain
Credit Cards ① ② ③

★Alpenrose ☎(036)221024
:Rest closed Tue
rm29(⇥♠19) P25 Mountain

★Viktoria ☎(036)221670
Closed Nov
rm12(♠5) P10 Mountain
Credit Cards ① ③

WILDHAUS
St-Gallen

★★★Acker (Amb) ☎(074)884138 tx 71208
⇥♠100 A50rm ♨ P Lift (⌒ Mountain

★★Hirschen ☎(074)52252 tx 884139
rm78(⇥♠75) ♨ P34 Lift ⌄ Mountain
Credit Cards ① ② ③ ⑤

WILEN
See **SARNEN**

WINTERTHUR
Zürich

★★★★Garten (Amb) Stadthausstr 4 ☎(052)847171 tx 896201
⇥♠60 ♨ P32 Lift (
Credit Cards ① ② ③

★★★Krone Marktgasse 49 ☎(052)232521
rm40(⇥♠35) P9 Lift
Credit Cards ① ② ③ ④ ⑤

♠ *Eulach* Technikumstr 67 ☎(052) 222333 Ope

♠ *Riedbach* Frauenfeldstr 9 ☎(052) 272222 P AR BMW Ren

♠ *A Slegenthaler* Frauenfeldstr 44 ☎(052) 272900

YVERDON
Vaud

★★Prairie av des Bains 9 ☎(024)231330
6 Jan-25 Dec
⇥♠36 P40 Lift (९ Mountain
Credit Cards ① ② ③ ⑤

ZERMATT
Valais
No road connection; take train from **TÄSCH** or **VISP**

★★★★Mont Cervin Seiler Bahnhofstr ☎(028)661122 tx 472129
Closed May, Oct & Nov
⇥♠132 Lift (⌒ Mountain
Credit Cards ① ② ③ ⑤

★★★Grand Zermatterhof ☎(028)661100 tx 472145
Dec-Oct
⇥♠89 Lift (९ ⌒ Mountain
Credit Cards ① ② ③ ⑤

AA Road Map – Austria, Italy and Switzerland

Featuring:

- **Up-to-date road information**
- **Scenic routes and viewpoints**
- **Contours and gradients**
- **Distances between towns**
- **Full colour, 16 miles to 1 inch**

An ideal map for route-planning and touring — available at good bookshops and AA Centres

Don't leave the country without one

★★★**Julen (ROM) DPn** ☎(028)672481 tx 472111
⚞⚟37 Lift ℂ ℆ ⬚ Mountain
Credit Cards ① ② ③ ④ ⑤

★★★**Parkhotel Beau Site** ☎(028)671271 tx 472116
21 May-2 Dec
⚞⚟66 A7rm ☎ P75 Lift ℂ ℆ ⬚ Mountain
Credit Cards ① ② ③ ④ ⑤

★★★**Schweizerhof** ☎(028)661155 tx 472101
17 Dec-26 Sep
⚞⚟103 Lift ℂ ⬚ Mountain
Credit Cards ① ② ③ ⑤

★★**Dom** (n.rest) ☎(028)671371 tx 472171
Dec-Sep
⚞⚟40 Lift Mountain
Credit Cards ① ② ③ ⑤

ZERNEZ
Graubünden

★★**Baer & Post** Curtinstr ☎(082)81141
Dec-Oct
⚞⚟19 A12rm ☎ ⌿

ZUG
Zug

★★★**City Ochsen** Kolinpl ☎(042)213232 tx 865249
⚞⚟47 Lift ℂ
Credit Cards ① ② ③ ⑤

★★**Guggital** Zugerbergstr ☎(042)212821 tx 865134

:Rest closed Mon
rm33(⚞⚟32) ☎ P50 Lift Mountain Lake
Credit Cards ① ② ③

★**Rössli** Vorstadstr 8 ☎(042)210394
15 Jan-20 Dec
rm18(⚞⚟10) P Lift Mountain Lake

⚟ **Kalser** Baarrestr 50 ☎(042) 212424 Fia Lan Mer

⚟ **C Kelzer** Grabenstr 18 ☎(042) 218148 **P** Ren

ZUOZ
Graubünden

★★★**Engladina** Hauptstr ☎(082)71021 tx 852100
16 Jun-14 Oct & 16 Dec-14 Apr
rm40(⚞⚟20) P20 Lift ℆ ⌿ Mountain
Credit Cards ① ② ③ ⑤

ZÜRICH *Zürich*

See Plan page 410

Switzerland's largest city boasts all the advantages of an international metropolis together with an attractive location at the northern end of Lake Zürich. Three old churches - the *Grossmüster*, St Peter's and the *Fraumünster* - dominate the skyline.

Among more than 30 museums with a great variety of exhibitions, the Swiss National Museum provides a lively demonstration of Swiss history. The Municipal Theatre, Opera House. Concert and various smaller theatres offer a varied selection of cultural events. The annual June Festival presents many events based on a common theme. Fifteen minutes from Zürich lies the industrial city of Winterhur, noted for its impressive art collections.

EATING OUT Zürich offers an enormous range of restaurants catering for most tastes and pockets. Specialities to look out for include *fondue* and *raclette*, game in season, noodle-like dumplings known as *spatzli*, and *Züri-Gschnatzlets*, diced veal with mushrooms in a cream and wine sauce.
At the upper end of the price range the *Agnes Amberg* in Hottingerstrasse and the *Kronehalle*, in Raemistrasse, are both outstanding. Of the less expensive restaurants, the *Bunderstube* at the Carlton has its devotees, as do *Le Pavilion* in the Globus department store and the *Bierhalle Kropf*, at In Gassen, which serves simple but hearty Swiss fare. For pastries and atmosphere, the *Schober*, in Napfgasse, is extremely popular.

ZÜRICH

★★★★★**Baur au Lac** Talstr 1 ☎(01)2211650 tx 813567
⚞⚟139 ☎ P140 Lift ℂ Lake
Credit Cards ① ② ③ ⑤

★★★★**Dolder** (Amb) Kurhaus-Str 65 ☎(01)2516231 tx 816416
⚞⚟200 ☎ P Lift ℂ ℆ ⌿ ♄♄ Mountain Lake
Credit Cards ① ② ③ ⑤

★★★★**Eden au Lac** Utoquai 45 ☎(01)2619404 tx 816339
⚞⚟54 P15 Lift ℂ Lake
Credit Cards ① ② ③ ④ ⑤

★★★★**Savoy Baur en Ville** Poststr 12 ☎(01)2115360 tx 812845
⚞⚟112 ☎ Lift ℂ
Credit Cards ① ② ③ ⑤

★★★★**Ascot** Tessinerpl 9 ☎(01)2011800 tx 815454
⚞⚟73 ☎ P30 Lift ℂ
Credit Cards ① ② ③ ④ ⑤

★★★★**Bellerive au Lac** Utoquai 47 ☎(01)2517010 tx 816398
⚞⚟53 P Lift ℂ Mountain Lake
Credit Cards ① ② ③ ⑤

★★★★**Carlton Elite** Bahnhofstr 41 ☎(01)2116560 tx 812781
;Rest closed Sun
rm72(⚞⚟71) P6 Lift ℂ
Credit Cards ① ② ③ ⑤

★★★★**Engematthof** Engimattstr 14 ☎(01)2012504 tx 56327
⚞⚟79 ☎ P20 Lift ℂ ℆
Credit Cards ① ② ③ ④ ⑤

★★★★**Zum Storchen** Weinpl 2 ☎(01)2115510 tx 813354
⚞⚟77 Lift ℂ Lake
Credit Cards ① ② ③ ⑤

★★★**Central** Central 1 ☎(01)2515555 tx 54909
⚞⚟99 ☎ P30 Lift ℂ
Credit Cards ① ② ③ ⑤

★★★**Excelsior** (GT) Dufourstr 24 ☎(01)2522500 tx 59295
⚞⚟50 P Lift ℂ
Credit Cards ① ② ③ ⑤

★★★**Glockenhof** (Amb) Sihlstr 31 ☎(01)21156502 tx 812466
⚞⚟106 P Lift ℂ
Credit Cards ① ② ③ ④ ⑤

★★**Burma** Schindlerstr 26 ☎(01)361108
rm32(⚞⚟8) P Lift ℂ

⚟ **AMAG Auto & Motoren** Uberlandstr 166 ☎(01) 412222

⚟ **E Frey** Badenerstr 600 ☎(01) 4952411 **P** AR DJ

⚟ **J H Keller** Vulkanstr 120 ☎(01) 4322410 Hon

⚟ **Riesbach** Dufourstr 182 ☎(01) 552211 **P** Ope

At ADLISWIL(4km SE on N4)

★★★**Jolie Ville Motor Inn** (Mövenpick) Zürichstr 105 ☎(01)7108585 tx 826760
⚞⚟60 P70 ℂ
Credit Cards ① ② ③ ⑤

At OERLIKON(4Km N)

★★★**Sternen Oerlikon** Schaffhauserstr 335 ☎(01)3117777 tx 823265
rm51(⚞⚟47) ☎ P18 Lift ℂ
Credit Cards ① ② ③ ⑤

At REGENSDORF(8km NW)

★★★★**Mövenpick** (Mövenpick) ☎(01)8402520
⚞⚟149 Lift ℂ ⬚
Credit Cards ① ② ③ ④ ⑤

ZÜRICH AIRPORT
At GLATTBRUGG(8km NE on N4)

★★★★★**Hilton International** Hohenbühlstr 10 ☎(01)8103131 tx 825428
⚞⚟287 ☎ P250 Lift ℂ ⬚
Credit Cards ① ② ③ ⑤

★★★★**Airport** Oberhauserstr 30 ☎(01)8104444 tx 825416
⚞⚟48 ☎ P200 Lift ℂ
Credit Cards ① ② ③ ⑤

★★★★**Mövenpick** (Mövenpick) W-Mittelholzerstr 8 ☎(01)8101111 tx 57979
⚞⚟335 P300 Lift ℂ ⬚
Credit Cards ① ② ③ ⑤

ZWEISIMMEN
Bern

★★**Krone** Lenkstr ☎(01)22626
Closed Nov
rm40(⚞⚟36) ☎ Lift

★**Sport** Saanenstr ☎(300)21631
⚞⚟20 P60 Mountain
Credit Cards ① ③

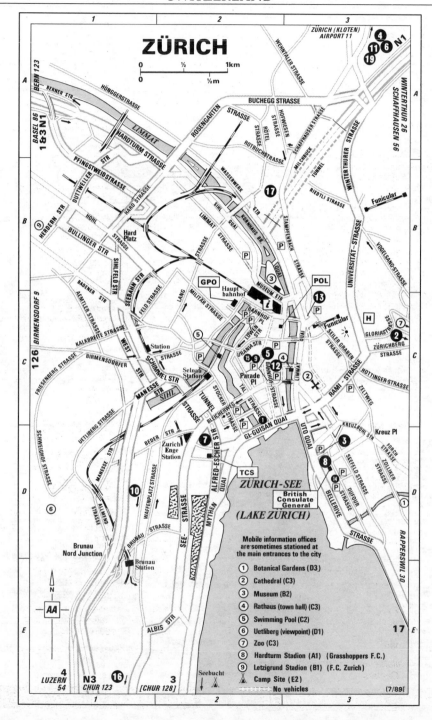

ZÜRICH

0   ½   1km

0   ½ m

Mobile information offices are sometimes stationed at the main entrances to the city

1. Botanical Gardens (D3)
2. Cathedral (C3)
3. Museum (B2)
4. Rathaus (town hall) (C3)
5. Swimming Pool (C2)
6. Uetliberg (viewpoint) (D1)
7. Zoo (C3)
8. Hardturm Stadion (A1)   (Grasshoppers F.C.)
9. Letzigrund Stadion (B1)   (F.C. Zurich)
△ Camp Site (E2)
------- No vehicles

ZÜRICH-SEE

British
Consulate
General

(LAKE ZÜRICH)

(7/89)

ZÜRICH

1	★★★★★ Baur au Lac	6	★★★★ Airport (At Glattbrugg)
2	★★★★★ Dolder	7	★★★★ Ascot
3	★★★★★ Eden au Lac	8	★★★★ Bellerive au Lac
4	★★★★★ Hilton International (At	9	★★★★ Carlton Elite
	Glattbrugg)	10	★★★★ Engematthof
5	★★★★★ Savoy Bauer en Ville	11	★★★★ Mövenpick (At Glattbrugg)
		12	★★★★ Zum Storchen

13	★★★ Central
14	★★★ Excelsior
15	★★★ Glockenhof
16	★★★ Jolie Ville Motor Inn (At Adliswil)
17	★★ Burma
19	★★ Sternen Oerlikon (At Oerlikon)

LIECHTENSTEIN

Liechtenstein was founded in 1719, when the domain of Schellenberg and the country of Vaduz were welded into an independent principality - a tiny country only 25km long and 6km wide, with just under 30,000 inhabitants. The two political regions are divided into a total of 11 autonomous communities, which together offer an extensive range of attractions: museums, boutiques, historical sites, vineyards and endless sporting activities, while retaining its very own individual charm and appeal.

Vaduz is the capital and also the main tourist centre. Located close to the right shore of the Rhine, it is dominated by Vaduz Castle, built around 1300 but not open to the public.

EATING OUT The cuisine here tends to be Swiss with Austrian overtones. In Vaduz the *Torkel*, owned by the ruling prince, enjoys a good reputation, as does the restaurant of the Engel Hotel.

LIECHTENSTEIN
SCHAAN

★★**Linde** Feldkircherstr 1 ☎(075)21704
15 Jan-15 Dec :Rest closed Sun
➡23 P25 Mountain
Credit Cards ⑴ ⑵ ⑶
❧ *Fanal* Feldkircherstr 52 ☎(075) 24604

TRIESENBERG

★*Masescha* Masescha ☎(075)22337
rm7(➡4) ⌂ P10 Lift Mountain

VADUZ

★★★**Park Sonnenhof** (Amb/Relais et Châteaux)
Mareestr 29 ☎(075)21192 tx 889329
Closed 10 Jan-28 Feb & 23-26 Dec
➡29 ⌂ P30 Lift ⊂ ⊠ Mountain
Credit Cards ⑴ ⑵ ⑶ ⑷ ⑸
★★**Real** ☎(075)222222 tx 889484
➡11 Lift Mountain
Credit Cards ⑴ ⑵ ⑶ ⑸
★**Engel** ☎(075)20313
➡17 P15 Lift ⊂ Mountain
Credit Cards ⑴ ⑵ ⑶ ⑸
❧ *Muhholzgarage* Landstr 126 ☎(075) 21668 **P**
Alf Ren

AA

BED AND BREAKFAST IN EUROPE 1990

Budget accommodation and lots of practical information for touring in 19 European countries. This book features 'insider' information to help you feel at home in major cities, and contains advice from the AA's experts on motoring abroad.

Available at good bookshops and AA Centres

Another great guide from the AA

AA

CAMPING AND CARAVANNING IN EUROPE 1990

This comprehensive guide for the outdoor European traveller lists about 4,000 camping and caravanning parks in 19 countries, and offers the AA's expert advice on motoring, documentation and equipment requirements.

Available at good bookshops and AA Centres

Another great guide from the AA

For most people, the word Yugoslavia is synonymous with the Adriatic coast, although in fact this is a country of mountains, plains, rivers, lakes, national parks and picturesque towns and villages. Certainly the lovely coast, with its countless coves, bays and islands, sandy and rock beaches and numerous holiday resorts, is ideal for those who enjoy water sports, cruises, sailing and fishing. An added bonus is that it has preserved many important monuments which testify to a stormy history: the remains of ancient Greek and Roman towns, medieval fortresses and palaces, churches and monasteries, and hundreds of picturesque fishermen's villages and hamlets.

But if you are in search of historical and cultural monuments it is to the large cities that you must look: Belgrade, Yugoslavia's capital, Zagreb, Ljubljana, Sarajevo, and the other capitals of the six Yugoslav republics and two provinces. Many of the smaller towns are often treasure-houses of historical monuments, too.

Modern roads now give access to even the most remote corners of the country, there are airports near all major cities, and the railway network links up major parts of the country.

YUGOSLAVIA

Language
Serbo-Croat is widely used, but minority languages include Macedonean, Slovene and Albanian. Many official documents are bilingual.

Local Time
GMT + 1 hour (Summer GMT + 2 hours)

Currency
Yugoslav dinar, divided into 100 *para*.
At the time of going to press
£1 = Din35,423
US$1 = Din21,339

Emergency numbers
In main towns:
Fire ☎93   Police ☎92
Ambulance ☎94
Elsewhere the number will be found in the front of the local telephone directory.

Information in Britain
Yugoslav National Tourist Office, 143 Regent Street, London W1R 8AE
☎01-734 5243 and 01-439 0399
(01-734 5243 and 071 439 0399 from 6 May 1990)

Information in the USA
Yugoslav National Tourist Office, 630 Fifth Avenue, New York, NY 10020
☎212 757 2801

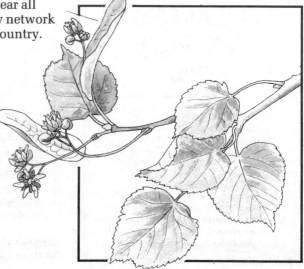

HOW TO GET THERE

Via Belgium: through Germany (*Köln/ Cologne* and *München/Munich*) and Austria (*Salzburg*).

Via France through Switzerland and Italy (*Milano/Milan*) and *Trieste*.

But see 'Motorways' in the Switzerland section for details of motorway tax.

Distance

from Calais to Beograd (Belgrade) is just over 2,300km (1,200 miles), a distance normally requiring 3 or 4 overnight stops.

Car sleeper trains

During Summer, services are available from Brussels and 's Hertogenbosch to *Ljubljana* and from Boulogne, Brussels, 's Hertogenbosch and Paris to *Milan*.

MONEYMATTERS

A maximum of *Din*1,000,000 per person in Yugoslav currency may be taken into or out of the country on a first journey in the course of a calendar year; for each subsequent journey during that year, a maximum of *Din*500,000 is allowed. However, it is forbidden to take into the country bank notes of a denomonation larger than *Din*100,000. There are no restrictions on the amount of *foreign* currency that may be taken in or out.

Banking hours

generally Monday–Friday 07.30–19.00hrs (13.00hrs in small towns).

You can exchange foreign currency at all exchange offices, banks, hotels, tourist offices, and some offices of the Yugoslav motoring organization, into *dinar* bank notes or *dinar*-denominated cheques. The *dinar* cheques may be used to pay for certain goods and services entitling the holder to a discount. They are easily reconverted into foreign currency, unlike *dinar* bank notes and coins. All exchange receipts should be retained until you leave the country.

Postcheques

may be cashed at all post offices up to a maximum of *Din*800,000 per cheque (current maximum will be displayed at post office counters). Go to a counter which displays a **Postcheque** sticker.

MOTORING REGULATIONS AND GENERAL INFORMATION

The information given here is specific to Yugoslavia. It **must** be read in conjunction with the European ABC at the front of the book, which covers those regulations which are common to many countries.

Accidents*

It is obligatory for the driver of a passing vehicle to assist anyone who has been injured in a traffic accident. The driver of a vehicle involved in an accident should inform the traffic police (*Saobracajna Milicija*) immediately, and wait for an on-the-spot investigation and the completion of a written report on the accident and damage. See also *Warning triangle* below.

Any damage to a vehicle entering Yugoslavia must be certified at the time of entry at the frontier. When leaving the country, certificates must be produced to cover any visible damage, otherwise the vehicle and driver will be detained until the circumstances of the damage have been ascertained.

Breakdown*

The Yugoslav motoring club *Auto-Moto Savez Jugoslavije* (AMSJ) operates a breakdown and road information service which covers the whole of the country ☎987 for assistance. See also *Warning triangle* below.

British Embassy/Consulates*

The British Embassy together with its consular section is located at 11000 Beograd, Generala Zdanova 46 ☎(011) 645-055. There are British Consulates with Honorary Consuls in Dubrovnik, Split and Zagreb.

Children in Cars

Children under 12 are not permitted to travel in a vehicle as front-seat passengers.

Dimensions

Private **cars** and towed **trailers** or **caravans** are restricted to the following dimensions – height, 4 metres; width, 2.50 metres; length†, 6 metres.

*Additional information will be found in the European ABC at the front of the book.

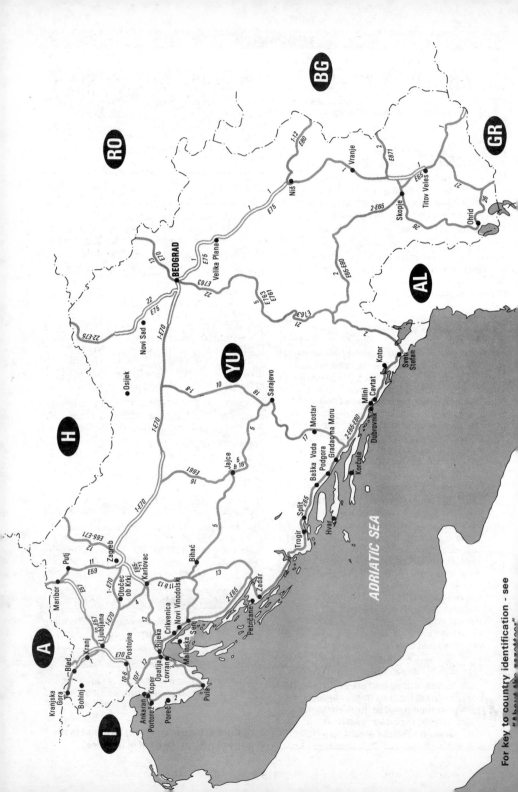

For key to country identification - see

The maximum permitted overall length of vehicle/trailer or caravan combinations is 15 metres.

†Trailers with two axles, 10 metres (including tow-bar)

Driving licence*

A valid UK or Republic of Ireland licence is acceptable in Yugoslavia. The minimum age at which a visitor may use a temporarily imported motorcycle (exceeding 125cc) or car is 18 years.

Emergency message to tourists*

Emergency messages to tourists are broadcast by the Yugoslav radio network.
Radio Beograd transmitting on 439 metres medium wave broadcasts the messages in English, French and German every day from 15 June to 15 September at 12.03–12.16hrs.
Radio Ljubljana transmitting on 537.6, 326.8, 202 and 189.4 metres medium wave broadcasts the messages in English, German and Italian every day, except Sunday, from 25 May to 26 September at 09.35–10.00hrs.
Radio Yugoslavia transmitting on 5955, 5980, 6005, 6040, 6100, 7130, 7250, 7140, 7220, 7240, 7165, 9620, 9660, 15325, 15380, 11735 and 11835KHz broadcasts the messages in English every day throughout the year at 15.30, 18.30, 20.00 and 22.15hrs GMT.

First-aid kit*

It is **compulsory** for visiting motorists to carry a first-aid kit in their vehicles.

Lights*

Dipped headlights must be used by motorcyclists during the day, when travelling outside built-up areas. It is **compulsory** for visiting motorists to equip their vehicle with a set of replacement bulbs.

Motoring club*

The **Auto-Moto Savez Jugoslavije** (AMSJ) has its headquarters at 11000 Beograd, Ruzveltova 18 ☎(011) 401-699 and is represented in most towns either direct or through regional and associated clubs.

Motorways

Several single and dual-carriageway sections of motorway (*autoput* or *avtocesta*) are now available. There are 560 miles open in all and further stretches are under construction. Tolls are charged on most sections.

Parking*

Between 08.00 and 19.00hrs (Mon–Sat) parking meters are in use in some towns.

Petrol

Credit cards Petrol stations do not accept credit cards.
Duty-free petrol The petrol in a vehicle tank may be imported free of customs duty and tax.
Petrol cans A reasonable quantity of petrol in a can may be imported provided customs duty is paid.
Petrol coupons Tourist coupons provide a discount on pump prices and may be purchased at road border crossings, but only with freely convertible currency. They cannot be purchased in Yugoslavia. The border crossings at Skofije, Kozina, Fernatiči, Nova Gorica, Rateče, Korensko sedlo, Ljubelj, Vič, Sentilj and Gornja Radgona provided tourist services on a 24-hour basis. However visitors arriving by *Motorail* cannot purchase tourist petrol coupons at Jesenice (the border crossing for rail traffic), but may obtain them in Ljubljana from the *Kompas* agency in the airport bank.
Petrol (leaded) Normal Benzin (86 octane) and Super Benzin (98 octane) grades.
Petrol (unleaded) is sold in Yugoslavia as bezolovni benzin (95 octane). The octane rating is displayed on pumps dispensing unleaded petrol.

Postal information

Mail Postcards Din600; Letters Din700.
Post offices There are 3,500 post offices in Yugoslavia. Opening hours in major cities are 07.00–20.00hrs Monday to Friday; elsewhere, 07.00–15.00hrs or 08.00–12.00hrs and 17.00–19.00hrs Monday to Friday. Most offices are open Saturdays 07.00–15.00hrs.

***Additional information will be found in the European ABC at the front of the book.**

Priority*

Trams have priority over all vehicles at all times.

Public holidays*

Official Public holidays in Yugoslavia for 1990 are given below.

January 1/2 (New Year)
April 27 (National holiday in Slovenia)
May 1/2 (Labour Day)
July 4 (Veteran's Day)
July 7‡ (National holiday in Serbia)
July 13† (National holiday in Montenegro)
July 27 (National holiday in Croatia and Bosnia-Herzegovina)
August 2 (National holiday in Macedonia)
October 11 (National holiday in Macedonia)
November 1 (National holiday in Slovenia)
November 25† (National holiday in Bosnia-Herzegovina)
November 29/30 (Republic Day)

Where a two-day holiday includes Sunday, the following Monday will be a holiday.
‡Saturday   †Sunday

Registration documents*

If the vehicle is not registered in your name, you should have a letter from the owner authorising you to use it; this letter must be countersigned by a motoring organisation.

Roads

Roads have improved considerably in the last few years, and many have been rebuilt. All the international transit routes are mainly in good condition, and so is the coast road from Rijeka to Dubrovnik and beyond. It is wise, when making a tour off the beaten track, to enquire at the local tourist agencies for the latest information on the next stage of the journey. Make sure your car is in good order before you go, as telephones and service stations are far apart.

Road signs*

The words *Jedan Smer* on a blue and white arrow indicate a one-way street in the direction the arrow is pointing.

Shopping hours

Generally, shops are open 08.00–12.00hrs and 16.00–20.00hrs Monday to Friday, and 08.00–15.00hrs on Saturday. Some *food shops* also open on Sunday, 06.00–10.00hrs.

Speed limits*

In *built-up areas*, 60kph (37mph); *outside built-up areas*, 80kph (49mph), but 100kph (62mph) on *dual-carriageways* and 120kph (74mph) on *motorways*. Vehicle caravan or trailer combinations are restricted to 80kph (49mph), *on all roads outside built-up areas*.

Spiked or studded tyres*

The use of *spiked tyres* is prohibited.

Telephone*

Insert coin **after** lifting the receiver; the dialling tone is long and short tones. When making calls to subscribers *within* Yugoslavia, precede the number with the relevant area code (shown in parentheses before the hotel/garage enquiry number in the gazetteer). Use *Din*50 or 100 coins for local calls, and the higher value coins for national and international calls.

International callbox identification Payphones with 3/4 coin slots.

Telephone rates A direct call to the UK costs Din1,580 per minute.

Telephone Codes

UK to Yugoslavia	010 38
Yugoslavia to UK	99 44
Yugoslavia to Republic of Ireland	99 353
Yugoslavia to the USA	99 1

Warning Triangles*

The use of warning triangles is compulsory in the event of an accident or breakdown. The triangle must be placed on the road 50 metres (55yds) behind the vehicle to warn following traffic of any obstruction. Two triangles (placed side by side) are required for vehicle/trailer combinations.

Wheel chains*

The use of winter equipment is compulsory between 15 November and 15 April in the Republic of Bosnia-Herzegovina and, between 15 November and 15 March, in Macedonia and the Kosovo region of Serbia. Elsewhere, the use of winter equipment depends on the weather and road conditions.

ACCOMMODATION

Many good hotels will be found in the tourist centres and main towns; the majority of those on the coast are relatively new. There is also a good coverage of motels along the country's main roads.

The summer tourist season generally lasts from mid-June to mid-September and the winter sports season from December to March, with local differences and variations in hotel prices. Rates normally include a service charge, but a motorist tax is payable per person, per day, which varies according to locality and period of stay. Special reductions are allowed for children under 7 years. Accommodation in private homes is available in every resort, and may be booked locally at tourist offices (**Turisticki Biro**).

Because of fluctuations in the value of the *Yugoslav dinar*, prices below are shown in *US Dollars*.

The prices shown below are an average for each classification. Accommodation is likely to be more expensive in Belgrade and some of the more popular tourist areas. You are advised to confirm the current rate of exchange before your departure as there is likely to be some fluctuation, but at the time of going to press. *£1 Sterling = $1.66.*

AVERAGE PRICES

	Single Room	Double Room	Breakfast	Lunch/Dinner
★★★★★	$93–$216	$133–$160	—	from $12
★★★★	$56–$88	$75/$95	—	$25/$34
★★★	$68–$89	$89–$126	—	from $16
★★	$21–$31	$27–$46	$5	from $6
★	—	—		—

Abbreviations
pl   plaza
The province names are as follows with their better known forms:
Bosna I Hercegovina-Bosnia and Herzegovina
Crna Gora-Montenegro
Hrvatska-Croatia
Makedonija-Macedonia
Slovenija-Slovenia
Srbija-Serbia

ANKARAN
Slovenija
★★*Bor* ☎(066)51815
Apr-Oct
➔🏠96 🏖 Beach

BAŠKA VODA
Hrvatska
★★*Slavija* ☎(058)620155 tx 26326
➔🏠72 P20 Lift ℂ Sea
Credit Cards ① ② ③ ⑤

BEOGRAD *(BELGRADE)*

See Plan pages 420–421 *Population* 1,572,000 *Local tourist office* Terazije (underpass at Albanija Building) ☎ (011) 635622

Capital of Yugoslavia and of the Socialist Republic of Serbia, Beograd is situated at the confluence of two large rivers, the Sava and the Danube, and occupies a commanding site on a ridge. It is a modern city with an active and varied cultural and sporting life. In addition to being the administrative and legal headquarters of Yugoslavia, it is the residence of the metropolitan of the Serbian Orthodox church and of the Jewish grand rabbi. Its university is the largest in the country and is mainly concerned with legal studies.

Beograd is an important centre of commerce and industry, as befits a town located on one of the finest sites in the Danubian lands. With the construction of road and rail bridges across the Danube and Sava, it was inevitable that Beograde should become the collecting and distributing centre of the commerce of a rich area. The navigable waterways of the two rivers are of first importance in this connection, and Beograd is easily the chief river port of Yugoslavia. At the same time, the city is the chief railway centre of the country, with several main lines and important roads, including a fast road to Zagreb.

Its many museums, art galleries, cultural institutions and restaurants are a delight, while the atmosphere of the city's old Bohemian quarter can be relived in Skadarska Street whose restaurants and cafés serve local specialities.

Yugoslavia's most famous 'son', Marshal Tito, was buried in Beograd in 1980, and the Josip Broz Tito Memorial Centre is today the most visited sight in Yugoslavia.

EATING OUT Grilled meats - especially lamb - and fresh fish are among the specialities the visitor will encounter in many of Beograd's restaurants. Specialities include *raznjici* (meat grilled on a skewer) and *cevapcici* (charcoal grilled minced meat). In the upper price bracket, *Dva Jelena*, in Skadarska, continues to attract an enthusiastic clientele, while for moderately priced meals the *Klub Knjizevnika*, in Francuska, serves what is often hailed as the best food in Belgrade.

BEOGRAD (BELGRADE)

★★★★★**Beograd Inter Continental** Vladimira Popovica 10 ☎(011)134760 tx 12009
⏺420 P100 Lift (९ ⌷
Credit Cards ① ② ③ ④ ⑤

★★★★★**Metropol** Bulevar Revolucije 69 ☎(011)330911 tx 11364
⏺218 ⍰ P Lift (
Credit Cards ① ② ③ ④ ⑤

★★★★**Excelsior** Kneza Miloša 5 ☎(011)331381 tx 12299
⏺86 P10 Lift (
Credit Cards ① ② ③ ⑤

★★★★**Jugoslavia** (SRS) Bulevar E-Kardelja 3 ☎(011)600222 tx 11777
⏺500 ⍰ P Lift (⌷

★★★★**Majestic** ☎(011)636022 tx 11345
⏺92 P10 Lift (
Credit Cards ① ② ③ ④ ⑤

★★★**Balkan** ☎(011)687466 tx 72224
rm95(⏺47) Lift (
Credit Cards ① ② ③ ⑤

★★★**Kasina** pl Terazi 25 ☎(011)335574 tx 11865
⏺96 Lift

★★★**National** ☎(011)601122 tx 11774
⏺70 P (
Credit Cards ① ② ③ ⑤

★★★**Putnik** ☎(011)697221
⏺118 Lift

★★★**Slavija** Svetog Save 9 ☎(011)450842 tx 11545
⏺509 ⍰ P100 Lift (
Credit Cards ① ② ③ ④ ⑤

★★★**Toplice** ☎(011)626426
⏺100 P Lift (

👁 **Auto-moto Turing Drutvo** Ruzveltova 19-21 ☎(011) 987 All makes

Dvadesetpvi MAJ Patrijarha Dimitrija 24 ☎(011) 592111 Fia

Interkomerc-Kontinental Omiadinskih Brigada 31 ☎(011) 154660 For Ren

Zastava-Auto Mije Kavacevia 6 ☎(011) 754899 Fia

BIHAĆ
Bosna I Hercegovina

★★**Park** ☎(077)229042 tx 45851
rm110(⏺76) ⍰ Lift Sea

BLED
Slovenija

★★★★**Golf** Cankarjeva 4 ☎(064)77591 tx 34531
⏺150 P Lift (⌷ Mountain Lake

★★★★**Grand Hotel Toplice** (SRS) ☎(064)77222 tx 34588
⏺121 Lift ⌷

★★**Jelcvica** Cesta Svobode 5 ☎(064)78078 tx 34635
rm146(⏺139) A30rm P30 Lift Lake
Credit Cards ① ② ③ ⑤

★★**Park** ☎(064)77945 tx 34504
⏺86 P Lift (⌷ Mountain Lake

★**Krim** Ljubljanska Cesta 7 ☎(064)77418 tx 34674
rm99(⏺69) ⍰

BOHINJ
Slovenija

★★**Zlatorog** ☎(064)723381 tx 34619
⏺74 A30rm P Lift (९ ⌷
Credit Cards ① ② ③ ⑤

BORIK
See **ZADAR**

CAVTAT
Hrvatska

★★★**Croatia** ☎(050)78022 tx 27530
Closed 5 Dec-1 Feb
⏺481 P200 Lift (९ ⌷ ⌷ Beach Sea Mountain
Credit Cards ① ② ③ ⑤

★★★**Epidaurus** ☎(050)78144 tx 27523
rm192(⏺175) Lift Beach Sea

CRIKVENICA
Hrvatska

★★★**Esplanade** Stonsmajerovo Setalitše ☎(051)781133
Apr-Oct
⏺89

★★★**International** Setalitše Vi Bakarica ☎(051)781324
⏺53 Lift

★★**Therapia** ☎(051)781511
⏺115 Lift ⌷

Automehanika Selska 1 ☎(051) 782197

DUBROVNIK
Hrvatska

Dubrovnik is one of the most important Yugoslav ports and holiday resorts on the Adriatic coast. Of ancient origin, it has changed hands frequently but reached its highest development as an independent small state in the 16th and 17th centuries when it rivalled Venice and gave the name *argosy* to the English language.
The old walled town is arguably the loveliest and most interesting resort in Yugoslavia, offering a multitude of fascinating monuments, churches, museums, towers and old patrician houses. By contrast, there are modern hotels with beaches and swimming pools, good sports and entertainment facilities, and a casino and congress centre. The nearby island of Lokrum, a national park, is a favourite bathing spot, or a cable car ride will take you to Mount Srdj (413m), which offers a magnificent view of the Adriatic coast.

EATING OUT Fresh fish is usually on the menu at the atmospheric *Amfora*, is situated at Gruz Harbour, and *Dubravka*, near Pile Gate, where specialities often include octopus and squid.

DUBROVNIK
Hrvatska

★★★★**Argentina** Frana Supila 14 ☎(050)23855 tx 27558
⏺151 A28rm ⍰ P30 Lift (९ ⌷ ⌷ Beach Sea
Credit Cards ① ② ③ ⑤

★★★★**Excelsior** Put Frana Supila 3 ☎(050)23566 tx 27523
⏺211 Lift ⌷ Beach Sea

★★★★**Holiday Inn** Frank Supila 28 ☎(050)28655 tx 27588
⏺209 P70 Lift (⌷ ⌷ Beach Sea
Credit Cards ① ② ③ ④ ⑤

★★★★**Libertas** Bratstva i jedinstva 3 ☎(050)27444 tx 27588
rm289(⏺53) A88rm P70 Lift (९ ⌷ ⌷ Beach Sea
Credit Cards ① ② ③ ⑤

★★★**Imperial** Mise Simoni 2 ☎(050)23688 tx 27639
⏺138 A28rm P10 Lift Sea
Credit Cards ① ② ③ ⑤

★★★**Neptun** Dalmatinski Put ☎(050)23755 tx 27523
Apr-Oct
⏺220 Lift Beach Sea

★★★**Splendid** ☎(050)24733
Apr-Oct
⏺61 Lift Beach Sea

★★★**Sumratin** Aleja Ive Lole Ribara ☎(050)24722
⏺70 A26rm Lift Sea

★★★**Villa Dubrovnik** Vlaha Bukovca 8 ☎(050)22933 tx 27523
Apr-Oct
⏺56 A9rm P Lift Beach

★★**Bellevue** put Pera Cingrie ☎(050)25075
Apr-Oct
rm51(⏺47) Lift Beach Sea

Auto-Dubrovnik Mihaila ☎(050) 23728 Cit For Ope Ren Fia

Dubrovkinja OOUR Auto-servis Masarikov 3 ☎(050) 28940 Aud VW

GORICA
See **OHRID**

GRADAC NA MORU
Hrvatska

★★**Laguna** ☎(058)70614
⏺70 P Lift Beach Sea

HALUDOVO
See **MALINSKA**

HVAR, ISLAND OF
Hrvatska

★★★**Adriatic** ☎(058)74028 tx 26235
⏺63 Lift ⌷ Sea

★★Dalmacija ☎(058)74120
◀♠70 Beach Sea
★★Pharos ☎(058)74026
◀♠175

JAJCE
Bosna I Hercegovina
★★Turist ☎(070)33268
rm54(◀♠20)

KARLOVAC
Hrvatska
Automehanika liovac ☎(047) 23844 VW

KOPER
Slovenija
Trgoavto Tozd Servis Istarska Cesta 12 ☎(066) 32201 Mer Ren

KORČULA, ISLAND OF
Hrvatska
★★★Marko Polo ☎(050)711100 tx 27556
◀♠113 P Lift ⚲ Beach Sea
★★★Park ☎(050)711005 tx 27556
15 Apr-25 Oct
◀♠161 P40 (⚲ ⌂ ⌐ Beach Sea Mountain
Credit Cards ① ② ④ ⑤

KOTOR
Crna Gora
Autoremont put Prvoboraca 188 ☎(082) 13388
Fia Ren

KRANJ
Slovenija
★★★Creina Koroska 5 ☎(064)23650 tx 34556
◀♠93 P50 Lift Mountain
Credit Cards ① ② ③ ④ ⑤
Gasilsko Resevaina Sluzba Oldhamska Cesta 4
☎(064) 21060

KRANJSKA GORA
Slovenija
★★Kompas (9km on Ratce-Jessenice road)
☎(064)88661
◀♠155 ⌂ Lift ⌐
★★Prisank ☎(064)88472 tx 34636
◀♠64

LJUBLJANA
Slovenija

Ljubljana is the capital of Slovenia, one of the most progressive parts of Yugoslavia. The old town lies in a loop of the Ljubljanica tributary of the Sava where a hill, 600ft above the river level, gives a defensive site near the river crossing. Here the Romans established Emona on the way from Italy to Pannonia. Immediately around Ljubljana is the basin of the same name which is hemmed in by the Julian and Karawanke Alps to the west and north, and by the Slovene Ksarst to the south-west. The cultural influence of the town is of particular importance, the Slovenes being proud of their literary achievements; in addition to the university there are several publishing houses.
The city is dominated by its castle, at whose feet is the most interesting part of the city, especially near the river, around Mestintrg. Napoleon stayed at the Bishop's Palace, next to the cathedral. Treasures in the National Museum include a magnificent bronze urn.

EATING OUT Home cooking is the speciality of the *Na Brinju*, in Vodovodna, which has a pleasant garden for summer dining *al fresco*.

LJUBLJANA
Slovenija
★★★★Lev Vosnjakova 1 ☎(061)310555 tx 31350
◀♠214 ⌂ P50 Lift (Mountain
Credit Cards ① ② ③ ⑤
★★★★Slon Titova 10 ☎(061)211232 tx 31254
◀♠185 P10 Lift (
Credit Cards ① ② ③ ⑤
★★★Grand Union Miklosiceva Cesta 1
☎(061)212133 tx 31295
◀♠264 P20 Lift (
Credit Cards ① ② ③ ④ ⑤
★★★Turist Dalmationova 15 ☎(061)322043 tx 31317
rm192(◀♠140) Lift (
Credit Cards ① ② ⑤
★★Ilirija Trg Prekomorskin Brigad 4
☎(061)551245 tx 31574
rm136(◀♠86) P Lift (
Credit Cards ① ② ⑤
Agrostroj Koseska 11 ☎(061) 555366
Automontaza Celovska Cesta 180 ☎(061) 556455 Alf
Autotehna Celovska 228 ☎(061) 573555 Ope Vau
Cimos-Citroën Servis Cilenskova 13 ☎(061) 442917 All makes
PAP Autoservis Celovska 258 ☎(061) 572640 BMW

LOVRAN
Hrvatska
★★★★Excelsior ☎(051)712233 tx 24666
◀♠188 ⌂ P80 Lift (⌐ Beach Sea
Credit Cards ① ② ③ ⑤
★★Beograd ☎(051)731022
◀♠102 A30rm ⌂ P20 Lift ⚲ Beach Sea

MALINSKA
Hrvatska
At **HALUDOVO**(0.5km N)
★★★★Palace ☎(051)859111
Mar-Nov
◀♠214 P100 Lift (⚲ ⌐ ⌐ Beach Sea
Credit Cards ① ② ③ ⑤
★★★Tamaris ☎(051)885566
May-Oct
◀♠289 Lift Beach

MARIBOR
Slovenija
★Orel Grajski Trg 3 ☎(062)26171 tx 33244
rm150(◀♠100) P50 Lift (Mountain
Credit Cards ① ② ③ ⑤
★★Slavija Vita Kraigherja 3 ☎(062)23661 tx 33141
◀♠122 ⌂ P Lift (
Credit Cards ① ② ③ ④ ⑤
Auto-Servis Cesta X1V Divizije 89 ☎(062) 513092
Ferromoto Zagrebka 85 ☎(062) 414711

Ferromoto Minska Cesta 13 ☎(062) 912125 Fia

MLINI
Hrvatska
★★Mlini ☎(050)86053
◀♠90 ⌂ Beach Sea

MOSTAR
Bosna I Hercegovina
★★Bristol ☎(088)32921 tx 46136
rm56(◀♠45) Lift
★★Mostar ☎(088)32941 tx 46136
◀♠27 P
★Neretva ☎(088)3230 tx 46136
◀♠35 (Mountain
Credit Cards ① ② ③ ⑤
Auto-Moto Drustvo Splitska BB ☎(088) 987 All makes

NIŠ
Srbija
★★★Ambassador ☎(018)25833 tx 16256
◀♠171 P25 Lift
Credit Cards ① ② ③
★★Nais ☎(018)701030 tx 16256
◀♠87 P Lift
Credit Cards ① ② ③ ⑤
★★Niš Voždova 12 ☎(018)24643 tx 16256
◀♠80 ⌂ P10 Lift
Credit Cards ① ② ③ ⑤
Auto-Moto Drustvo Marka Oreskovica 115
☎(018) 987 Fia
Zastava-Auto Kragujevac N Stojanovica ☎(018) 63055 Fia

At **NIŠKA-BANJA**
★★Partizan ☎(018)860317 tx 16256
◀♠50 P Lift
Credit Cards ① ② ③ ⑤

NIŠKA-BANJA
See **NIS**

NOVISAD
Srbija
★★★Park Hadjuk Veljkova 2 ☎(021)611711 tx 14153
◀♠315 P400 Lift ⌐ ⌐
Credit Cards ① ② ③ ⑤
Autovojvodina Kosovska 54 ☎(021) 27353 Aud VW Mer
Auto-Moto Drustvo Lenjinov trg 10 ☎(021) 29389 All makes

NOVI VINOLDOSKI
Hrvatska
★★Lisanj ☎(051)791022 tx 24707
◀♠24 A56rm P100 Lift (⚲ ⌐ ⌐ ⌂⌂ Beach Sea
Credit Cards ① ② ③ ⑤

OHRID
Makedonija
At **GORICA**(2.5km S)
★★★Inex Gorica ☎(096)22020
Apr-Oct
◀♠110 A20rm P (Beach

OPATIJA
Hrvatska
★★★★Ambasador ☎(051)712211 tx 24184
◀♠260 ⌂ P300 Lift (⌐ ⌐ Beach Sea
Credit Cards ① ② ③ ⑤
★★★★Kvarner Park 1,Maja 4-6 ☎(051)711211
◀♠86 A30rm P Lift (⌐ Beach Sea
★★★Belvedere Marala Tita 89 ☎(051)712433
May-Oct
rm171(◀♠100) Lift ⚲ ⌐ Beach Sea
★★★Slavija Marala Tita 200 ☎(051)711811 tx 24476
◀♠120 P20 Lift ⌐ Sea
Credit Cards ① ② ③ ④ ⑤

★★Dubrovnik Marala Tita 201 ☎(051)711611
➡☎120 P20 Lift ⌂ Sea
Credit Cards ①②③④⑤

★★Palme Marala Tita 166 ☎(051)711433 tx 24585
rm105(➡☎61) Lift ℂ Sea
Credit Cards ①②③⑤

40 Box Spinčiceva 21 ☎(051) 711439 Aud VW

OSIJEK
Srbija

Remontservis Vinkovacka 7 ☎(054) 24366 Fia

OTOČEC OB KRKI
Slovenija

★★Otočec ☎(068)21830 tx 35740
➡☎90 A64rm P150 Lift ℂ ⚲ ▭ ∪ Mountain
Credit Cards ①②③④⑤

PETRČANE
Hrvatska

★★★Pinija ☎(057)73062 tx 27136
Apr-20 Oct
➡☎131 P300 Lift ℂ ⚲ ⌂ ▸▸ Sea
Credit Cards ①②⑤

PODGORA
Hrvatska

★★★Mediteran ☎(058)6205155 tx 26322
Apr-Oct
➡☎131 Sea

★★Podgorka ☎(058)625266
Apr-Oct
rm19

POREČ
Hrvatska

★★Riviera Obala Marala Tita 25 ☎(053)32422 tx 25123
Closed 21 Oct-24 Apr
rm136(➡☎82) A52rm Lift Sea
Credit Cards ①②③⑤

Riviera Autoremont M Vlasica ☎(053) 31344 Cit Fia Ren

PORTOROŽ
Slovenija

★★★Palace ☎(066)73541 tx 34156
:Rest closed May-30 Aug
➡☎608 Lift ℂ ▭ Beach
Credit Cards ①②③④

POSTOJNA
Slovenija

★★Kras Titov Trg ☎(066)73541 tx 34156
May-Dec
rm108(➡☎54) P Lift

PTUJ
Slovenija

★★Poetovio ☎(062)772640
rm33(☎13) ☎

PULA
Hrvatska

★★★Verudela ☎(052)24811
Apr-Oct
rm376(➡☎328) Beach Sea

Auto-Servis Takop Beruda 39 ☎(052) 22450 Aud Ren VW

BEOGRAD (BELGRADE)

1	★★★★★	Beograd Inter Continental
2	★★★★★	Metropol
3	★★★★	Excelsior
4	★★★★	Jugoslavia
5	★★★★	Majestic
6	★★★	Balkan
7	★★★	Kasina
8	★★★	National
9	★★★	Putnik
10	★★★	Slavija
11	★★★	Toplice

BEOGRAD (BELGRADE)

Scale
0 — ½ — 1km
0 — ½mile

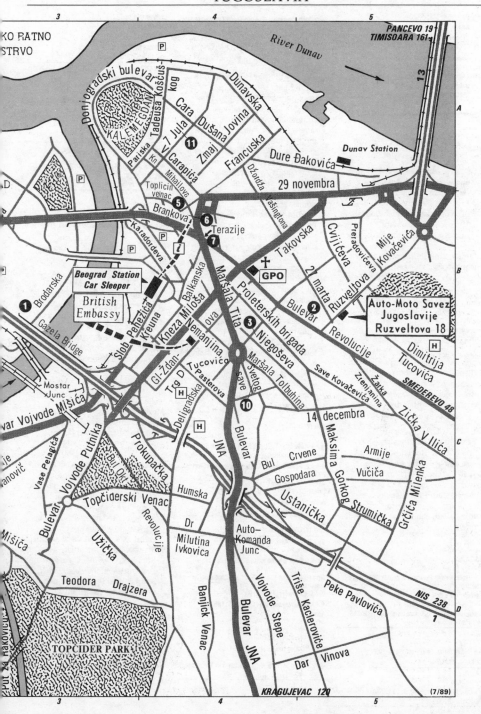

KO RATNO
STRVO

PANCEVO 19
TIMISOARA 161

River Dunav

Donjogradski bulevar
Cara Dušana
Dunavska
Jovina
KALEMEGDAN
Pariska
Tadeuša Košćuš
kog
7 Jula
Zmai
Francuska
V. Carapića
Kn.
Mihailova
Dure Đakovića
Dunav Station
29 novembra
Toplicin
venac
Brankova
Terazije
Karađorđeva
Takovska
Cvijićeva
Džordža Vašingtona
Preradovićeva
Mije Kovačevića
Beograd Station
Car Sleeper
British
Embassy
Balkanska
Maršala Tita
Proleterskih brigada
GPO
27 marta
Bulevar
Revolucije
Ruzveltova
Auto-Moto Savez
Jugoslavije
Ruzveltova 18
Brodarska
Gazela Bridge
Slob. Penezića
Krcuna
Kneza Miloša
Nemanjina
Njegoševa
Maršala Tolbuhina
Save Kovačevića
Zrenjanina
Žatka
Dimitrija
Tucovića
SMEDEREVO 48
Mostar
Junc
Gl. Ždan-
Trg D
Tucovića
Pasterova
Deligradska
Sveti
Svetog
14 decembra
Maksima Gorkog
Zička V Ilića
var Vojvode Mišića
vase Pelagića
Vojvode Putnika
Bul Okt
Prokupačka
JNA
Bulevar
Bul
Crvene
Gospodara
Armije
Vučića
Strumička
Grčića Milenka
Topčiderski Venac
Revolucije
Humska
Ustanička
NIS 238
Užička
Dr
Milutina
Ivkovica
Auto-
Komanda
Junc
Peke Pavlovića
Mišića
Teodora
Drajzera
TOPCIDER PARK
Banjick Venac
Bulevar
JNA
Vojvode Stepe
Triše Kaclerovića
Dar
Vinova
KRAGUJEVAC 120
(7/89)

YUGOSLAVIA

RIJEKA
Hrvatska

★★★*Bonavia* ☎(051)33744 tx 24129
🛏161 Lift

★★★*Jadran* ☎(051)421600 tx 24396
rm83(🛏72) P50 Lift Beach Sea
Credit Cards ①②③④⑤

★★*Park* ☎(051)421155 tx 24396
rm47(🛏16) P20 Lift Beach Sea
Credit Cards ①②③④⑤

Autoservis Barciceva 3 ☎(051) 30388 Cit Fia For

SARAJEVO
Bosna I Hercegovina

Sarajevo, encircled by mountains, is located on both banks of the river Miljaca, tributary of the Bosna. The old city (*Stari Grad*), with its market, Turkish houses and narrow streets, stands on the right bank, its core the *Bascsarsija* (old bazaar). This area also contains the 16th-century *Begova Dzamaja* (Mosque of the Bey), considered the finest of the city's 73 mosques.
On a street corner by Princip Bridge are two footsteps sunk into the pavement, marking the spot from which a student fired the fatal shots at Archduke Franz Ferdinand of Austria, that precipitated the First World War. Interesting excursions can be made into the mountains and to the spa of Ilidza, where Archduke Ferdinand spent the evening before his assassination.

EATING OUT Many of Sarajevo's restaurants reflect the centuries of Turkish influence, and you are likely to encounter such Turkish specialities as stuffed vine leaves and grilled meats. *Daire*, in Halaci, is one such establishment. Converted from a 17th-century warehouse, it offers both character and reliable cuisine.

SARAJEVO
Bosna I Hercegovina

★★*Evropa* Vase Pelagica 5 ☎(071)532722 tx 41219
🛏225 P60 Lift
Credit Cards ①②③④⑤
Bosna-Auto Obala 27 jula 35 ☎(071) 210256 Mer Ren

SENJ
Hrvatska

★★*Nehaj* Titova Obala ☎(051)881285
rm43(🛏21) Lift Sea

SKOPJE
Makedonija

★★*Continental* ☎(091)220122 tx 51318
🛏200 P100 Lift
Credit Cards ①②③⑤

Gradska Zaednica & Auto-Moto Drustvata Ivo Lola Ribar 51 ☎(091) 237305

SPLIT
Hrvatska

The city of Split is Yugoslavia's second largest sea port, an important traffic artery and the economic, administrative and cultural centre of Dalmatia. It is famous for its palace which was built by the emperor Diocletian at the end of the 4th century as a summer residence and whose dimensions and excellent condition make it one of the most important monuments of Roman architecture on the east coast of the Adriatic. Every year the Split Summer Festival takes place on the perstyle of the palace, by the cathedral, serving as the backdrop for opera, ballet and concert performances.
In addition to its many museums, Split also boasts the Ivan Mestrovic art gallery. Mestrovic was one of Yugoslavia's most famous sculptors.
The mild climate, modern hotels, ferryboat connections with Italian and Dalmatian ports, marinas, airport and countless cultural events year round make Split a popular resort in both summer and winter.

SPLIT
Hrvatska

★★★★*Marjan* Obala jna 8 ☎(058)42866 tx 26102
🛏331 P100 Lift Sea

★★★*Park* Setaliste 1-Maja 15 ☎(058)515411 tx 26316
🛏58 P16 Lift Sea
Credit Cards ①②③⑤
Auto-Diamacija Mosorskog Odreda 1 ☎(058) 47277 Fia Ren VW

STOBI
See **TITOV VELES**

SVETI STEFAN
Crna Gora

★★★★*Sveti Stefan* ☎(086)62090 tx 61188
1 May-25 Oct
🛏118 P160 Lift Beach Sea Mountain
Credit Cards ①②③④⑤

★★★*Maestral* ☎(086)41333 tx 61188
Apr-Nov
🛏157 P60 Lift Beach Sea Mountain
Credit Cards ①②③④⑤

★★★*Milocer* ☎(086)41411 tx 61188
May-Oct
🛏20 A6rm P25 Beach Sea Mountain
Credit Cards ①②③④⑤

TITOV VELES
Makedonija
At STOBI(26km SE)

★*Stobi* ☎(093)23255
🛏40 A50rm Mountain

TROGIR
Hrvatska

★★★*Medena* ☎(058)73222 tx 26204
🛏663 Lift Beach Sea

VELIKA PLANA
Srbija

★*Velika Plana* ☎(026)52253
🛏30 A5rm P

VRANJE
Srjiba

★★*Vranje* ☎(017)22366 tx 16781
🛏70 P30 Lift
Credit Cards ①②③⑤

ZADAR
Hrvatska
At BORIK(4km NW)
Autovatska Benkovacka BB ☎(057) 22690 Aud Cit Fia Mer Ren

ZAGREB
Hrvatska

Zagreb, the capital of the Socialist Republic of Croatia and the second largest city in Yugoslavia, lies on the banks of the Sava River. Its well preserved old city quarter, with a fine cathedral and impressive churches, is a special attraction, but the city also boasts lovely Baroque buildings, a rich and varied cultural and entertainment life, good restaurants and excellent hotels. Opera has a long-standing tradition here, and the world-renowned Hlebine school of naïve painting is located near by. In addition to Zagreb's many museums and art galleries there are numerous festivals, one of the most popular of which is the traditional festival of folklore, while the Zagreb Fair is one of the largest in Europe. The city is well located for excursions: within its vicinity are Marshal Tito's birthplace of Kumrovec, the old Trakoscan and Ptuj castles, many spas, Tuheljske Springs, and the Plitvice national park with its 16 delightful lakes.

EATING OUT Local specialities include *pohovano pile*, a type of breaded chicken. This is usually available at *Gradski Podrum* in Republic Square, which is one of Zagreb's best known and most fashionable restaurants.

422

ZAGREB
Hrvatska

★★★★**Esplanade** Mihanoviceva 1 ☎(041)435666
tx 21395
:Rest closed on Sun
⇥♠236 P30 Lift ℂ
Credit Cards ① ② ③ ⑤

★★★*International* Miramarka ☎(041)511511 tx
21184
⇥♠420 ⚘ Lift
★★*Dubrovnik* Gajeva 1 ☎(041)424222 tx 21670
⇥♠269 Lift ℂ
Credit Cards ① ② ③ ④ ⑤
Autosanitarija Planinska 7 ☎(041) 212622 Ren

Autoservis-Borongaj Borongajska 75 ☎(041)
215333
Opel Servis Samoborska 222a ☎(041) 155343
Ope
Skolski Centar za Cestovni Saobracaj
Kraljevicava 24 ☎(041) 210320 Peu Tal

INDEX

ACCOMMODATION REPORT

Town, country, hotel

Your star rating	Location	Date of stay
Food	Room(s)	
Service	Sanitary arrangements	Value for money

General remarks

Town, country, hotel

Your star rating	Location	Date of stay
Food	Room(s)	
Service	Sanitary arrangements	Value for money

General remarks

Town, country, hotel

Your star rating	Location	Date of stay
Food	Room(s)	
Service	Sanitary arrangements	Value for money

General remarks

Town, country, hotel

Your star rating	Location	Date of stay
Food	Room(s)	
Service	Sanitary arrangements	Value for money

General remarks

Name (block letters)

Address (block letters)

Membership no. (if any)

(For office use only)   Recorded
Acknowledged

ACCOMMODATION REPORT

Town, country, hotel

Your star rating	Location	Date of stay

| Food | Room(s) | |

| Service | Sanitary arrangements | Value for money |

General remarks

Town, country, hotel

Your star rating	Location	Date of stay

| Food | Room(s) | |

| Service | Sanitary arrangements | Value for money |

General remarks

Town, country, hotel

Your star rating	Location	Date of stay

| Food | Room(s) | |

| Service | Sanitary arrangements | Value for money |

General remarks

Town, country, hotel

Your star rating	Location	Date of stay

| Food | Room(s) | |

| Service | Sanitary arrangements | Value for money |

General remarks

Name (block letters)

Address (block letters)

Membership no. (if any)

(For office use only)
Acknowledged   Recorded

GARAGE REPORT
HOTELS AND RESTAURANTS IN EUROPE 1990

To: The Automobile Association, Hotel and Information Services,
Fanum House, Basingstoke, Hants RG21 2EA.

Town, country, garage

Address

Telephone no.

Agents for | Were AIT vouchers used for payment? | Recommended

Remarks

Town, country, garage

Address

Telephone no.

Agents for | Were AIT vouchers used for payment? | Recommended

Remarks

Town, country, garage

Address

Telephone no.

Agents for | Were AIT vouchers used for payment? | Recommended

Remarks

Town, country, garage

Address

Telephone no.

Agents for | Were AIT vouchers used for payment? | Recommended

Remarks

Town, country, garage

Address

Telephone no.

Agents for | Were AIT vouchers used for payment? | Recommended

Remarks

GARAGE REPORT

Town, country, garage

Address

Telephone no.

Agents for   Were AIT vouchers used for payment?   Recommended

Remarks

Town, country, garage

Address

Telephone no.

Agents for   Were AIT vouchers used for payment?   Recommended

Remarks

Town, country, garage

Address

Telephone no.

Agents for   Were AIT vouchers used for payment?   Recommended

Remarks

Town, country, garage

Address

Telephone no.

Agents for   Were AIT vouchers used for payment?   Recommended

Remarks

Name (block letters)

Address (block letters)

Membership no. (if any)

(For office use only)   Recorded
Acknowledged

ROAD REPORT
HOTELS AND RESTAURANTS IN EUROPE 1990

To: The Automobile Association, Hotel and Information Services,
Fanum House, Basingstoke, Hants RG21 2EA.

Section of road
From   To

Passing through
                                            Road no.

Names shown on signposts

Remarks: ie surface, width, estimated gradient, description of landscape

---

Section of road
From   To

Passing through
                                            Road no.

Names shown on signposts

Remarks: ie surface, width, estimated gradient, description of landscape

---

Section of road
From   To

Passing through
                                            Road no.

Names shown on signposts

Remarks: ie surface, width, estimated gradient, description of landscape

ROAD REPORT

Section of road
From   To

Passing through

Road no.

Names shown on signposts

Remarks: ie surface, width, estimated gradient, description of landscape

Section of road
From   To

Passing through

Road no.

Names shown on signposts

Remarks: ie surface, width, estimated gradient, description of landscape

Name (block letters)

Address (block letters)

Membership no. (if any)

(For office use only)   Recorded
Acknowledged